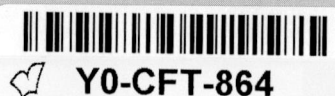

Query Designer Window Speedbar

1 2 3 4 5 6 7 8 9 10 11 12 13 14 15 16 17

Button	Function
1 New File	Create new file
2 Open File	Open existing file
3 Save File	Save query to disk
4 Print	Print query
5 Cut	Cut text to Clipboard
6 Copy	Copy text to Clipboard
7 Paste	Paste text from Clipboard
8 Run	Run query
9 Design	(n/a)
10 Add Table	Add another table
11 Delete Table	Delete currently selected table
12 Add Relation	Add new relation
13 Delete Relation	Delete selected relation
14 Navigator	Open Navigator
15 Command	Open Command window
16 Expert	Choose Expert
17 Tutor	Run interactive tutorial

See back inside cover for Table Structure, Table Records, and Form Designer Speedbars.

For every kind of computer user, there is a SYBEX book.

All computer users learn in their own way. Some need straightforward and methodical explanations. Others are just too busy for this approach. But no matter what camp you fall into, SYBEX has a book that can help you get the most out of your computer and computer software while learning at your own pace.

Beginners generally want to start at the beginning. The **ABC's** series, with its step-by-step lessons in plain language, helps you build basic skills quickly. For a more personal approach, there's the **Murphy's Laws** and **Guided Tour** series. Or you might try our **Quick & Easy** series, the friendly, full-color guide, with **Quick & Easy References**, the companion pocket references to the **Quick & Easy** series. If you learn best by doing rather than reading, find out about the **Hands-On Live!** series, our new interactive multimedia training software. For hardware novices, there's the **Your First** series.

The **Mastering and Understanding** series will tell you everything you need to know about a subject. They're perfect for intermediate and advanced computer users, yet they don't make the mistake of leaving beginners behind. Add one of our **Instant References** and you'll have more than enough help when you have a question about your computer software. You may even want to check into our **Secrets & Solutions** series.

SYBEX even offers special titles on subjects that don't neatly fit a category—like our **Pushbutton Guides**, our books about the Internet, our books about the latest computer games, and a wide range of books for Macintosh computers and software.

SYBEX books are written by authors who are expert in their subjects. In fact, many make their living as professionals, consultants or teachers in the field of computer software. And their manuscripts are thoroughly reviewed by our technical and editorial staff for accuracy and ease-of-use.

So when you want answers about computers or any popular software package, just help yourself to SYBEX.

SYBEX is committed to using natural resources wisely to preserve and improve our environment. As a leader in the computer book publishing industry, we are aware that over 40% of America's solid waste is paper. This is why we have been printing the text of books like this one on recycled paper since 1982.

This year our use of recycled paper will result in the saving of more than 15,300 trees. We will lower air pollution effluents by 54,000 pounds, save 6,300,000 gallons of water, and reduce landfill by 2,700 cubic yards.

In choosing a SYBEX book you are not only making a choice for the best in skills and information, you are also choosing to enhance the quality of life for all of us.

Understanding dBASE® 5 for Windows™

First Edition

Alan Simpson
Martin Rinehart

San Francisco ▲ Paris ▼ Düsseldorf ▲ Soest

ACQUISITIONS EDITOR: Joanne Cuthbertson
DEVELOPMENTAL EDITOR: David Peal
EDITOR: Marilyn Smith
PROJECT EDITOR: Valerie Potter
TECHNICAL EDITOR: Frank Seidel
BOOK DESIGNER: Helen Bruno
DESKTOP PUBLISHERS: Stephanie Hollier, Deborah Bevilacqua
PRODUCTION ASSISTANTS: Marc Duro, Kate Westrich
SCREEN GRAPHICS ARTIST: Dan Schiff
INDEXER: Nancy Guenther
COVER DESIGNER: Design Site
COVER PHOTOGRAPHER: David Bishop

Library of Congress Card Number: 94-61360

ISBN: 0-7821-1208- 0

Manufactured in the United States of America

10 9 8 7 6 5 4 3 2 1

To Susan, Ashley, and Alec
–A.S.

To Amanda, partly for her help and mostly for herself
–M.R.

▸▸ Acknowledgments

First, we want to thank the entire crew at Borland who brought you dBASE for Windows. Ray, Michael, Randy, Lloyd, and all the other dedicated team members have a lot to be proud of. dBASE for Windows is a superb product.

Thanks also go to the SYBEX team who helped to put the book together: developmental editor David Peal, editor Marilyn Smith, project editor Val Potter, technical editor Frank Seidel, desktop publishers Stephanie Hollier and Deborah Bevilacqua, production assistants Marc Duro and Kate Westrich, book designer Helen Bruno, screen graphics artist Dan Schiff, and indexer Nancy Guenther.

We would also like to thank the crew at Waterside Productions who put this project together.

Finally, we want to thank our families who put up with our long hours in front of our computers. They make it all worthwhile.

Contents at a Glance

Introduction *xxvii*

PART ONE ▶ *We Get Started*

1 Master the Basic Concepts 3

2 dBASE for Windows in an Evening 27

3 Design Your Database 67

PART TWO ▶ *Running dBASE for Windows*

4 Manipulating Your Data 103

5 The Two-Way Query Designer 155

6 Building Forms with the Two-Way Form Designer 199

7 Producing Database Reports 253

PART THREE ▶ *Master Classes*

8 Mastering the Menus, Navigator, and Command Window 289

9 Mastering Table Tools 349

10 Mastering Crystal Reports 393

11 Mastering Cross-Tab Reports, Labels, and Form Letters 457

PART FOUR ▶ *Programming Basics*

12 Working with Expressions and Functions 497

13 Using Command Window Commands 575

14 Basics of Programming Statements 663

15 Designing Forms and Menus 693

PART FIVE ▶ *Working with Forms*

16 Working with Static Form Objects 743
17 Working with Data-Entry Form Objects 797
18 Working with Advanced Form Objects 859
19 Putting the System Together 925

APPENDICES ▶

A Installing dBASE for Windows 969
B The Common Dialog Boxes 983
C Configuring with DBASEWIN.INI 1009
D Other dBASE for Windows Commands 1047
E Other dBASE for Windows Functions 1063
F Properties of DDE and OLE Objects 1085
G A Quick Reference to Object Properties by Object 1097
H A Quick Reference to Object Properties by Property 1113
Index ***1131***

Table of Contents

Introduction *xxvii*

PART ONE ▶ *We Get Started*

1 Master the Basic Concepts 3

Database Basics 6
Database Origins 6
Relational Databases 5
Arranging Data in Tables 7
An Overview of dBASE for Windows 8
Features of dBASE for Windows 9
The Navigator and the Command Windows 10
The Top Line 10
dBASE for Windows Menus 11
Speedbars 15
The Status Bar 17
dBASE for Windows Tools and Experts 17
Design and Run Modes 20
Speed Menus 21
Object Properties Inspectors 21
Your Job with dBASE for Windows 22
Summary 23

2 dBASE for Windows in an Evening 27

You Get Ready to Work 28
Menu Choices and Mouse Clicks 29
We Make a Test Run 30
Making a Working Directory 32
Lesson 1: You Create a Table 35
Navigating with the Navigator 36
Designing Offline 37
Using the Table Structure Tool 37
Rearranging and Deleting Fields 39

Leaving Your Work Safely Filed 40
Lesson 2: You Add and Change Data 40
Using the Table Records Tool 41
Entering Some Data 41
Taking a Different Look 42
Customizing the Browse Layout View 43
Getting Around in the Table 44
Changing Data 44
Printing the Table 45
Lesson 3: You Query Your Data 46
Using the Query Designer Tool 47
Leaving the Query Designer Tool 49
Lesson 4: You Create a Custom Form 50
Using the Form Expert 50
Using the Form Designer 52
Improving the Form 55
Using Your New Form 56
Lesson 5: You Write a Report 57
Picking Fields 58
Adding a Title 60
Previewing the Report 63
Sorting the Data 63
Summary 65

3 Design Your Database 67

The Art and Science of Database Design 68
Bad Database Design 69
The Art of Database Design 71
The Science of Database Design 72
TED Lets You Master Database Design 74
Things 74
Events 75
Designing with Things and Events 76
Details 78
TED in Action 78
You Master the Keys to Database Integrity 90
Principle Integrity Constraints 90
Assigning Unique Keys 91
Maintaining Relational Integrity 92
Summary 98

PART TWO ▶ *Runnig dBASE for Windows*

4 Manipulating Your Data 103

Improving the People Table 104
Adding an ID Field to the Structure 105
Letting dBASE Fill in the ID Field 107
Customizing the Table Records Tool 109
Organizing People Alphabetically 113
Putting Your Data in Order 116
What Is an Index? 116
Storing Your Indexes 117
Managing Your Production Index 119
Physical Sorting 123
Fast Updates for Groups of Records 126
Locating and Updating Data Groups 128
Finding Individual Records 131
Finding and Replacing in a Group of Records 134
Deleting and Recovering Groups of Records 140
Having dBASE Count for You 144
Letting dBASE Calculate for You 146
Sharing Data by Importing and Exporting 148
Exporting Data for Other Programs 148
Importing Data 151
Summary 152

5 The Two-Way Query Designer 155

You Query a Single Table 157
You Begin at the Beginning 157
Selecting Fields for a Query 162
Managing Indexes from the Query Designer 164
Selecting Relevant Records 169
Adding Calculated Fields 178
You Build a Database with Two Tables 179
Preparing a Two-Table Database 180
Relating the Tables with a Query 185
Using the Related Tables 188
You Edit the Program 194
Summary 196

6 Building Forms with the Two-Way Form Designer 199

You Build a Modal Form 201
Creating the Form 201
Attaching a Pushbutton 212
Adding a Memory Report 218
You Create a Main Form with a Menu 226
Building a Menu for a Form 227
Attaching Actions to Menu Choices 231
Attaching a Shortcut Key 234
You Build the People Form 236
Building the Query 236
Building the Base Form 237
Adding a Browse 237
Running the Completed Form 240
Putting Your Form into Your System 241
You Build the Orgs Form 242
Adding Pushbuttons 242
Adding Input Templates 244
Attaching the Form to the Fon_Main System 246
You Build the Combined Form 247
Building an Inverted Query 247
Creating the Form 249
Putting the Form in the Fon_Main System 250
Summary 250

7 Producing Database Reports 253

You Create a Two-Table Report 254
Building Your Query 254
Beginning the Report Definition 255
Adding the Other Fields 258
Previewing Your Work 261
Adding Headers and Footers 261
You Produce a Two-Table Grouped Report 264
Creating a Group 264
Putting the Employer Data into the Group Header 265
Previewing the Improved Report 266
Preventing Section Splitting 267
You Add Embellishments to Your Report 269
Manipulating Font Sizes and Styles 269
Drawing on Your Report 270

Formatting the Box 271
Emphasizing Names 273
Running the Report from the Navigator 274
Running the Report from Fon_Main 275
Handling Inverted Relationships 276
You Create Mailing Labels 278
Generating a Single-Table Label Set 278
Generating a Multiple-Table Label Set 282
Summary 284

PART THREE ▶ *Master Classses*

8 Mastering the Menus, Navigator, and Command Window 289

Using the File Menu 290
Using the Edit Menu 292
Using the Properties Menu 292
Setting Country Properties 293
Setting Table Properties 294
Setting Data Entry Properties 296
Setting File Properties 298
Setting Application Properties 300
Setting Programming Properties 302
Using the Window Menu 304
Arranging Your Windows 305
Closing and Opening Windows 305
Using the Help Menu 308
Working with the Navigator 310
The Directory Area 312
The File Types Menu 313
The Files List 313
Using the Navigator Main Menu 315
Using the Navigator's Properties Menu 318
The Navigator Speed Menus 319
The Other Navigators: Catalogs 321
The Catalog Window 321
Building a Catalog 323
Adding Items to the Catalog 324
Using a Catalog 325
The Catalog Is a Table 325

Working in the Command Window 326
Entering Commands in the Input Pane 327
Checking the Output in the Results Pane 330
The Command Window Speedbar 331
The Command Window's Main Menu 332
Using the Edit Menu 332
Using the Program Menu 334
Using the Table Menu 335
Using the Properties Menu 336
The Command Window's Speed Menu 337
The Results Pane Speed Menu 338
Using the Expression Builder 338
Building Simple Expressions 339
Using the Category, Type, and Paste Options 340
Editing Constants in the Expression 342
Adding a Date Operator Expression 343
Pasting to and from the Command Window 345
Summary 345

9 Mastering Table Tools 349

Using the Table Structure Tool 350
A Browse for Your Table Structure 350
Adding the Fields 351
Working in the Browse Area 354
Looking Above the Browse Area 354
Using the Table Structure Menus 355
Right-Clicking for the Table Structure Speed Menu 356
Using the Table Structure Speedbar Buttons 357
Avoiding Data Loss from Restructuring 358
Using the Table Records Tools 362
Using the Table Records Menus 362
Using the Table Records Speedbar Buttons 366
Setting Table Records Properties 368
Using Table Utilities 375
Working with Indexes 376
Closing Tables 379
Minimizing Waste and Recovering from Mistakes 379
Sharing Your Data with Other Applications 382
Analyzing Your Data 387
Summary 390

10 Mastering Crystal Reports 393

Using the File Menu 395
Printing Files 396
Setting Up the Printer and Page Margins 399
Setting File Options 400
Using the Edit Menu 412
Object Linking and Embedding through Paste Special 412
Deleting and Selecting Fields 414
Editing Formulas 415
Editing Text Fields 415
Editing Summary Fields 415
Hiding Report Sections 417
Editing Report Groups 418
Deleting Report Sections 418
Browsing the Selected Field's Data 419
Showing Field Names 419
Editing Objects 420
Managing Links 420
Using the Insert Menu 421
Inserting a Database Field 421
Inserting a Text Field 422
Inserting a Formula Field 422
Inserting a Summary Field 423
Inserting Lines and Boxes 426
Inserting Graphics and Objects 426
Inserting a Special Field 427
Inserting a Group Section 428
Using the Format Menu 428
Formatting Fields 429
Formatting Borders and Colors 430
Formatting Graphics 431
Formatting Lines 433
Formatting Boxes 433
Formatting Sections 434
Formatting Report Titles 435
Restacking Items 437
Using the Database Menu 437
Changing the Database File Location 437
Verifying Your Databases 437
Using the Report Menu 438
Specifying Record or Group Selection Formulas 439

Specifying Record or Group Sort Order 439
Refreshing and Saving Report Data 440
Specifying a Print Date 440
Using the Window Menu 441
Using the Help Menu 441
Using the Crystal Speedbar 442
Formatting with the Format Bar 444
Formatting Fonts 445
Aligning Fields 445
Formatting Numbers 446
Using the Preview Window's Speedbar 447
Using the Speed Menus 448
Speed Menus for the Report Bands 449
The Field-Related Speed Menus 450
The Special-Item Speed Menus 451
Summary 453

11 Mastering Cross-Tab Reports, Labels, and Form Letters 457

Generating Cross-Tab Reports 458
Sample Data for Cross-Tab Reporting 459
Building Your First Cross-Tab Report 460
Viewing Your Report 463
Adding Page Headers and Footers 464
Previewing the Report 464
Formatting a Cross-Tab Report 464
Adding Another Dimension 467
Creating Labels 473
Choosing a Label Type 474
Specifying the Printing Direction 476
How Crystal Determines the Number of Labels 477
Defining the Mailing Label Layout 477
Leaving and Returning to the Mailing Labels Dialog Box 479
Tips on Printing Labels 479
Producing Form Letters 480
Database Design for Form Letters 481
Creating Your Form Letter 483
Adding the Name and Address Fields 485
Using Formula Fields to Improve Your Letters 486
Summary 491

PART FOUR ▶ *Programming Basics*

12 Working with Expressions and Functions 497

Forming Expressions 499
Using Operands 500
Using Operators in Expressions 509
Calling Functions 517
Using Functions in Expressions 518
Function Categories 519
Alphabetic Reference to Common Functions 526
Summary 572

13 Using Command Window Commands 575

Commands versus Statements 577
Commands Listed by Topic 577
Alphabetical Reference to Commands 581
Summary 659

14 Basics of Programming Statements 663

Block Statements 664
Conditional Execution 664
Looping 667
Nesting 671
Intra-file Program Structure 673
Subroutine Declarations 673
Other Subroutine Statements 675
CLASS Blocks 680
Inter-file Program Structure 682
The SET PROCEDURE Command 682
The SET LIBRARY Command 683
The DO Command 683
Variable Declarations 685
LOCAL Variables 685
STATIC Variables 686
PRIVATE Variables 686
PUBLIC Variables 687
DECLARE Declarations 687
Adding Comments 688
Other Statements 688
The PRINTJOB Command 688

The SCAN Command 689
The TEXT Command 689
Summary 689

PART FIVE ▶ ***Working with Forms***

15 Designing Forms and Menus 693

Is It Programming? 694
Working with the Form Designer 696
Lassos and Layouts 696
Ordering Your Controls 700
Form Designer Properties 709
Using the Form Designer and Menu Designer Tools 711
Setting Properties with the Object Properties Inspector 712
Adding Controls with the Controls Palette 716
Working with the Procedure Editor 717
Using the Menu Designer 725
The Menu Designer Menus 726
The Menu Designer Speedbar 727
Form and Menu Object Properties Reference 727
Form Object Properties 727
Menu Object Properties 737

16 Working with Static Form Objects 743

Working with Image Objects 744
Aligning Images 745
Visible and Invisible Objects 749
Working with Line Objects 753
Exploring the Line's Possibilities 753
Exploring the Shape of the Line 756
Drawing a Circle 759
Setting the Colors 761
Working with Rectangle Objects 762
Adding a Label with the Text Property 762
Checking Out the OldStyle Property 764
Adding Border Styles 765
Adding a Pattern 767
Working with Text Objects 768
Adding a Border to a Text Object 768

The Many Ways to Align a Text Object 769
Choosing Fonts and Type Families 769
Static Form Object Properties Reference 773
Image Object Properties 773
Line Object Properties 778
Rectangle Object Properties 781
Text Object Properties 787

17 Working with Data-Entry Form Objects 797

Working with Checkbox Objects 798
Linking the Checkbox Object 799
Improving Checkbox Labels 802
Adding Checkbox Object Values 803
Working with Entryfield Objects 805
Changing the Entryfield Object Border 808
Setting the Entryfield Object's Maximum Length 809
Selecting All the Entryfield's Contents 810
Controlling Valid Values in Entryfields 811
Controlling When an Entryfield Object Is Available 814
Working with Radiobutton Objects 815
Working with Spinbox Objects 817
Choosing the Spinbox Object's Border 817
Setting the Spinbox Object's Range 819
Allowing Spinning Only 820
Using the Spinbox Object's Picture Property 820
Increasing the Spin Steps 820
Data-Entry Form Properties Reference 821
Checkbox Object Properties 821
Entryfield Object Properties 829
Radiobutton Object Properties 839
Spinbox Object Properties 847

18 Working with Advanced Form Objects 859

Working with Browse Objects 860
Using Aliases with Browse Objects 861
Editing Properties of Browse Objects 861
The Browse Object's Field Properties 862
Setting the Browse Object's Mode and Toggle Properties 863
Showing Items in Browse Objects 865
A Browse Example 865

Working with Combobox Objects 868
Setting the Combobox Object's Data Properties 868
Putting Combobox Entries in Order 872
Choosing Combobox Object Styles 873
Setting the Combobox Object's Value 874
Working with Editor Objects 874
Working with Listbox Objects 882
Advanced Form Objects Properties Reference 888
Browse Object Properties 888
Combobox Object Properties 897
Editor Object Properties 905
Listbox Object Properties 914

19 Putting the System Together 925

Working with Pushbutton Objects 926
Assigning OnClick Event Handlers 926
Pushbuttons and the Speedbar Property 928
Adding Conditions with the When Property 930
Working with Scrollbar Objects 930
Using What You've Learned 932
Automating Key Assignments 933
Automating Foreign Key Entry 940
Where Do We Go from Here? 950
Pushbutton and Scrollbar Properties Reference 951
Pushbutton Object Properties 951
Scrollbar Object Properties 960

APPENDICES

A Installing dBASE for Windows 969

Preload Your Hard Disk to Save Time 970
The Installation Questions 971
Pick an Appropriate Installation 971
Direct Installation to Your Drive 972
Claiming Ownership of Your Copy 972
Customizing Your Installation to Save Space 973
IDAPI Needs Space, Too 976
The Installation Process 977
Post-Installation Choices 978

B The Common Dialog Boxes 983

Dialog Box Types 984
Parent Windows 985
Modal Child Windows 986
MDI Child Windows 987
The Open File Dialog Box 988
Tabbing Order 989
File Name Entry Field and Rectangle 990
The Directory Rectangle 990
Available File Types 990
The Disk Drive Drop-down List 992
The Radio Buttons 992
The Choose Directory Dialog Box 992
The Font Dialog Box 993
Select Window Dialog Box 994
Manage Indexes Dialog Box 994
Index Dialog Box 996
Name and Key Expression 996
For and Unique Records Options 997
The Order Options 998
The Scope Panel 998
The Choose Template Dialog Box 1000
The Choose Template Panels 1000
Available Functions and Symbols 1001
Field Selectors 1004
Using the Pushbuttons 1005
Selecting to Control Order 1005

C Configuring with DBASEWIN.INI 1009

What Can You Do with DBASEWIN.INI? 1010
Multiple DBASEWIN.INIs for Multiple Projects 1010
Recovering the Original DBASEWIN.INI 1011
Things You Can't Do Without Editing DBASEWIN.INI 1011
Using Multiple Copies of DBASEWIN.INI 1011
DBASEWIN.INI in Detail 1013
The Structure of DBASEWIN.INI 1013
The Fonts Section 1014
The CommandSettings Section 1014
The CustomClasses Section 1020
The Install Section 1021

The Desktop Section 1021
The CommandWindow Section 1025
The Navigator Section 1026
The MRU_Files Section 1029
The OnOffCommandSettings Section 1030
The ObjectProperties Section 1031
The ControlsWindow Section 1033
The FormDesigner Section 1034
The TableRecords Section 1037
The ProgramEditor Section 1038
The Dialogs Section 1041
The Catalog Section 1042
The TextEditor Section 1042
The MemoEditor Section 1043
The QueryDesigner Section 1043
The ProcedureEditor Section 1044

D Other dBASE for Windows Commands 1047

E Other dBASE for Windows Functions 1063

F Properties of DDE and OLE Objects 1085

DDELink Object Properties 1094
DDETopic Object Properties 1088
OLE Object Properties 1090

G A Quick Reference to Object Properties by Object 1097

H A Quick Reference to Object Properties by Property 1113

Index 1131

▸▸ Introduction

Welcome to dBASE for Windows. If you've worked with dBASE IV or an earlier version, or another Xbase system, you'll find dBASE for Windows familiar. Whether or not you know how to use an earlier dBASE version, you'll find that dBASE for Windows is an exciting, powerful, and flexible database system.

The Windows version of dBASE has been reworked and rethought from the ground up. It is an object-oriented and event-driven database management system that lets you create custom applications without any programming. If you can point and click, you can build database systems that meet your needs.

▸▸ Who Should Read This Book?

We don't assume that you know an earlier version of dBASE. If you've worked with dBASE before, you'll learn dBASE for Windows that much more quickly. We do assume that you want to master the use of dBASE for Windows, from simple data-entry applications through building sophisticated forms, menus, and reports.

We assume that you already know the basics of operating an industry-standard computer. That includes getting around in DOS and in Microsoft Windows.

We don't assume that you're an expert at running database systems. We'll begin at the beginning, starting with how to design your own databases using tables to organize your data. You'll learn to manipulate these tables singly and in combinations as a complete database.

If you do have some experience with database systems, you'll be able to progress through the first chapters more quickly.

The user-interface components of dBASE for Windows are all completely new, since this is the first dBASE to run in a true graphical user interface (GUI) environment. These elements include pull-down menus, dialog boxes, speedbar buttons, and even Speed menus (accessed with a right mouse-click). dBASE for Windows provides several alternative ways to get to the features you need. We'll explain how to use the mouse and keyboard to give commands, and you can pick the methods that suit your own style of working.

►► What's in This Book?

The manuals that came with your dBASE for Windows are an excellent source of information, and the on-line help is even more exhaustive. But this book provides all the information you need, organized so that you can learn dBASE for Windows as quickly as possible. In Part 1, you'll get started using dBASE for Windows for practical work in just one evening. The chapters in Part 2 give you more details on each of the key portions of the program.

After you've finished reading and following the examples in Part 2, you'll be able to design multiple-table databases, prepare forms that guide your data entry and editing, build queries that let you view portions of your data, and prepare custom reports from your database. For example, if you can click a pushbutton labeled OK today, before you're finished with Chapter 6, you'll know how to add pushbuttons on your own forms.

Part 3, Master Classes, goes into every area of dBASE for Windows in depth. After you complete Part 2, you'll find that your work directs you into one or more of the topics covered here. Some of you may want to learn more about the data-entry tools, while others will be more interested in sophisticated reporting. The details are here, to be explored as your needs dictate.

In Part 4, we'll introduce you to the basics of programming. We'll treat dBASE programming at the beginning level. You'll find that as you get into building your own forms, you'll be adding simple programs (often just one line long) to handle the user-interface events, such as button clicks. These chapters serve both as an introduction and as reference. On a quick reading of Chapter 12, for instance, you'll meet all the most commonly used functions in the dBASE language. We don't expect you to memorize the facts you need to supply to calculate a mortgage payment, but we do hope you'll know that there is a function for this, and you'll be able to refer here when you need it.

The final part, Part 5, describes how to design your own data forms to make your database systems efficient and reliable. As you'll see, there are many different types of objects that you can place on a form, such as text, pushbuttons, and entry fields, as well as a substantial number of Windows objects, such as drop-down lists and comboboxes. The chapters in Part 5 provide examples you can work through to see what can be done with these objects. You can decide which are useful for your own systems. Then you can easily find just the details you need in the reference sections at the end of the chapters.

►► How Do You Read This Book?

Read Chapter 1 in your favorite easy chair, or on the train as you commute to work. But for Chapter 2 and all of Part 2, you'll need to be in front of your computer, typing and clicking as you go along. Actually, although we strongly recommend a mouse, there is nothing in dBASE for Windows that you can't access from the keyboard, so the clicking is not strictly necessary. But it's very, very helpful.

Chapter 1 is for beginners and those new to dBASE for Windows. It's relatively short, so we suggest you go through it, even if you think you know the basics.

Chapter 2, Use dBASE for Windows in an Evening, is just what it says. If you've never used dBASE, or any database for that matter, go through Chapter 2 thoroughly. By the time you're finished, you'll be able to enter a table definition, enter and edit data, query your data, and print simple reports. If you know a little about dBASE for Windows, skim this chapter quickly, slowing down for new topics.

Chapter 3 provides critical information about designing a database. The more you know about database work, the more you'll benefit from a careful reading of Chapter 3.

Part 2, Running dBASE for Windows, is four chapters of tutorials. Get in front of your computer and start using dBASE for Windows. We'll dive right into the use of multiple tables in a single database. Before you're finished, you'll have put together a single system with two tables plus forms and reports.

Part 3, Master Classes, is for those who want to get to know the tools thoroughly, leaving no stone unturned, no click unclicked, no menu choice unexamined. You can read it in front of your computer, trying every single feature, or you can skim it while you're waiting for the train, looking for helpful tricks.

Part 4, Programming Basics, should get dog-eared as you tack down corners pointing to useful commands and functions. You'll want to at least skim these chapters to get the most out of Part 5.

Part 5, Working with Forms, should also get dog-eared as you flag the parts that are most useful to you. You can experiment with the items that seem interesting, then return to the reference sections whenever you need specific information.

▸▸ Conventions You'll See in This Book

Throughout this book, you'll see in-text notes, marked by icons in the margin. You'll also see our particular style of referring to keyboard keys and menu selections.

▸ Book Notes

When there's a way to get in trouble, we'll alert you in the form of a warning note, as you see at the top of the next page.

▶▶ **WARNING**

This is a sample warning note. Don't overlook these warnings!

When there's a way to speed your work or an extra tidbit about how to accomplish something more efficiently, we'll tell you about it in a tip, like the one you see here.

▶▶ **TIP**

This is a sample tip. Read these for time-savers and other helpful hints.

Occasionally, we'll want to note something that is neither a warning nor a helpful hint. For example, we might supply some additional background material that we find interesting. This type of information is provided in a note.

▶▶ **NOTE**

This is something we think you may want to note.

▶ Keyboard and Menu Conventions

Arrow keys are shown as ←, ↑, →, and ↓. The Home, End, PgUp, PgDn, Ins, and Del keys are named in the style of the original IBM keyboard. Your keyboard may show the latter four spelled-out as Page Up, Page Down, Insert, and Delete. We call the Enter key *Enter*, although it is labeled *Return* on some keyboards.

Combination keys are labeled by specifying the shifting key (Shift, Ctrl, or Alt), a hyphen, and the other key in the combination. For example, one way to enter Design mode is with Shift-F2, which means to hold down the Shift key and press F2.

Menu choices are indicated by underscoring the hot keys and separating multiple menu choices with a ➤ symbol. For example, File ➤ Print… means choose the File option on the main menu. Then, from the pull-down menu, choose the Print… option.

►► How to Use This Book: Planning for Understanding

We already know a bit about you, so we feel that some words of advice on working with this book are in order. But let us introduce ourselves, first.

Alan Simpson is a software consultant and prolific author of a variety of books. His dBASE books have been best sellers since 1982. Martin Rinehart is a consultant and author who specializes in dBASE. He is a frequent contributor to *DataBased Advisor*, *dBASE Advisor*, *dBASE Informant*, and *Reference dBASE* magazines, as well as the author of three other books on dBASE.

What we know about you is that you have probably looked at a shelf of dBASE books and passed right by the little ones to pick out this oversized work. We know that you are interested in understanding dBASE for Windows, and you aren't about to settle for a superficial, enough-to-get-by approach.

So let us give you some advice. Start with Chapter 1. Find a place where you can really concentrate and time yourself. Then make a plan, setting aside the time that you can afford, to work steadily for an hour each evening, or a half hour every morning, or whatever suits your schedule.

Plan on working steadily, at whatever pace suits you, through Part 1 and Part 2. If you do one chapter a day, that will take a week. If you do one chapter a week, that will take the better part of two months. Whatever way you do it, do it with a plan. Just the first seven chapters will get you to an above average level of productivity with dBASE for Windows.

Then, when you have completed Chapter 7, go to work on your own database problems. Use the rest of the book as you solve the problems that made you decide to turn to a database management system in the first place.

Welcome to *Understanding dBASE 5 for Windows*.

We Get Started

PART ONE

In Chapter 1, Master the Basic Concepts, we'll introduce beginners to the basic concepts of database management, concentrating on relational databases. In this chapter, we also go through the basic concepts of the dBASE for Windows program, preparing you for rolling up your sleeves and getting to work in Chapter 2.

In Chapter 2, dBASE for Windows in an Evening, we show you how to design a table and enter that design in the Table Structure tool. Then you'll proceed to use the Table Records tool to enter and edit your data. You can also print simple reports directly from the Table Records tool.

We'll stop briefly at the Query Designer tool to ask questions about your data. Then you'll meet the Form Expert, and use it to generate a custom form for your table. Finally, we'll take a quick tour of Crystal Reports, designing and running a simple report.

Chapter 3, Design Your Database, is both the simplest and the most critical chapter in this book. If we needed to apportion the ingredients for successful database systems, we would say good design is three-quarters of the battle, and the other quarter is being proficient with dBASE for Windows. We can't overstate the importance of understanding the material in Chapter 3 as you go forward into the rest of the dBASE for Windows product.

▶ ▶ CHAPTER 1

Master the Basic Concepts

▸▸ **W***e* know that you want to get to your computer and get go ing. But one of the oldest and wisest pieces of advice ever given to computer programmers also applies to database users. It's this: The first step in building a computer system is to turn your computer off.

And that's just what we're going to do. Before we get started with dBASE for Windows, we'll talk about what you need to know to use a relational database system. This chapter is about the basics. First we'll discuss the fundamentals of databases, and then we'll give you an overview of the components of dBASE for Windows.

▸▸ *Database Basics*

Let's begin with databases in general before we get to relational databases in particular. If you are familiar with databases already, turn ahead a few pages and study Figure 1.2. If it makes perfect sense to you, skip this section. Or read on, and we'll give you a short history and overview of database systems.

▸ *Database Origins*

In the 1950s, the first computers could only read data one item at a time. Data was stored on punched paper tape, then punched cards used in pre-computer business data processing. Magnetic tape was an early improvement, but the computer still would start reading at the beginning and continue reading one item at a time. This is referred to as *serial* data access. For example, your computer probably has serial ports, which transmit and receive data one bit (an individual 0 or 1) at a time. (Parallel ports handle multiple bits at once.)

In data storage, the alternative to serial storage is random-access storage. Floppy disks, hard disks and CD-ROMs are random-access devices. It was the development of the hard disk that made random-access storage a reality.

Of course, reading "randomly" would not be useful in data processing. *Random access* means that if you have a million items of data on your disk, you can read item 654321 first, item 1 second, and item 999999 third. You don't need to read item 1, then item 2, and so on.

Serial storage limited the computer to processing files. Random-access storage made computerized database systems possible. The fundamental goals of a database system are to record different types of information in sensible groupings and to bring that information together in useful ways on demand.

Let's consider a typical example of a database. You probably have a personal phone list. For some people, you list a single number; for others, you list a home number and a separate work number. This phone list is a data file.

Let's say that you have three people in your list that work for BigCo, which is reached at 555-1234. One problem with a simple data file is that data gets repeated. If BigCo's phone number changes to 123-4567, you have three people whose work number needs changing. Will you remember them all?

With a database system, you don't need to worry about finding repeated items and changing each one. When you enter the data, you can note that each of your three friends works for BigCo. When you need a work number, the computer will look up the person, see that he or she works for BigCo, and then find BigCo's phone number. You'll see how this works in the next chapter, in which we'll implement a database of phone numbers and addresses.

▶ Relational Databases

Strangely, the word *relational*, as applied to databases, has nothing to do with the relationships that a database tracks. For example, one relationship that a database might track is that Fred and Judy both work for BigCo. If the database "knows" this, we can get the correct work number for either Fred or Judy. When BigCo changes its phone number, we'll enter that change as the new number for BigCo. We'll then get the new number if we look up either Fred or Judy's work number. This works because we tell the computer that there is a relationship between BigCo and Fred, and a similar relationship between BigCo and Judy.

But that's not what *relational* means. The term comes from what once was an obscure branch of mathematics: relational algebra and relational calculus. In the mathematics terminology, a *relation* is a table. A *relational database* is simply one that stores its data in tables—familiar rows and columns. Figure 1.1 shows a simple, two-table database.

FIGURE 1.1 ►

Relational means data in tables

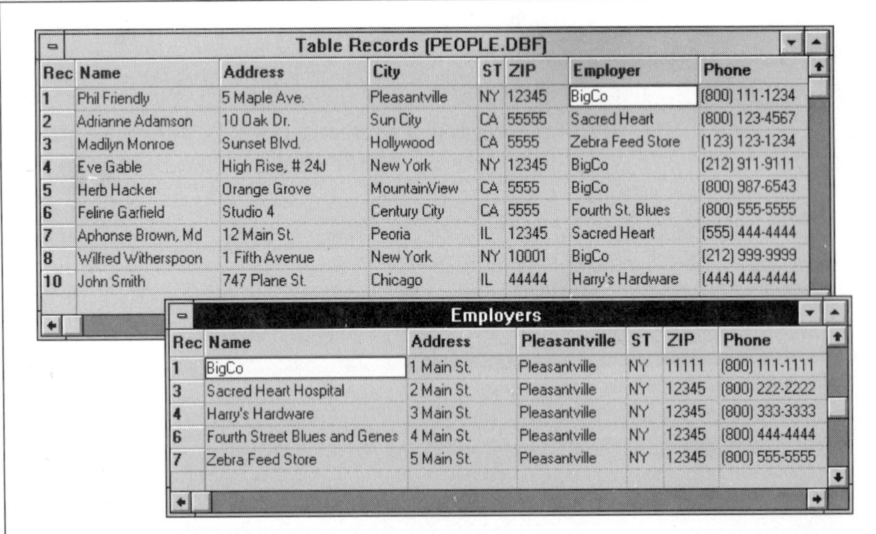

Table Records (PEOPLE.DBF)

Rec	Name	Address	City	ST	ZIP	Employer	Phone
1	Phil Friendly	5 Maple Ave.	Pleasantville	NY	12345	BigCo	(800) 111-1234
2	Adrianne Adamson	10 Oak Dr.	Sun City	CA	55555	Sacred Heart	(800) 123-4567
3	Madilyn Monroe	Sunset Blvd.	Hollywood	CA	5555	Zebra Feed Store	(123) 123-1234
4	Eve Gable	High Rise, # 24J	New York	NY	12345	BigCo	(212) 911-9111
5	Herb Hacker	Orange Grove	MountainView	CA	5555	BigCo	(800) 987-6543
6	Feline Garfield	Studio 4	Century City	CA	5555	Fourth St. Blues	(800) 555-5555
7	Aphonse Brown, Md	12 Main St.	Peoria	IL	12345	Sacred Heart	(555) 444-4444
8	Wilfred Witherspoon	1 Fifth Avenue	New York	NY	10001	BigCo	(212) 999-9999
10	John Smith	747 Plane St.	Chicago	IL	44444	Harry's Hardware	(444) 444-4444

Employers

Rec	Name	Address	Pleasantville	ST	ZIP	Phone
1	BigCo	1 Main St.	Pleasantville	NY	11111	(800) 111-1111
3	Sacred Heart Hospital	2 Main St.	Pleasantville	NY	12345	(800) 222-2222
4	Harry's Hardware	3 Main St.	Pleasantville	NY	12345	(800) 333-3333
6	Fourth Street Blues and Genes	4 Main St.	Pleasantville	NY	12345	(800) 444-4444
7	Zebra Feed Store	5 Main St.	Pleasantville	NY	12345	(800) 555-5555

Relational theorists have built our databases on a strong, theoretical foundation. In 1969, E. F. Codd, then a scientist at IBM, published the first of many papers on the application of relational mathematics to databases. He showed how joining data from one table to data in another provided a precise description for, getting the BigCo phone number when you want to call Judy at work (as one example).

You can't add and subtract tables, but you can perform other interesting operations on them, such as selecting a set of rows or joining columns from a row in one table with columns from a row in another table.

Although many people are working on different database forms, such as object-oriented databases, the relational database is the most popular choice today.

▶ Arranging Data in Tables

Tables are a common structure for arranging data. You decide that you will need data about people, so you create a table to store this data. At the outset, you decide that you will need the person's name, address, phone number, and employer. You put a column into your table for each of these items.

The columns in a relational database are considered fixed; the rows are variable. As you add new people to your table, it gets longer. If you delete people, your table gets shorter, but it retains the same columns.

Of course, as your needs change, you'll add new columns and delete ones that you don't use. And you'll change the column definitions, too. Perhaps you'll find that your Name column just isn't wide enough; or maybe it's too wide, and it would be a lot more convenient if it didn't waste so much space. You can make these adjustments as often as you need, but they will be far less frequent than the routine process of adding and deleting rows.

Each row in a relational database table is called a record. (If you are a relational theorist, you call it a *tuple*, which rhymes with *couple*.) The term *record* was borrowed from record keeping in the early days of computers and has been with us ever since.

In a relational database, the word *field* has two distinct meanings. If you speak of the fields in a table, you are referring to the table's columns. On the other hand, if you speak of the fields in a record, you refer to the individual entries in each column in a particular row.

When that ambiguity might be a problem, we'll be specific about referring to the field's definition or the field's value. For example, our table of people has a Name field. The field might be defined as a character data field, 32 characters wide. The value of the name field in a particular record might be "John Smith."

In dBASE, a field can contain character data, numbers, dates, and other data types. When you define your tables, you'll pick an appropriate type for each field. dBASE will make sure that only the selected type of data is allowed in each field. For example, you can't enter "Smith" into a numeric Weight field.

As you'll see, you can put further restrictions on the values allowed in a field. For example, you could have a rule that the value in the Ship_Date field is a date that doesn't come before the value in the Order_Date field. Restricting the values that get into your table fields helps ensure that you have valid information in your database. (The restrictions we put on the values that can go into a field define what the theorists call the field's *domain*.)

For a quick summary of these terms and concepts, take a look at Figure 1.2. It shows that a relational database is built of tables. The table rows are called records, and the columns are called fields. The field has a definition, and it has values in each record that match its definition.

FIGURE 1.2 ▶

Relational database terms

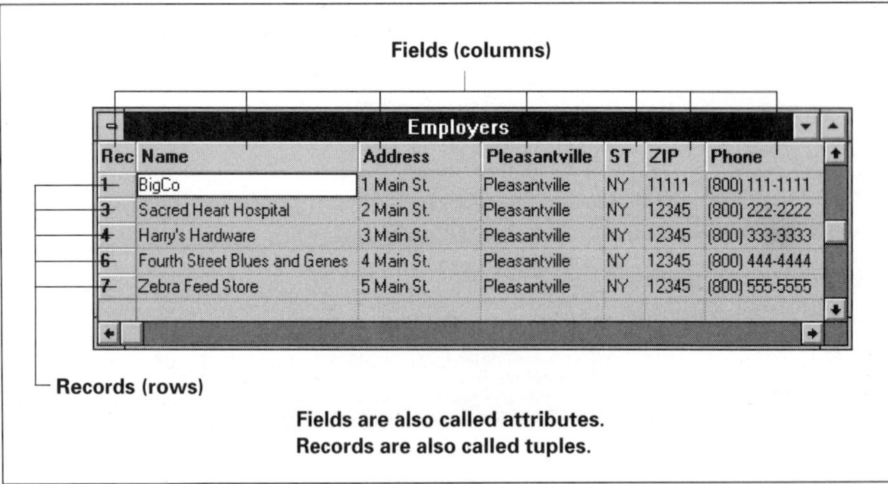

▸▸ An Overview of dBASE for Windows

How does dBASE for Windows work? Any relational database management system (RDBMS) works mostly behind the scenes. Its job is to get data from the keyboard and convert it into appropriate 1s and 0s on disk. Then, on demand, to return these 1s and 0s in the form of text and numbers that are meaningful to us. What we see is the surface through which this data management takes place.

▶ Features of dBASE for Windows

Figure 1.3 shows dBASE for Window's main features. The main window's *client area* is the space between the bar with icons (called the *speedbar*) at the top and the bar with status information (called the *status bar*) at the bottom. In the figure, this area contains the Navigator and Command windows.

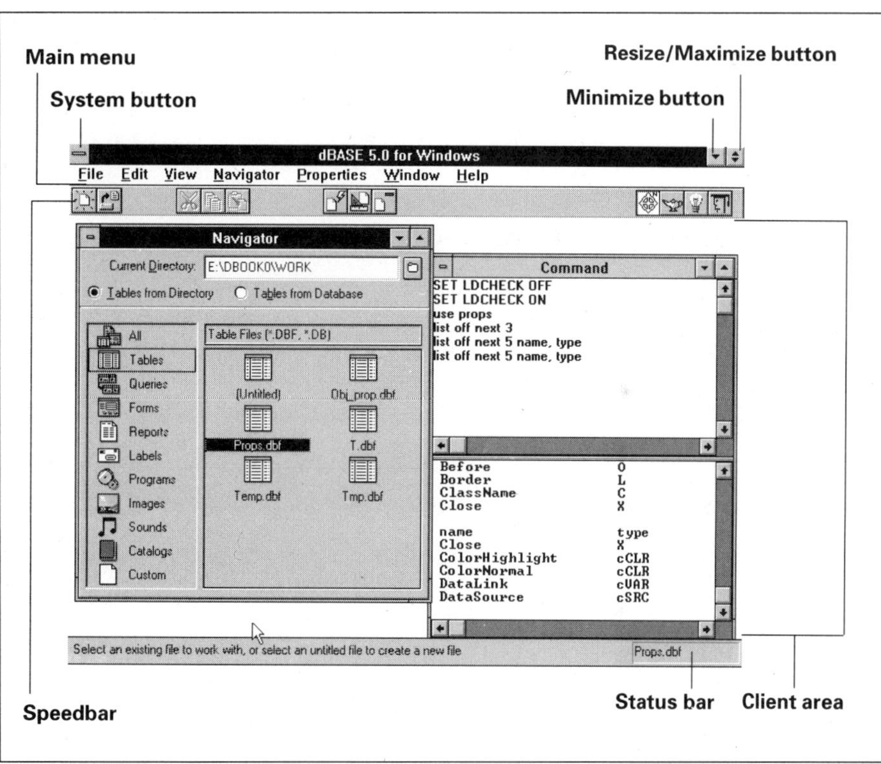

FIGURE 1.3 ▶

Main dBASE for Windows features

► The Navigator and the Command Windows

The Navigator and Command windows are the alternate control windows. Both are capable of fully controlling dBASE for Windows. We'll work mostly with the Navigator until we get to the more advanced topics.

As you'll see, as you point and click in the Navigator, your actions are translated into program commands in the Command window. Typing the commands in the Command window achieves exactly the same results as pointing and clicking in the Navigator.

Once you know your way around dBASE for Windows, you may find that some actions are easier to initiate from the Command window. If you are used to the dot prompt in dBASE IV and earlier, the Command window will be an old friend. On the other hand, if you prefer point-and-click actions, you may use the Navigator almost exclusively. Just remember that everything that you can launch in the Navigator can also be launched from the Command window.

► The Top Line

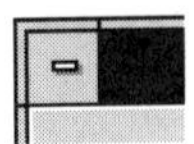

At the very top of the screen are the standard Windows buttons and the name of the Windows application. In the upper-left is the System button (shown in the margin). Click on the System button to see the standard System menu choices:

Double-clicking on the System button closes dBASE for Windows.

Note that you don't need a mouse (or other pointing device) to use the System menu. From the keyboard, press Alt-spacebar to get to this menu.

TIP

As is the case with most Microsoft Windows applications, being able to work from the keyboard and with the mouse will greatly increase your productivity in dBASE for Windows. You will benefit by taking the time to learn both the keyboard and mouse actions.

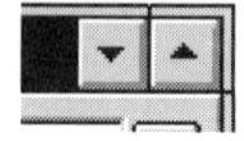

In the top-right corner of the main window are the Minimize and Resize/Maximize buttons (shown in the margin). The default startup size is maximized (full screen). Clicking on the Resize button (double-headed arrow) reduces the size.

You can drag the sides and corners to change dBASE's window size, but there's a problem. If you're running dBASE for Windows on a standard 14-inch monitor, you'll probably want to use 640 × 480 resolution. At higher resolutions, the icons and text become too small to read. At 640 × 480, you'll want to use most of the screen because there's a lot to put inside dBASE for Windows' client area.

NOTE

Your screen resolution is determined by Windows when it is started. You can change the resolution through the Windows Setup program.

Of course, the higher resolutions are great if you have a 17- or 21-inch monitor. On a 14-inch monitor, you may go to 800 × 600 resolution after you know dBASE's icons very well.

Under the top line comes the main menu.

dBASE for Windows Menus

Most of what you will do in dBASE for Windows is done by clicking on objects visible in the client area. When you begin with dBASE for Windows, you'll find that you don't use the menus much. As you get to more advanced uses, however, you'll find that the menus cover a wealth of operations that are difficult or impossible to find elsewhere.

The File Menu

The main menu starts with the IBM's Common User Access (CUA) standard menus. The File menu is on the left. This menu changes to reflect the active child window (the active window inside dBASE for Windows). For example, if you are working in a data table, it includes options to save your data, print your data, and close the table:

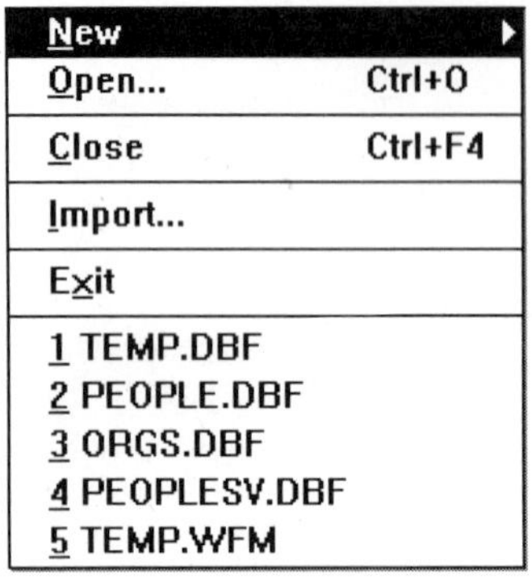

New ►
Open... Ctrl+O
Close Ctrl+F4
Import...
Exit
1 TEMP.DBF
2 PEOPLE.DBF
3 ORGS.DBF
4 PEOPLESV.DBF
5 TEMP.WFM

With the Navigator or Command window active, the File menu includes options to open tables or import data, as well as to close the active tool. If a child window isn't open, the File menu includes options to open a file or to exit from dBASE for Windows.

The Help Menu

Again conforming to the CUA convention, the Help option is on the far right. A Windows Help menu drops down when you click on Help (or press Alt-H).

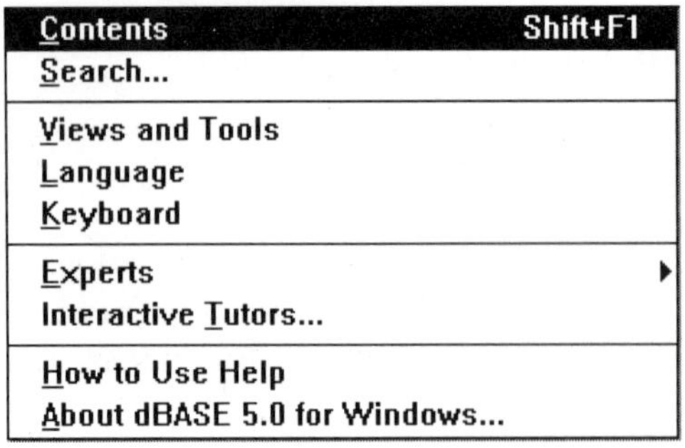

Contents Shift+F1
Search...
Views and Tools
Language
Keyboard
Experts ►
Interactive Tutors...
How to Use Help
About dBASE 5.0 for Windows...

As you can see, the Help menu includes the various Help options, plus the About dBASE 5.0 for Windows choice, which displays information about your machine and your version of dBASE for Windows.

The Edit Menu

The Edit menu, with the normal selection of cut, copy, and paste operations, is near the left, next to the File option. It performs the usual functions via the Windows Clipboard:

Undo	Ctrl+Z
Cut	Ctrl+X
Copy	Ctrl+C
Paste	Ctrl+V
Delete	Del
Select All	

This menu provides convenient ways to move data or other information around within dBASE for Windows, and between dBASE and other Windows programs.

The Window Menu

The Window menu is near the right, next to the Help option. It lets you cascade or tile your windows, and lists all the windows you have available, as in this example:

Cascade	Shift+F5
Tile Horizontally	
Tile Vertically	Shift+F4
Arrange Icons	
Close All Windows	
√ 1 Navigator	
2 Command	

You can choose any window in the list, and this can be important when the rich collection of tools here encourages you to make quite a mess of your computer's desktop.

The Properties Menu

The Properties option is always just to the left of the Window option. Clicking on it (or pressing Alt-P) pulls down a short menu, which always begins with the Desktop choice:

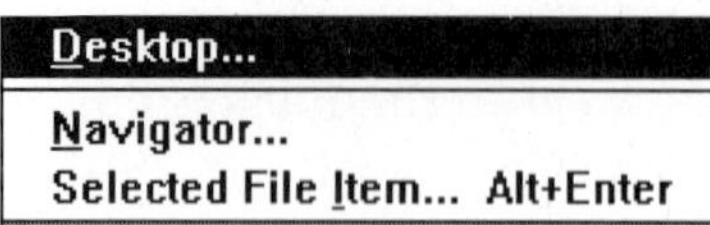

Choosing Desktop brings up a multi-tab form that lets you select your preferences in the following categories:

- Country
- Table
- Data Entry
- Files
- Application
- Programming

In addition to the Desktop properties, the menu includes any other properties relevant to the currently active tool. For example, if the Navigator is selected, a Navigator option is available to set your preferences for the Navigator.

Other Menus

The rest of the menu choices vary, depending on your location in dBASE for Windows. They are always appropriate to the active tool. Figure 1.4 shows menu choices available when the Table Records tool is active. As you'll see in Chapter 2, the Table Records tool is the basic tool for entering and maintaining data.

As you can see, the menu has View and Table choices, along with the standard File, Edit, Properties, Window, and Help options. In this case, the View menu lets you select from different ways to view your data. The Table menu offers a wealth of choices for manipulating your data. It is

FIGURE 1.4

dBASE for Windows browsing a table

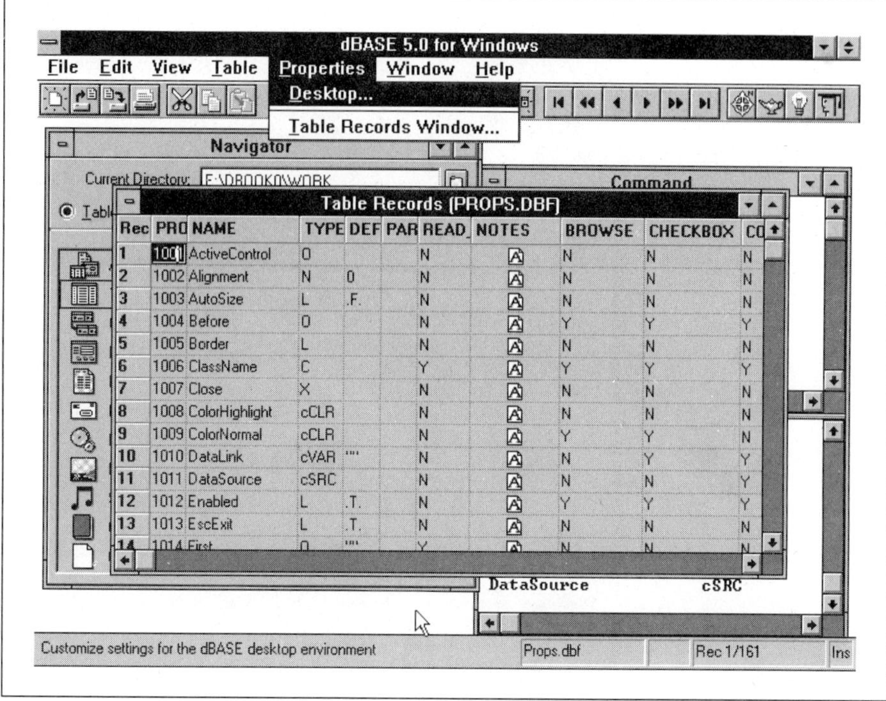

often true that the menu option that matches the active tool's name (Table for the Table Records tool) accesses the key operations for that tool.

▶ *Speedbars*

Below the menus are the speedbars. Like the menus, they vary with the tool you are using. For example, Figure 1.5 shows the speedbar when the Table Structure tool is active.

These four speedbar buttons appear on the left:

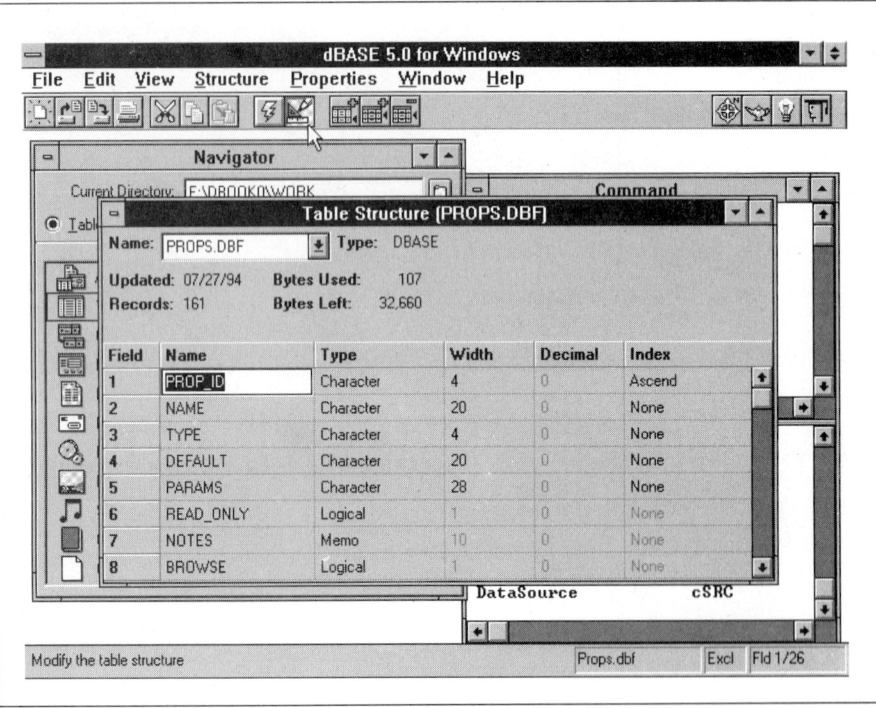

FIGURE 1.5 ▶

Using the Table Structure tool

These buttons are for performing common file and print operations.

To the right of these are the buttons for Clipboard (cut, copy, and paste) operations:

These four buttons appear on the far right:

They provide access to special dBASE for Windows features: the Navigator window, the Command window, Experts, and Tutors.

In between are buttons specific to the tool in use. The run and design icons are available in many places in dBASE for Windows. The run icon is a lightning bolt, and the design icon shows drafting tools:

The three other speedbar buttons for the Table Structure tool look like this:

These allow you to choose one of the standard layouts for your data.

Once you become familiar with dBASE for Windows, you'll find yourself doing a lot of work by simply clicking on the appropriate speedbar choice.

▶ The Status Bar

At the bottom of the dBASE for Windows window is the status bar. This provides information that is continuously changing. For example, as you move your mouse pointer over the speedbar buttons, an explanation of the active button's function appears in the left side of the status bar.

In an Editor, you'll see your current line and column position, a notation regarding whether you're in Insert or Overstrike mode, and other status information.

▶ dBASE for Windows Tools and Experts

Most of dBASE for Windows work is done with tools that Borland provides, or with the tools that you build using the tools that Borland provides. For example, Figure 1.6 shows the Form Designer with its Controls palette of standard and custom form objects.

Everything on a form—an entry field, a list box, a check box, and so on—is an object. In fact, all the dBASE for Windows user interfaces are built from objects. This includes the built-in tools that you see and the forms that you can build.

FIGURE 1.6

The Form Designer's Controls palette

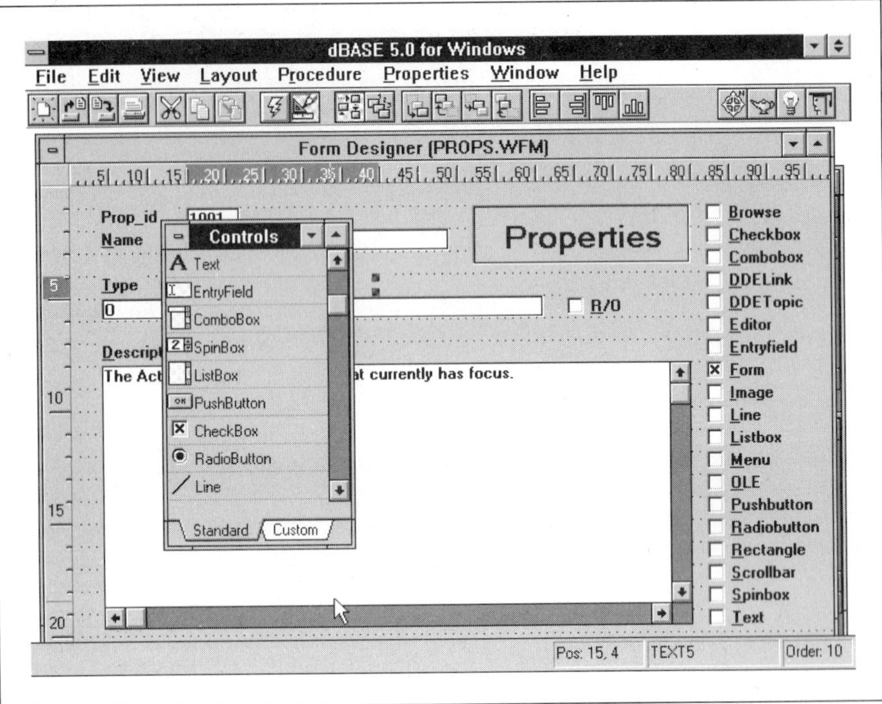

When you build your own forms, you'll start with a Form object. Then you'll add other objects as properties of the Form object. You might add Entryfield, Pushbutton, Listbox, and Radiobutton objects, as well as the other objects you need for a modern Windows interface.

These objects are described by properties which you can examine and change with the Object Properties Inspector (discussed later in this chapter). Properties include data (such as Top, Left, Height, and Width) and code for events (such as OnClick for pushbuttons and OnOpen for forms).

Using the Form Designer, we created the form shown in Figure 1.7. We use this form to access data in our People table. Note that this form would have required expensive, custom programming—many hours worth—just a few years back.

Building a form could still be a time-consuming activity, especially if your database has many fields. This is why we use the built-in Form Expert. For example, we always use this Expert to get an almost instantaneous form, once we've defined the fields in a table.

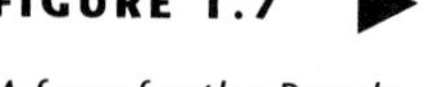

FIGURE 1.7

A form for the People table

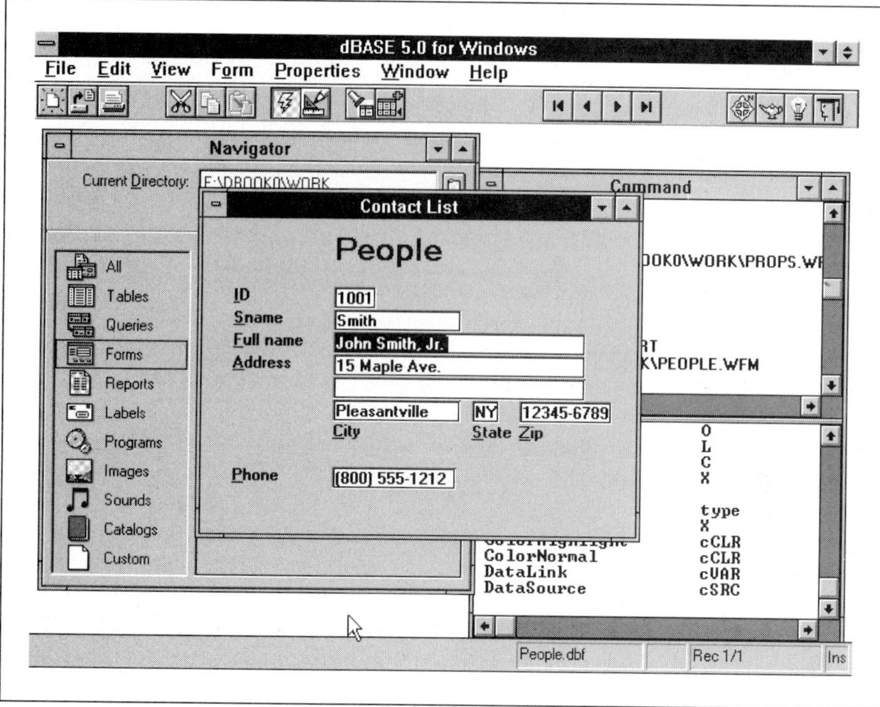

We built the preliminary version of the form in Figure 1.7 in less than a minute. More exactly, we answered the questions that the Form Expert asked, which took about half a minute, and then it built the form in another few seconds.

It took us about three minutes using the Form Designer to make a handful of changes, such as inserting proper formatting for a North American telephone number.

The components you see here are all objects selected from the Form Designer's Controls palette. If you want a check box, radio button, field, or edit box, you just click on that element in the Controls palette and drop it into place on your form.

Using the Form Expert, you'll be asked some questions about your preferences. As you see in Figure 1.8, the Form Expert wants to know how we want to lay out the form. You answer this question and some others, and the Form Expert builds the form to your specifications.

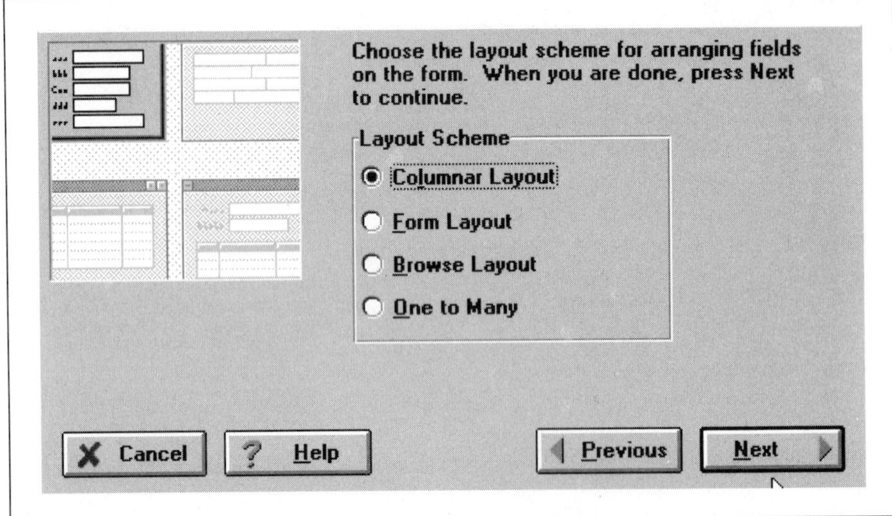

FIGURE 1.8 ▶

The Form Expert asking which layout we want

If you're not satisfied with the way the form looks, just run the Expert again. You can try a form in two or three ways in minutes. When you get one you like, you can begin to customize it with your favorite objects from the Form Designer's Controls palette. You'll see how the Form Designer and Expert work in the next chapter and get details in Chapter 6.

▶ Design and Run Modes

As you build forms, reports, or other components, you can switch between Design mode and Run mode. In Run mode, you'll actually be using the tool you're creating. This is wonderful for building a form, for example, because you can try it in operation just by clicking on a speedbar icon.

As you work, you'll click on the design icon (or press Shift-F2) to make improvements in a form, and then click on the run icon (or press F2) to test it. It makes creating reports, forms, and data tables fast and fun.

▶ Speed Menus

As with many Borland products, clicking with the right mouse button brings up a Speed menu. For example, here's the Speed menu for a table in the Navigator:

Navigator Properties...	
Cut	Ctrl+X
Copy	Ctrl+C
Paste	Ctrl+V

You just point at the table and click the right button to see this menu. Then, with one more click, you can choose to look at the table's properties, delete the table, add or edit records, or modify the table's structure.

▶ Object Properties Inspectors

The Object Properties Inspectors are key to much of your work. An Object Properties Inspector maintains an extensive list of properties. For example, Figure 1.9 shows the list for a simple Text object on a form.

As you can see, there's a lot to know about a Text object. dBASE for Windows wants to know what form it's attached to, where the form is located, what font we're using, if we want normal or boldface or italic text, what color to use, and so on.

In fact, in Figure 1.9, we've moved the speedbar to the left of the screen and turned the status bar off to get all the vertical room possible, and we still haven't shown all the text properties. Each entry on the Properties list that has a plus sign (+) next to it is a group entry, contracted to hide its details. The minus sign (–) entries are groups that are expanded to show all their details. For example, in the figure, you can see the position properties, but not the identification properties.

FIGURE 1.9 ▶

Properties of a text object

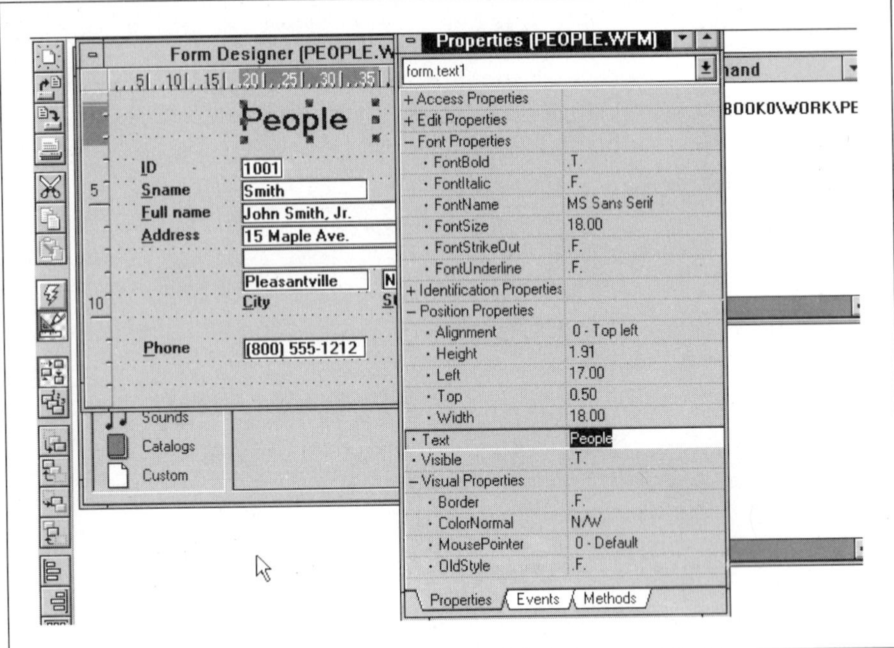

▶▶ **TIP**

You can reposition the speedbar and turn the status bar on and off through the Desktop Properties window. Choose Desktop from the Properties menu, and then click on the Application tab to change the speedbar and status bar settings.

Don't assume that you'll need to make all these decisions for every object you use. Each property has a default, so you can skip almost all of this. However, the default text for your first Text object is *text1*, so you'll need to enter something here. Otherwise, all these controls are here to satisfy your creative urges, not to make you do a lot of work.

▶ Your Job with dBASE for Windows

To build a system with dBASE for Windows, you'll start by defining your tables. Then you can use the Query tool to describe how your tables are related. As you'll see when we get there, this is almost no work at all. (For the simplest single-table system, the Query step isn't needed.)

With a query that defines how your tables are related, you can build one or more forms. One form can handle several tables, or you can have a separate form for each table. If you're in a big hurry, you can skip the forms altogether and use dBASE for Windows defaults. But with the Form Expert, creating forms is quick and simple, so you'll probably want to use forms.

Now you have the tools you need to enter, browse through, and edit your data. After you enter some data, you'll go back to the Query tool to define other queries. Queries allow you to select and work with subsets of your table. For example, queries let you locate your biggest spending customers and your lowest paid employees.

Finally, you'll use the Crystal Reports report writer to create reports, so you can get your data on paper. Like forms, reports can be created virtually instantaneously with the aid of Experts. Even a complex crosstab report can be created in minutes. dBASE for Windows provides a rich selection of report tools, so that once you decide to get creative, you have almost unlimited power to produce anything from intelligent form letters to complex catalogs.

For really polished work, you can wrap all your other tools into an application with its own menus, courtesy of the built-in menu maker. If you want to go further, you can begin programming in dBASE's built-in programming language.

►► Summary

You've learned that a relational database is a database that stores all its data in tables. A table is made up of rows and columns. The columns, called fields, are predefined (by you).

The rows, called records, are what you insert to add data or delete when your data is obsolete. Each record's fields contain values appropriate to the column type: text in the Name field, a date in the Ship_Date field, and so on.

dBASE for Windows provides the underlying database layer that makes a relational database work, but most of what we see is the interface layer that lets us work with our data in our own way.

dBASE for Windows has the features (buttons and menus) common to most Microsoft Windows applications. In its client area, it sports a large number of tools, including Experts that speed you through your work.

At the top level, you can do useful work very quickly with dBASE. As you delve more deeply into each tool, you'll find that there are no serious limits to get in the way of building systems that provide you with powerful, flexible databases.

In Chapter 2, we'll get started on a simple system in just one evening's work. We hope you enjoy it.

If you haven't done so yet, it's time to turn your computer back on!

► ► CHAPTER 2

dBASE for Windows in an Evening

▶▶ **In** this chapter, we'll introduce you to dBASE for Windows and dive right into some useful work. We'll define a data table, enter some data, edit the data, query the table for a summary, and finally write a report. Although you won't become an advanced dBASE for Windows user in a single evening, you'll be able to use many of the program's tools.

This chapter is like the guided tour you might take on your first visit to Paris. From the tour bus, you can learn the general layout of the city—see the Seine, Notre Dame, the Arc de Triomphe, and so on. But to get to know Paris, you need to set off on foot and spend some time in every part of the city. In Part 2 of this book, we'll be touring each section of dBASE for Windows on foot (in detail). For now, we'll just look at the highlights.

And this guided tour has one advantage over any you can find in Paris (or any other city): if you see something interesting, you can stop and poke around. Try some menu choices or click some speedbar buttons. We'll wait patiently until you're ready to get back on the bus.

▶▶ *You Get Ready to Work*

You'll need three things to be ready to work: basic Microsoft Windows skills, the dBASE for Windows software, and a working directory.

If you're new to Windows, you'll need skills outside the scope of this book. Please don't try to plow forward here, hoping to learn Windows along the way. You'll either get mad at us, or worse, you'll get mad at yourself.

Windows comes with a *Getting Started* manual, and there are lots of books on this subject. Alan might be biased, but we'll still recommend his book, *Windows Running Start* (also from SYBEX). If you do not have a manual and can't get to a bookstore, press Alt-H (for Help) in Windows 3.1 and choose the Windows Tutorial from the Help menu.

If you haven't installed dBASE for Windows, you'll need to do that first. Instructions are in Appendix A. Even if you've already installed the software, you might want to look at Appendix A. The method we suggest there is a lot faster than the standard installation procedure.

Those of you who are using dBASE for Windows on a network will need to ask your network administrator for installation instructions.

If you followed the default installation procedure, dBASE for Windows is available in a Program Manager group called dBASE for Windows. The default group looks like the one in Figure 2.1.

FIGURE 2.1

The dBASE for Windows group in the Program Manager

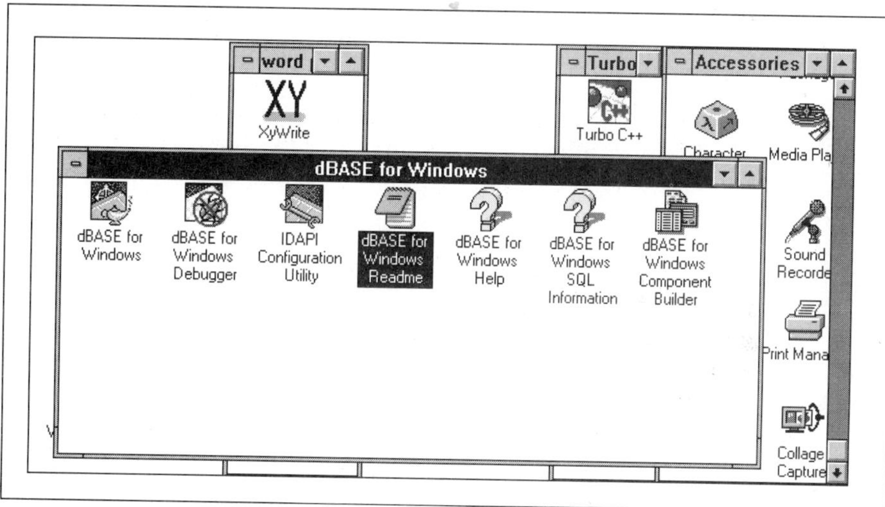

▶ Menu Choices and Mouse Clicks

Throughout this book, we'll frequently tell you to choose something like the following: Help ➤ Windows Tutorial. This means choose the Help menu. Then, from the drop-down menu, choose Windows Tutorial. The underscored characters are the ones you press if you're using the keyboard. For this example, you could press F10 (or Alt) to get to the main menu, and then press H to see the Help menu. In the Help menu, press W for the Windows Tutorial. Or you could press Alt-H, to skip over the F10 or Alt step. Of course, mouse clicks work, too.

Windows users usually click their mouse with the index finger. This is the left button if you have a two-button mouse and are right-handed. It's also the left button if you're left-handed and don't reverse the mouse buttons. If you're a lefty who has reversed buttons, you'll need to remember that what we call "left" is really right, and vice-versa.

dBASE for Windows, like many Borland products, also uses the right button. If your mouse cursor is over an object and you click the right button, you typically get a pop-up menu, called the Speed menu. This menu lists the most common operations for that object. For example, if your cursor is over a form in the Navigator, clicking the right mouse button brings up a Speed menu with choices to use the form, delete the form, or modify the form's design.

dBASE for Windows does not use the middle button of three-button mice. dBASE's programming language has support for the middle button, so programmers can build special applications that use the middle button. For our purposes, we assume (as does dBASE for Windows) that you probably have just two buttons on your mouse. If your mouse has only one button, you'll miss the convenience of the Speed menus, but all their functions are available from the other menus and speedbars, too.

▸ We Make a Test Run

Before the first lesson, let's make sure that everything is in working order. In Windows' Program Manager, double-click on the dBASE for Windows icon, shown in Figure 2.1.

After a brief pause, you'll see the dBASE for Windows screen, which should look something like the one shown in Figure 2.2.

You now have dBASE for Windows up and running. Let's say goodbye to it, for now. Click on the System button in the upper-left corner (at the very top) to display the System menu, and then click on Close, or press C, and you are out of the program. Of course, as the menu suggests, you could have pressed Alt-F4 instead of going through the menu.

FIGURE 2.2

dBASE for Windows' Navigator and Command windows

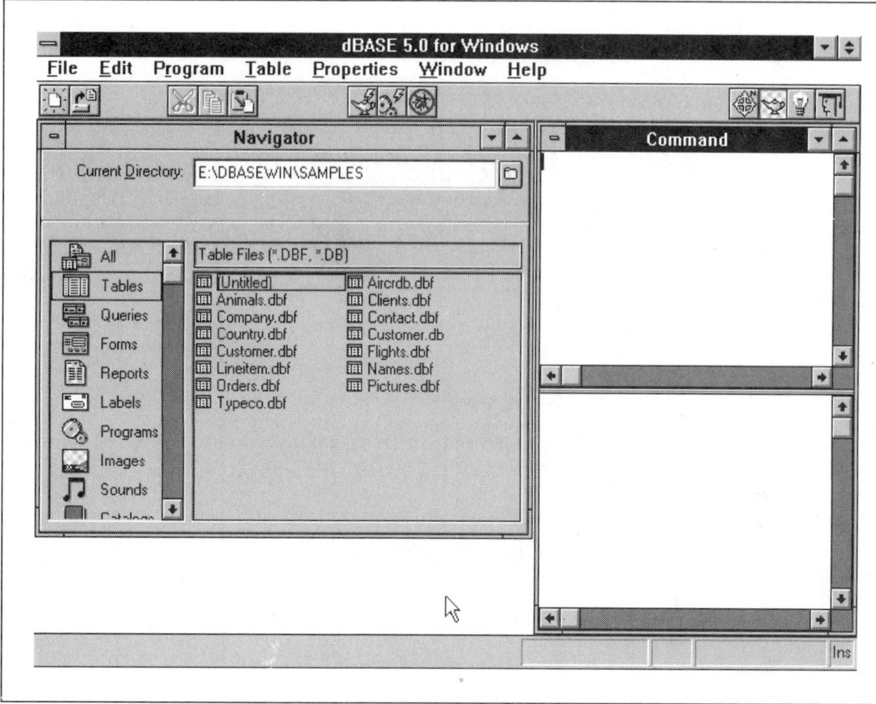

NOTE

As with all standard Microsoft Windows programs, you can also double-click on the System button or choose the eXit option from the Files menu to exit the application.

Now, let's reenter dBASE for Windows, with keyboard commands. Sooner or later, your mouse will break, or you'll be using a mouseless laptop on a plane trip, or whatever. It pays to know the keyboard alternatives.

In the Program Manager, press Ctrl-Tab to cycle from one group to the next. Press Ctrl-Shift-Tab to cycle in the other direction. Don't be surprised if the "cycle" doesn't make much sense; you could go in a logical pattern or hop around quite crazily. Stop when you get to the dBASE for Windows group. In a group, the arrow keys select a program. Use yours to select dBASE for Windows.

With dBASE for Windows selected, you can choose File ➤ Run to start dBASE for Windows (Alt-F then R, or F10, F, and then R). You can also press Enter. Your Enter key may be labeled Return. At any rate, it's located on the right, where an electric typewriter's carriage-return key is found.

Are you back in dBASE for Windows, looking at a screen similar to the one in Figure 2.2? Good. Now press Alt-F4 to exit back to the Program Manager. Throughout the book, we'll repeat a lot of operations with both mouse and keyboard methods, as we just did.

▸▸ TIP

If you want to be a real WinMeister, get Robert Cowart's *Mastering Windows,* also from SYBEX. See how many times you can get into and out of dBASE for Windows without repeating your keystrokes and mouse clicks.

▸ Making a Working Directory

You can make your working directory on any hard disk drive (or floppy disk drive, but it will be slow) where you normally store your work. It doesn't need to be on the drive that holds dBASE for Windows.

In this example, we'll show you how to make a \DBWORK directory on the D: drive. If D:\DBWORK is convenient for you, copy us exactly. If you want to put it somewhere else, that's fine, too. Just makeyour own adjustments to these instructions. If you're working on a network and you don't have a local disk, you'll need advice from your network administrator.

Follow these steps to create a working directory:

1. In Windows, run the File Manager (its default location is in the Main group).
2. Choose File ➤ Create Directory ..., and you'll see a dialog box.
3. At the Name prompt, enter **D:\DBWORK**.
4. Press Enter or click on OK. Now your directory is ready.
5. Press Alt-F4 to exit the File Manager.

With your new work directory ready, let's tell dBASE for Windows where we'll be working. Start dBASE for Windows and then choose Properties ➤ Desktop. You'll see the display shown in Figure 2.3.

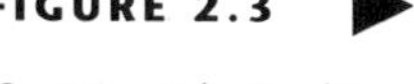

FIGURE 2.3

Country tab, Desktop Properties dialog box

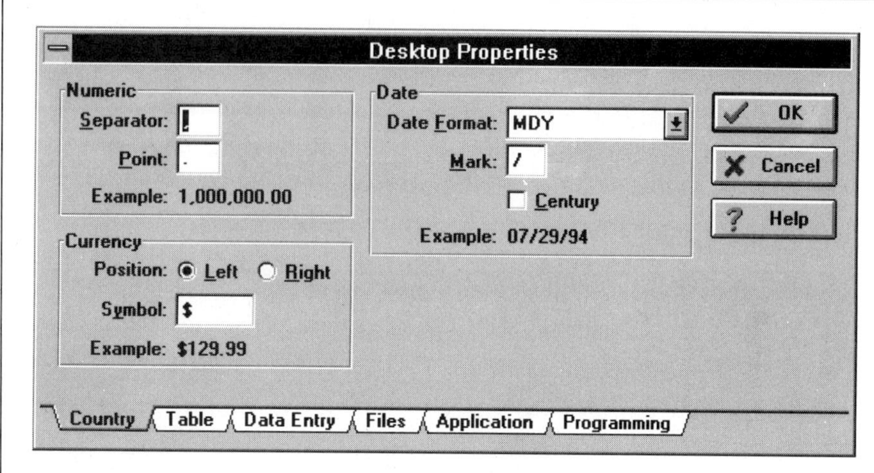

One of the settings that dBASE for Windows remembers between sessions is the last tab you used in the Desktop Properties dialog box. Your dBASE for Windows might open on another tab. If it did, click on the Country tab.

As you can see, the Country tab of the Desktop Properties dialog box gives you choices related to national preferences. dBASE for Windows defaults to local settings in many countries; it has been an international product for many years. If your defaults are not appropriate for your country, you'll want to look at the settings you can choose from here.

Of course, we said that we were going to tell dBASE for Windows where we were working, but we meant where on the disk, not where in the world. Look at the bottom of this dialog box, and you'll see a series of tabs:

Click on these tabs to look at some of the options available to you.

►► **NOTE**

You can change the Desktop Properties tabs using the keyboard, although it's inconvenient. Press the Tab key until your current tab is highlighted, and then use the ← and → keys, followed by Enter, to change tabs. We'll assume you have a mouse for these instructions.

Click on Files to see the dialog box shown in Figure 2.4.

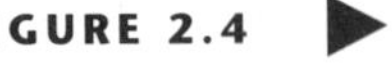

FIGURE 2.4

Files tab, Desktop Properties dialog box

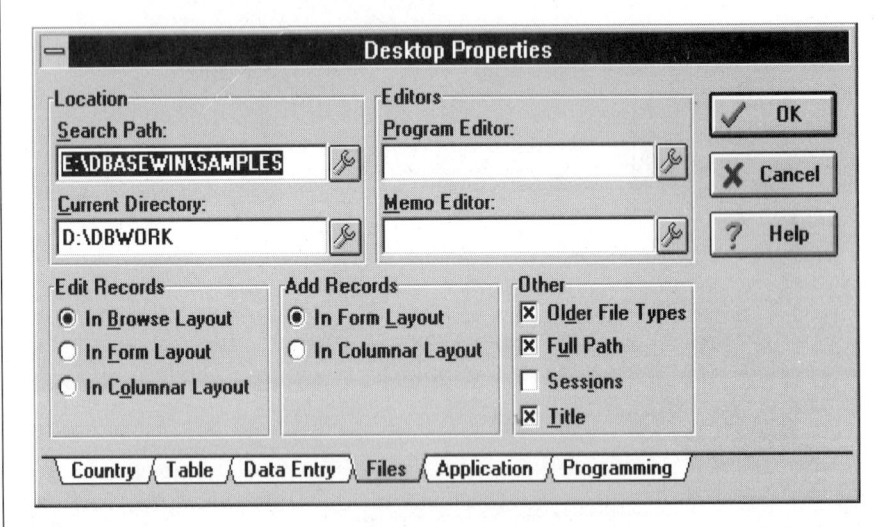

Enter **D:\DBWORK** (or the drive and directory you selected) in the Current Directory box, as you see in Figure 2.4. Then click on OK or press Enter. You'll now be back to the main dBASE for Windows screen, probably showing the Navigator and Command windows. We're ready to begin.

▶▶ Lesson 1: You Create a Table

If you aren't in dBASE for Windows, start it now. We'll need the Navigator. If it's not on your screen, choose Window ➤ 1 Navigator. The Navigator is shown in Figure 2.5.

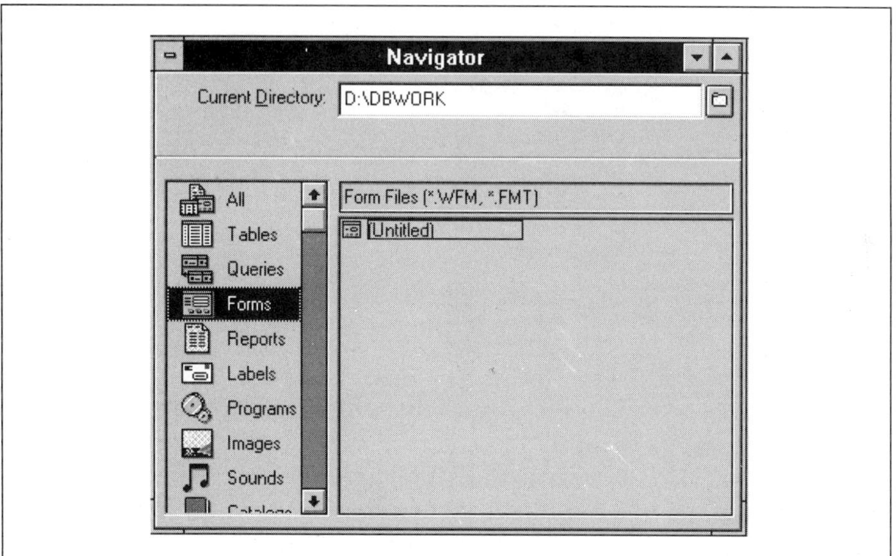

FIGURE 2.5 ▶

The Navigator set to \DBWORK

If you weren't able to enter your working directory via the Properties ➤ Desktop dialog box, you can click on the button to the right of current directory name:

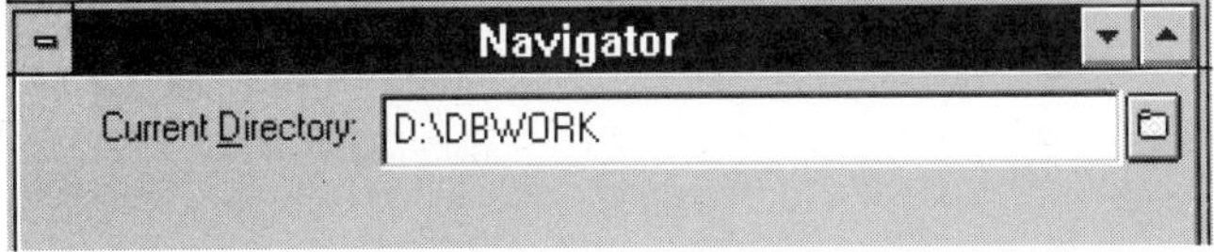

Clicking on this button displays the Choose Directory dialog box. You can select a drive by clicking the down button next to the drive (in the lower-right area of the dialog box) and a directory by clicking on the directory in the left window. Press Enter or click on OK when your directory is set. With that done, let's take a good look at the Navigator.

► Navigating with the Navigator

The Navigator can be your main control tool, from which you get around in dBASE for Windows. As you see, the Navigator has entries for all the main dBASE for Windows file categories:

Use the ↑ and ↓ keys to move through these selections. In each case except All, you'll see a single entry, named Untitled. When you select All, you see one Untitled icon for every file type. (We're assuming that you haven't starting adding files to your \DBWORK directory.)

►► TIP

The default path is set to the \DBASEWIN\SAMPLES directory. You can leave this setting (Properties\ Desktop, Files tab) but change the current directory in the Navigator to D:\DBWORK. With the Navigator selected, use Properties ➤ Navigator and uncheck the Use Supplemental Search Path option.

Having just Untitled entries shows that you have switched dBASE for Windows into your new, empty \DBWORK directory. Now let's consider the job at hand.

We want to create a data table to hold a list of people. We're starting with a list of people since almost every system we have ever seen has at least one list of people: employees, customers, sales contacts, or whatever. We're fairly sure that for the work you're doing, you'll want a list of people, too.

▶ Designing Offline

The first step in defining a table doesn't involve your computer. Working in your mind's eye, or on your favorite doodle pad, ask yourself what problem or problems you want your database to solve. Then consider the different types of things you need to have some data about.

Let's assume that one type of thing about which you want data is people. Now, for each type of thing, such as people, consider the detailed data you'll want. Remember that collecting data is expensive. Separate the data you would like to have from the data that you need. When you have a list of the data you really need, you're ready to turn your computer on and start up dBASE for Windows.

▶▶ **NOTE**

Actually, dBASE's Table Structure tool is flexible and visual. You might want to use it right from the start for designing your tables. But every time you enter a field, think about the expense of collecting and maintaining the data, even if the only expense is your own time.

▶ Using the Table Structure Tool

We've already thought through the data we want in our People table, and we suggest you follow our recommendations for this short course. But as we work, bear in mind that we're using an American address and telephone format. Use fields and field sizes that correspond to your own country. Add a Country field if you'll be keeping track of an international group of people.

You use the Table Structure tool to create a list of the fields in your table. Figure 2.6 shows the field list for our People table. You can make whatever adjustments are necessary for your own data.

FIGURE 2.6 

Field definitions for the People table in the Table Structure tool

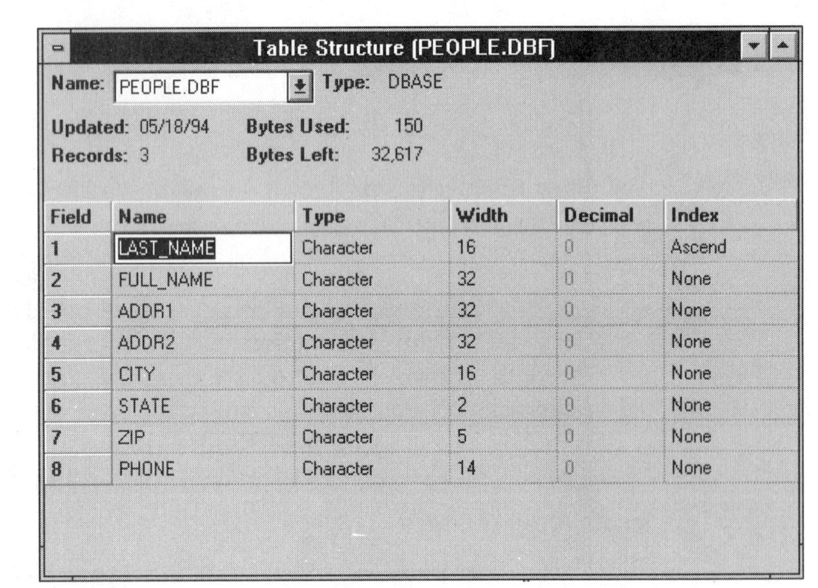

Field	Name	Type	Width	Decimal	Index
1	LAST_NAME	Character	16	0	Ascend
2	FULL_NAME	Character	32	0	None
3	ADDR1	Character	32	0	None
4	ADDR2	Character	32	0	None
5	CITY	Character	16	0	None
6	STATE	Character	2	0	None
7	ZIP	Character	5	0	None
8	PHONE	Character	14	0	None

Follow these steps to create a field list:

1. In the Navigator, select Tables. Press Enter, or double-click on Untitled. This brings up the Table Structure tool.
2. Type **LAST_NAME**. Note that you can only have letters, digits, and underscore characters in a field name. No spaces or other punctuation are allowed. Press Tab to move to the next field.
3. All our fields are for Character data, so just press Tab to move from the Type field to the Width field.
4. In the Width field, type **16**. You can also spin this number higher or lower by clicking the mouse on the up or down arrow. Holding the left mouse button down while the cursor is on either of these arrows will spin the number quickly. Press Tab to move to the next field.

5. You skipped right over the Decimal field (since decimal places do not apply to character data). You are now at the Index field. Press Tab again; we won't be using indexes in this chapter.
6. Continue entering the field names and widths shown in Figure 2.6 (with whatever changes are necessary for your own data). You can use the Backspace key to correct typing mistakes. If you don't notice a mistake until you have left a field, you can use Shift-Tab to back up or Tab to move forward. Note that Tab and Shift-Tab won't leave an empty name field. Use the ↑ key to move out of the last, unwanted field name.
7. After you've finished creating the field list, press Ctrl-W (as in Write to disk) to save your table definition. You get the Save Table dialog box.
8. Type **People** in for the name, and then press Enter or click on OK. The extension .DBF is supplied for you. (Without this extension, dBASE wouldn't know that the file was a dBASE table.)
9. Tell the Add or Generate Records dialog box that you're Done.

Before we leave the Table Structure tool to add some data, let's have some fun.

▶ Rearranging and Deleting Fields

Use the Navigator to select the People table. Press Shift-F2 or right double-click to return to the Table Structure tool.

Press Tab or press ↓ to get to the last field. Then press ↓ to add a new row. Type a dummy name, like **DUMMY**. Don't bother tabbing out of the Name column.

Now, with the mouse, move the pointer to the field number (just to the left of the name you just typed). Press and hold down the left button. The mouse pointer turns into a hand (as shown in the margin). This grabs the field. Holding the mouse down, move this field up and down with the mouse. You can drag the field anywhere you like.

Put it into the middle of your table structure and release the mouse button. It drops right in, and the other fields are renumbered appropriately. You can use this technique to add new fields anytime you want. Of course, now you have a field you don't want in the middle of your table structure. Is this a problem? No.

Use the same technique to grab the extra field and drag it to the bottom of the table. With the cursor in the Name column, use Backspace to erase the field name. Then press ↑, and the field is gone.

With this technique, do any serious arranging that you want. When you're satisfied with your table structure (it should look like Figure 2.6, adjusted for your country), choose File ➤ Save. (This is the same as Ctrl-S.)

This time your work was just saved; you didn't see the Save Table dialog box because dBASE for Windows now knows the name of your table.

Exit from the Table Structure tool by pressing Ctrl-F4 or by double-clicking on the Table Structure System button (the button in the Table Structure window, not dBASE's main window System button).

Back in the Navigator, you now see Untitled and People files. You've defined and created your first dBASE for Windows table. Ready for a break?

▸ Leaving Your Work Safely Filed

To take a break, exit from dBASE for Windows. dBASE will remind you if you have any unsaved work. If you exit with a new table structure defined but not saved, for example, dBASE for Windows will give you a chance to save it before exiting. This ensures that all your data is written to files and that the files are properly closed.

Actually, that's not quite true. dBASE has told Windows and DOS about all the data that it wants written and which files to close. But Windows and DOS may still have them open, with data cached for performance reasons. To be sure you work is safely filed, exit from Windows and wait several seconds before turning your computer off.

▸▸ Lesson 2: You Add and Change Data

Ready to use the People table? We'll continue to navigate with the Navigator. We'll open the table and work with the Table Records tool to add our data.

▶ Using the Table Records Tool

Internally, dBASE for Windows stores your table definitions as a table. This means that the Table Structure tool you used to define your table is just a specialized version of the Table Records tool. So you've already got the basics of entering and changing data.

To get started, if the table isn't already open, follow these steps:

1. Return to the Navigator (if you aren't already there) and select Tables.
2. Tab into your list of tables. It should have Untitled and People. Using the arrow keys, select People and press Enter.
3. Open the table for adding records. Either choose Navigator ➤ Add Records from the menu, or right-click and choose Add Records from the Speed menu.
4. You're now looking at the Table Records tool, but it might not look familiar. The Table Structure tool used the Browse Layout view. If your view is not familiar, select View ➤ Browse Layout. Your table should look similar to the one in Figure 2.7.

FIGURE 2.7 ▶

The empty People table in Browse Layout view

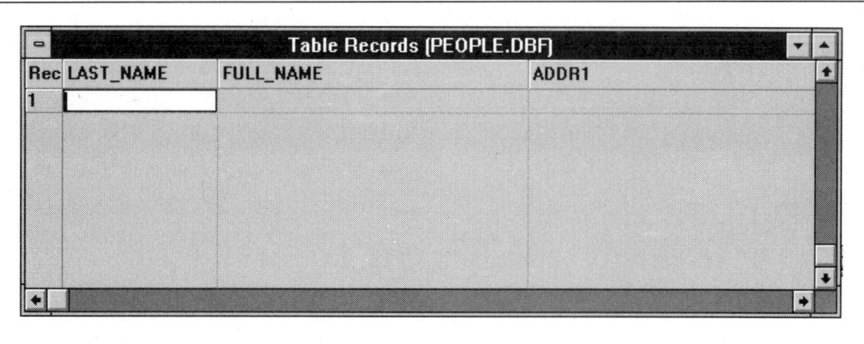

▶ Entering Some Data

Enter a few records, using Tab and the other keys and clicks you used in the Table Structure tool. The columns will scroll in the Browse Layout view as you move from one to the next.

Do you feel cramped? Click on the Maximize button in the upper-right corner of the Table Records window. This gives you a little more room, but all the data still doesn't fit inside a single screen.

Here are some ways to speed up your data entry:

- Type as fast as you can. Backspace corrections are easy to make on the fly. You'll make other corrections easily when you proofread your work.
- dBASE for Windows saves your data as you enter it. Starting a new record automatically saves the old one. So just keep going.
- Put the data in whatever order is most convenient. Later, you can use indexes to get the data in alphabetical or any other order you want.

Here are some ways to slow down your data entry:

- Don't look at the column headings. Type the right data into the wrong fields.
- Go so slowly that you never, ever make a mistake.

Here are some ways to make sure that your data is correct:

- Proofread everything carefully.
- Get a second opinion. A co-worker will catch mistakes that you miss.

With these tips in mind, enter several records. Use your own Rolodex or card file.

▸ Taking a Different Look

Now that you've got some data, let's look at it in different ways.

To see a single record, choose View ➤ Columnar Layout. That's a better view of a single record. While we're checking, try View ➤ Form Layout, too. (This is very different from the great-looking forms we'll create with the Form Designer tool.)

These views are also available directly from the speedbar. Click on each of these three icons to switch to the different views:

When you are comfortable with the different views, return to the Browse Layout view (click on the leftmost of the speedbar view icons or choose View ➤ Browse Layout).

▶▶ **NOTE**

As you move your mouse pointer through the speedbar buttons, descriptions of the buttons appear on the status bar at the bottom of the window.

▶ Customizing the Browse Layout View

There's an inherent conflict here that no amount of clever programming can get around. If you want to view lots of records, you need a browse-type view. But if you show your records this way, each whole record probably won't fit across the screen. However, dBASE for Windows does what it can to help by letting you adjust field widths manually.

With your mouse in a record, move slowly to the vertical bar between two fields. When you are right on the bar, the cursor shape changes:

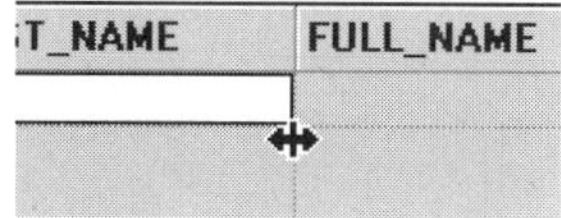

This is the field width adjustment cursor shape. Now you can drag to change the field width. Hold the left mouse button down and slide the mouse either left or right. Use this technique to shrink each of your fields.

With the Browse Layout view maximized (press Alt-hyphen ➤ Maximize or click on the window's Maximize button), make each column smaller, working from left to right. You should be able to fit most of the record within the width of your screen.

►► **NOTE**

Skinny columns don't lose data. The size of the underlying data field isn't changed when you adjust the visible field width.

► Getting Around in the Table

In each of the record layout views, new navigation buttons appear on the speedbar:

These move you one record at a time, one page of data at a time, or to either end of the file, as the icons suggest.

In the Browse Layout view, try these buttons. You'll see that they work just as you think they would in most cases. If you're already on the last record and you click on the right arrow icon, you'll be asked if you want to add more records. Choose No for now.

Click on the speedbar button for the Columnar Layout view (or choose View ➤ Columnar Layout) and try these buttons again. You should be moving around with ease. You'll see that the same question about adding data appears in the same situation as in the Browse Layout view. You can also test this in the Form Layout view if you like.

► Changing Data

Did you notice that the address of the third person in your table is wrong? (Actually, it's probably just fine, but bear with us for a moment.) If you could get to the address field of the third record, you could fix it.

Here are some ways to get to the field you want to correct:

- In Columnar or Form Layout view, click on the speedbar button for the beginning of file, then click on the speedbar button that moves to the next record, twice. Click on the address field.
- In Columnar or Form Layout view, press Ctrl-PgUp to get to the first record in the table. Then press PgDn twice to get to the third record. Press Tab until you are in the address field.
- In Browse Layout view, click on the page up or page down speedbar buttons to get the data that you want to change on the screen. Then click on the erroneous field. For the third record, of course, click on the speedbar button for the beginning of file.
- In Browse Layout view, use the PgUp or PgDn keys to get the erroneous data on the screen. Then use the ↑ and ↓ keys to change from record to record. Use Tab and Shift-Tab to navigate left and right among the fields.

Whatever method you use to get to the field, you can use the ← and → keys to position your cursor within the field. You can use the Del key to delete characters. The new characters you type will either overstrike existing characters or be inserted in front of the characters that are already there. Pressing Ins toggles between Overstrike and Insert modes. Your current mode is shown in the status bar, in the lower-right corner of the screen.

▶ Printing the Table

In Lesson 5 later in this chapter, we'll use the Crystal Reports tool to make a nice-looking report. But in some cases, you may just want dBASE for Windows to print your table quickly, without any work on your part. There are two ways to do this:

- The fourth speedbar icon shows a printer with paper coming out. Click on this icon (shown in the margin) to see the Print Records dialog box.
- Choose File ➤ Print to get to the same dialog box.

To print all the records, click on OK or press Enter in the Print Records dialog box.

When you print your records this way, if your fields don't fit on a single line, dBASE for Windows prints as many pages as required. You can tape the pages together to show the full table. (Perhaps wrapping the records to fit on a single page would have been a better choice; having the program ask would be better still.)

To save all your work (or at least to get close; as we said before, Windows and DOS have something to say about this, too), leave the Table Records tool by any of the standard Windows exits:

- Double-click on the Table Records System button.
- Click on the Table Records System button and choose Close.
- Get to the System menu by pressing Alt-hyphen and choose Close.
- Press Ctrl-F4.

Or you can exit from dBASE for Windows without bothering to first leave the Table Records tool, by any of the following standard exits:

- Double-click on the dBASE for Windows System button.
- Click on the dBASE for Windows System button and choose Close.
- Choose File ➤ Exit.
- Press Alt-F4.

►► Lesson 3: You Query Your Data

With only a small amount of data, the ability to do fast queries (find all the people in your list who live in California, for example) is not important. But as the size of your table grows, query time becomes critical. This is one place the Query tools come into play.

But there's another use for the Query Designer and Query Results tools. We think that the use of the name *Query* is misleading. Perhaps the more important use of the Query Designer is to establish different views of your data.

▶ Using the Query Designer Tool

For this lesson, let's establish a view of our People table that skips the address information. This will be a handy one when you want to find a phone number. These are the steps to get to the Query Designer to create this view:

1. From the Program Manager, start dBASE for Windows.
2. Open the Navigator (choose Window ➤ 1 or click on the compass icon on the speedbar) if it isn't already on your screen.
3. Select Queries (click on it, or tab to the list of file types and use the ↓ key to highlight Queries).
4. Click on Untitled in the file window, or press Tab to enter the file window and press Enter to select Untitled.
5. In the Open Table Required dialog box, choose PEOPLE.DBF and click on OK or press Enter. You are now in the Query Designer, which should look like the window in Figure 2.8.

FIGURE 2.8 ▶

Query Designer with PEOPLE.DBF loaded

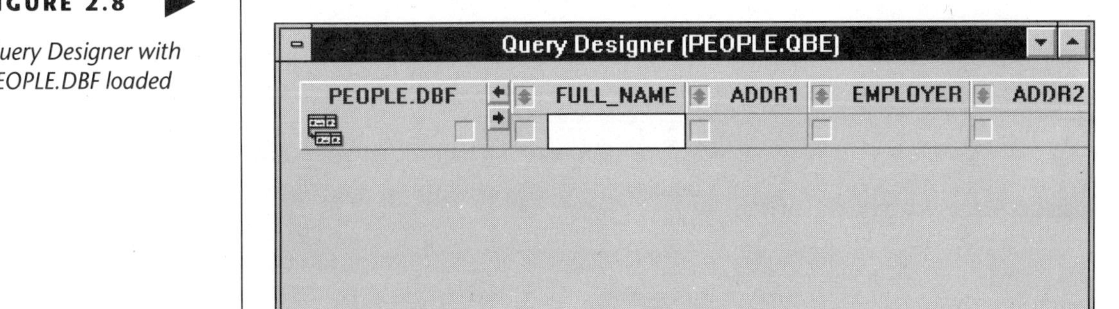

We love the Query Designer, but if you can't make head or tail of it at first, you're not alone. It's powerful and fast once you get used to it, but it's a bit short on description at first.

To begin with, you see a list of fields (as many as will fit), starting with the first one. Begin by clicking on the left and right arrows just to the right of PEOPLE.DBF. These arrows scroll the list of fields, which gives you access to your whole table.

Click on the little check box just to the left of these arrows. If you got the right one, every field in your table is now checked. Click on this box again to remove the check marks from every field.

Creating Views

Now we're ready to create a view.

1. Click on the check box (that's the lower of the two squares in each field, as shown in the margin) in the LAST_NAME field. It is now checked.
2. Using the arrows to shift your columns as needed, click on the check box to select FULL_NAME, CITY, and HOME_PHONE.

3. Click on the lightning icon in the speedbar (shown in the margin) to run this query. You should now be looking at the Query Results Table view, similar to the one in Figure 2.9.

FIGURE 2.9

Query Results for selected fields in PEOPLE.DBF

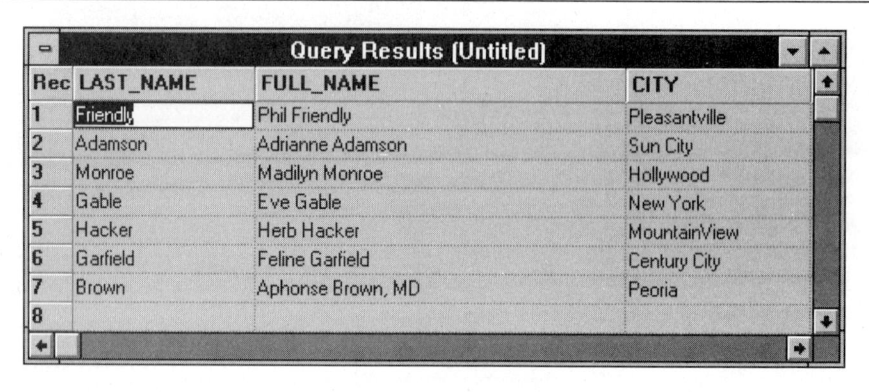

Query Results (Untitled)

Rec	LAST_NAME	FULL_NAME	CITY
1	Friendly	Phil Friendly	Pleasantville
2	Adamson	Adrianne Adamson	Sun City
3	Monroe	Madilyn Monroe	Hollywood
4	Gable	Eve Gable	New York
5	Hacker	Herb Hacker	MountainView
6	Garfield	Feline Garfield	Century City
7	Brown	Aphonse Brown, MD	Peoria
8			

Your query established a view that selected some pertinent fields from PEOPLE.DBF. This view is convenient for searching for home phone numbers. Next, we'll query this view to find all the people in our table who live in New York.

4. To switch back to the Query Designer, click on the drafting tools icon (shown in the margin), to the right of the lightning icon.

Back in the Query Designer, we want to query our PEOPLE.DBF file to find just the people who live in New York. (Pick a city where you have more than one person in your own table.) For this, you can work from the keyboard.

5. Press Tab enough times to get to the CITY field. In the empty box, type = "**New York**". (Use your own city, of course.)

For this query, you type a relational operator first. In this case, the = operator selects values that are equal. You'll meet the other relational operators in Chapter 12. The relational operator is followed by a value or expression. In this case, the value is a character string, which you must enclose in quotation marks in dBASE for Windows.

6. Choose View ➤ Query Results. You'll be looking at just the people who live in New York.

►► **NOTE**

As you see when you do choose View ➤ Query Results, pressing F2 is a shortcut. So, you can use the menu command, the keyboard shortcut, or the speedbar button with the lightning icon to run your queries.

7. If you would like a printed list, click on the printer icon, press Ctrl-P, or choose File ➤ Print. In the last lesson, we'll make a nicer looking report.

► *Leaving the Query Designer Tool*

When you exit from the Query Designer, you'll be asked if you want to save your query. Before you do this, remove the city restriction from the table. To do this, follow these steps:

1. Press Shift-F2 (or click on the speedbar button with the drafting tools icon) to switch from Query Results back to the Query Designer.

2. Press Tab until you are in the CITY field.
3. Hold down the Del key until the field is empty.
4. Press Ctrl-F4 to leave the Query Designer. You'll be asked if you want to save the query. Choose Yes.
5. In the Save File dialog box, call this query **Phones**. just type it into the file name field. dBASE for Windows will add the extension .QBE.
6. Press Enter or click on OK, and you're back in the Navigator, ready for our next lesson.

►► Lesson 4: You Create a Custom Form

dBASE for Windows has a marvelous Form Designer. Working with the Form Expert, you can design a good-looking form for your data entry in a matter of minutes. More important, it is the Form Designer that lets you add rules that reject invalid data. This is a key tool for building database systems.

For this lesson, however, we are going to settle for creating an attractive form. We'll begin by asking the Form Expert to do the bulk of the work for us.

► Using the Form Expert

The Form Expert will introduce itself every time you create a new form. To get into this Expert, follow these steps:

1. In the Navigator, select Forms. (Click on Forms or press Tab to reach the file type column and then use the ↑ or ↓ key to get there.)
2. In the file list, select Untitled. (Double-click on the Untitled item or press Tab, then Enter.)
3. You are now in the Form Expert. You see a pair of radio buttons that let you choose Expert Assistance or Blank Form. The default choice, Expert Assistance, is precisely what we want, so you can proceed. Click on the Next button or press Alt-N.

The Form Expert will now ask you some questions, and then prepare a default form based on those answers. Once it has finished its work, you'll have a preliminary form in the Form Designer, ready for minor touch-up work.

4. You are first asked to choose a file. To get all the fields in the file, choose PEOPLE.DBF. (Type the name in the file name field or double-click on the name.) If you chose PEOPLE.QBE, you would have only those fields that you checked in the Query Designer.
5. Choose Next to proceed.
6. You are now at the field selection panel, as shown in Figure 2.10.

FIGURE 2.10

Selecting fields in the Form Expert

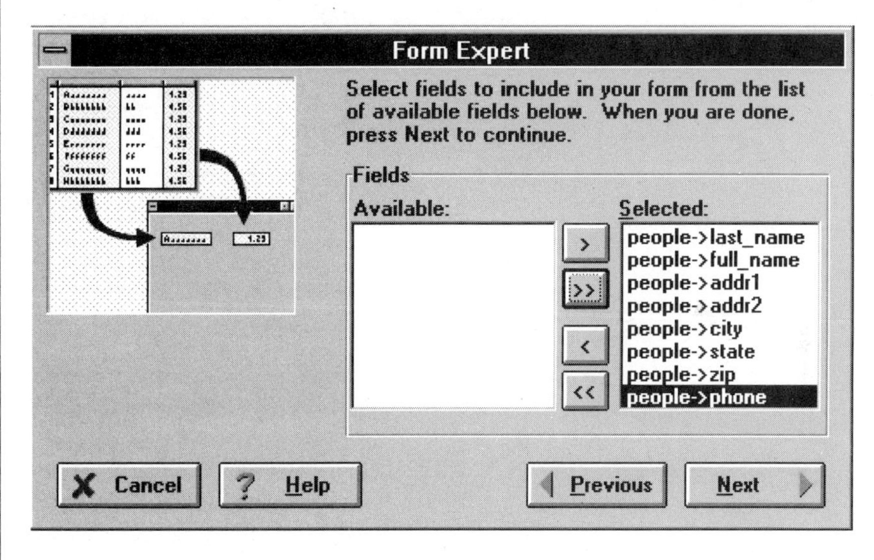

This panel is not as self-explanatory as the others. You run it by clicking the arrow buttons to send fields from the Available box to the Selected box.

7. Click on the **>>** button to select all fields. (The **<<** button deselects all fields; the **>** and **<** buttons move one field at a time in the indicated direction.)

8. Choose Next to proceed. (Next is not enabled if there aren't any fields in the Selected box.)
9. The next panel asks you to choose a layout. The default choice is Columnar Layout, which is usually just right. Just choose Next and proceed.
10. The final panel allows you to select fonts and colors. Choose any that you like. Note that the location of the Next button is now taken by a Build button with a lightning icon. Choose it when you have made your choices.

The best-looking forms use color sparingly (unlike the Form Expert defaults!), and we suggest that you adopt this policy. We like black text on a light-gray background, with white entry fields. With these choices, any colored icons or text will really stand out. On the other hand, the default font choices that the Form Expert suggests are good ones. We accept the defaults and use other fonts only for decorative effects.

► Using the Form Designer

You are now in the Form Designer, looking at a setup like the one shown in Figure 2.11. You see the Form Designer in the foreground, with its two related tools: the Object Properties Inspector and the Controls palette.

If you don't have these windows on your screen, choose View ➤ Object Properties. You'll see these choices:

Form Designer Properties...	
Cut	Ctrl+X
Copy	Ctrl+C
Paste	Ctrl+V
√ Controls	
√ Object Properties	
Procedures	

FIGURE 2.11

Form Designer with the People form

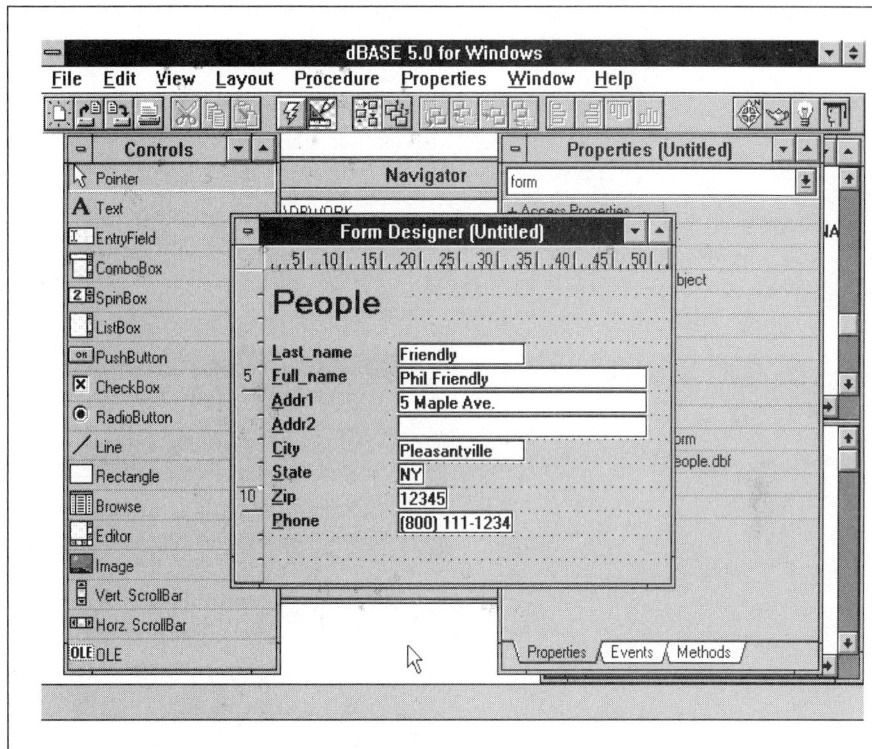

You want Controls and Object Properties checked, and Procedures left unchecked. If this isn't the case, click on the unchecked one(s) to get them checked. Click on Procedures, if it is checked, to get it unchecked. On each click, the named item will be activated (or deactivated). Click on the Form Designer and right-click again to return to the Speed menu.

WARNING

The Form Designer is a very graphical tool. It's only barely possible to use a few of its features without a mouse or other pointing device. We recommend that you don't use it if you don't have access to a mouse.

A Form (we'll capitalize the names of the dBASE for Windows built-in objects and their properties) is an object that contains other objects.

The title *People*, for example, is a Text object. All the Form's objects can be moved and sized in the same way.

Let's start by moving the title Text object over to the center. Position your mouse pointer over the *People* title. Click once, and you'll see a standard selection border surround the object. This forms a rectangle with black squares, called *handles*, at the corners and in the middle of each of the sides, as shown in Figure 2.12.

FIGURE 2.12 ▶

Selecting the People Text object

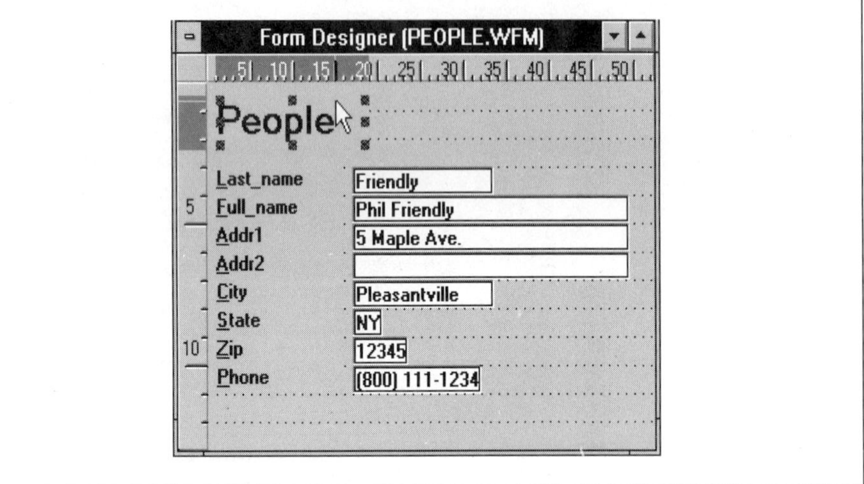

To move the object, place your mouse pointer within this border and drag the object to the top center of your form. As you drag, the mouse pointer changes into the hand icon you've already seen in the Table Structure tool.

If you drag on any of the black squares that appear around a selected object, you can resize the object, just as you can resize a window.

▸▸ **NOTE**

Entryfield objects are automatically sized to fit the fields in your database. See Part 5 for details.

Text objects from the Form Expert are often larger than the text they contain. This makes it easy to change to a larger font. It also means that you'll need to reduce some of your Text objects to avoid overlap. The text will be adjusted automatically within the object, as long as it still fits.

▶ Improving the Form

Not all of our fields conveniently fit, because we asked the Form Expert to build a Columnar Layout form. (If you try a Form Layout form, you'll find that dBASE's choices for positioning are probably not what you would select.) We can make a better-looking form by first stretching the form itself, and then moving the fields and Text objects around.

Try to make your form look something like the one shown in Figure 2.13.

FIGURE 2.13

People form with manual changes

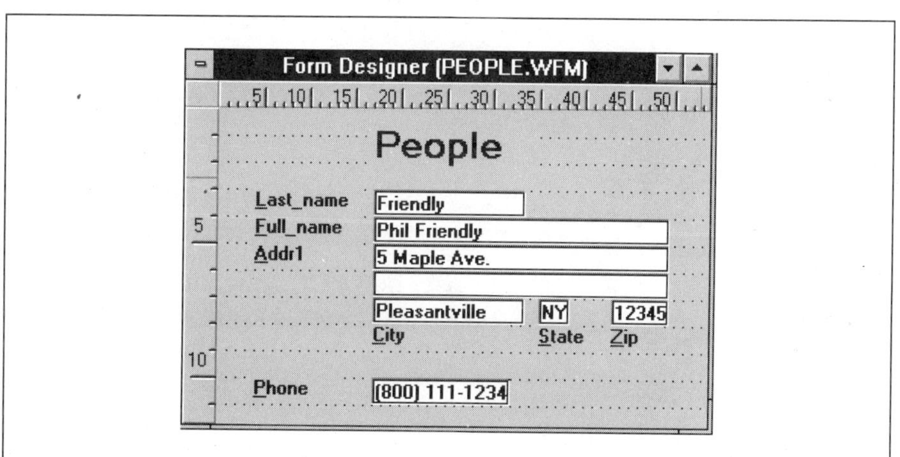

As you work, press Ctrl-S occasionally to save your work. The first time you press Ctrl-S, you'll be asked to choose a file name. Choose People, and your form will be stored as PEOPLE.WFM (Windows ForM). The next time you press Ctrl-S, this file will be resaved under the same name.

You can use the File ➤ Save As choice to save your form under a new name.

► *Using Your New Form*

Like the other dBASE for Windows tools, the Form Designer lets you alternate between Run and Design modes. Again, as with the other tools, you can use F2 and Shift-F2, or you can click on the lightning and design icons on the speedbar.

To use this form, just click on the lightning icon. You're now looking at your data one record at a time in a good-looking form. You can use the same buttons as before to navigate in your table and to add new records. These speedbar buttons are the run and design buttons, the record search and record append buttons, and the four navigation buttons:

In a form layout, there are no full page-movement buttons. Each record is a page on the form.

You can alternate between Design and Run modes as often as you wish to make adjustments to your form. When you're finished, press Ctrl-W in either mode to return to the Navigator.

Your latest changes are saved automatically when you switch from Design mode to Run mode. You don't need to explicitly save your work when changing modes.

▶▶ Lesson 5: You Write a Report

We've already seen that it's simple to print your data. But the results don't win any prizes for appearance. For prize-winning, world-class documents, you can use Crystal Reports. Crystal Reports is a third-party reporting program, licensed by Borland for inclusion in dBASE for Windows.

▶▶ **NOTE**

After licensing Crystal Reports, Borland bought the whole company that made the ReportSmith report writer, which is also a superb reporting program. We expect to see Crystal Reports replaced with ReportSmith in later versions of dBASE for Windows.

Now let's get started. First, in the Navigator, select Reports and double-click on Untitled. This will launch Crystal Reports, a separate program that runs under Windows, outside dBASE for Windows.

Unless you already have a table open, you'll first see the Open Table Required dialog box, shown in Figure 2.14.

FIGURE 2.14 ▶

Choosing a table for Crystal Reports

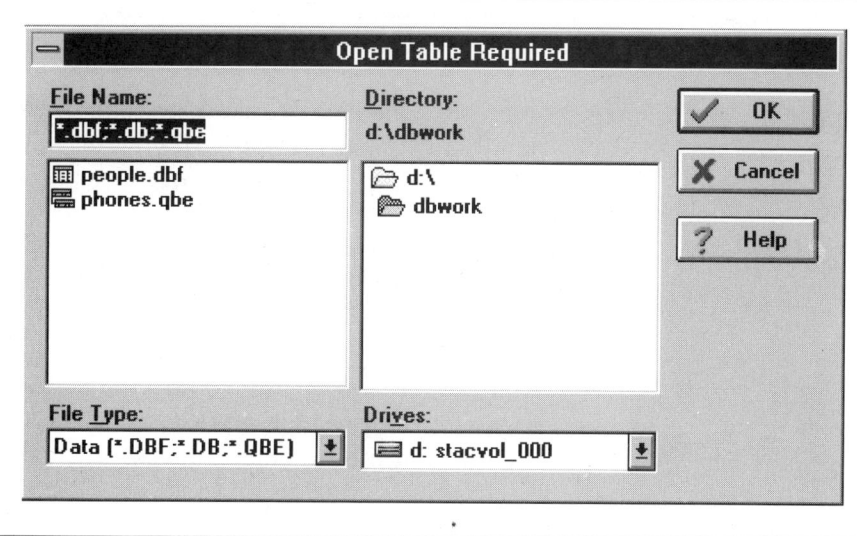

As Figure 2.14 shows, you can choose either a .DBF or a .QBE file. If you were using Paradox tables, you would have .DB files. If your tables were coming from an SQL database, those tables also would be available.

For this lesson, choose PEOPLE.DBF. After you choose the table, Crystal Reports is launched, and you're faced with the somewhat intimidating screen shown in Figure 2.15.

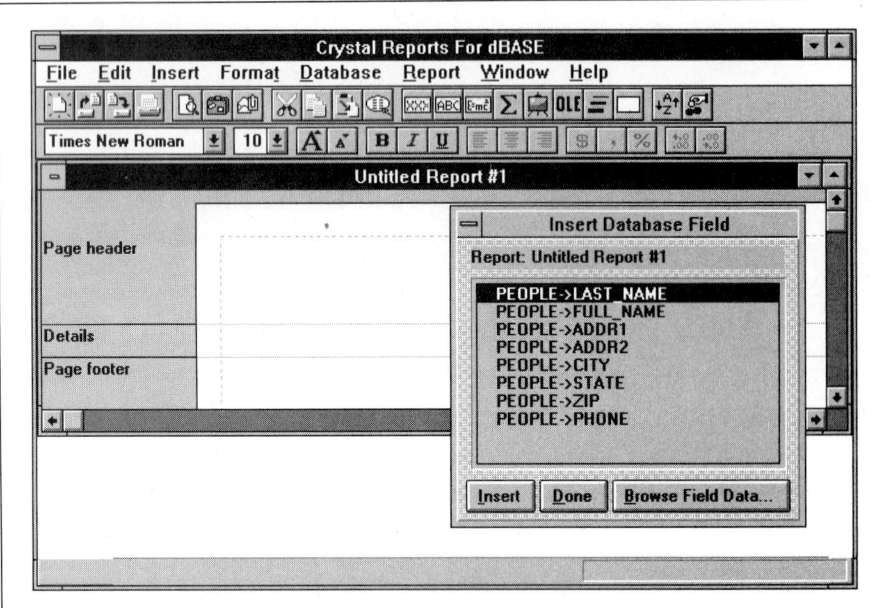

FIGURE 2.15

Crystal Reports opening look

Don't be too worried by what you see here. Crystal Reports is a reasonably friendly, as well as very powerful, reporter. (It was originally marketed as an add-on, so the appearance of sophistication was a selling point.)

▸ Picking Fields

Your first task is to pick the fields you want. Let's do a simple phone list.

1. Start with the LAST_NAME field. Click on the field in the field list, and your mouse pointer turns into a rectangle. When you

move the mouse pointer into the report area, the rectangle expands to reflect the size of the field.

2. Position the LAST_NAME field on the left in the Details band, as shown in Figure 2.16.

FIGURE 2.16

Putting the LAST_NAME field in the Details band

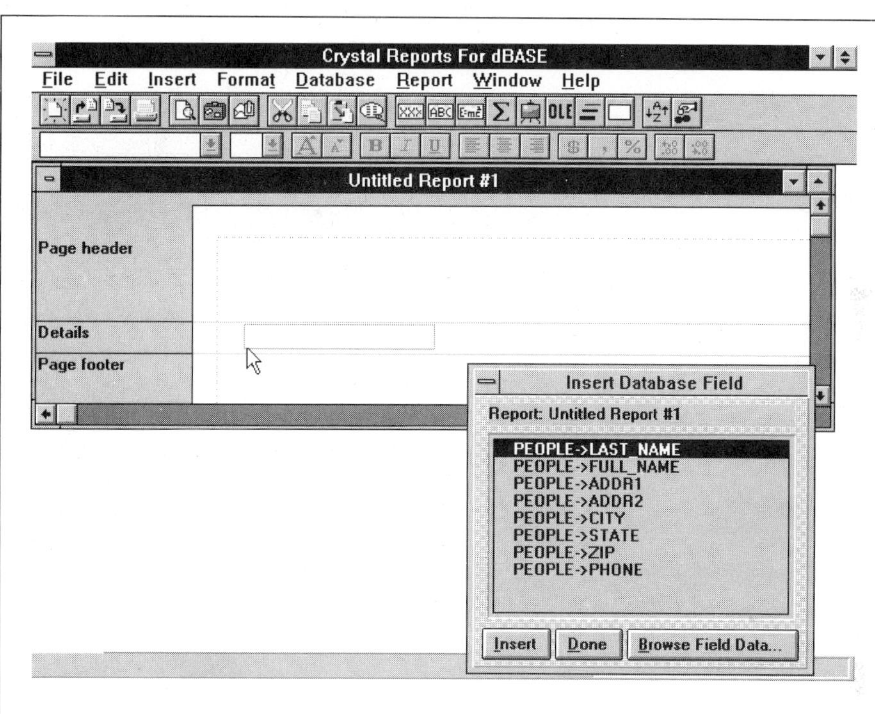

3. When you have the field in place, click the mouse to drop the field. When it drops, you'll see the text *LAST_NAME* hop into the report's Page header area, and the field, also reading *LAST_NAME*, drop into the Details area. When we begin the report, the Page header area will have the text, and the Details area will have data from our table.

4. Continue by placing the fields PHONE and FULL_NAME in the Details band.

5. Click on the Done pushbutton in the Insert Database Field box. Your screen should look like what you see in Figure 2.17.

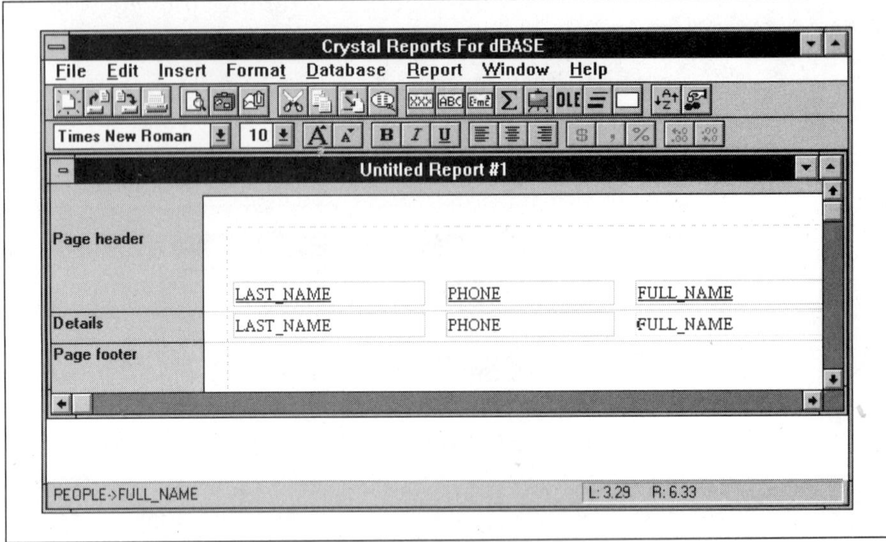

FIGURE 2.17 ▶ *Fields selected in Crystal Reports*

▶ Adding a Title

Now that we have some fields, let's add a title.

1. Choose Insert ➤ Text Field … from the menus, or click on the speedbar icon that says ABC (shown in the margin). You'll see a dialog box titled Edit Text Field.
2. Type **Telephone List** in this box, and then click on Accept or press Alt-A.
3. As when you're placing fields, your mouse pointer now turns into a rectangle. Position it in the Page header area of the report, somewhere near the top center. Click to drop the text field.
4. When you drop the text field, it is selected (outlined in yellow) and has resize handles on both ends. Grab one of the handles and drag it until the field is about twice as wide as it was originally. The title text field should look similar to the one shown in Figure 2.18.

Now we're ready to make that field look like a proper title. In the upper-left area of the Crystal Reports window, you'll see two comboboxes. One selects the font (it says Times New Roman, by default); the one to its right selects the point size. The default size is 10 points.

FIGURE 2.18

The title text field positioned

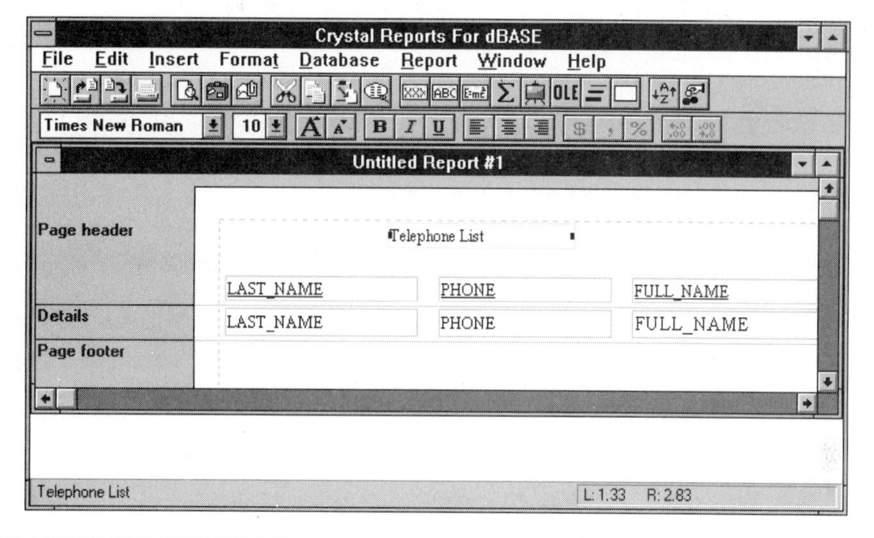

5. Change the point size to something dramatic. We'll use 24 in this lesson.

6. Let's also center the title and use boldface for added emphasis. Click on the speedbar icon with a capital **B** for boldface, and then click on the speedbar icon for centering. These icons (shown in the margin) are in the center of the second speedbar row.

7. Your title should look like the one you see in Figure 2.19. If the title field is not centered above the report, use the mouse to drag it into position, just as you did in the Form Designer. When you drag a field in Crystal Reports, you don't see the mouse pointer turn into the hand icon, but it has the same effect.

FIGURE 2.19

An assertive report heading

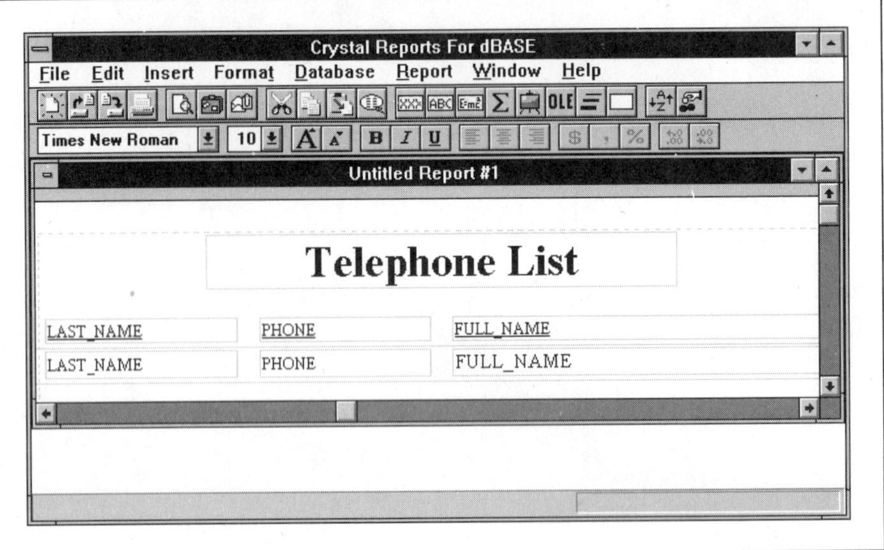

▸▸ **NOTE**

The Crystal Reports speedbar icons in the center of the second row are used to format text. If you use a Microsoft Windows word processor, you're probably using similar buttons. They let you choose boldface, italic, underscored, left-justified, centered, and right-justified formatting.

8. Let's use boldface for our column headings, too. Move the mouse pointer over the LAST_NAME heading and click to select it.
9. Move the mouse pointer to the next column heading, press and hold down the Shift key, then click.
10. Repeat step 9 for the final column. You now have three fields selected.
11. Click on the boldface speedbar icon to convert all three to **boldface.**

Now let's see what our finished product will look like.

▶ Previewing the Report

Before sending the report to the printer, let's look at a sneak preview. Choose File ➤ Print ➤ Window from the menus. This prints the first page of the report in a Preview window. Ours is shown in Figure 2.20.

FIGURE 2.20 ▶

Previewing the report before printing

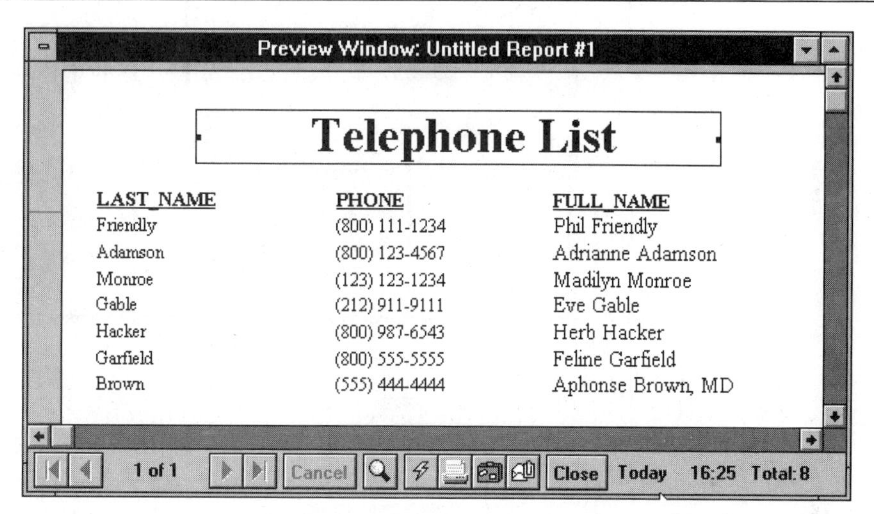

One of the best features of Crystal Reports is that you can manipulate the items in the Preview window, just as you can while defining the report. For example, you can click on an object and drag it to adjust its position. Select an object or group of objects and change the font or style. This is a wonderful capability for working directly with the report exactly as it will appear when printed.

Have everything looking good? One more item to take care of, and then we'll call it an evening.

▶ Sorting the Data

Our telephone list looks good, but it's not in order. There are lots of ways to keep your data in order in dBASE for Windows. Probably the least frequently used way is to have Crystal Reports do it for you, but right now, that capability is just what we need. Follow these steps:

1. From the menus, choose Report ➤ Record Sort Order .... The dialog box shown in Figure 2.21 appears.

FIGURE 2.21

Choosing fields for sorting

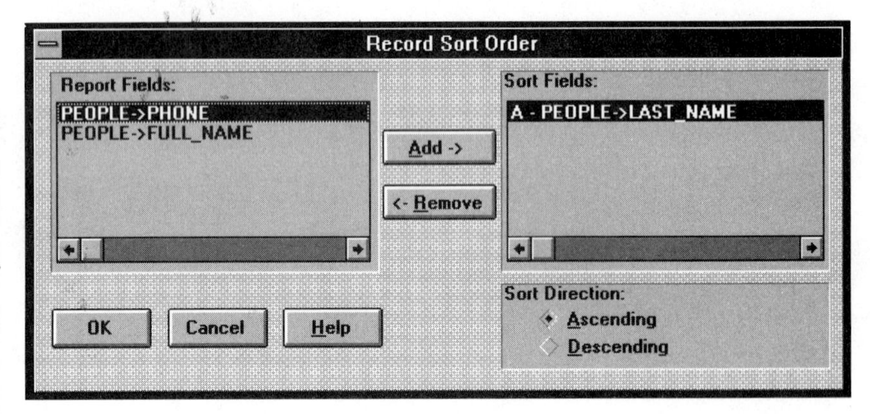

2. With the LAST_NAME field highlighted in the left rectangle, click on the Add button. It pops over to the right, as in Figure 2.21. We only need to sort on this one field.
3. Below the Sort Fields box, you see that you can choose to sort in ascending or descending order. The ascending order default is just what we want. Click on the OK button and wait patiently for a few seconds.

When your report preview is repainted, it is now in properly sorted order. If you are hooked to a printer, you can go ahead and print the report. Of course, we've just scratched the surface, but you should already have something fairly good looking.

4. Exit from Crystal Reports. (Press Ctrl-F4 or choose File ➤ Exit.)
5. Before closing, Crystal Reports will ask you if you want to save your data in your Untitled report. Choose Yes.
6. Finally, since you haven't chosen a title yet, you'll be asked to select one in the File Save As dialog box. We called ours Phone, and it was saved in PHONE.RPT.

►► Summary

Congratulations! You've gone from ground zero through using each of the main tools of dBASE for Windows. You know enough now to go off on your own and use dBASE for Windows for basic database tasks.

You learned that the Navigator and the Command window are complementary control tools. You've used the Navigator in this chapter.

After that, you used the Table Structure tool to define a table. When you were finished, you saw that the Design and Run modes complement each other. You entered Run mode to use your new table definition.

In the Table Records tool, you saw that you can look at your data in Browse, Form, or Columnar Layout view. Using the Browse Layout view, you adjusted your data to fit and then added and edited data.

You used the Query Designer to build a Query view that included only some of your fields. Then you used the Query Designer to select only a portion of your records.

Next, you went into the Form Designer, letting the Form Expert do most of your work in laying out a custom form. You looked at the Object Properties Inspector and the Form Designer's Controls palette. As before, you alternated between Design and Run modes.

Finally, you used Crystal Reports to design and print an attractive, properly sorted report.

Is there anything left? Yes and no. You've met each of the main tools. There are others, such as the Menu Designer, still waiting to be explored.

More important, you've worked with data in a single table. As you'll see in Part 2, the real art of database management comes into play when you draw together data in multiple tables.

Sure, there's lots more, but we're definitely on our way.

▶ ▶ CHAPTER 3

Design Your Database

▸▸ **For** the second and last time, we're going to start with some theory before we dive back into dBASE for Windows. In this chapter, we're going to explain the art of database design.

Of course, we mean the art of relational database design, since dBASE for Windows is built for relational databases. A relational database is a collection of one or more tables of data devoted to a common purpose. The art of database design is the art of using exactly as many tables as you need and filling them with well-chosen fields.

▸▸ *The Art and Science of Database Design*

Nothing else in this book is as important as mastering database design. If you mastered every nook and cranny of dBASE for Windows but couldn't set up good database designs, you wouldn't be able to get good results. You could be able to whip up table structures faster than Julia Child whips up an omelette. You could do three-table queries with as much grace as Michael Jordan doing a lay-up. Your forms could be as elegant as Fred Astaire dancing. It wouldn't matter.

Without a sound database design, the rest of your skills are meaningless. You might as well give Julia Child the basketball.

Without a sound database design, you'll delete one record and others will mysteriously disappear. You'll update one fact, and it will still be wrong on another report. You'll be meticulously careful about entering invoice data, but you'll end up sending an accurate invoice to the wrong customer.

With a sound database design, you can always add another table to your query or improve your forms. Your forms don't need to be elegant; they just need to work for your application.

In this section, we'll discuss the art and science of database design. You'll see that our art builds on the underlying science, as good engineering does in every discipline.

▶ Bad Database Design

Let's begin with the story of Mack, the owner of Peter Bilt Trucking. Mack owns his own tractor with which he hauls other people's trailers from one depot to another in North America.

Mack paid his accountant $5,000 last year. His accountant, who uses Lotus 1-2-3, assured him that he could save about half his fee if he provided his data in a computerized form that could be read into his spreadsheets.

Mack figured that a laptop and dBASE for Windows together cost less than the annual savings, so he decided to computerize. He followed us through Chapter 2, and decided he could dive right in immediately. The design he came up with is shown in Figure 3.1.

FIGURE 3.1 ▶

Mack's table design

Field	Name	Type	Width	Decimal	Index
1	DEPOT_PKUP	Character	32	0	None
2	DATE_PKUP	Date	8	0	None
3	WEIGHT	Numeric	6	0	None
4	DEPOT_DROP	Character	32	0	None
5	DATE_DROP	Date	8	0	None
6	DISTANCE	Numeric	4	0	None
7	INCOME	Numeric	8	2	None
8	FUEL	Numeric	7	2	None
9	OTHER_EXP	Numeric	7	2	None
10	GROSS_PRFT	Numeric	7	2	None

Mack's depot names are enough for Mack. He knows where each one is. He can give his accountant a list of the couple dozen depots where he picks up and delivers. A better system would include a table that showed the depots, but this solution is fine for a personal database.

But Mack has just reinvented a classic in the history of bad database design. It's in the Distance field. Mack's going to make some pickups south of Los Angeles and drop off just outside New York City. That's about 2800 miles. In New York, Mack might make a pickup heading 250 miles to Boston.

The problem is that the distance from the New York depot to the Boston depot never varies. Mack will be keying this distance into every record for a New York to Boston run. The same applies to every other run. There is just about zero probability that Mack will always enter the same distance for the same run.

Mack is going to start recording data in his table at the start of the year. He'll back up the table at the end of the year, then clear it out to start fresh next year.

When he starts, the database has no idea of the length of the Los Angeles to New York run, nor of the New York to Boston run. By the end of the year, it will probably have several different ideas of the lengths of these runs. Mack should really have another table, like the one shown in Figure 3.2.

FIGURE 3.2

The Route table Mack needs

Field	Name	Type	Width	Decimal	Index
1	DEPOT_PKUP	Character	32	0	None
2	DEPOT_DROP	Character	32	0	None
3	DISTANCE	Numeric	4	0	None

With this table, Mack would never put the distance data into his individual run records. The length of each run would be entered just once, and that would be it. The table would be there every year.

But there's a complication introduced when Mack does this. To get the distance for a run combined with the other run data (to compute fuel mileage, for example), Mack will need to join this table to his main table. The design shown here doesn't make that easy.

If Mack had read the rest of this chapter, he would see just how easily joining these tables could be accommodated. He would have his two tables and the correct cross-referencing technique, so that joining them would just take a couple simple mouse clicks in the Query Designer.

Let's learn how to do it right.

▶ The Art of Database Design

There's nothing complex about database design. Your grandmother probably said, "A place for everything, and everything in its place." That simple axiom is exactly what we'll be driving at here.

Suppose you work for a company that sells to other companies. One table in your database will probably be for customers. Now let's consider the art.

Suppose our employer is a company with three divisions. One sharpens knives for butchers, the second provides flour for bakers, and the third sells brass to candlestick manufacturers. Clearly, the data needs are very different.

In the knife-sharpening business, we'll need to know how many knives each butcher has, how frequently each type needs sharpening, and so on. The bakery supply business needs to know how much white flour is sold, how much whole wheat flour is sold, and so on. Similarly, the candlestick manufacturing supply business has its own requirements.

So, we'll want three separate tables: one each for butchers, bakers, and candlestick makers. Or will we?

For each customer, regardless of type, there is some basic information we'll want. We need a name, address, phone number, and other identification details. For each customer, we'll have a credit limit, an outstanding balance, and other common accounting information.

Perhaps we need just one table for customers, but with enough fields so that we can accommodate each of the individual types. (For butchers, we'll skip the entry for whole wheat flour, for example.) Perhaps we need three tables: one for each type of customer. Or perhaps we need a single customer table, and then three other tables geared to the specific needs of each type. Any of these ideas might be right. They'll each provide a sound database design, within the known limits of the science of database design. Next, we'll consider that science and its relationship to the TED method of database design, which we'll explain later in this chapter.

► The Science of Database Design

In this section, we'll introduce the science of database design. If you're totally practical, in a hurry, and want to just get on with it, go ahead and skip this material. You're not going to become a computer scientist by reading this, and we'll necessarily be compressing a large subject into a short space.

In the next section, we'll present a practical, in a hurry, and "let's get on with it" method for designing databases. This section is for those of you who always want to know more about everything and who aren't willing to believe that hurry-up methods are sound unless you've looked at the underlying reasons.

The science of relational database design involves a process called *normalization*. Normal forms, beginning with First Normal Form and ending with Fifth Normal Form, represent progressively better database designs. By "better" we mean less subject to what the scientists call *update anomalies*. For example, in Mack's database (Figure 3.1), deleting a record about an individual run could delete the only record of the distance for a route. Adding a new record may add a duplicated (and not necessarily consistent) distance fact.

First, Second, and Third Normal Forms

If all your data is put into tables, it's in First Normal Form. Since dBASE for Windows defines its data in tables, all .DBF file data is in First Normal Form automatically.

Second and Third Normal Forms define some complex concepts, including functional dependency, full-functional dependency, and transitive dependencies. Fortunately for us, another Normal Form was discovered between the Third and Fourth Normal Forms. This form, called the Boyce-Codd Normal form, lets us skip right over these steps.

Boyce-Codd Normal Form

Until recently, most data analysts struggled with the dependency concepts of Second and Third Normal Forms. Luckily for us, the scientists have proven that a database which is in Boyce-Codd Normal Form is already in Third Normal Form. In fact, it's also been proven that Boyce-Codd Normal Form is superior to Third Normal Form.

A database is in Boyce-Codd Normal Form if it uses only First Normal Form tables and each record in each table has a unique key that identifies each item in the record.

A large body of normalization literature is devoted to the process of selecting record *keys*, which are identifiers that uniquely specify a particular record. These unique identifiers are called *primary* or *candidate* keys. Database scientist Chris Date proposed a system, which we follow here, that greatly simplifies this.

The TED design method, which we'll explain soon, does precisely what Boyce-Codd Normal Form prescribes. It puts data into tables where each record has a unique key that identifies each item in the record.

Higher Normal Forms

The higher Normal Forms include Fourth Normal Form, Projection-Join Normal Form, Domain-Key Normal Form, and Fifth Normal Form. Each eliminates additional possible update anomalies.

Fifth Normal Form was proven to be the highest possible Normal Form. The proponents of Domain-Key Normal Form argue that Fifth Normal is highest in only a limited sense, and that there are entirely different avenues to explore, which may yet yield higher forms.

We think this is true, although the associated mathematics get quite abstract. We're happy to report that designs in Third Normal Form are generally considered adequate for practical software engineering. Our TED system gets to the Boyce-Codd Normal Form, so it is even better.

▸▸ TED Lets You Master Database Design

We use the acronym TED as an *aide memoire* for the three items in our very short list of table types:

- Things
- Events
- Details

These are the three types of tables that together will account for about 90 percent of the tables that you'll see if you spend your entire working life designing databases.

In brief, *Things* are items that you can kick. People, buildings, and products are examples of Things.

Events are not kickable. They happen at a point in time. For example, you sell products to your customers. A patient is admitted to the hospital and assigned a bed.

Details are a necessity of table-based data. If you have more than one of a Thing involved in an Event, you'll need a separate table to record Details. For example, a customer buys several products in one sale. That's one sale Event, but you need a Detail table to keep track of the quantity and price of each Thing purchased.

▸ Things

The easiest way to find out if something in your database is a Thing is to ask if it can be kicked. If the answer is Yes, it's definitely a Thing.

But that's not the real distinguishing characteristic. What really distinguishes Things from other items in our universe is that the Thing is relatively permanent. By relatively permanent, we mean it will have a long duration in the life of your system.

Employees come and go, but they generally are part of your database's universe for a long time once they are hired. The hospital's patients come and go, too, and much more rapidly than employees. Still, you hope that they are still around after getting out of the hospital (when it's time to pay the bill, for instance).

Here are some Things that are quite permanent, but definitely aren't kickable:

- Musical compositions
- Mathematical theorems
- Patents
- Leases
- Philosophical schools of thought

You may have noticed that some of these Things are written on paper. When you design a database, be careful to ignore the pieces of paper and look at the underlying reality. Pythagoras' theorem will be just as true when the last piece of paper on which it was ever written crumbles into dust.

A lease is a contract between parties, which exists in the abstract, even if the paperwork is lost. (Of course, hanging onto the paper can be distinctly helpful if a dispute arises.)

▶ Events

In contrast to a Thing, an Event is instantaneous. It happens at a moment in time. Actually, events are no more instantaneous than Things are permanent. But for the purposes of our database, we can treat them as if they were.

Here are some typical events:

- A customer *purchases* a product
- A patent is *issued*
- A hotel guest *registers*
- An insurance premium is *paid*

You probably see that Events are named by verbs. Things are all nouns. This is another good way of thinking about the items about which you'll be collecting data. Put the nouns in one group and the verbs in another.

Some perfectly useful systems exist without Events. For example, the phone list that we'll be putting together links a set of people (definite Things) to their employers (also Things).

In contrast, Events depend on Things. Let's revisit our list of events, but this time we'll emphasize the Things that participate in each event:

- A *customer* purchases a *product*
- A *patent* is issued (to an *applicant*)
- A *hotel guest* registers
- An insurance (*policy's*) premium is paid (by the *insured*)

Note that sometimes you'll explicitly record the Things that participate in an Event. A *customer* purchasing a *product* is a common example.

Other times, one or more of the Things are implied by your system. For example, if you are keeping a list of patents that your organization has been issued, the applicant is implied—it's your organization.

The same is true of guest registrations at a hotel. If you're creating a registration system for the Regency, each registration by a guest implies that the guest is registering at your hotel. On the other hand, if your system is for a chain of hotels, you'll always include the particular hotel in your registration Event.

Whether the Things are recorded or implied, every Event is an interaction between Things, at a point in time.

▶ Designing with Things and Events

The first step in database design is to make a list of the Things and Events that are important to your system. Remember that collecting data is expensive, even if (or especially if) it's your time at stake. Firmly reject your urge to include "nice to have" Things and Events. Stick to absolutely necessary Things and Events.

Each Thing and Event is a table. Your list of Things and Events is your preliminary overall database design. The first choice is to pick a name. If you're using .DBF or .DB files to store your tables, you're limited to DOS's eight characters. Within that limit, pick the most descriptive name possible.

Then start to work on your field lists. The first field you'll place in each table is an ID field, but postpone that until we begin considering keys.

For each table, carefully list the characteristics that you'll need to record. These are your fields. As you list your fields, note the type and, if necessary, the length and number of decimal places.

TIP

It used to be important to allocate no more space than needed for fields, especially for character fields such as names. With today's disk-compression technology, our fixed-length character fields don't actually take much space if they are mostly blank. So err on the wide side initially.

You'll see in practice that oversized character fields are a nuisance, even if they don't cost much in disk space. For example, a field that is 40 characters wide takes about half the screen's width in a Browse Layout view in the Table Records tool.

You already know that you can drag the bars dividing fields in the Browse Layout view to reduce space. You can still type to the full width of the field, even with the visible width reduced. Later on, you'll meet more ways for bringing this problem under control. So again, err on the high side for widths, but don't overdo it. You can always add more space or take away space you find you don't need.

In Event tables, we'll have a specific technique for referring to the Things that participate in the Event. For now, just note that you need to know, for example, which patient is being admitted in your Admssion table.

▶ Details

There's one more letter in TED: D for Details. When you list your Thing and Event characteristics, sometimes you may note that you need to allow for one (or zero) or more of an item. In a sale, for example, a customer will buy one or more products. (Zero products isn't a sale.)

Zero or more also crops up frequently. Your health insurance plan probably wants to know facts about your employees' dependents. Here you must allow for zero or more dependents per employee.

Whenever you have an indefinite number (zero or more, or one or more), you need to create a Detail table. The most typically cited Detail table is the line-item table for a sales system. In this table, you would have one record for each product. It would include a product identifier (we'll get to that soon), the number sold, and the unit price. The record would also include a reference to the sale which it is part of. We'll get to these references soon.

▶ TED in Action

In this section, we'll take a look at a few databases, so you can get an idea of how TED can be applied. First, we're going to sneak ahead and steal from the next section to introduce you to record identifiers. We'll call these *record IDs*, or just *IDs*. We'll put a column in each table for a record ID. We'll name it after the table and append the two letters *ID*. We'll use an underscore character when it fits. Here are typical examples:

Table	ID Field
Sales	SALES_ID
Admsion	ADMSION_ID
Employee	EMPLOYEEID
People	PEOPLE_ID

In the next section, we'll explain exactly how these fields work. For now, the value in an ID field will uniquely identify a record in the table for which it is named. Each record in the Sales table will have a unique SALES_ID value.

Now let's design some tables. First, we'll want a pair of tables to keep track of our contacts and the organizations where they are employed. With these tables, and with all the others, there is really no end to the data which we could collect. People have home phones, car phones, company phones, private lines through the company switchboard, private extensions from the company number, and so on. Here, we'll concentrate on the basics.

▶▶ **TIP**

Add fields like a backpacker adds gear to a pack: "When in doubt, leave it out."

A Phone and Mail List Example

Figure 3.3 shows the structures of two tables in a phone and mail list system. Note that each table starts with an ID field. For cross-referencing people to employers, you simply add the EMPLOYERID field to the People table.

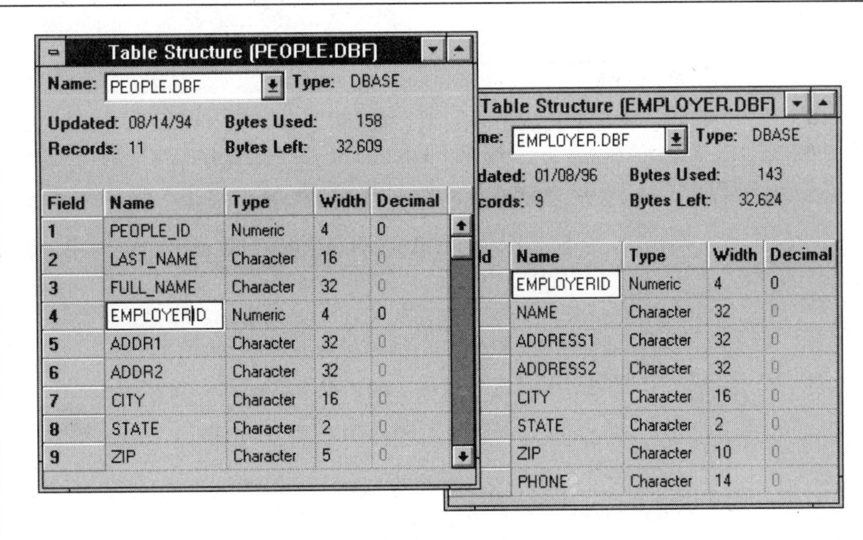

FIGURE 3.3 ▶

Structures of People and Employer tables for a phone and mail list system

Figure 3.4 shows how a simplified version of this database might look in practice. Although our real ID fields are numeric, in these examples, we'll use names as if they were IDs. You can't do this in practice, but it helps make these examples easy to follow. You'll learn all about this later in this chapter.

FIGURE 3.4 

Some data in the People and Employer tables

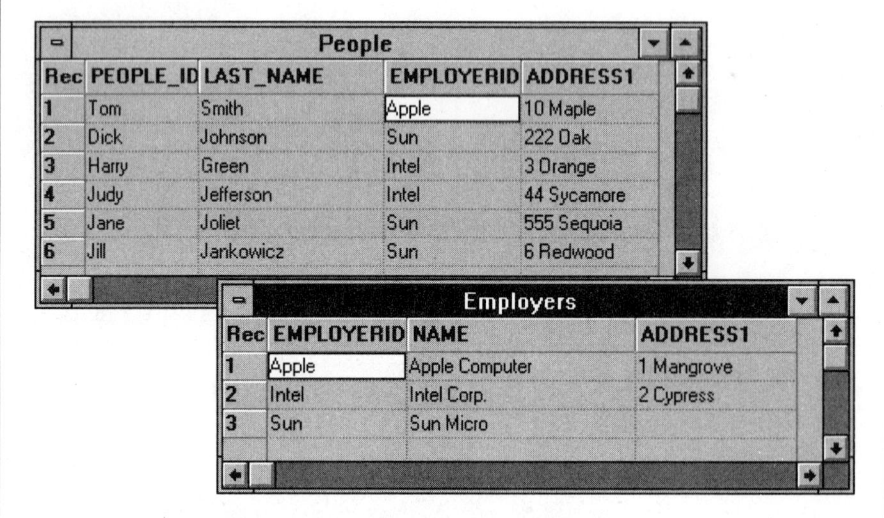

People

Rec	PEOPLE_ID	LAST_NAME	EMPLOYERID	ADDRESS1
1	Tom	Smith	Apple	10 Maple
2	Dick	Johnson	Sun	222 Oak
3	Harry	Green	Intel	3 Orange
4	Judy	Jefferson	Intel	44 Sycamore
5	Jane	Joliet	Sun	555 Sequoia
6	Jill	Jankowicz	Sun	6 Redwood

Employers

Rec	EMPLOYERID	NAME	ADDRESS1
1	Apple	Apple Computer	1 Mangrove
2	Intel	Intel Corp.	2 Cypress
3	Sun	Sun Micro	

Now let's consider some other examples.

Hotel Guest Registration

Our hotel started with a dozen rooms. The price was moderate, and the service was exceptional. We are now just about ready to open rooms 32 through 56. The old manual system has got to be replaced. Let's think through the Things and Events relevant to a registration system.

The Things are fairly obvious: our guests and the rooms they stay in. There are two significant Events: arrivals and departures. Our first cut is this:

Things: Guests
 Rooms
Events: Arrival
 Departure

Now let's sketch in the characteristics of each:

Things: Guests
- Name
- Address data
- Number in party
- Method of payment
- Special requests?

Rooms
- Number
- Floor
- Maximum occupants
- Special features?

Events: Arrival
- Which guest
- Which room
- Date
- Length of stay

Departure
- Which guest (or room)
- Date

At this point, it's not necessary to spell out exactly which specific fields, such as address data, are required. We generally leave this until we get to the Table Structure tool.

Note that there are "Special requests?" possible for our guests. Impeccable service is what has made our reputation. If Mr. Johnson likes coffee and fresh juice at 6:45 a.m., let's not start forgetting now that we're successful.

The same is true for the rooms. We have "Special features?" that don't lead to easy classification. One room may have especially nice decor, another faces the courtyard and is very quiet, and another has a good view. Wouldn't you want to be asked, "Would you prefer a quiet room on the courtyard or do you want a view?" (The first computer systems forced you to make everything impersonal; today's smart computer systems help you do just the opposite.) Both these items are free-form, so we can use Memo fields to record a sentence or two.

Now let's look at the Events. The departure could note which guest or which room. We could note that Smith has gone. Checking registrations we'll see that Smith was in room 26. Or we could note that the party in room 26 has departed. Checking registration, we'll see that it was Smith.

Either way, our guest is gone, and that room is available. Don't record both! That would be redundant data, and redundant data is bad design. You'll get mistakes soon enough.

There is another possibility. Stare at those two Events for a moment and see if you can simplify the design.

Here's what we would do:

Events: Stay

- Arrival date
- Which guest
- Which room
- Departure date

We'll have a Stay Event. The arrival and departure are characteristics of that Event. That eliminates a table, but fits our data quite naturally.

Finally, we studied our fields for any evidence of a zero or more, or one or more, condition. We don't see any, so we don't need a table for Details.

Now here's our design, in enough detail so that we would be comfortable sitting down with the Table Structure tool, filling in the final details as we go:

Things: Guest

- GUEST_ID
- NAME
- Address data
- PARTY_SIZE
- HOW_PAY
- SPECIAL (memo)

Room

- ROOM_ID
- FLOOR
- MAX_IN_RM
- SPECIAL (memo)

Events: Stay

- DATE_IN
- GUEST_ID
- ROOM_ID
- DATE_OUT

A common choice in databases is whether we should have just one item, as in DATE_OUT, or an estimate and an actual. Here we chose just one. If we felt it was important to be able to accurately project actual departures based on original estimates, we would keep both.

Note that the room number became the ROOM_ID field. The room number in hotels has always been the sort of unique identifier that we need in our systems. Each number is assigned to exactly one room. No

two numbers are the same. Since the hotel employees already are familiar with these numbers, we'll retain them.

As a final note, our Stay Event is much less instantaneous than our original Arrival and Departure Events. It still captures the same information, so nothing is lost by simplifying. Always eliminate tables when there is a natural way to do so.

TIP

Never eliminate tables if you have to force the data to fit into the new structure. Always eliminate tables if there is a natural way to simplify.

This isn't complicated, is it? We're just creating a place for everything, and keeping everything in its place.

A Wholesale Supplier

Let's look at another example of a simplified system for a wholesale supplier of computer software. This is not a trivial database, even though we're eliminating a lot of details.

Our supplier is shipped software by software companies. From its warehouse, our supplier ships software to computer and office supply dealers and to software retailers.

Here's a first cut at Things and Events:

Things:	Software Packages
	Software companies
	Computer dealers
	Office-supply dealers
	Software retailers
Events:	Receiving stock
	Shipping stock

Don't those events remind you of our hotel example. Could we just record the software's "stay" in our warehouse?

No, don't do it. Remember our rule: Only simplify if the result is a natural fit. The product is not a natural guest in our supplier's warehouse. There's a critical difference that would cause all kinds of problems if we ignored this rule.

The difference is that a guest (or party) checks into a hotel and subsequently checks out. In a wholesale business, we check our product in by the caseload, and it checks out one or a few units at a time. When we ship two units to a dealer, we might be shipping the last of the case we got last month and the first of the case we got this month.

But let's look at the Things in our rough design. Do we really need to differentiate between computer and office-supply dealers and software retailers? We need the same data for each one, and for purposes of our system, it doesn't really matter which they are. Those three could be put together and all called customers.

We might want to add a field for the customer type, so we can break our sales down into each of these customer categories.

Here's our new version, with the first details filled in:

Things: Product

- PRODUCT_ID
- NAME
- SOFT_CO_ID
- LIST_PRICE
- Other

Soft_Co

- SOFT_CO_ID
- NAME
- Address and phone
- Other

Custmer

- CUSTMER_ID

Type (computer, office, software only)
Address and phone
Credit and balance data

Events: Receive
RECEIVE_ID
SOFT_CO_ID
DATE_RECD
Product(s)
Quantity(s)
Ship
SHIP_ID
CUSTMER_ID
DATE_SHIP
Product(s)
Quantity(s)

Here we meet our first fields calling for one or more entries. In both receiving and shipping, it is likely that multiple units will come and go. So we need to add details.

Here is the new breakdown:

Things: Product
PRODUCT_ID
NAME
SOFT_CO_ID
LIST_PRICE
Other
Soft_Co
SOFT_CO_ID
NAME

Address and phone
Other
Custmer
CUSTMER_ID
Address and phone
Credit and balance data

Events: Receive
RECEIVE_ID
SOFT_CO_ID
DATE_RECD
Ship
SHIP_ID
CUSTMER_ID
DATE_SHIP

Details: Rec_Dtl
REC_DTL_ID
RECEIVE_ID
PRODUCT_ID
QUANTITY
Shp_Dtl
SHP_DTL_ID
SHIP_ID
PRODUCT_ID
QUANTITY

There will be other data, such as for special terms from suppliers or granted to customers. But for this example, we'll skip these to concentrate on the main point.

When we break out a Detail table, we start it with its own ID, as we do every other table. We continue with the ID of the table from which it was broken out. Then we add the repeating item and any data about the repeating item. In this case, the repeater is which product and how many of each.

Figure 3.5 shows an example of the details of a receipt Event. Again, the example uses phony ID values that make it easy to read. In the next section, we'll discuss the real key details.

FIGURE 3.5

Details of a receipt Event

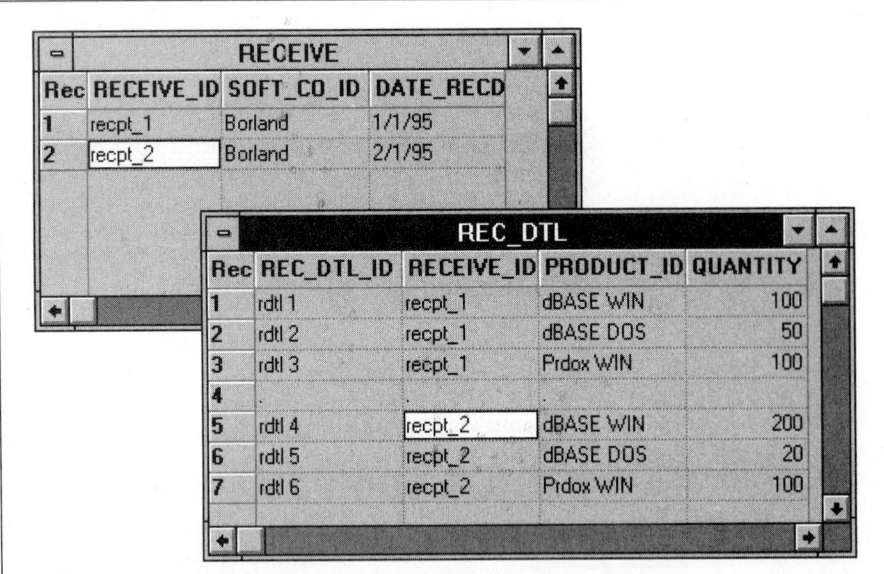

RECEIVE

Rec	RECEIVE_ID	SOFT_CO_ID	DATE_RECD
1	recpt_1	Borland	1/1/95
2	recpt_2	Borland	2/1/95

REC_DTL

Rec	REC_DTL_ID	RECEIVE_ID	PRODUCT_ID	QUANTITY
1	rdtl 1	recpt_1	dBASE WIN	100
2	rdtl 2	recpt_1	dBASE DOS	50
3	rdtl 3	recpt_1	Prdox WIN	100
4	.	.	.	
5	rdtl 4	recpt_2	dBASE WIN	200
6	rdtl 5	recpt_2	dBASE DOS	20
7	rdtl 6	recpt_2	Prdox WIN	100

In this example, we received two shipments from Borland. The first was for 100 units each of dBASE for Windows and Paradox for Windows, with 50 units of dBASE for DOS.

For clarity, we've used a blank line in the Rec_Dtl table to separate the details of the first receipt from the second. The second receipt was for 200 units of dBASE for Windows, 20 units of dBASE for DOS, and 100 units of Paradox for Windows.

Figure 3.6 shows a similar example of a shipment. As you can see, the SHIP_ID field in the Detail table lets us tie the individual items back to the Ship table record of which they were parts. The PRODUCT_ID field tells us which product was shipped. Actually, it tells us this by referring back to a record in the Product table, not by using a name as we show here for simplicity's sake. By referring back to a record, we have access to the product's name, shipping weight, list price, discount structure, and whatever other information you stored in the fields.

FIGURE 3.6

Details of a shipment Event

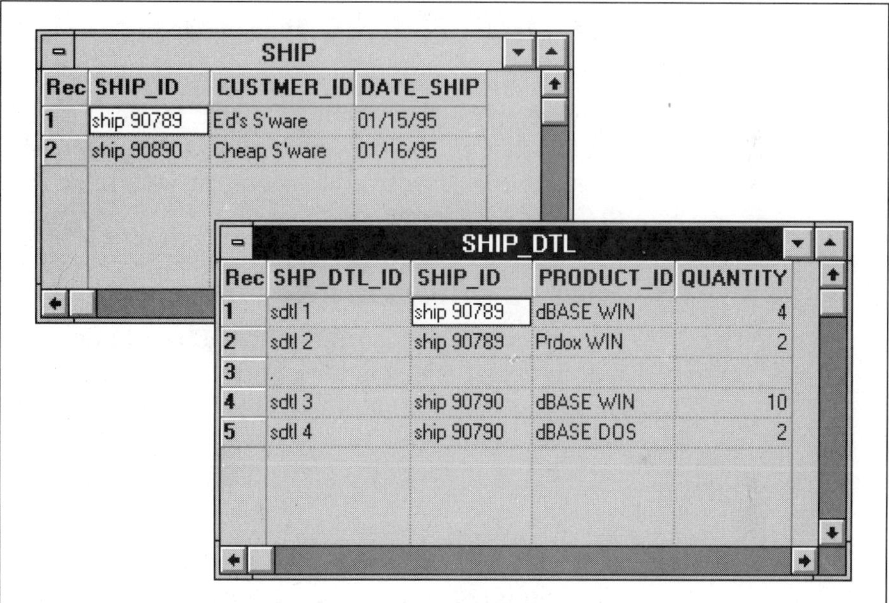

SHIP

Rec	SHIP_ID	CUSTMER_ID	DATE_SHIP
1	ship 90789	Ed's S'ware	01/15/95
2	ship 90890	Cheap S'ware	01/16/95

SHIP_DTL

Rec	SHP_DTL_ID	SHIP_ID	PRODUCT_ID	QUANTITY
1	sdtl 1	ship 90789	dBASE WIN	4
2	sdtl 2	ship 90789	Prdox WIN	2
3	.			
4	sdtl 3	ship 90790	dBASE WIN	10
5	sdtl 4	ship 90790	dBASE DOS	2

You have seen three examples of how the TED method works to organize your design process. It helps you get a place for everything, and to put everything in its place. Now let's get to the full details about those keys.

►► You Master the Keys to Database Integrity

Database integrity is what the computer scientists call a database with no fundamental flaws. It doesn't happen often, but in this case, the term means just what you might think. The scientists tell us that we want several kinds of integrity.

► Principle Integrity Constraints

We'll consider four types of integrity that our TED design method and consistent use of keys will maintain for you. The first two are so closely related that we'll consider them together. Don't let the size of the words in this scientific jargon throw you; the concepts are as simple as the words are large.

Entity and Primary Key Integrity

If every record has an ID field, and the value in every ID field is unique within each table, you have entity and primary key integrity. In the TED method, we automatically give each table an ID field, so part one is done. In the work that follows, we'll show you how to be sure that each key is unique. It's really not hard.

Domain Integrity

Domain integrity specifies that each field's value is a legal value for the field. At its simplest, this means that a Date field must contain a valid date (not a number or a name or a bitmap). dBASE for Windows maintains this simple level of domain integrity for you.

For better or worse, the concept of domain integrity is as complex as the data you are modeling. For instance, the domain of values for a salary field would be a range of numbers. Presumably, the exact range would depend on the size of the organization and on the responsibilities of the employee. Without setting any hard rules, you would expect the salary of the CEO of an international bank to be higher than the salary of a clerk in a small hardware store.

dBASE for Windows supports domain integrity rules of arbitrary complexity through its VALID handlers. If the rules can be expressed rigorously (not vaguely, as in the preceding paragraph), they can be programmed and dBASE for Windows will enforce them.

Relational Integrity

Relational integrity, or just RI, is the requirement that every ID value refer to exactly one record. If you have a PRODUCT_ID value in a Ship_Dtl table record, for example, there must be exactly one Product table record identified by this ID. Zero is unacceptable; so is two.

Relational integrity cannot be maintained if you don't have primary key integrity. A product has a unique ID number. Receiving and shipping records record that ID appropriately.

If you added a new product and assigned it a duplicate of that ID number (violating primary key integrity), you would lose your relational integrity. The IDs in the detail table records would ambiguously refer to two different products.

We'll elaborate on this rule when we get to assigning and using IDs. These IDs are called *keys* in the relational literature.

▶ Assigning Unique Keys

All sorts of systems have been used for assigning unique keys. One common system is to pick a large random number (dBASE for Windows has a RANDOM function that will do this). After you pick the number, you search your table to be sure that you haven't already used that number. If the number isn't there, you go ahead and assign it. If it's already in use, you discard it, get another random number, and try again.

This system has problems, which we'll discuss shortly. Fortunately, a much simpler system works: assign the first ID the number 1, the second ID the number 2, and so on.

For an ID field, start by guessing the largest number of records you might ever have in your table. Make the ID field one or two digits wider than necessary for that number. For example, if you think you might have hundreds of people in your phone list, use at least a four-digit ID field.

In practice, we use a little trick that can simplify things. We don't start with 1 as the first ID number. If we have a four-digit ID, we start with 1001. This means that every ID field will be four digits wide. With this method, all sorts of quickly printed lists line up neatly, no matter what software we might be using to read the table.

Another trick we use is to accept some unique keys as IDs. The hotel room numbers in the example in the previous section are one good example. However, before you use such keys, make sure that they are appropriate.

For example, each working American has an assigned tax identification number, called the Social Security number. These are suitable unique identifiers for database work. Actually, they are far too suitable. Privacy legislation restricts the use of these numbers to their intended purpose: providing tax information to the government.

If there are no legal impediments and the IDs are naturally occurring, definitely unique identifiers, go ahead and use them.

It's simple enough to type in a new ID number each time you add a record. It is also error-prone in a high-volume environment. In Chapter 4, we explain a short routine that automatically supplies a new ID for each new record created. For now, you can just type the IDs in.

Do not reuse IDs after records have been deleted. The word we have been using is *unique*. This means forever and permanently unique. If you delete an inactive customer, you don't want to reassign that customer's ID. You might find that you want to reconstruct last year's billing, for example. You won't be able to do it if you have given an old ID to a new customer.

The deleted record problem is the one that causes the random ID system problems we mentioned earlier. Just because an ID is not in the table doesn't mean that it wasn't there at some time in the past.

▸ Maintaining Relational Integrity

The first step in maintaining relational integrity is to maintain entity and primary key integrity. If you assign each record a unique ID as we have discussed, you'll meet these two integrity constraints.

Now we're ready for the three cases where we must consider relational integrity:

- When you add a record
- When you edit a record
- When you delete a record

One-to-Many Relationships

In our phone list system, each employer can have many employees. This is known as a *one-to-many relationship*. One employer can have many employees.

From the opposite perspective, we could say that there is a many-to-one relationship between employees and employers. Many employees work for one employer.

Many-to-many and *one-to-one* relationships are also possible. For example, if your system is keeping track of consultants and their employers, you might have one employer using many consultants, and one consultant working for many employers. If your software company has a product manager for every product, that is a one-to-one relationship.

The way we will most commonly look at relationships is the one-to-many perspective.

Parent and Child Records

A one-to-many relationship is also called a *parent-child relationship*. For instance, in the example of a wholesale supplier database presented earlier in this chapter, we had a Ship table and a Ship_Dtl table. This is a one-to-many relationship: each Ship table record can have many Ship_Dtl records.

We call the Ship record the *parent* of the Ship_Dtl record. Let's reconsider the way we use IDs in a parent-child relationship.

As you can see, the SHIP_ID field is placed in the child record to identify its parent. The SHIP_ID is, by definition, unique for each Ship table record. When we use it in the Ship_Dtl table, we will reuse it once for every child record attached to the parent Ship table record.

Foreign Keys

When the Ship table record is identified by the SHIP_ID key, the key is called a *primary key*. When the SHIP_ID field is used in a child record to select the parent, it is called a *foreign key*. Those SHIP_ID fields in the Ship_Dtl table are foreign keys. They are sometimes called foreign keys *into* the Ship table.

Other people say that the foreign key *points to* the parent record. This usage bothers the scientists, but we still use it. To give the science its due, remember that the ID doesn't point to a particular place in the parent table. You could shuffle the parent table's records like a deck of playing cards. The foreign key doesn't specify "card 24." It specifies "3 of spades," wherever that might be located.

Relational integrity is all about the maintenance of foreign keys.

Relational Integrity and Adding Records

Let's begin with another look at our phone list system, but this time we'll use real keys as they'll appear in our database. Figure 3.4, shown earlier in this chapter, portrays the system as you might think about it. But the way a database with relational integrity would represent it is shown in Figure 3.7.

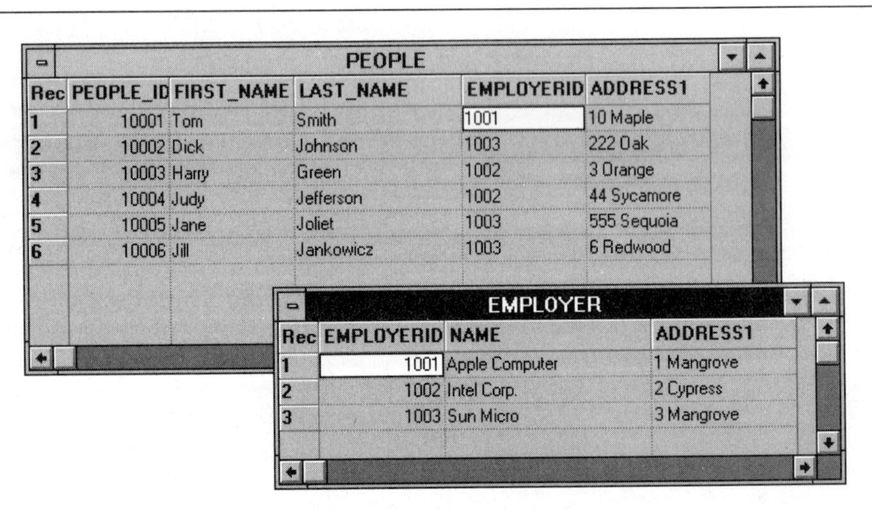

FIGURE 3.7 ▶

Database representation of People and Employer system

Now let's add a record to the Employer table. This has a primary key and no foreign keys. All we need to do is make sure that our new record uses the next higher key:

EMPLOYER

Rec	EMPLOYERID	NAME	ADDRESS1
1	1001	Apple Computer	1 Mangrove
2	1002	Intel Corp.	2 Cypress
3	1003	Sun Micro	3 Mangrove
4	1004	Compaq	4 Live Oak

There are no relational integrity problems, because no other record has an EMPLOYERID of 1004.

Adding a record to the People table has an additional consideration. We'll pick the next higher primary key, but when we pick a foreign key, we must make sure that it exists in the appropriate table. Here we'll add the first employee working for Compaq:

PEOPLE

Rec	PEOPLE_ID	FIRST_NAME	LAST_NAME	EMPLOYERID	ADDRESS1
1	10001	Tom	Smith	1001	10 Maple
2	10002	Dick	Johnson	1003	222 Oak
3	10003	Harry	Green	1002	3 Orange
4	10004	Judy	Jefferson	1002	44 Sycamore
5	10005	Jane	Joliet	1003	555 Sequoia
6	10006	Jill	Jankowicz	1003	6 Redwood
7	10007	Fred	Furrier	1004	747 Plane

To maintain relational integrity when you add records, you need to be sure that your primary key is new, and that any foreign keys are *not* new.

When we get to Part 4, you'll see that this can be done by a simple bit of event-handler programming. If you're working on a personal system, use the Navigator to launch your table, and then launch browse views of any tables where you'll pick foreign keys.

Relational Integrity and Editing Records

If you assigned a primary key correctly, it should never be changed. Other records may be using the primary key's value as a foreign key. Changing it could "orphan" those child records.

You could, if necessary, carefully change the primary key in the parent record, and then find each child record that was attached and change the children's foreign key values. This would maintain relational integrity.

However, the simple way to maintain integrity is to never change the primary key. When you add records, enter the primary keys, check them carefully, and fix any mistakes. Then go on to the next record; never go back to that primary key.

TIP

You can use the Table Records Properties dialog box to make your primary keys Read Only. When you're ready to add records, use this tool to reverse this setting.

You won't often need to edit foreign keys, either. For example, all our Ship_Dtl table records will be permanently attached to their parent Ship table record. One exception is in correcting errors. You may discover that those copies of dBASE for Windows were, in fact, shipped to a different dealer, for example.

In some cases, you'll need to edit foreign keys because facts have changed. For example, we'll need to change a key in our phone list when one of our acquaintances changes jobs.

The rule for changing a foreign key is the same as the rule for adding a new one. You must check that it exists. For example, a correct change for our phone list when Tom leaves Apple and goes to work for Compaq is shown on the next page.

PEOPLE

Rec	PEOPLE_ID	FIRST_NAME	LAST_NAME	EMPLOYERID	ADDRESS1
1	10001	Tom	Smith	1004	10 Maple
2	10002	Dick	Johnson	1003	222 Oak
3	10003	Harry	Green	1002	3 Orange
4	10004	Judy	Jefferson	1002	44 Sycamore
5	10005	Jane	Joliet	1003	555 Sequoia
6	10006	Jill	Jankowicz	1003	6 Redwood
7	10007	Fred	Furrier	1004	747 Plane

Just be sure that the new foreign key correctly attaches the child record to another parent record. Again, if you're working from the Navigator, launch the parent table and choose a Browse Layout view.

Relational Integrity and Deleting Records

Deletions follow a very simple rule: never delete a parent record.

Before deleting a record, you must check every table that is a child of that parent. Search the foreign key field for that parent's ID value. If you find one, you cannot delete the parent record.

In relational jargon, we talk about *refuse deletes* and *cascade deletes*. What we just described is the refuse deletes system. Never delete a parent record.

The other alternative does not violate this rule. A cascade deletes system searches for all child records. It deletes every child record. Once all the children are gone, it deletes the parent record.

This is called *cascade* because the child records themselves could be parents of other records. Deleting a child record requires that you repeat the process: find all its children and delete them first. This could proceed down several levels.

For example, in our software distributor system, deleting a customer requires that we delete all Ship table records for that customer. Deleting the Ship table records requires that we delete each Ship_Dtl table record for that shipment.

The cascade deletes method requires a program set up for that purpose. If you think that cascade deletes has the potential for disastrous consequences, you're right. For example, if we cascaded the deletion of an employer in our phone list, all the people employed by that employer would be deleted. Even if the employer went out of business, you probably wouldn't want to lose all the other data about those people.

There is one place where a cascade delete is helpful. If your tables are backed up to suitable permanent storage media (tape, removable disk, or something similar), you may want to delete the records for inactive customers. In this case, a cascade delete would remove all the sales and sales detail records for that customer. This would be appropriate if, for example, all these sales were made last year and last year's books are closed.

▸▸ Summary

We've considered the art and science of database design. Ultimately, it is an art, with many "correct" ways to design a database.

The science of database design works through normal forms, beginning with First Normal Form, progressing through Fifth Normal form. Most software engineers consider Third Normal Form adequate. We use the TED method, which is simple and always generates a Boyce-Codd Normal Form design, which is proven to lie between Third and Fourth Normal Forms.

The TED method is to break down your target database into a list of Things (long-duration, often kickable) and Events (instantaneous interactions among Things). For each Thing and Event, you list the important characteristics. For repeating characteristics, you create Detail tables.

We use ID fields for each record. These become our records' primary keys, ensuring entity and primary key integrity.

We assign the first record an integer value that fills its width, such as 1001 for a four-digit field. With each new record, we assign the next integer in sequence: 1002, 1003, and so on. These IDs, or keys, are certain to be unique, which is the main requirement.

We use these ID fields as foreign keys in the *many* part of one-to-many relationships, which are also called *child* records in a parent-child relationship.

We maintain complete referential integrity by always adding new, unique primary keys when we add records and by adding existing foreign keys.

We don't edit the primary keys. Occasionally, we may change an existing foreign key in a child record to "point to" a new parent record.

We don't ever delete parent records if there are child records referring to them.

Running dBASE for Windows

PART TWO

dBASE for Windows is one of those products that you can run at a very simple level, as you learned to do in Chapter 2. Here in Part 2, we'll bring you from that beginning up to a strong intermediate level.

In Chapter 4, Manipulating Your Data, we'll cover the use of the Table Records tool in depth. You'll use the Table Utilities for chores such as setting up indexes. dBASE for Windows' indexes allow you to sort your data on various criteria.

In Chapter 5, The Two-Way Query Designer, you'll use the Query Designer to not only query your data, but to organize multiple tables into a database system. The "Two-Way" part of this tool means that it creates programs for you. You can edit these programs directly, or use the Query Designer. You'll discover that the Query Designer writes programs that are consistently error-free, and being able to edit those programs gives you additional power. You can do this type of editing long before you get into even the beginnings of dBASE for Windows programming.

In Chapter 6, Building Forms with the Two-Way Form Designer, you'll use the Form Expert, which we met in Chapter 2. You'll also do your own work with blank forms. You'll use the Menu Designer to create a menu program that will tie together a two-table phone list system, with one table for employees and another for employers. You'll be able to access your tables either individually or in a combined view.

You'll also use the Form Designer to add custom touches, such as Browse and Pushbutton objects. As we do this work, you'll use the Procedure Editor to add programs that run when triggered by user-interface events. (These programs are either one or two lines long—not over the head of even a determined nonprogrammer.)

In Chapter 7, Producing Database Reports, you'll start with a two-table report to tie together your employer and employee data. Beginning with a simple listing, you'll work forward to a sophisticated grouped report, which will include a variety of decorative effects highlighting information.

Before leaving Chapter 7, you'll return to the menu you developed in Chapter 6 and tie in a report as part of your phone list system. We finish the tutorial sections in Part 2 with a discussion of mailing label generation using the Crystal Reports tool.

▶ ▶ CHAPTER 4

Manipulating Your Data

▶▶ **I**n this chapter, we'll work on single table operations. To begin, we'll apply what we discussed in Chapter 3 to add an ID (key) field to our People table. We'll have dBASE for Windows fill in every ID in a single stroke. Next, we'll use an index to sort the People table by last name. You'll learn more about using indexes to maintain multiple orders continuously and to permit virtually instantaneous searches for last names or record IDs.

Then we'll go on to take a closer look at searching and modifying our data in bulk operations. Just as the Table Record tool lets us edit individual records, the Table menus let us apply edits across large groups of records.

Finally, we'll cover importing and exporting data from a variety of formats. These operations will give us instant tables, filled from existing sources. Going the other way, they'll instantly fill our spreadsheets and other files with data culled from our tables.

We'll begin by updating our People table to the design standards discussed in Chapter 2.

▶▶ *Improving the People Table*

For starters, the People table doesn't have the ID field that it will need when we get to the next chapter, where we'll add a related table. For this task, we'll use the Table Structure tool again. We used that tool to create the People table; now we'll use it to improve that table.

▶ Adding an ID Field to the Structure

We'll need a field, PEOPLE_ID, to hold identifiers for each record in the table. Adding this field is not difficult. Follow these steps:

1. Launch dBASE for Windows and open the Navigator, if you haven't already done so. Select the D:\DBWORK directory (or whatever directory you're using). This is the way dBASE for Windows will start itself if you haven't done additional work since Chapter 1.
2. Select Tables from the list of file types, and then choose People from the list of tables. (It's the only table if you haven't added more on your own.)
3. Right double-click on People or press Shift-F2 to launch the table in Design mode. You should now be in the Table Structure tool, looking at the structure of your People table, as you see in Figure 4.1.

▶▶ NOTE

For every file type in the Navigator list, you can left double-click or press F2 to launch a file in Run mode, or right double-click or press Shift-F2 to launch a file in Design mode.

4. We want to add a new field at the beginning or the table. Be sure the currently highlighted record is the first one, then press Ctrl-N, or choose Structure ➤ Insert Field. This inserts a new record immediately above the previously selected one.
5. Type **PEOPLE_ID** for the field name.
6. Press Tab or Enter to move to the Type field. With the mouse, click on the down arrow and then click on Numeric. From the keyboard, just press N. You can't pull down the list of types from the keyboard—a design oversight. You can use the ↓ and ↑ keys to scroll through the options.

▶▶ TIP

Most table operations are quicker from the keyboard. Don't get your hand glued to that mouse.

FIGURE 4.1 ►

Ready to add a new field to PEOPLE.DBF

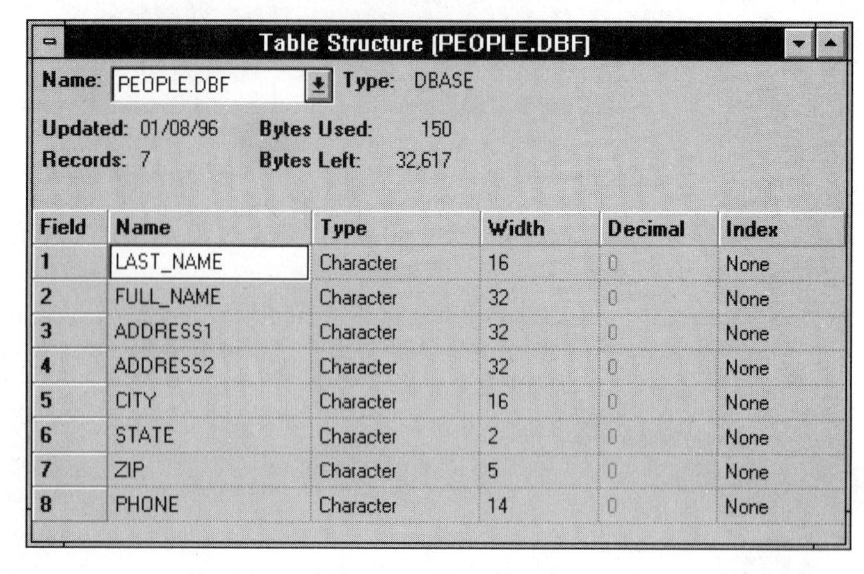

7. Press Tab or Enter to move to the Width field. Enter **4** or higher number. If your personal phone list is not likely to get to 1000, 4 is adequate. If you're a professional in a people field (employment agent, perhaps), you may want to make the field wider.
8. Press Tab or Enter twice to pass over the Decimals field (the default 0 is just what we want) and reach the Index field. Press A for an ascending index.
9. If you haven't already done so, specify A for an ascending index for the LAST_NAME field. Your first two records should specify A, and the rest N (for None). You'll be learning all about indexes later in the chapter.
10. Choose Structure ➤ Manage Indexes … from the menus. Before you get to the Manage Indexes dialog box, you'll see the Changes Made - Table Structure dialog box. Tell it Yes, you do want to save your changes.

Take a good look at the Manage Indexes dialog box. For the moment, we won't make any selections. Just remember that this dialog box is available from the Table Structure tool. Later in this chapter, we'll use this same dialog box from the Table Records tool (in Run mode). In the future, you'll find it convenient to specify your indexes when you design your tables (from the Table Structure tool).

11. Choose Cancel to exit the Manage Indexes dialog box.

12. To run the new table structure, press F2 or click on the lightning icon on the speedbar. Don't start typing!

WARNING

If you've been experimenting on your own and you've used the Table Properties dialog box, you've created a custom Fields list. When you change from the Table Structure tool to the Table Records tool, dBASE for Windows ignores previous Fields lists. This means that the next time you browse your table from the Navigator, you won't see the fields you added. To add the new fields to your Fields list, return to the Table Properties tool (choose Properties ➤ Table Records Window …) and add the new fields.

Letting dBASE Fill in the ID Field

We think you'll be surprised at how easy it is to add the data to our new field. (No, we're not going to type IDs one at a time!)

If you aren't in the Browse Layout view, select it by clicking on its icon on the speedbar or by choosing View ➤ Browse Layout from the menus. Your table should look like the one in Figure 4.2.

Now we want to explain to dBASE that it should put the number 1001 (use more zeros if you have a field wider than four characters) in the first record's PEOPLE_ID field, 1002 in the second, and so on.

The more records you have in the table, the more valuable this technique will be. If you have only a handful of records, just imagine that you've added several hundred and need to fill in all those PEOPLE_ID numbers.

FIGURE 4.2

People table, with blank PEOPLE_ID fields

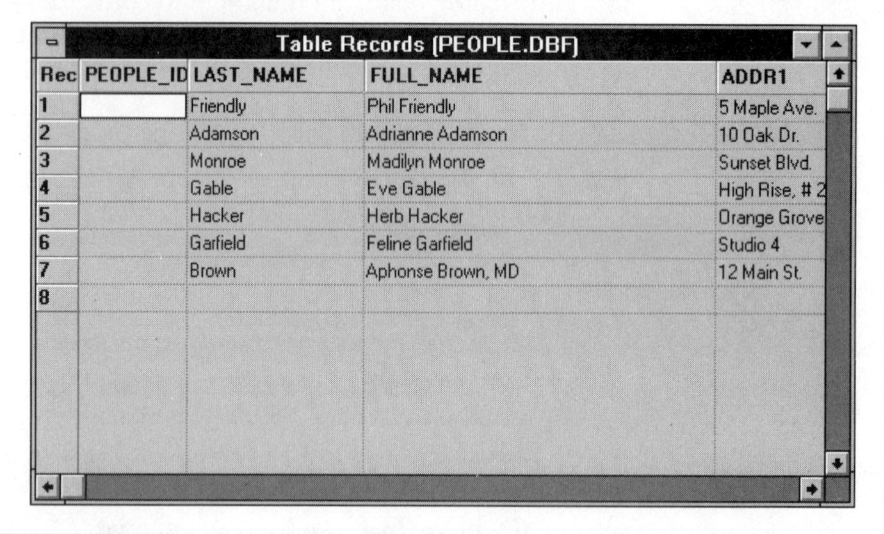

Table Records (PEOPLE.DBF)

Rec	PEOPLE_ID	LAST_NAME	FULL_NAME	ADDR1
1		Friendly	Phil Friendly	5 Maple Ave.
2		Adamson	Adrianne Adamson	10 Oak Dr.
3		Monroe	Madilyn Monroe	Sunset Blvd.
4		Gable	Eve Gable	High Rise, # 2
5		Hacker	Herb Hacker	Orange Grove
6		Garfield	Feline Garfield	Studio 4
7		Brown	Aphonse Brown, MD	12 Main St.
8				

This operation, and many others, is available from the Table drop-down menu. Choose the Replace Records … choice:

Find Records...	Ctrl+F
Replace Records...	Ctrl+R
Create Query	
Table Utilities	▸
Add Records	Ctrl+A
Delete Selected Record	Ctrl+U
Lock Selected Record	Ctrl+L
Blank Selected Record	
Go to Record Number...	Ctrl+G
Previous Record	Up Arrow
Next Record	Down Arrow
Previous Page	PgUp
Next Page	PgDn
Top Record	Ctrl+PgUp
Bottom Record	Ctrl+PgDn

This brings up the Replace Records dialog box, which lets you search for a value in one field and replace values in a field for every record that matches. In a word processor, this would be the global search and replace function. In a data table, it works with text, numbers, dates, and the other data types.

We want to look for all the PEOPLE_IDs that contain a zero value. Type a **0** in the Find What entry field. Press Tab to reach the Replace With entry field, and type this expression:

recno() + 1000

We'll cover expressions in detail in Chapter 12. For now, we'll jump ahead to explain this one. The RECNO() function (the trailing parentheses identify it as a function) returns the record number. It will be 1 for the first record, 2 for the second, and so on.

dBASE will evaluate the Replace With expression once for every record that matches the Find What expression. In this case, every record will match. On the first record, the expression will evaluate to 1001; at the second record, it will evaluate to 1002, and so on.

Your Replace Records dialog box should look like the one shown in Figure 4.3. From the pushbuttons on the right, choose Replace All. This will fill our PEOPLE_ID fields with exactly the unique key values that we want.

When you're finished, choose Close. When you're asked if you want to keep your changes, respond Yes. Now all the PEOPLE_ID fields in our table are filled in with ascending numbers beginning with 1001. Next, we'll customize our view to match our table.

▶ Customizing the Table Records Tool

Let's make more of the People table visible in a Browse Layout view. Follow these steps:

1. Launch the People table and choose the Browse Layout view.
2. From the Table Records tool, choose Properties ➤ Table Records Window .... This opens the Table Records Properties dialog box.

The default selection is all fields. Let's start by removing the second line of address data. Note that this doesn't change the table or its data; it just controls what fields you'll see in the Table Records tool.

FIGURE 4.3 ▶

Filling PEOPLE_IDs with the Replace Records dialog box

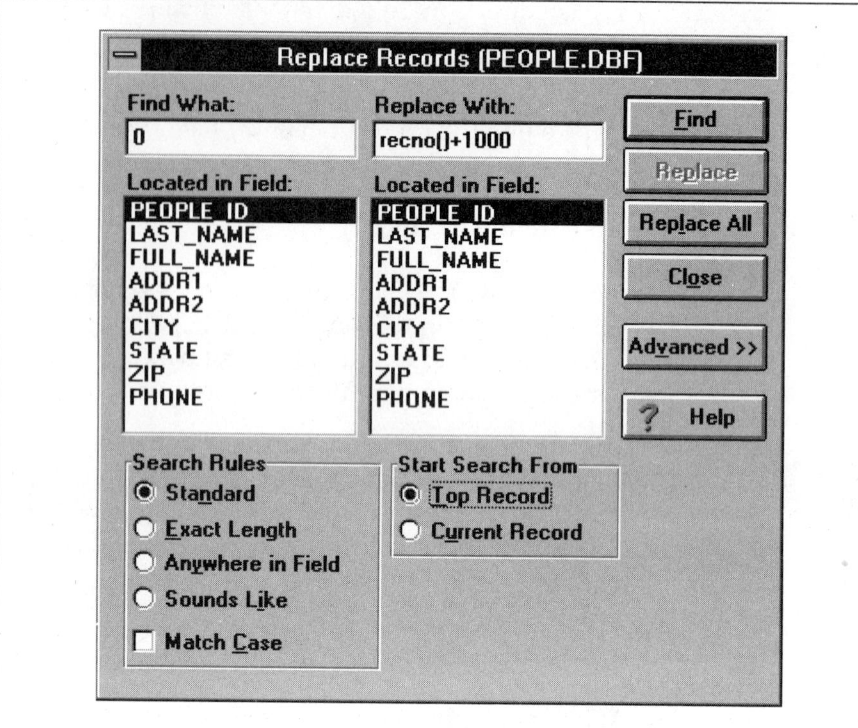

3. Click on the ADDR2 field, or tab to the Selected Fields box and use the ↓ key to select this field.
4. Click on the < pushbutton. This shoots just the selected field back to the Available Fields box, as shown in Figure 4.4.

Now let's customize the other fields. We'll change their width and give the PEOPLE_ID field a shorter name. Remember, these changes affect only the appearance of the table in Browse Layout view.

5. Highlight the PEOPLE_ID field in the Selected Fields box and click on the Properties … pushbutton at the bottom of the dialog box. You'll see the Field Properties dialog box.
6. In the Heading box, enter **ID**. Use the down arrow for the Width box to change the width to 4. These entries are shown in Figure 4.5.

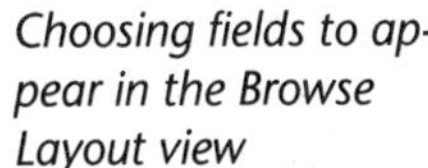

FIGURE 4.4

Choosing fields to appear in the Browse Layout view

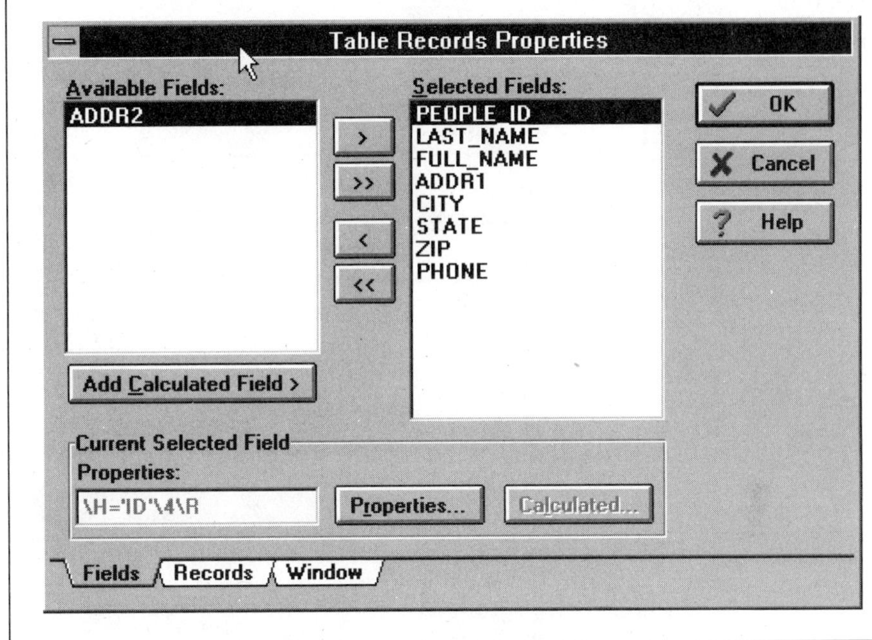

7. Choose OK in the Field Properties dialog box, then again in the Table Records Properties dialog box. Now you're back in your Browse Layout view. This should show the PEOPLE_ID field nicely sized and titled ID.
8. Return to the Table Records Properties dialog box. For each of the remaining fields, except the PHONE field, use Properties… to set a width two-thirds or less of the field's actual width. When you're finished, return to your Browse Layout view. Ours is shown in Figure 4.6.

Adjust your view as needed, until you can comfortably view your People table. When you leave the Table Records tool, these settings are stored in a Fields record in your DBASEWIN.INI file. They will be recalled each time you run the Table Records tool for the People table.

FIGURE 4.5 

Setting properties for the PEOPLE_ID field

Field Properties (PEOPLE->PEOPLE_ID)

Options

Heading: ID

Width: 4

Template:

Read Only

When:

Valid

Expression:

Error Message:

Required

Range

Lower Limit:

Upper Limit:

Required

OK Cancel Help

FIGURE 4.6 

A Browse Layout view with the whole record visible

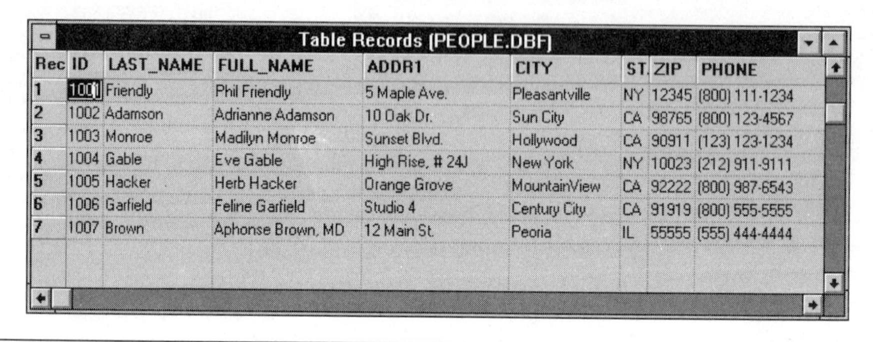

Table Records (PEOPLE.DBF)

Rec	ID	LAST_NAME	FULL_NAME	ADDR1	CITY	ST.	ZIP	PHONE
1	1001	Friendly	Phil Friendly	5 Maple Ave.	Pleasantville	NY	12345	(800) 111-1234
2	1002	Adamson	Adrianne Adamson	10 Oak Dr.	Sun City	CA	98765	(800) 123-4567
3	1003	Monroe	Madilyn Monroe	Sunset Blvd.	Hollywood	CA	90911	(123) 123-1234
4	1004	Gable	Eve Gable	High Rise, # 24J	New York	NY	10023	(212) 911-9111
5	1005	Hacker	Herb Hacker	Orange Grove	MountainView	CA	92222	(800) 987-6543
6	1006	Garfield	Feline Garfield	Studio 4	Century City	CA	91919	(800) 555-5555
7	1007	Brown	Aphonse Brown, MD	12 Main St.	Peoria	IL	55555	(555) 444-4444

TIP

If you start in Design mode (Table Records Structure tool) and switch to Run mode, the stored Fields list is ignored. This lets you see the structure changes you just made. For a quick look that ignores your Fields list, launch the Table Records Structure tool before you switch to Run mode.

See Chapter 9 for a full explanation of all the features of the Table Records Properties tool.

Let's finish up by putting our people into alphabetical order by last name.

▶ *Organizing People Alphabetically*

Remember the Manage Indexes dialog box that we looked at, but didn't use, from the Table Structure tool? That's where we're heading next. We wanted to get those IDs in place and have a nice Browse Layout view to see the effects of the indexes.

Launch your People table and choose a Browse Layout view. Choose Tables ➤ Table Utilities from the menus.

Table Properties Window Help

Find Records... Ctrl+F
Replace Records... Ctrl+R

Create Query
Table Utilities

Manage Indexes...
Reindex

Close Table
Close All Tables

Delete Records...
Recall Records...
Pack Records
Zap Records

Append Records from File...
Export Records...
Sort Records...
Generate Records...

Count Records...
Calculate Records...

As you see, the first choice here is Manage Indexes .... Select that option to get to the Manage Indexes dialog box.

In the Manage Indexes dialog box for the People table, you should see three choices:

- [Natural Order]
- PEOPLE_ID
- LAST_NAME

When you first use the Manage Indexes dialog box, the default index highlighted is Natural Order. Actually, that means no index is in use.

►► **NOTE**

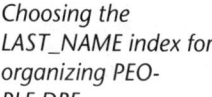

Natural Order may not be the best choice of words. For us, a phone list is most natural when it's in alphabetic order. Remember that Natural Order really means no index at all. The records are in the order in which they were added to the table.

Choose the LAST_NAME index, as shown in Figure 4.7. Then click on OK.

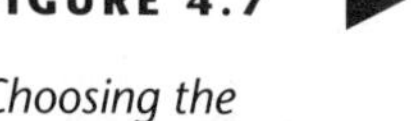

FIGURE 4.7

Choosing the LAST_NAME index for organizing PEOPLE.DBF

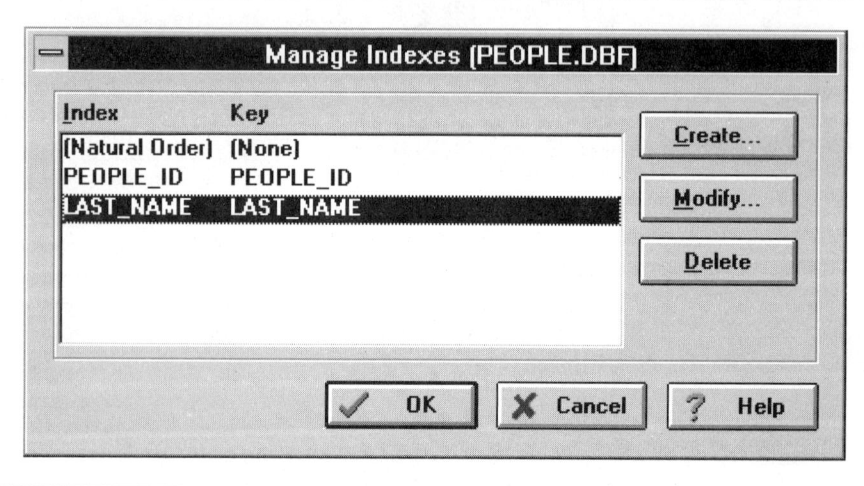

When dBASE for Windows redisplays your table, your records will be ordered alphabetically by last name. You might see two problems in this view, depending on your data.

Retrieving Disappearing Records

You may see that you've lost some of your records. Actually, they're not lost at all. When dBASE redisplays your table, it begins its display at record 1. Record 1 is your first physical record, but the index reorders the table. (It doesn't actually sort the records, which we will discuss later in this chapter.) Unless your first record happens to be first in alphabetical order, this will "hide" the records that come before it.

Click on the beginning of file speedbar icon, or press Ctrl-PgUp, and you'll go to the first record in the alphabetic order that your index specifies.

WARNING

In the first release, there is a bug in the vertical elevator. It may not show you that you're not looking at the top of the Browse Layout view.

True Alphabetic Sorting

If your LAST_NAME fields begin with a capital letter and continue with lowercase letters, your sort will be acceptable. But it isn't a true alphabetic sort; it's an ASCII collating sequence sort.

In the ASCII character set, the capital letters *A* through *Z* come before the lowercase letters *a* through *z*. This means that *Zebra* sorts before *aardvark*.

Later in this chapter, we'll explain the technique for doing a true alphabetic sort. If you have simple LAST_NAME field values, you'll have no problem so far. But consider some of these:

- Zenith will sort before adams.
- LeBeouf will sort before Lebatt.
- LeValley will sort before Leanne.
- DePres will sort before Deparne.

- McPhee will sort before Mcmanus.
- Smith, PID will sort before Smith, PhD.

The default ASCII sort won't be satisfactory in the long run.

Now let's dig into these topics in more detail, starting with sorting.

▸▸ Putting Your Data in Order

For most applications, you want your data to appear in a sensible order. The order that makes the most sense is seldom the order in which you enter the data. If you meet a new supplier, named Adams, you'll enter a new record in your phone list. You'll want to see Adams name appear between Adam and Addams when you look at your phone list.

Putting a small table into order is not a problem. But dBASE doesn't handle just small problems. It can handle up to a billion records in a single table. Real tables frequently run into the millions of records.

Sorting a table of 10,000 records takes several seconds. Sorting 100,000 records takes minutes; 1,000,000 records would need hours.

Consider also that many applications require that the data be organized in more than one way. When we look at our lists, alphabetic order often makes sense. When our system wants to relate two records, it will be looking for an ID value, so it needs the table sorted by ID. Often, both needs must be accommodated at the same time.

This is where indexes come in.

▸ What Is an Index?

This book has an index. If you need to find information about sorting your data, you could look in the index, find the page number, and then turn to that page. Without the index, you could start reading at page 1 and keep reading until you arrived here. Obviously, indexed access is much more efficient.

Computer indexes serve the same purpose, except that they have record number entries, not book page numbers. Actually, the computer indexes are themselves indexed.

If the computer is looking for the name Smith, it will first look in its index of the last names. That might tell it that the *S* entries start on page 17 of the index. Page 17 might be the place where the *S* entries start, or it might have another index. On page 17, the computer might learn that the *Sm* entries start on page 24.

These indexed indexes are called *B-trees* by computer scientists. For our purposes, we can just call them lightning fast. Borland and its main database rival, Microsoft, compete fiercely in trying to produce ever more effective (fast) indexes.

The exact details of each release's indexes keep changing as Borland keeps discovering more effective indexing techniques. From our perspective, this means that each relase will run more quickly than the last.

On our test machine (a generic 33 MHz 486), finding one entry from 10,000 in a sample PEOPLE.DBF file takes only a small fraction of a second.

▶ Storing Your Indexes

If you use the Table Structure tool and the Manage Indexes dialog box to specify your indexes, dBASE for Windows automatically creates and maintains an index file whose name is the same as your table name, giving it the extension .MDX.

Your Production Index

The .MDX file whose name matches your table's name is called the *production index*. Older versions of dBASE used single index files, with the extension .NDX. The .NDX file stored only one index; the .MDX file can store up to 47 separate indexes.

This means that PEOPLE.MDX can conveniently store all the indexes you'll need for PEOPLE.DBF, for one example.

Your Master Index

When you selected an index other than Natural Order, you were choosing a *master index* for your table. The master index is the index that you're using. As you browse through your data, or scroll through it in any layout, it appears to be ordered by the master index.

You can choose a different master index at any time. This will change the apparent order of the records in your table. In fact, you can launch two or more separate instances of the Table Records tool and set a different master index for each. Figure 4.8 shows two simultaneous views of the People table, set to different indexes.

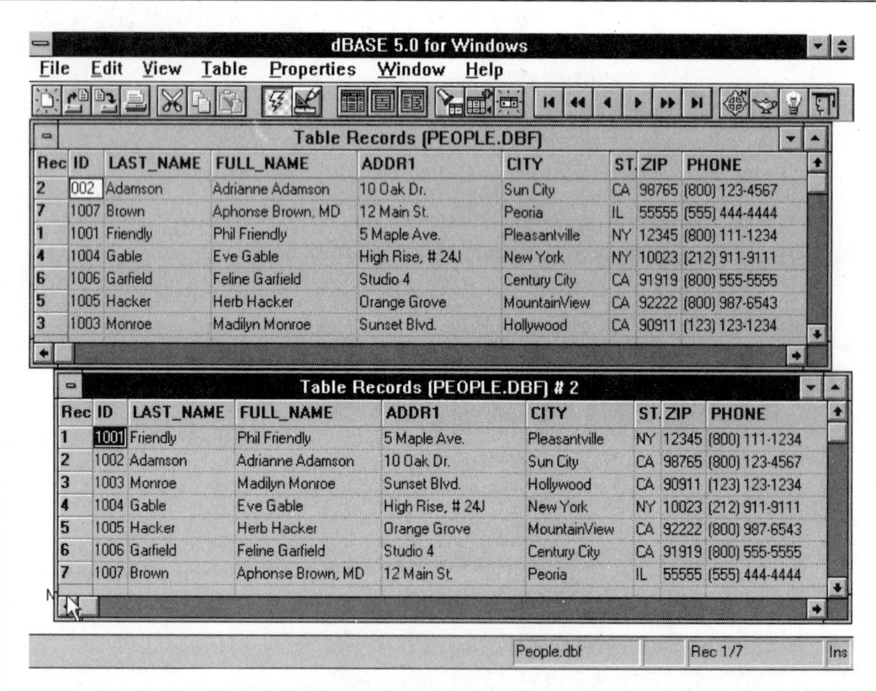

FIGURE 4.8 ►

PEOPLE.DBF sorted by the ID and LAST_NAME fields

The index that is highlighted in the Manage Indexes dialog box is your master index for the currently active Table Records tool or custom form.

Each index is given a name, called a *tag*, that can be used in the Command window when you open a table. From the Navigator, you can't specify a master index until you have launched a form or a Table tool. dBASE for Windows doesn't record your choice for a master index in DBASEWIN.INI, either. You must reselect the field for indexing each time.

There is a partial solution to this minor problem. If you have only one index as the production index, dBASE will always choose that index as the default master index. With multiple tags, dBASE defaults to the Natural Order choice (no index).

▶ Managing Your Production Index

When you choose an ascending or descending index in the Table Structure tool, an appropriate index tag and expression is created in the production index (.MDX) file. After your table is created, you can use the Manage Indexes dialog box to edit, create, and delete indexes.

So far, you've just used your tables and not worried about the possibility that others might want to use them, too. The default access that you've been using is *shared*. Shared access lets others use your tables, and it lets you use a table in several different windows simultaneously. However, some operations don't work if you are sharing access. For these you'll need *exclusive* access.

One operation that requires exclusive access to your table is index manipulation. If you're using the default shared access, dBASE for Windows will point this out and offer to correct the situation for you. Accept its offer of exclusive use if it asks you.

When you first display the Manage Indexes dialog box, the Modify … and Delete pushbuttons are grayed. (Remember, you can access this dialog box from the Structure menu of the Table Structure tool, or from the Table ➤ Table Utilities menu of the Table Records tool.) These pushbuttons aren't available because the default first index is Natural Order, which is no index at all. If you select an index, the Modify … and Delete pushbuttons become available.

Modifying an Index

We want to change the index expression to one which will cause the order for the LAST_NAME index to be truly alphabetic, as opposed to being in ASCII collating sequence.

Go ahead and select the LAST_NAME index and click on Modify … to reach the Modify Index dialog box.

The indexes you created by choosing Ascending or Descending in the Table Structure tool have the simplest possible index expression: just the name of the field. Any dBASE expression, from the simplest to the most complex, can be used.

We'll apply the dBASE UPPER() function to the LAST_NAME field. UPPER() converts all the alphabetic characters in a string to uppercase characters. (It leaves other characters unchanged.) Recall that the problem with the ASCII collating sequence is that A–Z comes before a–z. These are a couple of the problems we cited:

- Zenith will sort before adams.
- LeBeouf will sort before Lebatt.

If you convert all letters to uppercase, then your problem is solved:

- ADAMS sorts before ZENITH.
- LEBATT sorts before LEBEOUF.

To use UPPER(), just use the function name, putting whatever it is to get UPPER()ed inside the parentheses. In this case, it is the LAST_NAME field, so you want the expression to be:

```
UPPER(LAST_NAME)
```

Figure 4.9 shows the correct expression added to the Modify Index dialog box.

▸▸ **NOTE**

dBASE expressions are not case-sensitive. You can use any combination of uppercase and lowercase letters. By tradition, dBASE's built-in functions, such as UPPER(), are written in all capital letters.

Enter the expression in the Modify Index dialog box, just as you see it in Figure 4.9, then click on OK. There will be a brief pause while the new expression is written to the production index file and your table's index is re-created with the new expression. You'll return to the Manage Indexes dialog box.

FIGURE 4.9

Using UPPER() for true alphabetic sorting

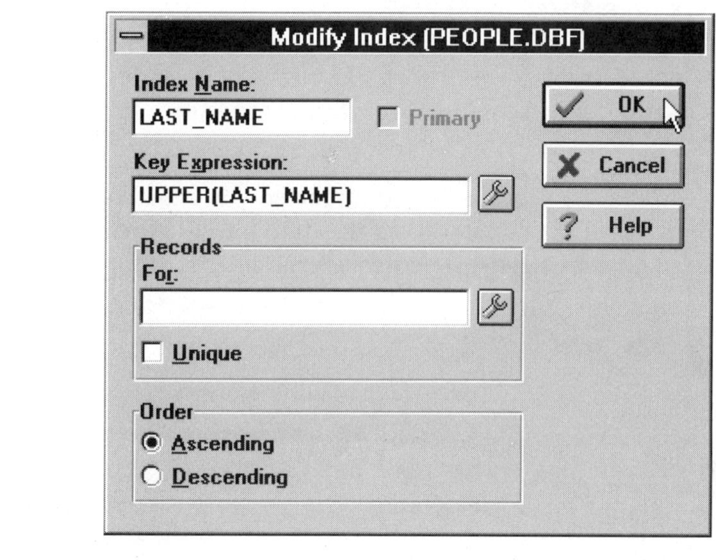

Adding and Deleting Indexes

From the Manage Indexes dialog box, you can also add and delete indexes. Deleting is a simple matter of selecting an index and clicking on the Delete pushbutton (or pressing Alt-D).

WARNING

The Delete option will delete the index without giving you a chance to reconsider. Be sure you want to delete the highlighted index before you click this button or press Alt-D.

To add a new index, simply click on Create .... This launches the Create Index dialog box, which is identical to the Modify Index dialog box, except that it's not filled in. You enter a name and expression, and your index is created.

See Chapter 12 for a full discussion of dBASE for Windows' expressions.

Date Sorting

Unfortunately, choosing to index on a Date field in the Table Structure tool doesn't work like choosing to index on a Character field. The Date field is held in an internal structure, and a default sort on a Date field uses that structure.

To sort dates in date order, you must use the DTOS() function. DTOS() converts the date into the form *YYYYMMDD*. By using this form, sorting dates as character strings puts them into order by date.

▸▸ **NOTE**

Sorting this way ignores the SET DATE TO and SET CENTURY settings, which is exactly what you want in this case. See Chapter 13 for a discussion of the SET settings.

The following expression correctly sorts records based on the date in the START_DATE field:

```
DTOS(Start_date)
```

Logical Sorting

For many purposes, an index on a logical variable is helpful. This type of index organizes a table into two parts: True and False. For example, your database of attorneys includes a logical field which is True if the attorney is licensed to practice in California. An index on this field would sort those who were licensed in that jurisdiction together, which would be helpful if you needed an attorney for a California legal matter.

You cannot index directly on a logical variable, however. Indexing is only permitted on Character, Numeric, Float, and Date fields. You can use the IIF() expression to convert logical values to character data when you want a logical sort.

This expression will convert the logical field LIC_IN_CA to a single character:

```
IIF(lic_in_ca, "Y", "N")
```

The result is either a Y or an N, depending on the value of the LIC_IN_CA field. (If you want to sort the True values to the top of the table, use descending sequence.)

▶ *Physical Sorting*

The last, and least used, option for putting your records in order is actually sorting the table. In fact, dBASE does not really have an option for sorting a table. It will write a new, sorted table, based on your original (presumably unsorted) table. You can, if you wish, copy this table over the original to get a truly sorted table.

The steps here are not as simple as you might wish. But there's a reason for this. It's to discourage you from doing physical sorts.

TIP

You should almost always use indexes or queries to put your data in the order you want. Physical sorting has almost no place in modern data management.

There is one special case where a physically sorted table makes sense, which is why we're going to show you the steps here. Remember that this process is only for this one special case.

The situation that sometimes justifies physical sorting is that static data table. You sometimes meet situations where your data will never change, or change very rarely. In this case, it may be worth the trouble to physically sort your table and dispense with the indexes.

In preparing this book, for example, we built a table of all the object properties available in dBASE 5 for Windows. We don't expect this list to change until dBASE 6.0 for Windows is released. So we waited until we were sure our list was complete, and then we sorted it into name order. We didn't assign IDs until it was sorted.

In the end, we had the table sorted so that the Natural Order, the ID order, and the alphabetic name order were all the same. However, you may find that sorting is enough trouble so that, even in this situation, you go right on using indexes. That's what the dBASE designers had in mind.

Now let's sort the People table. (Sorting is the easy part; the hard part comes next.) We chose the Sort Records … option from the Table ➤ Table Utilities menu.

Selecting Sort Records … displays the Sort Records dialog box. In Figure 4.10, we've typed the name of the new table into the Name entry field for the Target Table. We always use the name TEMP for the file that gets the sorted data.

FIGURE 4.10 ▶

Choosing LAST_NAME to sort to TEMP.DBF

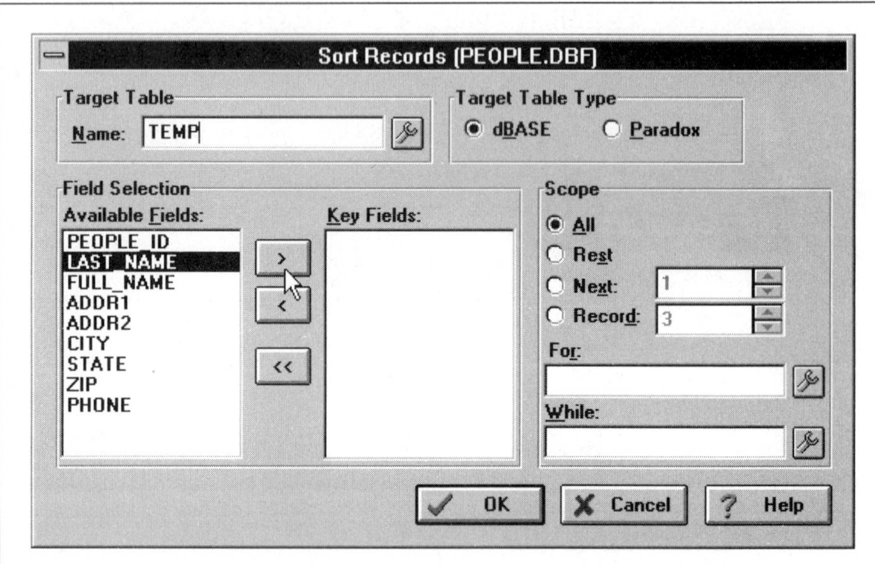

▶▶ **TIP**

If you always sort into the same .DBF file, each sort will overwrite the last one. If you use different names for each sort, you'll have a hard time telling your real .DBFs from the temporary ones.

After you enter a name, select one or more sort fields. The first field is the main sort order. For example, you could sort sales orders by date and then by customer name. The second field would sort records where the first field's value matched (all the orders for one date, for example).

Highlight the field on the left, and click on the > pushbutton to shoot it from the Available Fields box into the Key Fields box. After you move a field across, an up arrow icon appears next to it in the Key Fields box.

Click on this arrow and, for a Character field, you will be given four choices: ascending or descending, both with or without case. Choose without case for a true alphabetic sort.

After you've specified your sort and chosen OK, in a very few seconds, the sort will be completed. You'll have a new table, in our case TEMP.DBF, that has the records in the order you specified.

If you had any memo fields, you now have a new copy of the memos in TEMP.DBT. There is no production index for TEMP.

You also have your original .DBF, .DBT (if any), and .MDX files, and probably a .DBK (backup) file as well. Exit from all copies of the Table Records, Table Structure, and Form tools that are manipulating your original file.

In the Navigator, highlight your original .DBF file and right-click to get the Speed menu. From the Speed menu, select Delete. Alternatively you could choose Edit ➤ Delete from the menus, or just press the Del key. You'll see the Delete File dialog box, which will remind you that you will be deleting all the associated files, as well as the .DBF file.

▶▶ TIP

The Delete File process forgets the .DBK extension. This gives you the opportunity to recover from serious mistakes. On the other hand, it gives you one more cleanup chore to remember.

Once you delete the original file, you can rename the TEMP.??? files to the old name. In the Command window, type

```
rename TEMP.DBF TO oldname.DBF
rename TEMP.DBT TO oldname.DBT
```

With that chore out of the way, you only need to launch the renamed table into the Table Records tool and choose Table ➤ Table Utilities ➤ Manage Indexes. In the Manage Indexes dialog box, you can re-create any indexes you want in your production index.

▸▸ **TIP**

If re-creating your indexes is a major job, use the Command window (not the Navigator) to delete your old files one at a time. Don't delete the .MDX file. After you rename your TEMP files to the old name, your old .MDX file has the correct index expressions, but the wrong indexes. Use the Table ➤ Table Utilities ➤ Reindex option to fix the indexes.

Does this seem like a lot of work? Well, again we remind you that you never need to do it, and that you should do it only in the rare instance of a static file. Even in that instance, you could just use an index and not bother physically sorting.

▸▸ Fast Updates for Groups of Records

Sometimes, updating a record is a simple matter of typing a new value over an old one. An acquaintance moves, so you enter a new address in your People table.

Other times, and they are numerous, you want to update a group of records. We just did this when we added ID fields to our People table. In this section, we'll look at some more ways to work with groups of records.

Before we do that, we'll need to have a fair-sized table to work with. For the moment, we'll assume that you have ten records in your People table. If you have a different number, adjust these instructions to fit.

WARNING

If you have a substantial number of live records, copy PEOPLE.* to a backup disk, so that you can restore your files later.

dBASE for Windows will be happy to supply you with data in bulk. This is very helpful for testing. Let's expand our People table to 1000 records. Here's how:

1. From the Navigator, select and launch your People table. (Double-click the table, or select the table and press F2.)
2. If you're not in the Browse Layout view already, select it. (Choose View ➤ Browse Layout, or click on the icon for that view in the speedbar.)
3. Choose Table ➤ Table Utilities ➤ Generate Records ....
4. In the Generate Records dialog box, enter 990 (or as many as you need to get to 1000).

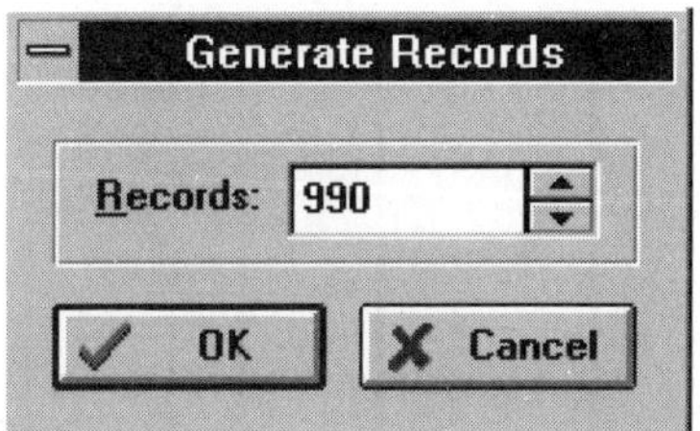

Then click on OK or press Enter.

dBASE for Windows reports its progress in this operation with the color bar at the bottom of the screen in the center of the status bar. When it fills its rectangle, the operation is complete. Bear in mind that dBASE is not just adding records; it is updating its indexes as it goes. This product is fast!

►► **WARNING**

In version 5.0, there is a harmless but annoying bug. The record number column in the Browse Layout view is not wide enough for four or more digits if you start with fewer than 1000 records. dBASE itself can handle millions of records. This is just a display problem.

Now we have a moderate-size table to work with. Ours is shown in Figure 4.11. As you see, dBASE for Windows has supplied random numbers and text to fill your table. This is the data we will begin to manipulate.

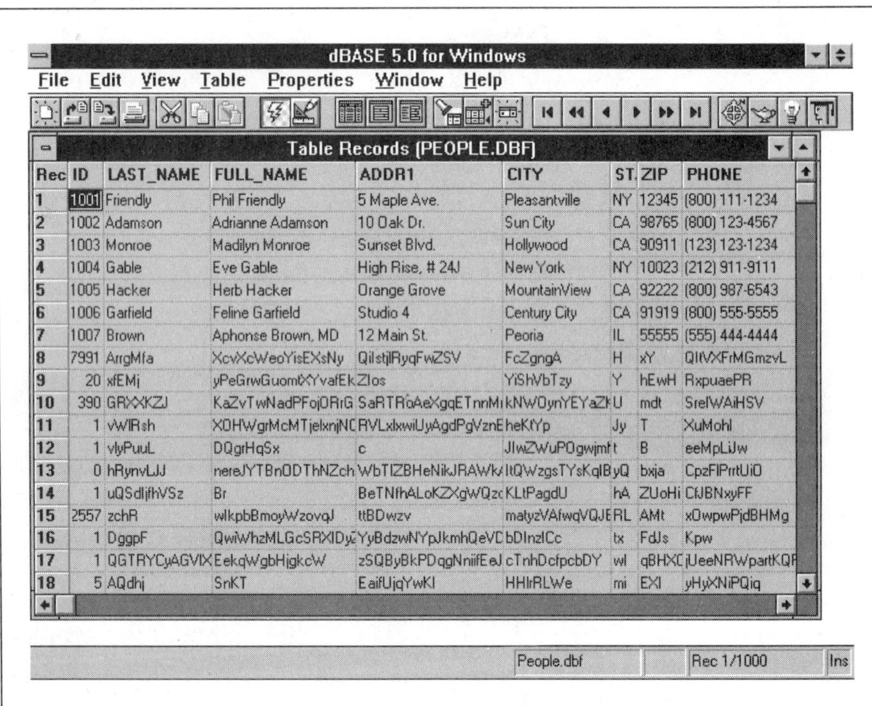

FIGURE 4.11 ►

dBASE's generated PEOPLE data

► Locating and Updating Data Groups

Before we do anything else, the fact that our ID fields are sporting nonunique values bothers us. We hope it bothers you, too. Let's fix that right away. We'll do this from the Command window, because it's the easiest way.

Reestablishing Unique ID Values

First, close any open windows accessing the People table. Then open the Command window. To do so, click on the icon showing Aladdin's lamp on the speedbar (shown in the margin), or choose Window ➤ 2 from the menus.

In the Command window, we'll do three things:

- Open the People table and its production index.
- Set unique values in the PEOPLE_ID field and reindex on these values.
- Close our table and index.

Fortunately, none of these is difficult to do. These three commands will do the trick:

```
USE People
REPLACE ALL People_ID WITH RECNO()+1000
USE
```

The first command is USE People. When you USE a table, it's associated production index (if it has one) is automatically opened. As in the Table Records tool, Natural Order (no index) is chosen if there are multiple index tags. (The USE command also opens associated memo, .MDT, files.)

The second command is REPLACE. The ALL keyword specifies the scope, which in this case is every record. The People_ID specifies the field to be replaced. The WITH clause, including the expression, specifies the value to use as a replacement.

Any replacement that affects an indexed field automatically causes the index to be updated, so we don't need to worry about reindexing. This operation would be virtually instantaneous if it were not updating the index every time it replaces the PEOPLE_ID field.

The third command, USE with no table name, closes any open table and its associated files.

Figure 4.12 shows how we entered these commands.

FIGURE 4.12

Reestablishing unique ID fields for the People table

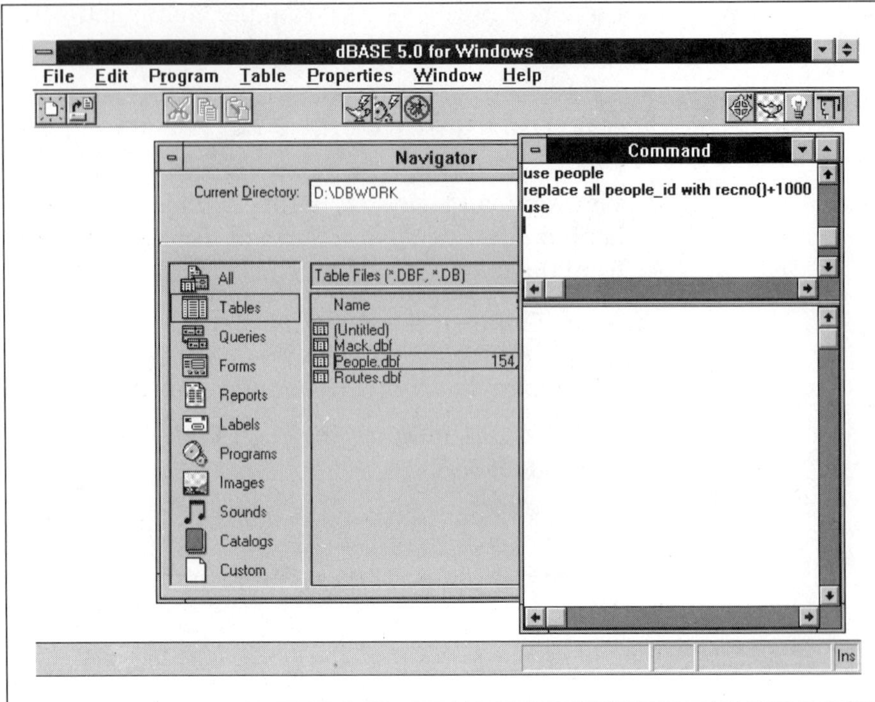

As you can see, we type commands in all lowercase, because it's faster. If we are writing a program (or a book) we use uppercase and lowercase conventions to distinguish dBASE functions and keywords from other elements. dBASE doesn't care either way.

We feel better now that our ID fields are filled with unique values. So much better that we'll allow a little digression right here.

We just did that operation the slow way. If you want to change all, or substantially all, the values in an index, it's better to make the changes with the index turned off, and then reindex when you're finished. For 1000 records, it's faster to forget this and make the change the way shown here. For 100,000 records, do it this way:

```
USE People
SET INDEX TO
REPLACE ALL People_ID WITH RECNO()+1000
USE People EXCLUSIVE
REINDEX
USE
```

The first command, USE People, works as before. The next command, SET INDEX TO, is normally followed by the name of an index file. (You can use this command to have other .MDX files in addition to the production index.) Without a file specification, it turns the indexes off.

The REPLACE command is the same as before. Next, we USE People again, this time specifying EXCLUSIVE use. Then the REINDEX command does just what its name suggests. Finally, the plain USE command closes everything for us.

▶ Finding Individual Records

The first choice on the Table menu is for finding records. The Find Records option lets you locate an individual record. The Find tool is also used as part of a find and replace operation to specify a group of records. Let's begin by using Find Records ... to locate a particular record in our People table.

From the Navigator, launch the Table Records tool for your People table. For this example, we'll want the master index to be our UPPER (LAST_NAME) index. Choose Table ➤ Table Utilities ➤ Manage Indexes ....

In the Manage Indexes dialog box, select the LAST_NAME index, and then click on OK or press Enter.

▶▶ **TIP**

Picking a master index is fastest from the keyboard: press Alt-T for Table, then T and M to get the Manage Indexes dialog box. Press End (assuming your LAST_NAME index is the last index in the list) and Enter. This requires just five keystrokes.

Press Ctrl-PgUp (or choose Table ➤ Top Record, or click the beginning of file speedbar button) to get to the start of the list.

Now, let's find the first record for a person whose last name starts with the letter *M*. Follow the steps on the following page.

1. Open the Find Records dialog box. There are several ways to get to this dialog box: press Ctrl-F, click on the flashlight icon (shown in the margin) on the speedbar, choose Table ➤ Find Records …, or right-click to get the Speed menu and choose Find Records ….
2. Type the letter **m** in the Find What entry field.
3. Highlight the LAST_NAME field in the Located in Field box by pressing Tab to reach the box and pressing ↓, or by clicking on that field.
4. Specify that you want the search to start from the top by clicking on the Top Record radio button, or by pressing Alt-T.
5. Begin the search by pressing Enter or by clicking on Find.

You'll now be positioned on the first record where the last name starts with *m* or *M*. If you look at the buttons in the Search Rules box, you'll see that the Standard search is selected. Figure 4.13 shows our search, after execution.

FIGURE 4.13

Finding the first last name starting with m

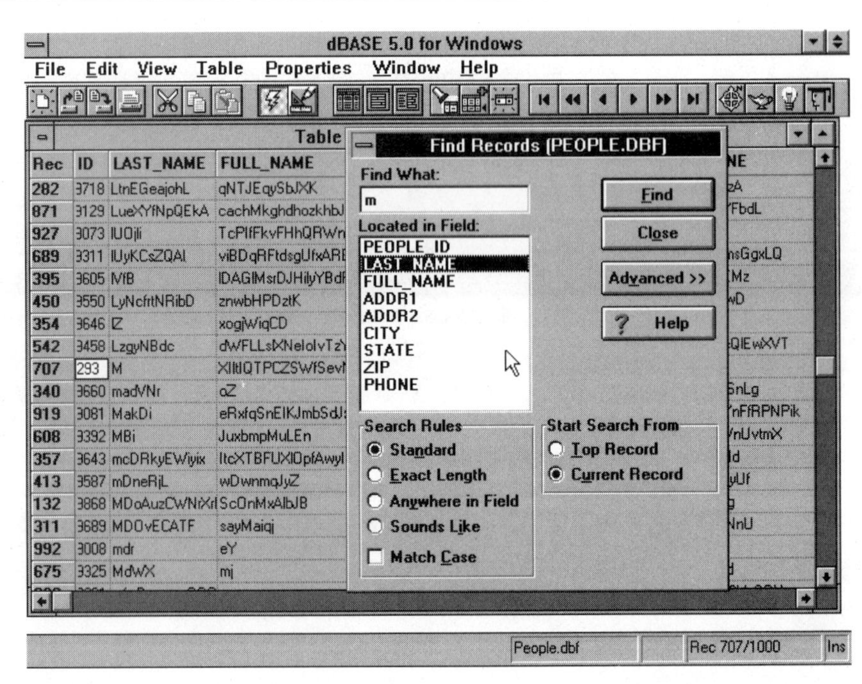

If you look in the Start Search From box now, you'll see that the Top Record radio button is no longer selected. Instead, Current Record is chosen. This is done so that if you click on Find again (or press Enter), you'll find the next record that begins with *m*.

Pressing Alt-O or Esc, or clicking on Close, removes the Find Records dialog box.

We recommend using the keyboard for fast searching. Here's a rundown, one keystroke at a time, of the search for the first *m*:

- Ctrl-F opens the Find Records dialog box.
- M places the search target in the Find What entry field.
- Tab switches to the Located in Field box.
- ↓ highlights the LAST_NAME field.
- Enter executes the search.
- Esc removes the Find Records dialog box.

Of course, if you wanted to search for *Masters*, you could type a few more letters into the Find What entry field.

The value you enter in the Find What entry field is the value that dBASE for Windows will look for in the table. It must match the type of field being searched. (Text goes in a Chartacter field, dates for a Date field, Numbers for a numeric field, and so on.)

You may use a dBASE expression in this field, too. Enclose the expression in parentheses, to tell dBASE that it should evaluate the expression before searching. For example, the DATE() built-in function returns today's date. If you wanted to find the first invoice from a week ago, you could type this into the Find What entry field:

```
(DATE()-7)
```

Subtracting 7 from a date backs up exactly one week.

Entering text in the Find What entry field actually is a form of an expression. You're really telling dBASE for Windows to search for a match on the left side of the search field and that the search is not case-sensitive (unless you select otherwise through the Search Rules choices).

In dBASE for Windows, literal strings are enclosed in quotation marks. This is another way you could provide an *m* string:

('m')

You can use either single or double quotation marks, but you must use them in pairs. This is certainly an inconvenient way to do what is simple, but the technique has a very practical use, as you'll see when we come to replace all records operations.

If you look at the buttons in the Search Rules panel, you'll see that you can override these defaults. The search could be for a value that exactly matches the length of your search string. Alternatively, dBASE could search for your string anywhere within the field. It could be a SOUNDEX search (where Smythe and Smith are a match), and it could be case-sensitive.

▸ Finding and Replacing in a Group of Records

The second place where you'll use the Find operation is from the Replace Records dialog box, which appears when you choose Table ➤ Replace Records ... (or press Ctrl-R). Figure 4.14 shows this dialog box.

As you can see, the Find What entry field, the Located in Field box, and the Search Rules choices are identical to those in the Find Records dialog box.

Replacing in Every Record

There is no direct way to specify that you don't want to find particular records; that you just want to do a replace operation in every record in your table. Fortunately, it's simple enough to trick dBASE for Windows into doing exactly what you want.

Recall that the default is to match the length of the string that you type in the Find What entry field. Now if you could type zero characters, then every field would match. If you experiment with typing in this box, you'll see that the very first letter you type enables the grayed Find and Replace All options. If you use the Backspace key to delete the first letter, those options are grayed again.

FIGURE 4.14

Finding and replacing through the Replace Records dialog box

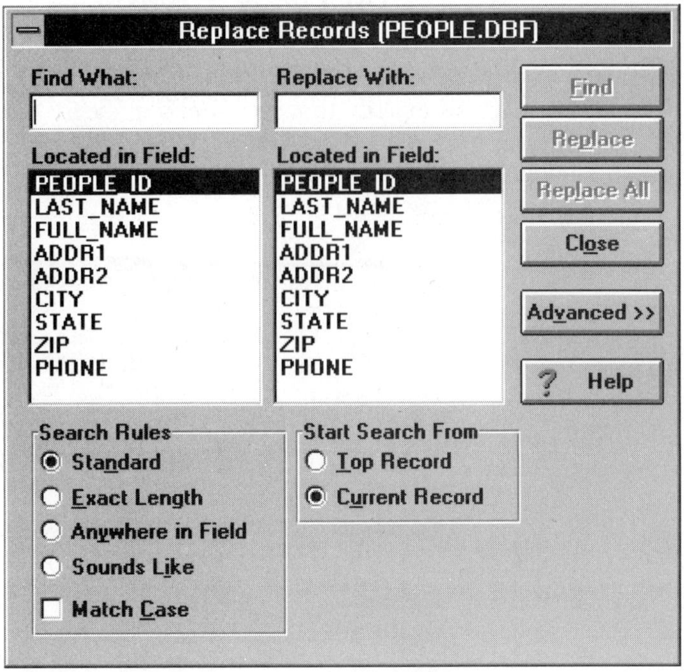

Similarly, if you type any text, and then use the Del key to delete the last letter, those options are also returned to gray. dBASE for Windows knows that nothing is in the Find What entry field.

This is where we outsmart it. Type in this expression:

('')

That's two adjacent single quotation marks, with no space in between. Since the text is in parentheses, dBASE knows that it's an expression. The quotation marks tell dBASE that this is a character string. The fact that there is nothing between the opening and closing quotation marks tells dBASE that we have a zero-length string. If the Exact Length radio button isn't selected, every text field will match this string.

Now that we know how to do a "can't miss" match, let's go on to making some improvements in the test data that dBASE for Windows gave us. While you do this, you'll master this important tool.

A PROPER( ) LAST_NAME

Last names generally begin with a capital letter and are followed by lowercase letters. In dBASE, the PROPER( ) function capitalizes words exactly that way. Let's make all our LAST_NAMEs PROPER( ). Figure 4.15 shows the Replace Records dialog box we used to do this.

FIGURE 4.15

Making our last names propercase

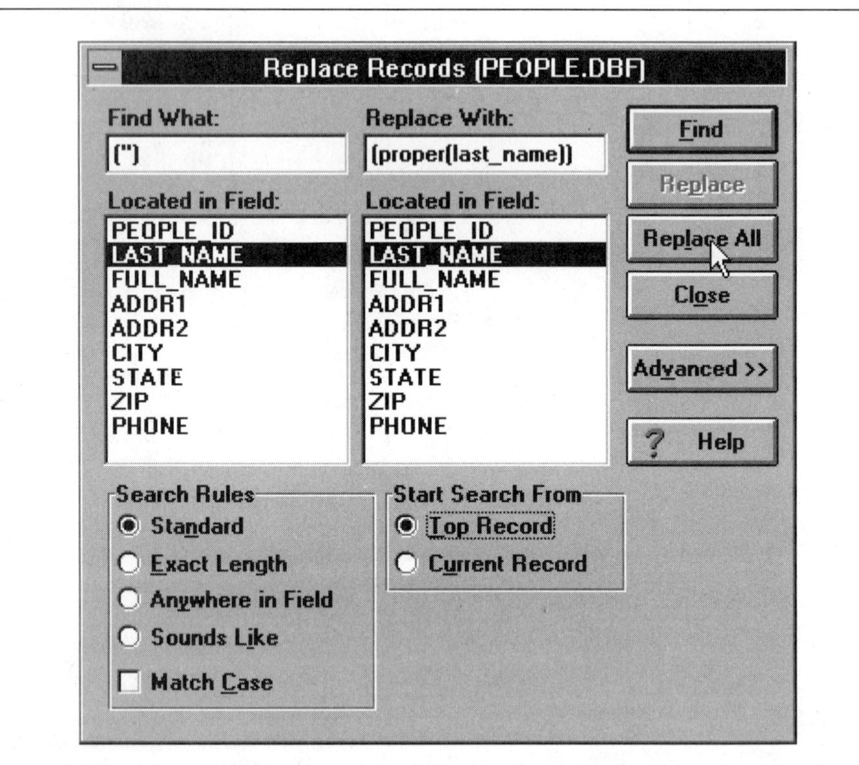

We're searching a text field (it doesn't need to be the LAST_NAME field; any text field will do) for a zero-length string, which will find every record.

Make sure that you put the PROPER( ) function in parentheses:

```
(PROPER(LAST_NAME))
```

This makes dBASE for Windows evaluate the expression. Without the parentheses, it will type the text itself as the replacements. In this case, every field would be replaced with the text *(PROPER(LAST_NAME))*.

When your Replace Records dialog box looks like the one in Figure 4.15, choose Replace All to make the changes.

Fixing the State Codes

We're about to go on to the advanced options for replace operations. Before we do, we'll need to group our data. The states provide a way to do this. First, make the replacement shown in Figure 4.16 to convert all the state codes to capital letters.

FIGURE 4.16

Capitalizing the two-letter state codes

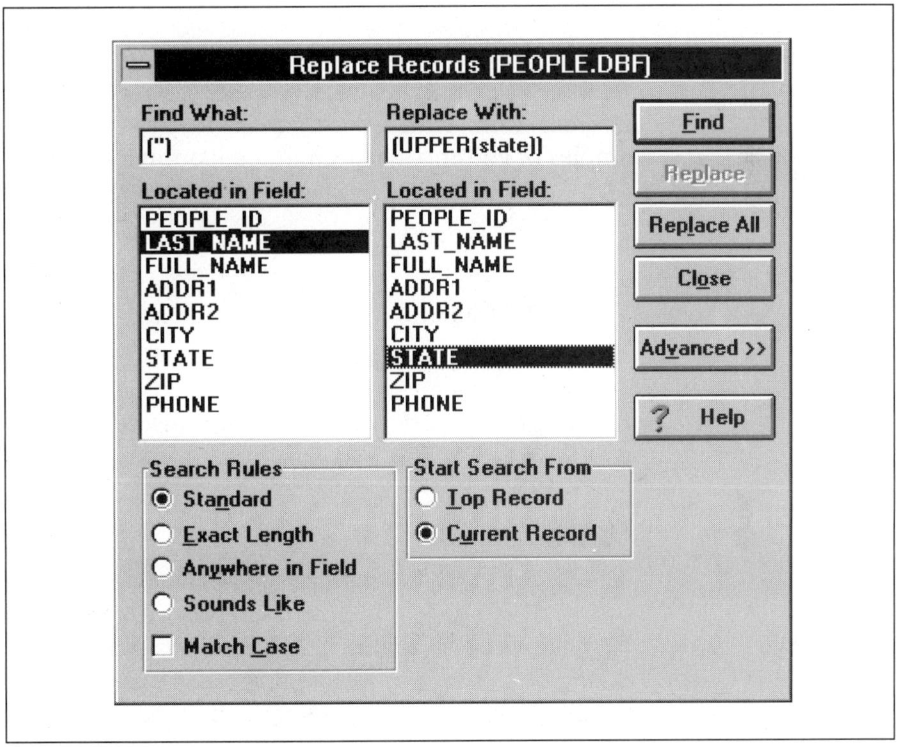

Replace Records (PEOPLE.DBF)

Find What: (")
Replace With: (UPPER(state))

Located in Field: PEOPLE_ID, LAST_NAME, FULL_NAME, ADDR1, ADDR2, CITY, STATE, ZIP, PHONE
Located in Field: PEOPLE_ID, LAST_NAME, FULL_NAME, ADDR1, ADDR2, CITY, STATE, ZIP, PHONE

Find | Replace | Replace All | Close | Advanced >> | Help

Search Rules: Standard, Exact Length, Anywhere in Field, Sounds Like, Match Case
Start Search From: Top Record, Current Record

If you look closely, you'll see that the radio button for Current Record is selected. When you choose Replace All, this setting is ignored.

Make this change, and your state codes will begin to look a little more like U.S. state codes (two-letter codes, always capitalized, identifying the 50 states and a handful of other American territories, such as the U.S. Virgin Islands). The remaining problem, which we'll take as an opportunity, is that dBASE used a mixture of one- and two-character strings. We'll convert all the one-letter strings to CA, to get a generous supply of people living in California.

For this change, the Command window will be handy. Close the Table Records tool and open the Command window. You'll see that the instructions you've been giving are echoed here as if you had typed in equivalent dBASE language commands. These are the commands to type to change the single-letter state codes to CA:

```
USE People
REPLACE ALL State WITH 'CA' FOR 1 = LEN(RTRIM(State))
USE
```

The LEN( ) function returns the length of a character string. The State field is two characters wide, whether it is filled in or not. The RTRIM( ) function trims blank spaces off the right side of a string. Here are some examples of commands given in the Command window and their results:

? state	Reports "X"
? LEN(state)	Reports 2
? RTRIM(state)	Reports "X"
? LEN(RTRIM(state))	Reports 1

If you used an address format appropriate to your country, pick one of your own fields and make a similar change.

Using the For Clause

Now we're ready to explore the advanced options of the Replace Records tool. To get to them, click on the Advanced >> pushbutton in the Replace Records dialog box. This pops out an additional portion of the dialog box. To make a change for all the records where the state is CA, use the For entry field, as shown in Figure 4.17.

The For entry field accepts a logical expression, which is one that evaluates to True or False. The expression

```
state = 'CA'
```

is one example.

Here we've replaced the zip codes with a distinctive value, so we can check the results. Be sure that you've selected the All radio button under Scope.

FIGURE 4.17

Replacing records with the For clause

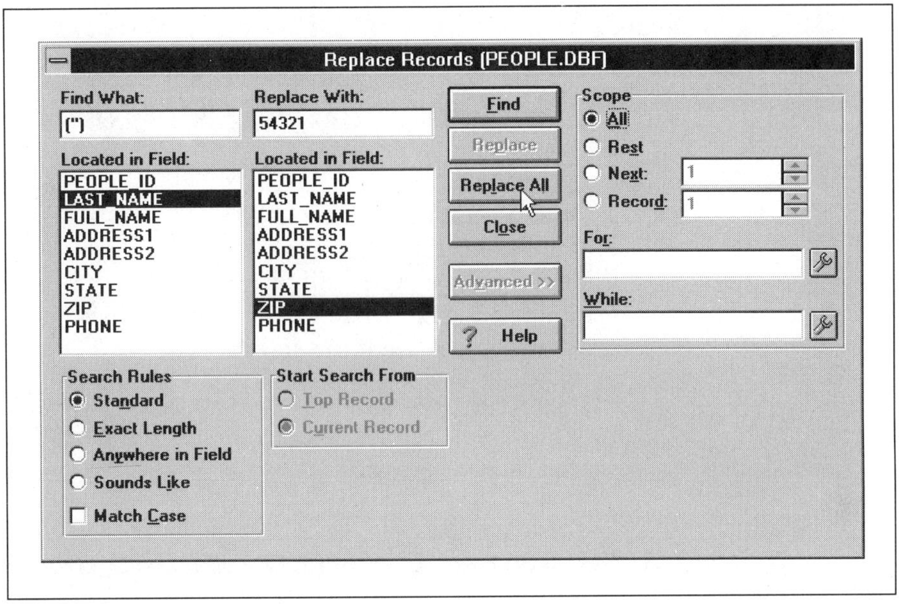

Using the While Clause

Try this change again, but use another replacement value and put the expression into the While entry field. Make sure that your currently selected record is one where the state is CA before you start.

This operation changes only a handful of states. As its name implies, a While selection does its replacements while the condition is true. As soon as it comes to a state that is not CA, it stops.

As you've noticed, running replacements such as these through a 1000-record table is quite quick. However, if you were working with a really large table, it could be important to take advantage of the While clause.

You could create an index on the STATE field and select that index as your master index. Then you could find the first record that has CA in the STATE field. Using

```
State = 'CA'
```

for the While expression will process every record where the state is CA. It will stop on the first record where the state exceeds CA.

►► **TIP**

Using While expressions with an indexed (or sorted) database can save time if your tables are large.

In the U.S., about one in eight people lives in California. For a representative collection of Americans, indexing by state and replacing While the state is 'CA' will process about one-eighth of your records. Without an index, the For expression will evaluate every record in your table to check to see if the state is CA.

When you do this, click on the Rest radio button for Scope, so dBASE knows that you want to search the rest of the table, starting from the current record forward.

► *Deleting and Recovering Groups of Records*

When you delete a record in dBASE, the record is not physically removed from the file. Its Deleted flag is set and, if you have set Deleted on, your records are not shown in the Table Records tool or in forms.

To see how this works, follow these steps:

1. Launch the People table in the Table Records tool. Choose a Browse Layout view.
2. Choose Properties ➤ Desktop, Table tab. In the Other box, make sure that Deleted is checked.
3. Return to your Browse Layout view.
4. Select a record somewhere in the middle of the window and press Ctrl-U or choose Table ➤ Delete Selected Record. The deleted record disappears.
5. Return to the Properties ➤ Desktop, Table tab. Now remove the check from Deleted and close the dialog box by clicking on OK or pressing Enter.

When you return to your table, you'll see the deleted record. dBASE has added a Del column with a check box to your table to show the deletion status of your records, as you can see in Figure 4.18.

FIGURE 4.18

People table with Deleted turned off

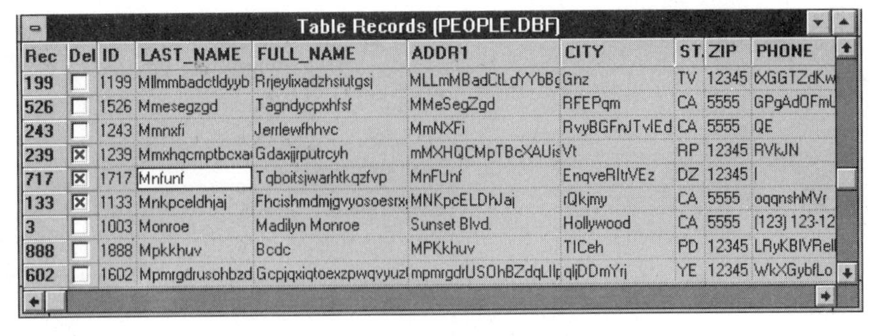

Table Records (PEOPLE.DBF)

Rec	Del	ID	LAST_NAME	FULL_NAME	ADDR1	CITY	ST.	ZIP	PHONE
199		1199	Mllmmbadctldyyb	Rrjeylixadzhsiutgsj	MLLmMBadCtLdYYbBg	Gnz	TV	12345	tXGGTZdKw
526		1526	Mmesegzgd	Tagndycpxhfsf	MMeSegZgd	RFEPqm	CA	5555	GPgAdOFmL
243		1243	Mmnxfi	Jerrlewfhhvc	MmNXFi	RvyBGFnJTvlEd	CA	5555	QE
239	X	1239	Mmxhqcmptbcxa	Gdaxjjrputrcyh	mMXHQCMpTBcXAUis	Vt	RP	12345	RVkJN
717	X	1717	Mnfunf	Tqboitsjwarhtkqzfvp	MnFUnf	EnqveRltrVEz	DZ	12345	I
133	X	1133	Mnkpceldhjaj	Fhcishmdmjgvyosoesrx	MNKpcELDhJaj	rQkjmy	CA	5555	oqqnshMVr
3		1003	Monroe	Madilyn Monroe	Sunset Blvd.	Hollywood	CA	5555	(123) 123-12
888		1888	Mpkkhuv	Bcdc	MPKkhuv	TICeh	PD	12345	LRyKBIVRel
602		1602	Mpmrgdrusohbzd	Gcpjqxiqtoexzpwqvyuzl	mpmrgdrUSOhBZdqLIIp	qljDDmYrj	YE	12345	WkXGybfLo

With Deleted turned off, all you need to do to delete a record is check the Del box. To see this, place some checks in the Del boxes, and then use Properties ➤ Desktop to check the Deleted feature. When you return to your Browse Layout view, the deleted records will be gone.

Return to Properties ➤ Desktop and remove the check from Deleted. When you return to your table, the deleted records will reappear.

For the rest of this section, leave the Del column visible so you can see your records' deleted status.

Deleting a Group of Records

Let's delete a handful of records with the Delete Records dialog box. Move to the middle of your People table and select a record somewhere near the middle of your Browse window. From the menus, select Table ➤ Table Utilities ➤ Delete Records ....

As shown in Figure 4.19, in the Delete Records dialog box, choose to delete the Next 4 records. Then choose OK. You'll see that the selected record and the following three are deleted.

Recovering the Deleted Records

Let's retrieve these records, along with any others you may have deleted. From the menus, choose Table ➤ Table Utilities ➤ Recall Records .... This dialog box, shown in Figure 4.20, is similar to the Delete Records dialog box.

FIGURE 4.19

Delete the selected record and three more

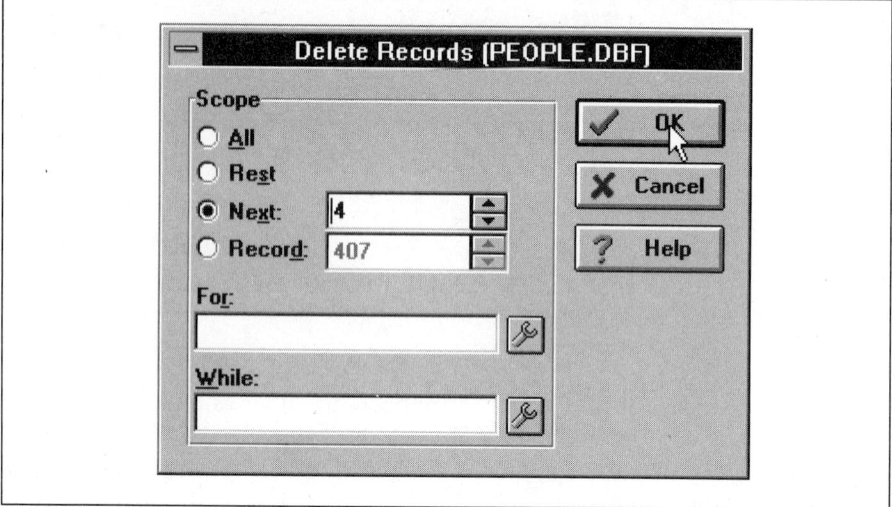

FIGURE 4.20 

Recalling all deleted records

The default for recalling records is All. Accept the default by choosing OK, and all your deleted records are now returned to nondeleted status.

This is certainly useful for recovering from mistakes, but it can also be used in many other ways.

Using Deletions to Control a Mailing

Suppose you have a mailing which you want to send to all your customers in California. You have used Crystal Reports to prepare a mailing label program. Now it's time to run the labels. One way to make sure you generate just the labels you want is to delete all the customers who are not in California.

Figure 4.21 shows the expression in the For: entry field of the Delete Records dialog box that will delete those customers. The expression uses the dBASE operator **<>**, which represents "not equal to." Here we are deleting all the records where the STATE field's value is not equal to CA.

FIGURE 4.21

Temporarily eliminating non-California addresses

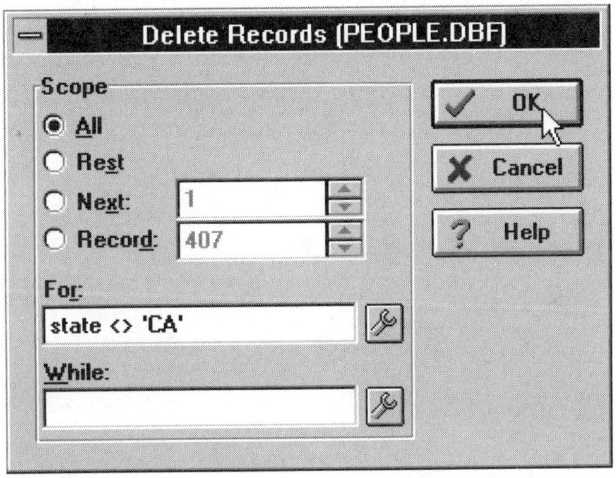

Delete Records (PEOPLE.DBF)

Scope: (•) All ( ) Rest ( ) Next: 1 ( ) Record: 407

For: state <> 'CA'

While:

OK | Cancel | Help

After you print your mailing labels, choose Table ➤ Table Utilities ➤ Recall Records … and recall all your records.

Making Deletions Permanent

In some cases, you'll want to permanently delete unwanted records. The PACK command performs this function. You can enter the command in the Command window, or with the Table Records tool active, you can choose Table ➤ Table Utilities ➤ Pack Records.

▸▸ **WARNING**

The Table ➤ Table Utilities ➤ Pack Records selection does not give you any warning prompt or other dialog box. It executes immediately.

Experienced database users develop routine data-maintenance procedures. A common maintenance task is to back up tables first, and then pack them. Backing up your tables outside dBASE guarantees that all records, deleted or not, are backed up. This lets you recover from an eventual Pack mistake.

If you use the PACK command or Pack Records menu option, you'll see that this is a relatively slow, disk-intensive process. It requires physically rewriting the entire table.

You may want to delete every record in a table, to start a fresh table. The ZAP command does this operation in a single, highly efficient step. You can enter the command in the Command window, or with the Table Records tool active, you can choose Table ➤ Table Utilities ➤ Zap Records.

▸▸ **WARNING**

Zapping your table deletes every record, permanently. Before you use the ZAP command, back up your data!

▸ Having dBASE Count for You

For this section, recall all your records that are marked for deletion (Table ➤ Table Utilities ➤ Recall Records …), go anywhere in the People table above the bottom of the table, and delete ten records. Use Table ➤ Table Utilities ➤ Delete Records …, setting Next: to 10.

We assume that you have 1000 records, of which 10 are now deleted. If you were at or near the bottom of your table when you deleted Next: 10, there might not have been 10 records to delete. Take a good look to be sure.

How many records are in your table? There are two correct answers: there are 1000 records and there are 990 active (not deleted) records.

The answer dBASE gives you depends on the setting of the Deleted flag. Let's go for a count. Here we assume that your Deleted box in Properties ➤ Desktop, Table tab, is not checked, and that the Del column appears in your Browse Layout view.

Counting the Total Records in Table

Choose Table ➤ Table Utilities ➤ Count Records … to get a count. To select the default All, just press Enter or click on OK. The Counted Records dialog box will report that you have 1000 records:

Counting Active Records

Now return to Properties ➤ Desktop, Table tab and check the Deleted box. Press Enter or click on OK. When you return to Table ➤ Table Utilities ➤ Count Records …, the count of All records will report that there are 990 records.

TIP

Normal operations are done with the Deleted flag left on. You'll seldom find that counts which include deleted records are useful.

Counting Records that Match a Condition

How many people in this table are in California? Like the Delete Records and Recall Records dialog boxes, the Count Records dialog box provides For: and While: entry fields, which function the same way.

To count your records for people in California, enter this in the For: entry field:

```
state = 'CA'
```

Be sure the scope is All, and click on OK to count those records.

Counting Contiguous Records

Similarly, the While: entry field will count only as long as the condition you enter there is True. If your LAST_NAME index is the master index, you can find the first person whose last name starts with *S*, for example. Then you can count While:

```
last_name = 'S'
```

This will tell you how many people you have whose last name starts with the letter *S*.

Counting a Condition in a Range

You can use For and While conditions together. As an example, repeat the previous count, adding this For condition:

```
state = 'CA'
```

You'll get a count of all the people whose last name starts with the letter *S* and who are in California. You can use the While condition to specify a range of records, and the For condition to select some of the records in the range.

▸ Letting dBASE Calculate for You

dBASE for Windows can perform any sort of calculations you may require. These half dozen common calculations are defined for you and can be done with only a few mouse clicks (or keypresses):

- Average
- Minimum
- Maximum
- Standard deviation
- Sum
- Variance

Other calculations require programming.

Calculations apply only to Numeric fields. Our People table's only Numeric field is its PEOPLE_ID field, for which these calculations are not meaningful. However, for now, the ID values will be adequate for demonstrating how the calculations are performed.

Let's start by finding the average of our ID values. Choose Table ➤ Table Utilities ➤ Calculate Records .... Figure 4.22 shows the Calculate Records dialog box set to calculate the average of all records in the PEOPLE_ID field.

FIGURE 4.22

Finding an average value

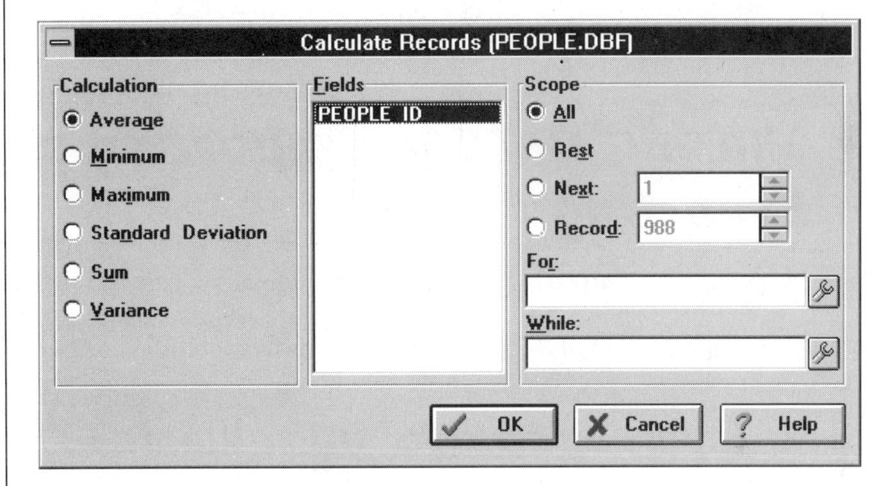

When you click on OK or press Enter, you'll get the Calculation Results dialog box:

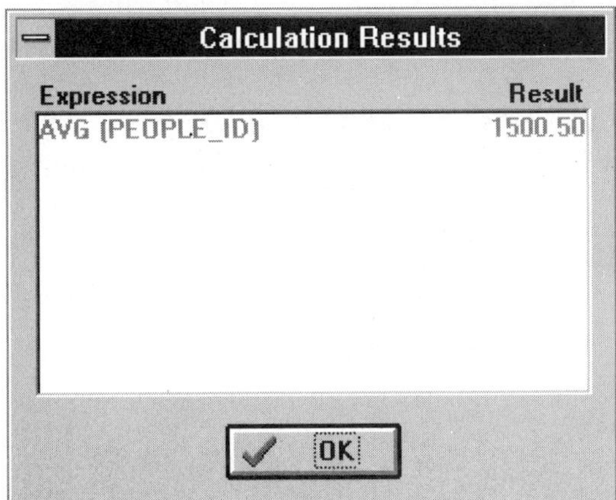

The process is lightning fast.

dBASE for Windows will perform the specified calculation for several fields at once. The Fields box in the Calculate Records dialog box lists all your numeric fields. You select the first field you want by clicking or by using the ↓ and ↑ keys. To select a range, hold down the Shift key and use ↓ or ↑, or click at the end of your range. The Calculations Results dialog box will show all the results at once. Go ahead and experiment with the other calculations.

The Scope box provides the same controls over the scope of the calculation that you can use to control the deletion of records. You can specify a particular number of records as well as For and While conditions.

▸▸ Sharing Data by Importing and Exporting

Many modern programs, such as major word processors and spreadsheets, can read .DBF format files directly. For other programs, dBASE for Windows provides capabilities to share its data.

▸ Exporting Data for Other Programs

Although many programs can directly read data in .DBF files, you'll find it handy to be able to export your data to other dBASE and Paradox tables, or in standard system formats for programs that don't read .DBF files.

To export data, choose Table ➤ Table Utilities ➤ Export Records .... Figure 4.23 show the Export Records dialog box. In this example, we've chosen the TEMP file, with the SDF (System Data Format) file type. All our fields are selected, and we are exporting the Next 10 records. This will create the file TEMP.TXT in our working directory.

Files and File Types

The file name's default extension is based on the File Type value, which can be one of the following:

- dBASE

FIGURE 4.23

Exporting ten records to TEMP in System Data Format

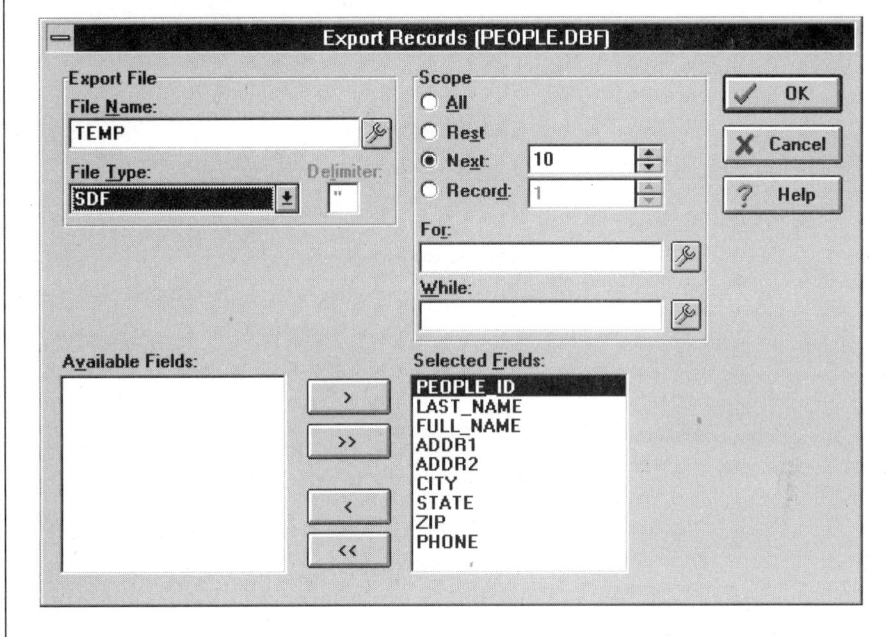

- Paradox
- SDF
- Delimited
- DBMEMO3

Specifying dBASE or DBMEMO3 exports to a .DBF file. The DBMEMO3 type provides compatibility with dBASE III Plus files. Paradox output is directed to a .DB file type. The other two options create .TXT files.

An SDF file is a text file with each field written according to its width. Text fields are left-aligned within their width; numbers are aligned on the right, based on their specified width and decimal places. No extra space is provided between fields.

Delimited data files use delimiters to separate fields in a manner that is compatible with old BASIC program's requirements. Numeric fields are written in whatever width is needed. Character data is enclosed in quotation marks. All fields are separated by commas. (Delimited data is seldom used today.)

The Field Picker

The default selection for exporting records is all fields. You can adjust this to suit your requirements with the field selection pushbuttons.

The **>>** and **<<** buttons send every field in the direction indicated. The **>** and **<** buttons move just the highlighted field in the direction indicated.

In addition to letting you select fields, you can use these buttons to order your fields in whatever way you like. When you use the single-character buttons (**>** and **<**), the field that you're moving will be placed immediately below the field that is highlighted in the destination box.

To export a very simple phone list, for example, you could start by clicking on the **<<** button to move all the fields from the Selected Fields box back to the Available Fields box. Then click on the FULL_NAME field to select it and click on the **>** button to send it to the Selected Fields box. Next, use the same technique to move the PHONE field.

If you wanted to add the CITY field next, you could highlight either of the two fields (FULL_NAME or PHONE) already in the Selected Fields box. Highlighting the first one before you move the CITY field will place the CITY field as the second one in the Selected Fields list. Highlight the last one to put the new field at the bottom of the Selected Fields list.

Setting the Export Scope

The Scope choices in the Export Records dialog box provides the same tools that we've been using throughout this chapter. You can pick All or a limited record range, such as Next: 10.

You can also use For and While clauses to select the records you want. As in the other dialog boxes, you can use these clauses together to select a portion of the records in a range.

▶ Importing Data

dBASE for Windows has a limited ability to import data through the Import choice on the File menu. However, it has an almost unlimited ability to import data through the Append Records from File choice on the Table Utilities menu. Any data that you can get in neat columns in a file (such as by printing to file from a word processor or spreadsheet program) can be directly read into a dBASE table.

To import data this way, choose Table ➤ Table Utilities ➤ Append Records from File .... The Append Records from File dialog box supports the same file types as the Export Records dialog box. DBMEMO3 is not listed in the File Type selection list, because dBASE for Windows can read dBASE III Plus files if you simply select dBASE as the file type.

In Figure 4.24, we're using this tool to import the records that we exported in Figure 4.23.

FIGURE 4.24 ▶

Importing System Data Format records

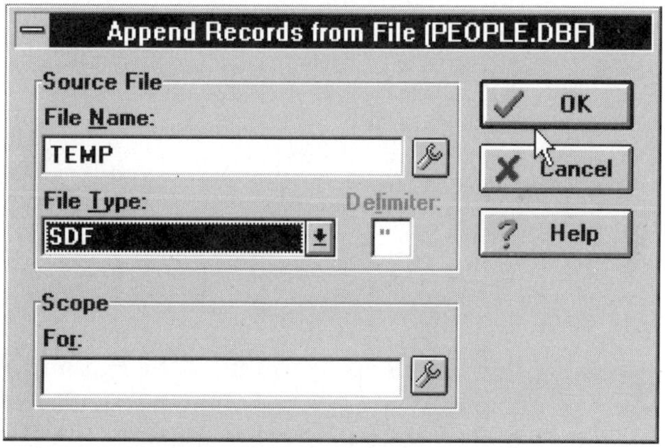

If you choose the Delimited file type, you can also select the delimiter character, which defaults to a double quotation mark.

The For entry field provides a limited means for selecting only a portion of the records in the import file.

▸▸ Summary

We've covered a lot of ground in this chapter! We hope you've become comfortable with some of the capabilities dBASE for Windows offers for manipulating your data.

You started by adding a record ID field to your People table and using dBASE's update capabilities to fill in appropriate unique values. Before you dove into the rest of the chapter, you used the record-generation capability to expand your table to 1000 records.

You also used the Properties ➤ Table Records dialog box to customize your view of your table.

You used indexes to organize your data, and you learned the difference between an ASCII sort and a true alphabetic sort. You also learned how to use indexes instead of physically sorting your table.

You used the Find Records dialog box to quickly locate individual records. Then you used the Replace Records dialog box to do mass updates. You saw how the Find Records capabilities were built into the Replace Records dialog box.

You learned to delete records by groups, for a range of records, for a logical condition, and while a condition was True. You learned that these deletions are not permanent, and you saw that you could use group deletions to temporarily restrict the visible contents of your table. You learned to recall deleted records.

You used dBASE to count records, both all records and just non-deleted records. You used the For and While clauses of dBASE's scope to count records matching particular conditions. You used dBASE's built-in calculation capability to get quick answers to numerical questions.

Finally, you saw how dBASE could export data to other programs and import data from other programs.

As a closing exercise, go back and clean out your People table. First, go back to Natural Order for the index. Then select the first of your generated records. Use the Delete Records dialog box to delete from the selected record through the end of your table. Finally, pack the table (with the Table Records tool active, choose Table ➤ Table Utilities ➤ Pack Records), because you no longer need the test data dBASE generated for you.

Now that you've become adept at manipulating the data in a single table, in the next chapter, you'll use the Query tool to tie together data from multiple tables. This will lead you further into mastering dBASE for Windows.

▶ ▶ CHAPTER 5

The Two-Way Query Designer

▶▶ In this chapter, we'll explore the Query Designer. The Query Designer is useful for querying tables, as its name suggests. Perhaps more important, the Query Designer is the tool you use to describe your database when you use .DBF or .DB form tables.

With the Query Designer, you tell dBASE for Windows which tables are involved in your database and how these tables are related. This information, called a *view* in earlier dBASE versions, is available to the Table Records tool, to your forms, and to Crystal Reports.

Borland calls the Query Designer a Two-Way-Tool. This means that you can work in a graphical design surface to specify your query. When you save your work, it is written as dBASE program code. If you return to the Query Designer (to add another table, for example), the design surface reads the program to reconstruct its state where you left off.

What this means is that, within limits, you can edit the program generated by the Query Designer, and your changes will be remembered the next time you return to the graphical design surface.

We assume that you have no experience with dBASE program code except, perhaps, for what you've seen pass by in the Command window. You'll find that by letting the Query Designer write your dBASE programs, you can make minor changes quite easily.

As we go through this chapter, we'll explain each dBASE for Windows command that we meet. Don't try to memorize them! Most dBASE commands are quite readable, and they're documented in Chapter 13. The commands that you start using are the ones you'll remember, and they're the only ones you need for now.

Understanding the programs written by the Query Designer won't make you an ace dBASE programmer, but it will extend your control over dBASE for Windows.

▸▸ You Query a Single Table

In this section, we'll use the Query Designer with just one table. This will let us do the following:

- Use a table.
- Use selected fields from a table.
- Use indexes to order our table.
- Use logical expressions to find selected records.
- Use calculated fields not actually in the table.

Let's get started with the simplest possible query.

▸ You Begin at the Beginning

Let's get started at the beginning. If you have queries from our work in Chapter 2, delete them. In the Navigator, highlight the query and press Del (or right-click and choose Delete from the Speed menu). dBASE for Windows will pop up its Delete File dialog box, asking if you really want to delete the .QBE file from your disk. Tell it Yes. Then dBASE for Windows will ask you if you want to delete the .QBO file. Go ahead and say Yes to that one, too.

With all program files (such as .PRG programs, .WFM Windows' form files, and .QBE query-by-example files), dBASE for Windows must first compile the program into an internal executable form. Whenever it does this, it writes a new file with the last letter of the file extension changed to an *O*. The *O* stands for Object form. Programmers speak of their programs as *source* code, and the 1s and 0s that the compiler writes (which actually drive the computer) is the *object* code. In our case, the .QBE files will be written by dBASE for Windows from our specifications, but they still qualify as source code.

You Build a Plain Query

Now let's build the simplest possible query, using our People data table. From the Navigator, launch the Query Designer for a new query. Select the Untitled query and press Enter, or press Shift-F2, or double-click the mouse. In the Open Table Required dialog box, shown in Figure 5.1, choose the People table.

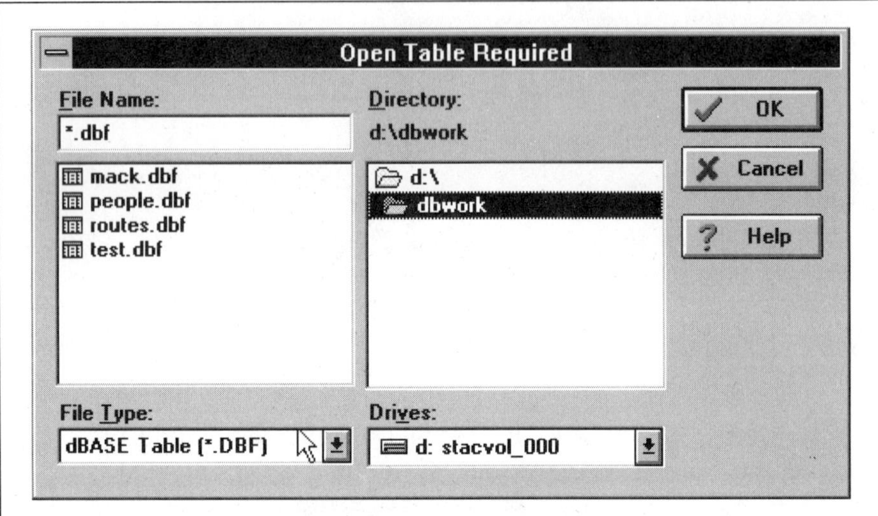

FIGURE 5.1 ▸ *Choosing a table for the Query Designer*

▸▸ **WARNING**

There's a minor bug lurking here. If you press Esc or otherwise don't select a table, you'll still be in the Query Designer. If this happens, right-click and select Add Table ... from the Speed menu.

After you pick the table, you'll be in the Query Designer, shown in Figure 5.2.

Once you're in the Query Designer, press F2 or click the speedbar's lightning icon to run your query. (That's right, do absolutely nothing first—we said we wanted to start plain!)

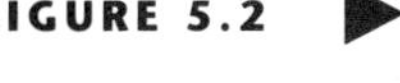

FIGURE 5.2

The Query Designer left plain

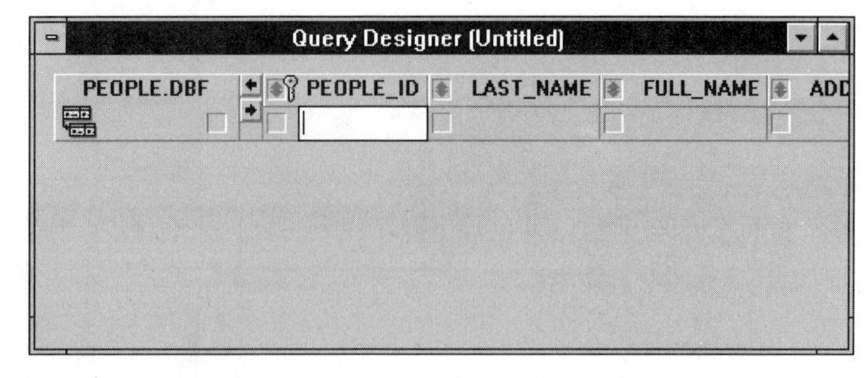

You'll be in a Browse Layout view similar to the first time you browsed your People table. If you're not in a Browse Layout view, choose Properties ➤ Desktop, Files tab. In the Edit Records box, select In Browse Layout. Press Enter or click on OK to commit this change.

After you've taken a look at your data, exit to the Navigator. Let's take a look at the program we just wrote (or, more exactly, that dBASE for Windows wrote for us).

NOTE

We named our query file People. We find it helpful to make the query and table names the same.

The Program Editor is the tool for working with program code. In the Navigator, select the People query and right-click for the Speed menu. Choose Edit as Program to open the file in the Program Editor.

If you are mouseless, open the Command window and enter this command:

MODIFY COMMAND People.qbe

You can set various properties for the Program Editor by choosing Properties ➤ Program Editor. (This choice is only available when the Program Editor is active.) Figure 5.3 shows the Program Editor Properties dialog box, with the PEOPLE.QBE file in the Program Editor in the background.

FIGURE 5.3

A typical Program Editor setup

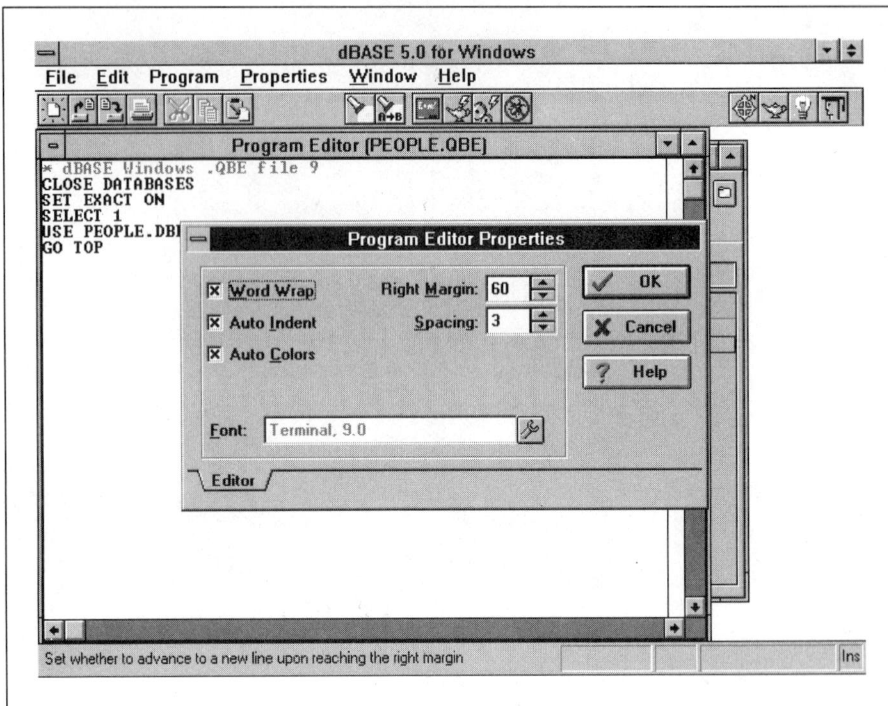

Our PEOPLE.QBE file contains this program:

```
* dBASE Windows .QBE file 9
CLOSE DATABASES
SET EXACT ON
SELECT 1
USE PEOPLE.DBF
GO TOP
```

The first line is a comment. The asterisk (*) at the beginning of the line identifies it as a line of commentary, not program code, to both you and the dBASE for Windows system.

The line CLOSE DATABASES closes any databases that you may have open in the current session (you might have several tables open).

We'll learn more about the SET EXACT command when we get to using logical expressions to find selected records.

The SELECT 1 command picks the dBASE for Windows work area for the PEOPLE.DBF file. Available work areas are from 1 to 225.

Since each session has its own set of work areas, we doubt that you'll ever run out.

The USE PEOPLE.DBF command is the one that actually opens the People table. Finally, GO TOP positions the record pointer at the start record. This will be the record selected when your browse begins.

Now exit the Program Editor by pressing Ctrl-Q or by choosing File ➤ Abandon and Close. We'll use the Command window next.

The .QBE file sets the environment for the following command. To simulate the effect of running the query, type these commands in the Command window:

DO People.qbe

BROWSE

After you enter the BROWSE command, control passes to the Table Records tool. Click in the Command window and type the final line:

CLOSE DATABASES

Actually, you can use lowercase, and abbreviate the dBASE for Windows commands to four letters. Here's what that looks like:

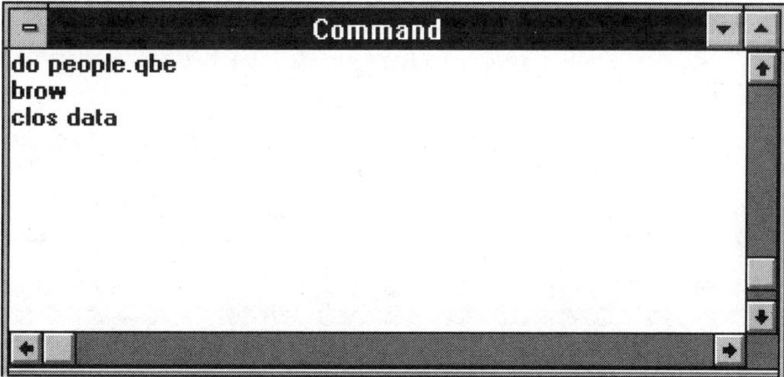

Note that you can shorten dBASE commands to four characters, but you can't shorten dBASE function names. They must be spelled out.

Whatever way you type it, you're letting the query you just built set up your environment. Then the BROWSE command launches the Browse Layout view. Finally, you need to clean up after yourself. When you close a form, you end its session, so this cleanup is done for you. The

Command window is the exception; it is its own session, and it's up to you to do proper cleanup.

TIP

You'll see lots of other commands in the Command window. As you work, each dBASE for Windows surface echoes the dBASE commands that it's executing to the Command window. If you watch this window, it will teach you a lot about dBASE commands.

▶ *Selecting Fields for a Query*

With that introduction, let's start building more complex queries. First, let's select some fields. Follow these steps:

1. Launch the People query in the Query Designer. If you're still in the Command window, try entering:

   MODIFY QUERY People.qbe

2. Tab to the LAST_NAME field and press F5 to select it.
3. Tab to the CITY and PHONE fields and press F5 to select them.
4. Press F2 to run the query. You've now specified a query on just three of the fields, which fit nicely in your Browse Layout view. Figure 5.4 shows the view that this launched for us.

FIGURE 5.4 

A restricted Browse Layout view created by a query

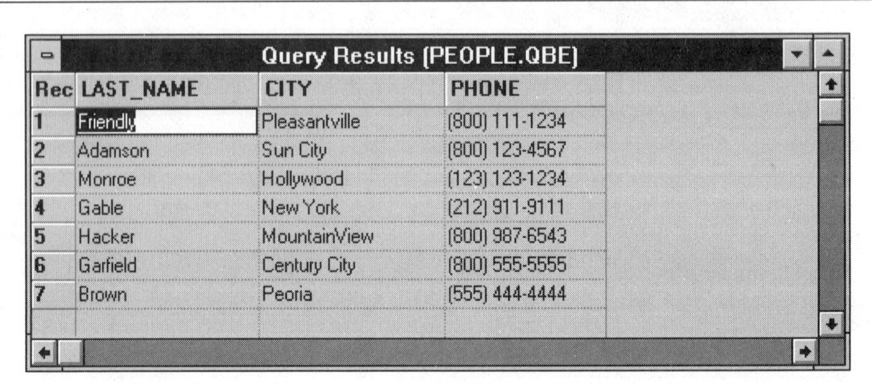

Query Results (PEOPLE.QBE)

Rec	LAST_NAME	CITY	PHONE
1	Friendly	Pleasantville	(800) 111-1234
2	Adamson	Sun City	(800) 123-4567
3	Monroe	Hollywood	(123) 123-1234
4	Gable	New York	(212) 911-9111
5	Hacker	MountainView	(800) 987-6543
6	Garfield	Century City	(800) 555-5555
7	Brown	Peoria	(555) 444-4444

5. Press Ctrl-F4 to exit from the view. The Changes Made - Query Designer dialog box will ask you if you want to save your changes. Tell it Yes.

Now let's launch the Program Editor to examine the code that the Query Designer wrote for you.

6. Choose Edit as Program from the Speed menu in the Navigator, or enter **MODIFY COMMAND People.qbe** from the Command window.

Our program looks like this:

```
* dBASE Windows .QBE file 9
CLOSE DATABASES
SET EXACT ON
SELECT 1
USE PEOPLE.DBF
SET FIELDS TO LAST_NAME, CITY, PHONE
GO TOP
```

There's one new line, which contains the SET FIELDS command. This matches the fields you've selected.

7. While you're in the Program Editor, add the FULL_NAME field to that list of fields. Put the field where you want it to appear when you browse. Ours is shown here:

```
SET FIELDS TO LAST_NAME, full_name, CITY, PHONE
```

NOTE

dBASE for Windows will put the commands in capital letters the next time you run the Query Designer. You don't need to worry about it.

8. After making this change, press Ctrl-W to write the new version of the file to disk.
9. Reenter the Query Designer, and you'll see the check mark in the FULL_NAME field.

If you're not satisfied with the order of the fields in your query, you can edit the SET FIELDS command in the .QBE file with the Program Editor. Alternatively, you can grab the field with your mouse when you're in the Query Designer. As Figure 5.5 shows, holding the left button down lets you drag your fields into an order you prefer.

FIGURE 5.5 

Dragging a field in the Query Designer

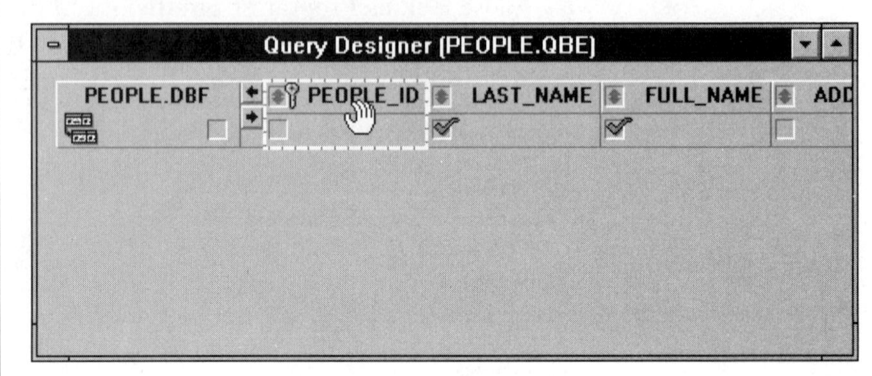

Now let's put an index into use.

▸ Managing Indexes from the Query Designer

It would be nice if our list of names was prepared in alphabetical order, wouldn't it? In the Query Designer, choose Query, and then select Manage Indexes.

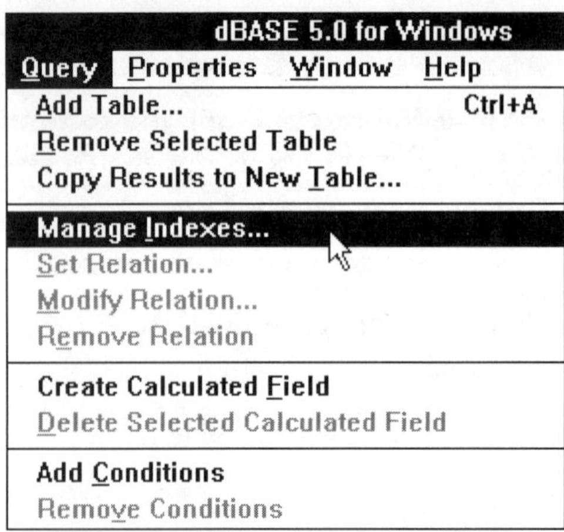

In the Manage Indexes dialog box, select the LAST_NAME index and click on OK or press Enter. Then run the query (press F2 or click on the speedbar's lightning icon). Now you can see your table in alphabetical order. There's a problem here, though.

Exit from the Browse Layout view. Then double-click on the People query in the Navigator to return to browsing the query results. You've lost your index selection, as you see.

Selecting a Single Index Tag

What you really want is a permanent selection (or at least one that lasts until you change your mind). Click on the speedbar's design icon or press Shift-F2 to return to the Query Designer. Now press Tab to reach the right end of the table, or click and hold the right-pointing arrow near the file name until you get to the right end. You'll see an unexpected field there, as Figure 5.6 shows.

FIGURE 5.6

An extra field at the end of the table

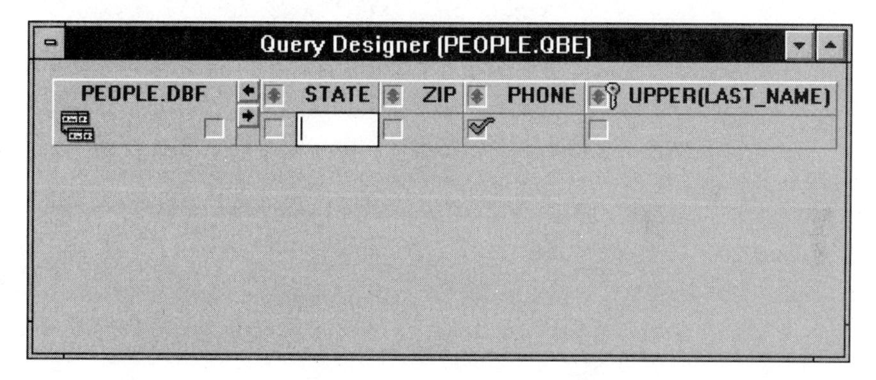

The "field" is actually our index tag expression: UPPER (LAST_NAME). The key that appears in the upper-left corner of the field tells you that there is a tag for this expression in the production index. Next to the key is a box with a smudge mark.

The smudge mark appears when no index order is selected. (Actually, that smudge is a double-headed vertical arrow.) Here's what happens when we click and hold this box for the STATE field:

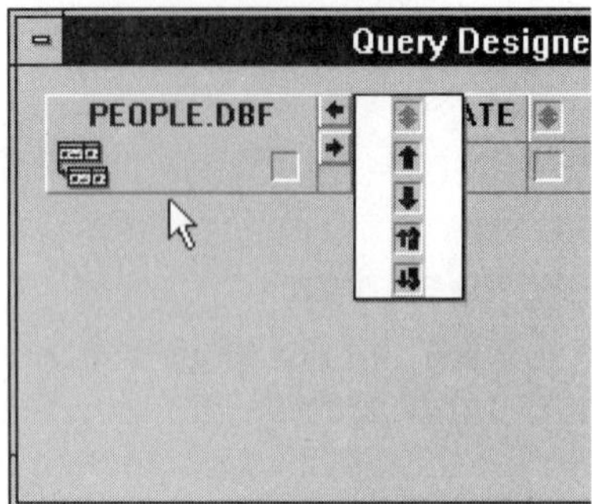

There are five choices here:

- No order (the smudge)
- Ascending, ASCII order (up arrow)
- Descending, ASCII order (down arrow)
- Ascending, alphabetically (double up arrows)
- Descending, alphabetically (double down arrows)

We want to choose the UPPER(LAST_NAME) index. Since this actually is a tag in our production index, when you click on the smudge in this field, there are only two choices: an arrow (the index order) and the smudge (no order). Clicking the box toggles between the smudge and the arrow. Pressing and holding lets you drag to your choice.

Choose the arrow to use the index tag. Now when you run your query (press F2 or click the lightning icon), your records are again in alphabetical order by last name. When you exit from the query, tell dBASE for Windows to save the new design.

If you return to the Program Editor, you'll see that this is what the Query Designer wrote:

```
* dBASE Windows .QBE file 9
CLOSE DATABASES
SET EXACT ON
SELECT 1
```

```
USE PEOPLE.DBF ORDER TAG LAST_NAME OF PEOPLE.MDX
SET FIELDS TO LAST_NAME, FULL_NAME, CITY, PHONE
GO TOP
```

The USE PEOPLE.DBF line has expanded with our new order specification. Actually, this is a more complex form than is needed. This would have been sufficient:

```
USE PEOPLE.DBF ORDER LAST_NAME
```

The OF PEOPLE.MDX clause can be dropped because the production index will be chosen by default. The word TAG only serves to remind us that LAST_NAME is a tag in the production index.

►► **NOTE**

You need a mouse (or other pointing device) to manipulate the order box (smudge or arrow) in the Query Designer. Without a mouse, you must use the Program Editor to add an ORDER clause to the USE command or to edit this clause to change the order.

Selecting Multiple Index Tags

Sometimes, you may want a primary order and a suborder. For instance, you might want your People table sorted by state, and sorted by last name within each state.

The documentation suggests that you can select more than one index tag by clicking the appropriate order boxes. They are, it says, used in left-to-right order. Unfortunately, this simply isn't true. Fortunately, you can work around this limitation.

When you choose an index by clicking the order box, the Query Designer sets any other index that was specified back to the no index state. You can have only one index tag at a time active as the master index.

The ORDER clause of the USE command does not accept a list of tags. It takes exactly one tag and reports an error if you try to use more than one.

However, even though you can't use multiple tags, you can get exactly the effect you want by using multiple fields in a single index tag. In dBASE for Windows, the **+** operator concatenates (joins together) strings. (It does addition for numbers, too, of course.)

Test these commands in the Command window:

```
USE People
? LAST_NAME
? STATE
? STATE + LAST_NAME
SKIP
? STATE + LAST_NAME
CLOSE Data
```

The **?** command sends the result of an expression to the results pane of the Command window. (Think of the ? as "What is ...?") You can use it to test any expression, which is exactly what we're doing here.

The SKIP command here is also new. It moves the record pointer. A plain SKIP is equal to SKIP 1. You could SKIP 5 to go ahead 5 records, or SKIP –1 to back up a record, too.

If you examine enough records, you'll see that sorting on the STATE + LAST_NAME combination is the same as sorting on STATE, and then sorting on LAST_NAME within state. This is exactly what we wanted to achieve.

Let's create an index for this combination. To get to the Manage Indexes dialog box from the Query Designer, choose Query ➤ Manage Indexes. If you're running your query (not designing), choose Table ➤ Table Utilities ➤ Manage Indexes.

In the Manage Indexes dialog box, choose Create ... to display the Create Index dialog box. You'll probably be presented with the Exclusive Access Required dialog box. This offers to open the table for exclusive access, which you need to adjust the production index, so accept the offer. Figure 5.7 shows the Create Index dialog box we used to add an index combining the STATE and LAST_NAME fields.

After you create that tag, leave it selected when you exit the Manage Indexes dialog box. For the query, check STATE, but deselect CITY. Figure 5.8 shows our Browse Layout view, with people sorted by last names within each state.

FIGURE 5.7

Making an index combining STATE and LAST_NAME fields

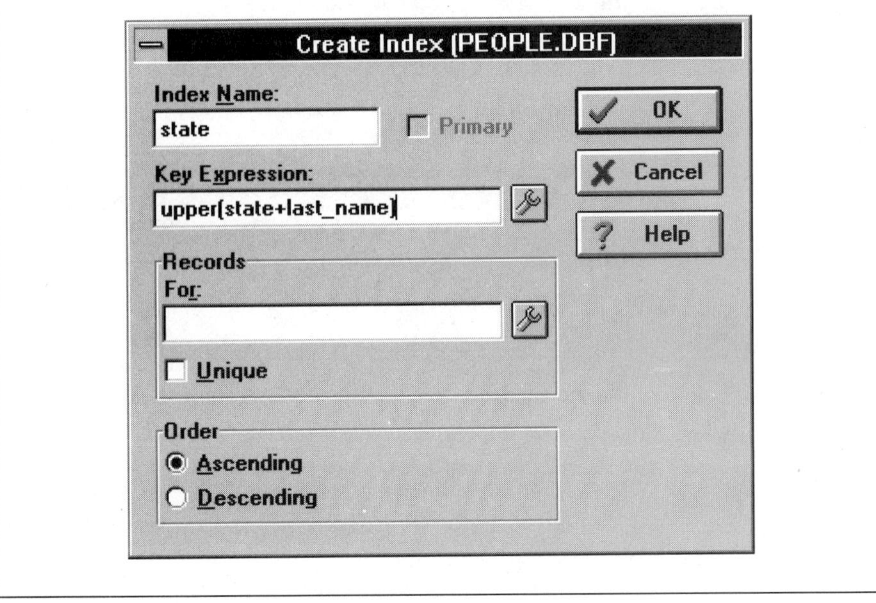

FIGURE 5.8

The People table sorted on two fields at once

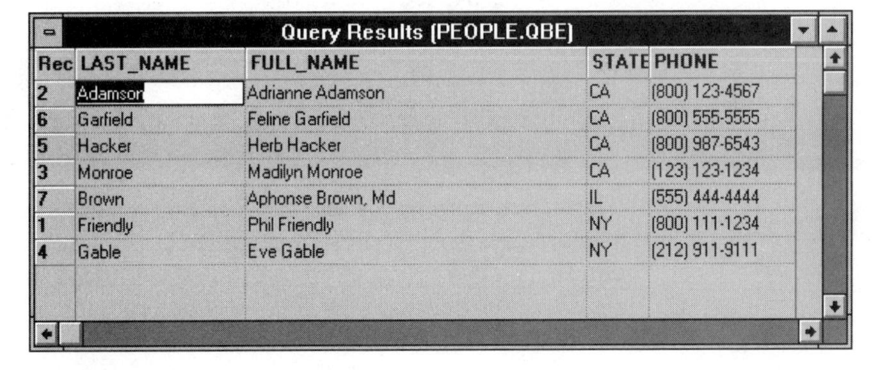
Query Results (PEOPLE.QBE)

Rec	LAST_NAME	FULL_NAME	STATE	PHONE
2	Adamson	Adrianne Adamson	CA	(800) 123-4567
6	Garfield	Feline Garfield	CA	(800) 555-5555
5	Hacker	Herb Hacker	CA	(800) 987-6543
3	Monroe	Madilyn Monroe	CA	(123) 123-1234
7	Brown	Aphonse Brown, Md	IL	(555) 444-4444
1	Friendly	Phil Friendly	NY	(800) 111-1234
4	Gable	Eve Gable	NY	(212) 911-9111

▶ Selecting Relevant Records

So far, we've worked with fields, selecting the ones we want and putting them in the order we want. Now we'll go on to selecting sets of records that match our specifications.

A Single Field Selection

The simplest record selection is done by placing a criterion in the condition area below a field's name in the Query Designer. Here's how you could select the records where the STATE field was equal to CA:

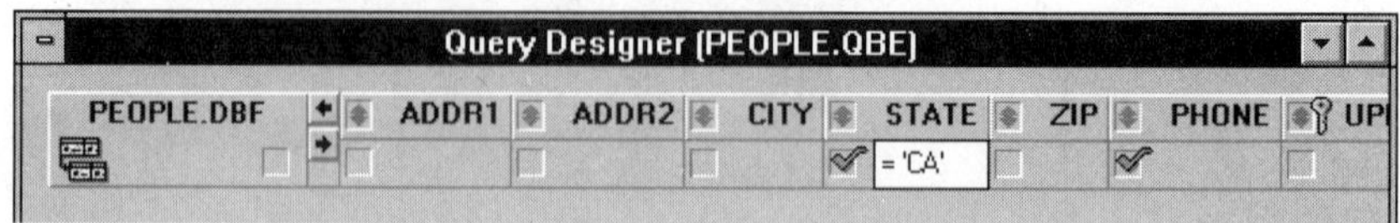

The entry below the record is actually a logical expression, where the name of the field is implied on the left. You enter

='CA'

and dBASE for Windows fills in the complete expression:

```
STATE = 'CA'
```

Here's the PEOPLE.QBE program that the Query Designer wrote:

```
* dBASE Windows .QBE file 9
CLOSE DATABASES
SET EXACT ON
SELECT 1
USE PEOPLE.DBF ORDER TAG STATE
SET FILTER TO STATE='CA'
SET FIELDS TO LAST_NAME, FULL_NAME, STATE, PHONE
GO TOP
```

The new line is SET FILTER TO STATE='CA'. A *filter* restricts the available records to the ones that meet the filter condition. The filter condition is a logical expression. If it evaluates to True, the record is accepted. Otherwise, the record is not shown.

NOTE

Actually, we worked with our first filter in Chapter 4, when we discussed deleting records. The Deleted flag, when set, filters out deleted records. The SET FILTER command adds additional restrictions. Neither one actually deletes any records; they just restrict what you can see when they are in effect.

Setting Conditions on Multiple Fields

You can use logical conditions on as many fields as you like. The records that appear in your Query Results window will be the ones that meet all the criteria you have established. In Figure 5.9, we show both the Query Designer and the Query Results windows.

FIGURE 5.9

A query with conditions on two fields

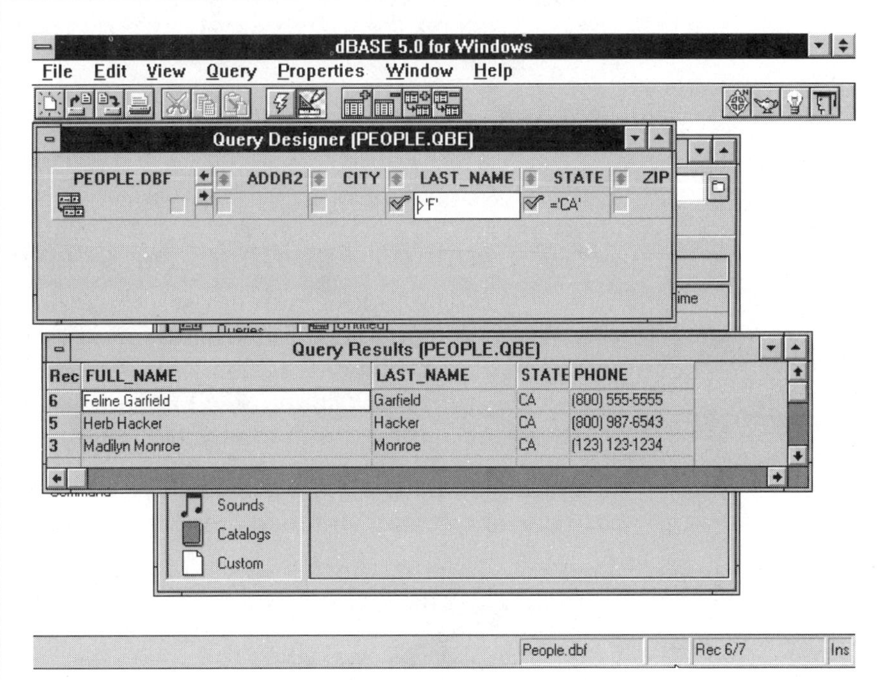

In the Query Designer, we've grabbed the LAST_NAME field and dragged it next to the STATE field, so that you can see both conditions at once. Here, we've selected the records where the state is equal to CA and the LAST_NAME is greater than F.

In an alphabetic sort, *Fa* sorts after (is greater than) *F*, so specifying >'F' includes all the last names beginning with *F* as well as the higher letters. This type of sort has some practical uses. For example, suppose that you're mailing your new price list to your customers. Yesterday afternoon you sent out the mailing for names that begin from *A* through *E*. Today you're finishing the rest.

This is the PEOPLE.QBE program that the Query Designer wrote with conditions on two fields:

```
* dBASE Windows .QBE file 9
CLOSE DATABASES
SET EXACT ON
SELECT 1
USE PEOPLE.DBF ORDER TAG STATE
SET FILTER TO (LAST_NAME>'F' .AND. STATE='CA')
SET FIELDS TO FULL_NAME, LAST_NAME, STATE, PHONE
GO TOP
```

As you can see, the conditions are ANDed together. Note the periods around the AND operator (and the OR operator discussed in the next section).

Setting Multiple Conditions for One Field

You can place multiple conditions in a single field. The records that are available in the Query Results window are the records that meet any of these conditions. Figure 5.10 shows the Query Designer with the conditions ='CA' and ='NY'in the STATE field. You can see the people that match either of these conditions in the Query Results window.

To place multiple conditions in a field, click on the condition area of the field, or tab to it, and then press the ↓ key.

This is the PEOPLE.QBE program that the Query Designer wrote with two conditions on one field:

```
* dBASE Windows .QBE file 9
CLOSE DATABASES
SET EXACT ON
```

FIGURE 5.10

A query with two conditions on one field

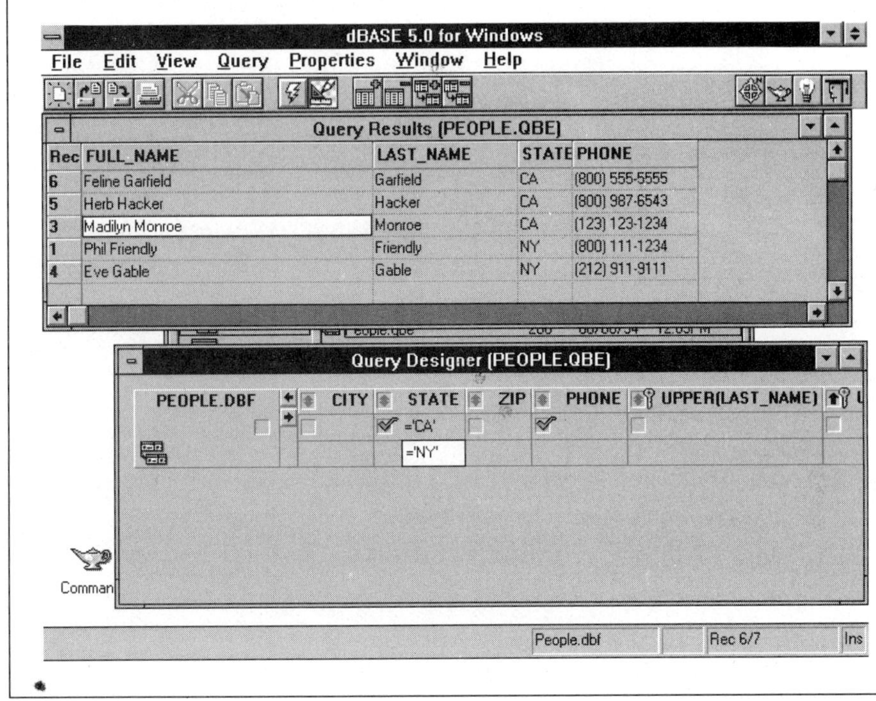

```
SELECT 1
USE PEOPLE.DBF ORDER TAG STATE
SET FILTER TO (STATE='NY' .OR. STATE='CA')
SET FIELDS TO FULL_NAME, LAST_NAME, STATE, PHONE
GO TOP
```

As you see, the conditions are ORed together.

Setting Multiple Conditions for Multiple Fields

You've seen that conditions placed in multiple fields are ANDed together and that multiple conditions in one field are ORed together. The records that pass must meet each condition when you have conditions in multiple fields. When you have multiple conditions for a single field, they pass if they meet any condition.

This was not, in fact, precisely stated. More correctly, the conditions in any row are ANDed together, and the conditions from each row are ORed together.

Figure 5.11 shows conditions accepting any record where the state is NY or the city is Hollywood. Because these conditions are on separate lines, records meeting either one are accepted. If they were on one line, no record would pass (Hollywood is not in New York).

FIGURE 5.11 ►

Finding records in STATE = 'NY' or CITY = 'Hollywood'

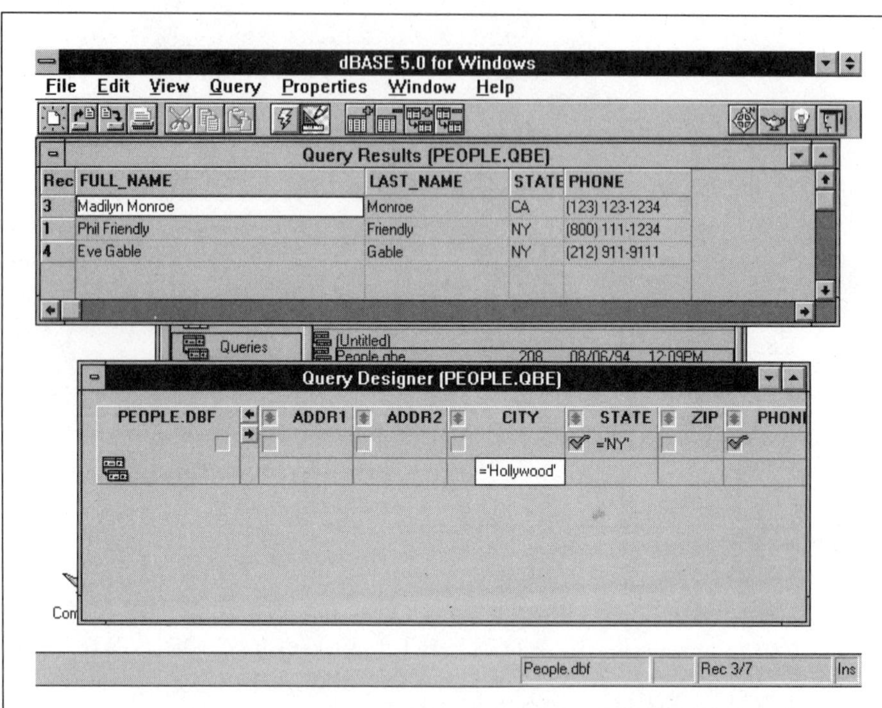

►► **TIP**

If you look closely at Figure 5.11, you can see that we did not include the equal sign (=) in front of the value. If you don't include a relational operator, dBASE for Windows assumes that you mean "equal to." However, we think it's good practice to include the = to be explicit.

This is the PEOPLE.QBE program that the Query Designer wrote with two conditions on separate lines in their fields:

```
* dBASE Windows .QBE file 9
CLOSE DATABASES
SET EXACT ON
SELECT 1
USE PEOPLE.DBF ORDER TAG STATE
SET FILTER TO (STATE='NY' .OR. CITY='Hollywood')
SET FIELDS TO FULL_NAME, LAST_NAME, STATE, PHONE
GO TOP
```

As before, those conditions are ORed together. You can see how the Query Designer completes your logical expressions for you.

In this example, we specified > 'F' for LAST_NAME on the same line as we specified 'NY' in the STATE field. On a separate line, we specified 'Hollywood' for the CITY field. Here's the PEOPLE.QBE program that was generated:

```
* dBASE Windows .QBE file 9
CLOSE DATABASES
SET EXACT ON
SELECT 1
USE PEOPLE.DBF ORDER TAG STATE
SET FILTER TO (LAST_NAME>'F' .AND. STATE='NY' .OR.
CITY='Hollywood')
SET FIELDS TO FULL_NAME, LAST_NAME, STATE, PHONE
GO TOP
```


The AND operator has a higher precedence than the OR operator. This means that in an expression mixing ANDs and ORs, the AND operators will be applied first. Tied back to our .QBE specification, this means that all conditions on a single line will be evaluated first. If any single line evaluates to True, the record passes.

WARNING

The early documentation stated that AND and OR have equal precedence. This is incorrect. If they had equal precedence, these queries would not have worked whenever there were two or more conditions on any line after the first.

The following are some simple expressions and their results. In these examples, we use values instead of field names, so you can see exactly what this means:

T = .T.	True
F = .F.	False
? T .AND. F	False
? T .OR. F	True
? F .OR. F .AND. T	False
? F .OR. (F .AND. T)	False (same as above)
? (F .OR. T) .AND. T	True

An AND operation is True only if both its parts are True. The OR operation is True if either of its parts are True. The compound expression

```
F .OR. F .AND. T
```

evaluates to False, because the AND operation is done first. If you did ORs first (or just go left to right), the answer would be the opposite.

When we write expressions that combine ANDs and ORs, we always use parentheses to group the evaluation precisely as we intend it: (A .AND. B) .OR. (C .AND. D), for example.

Adding More Conditions

When you place a condition in a field, the field name is implied as the left-hand part of the logical expression. This limits the kinds of expressions you can build.

For unlimited possibilities, you can use the Query Designer's Conditions box. This is added or removed via the Query pull-down menu, which is available when the Query Designer is active. Choose Add Conditions from this menu:

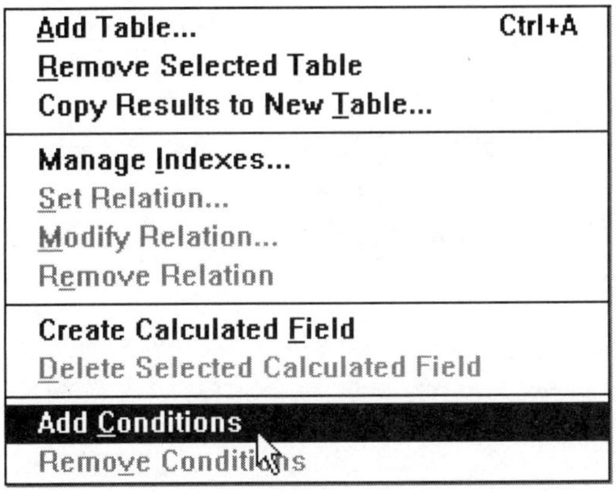

Add Table...	Ctrl+A
Remove Selected Table	
Copy Results to New Table...	
Manage Indexes...	
Set Relation...	
Modify Relation...	
Remove Relation	
Create Calculated Field	
Delete Selected Calculated Field	
Add Conditions	
Remove Conditions	

Like the conditions for individual fields, the Conditions box originally opens with space for a single line of conditions. You must specify full logical expressions in the Conditions box. For example, 'NY' or ='NY' is not acceptable, because the Conditions box has no idea what is to be equal to NY.

Full dBASE expressions must be used, such as these:

```
STATE = 'NY'
LAST_NAME > 'F'
```

Complex expressions, using AND and OR to connect conditions, may also be used:

```
LAST_NAME > 'F' .AND. LAST_NAME < 'K'
```

Figure 5.12 shows the Conditions box being used to search for records where the state equals NY or the city equals Hollywood.

As with the condition areas under your fields, you can add more conditions by pressing the ↓ key. You can also add multiple conditions on a single line, separating them with commas. These are interpreted the same way as the other field conditions: if they are on one line, all the conditions must be met; if they are on separate lines, records pass if they meet any one of the conditions.

FIGURE 5.12

Using the Query Designer's Condition box to search for STATE = 'NY' or CITY = 'Hollywood'

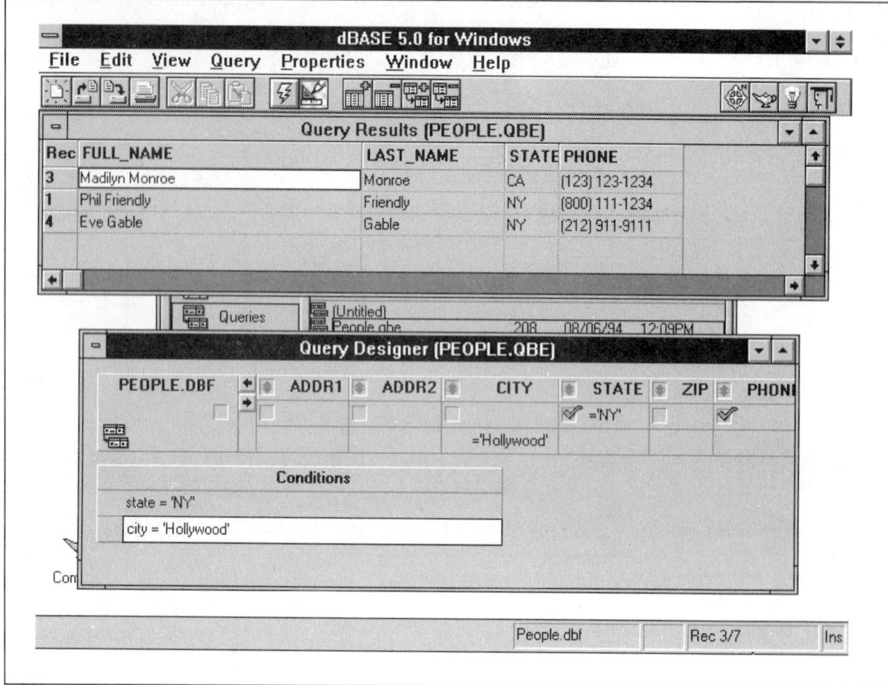

▸ Adding Calculated Fields

Along with the fields in your table, you can use additional fields calculated from the values in your records. Use Query ➤ Create Calculated Field.

When you select this menu choice, a Calculated box, with additional fields, appears. These function in the same way as your original fields in the Query Designer, except that you type in a name and an expression for each field. The width of each field in the Calculated box expands to accommodate the field's name or its expression (whichever is larger).

You can use any valid dBASE expressions, such as numeric and character expressions. In Figure 5.13, we've added three calculated fields and checked two of them for inclusion in the results table. We've used numeric expressions in this example.

Once you have added calculated fields, they function much like your other fields, except that they cannot be used as part of expressions in other calculated fields. Otherwise, you can work with them in the

FIGURE 5.13

Calculated fields added to the Query Results window

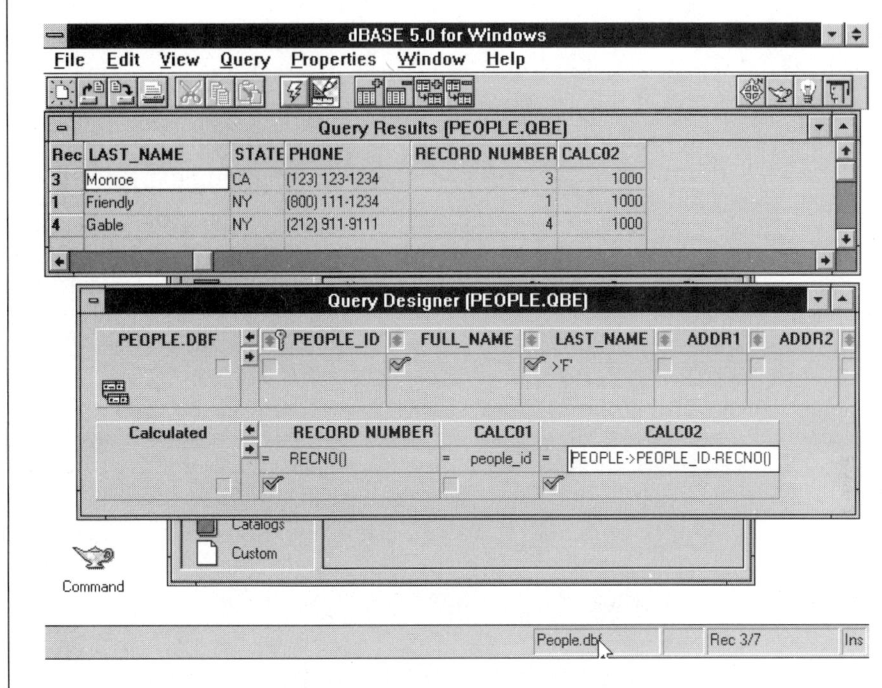

same way as you work with your other fields. Pressing Ctrl-F5 selects (or deselects) all the calculated fields, for example.

Now that you can use the Query Designer on one table, it's time to extend those techniques to building databases with multiple tables.

►► You Build a Database with Two Tables

Beginning with dBASE III Plus, a new feature, called the *view*, came into play. This was a powerful concept that never got fully implemented. The basic concept was that a database is built from one or more tables. When there is more than one table, the database needs to know how the tables work together.

Views have now been replaced by queries. The Query Designer lets you describe a database to dBASE for Windows. We'll build a two-table database in this section.

As we work with this powerful capability, bear in mind that you can create as many queries as you like for a single combination of tables. One query might include all the available fields of the related tables, which will be useful for entering and editing data. Another query for the same table might use just the most important fields, which could easily fit into a single Browse Layout view for conveniently examining your data.

► Preparing a Two-Table Database

We've already got a People table. If we add a table for employers, we can go on to build the phone number capability that we discussed back in Chapter 1 (remember the BigCo example?). In the two-table system we develop, we can change the phone number for a company in just one place, and the new phone number will appear in the records of all the people in our list who work for that company.

Creating the Orgs Table

We like descriptive file names, but we'll make an exception here. We want a table of organizations, not just companies, since our acquaintances work for companies, schools, hospitals, government agencies, and so on. We don't like any eight-letter abbreviation for *organizations*, so we decided to just use Orgs for our table name.

Figure 5.14 shows the structure of our Orgs table. Build your own using the Table Structure tool (double-click on the Untitled table in the Navigator or select it and press Enter). As with the People table, you can adjust the address fields to suit your national or international needs.

After you set up your table structure, add a handful of organizations to it. Figure 5.15 shows our collection of organizations on a local Main Street.

The importance of the ID field cannot be overstated, as you will see when we relate the People table to the Orgs table. Make sure that you have your own BigCo company (one that several people work for) available for the work that follows. You can change the name to suit yourself, but we recommend that you stick with ID 1001.

FIGURE 5.14

The structure of the Orgs table

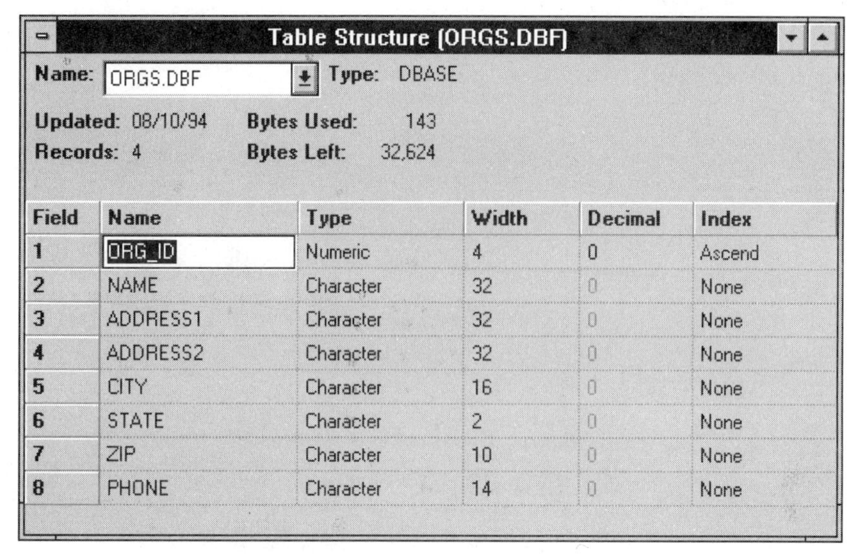

Table Structure (ORGS.DBF)

Name: ORGS.DBF Type: DBASE

Updated: 08/10/94 Bytes Used: 143

Records: 4 Bytes Left: 32,624

Field	Name	Type	Width	Decimal	Index
1	ORG_ID	Numeric	4	0	Ascend
2	NAME	Character	32	0	None
3	ADDRESS1	Character	32	0	None
4	ADDRESS2	Character	32	0	None
5	CITY	Character	16	0	None
6	STATE	Character	2	0	None
7	ZIP	Character	10	0	None
8	PHONE	Character	14	0	None

FIGURE 5.15

Some organizations in Pleasantville

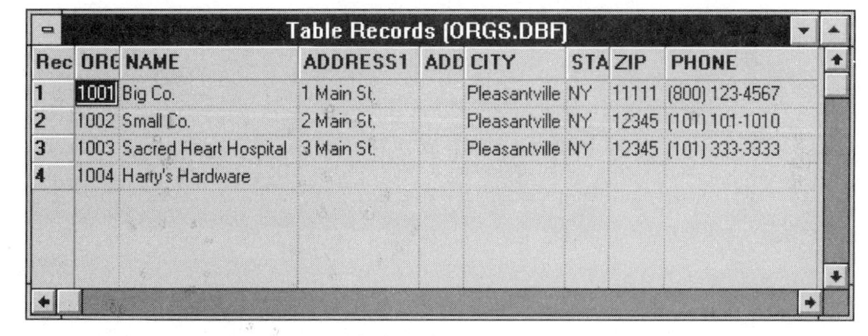

Table Records (ORGS.DBF)

Rec	ORG	NAME	ADDRESS1	ADD	CITY	STA	ZIP	PHONE
1	1001	Big Co.	1 Main St.		Pleasantville	NY	11111	(800) 123-4567
2	1002	Small Co.	2 Main St.		Pleasantville	NY	12345	(101) 101-1010
3	1003	Sacred Heart Hospital	3 Main St.		Pleasantville	NY	12345	(101) 333-3333
4	1004	Harry's Hardware						

Updating the People Table

Before we can begin doing two-table work, we'll need to have a linking field, called ORG_ID, in the People table. Figure 5.16 shows the added field, which serves as the foreign key, in the People table.

We make a habit of adding our foreign keys just after the primary key, as you see here. This lets us see our table's parents at a glance. Make sure that the ORG_ID field in the People table matches the one in the

FIGURE 5.16

Adding a foreign key (the ORG_ID field) to PEOPLE.DBF

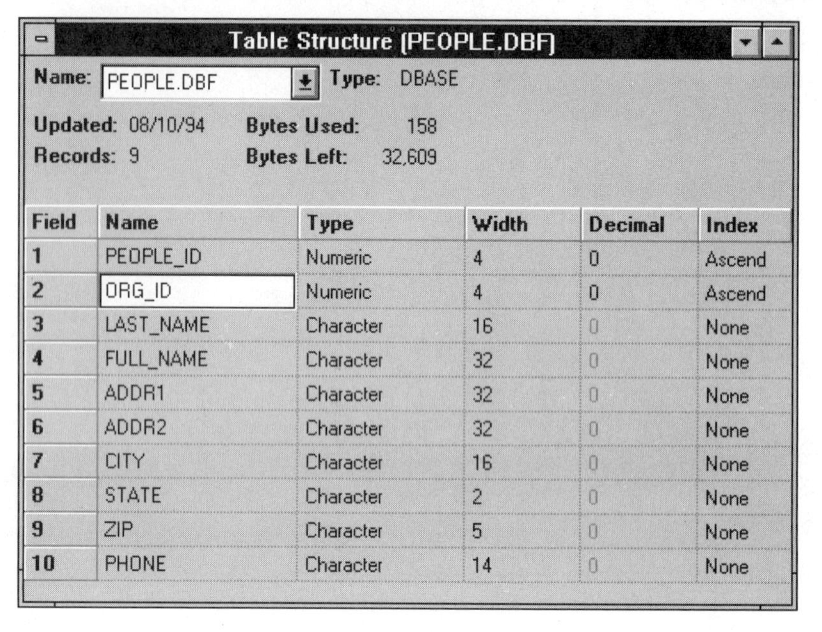

Field	Name	Type	Width	Decimal	Index
1	PEOPLE_ID	Numeric	4	0	Ascend
2	ORG_ID	Numeric	4	0	Ascend
3	LAST_NAME	Character	16	0	None
4	FULL_NAME	Character	32	0	None
5	ADDR1	Character	32	0	None
6	ADDR2	Character	32	0	None
7	CITY	Character	16	0	None
8	STATE	Character	2	0	None
9	ZIP	Character	5	0	None
10	PHONE	Character	14	0	None

Orgs table. Both must be numeric and 4 characters with 0 decimals. You need an ascending index on every foreign key, too.

After you add the foreign key, you need to enter data to tie your people to your organizations. When you enter the Table Records tool for your People table, you won't see the new field you added. This is because we created a Browse Layout view that selects specific fields. Start by updating this layout to include the new field.

Figure 5.17 shows the Table Records Properties dialog box for adding the new foreign key field into our layout. To access this dialog box, choose Properties ➤ Table Records Window ... from the menus.

Remember that the fields you move from the Available Fields box are placed immediately under the highlighted field in the Selected Fields box. Before you select the ORG_ID field and click the > button, highlight the PEOPLE_ID field in the Selected Fields box so the new field will be inserted after it.

FIGURE 5.17

Adding the new foreign key to our layout

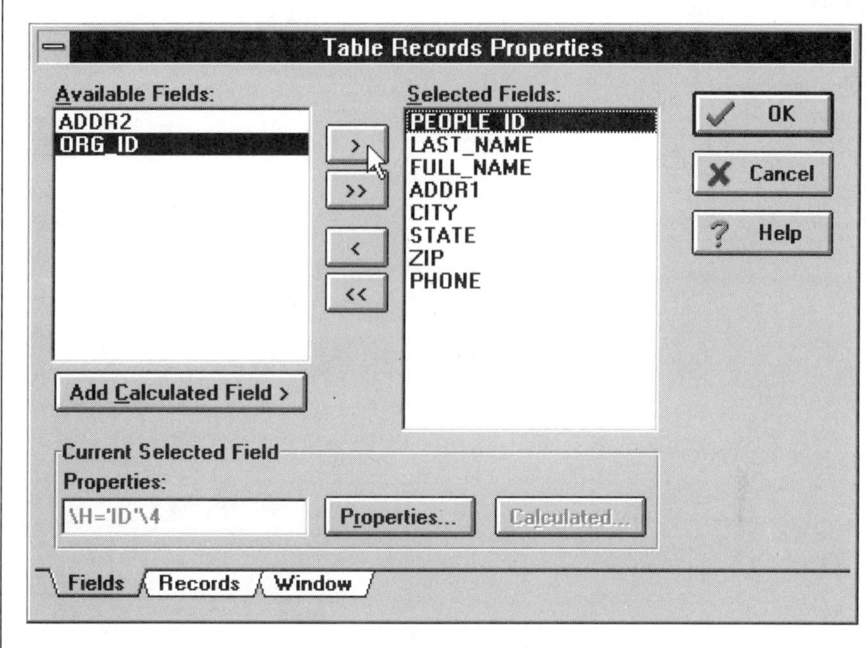

After you add the field, you need to set its properties. Choose the ORG_ID field in the Selected Fields box and click on the Properties … buttton. Figure 5.18 shows the Field Properties dialog box for the field. We've given it the heading ORG and set the width to 4.

With this setting, we're ready to add data. Figure 5.19 shows the data we added. When you fill in these fields, make sure that the values here match the ID values in the Orgs table.

Now we have a table of organizations and a table of people with data specifying which organization each person works for. (If you look closely, you'll noticed that our people live all around the country, but they all work in Pleasantville—they're modern telecommuters.)

What we haven't done is tell dBASE for Windows that these two tables together form a database. That's our next job.

FIGURE 5.18 

Setting the properties for the new field

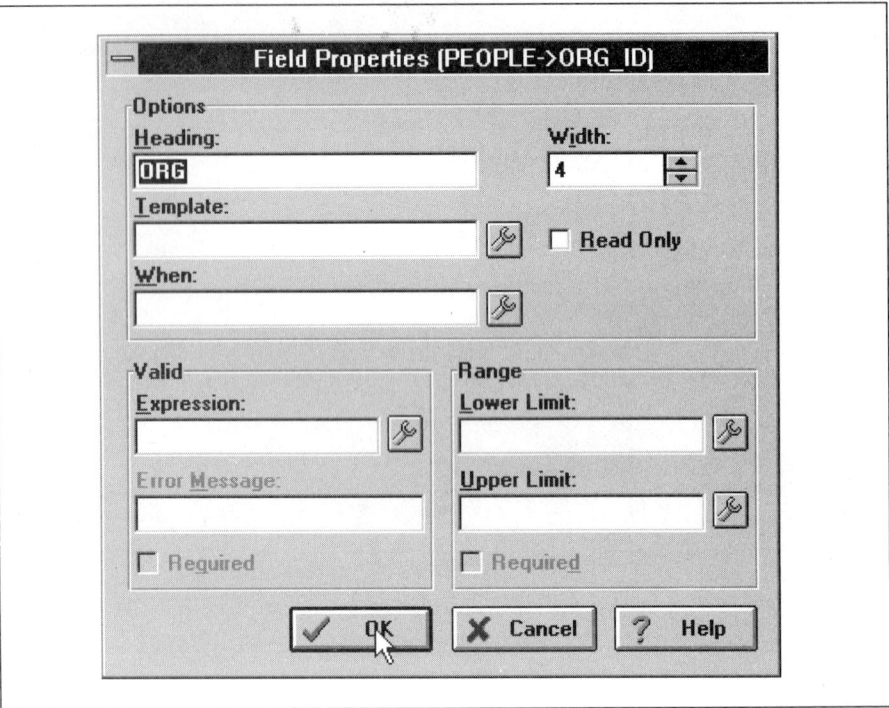

Field Properties (PEOPLE->ORG_ID)

Options
Heading: ORG
Width: 4
Template:
Read Only
When:

Valid
Expression:
Error Message:
Required

Range
Lower Limit:
Upper Limit:
Required

OK Cancel Help

FIGURE 5.19 

Filling in the ORG_ID fields to specify employers

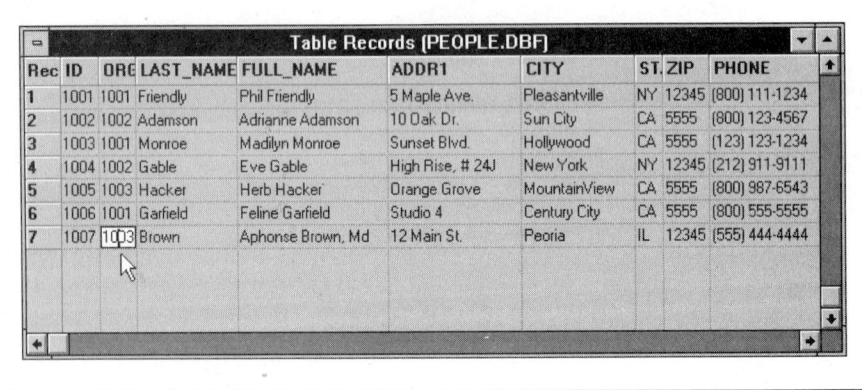

Table Records (PEOPLE.DBF)

Rec	ID	ORG	LAST_NAME	FULL_NAME	ADDR1	CITY	ST	ZIP	PHONE
1	1001	1001	Friendly	Phil Friendly	5 Maple Ave.	Pleasantville	NY	12345	(800) 111-1234
2	1002	1002	Adamson	Adrianne Adamson	10 Oak Dr.	Sun City	CA	5555	(800) 123-4567
3	1003	1001	Monroe	Madilyn Monroe	Sunset Blvd.	Hollywood	CA	5555	(123) 123-1234
4	1004	1002	Gable	Eve Gable	High Rise, # 24J	New York	NY	12345	(212) 911-9111
5	1005	1003	Hacker	Herb Hacker	Orange Grove	MountainView	CA	5555	(800) 987-6543
6	1006	1001	Garfield	Feline Garfield	Studio 4	Century City	CA	5555	(800) 555-5555
7	1007	1003	Brown	Aphonse Brown, Md	12 Main St.	Peoria	IL	12345	(555) 444-4444

▶ Relating the Tables with a Query

Using the Query Designer to link two tables takes a great deal more explaining than actual work. In practice, you'll find that you can dispense with this chore in a small part of a minute, once you become proficient with multi-table work.

For the first one, however, we'll go very slowly and try not to skip anything.

A Simple Table-Relating Query

To begin, we'll create the simplest possible query that relates our two tables. Begin by launching the Query Designer to build a new query (double click Untitled or select it and press Enter). Now follow these steps:

1. In the Open Table Required dialog box, select the Orgs table.
2. With Orgs in your Query Designer, choose Query ➤ Add Table … (or press Ctrl-A, or right-click and pick Add Table … from the Speed menu). Figure 5.20 shows this step.

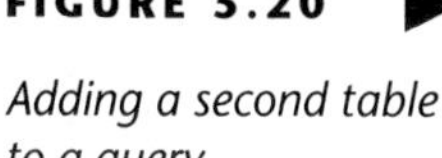

FIGURE 5.20 ▶

Adding a second table to a query

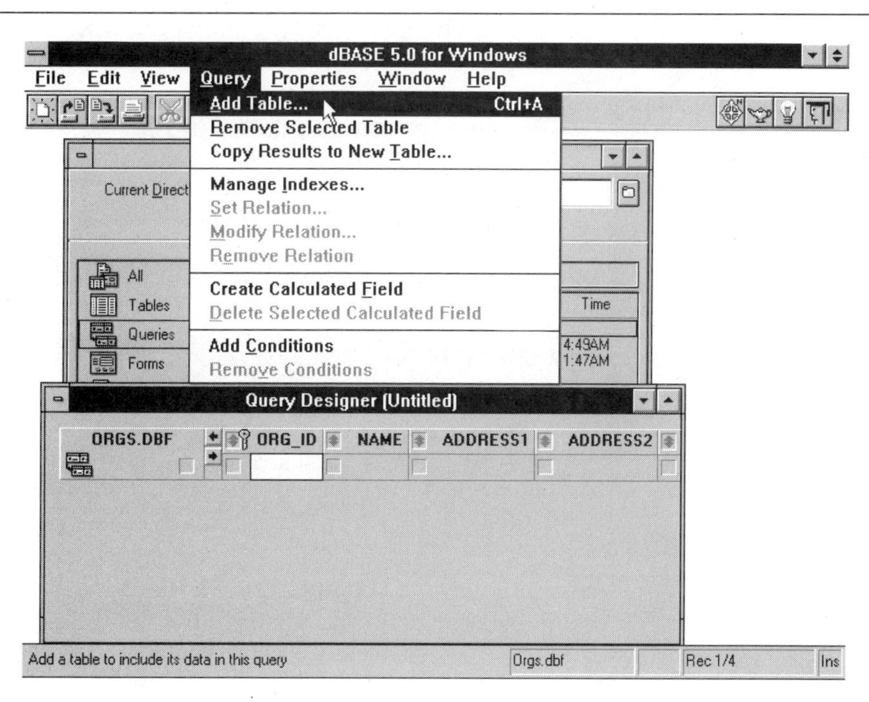

3. Choose the People table from the Open Table Required dialog box.
4. Put your mouse pointer over the relation Set Relation icon in the Orgs table. Press the left button down and drag to the Set Relation icon in the People table, like this:

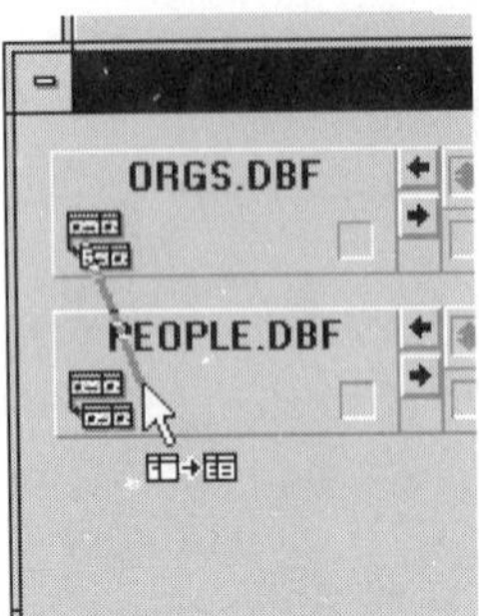

When you drag this icon, you will see the Relation cursor (as shown above). Be sure to start at the Orgs table (our parent table) and drag to the People table (the People records will be *children* of the organization records).

5. In the Define Relation dialog box, which pops up in response to step 4, click on the ORG_ID field in the Child Table box. dBASE for Windows will automatically select the same named field in the Parent Table box, as shown in Figure 5.21. (If you start by selecting the field in the Parent Table box, you will also need to select it in the Child Table box.)
6. Click on OK or press Enter, and you'll return to the Query Designer, with your relationship in place. It will look like this:

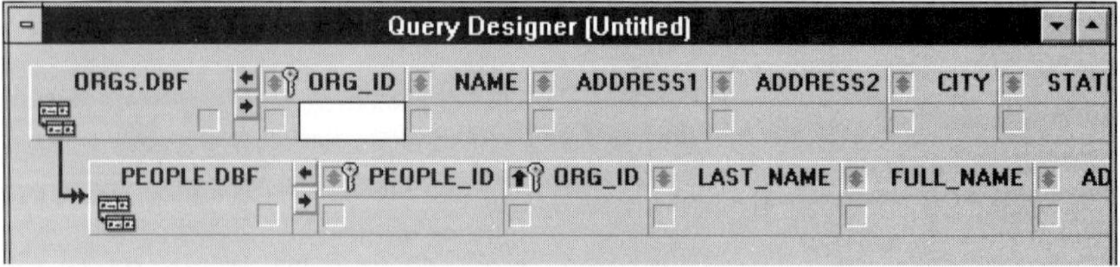

As you can see, the child table, PEOPLE.DBF, is offset to the right, and a double-headed arrow points from the Set Relation icon in the Orgs table

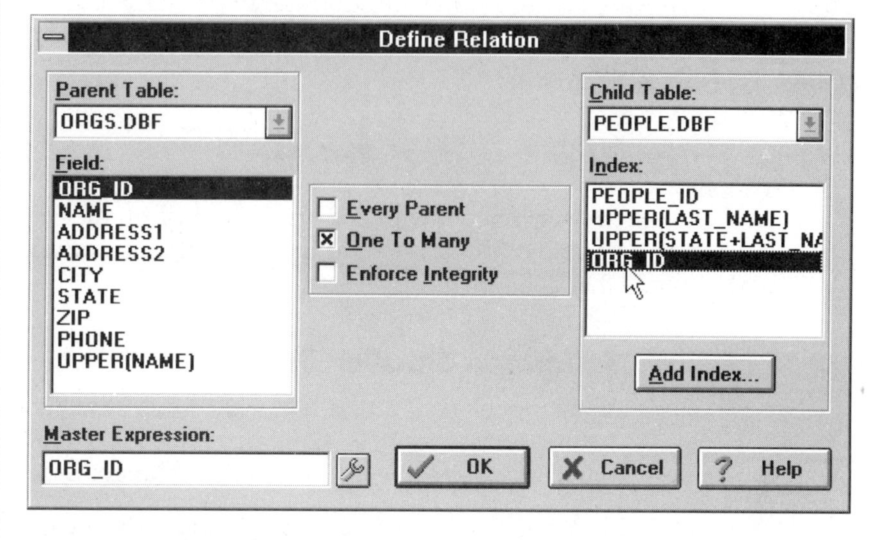

FIGURE 5.21

Selecting the foreign field in the child table

to the People table. This shows that you've properly established the one-to-many relationship.

We're now ready to run the query. But first, save your query. We call ours Orgs1. Before we start running it, take a moment to look at the ORGS1.QBE program that the Query Designer wrote:

```
* dBASE Windows .QBE file 9
CLOSE DATABASES
SET EXACT ON
SELECT 1
USE ORGS.DBF
SELECT 2
USE PEOPLE.DBF ORDER TAG ORG_ID OF PEOPLE.MDX
SELECT 1
SET RELATION TO ORG_ID INTO PEOPLE CONSTRAIN
SET SKIP TO PEOPLE
SET FILTER TO FOUND(2)
GO TOP
```

As you see, it opens the Orgs table in work area 1, with no index. It then opens the People table in work area 2, using the ORG_ID field index. Next, it switches back to work area 1 (the parent table) and sets the relation.

FOUND(2) specifies that the FOUND() function returns True in work area 2. Let's go on to use this query, which will show you what all this code means.

▶ Using the Related Tables

We won't begin with the query we just built. We'll take a little more trouble to build one that has less data, so we can clearly see exactly what is happening.

Building a Smaller Query

Again, open an Untitled file in the Query Designer. Repeat the steps in the previous section, so that your new query looks just like the old one. (This only takes a few seconds after you get used to the process.)

Now, what we want is a lot less. Check five fields. In the Orgs table, check the ORG_ID and NAME fields. In the People table, check the PEOPLE_ID, ORG_ID, and LAST_NAME fields, like this:

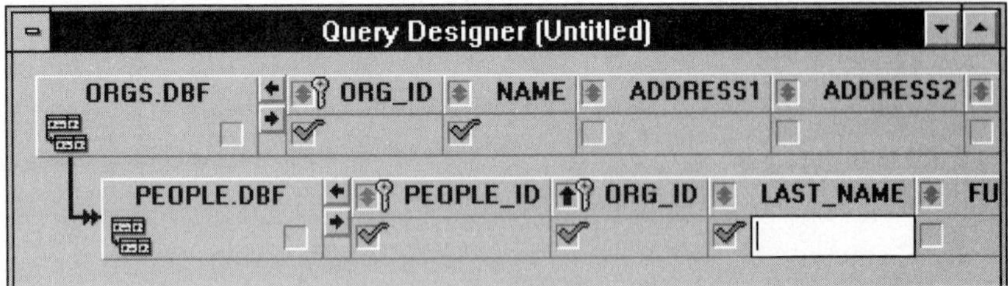

These are the ID fields that the computer will use for identification, and the name fields that we use for identification. Now run the query (click on the lightning icon on the speedbar, choose View ➤ Query Results, or just press F2).

Our results are shown in Figure 5.22. As you can see, the people are now neatly organized by organization. You'll get from no relation to this point in about 30 seconds. Using the ID fields makes this very fast.

FIGURE 5.22

People related to employers

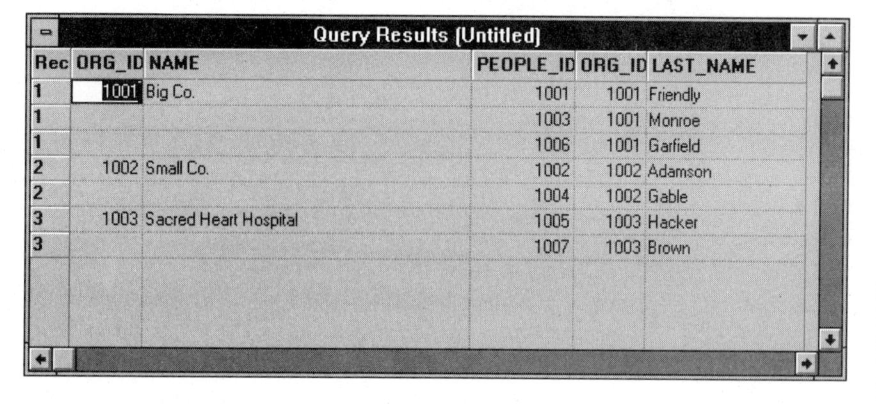

Query Results (Untitled)

Rec	ORG_ID	NAME	PEOPLE_ID	ORG_ID	LAST_NAME
1	1001	Big Co.	1001	1001	Friendly
1			1003	1001	Monroe
1			1006	1001	Garfield
2	1002	Small Co.	1002	1002	Adamson
2			1004	1002	Gable
3	1003	Sacred Heart Hospital	1005	1003	Hacker
3			1007	1003	Brown

Using the Query

With this query view, you see data from both tables together. Normally, a restricted view such as this one won't be a good choice for data entry. You won't be able to enter data in any of the fields that you didn't include in the query, of course.

However, for our present purposes, let's go ahead and use it anyway. You can learn from it.

First, change your view to either the Form or Columnar Layout (click on the speedbar button, or choose View ➤ Columnar Layout or Form Layout). Go to the beginning of the file and then move down from one record to the next.

In every case, you'll see that each of your fields is filled in. As you go down the Query Results table, you are actually working your way down the child table (in this case, PEOPLE.DBF) of all the children of the first parent. When you finish with the children of the first parent record, dBASE for Windows goes to the parent table (in this case, ORGS.DBF) and advances to the next parent record. It then starts with the first child of the new parent.

If you return to the Browse Layout view, you'll see that the repeated occurrences of the parent data are not filled in (as in Figure 5.22). This is a visual convenience. As far as the database is concerned, the situation is the one you see in the Form or Columnar Layout: each child is matched to its parent's related data. With that in mind, let's edit our data.

First, try editing the ORG_ID field in the Orgs table (change 1001 to 999, for example). You'll see that this change destroys the relationship between the child records and the parent, but dBASE doesn't seem to mind.

Put the correct value back in the ORG_ID field for the parent, and then try changing one of the values in the ORG_ID field of the People table. Again, you're damaging a relationship, but dBASE doesn't seem to mind.

What's lacking is what the relational database scientists call referential integrity.

Enforcing Referential Integrity

Referential integrity means that every ID of an employer in the People table matches one and only one ID in the Orgs table. To achieve referential integrity, you must make sure that you use a proper value when you add the ORG_ID value to the People table, and you must be sure that you change it to another proper value when you edit it.

On the parent table side, you must be sure that each ORG_ID value is unique when you add a new record. You must never edit or delete the value in the parent table if there are child records that match that value.

Fortunately, dBASE for Windows has considerable intelligence. Let's ask it to help.

Switch from Run mode to Design mode (click on the design icon on the speedbar or press Shift-F2). From the Query Designer, we want to get back to the Define Relation dialog box. Select any field in the child table and choose Query ➤ Modify Relation …. (This choice is also available from the Query Designer's Speed menu.)

In the Define Relation dialog box, check the Enforce Integrity box, as shown in Figure 5.23.

With that box checked, click on OK or press Enter and then return to Run mode (click on the lightning icon on the speedbar or press F2). Now try those changes again.

FIGURE 5.23

Asking dBASE for Windows to enforce referential integrity

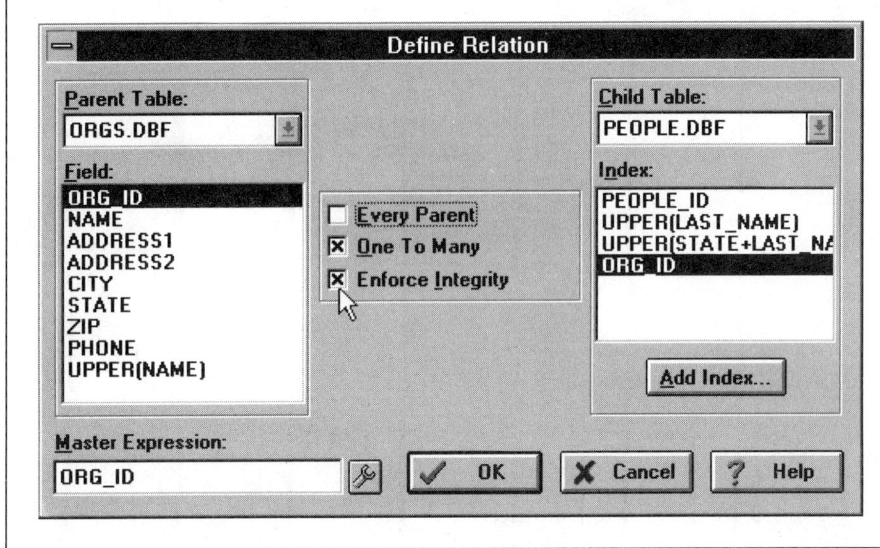

When you try to change the parent key to a new value, dBASE for Windows warns you that records are still attached to that key, and asks you if it should cascade delete these records, with this Alert box:

When you get to the ORG_ID values in the People table records, you'll find that these values have become read-only—you can't change them.

Now try appending new records. If you are in a field from the parent table when you press Ctrl-A, you'll be adding new parent data, in this case, the ID and name. dBASE for Windows will insist that the ID be unique. When you're appending data to the parent, dBASE won't let you add child records.

If you have a child field active when you press Ctrl-A, you'll see the Append to Alias dialog box, shown in Figure 5.24. If you select ORGS here, it will be as if you had pressed Ctrl-A when you were in an Orgs

FIGURE 5.24

Selecting parent or child tables for appending

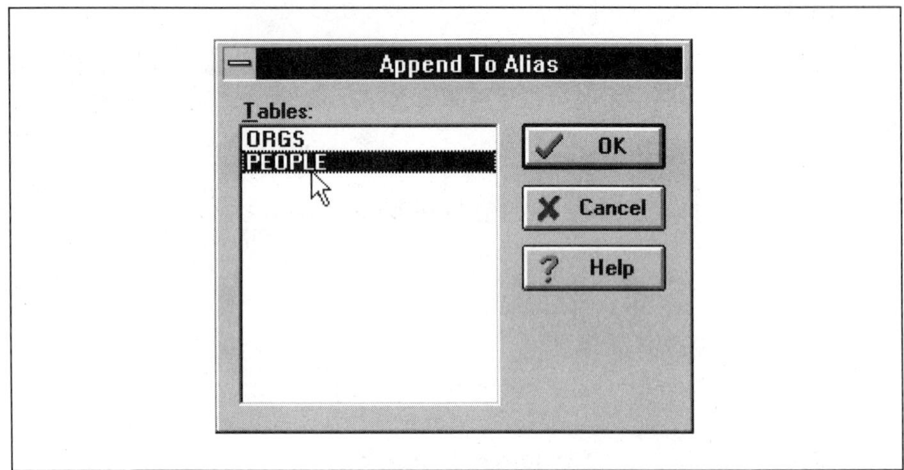

table field.

If you select PEOPLE, you'll be adding people automatically related to the currently selected parent record. dBASE for Windows will automatically fill in the ORG_ID value with the correct parent ORG_ID value. This field will still be read-only, so you won't be able to get it wrong.

Showing Every Parent

Select any organization and change its ID value. (In practice, you will *never* change this value.) When the Cascade Delete Alert box pops up, say Yes.

All the children of that record are deleted, and the parent also disappears. Why?

The default setting for the Every Parent question is unchecked. Unless this box is checked, only those parents that have attached children appear in the Query Results window.

To restore your childless parents (Orgs without associated People) return to the Define Relationship dialog box (press Shift-F2 for Design mode, then click on any field in the People table and choose Query ➤ Modify Relation …). In the dialog box, check the Every Parent box. Select OK and return to Run mode. You'll see that all parents (Orgs) are shown, including the ones that have no related children.

TIP

When we build a relation, we make a habit of checking all three center boxes in the Define Relation dialog box.

When you exit from the Query tools, dBASE for Windows will ask you if you want to save your query. Tell it Yes, and save the query as Orgs2.

This is the program that the Query Designer wrote for our ORGS2.QBE:

```
* dBASE Windows .QBE file 9
CLOSE DATABASES
SET EXACT ON
SELECT 1
USE ORGS.DBF
SELECT 2
USE PEOPLE.DBF ORDER TAG ORG_ID
SELECT 1
SET RELATION TO ORG_ID INTO PEOPLE CONSTRAIN INTEGRITY
SET SKIP TO PEOPLE
SET FIELDS TO ORG_ID, NAME
SELECT 2
SET FIELDS TO People_ID, ORG_ID, LAST_NAME
SELECT 1
GO TOP
```

CLOSE DATABASES closes any data tables or SQL databases (linked through the IDAPI Configuration Utility).

With EXACT off, character strings are considered equal in an expression if the one on the left matches the one on the right to the length of the one on the right. For example, *Mitchell* equals *M*, as do *Morris* and *Mary*. With EXACT ON, strings must match exactly, so *Mary* does not equal *M*.

The next four lines open Orgs and People in work areas 1 and 2. The master index on People is the ORG_ID value.

Returning to work area 1, the parent table's area, the relation is set. CONSTRAIN eliminates any child records whose foreign keys (ORG_ID in the People table) don't match primary keys in the parent table (ORG_ID in the Orgs table). The INTEGRITY clause is added when you check Enforce Integrity. We've seen it in action.

SET SKIP TO PEOPLE controls the way the records are presented as you move through the table. It specifies that the each child record (in the People table) attached to a parent (in the Orgs table) will be shown before skipping to the next parent record.

Finally, the SET FIELDS commands specify the fields that we checked in the Query Designer.

▸▸ You Edit the Program

Normally, using the Query Designer has dBASE for Windows do the programming for us. We work with tools that make visual sense and let dBASE for Windows handle the rather exacting task of creating program statements.

However, the Query Designer is a Two-Way-Tool, so we can also edit the program. This provides a convenient way for us to overcome any limitations that we perceive in the design tool.

One limitation (we actually think it's a bug, but you could argue otherwise) is that the Query Designer always sets EXACT ON. Try this:

1. Launch the Query Designer for your Orgs2 query. (Select the Orgs2 query in the Navigator and right double-click, or press Shift-F2.)
2. In the conditions area of the LAST_NAME field of the People table, type **M**. If EXACT is OFF, this will select all last names starting with *M*. If EXACT is ON, as it always is through the Query Designer, this will only select a person whose last name is the single letter *M*.
3. Launch Run mode. (Press F2 or click the lightning icon in the speedbar.)

Unless one of your people has the a last name *M*, one-letter long, you'll see an Alert box telling you that no records were found. Before the next step, make sure that you use a letter, such as *M* that does, in fact, start at least one last name in your People table.

4. Exit from the Query Designer, saving your query in the ORGS2 file.

Since the Query Designer sets EXACT ON, we need to edit the query as a program and run it from the Command window.

5. In the Navigator, select the Orgs2 query and choose Edit as Program from the Speed menu (right-click on the file).
6. In the Program Editor, change the word ON to **OFF** in the SET EXACT command.
7. Run the .QBE program by pressing Ctrl-D in the Program Editor. This will run all the lines in your Program Editor, and turn control over to the Command window.
8. Give the BROWSE command in the Command window. Figure 5.25 shows our Program Editor and Command window after doing these steps.

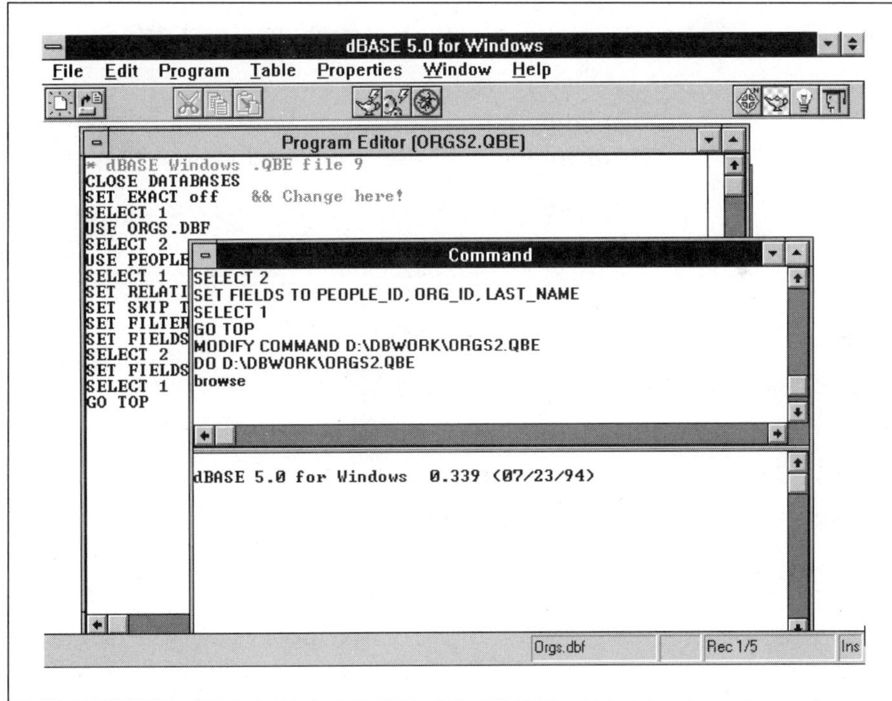

FIGURE 5.25

Launching a query with EXACT OFF

If you look closely in the Program Editor window, you'll see that we have added a comment, starting with two amerpersands (&&), in the program. dBASE lets you add notes to yourself in a program. Just be sure to start the comment line with **.

This time, your Browse Layout view will show all the people whose last names start with *M*.

In general, we let the Query Designer handle the programming for us, but there are occasions when we find that we need to take over. As you see, it's not too complex to make your own changes to the code that the Query Designer wrote.

►► Summary

In this chapter, you started by doing some cleanup work. You learned that program files, such as the .QBE files written by the Query Designer, are compiled into object files, which have the last letter of their extension replaced with *O*, such as .QBO.

Then you went into the Query Designer to create a simple query. Building from the simplest query, you used the field check marks to control the fields that appeared in your Query Results window.

Then you went on to indexes. You used simple indexes on a single field, and then used index expressions. You used the UPPER( ) function to change ASCII sorting into true alphabetic sorting.

You discovered that it wasn't possible to use more than a single field in an index. But we worked around that limitation by including multiple fields in an index expression.

You then went into selecting records matching your criteria. You used individual field conditions and then you ANDed conditions together across multiple fields. Next, you added multiple conditions on a single field, ORing them with other conditions.

Then you used combinations of AND (across the condition line horizontally) and OR (vertically) conditions for precise control. You also saw that there is a separate Conditions box with similar AND and OR capabilities for the ultimate in selection control.

You then went on to adding calculated fields. You built a separate file skeleton showing calculated fields, and you used it as if it were a normal table-based file skeleton.

After calculated fields, we moved on to relating two tables. You added an Orgs table, and a relating ID field in the People table. With the records related, you built a query that organized your People table by the employing organizations.

Then you created a small (showing only a few fields) query that you used to examine referential integrity. You saw that relational integrity is provided by dBASE for Windows when you check the Enforce Integrity box in the Define Relation dialog box.

Before you left the Define Relation dialog box, you learned to use the Every Parent property to include or exclude Orgs table records that did not have related People table records in your Query Results window.

Finally, you modified the program code to make a change that you could not otherwise get from the Query Designer. You used the Program Editor to edit the code, and launched your own BROWSE command from the Command window.

As you go on in your database work, you'll see that the ability to relate and control multiple tables through the Query Designer is a key to building powerful, flexible databases.

In the next chapter, you'll continue to use your queries when you build your own custom forms.

▶ ▶ CHAPTER 6

Building Forms with the Two-Way Form Designer

▶▶ **There's** a secret we want to let you in on, but we don't want it passed along: dBASE for Windows forms are fun. If building Windows forms is part of your job, you'll need to do your best to make it look like a serious, difficult business.

It will help if you talk about all the programming that you need to do in order to really build forms. Let's keep it just between ourselves that these "programs" generally run about one line long.

The Form Designer is a vast tool that addresses all the facets of Microsoft Windows user interface programming. To give it thorough coverage, we've used Part 5 of this book. In this chapter, we'll build MDI (Multiple Document Interface) and non-MDI forms to create a system for our phone lists.

You've already used the Form Expert to build an MDI Windows child form. We'll start by bypassing the Form Expert to create a modal window and then we'll go on to menu building and multi-table forms.

▶▶ **WARNING**

Like any new Windows program, dBASE for Windows has some bugs. You're more likely to meet them when you are building new systems than when you're running existing systems.

Before we continue, we'll warn you about one of the most annoying bugs in dBASE for Windows. We assume that it will be eradicated in one of the next releases, but it may still show up. You should be prepared for it.

When you build a form, the Form Designer is writing a program for you. When you run the form, dBASE compiles the form (in a .WFM file) into object code (in a .WFO file). It then runs the object code. The problem is that it does not *always* realize that it needs to replace its in-memory copy of the object code when it recompiles. It can go right on running an obsolete copy, even while you're making changes to the form.

The visible effect of this is that you will make changes and your changes won't show up when you run the form. When this happens, you need to exit dBASE for Windows and restart it. (This bug affects only the form design phase; it has no effect when you run the form.)

With that word of warning, let's get started.

►► You Build a Modal Form

In Microsoft Windows programs, *modal forms* are those that must be processed by the user before going on to any other part of the system. For example, Alert boxes are modal forms. Frequently, the only processing required is a button click.

One common modal form is the About box, which can be selected from most Help menus. As a simple starter, let's build a modal About box for our phone system.

► Creating the Form

To begin, from the Navigator select the Untitled form and launch the Form Designer (press Shift-F2 or double-click the icon). When the Form Expert asks its first question, tell it you want a Blank Form, as you see in Figure 6.1.

This will launch the Form Designer with a blank form. Before we proceed, let's spend a couple minutes organizing the Form Designer so we can work efficiently.

Laying Out the Form Designer Desktop

After many hours in the Form Designer, we've arrived at a layout that is very productive. First select all three of the auxiliary surfaces:

- The Controls palette
- The Object Properties Inspector

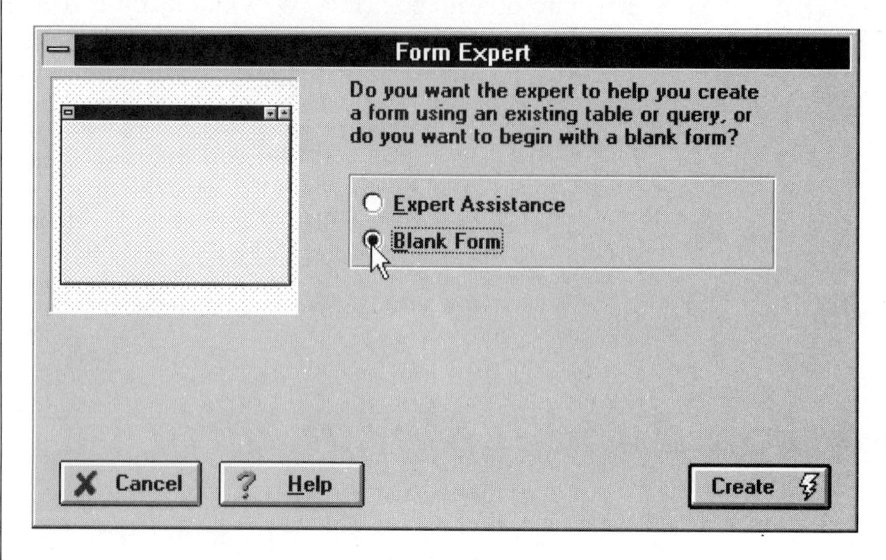

FIGURE 6.1

Using a blank (not Expert-generated) form

- The Procedure Editor

These tools are available through the View menu pull-down menu or the Speed menu. Figure 6.2 shows them selected through the View menu.

Note the position of the Procedure Editor in Figure 6.2. We'll leave it here, but you won't be able to see its window clearly in the next figures.

The challenge in laying out your Form Designer desktop is to give yourself convenient access to all the tools, all the time. We've solved that problem with the setup shown in Figure 6.3:

- The Controls palette is full height, on the left.
- The Object Properties Inspector is full height, on the right.
- The Procedure Editor is full width, at the bottom.
- The form we're working on is centered, but not so low that it covers the tabs of the Controls palette or the Object Properties Inspector.

FIGURE 6.2

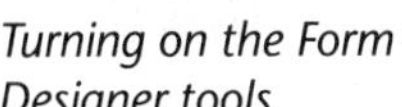
Turning on the Form Designer tools

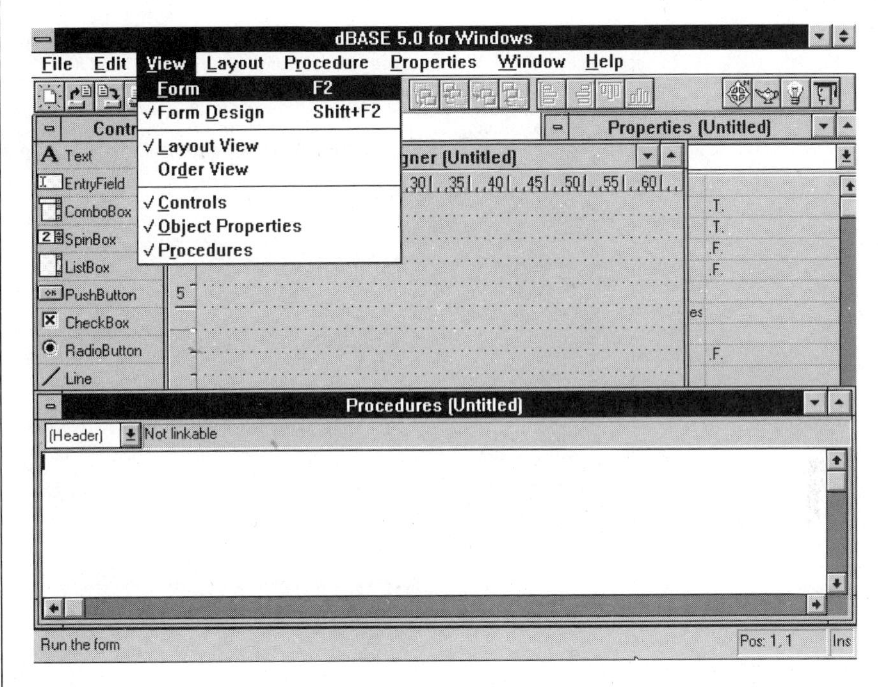

The key points to observe here are that the tabs of the Controls palette and the tabs of the Object Properties Inspector are available with just a click. If you lay out your window this way, the Procedure Editor is also available by clicking in the bottom center, between the Controls palette and the Properties window.

You'll see that the forms we design aren't full height, because that would make working with the three tools extremely difficult.

TIP

We don't consider the keyboard a viable option for Form Designer work. If you're on a plane without your trackball, use the Form Expert to create its default forms, and then enjoy the in-flight movie.

FIGURE 6.3 ►

An efficient Form Designer layout

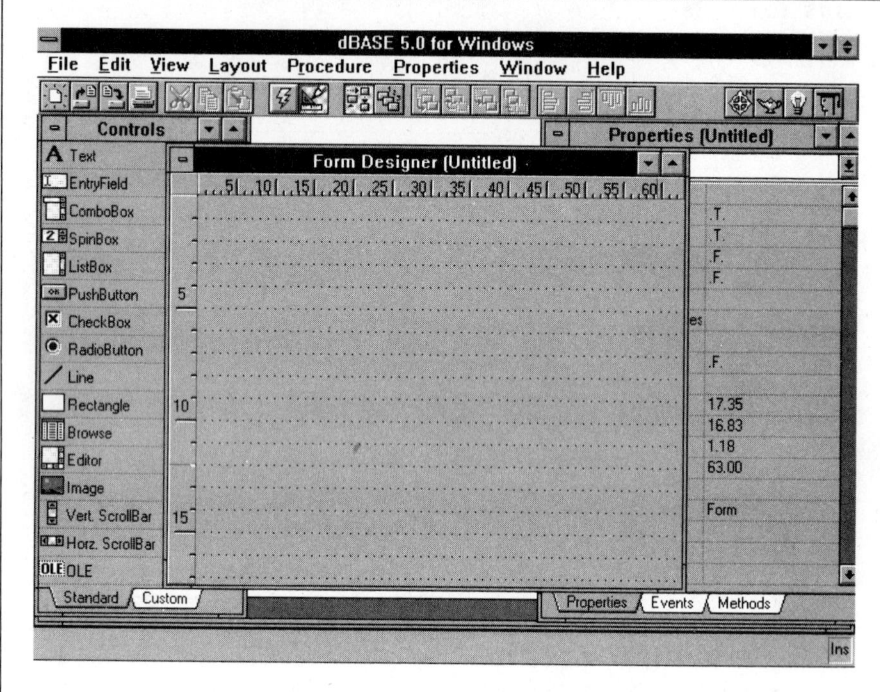

Now that we have a plain form and a good working setup, let's build an About form.

Adding Text Objects

First, let's add the form's title. These are the steps:

1. Click on the Standard tab of the Controls palette, to access this tool.
2. Click on the Text object, like this:

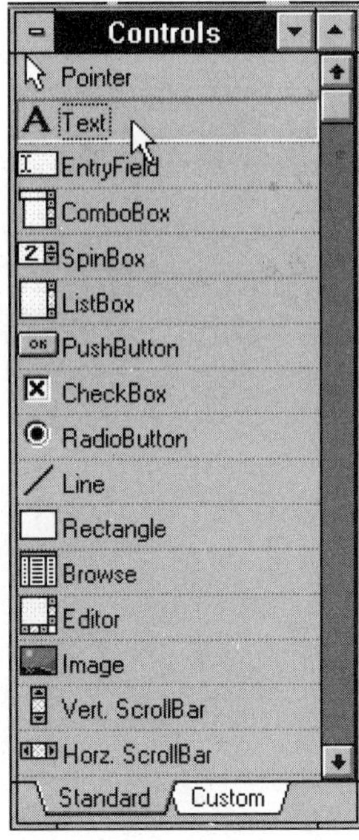

3. Press the left button and drag a large Text object on your form. At this point, don't be too fussy about this object's size or placement.

After you drag the Text object, the form becomes the active window. The text you just placed is selected, with resize handles at each of the sides and corners.

4. Use the object's handles, or drag, to make your Text object look like the one you see in Figure 6.4.

FIGURE 6.4

A large Text object for the form's title

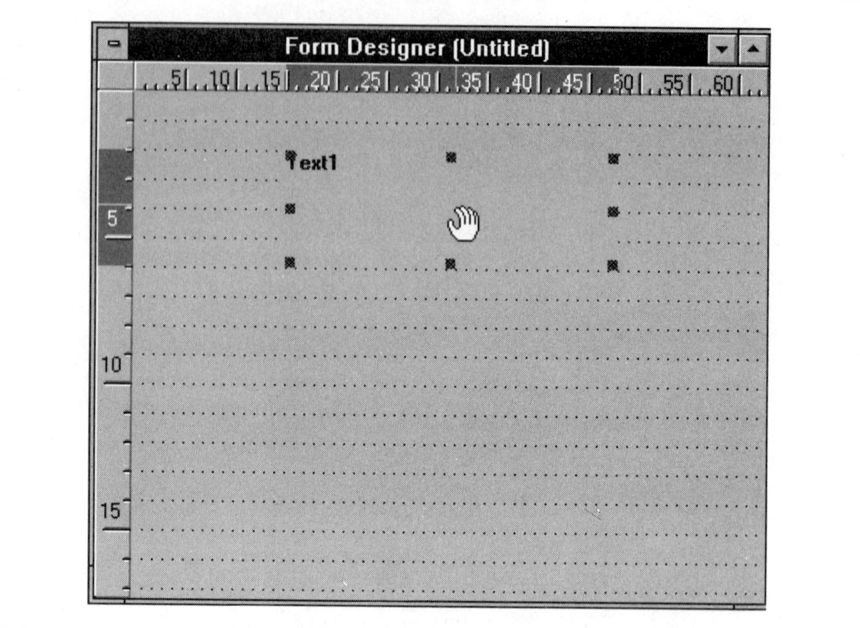

Now you have a large Text object with a tiny *text1* up in the corner. That's not what we want to say, and it's not how we want to say it. To fix those problems, we'll work with the Object Properties Inspector.

5. Click on the Properties tab of the Object Properties Inspector.

▸▸ **NOTE**

Objects have data properties, event properties, and method properties. The Properties tab of the Object Properties Inspector refers to just the data properties.

6. Click on the Text property to select it:

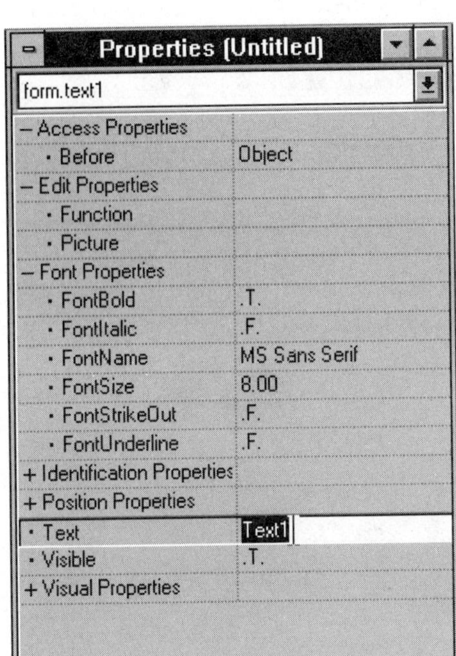

7. Press Backspace to clear the field, and then type **Phone List** (or whatever title you like).
8. If the Position Properties list is not expanded (it shows a + sign), double-click on it to expand it. (It shows a – sign when it's expanded; another double-click reduces it.)

9. Click on the down arrow next to the Alignment property. Then select 4 - Center from the pop-up menu:

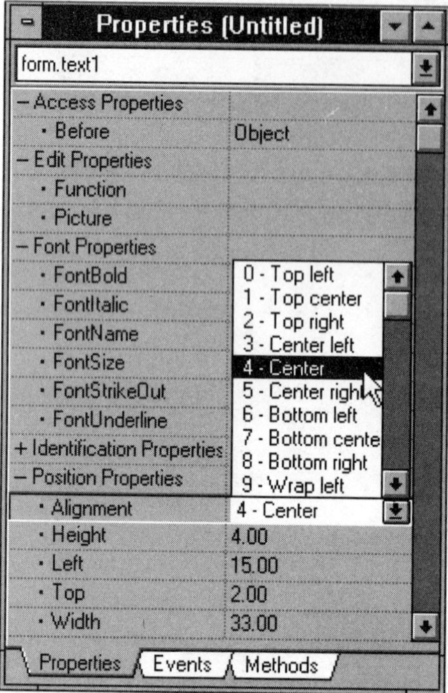

10. If the Font Properties are not expanded, double-click to expand them.

11. Use the spinbutton next to the FontSize property to select a large font.

As you click on higher sizes, you'll see the text (or at least most of the text) grow in your form. You'll also see that some sizes are very readable, and some are not. Multiples of 4 seem to work best.

We now have a big, centered title, as you can see in Figure 6.5.

With that done, add another Text object underneath with your copyright notice. (If you're working for your employer, add your employer's copyright notice, but be sure to sneak in credit for yourself, somewhere.) Figure 6.6 shows our form with the copyright notice added.

FIGURE 6.5

A suitable title on our About form

FIGURE 6.6

A second font for the copyright line adds visual interest.

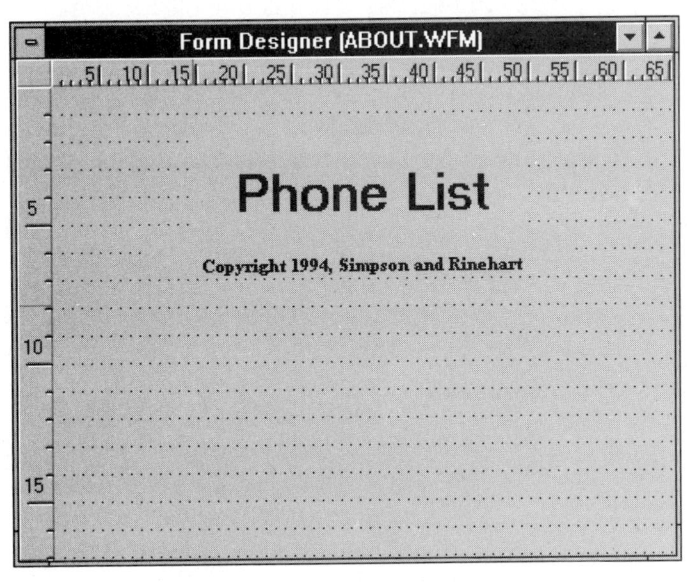

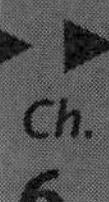

The copyright line is a good place to be creative with your choice of fonts. We used Times New Roman—an exception to our rule about not choosing serifs for on-screen fonts.

Making the Form Modal

Now we're ready to turn this form into a modal form. If you haven't done so yet, run the form. Before it runs, you will get the Save Form dialog box. We called our form About. The Save Form dialog box will supply the file extension .WFM.

Note that you can resize the form, minimize or maximize it, and so on. But this is not what we want. We want a form that provides its information and exits when the user tells it to.

Return to the Form Designer (press Shift-F2 or click on the design icon on the speedbar) to change this.

To make the form modal, we need to change the MDI property from True to False. MDI is one of the Window Properties (on the Properties tab), which you will need to expand before you can access the MDI property.

To change MDI to False, click on the MDI property, click on the drop-down arrow, and then click on .F. in the list. Run the form again. It looks the same, but it's very different. Start by minimizing the form.

If your dBASE for Windows is maximized (full screen), your form disappears. It's not a child form anymore. To return to it, press and hold down the Alt key while you press Tab to cycle through all your active Windows applications. You will come to your About form.

When you come to the form, release the Alt key, and your form is selected again. Double-click on the System button or press Alt-F4 to close the form.

▶▶ NOTE

The Alt-F4 combination is for closing non-MDI forms. Ctrl-F4 works for MDI forms.

Our form is still sizable, and can be minimized and maximized, which is what we want.

Return to the Form Designer and set these additional Window properties to False (click on .F):

- Maximize
- Minimize
- Sizeable

Now when you run the form, it's a modal, information-type form.

▶▶ WARNING

A bug in an early version of dBASE for Windows may or may not still be in your version. The Form Designer did not read the settings of Maximize, Minimize, and Sizeable. We needed to reset these to False each time the Form Designer took over in Design mode. If you save the form first, however, you'll avoid this bug.

The EscExit property should get a bit of your thought. If you are used to pressing Esc to exit a form, this is the default behavior of dBASE for Windows forms. Pressing Esc to exit is *not* part of the CUA (Common User Access) specification, however. If you want to follow the CUA conventions, set the EscExit property to False.

Now let's attach an OK pushbutton to our form, so that we can click this familiar button.

► Attaching a Pushbutton

The dBASE Custom Control named OKBUTTON (on the Custom tab of the Controls palette) is precisely what we want. It says OK and it has the distinctive Borland check mark. You could just grab the prebuilt one and use it. However, you'll learn more if you do it yourself. It's not difficult.

Adding a Pushbutton

Start by clicking on the Standard tab of the Controls palette. Then choose the Pushbutton object. On your form, drag a button about 2 lines high and 15 characters wide. Note the shadowed area on the form's rulers (along the top and side of the window). If you adjust your form to a precise width, you can use the rulers for centering objects.

Our button is shown in place in Figure 6.7. Notice that we used the rulers to set the form to 65 characters wide, which makes it easy to position a 15-character pushbutton.

FIGURE 6.7 ►

A pushbutton centered on our form

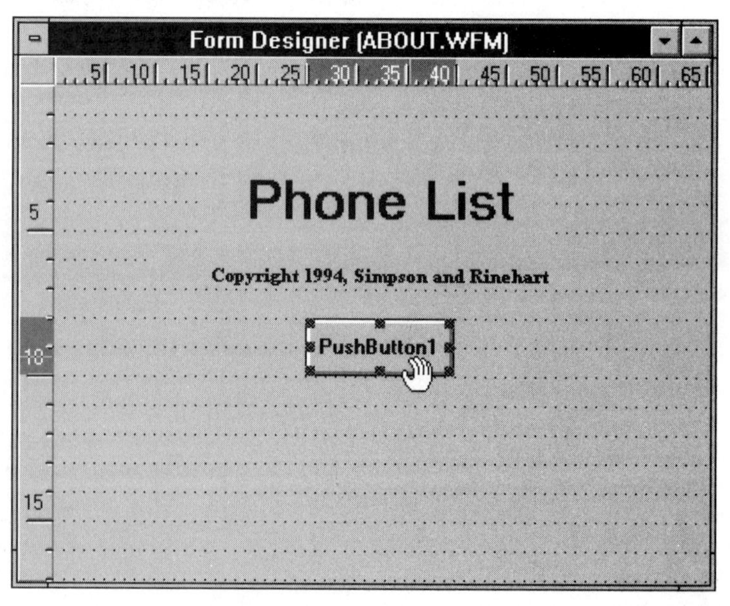

Setting the Text Property

Once again, the Form Designer has chosen the object's class name and added a digit to create a default name (Pushbutton1). As with Text objects, our first order of business is to change the default object to something reasonable.

Click on the Properties tab of the Object Properties Inspector, and then choose the Text property. Replace the text with **OK**. Unlike the Text property of a Text object, there is no Alignment property to set; the pushbutton's alignment works just fine.

Making the Button Work

When you test this form, you'll see that the button is a fine addition, except for one thing: it doesn't do anything.

WARNING

Be sure that you close non-MDI windows and return to the Form Designer from the Navigator. If you simply click on the design icon or press Shift-F2, your form will still be in Windows' list of active applications.

To make a working button, we need to use the Procedure Editor to build an event-handling program that calls the form's Close method. All of this is easier to do than it is to say, fortunately.

So far, we've worked with the Object Properties Inspector's Properties tab. For this task, we'll use the other tabs.

First, select the About form. (Click anywhere in the form outside the objects on the form.) Then click on the Methods tab of the Object Properties Inspector to see these properties:

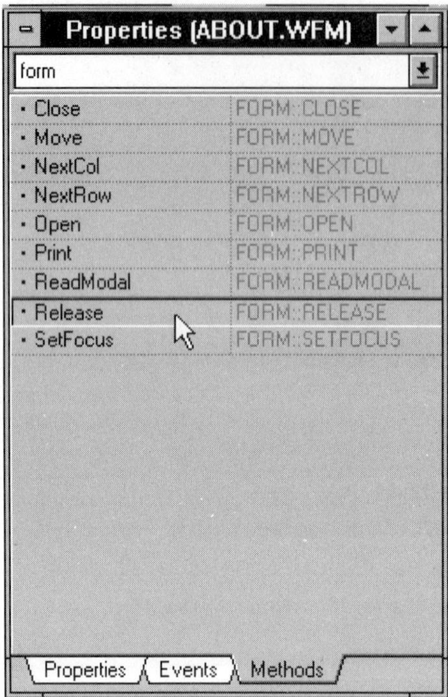

An object's methods are things that it knows how to do. As you can see in the Methods list, a form knows how to open and close itself, how to move and print, and so on.

Let's look at the Event properties of a Pushbutton object. To do this, click the pushbutton, then the Events tab of the Object Properties Inspector.

You'll see the list of events which a pushbutton can respond to. For now, we'll be attaching an event handler to the OnClick event. Click on this event, and then click on the tool icon to the right of the OnClick entry field:

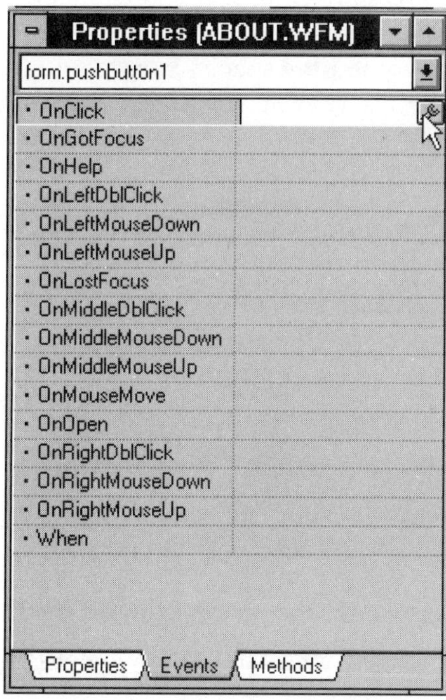

The tool that pops up now is the Procedure Editor. This is another text editor, like the Program Editor, but with a special knowledge of where you called it and how it should organize the programs you enter.

Figure 6.8 shows the Procedure Editor after we entered this program line:

```
Form.Close()
```

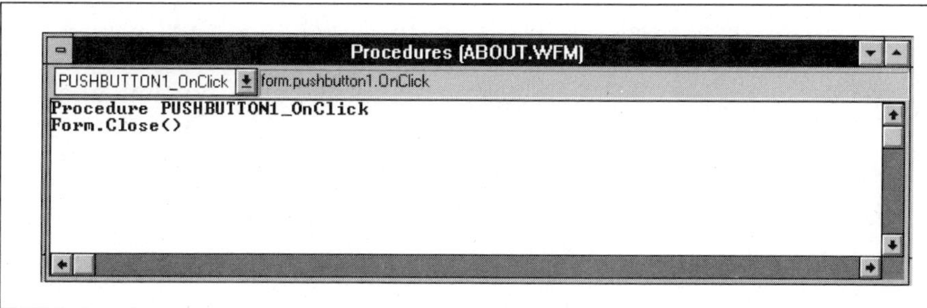

FIGURE 6.8

Calling the Close method from the OnClick event

This specifies that we want to invoke the Close method of the Form object.

Enter that line into your own Procedure Editor and then switch to Run mode. This time, when you click on the OK button, your form is closed.

Obviously, this capability would let you write a long, complex program to handle any of the events to which your pushbutton can respond. If you want it to do something special in response to a right double-click, for instance, select the OnRightDblClick event and click on the tool icon. The Procedure Editor will appear and let you enter whatever commands you like.

However, the event handler we just entered is very typical. A simple line of code is often all that is required.

Adding an Icon to the Pushbutton

So far, our form is functional but a bit utilitarian. Let's make a couple improvements.

The Borland buttons all have those decorative images that reinforce the meaning of each button. Let's add one to our pushbutton. Follow these steps:

1. Select (single-click) the pushbutton on the form.
2. Click on the Properties tab of the Object Properties Inspector.
3. Double-click on Bitmap Properties if these properties are not already expanded.

4. Click on the UpBitmap property, and then click on the tool icon (shown in the margin) on its right.

These steps open the Choose Bitmap dialog box you see in Figure 6.9. The Location drop-down list lets you choose between Resource and Filename options. The standard Borland bitmaps are all Resource choices. You can choose the Filename option to use a custom bitmap that you have in a .BMP file.

5. With Resource selected for Location, click on the tool icon at the right of the Bitmap entry field. You'll see the dBASE for Windows Bitmaps dialog box, shown in Figure 6.10.

FIGURE 6.9 

Choosing a bitmap for a pushbutton

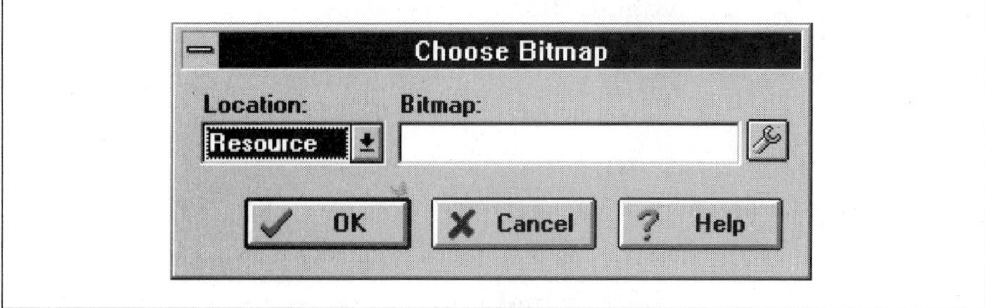

FIGURE 6.10 

The dBASE for Windows Bitmaps dialog box

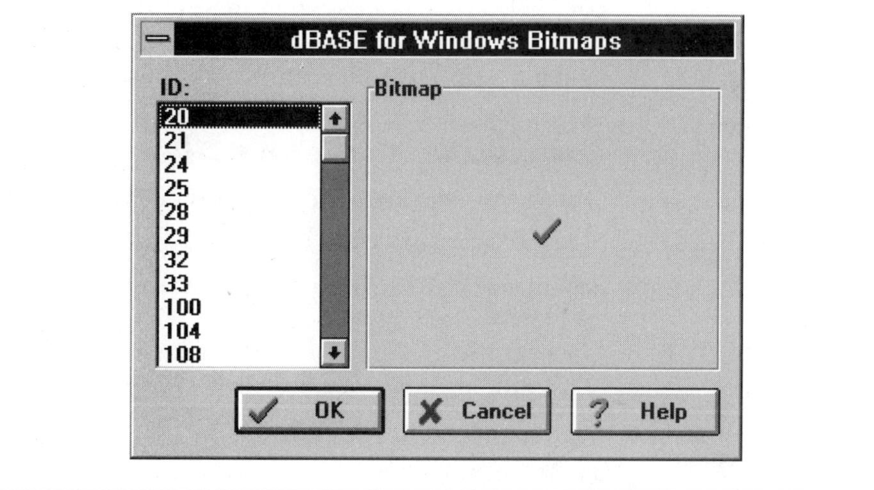

Of the large collection of available icons, it turns out that the first one is exactly the one we want. Before continuing, you'll probably want to look through the icon collection to see what's available. As you scroll through the icon numbers on the left, the icon is displayed on your right.

6. When you're finished taking a look at the icons, return to ID: 20, the small check mark, and press Enter or click on OK. You will be returned to the Choose Bitmap dialog box, showing #20 in the Bitmap entry field.
7. Again, click on OK or press Enter, and you'll return to the Object Properties Inspector.

RESOURCE #20 now appears in the UpBitmap property's entry field. But you probably overlooked that detail, since your eye is drawn immediately to the check mark on your bitmap! We think these little bits of color add a lot to a form.

If you keep your forms mostly monochrome, the colors stand out.

As you've seen, UpBitmap is only one of the possible bitmaps. You could also have selected a bitmap to show when the button was disabled, pushed down, and selected (received focus). In many cases, just assigning an UpBitmap property is adequate.

Customizing the Form's Title

Our form is looking better now, isn't it? Its title in the title bar just says OK, however. We really want that to be something a bit more descriptive.

Again, select the form (click anywhere outside the on-form objects) and click on the Properties tab of the Object Properties Inspector. Click on the Text property. A Form object's Text property refers to the text in the window title bar.

Enter **About My Phone List** (or whatever text you would like to see as the form window's title), and then run your form again. It's looking good, isn't it?

► *Adding a Memory Report*

If you choose Help ➤ About dBASE 5.0 for Windows ..., you'll see the great splash screen with dBASE's transparent globe. To make one of those for your own About message requires a good paint program and considerable skill as an artist. We don't recommend adding those big bitmaps, because they are real resource hogs.

What we do like is the report at the bottom of the About box that shows how much memory is available. Let's add that to our own About form.

Adding More Text Objects

We'll need two Text objects: one to say *Memory:* and the other to actually report the available memory. (Actually, you could do it with just one object, but it wouldn't be as direct a solution.)

With your About form launched in the Form Designer, grab the Text object from the Controls palette and drag a Text object on your form, beneath the pushbutton. Repeat this procedure to place a second Text object. Figure 6.11 shows the two Text objects we added to our form, both selected.

FIGURE 6.11

Two Text objects just added to our About form

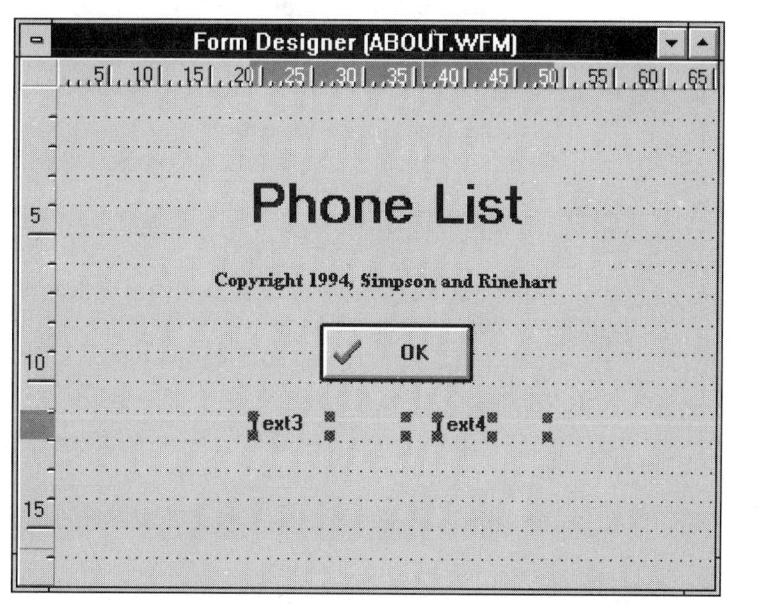

To select multiple objects on your form, click on the first one, then hold a Shift (or Ctrl) key down while you click on the other objects. This is useful, for example, for moving a group of objects. With multiple objects selected, dragging with the left button moves all the selected objects together.

Adjusting the Text Objects

For both Text objects, change the Alignment property to 3, Center left. Do each object separately. Remember, the Alignment property is listed under Position Properties.

Change the first object's Text property to read **Memory:**. Then shrink the Text object so that it is just slightly larger than the text. Position the two Text objects so that they are close enough to make a pleasing display.

For the second Text object's Text property, enter **123456**. You'll see why when we start working with the Picture and Function properties to display the actual memory report.

Using the MEMORY( ) Function

dBASE has a built-in function, MEMORY( ), that returns the available memory in kilobytes. In the Command window, ask

? MEMORY( )

The MEMORY( ) function gives us the information we want. (Remember, the ? command asks "What is?") You'll see the number of kilobytes available reported in the results pane of your Command window.

But there's a problem with using this function: the value reported by MEMORY( ) is a number, and the Text property of a Text object is a text string. How do we get this information into our second Text object?

Enter these lines in the Command window to see how they work:

```
x = MEMORY( )
? x
? TYPE('x')
? STR(x,6)
? TYPE('str(x,6)')
```

Our results for these commands are shown in Figure 6.12.

In this example, *x* is a variable that holds the number of kilobytes of available memory, as reported by the MEMORY( ) function. The

FIGURE 6.12

Assigning MEMORY( ) when the form is opened

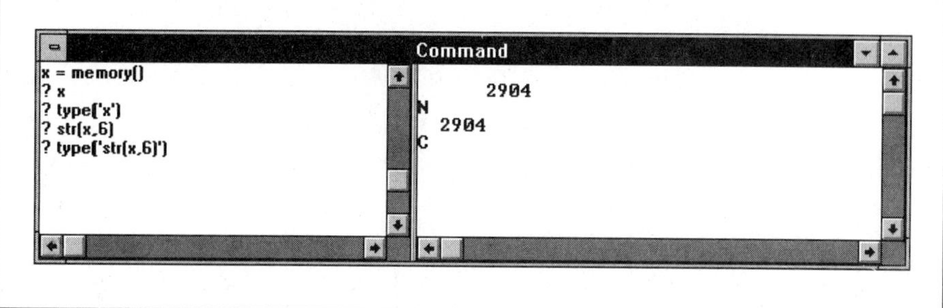

TYPE( ) function reports a variable's type. (See Chapter 12 for a discussion of TYPE( ) and other functions.)

Among other values, TYPE( ) reports 'N' for a numeric value and 'C' for a character string. As you see in Figure 6.12, *x* is a number. The STR( ) function converts a number to a string. In addition to giving the function the number variable that you want to convert, you can give it a second argument that specifies the number of places to include. In our example, the function STR(*x*,6) specifies six places for the result. The actual *x* value converts to a four-place number.

By default, the Command window's results pane will format a number to ten places. This is why the responses to ? *x* and to ? STR(*x*,6) are positioned differently, even through the resulting value is the same.

Now you know how to use the STR( ) function to convert a number to a character string, whose width you control. Next, we need to figure out how to get this string assigned to the Text property at the right time. This isn't something you can precalculate. Your system must query the MEMORY( ) function immediately before displaying the About form. The proper timing will depend on how many other things you have going on.

Using the OnOpen Event Handler

One of the events that almost every object can respond to is the OnOpen event. The code in an OnOpen event handler is called when the form to which the object is attached is opened. So all we need to do is to assign our Text object's Text property when the About form is opened.

Again, all of this is a lot more trouble to explain than it is to program. As you've probably guessed, to assign this at the right time, select your second Text object, then click on the Events tab of the Object Properties Inspector. Choose the OnOpen event and click on the tool icon at the right of its entry field.

This launches the Procedure Editor, which has the built-in intelligence to properly attach the program you write to the correct event. a simple, one-line program:

This.Text = STR(MEMORY( ),6)

Figure 6.13 shows the program in the Procedures window.

FIGURE 6.13

Numbers and character strings in the Command window

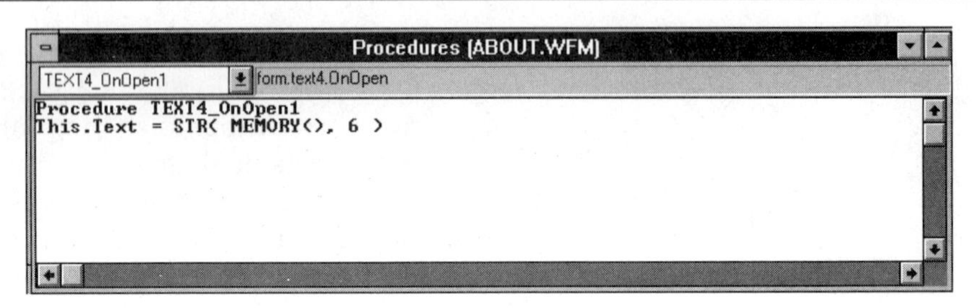

The *This* object in that line refers to the object handling the event. Because we selected the Text object in which we wanted the text, *This* is that Text object. The period (.) operator separates an object from one of its properties. This.Text is the Text property. We assign it the STR( ) function (for character string conversion) of the number that MEMORY( ) reports.

Select your constants, such as using six places for the result of MEMORY( ), very carefully. You want to allow enough room for growth so that you won't run into your own limits during the life of your system.

Using a six-character string will suffice until our desktop computer's memory exceeds a million kilobytes (just under a gigabyte). Our desktop PC's memory is expanding tenfold every seven years or so; six places should carry us at least through the end of the century.

When you run this version, you'll see that your form now reports available memory, in kilobytes.

Formatting the Memory Report

Now we're going to format our memory report with a comma to separate the number into groups of three digits. This is a nice touch with smaller numbers; it becomes increasingly vital as you look at longer numbers. If your national convention isn't a comma, use your own separator.

WARNING

In an early version of the Form Designer, there is a bug in the handling of the Function and Picture properties, Because of this bug, the Two-Way feature doesn't quite work. These changes in the program code would get lost if you returned to Design mode.

We can make this change by using the Program Editor to edit the form as a program. The objects we attached to our program are written into our program file (.WFM for forms) in the order we introduced them as we built our form. This means that our second Text object is the last one in the code, which is very convenient for editing it in the Program Editor.

From the Navigator, right-click on your About form and choose Edit as Program from the Speed menu. Press Ctrl-PgDn to get to the end, and then go up a bit. You'll see the code shown in Figure 6.14.

In a dBASE program, the semicolon at the end of a line means that the line continues. For example, this line:

```
DEFINE Text Text1 PROPERTY Top 1, Left 2, ...
```

is the same as these lines:

```
DEFINE Text Text1;
  PROPERTY;
    Top 1,;
    Left 2,;
    ...
```

FIGURE 6.14

The bottom part of ABOUT.WFM in the Program Editor

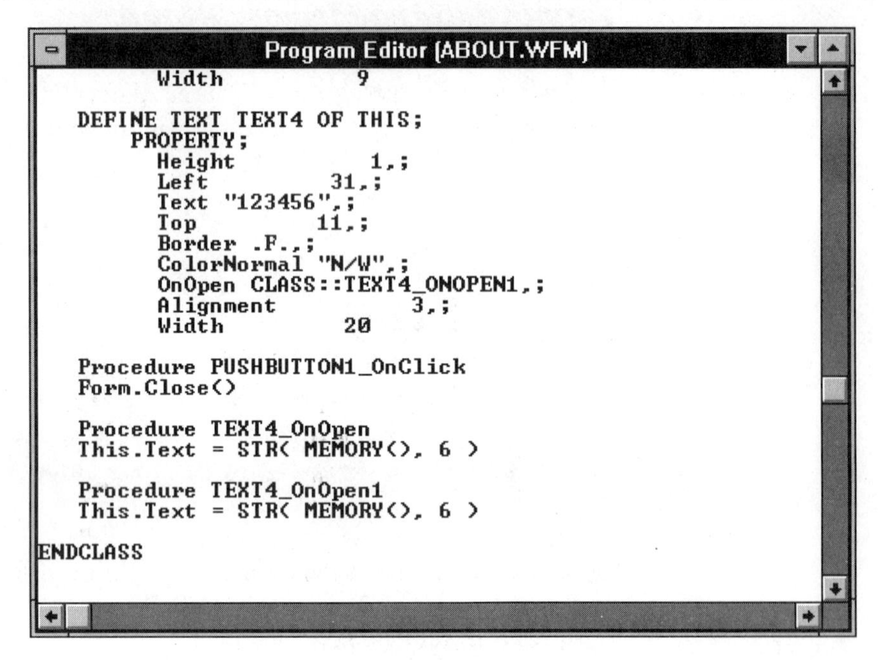

With that in mind, we want to add two new properties to the Text4 object:

```
Function "R", ;
Picture "999,999k", ;
```

The "R" function specifies that the text string does not contain the special characters in the Picture property. The "9"s in the Picture property are places where dBASE will substitute digits. The comma and the letter k are special characters that dBASE will just copy.

To test this thoroughly, use the test string "123456" (it should appear as "123,456k"), not the shorter string that your MEMORY( ) function will report. To do this, you "comment out" the OnOpen event handler that gets the real value. To comment out OnOpen, put a semicolon (meaning the line continues) and two ampersands (meaning that what follows is a comment) to the left of the code.

Figure 6.15 shows the two new lines and the commented out change in our Program Editor window. You don't need to add the comments that we used to point out the location of the changes. However, you do

FIGURE 6.15 

Two lines added, one line commented out in ABOUT.WFM

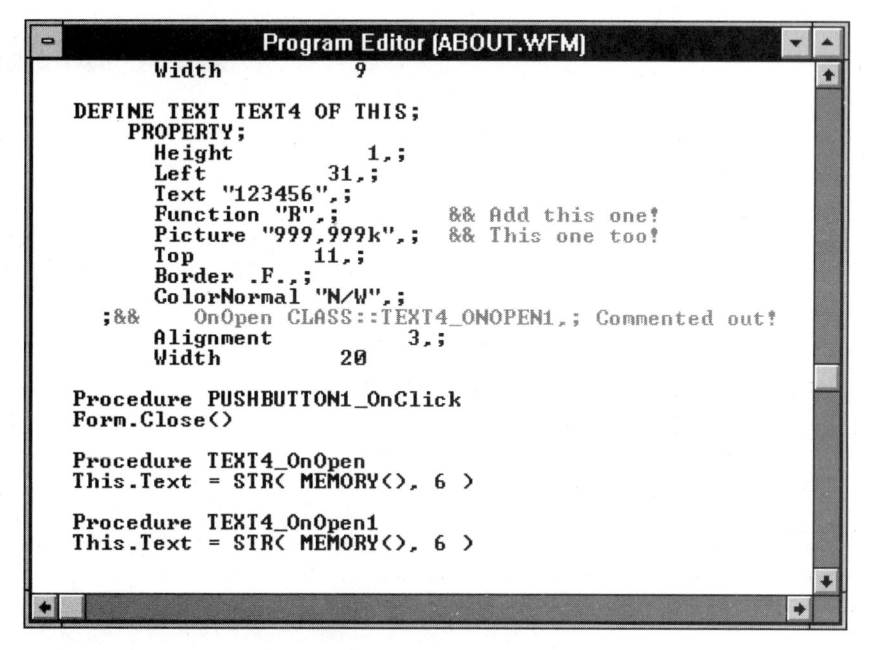

need the semicolon and two ampersands (**;&&**) on the line that is commented out.

Now if you press Ctrl-D, your program runs, and your About form looks very good. You should see the Memory value display as 123,456k. Two more changes, and we'll call this complete.

First, "uncomment" (remove the semicolon and asterisks) the line that you commented out, so your program goes ahead and gets the real amount of memory. Second, move the top of the object down a few lines. The default placement is way up there at line 1, which obscures the speedbar and the menus. Figure 6.16 shows that location changed to 4.

Make sure you make the Top setting change at the correct place in the program. Every object on your form, as well as the form itself, has a Top property. You want to change the form's top. All the other Top settings are relative to the top of the form. Move the form, and everything in it moves along with it.

Press Ctrl-D again, and your About form should have a polished look. What we need now is a form that has a menu with a Help ➤ About choice to launch this form.

FIGURE 6.16

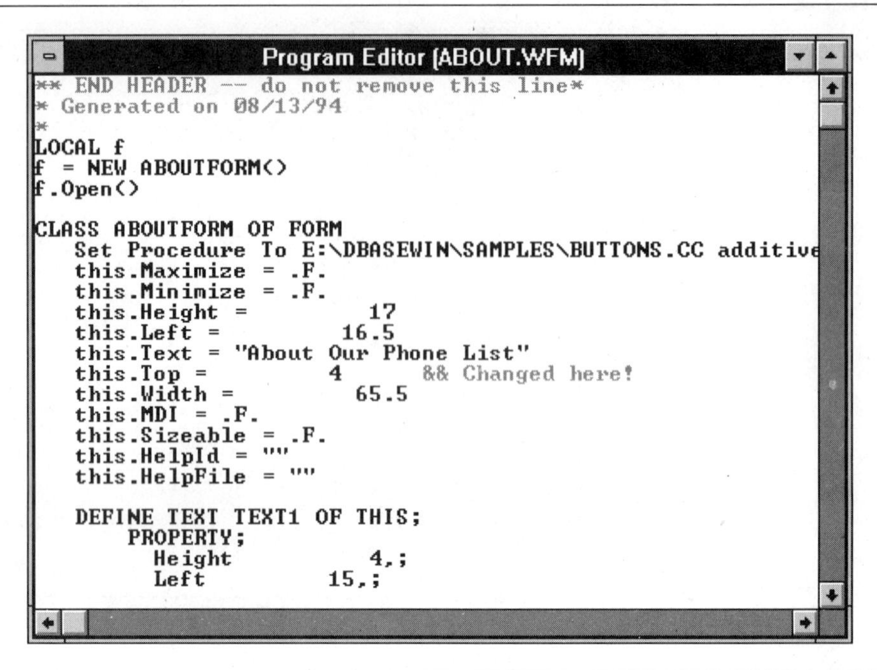

Moving the About form down three lines

▸▸ You Create a Main Form with a Menu

We've built an About form. Now it's time to build a form that About can be about.

We'll design a menu with the options File, People, Organizations, Phone List, and Help. The File menu can let us choose a working disk and directory (so you can keep different lists in different directories) and have the expected Exit option. The middle menu choices will launch three forms: one for the People table, one for the Orgs table, and another for a view that shows phone numbers selected from a combination of both files. Help will only have one choice: About.

With older software, all this would have take an experienced programmer a day or more to program. With dBASE for Windows, it will happen in just a few minutes once you master the Menu Designer. Now we'll show you how that tool works.

▶ Building a Menu for a Form

First, we'll need another form for our system. Menus for MDI and non-MDI forms are handled differently. If you have an MDI form, its menu replaces the menu in dBASE for Windows. The dBASE menus return when you close the form. A non-MDI window has its own menu in the standard location. We'll use the non-MDI form for our phone list work.

Creating the Menu

To begin, let's create a blank form and attach a menu. Follow these steps:

1. Launch the Untitled form from the Navigator's list of forms. Tell the Form Expert that you want a Blank Form and click on Create.
2. With the blank form in the Form Designer, set the MDI property to False. To do this, expand the Window Properties if they aren't already expanded, and then click on the MDI property and type **.F.** in the entry field, or click on the tool icon and click on .F. in the list.
3. Select the MenuFile property and Type the word **phone** into its entry field. (You can't create a new file by just clicking on the tool icon.) Then click on the tool icon. The Modify Menu Property dialog box pops up.
4. Choose Design Current Menu, as shown here:

►► NOTE

If you forget to enter a menu name for the MenuFile property before you select the Choose Menu option (or click on the tool icon), you'll see the Choose Menu dialog box. This dialog box doesn't include a choice for creating a new menu file.

You should now be in the Menu Designer, with the insertion point in the upper-left corner, waiting for you to type in your first Menu object.

Entering the Main Menu

The Menu Designer is another of the Two-Way-Tools. It creates an .MNU file of program code, which is a collection of Menu objects. Each Menu object corresponds to one of the prompts on a menu.

Begin by typing **&File**. By preceding the *F* with an ampersand, you tell the Menu Designer to put an underscore under that character. Figure 6.17 shows the first option added in the Menu Designer window.

Note the Object Properties Inspector to the right of the Menu Designer. It is *not* showing the properties of the form from which you launched the Menu Designer. What you see are the properties of the currently selected Menu object (menu option).

What you have, at the point shown in Figure 6.17, is a single Menu object, which would give you a menu system with exactly the one option you've created. Let's continue to add some more.

To switch to the next menu option to the right, press Tab. Then type **&People**. Press Tab again and continue. Use the same procedure to add the other options: **&Organizations**, **Phone &List**, and **&Help**. (Note that for the Phone List Menu object, you type the ampersand in front of the *L*, not at the start of the first word.) Your menu should look like the one in Figure 6.18.

When you have the focus on the final Help Menu object, check your work. Correct any mistakes (use Shift-Tab to back up; Tab to move forward), and then return to the Help choice. If you Tab past the Help option, simply Shift-Tab to back up without typing anything. When you

FIGURE 6.17

Entering your first menu option

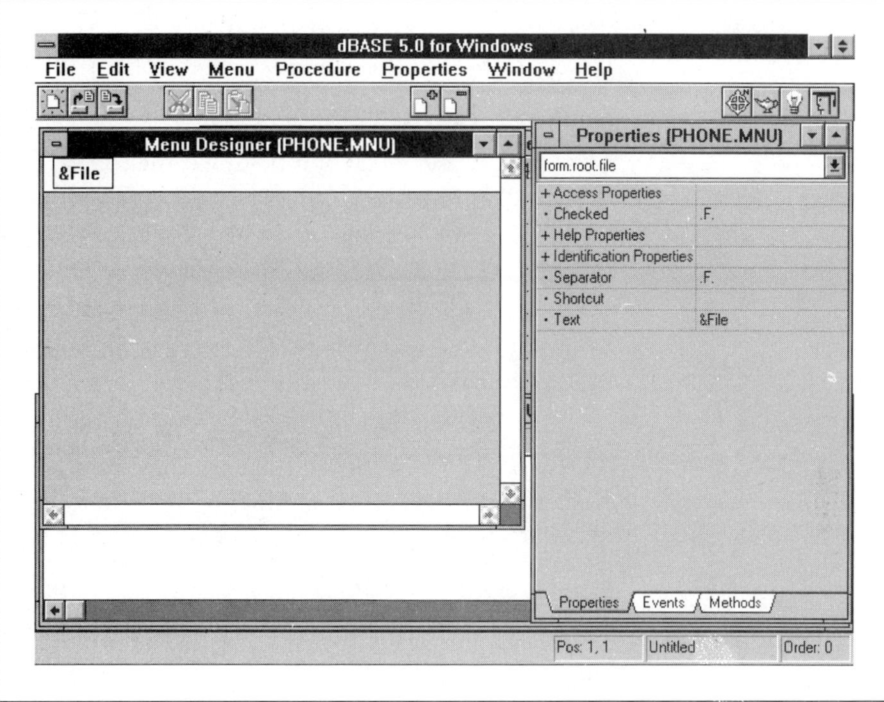

FIGURE 6.18

Finishing the main menu

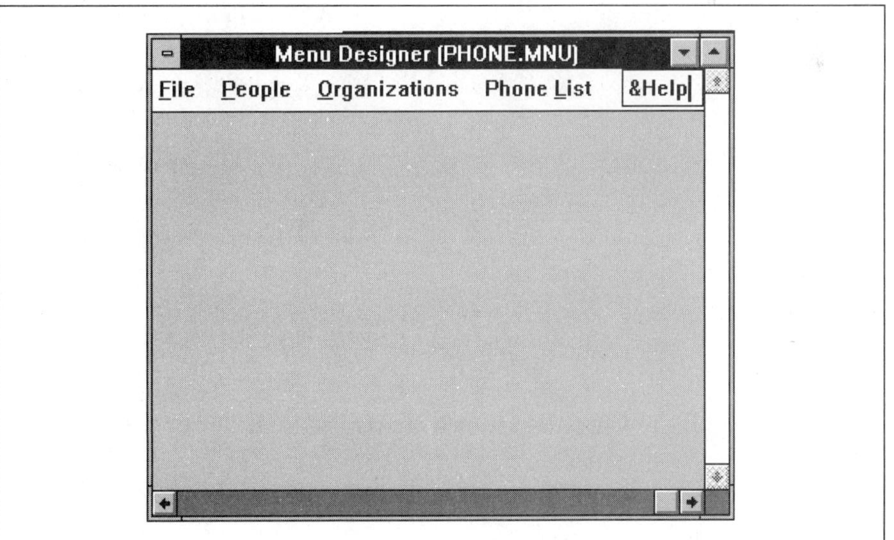

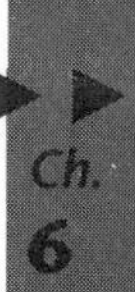

exit a trailing menu choice with no text, the Menu Designer does not create a Menu object.

Making Pull-down Menus

Now we want to make a pull-down menu that will have the About option. To start a pull-down menu, just press the ↓ key. This gives you a new Menu object below the current one. Type **& About Phone List** … (include the three dots, to show that a dialog box follows).

With the About Menu object entered, press ↑ or Shift-Tab to return to the Help Menu object. Then press Shift-Tab until you have returned to the File Menu object.

Again, press the ↓ key to create a pull-down menu. Enter **Change &Directory** … in the first Menu object. Press ↓ again and enter **E&xit**. Since these two are logically distinct, you should draw a line between them.

Lines (menu separators) are available from the Menu option of the Menu Designer. Separators are inserted above the currently selected choice. Make sure the Exit Menu object is selected and choose Menu ➤ Insert Separator:

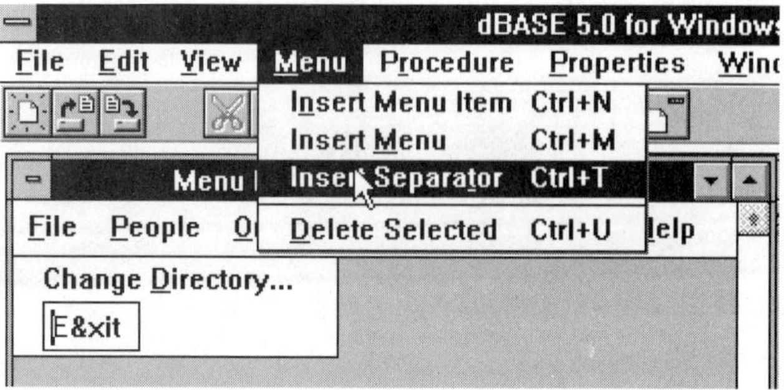

Making a Cascading Menu

Our needs are met without a third-level, cascading menu. But we'll add one anyway, just so you'll know how to make one if you need this type of menu for your own systems. They are as simple to create as the other menus.

Start at the Exit option and press Tab to move to the right. This creates a cascading menu. Type the first item, **&Right Now**, and then press ↓ to add the second: **&Soon**. When you have added the third, **&Whenever**, it should look like this:

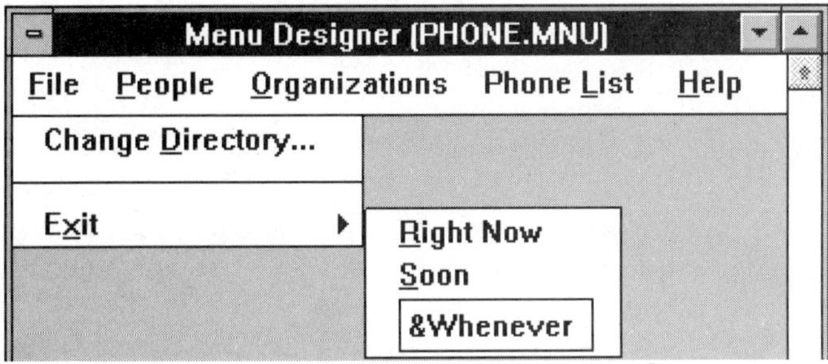

Of course, this menu is total nonsense. Now that you know how simple it is to create a cascading menu, let's get rid of it. With one of the cascaded Menu objects selected, choose Menu ➤ Delete Selected. To get rid of the other two, select them and use the shortcut key, Ctrl-U.

Close the Menu Designer. It will save your work as program code in the PHONE.MNU file. Now run the form you are designing. We named ours Fon_Main.

When you run it, you'll get a form with the menu you just designed. It responds appropriately to pressing Alt with the designated letters, or to mouse clicks. Unfortunately, it does absolutely nothing except handle its menus. They haven't been attached anywhere.

That's our next step.

► Attaching Actions to Menu Choices

Attaching actions to menu selections is similar to adding an event handler for a pushbutton's OnClick event. Let's begin with the File ➤ Exit menu option.

Making Exit Work

We want the Exit selection to close and release the form. To make it work, follow these steps:

1. Launch the Form Designer with the Fon_Main form. In the Navigator, right double-click on the Fon_Main file, or select it and press Shift-F2.
2. From the Form Designer, launch the Menu Designer for the PHONE.MNU file. (Click on the Properties tab of the Object Properties Inspector, click on the MenuFile property, click on the tool icon, and choose Design Current Menu from the Modify Menu Property dialog box.)
3. Select the Exit Menu object. Navigate with ↓ and ↑ vertically, Tab and Shift-Tab horizontally, or just click on it with the mouse.
4. Click the Events tab of the Object Properties Inspector. A menu item can only respond to two events, as you see:

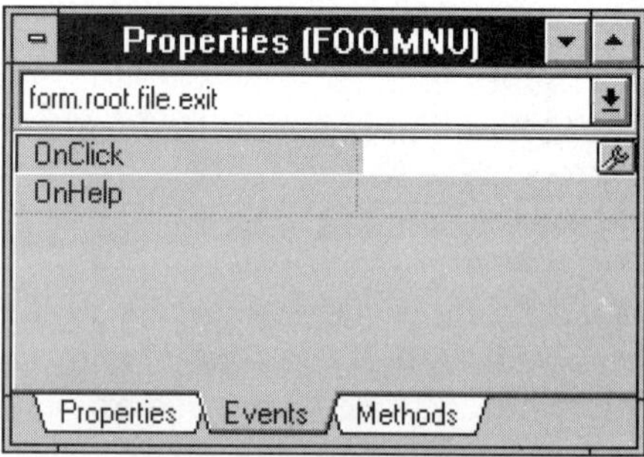

5. Click on the OnClick property, and you'll be in the Procedure Editor. Enter this line:

Form.Release( )

Your Exit Menu object now knows how to respond to a click (or to a selection from the keyboard). This involved traveling a long way from the Navigator to get to the right point at which to add that one line.

A much more efficient way to operate is to add menu event handlers as you build your menu. The method we're using is good practice while you're learning, however.

Let's run the menu and see if it works. Press Ctrl-W to exit the Procedure Editor and the Menu Designer. Then press F2 or click on the lightning icon on the speedbar to run your form. Try pressing Alt-F, then X to close your form.

Now that you've got the Exit choice working, let's get on to launching our About form from the Help ➤ About Phone List… menu choice.

Launching a Form from a Menu Object

First, you need to know how to launch a form by giving a dBASE command. (Obviously, you aren't going to be able to put appropriate mouse movements into the Procedure Editor.)

A form is stored in a .WFM file, which is one type of program file. You execute a program with the DO command. Try typing this in the Command window:

DO About.wfm

This command launches your About form. Since About is a modal form, it will remain on your screen until you click on OK or otherwise close the form, which is what you want for an About form.

Now the only chore that remains is to put that command into the menu. These are the steps:

1. Launch the Fon_Main program in the Form Designer.
2. Using the Object Properties Inspector, MenuFile property, launch the PHONE.MNU file in the Menu Designer.
3. Select the Help ➤ About menu choice in your menu.
4. Click on the Events tab of the Object Properties Inspector and choose the OnClick event. Click the tool icon to get to the Procedure Editor.
5. Enter the line **DO About.wfm** in the Procedure Editor.

Now when you run your Fon_Main file, choosing Help ➤ About Phone List… will launch your About form. Before we leave our menu, lets assign a shortcut key so that we can press Ctrl-D to select a directory.

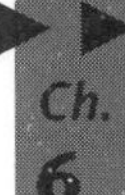

► Attaching a Shortcut Key

Attaching a shortcut key (one you can press to go directly to a Menu object's OnClick handler) is straightforward. You simply put the name of the key into the Shortcut property of the Menu object.

Let's try assigning the Ctrl-D keypress to the Change Directory … choice in our File menu. While we're there, we might as well program this Menu object to actually change directories.

Before you get to the menu's Procedure Editor, try out these commands in the Command window:

```
x = GETDIRECTORY( )
? x
CD &x
```

As you can see, the built-in GETDIRECTORY( ) function pops up the appropriate dialog box and lets you choose a directory. The line ? x lets you see your choice in the Command window's results pane.

The CD command in dBASE is similar to the same command in DOS. It changes to the named directory. The ampersand in front of the variable name *x* tells dBASE to substitute the value of the variable, not to use it as the letter *x*.

Now that you know which commands to use, launch the Fon_Main form in the Form Designer, and then open the PHONE menu in the Menu Designer.

Click on the Change Directory … option to select it and then click on the Events tab of the Object Properties Inspector. Choose the OnClick property, and then click on the tool icon to get to the Procedure Editor.

Add these two lines:

```
d = GETDIRECTORY( )
CD &d
```

Your Procedures window should look like this:

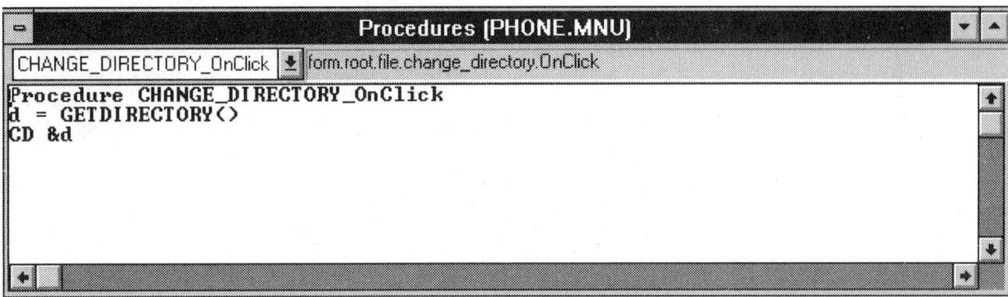

Now we have a program that will change directories based on our selection, so it's time to provide convenient access via the Ctrl-D key.

Click on the Properties tab of the Object Properties Inspector. Then click on the Shortcut property. In its entry field, type **Ctrl-D**. When you start typing, the field turns a warning yellow color. When you're finished, press Enter. The field will return to white. If you make a mistake, you'll get an appropriate warning message.

You can use Ctrl, Alt, and function key combinations for your shortcut keys, although function keys higher than F10 are not supported. The following are some valid entries:

- Ctrl-A through Ctrl-Z
- Ctrl-0 through Ctrl-9
- Alt-any letter or number
- F1 through F10
- Ctrl-F1 through Ctrl-F10
- Alt-F1 through Alt-F10
- Shift-F1 through Shift-F10

▸▸ **WARNING**

The error trapping does *not* detect conflicts with Microsoft Windows special keys, such as Alt-F4 for closing a form. You must be careful not to use these as shortcut keys.

If you haven't done so yet, go ahead and run your modified program. You should be able to choose directories by pressing Alt-F then D, or just by pressing Ctrl-D.

We hope that you don't mind that this program is twice as long as the ones we've used so far!

A final item to fix is the Text property of the Fon_Main form. Change this property's value to **My Phone List** (or something else that's more descriptive than the default *Form*).

Now it's time to go on and use this framework with some real forms that access our tables.

▸▸ You Build the People Form

For our phone list system, we'll make a special form that incorporates the best features of a human-assisted form layout and a browse view. Let's begin by letting the Form Expert build a starting form for us, as we did in Chapter 2.

For this form, let's start with a query that has all the People table data, except the employer link, arranged in alphabetical order by last name.

▸ Building the Query

The Query Designer will let us get this result quickly. Follow these steps:

1. Launch the Query Designer on the Untitled query.
2. Choose the People table from the Open Table Required dialog box.

3. Click on the All Fields selection box, like this:

4. Click on the field selection box in the ORG_ID field to remove it from the selected set.
5. Tab to the end of the file skeleton, or hold the right arrow to shift the list toward the end. In the UPPER(LAST_NAME) field, click on the smudge. It will turn into an up arrow, indicating an ascending index on last name, using a true alphabetic sort.
6. Press Ctrl-W to save your work. Give it the name **People_A**.

▶ Building the Base Form

With the query built, it's time to build the basic form. For this, use the Form Expert. Launch the Untitled form and accept the offer of Expert assistance. Choose PEOPLE_A.QBE for your view.

Select all the fields, then send back the two tags (the indexes that are labeled TAG01 and TAG02). Adjust the colors to suit yourself, and then generate the form.

After your form is generated, make some changes. First, stretch it to be about as wide as our sample, which is shown in Figure 6.19.

As you see in Figure 6.19, we've made small adjustments for a better-looking form. For example, we don't use underscores in the Last name and Full name labels.

Make similar improvements in your own form. When you are finished, we'll go on to add a Browse object, which will simplify navigating in the form.

▶ Adding a Browse

We like a form type of layout (really, a Columnar Layout view with some human adjustments—not the built-in Form Layout view) for data entry. We like the Browse Layout view for looking through our data. In this form, we're going to have both!

FIGURE 6.19

A base form with some adjustments

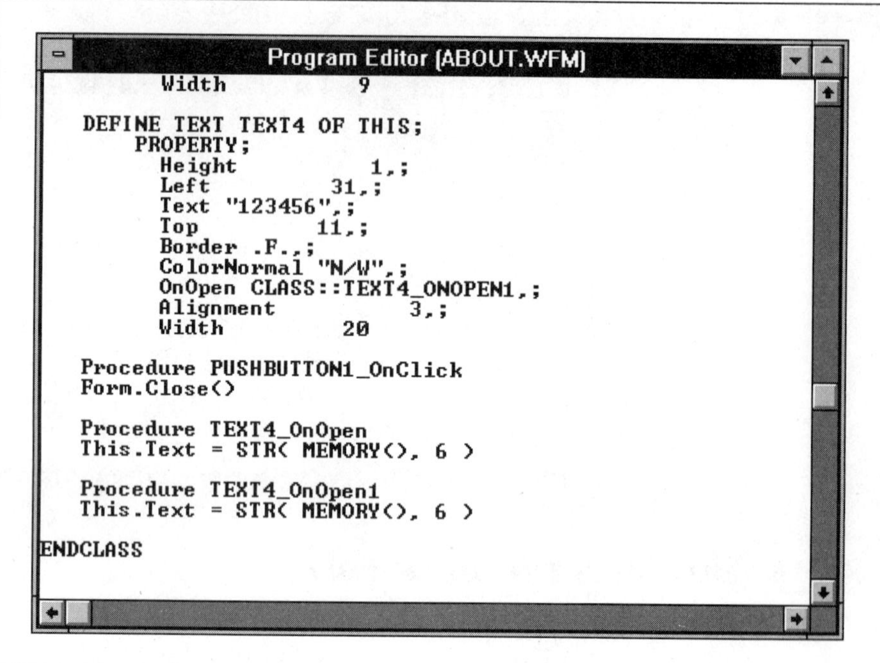
```
Program Editor (ABOUT.WFM)
        Width            9

    DEFINE TEXT TEXT4 OF THIS;
        PROPERTY;
          Height           1,;
          Left          31,;
          Text "123456",;
          Top          11,;
          Border .F.,;
          ColorNormal "N/W",;
          OnOpen CLASS::TEXT4_ONOPEN1,;
          Alignment          3,;
          Width          20

    Procedure PUSHBUTTON1_OnClick
    Form.Close()

    Procedure TEXT4_OnOpen
    This.Text = STR( MEMORY(), 6 )

    Procedure TEXT4_OnOpen1
    This.Text = STR( MEMORY(), 6 )

ENDCLASS
```

From the Form Designer's Controls palette, click on the Browse object. Then drag it onto your form in the empty space you've got on the right. Figure 6.20 shows us adding the Browse object to our form.

Now that the Browse object is on the form, we need to set some properties. Click on the Properties tab of the Object Properties Inspector.

Setting Access Properties

In the Access properties, you can set the TabStop property to .F. for efficient data entry. This means that you will tab from field to field, but not tab into the Browse object. The problem with this is that there will be no access to the Browse object if you don't have a mouse or some other pointing device.

FIGURE 6.20

Adding a Browse object

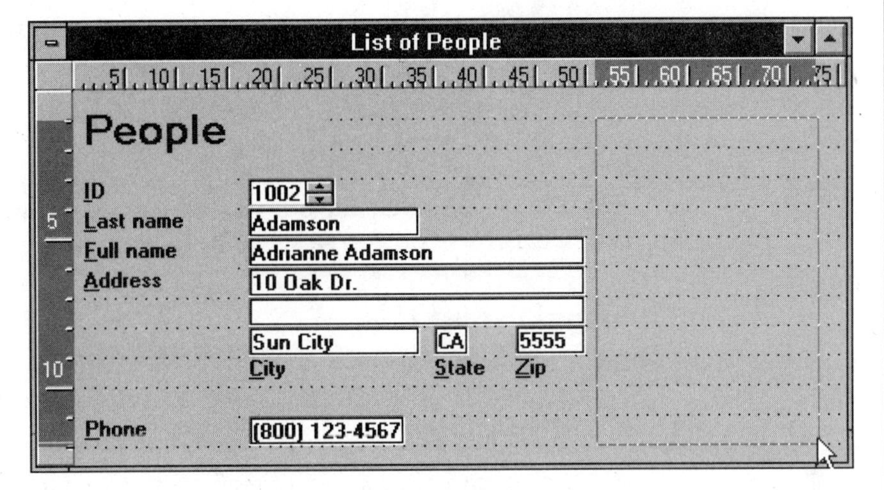

TIP

Set the TabStop property for your normal situation. If you set it to .F., for instance, you can always change it to .T. when you find yourself without a mouse.

Data-Linkage Properties

You need to select an Alias property. With the People_A query selected, the only choice when you click on the tool icon is People, which is exactly what you want. Choose that, and then click on the tool icon for the Fields property.

We deselected all the fields, then clicked just the LAST_NAME field back into the Browse object. We use this browse to locate the person we want. As we move through the list of last names, every data field about the one we're selecting appears just to the left of the browse, so this arrangement is just right for our purposes.

Edit Properties

If you set the Modify property to False, you'll automatically turn off the Append and Delete properties. This is what we want. Editing will be done in the form layout.

The Toggle property, when True, lets you change between Browse, Form, and Columnar Layout views. You don't want this capability inside this Browse object, so set it to False.

Visual Properties

Set the ShowDeleted property to .F. to turn it off. This eliminates the deleted column, even if the deleted setting in the Desktop Properties dialog box allows showing deleted records.

Also turn off the ShowHeading and ShowRecNo properties. The first eliminates the field names above the data. (It's obvious that w're looking at last names.) The second eliminates the record number column on the left.

▶ Running the Completed Form

After you've finished setting the properties for the Browse object, you can run the completed form. Ours is shown in Figure 6.21.

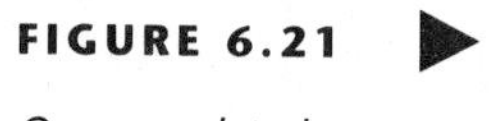

FIGURE 6.21 ▶

Our completed People_A form

You can navigate in this form with the standard tools (such as the speedbar buttons and PgUp and PgDn keys), as well as with the vertical elevator on the Browse object.

The form layout portion lets you enter and edit the data. We think this type of form gives you the best of both worlds.

▶ Putting Your Form into Your System

Now that we have a completed PEOPLE.WFM, we have something to launch when we choose People from the Fon_Main form. It's time to tie the new form into our system. Follow these steps:

1. Launch the Fon_Main form in the Form Designer.
2. Open the PHONE.MNU menu in the Menu Designer.
3. Launch the Procedure Editor for the OnClick event of the People Menu object.
4. Add a single line that says **DO People.wfm**, and then save your program.

Now you can switch to Run mode from the Form Designer to test our system. When you choose People from your Fon_Main menu, the People_A form we just created will be launched.

Once the People_A form is closed, you may "lose" your Fon_Main window. If this happens, hold the Alt key down and press Tab to cycle through the list of active applications. When you find that window, release the Alt key, and the window will be active again.

If you don't like this behavior, change the Fon_Main form's MDI property back to True. When you do this, the Fon_Main window will still be visible after you open and then close your People form.

Unlike the non-MDI window, an MDI window does not have a menu. Your menu replaces the dBASE for Windows menus. When you close the Fon_Main form, the dBASE for Windows menus return.

►► You Build the Orgs Form

To begin building the Orgs form, let's repeat the process we went through in the last section. Build a query, ORGS_A.QBE, that includes all the fields in the Orgs table and indexes in ascending, true alphabetical order.

Have the Form Expert build a form for you. Then change the appearance and text as you like to improve the form.

Next, add a Browse object on the right. Select just the NAME field, and turn off headings and record numbers. Set the Modify property to .F. for this field. Do the same for the TabStop property (unless you'll frequently run this form without a mouse). Our form is shown in Figure 6.22.

FIGURE 6.22 ►

A form for the employers

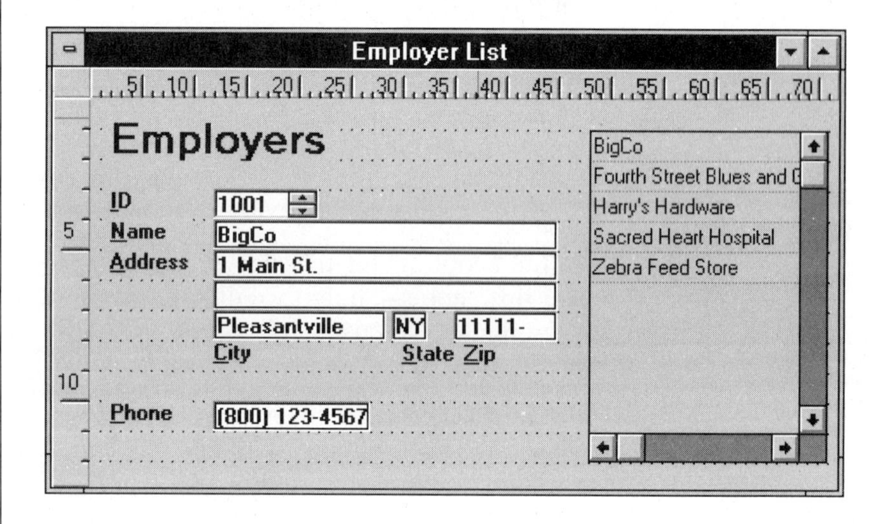

► Adding Pushbuttons

If the form has room, we like to include pushbuttons. They provide another option for choosing the most common activities. Let's add a pair of these buttons to our Orgs_A form.

Start by adding more space at the bottom of the form to accommodate the pushbuttons. Then click on Pushbutton in the Controls palette and drag it on your form. In the Object Properties Inspector, change the Pushbutton object's Text property to **Append**.

Repeat the procedure to create a **Close** pushbutton. Figure 6.23 shows our form with these buttons.

FIGURE 6.23

A form with push-buttons added

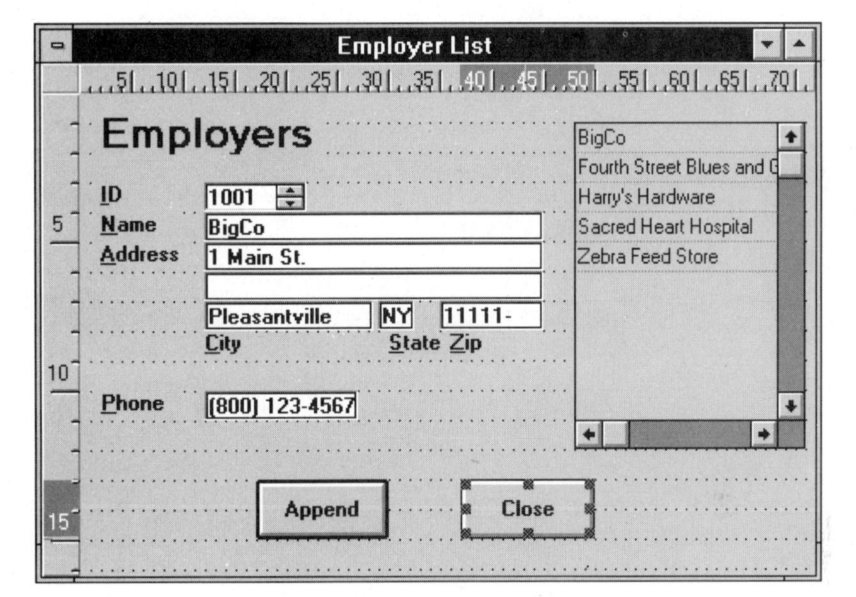

Now let's attach appropriate code to their OnClick events.

For the Append button, enter a one-line program:

```
APPEND BLANK
```

The APPEND BLANK command adds a single, blank record at the end of the table. It also switches the record pointer to this record, which is exactly what you need to add a record.

For the Close button, you want to release the form. Enter this line:

```
Form.Release( )
```

With those two event handlers attached, we're ready to test our improved form.

▸ Adding Input Templates

When you try your Append button, you'll get a new, blank record, just as we wanted. However, the spinbutton for the ORG_ID field doesn't behave as we wanted.

Spinbuttons default to spinning from 1 to 100 in increments of 1. This is not at all what we want for our ID fields. Let's fix that and make some other improvements.

First, select the spinbutton and click on the Properties tab of the Object Properties Inspector. If it is not expanded, double-click on the Edit Properties category. Set the RangeMin property to 1001 and the RangeMax property to 9999.

Spinbuttons have another bad habit: they may report the number right-justified under the spinbuttons, so you can't see your whole entry. To prevent this, use a Picture property.

The Picture property is a template that controls input. A Picture template is built with special symbols and other characters. The special symbols allow entry of characters where they appear in the template. Regular characters are repeated as they are. The following are some common special characters:

Character	Meaning
A	Alphabetic characters only
9	Numeric digits only
!	Capital letters (no need to press Shift)

The following Picture property will format ten digits in the common North American phone number format:

```
(999) 999-9999
```

As you type digits, each one is placed where the 9s occur in the template. The other characters (the parentheses, hyphen, and blank space) do not accept input, so they remain unchanged.

To be sure the spinbutton aligns its digits on the left, use the Picture property **9999**, like this:

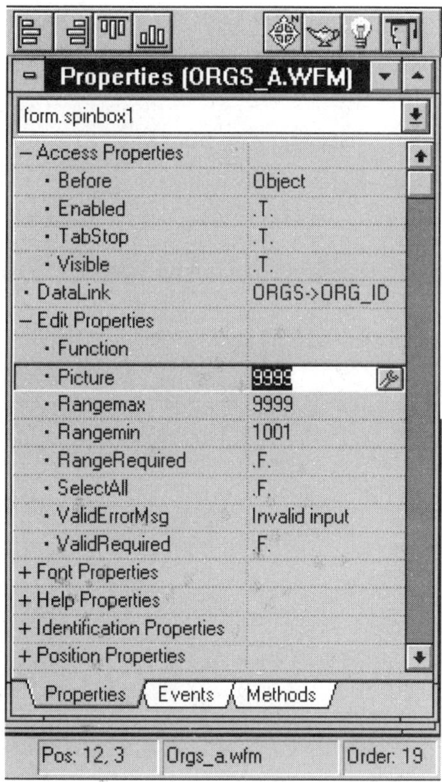

You can also add the Picture format we suggested above—(999) 999-999—for your PHONE field. (Or add a different format if it's appropriate for your national conventions.)

WARNING

If your list is limited to one country, you can be quite specific about formatting phone numbers, postal codes, and so on. However, if you will be maintaining an international list, you shouldn't use any formatting, because conventions vary from country to country.

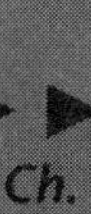

▸ Attaching the Form to the Fon_Main System

Once you're satisfied with the Orgs_A form, you'll want to attach it to your Fon_Main system. In this section, we'll show you how to sneak into the Menu Designer without going through the Form Designer.

Click the Custom file type in the Navigator. In the Custom Files entry field, enter ***.MNU**, as you see in Figure 6.24.

FIGURE 6.24

*Adding *.MNU files to the Navigator*

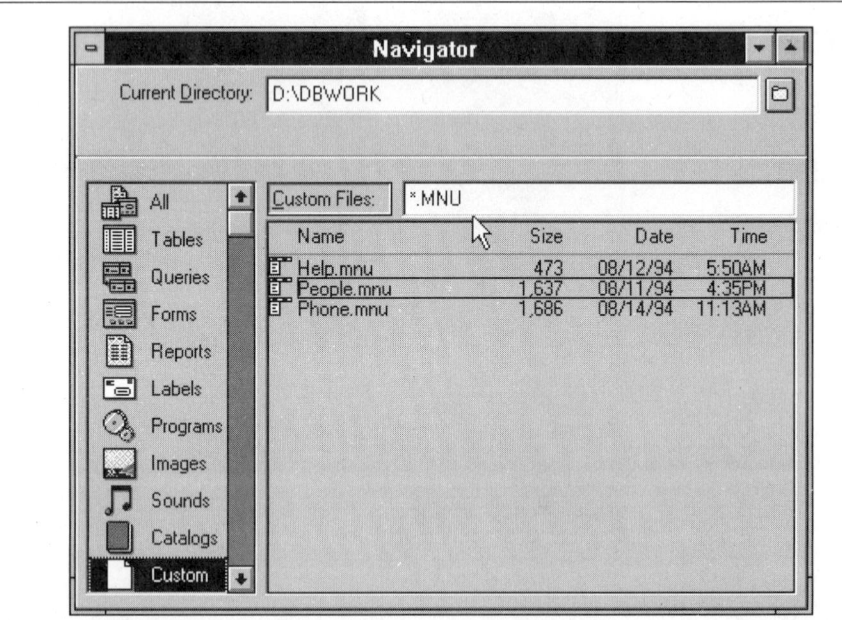

Now you can get to your menus just by choosing Custom and clicking on the files. A right click on the PHONE.MNU file opens its Speed menu, from which you can choose Design Menu. Alternatively, you can right double-click or press Shift-F2 to launch the Menu Designer.

With this trick, enter the Menu Designer and select the Organizations Menu object. On the Object Properties Inspector, click on the Events tab, and then click on the OnClick property. In the Procedure Editor, add this line:

```
DO Orgs_a.wfm
```

Save and test your work by running Fon_Main. Your system is now complete, except that it doesn't have the combined people and employer phone list capability.

This is what we will work on in the next section. Before going on, this would be a good time for you to go back to the People_A form and improve it. Add pushbuttons, adjust the ID field, and add Picture properties, as we did in the Orgs_A form.

►► You Build the Combined Form

You've seen how to build a query that relates people to their employers. However, the query that we built in Chapter 5 won't serve our purposes here. That query related employers to their employees. It showed people in alphabetical order within each employer. For a phone list, you need people in alphabetical order, regardless of their employer. Otherwise, you would have a hard time locating people if you did not already know their employer.

► Building an Inverted Query

For this query, we'll invert the normal order of parent and child. Normally, you would treat the employer record as the parent, since many employees could be attached to each employer.

But you can do that the other way, too. If you call the People table record the parent, dBASE for Windows will find "every" employer record that matches. Of course, we know that there will only be one, but computers don't have our human knowledge.

One thing we'll lose when we do this is the ability to change an employee's ORG_ID field value, which we would need to do if a person switched employers. But we can still do this through direct access to the People table record in our other forms.

Figure 6.25 shows the query, as we specified it in the Query Designer. Start with the People table, and click on the select all fields check box. Then move to the right and click the smudge mark on the UPPER(LAST_NAME) index to get people in true alphabetic order.

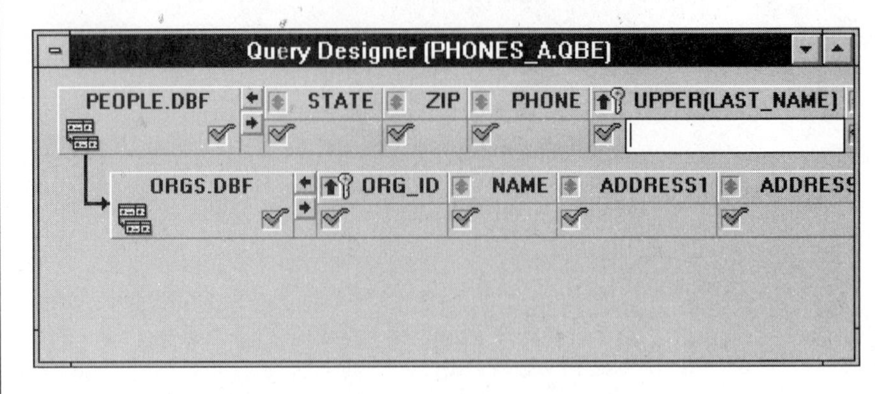

FIGURE 6.25

Using an inverted query, keeping people alphabetized

Next add the Orgs table and drag a relation from People to Orgs. Figure 6.26 shows the details of this relationship, in the Define Relation dialog box.

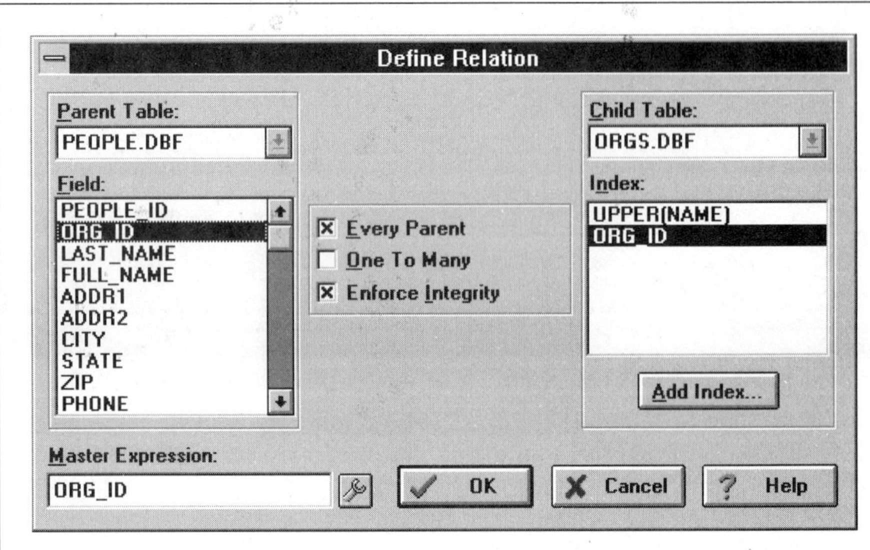

FIGURE 6.26

The details of the inverted relationship

After you've created the relationship, save the query as Phones_A. Now we can get on to building a form.

▶ Creating the Form

Launch the Untitled form and accept the Form Expert's offer of assistance. Pick the PHONES_A.QBE view, which we just created.

Pick all the fields, and then reject the three tag fields that are associated with indexes. From here, the process is the same as the one we've used for building the individual table forms. Adjust the display of the items until it looks pleasing, and then add a Browse object on the right.

The Alias property of the Browse object is set to PEOPLE. The Fields property is set to just LAST_NAME. The other adjustments are the same ones we made for the Browse objects on the single-table forms.

Our finished form is shown in Figure 6.27.

FIGURE 6.27 ▶

Our completed phone list form

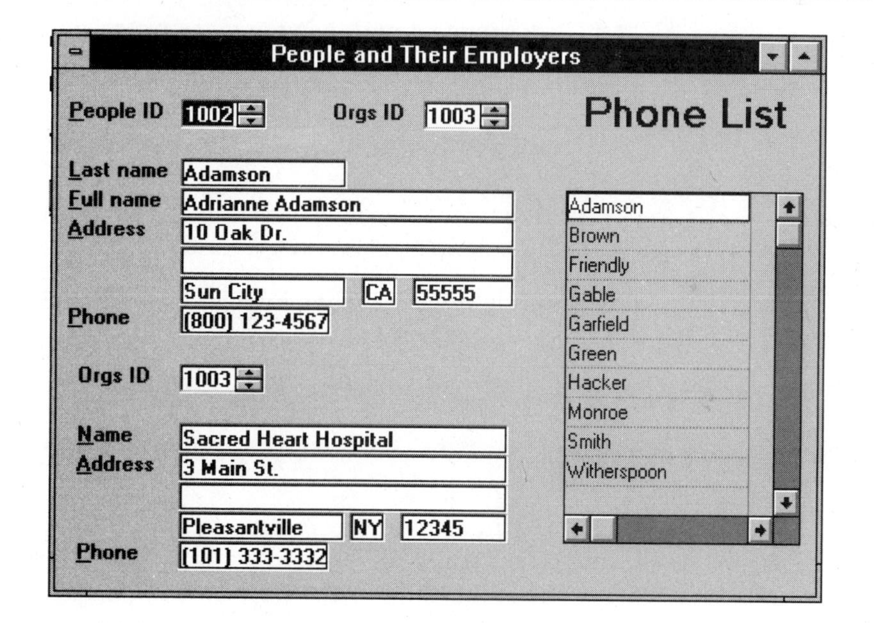

When you run this form for the first time, give it the name Phones_A.

Don't forget to set the title on the form. Also, since you can't change the ORG_ID value in either the People or the Orgs table, you should change these two fields' TabStop properties to False.

When your form satisfies you, give it a test run. Now as you move through the form, your employer data is constantly updated to match the person you've selected.

If you change the BigCo phone number, that change is correctly reflected whenever you look at a person who works for BigCo.

Your system is open for business. The last detail is to bring it in as part of the Fon_Main system.

► Putting the Form in the Fon_Main System

From the Navigator, select Custom tables. Right double-click the PHONE.MNU file to launch it in the Menu Designer.

In the Menu Designer, click on the Phone List menu object and then click on the Events tab of the Object Properties Inspector. Click on the OnClick property, and then the tool icon, to get to the Procedure Editor.

Enter this line in the Procedure Editor:

```
DO Phones_a.wfm
```

Now save your work and return to the Navigator. In the Forms file list, double-click on Fon_Main to launch your finished system.

Congratulations! If you've followed this far, you've built some very nice forms and integrated them in a system.

►► Summary

You've come a long way in this chapter. First, you learned about modal and MDI forms. You created a modal About form. You added a push-button, decorated it with a bitmap from the resource file, and added an appropriate event handler to close the form when the button is clicked.

You used a Text object, supported by the MEMORY( ) function, which you called in the OnOpen event handler, to report memory available. You used Function and Picture properties to format the number appropriately.

Next you went into the Menu Designer. You built a main menu, pull-down menus, and even a cascading menu. You underscored the hot keys and learned to assign shortcut keys. You hooked your Menu objects, through their OnClick events, to the other forms you were building.

For the tables, you learned to start with a query, built in the Query Designer, that you later used as input to each form's design through the Form Expert.

For the People table, you combined the Form Expert and your own work to produce a sophisticated form that combined a Browse object with the basic form layout.

For the Orgs table, you created another combined form. Then you went on to adding pushbuttons. You also used Picture properties to help with entering individual fields on the form.

For the combined table, showing both People and Orgs data, you specified a query that inverted the normal parent-child relationship. This lets you look at each employer attached to the employee's record.

Through this view, you were able to build another form that integrated a Browse object with form layouts from both tables. Changing an employer's phone number in one record effectively changes it for all the employees who work for the same employer.

As you built your forms, you added them to your system through the Menu Designer. You added the .MNU type into your Navigator's Custom table list, to get convenient access to this tool.

In the next chapter, we'll conclude our series of tutorials with a study of the Crystal Reports tool.

▶ ▶ CHAPTER 7

Producing Database Reports

▶▶ **In** this chapter, we'll complete our tutorials with a closer look into the Crystal Reports tool, which we'll call Crystal for short. Crystal is a third-party, add-on report writer that has been bundled by agreement between Seagate (owner of Crystal Computer Services) and Borland.

After Crystal was licensed, Borland acquired the ReportSmith company and software, which was a direct competitor to Crystal. ReportSmith reporting software is now being sold by Borland, and we expect a future version of dBASE for Windows to replace Crystal with ReportSmith.

However, for now, we have Crystal Reports, which is a rich and powerful reporting environment. As you'll see, Crystal makes multi-table reporting simple, and lets you create reports that take advantage of the Microsoft Windows' graphical environment.

▶▶ You Create a Two-Table Report

To begin, we'll start with a two-table report. We'll list our People table data, grouped by employers. To start, we'll need a query that structures the two tables.

▶ Building Your Query

Follow these steps to build the query for the tables:

1. Launch the Untitled query from the Navigator, and select the Orgs table as your first table.
2. In the Query Designer, choose Query ➤ Add Table (or press Ctrl-A) and add the People table.

3. For both tables, click on the select all fields check box, and then deselect each of the ID fields. Your query should now look like the one shown in Figure 7.1.

FIGURE 7.1

Building a query for your report

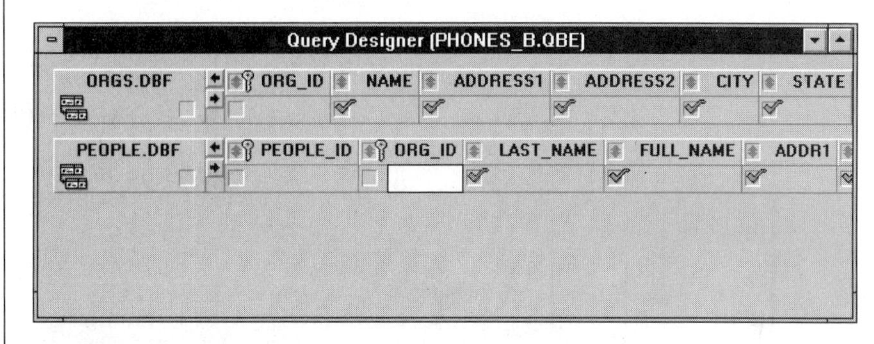

4. With the tables and fields selected, the next step is to establish the relationship between the tables. Drag a line from the set relation icon in the Orgs table skeleton to the set relation icon in the People table skeleton.
5. In the Define Relation dialog box, click on ORG_ID in the child table's Index list, and then click each of the three check boxes in the center. Your relationship should look the same as the one shown in Figure 7.2.
6. With the relationship specified, click on OK or press Enter to return to the Query Designer.
7. Press Ctrl-F4 or Ctrl-W to exit. dBASE for Windows will ask if you want to save your query. Save it as **Phones_B**. (The Phones_A query is the inverted query we did for our Fon_Main system; our _B series will be for noninverted work.)

Beginning the Report Definition

With our query defined, it's time to enter Crystal Reports and define our report. Follow these steps:

1. From the Navigator, click on the Untitled report. This launches the Crystal Reports program.

FIGURE 7.2 ▶

Establishing the relationship between the Orgs and People tables

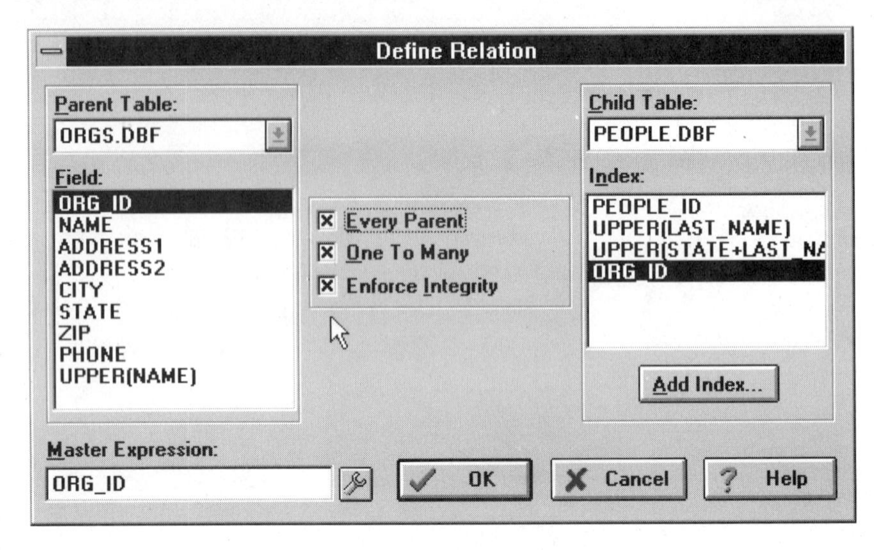

2. Select PHONES_B.QBE in the Open Table Required dialog box. After a moment, Crystal will be loaded, as shown in Figure 7.3. (Crystal is easiest to use if you start by maximizing its window, and then open the report window.)

▸▸ **WARNING**

If you have any open tables, Crystal will use the open table; it won't prompt you for a table or query selection. If this happens, exit Crystal. Then go to the Command window and type CLOSE ALL before returning to the Navigator. With everything closed, you'll be prompted for a table or query name when you launch the Untitled report.

You should see the insertion point flashing in the Details area of the report design screen. (If it isn't there, move the mouse pointer into this area and click the left mouse button.)

FIGURE 7.3

Crystal Reports, ready to accept report fields

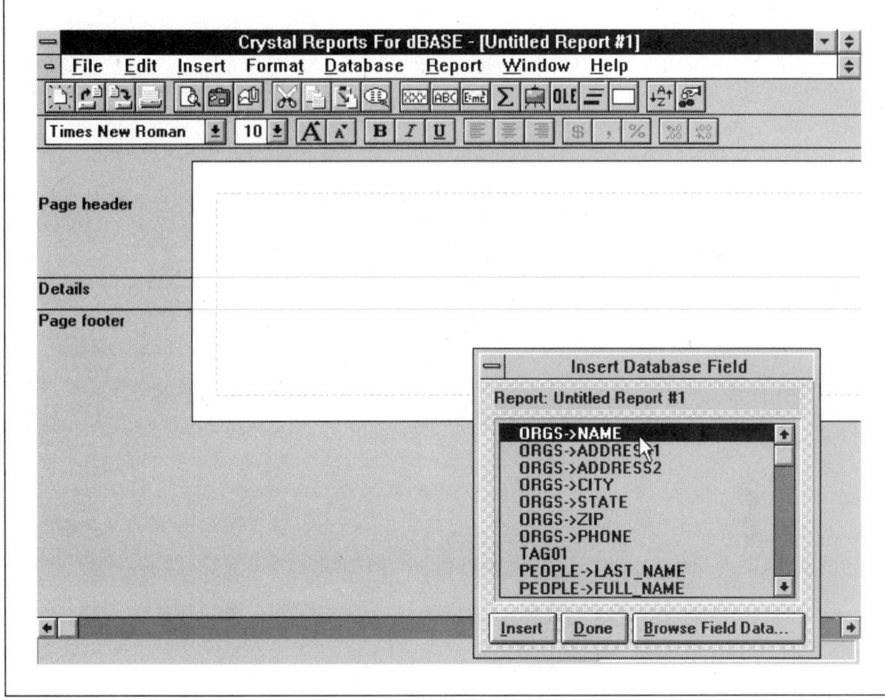

3. In the Details area of our report, we want more space than just one line, so press Enter several times. Give yourself about a dozen lines, but don't worry about counting them. You can add or delete detail lines whenever you like.
4. Click on the NAME field in the Insert Database Field window, and then click on the Insert pushbutton in that window. (A shortcut is to just double-click on the field in the Insert Database Field window.)
5. Your cursor will turn into a rectangular shape. Move back to the first line of the Details area, and click to drop your field near the left margin.

After you have placed this field, your report will look like Figure 7.4.

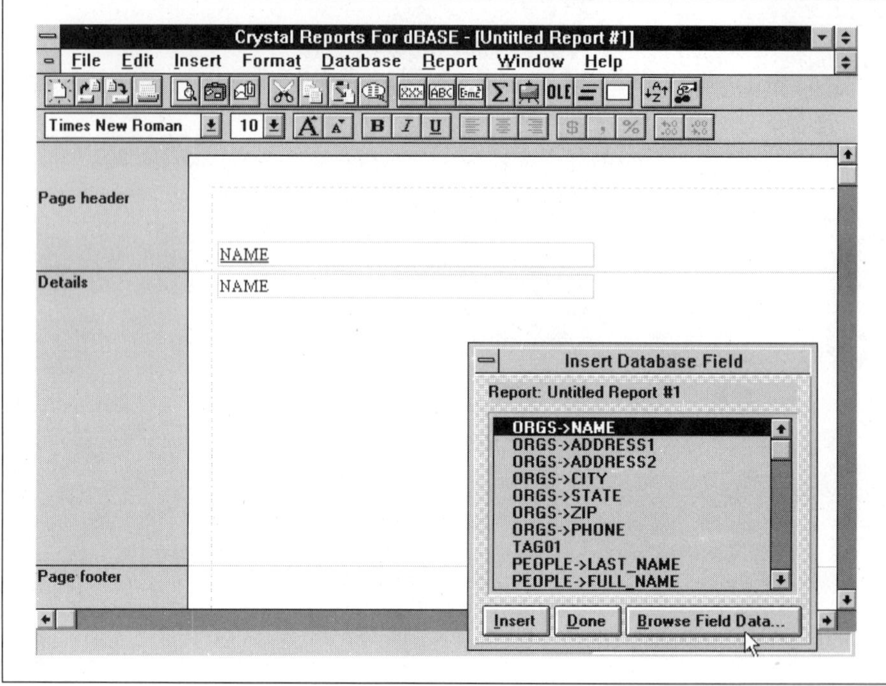

FIGURE 7.4 ▶

The Details area expanded, with its first field

▶ Adding the Other Fields

When you add a field, Crystal helps you out by adding its name above the field in the Page header area. This is fine when your report has multiple fields that run across the page. However, we're building a report of names and addresses, so each column will be a stack of fields.

Unfortunately, when Crystal inserts another field, it stacks the field headings. To see this, add the PHONE field under the NAME field.

▶▶ **WARNING**

When you have more than one table, you can have duplicate field names. Be sure you pick the Orgs table PHONE field when it's appropriate, and the People table PHONE field when it's the right one.

As you can see, you now have two column headings disagreeing about who has the right to occupy the heading space. Click on the argument and press Del. A heading will be deleted. Press Del again, and the argument is settled. They're both gone.

Fortunately, the Crystal Reports authors anticipated work such as we are doing. Choose File ➤ Options.... In the Options dialog box, shown in Figure 7.5, you'll see these four categories:

- General
- Database
- Format
- Fonts

FIGURE 7.5

Setting Crystal Reports options

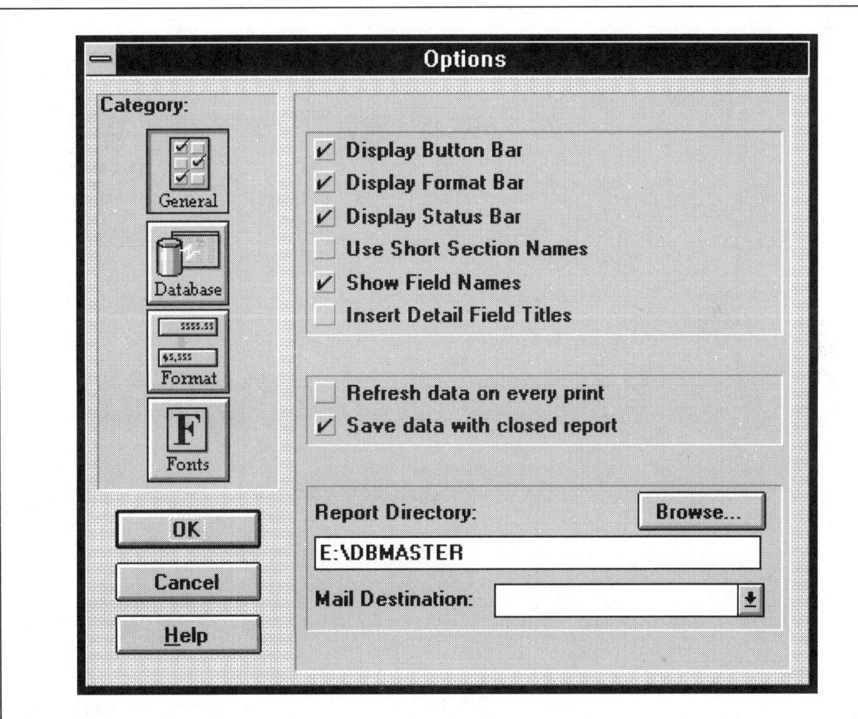

The General option is the default. The last check box in the upper-right section of the dialog box is Insert Detail Field Titles. Click on it to remove the check mark, and then press Enter or click on OK. From now on, Crystal will *not* put those column headings up for you.

▶▶ TIP

Sometimes computer programs put labels on everything. Human beings are smarter than computers—we don't need a label that says "Address" if we're looking at an address. Skip unnecessary labels.

Now shift the report design window a bit to the right and add the address information from the Orgs table. Place the fields to the right of the name and phone number. Figure 7.6 shows our report at this stage. As you can see, we moved the Insert Database Field window to a location that was more convenient.

FIGURE 7.6 

The Orgs table details in place

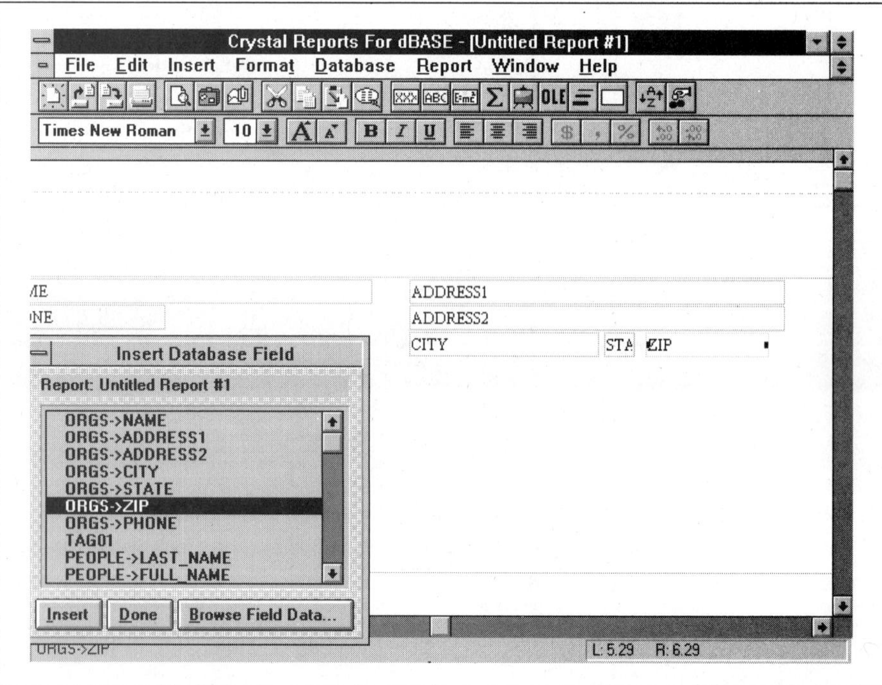

When you're finished adding data from the Orgs table, add the data from the People table in a similar fashion, but offset it to the right by an inch or so (about 3 centimeters). We put the LAST_NAME field above the PHONE field. To the right of these, we put the full address, starting with the FULL_NAME field.

If you don't have enough space in the Details band, put the insertion point into this band and press Enter. Pressing Backspace on a blank Details line deletes the line.

▶ *Previewing Your Work*

After you have these fields in place, click on the looking glass icon (shown in the margin) on the speedbar, which is the fifth from the left, to preview your report. This button launches the Preview window, where you can look at your report.

Actually, the Preview window could also have been correctly called the Report to Screen window, because it lets you look at your whole report.

The default preview is full size. If you click on the looking glass (shown in the margin) on the Preview window's speedbar (at the bottom of the window) you can zoom out to two smaller sizes. Two clicks put the whole page on the screen, as shown in Figure 7.7.

If you click on the looking glass again, you return to the full-size view. In this view, you'll see that you have repeated the name of the employer with every employee record. It would be better to have the employer data just once, and have each employee listed below the employer's listing.

We'll make that improvement soon. For now, let's add a page header and footer to our report.

▶ *Adding Headers and Footers*

When we started Crystal, we were in the Details band of a three-band design surface. The other two bands are for a page header and footer. What we put in these bands will be part of each page of our report.

Let's add a title and a page number.

FIGURE 7.7

The full-page view in the Preview window

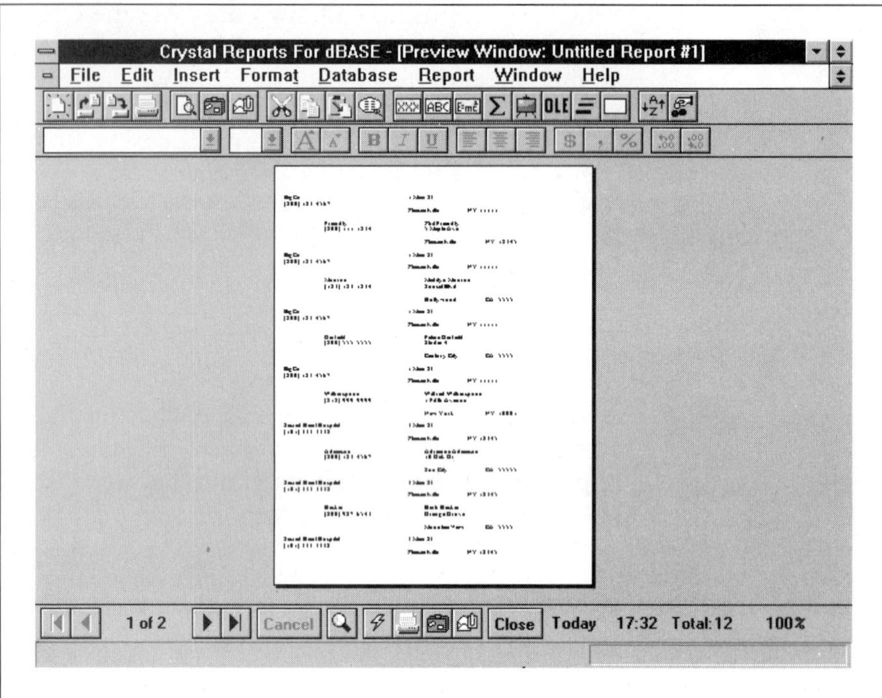

Putting a Title in the Page Header Area

Move the mouse pointer into the Page header area and click. The insertion point will be located to the far left of this area, where you could begin typing the header text directly into that band. Actually, you can type text directly in any area of the report. However, we recommend that you always use text fields for fixed text.

To insert a text field, choose Insert ➤ Text Field … from the menus. The Edit Text Field window pops up.

Enter your text in this box. Obviously, you could write an extended essay here, but we used a simple, two-word title:

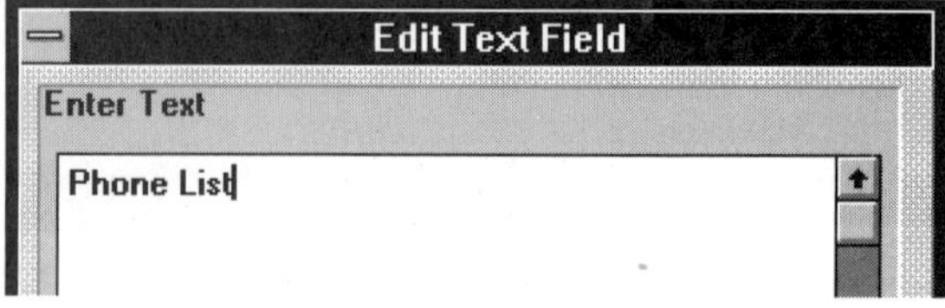

When you click on the Accept pushbutton (pressing Enter is interpreted as part of the text you're entering, not an Accept action), your cursor again becomes the field-placement rectangle. Put the rectangle in the center of your report's Page header section and click to drop it.

Now we have a rather unimposing title, to say the least. When you dropped your title, it was selected; it was outlined in yellow and had resize handles at the left and right sides.

If the title is not still selected, click on it. Now go to the fonts bar and click on the down arrow next to the point size box. This will drop down a menu of font sizes:

Use the elevator to scroll to something a bit larger than the default size. We use 24 points for a title.

To the right of the point size box are big and small *A*s, which tighten and loosen the kerning. To the right of these are three icons that specify font style information:

These are for boldface, italics, and underlining.

For our title, we chose all three: bold, italic, and underlined. Our selections look like this:

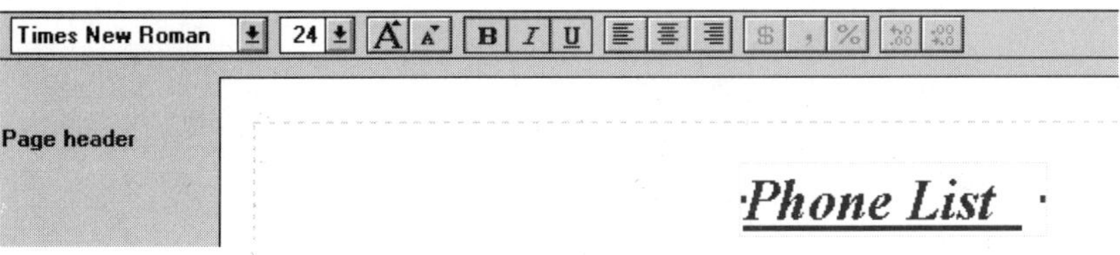

Numbering the Pages in the Page Footer

Numbering your report pages is simple. Choose Insert ➤ Special Field to see a menu of special items. Each of these is a field that you can insert, just as you would add a database or text field. For our work, click on Page Number. Your cursor again turns into the rectangular field-insertion cursor.

Position it in the Page footer area and click in the center. This gives the report a page number centered at the bottom of every page. If you like, you can leave it selected and adjust the font size and style to suit your tastes.

▸▸ You Produce a Two-Table Grouped Report

Most multi-table reports benefit from grouping the data, and our list is no exception. What we want are detail records for employees grouped by employer. We don't really want to repeat the employer data once for each employee.

▸ Creating a Group

To create a group, choose Insert ➤ Group Section … from the menus. This will pop up the Insert Group Section dialog box, shown in Figure 7.8. The default setting is for the employer name, in ascending sequence. This

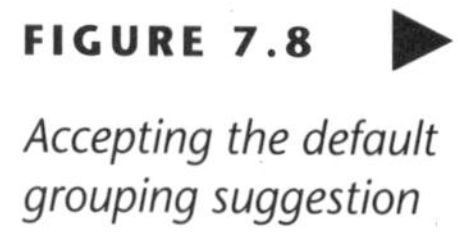

FIGURE 7.8 ▸

Accepting the default grouping suggestion

dialog box will let you pick a field and sequence to suit your needs. But in this instance, the defaults are precisely right. Just click on OK or press Enter.

Groups have a Group header and Group footer area. In this case, since we're grouping on the NAME field, the report design screen labels these areas NAME. They appear above and below the Details section.

But we want to put the employer data into the Group header area, so that it precedes the details about each employee. (The Group footer area prints after all the details about the group.)

▶ *Putting the Employer Data into the Group Header*

Begin by clicking in the Group header area to position the insertion point there. Press Enter twice to expand this area to three lines, so that it will accommodate all the employer data.

You can move fields in Crystal Reports by selecting them and dragging them, just as you move objects in the Form Designer. (The cursor doesn't change into the little hand, but the operation is the same.)

However, for moving a group of fields, the lasso is the best tool. The lasso (shown in the margin) is available on the speedbar. It's the one that looks a little like a squashed baseball, under the *base* part of the Database menu selection.

Click on the lasso on the speedbar. Your cursor changes to cross-hairs. Position the cross-hairs at the top and to the left of the first Orgs table field. Then click and hold the mouse button down while you drag to the lower-right corner of the area that holds all the Orgs table fields.

When you release the mouse button, all the fields within the rectangle you just sketched are selected. Again as in the Form Designer, with multiple fields selected, you can move the fields by dragging with the mouse.

Put the mouse pointer over any one of the selected fields, and press and hold the mouse button while you drag the fields into the Group header area. When they are in position, release the mouse button.

Now return to the Details section of your report and click to position the insertion point in the blank space above the People table data. Use the Del and Backspace keys to delete the blank lines. These keys remove characters in the same way that they do in any text editor.

The result we want is shown in Figure 7.9.

FIGURE 7.9 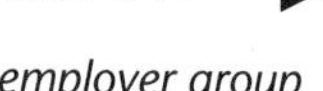

The employer group with employee details

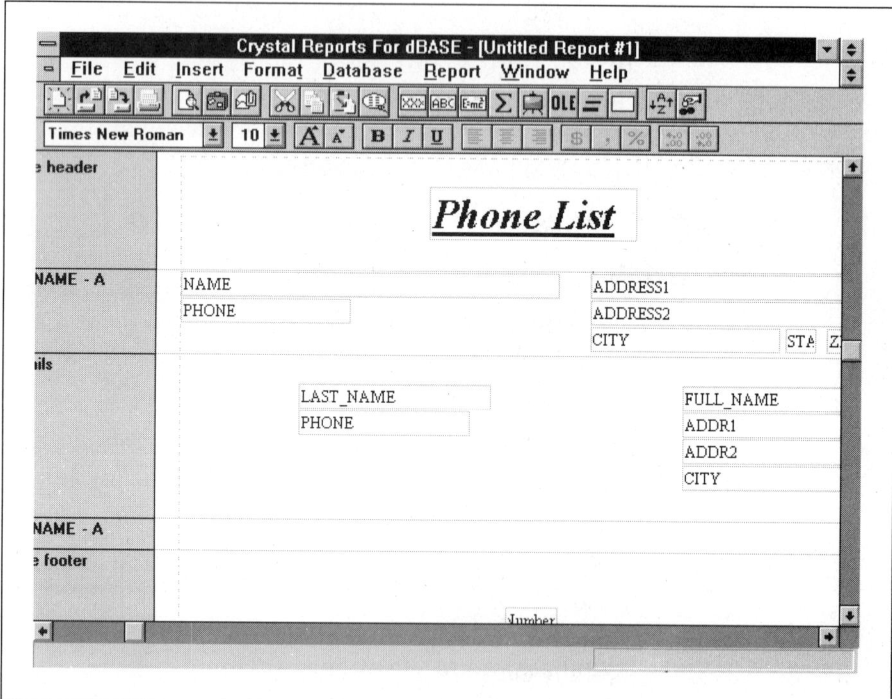

▶ Previewing the Improved Report

With the employer data in the Group header area and the space adjusted in the Details area, click on the Preview window button (the looking glass icon) to preview your report again.

Crystal makes its own copy of your reports data. The second and subsequent times that you preview your report, Crystal asks if you want to use the saved data:

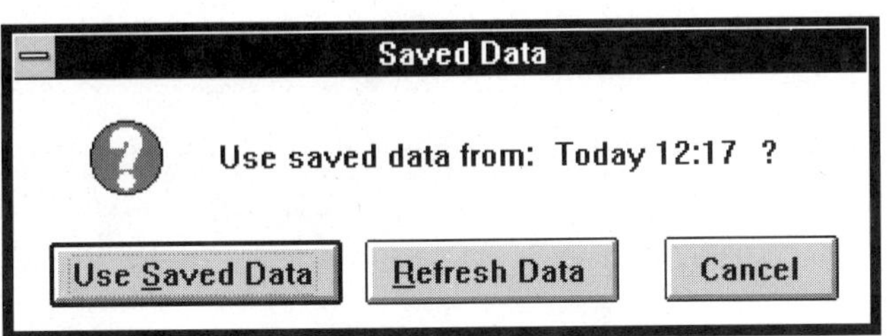

This dialog box tells you the time and date when it last saved the data. Unless you change the default setting, when you save a report, you also save a copy of the data. Using the copy is faster and avoids the problems possible in a multi-user environment, where one person could be updating data as another is running a report.

Make a choice. Normally, you'll accept the default choice to reuse the saved data. Click on the button reflecting your choice, or press Enter to accept the default. In the Preview window, click on the glass at the bottom to zoom out to a full-page view of your report.

You may or may not see a problem, depending on your data. Crystal may have come to the bottom of the page in the middle of printing data about an employee or employer, and split the address between two pages. Use the navigation buttons on the bottom speedbar to page through your report to see if this happens in your report.

▶ *Preventing Section Splitting*

To make sure the address lines appear on the same page, you need to tell Crystal that you don't want it to start a detail group or a section header if it can't finish it on the current page. To do this, choose Format ➤ Section … from the menus. In the Format Section dialog box, choose Details, as shown in Figure 7.10.

After you choose a section, Crystal launches another dialog box, also titled Format Section, where you can provide formatting details about the section you have chosen. In Figure 7.11, we're choosing the Keep

FIGURE 7.10

Choosing to format the Details section

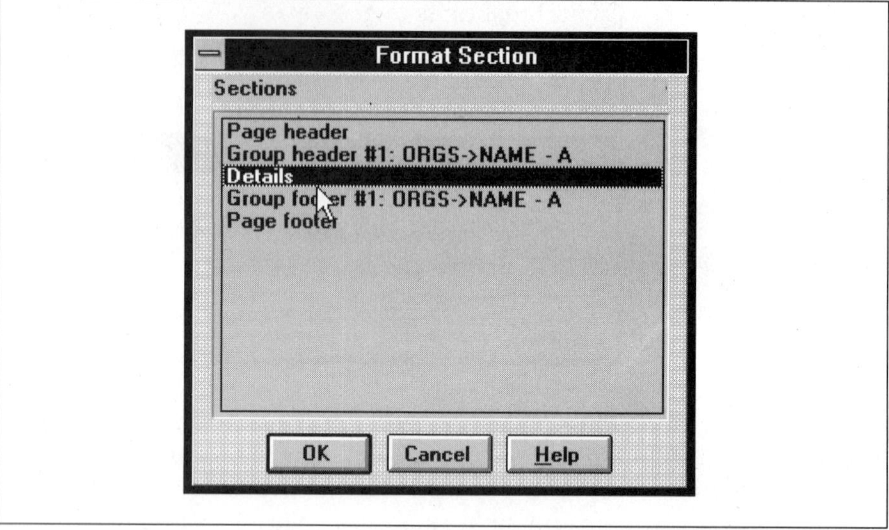

FIGURE 7.11

Choosing to print only complete Details sections

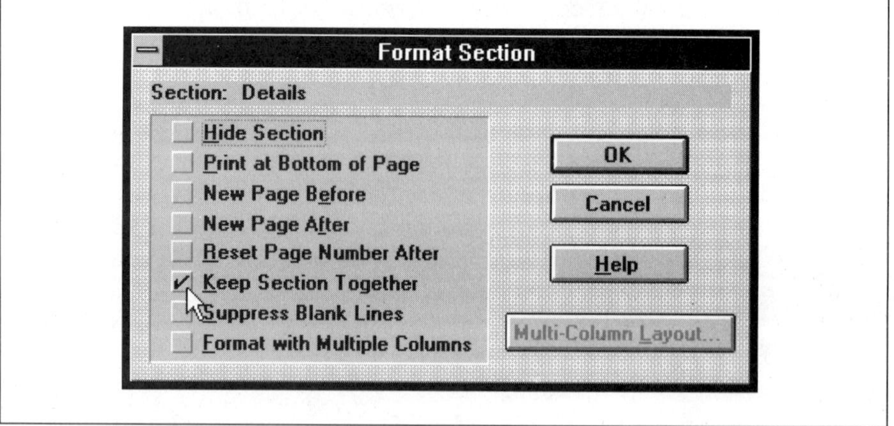

Section Together option for the Details section. This choice tells Crystal that we don't want it to start the section if it can't fit the whole section on the current page.

After choosing this option for the Details section, go back and repeat the process for the Group header section. Note that although this keeps the Group header section together, it doesn't keep all the details together with the header. Keeping the entire group together is not an option in Crystal Reports.

You Add Embellishments to Your Report

One of the best features of Crystal is that it lets you work in the Preview window, where you see the results of your work on live data. When you get to the position we are now in—you have the right data in the right order—you begin to address the appearance of the report. Being able to do this in the Preview window is invaluable.

TIP

Make regular use of the zoom icon spy glass at the bottom of the page as you make improvements.

You will need to be in the full-size view to select fields. Your selections remain in the other views, but you can't select different fields unless the window is full size.

Manipulating Font Sizes and Styles

The simplest, and one of the most effective, ways to dress up a report is to vary your font sizes and styles. To begin, let's make the employers' names stand out.

Click on an employer's name to select this field. You'll see that every occurrence of the field in the Preview window is selected. With the name selected, set the font size to 16 points and choose boldface. To change the font size, click on the font size box and use the elevator to select a size. To boldface the text, click on the B button for boldface.

▸▸ TIP

Varying font sizes and styles adds emphasis. Using multiple fonts makes reports look garish. Stick with one font for most of your work. Used with discretion, using two fonts sometimes works. Using three or more fonts almost always looks foolish.

We've used a 16-point, boldface font for the employers' names, and a 16-point, regular font for their phone numbers. Now try a 12-point, boldface font for the employees' names and a 12-point, regular font for their phone numbers.

▸ Drawing on Your Report

You can use lines and boxes to dress up your report. Before we go on, however, let's save what we've got. If you haven't saved your work yet, you'll see that your report is untitled (look in the Crystal Reports main window's title).

Choose File ➤ Save or File ➤ Save As … to save your work. (Crystal will ask for a name if your report is untitled.) We saved our report as Phones_B.

Now let's put a box around the employer's data. Choose Insert ➤ Box from the menus. Your mouse pointer will turn into a pencil (as shown in the margin). From the upper-left area, above the employer's name, drag to the lower-right, area, just below the end of the employer's address. Your box should surround all the employer data.

When you release your mouse button, you might get the mixed-up result shown in Figure 7.12.

What's going on here? The answer is simple. The box you just drew is covering some of the Details section, as well as the Group header section. The portion in the Details section is repeated for every detail.

Close the Preview window (click on the Close button at the bottom) to go back to the report design window. Click on the box you just added to select it, and drag any convenient handle back into the Group header section.

FIGURE 7.12

A box causing problems

Phone List

BigCo (800) 123-4567	1 Main St. Pleasantville	NY	11111
Friendly (800) 111-1234	Phil Friendly 5 Maple Ave. Pleasantville	NY	12345
Monroe (123) 123-1234	Madilyn Monroe Sunset Blvd. Hollywood	CA	5555
Garfield (800) 555-5555	Feline Garfield Studio 4 Century City	CA	5555
Witherspoon	Wilfred Witherspoon		

NOTE

You may find that trying to grab a box handle selects a field instead. Drag the field out of the way before you adjust the box.

With the box located in the Group header section, you can return to the Preview window. Your box is now well-behaved, neatly enclosing the employer data, as shown in Figure 7.13.

▶ Formatting the Box

With the box in place, we can add decorative effects. Click on your box, then choose Format ➤ Box … from the menus. (You can't access the Box option of the Format menu unless you've selected a box first.) You'll see the Box Format dialog box. Figure 7.14 shows this dialog box with our settings.

We chose a gray fill color (which Crystal calls Silver). For our border, we used a 3-point, solid-black line. Choose whatever combinations you like.

FIGURE 7.13

A well-behaved box

Phone List

BigCo (800) 123-4567	1 Main St. Pleasantville	NY	11111
Friendly (800) 111-1234	Phil Friendly 5 Maple Ave. Pleasantville	NY	12345
Monroe (123) 123-1234	Madilyn Monroe Sunset Blvd.		

FIGURE 7.14

Choosing box formatting options

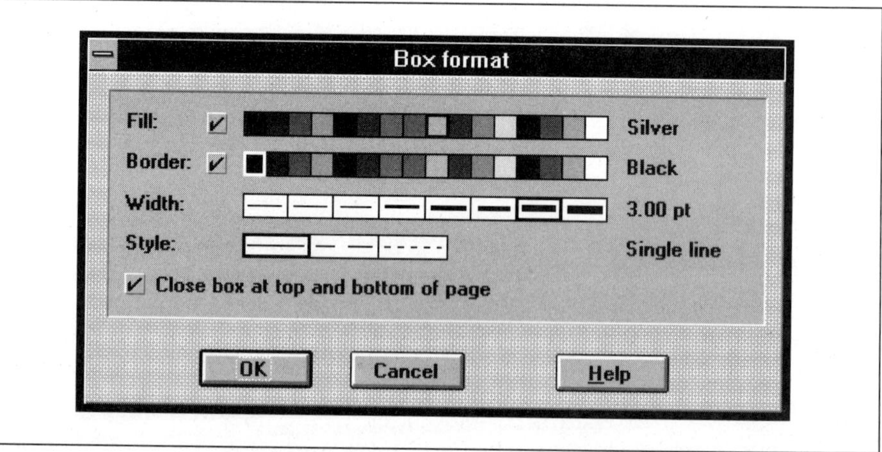

▸▸ **WARNING**

Adding gray areas can increase the print time dramatically. An eight-page-per-minute printer can be slowed to one or two pages per minute.

As you add decorative effects, remember that individual characters are transmitted to your printer 8 bits per character. Bitmaps and gray areas are transmitted at 300 dots per inch (dpi). (Both lower and higher densities are available, but 300 dpi is the most common.)

A square inch of gray area takes 90,000 bits. For pure character information, 90,000 bits would handle 11,250 characters (about four pages of single-spaced text). You might consider two versions of your reports: one with embellishments and one that prints quickly.

▶ Emphasizing Names

With our employers standing out so clearly, we need to do something to add emphasis to the employees' names. The work we are about to do should be done with discretion. If you use too much emphasis, nothing will stand out.

The potential to abuse, rather than use, the field-emphasis features may have led the designers of Crystal to place these capabilities in an obscure portion of the product.

To add emphasis, select a field (we chose the last name field), and then choose Format ➤ Borders and Colors .... Figure 7.15 shows our choices in the Format Borders and Colors dialog box.

In this dialog box, we've chosen to place a border line on all four sides of the field. We've also asked for a Drop Shadow, to really pop the field up off the page.

FIGURE 7.15

Boxing and shadowing last names

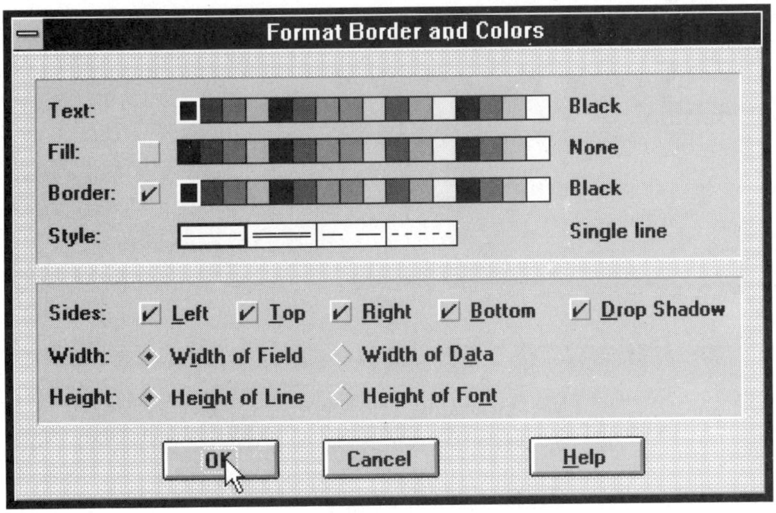

With these improvements made, it's time to preview the report again. Our Preview window now shows the report as it appears in Figure 7.16.

FIGURE 7.16 ▸

Previewing a handsome report

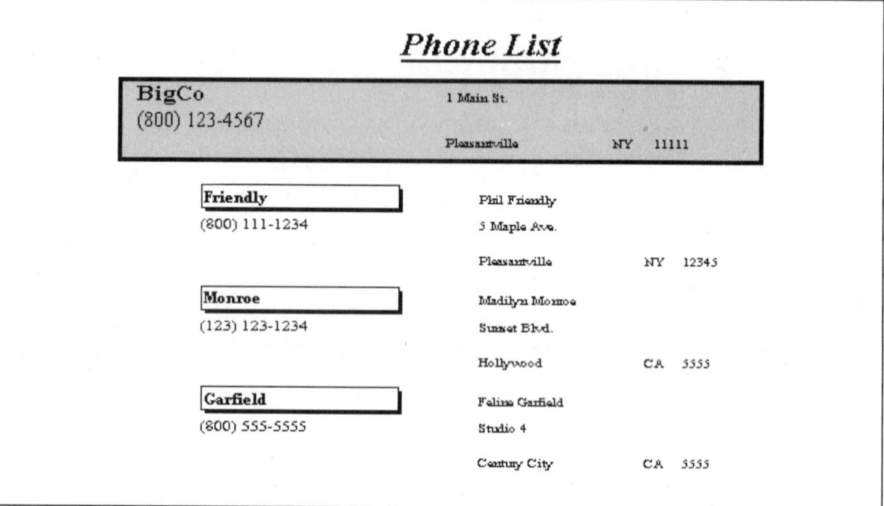

If your report looks something like ours, you'll probably be pleased with the results. This is just one example of the results you can achieve with Crystal Reports, with very little effort.

Now you can exit from Crystal Reports. You'll return to dBASE for Windows.

▸▸ **WARNING**

Don't close dBASE for Windows while you're in Crystal Reports. Crystal Reports runs partly under Windows independent of dBASE for Windows, and partly as a child of dBASE for Windows.

▸ Running the Report from the Navigator

You now can choose your new PHONES_B.RPT file in the Navigator's Reports area and launch it with a double-click or by pressing F2. This will *not* return you to Crystal Reports. That tool is only for designing reports, not running them.

The Report window, shown in Figure 7.17, is the tool for running your reports. As you can see, it's a child window in dBASE for Windows.

The navigation buttons on the speedbar let you browse through your report. Clicking on the print button (or pressing Ctrl-P) sends your report to the printer. When you choose to print, the Printing Reports dialog box appears. It reports on the progress of your print job and gives you a chance to cancel it.

FIGURE 7.17

Running your report inside dBASE for Windows

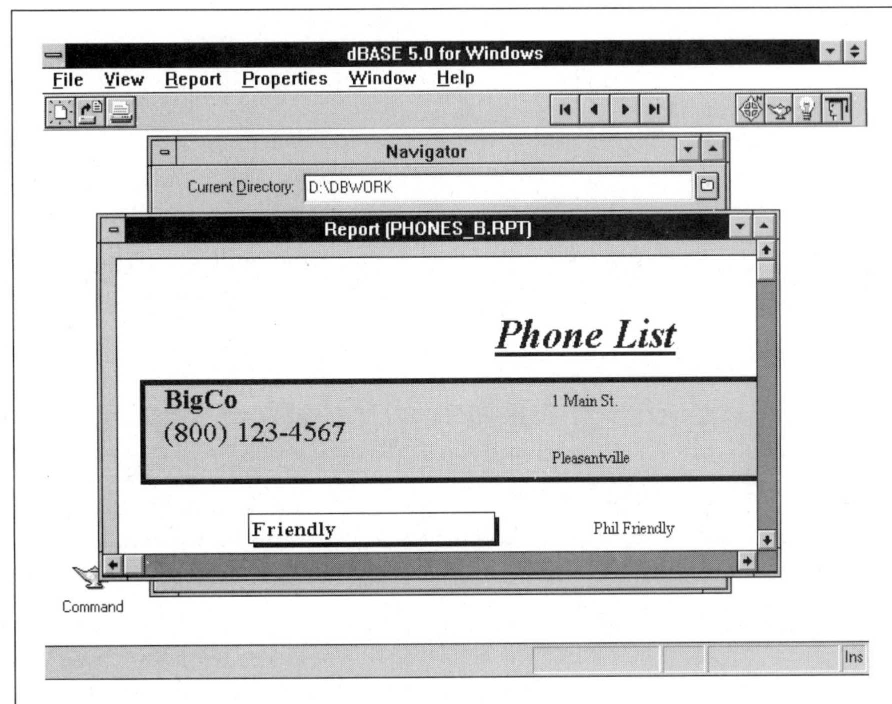

▶ Running the Report from Fon_Main

Now that we have a report that can be run from the Navigator, we also have a report that should be added to the Fon_Main File menu, as the Print ... option.

Choose the Custom file type in the Navigator and launch the Menu Designer on the PHONE.MNU file. (Right double-click or press Shift-F2 after selecting it.)

Press the ↓ key from the File choice to get to the Exit menu item. Choose Menu ➤ Insert Menu Item, or press Ctrl-N, to put a new Menu object above the Exit choice. Its text should read **Print** ....

Now add the OnClick property for this option. Choose the Events tab of the Object Properties Inspector, click on the OnClick property, and then click on the tool icon to get to the Procedure Editor. Add this two-line program:

```
SET VIEW TO Phones_b
REPORT FORM Phones_b
```

The first line uses the view we've created, and the second line runs the report we've created.

As a final touch, add another menu separator between the Print ... and Exit options. Then save your work.

From the Navigator, choose Forms and launch Fon_Main. You should be able to choose File ➤ Print ... and have dBASE for Windows launch your new report.

▸ Handling Inverted Relationships

With the 5.0 release, there is a bug in Crystal Reports that won't let it correctly run a report with an inverted relationship. However, this doesn't mean that you can't use an inverted list, such as our PHONES_A.QBE file. It just means that you must work around the problem.

One way to get your inverted relationship to Crystal is by preparing a single table. Then with the data correctly drawn together into a single table, you can design a single-table report in Crystal.

Preparing a Single Table

To build a consolidated results table from your query, first launch the inverted query by double-clicking on it or selecting it and pressing F2. Choose Table ➤ Table Utilities ... ➤ Export Records .... You'll see the Export Records dialog box, shown in Figure 7.18.

Type a name for your new table and click on OK or press Enter. The export defaults are all exactly what you want. You will get all records and all fields in the exported file. It will be another dBASE data table.

After you have exported your data to a new, single table, select the Untitled report in the Navigator and open it. In Crystal, you can just go ahead and create an attractive report for your single table.

FIGURE 7.18

Exporting the PHONES_A file into a single table

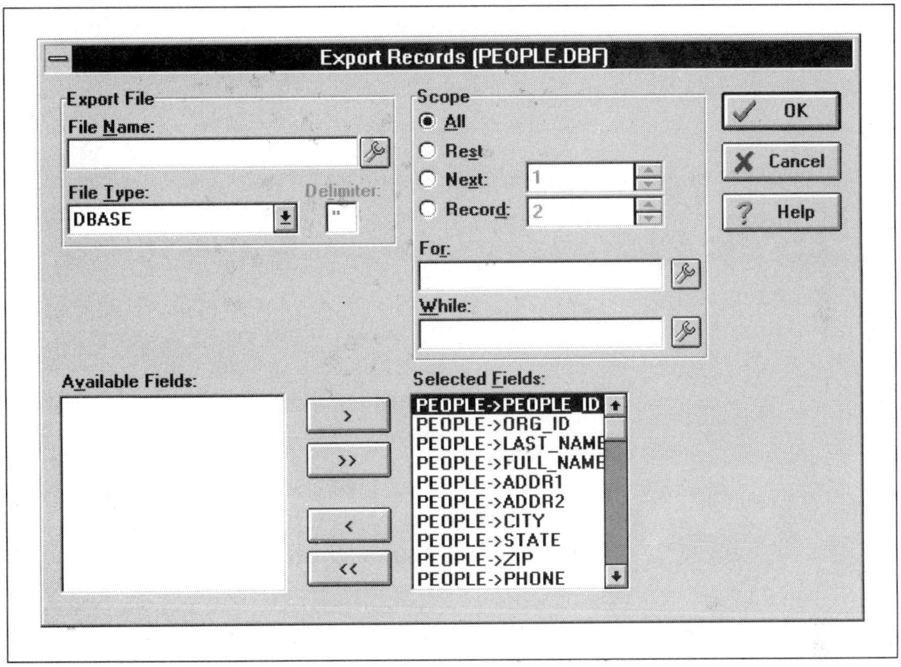

There is one problem in this procedure that has been solved for you. In Phones_A, our People and our Orgs tables have fields with the same names; for example, they both have a field named PHONE.

As you scroll through the field list in Crystal, you'll see that the second PHONE field (in the Phones_A query, the fields in the Orgs table are second) has been named PHONE_1. This gives you all the fields, without name conflicts.

▸▸ You Create Mailing Labels

Crystal Reports makes the mailing label generation process as simple as it can possibly be. However, there are some tricks of the trade that you may want to use.

For these instructions, we assume that you'll be doing relatively low-volume work, using peel-and-stick labels. For high-volume runs, you would use continuous-form labels suited to automated mailing equipment. The techniques here are still applicable.

To begin with, mailing label work depends on a precise knowledge of the placement of the labels on the label sheet. Specifically, your printer needs to know exactly how far from the paper edge the first label should be placed.

Crystal makes this easy by including a database of the most common label types. If you have Avery (or compatible) labels, you just need to look at your label number, and Crystal will take it from there.

Unfortunately, Crystal cannot look at your hardware, which is a key variable. Your paper-feed path determines the actual placement of text on your label stock. Your labels may be feeding a bit more to the right or left than our labels. You'll need to print test labels to be sure.

The last time we bought labels, each sheet (three across, ten down) cost about 40 cents. That's just over a penny a label, which is not a lot. However, it may take you five or ten test runs to get your labels positioned exactly.

We take a single sheet of labels and make photocopies. If you use a dark setting, you'll be able to see the label borders on your copies. These copies will substitute for the real labels when you do your test printing.

With photocopies loaded in your printer to test your labels, let's get started.

▸ Generating a Single-Table Label Set

If you've been running other reports and forms, begin by giving a CLOSE ALL command in the Command window. If any of your data tables are open, Crystal Reports will use those tables, rather than asking you to choose a table or query.

Without any tables open, choose the Untitled option in the Labels file type in the Navigator. Double-click on it or press F2 to launch it in Crystal Reports.

On your way to Crystal, dBASE for Windows will prompt you with an Open Table Required dialog box. Choose your basic People query, PEOPLE_A.QBE.

TIP

In the U.S., you can get a reduced postage rate by presorting your mail on the postal codes. For high-volume work, check with your postal authorities and prepare a modified .QBE file to take advantage of any savings.

Choosing a Label Type

When you enter Crystal Reports from the Labels section of the Navigator, you begin with the Mailing Labels dialog box. The default type is User Defined Label, which lets you describe a nonstandard type of label. The Choose Mailing Label Type drop-down list gives you a selection of the most common Avery labels. If you're using Avery or compatible labels, pick your type from this list, and the rest of the data will be filled in for you. We choose the Avery 5260 type, as shown in Figure 7.19.

Before you leave this dialog box, take a good look at the options you have. Even though Crystal's label database has the correct setting for the left margin, for example, you may need to change it because your printer is feeding paper a little to the right or left of center.

When you click on OK or press Enter, you'll proceed to the Crystal label design screen.

Designing Your Labels

On the design screen, pick your fields from the Insert Database Field dialog box (double-click for quick picking) and position them in the Details band.

FIGURE 7.19

Choosing Avery 5260 labels

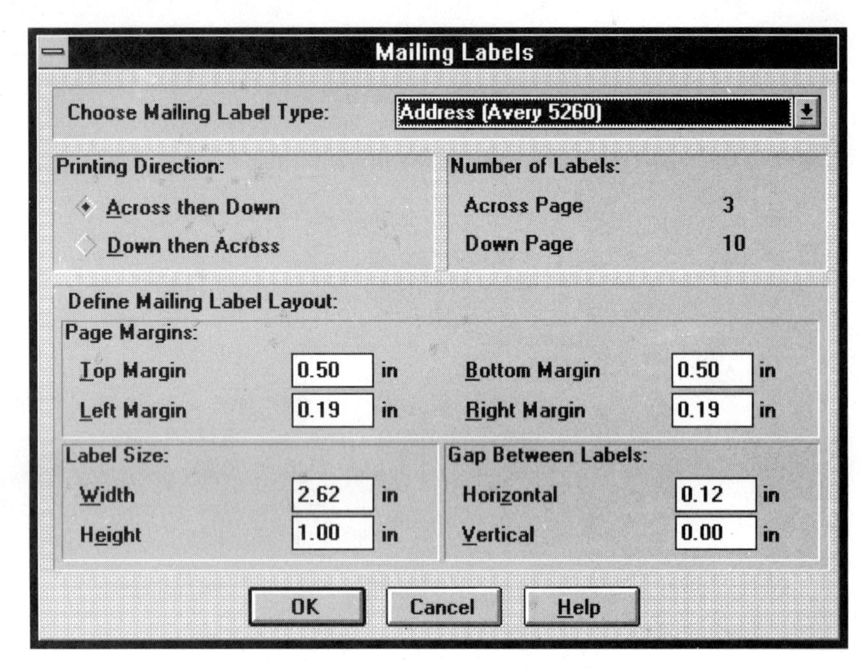

 **TIP**

Stay to the right of the left margin by two or three characters, to avoid paper-path alignment problems.

Crystal will repeat each Details section across the page according to the number of labels specified in the Mailing Labels dialog box. For example, the 5260 type is three labels across and ten down. You don't need to worry about this; just position your fields to print correctly on a single label.

Here's the Details section for our Avery 5260 labels:

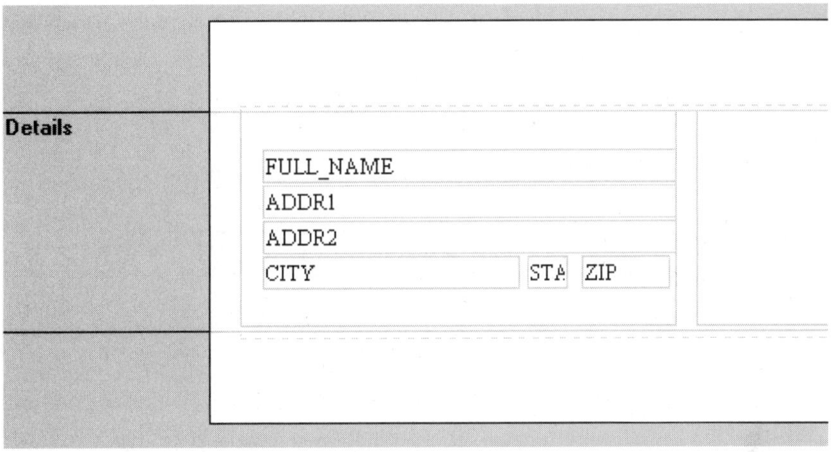

You can see that we've avoided the left margin and stayed away from the very top and bottom of the label. Our fields have been moved in on the right to stay within the boundary of the label.

Checking Your Labels

For a quick check of what Crystal intends to do with your specifications, look at your label design in the Preview window. If it looks reasonable, print a test sheet. (Just one sheet—there's no need to run your whole table.)

You may find that your data is slightly off to the left or right, or slightly too high or low on your label. If necessary, return to the Mailing Labels dialog box and adjust the top and left margins appropriately. You can get to this dialog box by choosing File ➤ Set Label Layout ….

Running Your Labels

Once you are satisfied with the label layout, you can begin to print the real labels from Crystal Reports. Alternatively, you can return to dBASE for Windows and run the labels from there.

When you exit, you'll be given a chance to save your layout. We chose to save it under the file name PEOPLE_A.RPL (the .RPL extension is added automatically), to correspond to the query we use with the labels.

From dBASE for Windows, launch the People_A label file in Run mode. Your labels will appear in the Labels window, just as reports run in the Reports window. From here, you can print them (from the File menu or by clicking on the speedbar icon).

Remember that you can modify the People_A query before you run your labels in dBASE for Windows. For example, you may need to select only the first half of your table.

▸ Generating a Multiple-Table Label Set

Generating labels from a multi-table query is generally no more difficult that generating labels from a one-table query. However, there are some special considerations.

To illustrate these, let's prepare a mailing label job that will send mail to all the people in our People table at the business addresses in our Orgs table.

Selecting the Query and Label Type

If you simply return to Crystal Reports at this point, it will continue to use the last tables you had open. You need to issue a CLOSE ALL command in the Command window before you launch the Untitled file in the Navigator's Labels file type.

When you get the Open Table Required dialog box, choose the PHONES_B.QBE query that we prepared earlier for our multi-table report. This has all the data we need.

Again, you could modify this query to suit your mailing. For example, if you were doing a high-volume mailing, you could sort the table by zip code to take advantage of discounted postal rates.

Launch Crystal Reports and make your selections in the Mailing Labels dialog box (pick the type of label you will be using, or enter custom coordinates for a User-Defined label).

Designing for More Fields

Next, lay out your fields on the label design screen. The only special consideration here is that you'll certainly have more data when you combine employee names with employer names and addresses.

Here's our design for these labels:

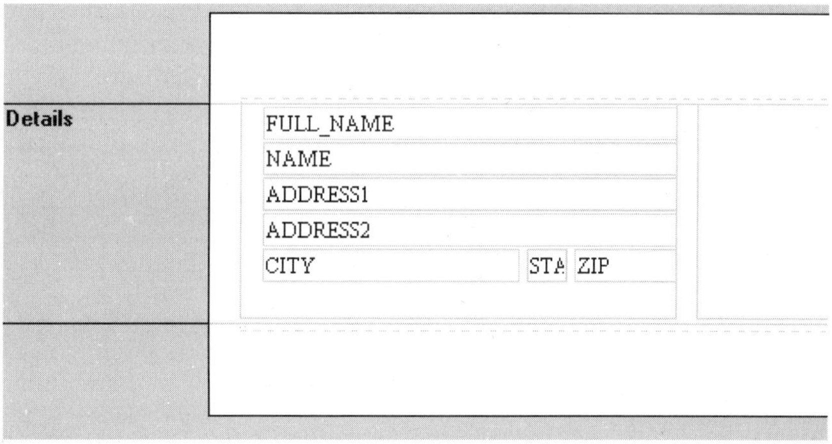

Details
FULL_NAME
NAME
ADDRESS1
ADDRESS2
CITY STA ZIP

It includes the full name from the People table, along with the name and three lines of address data from the Orgs table.

In our single-table label design, we avoided problems with the data printing too high or low on the label sheet by not using the first or last label line. With five lines, we recommend using half-line spacing.

The setting for the top margin depends on the size of the font you're using. With a 10-point font size, you're printing six lines per inch. Each line is one-sixth inch—about 0.1666 inch tall. To get a half line vacant at the top of the label, set the top margin at 0.0833 inch.

If your printer's top margin is 0.50 inch, change it to 0.58. That will start the first label line down a half line. The sixth label line (the one we don't use in a five-line label) would be half on the current label and half on the top of the next label.

In some cases, you may find that you need to use a full, six-line label. The simplest way to accommodate this is to switch to a larger label size. If you must put six lines on a ten-deep set of labels, you'll need to experiment with your equipment.

It may work, if your paper feed is extraordinarily accurate, to just use all six lines. More likely, you'll need to bump the top margin up a bit and print with a smaller type size.

Testing and Printing Your Labels

The testing and printing processes for mutiple-table labels are the same as with single-table labels, except that you should be aware of a possible subtle problem with your test sheets. When you photocopied from the labels to test sheets, the copying process could have introduced slight errors. You might, for example, have not adjusted the labels in the precise center of your copying area.

If you've designed a full, or nearly full, label, there is no substitute for doing your final testing on actual label stock.

Once you are satisfied that your labels print correctly, exit Crystal Reports. On the way out, save your new label job as Phones_B (the extension .RPL is automatically applied) to match the query it runs on.

▸▸ Summary

You began your work with Crystal Reports by preparing a new query tying the People table to the Orgs table. With the results of this query, you built a simple report, showing employer and employee data. You used the Preview window and its zoom feature to check your results.

Moving out of the Details area of the Crystal Reports design window, you added a text field in the Page header area for a report title. You adjusted the font size and style to make the title stand out.

In the Page footer area, you used the Insert menu to insert a special field. You chose the Page Number option as a Page footer field.

Your first report repeated the employer data with each employee's data. You improved this by creating a group, grouping on the employer's name field in ascending order. You moved the employer data from the Details section into the Group header section, to have it print before any employee data. This report showed the employer data once, preceding as many employees as needed.

Again, you used the Preview window to check and to edit the results. You used the Format ➤ Section … menu choice to tell Crystal Reports that your data in each section should be printed together, not split across pages.

With the content of your report set, you went on to improve its appearance. You started with varying the font sizes and styles, highlighting the most important fields.

You added a box around the employer data. You used the Insert ➤ Box choice to add the box and then the Format ➤ Box … choice to select fill and border characteristics.

You added emphasis to the employee's last name field with the Format ➤ Borders and Colors … choice. In the Borders and Colors dialog box, you specified a single line around all four sides of the field and added a drop shadow beneath it.

After creating an attractive report, you saved your work and returned to dBASE for Windows, where you ran your finished report in the Reports window, launched from the Navigator. You set up this report as a Print … choice, which you added to your Fon_Main system.

You learned that a problem in Crystal Reports prevents the current version from handling inverted queries directly. For these queries, you learned to use the Table Utilities tools to export your data into a single table, and then report from that table.

Finally, you went on to create mailing labels. You learned to use the Mailing Label dialog box to select an appropriate label type, and then use the design surface to paint labels in the Details area.

You tested your labels on photocopies of the real label stock. You learned to adjust the margins to compensate for the characteristics of your printer.

Finally, you used the label capability to generate labels drawing data from two tables. You learned to adjust the margins to center five lines of text in a six-line label.

Congratulations! You have finished the tutorial section of this book. Now we'll go on to more advanced topics. At this point, you can pick and choose the topics that are most relevant to your own work with dBASE for Windows.

Master Classes

PART THREE

In this part, we'll examine all the tools and surfaces of dBASE for Windows in depth. Our goal in Part 2 was to be good teachers. We selected the features that we thought were most important and showed you how to use them.

Our goal in this part is to be totally exhaustive, even if we risk being exhausting in the process. We'll cover every menu choice, every mouse-click possibility, and every combination in dBASE for Windows.

Obviously, not all of this information is relevant. In fact, a great deal of it may be irrelevant to your daily use of dBASE for Windows. On the other hand, we think that every bit of it will be relevant to at least someone, doing something. The designers of dBASE for Windows went to the trouble of adding all these features so that they could meet real, working database needs.

In Chapter 8, Mastering the Menus, Navigator, and Command Window, we'll look at the control surfaces for dBASE for Windows. You can drive almost every feature in dBASE for Windows from all three control surfaces, and we explore them all in depth. The menus are particularly fascinating to track down. The menus of dBASE for Windows are constantly changing to reflect the capabilities of the active design or run surface.

In Chapter 9, Mastering Table Tools, we'll cover the Table Structure tool, the Table Records tool, and the Table Utilities in depth. When you get tired of grabbing the bars separating your fields and want dBASE for Windows to remember how wide you like each column, this is the place to turn for help. If you must export selected records and fields to your spreadsheet or word processor, here's where you'll find out how.

In Chapter 10, Mastering Crystal Reports, we'll continue our exploration of the report writer, covering all of its menus, dialog boxes, and speedbars.

In Chapter 11, we complete the Master classes with a thorough treatment of the remaining Crystal Reports topics. We'll look at the cross-tab and mailing label topics that we passed by in Chapter 10, and also study the use of Crystal Reports for generating form letters.

▶ ▶ CHAPTER 8

Mastering the Menus, Navigator, and Command Window

▶▶ In Parts 1 and 2 of this book, we've covered the basics of using dBASE for Windows to design tables, manage and manipulate your data, and create reports. Now we'll begin to go into detail about the great variety of features offered by dBASE. This chapter covers the main menus, the Navigator, catalogs, the Command window, and the Expression Builder. Yes, we know you've already worked with some of these features. But here we'll discuss every nook and cranny of these elements, so you'll know where to find whatever options and settings you need.

We'll start with the dBASE for Windows main menus. As you've seen, the menu choices vary depending on the active child window. Here we'll cover the parts that are common to all child types.

▶▶ Using the File Menu

The File menu choices vary depending on the type of object that is active. However, the following options are always available when an object of some type is active:

- New (Ctrl-N)
- Open … (Ctrl-O)
- Save (Ctrl-S)
- Close (Ctrl-F4)
- Print … (Ctrl-P)
- Printer Setup …
- Exit
- 1, 2, 3, 4 and 5

Choosing File ➤ New displays this submenu of dBASE file types:

Table
Query
Form
Report
Cross-Tab
Labels
Program
Catalog...

These options work as follows:

- Table launches the Table Structure tool.
- Query invokes the Query Designer.
- Form starts the Form Expert.
- Choosing Report, Cross-Tab or Labels enters Crystal Reports.
- Program starts the Program Editor.
- Catalog starts the Create Catalog process.

Choosing File ➤ Open displays the Open File dialog box. This is a common dialog box that you've seen in one form or another during your work with dBASE for Windows. Appendix B provides a complete discussion of its options.

Items 1 through 5, at the bottom of the menu, are the Most Recently Used (MRU) files: the five files you've used most recently. So, for example, you could choose File ➤ 1, and get to the appropriate file immediately. You can choose to have more or less than five files in the MRU list, via the Application tab in the Properties ➤ Desktop window.

When you use one of the MRU options, the file automatically opens in Run mode, not Design mode. If you choose File ➤ Open, radio buttons give you a choice between modes for most file types.

TIP

For Design mode, open a file through the Navigator. Use the Speed menu or press Shift-F2.

The other options, including Close, Print, Printer Setup, and Exit, do precisely what they say.

▸▸ Using the Edit Menu

The Edit menu always includes the following options:

- Undo (Ctrl-Z)
- Cut (Ctrl-X)
- Copy (Ctrl-C)
- Paste (Ctrl-V)
- Delete (Del)

For most operations from the Navigator, all of the Edit menu choices are dimmed (unavailable). Other times, this menu will contain different options, depending on the active object. For example, when the Command window is active, Edit menu options include copying to and from files and using the Expression Builder.

▸▸ Using the Properties Menu

The Properties menu always includes the Desktop ... choice. Its other options depend on where you are in dBASE for Windows.

Selecting Properties ➤ Desktop brings up a form with six tabs:

- Country
- Table
- Data Entry
- Files
- Application
- Programming

▶ Setting Country Properties

The Country tab (Properties ➤ Desktop ➤ Country), shown in Figure 8.1, offers Numeric, Currency, and Date settings. Each group of choices also includes an Example display, which shows how the current selection appears.

FIGURE 8.1 ▶

Properties ➤ Desktop, Country tab

The two Numeric choices are Separator and Point. The Separator is the character that separates whole numbers into groups of three digits (as in one million: 1,000,000). Point refers to the character that separates the whole part from the fractional part (as in 1.23).

The Currency choices include the location of the currency symbol (radio buttons for Left or Right) and an entry field to select a Symbol.

The Date selections give you a choice of Date Format (GERMAN, JAPAN, USA, YMD, MDY, and DMY) and the Mark to separate the components or the date (such as a /, as in 1/1/96). You can also check the Century check box if you wish the full four-digit version of the century to be displayed (1996 if checked; 96 if unchecked).

▶▶ **NOTE**

In all the Desktop Properties tabs, the OK, Cancel, and Help pushbuttons perform their standard functions.

► Setting Table Properties

The Table tab (Properties ➤ Desktop ➤ Table), shown in Figure 8.2, offers Multiuser, Default Table Type, Block Sizes, and Other settings.

FIGURE 8.2 ►

The Properties ➤ Desktop, Table tab

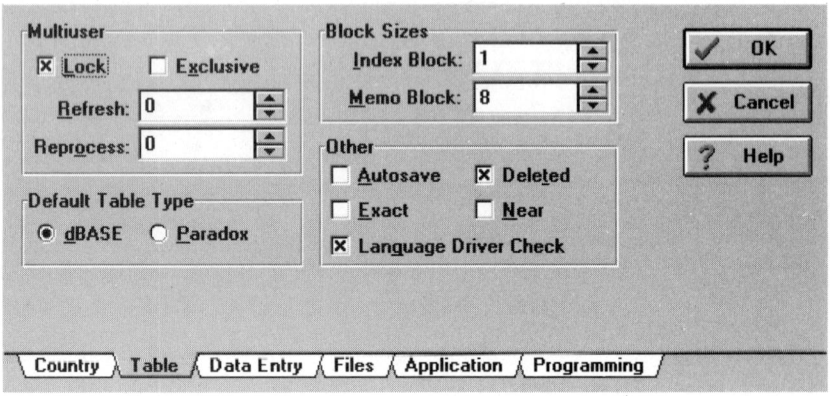

Multiuser Choices

The Table tab's Multiuser selections include check boxes for Lock and Exclusive. With Lock (the default) selected, your table records are locked when you add or update them. When Exclusive is checked, you have exclusive access, which means that no one else can use the table when you are using it.

The Refresh counter lets you set the number of seconds that elapse before any change one user makes in a database is reflected on all other users' screens (when dBASE for Windows is running on a server). The default setting, 0, does no refreshing.

The Reprocess button sets the number of times dBASE for Windows will retry access to a record or table before reporting an error. It defaults to 0, for no retries.

Default Table Type Options

You can choose either dBASE or Paradox as the default table type for dBASE for Windows. With dBASE (the default) selected, if you ask for access to your People table, for example, dBASE for Windows will get data from the PEOPLE.DBF file. If Paradox was selected as the default type, data would be read from the PEOPLE.DB file.

Choosing Block Sizes

The Block Sizes choices let you adjust the size of blocks for indexes (Index Block) and memo files (Memo Block). These adjustments allow you to make performance tradeoffs. Larger block sizes can improve performance, at the cost of wasting disk space.

Your Other Table Choices

The Other section of the Table tab includes the following check boxes:

- Autosave, which saves additions, changes, and deletions to disk after each record is processed. This helps to ensure against data loss (in case of a power outage or computer crash), but it can slow down processing.
- Exact, which determines when one character string is equal to another. If the language driver is French, for example, the letter *e* may or may not have an accent. If Exact is not checked, all the *e*'s are considered equal, regardless of accent. If Exact is checked, the letter and the accent must match.
- Language Driver Check, which warns you if your table was created with a language driver that is incompatible with the ones you have available.
- Deleted, which determines how deleted records are handled. If Deleted is checked, deleted records are not shown in your tables. If it is not checked, deleted records remain visible, with their deletion status shown in a Del column.
- Near, which controls where dBASE for Windows stops after it can't find something you've asked it to look for (with a SEEK or FIND command, for example). When Near is checked, the operation will stop at the first index entry after the target if the target cannot be found. For example, you could SEEK for "Simp" and the SEEK might stop at "Simpson." When Near is not checked, the operation will stop at the end of the file.

▶ Setting Data Entry Properties

The Data Entry tab (Properties ➤ Desktop ➤ Data Entry), shown in Figure 8.3, offers Keyboard, Delimiters, and Bell settings.

FIGURE 8.3 ▶

The Properties ➤ Desktop, Data Entry tab

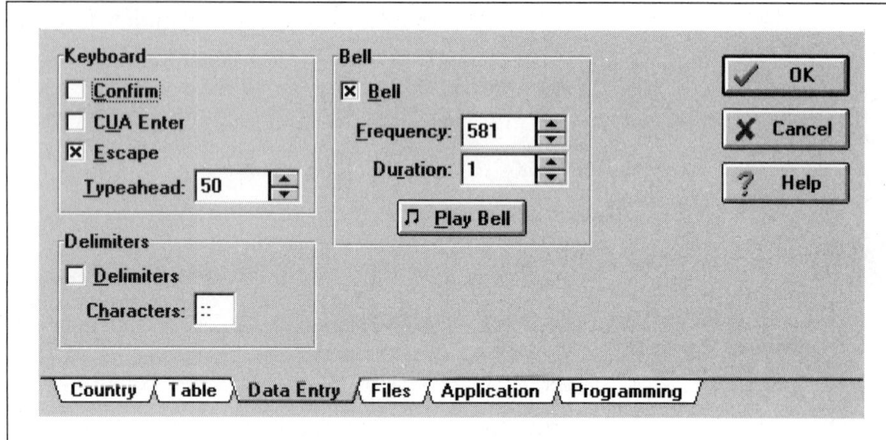

Keyboard Options

The Keyboard options include the following selections:

- Confirm, which controls whether or not the user must press a key to leave an entry field. If Confirm is checked, the user must press a key, such as Tab, after typing the last character in an entry field. If it is not checked, typing the last character immediately moves the entry point to the next entry field or next control.
- CUA Enter, which controls the effect of pressing the Enter key. Checking CUA Enter enforces the CUA default meaning for Enter, which is the same as clicking an OK pushbutton. When it is not checked, the Enter key is used to complete a field and move to the next field, which is consistent with older dBASE applications.

▶▶ **NOTE**

Checking CUA Enter maintains consistency with other Microsoft Windows applications at some cost in convenience and in breaking with dBASE's older behavior. Leaving this box unchecked is consistent with older dBASE applications and very convenient, but not consistent with other Windows applications.

- Escape, which controls the effect of pressing the Esc key. If Escape is checked, pressing the Esc key exits from the current dialog box. This is consistent with dBASE's former behavior, but is not defined to work in Windows. If this box is not checked, one of the Windows exits (such as Ctrl-F4) must be selected.
- The Typeahead spinbutton, which sets the size of the keyboard typeahead buffer.

Your Choice of Delimiters

The Delimiters choices include a check box for Delimiters and an entry field where you can specify the delimiter Characters. In dBASE IV and earlier, setting Delimiters on made dBASE put the specified characters before and after an entry field. Checking the Delimiters box here does not have this effect in dBASE for Windows forms.

Bell Selections

The selections in the Bell area set the bell's characteristics. If the Bell check box is unchecked, the bell is turned off. The Frequency spinbutton lets you choose a higher or lower note. (Middle C on a piano is about 256.) The Duration spinbutton lets you select the length of time that the bell sounds, in DOS clock ticks. A DOS clock tick happens about 18.2 times every second.

▶▶ **TIP**

We like the bell—it rings when you come to the end of an entry field, among other places. But a short, high bell (1 tick at 1000 Hz) is all it takes.

The Play Bell pushbutton lets you test the choices you have made.

▶ Setting File Properties

The Files tab (Properties ➤ Desktop ➤ Files), shown in Figure 8.4, offers Location, Editors, Edit Records, Add Records, and Other settings.

FIGURE 8.4 ▶

The Properties ➤ Desktop, Files tab

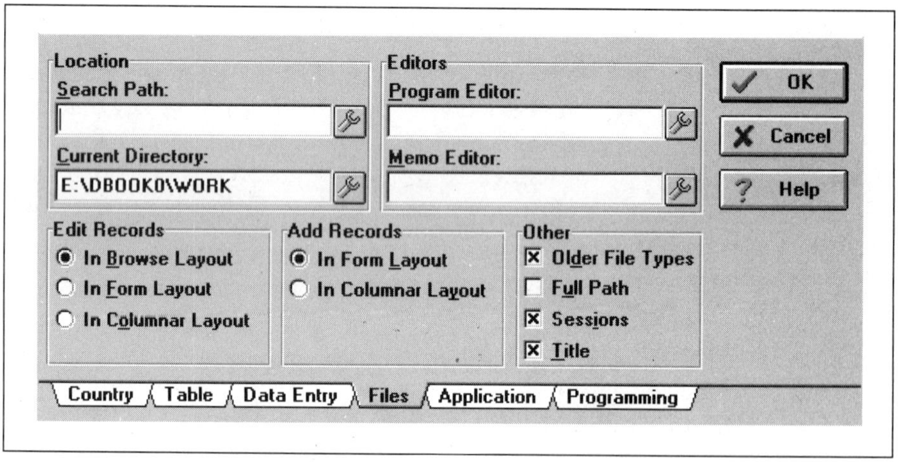

Choosing Locations

The Location section has two entry fields: Search Path and Current Directory. Each entry field has a pushbutton with the tool icon to its right. You can click on this button if you want to go into the Choose Directory dialog box. Alternatively, you can simply type the directory (with optional drive specification) in the entry field.

dBASE for Windows will look for files that are not qualified with a directory specification in the current directory first. If it does not find them, it will continue looking through any directories in the search path, in the order you specify them.

Choosing Editors

The Editors area has two entry fields: Program Editor and Memo Editor. As with the Location selections, each field has the tool icon pushbutton to its right. Clicking on the icon takes you to a Choose File dialog box. Alternatively, you can type the name of the editor in the entry field.

Edit Records Choices

The Edit Records section lets you select the default way to look at a table in Run mode. The three radio buttons show your choices:

- In Browse Layout
- In Form Layout
- In Columnar Layout

Add Records Choices

The Add Records section lets you choose the default view for adding new records. The two radio buttons show your choices:

- In Form Layout
- In Columnar Layout

The Form Layout choice is generally better, unless you normally have more fields than will fit on a screen.

Other Selections

The Other selections include four check boxes:

- Older File Types, which controls the file types that appear in file lists.
- Full Path, which is useful to dBASE programmers. If checked, it tells functions that return a file name to return the full path along with the name.
- Sessions, which can be turned off if you need to emulate a dBASE III or older dBASE version. With Sessions on, each table you launch runs in a separate session, as if you were multiple users.
- Title, which turns on prompting for item descriptions when you use a catalog.

If Ol<u>d</u>er File Types is checked, the list of dBASE file types includes the following:

- View (*.VUE)
- Filter (*.QRY)
- Format (*.FMT)
- dBASE/DOS Report (*.FRM)
- dBASE/DOS Label (*.LBG)
- dBASE/DOS Label (*.LBL)
- dBASE/DOS Report (*.FRG)

These types are included to support dBASE IV and earlier systems. They are not used in Microsoft Windows programs. If this box is not checked, these file types are not shown in the file lists.

▶ Setting Application Properties

The Application tab (Properties ➤ Desktop ➤ Application), shown in Figure 8.5, offers Speedbar Position, Status Bar, and Other settings.

FIGURE 8.5

The Properties ➤ Desktop, Application tab

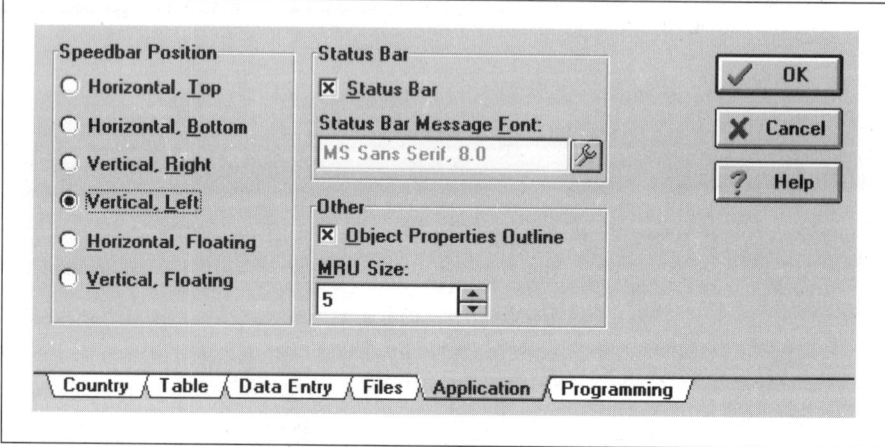

Speedbar Position Choices

For Speedbar Position, you have six choices for positioning the speedbar:

- Horizontal, Top
- Horizontal, Bottom
- Vertical, Right
- Vertical, Left
- Horizontal, Floating
- Vertical, Floating

Vertical speedbars lose the end icons: Tutor, Expert, Command, and Navigator. (You can use Window ➤ 1 for the Navigator and Window ➤ 2 for the Command window.) The floating speedbars can be dragged with the mouse.

▶▶ TIP

We prefer a horizontal speedbar for most use. The one exception is when we are programming. Then we use a vertical speedbar, because it gives us a few more lines of code in the Program Editor.

Status Bar Choices

The Status Bar check box controls whether not the status bar appears. You can uncheck it if you want to turn the status bar off. The entry field, Status Bar Message Font, shows the currently selected font. You can select another font for the status bar. Clicking on the tool pushbutton to the right of this field opens the Font dialog box.

Other Selections

The Object Properties Outline check box in the Other section controls the appearance of the Object Properties Inspectors. Unchecking it turns the outlining feature off in the Object Properties Inspector. All the object's properties (and events and methods) are shown in a single, long list.

TIP

Turning off the outlining feature might be useful if you're teaching a class and want to simplify the Object Properties Inspector tool for beginners.

The MRU Size spinbutton controls the number of MRU files that you can access as 1, 2, and so on in the File menu.

▶ Setting Programming Properties

The Programming tab (Properties ➤ Desktop ➤ Programming), shown in Figure 8.6, offers Command Output, Program Development, and Other settings.

FIGURE 8.6 

The Properties ➤ Desktop, Programming tab

Command Output
Decimals: 4
Precision: 16
Margin: 0
[X] Space
[ ] Talk
[X] Headings
Program Development
[ ] Coverage
[X] Ensure Compilation
Other
[X] Design
[X] Safety
OK
Cancel
Help
Country | Table | Data Entry | Files | Application | Programming

Command Output Choices

The Command Output area has the following spinbutton choices:

- Decimals, which specifies the number of decimals to display when showing numbers. The default is 2, and the range is 0 to 18. Internally, dBASE for Windows stores floating-point numbers accurate to 15 decimal places, regardless of the setting of Decimals.

- Precision, which sets the number of decimal places dBASE for Windows stores for Numeric data (not for Float data). This defaults to 16 and ranges from 10 to 20.
- Margin, which establishes a default left margin for printed output. It defaults to 0 and ranges from 0 to 254. Crystal Reports handles margins when you use that tool. This setting affects your dBASE for Windows File ➤ Print printouts.

The Command Output section also includes three check boxes:

- Space, which determines whether the output of ? and ?? commands inserts a space between items in the command's parameter list (for example, between names when you give the command `? First_name, Last_name`). This setting is retained for compatibility with dBASE IV and earlier programs.
- Talk, which controls whether or not results are shown in the Command window's results pane. It is on by default. If it is checked, it directs the results of assignment statements in programs and in the Command window to the results pane of the Command window. For example, if you entered x=2+2 in the Command window, the number 4 would show in the results pane if this option is checked.
- Headings, which controls the use of field names over columns displayed with commands such as LIST and SUM. By default, it is on, and field names are used as column headings.

Program Development Choices

The Program Development section has two check boxes. Coverage turns on the program coverage feature, which programmers use to get a detailed analysis of which parts of their programs are most heavily used.

The Ensure Compilation setting is also used by programmers. With this box checked, dBASE for Windows will always check to see if a program source file (such as a .PRG or .WFM file) has been modified since the corresponding object file (.PRO or .WFO file) was created. If the program source has been changed, dBASE for Windows will recompile the source, creating a new object version.

If you are not developing programs by directly editing .PRG files, leaving Ensure Compilation checked only slows down dBASE for Windows. The tools that create programs for you, such as the Form Designer, handle compilation.

Other Choices

The Other section has Design and Safety check boxes, which are both checked by default. If Design is not checked, the Design abilities of dBASE for Windows are turned off (presumably, for users who only run a system created by others). With Safety checked, operations that could destroy existing data (creating a new file which has the same name as an existing file, for instance) trigger a warning dialog box.

▸▸ WARNING

Always leave Safety checked, for safety's sake! Sometimes programs will turn safety off temporarily (for example, to create a TEMP.DBF for some temporary data, deliberately overwriting the previous TEMP.DBF) but Safety will save you from a lot of mistakes.

▸▸ Using the Window Menu

The Window menu has these options:

- Cascade (Shift-F5)
- Tile Horizontally
- Tile Vertically (Shift-F4)
- Arrange Icons
- Close All Windows
- 1 Navigator
- 2 Command
- 3 (and higher) your windows

▶ Arranging Your Windows

The Cascade, Tile Horizontally, and Tile Vertically options make neat (if not always helpful) arrangements of your windows. If you have not used this feature in other Microsoft Windows programs, open several windows and try it. Figure 8.7 shows cascaded windows. Figures 8.8 and 8.9 show tiled arrangements.

FIGURE 8.7 ▶

Cascaded windows

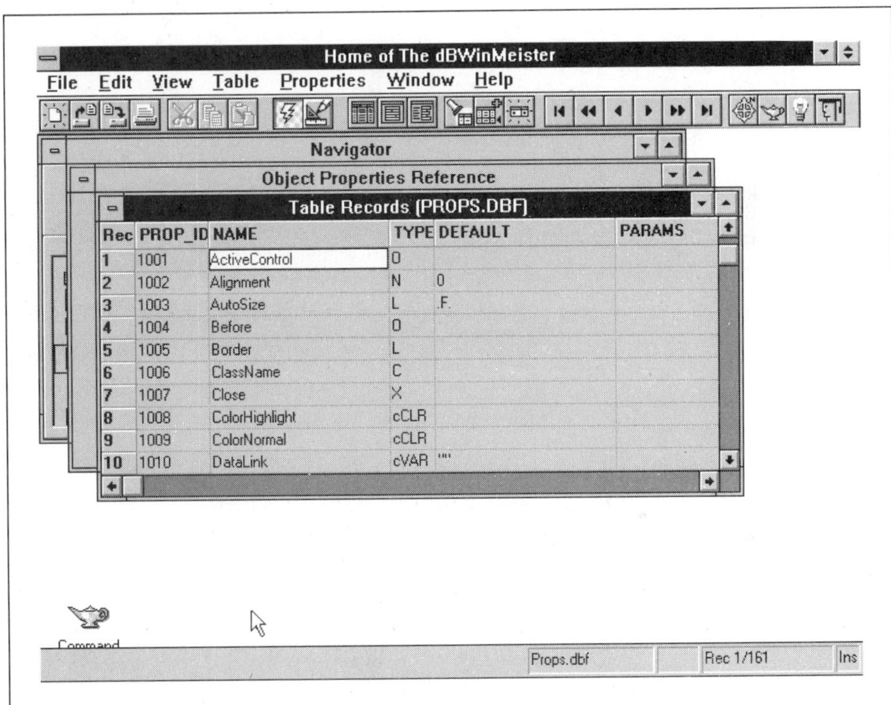

The Arrange Icons option makes a neat arrangement of your icons. Figures 8.10 and 8.11 show a before-and-after example of using this option.

▶ Closing and Opening Windows

The Close All Windows option does just what it says. You don't need to worry about saving your work. If any window contains new or changed

FIGURE 8.8 ▶

Horizontally tiled windows

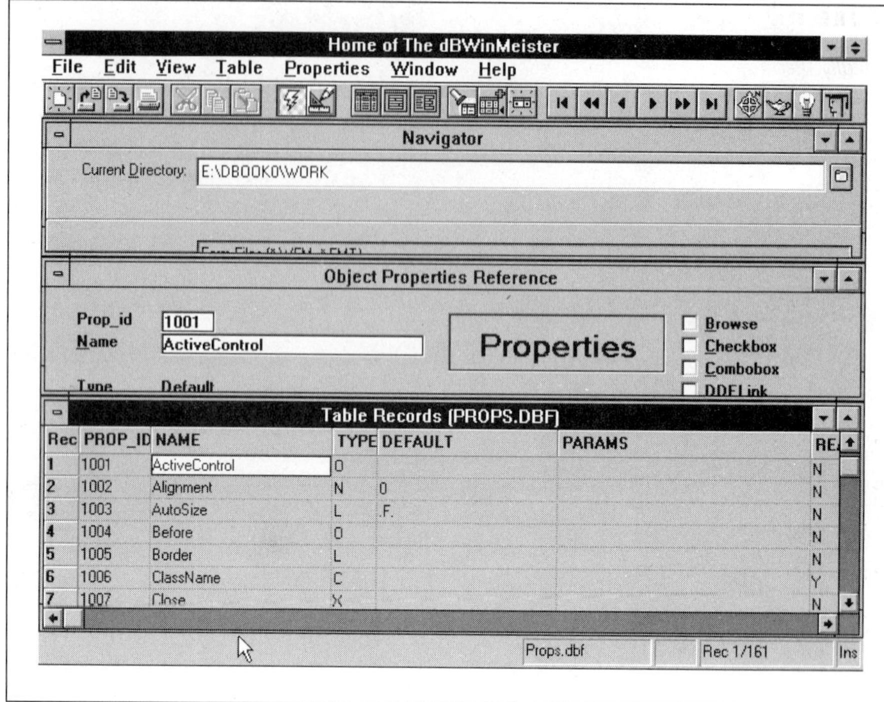

data, dBASE for Windows will ask you if you want to save the file before closing. This is the same close procedure that takes place when you exit from dBASE for Windows.

Window 1 is always the Navigator window. Choosing Window ➤ 1 brings the Navigator into focus on top of any other open windows. Similarly, window 2 is the Command window, which can be given focus by choosing Window ➤ 2.

The remaining numbers are for your open child windows. If you have more than seven child windows (nine, including Navigator and Command), an additional menu option appears: More Windows. Selecting

FIGURE 8.9

Vertically tiled windows

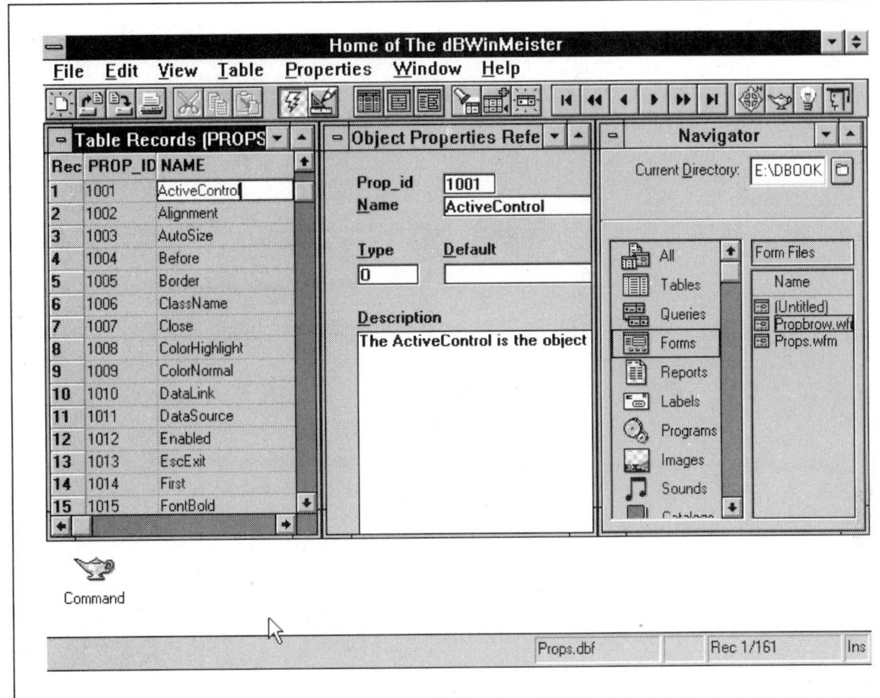

this option opens the Select Window dialog box, which will look something like this:

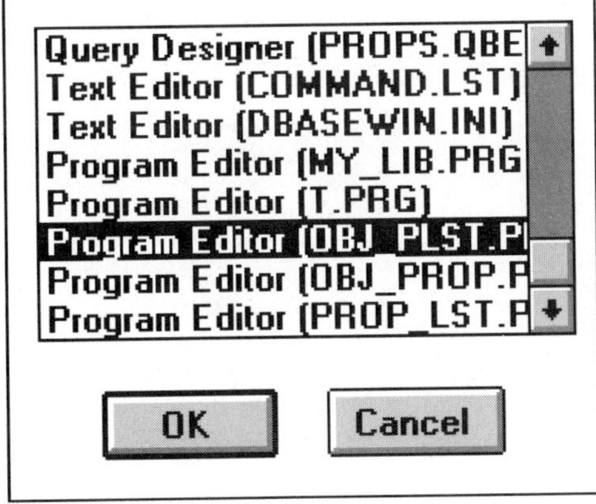

FIGURE 8.10

Before Arrange Icons

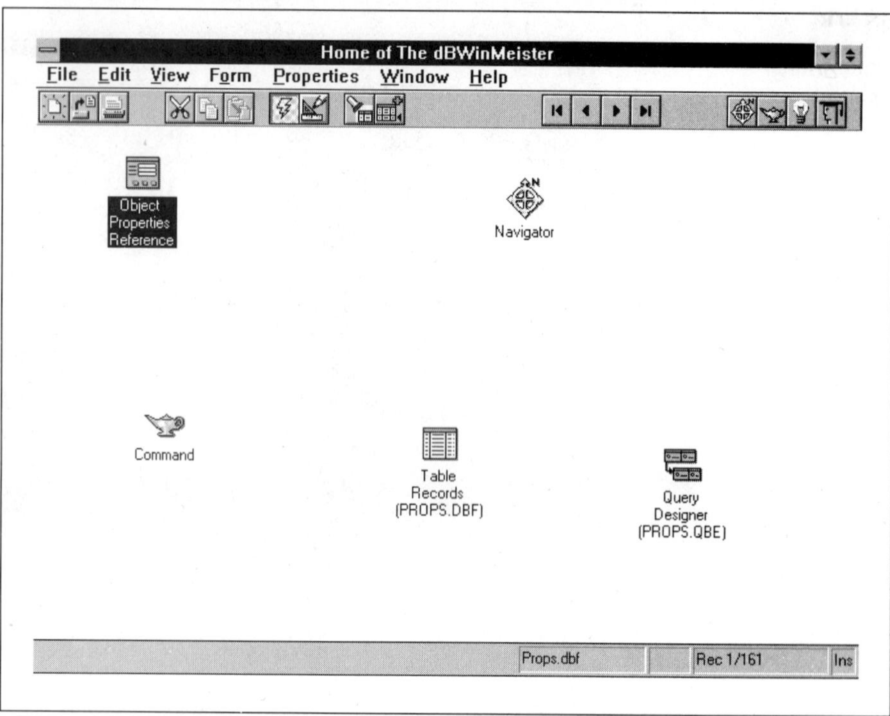

▸▸ Using the Help Menu

The Help menu has these options:

- Contents (Shift-F1)
- Search ...
- Views and Tools
- Language
- Keyboard
- Experts
- Interactive Tutors ...
- How to Use Help
- About dBASE 5.0 for Windows ...

FIGURE 8.11

After Arrange Icons

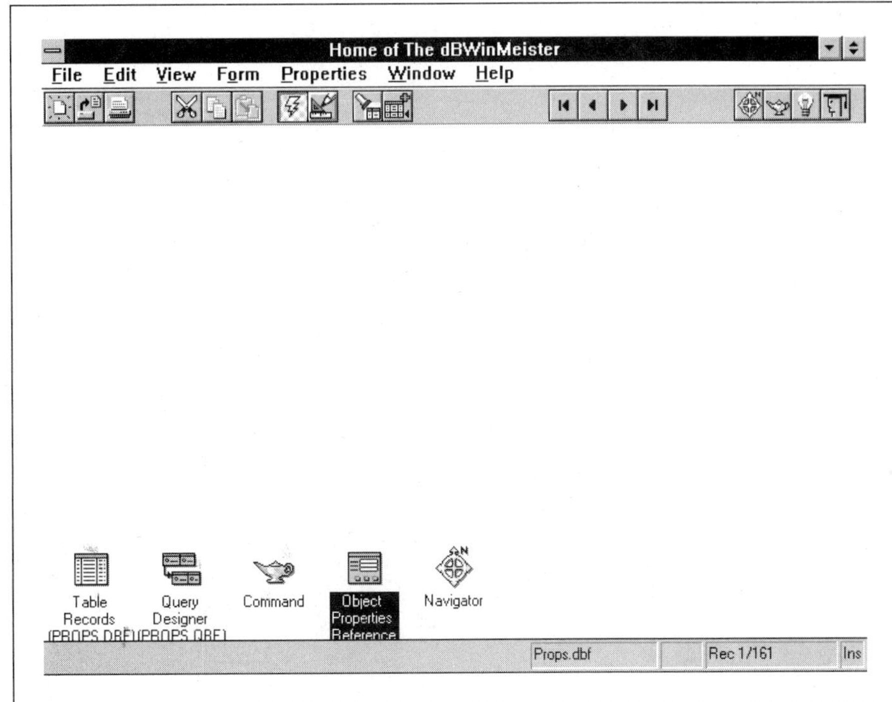

You can go immediately to the Table of Contents by choosing the Contents option (or by pressing Shift-F1). The Search … option brings up Windows' Search dialog box.

The Views and Tools, Language, and Keyboard options name three of the most commonly accessed sections in the Table of Contents. Choosing Keyboard, for example, is the same as choosing the Keyboard topic from the Table of Contents.

The Experts option brings up the Experts submenu. From this menu you can choose the Form Expert.

The Interactive Tutors … choice takes you to the main menu of the Tutors. This is the same as clicking on the tutor button on the speedbar (the one on far right).

The How to Use Help choice takes you into this topic in Windows' Help system.

The About dBASE 5.0 for Windows … brings up an information window, such as the one shown in Figure 8.12.

FIGURE 8.12

About dBASE for Windows

▸▸ Working with the Navigator

The Navigator, an MDI child window, is a simple, powerful tool for directing all your work in dBASE for Windows. You can operate it fully with only a mouse, and you can operate it fully with only a keyboard. (In fact, there are two different ways to drive it from the keyboard!) Of course, you can combine the two.

There are three main areas in the Navigator window:

- Directory area
- File Types menu
- Files list

Changes in Navigator settings can substantially impact the appearance of your Navigator. Compare the Navigators shown in Figures 8.13 and 8.14 to see just how different these can be. You can control the appearance of

FIGURE 8.13

One Navigator

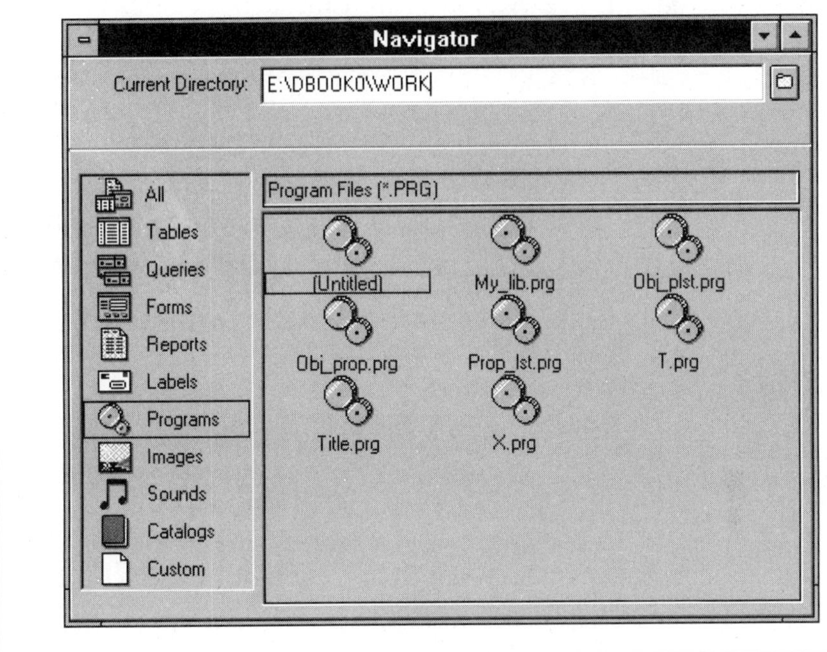

FIGURE 8.14

A different Navigator

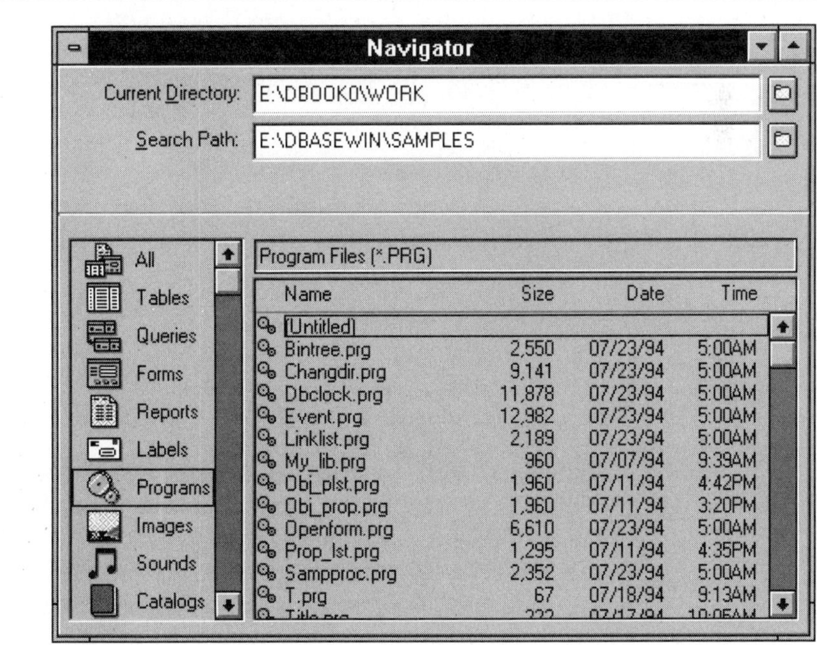

the Navigator window through the Properties ➤ Navigator choice, as discussed later in this chapter.

▶ The Directory Area

The directory area, the top part of the Navigator, has one or two entry fields, Current Directory and Search Path. The pushbuttons to the right of each entry field access the Choose Directory dialog box, which lets you choose a different directory than the current one. Its icon is a file folder (we think; we're not sure that miniscule icons are terribly helpful).

The Current Directory

The current directory is the directory in which you're storing your work for a particular project. If you're working on multiple projects, you simply switch from one current directory to another, to switch projects. The Navigator will change all its files accordingly. (See Appendix C for information about using multiple DBWIN.INI files for different projects.)

You can type the directory into the entry field, or choose the pushbutton to access the directory list. You can click the pushbutton, or tab to it and press the spacebar (or Enter).

▶▶ TIP

In the directory list, the spacebar functions like a mouse click, and the Enter key functions like a double-click. For example, pressing the spacebar will expand a directory or, if the directory is expanded, hide the subdirectories.

The Search Path

The Search Path entry field and pushbutton are shown if the Use Supplemental Search Path check box is selected in the Navigator's Properties dialog box. dBASE for Windows will look at all files in the current directory, and in the Search Path directory. One common use for a supplemental path is to use local programs to access data on a network drive.

You can have more than one supplemental directory. Type them into the entry field, separated by commas. (Don't use the Choose Directory dialog box, because that overwrites anything in the entry field with a single choice.)

▶ The File Types Menu

The file types list on the left side of the Navigator window is a custom menu (a slick, Borland-designed menu, not standard Windows) that lists the different types of files you can manipulate:

- All
- Tables
- Queries
- Forms
- Reports
- Labels
- Programs
- Images
- Sounds
- Catalogs
- Custom

Since each type of file corresponds to a major functional area of dBASE for Windows, this lets you control your dBASE for Windows work by picking files.

You can select a file type by clicking on it in this menu. With the keyboard, you can press Tab to reach this menu, then use the ↑ and ↓ keys to select a particular type, or type the first letter in the file type to move to that type.

▶ The Files List

The files list is in the area to the right of the file type menu. This has two parts: a title line and the list itself.

The title line reflects the choice you made in the file type menu. The file name extensions that appear depend on whether or not the Older File Types check box in the Desktop Properties Files tab is checked, as follows:

File Types	**With Older File Types On**	**With Older File Types Off**
dBASE files	All	All
Table files	*.DBF, *.DB	*.DBF, *.DB
Query files	*.QBE, *.VUE, *.QRY	*.QBE
Form files	*.WFM, *.FMT	*.WFM
Report files	*.RPT, *.RPC, *.FRM, *.FRG	*.RPT, *.RPC
Label files	*.RPL, *.LBL, *.LBG	*.RPL
Program files	*.PRG	*.PRG
Image files	*.BMP, *.PCX	*.BMP, *.PCX
Sound files	*.WAV	*.WAV
Catalog files	*.CAT	*.CAT

If you have selected Custom files, an entry field follows the text *Custom Files:*. You can enter any other file type(s) you wish here. Enter them as DOS file masks (for example, in the format *.*XXX*). You can enter multiple types, separated by commas.

The list itself includes your files, of whatever type you chose. The appearance of this listing is determined by your selection in the View menu. Here's the list with large icons:

Here's the same list with small icons:

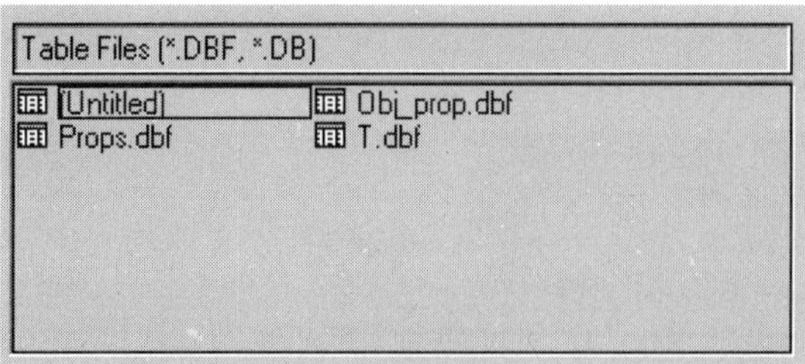

And here's what it looks like when Details is selected:

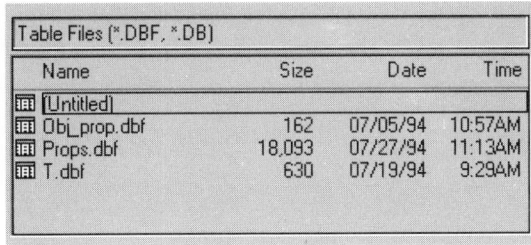

Table Files (*.DBF, *.DB)

Name	Size	Date	Time
(Untitled)			
Obj_prop.dbf	162	07/05/94	10:57AM
Props.dbf	18,093	07/27/94	11:13AM
T.dbf	630	07/19/94	9:29AM

As you can see, each option shows an icon and file name. The details version adds file size, and the date and time of last update, as well.

In this list, you can choose a file by clicking on it or by moving to it using the arrow keys. Alternatively, you can type the first letter of the file name to move to it. (Tab and Shift-Tab move from the file types menu to the files list.)

Double-clicking on a file launches it in Run mode. For example, double-clicking on a form (.WFM file) runs the form. Double right-clicking brings up a file in Design mode. Right-clicking brings up a Speed menu. You can press F2 to run the selected file. Pressing Shift-F2 launches the file in Design mode.

▶ Using the Navigator Main Menu

The File, Window, and Help menus are not changed in the Navigator. Two new menu choices are added, and the Edit and Properties choices are changed. The new menu options are View and Navigator.

The Edit menu has one additional choice in the Navigator: Delete, with Del as the shortcut key. When an Untitled file is selected in the files list, this choice is grayed (not available). When a named file is selected, choosing this option will delete the selected file.

Files can also be deleted from the Speed menu. Right-click on the file, then click on Delete.

Using the View Menu

The Navigator's View menu looks like this:

The choice corresponding to the currently selected file type is checked. A second check indicates which of the display options (Large Icons, Small Icons, or Details) is currently selected.

View gives you a keyboard shortcut for selecting a file type. For Queries, for example, press Alt-V, then Q.

The last three choices control the files list display, selecting the displays shown earlier, in the section about the files list.

The Sort choice displays this submenu:

√ by Name
by Type and Extension
by Size
by Date and Time

These options control the order in which your files are displayed in the files list.

Using the Navigator Menu

The Navigator menu generally has a New option, and it always has a Refresh Items option. The Refresh Items option forces the Navigator to reexamine the current and search path directories for files that may have appeared since the last time the Navigator looked. For example, you might use this option after you run a form that creates or deletes other files.

The New choice depends on the type of file selected in the files list, and whether it is a named file or Untitled. For untitled files, the new choice is the type of file, such as New Table when the Table type is selected, or New Query when the Query type is selected. The shortcut key is Shift-F2 for all the new file types. When the type is Reports, an additional choice is New Cross-Tab. The New Catalog choice leads to the Create Catalog dialog box. The default type is *.CAT. For the Custom type, the choices are Design Menu (Shift-F2) and Edit As Program.

For named files, the Navigator menu choices are as follows:

- **Tables:** Edit Records (F2), Add Records, and Design Table Structure (Shift-F2)
- **Queries:** Run Query (F2), Design Query (Shift-F2), and Edit as Program
- **Forms:** Run Form (F2), Design Form (Shift-F2), and Edit as Program
- **Reports:** Run Report (F2) and Design Report (Shift-F2)

- **Labels:** Run Labels (F2) and Design Labels (Shift-F2)
- **Programs:** Do (F2), Debug, and Design Program (Shift-F2)
- **Images:** Display Image (F2) and Design Image (Shift-F2)
- **Sounds:** Play Sound (F2) and Design Sound (Shift-F2)
- **Catalogs:** Open Catalog (F2)
- **Custom:** The choices vary depending on the file extension.

► Using the Navigator's Properties Menu

In the Navigator, the Properties menu has the standard Desktop choice (discussed earlier in the chapter) plus the Navigator … and Selected File Item … (Alt-Enter) choices.

Setting Navigator Properties

Choosing Properties ➤ Navigator displays the Navigator Properties dialog box. This is a single tab with three sections: Large Icons, Small Icons, and Details.

The Large Icons choices include two spinbuttons. One lets you adjust the X Spacing (horizontal), and the other is for adjusting the Y Spacing (vertical). These spacings are in pixels. The X default is 100; the Y default is 47.

The Small Icons choices are similar. Its two spinbuttons are X Spacing and Y Spacing. These default to 117 and 13, respectively. The small icons are wider, but very short, because the file name appears to the right of the small icon.

The Details section has just one spinbutton, for Y Spacing, which defaults to 13. If you have lots of files to list, it can be reduced to its minimum: 12.

The Navigator Properties dialog box also has a Use Supplemental Search Path check box. As discussed earlier, checking this box enables the supplemental path and adds the Search Path entry field to the Navigator window.

In addition to the three normal pushbuttons (OK, Cancel, and Help), a fourth pushbutton, Reset, is added. This lets you reset the spacings to their original default values.

Selected File Items

When you choose Properties ➤ Selected File Item, you see a dialog box giving details about the file. A sample is shown in Figure 8.15. This dialog box is also available from the Speed menu and by selecting a file and pressing Alt-Enter.

FIGURE 8.15 ▶

File Item Properties dialog box

▶ The Navigator Speed Menus

The Navigator has a Speed menu that you can access by right-clicking in the Navigator window, anywhere outside the files list rectangle. This Speed menu has the following choices:

- Navigator Properties ...
- Cut (Ctrl-X)
- Copy (Ctrl-C)
- Paste (Ctrl-V)

Choosing Navigator Properties is just like choosing Properties ➤ Navigator from the main menu. It accesses the Navigator Properties dialog box.

The Clipboard-related choices apply to text in the three entry fields (Current Directory, Search Path, and Custom Files).

Navigator Files List Speed Menus

If you right-click on any file in the Navigator's files list, you'll see a Speed menu for the type of file you have selected. There are separate Speed menus for the Untitled and for the named files in the files list.

With an Untitled choice, the only option on its Speed menu is to create one. For example, when the file type is Tables, the Speed menu will have the choice New Table (Shift-F2).

The Speed menus for named files have the following choices:

- **Tables Speed menu:** Table Properties … (Alt-Enter), Delete (Del), Edit Records (F2), Add Records, and Design Table Structure (Shift-F2)
- **Queries Speed menu:** Query Properties … (Alt-Enter), Delete (Del), Run Query (F2), Design Query (Shift-F2), and Edit as Program
- **Forms Speed menu:** Form Properties … ((Alt-Enter)), Delete (Del), Run Form (F2), Design Form (Shift-F2), and Edit as Program
- **Reports Speed menu:** Report Properties … (Alt-Enter), Delete (Del), Run Report (F2), and Design Report (Shift-F2)
- **Labels Speed menu:** Label Properties … (Alt-Enter), Delete (Del), Run Labels (F2), and Design Labels (Shift-F2)
- **Programs Speed menu:** Program Properties … (Alt-Enter), Delete (Del), Do (F2), Debug, and Design Program (Shift-F2)
- **Images Speed menu:** Image Properties … (Alt-Enter), Delete (Del), Display Image (F2), and Design Image (Shift-F2)
- **Sounds Speed menu:** Sound Properties … (Alt-Enter), Delete (Del), Play Sound (F2), and Design Sound (Shift-F2)
- **Catalogs Speed menu:** Catalog Properties … (Alt-Enter), Delete (Del), and Open Catalog (F2)
- **Custom Speed menu:** Depends on the type of file selected

►► The Other Navigators: Catalogs

Some work can be organized conveniently in disk directories. We've used our \DBWORK directory to organize our phone list system by keeping it all in one place. There are times when this works well, and there are times when it doesn't work. Here are a few examples of situations in which you wouldn't be able to keep all your system's files in the same directory:

- You may have tables that are critical to several systems. If the systems each have several forms and reports, keeping them all together in a single directory leads to a situation that is, at best, difficult to manage. (Take a look at your \WINDOWS directory to see what happens when you have far too many files in one place.)
- You may develop or acquire libraries of useful routines and functions that you want to use in several systems. Again, you'll need to draw work from multiple directories into a single system.
- If you're working on a network, your forms may be local while your tables are remote.

In each of these situations, the catalog is your answer.

You can think of a catalog as a Navigator that is not built from the files in a directory (or a directory plus a search path). A catalog is assembled from whatever components you choose. With a catalog, you can have forms in one location, library routines in another place, and data spread over one or more local and remote drives. Whatever organization makes sense for your work makes a fine catalog.

► The Catalog Window

Figure 8.16 shows a catalog that we constructed for our phone list system, active over the Navigator.

Our Navigator is using a default working directory on the E: drive. As you can see, the catalog does not depend on the current directory or supplemental search path setting.

FIGURE 8.16

The catalog is a type of Navigator

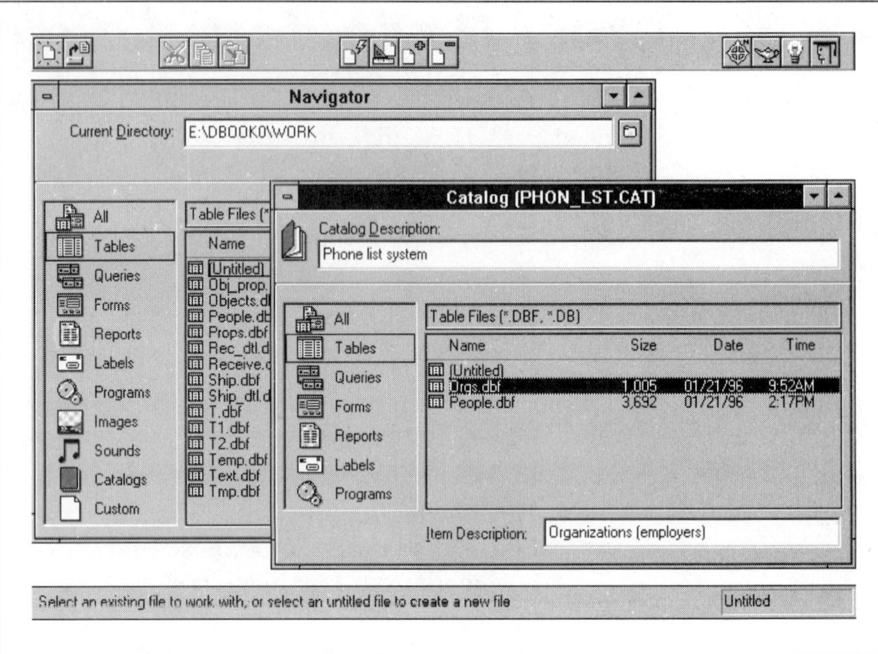

The catalog itself shows a system description where the Navigator shows a directory. On the lower right, it shows a description of the individual catalog item.

You can see that the Navigator includes more file types than the catalog does. The following types are not available in a catalog:

- Images
- Sounds
- Catalogs
- Custom

When you include images and sounds in your forms or reports, they are linked with the item to which you attach them, so they can be part of your system, even though they are not listed in the catalog.

▶▶ **NOTE**

You obviously don't need a Catalog file type inside a catalog, but we do miss the Custom file type. We like including *.MNU or whatever else is needed in the Custom section, a capability that you lose with a catalog.

▶ Building a Catalog

Creating a catalog is no different than creating any other item from the Navigator. Pick the Catalog type, select the Untitled entry, and press F2 or double-click.

This launches the Create Catalog dialog box. You enter a name (optionally changing the drive and directory), and press Enter or click on OK.

Next, you go to the Catalog Item Description dialog box, shown in Figure 8.17. This dialog box appears, appropriately labeled, for the catalog and for every item that you enter in the catalog. Type in a description and select OK.

FIGURE 8.17 ▶

Entering a description for the catalog

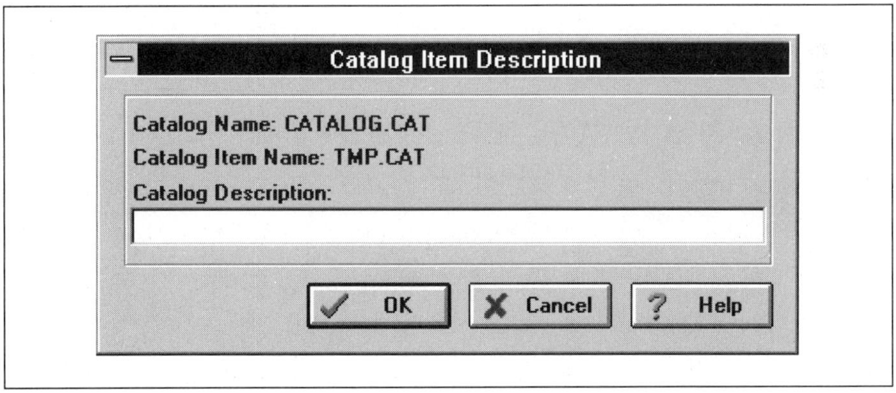

TIP

Don't labor over the descriptions. The catalog fields that display the catalog and item descriptions are entry fields, so you can add to or change the descriptions whenever you see them.

▸ *Adding Items to the Catalog*

There are several ways to add items to the catalog. The simplest way is to open the catalog and leave it open as you continue your work. You can minimize it to an icon so that it doesn't get in your way.

As you open tables, queries, and so on, each one is added to your catalog. If the item is not part of the catalog, the Catalog Item Description dialog box is launched so you can add a description.

You can click the Cancel pushbutton if you do not want to add a description, but the selected item will still be added to your catalog. We're not sure if this is a bug or a feature. If you don't want an item in your catalog, select it and choose Delete from the Speed menu.

After you choose Delete from a catalog, you'll see two dialog boxes in succession. The first one asks you if you want to delete the item from the catalog. If you say yes, the next dialog asks you if you want to delete it from your disk. Obviously, you can say no in the second dialog box if you want to save the item but remove it from the current catalog.

With your catalog active, these are the other ways you can add an item to that catalog:

- Click on the add a file speedbar button (shown in the margin).
- Choose Catalog ➤ Add Item ....
- Press Ctrl-A.
- With the mouse, drag the file from the Navigator to the catalog.

Each of these actions launches the Add Catalog Item dialog box. Select a file from this dialog box, and dBASE for Windows will open the Catalog Item Description dialog box so you can add a description.

▶ Using a Catalog

Using a catalog is essentially the same as using the Navigator. There are some minor differences, however. First, the Navigator menu choice is replaced by the Catalog menu choice. The choices in the Catalog menu are the ones that are appropriate to the item selected in the catalog. For example, here are the choices that are available when the Tables file type is selected:

Edit Records	F2
Add Records	
Design Table Structure	Shift+F2
Add Item...	Ctrl+A

When a catalog is active, the Properties menu has the Catalog Window... choice. If you select this choice, it launches the Catalog Properties dialog box, which is identical, except for the title and the absence of the Use Supplemental Search Path check box, to the Navigator Properties dialog box.

Another difference is that the add a file speedbar button is located just to the left of the delete file button. With the Navigator active, you add files by creating them. With a catalog, you add existing files (or create new ones).

▶ The Catalog Is a Table

The catalog that is created is stored as a table on your disk, like any other dBASE for Windows table, except that the extension is .CAT, not .DBF. To launch a catalog as a table, in the Command window, give these commands:

```
USE catalogname.cat
BROWSE
```

You must provide the .CAT extension to the USE command, because it defaults to a .DBF of .DB table.

When you give these two commands, the Table Records tool is launched with your catalog data. Ours is shown in Figure 8.18.

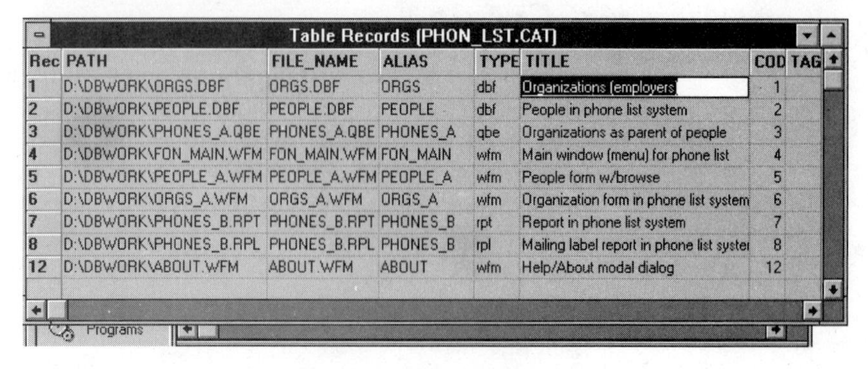

Table Records (PHON_LST.CAT)

Rec	PATH	FILE_NAME	ALIAS	TYPE	TITLE	COD	TAG
1	D:\DBWORK\ORGS.DBF	ORGS.DBF	ORGS	dbf	Organizations (employers)	1	
2	D:\DBWORK\PEOPLE.DBF	PEOPLE.DBF	PEOPLE	dbf	People in phone list system	2	
3	D:\DBWORK\PHONES_A.QBE	PHONES_A.QBE	PHONES_A	qbe	Organizations as parent of people	3	
4	D:\DBWORK\FON_MAIN.WFM	FON_MAIN.WFM	FON_MAIN	wfm	Main window (menu) for phone list	4	
5	D:\DBWORK\PEOPLE_A.WFM	PEOPLE_A.WFM	PEOPLE_A	wfm	People form w/browse	5	
6	D:\DBWORK\ORGS_A.WFM	ORGS_A.WFM	ORGS_A	wfm	Organization form in phone list system	6	
7	D:\DBWORK\PHONES_B.RPT	PHONES_B.RPT	PHONES_B	rpt	Report in phone list system	7	
8	D:\DBWORK\PHONES_B.RPL	PHONES_B.RPL	PHONES_B	rpl	Mailing label report in phone list syste	8	
12	D:\DBWORK\ABOUT.WFM	ABOUT.WFM	ABOUT	wfm	Help/About modal dialog	12	

FIGURE 8.18

Browsing a catalog

▸▸ Working in the Command Window

The Command window is always available from the speedbar, via the Aladdin's lamp button, or from the keyboard as Window ➤ 2. A sample Command window is shown in Figure 8.19.

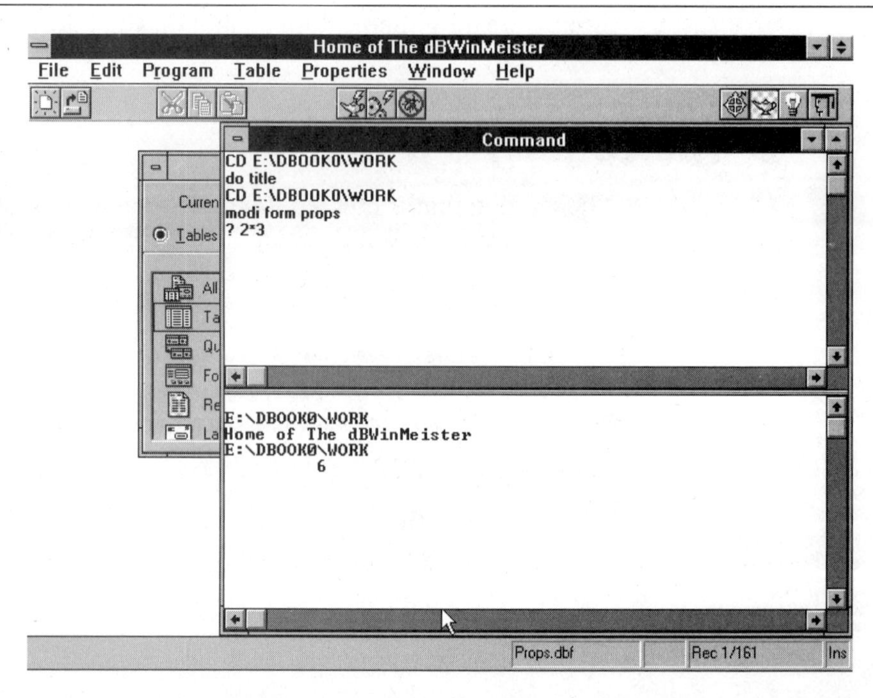

FIGURE 8.19

One Command window setup

The Command window provides an alternative to the Navigator for driving dBASE for Windows. Most dBASE for Windows users will operate from the Navigator for most operations, because it's a much friendlier tool. On the other hand, while the Navigator provides ease of use, the Command window provides *total* power for the true dBASE for Windows master.

The end result of most dBASE for Windows operations is a command given to the dBASE engine. These commands are echoed, as native dBASE commands, to the Command window, as you may have noticed while you worked in the Navigator.

The Command window has two panes, which default to the arrangement shown in Figure 8.19. The top pane is for input, and the bottom pane shows the results of commands given in the input pane.

You can drag the bar between the panes to divide the window into proportions that suit your requirements. The window can be mostly commands, with a tiny results pane, or vice versa. When a dBASE for Windows program (.PRG file) is running, the input pane disappears, and the results pane shows all non-Windows output.

NOTE

dBASE IV and older systems run in the results pane of the Command window.

Entering Commands in the Input Pane

The input pane is a memory-only text editor. You type a command, and it executes immediately. As you accumulate commands, you add text. This text can be cut or copied into the Clipboard, and commands can be pasted in from the Clipboard. Through the Command window menus, you can bypass the Clipboard, reading and writing directly from .PRG files or other files.

When the Command window is active, the input pane is active by default. If you switch focus to the results pane (for example, by selecting results to copy into the Clipboard), you can just click in the input pane to position the insertion point (I-beam) wherever you want.

The ? Command

One of the simplest dBASE for Windows commands is the ? command, which you've met in earlier chapters. The ? command writes the results of any valid dBASE for Windows expression into the results pane. Here are some expressions you can try typing in the input pane:

```
? 2+2
? 'John ' + 'Smith'
? DATE()
? DATE()+1
? LEFT('abcdefg',3)
? 'Mary' + 1
```

The last one gives you an error.

▸▸ **NOTE**

You can build expressions in the Expression Builder, which is covered later in this chapter, or just type them in directly.

Most of today's dBASE programmers got started programming by typing simple commands in the dBASE dot prompt environment, which was the predecessor to the Command window. Most of tomorrow's dBASE programmers will get their start typing commands in the Command window. It's a wonderful place to try things out. The ? command is used constantly by experienced dBASE users and programmers to try expressions out.

The MODIFY Command

Another command commonly used in the input pane is MODIFY. The full command is:

MODIFY *<file type>* *<file name>*

For example, you could give any of the following commands (assuming you have file with these names):

```
MODIFY FORM people.wfm
MODIFY QUERY people.qbe
MODIFY REPORT people.rpt
MODIFY LABEL people.rpl
```

```
MODIFY COMMAND people.prg
MODIFY FILE any.txt
```

dBASE for Windows commands are not case-sensitive. They can all be abbreviated to just their first four letters. Additionally, most of the file extensions above are implied by the object type. These are the commands as a dBASE master would really enter them:

```
modi form people
modi quer people
modi repo people
modi labe people
modi comm people
modi file any.txt
```

The USE Command

To use a data table in the Command window, you give a USE command. Your subsequent table commands apply to that table. These are some typical examples:

```
USE e:\dbmaster\people.dbf
MODIFY STRUCTURE
BROWSE
DO people.wfm
```

The DO command runs a program, form, or report.

If your current directory includes the file, you don't need the drive and directory specification. Additionally, the USE command implies the .DBF file type, so you can omit the extension. Again, you can abbreviate to four letters and use lowercase letters. Here are the more likely versions of those commands:

```
use people
modi stru
brow
do people.wfm
```

Note that you cannot abbreviate the file name. The default file type for the DO command is .PRG, so the .WFM is needed here.

Running Commands from the Input Pane

If you've tried any of these examples, you've seen that you type a command and then press Enter. The command then runs. But that's not the only option.

If you select any set of one or more commands (drag the mouse to select text), pressing Enter causes the currently selected set to execute. If there is no selected text, the command that has the insertion point, before you press Enter, is executed. This latter is the case when you type a command and press Enter.

But there's more to that last option. If you want to repeat a command that is anywhere in the input pane, simply use the ↑ or ↓ key to move the insertion point to the line that has the command, and press Enter. Alternatively, click anywhere on the command and press Enter.

This means that sometimes its easier to repeat operations from the Command window than it would be in the Navigator.

For more on commands, refer to Chapter 13.

▸▸ **WARNING**

With the exception of the ? command, all the commands that direct output to the results pane are supported only so that dBASE for Windows can still run dBASE IV and earlier applications. dBASE for Windows uses objects and properties on forms outside this window. Don't use commands that write to or read from the results pane, except for the ? command.

▸ Checking the Output in the Results Pane

You don't do any operations in the results pane, except for copying results to the Clipboard and the input operations for legacy (dBASE IV and earlier) applications. dBASE 5.0 and later programs all use windows outside the results pane.

We think the results pane, combined with the input pane, is invaluable for testing commands and expressions, so we expect this use of the results pane to have a very long future.

▶ The Command Window Speedbar

When the Command window is active, its speedbar looks like this:

Table 8.1 shows the functions of the speedbar buttons in the Command window.

TABLE 8.1: *Command Window Speedbar Buttons*

BUTTON	FUNCTION
	Create one of the primary types of files
	Open one of the primary types of files
	Cut selected text to the Clipboard
	Copy selected text to the Clipboard
	Paste the contents of the Clipboard at the insertion point
	Run the currently selected commands
	Run a program
	Launch the dBASE for Windows Debugger
	Launch the Navigator
	Launch Command window (current selection)
	Run an Expert
	Run a Tutorial

▶ The Command Window's Main Menu

The File, Window, and Help menus are not changed in the Command window. Two new menus are added, and the Edit and Properties menus are changed. The new menus options are Program and Table.

▶ Using the Edit Menu

The Edit Menu always includes the following standard options:

- Undo (Ctrl-Z)
- Cut (Ctrl-X)
- Copy (Ctrl-C
- Paste (Ctrl-V)
- Delete (Del)

It also includes these options:

- Select All
- Clear Results
- Insert from File …
- Copy to File …
- Search ➤
- Build Expression … (Ctrl-E)
- Execute Selection

These new options are discussed in the following sections.

Edit ➤ Select All

The Select All option selects (highlights) all the text in the input pane. (You can also do this by dragging with the mouse.) This is useful to either reexecute the commands or to cut or copy the commands to the Clipboard or another file.

Edit ➤ Clear Results

The Clear Results option clears the results pane. This choice is the same as issuing a CLEAR command in the input pane.

Edit ➤ Insert from File ...

The Insert from File option is used to copy in the contents of a file (normally a .PRG or .WFM file). It brings up an Insert from File dialog box, in which you specify the file you want to insert. The default file type is Text (*.TXT).

Edit ➤ Copy to File ...

The Copy to File option is used to copy the contents of the input pane to a program file (normally a .PRG or .WFM file). It displays a Copy to File dialog box, in which you specify the file you want to write. The default file type is Text (*.TXT).

Edit ➤ Search ➤

Choosing Edit ➤ Search choice displays this text search submenu:

Find Text...	Ctrl+F
Find Next Text	Ctrl+K
Replace Text...	Ctrl+R

Edit ➤ Build Expression ...

The Build Expression choice launches the Expression Builder. You can build your expressions using this tool and then paste them into the Command window input pane. The Expression Builder is discussed later in this chapter.

Using the Expression Builder is much slower, but much more reliable, than typing expressions directly into the input pane. You'll want to try both methods to find which one gets your results most quickly.

▶▶ **TIP**

Don't use the Expression Builder just to avoid mistakes. The Command window will trap mistakes and you can try again, editing the erroneous line. Your data is not at risk from a syntax error.

Edit ➤ Execute Selection

The Execute Selection option gives mouse users a convenient substitute for pressing the Enter key. Is this worthwhile? We think so. How else can you sip your coffee without stopping your work?

▶ *Using the Program Menu*

The Command window's Program menu has four options:

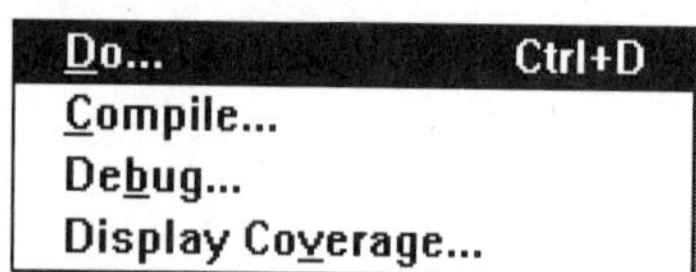

These options are discussed in the following sections.

Program ➤ Do

The Do option opens an Execute Program dialog box, which is like the other Open File dialog boxes. The available file types are *.PRG, *.PRO, and *.WFM. The program you select is run when you choose OK in this dialog box.

▶▶ **NOTE**

There are no radio buttons, so you cannot choose Design mode here.

Program ➤ Compile

The Compile option opens the Compile Program dialog box, which is similar to the Execute Program dialog box. The only difference between this dialog box and the one displayed by Edit ➤ Do is that is that the compiled file type *.PRO is not available here.

Unlike the Do option, this choice compiles the source program into an executable form, but does not run it. This choice is used during programming to check that your syntax is all correct, without actually starting your program.

Program ➤ Debug

The Debug choice opens the same Execute Program dialog box as the Do option. However, once you have chosen the program, it then starts the dBASE for Windows Debugger.

This is a tool primarily useful to advanced programmers. It lets you examine and tinker with the inner workings of a dBASE for Windows program while it is running.

Program ➤ Display Coverage

The Display Coverage option opens a Display Coverage dialog box. This lets programmers choose a coverage file (the only extension is .COV).

Coverage files are an option available to programmers. They show how often each section of a program is used. This information lets the programmer focus on the most frequently used portions of the code in tuning for optimum perfomance.

▶ Using the Table Menu

The Table choice on the Command window's main menu displays this menu:

Find Records...
Replace Records...
Table Utilities ▸
Edit Records
Add Records

These choices are all documented in Chapter 9, which covers the Table tools.

▸ Using the Properties Menu

The Properties menu choice adds one new choice to the universal Desktop choice: Command Window .... This option displays the Command window Properties dialog box, which is shown in Figure 8.20.

This dialog box lets you adjust the look of the Command window to suit your tastes and work habits. It has two sections: Input Pane Position and Fonts.

FIGURE 8.20 ▸

Command Window Properties dialog box

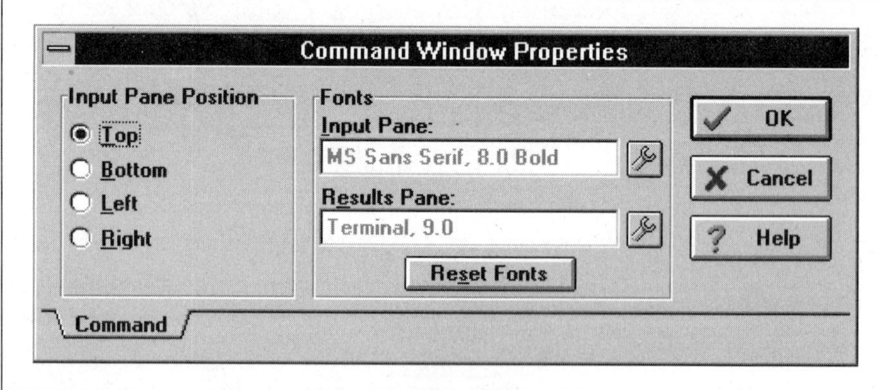

Input Pane Position Choices

The Input Pane Position section has four radio buttons:

- Top
- Bottom
- Left
- Right

Top is the default choice. (We fiddle with this occasionally, just to keep from getting bored.)

Font Choices

The Font section has two pseudo entry fields, Input Pane and Results Pane, with associated tool pushbuttons. These name the font used for the respective panes. Clicking on the tool pushbutton (or tabbing to it and pressing the spacebar) brings up the Windows Font dialog box, where you can select your fonts.

These are pseudo entry fields. You cannot type in them, though they look like you can. Their information is taken from the Font dialog box. They report the font name, size, and style.

▶ The Command Window's Speed Menu

If you right-click in the input pane, you bring up the Command window Speed menu. It offers six options:

- Command Window Properties …
- Cut (Ctrl-X)
- Copy (Ctrl-C)
- Paste (Ctrl-V)
- Build Expression … (Ctrl-E)
- Execute Selection

The Command Window Properties choice opens the Command Window Properties dialog box—the same one that you see when you choose Properties ➤ Command Window.

The Cut, Copy, and Paste options provide access to and from the Clipboard for text selected in the input pane.

The Build Expression option starts the Expression Builder.

The Execute Selection option provides another way for you to work without touching the keyboard. (This is Enter on the keyboard.)

▸ The Results Pane Speed Menu

If you right-click in the results pane, you bring up another Speed menu. Its three options are:

- Command Window Properties…
- Copy (Ctrl-C)
- Clear Results

The first choice launches the Command Window Properties dialog box.

The Copy choice lets you copy to the Clipboard after you have selected a rectangle by dragging.

The Clear Results choice clears the results panc. It is the same as giving the CLEAR command in the input pane.

▸▸ Using the Expression Builder

The Expression Builder lets you build dBASE expressions that you can use throughout dBASE for Windows. Whenever you see the tool icon next to a field that accepts expressions, the Expression Builder is just a click away. If the Command window is active, the Expression Builder is also available from the Edit menu.

In the Command window and in the editors, the Expression Builder is launched when you press Ctrl-E. From the Program Editor, you can click on the Einstein button (shown in the margin) to launch it. You'll see the Build Expression dialog box.

After you create an expression in the Build Expression dialog box and choose OK, dBASE for Windows pastes your expression into the tool you were using when you launched the Expression Builder.

▶ Building Simple Expressions

Let's start by entering a simple expression. Launch the Expression Builder from the Command window (choose Edit ➤ Expression Builder…). Notice the Safety Net check box at the top of the Build Expression dialog box. When Safety Net is checked, you can't type in the expression itself. For now, let's begin with Safety Net off. Make sure that the Safety Net check box is *not* checked, and type this expression: **2 + 2**. Figure 8.21 shows this expression entered in the dialog box.

FIGURE 8.21 ▶

Adding two and two in the Expression Builder

Build Expression
Expression: Safety Net Undo [Group] Evaluate
2+2
Type your expression directly or choose elements to be pasted into the expression from the Paste list box.
Category: Constant Field Function Operator Variable
Table: TEMP
Paste: NAME NOTES
TEMP->NAME: Character 10
OK Cancel Help

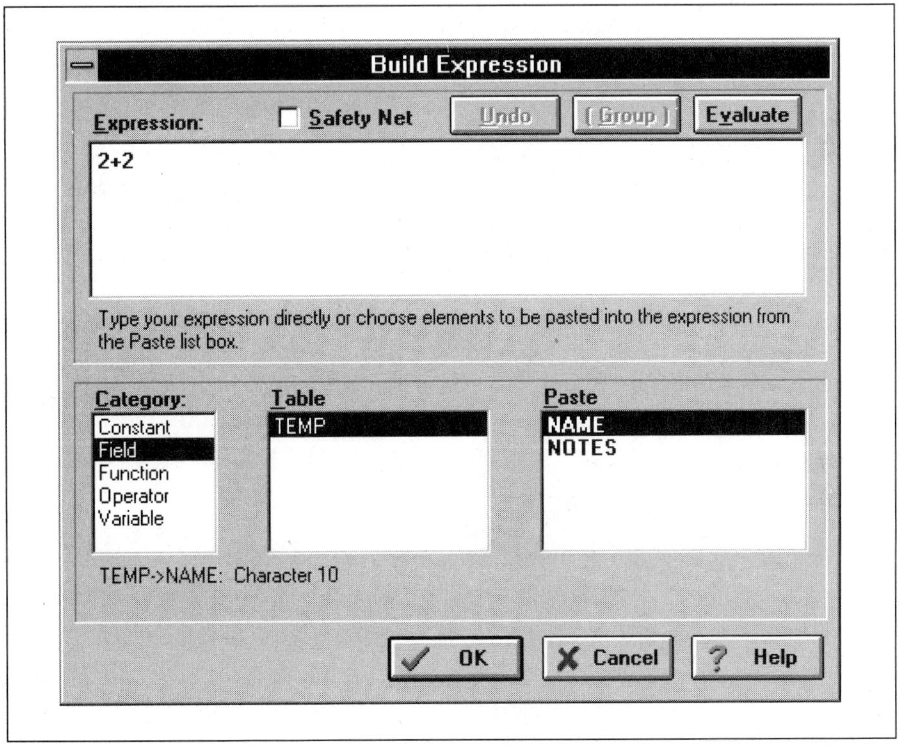

With this trivial expression entered, click on the Evaluate pushbutton at the top of the dialog box. Below your expression, the Expression Builder will report Result: 4.

Now let's go for a small increase in complexity. Delete the 2+2 expression and add this one: **2 + 3 * 4**. (You can use spaces freely within your expressions; they can be a big help when you get to more complex expressions.)

▸▸ **NOTE**

If you're like us, you'll press Enter when you didn't mean to in the Expression Builder. Simply select the expression and press Ctrl-E to return to the Expression Builder with the expression exactly where you left it.

Can you predict the result of this expression? Give it a guess, and then click on Evaluate. The result is 14, because multiplication is done before addition, unless you specify otherwise. If you added 2 and 3, then multiplied by 4, the answer would be 20. Let's get this done next.

Click on the Safety Net check box to turn this feature on. Then drag to select 2 + 3 and click on the Group button at the top of the dialog box. It should look like this:

After you click on the Group button, the Expression Builder inserts parentheses around the sum, turning the expression into:

```
( 2 + 3 ) * 4
```

Now click on Evaluate. The Expression Builder will report 20 as your result.

▸ Using the Category, Type, and Paste Options

The three lists near the bottom of the dialog box are labeled Category, Type, and Paste, unless the Field choice is highlighted in the Category list. In this case, the middle list is labeled Table. We'll call it the Type list, since this is the most common name.

So far, you've discovered that the Expression Builder can be used as a clumsy calculator. Let's go beyond this for our next example.

We're approaching the turn of the century. At midnight at the end of December 31, 1999, we'll usher in a new century. (Some will say that the twentieth century actually ends on 12/31/2000, but this detail won't stop us from having a big party on 12/31/1999.) Let's start getting ready to celebrate by finding out what day of the week 12/31/99 is.

dBASE for Windows has a function that returns the day of the week, given any date. We presume that you don't know the name of that function (do your best to forget, for the moment, if you do know). Begin by deleting any expression (drag to select the current expression and press Del) and turning Safety Net on.

Often, a rough idea of what you want is enough to find the exact expression that will do the job. Start in the Category list and click on Function, since you know you want a function. Now the Type list will show the various types of functions. One of the choices is Date/Time data, which seems promising.

Click on Date/Time data and look in the Paste list. This list shows the actual functions from which you can choose. Underneath the Category, Type, and Paste lists, the highlighted function is explained, very briefly.

As luck would have it, the first of the Date/Time data functions is CDOW. As you see at the bottom of the dialog box, this function returns the day of the week for the given date expression, which is exactly what we want to know. Figure 8.22 shows our selections in the lists.

FIGURE 8.22

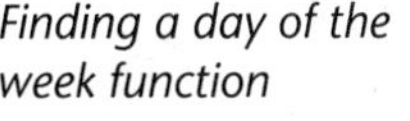
Finding a day of the week function

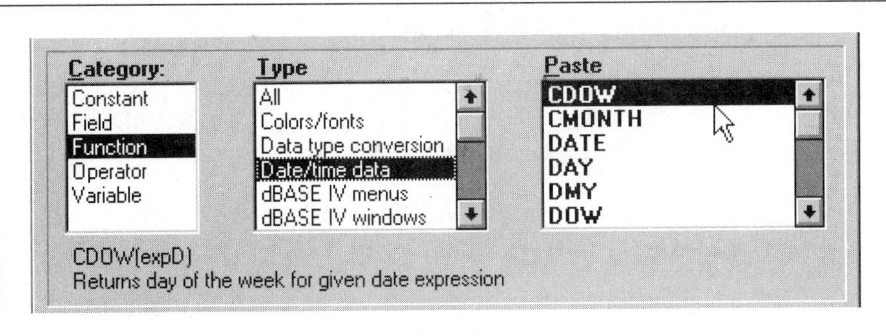

The last list is called Paste because this is what you do when you find what you're looking for: you paste the result into the expression. Paste the CDOW( ) function into the expression by double-clicking on the function, or by dragging it into the Expression area, like this:

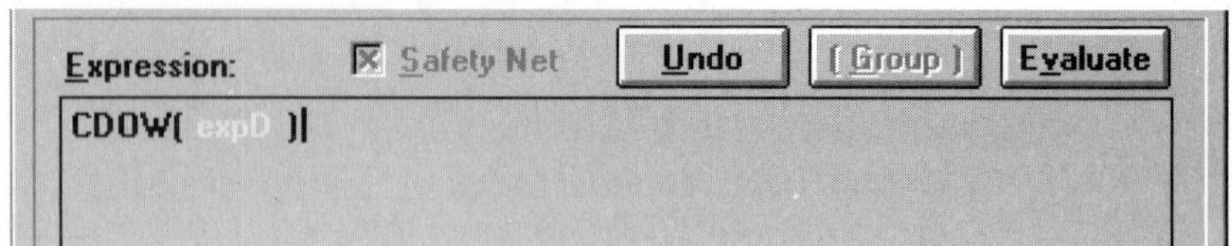

When you put a function into the Expression area, it is shown in black, but its arguments (the values you supply for its operation) are shown in yellow. In this case, its argument is *expD*, which means that it needs a date expression.

We want to know what the day of the week will be on 12/31/99. This is a date constant, so return to the Category list and click on Constant. One of your Type choices is now Date, which is the one that we want.

Click on Date in the Type list. Now your choices in the Paste list are LastWeek, NextWeek, Today, Tomorrow, and Yesterday. If you don't happen to be reading this book in late December 1999, these choices aren't what you want.

Don't worry; you'll be able to get the correct constant in there. For now, drag any one of these date constants from the Paste list to the expression and drop it right on top of the *expD* value. Don't double-click, because that would made it a separate expression. (If you had selected a numeric constant, your only choice would be zero; it's just a place to start.)

Your expression is now all black, and you can click on Evaluate. We dragged LastWeek to the *expD*. Since today is Wednesday, the Expression Builder reported Wednesday when we clicked on Evaluate.

▶ Editing Constants in the Expression

The important result you have is that you are now looking at a correctly formed expression that will evaluate a date constant and return the day of the week. The last item to be done is to type 12/31/99 where it is reporting the date constant. Just click on the date and start typing.

An entry field will open underneath the date constant, like this:

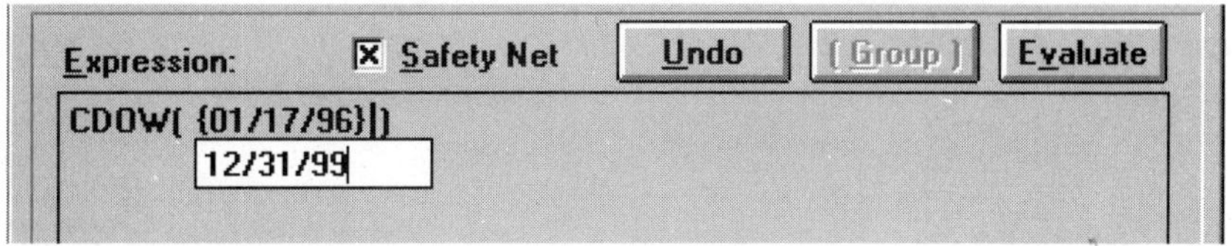

Don't enter the { } delimiters around a date constant (and don't enter the quotation marks that surround a character string constant, either).

Once you have 12/31/99 entered in the CDOW( ) function, click on the Evaluate button. You'll find that this important New Year's Eve is on Friday. That means that we'll have the whole weekend to clean up and recover from our big party.

▶ Adding a Date Operator Expression

Of course, Friday might not be the best choice for the widest number of people. If this will put a damper on your celebration, perhaps you want to think about having your big celebration on 12/31/2000, which will be, after all, the last day of the century.

If you recall, the argument to the CDOW function was *expD*, a date expression. Let's try to add 366 days to 12/31/99 to get the day of the week a year later. (Sure, you could just change the 1999 to 2000, but that wouldn't teach you about using the Expression Builder, which is our real point.)

Start by clicking near the right side of the date constant in the CDOW expression. Your insertion point (vertical bar) will appear to the right of the date, just to the left of the closing parenthesis. Here you want to add 366 to get the date one year later (2000 a leap year).

Return to the Category list and click on Operator. The Type list now shows the types of operators you can choose. Select Numeric, and the Paste list will show a menu of numeric operators. Select the plus sign to add the value. Figure 8.23 shows these selections in the Category, Type, and Paste lists.

FIGURE 8.23

Choosing the add operator

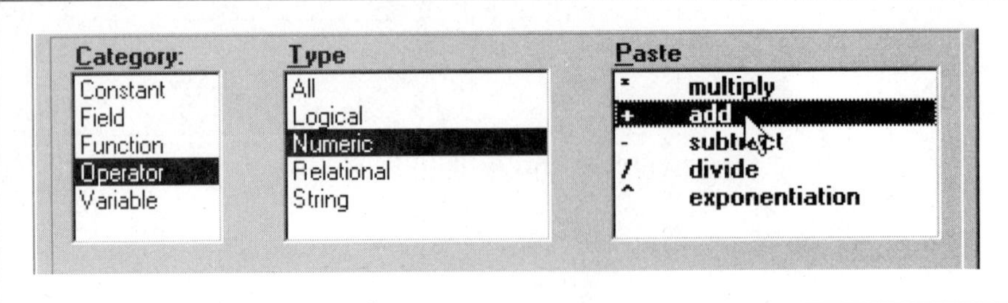

When you choose an operator, the Expression Builder also adds any needed operands. In this example, an operand called *Value* has been added, waiting for our action:

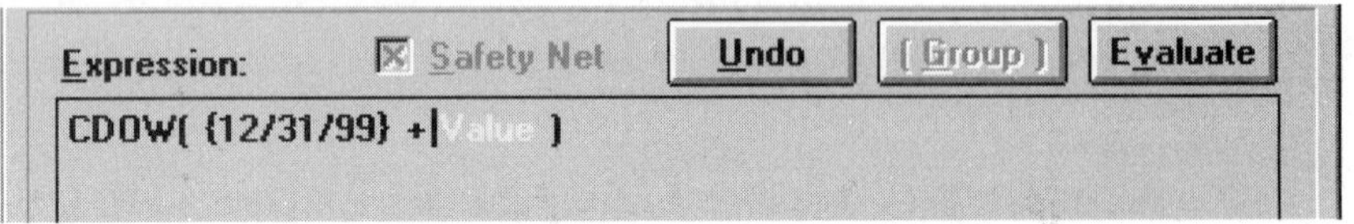

This *Value* could be replaced by anything that will create a numeric value. We want the numeric constant 366. Return to the Category list and select Constant, and then choose Numeric in the Type list. The Paste list will show the constant zero. Drag the zero over the value operand and drop it. *Value* will be replaced by the 0.

Just as we did with the date, click on the 0 and start typing. An entry field will open beneath the constant. Type in **366, as shown here:**

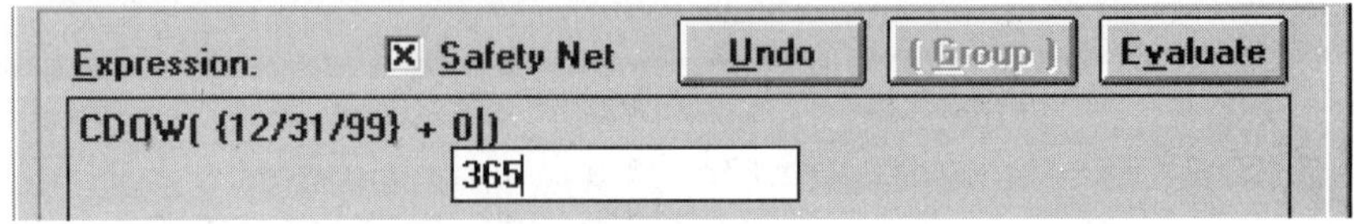

Now the value 366 replaces the 0.

With that value inserted, we can now ask for an evaluation of the expression:

```
CDOW( {12/31/99} + 366 )
```

This is the day of the week that New Year's Eve falls on in the year 2000: a Sunday.

▶ Pasting to and from the Command Window

If you launched the Expression Builder from the Command window, you can press Enter (or click on OK) to paste your expression back into the Command window. When you send an expression to the Command window, it is automatically written at the location of the insertion point in the Command window. The expression is not a complete command, but you can use the ? command to see the value of an expression.

To reverse the process—paste an expression from the Command window into the Expression Builder—select an expression (drag from the first character to the last) in the Command window and press Ctrl-E. This launches the Expression Builder with the expression already in place.

▶▶ Summary

In this chapter, you examined the dBASE for Windows menus, the Navigator, and the Command window. You also learned about catalogs and the Expression Builder.

You started with the menu options that are available for most file types, including the File, Edit, Properties, Window, and Help menus. You reviewed the Properties ➤ Desktop option, which is available from anywhere in dBASE for Windows.

Then you moved onto the Navigator. You learned about the features for selecting directories, file types, and files. You also explored the Navigator menus, including the Navigator menu and the Properties ➤ Navigator choices, as well as the Speed menu.

Next, you became acquainted with catalogs, which work like the Navigator, but for files that aren't in the same directory. You learned that you can build a catalog simply by picking the Catalog type from the Navigator and then opening the files that you want the catalog to contain.

Then you learned how to work in the Command window. You saw that the Command window has an input pane, in which you enter commands, and a results pane, which shows the results of your commands.

You tried out a few of the more commonly used commands. You also explored its menus, including the Speed menus for the results and input panes.

Finally, you took a look at the Expression Builder, which helps you create expressions. The Expression Builder provides one way to put expressions in your commands.

In the next chapter, you'll get thorough coverage of the Table tools, including Table Structure, Table Records, and Table Utilities.

▶ ▶ CHAPTER 9

Mastering Table Tools

▶▶ **I*n*** this chapter, we'll dissect the table-related tools. Table Records tools let you examine, edit, add, and delete data in one of the Browse, Form, or Columnar Layout views. A tool with a lower profile is Table Properties, which is a design tool that lets you customize your Table Records tools.

Finally, we'll examine the other Table tools. These are accessed through the Table Utilities menu, which presents a collection of data-manipulation tools.

▶▶ *Using the Table Structure Tool*

As you've seen in your earlier work, the Table Structure tool lets you design tables and modify the design of tables. Here, we'll examine every feature of the tool. We'll also consider the key problems and solutions when it comes time to use this tool to modify a table with live data.

▶ *A Browse for Your Table Structure*

The main part of the Table Structure tool is a specialized Browse window. A sample is shown in Figure 9.1.

The columns are the same columns that you find in a structure-extended file:

- Name, for the field's name
- Type, for the field's type

FIGURE 9.1

Browsing in a Table Structure window

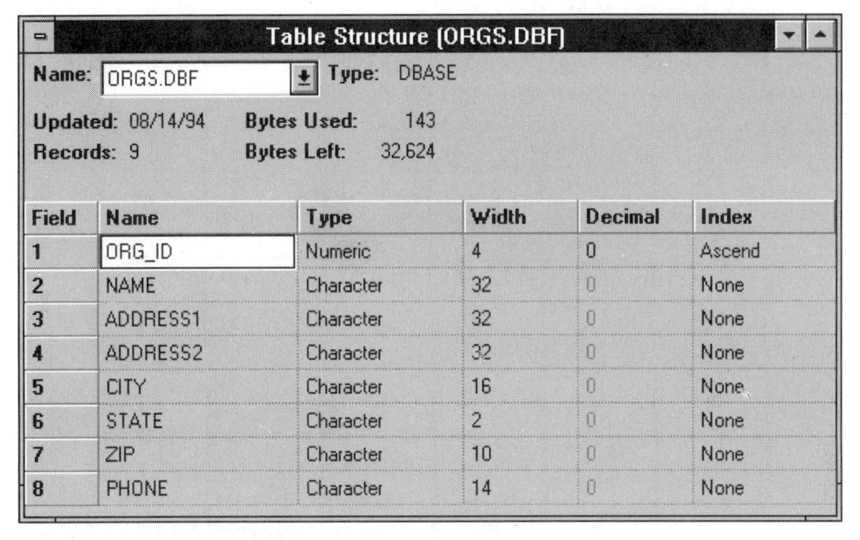

- Width, for the field's width, in characters
- Decimal, for Numeric or Float fields, the number of places to the right of the decimal point
- Index, for the type of index (if any)

► *Adding the Fields*

The data-entry characteristics of this Browse window are tailored to the requirements of designing a table structure. The requirements discussed in the following sections may give you some ideas for your own work.

Field Name

The Name field restricts entry to valid field names. The first character must be alphabetic (you get a beep when you try anything else). The remaining characters must be alphabetic, numeric, or underscore characters. Invalid keystrokes are simply ignored.

Field Type

The Type field choices are given in a drop-down list box:

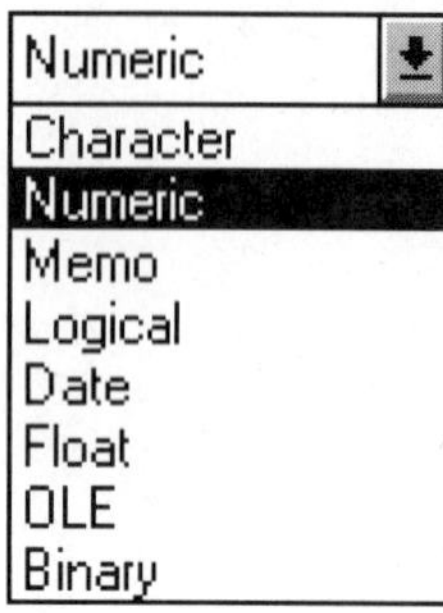

With the mouse, click on the down arrow next to the field, and then click on your choice. From the keyboard, the first letter of your choice is adequate. Pressing the down arrow cycles through the choices.

dBASE for Windows supports the following field types:

- Character fields hold text (for names, addresses, and so on).
- Numeric fields store numbers, usually for business data.
- Memo fields are used for memoranda, notes, and other long blocks of text.
- Logical fields contain True/False or Yes/No data.
- Date fields store dates.
- Float fields store numbers, usually for scientific and engineering data.
- OLE fields are used to link to OLE (Microsft's Object Linking and Embedding protocol) objects, such as spreadsheets or word processing documents. (OLE lets you access one application when you are working in another one.)
- Binary fields hold data that cannot be entered from the keyboard, such as sounds and pictures.

Field Width

The Width field is a spinbutton. It is available for Character, Numeric, and Float data types. Memo, OLE, and Binary fields are 10 characters wide, which is the width needed to link to those data types. Date fields are 8 characters wide. Logical fields are 1 character wide.

Field Decimals

The Decimal field is a spinbutton available for Numeric and Float fields. For both those types, its range is 0 through 8.

Field Index

The Index field is a drop-down list box:

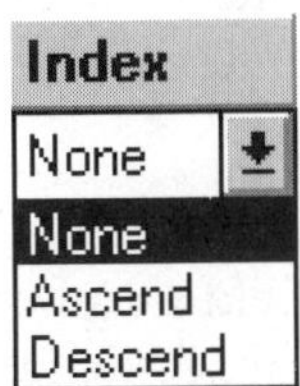

The default choice, None, does not index the field. The other two choices, Ascend and Descend, create an index from low to high, or high to low, respectively.

TIP

Almost never index a character field. The default index is based on the ASCII collating sequence, in which A–Z come before a–z. This will sort *Zebra* before *aardvark*, which is seldom what you want. Use the Manage Indexes dialog box (choose Structure ➤ Manage Indexes) and index on UPPER (or LOWER) of the character field, for an alphabetic sort.

With the mouse, click on the down arrow, and then click on your choice. From the keyboard, press A or D to override the default None selection.

If you choose indexing on a single field, that index will be the main index, by default. If you choose indexing on more than one field, the dBASE does not pick one for you. Instead it defaults to the physical order. You must use the Manage Indexes dialog box (choose Structure ➤ Manage Indexes) to select the primary index.

► Working in the Browse Area

As in the Table Records tool's Browse Layout view, placing the mouse pointer at the top (title) of a column turns the mouse pointer into the hand (grabber) icon. By pressing down and holding, you can drag the columns into a different order.

As is also true in the Table Records tool's Browse Layout view, placing the mouse pointer on the line between columns gives you the double-headed arrow that lets you drag the column separator left or right. In the standard setup, you can see all of each column, so this is seldom used.

Unlike the behavior of the Browse Layout view in the Table Records tool, moving the mouse pointer to the field number column turns it into the grabber hand. You can grab your records here and move them up and down. This will change the order of the columns in your table.

In a Table Records Browse window, clicking on the record number selects the field, letting you copy or cut it to the Clipboard. Pasting it elsewhere gives you a similar capability. The Table Records Browse window is more useful in large tables. The grabbing capability in the Table Structure tool is convenient for smaller tables, which table structures generally are.

A vertical elevator appears when you have more rows of data than fit in the window.

►► **NOTE**

Perhaps it was an oversight, but no horizontal elevator appears if you reduce the width of the Table Structure window to the point that not all columns fit. Data on the right is just not accessible.

► Looking Above the Browse Area

The combobox above the Browse area shows the file name. The default type (also shown) is dBASE. The other types available depend on the choices made in your IDAPI configuration installation. (If your organization is not using Paradox tables or remote relational database management systems, this will not be relevant to you.)

A continuous display shows you four items: the date the table was last updated, the number of records in the table, the bytes used, and the bytes available. The bytes available are 32,767 minus the amount of bytes you have used. (This is the space for your table structure; data space is limited by your disk space.) Since each record takes 10 to 14 bytes, this gives you space for a table with 2500 to 3000 columns—more than anyone should ever need.

▶ Using the Table Structure Menus

The File and Edit menus in the Table Structure tool are standard, as described in Chapter 1.

The View menu includes two options:

- Table Records (F2)
- Table Structure (Shift-F2)

The Structure menu has five choices:

- Add Field (Ctrl-A)
- Insert Field (Ctrl-N)
- Delete Selected Field (Ctrl-U)
- Go to Field Number … (Ctrl-G)
- Manage Indexes …

The first three choices let you add a new field, insert a field, and delete the selected field.

The Go to Field Number … choice opens the Go to Field dialog box. This dialog box contains a spinbutton that ranges from 1 to the number of fields you have, plus OK and Cancel buttons.

The Manage Indexes choice launches the Manage Indexes dialog box. If you've made changes to the table structure, it begins with the Changes Made dialog box, which gives you a choice of saving or discarding those changes. Whether you save your changes or not, the next step is the Manage Indexes dialog box. This dialog box is discussed later in this chapter, in the section about Table Utilities.

The Table Structure tool's Properties menu has two choices:

- Desktop
- Table Structure Window …

The Desktop choice offers the standard multi-tab form, which you've learned about in earlier chapters. Choosing Properties ➤ Table Structure Window … opens the Table Structure Properties form. This form has a single tab, Table Structure, with only two choices: Horizontal Grid Lines and Vertical Grid Lines. These check boxes turn the specified grid lines on or off.

▸▸ NOTE

In all the dialog boxes, the OK, Cancel, and Help pushbuttons perform their normal duties.

▸ Right-Clicking for the Table Structure Speed Menu

Right-clicking with your mouse in the Table Structure window brings up a Speed menu, with the following choices:

- Table Structure Window Properties …
- Cut (Ctrl-X)
- Copy (Ctrl-C)
- Paste (Ctrl-V)
- Add Field (Ctrl-A)

- Insert Field (Ctrl-N)
- Delete Selected Field (Ctrl-U)

The Table Structure Window Properties choice launches the Table Structure window (the same result as choosing Properties ➤ Table Structure).

The three editing choices—Cut, Copy, and Paste—work on the contents of the Name field or the numbers in the Width and Decimal fields. (If you're wondering if this might be less than overwhelmingly useful, we agree.)

The Add, Insert, and Delete options are the same as the Structure pull-down menu's Add Field, Insert Field, and Delete Selected Field choices.

▶ Using the Table Structure Speedbar Buttons

The speedbar for the Table Structure tool looks like this:

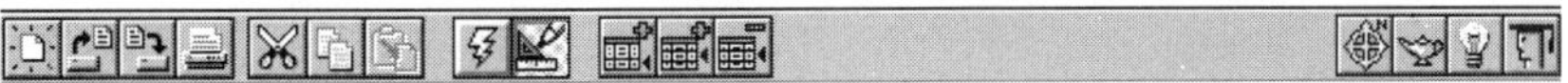

Three special buttons appear on the speedbar when the Table Structure tool is active:

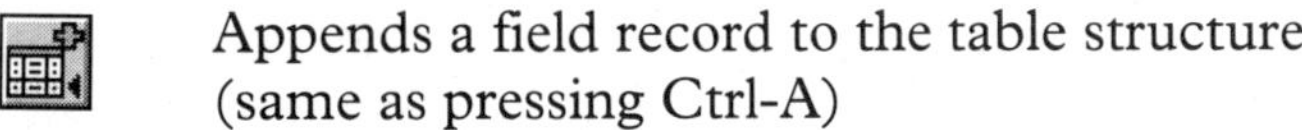

Appends a field record to the table structure (same as pressing Ctrl-A)

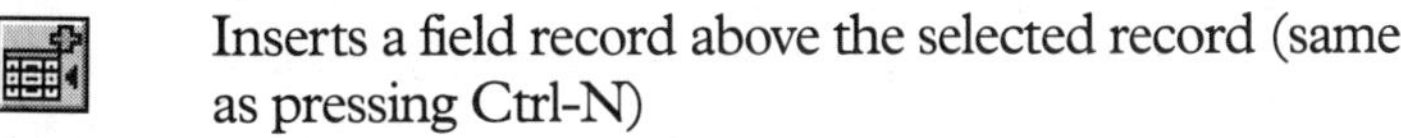

Inserts a field record above the selected record (same as pressing Ctrl-N)

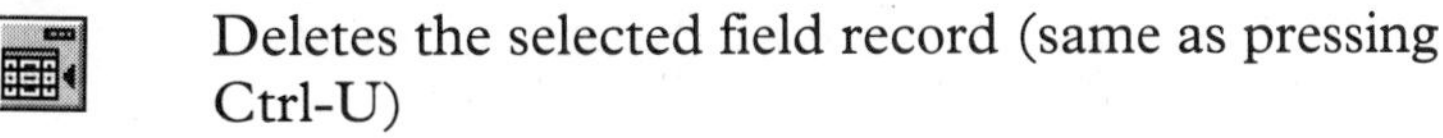

Deletes the selected field record (same as pressing Ctrl-U)

These choices are also available on the Speed menu and from the Structure pull-down menu.

▶ Avoiding Data Loss from Restructuring

This warning box might appear when you're using the Table Structure tool to modify the structure of an existing table:

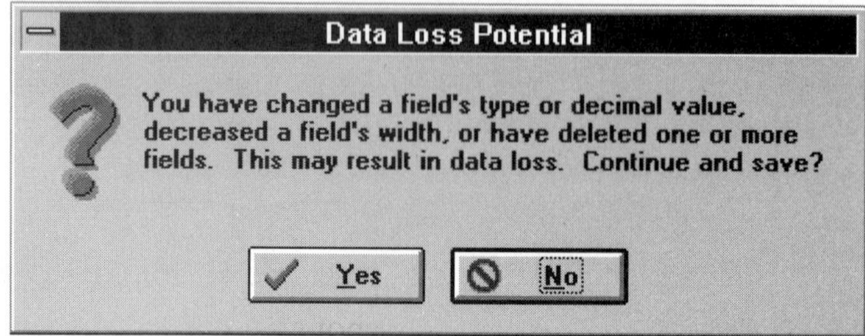

The two pushbuttons in the Data Loss Potential warning box let you choose a Yes or No response. Often, you can simply ignore this dialog box—just click on Yes and proceed. But not always. The following sections give the rules for making successful changes.

Make a Backup Copy

Before editing a table structure, make a backup copy of the table. With a backup copy, you can proceed to make any changes you want. If you've made a mistake, there's no harm done.

Sometimes, you'll find yourself working with a very large table—too large to back up on disk. (We presume that you have backed up on tape or some other backup medium.) When this happens, copy the first few dozen records to a temporary table. Make your changes on the temporary table and test the result. If there's a problem, try again with another copy of a dozen records. When you have a set of changes that work, apply them to the full table.

Make Multiple Passes

Changing field names and reordering fields never triggers the Data Loss Potential dialog box. Do these changes first.

Increasing field widths is also never a problem. Make these changes second.

Increasing a Numeric or Float field's decimal places might leave too little space to the left of a decimal point. If you know that all your data will continue to fit, or if you have increased the field's width so that this will not be a problem, go ahead with this change. You *will* trigger the Data Loss Potential dialog box, but you'll know that you can safely continue.

Similarly, decreasing a field's width will trigger the Data Loss Potential dialog box, but if you know that you've allowed enough space, you can select Yes and continue.

Check Maximum Widths

To be sure that you allow enough space for the largest number in a Numeric or Float field, choose Table ➤ Table Utilities ➤ Calculate. Use the Calculate Records dialog box to find the highest value. (The Calculate Records dialog box is discussed later in this chapter.)

►► **WARNING**

If you have mixed positive and negative values, you must check both the maximum (largest positive number) and minimum (largest negative number) to be sure you allow for the widest number in your table.

To find the width of the widest character field, use the CALCULATE MAX( ) command in the Command window. For the expression, you want the LEN( ) of the TRIM( ) of the field. (Without the TRIM( ), the LEN( ) of the field is its width as defined in the table's current structure.) This will work in the Command window for a character field named LAST_NAME:

```
CALCULATE MAX( LEN(TRIM(Last_name)) )
```

►► **TIP**

The extra blank spaces inside the parentheses are discarded by dBASE for Windows, but we like them since they help make nested function calls, like this one, more readable.

That command will show its answer in the Calculation Results dialog box.

Read the Dialog Box Message

The message explicitly states the conditions that trigger the Data Loss Potential dialog box:

- Changing a field's type
- Changing a field's decimal value
- Decreasing a field's width
- Deleting a field

Changes to the field's type may or may not cause problems. dBASE does its best to preserve your data. It works extra hard when you change a field's type. These are the changes:

- **Numeric to Float:** The internal representation of the number is changed. This may make a difference in round-off error, but is probably negligible.
- **Float to Numeric:** With any difference in precision between the Float field's decimal places and the Numeric field's decimal places, dBASE for Windows rounds the number to the nearest value that fits (for example, 0.04 rounds to 0.0 at one decimal place; 0.05 rounds to 0.1). This will cause significant loss of precision, which may or may not be important, depending on your application.

▸▸ NOTE

As an example of changing a Float field to a Numeric field, suppose that your Float field contained the fraction ⅓, stored to eight decimal places (the default for Float field data). Converting to a numeric with two decimal places will truncate 0.00333333 (to .00). Then again, this truncation may actually improve the accuracy of your calculation if, for example, you are dealing with currency amounts that should be rounded.

- **Character to Memo:** The character data will be moved into the Memo field. Ignore the Data Loss Potential dialog box. There is no data loss.
- **Memo to Character:** As much of the Memo field text that will fit is moved into the Character field. Any memo longer than the field is truncated.
- **Numeric or Float to Character:** The number is written as a character string into the Character field. It is left-justified. Precision or data may be lost if the number does not fit in the Character field.
- **Character to Numeric or Float:** The VAL( ) of the Character field is moved into the Numeric field if, and only if, the entire character string can be converted to a number. For example, "123" is converted to the number 123; "123a" is not entirely numeric, so the Numeric field is blanked. (A blank field is treated as a zero in most dBASE for Windows operations.)
- **Date to Character:** The DTOC( ) of the date is written into the Character field. There is no data loss as long as the Character field is wide enough to fit the date as a string.
- **Character to Date:** The Character field data is interpreted as a date constant and placed in the Date field. If the character string is not a valid date, the Date field is blanked.
- **Logical to Character:** .T. values are converted to Y, and .F. values are converted to N.
- **Character to Logical:** If the Character field data is an acceptable input to a Logical field, the appropriate value is entered into the Logical field. Y, y, T, and t are .T.; N, n, F and f are .F. The character string ".T." is *not* recognized as True. All other character strings are converted to .F. values.
- **Numeric or Float to Logical:** Zeros are converted to .F. values. Nonzeros (positive or negative) are converted to .T. values. Blank Numeric fields are converted to .F.
- **Logical to Numeric or Float:** .T. values are converted to 1. .F. values are converted to 0.

No other conversions are attempted. The existing data is discarded and the new fields are blanked.

We've already considered the impacts of changing the data decimal value or decreasing a field's width. If you delete a field, the data in it will be lost, of course. If this is what you have in mind, you can proceed.

Remember that your computer is not as smart as you are. You may have just looked at the data and know that you have plenty of room to increase the decimals from 2 to 4, for instance. dBASE for Windows doesn't check; it just displays the Data Loss Potential dialog box and lets you decide.

▸▸ Using the Table Records Tools

The Table Records tools are the primary tools for entering and editing data (unless you build custom forms).

▸ Using the Table Records Menus

In the Table Records views, the only standard menus are Window and Help. The other menus have custom options or are entirely new.

File Menu

The File menu has two changes from the standard File menu: the Save section has modified options, and there is a new section for importing spreadsheet data.

The Save section has the following options:

- Save Record (Ctrl-S)
- Save Record and Close (Ctrl-W)
- Abandon Record
- Abandon Record and Close (Ctrl-Q)
- Close (Ctrl-F4)

The two Abandon options eliminate any changes made to an existing record or they discard a record that you were appending.

The new option for importing a spreadsheet is Import .... This option opens the Import dialog box, shown in Figure 9.2.

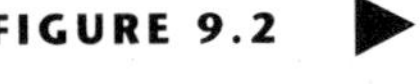

FIGURE 9.2

Importing data with File ➤ Import

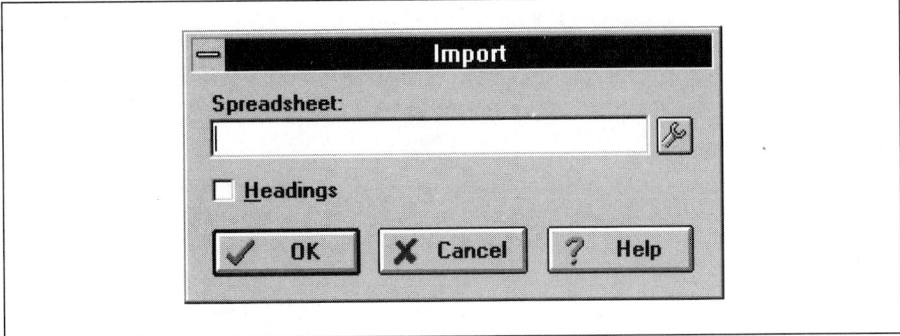

The tool button next to the entry field launches an Open File dialog box titled Choose Spreadsheet. Its available file extensions are .WB1 for Quattro Pro spreadsheets and .WK1 for Lotus 1-2-3 spreadsheets. (See Appendix B for more information about Open File dialog boxes.)

Importing a spreadsheet creates a new table with each field in the table corresponding to a column in the spreadsheet.

If the Headings box is checked, the data in the first row of the spreadsheet is used for field names. The data is adjusted as needed. For example, blanks are converted to underscores, and text is truncated to 10 characters.

The import process is *not* intelligent. Except for row 1 (when Headings is checked), all data in each column is read into your table, so you must have exactly zero or one row of header in the spreadsheet.

Only Lotus 1-2-3 and Quattro Pro spreadsheets are supported.

Edit Menu

You can use the Clipboard to copy field contents (including Memo fields). You can select text by either dragging with the mouse or holding down the Shift key while using the ← or → key.

In the Browse Layout view, you can also click on the record number to select the entire record. Doing this lets you copy the whole record to the Clipboard.

►► NOTE

The Cut option is not available; you can only Copy a record to the Clipboard.

You can't Shift-click to select multiple records. However, dragging with the left button over the record numbers lets you select a range of records in the Browse Layout view.

When you paste from the Clipboard, the current field is overwritten with the Clipboard's contents. If you have copied a record, the entire current record is overwritten. (Picture all paste operations as if you were using an editor in overstrike mode.)

If you've copied multiple records to the Clipboard, each record from the Clipboard overwrites one record in the table, beginning with the currently selected record.

Pasting from the Clipboard will *not*, however, add records to the table. The paste operation stops when it reaches the end of the file.

The only non-overwrite option is the new choice added to the Edit menu: Paste Add Records. This option appends enough blank records to fit the Clipboard's contents, and then pastes the Clipboard's record(s) into the new record(s).

View Menu

The View menu is divided into three sections. In the first, you choose one of the following:

- Table Records (F2)
- Table Structure (Shift-F2)

The current choice is checked.

The second section has three options:

- Browse Layout (F2)
- Form Layout (F2)
- Columnar Layout (F2)

Again, your current choice is checked. You can press F2 to switch between these layouts.

A Browse object may disable toggling between the different layouts, in which case these options are grayed. (This is the Toggle property of the Browse object, discussed in Chapter 18, which can also be set for a Browse in the Table Properties dialog box, discussed later in this chapter.)

The last section has a single choice: Field Contents (F9). This choice is available when you have selected a Memo, Binary, or OLE field. It activates the text editor for a Memo field, or the appropriate editor for Binary and OLE fields.

Table Menu

The Table menu has four sections. The first one has two choices:

- Find Records … (Ctrl-F)
- Replace Records … (Ctrl-R)

These are covered in Chapter 4 of this book.

The next section also has two choices:

- Create Query
- Table Utilities

The Create Query choice launches the Query Designer, which is covered in Chapter 5. The Table Utilities choice is one of the routes to the Table Utilities menu, discussed later in this chapter.

The next section has four choices:

- Add Records (Ctrl-A)
- Delete Selected Record (Ctrl-U)
- Lock Selected Record (Ctrl-L)
- Blank Selected Record

You've probably been using the Ctrl-A and Ctrl-U shortcut keys in your Table Records work. We don't recommend using the Ctrl-L method for coordinating multiple, simultaneous table users. If you're updating the table while others are also updating it, pressing Ctrl-L is *not* a reliable way of coordinating multiple users. This should be done under control of a program designed for this purpose.

If you have the Deleted flag off (the view shows deleted records) and the current record is deleted, the Delete Selected Record choice is replaced by its opposite: Recall Selected Record (Ctrl-U).

The last section of the menu provides record-navigation options:

- Goto Record Number … (Ctrl-G)
- Previous Record (Up Arrow)
- Next Record (Down Arrow)
- Previous Page (PgUp)
- Next Page (PgDn)
- Top Record (Ctrl-PgUp)
- Bottom Record (Ctrl-PgDn)

Properties Menu

The Properties menu adds one choice: Table Record Properties …. The Table Records Properties dialog box is accessed from this menu choice (as well as from the Speed menu). This dialog box is a form with three tabs:

- Fields
- Records
- Window

These tabs are discussed in the section about setting Table Record properties, later in this chapter.

▸ Using the Table Records Speedbar Buttons

The speedbar for the Table Records tool looks like this:

Up to 12 special buttons appear when you run the Table Structure tool. Table 9.1 shows the functions of this speedbar.

TABLE 9.1: *Speedbar Buttons for the Table Records Tool*

BUTTON	FUNCTION
	Changes to the multicolumn Browse Layout view (same as choosing View ➤ Browse Layout or pressing F2 to cycle through the available layouts).
	Changes to the single-record Form Layout view (same as choosing View ➤ Form Layout or pressing F2 to cycle through the available layouts).
	Changes to the single-column Columnar Layout view (same as choosing View ➤ Columnar Layout or pressing F2 to cycle through the available layouts).
	Opens the Find Record dialog box (same as choosing Table ➤ Find Records … or pressing Ctrl-F).
	Appends a new record (same as pressing Ctrl-A or attempting to navigate to the record past the end of the table).
	Launches the Query Designer for this table.
	Goes to the first record in the table (same as pressing Ctrl-PgUp).
	In Browse Layout view, goes to the previous page of records (same as pressing PgUp).
	Goes to the previous record (same as pressing ↑ in Browse Layout view; PgUp in Form and Columnar Layout views)
	Goes to the next record (same as pressing ↓ in Browse Layout view; PgDn in Form and Columnar Layout views)

TABLE 9.1: *Speedbar Buttons for the Table Records Tool (continued)*

BUTTON	FUNCTION
	In Browse Layout view, goes to the next page of records (same as pressing PgDn).
	Goes to the last record in the table (same as pressing Ctrl-PgDn).

►► NOTE

In Form or Columnar Layout view, there are four record-navigation buttons on the Table Records speedbar. Since there's more to move through in the Browse Layout view, that window has six record-navigation buttons on its speedbar.

► Setting Table Records Properties

You can adjust the properties of field, records, and the Table Records window as a whole through the Table Records Properties dialog box. This dialog box can be accessed by selecting Properties ➤ Table Records Properties … from the pull-down menu, or by choosing Table Records Window Properties from the Speed menu.

Fields Tab Properties

The Fields tab of the Table Records Properties dialog box is shown in Figure 9.3.

The main part of the upper-left portion of this dialog box is a field selector. Using the field selector, you can choose the fields to include, as well as the order of those fields. (See Appendix B for more information about using the field selector.)

FIGURE 9.3

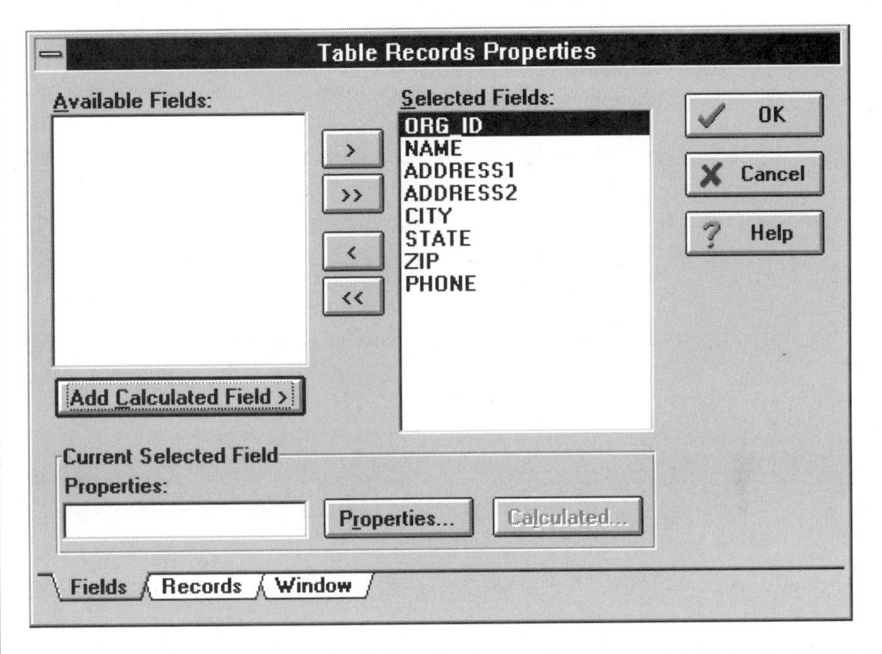

Table Record Properties, Fields tab

Calculated Fields Beneath the field selector on the left is the Calculated Field pushbutton. Pushing this button launches the Calculated Field dialog box, shown in Figure 9.4.

FIGURE 9.4

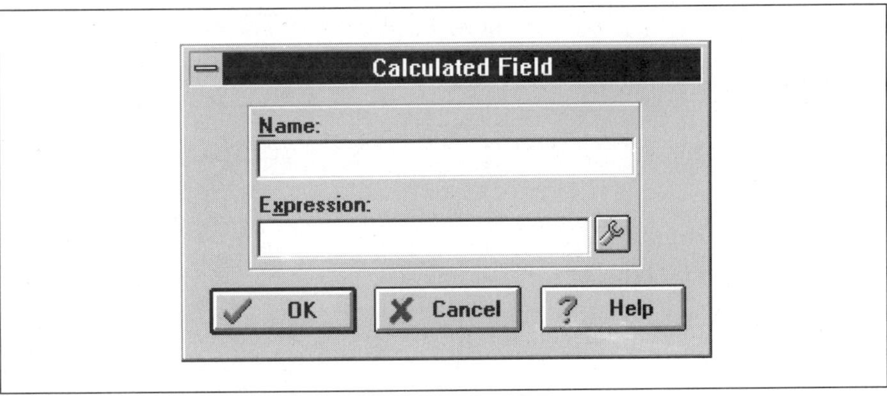

Calculated Field dialog box

To add a calculated field, enter a name and then an expression. If you fill in these two fields and click on OK or press Enter, your new calculated field is added to the Selected Fields list in the Table Records Properties dialog box.

Clicking on the tool icon next to the Expression: entry field launches the Expression Builder, which lets you build a dBASE expression. (See Chapter 8 for information about using the Expression Builder.)

To edit the characteristics of a calculated field, select it in the Selected Fields list to make the Calculated ... pushbutton at the bottom of the Fields tab available. Clicking on this button returns you to the Calculated Field dialog box for the selected field.

Field Properties To set field properties, click on the Properties ... pushbutton, just to the left of the Calculated Field ... pushbutton. You'll see the Field Properties dialog box, shown in Figure 9.5.

FIGURE 9.5

The Field Properties dialog box

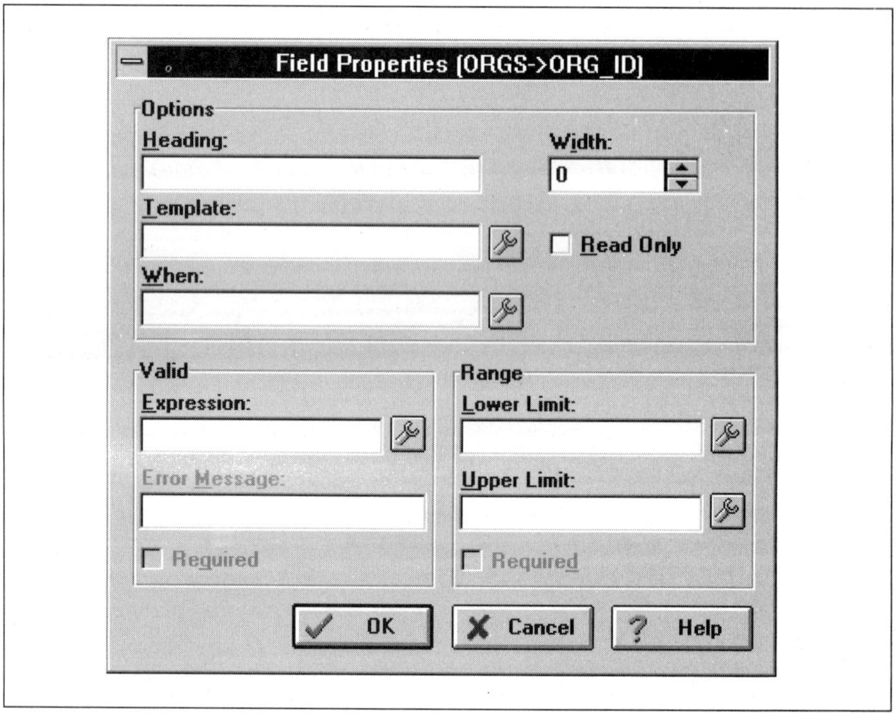

The Heading entry field accepts a column or field heading that replaces the default field name heading. The Width spinbutton sets the visual width. If the field width is wider than the visual width, the field will scroll as you enter data.

The Template entry field lets you enter formatting information, just as you can with the Picture property. Clicking on the tool icon launches the Choose Template dialog box.

The Read Only check box can make the field read-only (so that it cannot be modified). This can be very useful for ID fields.

The When entry field is a more sophisticated version of the Read Only check box. It allows editing the field when the contents of the When expression evaluate to True. Clicking on the tool icon launches the Expression Builder.

The Valid and Range settings have a similar function: to allow entry of only allowable values into the field. You can enter a logical expression into the Valid Expression entry field. You can enter numbers or dates, depending on your field's type, in the Limit (Lower Limit and Upper Limit) entry fields. A number or date must be within the specified range, or the entry will be rejected. For any field type, the Valid expression must evaluate to True, or the entry won't be accepted. For each of these fields, clicking on the tool icon launches the Expression Builder.

Normally, the Valid Expression and Range entries are evaluated when you enter data. If you select the Required check box for either field, every field that you navigate over is checked for these conditions. If you get to a field that doesn't meet the conditions, you will not be able to go past it without entering an acceptable value.

After you use the Field Properties dialog box to set values for each field, the Properties reporting field (it looks like an entry field, but you can't type in it) in the Table Records Properties dialog box is updated with a compressed version of the data you entered.

▸▸ **NOTE**

All your work in the Field Properties dialog box will be entered into your DBASEWIN.INI file, for use in later dBASE for Windows sessions. See Appendix C, which is about the DBASEWIN.INI initialization file, if you want to try your hand at entering this data as a compressed text string.

Records Tab Properties

The Records tab of the Table Records Properties dialog box is shown in Figure 9.6. It includes three sets of choices:

- Editing Options
- Scope
- Index Range

FIGURE 9.6 

Table Record Properties, Records tab

In the Editing Options choices, if Append is checked, you can add new records to the table. If the Edit option is checked, you can modify the values in your fields, in accordance with any other specifications you've made for particular fields. If it isn't checked, every field is read-only, overriding any other field settings you've made.

The Delete option, if checked, lets you delete records. For some tables, such as a table of U.S. two-letter postal codes, you would not normally want to allow deletion of records, so you would not check this option.

The Follow Index option selects one of two behaviors, either of which can be confusing at times. Assume that your master index is on the Name field and you're correcting the invalid entry Zenith, changing it to Azimuth. The question is, what should dBASE for Windows do when you make this change?

If you choose Follow Index, when you change the master index value, dBASE for Windows will relocate its position in the table. In the example above, it would change from the *Z*'s to the *A*'s. If Follow Index were not checked, when you changed the master index value to Azimuth, your record would disappear from the page full of *Z*'s that you could see. Your position in the table wouldn't change. For most applications, you'll want Follow Index checked.

The Index Range selections are available whenever a master index is selected. You enter expressions in these fields that evaluate to the same data type as your master index. If the current record is between the Low Key and High Key values, it is shown. If it is not in range, it disappears.

This is a method for limiting the table to a portion of the available data. For instance, on Monday, you might be updating data from *A* through *E*, so you use this range to make the rest of your table disappear (it is masked out until you change the range).

The Exclude check box specifies whether the end points of the range are considered in range. If your range is dates between 12/1/95 and 12/31/95, checking Exclude would eliminate the start and end dates. Only records from 12/2/95 through 12/30/95 would be accepted. If it isn't checked, records exactly matching the end values are considered part of the range.

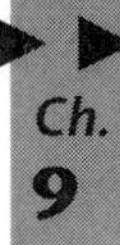

Window Tab Properties

The Window tab of the Table Records Properties dialog box controls settings that affect the whole window. It is shown in Figure 9.7.

FIGURE 9.7

Table Record Properties, Window tab

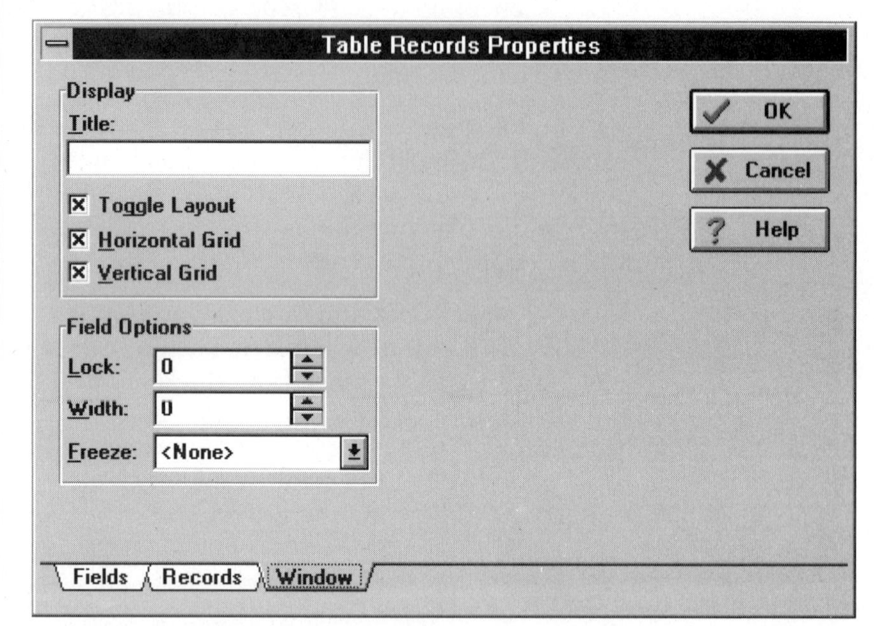

The Title entry field lets you replace the default window title (Table Records, followed by your table name in parentheses) with one of your own choosing.

The Toggle Layout check box, if checked, lets you toggle between Browse, Form, and Columnar Layout views. The Horizontal Grid and Vertical Grid check boxes let you turn these grid lines on or off.

The Field Options choices let you set the number of fields that will be frozen on the left (Lock), the maximum display width of fields (Width), and a single field to take all data entry (Freeze).

The Lock spinbutton locks the specified number of fields into the left side of a Browse Layout view. It's handy when, for example, you have a name on the left and want it to stay in place while you scroll through the other fields.

The Width setting is the second place dBASE for Windows looks when deciding on the display width for your fields. It starts with width settings specified for individual fields, which take top priority. Without a setting for the individual field, the setting here applies, if it is smaller than the actual field width. Finally, the field's width is used if this Width setting is equal to 0 or the field is smaller than the width set here. This is a convenient way to make a large number of wide columns temporarily shrink.

The Freeze drop-down list lets you pick a single field that will be the only one available for data entry. It will remain in your Browse window regardless of your horizontal scrolling, and all your other fields will be read-only.

►► *Using Table Utilities*

To get to the Table Utilities, you must go through the Table pull-down menu, which is available in the Command window or when the Table View tool is active. In both cases, choose Table ➤ Table Utilities Alt-T, then T) to access the Table Utilities.

►► **NOTE**

One of the design changes we would make if dBASE for Windows were our product is to not hide the Table Utilities. As you'll see, this is a powerful set of data-manipulation tools. We think it deserves a place on the main menu and on the speedbar. Maybe in a later version...

This selection displays the Table Utilities menu:

Manage Indexes...
Reindex

Close Table
Close All Tables

Delete Records...
Recall Records...
Pack Records
Zap Records

Append Records from File...
Export Records...
Sort Records...
Generate Records...

Count Records...
Calculate Records...

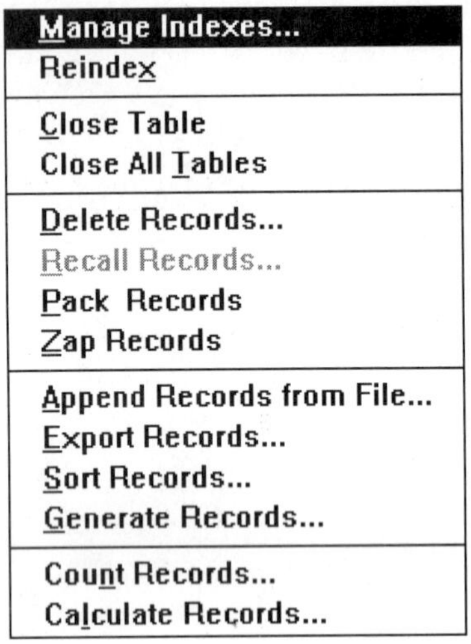

As you can see, the utilities themselves are divided into five groups:

- Index Management
- Table Closing
- Record Deleting and Recalling
- Record Import and Export, Sorting and Generating
- Counting and Calculation

The five sections that follow discuss each of these capabilities in detail.

▸ Working with Indexes

The two index-related utilities are represented by the Manage Indexes and Reindex choices in the Table Utilities menu.

Managing Indexes

The Manage Indexes choice lets you control the indexes in the production index (the .MDX file with the same name as the table). You can create, modify, and delete indexes, and you can select the current master index (the one which controls the apparent order of the records). Figure 9.8 shows the Manage Indexes dialog box being used to select a master index.

FIGURE 9.8 

Managing a master index

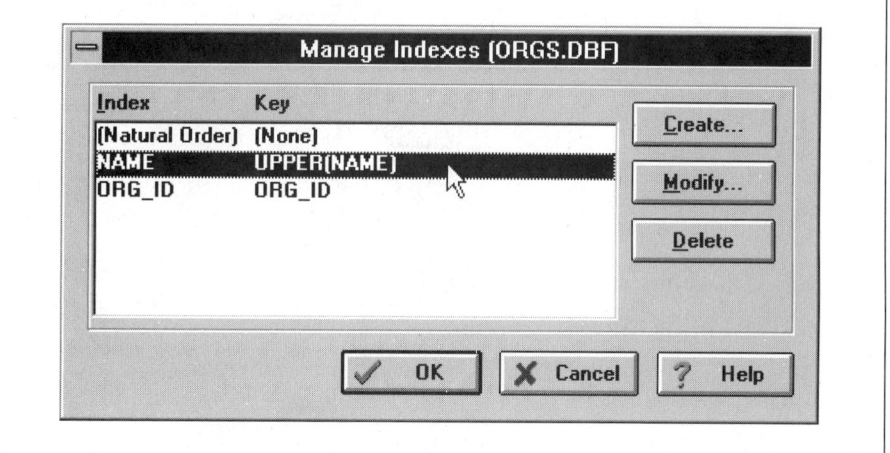

NOTE

The Manage Indexes dialog box is also available from the Structure menu of the Table Structure tool and the Query menu of the Query Designer tool.

The dialog box presents three choices:

- Create …
- Modify …
- Delete

If the (Natural Order) index is highlighted, the Modify and Delete choices are grayed (not available). When an index is highlighted, those choices become available.

Choosing Create … allows you to specify a new index (see Chapter 4). To remove an index, highlight it and choose Delete. Selecting an existing index and clicking on the Modify … button takes you to the Modify Index

dialog box, as shown in Figure 9.9. This looks just like the Create Index dialog box, except that it shows the current settings for the index you chose. You can change the settings for this index, and then choose OK to put those changes into effect.

FIGURE 9.9 

The Modify Index dialog box

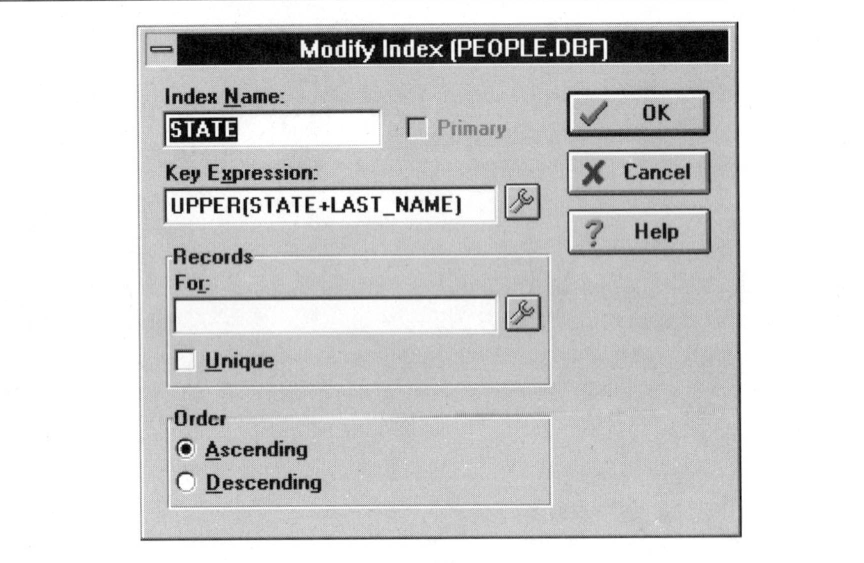

Reindexing

Choosing Reindex rebuilds the production index. The production index is maintained automatically as you add, edit, and modify your data, so this choice is only necessary if you need to recover from a hardware or software failure.

However, rebuilding the indexes periodically can lead to faster operation. The internal index structure, called a B-tree, depends on spreading the index data evenly over the index pages (called *balancing* the index) for maximum efficiency.

dBASE for Windows balances indexes as it builds them. However, the index can become unbalanced over time as data is added, changed, and deleted. So reindexing is a sensible maintenance procedure.

The reindex process should be run on the machine that holds the data, as it involves reading every record in the table multiple times. You should plan to reindex when you have exclusive use of the table and don't object to a time-consuming process.

▶ Closing Tables

There are two table closing choices: Close Table and Close All Tables. Selecting Close Table is equivalent to choosing Close from the Table Records tool's System menu or pressing Ctrl-F4. It closes the current table. If you have multiple related tables open, it closes all of them. It also closes any related .MDX and .DBT files.

The Close All Tables choice closes all open tables and related .MDX and .DBT files. If sessions are on, it closes all the tables in the current session, which also ends the session. If sessions are off, all open tables are closed.

▶ Minimizing Waste and Recovering from Mistakes

The next section of the Table Utilities menu deals with deleting and recalling records. It includes four choices:

- Delete Records ...
- Recall Records ...
- Pack Records
- Zap Records

Deleting Records

The Delete Records dialog box is shown in Figure 9.10. As you can see in that example, the Delete Records dialog box is simply a Scope panel plus the three standard pushbuttons. The default scope is Next 1. Next starts counting at the current record. (The Scope panel is the same as the one that appears in the Find and other dialog boxes; see Appendix B for more information.)

The default settings in this dialog box delete a record in the same way that selecting Table ➤ Delete Selected Record (or pressing Ctrl-U) deletes a record.

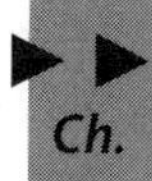

FIGURE 9.10

Removing California records from the table

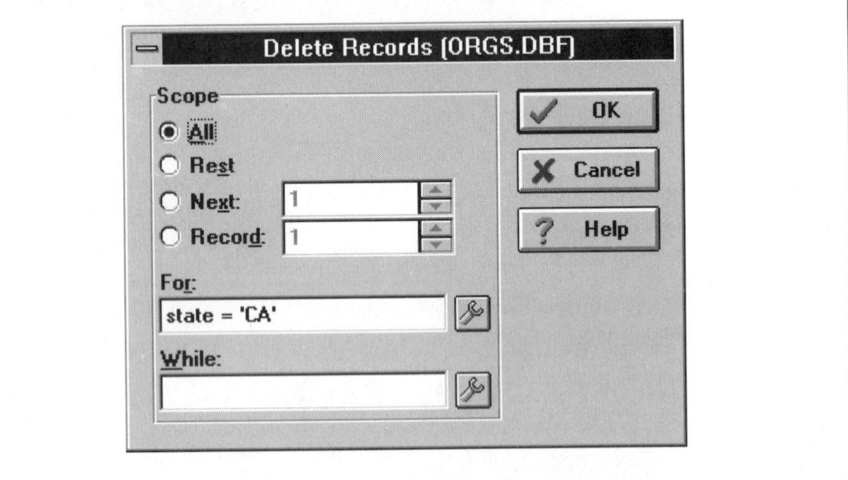

▸▸ **WARNING**

The Delete Records dialog box does *not* recall records. Unlike when you use Ctrl-U on a record that has been deleted (its Delete flag is on), the record does not become "undeleted." Any record in the scope of the deletion that is already deleted simply stays deleted.

Recalling Records

dBASE for Windows tables use a single byte to indicate a record's deletion status. This Deleted flag is set when the record is deleted (or, more correctly, marked for deletion). Deleting the record sets this flag. If the Deleted setting is on, the record disappears from view. If the Deleted setting is off, the record stays in view but the Deleted flag is set.

▸▸ **WARNING**

Deletion status does not apply to Paradox .DB or SQL records, which are physically deleted when you delete them. They cannot be recalled.

Figure 9.11 shows the operation performed in Figure 9.10 being reversed. All the records where the state is California are being recalled.

FIGURE 9.11

Recalling deleted records

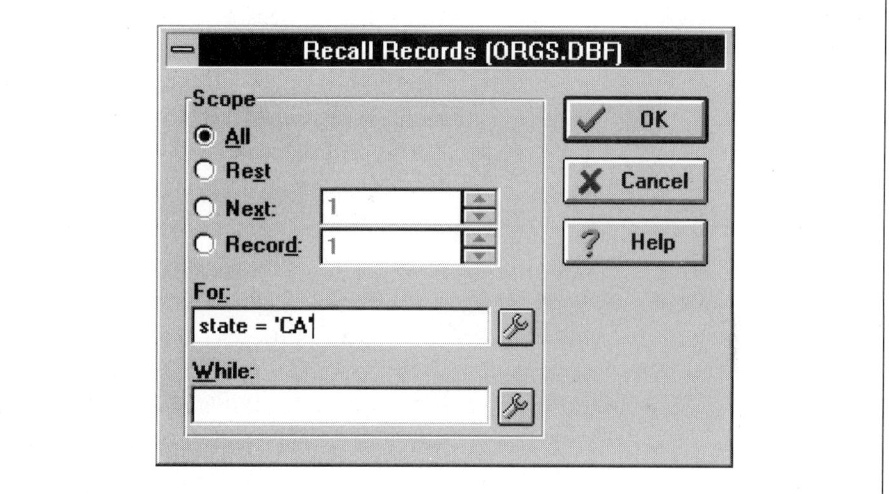

Packing Records

The Pack Records choice physically deletes records from a .DBF file. After packing, the .DBF file contains only records that do not have the Deleted flag set. (Paradox .DB tables and SQL tables are continuously packed.)

If you're responsible for maintaining your tables, we recommend the following routine maintenance procedure:

- Make backups of your tables.
- Pack your tables.
- Reindex your tables.

Note that the backup must come before the pack operation. If your data is auditable, your auditors will require that you do it this way. If you are your own auditor, you should require it of yourself.

There is no way to recover data that has been packed out of existence. The nondeleted records overwrite the locations of the deleted records. Except for deleted records at the very end of the table, other deleted records cannot be recovered records after a pack operation, unless you have a backup copy.

Zapping Records

Zapping a file kills every record in the file—quickly! Zap resets the internal record count in the table to 0, and it tells DOS that the end of the file is the end of the header area. The portion of the file that holds the records is returned to DOS's free space pool.

This process is virtually instantaneous. The equivalent process is deleting all records, then packing the table. To delete all the records, every record's Deleted flag must be written. Since the pack operation does not know what you have been doing before you tell it to start, it will read every record to check the Deleted status. This means that the process must first write every record, and then read every record. Obviously, with a large table, this can be a long process.

If the safety setting is on, the Zap Records dialog box will prompt you to confirm that you want to empty your file.

If you have not opened the table for exclusive use, dBASE for Windows will ask you if you want to open the table for exclusive use. (Obviously, you cannot zap a file if others are accessing it.)

▸ Sharing Your Data with Other Applications

There are four data-sharing and file-manipulating choices on the Table Utilities menu:

- Append Records from File …
- Export Records …
- Sort Records …
- Generate Records …

Appending Records from a File

The Append Records from File … selection opens the Append Records from File dialog box, shown in Figure 9.12.

FIGURE 9.12

Appending records from a temporary table

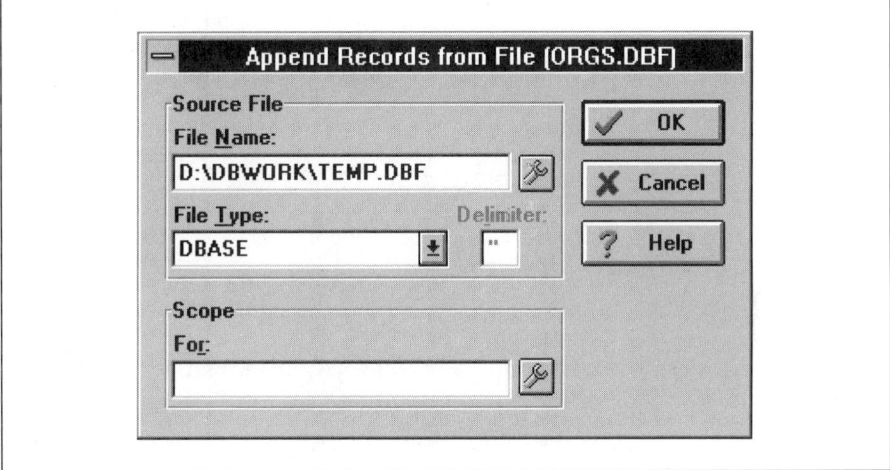

The File Type selection in the Source File section lists the type choices on a drop-down list:

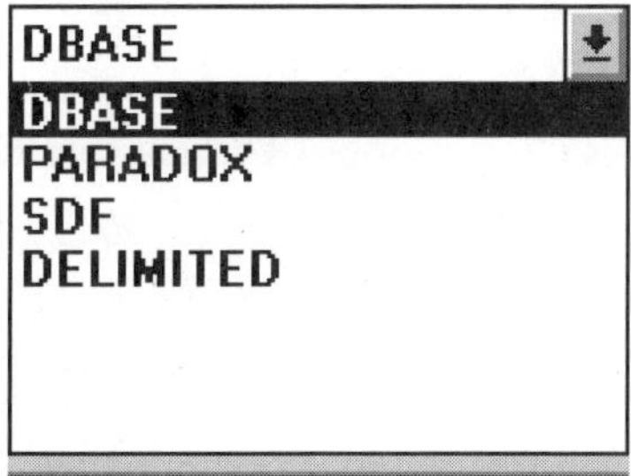

Clicking on the tool icon next to the File Name entry field launches an Open File dialog box titled Import File. For dBASE files, the default file type is .DBF. For Paradox files, the default is .DB. For SDF (System Data Format) and delimited files, the default type is .TXT.

SDF files are text files with the columns lined up (also known as fixed field lengths):

```
Friendly    Phil Friendly          Pleasantville    NY12345(800) 111-1234
Adamson     Adrianne Adamson       Sun City         CA55555(800) 123-4567
Monroe      Madilyn Monroe         Hollywood        CA55555(123) 123-1234
Gable       Eve Gable              New York         NY12345(212) 911-9111
Hacker      Herb Hacker            Mountain View    CA55555(800) 987-6543
```

Delimited files use delimiters:

```
"Friendly","Phil Friendly","Pleasantville","NY","12345","(800) 111-1234"
"Adamson","Adrianne Adamson","Sun City","CA","55555","(800) 123-4567"
"Monroe","Madilyn Monroe","Hollywood","CA","55555","(123) 123-1234"
"Gable","Eve Gable","New York","NY","12345","(212) 911-9111"
"Hacker","Herb Hacker","Mountain View","CA","55555","(800) 987-6543"
```

The Delimiter entry field lets you choose your own delimiter if the default is not suitable. It is only available when the File Type is DELIMITED.

The Scope choices let you establish a logical condition that limits the records appended. The For condition only applies when you are importing from dBASE tables.

When you import from dBASE tables, the Deleted setting controls the import of records marked for deletion. If Deleted is checked, only non-deleted records are imported. If Deleted is not checked, all records are imported.

Exporting Records

The Export Records ... choice opens the Export Records dialog box, shown in Figure 9.13.

The Export File section is similar to the Source File section in the Append Records dialog box. The only difference is that a fifth file type is available: DBMEMO3.

The default file extension for DBMEMO3 data is .DBF. This type is a dBASE III+ compatible .DBF format.

The dialog box offers the full range of Scope choices. You can select and order fields through the field selector at the bottom of the dialog box. (The Scope options and field selector are described in Appendix B.)

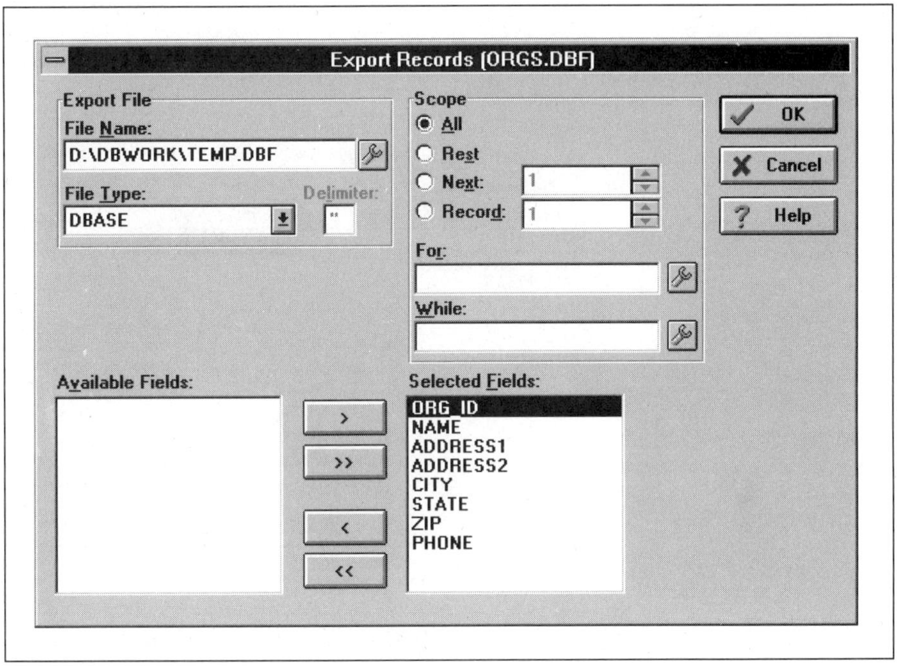

FIGURE 9.13

Exporting data to a temporary table

Sorting Records

The Sort Records … choice opens the Sort Records dialog box, shown in Figure 9.14.

The sorting process does not sort a table's records. Rather, it sorts from the active table into another table.

The Name field is used to enter the .DBF or .DB file into which you will sort the records of the current table. Clicking on the tool icon launches an Open File dialog box titled Save File.

The Target Table Type box lets you choose between dBASE (.DBF) and Paradox (.DB) tables. Your choice determines the default extension in the Open File dialog box.

The Field Selection box is a modified field selector. There is no **>>** button in this selector, because moving every available field into the Key Fields list would not normally be a sensible operation.

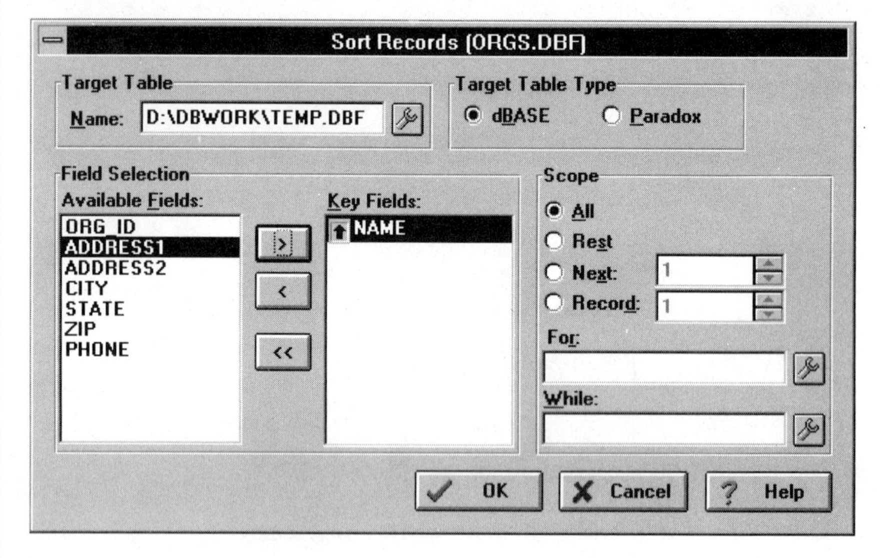

FIGURE 9.14 *Sorting to a temporary table on the Name field*

The field or fields that you select are the ones on which the result table will be sorted. Using multiple fields sorts on each, in order. For example, if you sort on State and Name, the data will be ordered by State and, within each state, by Name.

When you select a field for sorting, an up arrow appears next to its name. If you click on this arrow, you get a drop-down list of sort choices:

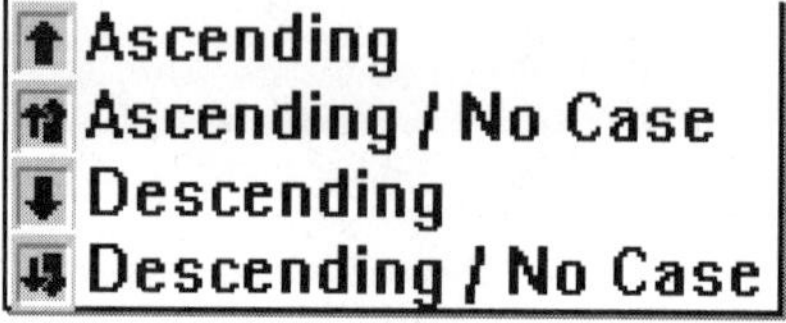

The arrows indicate your choice (just as they do in the Query Designer). The Scope choices are the standard ones.

Generating Records

The Generate Records … choice launches the Generate Records dialog box, which allows you to enter the number of records you want to generate (as we did in Chapter 6 to get some test data).

Generating records is very useful when you are designing a system and need to check possible response times. Test files of a few records give you no idea of what your performance will be with tens of thousands of records. The dBASE for Windows record-generation feature lets you test your system on a filled file.

This dialog box is simple. Just spin the button or, for larger values, type the number of new records you want generated, then click on OK or press Enter.

dBASE for Windows' progress is reported in the center of the status bar by a colored area that moves from left to right, showing the proportion of the new records that have been generated. A percentage figure is also displayed in this area.

To generate a lot of records (10,000 or more), eliminate all tags from your production index, then generate. Add the indexes after your table is filled.

▶▶ **WARNING**

Before you use the Generate Records dialog box for a substantial number of records, check that you have disk space available. Multiply the record length by the number of records that will be generated. The record length is given in the Table Structure tool.

▶ *Analyzing Your Data*

There are two Table Utilities menu choices for data analysis: Count Records … and Calculate Records ….

Counting Records

The Count Records … choice launches the Count Records dialog box, shown in Figure 9.15.

One of the most frequently asked questions of any database is, "How many …?" In Figure 9.15, we are asking how many of our records are for California.

FIGURE 9.15

Counting the records in California

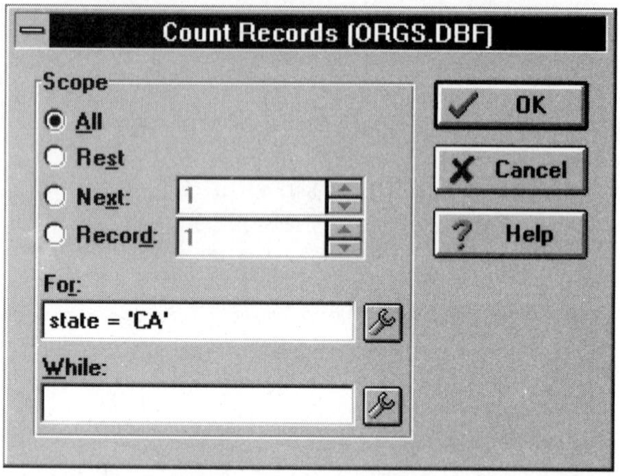

The Count Records dialog box answers these questions. It reports its results in the Counted Records dialog box, which shows your answer and waits for an OK click or Enter press.

You can use the Scope panel to set your criteria and proceed to click on OK or press Enter. If you're counting in a small table, your answer will be virtually instantaneous. If your count is For or While a condition that matches an index expression, the answer will be pulled from the index, and will also be virtually instantaneous, even on very large tables.

Counting for a nonindexed condition on a large file requires reading every record, which may take some time.

If you give the command

```
? RECCOUNT( )
```

in the Command window, you get an immediate response in the results pane, showing the total records in the file. If the Deleted setting is off, this will match the Count Records results (when your Scope is All).

If the Deleted flag is on, the Count Records dialog box will exclude deleted records from its count, so it may be lower than RECCOUNT( ).

Calculating on Records

The Calculate Records … choice launches the Calculate Records dialog box shown in Figure 9.16. The following calculations are available:

- Average
- Minimum
- Maximum
- Standard Deviation
- Sum
- Variance

FIGURE 9.16

Performing calculations

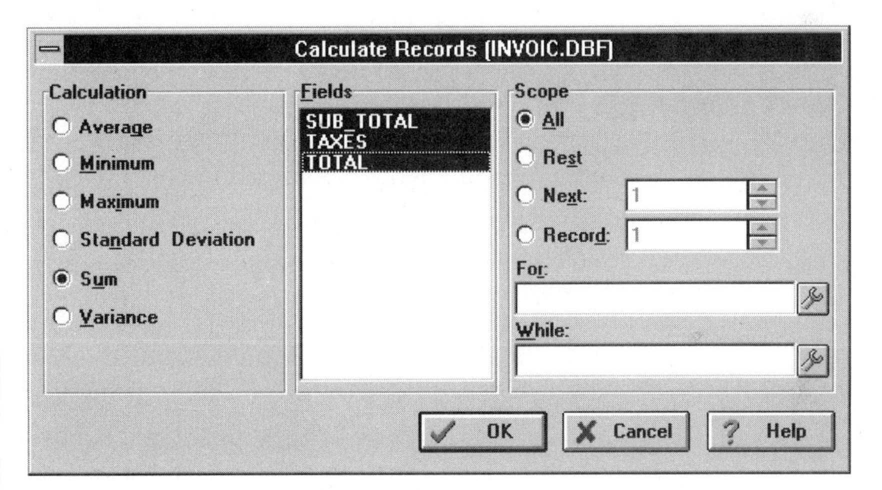

For those of you who are not statisticians, the standard deviation of a set of data points measures the amount by which they vary from the arithmetic average (mean). It is the square root of the average of the square of the deviations from the mean. Variance is the square of the standard deviation.

In the Fields box, you'll see a list of all the Numeric and Float fields in your active table. You can select one by clicking on it. You can select a range of fields by clicking on the first field and Shift-clicking at the other end of the range. If you want to select multiple fields, but not a range, use Ctrl-click.

▸▸ TIP

All the calculations require far more time spent reading records than actually calculating, so you might as well get your answer for all Numeric fields.

On our test machine, a generic 33 MHz 80486, we calculate the standard deviation of a single Float field in a 1000-record database in a little under two seconds. We calculate the standard deviation of all six Float fields in the same table in a little under two seconds, too. (The time difference is not measurable with a stopwatch.)

The dialog box has a Scope panel, so you can limit your calculations to a subset of your available records.

▸▸ Summary

In this chapter, you've reviewed the features of the Table Structure and Table Reports tools.

You started with the Table Structure tool, which is a special Browse window for table structures.

You looked into every part of what you could do in the fields, between and outside the fields, with the menus, and with speedbar buttons.

You studied the Data Loss Potential dialog box. Some changes to table structures can lose data, and dBASE warns you. However, it warns you about the *potential*. You learned about what type of loss you might expect, and what could be done to prevent it.

Next you went on to the Table Records tool. You examined every new choice menu choice. You spent a lot of time on the Properties menu's Table Records Window … choice, which launches a three-tab form.

You learned to use the Table Properties dialog box to customize your Table Records tool for your forms, and you learned that these customized settings were saved for you in the DBASEWIN.INI file.

After going into every aspect of the Table Records tool, you went on to the Table Utilities menu choices. This menu lets you control your indexes, close tables, delete and recall records (in .DBF files), share data with other applications, and perform data analysis.

In the next chapter, you'll begin taking an equally comprehensive look at Crystal Reports.

CHAPTER 10

Mastering Crystal Reports

▶▶ **This** chapter and the next cover the Crystal Reports tool. In this chapter, we'll go through every menu choice, dialog box, and speedbar button in detail. We'll attempt to treat Crystal Reports (Crystal, for short) exhaustively, at the risk of getting exhausting.

Here, we'll cover every tool at your disposal, so you'll know just how much you can do with Crystal. This will prepare you for getting creative, as we'll do in the next chapter.

Unlike dBASE for Windows, which changes menu options for the different tools, Crystal has a single main menu. Each pull-down menu has a single list of options, which are grayed or active, as appropriate to your work. The main menu for Crystal has eight choices:

File Edit Insert Format Database Report Window Help

We'll go through each of these pull-down menus and the options they offer. Then we'll cover the speedbar, the format bar, and the Preview window's speedbar. We'll complete the chapter with a discussion of Crystal's Speed menus.

▶▶ NOTE

In Chapter 11, we'll treat some special types of reports that you can create using what you'll learn here. Frankly, Chapter 11 is more fun, and we won't mind if you turn right past this chapter to get to it. If you're stuck on a particular report you want to create, go right ahead and try to find something similar in Chapter 11. But you'll still need the information in this chapter. As you go through Chapter 11, you can flip back to this chapter to pick up on all that you've missed.

▶▶ Using the File Menu

The File pull-down menu includes choices for opening, saving, printing, and closing files, as well as setting file options.

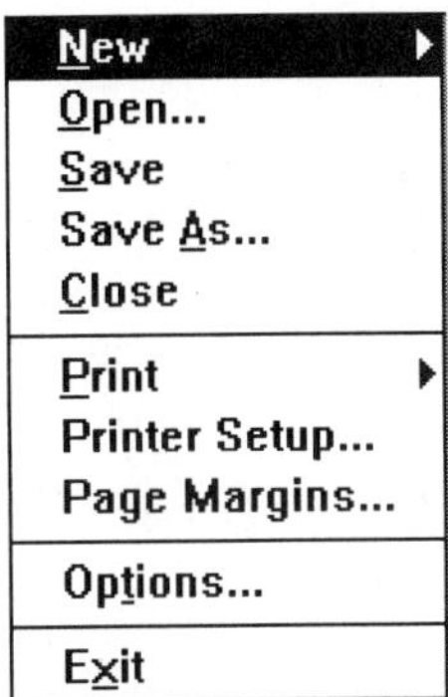

We'll cover the New choice in the next chapter, when we discuss crosstabs and labels. The Open …, Save, Save As …, and Close menu choices work as you would expect.

▸ Printing Files

The File ➤ Print menu let's you print to a printer, to the Preview window, or to a file:

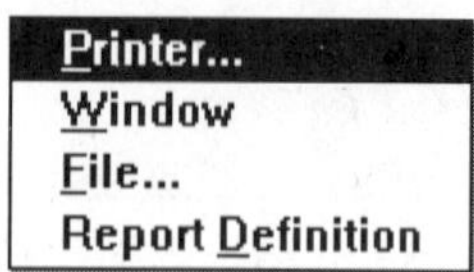

You can also print the report's definition—a text file that documents your report.

The Saved Data Dialog Box

Once your data has been saved, any of the first three File menu choices launch the Saved Data dialog box, shown in Figure 10.1.

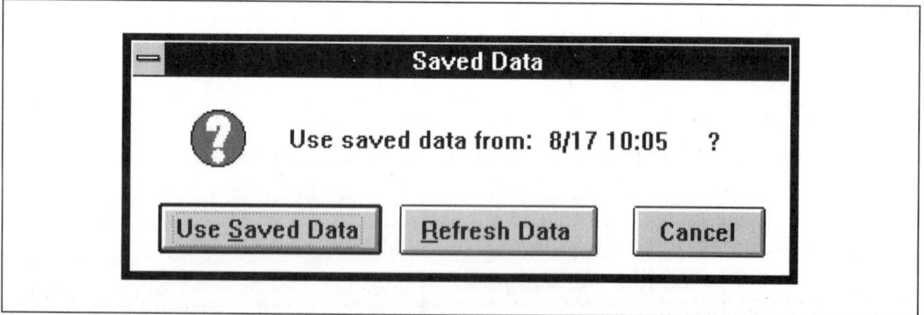

FIGURE 10.1 *The Saved Data dialog box saves your time*

When Crystal is launched with a view or .DBF file selected, it will make a copy of the data that it will use in a temporary .DBF file. This can be a time-consuming process, especially if your tables are large and your view is complex. Once the temporary data table is created, its use is almost instantaneous.

Most of the time, you will use your saved data. For a final report, you may refresh your data to make sure that you have the latest information. If you are not on a network with multiple users, your saved data will be identical to the result from refreshing your data (unless you are running dBASE for Windows in another session and editing your data while your work in Crystal).

Printing and Previewing Files

The File ➤ Print ➤ Printer ... choice launches the Windows Print dialog box. From this dialog box, you can choose to print your entire report or a range of pages.

The File ➤ Print ➤ Window choice launches your report in the Preview window (see Chapter 7).

Exporting by Printing to a File

The File ➤ Print ➤ File choice launches the Export dialog box, shown in Figure 10.2. This is an important dialog box, because it provides a backdoor export facility that is much more robust than the export facilities built into dBASE for Windows.

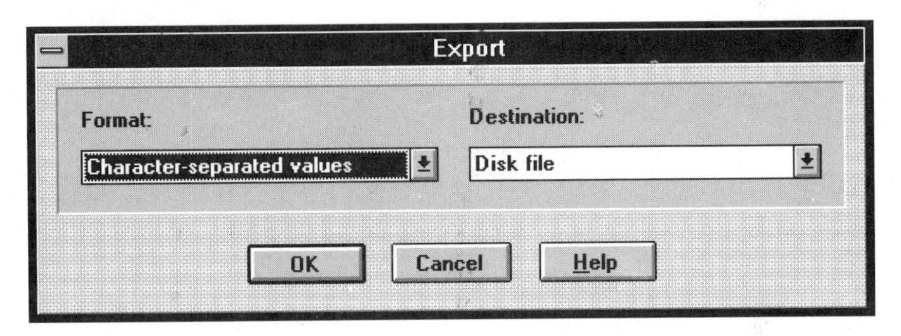

FIGURE 10.2 ▶

The Export dialog box

▶▶ **NOTE**

As any major software company does, Borland competes with Microsoft and Lotus, among others. It is not overly enthusiastic about providing links from its programs to competing programs. In contrast to Borland, Crystal sells add-ons, not major software. An add-on vendor's existence depends on good support for the software of major vendors, so it is not surprising that its list of supported products is much more extensive than Borland's.

The direct export support available from the pull-down menu on the left side of the Export dialog box includes the following:

- Character-separated values
- Comma-separated values (CSV)
- Crystal Reports (RPT)
- Data Interchange Format (DIF)
- Excel 2.1 (XLS)
- Excel 3.0 (XLS)
- Excel 4.0 (XLS)
- Lotus 1-2-3 (WK1)
- Lotus 1-2-3 (WK3)
- Lotus 1-2-3 (WKS)
- Quattro Pro 5.0 (WB1)
- Record style (columns of values)
- Rich Text Format
- Tab-separated text
- Tab-separated values
- Text

When you choose the Character-separated values option, you move to the Character-Separated Values dialog box, shown in Figure 10.3. In this dialog box, you can choose the character that will separate fields and the character to use to surround character fields (by default, the double-quotation mark).

FIGURE 10.3 ►

The Character-Separated Values dialog box

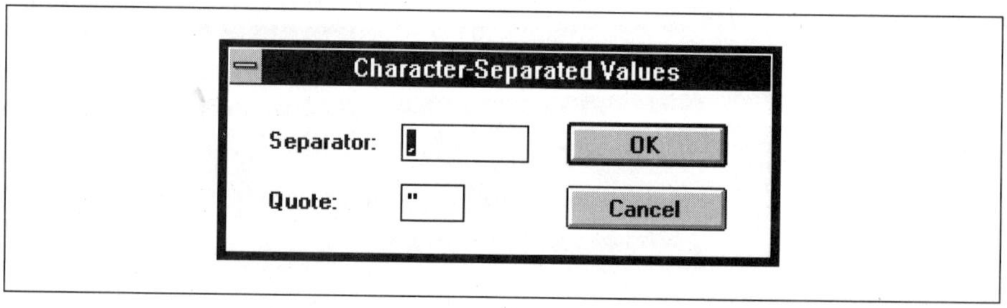

After you choose these characters, the Number and Date Format dialog box is launched, as shown in Figure 10.4.

FIGURE 10.4

The Number and Date Format dialog box

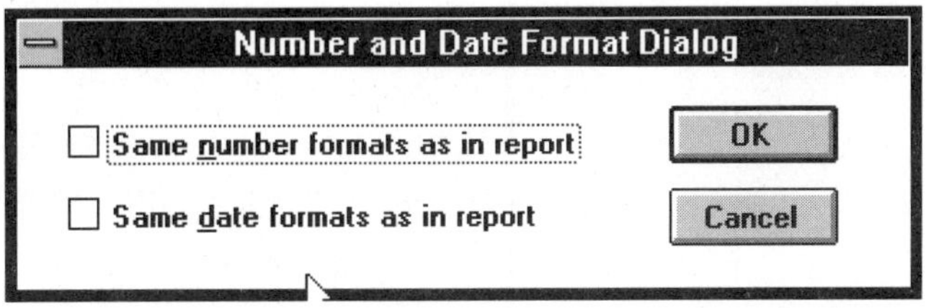

Next, the Choose Export File dialog box is launched. This is a standard Open File dialog box (see Appendix B). If you are attached to a network mail system, the destination may be a disk file or a network mail system. If you are not on a network, the destination is a disk file.

Getting a Report on Your Report Design

The File ➤ Print ➤ Report Definition choice prints documentation about the design of your report. This is a five-section report. The easiest way to get a feel for this report is to choose this option and examine its output.

The output is directed immediately to your default printer, without any prompts. Be ready to print a report before you choose this option.

▶ Setting Up the Printer and Page Margins

There are two additional choices in the printer section of the File pull-down menu: Printer Setup … and Page Margins ….

The Printer Setup … option launches the Print Setup dialog box, common to Windows applications. This lets you choose a default printer, portrait or landscape orientation, upper or lower paper trays, and the other options that your printer supports.

The Page Margins … choice launches the Printer Margins dialog box, shown in Figure 10.5.

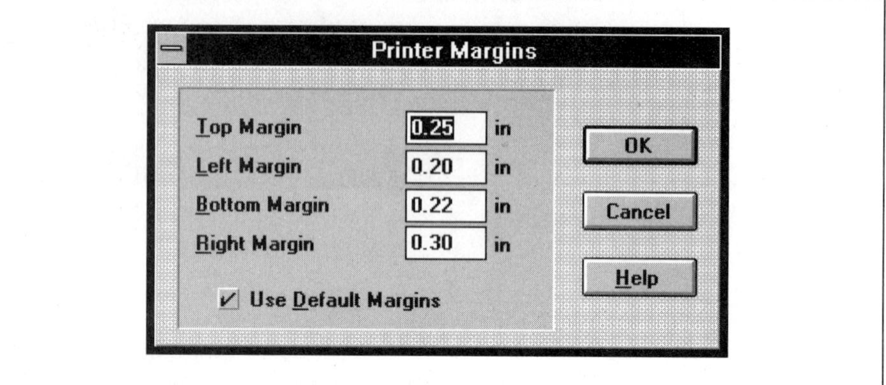

FIGURE 10.5 *The Printer Margins dialog box*

This dialog box lets you set margins for your printed pages (hence the difference in the names of the menu choice and the dialog box).

▸▸ **TIP**

Leave the default choices unless you know that your printer needs special choices. Click on the Use Default Margins check box to return to the standard setting if you are having problems.

▸ Setting File Options

The File ➤ Options ... choice launches Crystal's Options dialog box. The Options dialog box is functionally similar to the multi-tab dialog boxes in dBASE for Windows. As you click on the four choices in the Category section, the rest of the dialog box changes to reflect your choice. Figure 10.6 shows the Options dialog box for the General choice.

The Options Dialog Box General Options

The first three general options let you control the work surface for Crystal Reports. You can turn the button bar (speedbar) on or off, and do the same for the format bar and the status bar.

FIGURE 10.6

The Options dialog box, General category

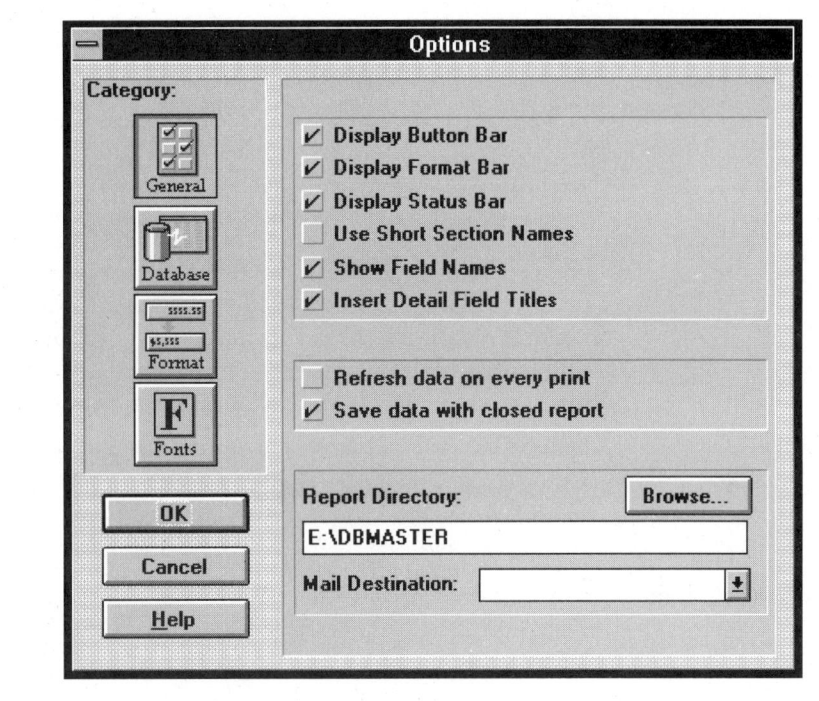

The Use Short Section Names choice abbreviates the section names to the left of the report to something that barely suggests the section. The Page header becomes PH, the Details band becomes D, the first Group header is GH1, and so on.

TIP

Don't choose Use Short Section Names until you are comfortable with Crystal Reports. Once you know the sections well, you may appreciate having more of your work surface available for the report you are working on.

The Show Field Names choice toggles between showing the field names in the report's fields or showing characters which suggest field contents. For example, without field names a character field will show *X*'s.

By default, as you add fields to the Details band, the field names are added over the Details band as field titles. If you don't want these default titles, remove the check from the Insert Detail Field Titles box.

The next panel lets you control the use of saved data. If you check Refresh data on every print, the Saved Data dialog box will not appear. Each time you print, your data will be retrieved from its tables. This option is a time-waster if you are not running on a network with multiple simultaneous users.

The Save data with closed report option, if checked, saves a copy of the temporary data when Crystal saves your report's definition. If your data is not time-consuming to pull together from multiple tables, of if your data takes lots of disk space, don't choose this option.

Clicking on the Browse ... pushbutton launches the Set Directory dialog box, shown in Figure 10.7.

FIGURE 10.7

The Set Directory dialog box

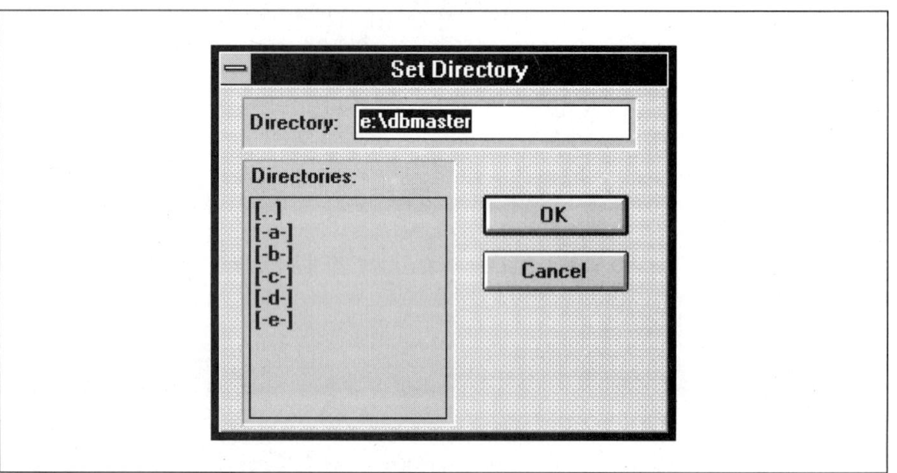

The Mail Destination choice in the Options dialog box has a drop-down list of the mail choices supported on your network.

The Options Dialog Box Database Options

The Options dialog box with the Database category selected is shown in Figure 10.8.

FIGURE 10.8

The Option dialog box, database category

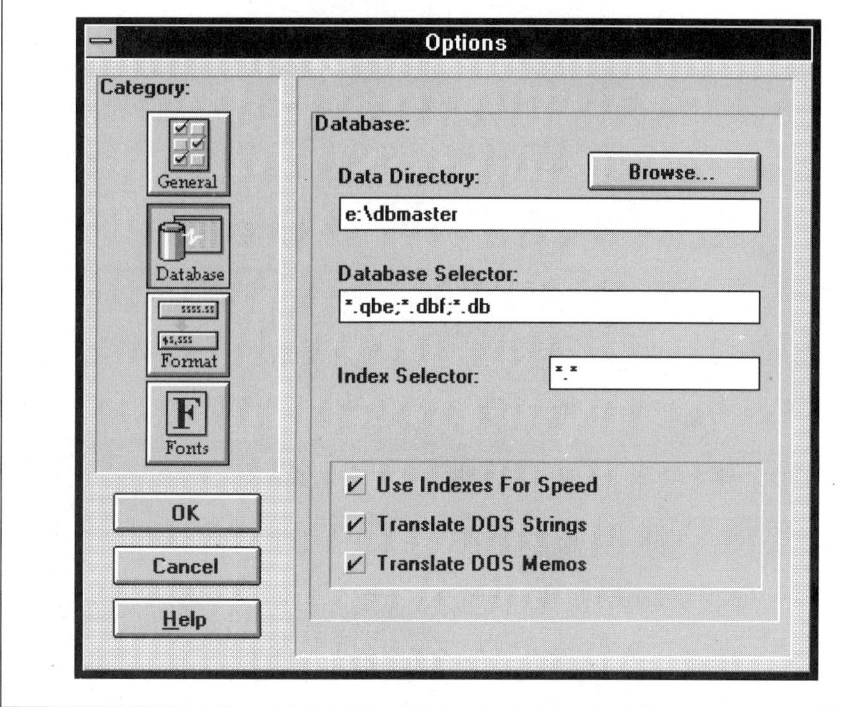

The first choice in this dialog box is Data Directory. This defaults to the same location as the Report Directory in the General category. Clicking on the Browse … button launches the Set Directory dialog box (Figure 10.7).

The Database Selector shows the choices from which your table or query will be chosen. The Index Selector shows the extensions used for finding indexes. When you call Crystal from dBASE for Windows, the exact names of your tables and their indexes are supplied by dBASE, so these choices are not relevant.

The Use Indexes For Speed choice should be left checked except in extraordinary circumstances. (You might not want an index used if you had inadvertently used an index that Crystal Reports needed to do a partial index, when you wanted a full report.)

The Translate DOS Strings and Translate DOS Memos check boxes let you use the characters you supplied in DOS applications in Character and Memo fields, respectively. This applies to the *hi-bit* characters (from 128 and up). In Windows, the hi-bit characters are different from those in DOS. Checking either of these boxes directs Crystal to translate the DOS characters to their Windows equivalents.

The Options Dialog Box Format Options

Figure 10.9 shows the Options dialog box for the Format category. The settings here are your general settings, which you can override for any or all fields in your report. Choosing one of the options in the Options dialog box's Field Format panel launches another dialog box for the type you selected.

FIGURE 10.9

The Options dialog box, Format category

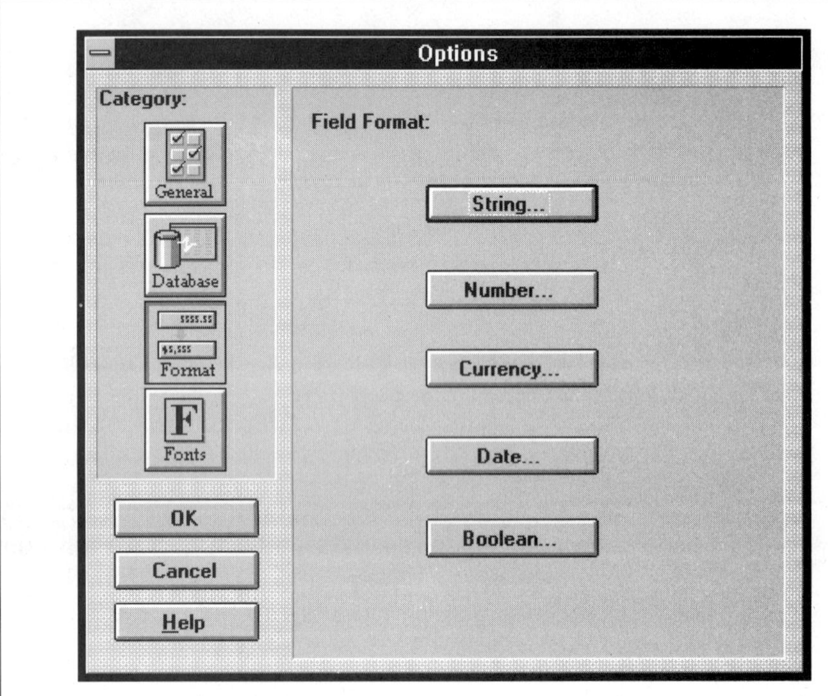

The Format String Dialog Box Choosing File ➤ Options ... Format category and pressing the String ... pushbutton launches the Format String dialog box, shown in Figure 10.10.

This dialog box controls the default formatting for character-based fields. In dBASE tables, for example, these are called *character strings*. In other databases, they are called by other names, such as *text* or *string fields*.

FIGURE 10.10

The Format String dialog box

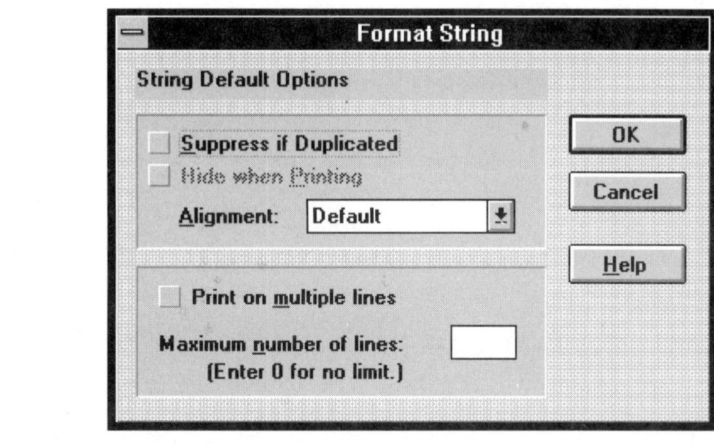

The Suppress if Duplicated option prevents a field's value from being repeated on successive lines of a report. The individual value will be printed only on the first line on which it occurs.

The Hide when Printing option is not available when you select Options … from the File menu, since this would not be a sensible general option. However, the Format String dialog box is also available when you format an individual field. For individual field formatting, the Hide when Printing Option is active. This lets you exclude the field from the printed report. For example, you might use this option for a column that does a calculation for the report, but does not need to appear in the printed version.

The Alignment choices are Default, Left, Centered, and Right. The Default alignment is right-justified for numeric data (columns of numbers line up) and left-justified for all other types (names line up on the left). You can override this here. For example, you could choose to center all dates.

The second section in the Format String dialog box lets you specify the treatment of text fields that are too long to fit on one line. The default is *not* to print long strings on multiple lines. If you check the Print on multiple lines box, the Maximum number of lines box applies. You can specify a maximum number, or leave it at zero, which will let Text fields take as many lines as needed.

▸▸ **NOTE**

Word wrapping is used to print text fields over multiple lines. If the text doesn't fit in the number of lines allowed (1 by default, or the number specified in the Maximum box), the text is truncated to fit.

The Format Number and Format Currency Dialog Boxes Choosing File ➤ Options … Format category and selecting the Number … pushbutton launches the Format Number dialog box, shown in Figure 10.11.

FIGURE 10.11 ▸

The Format Number dialog box

Format Number

Number Default Options

☑ Use Windows Default Format

☐ Suppress if Duplicated
☐ Suppress if Zero
☐ Hide when Printing
Alignment: Default

☐ Currency Symbol: $
☐ One Symbol Per Page
◇ Fixed ◇ Floating
Position: -$123

Decimals: 1.00
Rounding: 0.01
Negatives: -123

Decimal Separator: .
☑ Thousands Separator: ,
☑ Leading Zero

Sample: -5,555,555.56

OK
Cancel
Help

The Currency … pushbutton brings up the Format Currency dialog box, which looks just like the Format Number dialog box. The Format Number dialog box applies to dBASE Numeric and Float fields. The Format Currency settings apply to money type fields, such as those in Paradox.

The Use Windows Default Format check box has the formatting default to the specifications provided in the Windows Control Panel.

NOTE

Using the Windows defaults may limit your other choices in a way you don't want, or it may quickly adjust your formatting to your national standards. You can try it to see if it is helpful or limiting.

The Suppress if Duplicated option prevents a field's value from being repeated on successive lines of a report. The individual value will be printed only on the first line on which it occurs. Suppress if Zero prevents a field's value from being printed if it is zero. Hide when Printing is unavailable when you get to this dialog box from the File menu. When you are formatting an individual field, you can choose this option to prevent the field from appearing in the printed report. The Alignment choices are Default (right-justified for numbers and left-justified for other data), Left, Centered, and Right.

The currency-related choices let you choose a symbol (such as $) for currency. The rest of the options, such as printing the symbol just once on each page, apply when you are formatting currency fields, not when you access this dialog box through the Format Number choice.

Your choices in the Format Currency dialog box are to print the symbol only once, at the top of a column; to print the symbol in a fixed position (to the left or right of the number portion of the field, inside or outside optional parentheses for negative numbers); or to let it float, printing adjacent to the nearest digit.

To specify the number of decimals, you choose from a drop-down list that shows the alternatives. You can have from none through ten places to the right of the decimal point. Similarly, you choose rounding by picking a value between 0.01 and 1,000,000.

For negative values, you can have the number in parentheses or with the minus sign on the left or right. The decimal separator and thousands separators can be selected to meet your requirements. The thousands separator and leading zeros can be printed or suppressed.

The value in the Sample section shows what a number or currency field will look like based on the settings you've selected.

The Format Date Dialog Box Choosing File ➤ Options ... Format category and clicking on the Date ... pushbutton launches the Format Date dialog box, shown in Figure 10.12.

FIGURE 10.12

The Format Date dialog box

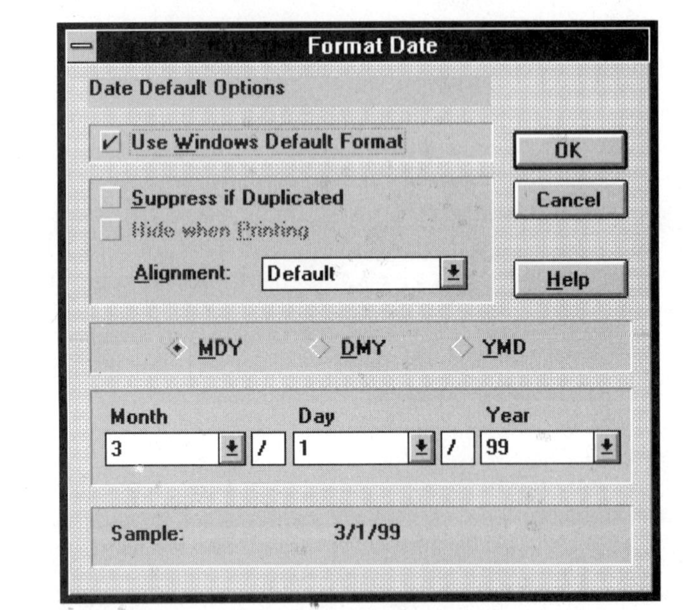

As in the dialog boxes for formatting numbers and currency, your first option in the Format Date dialog box is Use Windows Default Format. As with numbers, checking this box will conform your selection to the default set in the Windows' Control Panel.

The Suppress if Duplicated, Hide when Printing, and Alignment options work the same as they do in the other Format dialog boxes.

The next section lets you choose from MDY, DMY, and YMD orders for the month, day, and year in your date. The choice you make here is *not* reflected in the next section, where you choose specific options for Month, Day, and Year. However, it does control the output of your dates, as you can see in the Sample section.

The Month, Day, and Year options let you choose specific options for each component of your date. The month can be a single digit (if appropriate), a two-digit number, a three-letter abbreviation, or the month fully spelled-out. The day can be a one- or two-digit number. The year can be two or four digits long.

The separators between the three components specify the separation. The separation will be between the components you chose when you specified MDY, DMY or YMD—which may *not* be the order in which the three components are labeled in this section.

For a display such as 12/31/95, you can use the default / character or choose a different one. For a spelled-out date, such as December 31, 1995, you would type a single blank space for the first separator, and a comma followed by a blank space for the second separator.

The Sample section at the bottom shows the results of your choices (for the date March 1, 1999).

FIGURE 10.13

The Format Boolean dialog box

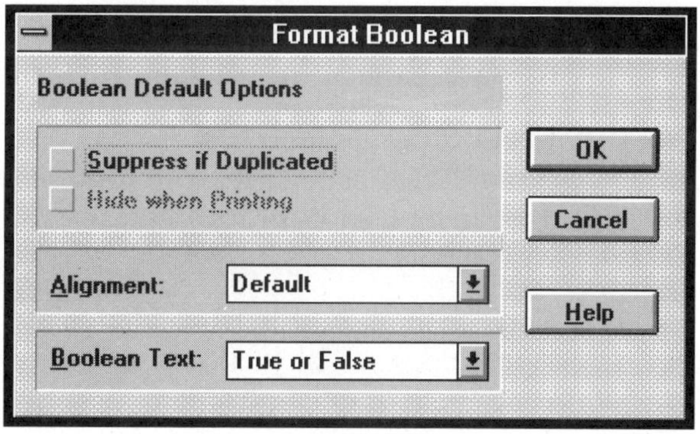

The Format Boolean Dialog Box Choosing File ➤ Options … Format category and choosing the Boolean … pushbutton launches the Format Boolean dialog box, shown in Figure 10.13.

In dBASE tables, Boolean fields are called Logical fields. Other databases could use other names, such as Bit fields. Whatever the name, these are the fields used for True/False or Yes/No answers.

All the options here are discussed above in the Format String dialog box section, except for the Boolean Text option, which provides the following choices:

- True or False
- T or F
- Yes or No
- Y or N
- 1 or 0

By convention, 1 is synonymous with True or Yes; 0 is synonymous with False or No.

The Options Dialog Box's Fonts Options

Figure 10.14 shows the array of choices that you are faced with when you select the Fonts category from the File ➤ Options … menu.

Here you can choose from each of the main bands, from headers through details to totals and footers. In each band, you can choose a font for the fields, or for the text you have typed in the band outside your fields.

Each of these pushbuttons launches the Windows Font dialog box (see Appendix B). This dialog box lets you choose a font name, a size, and a style (bold, italic, and so on).

FIGURE 10.14

The Options dialog box, Fonts category

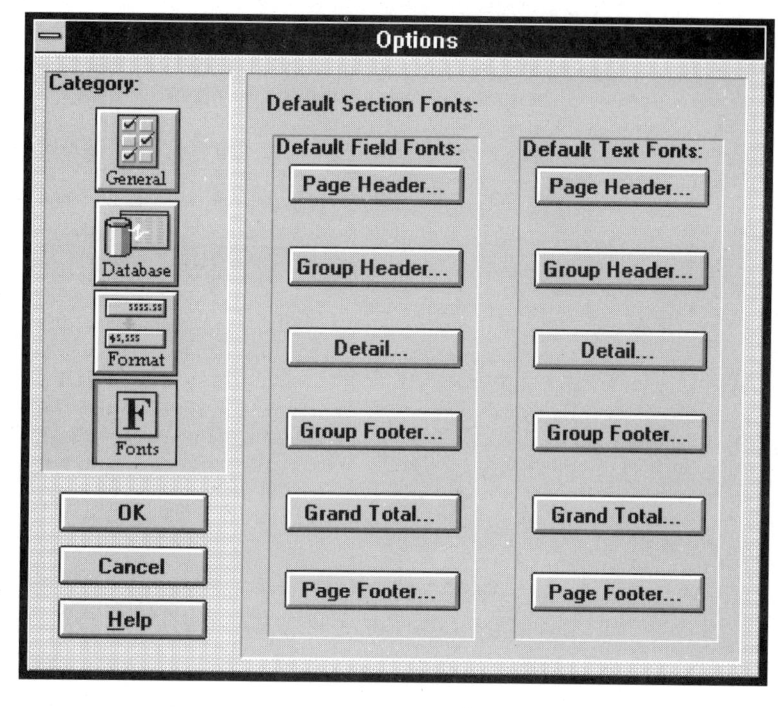

TIP

Critics of the overuse of fonts suggest that this many choices will lead to *ransom-note* typography. That name suggests what you would get by cutting individual letters from a newspaper or magazine and pasting them together. To avoid ransom-note typography, tread lightly here, if you tread at all.

Probably the best use of this set of choices would be either to ignore it or to replace every one of the choices with another font family. The default is Times New Roman, which is an excellent proportional font with serifs. The only reason that you might want to replace it is that it is very common. However, it has earned its popularity, since it is a well-designed, highly readable font. Don't change it unless you are sure that your alternative is better.

▸▸ Using the Edit Menu

The Edit menu provides the standard Clipboard-related options and an OLE-related choice:

Cut	Ctrl+X
Copy	Ctrl+C
Paste	Ctrl+V
Paste Special...	
Clear	Del
Select Fields	
Formula...	
Text Field...	
Summary Operation...	
Show/Hide Sections...	
Group Section...	
Delete Section...	
Browse Field Data...	
Show Field Names	
Object	
Links...	

The Cut, Copy, and Paste options allow standard interaction with the Windows Clipboard. The fourth menu item, Paste Special …, allows interaction with OLE applications.

▸ Object Linking and Embedding through Paste Special

If you activate an OLE-enabled application and copy to the Clipboard, the Edit ➤ Paste Special … menu choice becomes available. Choosing it launches the Paste Special dialog box, shown in Figure 10.15.

Through this dialog box, you can embed any of the following in your report:

- A graphic (or other OLE result)
- A graphic with a link to the program that created it

FIGURE 10.15

The Paste Special dialog box for OLE links

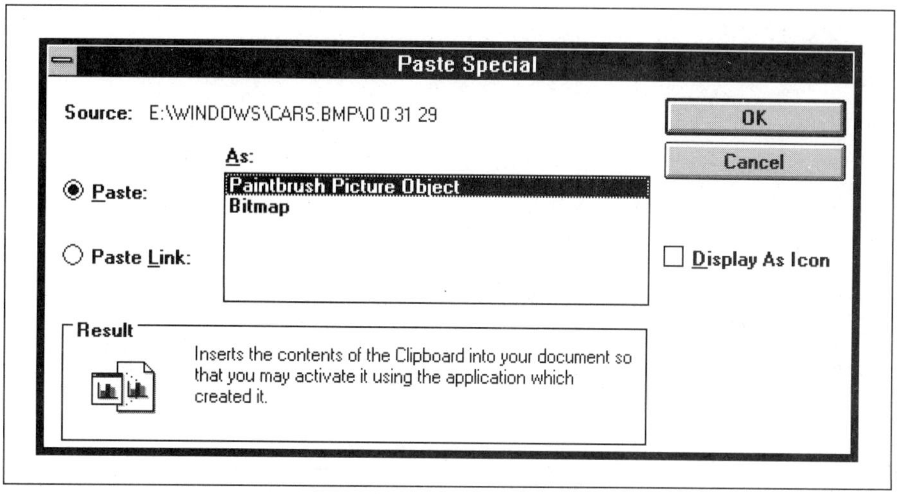

Paste Special

Source: E:\WINDOWS\CARS.BMP\0 0 31 29

OK

Cancel

As:

Paste: Paintbrush Picture Object

Bitmap

Paste Link:

Display As Icon

Result

Inserts the contents of the Clipboard into your document so that you may activate it using the application which created it.

- A link accessed by an icon in your report

If you choose the Paste radio button, you can then choose to paste the object, or just an image of the object. If you choose an image, you will have pasted an image into your report. If you choose the object, you will include an OLE connection to the program that created the object along with the object itself. Then you can use the program that created the image to edit the image from within your report.

If you choose the Paste Link radio button, you will have created an active link between the object's creating program and your report. If you change the object in the creating program, the change will be shown in your report.

When you choose Paste or Paste Link, the Display As Icon check box is activated. If you choose this option, your report will show an icon of the creating application.

If you have an icon for the creating application, an additional pushbutton, labeled Change Icon ..., appears in the lower-right corner of the Paste Special dialog box. Clicking this button launches the dialog box shown in Figure 10.16.

This dialog box lets you choose from among the icons available in an executable file. By default, this file is the creating object's executable file. If you choose the From File option in this dialog box, you can select icons from any Windows executable file on your system, such as Windows .EXE and .DLL files.

FIGURE 10.16

The Change Icon dialog box

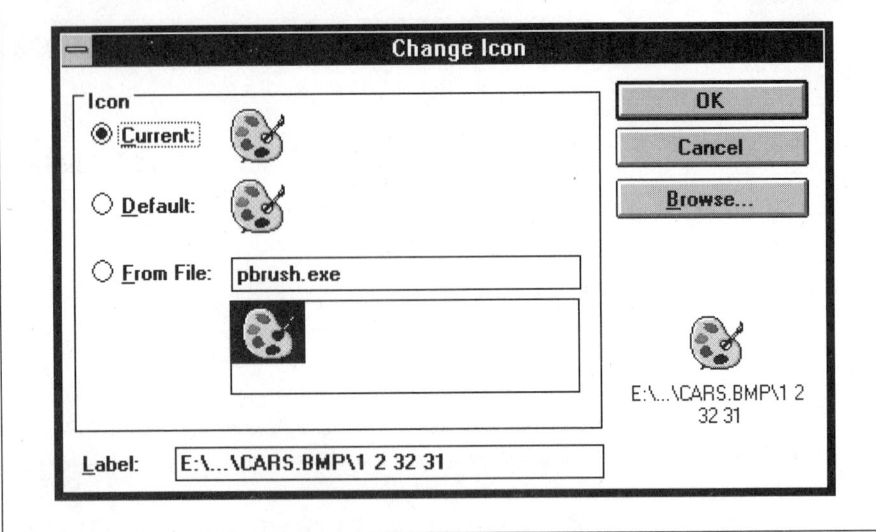

The icons available in the selected file are shown in the unlabeled rectangle below the From File choice. Clicking on the Browse … pushbutton launches the Browse dialog box, which lets you specify a file from which to choose icons.

▸ Deleting and Selecting Fields

The next two choices in the Edit menu allow additional keyboard access to two common functions: deleting and selecting.

The Clear choice has the same effect as pressing the Del key. If you select any report component, you can choose this option in lieu of pressing the Del key.

▸▸ **TIP**

While menu choices are often used as keyboard alternatives for mouse actions, the Clear choice also provides mouse access to a keyboard function. After you select your report element, clicking the Edit choice followed by clicking Clear is an alternative to pressing the Del key.

The Select Fields choice is an alternative way of selecting the lasso from the speedbar. After choosing this, you select report elements by dragging a rectangle on the report.

Note that the lasso in Crystal is *not* the same as the lasso in the Form Designer. First, you can start the lasso in the Form Designer simply by beginning a drag action anywhere that is not on top of a Form object. In Crystal, you must choose the lasso from the speedbar or by the Edit ➤ Select Fields menu choice.

Second, the lasso in the Form Designer selects only those fields that are entirely inside the lasso. The lasso in Crystal also selects all fields that are touched by the lasso. To put it another way, fields that are touched by the lasso are *not* selected in the Form Designer but *are* selected in Crystal Reports.

▶ Editing Formulas

The Edit ➤ Formula ... choice launches the Expression Builder (see Chapter 8) to edit the formula in a formula field. This choice is only available when you have a formula field selected. If you have more than one formula field selected, Formula launches the last selected formula field in the Expression Builder.

▶ Editing Text Fields

The Edit ➤ Text Field ... choice launches the Edit Text Field dialog box, shown in Figure 10.17.

This dialog box lets you enter extensive text in a field, which is not a practice we recommend. See Chapter 11 for information about form letters, which are one area where you will want extended text in a report.

Note that you can't exit the Edit Text Field dialog box with an Enter keypress, because this keystroke is interpreted as part of the text you are entering or editing.

▶ Editing Summary Fields

The Edit ➤ Summary Operation choice is available when you have selected a summary field, such as a subtotal or total. It launches the Summary Field dialog box, shown in Figure 10.18.

FIGURE 10.17

The Edit Text Field dialog box

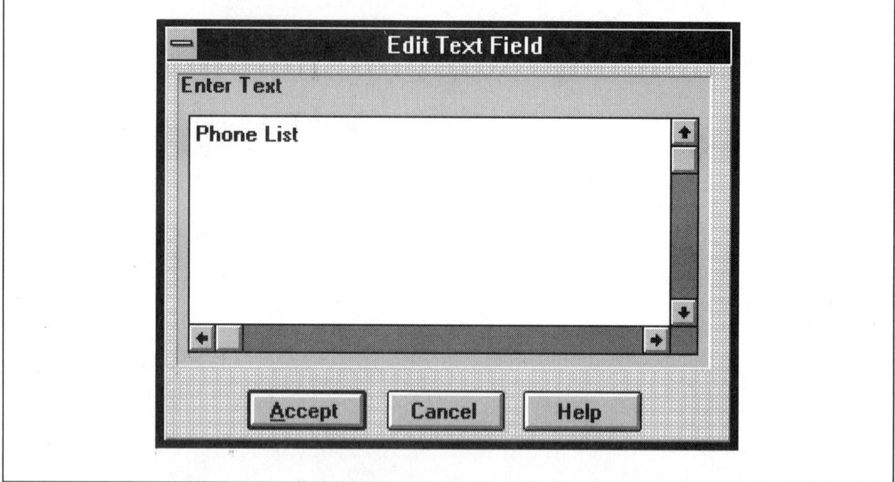

FIGURE 10.18

Selecting a summary field operation

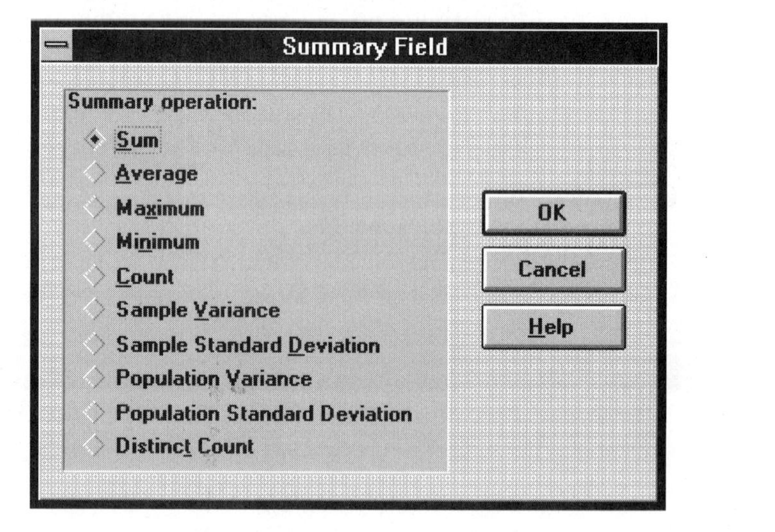

The Summary Field options are standard mathematical operations you can perform, such as calculating a sum or average. (See the Table Utilities section in Chapter 9 for definitions of the variance and standard deviation calculations.) For this dialog box, a *sample* is a portion of the total series, similar to a group subtotal. The *population* is the entire set of data, similar to a grand total.

▶ Hiding Report Sections

The Edit ➤ Show/Hide Sections … choice lets you temporarily suppress individual report sections. It launches the Show/Hide Sections dialog box, which lists all the available sections in your report.

In Figure 10.19, we chose to hide the Grand total section of a report. This section will not appear on the report layout surface, nor will it appear in the report itself.

FIGURE 10.19 ▶

Temporarily eliminating a report section

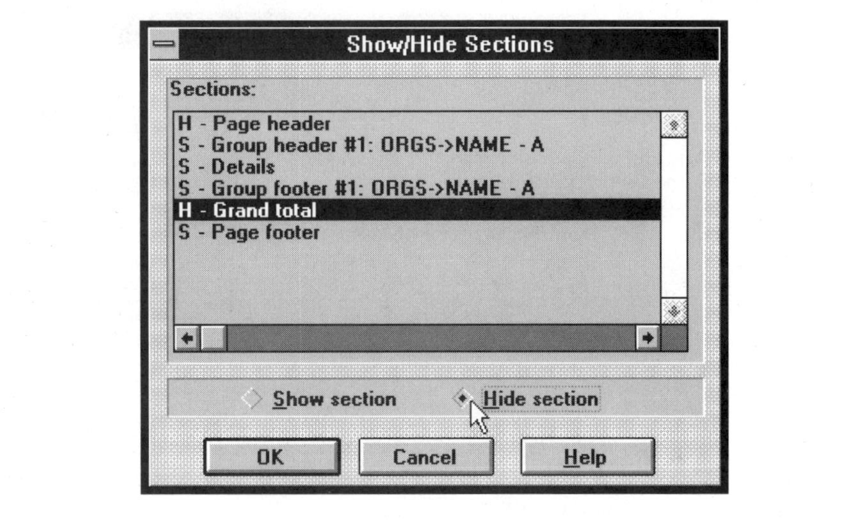

▶▶ **TIP**

If you're designing a report with lots of items, hiding sections is a good way to make room for your work. That way you can focus on only the sections of a report that need attention.

The radio buttons at the bottom of the dialog box, Show section and Hide section, reflect the current status of each section.

▶ Editing Report Groups

The Edit ➤ Group Section … option launches two successive dialog boxes, both titled Edit Group Section. The first dialog box lets you choose from a list of your report's group sections. You must select a group section before you can click on OK or press Enter to proceed to the second Edit Group Section dialog box.

The second Edit Group Section dialog box is shown in Figure 10.20.

FIGURE 10.20 ▶

The second Edit Group Section dialog box

Edit Group Section

When the report is printed, the records will be sorted and grouped by: ORGS->NAME

in ascending order.

The section will be printed on any change of: ORGS->NAME

OK | Cancel | Browse Field Data... | Help

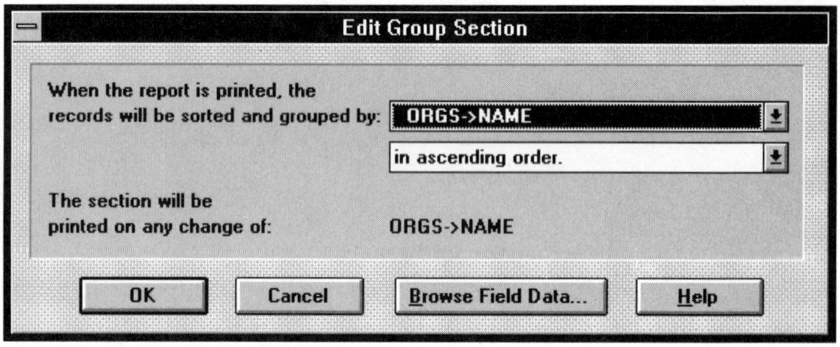

The first of the two drop-down lists lets you choose from any available data field. The second lets you choose between ascending and descending order.

The Browse Field Data … pushbutton lets you examine the contents of the selected field.

▶ Deleting Report Sections

The Edit ➤ Delete Section … option launches the Delete Section dialog box, shown in Figure 10.21.

This dialog box is another instance of the first Edit Group Section dialog box. It provides a list of your report's group sections so that you can choose a group section or total section for deletion.

Deleting all the fields from a section does not delete the section itself. Deleting the section gets rid of all the fields in the section.

FIGURE 10.21

Choosing a section to delete

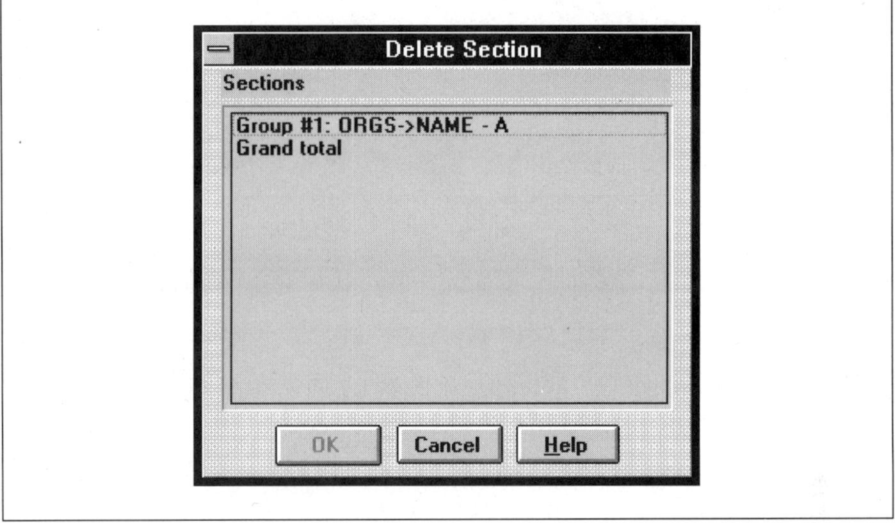

WARNING

There is no warning in Crystal Reports when you choose to delete a section that contains fields. All your fields will be deleted. Look carefully before you delete a section.

Browsing the Selected Field's Data

When you choose Edit ➤ Browse Field Data …, you see a dialog box, titled by the field you have selected, which shows the data in that field. You cannot choose this option until you have selected a field. If you have selected more than one field, the last field in the selection is used.

Showing Field Names

The Edit ➤ Show Field Names choice is documented to toggle between the display of letters and the display of field names in the fields in your report layout surface. It is not operable in the current release of dBASE for Windows. Choose File ➤ Options …, General category and check the Show Fields Name box to change this setting.

▶ Editing Objects

The next to last choice on the Edit menu is dimmed and labeled Object if you have not selected an object on your report. If you have selected an object, this choice is labeled according to the object you have selected. For example, here's the command when a Microsoft drawing object is selected:

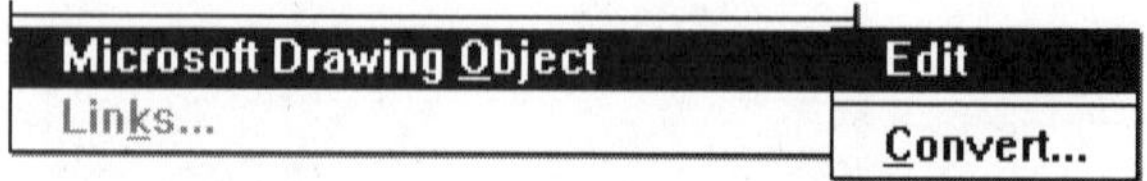

When you've selected an OLE object in your report, you can edit it (launch Microsoft Draw, in this case) or convert it (from an object link to just a graphic, for example). For more information, see the discussion of the Edit ➤ Paste Special choice.

▶ Managing Links

The Edit ➤ Links choice is available when you have established a link to an OLE object (see the discussion of Edit ➤ Paste Special). If you have selected a linked object, this choice launches the Links dialog box, shown in Figure 10.22.

FIGURE 10.22 ▶

Editing OLE links

The Links dialog box shows the link and provides options to update, open, or change the link's source. You can also break the link.

▶▶ Using the Insert Menu

The Insert pull-down menu is used to add items to your reports after you have finished your basic layout:

Database Field...
Text Field...
Formula Field...
Summary Field ▶
Line
Box
Graphic...
Object...
Special Field ▶
Group Section...

▶ Inserting a Database Field

Choosing Insert ➤ Database Field ... launches the Insert Database Field dialog box, shown in Figure 10.23. From this dialog box, you can add as many fields as you like to your report. This dialog box is in a modeless child window, so you can leave it open as you do other work on your report.

From this dialog box, you can select a field to place in your report in three ways:

- Select it and click on the Insert pushbutton.
- Double-click on the field.
- Drag the field from the dialog box to the report.

In addition to the Insert choice, the Browse Field Data ... pushbutton lets you look at the data in the field you have selected. When you're finished with this dialog box, choose the Done pushbutton.

FIGURE 10.23

The Insert Database Field dialog box

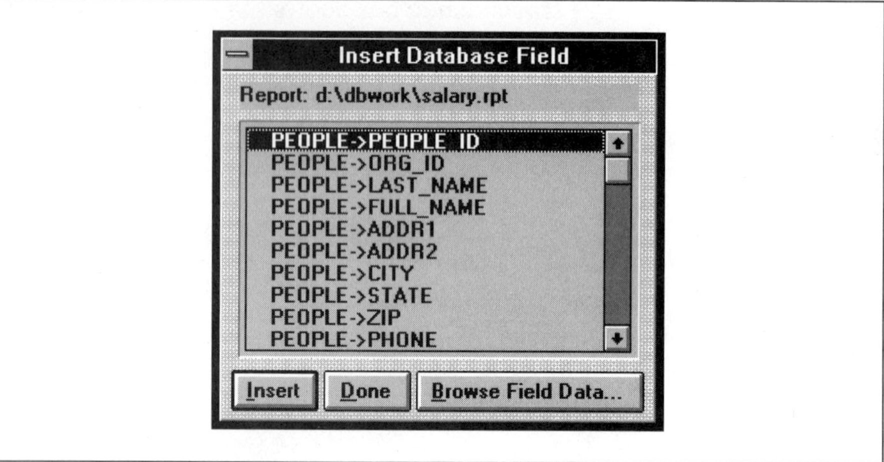

▸ Inserting a Text Field

The Insert ➤ Text Field … choice launches the Edit Text Field dialog box, shown earlier (Figure 10.17). You can create your text field in this dialog box.

When you're finished entering text, click on Accept. Your cursor will turn into the field-insertion rectangle. Position the field in the report and click to drop it.

▸ Inserting a Formula Field

Choosing Insert ➤ Formula Field … launches the Insert Formula dialog box, shown in Figure 10.24.

This dialog box lets you manage your list of formula fields. You can enter a new name in the top entry field, or click on one of the existing fields listed in the middle section to enter its name in the entry field automatically.

If you enter a new name in the entry field, clicking on OK or pressing Enter launches the Expression Builder (see Chapter 8). After you've created a new expression or selected an existing formula, your cursor turns to the field-insertion rectangle. Position the field and click to drop it into your report.

FIGURE 10.24

Managing your list of formula fields

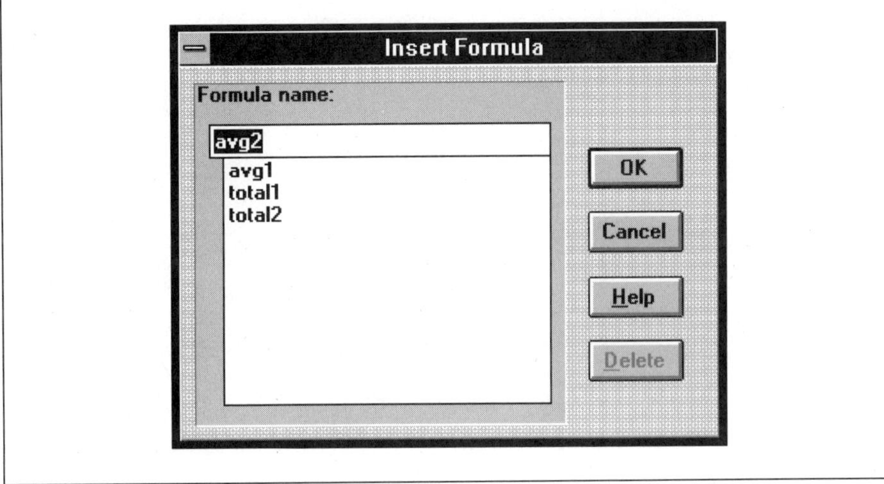

Inserting a Summary Field

To insert a summary field, you begin by selecting a Numeric or Date field to summarize. After you have selected one, choosing Insert ➤ Summary Field brings up this cascading menu:

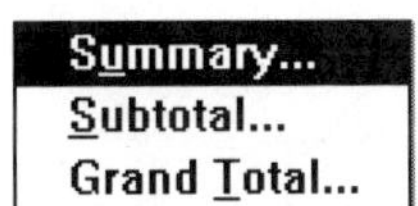

Adding a Summary Calculation

If you choose Insert ➤ Summary Field ➤ Summary ..., the Insert Summary dialog box, shown in Figure 10.25, is launched.

The summary choices are the same as those in the Summary Field dialog box (see the discussion of Edit ➤ Summary Operation ...). You can also choose the group if you've inserted multiple groups. The Browse Field Data ... choice launches a dialog box that shows you the data in your field.

FIGURE 10.25

Inserting a summary field

Insert Summary
Insert a field which calculates the
sum
of:
PEOPLE->SALARY
When the report is printed, the records will be sorted and grouped by:
Group #1: ORGS->NAME - A
OK
Cancel
Browse Field Data...
Help

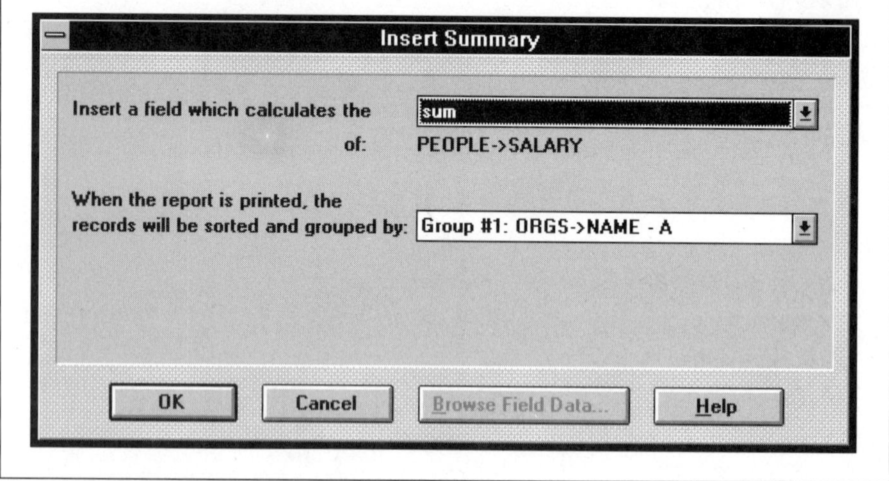

Inserting a Subtotal for a Data Field

If you've selected a data field (not a summary field), you can choose to insert a subtotal. The Insert ➤ Summary Field ➤ Subtotal … choice launches the Insert Subtotal dialog box, shown in Figure 10.26.

FIGURE 10.26

The Insert Subtotal dialog box

Insert Subtotal
Insert a subtotal for the field:
PEOPLE->SALARY
When the report is printed, the records will be sorted and grouped by:
ORGS->NAME
in ascending order.
The subtotal will be printed on any change of:
ORGS->NAME
OK
Cancel
Browse Field Data...
Help

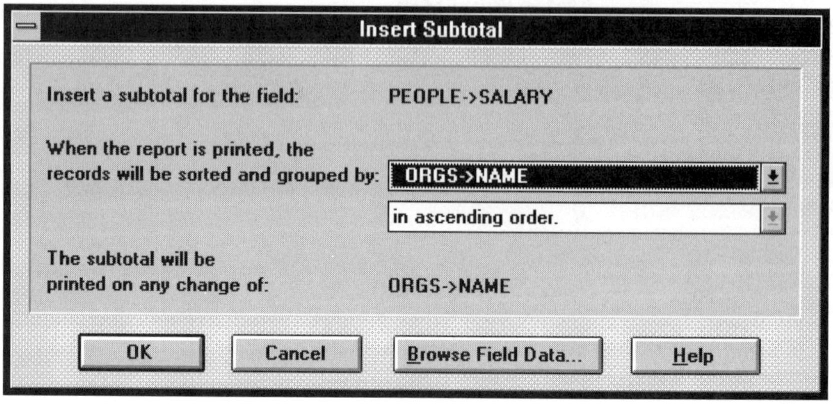

If you access the first drop-down list, the dialog box allows you to pick from all your data and calculated fields. If you drop down this list, you can choose a different grouping variable. The second drop-down list lets you choose ascending or descending sequence.

If you do not drop down the first list, you will be given an existing grouping as the default.

FIGURE 10.27

Inserting a grand total

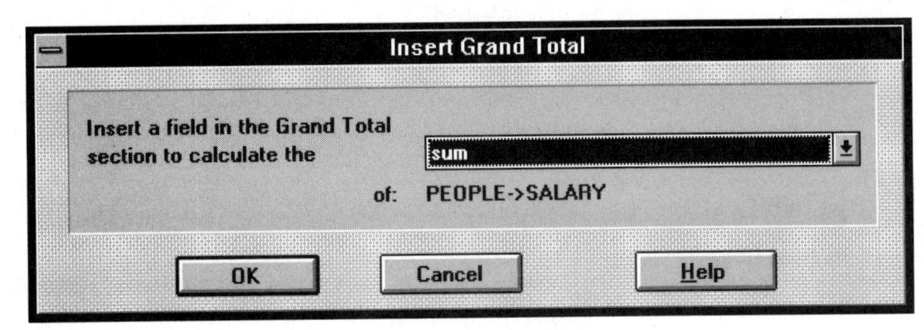

Adding a Grand Total

Choosing Insert ➤ Summary Field ➤ Grand Total … launches the Insert Grand Total dialog box, shown in Figure 10.27.

Inserting a grand total is simpler than inserting a subtotal, because it does not respect groups—it computes a grand total across all groups. Inserting a grand total adds an additional band to your report, titled Grand total. (If you are using short section names, it's GT.) The grand total field is automatically placed in this band.

TIP

It's almost always a good idea to add a text field to label the grand total field.

▶ Inserting Lines and Boxes

When you choose Insert ➤ Line or Box, the cursor changes to the pencil shape. To draw a line, you drag from one end of the line to the other end. You draw a box by dragging from any corner of a rectangle to the opposite corner.

For those who find the mouse a somewhat imprecise drawing instrument, you'll be happy to know that the designers of Crystal assumed that you would only use vertical and horizontal lines.

If your end is more or less to one side or the other of your starting point, you will get a perfectly horizontal line. Similarly, if you move more or less up and down, you get a perfectly vertical line.

▶▶ **TIP**

You can insert a graphic to add lines other than horizontal and vertical ones.

You can use Format ➤ Line … to add color to lines, to change line width, and to select line styles. Use Format ➤ Box … to change box widths and border styles, add colors to your box, and choose other features.

▶ Inserting Graphics and Objects

The Insert ➤ Graphic … choice launches the Choose Graphic File dialog box. In this dialog box, you can choose from .BMP, .GIF, .PCX, .TIF, and .TGA graphics files.

Choosing Insert ➤ Object … launches the Insert Object dialog box, shown in Figure 10.28. This dialog box lets you pick any OLE-enabled application to supply an object to place on your report.

You can create a new object of any of the specified types, or use one from a file. To display this object as an icon, check the Display As Icon check box (see the discussion of Edit ➤ Paste Special …).

FIGURE 10.28

Choosing to insert an OLE application

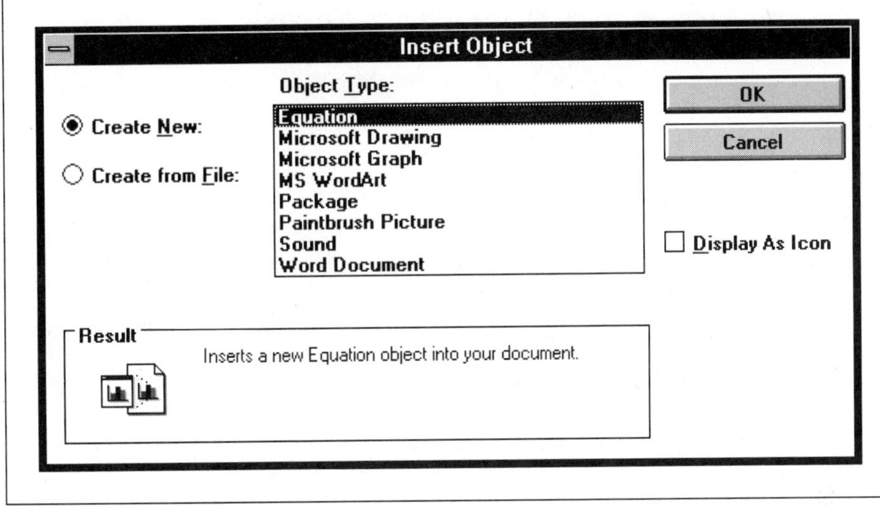

▶ *Inserting a Special Field*

The Insert ➤ Special Field choice displays this cascading menu:

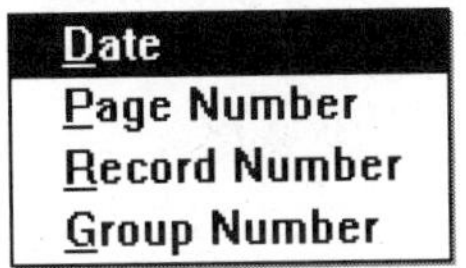

The Date choice is today's date (actually, the system date in your computer, which is probably today's date). This is frequently used in the Page header area.

The Page Number choice is used to number pages, as it is in any publication. This is commonly used in the Page footer or Page header area.

You can also choose to use record numbers and number your groups, with the Record Number and Group Number choices, respectively.

When you make any of these choices, your cursor turns into the field-insertion rectangle, which you position wherever you like and then click to drop the field.

To format these fields, choose Format ➤ Field … after selecting the special field. The Date special field is formatted as a date; the others are formatted as numbers.

▶ Inserting a Group Section

Choosing Insert ➤ Group Section … launches the Insert Group Section dialog box, shown in Figure 10.29.

FIGURE 10.29

Inserting a group section

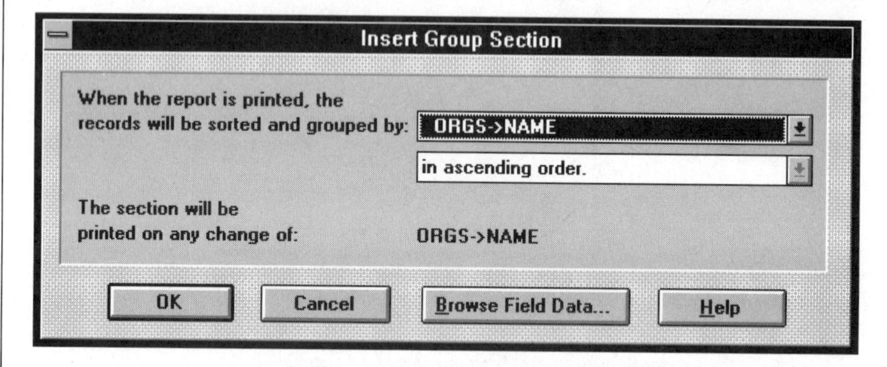

The default grouping field is the first field in the Details band. If you have a typical one-to-many relationship (one employer with many employees, for example), this is frequently the correct choice. You can access the other fields in your report and the other fields in your table or query through the drop-down list.

The default order is ascending. You can change this to descending through the second drop-down list. The section is printed every time the selecting grouping item changes.

Through the Browse Field Data … pushbutton, you can take a look at the data in the field that you selected for grouping.

▶▶ Using the Format Menu

Each element you add to your report is given a default format, which you can set with the File ➤ Options … choice. The Format menu lets you give specific format characteristics to each field and other object on your report.

Font...
Field...
Border and Colors...
Graphic...
Line...
Box...
Section...
Report Title...
Send Behind Others

TIP

A very light hand with the format features will yield more effective reports. Before you add any formatting, ask yourself if it will help the report communicate its message. When you add features, keep your final output device(s) in mind. The most effective use of color is useless if you are going to reproduce the report on a black-and-white photocopier.

Some of the Format menu choices, such as Section … and Report Title …, are always available. Other choices, such as Graphic …, Line …, and Box …, are only available when you have selected an object of the appropriate type.

The Format ➤ Font … choice lets you select a font, size, and font style for the text in the object you have selected. It launches the Windows Font dialog box (see Appendix B).

Formatting Fields

The Format ➤ Field … choice launches one of the following dialog boxes, depending on the field's type:

- Format String

- Format Number
- Format Currency
- Format Date
- Format Boolean

These are the same dialog boxes you can get to through File ➤ Options, Format category (Figures 10.10 through 10.14).

▶ Formatting Borders and Colors

Choosing Format ➤ Border and Colors ... launches the Format Borders and Colors dialog box, shown in Figure 10.30.

FIGURE 10.30 ▶

Setting field border and color characteristics

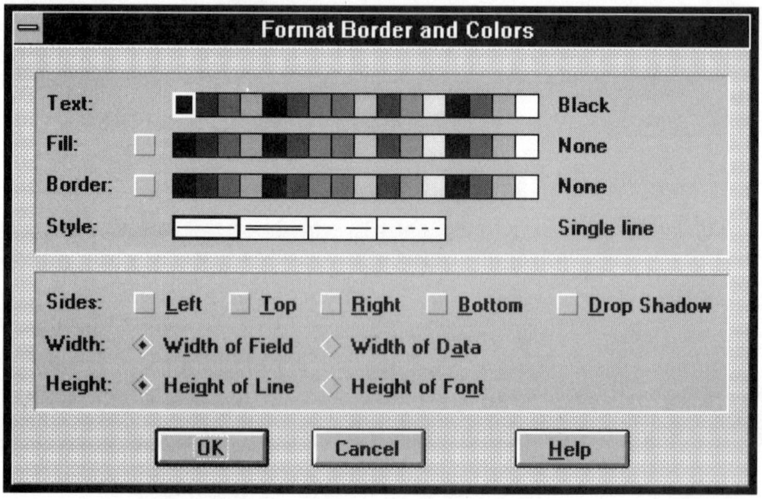

By default, your fields have black text and no fill color, which normally will mean printing with black ink on white paper. You can change the color of the text (the foreground color) and the fill color (the background color). The check box next to the Fill choice must be checked to choose a fill color other than None.

A border is not normally used. If you check the box next to the Border choice, it will trigger checks in the boxes for all four of the field's sides.

If you use a border, it will be drawn on the sides specified by these checks. Figure 10.31 shows some sample uses of the border.

FIGURE 10.31

Various border characteristics

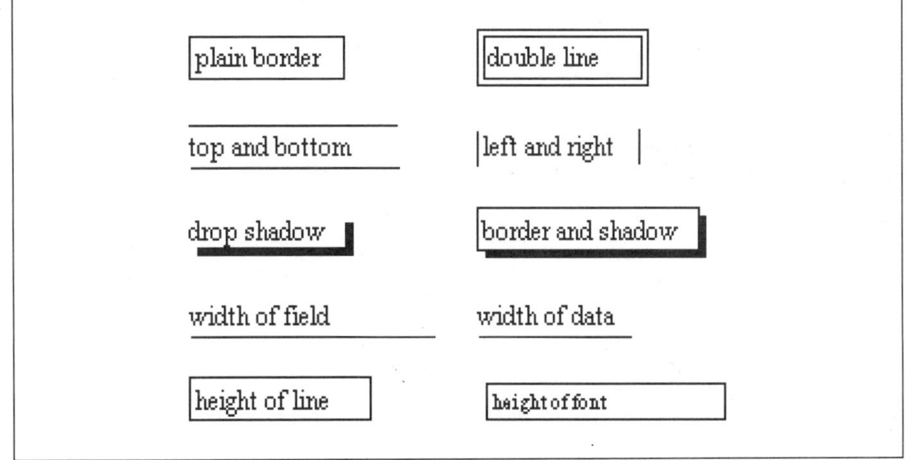

▶ Formatting Graphics

The Format ➤ Graphic … choice launches the Graphic Format dialog box, shown in Figure 10.32.

FIGURE 10.32

Cropping and scaling a graphic

Graphic format

Cropping of original:
Left 0.00 in
Top 0.00 in
Right 0.00 in
Bottom 0.00 in

Scaling:
Width 100 %
Height 100 %

Size:
Width 0.33 in
Height 0.33 in

Original size:
Width: 0.33 in
Height: 0.33 in

Hide when printing

OK
Cancel
Help
Position...

The Graphic Format dialog box provides options for cropping, scaling, and sizing graphics:

- Crop a graphic on any of its four sides.
- Set scaling in both the horizontal and vertical dimensions.
- Adjust the size of a graphic.

▸▸ **TIP**

If you adjust the scaling differently for width and height, you will change the aspect ratio. This lets you be creative about how you stretch an image.

The Hide when printing check box lets you show a graphic on the screen but not print it. (Printing graphics ranges from time-consuming to impossible, depending on its size and your printer's capabilities.)

Clicking on the Position … pushbutton launches the Graphic Position dialog box, shown in Figure 10.33.

FIGURE 10.33

Positioning the graphic

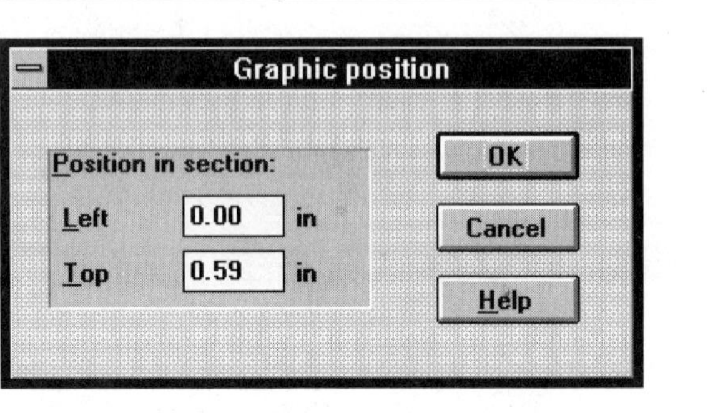

The values in this dialog box default to the position at which you drew the graphic. You can change the position by dragging the graphic or by adjusting the coordinates in this dialog box.

▶ Formatting Lines

Choosing Format ➤ Line … launches the Line Format dialog box, shown in Figure 10.34. This dialog box lets you adjust the color, width, and style of your line.

FIGURE 10.34 ▶

The Line Format dialog box

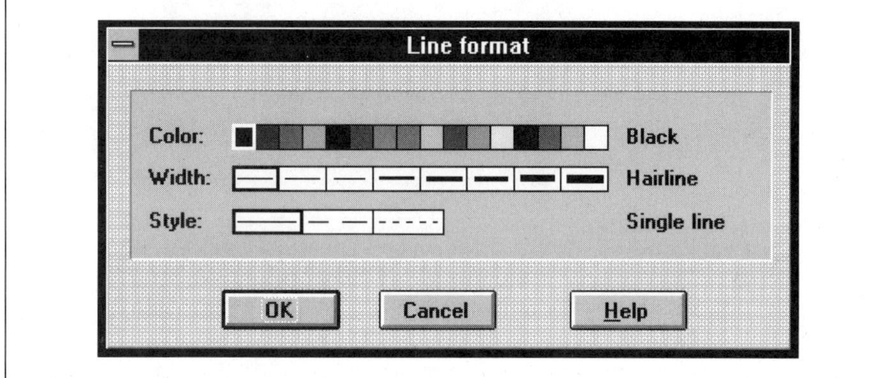

Here are some examples of lines in different widths, ranging from one pixel to the thickest available (3.50 points), and the dashed and dotted line styles:

Dashed and dotted line styles are not available if you have selected a thick line.

▶ Formatting Boxes

Choosing Format ➤ Box … launches the Box Format dialog box, shown in Figure 10.35. This is similar to the Line Format dialog box, but it adds a check box for closing the box at the top and bottom of pages. This applies when the printing would otherwise start a box on one page and finish it on another.

FIGURE 10.35

The Box Format dialog box

Box format

Fill: None

Border: ✔ Black

Width: Hairline

Style: Dashed line

✔ Close box at top and bottom of page

OK Cancel Help

Here are examples of a standard-width box, a thicker box, and boxes drawn with dashed lines and dotted lines:

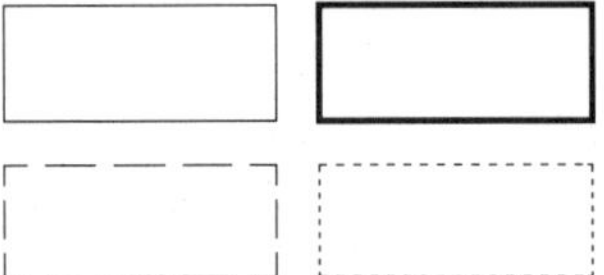

▸ Formatting Sections

The Format ➤ Section … choice launches two dialog boxes, both named Format Section. The first one lets you choose one of your report's sections. The second dialog box lets you choose formatting characteristics for the section you selected. Figure 10.36 shows the Format Section dialog box after the Details section was selected.

The Hide Section option hides the section you have selected (it doesn't show on the screen or in the printed version). For example, you might hide a section that includes calculated fields that you use in other sections but don't want to show in detail.

The Print at Bottom of Page option is used for group values, such as a subtotal section, which you want to appear at the bottom of a page. Invoices are a typical use for this feature.

The New Page Before option forces a new page to be started before starting the selected group. New Page After forces the page to be completed

FIGURE 10.36

Formatting a report's Details section

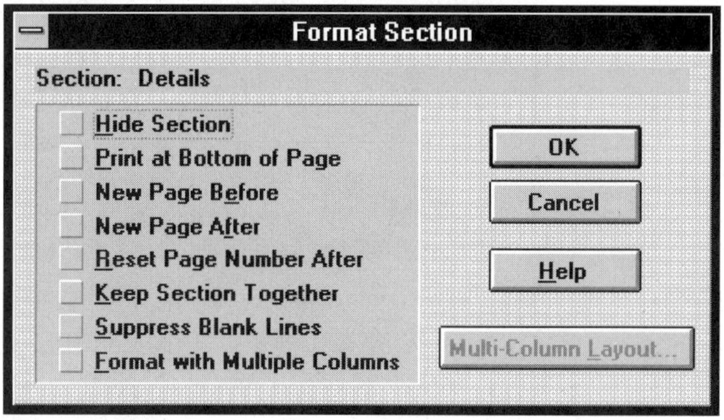

when this section is printed. (Pages still start and end with the normal Page header and Page footer sections.)

The Reset Page Number After option sets the page number back to 1 after printing the section. You would use this feature if you were printing long groups where you wanted each group numbered starting with 1.

The Keep Section Together option prevents the section from being split at the end of a page. Note that this does not support keeping a group together; only the selected section (such as a Group header section) is kept together.

Suppress Blank Lines suppresses those lines that have fields that are suppressed (for example, by using blanks for zero values). It does not suppress blank lines that you have included for spacing in your layout.

The Format with Multiple Columns option enables the Multi-Column Layout … pushbutton, which launches the Multi-Column Layout dialog box, shown in Figure 10.37.

This dialog box lets you specify formatting for a multiple-column (telephone book) style layout. This is the layout used for most mailing labels.

▶ Formatting Report Titles

The Format ➤ Report Title … choice launches the Edit Report Title dialog box, shown in Figure 10.38.

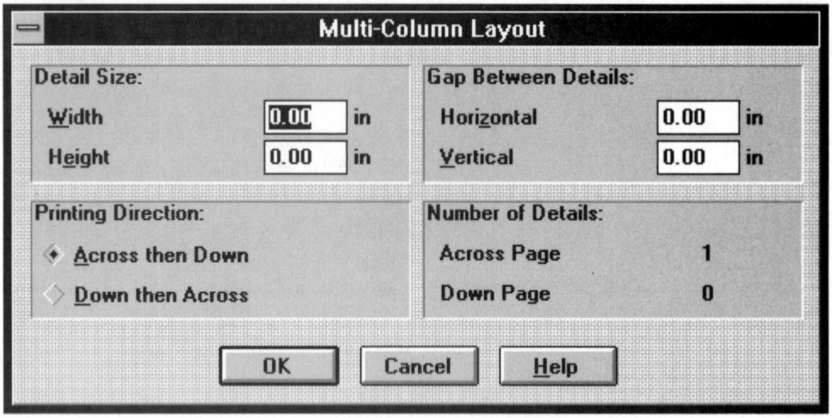

FIGURE 10.37

Setting a multiple-column layout

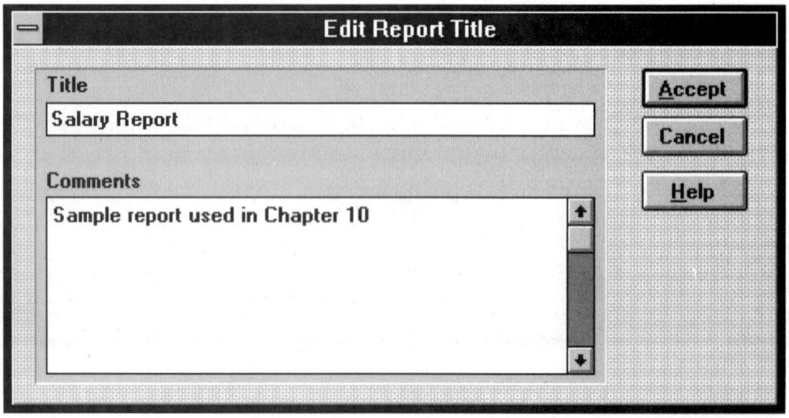

FIGURE 10.38

Entering a report title and description

The title you enter here (as well as the comments) is for your use in identifying the report. It does not appear in the Report window when you run the report in dBASE for Windows, nor does it appear on the printed report. (Use a text field with the same text to put a title on the printed report.)

The title, but not your comments, is printed as part of the report definition when you choose File ➤ Print ➤ Report Definition.

▶ Restacking Items

If you have multiple items stacked on top of each other, they are in what the Form Designer calls the z-order. In Crystal, you can use Format ➤ Send Behind Others to push the top item in the stack to the bottom.

▶▶ Using the Database Menu

The Database pull-down menu lets you specify the location of your data and verify that the report is consistent with the latest version of your tables.

File Location...
Verify Database
Verify Before Printing

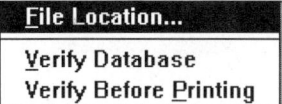

▶ Changing the Database File Location

If you want your report to use data from a different location than the one you specified when you created it, use the Database ➤ File Location ... option. This choice launches the Set Location dialog box, shown in Figure 10.39.

The Set Location dialog box does *not* let you move your data. It lets you specify the location of your data. For each database (SQL database, query, or table), you can choose the Set Location ... pushbutton. This takes you to the Choose New Location dialog box, in which you can specify another location.

The Same as Report pushbutton sets the location of the data to the same location as the report. This button is available only after you have saved your report.

▶ Verifying Your Databases

The Database ➤ Verify Database choice checks that your database tables exist in the location you specified. If the tables exist, it continues to check that they have the fields used to create your report.

FIGURE 10.39

Choosing a database location

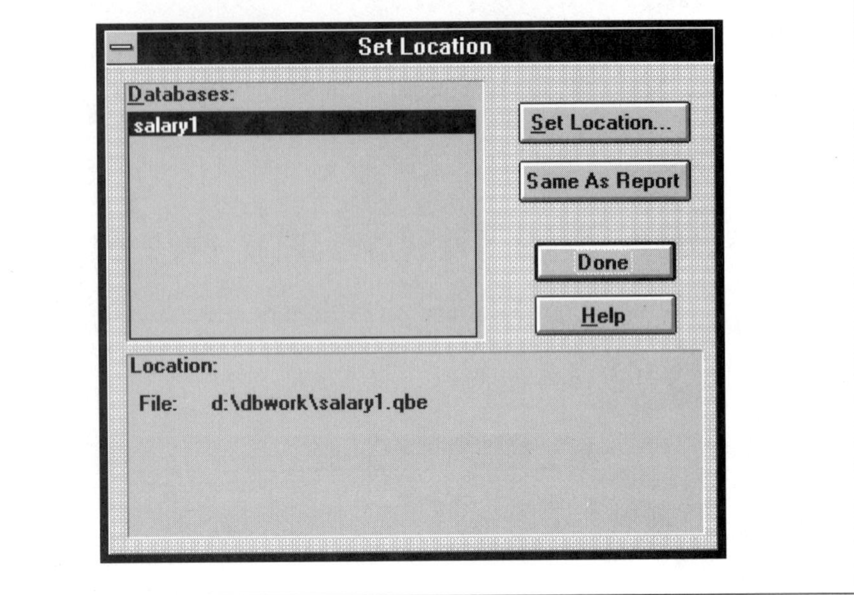

You are given appropriate messages if your tables are not found, or if they do not have all the fields used in your report.

Crystal will try to run a report with different fields. If you have added fields to the table since you built the report, Crystal will ignore them. If you have deleted fields used in the report, Crystal will also delete the field(s) from your report and run just the remaining portions. Alert boxes advise you if this is the situation.

The Database ➤ Verify Before Printing menu option is a toggle, which defaults to not checked. If you turn it on, each time you choose to print the report, Crystal will check that your database tables exist in the location you specified and that they have the fields used to create the report (like Database ➤ Verify Database).

▸▸ Using the Report Menu

The Report pull-down menu's choices let you filter and sort records, as well as specify how report data is handled.

Record Selection Formula...
Record Sort Order...
Group Selection Formula...
Group Sort Order...
Refresh Report Data
Save Data with Closed Report
Set Print Date...

▶ Specifying Record or Group Selection Formulas

The Record Selection Formula … and Group Selection Formula … choices both launch the Expression Builder. They require a logical expression. If you select Record Selection Formula … and enter an expression, only those records that evaluate to True are selected. This is the same as using a filter in dBASE for Windows. If you choose Group Selection Formula … and enter an expression, only the groups for which the formula is True are selected.

▶ Specifying Record or Group Sort Order

The Record Sort Order … option displays the Record Sort Order dialog box, shown in Figure 10.40.

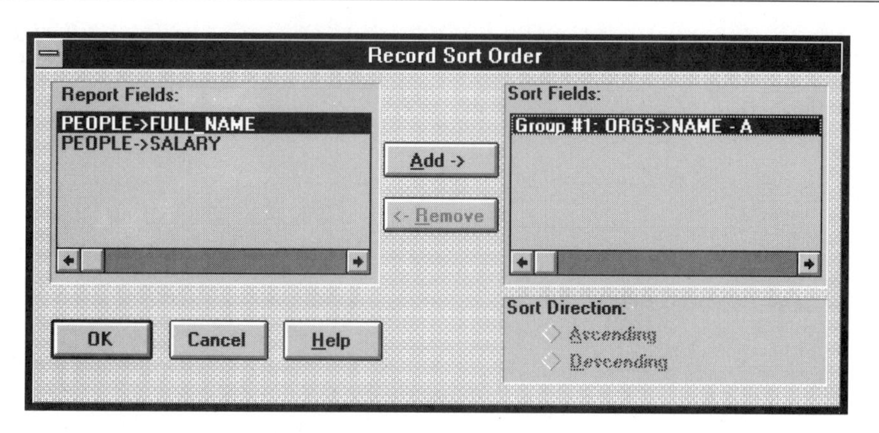

FIGURE 10.40 ▶

Choosing a record sort order

The default sorting is done by groups, as you specified when you added groups to your report. The Record Sort Order dialog box lets you sort the records within your groups. If you add fields from the list (the fields in your Detail band), the Sort Direction choices become available. These give you a choice between ascending or descending sort order.

If you choose the Group Sort Order … option, the Group Sort Order dialog box is launched. This dialog box is almost identical to the Record Sort Order dialog box. The difference is that the fields are those that are in your Group summary bands. Choosing one or more of these groups will sort your groups into the order you specify. Again, the Sort Direction choices are available after you choose a sort field.

▸ Refreshing and Saving Report Data

The Refresh Report Data option reads the report's data from the databases or tables you have specified, so that your report will reflect the latest changes to the data.

The Save Data with Closed Report is a toggle. When checked, this option saves a copy of the report's data with the report. This is a particularly useful option when you are building a report.

▸ Specifying a Print Date

The Set Print Date … choice launches the Print Date dialog box, shown in Figure 10.41.

The default choice is to use today's date (actually, the system date stored in your computer). If you check the Other box, you can add a date in the fields shown.

FIGURE 10.41

Setting the print date

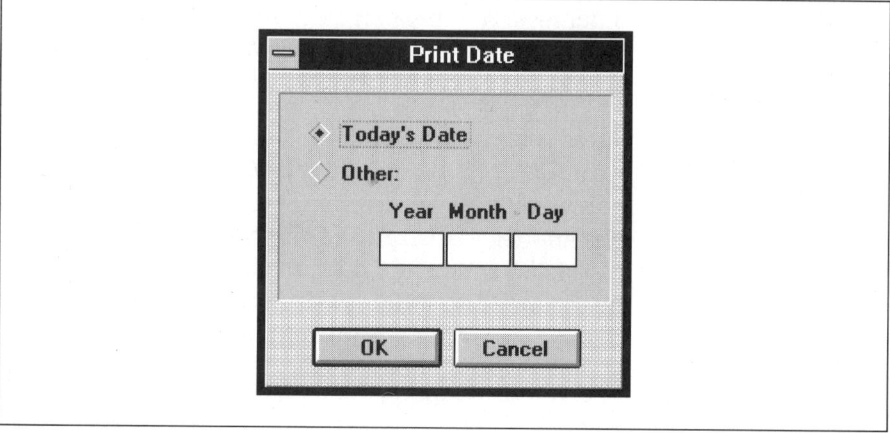

►► Using the Window Menu

The Window menu is a standard Microsoft Windows Window menu, with the same features as the dBASE for Windows Window menu.

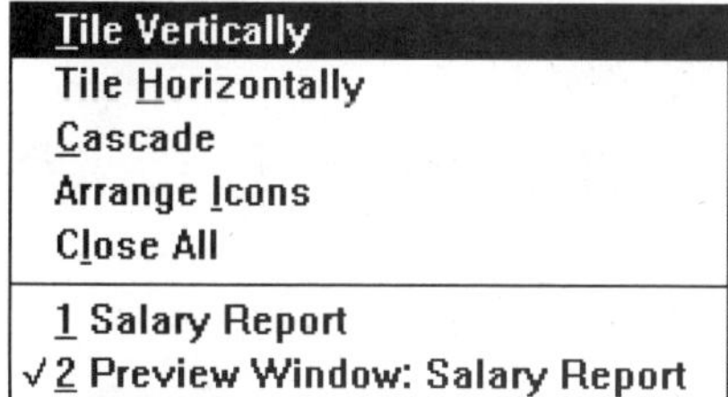

►► Using the Help Menu

The Help menu has the choices that are common to most Windows Help menus:

Contents F1
Search...
Using Help

Personal Trainer

Register / Change Address...
Technical Support Request...
Crystal Library...

About Crystal Reports For dBASE...

There is a notable extra capability here. Through Crystal's Help menu, you can register and change your registration information with Crystal Computer Services, the company that built Crystal Reports.

After you enter or update your name and address information, the registration options include registering via modem. If you have a modem, you select your modem's speed and COM port (Com1, Com2, and so on) and the registration software takes over. This Help option will dial Crystal's computer and transfer your registration information. It will inform you of its progress (it takes a minute or so), and it is totally automatic—a very nice feature.

If you want to change your registration information (you move, for instance), you can do so by choosing the appropriate choices on the Help menu and using your modem to automatically update your data in Crystal's database.

▸▸ Using the Crystal Speedbar

The speedbar in Crystal Reports looks like this:

The functions of the buttons are listed in Table 10.1.

TABLE 10.1: *Crystal Reports Speedbar Buttons*

BUTTON	FUNCTION
	Creates a new report (same as File ➤ New ➤ Report...)
	Opens an existing report (same as File ➤ Open...)
	Saves the report (same as File ➤ Save)

TABLE 10.1: *Crystal Reports Speedbar Buttons (continued)*

BUTTON	FUNCTION
	Prints the report (same as File ➤ Print ➤ Printer…)
	Previews the report (same as File ➤ Print ➤ Window)
	Exports the report (same as File ➤ Print ➤ File…)
	Mails the report (like File ➤ Print ➤ File … but the destination default is a network mail system, not a disk file)
	Cuts selected text to the Clipboard (same as Edit ➤ Cut, or Ctrl-X)
	Copies selected text to the Clipboard (same as Edit ➤ Copy, or Ctrl-C)
	Pastes text from the Clipboard (same as Edit ➤ Paste, or Ctrl-V)
	Selects (lasso) fields (same as Edit ➤ Select Fields)
 XXX	Inserts a database field (same as Insert ➤ Database Field…)
 ABC	Inserts a text field (same as Insert ➤ Text Field…)
 E=mc²	Inserts a formula field (same as Insert ➤ Formula Field…)

▸▸ Formatting with the Format Bar

TABLE 10.1: *Crystal Reports Speedbar Buttons (continued)*

BUTTON	FUNCTION
Σ	Inserts a summary field (same as Insert ➤ Summary Field ➤ Summary…)
	Inserts a graphic (same as Insert ➤ Graphic…)
OLE	Inserts an OLE object (same as Insert ➤ Object…)
	Inserts a line (same as Insert ➤ Line)
	Inserts a box (same as Insert ➤ Box)
	Selects the record sort order (same as Report ➤ Record Sort Order…)
	Allows you to enter or edit the record selection formula (same as Report ➤ Record Selection Formula…)

Crystal's format bar includes buttons for formatting your report. You can use these buttons instead of the Format menu choices.

▶ Formatting Fonts

The font name and size drop-down lists let you choose their respective properties (like Format ➤ Font...):

The two buttons to the right or this group let you increase and decrease the font size by one unit. Click on the large A to increase the size; click on the small A to decrease the size.

The font style buttons can be used in any combination you like:

The **B** button toggles the boldface style. The *I* button toggles the italic style. The U button toggles underlining. (The menu choice is Format ➤ Font....)

▶ Aligning Fields

The alignment buttons let you pick an alignment for your fields:

These buttons select left, center, or right alignment, respectively. (The menu choice is Format ➤ Field....)

▸ Formatting Numbers

The number formatting buttons are toggles:

Their current setting reflects the state of the highlighted number or currency field. (The menu option is Format ➤ Field ....)

Clicking on the $ button turns on (or off) the use of the currency sign. The default setting is to show the $ to the left of the number, but you can change the symbol and position through the File ➤ Options ... menu's Format choice.

The comma button toggles the display of commas (or the separator character you specified in the File ➤ Options ..., Format category) in the selected Numeric field.

The % button toggles the display of a percent sign to the right of the selected field. Note that the number 1 will display as 1%, not 100%—the assumption is that your number is already a percentage.

The decimal selection buttons control the decimal places shown:

The button on the left increases the number of decimal places displayed in the selected field. The button on the right decreases the number of decimal places. (The menu choice is Format ➤ Field ....)

►► Using the Preview Window's Speedbar

The speedbar at the bottom of the report Preview window looks like this:

Table 10.2 lists the functions of these buttons.

TABLE 10.2: *Preview Window Speedbar Buttons*

BUTTON	FUNCTION
[First page button]	Moves to the first page
[Previous page button]	Moves one page at a time toward the first page
[Next page button]	Moves one page at a time toward the last page
[Last page button]	Moves to the last page
Cancel	Cancels activity, during processes such as refreshing report data.

TABLE 10.2: *Preview Window Speedbar Buttons (continued)*

BUTTON	FUNCTION
	Toggles among three zoom levels
	Refreshes your report's data (same as Report ➤ Refresh Report Data)
	Prints the report (same as File ➤ Print ➤ Printer ...)
	Exports the report's data (same as File ➤ Print ➤ File ...)
	Mails the report (like File ➤ Print ➤ File ... but the destination default is a network mail system, not a disk file)
Close	Closes the report Preview window (same as Close from the Preview window's System menu)

►► Using the Speed Menus

Clicking the right mouse button launches a Speed menu from almost every point in Crystal Reports. The following sections describe the Speed menus, grouped as follows:

- Speed menus in report bands
- Field-related Speed menus
- Special-item Speed menus

► Speed Menus for the Report Bands

You access the Speed menus for report bands by right-clicking in the area to the left of the report, in either the report layout window or in the Preview window.

The following choices are available in the Speed menus for report bands:

- Hide Section
- Show ➤ Hide Sections …
- Format Section …
- Add Line
- Delete Last Line
- Cancel Menu

The Group header and Group footer Speed menus have two addtional options:

- Change Group …
- Delete Section

The Grand Total Speed Menu

The following choices are available in the Grand Total Speed menu:

- Hide Section
- Show ➤ Hide Sections …
- Format Section …
- Add Line
- Delete Last Line
- Delete Section
- Cancel Menu

The Page Footer Speed Menu

The Page Footer Speed menu offers the following options:

- Hide Section
- Show/Hide Sections …
- Format Section …
- Add Line
- Delete Last Line
- Cancel Menu

▶ The Field-Related Speed Menus

There are two similar Speed menus for fields. One is for database or table fields, and the other is for report fields, such as subtotals and grand totals. These Speed menus appear when you right-click over the related field type.

Database and Table Field Speed Menu

The Speed menu choices available for database and table fields are as follows:

- Change Font …
- Change Format …
- Change Border and Colors …
- Browse Field Data …
- Insert Subtotal …
- Insert Grand Total …
- Insert Summary …
- Send Behind Others
- Delete Field
- Cancel Menu

Text Field Speed Menu

The following choices are available for text fields:

- Change Font …
- Change Format …
- Change Border and Colors …
- Edit Text Field …
- Send Behind Others
- Delete Field
- Cancel Menu

Summary Field Speed Menu

The following choices are available for summary fields:

- Change Font …
- Change Format …
- Change Border and Colors …
- Change Summary Operation …
- Send Behind Others
- Delete Field
- Cancel Menu

► The Special-Item Speed Menus

Speed menus are also associated with the following:

- Text areas
- Special fields
- Lines
- Boxes
- Graphics
- Objects

The Speed Menu for Text Areas

Text areas are the areas of your report that are outside fields or other items but within the report itself.

The following Speed menu options are given for a text area:

- Change Font …
- Paste …
- Cancel Menu

The Speed Menu for Special Fields

Special fields are the fields added by the Insert ➤ Special Field choice: date, page number, record number, and group number. The Speed menu choices for these fields are as follows:

- Change Font …
- Change Format …
- Change Border and Colors …
- Send Behind Others
- Delete Field
- Cancel Menu

The Speed Menus for Lines and Boxes

The following choices are on the Speed menus for lines and boxes:

- Change Format …
- Send Behind Others
- Delete Line (or Box)
- Cancel Menu

The Speed Menus for Graphics and Objects

The following Speed Menu choices are available for graphics and objects:

- Change Format ...
- Change Position ...
- Send Behind Others
- Delete Graphic
- Cancel Menu

When you've selected an OLE object, the first choice of the Speed menu is the name of the object. Choosing this option displays a cascading menu that lets you edit or convert the object.

►► Summary

In this chapter, we explored almost every part of the Crystal Reports program. (We've saved a couple of the best parts, including cross-tab reports, for the next chapter.)

We started with the File menu, which has more choices than you might expect. The Print options in particular offer a wider range of choices. Exporting provides a richer set of export file types than the export option within dBASE for Windows.

The File ➤ Options dialog box provides a comprehensive set of default settings. It is roughly comparable to the dBASE for Windows Desktop Properties dialog box (although Crystal doesn't uses the multi-tab format).

Along wilth the standard Clipboard operations, the Edit menu covers many other operations, including controlling which sections of the form are visible and manipulating OLE links to other Windows programs.

The Insert menu lets you add items to your report. You can insert lines, boxes, graphics, and special fields, as well as summary fields such as subtotals and grand totals.

The Format menu lets you apply all kinds of formatting to the items on your report. You can change colors, draw lines around some or all of your items' sides, add drop shadows, and more.

The Report, Window, and Help menus provide typical Windows' program services.

After the menus, we discussed the speedbars, the format bar, and the Speed menus in Crystal Reports.

In the next chapter, we'll conclude Part 3 with a closer look at some specialized reporting, including building cross-tab reports.

▶ ▶ CHAPTER 11

Mastering Cross-Tab Reports, Labels, and Form Letters

In this chapter, we'll conclude Part 3 with an in depth look at three types of specialized reports: cross-tabs, mailing labels, and form letters.

Cross-tab reports are used when you want to look at your data in two or more dimensions simultaneously. This is a common requirement with, for example, sales data.

Mailing labels let you prepare mailing labels from your data, as we did in Chapter 7. In this chapter, we'll explore your choices and the label settings in detail. You'll find that you can use the mailing label feature for a lot more than simple mailing labels.

Form letters are the final type of report that we'll examine in depth. The way Crystal Reports lets you handle your text makes it an ideal tool for preparing form letters.

We'll begin with cross-tab reports, which are designed using another one of Crystal Report's design surfaces.

Generating Cross-Tab Reports

Cross-tab reports let you group your data on two criteria simultaneously, presenting a spreadsheet-style view. For example, with a cross-tab report, you could view your company's sales by product line within geographic regions.

In Crystal Reports, creating a cross-tab report is a simple matter of dragging your fields into the appropriate box.

▶ Sample Data for Cross-Tab Reporting

For our example of cross-tab reporting, let's suppose that we've built a database system for a seed company that does business in three states in the center of the U.S.: Indiana, Illinois, and Iowa (IN, IL and IA, respectively, in U.S. postal codes). Figure 11.1 shows the structure of the portion of an Orders table that we'll use. Create a similar ORDERS.DBF file for your own use.

FIGURE 11.1

A table structure for cross-tab reporting

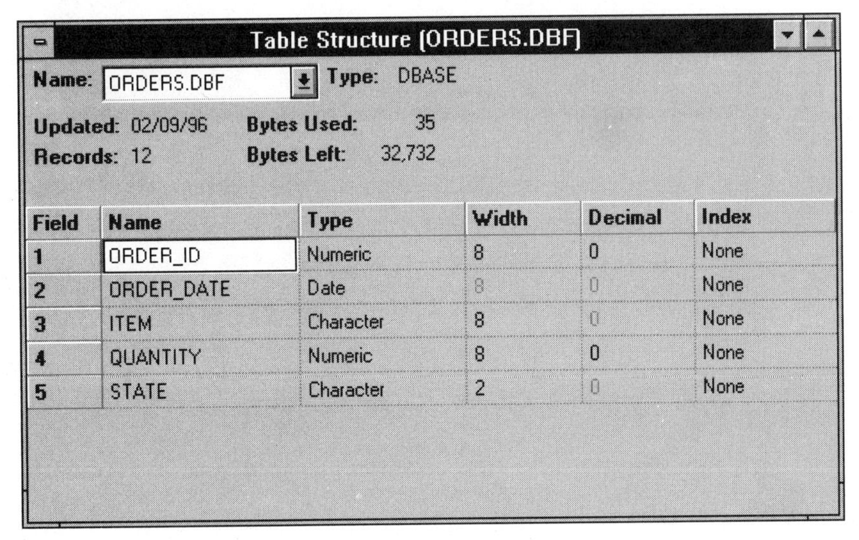

Figure 11.2 shows our Orders table filled in with some sample information. Fill in your own Orders table with data similar to that in Figure 11.2.

Note that we have taken some liberties here. In practice, we would have at least three tables. Through the Query Designer, we would link an Orders table to a Customer table. Assume that we've done this in the example, using the STATE field from the Customer table. Similarly, we would link the Orders table to a Product table. Again, assume that we've created this link, using the ITEM field from the Product table.

FIGURE 11.2 ►

Sample Orders table data

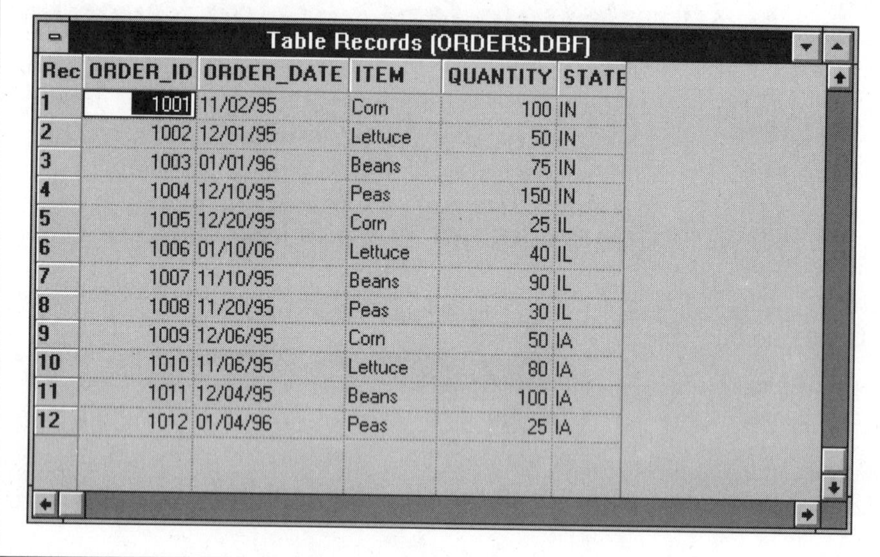

Table Records (ORDERS.DBF)

Rec	ORDER_ID	ORDER_DATE	ITEM	QUANTITY	STATE
1	1001	11/02/95	Corn	100	IN
2	1002	12/01/95	Lettuce	50	IN
3	1003	01/01/96	Beans	75	IN
4	1004	12/10/95	Peas	150	IN
5	1005	12/20/95	Corn	25	IL
6	1006	01/10/06	Lettuce	40	IL
7	1007	11/10/95	Beans	90	IL
8	1008	11/20/95	Peas	30	IL
9	1009	12/06/95	Corn	50	IA
10	1010	11/06/95	Lettuce	80	IA
11	1011	12/04/95	Beans	100	IA
12	1012	01/04/96	Peas	25	IA

► Building Your First Cross-Tab Report

You can create a cross-tab report from the Navigator, but it is much simpler if you use these commands in the Command window:

```
USE orders
CREATE REPORT CROSSTAB
```

This command sequence—USE orders and then CREATE REPORT CROSSTAB—selects the table and launches the Cross-Tab window in Crystal Reports, as shown in Figure 11.3.

The alternative method for getting to the Cross-Tab window is to select the Untitled report from the Navigator, which takes you into Crystal Reports. In Crystal, you'll be creating a standard banded report. Cancel that process and choose File ➤ New ➤ Cross-Tab.

In the Cross-Tab window, your first task is to pick the field that will contain your summary data. From our Orders table, we want to summarize the QUANTITY field by STATE and by ITEM.

With the mouse pointer, drag the QUANTITY field into the Summarized Field rectangle of the Cross-Tab window, as shown in Figure 11.4. As you drag the field, you'll see that your cursor turns from a "stop" shape circle

FIGURE 11.3

The Cross-Tab window in Crystal Reports

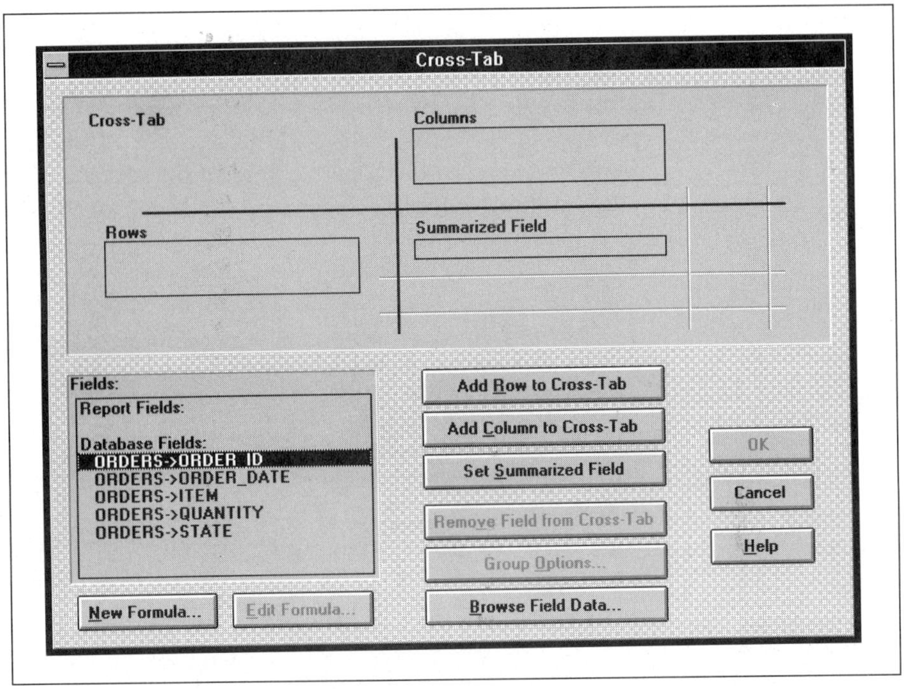

FIGURE 11.4

Dragging the QUANTITY field into position

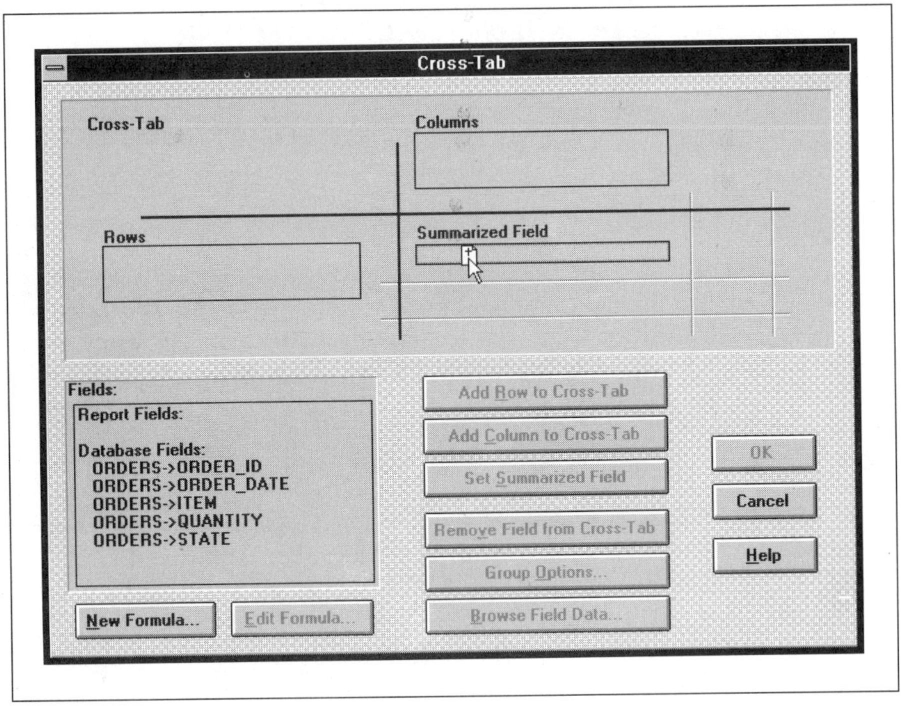

into a document marked with a cross (as in cross-tab report, we presume) when it is in a position where it can be dropped.

Now that the QUANTITY field is in the Summarized Field position, let's put the states across the top of our report and the items down the side. Start by dragging the STATE field to the rectangle marked Columns. Here we are beginning to drag that field out of the Fields rectangle:

Notice the cursor is still in its "stop" shape, which tells us that the field can't be dropped yet.

Next, drag the ITEM field to the Rows rectangle. When you have dragged the three fields into position, the top of the window should look like this:

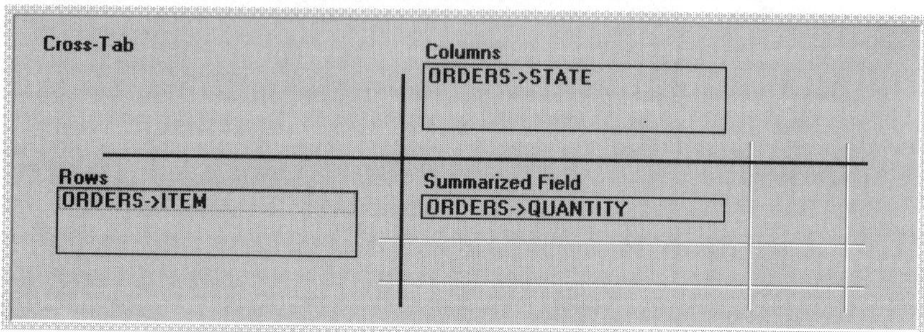

We've now completed the specification of a basic cross-tab report.

▶ Viewing Your Report

With your three fields in place, click on OK or press Enter. Your new cross-tab report is complete. Figure 11.5 shows our report in Crystal. For this figure, we maximized Crystal Reports itself and also maximized the child window labeled Untitled Report.

FIGURE 11.5 ▶

Our cross-tab report in Crystal Reports

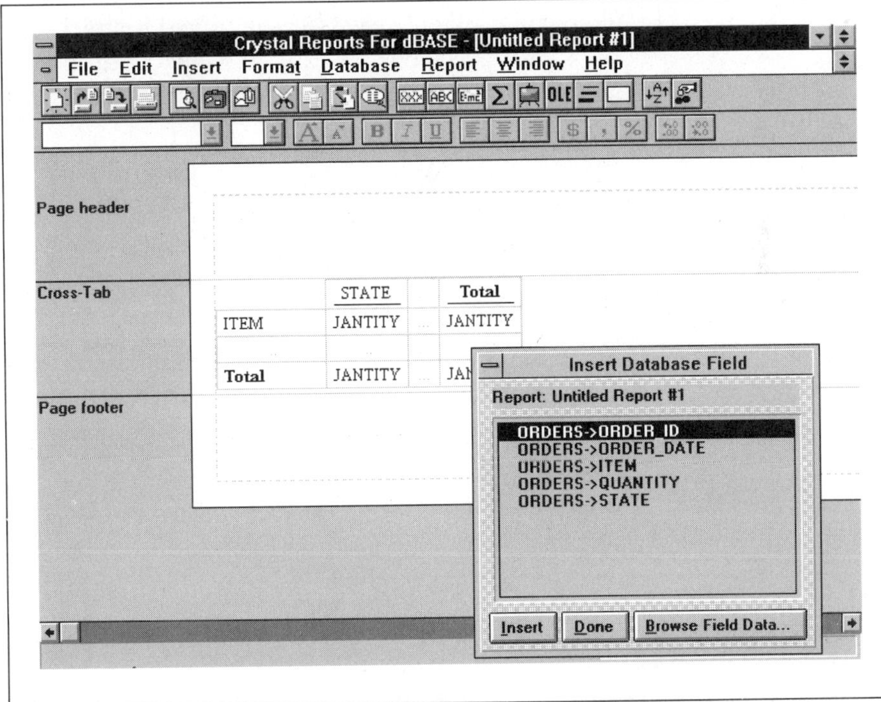

As you see in Figure 11.5, there are three bands in a cross-tab report:

- Page header
- Cross-Tab
- Page footer

▶ Adding Page Headers and Footers

The Page header and Page footer bands have their usual uses, and you can treat them as you would for any other report. For now, try adding a title in the Page header band and a page number in the Page footer band.

We've called our report Seed Sales. To add a title, choose Insert ➤ Text Field .... In the Edit Text Field dialog box, type the report title.

When you click on Accept, the text field is attached to your cursor. Position it in the Page header band and click to drop it. While the text field is still selected, set the point size to 24 (or something similarly emphatic).

To add the page number in the Page footer band, choose Insert ➤ Special Field ➤ Page Number. Again, the field is attached to your cursor. Drop it in the Page footer area.

▶ Previewing the Report

With these preliminaries completed, click on the spyglass icon to look at your report in the Preview window. Figure 11.6 shows our first version.

At this point, if we were preparing a banded report, we would start selecting individual fields to make the formatting improvements that transform a plain report into an elegant report. Unfortunately, you can't edit fields in the Cross-Tab band from the report's Preview window. You must close the Preview window and return to the Crystal design surface to make changes.

▶ Formatting a Cross-Tab Report

For this example, we'll make a few simple improvements. The column titles would look better if they were right-justified, and the totals would stand out if they were in boldface.

Formatting the Column Titles

To begin, click on the Close button in the Preview window's speedbar to return to the report design surface. Then click on the lasso icon or choose Edit ➤ Select Fields to get the cross-hair cursor that allows you to draw a rectangle around a group of fields.

▶▶NOTE

The Crystal Reports lasso is different from the Form Designer lasso. In Crystal Reports, every field that is touched by the lasso is selected. In the Form Designer, only fields that are fully enclosed are selected.

FIGURE 11.6 ▶

Previewing our cross-tab report

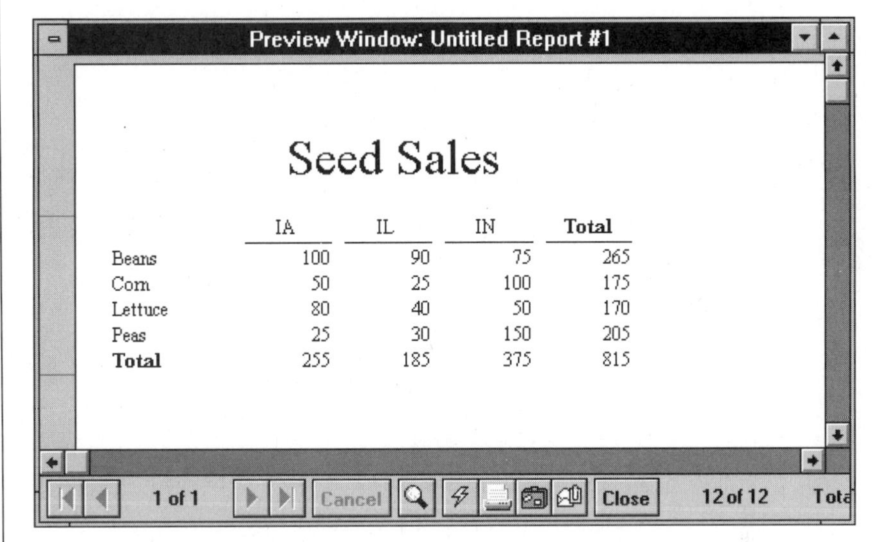

With the cross-hair cursor, drag from the upper left of the column-title fields to a point far enough down and to the right to touch both the STATE and Total column-title fields. Then choose Format ➤ Field … to launch the Format String dialog box.

In the Format String dialog box, set the Alignment to Right, and then click on OK or press Enter. Your two column-title fields will now be right-justified.

If both column-title fields are selected, click any field to deselect them and return to single-field selecting. With one field selected, we can consider the differences between the two column-title fields shown here.

Remember that there is a key difference between the STATE column-title field and the Total column-title field. To see this, click on the Total field and choose Edit ➤ Text Field .... This choice will let you edit the text.

Now try the same thing with the STATE field. When you choose Edit ➤ Text Field ..., you'll find that the selection is grayed; it's not available. Why?

The STATE field isn't really a column heading at all. It's a proxy for data that will come from the database. You will have one STATE field for each different state value in your table. In our report, we have IN, IL, and IA.

Formatting Row Labels

As you've seen, the column titles are actually made up of data from your tables, plus a Total column at the end. The rows are also built this way.

The ITEM field in your Cross-Tab band is the same as the STATE column title; you can't use Edit ➤ Text Field ... to change it. The values will be supplied from your database.

You can, however, use Edit ➤ Text Field ... on the Total row. You can also use Format ➤ Field on either the ITEM or Total row label.

Formatting the Bottom Totals

To format the totals at the bottom, use the lasso to select both of the QUANTITY fields at the bottom of the Cross-Tab band. As shown in Figure 11.7, our fields are right-justified (the default for numbers), and they don't quite fit. The Q in QUANTITY is chopped off.

FIGURE 11.7 ▶

Lassoing the QUANTITY fields

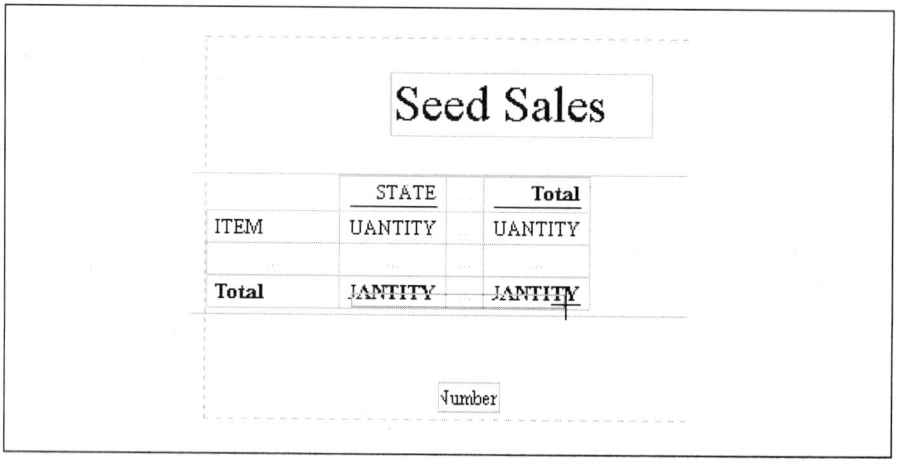

When these fields are selected, click on the **B** icon to convert them both to boldface. If you return to your Preview window, you'll see a more attractive report.

▶ Adding Another Dimension

As you may have noticed when we built the cross-tab report, you could put more than one field in the columns or rows of your cross-tab report. Putting additional fields here is similar to selecting multiple group levels in a banded report. We'll work through an example, breaking down our sales by month within item types.

Changing the Cross-Tab Layout

The Cross-Tab window lets you define and change the selection of your cross-tab report's fields. To return to the Cross-Tab window to make changes, choose Format ➤ Section …. In the first Format Section dialog box, you'll see the list of each band in your report, as shown in Figure 11.8.

FIGURE 11.8 ▶

The first Format Section dialog box for a cross-tab report

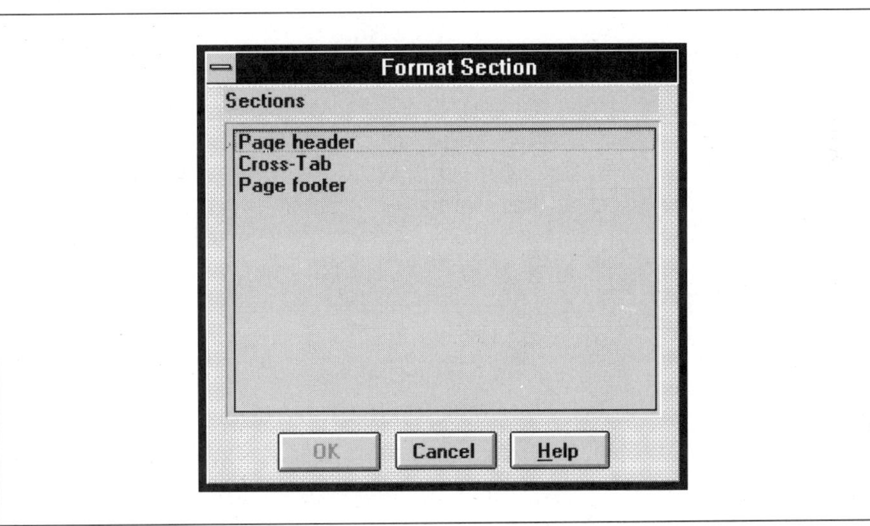

Choose the Cross-Tab section from the Format Section dialog box, and then click on OK or press Enter. This will launch the Format Section dialog box for the Cross-Tab section. From this second Format

Section dialog box, choose the Cross-Tab Layout … pushbutton, as you see us doing in Figure 11.9. This will return you to the Cross-Tab window, where you can modify your layout.

FIGURE 11.9

The Format Section dialog box for the Cross-Tab section

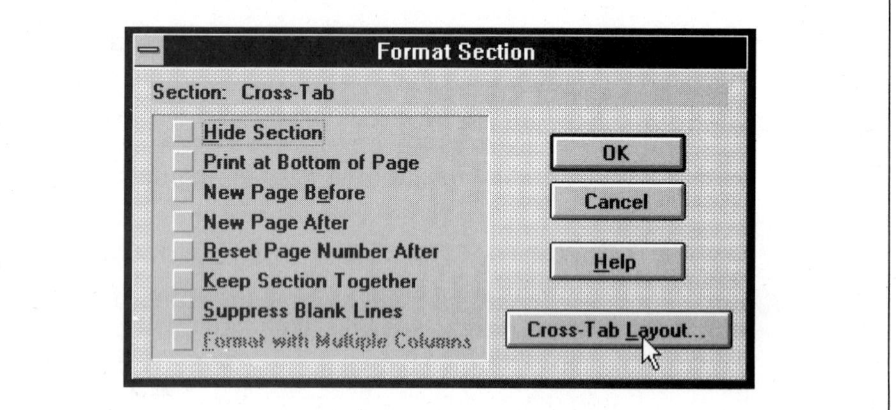

►► **NOTE**

The Cross-Tab Layout … pushbutton does not appear unless you have already built a cross-tab report.

In the Cross-Tab window, we could add the ORDER_DATE field as an additional row, but this would not give us what we want. Each field in either the rows or the columns is another grouping item. If we added the ORDER_DATE field, we would group our orders by individual days. This might be interesting for some purposes, but for our data, grouping the orders by month would be much more useful.

Adding a Formula to Group by Month

To group by month, we'll need to use a formula field, and enter a dBASE for Windows expression that will give us the month from the date data we have available. We'll cover dBASE for Windows expressions and functions in detail in Chapter 12. For now, we'll go over the ones we need for our sample cross-tab report.

dBASE for Windows has a built-in function, MON( ), which returns a month number, given a date. For example, MON({1/1/96}) returns 1, meaning January. We could use MON( ) as the base for our formula field's expression:

```
MON(Order_Date)
```

This function will return 11 for November orders, 12 for December orders, 1 for January orders, and so on. This will do a good job of sorting our orders by month, except for one problem: computers are stupid.

When you give Crystal an expression that returns a number, you and I may think about farmers ordering seeds during the winter, but Crystal only knows that it has some numbers used to group data. So it will do what it always does: put them in order.

The order of your data will come out like this:

January (1)
November (11)
December (12)

But we want a numbering scheme that will make the months come out like this:

November
December
January

We'll need to devise a trick that returns the months of late fall and early winter in a numeric sequence that will put January after December. As is frequently the case, the method is a lot more complicated to explain than it is to implement.

Another dBASE built-in function is INT( ), which stands for INTeger part. The INT( ) of any number is the whole part, with any fractional part chopped off. INT( ) doesn't do rounding.

If we asked for INT(1/30), we would get 0 (zero). If we asked for INT(29/30), we would still get 0. Similarly INT(30/30) would give the result 1 (one), and INT(59/30) also returns 1.

In dBASE for Windows, if you subtract one date from another, you get the number of days between the two dates. Here are two examples that evaluate to 30:

```
{11/1/95} – {10/2/95}
{12/1/95} – {11/1/95}
```

As you can see, dBASE does real date arithmetic. It knows that there are 31 days in October and that there are only 30 days in November.

Now that you know all this, here's what we can do. We'll subtract {10/2/95} from the order date. It will give us the following results:

- A number from 1 to 29 for any order in October
- A number from 30 through 59 for any order in November
- A number from 60 through 90 for any order in December
- A number from 91 through 121 for any order in January

If we divide these numbers by 30 and take the INT( ) of the result, we'll have 0 for October, 1 for November, 2 for December, and 3 for January.

You might have realized that December 31 will give us a 3, as if it were in January. Similarly, January 30 and 31 will give us a 4, as if they were in February. This is an approximation that gets sloppier as more months pass. But if you look at the data we have, it gets every order in our table right, so we can go with it.

Adding a Formula Field

To add a formula field to our report, click on the pushbutton labeled New Formula ..., under the Report Fields list in the Cross-Tab window. You'll see the New Formula dialog box. We called our formula field ord_month, as shown in Figure 11.10.

FIGURE 11.10

Entering a formula field's name

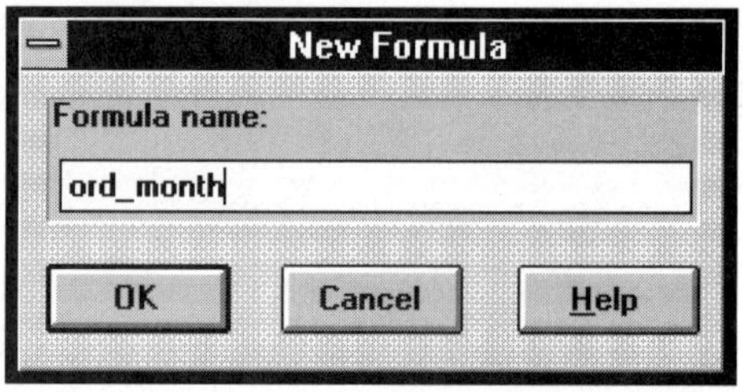

New Formula
Formula name:
ord_month
OK Cancel Help

After you enter the name and press Enter or click on OK, the Expression Builder is launched. We entered this expression:

```
INT( (Order_date-{10/2/95})/30 ) + 10
```

Adding 10 at the end converts November dates from a 1 to an 11, December dates from a 2 to a 12, and so on.

When you're finished entering your formula field's expression in the Expression Builder, click on OK or press Enter to return to the Cross-Tab window. (See Chapter 8 for details on using the Expression Builder.)

In the Cross-Tab window, your new formula field will be highlighted. You can drag it to the Rows rectangle and drop it underneath the ITEM field, but there is another way.

Specifying a Cross-Tab without Dragging

You may have noticed that the pushbuttons in the Cross-Tab window are enabled and disabled as you work with your layout. If you have a field selected in the Fields rectangle, the first three buttons are available:

- Add Row to Cross-Tab
- Add Column to Cross-Tab
- Set Summarized Field

Note that the first two choices are to *add* a field, but the third is to *set* the field. You can have multiple row or column fields, but only a single summarized field.

If you have any of the fields in the Cross-Tab section, the Remove Field from Cross-Tab pushbutton is available. This button lets you clear the selected field from the report.

With your formula field (Crystal labels it @Ord_month) selected in the Fields rectangle, click on the Add Row to Cross-Tab pushbutton. The formula field is added underneath the ITEM field.

Running the Revised Cross-Tab Report

With your date formula field added to the Rows section, click on OK or press Enter. You'll return to the Format Section dialog box. Again, click on OK or press Enter. Now you'll see your report layout, which should look like the one shown in Figure 11.11.

FIGURE 11.11

A date dimension added to the layout

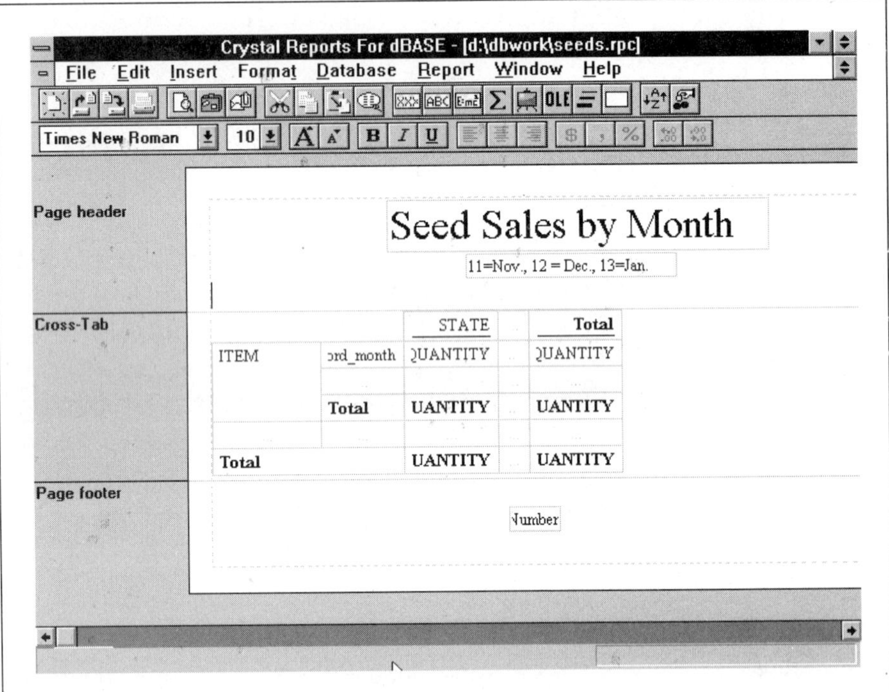

If you look carefully, you'll see that we changed our title text field and added another, explanatory field underneath the title. When you preview the report, your Preview window should look like the one in Figure 11.12.

As you can see, adding the months has added another dimension to the report. You can examine sales by month for individual items, for individual states, or for both. While our sample data is not going to help anyone who is in the seed business, it's enough for you to see that this type of report will go a long way toward helping you examine your own data for trends.

As you can also imagine from studying our sample report, adding more dimensions by adding more row or column fields will let you continue to break down your analysis to whatever degree is required.

FIGURE 11.12

Previewing the cross-tab report with months added

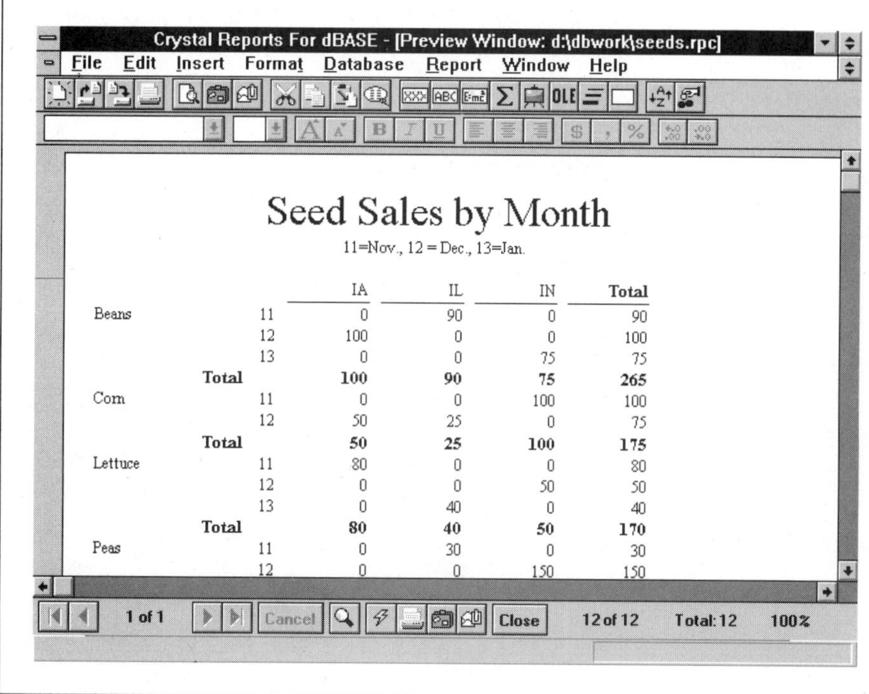

Seed Sales by Month

11=Nov., 12 = Dec., 13=Jan.

			IA	IL	IN	Total
Beans		11	0	90	0	90
		12	100	0	0	100
		13	0	0	75	75
	Total		**100**	**90**	**75**	**265**
Corn		11	0	0	100	100
		12	50	25	0	75
	Total		**50**	**25**	**100**	**175**
Lettuce		11	80	0	0	80
		12	0	0	50	50
		13	0	40	0	40
	Total		**80**	**40**	**50**	**170**
Peas		11	0	30	0	30
		12	0	0	150	150

TIP

If your cross-tab report runs to several pages, see if you can create a summary on a single page that shows the data aggregated in the most informative way possible.

A single-page cross-tab report is often worth more in providing information than the most detailed banded report. Use cross-tab reports whenever you can.

Creating Labels

In Chapter 7, we generated our first mailing labels. Crystal makes this simple, but the vagaries of our hardware make it a job that still takes a little human intelligence. Here, we'll consider the mailing label design tools in depth. You'll see that a wide variety of labels—ranging from standard Avery mailing labels to name tags to VCR labels—come under the heading mailing labels.

To specify a label layout, choose File ➤ New ➤ Mailing Label .... Crystal displays the Database File dialog box so that you can select a table or query. After you choose a file, the Mailing Labels dialog box appears, as shown in Figure 11.13.

FIGURE 11.13

Specifying mailing label layout

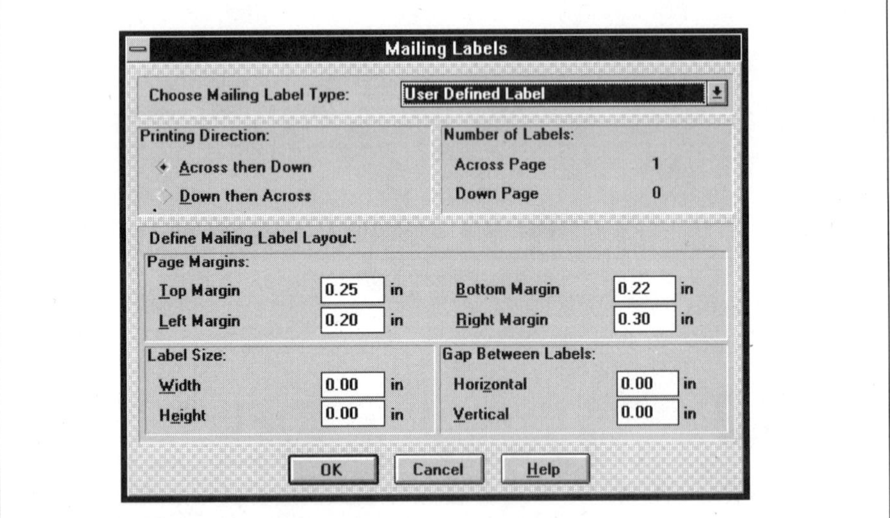

▸ Choosing a Label Type

The first option in the Mailing Labels dialog box is Choose Mailing Label Type. The following list gives the available types and counts (columns per page by rows per page). The counts give you a rough idea of the size of each label. For the exact size, select the label type and look at the Label Size section of the Mailing Labels dialog box, which will show the exact specifications of the selected type.

These standard labels are white, with other colors noted:

- Address (3×10, 3×6, 3×5, 2×10, 2×7, 2×3)
- Address/Shipping (2×5, 2×3, 2×2)

- Address, $5\frac{1}{4}$ diskette (2×6)
- Address, $3\frac{1}{2}$ diskette (3×3)
- Audio Cassette (2×6)
- Clear Address (3×10, 2×7, 2×6, 2×5, 2×3)
- Diskette, $3\frac{1}{2}$-inch (3×3) (also in red and blue)
- Diskette, $5\frac{1}{4}$-inch (2×6) (also in red and blue)
- Diskette, $3\frac{1}{2}$-inch (2×3)
- Diskette, $5\frac{1}{4}$-inch (1×7)
- File Folder (2×15)
- Full Sheet (1×1)
- Index Card (1×3)
- Index/Post Card (1×2)
- Mini Address (5×12) (also clear)
- Name Badge (2×4) (also in blue)
- Name Tag (2×4) (also in blue)
- Name Tag (2×2)
- Return Address (4×20)
- Rotary Index Card (2×4, 1×3)
- Round (3×4)
- Video Cassette Face (2×5)
- Video Cassette Spine (1×15)

As you can see, the range of labels is substantial, covering far more than just mailing labels.

One good use of mailing labels is for return addresses for yourself. Enter your name and address into a table and then copy your record to another record. Then copy the two records to two more. Then copy the four records, and so on. In short order, you'll have a table full of copies of your name and address.

Generate a few pages of labels for yourself and keep them handy. Even if you send most of your correspondence in preprinted envelopes, you'll find an amazing number of times when you can stick on a return address. They work on large envelopes, packages, and postcards. They are especially handy when you pay your bills, using the envelopes your creditors supply for this purpose.

You can test your creativity by trying to come up with the best use yet for the round labels. We think using a fancy graphic to make awards to give your kids for bringing home good test scores is one good idea. Have you got a better one?

Crystal has provided thorough coverage for the Avery label series; however, one important category it omits is Cheshire labels. In the mailing trade, Avery labels are known as *peel-and-stick* labels, since that is exactly what you do to apply one.

Cheshire labels are named after the brand of equipment that applies these labels (which don't peel) to envelopes. If you're doing large-volume mailings, your mail house will supply the exact specifications for its range of Cheshire labels. You can enter those specifications in the Mailing Labels dialog box. Either choose User Defined Label as the label type, or pick the closest type and edit the specifications.

▸ Specifying the Printing Direction

In the Printing Direction section, you can choose to print labels Across then Down, or Down then Across. In many applications, your choice here doesn't matter. However, in some cases, the printing order can be an important consideration.

If you're printing personalized letters and using mailing labels, you'll start with sheets of labels and a stack of letters, both in alphabetical (or some other) order. You'll want to be absolutely certain that the labels are applied in the same order as the envelopes are stuffed.

Decide beforehand which way makes it easiest to peel your labels from their backing and stick them onto the envelopes. You may find, for example, that 2-up labels (labels in 2 columns per page) are easiest to peel across and then down, but 3-up labels may be easier to peel down the columns. Whatever you decide, make your printing conform to your manual procedures.

▶ How Crystal Determines the Number of Labels

The Number of Labels section tells you how many labels you will get across the page and down the page. It does *not* let you enter these values. They are calculated from two sources:

- The values entered in the Mailing Labels dialog box
- The paper size Windows lists for your printer

The values in the Mailing Labels dialog box determine how many labels fit across and down on a page. The values that Crystal chooses are the maximum number of full labels that can be printed on a page. If, for example, your label specification would give you room for 3.9 labels across, Crystal would print only 3 across.

The page size is determined by the settings in the Windows Control Panel's Printer Setup dialog box (or Crystal's Printer Setup dialog box if you've filled that in).

▶▶ TIP

In some cases, you may want to use paper smaller than the maximum size that your printer can support. For example, you could be running 8½-inch-wide labels in a printer that supports up to 15-inch-wide paper. You can always reduce the available paper size by setting a large right or bottom margin value in the Mailing Labels dialog box.

▶ Defining the Mailing Label Layout

The Define Mailing Label Layout section is divided into three panels:

- Page Margins
- Label Size
- Gap Between Labels

Setting Page Margins

In the Page Margins panel, you enter the margins that are the greater of either of these:

- The area your printer cannot reach
- The margins on your label stock

For example, many laser printers that use $8\frac{1}{2}$-by-11-inch paper cannot print on the leftmost or rightmost $\frac{1}{2}$ inch, nor on $\frac{1}{6}$ inch at the top and bottom. (Your page dimensions may be given in centimeters, not inches, depending on your Windows setup's international settings.)

Your labels will also have margins. For example, the Avery 7664 labels for $3\frac{1}{2}$-inch diskettes have 0.71 inch (about 2 centimeters) left and right margins. These are the controlling margins for these labels.

If you're using paper that is smaller than the size listed for your printer, increase the bottom and/or right margins accordingly. For instance, a $4\frac{1}{2}$-inch right margin would let you run $8\frac{1}{2}$-inch-wide paper through a printer that can support 13-inch-wide paper.

Specifying the Label Size

In the Label Size section, you can enter the maximum width and height of your labels. For round or other odd shapes, measure the maximum width and height and enter those dimensions here.

Setting the Gap between Labels

In the Gap Between Labels section, enter the amount of space between your labels that is not available for printing. Bear in mind that the width of the first label plus the gap between labels must be the exact location of the left edge of the second column of labels.

Always compute the location of the left edge of the last column of labels from the dimensions you specify and compare that to an actual label measurement.

▶ Leaving and Returning to the Mailing Labels Dialog Box

After you select your label specifications from the Mailing Labels dialog box and click on OK or press Enter, you'll return to the report layout window.

In your label layout, the Details band is sized correctly, according to the settings in the Mailing Labels dialog box. The layout shows as many rectangles across the page as you have columns of labels. You only need to put your fields into the first label; the rest are filled in automatically.

If you need to make changes, or just want to review the settings, you can return to the Mailing Labels dialog box for your labels. From the layout window, choose Format ➤ Section ..., and then choose the Details section. In the second Format Section dialog box, click on the Label Layout ... pushbutton to launch the Mailing Label dialog box again.

▶ Tips on Printing Labels

Making your selections in the Mailing Labels dialog box and setting up the Details band in the layout window may be all that you need to do to print your labels. However, as we've mentioned, your printer may not print the labels correctly for one reason or another. Be sure to make some dummy labels with your photocopier and to run these samples before using your real label stock. If your printer doesn't print the labels properly, you can try some of the adjustments noted in the following sections.

Margin Variation

Some printers have an inherently imprecise margin mechanism. For example, feeding single sheets into a laser printer can provide quite a bit of error to the left or right.

To compensate for margin variation, specify a left margin that is slightly large, a gap between labels that is similarly oversized, and a label width that is undersized. For example, if your variability is 0.1 inch, you could specify a left margin that is 0.1 inch too large, a label width that is 0.2 inch too small, and a gap that is 0.1 inch too large.

Again, remember to calculate the location of the rightmost column of labels from your specifications, and compare it to an actual label measurement.

Labels and Field Sizes

Remember that your selection of labels has no effect on your table's field width. If you have chosen 60 character-wide names and addresses, you won't be able to fit them on 3-up labels on 8½-by-11-inch paper. You can, however, accommodate a reasonable variation in field widths by varying the point size of the field's font.

Lines per Label

If at all possible, leave at least one line unprinted to provide a margin between the printing and the edge of the label. Again, the number of lines that fit are a function of the size of the font you choose.

If you can leave, for example, 0.16 inch free between labels, set your label layout to begin at the top of the Details band in Crystal. Leave the blank space at the bottom of the label. Then, before you print, add 0.08 inch to the top margin of your paper in the Mailing Label dialog box. This will divide the free space evenly between labels.

▸▸ Producing Form Letters

Crystal Reports lets you put large amounts of text in any text field, and in any band of your report. Its limit is 32,000 characters per field (just a little shorter than this chapter, for example). While Crystal isn't going to replace your favorite word processor for text entry and manipulation, it is more than capable of handling your most demanding form letter requirements.

NOTE

To generate form letters, you can use Crystal or you can use the mail-merge capabilities of your word processor. If you're familiar with Crystal, it will be the simpler tool. If you've already been using the mail-merge features of your word processor, there's no reason to switch.

Database Design for Form Letters

Before you do any work on form letters, you need to design your database to support this application.

The first principle of database design for form letters is to assume nothing. Don't try to extend your letters past the edge of your actual knowledge.

Alan likes being known as Alan. If you wanted him to respond to your letter, you wouldn't begin with "Dear Al,"—he would know that you're a stranger, and he may be offended at your presumption. On the other hand, none of Marty's friends would ever send him a letter that began, "Dear Martin,"—he would know that it was a half-baked form letter and probably toss it without a second thought.

The second principle to observe is to never assume that anything about addressing a letter is simple.

Here in the U.S., we are a relatively egalitarian people. You correctly address both Joe Jones, the maintenance man at BigCo, and Sam Jones, the Chief Executive Officer of BigCo, as Mr. Jones.

However, a simple Mr. or Ms. will not work for Dr. Brown, Professor Green, or Senator Smith. Judges and clerics have their own forms of address. Some lawyers prefer an Esq. after their names. These are just a few of the many exceptions to Mr. or Ms.

Beginners generally start with a database design with fields like these:

- SALUTATION (for Mr., Ms., and so on)
- FIRST_NAME

- MID_INIT
- LAST_NAME

Then they build the address by combining the salutation, first name, middle initial, and last name on one line. For the salutation that comes after "Dear" in the letter, they often try the first name.

We suggest that you don't make these beginners' mistakes. The only method that is guaranteed to give sound results is to have one field for the individual's full name and a second field for the name you will use after "Dear" in your letters.

With those two fields, you could address a letter to "Ms. Mary Smith," and open it "Dear Mary," or you could address it to "The Hon. Mary Smith, M.S., J.D." and open it with "Dear Judge Smith."

For our example, we copied PEOPLE.DBF to MAILLIST.DBF and modified it for form letter application. Figure 11.14 shows our new structure.

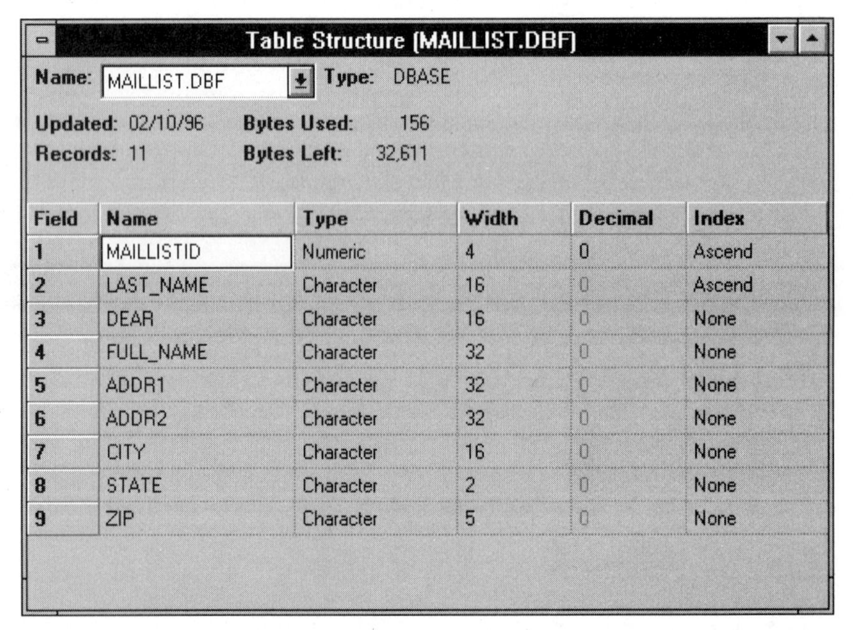

FIGURE 11.14

A mailing list table's structure

The field we've called DEAR is for the name that will come after the "Dear" in a letter. You could fill in Bill for "Dear Bill," or you could fill in Mr. President, for "Dear Mr. President."

After modifying the structure, we went through our PEOPLE.DBF data and modified it so that we can use it for form letters. As you see in Figure 11.15, we filled in our close personal friends' nicknames, but we've been safe and formal with our more remote acquaintances.

FIGURE 11.15

Data for mailing list applications

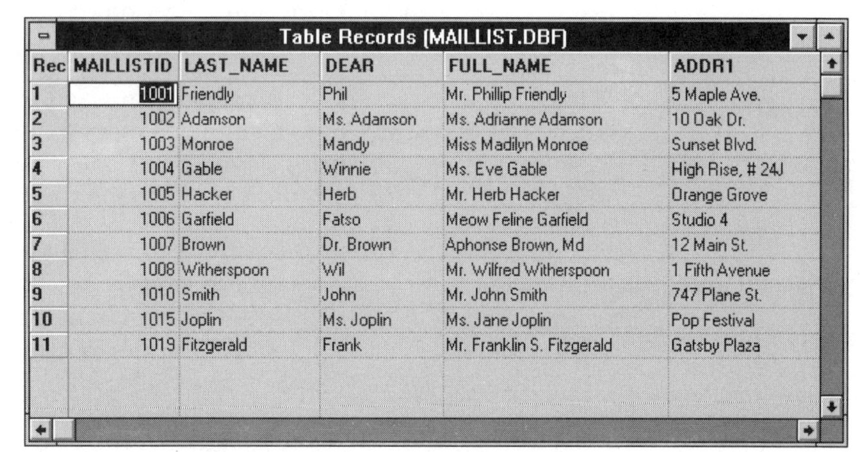

Table Records (MAILLIST.DBF)

Rec	MAILLISTID	LAST_NAME	DEAR	FULL_NAME	ADDR1
1	1001	Friendly	Phil	Mr. Phillip Friendly	5 Maple Ave.
2	1002	Adamson	Ms. Adamson	Ms. Adrianne Adamson	10 Oak Dr.
3	1003	Monroe	Mandy	Miss Madilyn Monroe	Sunset Blvd.
4	1004	Gable	Winnie	Ms. Eve Gable	High Rise, # 24J
5	1005	Hacker	Herb	Mr. Herb Hacker	Orange Grove
6	1006	Garfield	Fatso	Meow Feline Garfield	Studio 4
7	1007	Brown	Dr. Brown	Aphonse Brown, Md	12 Main St.
8	1008	Witherspoon	Wil	Mr. Wilfred Witherspoon	1 Fifth Avenue
9	1010	Smith	John	Mr. John Smith	747 Plane St.
10	1015	Joplin	Ms. Joplin	Ms. Jane Joplin	Pop Festival
11	1019	Fitzgerald	Frank	Mr. Franklin S. Fitzgerald	Gatsby Plaza

WARNING

When you fill in your data for a form letter application, be sure that you don't make any guesses. The great actor Leslie Howard would probably *not* respond to your appeal if you sent him a letter addressed to "Dear Ms. Howard."

Creating Your Form Letter

With your database designed and filled in for a mailing application, your next concern is the creation of the letter itself. Any text editor can be used with good results. One of your authors (we won't say who, but one of us is a bit old-fashioned) likes to use a DOS text editor. Even that works.

You can use the built-in dBASE editor, if you like. From the Command window, launch the text editor with:

```
MODIFY FILE t.let
```

Choose Properties ➤ Text Editor … to launch the Text Editor Properties dialog box, where you can set word wrap and an appropriate margin.

For more extensive writing, use the text editor or word processor you like best. You can even type your letter directly into Crystal (but editing text in a report writer is not our idea of fun).

Whatever editor you choose, prepare the fixed part of your letter and revise it as necessary. Finish all the changes before you go to Crystal Reports, where text editing is much less convenient. When you're finished, select all your text and copy it to the Clipboard.

From a Windows program, copying to the Clipboard is generally a one-button choice, or available by pressing Ctrl-C. If you're running a DOS editor under Windows, press Alt-Enter if you are running full-screen. With your letter in a DOS window under Windows, click on the System button or press Alt-spacebar to get the System menu. Choose Edit from this menu. From the cascading menu, choose Mark and use your mouse to select text as if you were in a Windows program. When you have selected your whole letter, press Enter to copy the text to the Clipboard.

When you have your letter in the Windows Clipboard, it's time to launch Crystal Reports. From the Navigator, select the Untitled report and press F2 or double-click. Or, from the Command window, type

```
CREATE REPORT
```

Pick your mailing list database and let Crystal start up. Once Crystal is launched, maximize it and the design window. Click in the Details band if your insertion point is not already there. Then choose Edit ➤ Paste or press Ctrl-V to paste your letter into the Details band. Figure 11.16 shows our form letter in Crystal.

We clicked on Done in the Insert Database Field dialog box, so it would get out of the way. You can leave yours in place, or do likewise.

FIGURE 11.16

A form letter in the Details band

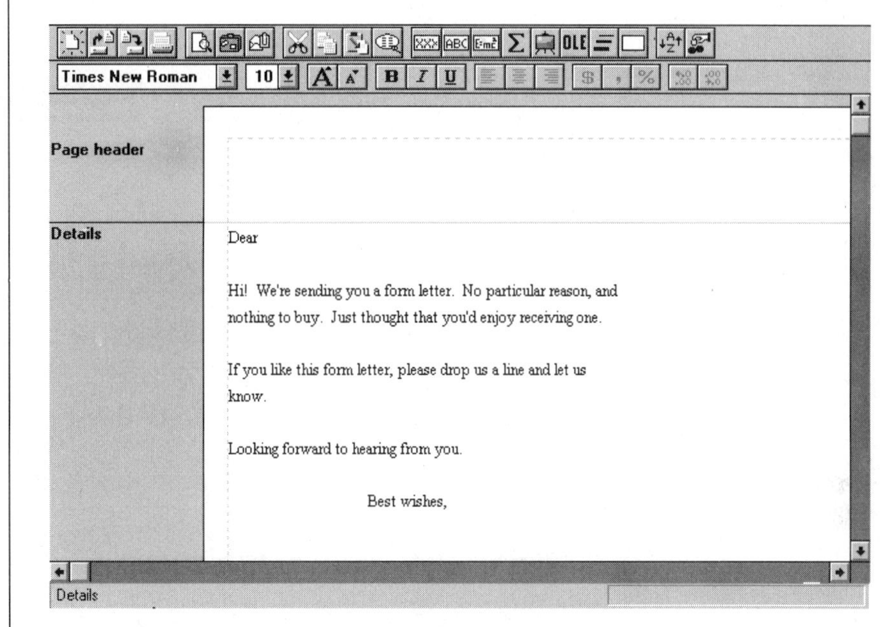

At this point, we recommend using the File ➤ Save As command to save your work.

▶ Adding the Name and Address Fields

With your letter safely saved in Crystal, put your insertion point in front of the *Dear* and press Enter several times to make enough space for the address. If you closed the Insert Database Field dialog box, choose Insert ➤ Database Field … to bring it back.

Drag the full name field and the address fields into the space you made. Also copy the Dear field after the word *Dear*. When you have done this much, your result should look similar to the Details band shown in Figure 11.17.

Now we're ready to run our report in the Preview window. Click on the spyglass icon and look at a few of your letters. Do you see what the biggest problem is?

FIGURE 11.17

The name, address, and Dear fields in place

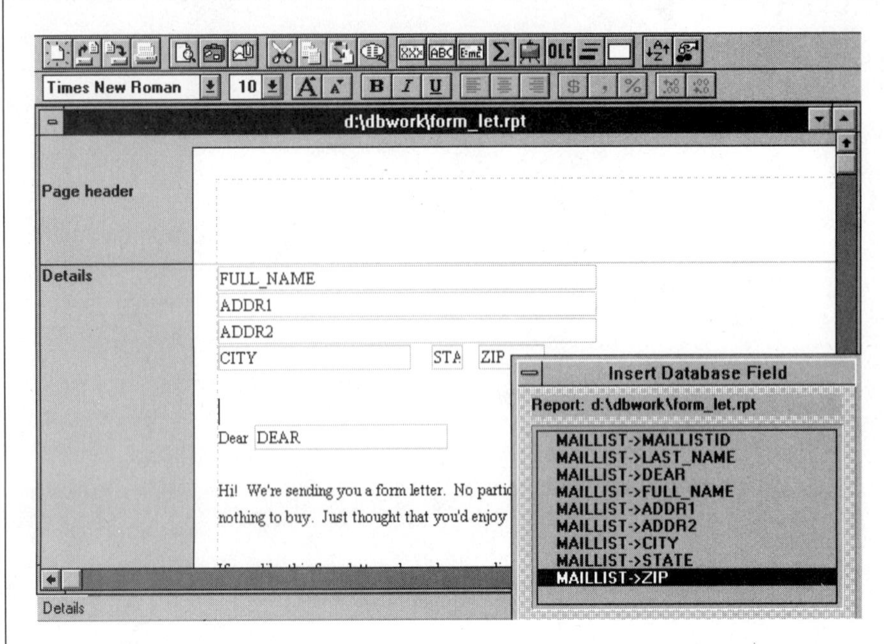

Crystal Reports has no idea that we are sending form letters. It repeats the Details band as many times as it can, including fractional times, on a page.

To get a new letter on each page, choose Format ➤ Section … and choose the Details band. In the second Format Section dialog box, check the New Page After option.

Now return to the Preview window. This time, you'll see that you have a separate letter on each page.

► Using Formula Fields to Improve Your Letters

Our first letter begins:

Dear Phil

There's no comma or colon after Phil's name.

If you were to simply add a colon (or comma) after the Dear field, you would have a letter that starts like this:

Dear Phil   :

The colon will come after the end of the Dear field. Of course, you allowed enough space in this field to hold the longest name you might include, so there is a lot of blank space after almost every name in your table.

Cleaning Up the Salutation Field

To print a comma or colon after the salutation, we need to replace the DEAR field from our data table with a formula field. We need an expression that will trim the trailing blanks from the DEAR field and append a colon. The RTRIM( ) function trims blanks from the right of a character field. The plus operator (+) puts two strings together. This is the expression that we want to use:

```
RTRIM(Dear)+":"
```

To add a formula field, click on the Einstein icon on the speedbar or choose Insert ➤ Formula Field .... Either one will launch the Insert Formula dialog box, where you enter the name of your formula field.

After you enter a name and click on OK or press Enter, the Expression Builder is launched. In the Build Expression dialog box, enter the expression above. If you like, you can double-click on the DEAR field instead of typing it in. (For our table, this entered MAILLIST->DEAR, which would help us get the correct DEAR field if we had a multiple-table view open.)

After you enter your expression, ask the Expression Builder to Evaluate it, just to check. Then click on OK or press Enter to return to Crystal's design window. Your field is now attached to your cursor.

Position it anyplace near the existing DEAR field and drop it. Then select the DEAR field and press Del to delete it. (If Del doesn't work, which is sometimes the case with our copy, choose Edit ➤ Clear.) With the old field gone, you can position the new one after the *Dear* in the letter, and get the result shown in Figure 11.18.

FIGURE 11.18

***Dear** handled correctly*

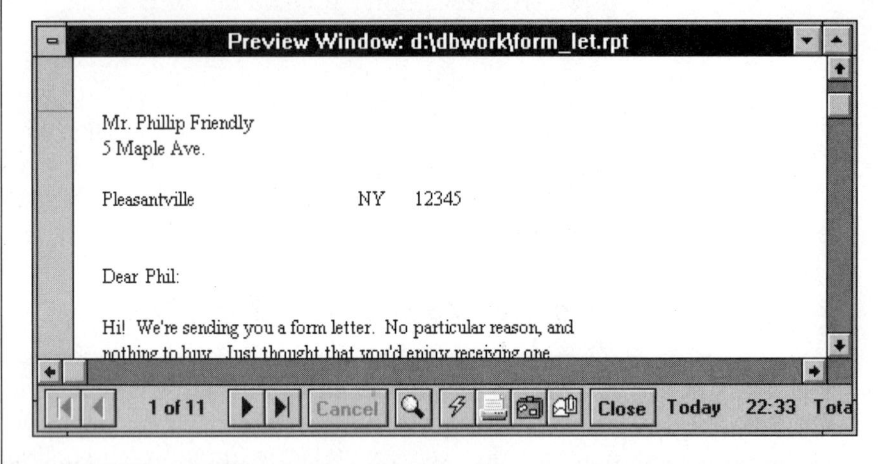

Handling the Address Fields

Figure 11.18 shows fine style in handling the *Dear* line, but take a look at the city, state, and zip code line in the address. You'll see a rather clumsy line with lots of extra space (it probably reminds you of every poorly programmed computer form letter you've ever seen). Let's fix this up next.

We want is to print the city, followed immediately by a comma and a single space, followed by the two-letter state code and another space, and then the zip code. (We assume that you'll adapt the methods we describe here as necessary to suit the address format appropriate to your country.)

Again, we need to replace the database fields with a formula field. Just as with the DEAR field, the RTRIM( ) function and + operator will work here. This is the expresson we need:

```
RTRIM(City)+", "+State+" "+Zip
```

This is going to become part of a more extensive formula when we address the next problem, so copy this one carefully.

Begin by adding a new formula field (choose Insert ➤ Formula Field … or click on the Einstein button). Name this formula **line4** (the reason will become apparent shortly). In the Build Expression dialog box, type the expression above, and then ask the Expression Builder to Evaluate your results. If you had our data, your result would be:

```
Pleasantville, NY 12345
```

Test our line4 expression by running your report in the Preview window. You should see that the city, state, and zip code line looks just fine. However, we still have a problem with the address.

Three- or Four-Line Addressing

The problem we face is that we have allowed for two address lines before the city, state, and zip code line. In many cases, the ADDR2 field will be blank, so we will be addressing the letter with something like this:

```
Mr. Phil Friendly
5 Maple Ave.

Pleasantville, NY 12345
```

If this letter were typed, we certainly wouldn't leave a blank line in Phil's address just because we might want another line in someone else's address. For the sake of this discussion, let's call the city, state, and zip code line the CSZ line. We want to print the CSZ line at line 3 if the ADDR2 field is blank. If the ADDR2 file is not blank, then the CSZ line should be the fourth line printed. Here's the algorithm we should follow:

```
Print the full name

Print the Addr1 value

IF the person has an Addr2 field value
      Print Addr2
   ELSE
      Print the CSZ line
ENDIF

IF the person had an Addr2 field value
      Print the CSZ line
   ELSE
      (do nothing -- the address is done)
ENDIF
```

As you see, we need a more complex expression for the third and fourth lines. As you've probably guessed, we'll call the third one **line3**.

We can use the IIF( ) function to make a choice. Here's an example of IIF( ) that returns "genius" or "normal" depending on whether or not the value of Person is "Einstein":

```
IIF(person="Einstein", "genius", "normal")
```

The IIF( ) function takes a logical expression and returns one of two values following that expression. If the logical expression is True, it returns the first value. In our example, if the person is Einstein, it returns "genius." If the expression is False, it returns the second value.

Using IIF( ) functions, here is our address algorithm:

```
Print the full name

Print the Addr1 value

IIF( .NOT. EMPTY(Addr2), Addr2, CSZ )

IIF( .NOT. EMPTY(Addr2), CSZ, "" )
```

In the last line, we use quotation marks with nothing in between for an empty string—it will print nothing.

Now our final point is that the CSZ expression must be spelled-out in full (Crystal Reports hasn't been reading this chapter). So here is the full expression for line 3:

```
IIF( .NOT. EMPTY(Addr2), Addr2, RTRIM(City)+", "+State+" "+Zip )
```

In Crystal, delete the third line field (ADDR2) and then create a new formula field named line3 with this expression. Use the Preview window to check your work.

When you have line 3 complete, edit the formula in line 4. Choose Edit ➤ Formula Field … after you select the line 4 formula field. This will launch the Expression Builder with the line available for editing. This is the formula we want to use:

```
IIF( .NOT. EMPTY(Addr2), RTRIM(City)+", "+State+" "+Zip, "" )
```

Now you have an address that will print without blank lines, as shown in Figure 11.19.

FIGURE 11.19

The correct address for Phil's letter

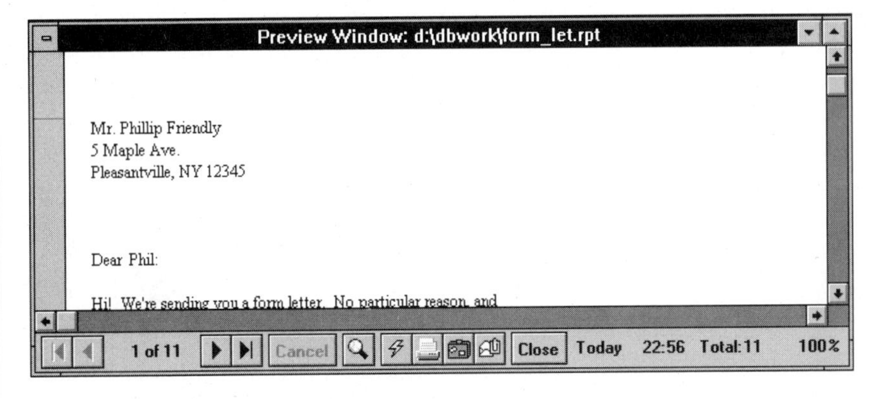

These same expressions can be used for other applications that require mailing addresses, such as for printing the envelopes or mailing labels for our form letters.

▶▶ Summary

In this chapter, we examined cross-tab reports, labels, and form letters. We started by developing a simple approximation of a sales data system for building sample cross-tab reports.

Launching Crystal from the Command window with a CREATE REPORT CROSSTAB command is a simple way to begin building a new cross-tab report. Alternatively, you can select the Untitled report in the Navigator, and then choose File ➤ New ➤ Cross-Tab in Crystal Reports. In the Cross-Tab window, we used our items as rows, our states as columns, and summarized our quantity field.

Crystal prepared a cross-tab report for us, after we added a title and page number in the Page header and Page footer bands.

We edited our report in the Crystal report design window, because you can't edit the Cross-Tab band in the Preview window.

After this, we added a formula to subgroup our data by the month of the sale. We used an approximation to get January to sort after December. This additional grouping added another dimension to our cross-tab report.

Next, we went on to discuss mailing labels. The first thing you saw was that a wide variety of label types are available. You can use the mailing label feature to produce far more than just standard mailing labels. We examined the Mailing Label dialog box settings in detail. You can make adjustments here to compensate for the variability in your equipment and to force Crystal Reports to use smaller paper than the maximum supported by your printer.

Finally, we went on to form letters. You saw that a simple database design, using one field for the recipient's full name and another for the data that comes after the word *Dear* in the letter is the best design to correctly address the people on your list.

You used your favorite word processor to create and edit your letter, and then used the Windows Clipboard to paste it into the Details band of Crystal's standard banded report. Setting the New Page After option for the Details band produces one letter per page.

You used your table to add name and address fields. You then used formula fields to place the punctuation after the *Dear* line; to correctly format the city, state, and zip line; and to correctly format the address, accommodating varying numbers of lines.

This concludes Part 3. The next part deals with programming basics. In Chapter 12, you'll learn more about using expressions and functions to get the results you want.

Programming Basics

PART FOUR

In this part, we'll go through some of the basics that you'll need to know to write simple dBASE for Windows programs. Actually, it would almost be correct to call this part Procedural Programming Basics, since most of it (though not all) is about the tools and techniques needed to write programs that run one step at a time, directly under your control.

In the next part, Working with Forms, you'll be working with dBASE for Windows' objects and object properties, including events. That is all about object-oriented programming, but we hesitate to use the word *programming*. You do most of that "programming" by clicking on tools from the Controls palette and by entering properties in the Object Properties Inspector.

As you learned in Chapter 6, event handlers that you attach to your objects are, indeed, programs. Many of them are only a line or two long, as all the examples in Chapter 6 were. Sometimes, however, you'll want to establish longer chains of commands. Other times, you'll find that something you're doing in the Table Records tool was interesting the first time, but has become boring by the sixth time, and you want to automate the task. For both these reasons, knowing a little bit about dBASE programming helps.

In Chapter 12, Working with Expressions and Functions, we'll dive into dBASE expressions in detail. Then we'll divide the functions into categories. We'll also provide an alphabetic reference to all the functions, which you can browse through to find ones that meet your needs.

In Chapter 13, Using Command Window Commands, we'll cover the commands that you can give in the Command window. The chapter doesn't include the commands that control the operation of dBASE programs or those that are in dBASE for Windows just to support dBASE IV and earlier applications (those are listed in Appendix D). Even so, there are still more than 200 commands here!

Our goal is to present the commands in a form that you can read through, getting an idea of the types of commands that are available. Then while you're working, you should recognize that what you want to do can be achieved by the right command. Turn to the listing by topic, and you should be able to find the right command. Then turn to the alphabetical listing, and you'll see it explained and, frequently, you'll see examples and tips or warnings about the command.

In Chapter 14, Basics of Programming Statements, we explain the commands, which we call *statements*, that control the operations of dBASE for Windows programs. These are the core of the dBASE language. You'll see that unlike the huge sets of functions and commands, the core statements comprise a small, easily mastered group.

With one reading of Chapter 14, you should be able to understand the way that the Form Designer structures its dBASE for Windows programs. And you'll be prepared when it comes time to create more elaborate event handlers as you work with the object-oriented tools presented in Part 5.

CHAPTER 12

Working with Expressions and Functions

▶▶ **dBASE** for Windows supports a wide variety of expressions and an even wider set of functions to use as part of those expressions. They are used everywhere. In an index expression, you might specify `UPPER(Last_name)` to get a true alphabetic sort. In a calculated field you specify `Price*Quantity` to compute a currency amount.

The list of rules for properly forming expressions is very long, and every one of those rules is given in this chapter. But don't be intimidated. If an expression seems reasonable to you, it's probably acceptable to dBASE, too.

dBASE's language designers have always had typical users, not programmers, in mind as their target audience. You may wonder, "Can I add 7 to a date to get the date a week later, or subtract 7 to get to last week?" The answer is yes.

If you subtract 7 from the 3rd of January, you'll get the 27th of December in the prior year (not the -4th of January). dBASE does its best to take good care of you.

We'll begin with expressions. Functions are a component of expressions, but they get their own section in the second part of this chapter.

▶▶ **TIP**

Read this chapter quickly to get an idea of the things you can do. Then use it for reference as you develop requirements for expressions in your database work.

Forming Expressions

dBASE expressions are built from operators and operands. Any dBASE expression can be evaluated in the Command window by using the ? command (to pose the question "What is …?"). In this example, the ? command outputs the value of the expression 2+2 to the results pane of the Command window:

```
? 2+2
```

This command contains two *2* operands and a + operator. Figure 12.1 shows several sample expressions in the Command window's input pane, along with their values in the results pane.

FIGURE 12.1 

Some expressions and their results in the Command window

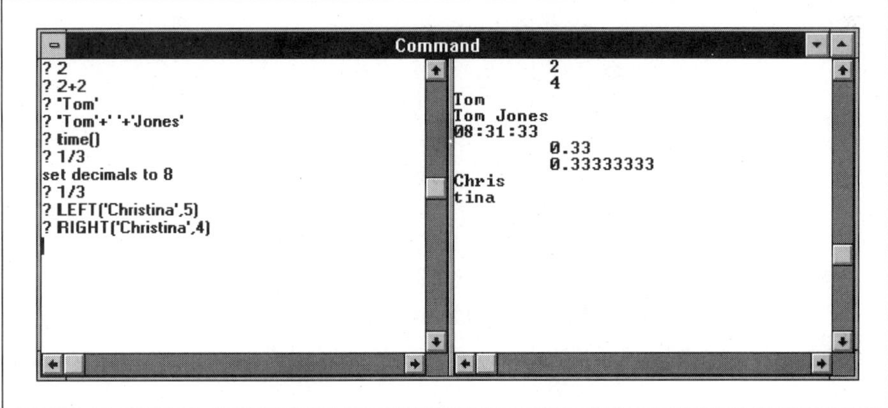

TIP

The left-to-right orientation of the input and results panes is our preference for evaluating expressions. Select Properties ➤ Command Window from the menus to change the window layout.

In the following sections, we'll discuss operands and operators in depth, beginning with operands.

▶ Using Operands

The following are the seven different types of operands, from the simplest to the most complex:

- Constants
- Memory variables
- Fields
- Object properties
- Object references
- Function calls
- Subroutine references
- Expressions

We'll cover each in turn.

Types of Constants

The five types of constants are numeric, character string, date, logical, and other.

Numeric Constants

Numeric constants begin with integers, which can be signed, such as the following numbers:

```
0
1
123456789
-5
```

Your numeric input cannot include grouping separators, such as commas. For example, `1,234,567` is not a valid numeric constant.

Numeric constants can include decimal fractions, as in these examples:

```
0.5
14.3456
-28.43210
```

dBASE for Windows defaults to carrying decimal numbers to 16 significant digits, so you don't need to worry about numeric accuracy except in extreme cases.

Leading zeros are not significant, and may be omitted. These are pairs of identical values:

```
0.5
.5

-0.456
-.456
```

You can also use integral exponents in scientific notation, as in these examples:

```
1E6
-1.4E-8
```

The scientists and engineers who understand scientific notation will comprehend that immediately. For you nonscientists, we offer the following tip.

TIP

Large numbers are sometimes better written in scientific notation. 1E6 is a million (1, followed by six zeros). 1E9 is a billion. 1000000000 is impossible to read without stopping to tick off the zeros in groups of three.

Character String Constants

Character string constants are any string of characters that you can type, delimited by single or double quotation marks or by square brackets. For example, these are all the same:

```
"Smith"
'Smith'
[Smith]
```

dBASE reads a string constant from the opening delimiter to the matching closing delimiter. This means that you need to decide if your

string should include one or more of the delimiters before forming your expression. These examples are correctly specified:

"Single 's inside doubles"
'Double "s inside singles'
"Brackets [inside] either"
'Brackets [inside] either'
[Brackets surrounding both: "Don't go," she said.]

Date Constants Date constants are written according to the settings of Desktop Properties Country tab (choose Properties ➤ Desktop, Country tab to check). They are enclosed in braces. The following examples assume the *M/D/Y* format:

{6/28/94}
{12/31/95}
{1/1/96}
{12/31/1999}
{1/1/2000}

(The first date above was the date that dBASE for Windows was officially launched.)

Logical Constants Logical constants are one of two values:

.T.
.F.

These mean True and False, respectively.

▸▸ **WARNING**

Although you can also use Y and N (or y and n) in logical entry fields, and you never include the surrounding dots, these forms are not permitted in expressions.

Other Types Other constant data types include binary types, such as sounds and images. These constants can be supplied to commands, but cannot be used in expressions.

Memory Variables

A memory variable is created, most simply, by assigning an expression to a variable name. A constant is the simplest form of expression. These are all statements that create memory variables:

```
days_per_week = 7
tax_rate = .0675
last_name = "Smith"
full_name = 'Ms. Jillian Smith, PhD.'
launch_date = {6/28/94}
is_project_complete = .F.
```

Memory variable names begin with an alphabetic character and continue with any combination of letters, digits, and underscore characters. Valid memory variable names include the following:

```
x
x_ray
product_1
P17_A40
```

dBASE does *not* consider differences in case to be significant. The following names are all identical:

```
on_hand
On_hand
On_Hand
ON_HAND
```

By convention, memory variable names are typed in lowercase.

The name `x-ray` is not valid because the – operator is not allowed in names. The names `01P47` and `_target` are not valid either, because variable names must start with a letter.

▶▶ **NOTE**

An exception to the rule for naming memory variables is the dBASE internal global variable names, which all start with an underscore character.

There are no formal restrictions on the sorts of names you can make up. However, it is good policy to make your name reflect the variable's contents. The following are perfectly acceptable to dBASE, but will make your job much harder than it should be:

```
days_per_week = "Smith"
tax_rate = 'Ms. Jillian Smith, PhD.'
last_name = .0675
full_name = {6/28/94}
launch_date = .F.
is_project_complete = 7
```

In dBASE IV and earlier, you could use only 10 characters in a variable name. (Actually, you could use 11 but only the first 10 were significant.) dBASE for Windows lifts this restriction. There is no limit to the length of variable names. Use names that are just long enough to describe the value they will hold, but are not unnecessarily verbose.

Field Names

A field name is an alphabetic character, followed by up to nine letters, digits, or underscore characters. For example, these are all valid field names:

```
Address1
Last_name
Ship_date
Qty_on_hnd
```

The field name width is limited to 10 characters. This is because the field name is written into a strictly formatted header in the .DBF file.

A field name may include an optional data table alias specification. The table's alias is the table's name, unless an alternative is specified with the USE command (see Chapter 13). We always use these table alias specifications to be sure we're getting the data we want. For instance, you could have tables for Company, Product, and Customer, each with a NAME field. The following field names would keep the name data *Amalgamated Widgets, Inc.*, *Large Widgets*, and *Fred Smith* sorted out:

```
Company->name
Product->name
Customer->name
```

If a field name matches a memory variable name, the field takes precedence. Choosing a different (longer always works) memory variable name can eliminate this conflict. You can also prefix a memory variable with `M->` as a pseudo table alias. For example if `name` is a field, `M->name` can be used as a memory variable.

Object Properties

Object properties can be referred to in expressions. Using the Properties tool in the Form Designer, you have assigned many properties. Properties can also be assigned with statements such as these:

```
my_form.Top = 2
pushbutton1.Left = my_form.Width - 12
my_form.Maximize = .F.
```

As you see in the second example, the property my_form.Width can be used as part of an expression. Since it is a number, it can be used like any other number.

You can create your own properties, just as you create your own memory variables. Property names follow the same rules as memory variable names, except that there is no M-> pseudo-table prefix. These are some examples using property names:

```
my_form.is_complete = .F.
my_form.start_date  = {12/31/95}
```

NOTE

dBASE for Windows uses mixed uppercase and lowercase names for properties, such as Left, OnClick, and ColorNormal. To keep our custom properties separate, we use the lower_with_underscores style you've seen above. Keep in mind that this is a convention; dBASE doesn't care about uppercase and lowercase.

Object References

If you examine your .WFM file output from the Form Designer, you'll see that it is dBASE program code, and that the vast majority of the lines of code define and assign properties to your form's objects. By default, the object that the Form Designer creates is named *f*.

This is known as an *object reference variable*. It can be used in expressions, although its usage is specialized. Examples are given later in this chapter, in the section about structure operators.

An object reference is at least one of the properties of most of the dBASE built-in objects. For example, all the objects that you attach to forms have a Parent property. That is an object reference to the parent form.

The parent form's First property is the first on-form object in the form's tabbing order. All the on-form objects that are tab stops (including buttons and entry fields, but excluding lines and rectangles) have a Before property, which is the on-form object that they precede in the tabbing order. (The Before property of the last object in the tabbing order is an object reference to the First object, so tabbing goes in a circle.)

▸▸ NOTE

Subroutine references can also be used to refer to procedures, functions, or code blocks. However, these references are seldom used outside advanced programs.

Function Calls

A function is a subroutine that returns a value. A function call is the function's name followed by parentheses enclosing the function's arguments, if any. All function calls require the parentheses. Arguments may or may not be needed, depending on the function.

A function call may be used as an operand anywhere that the appropriate result can appear in an expression. Here are some valid numeric function calls in ? commands that you can test in the Command window:

`? LEN("Smith")`	Returns 5
`? RECNO()`	Returns number of current record (or error if no table is in use)
`? PAYMENT(100000, .07/12, 30*12)`	Returns 665.3025
`? YEAR({12/31/95})`	Returns 1995

These are valid character string function calls:

`? CHR(65)`	Returns "A"
`? STR( 1/3, 5, 3)`	Returns "0.333"

These function calls return dates:

`? DATE()`	Returns today's date
`? CTOD('12/31/99')`	Returns date of big New Year's Eve

These function calls return logical results:

`? EOF()`	Returns .T. at end of table; .F. otherwise (or error if no table is open)
`? ISALPHA('9')`	Returns .F.
`? ISUPPER('A')`	Returns .T.

In these examples, some of the functions have no argument at all, such as DATE( ), EOF( ), and RECNO( ), and some have as many as three arguments, such as the PAYMENT( ) and STR( ) functions. Other functions can be called with varying numbers of arguments.

In each function that accepts one or more arguments, the arguments can always be expressions. Here we've shown constant values. These are some valid expressions called with expressions more complex than simple constants:

`? DTOS( DATE( ) )`	Returns a string for today, such as "December 31, 1995"
`? CHR(10*6 + 5)`	Returns "A"
`? ISUPPER( CHR(65) )`	Returns .T.

These examples all use dBASE for Windows built-in functions. By convention, these are typed in all uppercase letters; however, as with other names, dBASE is not case-sensitive.

You can also create your own functions. These participate in expressions exactly as the built-in ones do. See Chapter 14 for information about writing your own functions.

►► NOTE

By convention, your own functions, called UDFs (user-defined functions) are typed in lowercase (but again, dBASE doesn't care). Following the conventions makes it easy for you to distinguish calls to UDFs from calls to the dBASE built-in functions.

Expressions as Operands

You can build expressions using other expressions as operands. This is a simple example:

```
? 4 + 1/3
```

which returns 4.33. In this case, the value of the expression 1/3 (0.33) was used as the operand of the addition operator.

Expressions can be enclosed in parentheses. An expression in parentheses is evaluated fully before it is used as an operand. Consider these two expressions:

`? 4 + (1/3)`	Returns 4.33
`? (4+1)/3`	Returns 1.67 (that's 5/3)

In our first example, without parentheses, dBASE decided to do the division before the addition, because its internal rule is that division has higher precedence than addition. The precedence follows this order:

- Exponentiate first
- Multiply and divide second
- Add and subtract third

The rules of precedence also extend to all other types of operators. We're not going to present those rules here, and we recommend that you ignore them if you stumble across them. However, the one rule to remember is that expressions in parentheses are fully evaluated before being used as an operand. By using parentheses, you control the order of execution. In fact, your expressions will be more readable and less prone to errors if you always use parentheses.

▶▶ **TIP**

Here's one way to remember the order of precedence: "Please Excuse My Dear Aunt Sally," for Parentheses, Exponentials, Multiplication, Division, Addition, Subtraction.

▶ *Using Operators in Expressions*

You can use half a dozen different kinds of operators in your expressions:

- Arithmetic
- Date
- String
- Logical
- Structure
- Relational

The following sections discuss each one in turn.

Arithmetic Operators

Arithmetic operators include the big four: +, –, *, /. We'll start with these, then round out the set with the others.

The big four numeric operations do just what you would expect:

`? 2+3`	Returns 5
`? 2-3`	Returns -1
`? 2*3`	Returns 6
`? 2/3`	Returns 0.67

As you will see below, the + and – operators are also string and date operators. They examine their operands to pick an appropriate type of operation. The arithmetic operations are performed if both their operands are one of the numeric types.

You may have noticed that dBASE for Windows keeps two types of numbers: N and F. The N type is used for integers—numbers that have no decimal fraction part. The F type is used for numbers that do have a fractional part. dBASE picks the appropriate types and handles the conversion from one to the other automatically.

For instance, dBASE for Windows will add the integers 2 and 2 and produce an integer 4. It will divide integer 4 by integer 3 and produce a floating-point number: 1.33. The number of digits you display is set in the Desktop Properties Programming tab. The number of places kept internally is also set there. In most cases, you'll want to display only a small portion of the available digits.

The other arithmetic operators are –, for unary negation, and ^, for exponentiation.

The operators we have looked at so far have all been binary, meaning they take two operands—one on either side. The – operator can also be used in a *unary* fashion, meaning with a only a single operand (on its right).

The – sign can precede an expression, meaning to reverse its sign. Here are some examples:

```
x = 2
? -x        Returns –2
? -(2+3)    Returns –5
? -(2-3)    Returns 1
```

The **^** operator means "raise the operand on the left to the power on the right." Here are some examples:

```
? 3^2       Returns 9
? 3^3       Returns 27
? 3^4       Returns 81
```

Neither operand need be integral, as in these examples:

`? 1.2^2`	Returns 1.44
`? 3^2.5`	Returns 15.5885

The ** operator is a synonym for the ^ operator.

The arithmetic operators are used only with arithmetic operands and produce arithmetic results.

Date Operators

Unlike numeric operators, the date operations use mostly mixed operands and do not always produce date results.

▶▶ **NOTE**

Other authors classify operators by the type of result they return. For example, subtracting two dates yields a number, so it is categorized as a numeric operator. We call them date operators if one (or both) operands is a date.

The date operators are +, for date/number addition, and –, for date subtraction. The date/number addition operation adds a number to a date (or a date to a number) and produces a date result, as in these examples:

`? DATE( )+7`	Returns the date a week from today
`? 30 + {12/1/99}`	Returns {12/31/99}

Date subtraction has more rules. But if you ignore the rules and think about the operation, it all makes sense, as in these examples:

`? DATE( )-7`	Returns the date one week past
`? {12/31/99}-DATE( )`	Returns the number of days until the big New Year's Eve

`? 7-DATE( )`	Returns error (because it's meaningless)

Date operators are supplemented by a wide range of date functions.

String Operators

There are three string operations, two involving a form of string concatenation and the third performing a string search:

- +, for simple concatenation
- –, for concatenation, trimming blanks
- $, for search (member of)

Concatenation is the operation of putting two strings together to form a single, longer string. The simple concatenation operator (+) abuts two strings. The result is precisely the combined length of both strings.

The trimming operation (–) removes trailing blanks from the left argument string. Here are some examples:

`? 'John'+'Smith'?`	Returns 'JohnSmith'
`? 'John '+'Smith'?`	Returns 'John Smith'
`? 'John '-'Smith'?`	Returns 'JohnSmith'
`? 'John'-' Smith'?`	Returns 'John Smith'
`? 'John?'-' Smith'`	Returns 'John Smith'

The result of the – concatenation is the same as using the RTRIM( ) (right side trim) function on the right argument, then using the + operator for a simple concatenation. You may prefer that form, since it's more explicit.

The *member of* operator returns a logical result. It looks for the first string in the second, returning .T. if it is found. These examples show the operator in operation:

```
? 'a'$'abc'     Returns .T.
? 'at'$'abc'    Returns .F.
? 'at'$'Hat'    Returns .T.
```

The $ operator is case-sensitive. For example, this expression:

```
? 'A'$'abc'
```

returns the result .F.

For a case-insensitive search, use UPPER( ) or LOWER( ) on the operands, as in:

```
? UPPER('A')$UPPER('abc')
```

This expression returns .T.

Logical Operators

The following logical operators let you manipulate True and False results:

- .AND. returns True if both operands are True.
- .OR. returns True if either or both operands are True.
- .NOT. is a unary operator, which returns the reverse of the operand.

These are the operators that you will use constantly in expressions that test for two or more conditions. Here are some examples:

```
credit_limit = 500
balance = 450
frequent_buyer = .T.
buying_power =              Returns 50
credit_limit-balance
hi_buy_power = buing_       Returns .F.
power > 100

? frequent_buyer            Returns .T.
```

`? frequent_buyer .AND. hi_buy_power`	Returns .F.
`? frequent_buyer .OR. hi_buy_power`	Returns .T.
`? .NOT. hi_buy_power`	Returns .T.
`? .NOT. (frequent_buyer .OR. hi_buy_power)`	Returns .F.
`? .NOT. (frequent_buyer .AND. hi_buy_power)`	Returns .T.

▸▸ **WARNING**

Parentheses are vital when working with logical operators. You need to use them to force dBASE for Windows to evaluate the expression as you want it evaluated.

Structure Operators

There are three complex structures in dBASE for Windows: tables, arrays, and objects. The structure operators are **[ ]** (brackets), which is the subscript operator) and **.** (period), which is the "property of" operator.

▸▸ **NOTE**

The field value operator (->) is technically an operator, but it was covered earlier as part of a field name operand. We think of it as part of the name, despite its technical status.

The subscript operator can be applied to either an array or an object, as in these examples:

`? arr[10]`	Returns the tenth value in arr, or error if arr is less than 10 long

`? arr[2,3]`	Returns the value in second row, third column of arr; returns error if arr does not have two dimensions or if either subscript is too large
`? obj[10]`	Returns property number 10 of obj, or error if property 10 is not assigned

Arrays must be DECLARED before they can be used. See Chapter 14 for information about array declarations.

Objects come into existence by the NEW operator or by the DEFINE command. Numbered properties are created when you assign them a value. They cannot subsequently be unassigned. You can assign a value to obj[10], for example, without assigning any preceding property number. (obj[1] through obj[9] do not need to exist to have obj[10].)

►► **TIP**

You can use an object's .Parent dimensions to make resizable forms. For example, assign Line1.Parent.Width to Line1.Right. That way, the line will grow or shrink as the parent form is resized.

The . and [ ] operators may be used repeatedly in a single structure expression, as long as the value reached from left to right is appropriate to the operation. The following are examples:

`? Line1`	Returns object
`? Line1.Parent`	Returns object (form holding line1)
`? Line1.Parent.Width`	Returns width of parent form
`? Line1.Width`	Returns number (width of line, in pixels)

```
arr[1] = Line1
```

`? arr[1]`	Returns object (Line1)
`? arr[1].Width`	Returns width of Line1
`? arr[1].Parent.Width`	Returns width of parent form

►► **WARNING**

The Two-Way Form Designer is not totally two-way. It will replace any expressions you assign in properties with numeric constants. Get your form design right, then abandon the Two-Way tools to make final changes in the Program Editor.

Relational Operators

The following relational operators allow you to compare two values:

- <, for less than
- <=, for less than or equal to
- =, for equal to
- <> or #, for not equal to
- >=, for greater than or equal to
- >, for greater than

The operands must be matching types: numeric, character, date, or logical. Here are some examples:

`? 5.5 < 5.5`	Returns .F.
`? 5.5 <= 5.5`	Returns .T.
`? 'Smith' <= 'Smythe'`	Returns .T.
`? DATE( ) < {12/31/99}`	Returns .T. (as this is written)
`? .T. > .F.`	Returns .T.

All relational operators return results when applied to logical operators. .F. equals .F. and .T. equals .T.; .T. is greater than .F. (or .F. is less than .T.). A beginners mistake is writing:

```
buy_power = credit_limit - balance
hi_buy_power = buy_power > 100

? hi_buy_power = .T.      && silly!
? hi_buy_power      && same thing, good style
```

▶▶ **TIP**

We've never seen a good reason to use relational operators solely with logical operands.

That finishes covering the operators.

▶ Calling Functions

Technically speaking, the parentheses that follow a function name are also an operator: the function call operator. However, unlike any other operator, function calls may not contain any operand at all, or they may have one or more operands (up to a limit imposed by your equipment's available memory).

All syntax (ours, the on-line help, printed documentation, and other books) documents the arguments to functions as expressions of specified types. For example, the ABS( ) (absolute value) function takes a single numeric argument. Its syntax is

ABS(<*expN*>)

It takes one argument, which is any expression evaluating to a number. This is why we say that a constant is the simplest form of expression. This syntax then covers all of these possibilites:

```
ABS(-2.5)
ABS(total_due)
ABS(invoic->total_due)
ABS(arr[1])
```

```
ABS(Form.First.Top)
ABS(ASC(LEFT(UPPER(last_name),1))-100)
```

You "unpeel" deeply nested function calls, like the last one, from the inside out. Here's an example:

`last_name = "Smith"`	
`? UPPER(last_name)`	Returns "SMITH"
`? LEFT(UPPER(last_name),1)`	Returns "S"
`? ASC(LEFT(UPPER(last_name),1))`	Returns 83
`? ABS(ASC(LEFT(UPPER(last_name),1))-100)`	Returns 17 = ABS(83-100)

In a program, such as an event handler, it is better to provide named variables for the portions of the expression and build it in stages. (This is slightly less efficient, but massively less prone to error.) Here's an example:

```
last_name = "Smith"
uname = UPPER(last_name)
first_char = LEFT(uname,1)
...
```

Unfortunately, in many uses, such as in index expressions, you do not have this choice—you must provide a single expression. If you find yourself using more and more complex expressions, consider writing a user-defined function to hold the expression. See Chapter 14 for information about writing your own functions.

▸ Using Functions in Expressions

The rest of this chapter is devoted to the dBASE for Windows functions that are commonly used in expressions. It excludes those that are solely used to support obsolete dBASE IV syntax, functions used only in programming, and other functions that are not commonly used. (These other functions are listed in Appendix E.)

▶ Function Categories

Functions can be grouped into the following categories:

- Database-related
- Date manipulation
- Financial
- Low-level file I/O
- Miscellaneous

TABLE 12.1: *Database-Related Functions*

FUNCTION	RESULT
ALIAS([<*alias*>])	Name of table in work area
BINTYPE([<*field name*>])	Type of Binary field
BOF([<*alias*>])	True if attempted to move before first record
BOOKMARK( )	Alternative to RECNO( ) for SQL tables
CATALOG( )	Name of current catalog
DATABASE( )	Name of open SQL database
DBF([<*alias*>])	Name of current of specified table
DELETED([<*alias*>])	Is record deleted?
DESCENDING(…	Is index descending?
EOF([<*alias*>])	True if moved past last record
FDECIMAL(<*field number expN*> …	Number of decimals in field
FIELD(<*field number expN*>[…	Name of field, given number
FLDCOUNT([<*alias*>])	Number of fields in table
FLDLIST([<*field number expN*>])	Fields in SET FIELDS TO …
FOR([[<*.mdx filename*>,] …	FOR expression used to create tag
FOUND([<*alias*>])	Was last search successful?

TABLE 12.1: *Database-Related Functions (continued)*

FUNCTION	RESULT
ISTABLE(<*table name*> …	Is table in database?
KEY([<*.mdx filename*>,] …	Key expression of an index
KEYMATCH (<*exp*> …	Is there an index on the expression?
LUPDATE([<*alias*>])	Date of last update
MDX(<*index tag expN*> …	Name of .MDX file containing a tag
ORDER([<*alias*>])	Order # of master index tag
RECCOUNT([<*alias*>])	Number of records in database
RECNO([<*alias*>])	Number of current record
RECSIZE([<*alias*>])	Size of record
RELATION(<*expN*> …	Relation expression of specified relation
SEEK(<*expC*> …	Search index for expression
SELECT([<*alias expC or expN*>])	Select a [new] work area
SQLEXEC(<*SQL statement*> …	Execute an SQL statement
TAG([<*.mdx filename expC*> …	Return selected tag
TAGCOUNT([<*.mdx filename*> …	Number of tags in MDX file
TAGNO([<*tag name expC*> …	Index tag number
TARGET(<*expN*>[, <*alias*>])	Table that is target of relation
UNIQUE([[<*.mdx filename*> …	Is index UNIQUE?

TABLE 12.2: *Date-Manipulation Functions*

FUNCTION	RESULT
CDOW(<*expD*>)	Character day ("Sunday" …)
CMONTH(<*expD*>)	Character month ("January" …)
DATE( )	Today's date

TABLE 12.2: *Date-Manipulation Functions (continued)*

FUNCTION	RESULT
DAY(<*expD*>)	Day number (1 through 31)
DOW(<*expD*>)	Day of week (Sun.=1, ... Sat. = 7)
MONTH(<*expD*>)	Month number (1 through 12)
YEAR(<*expD*>)	Year number, two to four digits

TABLE 12.3: *Financial Functions*

FUNCTION	RESULT
FV(<*payment expN*> ...	Future value of constant stream
PAYMENT(<*principal expN*> ...	Mortgage-type payment
PV(<*payment expN*> ...	Present value of constant stream

TABLE 12.4: *Miscellaneous Functions*

FUNCTION	RESULT
FLENGTH(<*field number expN*> ...	File length from DOS (categorized as a low-level I/O function)
IIF(<*expL*>, <*exp1*>, <*exp2*>)	In-line IF test
INSPECT(<*object reference*>)	Inspect object properties
LOOKUP(<*return field 1*> ...	Look up value in table
SET(<*expC*>)	Set commands (on/off)
SETTO(<*expC*>)	Set commands (SET TO)

TABLE 12.5: *Mixed-Type Functions*

FUNCTION	RESULT
MAX(<*exp 1*>, <*exp 2*>)	Greater of two values
MIN(<*exp 1*>, <*exp 2*>)	Lesser of two values

TABLE 12.6: *Numeric Functions*

FUNCTION	RESULT
ABS(<*expN*>)	Absolute value
CEILING(<*expN*>)	Round up away from zero
EXP(<*expN*>)	Raise e to the power
FLOAT(<*expN*>)	Convert number to floating point
FLOOR(<*expN*>)	Truncate to integer nearest 0
INT(<*expN*>)	Integer portion of decimal number
LOG(<*expN*>)	Natural logarithm
LOG10(<*expN*>)	Logarithm, base 10
MOD(<*dividend expN*>, <*divisor expN*>)	Remainder after division
RANDOM([<*expN*>])	Get random number
ROUND(<*expN 1*>, <*expN 2*>)	Numeric roundoff
SIGN(<*expN*>)	–1, 0, 1 for negative, zero, positive
SQRT(<*expN*>)	Square root

TABLE 12.7: *String-Related Functions*

<table>
<tr><th>FUNCTION</th><th>RESULT</th></tr>
<tr><td>AT(<<i>search expC</i>> …</td><td>Search for substring in string</td></tr>
<tr><td>CENTER(<<i>expC</i>> …</td><td>Return centered string</td></tr>
<tr><td>DIFFERENCE(<<i>expC1</i>> …</td><td>SOUNDEX difference between strings</td></tr>
<tr><td>EMPTY(<<i>exp</i>>)</td><td>Is string all blank?</td></tr>
<tr><td>ISALPHA(<<i>expC</i>> | <<i>memo field</i>>)</td><td>Is character alphabetic?</td></tr>
<tr><td>ISBLANK(<<i>exp</i>>)</td><td>Is string all blank?</td></tr>
<tr><td>ISCOLOR(<<i>expN</i>>)</td><td>Does computer do color?</td></tr>
<tr><td>ISLOWER(<<i>expC</i>> | <<i>memo field</i>>)</td><td>Is character lowercase letter?</td></tr>
</table>

TABLE 12.7: *String-Related Functions (continued)*

FUNCTION	RESULT
ISUPPER(<*expC* > | <*memo field*>)	Is chararacter uppercase letter?
LEFT(<*expC*> …	Return characters from left side of string
LEN(<*expC*> | <*memo field*>)	Length of string
LENNUM(<*expN*>)	Length of formatted number
LIKE(<*skeleton expC* > …	Does string match skeleton?
LOWER(<*expC*> | <*memo field*>)	Convert to all lowercase
LTRIM(<*expC* > | <*memo field*>)	Trim leading blanks (left)
PROPER(<*expC*> | <*memo field*>)	Make SMITH into Smith
RAT(<*search expC*> …	AT( ), from right to left
REPLICATE(<*expC*> …	Repeat input string as specified
RIGHT(<*expC* > …	Return characters from right side of string
RTRIM(<*expC*> …	Trim trailing blanks (right)
SOUNDEX(<*expC*> …	Return SOUNDEX value (for comparisons)
SPACE(<*expN*>)	Return blank string to specified length
STUFF(<*target expC*> …	Put a substring into a string
SUBSTR(<*expC* > …	Return a substring of a string
TRANSFORM(<*exp*>, <*picture expC*>)	Format with Picture specification
TRIM(<*expC* > | <*memo field*>)	Same as RTRIM( )
UPPER(<*expC* > | <*memo field*>)	Convert to all uppercase

TABLE 12.8: *System-Related Functions*

FUNCTION	RESULT
FILE(<*filename expC* >)	Does file exist?
FUNIQUE(<*expC*>)	Create unique temp file name
RUN([<*is Windows expL1*> …	Run DOS or Windows application

TABLE 12.9: *Time-Related Functions*

FUNCTION	RESULT
ELAPSED(<*time expC 1*> …	Time between two events
SECONDS( )	Seconds elapsed since midnight
TIME([<*exp*>])	Current time

TABLE 12.10: *Trigonometric Functions*

FUNCTION	RESULT
ACOS(<*expN*>)	Arccosine of cosine
ASIN(<*expN*>)	Arcsine of sine
ATAN(<*expN*>)	Arctangent of tangent
ATN2(<*sine expN*> …	Alternate form, arctangent
COS(<*expN*>)	Cosine of angle
DTOR(<*expN*>)	Degrees to radians
PI( )	Pi (3.1415 …)
RTOD(<*expN*>)	Radians to degrees
SIN(<*expN*>)	Sine of angle
TAN(<*expN*>)	Tangent of angle

TABLE 12.11: *Type-Conversion Functions*

FUNCTION	RESULT
ASC(<*expC*>)	Convert single character to ASCII number equivalent
CHR(<*expN*>)	Convert ASCII number (0–255) to equivalent character
CTOD(<*expC*>)	Convert character string to date
DMY(<*expD*>)	Convert date to *DD/MM/YYYY*-type format
DTOS(<*expD*>)	Convert date to string (month spelled-out)
MDY(<*expD*>)	Convert date to *MM/DD/YY*-type format
STR(<*expN*> …	Convert number to character string
VAL(<*expC*>)	Convert string to number

- Mixed type
- Numeric
- String-related
- System-related
- Time-related
- Trigonometric
- Type-conversion

Tables 12.1 through 12.11 list the functions in these categories. The function's syntax is included in its entirety if it is simple, or truncated (with the truncated part replaced by …) if it is more complex. The table also provides a brief summary of the intended use of each function.

Look through these tables to see which functions you might use, and then look up those functions in the descriptions that follow.

▸▸ **WARNING**

You may find some differences between this listing and the on-line documentation. In case of differences, the safe approach is to test the alternatives in the Command window.

▸ Alphabetic Reference to Common Functions

The descriptions that follow include the use of the function, the function's syntax, and examples of the function in use (if examples clarify the use). The functions are listed in pure alphabetic order; they are not grouped in categories as they are in Tables 12.1 through 12.11.

For our examples, we've set decimals to four places. The syntax we've used has become standard in dBASE documentation, as well as in the documentation for other Xbase dialects. Functions are specified exactly as they should be typed, with these exceptions:

- <*item*>: Replace this with the suggested item. Do not type the angle brackets.
- [*item*]: The item is optional; do not include it if you do not need it. Do not type the square brackets.
- ...: The preceding item may be repeated as often as you need. Do not type the ellipses.
- ¦: This means this item **or** that item. Use the item on the left or the item on the right. Use only one or the other. Do not type the ¦ symbol.

The expressions for the functions are specified by type:

- <*exp*>: Any dBASE expression
- <*expC* >: Character expression
- <*expN*>: Numeric expression
- <*expD*>: Date expression
- <*expL*>: Logical expression

Here's an example:

AT(<*search expC*>, <*target expC*> ¦ <*target memo field*>[, <*nth occurrence expN*>])

The AT function takes two or three arguments. The first is a search expression, for which any character expression is permitted. The second argument is separated from the first by a comma (as are all arguments). It is a target character expression or Memo field. The third argument is optional. If specified, it must be a numeric expression. Note that the second comma is inside the square brackets. If you don't include the third argument, don't include that comma (the second one).

ABS

The ABS function returns the absolute value of a number. If the number is positive, ABS returns the number. If the number is negative, ABS returns the number, stripped of the negative sign.

Syntax

ABS(<*expN*>)

Examples

`? ABS(3.2)`	Returns 3.2
`? ABS(-27)`	Returns 27

ACOS

The ACOS function returns the arccosine (or inverse cosine) of a number from 0 to 1. It returns its answer in radians. Use RTOD( ) to convert radians to degrees. Use DTOR( ) to convert degrees to radians.

Syntax

ACOS(<*expN*>)

Examples

`? ACOS( 1 )`	Returns 0
`? ACOS( 0 )`	Returns 1.5708
`? RTOD( ACOS(0) )`	Returns 90

ALIAS

The ALIAS function returns the alias or name of the table in use in the current work area. It returns an empty string if no table is in use.

Syntax

ALIAS([<*alias*>])

Examples

```
* table in use: PEOPLE
? ALIAS( )                Returns PEOPLE
* table in use: PEOPLE
ALIAS LIST1
? ALIAS( )                Returns LIST1
```

ASC

The ASC function returns the number corresponding to a character in the ASCII character set.

Syntax

ASC(<*expC*>)

Examples

```
? ASC(" ")    Returns 32
? ASC("A")    Returns 65
```

ASIN

The ASIN function returns the arcsine (or inverse sine). It changes its argument, a sine, into an angle, in radians. Use RTOD to convert radians to degrees. Use DTOR to convert degrees to radians.

Syntax

ASIN(<*expN*>)

Examples

`? ASIN(0)`	Returns 0
`? ASIN(SIN( DTOR(90) ))`	Returns 1.5708

AT

The AT function returns the location of a substring in a string or Memo field. With the optional third parameter, it returns the location of the *n*th occurrence of a string in a string or Memo field. It returns zero if the string, or specified occurrence of the string, is not found.

Syntax

AT(<*search expC*>, <*target expC*> ¦ <*target memo field*>[, <*nth occurrence expN*>])

Examples

`? AT('Smith','John Smith')`	Returns 6
`? AT('at', 'Cat in hat', 2 )`	Returns 9
`? AT('x','abcde')`	Returns 0

ATAN

The ATAN function returns the arctangent (or inverse tangent) of a number. Given the tangent of an angle, it returns the angle, in radians. Use RTOD to convert radians to degrees. Use DTOR to convert degrees to radians.

Syntax

ATAN(<*expN*>)

Examples

`? ATAN(0)`	Returns 0
`? RTOD(ATAN(1))`	Returns 45
`? ATAN(TAN(DTOR(45)))`	Returns 0.7854

ATN2

The ATN2 function returns an arctangent given a sine and cosine of an angle.

Syntax

ATN2(<*sine expN*>, <*cosine expN*>)

Examples

`? ATN2(1, 1)`	Returns 0.7854
`? ATN2(1, 0)`	Returns 1.5708
`? ATN2(0, 1)`	Returns 0

BINTYPE

The BINTYPE function returns the type of a binary field.

Syntax

BINTYPE([<*field name*>])

The types are as follows:

0 to 32K-1	Available for user definition
32K	.WAV
32K + 1	.BMP
32K + 2	.PCX
32K + 3	.TIF
32K + 4	.GIF
32K + 5	.EPS

BOF

The BOF function returns .T. if the active table is at the beginning of the file.

Syntax

```
BOF([<alias>])
```

BOOKMARK

The BOOKMARK function is used for SQL tables that do not have record numbers. It returns an identifier that you may subsequently use in a GO command, as if it were a record number.

Syntax

```
BOOKMARK( )
```

CATALOG

The CATALOG function returns the name of the currently open catalog, if any. It returns an empty string if no catalog is open.

Syntax

```
CATALOG( )
```

CDOW

The CDOW function returns the day of the week of a date argument as a character string.

Syntax

```
CDOW(<expD>)
```

Examples

`? CDOW( DATE( ) )`	Returns "Monday" (if today is Monday)
`? CDOW( DATE( )+2 )`	Returns "Wednesday"

CEILING

The CEILING function returns a number rounded up to the next highest integer.

Syntax

CEILING(<*expN*>)

Examples

`? CEILING(1)`	Returns 1
`? CEILING(1.1)`	Returns 2
`? CEILING(-1.2)`	Returns –1

CENTER

The CENTER function returns a text string resulting from the centering of an input string in a given number of characters. If the length of the result string is not supplied, 80 is implied. You can supply a pad character to be used in lieu of the space character for left and right side padding.

Syntax

CENTER(<*expC*> ¦ <*memo field*>[, <*lengthexpN*> [, <*padexpC*>]])

Examples

`? CENTER('Title', 15)`	Returns 'Title'
`? CENTER('News!', 15, '*')`	Returns '*****News!*****'

CHR

The CHR function returns an ASCII character given a number in the range 0 to 255. This is the inverse of the ASC( ) function.

Syntax

CHR(<*expN*>)

Examples

`? CHR(33)`	Returns "!"
`? CHR(65)`	Returns "A"

CMONTH

The CMONTH function returns the month as a character string, given a date.

Syntax

CMONTH(<*expD*>)

Examples

`? CMONTH(DATE( ))`	Returns "June" (if the month is June)
`? CMONTH(DATE( )+60`	Returns "August"

COS

The COS function function returns the cosine of an angle, given in radians. Use DTOR to convert degrees to radians.

Syntax

COS(<*expN*>)

Examples

`? COS(0)`	Returns 1
`? COS(DTOR(45))`	Returns .7071

CTOD

The CTOD function converts a character string to a date.

Syntax

CTOD(<*expC*>)

Example

`? CTOD("12/25/95")+365`	Returns 12/24/96

DATABASE

The DATABASE function returns the name of the currently open database or an empty string if no database is open.

►► **NOTE**

.DBF and .DB files are not part of a database within the meaning of the DATABASE function. The DATABASE function applies to SQL databases.

Syntax

```
DATABASE( )
```

DATE

The DATE function returns today's date, as a date variable.

Syntax

```
DATE( )
```

DAY

The DAY function returns the number of the day in a date.

Syntax

```
DAY(<expD>)
```

Example

```
? DAY(CTOD("1/31/96"))
```
Returns 31

DBF

The DBF function returns the name of the table open in the current work area, or in a specified work area. It returns an empty string if no table is in use in the current or specified area.

Syntax

```
DBF([<alias>])
```

DELETED

The DELETED function returns .T. if the currently selected record is marked for deletion.

Syntax

DELETED([<*alias*>])

DESCENDING

The DESCENDING function returns .T. if the specified index is in descending sequence.

Syntax

DESCENDING([<*.mdx filename*>,] <*index position expN*> [, <*alias*>])

DIFFERENCE

The DIFFERENCE function returns the SOUNDEX difference between two strings. A difference of 4 is minimal; a difference of 0 is maximal. See the SOUNDEX function.

Syntax

DIFFERENCE(<*expC1*> | <*memo field* 1>, <*expC2*> | <*memo field* 2>)

Examples

`? DIFFERENCE('Smith','Smythe')`	Returns 4
`? DIFFERENCE('Aardvark','Zebra')`	Returns 1

DMY

The DMY function returns a string in *dd month yy* format, given a date. The *yy* portion is two or four digits, depending on the setting of CENTURY.

Syntax

DMY(<*expD*>)

Example

`? DMY( {12/31/95}+1 )` Returns "1 January 96"

DOW

The DOW function returns a number representing the day of the week, given a date variable. Sunday is day 1, and Saturday is day 7.

▸▸ **TIP**

To find weekends, take DOW(DATE-1). This command returns 1 through 5 for Monday through Friday, and 6 and 7 for Saturday and Sunday.

Syntax

DOW(<*expD*>)

Example

`? DOW(DATE( ))` Returns 2, which represents Monday (if today is Monday)

DTOR

The DTOR function converts degrees to radians.

Syntax

DTOR(<*expN*>)

Example

`? DTOR(45)` Returns 0.7854

DTOS

The DTOS function converts a date to a string in the form *YYYYMMDD*. It always uses this format, which is guaranteed to sort dates correctly. DTOS is the function to use when you want to set up indexes on dates combined with other strings.

Syntax

DTOS(<*expD*>)

Example

```
? DTOS({12/31/95})
```
Returns "19951231"

ELAPSED

The ELAPSED function returns the time difference, in seconds, of two time strings in *HH:MM:SS* format. This time format is the one returned by the TIME function.

Syntax

ELAPSED(<*time expC* 1>, <*time expC* 2>)

EMPTY

The EMPTY function returns .T. if its argument (often a field) is all blank.

Syntax

EMPTY(<*exp*>)

EOF

The EOF function returns .T. if the current table's record pointer is at the end of the file.

Syntax

EOF([<*alias*>])

EXP

The EXP function returns 2.7183 (the base of the natural logarithm) raised to the specified power. It is the inverse of the LOG function.

Syntax

EXP(<*expN*>)

Examples

`? EXP(1)`	Returns 2.7183
`? LOG(EXP(2))`	Returns 1.000

FDECIMAL

The FDECIMAL function returns the number of decimal places in a given field in the current table, or in a table specified by its alias.

Syntax

FDECIMAL(<*field number expN*>[, <*alias*>])

FIELD

The FIELD function returns the name of a field specified by its number in the table structure. It uses the current table unless an optional table alias is specified.

Syntax

FIELD(<*field number expN*>[, <*alias*>])

Example

`? FIELD(3)`	Returns name of third field in current table

FILE

The FILE function tests for the existence of a file. It returns .T. if the file exists.

Syntax

FILE(<*filename expC*>)

Example

```
? FILE("\DBASEWIN\BIN\DBASEWIN.INI")
```
Returns .T. (for us)

FLDCOUNT

The FLDCOUNT function returns the number of fields in the current table or, if an alias is supplied, to the table specified by the alias.

Syntax

FLDCOUNT([<*alias*>])

FLDLIST

The FLDLIST function returns the expression given in a SET FIELDS TO command. (This is the command issued by a query to restrict the fields in a view of a table.)

Syntax

FLDLIST([<*field number expN*>])

FLENGTH

The FLENGTH function returns the length of a field, given its number in the current table, or, if an optional alias is specified, in a specified table.

Syntax

FLENGTH(<*field number expN*>[, <*alias*>])

FLOAT

The FLOAT function converts a Numeric data type to a Float data type.

Syntax

FLOAT(<*expN*>)

Example

```
? FLOAT(5)
```
Returns 5.0000 (with decimals set to four places)

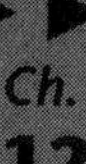

FLOOR

The FLOOR function returns a number rounded down to the next lowest integer.

Syntax

FLOOR(<*expN*>)

Examples

`? FLOOR(2)`	Returns 2
`? FLOOR(1.9)`	Returns 1
`? FLOOR(-1.5)`	Returns –2

FOR

The FOR function returns the FOR clause used to specify an index (as in FOR state = 'CA').

Syntax

FOR([[<*.mdx filename*>,] <*index position expN*> [,<*alias*>]])

FOUND

The FOUND function returns .T. if the last FIND, SEEK, or LOCATE was successful.

Syntax

FOUND([<*alias*>])

Example

`? SEEK 'Smith'`	
`? FOUND( )`	Returns .T. if there is a 'Smith'

FUNIQUE

The FUNIQUE function returns the name of a new file. You can use FUNIQUE repeatedly to create new file names that are guaranteed not to already exist.

Syntax

```
FUNIQUE(<expC>)
```

<*expC* > is a DOS-type file name mask, such as `????????.TMP` or `TEMP????.DBF`.

FV

The FV function calculates the future value of a stream of payments given a periodic interest rate and number of payments. The first payment is at time 0; the valuation is reported at time *n*–1.

Syntax

```
FV(<payment expN>, <interest expN>, <term expN>)
```

Example

`? FV(100, 0.05, 10)`	Returns 1257.79

IIF

The IIF function (immediate IF) evaluates a condition and picks one of two results, based on the condition. If the condition evaluates to .T., IIF picks the first result.

Syntax

```
IIF(<expL>, <exp1>, <exp2>)
```

Example

`? IIF(test_grade > 90, "Excellent!", "OK")`	Result depends on test_grade

INSPECT

The INSPECT function opens the Object Properties Inspector to examine the properties of an object, such as a form.

TIP

Although INSPECT is never used in the contexts of our other expressions (index expressions, scope expressions, and so on), it is invaluable from the Command window.

Syntax

INSPECT(*<object reference>*)

Examples

`?check_it = NEW my_form( )`	No result
`?INSPECT(check_it)`	Brings up Object Properties Inspector for your form

INT

The INT function chooses the integer part of a number. This rounds positive and negative numbers toward zero.

INT is commonly used for rounding by adding 0.5, as in

INT(*amount*+0.5)

However, adding 0.5 and taking INT( ) rounds positive numbers correctly, but not negative numbers. To round negative values, you must subtract 0.5. This expression rounds negative numbers correctly:

INT(*num* + IIF(*num* > 0, 0.5, -0.5))

▶▶ **WARNING**

The examples describe mathematically correct rounding. Different business practices prescribe different methods for treating numbers that end exactly in .5.

Syntax

INT(<*expN*>)

Examples

`? INT(1.49 + 0.5)`	Returns 1
`? INT(1.5 + 0.5)`	Returns 2
`? INT(-1.9)`	Returns –1
`? INT(-1.9 + 0.5)`	Returns –1
`? INT(-1.9 - 0.5)`	Returns –2

ISALPHA

The ISALPHA function returns True if the first character of the argument string is *a* through *z* or *A* through *Z* (if you're using an English language driver). Non-English language drivers may include additional characters.

Syntax

ISALPHA(<*expC*> | <*memo field* >)

Examples

`? ISALPHA('X')`	Returns .T.
`? ISALPHA('9')`	Returns .F.
`? ISALPHA(CHR(135))`	Result depends on code page and language driver

ISBLANK

The ISBLANK function is a synonym for EMPTY. It returns .T. if its argument is all blank.

Syntax

ISBLANK(<*exp* >)

Examples

`? ISBLANK("?")`	Returns .T.
`? ISBLANK("Smith")`	Returns .F.

ISCOLOR

The ISCOLOR function returns .T. if the computer is capable of including color in its display.

Syntax

ISCOLOR( )

ISLOWER

The ISLOWER function returns .T. if the argument character is a lowercase alphabetic character. Non-English language drivers may include additional lowercase alphabetic characters.

Syntax

ISLOWER(<*expC*> ¦ <*memo field*>)

Examples

`? ISLOWER('a')`	Returns .T.
`? ISLOWER('A')`	Returns .F.
`? ISLOWER('9')`	Returns .F.
`? ISLOWER(CHR(135))`	Result depends on code page and language driver

ISTABLE

The ISTABLE function is used to check if a table exists in an SQL database. It checks the currently open database, or, if one is specified, a named database. It returns .F. if no SQL database is open.

Syntax

ISTABLE(<*table name*> [, <*database name*>])

ISUPPER

The ISUPPER function returns .T. if the argument character is an uppercase alphabetic character. Non-English language drivers may include additional uppercase alphabetic characters.

Syntax

ISUPPER(<*expC*> ¦ <*memo field*>)

Examples

`? ISUPPER('A')`	Returns .T.
`? ISUPPER('a')`	Returns .F.
`? ISUPPER('9')`	Returns .F.
`? ISUPPER(CHR(135))`	Result depends on code page and language driver

KEY

The KEY function returns the key expression used to create the specified index. If no .MDX file name is specified, the selected table's production index is used. If no alias is specified, the current table is selected.

Syntax

KEY([<*.mdx filename*>,] <*index position expN*>[, <*alias*>])

KEYMATCH

The KEYMATCH function checks to see if an expression exists in an index. If nothing except the expression is specified, the current table's currently active index is used. The additional arguments let you specify an alternate index, an alternate index file, and an alternate table.

Syntax

KEYMATCH (<*exp*> [, <*index position expN1*> ¦?? [, <*.mdx filename*> ,] <*tag expN2*> [, <*alias*>]])

LEFT

The LEFT function returns a specified number of characters from the left side of a character string.

Syntax

LEFT(<*expC*> ¦ <*memo field*>, <*length expN*>)

Example

```
? LEFT('Sample',3)
```
Returns 'Sam'

LEN

The LEN function returns the length, in characters, of a character expression.

Syntax

LEN(<*expC*> ¦ <*memo field*>)

Example

```
? LEN('Smith')
```
Returns 5

LENNUM

The LENNUM function returns the width, including leading decimal places, of a number formatted for output using the current default settings. The default output width for an integer is ten characters.

▶▶ TIP

Use the STR function to gain more control over the output of numbers.

Syntax

LENNUM(<*expN*>)

LIKE

The LIKE function returns .T. if a skeleton expression with wildcard characters matches a target expression or Memo field.

Syntax

LIKE(<*skeleton expC*>, <*expC*> ¦ <*memo field*>)

Examples

`? LIKE('a?c', 'abc')`	Returns .T.
`? LIKE('a*d', 'axxxxd')`	Returns .T.
`? LIKE('a*d', 'AxxxxD')`	Returns .F. (LIKE is case-sensitive)
`? LIKE('abc', 'a*c')`	Returns .F. (* is a literal in target)

LOG

The LOG function returns the natural logarithm of its argument number. It is the inverse of the EXP function.

Syntax

LOG(<*expN* >)

Examples

`? LOG(10)`	Returns 2.3026
`? LOG(1)`	Returns 0.0000
`? LOG(EXP(1))`	Returns 1.0000

LOG10

The LOG10 function returns the log to the base 10 of its argument number.

Syntax

LOG10(<*expN*>)

Examples

`? LOG10(10)`	Returns 1.0000
`? LOG10(100)`	Returns 2.0000

LOOKUP

The LOOKUP function looks for a value in one column of a table. If it finds a match, it returns the value of a field in the row where it found the match.

Syntax

LOOKUP(<*return field 1*>, <*exp*>, <*lookup field 2* >)

Example

`? LOOKUP(emp_id, 'Smith', last_name)`	Returns emp_id of first 'Smith', or " if no 'Smith's'

LOWER

The LOWER function changes all alphabetic characters in the argument expression into lowercase characters. This can be used to force case-insensitive searching and ordering.

Syntax

LOWER(<*expC*> ¦ <*memo field*>)

Example

```
?INDEX ON
LOWER(last_name)
```

`?SEEK 'smith'`	Finds any 'Smith', 'SMITH', 'smith', etc.

LTRIM

The LTRIM function returns the argument string after removing any leading blanks.

Syntax

LTRIM(<*expC*> ¦ <*memo field*>)

Example

`? LTRIM("?mith")`	Returns "Smith"

LUPDATE

The LUPDATE function returns the date of the last update of the currently open table, or of one specified by an alias.

Syntax

LUPDATE([<*alias*>])

MAX

The MAX function returns the greater of two values. The input values most be of the same type (except that an N can be compared to an F). .T. is greater than .F. if you're comparing logical variables.

Syntax

MAX(<*exp 1*>, <*exp 2* >)

Examples

`? MAX(1.1*old_price, new_price)`	Returns larger amount
`? MAX({12/31/95},DATE( )}`	Returns later date

MDX

The MDX function returns the name of the .MDX file that contains the specified index. If an alias is not supplied, the current table is used. Otherwise, the table specified by the alias is used.

Syntax

MDX(<*index tag expN*>[, <*alias*>])

MDY

The MDY function returns a text string, in the format *Month dd, yy*, for a date. The year values are either two or four digits, depending on the setting of CENTURY.

Syntax

MDY(<*expD*>)

TIP

MDY is one of numerous reasons why we prefer to set and leave CENTURY turned on. This is particularly true since the end of the century is rapidly approaching.

Example

`? MDY({12/31/95})`	With CENTURY off, returns "December 31, 95"; with CENTURY on, returns "December 31, 1995"

MIN

The MIN function returns the smaller of two values. The input values most be of the same type (except that an N can be compared to an F). .T. is greater than .F. if you're comparing logical variables.

Syntax

MIN(<*exp 1*>, <*exp 2* >)

Examples

`? MIN(1.1*old_price, new_price)`	Returns smaller amount
`? MIN({12/31/95},DATE( )}`	Returns earlier date

MOD

The MOD function returns the remainder after division. This is commonly used for finding remainders of integral arguments, although the function is not restricted to integral arguments.

Syntax

MOD(<*dividend expN*>, <*divisor expN*>)

Examples

`? INT(DAY(my_date)/7)`	Returns number of whole weeks in the month (4)
`? MOD(DAY(my_date),7)`	Returns 0 or 1 for February, 2 or 3 for other months
`? MOD(6.4, 4.2)`	Returns 2.2

MONTH

The MONTH function returns the number of the month, given a date. January is 1; December is 12.

Syntax

MONTH(<*expD*>)

Example

`? MONTH({12/31/95})`	Returns 12

ORDER

The ORDER function returns the name of the master index tag (.MDX or .NDX) in the currently active table, or in the table specified by the optional alias argument.

Syntax

ORDER([<*alias*>])

PAYMENT

The PAYMENT function returns the payment required to repay a given principal amount at a fixed interest rate over a given number of payments. The interest rate is the periodic rate. The *n* payments are made at time 0 through time *n*–1.

Syntax

PAYMENT(<*principal expN*>, <*interest expN*>, <*term expN*>)

Example

`? PAYMENT(100000, .07/12, 30*12)`	Returns 665.3025; amortizes a $100,000 mortgage at 5833%/month over 360 months

PI

The PI function returns the value of PI, the ratio of the circumference of a circle to its diameter (3.141596…). dBASE for Windows stores floating-point numbers to 16 decimal places.

Syntax

```
PI( )
```

PROPER

The PROPER function returns a character string with first letters in uppercase and other letters in lowercase. This is used, for example, to take a list of names in all capitals and convert them to uppercase and lowercase.

►► **WARNING**

PROPER results aren't always proper. None of these will have the second capital letter: McPherson, LeBoeuf, DeVille. Doing human names requires human intelligence.

Syntax

PROPER(*<expC>* ¦ *<memo field>*)

Examples

`? PROPER("JOHN SMITH")`	Returns "John Smith"
`PROPER("Ms. Smith, MD")`	Returns "Ms. Smith, Md"
`PROPER("John Smith III, PhD.")`	Returns "John Smith Iii, Phd."

PV

The PV function returns the present value of a stream of constant payments at a fixed interest rate. The interest rate is the periodic interest rate. The n payments are made at time periods 0 through $n - 1$. PV is the inverse of the PAYMENT function.

Syntax

PV(<*payment expN*>, <*interest expN*>, <*term expN*>)

Examples

`? PAYMENT(100000, .07/12, 30*12)`	Returns 665.3025
`? PV(665.30, .07/12, 30*12)`	Returns 99999.6250

RANDOM

The RANDOM function returns a random floating-point number between 0 and 1. If seeded with a positive number, RANDOM returns the identical number each time it is called. If RANDOM is called without an argument—`RANDOM( )`—it returns the value of RANDOM(0) the first time it is called. Subsequent calls without an argument use the previous value of RANDOM as an argument, creating an apparently random series. This series will be the same each time you run dBASE for Windows.

If RANDOM is seeded with a negative number, as in `RANDOM(-1)`, it returns a value based on the precise state of the system clock, which approximates true randomness.

▶▶ TIP

Calling RANDOM without an argument is helpful in testing a calculation, because you know that the series of random numbers should be the same each time you run dBASE for Windows.

Syntax

RANDOM([<*expN* >])

RAT

The RAT function (reverse AT) finds the first occurrence of a substring in a string, searching from the right end toward the left.

Syntax

RAT(<*search expC*>, <*target expC*> ¦ <*target memo field* >)

Example

`? RAT('at', 'Cat in Hat')`	Returns 9 (using the AT function with the same arguments would return 2)

RECCOUNT

The RECCOUNT function returns the number of records actually in a table. If a table of 1000 records has 100 records deleted, and DELETED is on, the COUNT of records will return 900. RECCOUNT, on the other hand, will return 1000. Similarly setting a filter will affect the COUNT value, but not the value of RECCOUNT.

Syntax

RECCOUNT([<*alias*>])

RECNO

The RECNO function returns the number of the record pointed to by the record pointer in the currently active table, or, if an alias is specified, in the specified table.

Syntax

RECNO([<*alias*>])

RECSIZE

The RECSIZE function returns the number of bytes in each record in the currently active table or, if an alias is specified, in the specified table.

▶▶TIP

RECCOUNT( )*RECSIZE( )+1000 gives a quick, though imprecise, approximation of the size of a table on disk (not including indexes or memo files). The 1000 is for file overhead.

Syntax

RECSIZE([<alias>])

RELATION

The RELATION function returns the key expression of a selected relation in the current table or, if an alias is specified, the specified table.

Syntax

RELATION(*<expN >*[, *<alias >*])

REPLICATE

The REPLICATE function returns a character string that repeats the argument string the specified number of times.

Syntax

REPLICATE(*<expC>* ¦ *<memo field>*, *<expN >*)

Examples

`? REPLICATE('*',10)`	Returns '**********'
`? REPLICATE('*--*', 4)`	Returns '*--**--**--**--*'

RIGHT

The RIGHT function returns the specified number of characters from the right side of a character string.

Syntax

RIGHT(*<expC>* ¦ *<memo field>*, *<expN>*)

Example

`? RIGHT('Cat in Hat',3)`	Returns 'Hat'

ROUND

The ROUND function rounds numbers to a specified number of decimal places.

Syntax

ROUND(*<expN 1>*, *<expN 2 >*)

Examples

`? ROUND(1.249, 1)`	Returns 1.2000
`? ROUND(1.250, 1)`	Returns 1.3000
`? ROUND(3.49, 0)`	Returns 3.0000
`? ROUND(3.5, 0)`	Returns 4.000

RTOD

The RTOD function converts an angle specified in radians to an angle in degrees.

Syntax

RTOD(*<expN>*)

Examples

`? RTOD(1)`	Returns 57.2958
`? RTOD(PI( ))`	Returns 180.0000

RTRIM

The RTRIM (right TRIM) function returns a string after removing trailing blanks from the argument character string.

Syntax

RTRIM(<*expC*> ¦ <*memo field*>)

Example

`? RTRIM("Smith?)`	Returns "Smith"

RUN

The RUN function runs a DOS or Microsoft Windows program or a DOS command. If the first parameter is .T., a Windows program is run. If it is .F. or omitted, a DOS program or command is run. The optional second logical parameter is ignored.

Syntax

RUN([<*is Windows expL1*>,]<*command expC*> [, <*expL2*>])

Examples

`?RUN('chkdsk /f')`	Runs DOS chkdsk /f command
`?RUN(.T., '\windows\notepad.exe')`	Runs Windows Notepad

SECONDS

The SECONDS function returns the number of seconds, to the nearest two-hundredths, elapsed since midnight. Because SECONDS returns a number, it is useful when you need to do calculations.

TIP

The TIME function returns the same information as a character string. TIME is useful for reporting the time.

Syntax

SECONDS( )

SEEK

The SEEK function searches for the value of the expression in the current index in the current table, or, if the optional alias is specified, in the specified table. The type of expression must match the index expression.

Syntax

SEEK(<*expC*> ¦ <*expN*> ¦ <*expD*> [, <*alias*>])

Example

`?SEEK('Smith')`	Finds first 'Smith' (if there is one)

SELECT

The SELECT function returns the next available work area number (where you can open an additional table without closing any open tables) if you omit the optional alias. If you include the alias, SELECT returns the work area number of the alias. You can have up to 225 work areas in each session.

▸▸ **WARNING**

While dBASE for Windows would be happy to let you open a hundred tables in each of an unlimited number of sessions, the DOS file handle limit seriously restricts you. We'll need a better operating system to exploit this capability.

Syntax

SELECT([<*alias expC or expN*>])

Examples

`? SELECT( )`	Returns number of next available work area
`? SELECT('people')`	Returns number of work area for People table

SET

The SET function returns the value of the current setting of the features listed in Table 12.12.

TABLE 12.12: *Settings Reported by the SET Function*

SETTING	EFFECT IF ON
ALTERNATE	Echoes output to SET ALTERNATE TO device
AUTOSAVE	Automatic saving
BELL	Warning beeps
CARRY	Copy data from prior record on append
CATALOG	Add new files to active catalog
CENTURY	Use four-digit year format in dates
CONFIRM	Require keypress after typing last character in field
CONSOLE	Use results pane of Command window for output
COVERAGE	Do coverage analysis of running programs
CUA ENTER	Enter submits a form (if off, Enter completes a field)
CURRENCY	Position of currency symbol (left or right)
CURSOR	Show/hide cursor in dBASE IV-style applications
DELETED	Deleted records appear to be removed from tables
DELIMITERS	Mark start and stop of dBASE IV-style entry fields
DESIGN	Allow switching from Run mode to Design mode
DEVELOP-MENT	Check for more recent .PRG file before running .PRO file and other compiled programs (if off, always run .PRO file; no recompiles)
ECHO	Open the Debugger
ESCAPE	Pressing Esc interrupts a running program
EXACT	Matches are exact (if off, 'Smith' = 'S' is True)
EXCLUSIVE	All tables are opened for exclusive use
FIELDS	Fields are set (if off, SET FIELDS TO clauses are ignored)

TABLE 12.12: *Settings Reported by the SET Function (continued)*

SETTING	EFFECT IF ON
FULLPATH	Functions that return file names include full drive and directory specifications
HEADINGS	Show column headings over commands such as AVERAGE and LIST
INTENSITY	Affect display in dBASE IV-style applications
IDCHECK	Check language driver (if off, suppresses language-driver checking)
LOCK	File locking (if off, suppresses file locking during read-only processing, such as in computing averages or sums)
MOUSE	Mouse use (if off, the mouse pointer is turned off, and mouse actions are ignored)
NEAR	Failed SEEKs stop at the next highest record (if off, failed SEEKs stop at the end of file)
PRINTER	Streaming output (such as from ? commands) is sent to the printer
SAFETY	Prompt before deleting records or overwriting files
SPACE	Put spaces between fields in output lists
STEP	Open the debugger
TALK	Echo results of commands to the Command window's results pane
TITLE	When CATALOG is on, added files are prompted for title information
UNIQUE	Only the first record matching a key value is included in an index

You can abbreviate the setting names to the first four characters. For example, CENTURY can be written as CENT, and SAFETY can be input as SAFE.

Syntax

SET(<*expC*>)

Example

`? SET("TALK")`	Returns "OFF" (if the Talk setting is off)

SETTO

The SETTO function returns the values of the settings listed in Table 12.13, set by the SET TO command.

TABLE 12.13: *Settings Reported by SETTO Function*

SETTING	REPORT
ALTERNATE	Device or file to receive output
BELL	Frequency and duration of bell tone
BLOCKSIZE	Size of index blocks, in units of 512 bytes
BORDER	Style of dBASE IV-type windows
CARRY	List of fields where data gets carried
CATALOG	Name of catalog file
COLOR	Color settings for dBASE IV-style applications
CURRENCY	Currency symbol
DATABASE	Name of the current SQL database
DATE	*MDY* (American style; other styles are available)
DBTYPE	Either DBASE or PARADOX
DECIMALS	Number of decimal places to display
DEFAULT	Default disk drive
DELIMITERS	Field delimiters character
DEVICE	One of screen, printer, or file <*filename*>

TABLE 12.13: *Settings Reported by SETTO Function (continued)*

SETTING	REPORT
DIRECTORY	Current directory
DISPLAY	One of mono, color, ega, ega43, mono43, vga25, vga43, vga50
EDITOR	Default editor for program and text files
ERROR	Messages to precede/follow dBASE runtime error messages
FIELDS	Fields list specification
FILTER	Filter condition (only records matching the condition appear to be part of the table)
FORMAT	File name in dBASE IV-style applications
HELP	Help file name
IBLOCK	Size of index blocks, in multiples of 512 bytes
INDEX	One or more index files
KEY	Range of accepted values in master index
LIBRARY	Name of subroutine library file
MARGIN	Left margin of printed pages
MARK	Separator character in date displays
MBLOCK	Block size in memo files in units of 64 bytes
MEMOWIDTH	Display width for Memo fields
MESSAGE	Status bar message
ODOMETER	Units which will be displayed in the status bar as dBASE processes records
ORDER	Tag of the master index
PATH	Search path
PCOL	Next horizontal print position
POINT	Character separating the whole part from the decimal part of numbers

TABLE 12.13: *Settings Reported by SETTO Function (continued)*

SETTING	REPORT
PRECISION	Number of decimal digits used in numeric comparisons
PRINTER	Device or file to receive printer output
PROCEDURE	Name of a file of subroutines
PROW	Printer's vertical position
REFRESH	Number of seconds between refreshing client screens with new file server data
RELATION	Relation(s) between tables
REPROCESS	Number of tries attempted to access a locked file or record before returning an error
SEPARATOR	Character used to separate the whole part of numbers into groups of three digits
SKIP	Alias list controlling the advancement of the record pointer with related tables
TIME	One of HH, HH:MM, HH.MM, HH:MM:SS, HH.MM.SS
TOPIC	Help topic
TYPEAHEAD	Length, in bytes, of the typeahead buffer
VIEW	Name of a QBE file
WP	Name of the editor used for Memo fields

NOTE

As alternatives to the American-style date (*MM/DD/YY*), of SET TO's DATE setting, there are other styles available, such as ANSI (*YY.MM.DD*), British (*DD/MM/YY*), German (*DD.MM.YY*), and USA (*MM - DD - YY*).

Syntax

SETTO(<*expC*>)

Example

`? SETTO('DBTYPE')`	Returns "DBASE" or "PARADOX"

SIGN

The SIGN function returns 1 for positive numbers, -1 for negative numbers, and 0 for zero.

Syntax

SIGN(<*expN*>)

Examples

`? SIGN(1.5)`	Returns 1
`? SIGN(0)`	Returns 0
`? SIGN(-1.5)`	Returns –1

SIN

The SIN function returns the sine of an angle. The angle is in radians. Use DTOR to convert degrees to radians.

Syntax

SIN(<*expN*>)

Examples

`? SIN(1)`	Returns 0.8415
`? SIN(DTOR(45))`	Returns 7071
`? SIN(PI( )/2)`	Returns 1.0000

SOUNDEX

The SOUNDEX function returns the SOUNDEX value of a character string. The SOUNDEX value is a character representation approximating the sound of the string. Comparing SOUNDEX values yields .T. if the sounds of the two strings are equal.

WARNING

The SOUNDEX algorithm is far from perfect. "Alan" and "Allen" have equal SOUNDEX values. Unfortunately, the following also have equal SOUNDEX values: "Martin," "Morton," and "Martian."

Syntax

SOUNDEX(<*expC*> ¦ <*memo field*>)

Examples

`? SOUNDEX("Smith")`	Returns "S530"
`? SOUNDEX("Smythe")`	Returns "S530"

SPACE

The SPACE function returns a string of the specified number of spaces. This is useful in formatting outlines, for one example.

Syntax

SPACE(<*expN*>)

Example

```
? SPACE(4*indent_level)+outline_item
```

Indents an outline four spaces per indent level.

SQLEXEC

The SQLEXEC function executes a SQL statement in a SQL database. (See your SQL database documentation for its accepted SQL syntax.)

Syntax

SQLEXEC(<*SQL statement*> [, <*Answer table*>])

SQRT

The SQRT function returns the square root of a nonnegative number.

Syntax

SQRT(<*expN* >)

Examples

`? SQRT(9)`	Returns 3.0000
`? SQRT(2)`	Returns 1.4142

STR

The STR function returns a number in a character string. The length of the string and, optionally, the number of decimal places are given as arguments. The length is the total length, including decimals and the decimal point if the number of decimals is not zero. The default length is 10.

▸▸ **WARNING**

Don't forget to allow space for the minus sign (–), if negative numbers are possible in your application.

An optional fourth argument specifies the character used to pad the number on the left. (For instance, you might pad with "*" in a check-writing application.)

Syntax

STR(<*expN*>[, <*length expN*>?? [, <*decimals expN*>[, <*expC*>]]])

Examples

`? STR(4.5, 5, 2)`	Returns "4.50"
`? STR(4.5, 6, 1, "*")`	Returns "***4.5"

STUFF

The STUFF function returns a string made by stuffing one string into another at a specified location, optionally overwriting bytes in the "stuffee" string.

Syntax

STUFF(*<target expC>* ¦ *<target memo field>,?? <start expN>, <quantity expN>, <replacement expC>*)

Examples

`? STUFF("12345",4,0,"abc")`	Returns "123abc45"
`? STUFF("12345",4,1,"abc")`	Returns "123abc5"
`? STUFF("123abc5",4,3,"4")`	Returns "12345"

SUBSTR

The SUBSTR function extracts a substring from a string. You supply the string, the starting location of the substring, and the length of the substring.

Syntax

SUBSTR(*<expC>* ¦ *<memo field>,?? <start expN>*[, *<length expN>*])

Example

`? SUBSTR("Cat in Hat",5,2)`	Returns "in"

TAG

The TAG function returns the name of a specified index tag in the current .MDX file for the current table. Optionally, if you specify an .MDX file name, the tag name in that .MDX file is returned. If you specify an optional alias, the tag name is returned for the table specified by that alias.

Syntax

TAG([*<.mdx filename expC>*,], *<index number expN>*[, *<alias>*])

TAGCOUNT

The TAGCOUNT function returns the number of active indexes in the currently open table's open .MDX file. If you specify an .MDX file name, that file is used in lieu of the currently open one. If you specify an optional alias, the value is returned for the table specified by that alias.

Syntax

TAGCOUNT([<*.mdx filename*>[,<*alias*>]])

TAGNO

The TAGNO function function returns an index tag's number, given its name. Unless an optional alias is supplied, TAGNO applies to the table open in the current work area. Unless an optional .MDX file name is supplied, TAGNO applies to the current .MDX file.

Syntax

TAGNO([<*tag name expC*> [, <*.mdx filename*> [, <*alias*>]]])

TAN

The TAN function returns the tangent of an angle. The angle is given in radians. Use DTOR to convert degrees to radians.

Syntax

TAN(<*expN*>)

Examples

`? TAN(0)`	Returns 0
`? TAN(DTOR(45))`	Returns 1

TARGET

The TARGET function returns the name of the table linked by the specified relation number. If an optional alias is supplied, the value is returned for the work area specified by that alias. Otherwise, the value is returned for the table in the current work area.

Syntax

TARGET(<*expN*>[, <*alias*>])

TIME

The TIME function returns the time as a string in *HH:MM:SS* format unless an argument is supplied. If an argument is supplied, the time is returned in *HH:MM:SS.hh* format, where the *.hh* is in hundredths of a second. (DOS returns the time accurately to about two-hundredths of a second; in the form *HH:MM:SS.hh*, the last digit is provided, but it is only accurate plus or minus one-hundredth.)

►► **TIP**

You can used ELAPSED to find the difference between two time strings.

Syntax

TIME([<*exp*>])

Examples

`? TIME( )`	Returns "09:57:42"
`? TIME(0)`	Returns "09:52:44.83"

TRANSFORM

The TRANSFORM function returns an input string formatted with a picture string. The formatting is the same as the formatting the Function property applies to an entry field.

Syntax

TRANSFORM(<*exp*>, <*picture expC*>)

Example

`? TRANSFORM ('1234567890', '@R(999) 999-9999')`	Returns '(123) 456-7890'

TRIM

The TRIM function returns a string after removing trailing blanks from the argument character string. This is the same as the RTRIM function

Syntax

TRIM(<*expC*> ¦ <*memo field*>)

Example

```
? TRIM("Smith?)
```
Returns “Smith”

UNIQUE

The UNIQUE function returns .T. if the indicated index was created with the UNIQUE option. If the optional alias is specified, the table open in that work area is used; otherwise, the table in the currently open work area is used. If the optional .MDX file name is supplied, that file is used; otherwise, the current .MDX file is used.

Syntax

UNIQUE([[<*.mdx filename*>,] <*index position expN*> [, <*alias*>]])

UPPER

The UPPER function returns a string formed by turning all lowercase letters in the input string into uppercase letters in the output string. As with LOWER, you can use UPPER to be sure that sorts and comparisons are not sensitive to case.

▸▸ **WARNING**

In the ASCII collating sequence, *A–Z* come before *a–z*. This means that 'Zebra' sorts before 'aardvark.'

Syntax

UPPER(<*expC*> ¦ <*memo field*>)

Example

```
?INDEX ON UPPER(last_name)
? UPPER('Zebra') >
UPPER('aardvark')
```

Returns .T.

VAL

The VAL function returns a number given a string representation of a number.

▶▶ **WARNING**

VAL will skip leading blanks, but otherwise it stops evaluating as soon as it sees a nonnumeric character.

Syntax

VAL(<*expC*>)

Examples

`? VAL("1234.5")`	Returns 1234.5000
`? VAL("-2")?`	Returns -2.0000
`? VAL("??)`	Returns 3.0000
`? VAL("123abcde")`	Returns 123.0000
`? VAL("abcde123")`	Returns 0.0000

YEAR

The YEAR function returns the number corresponding to the year in a date input.

▶▶ **NOTE**

YEAR returns the full numeric value of the year, such as 1995 from 12/31/95. The setting of CENTURY only changes the representation of the date when it is shown as a character string.

Syntax

YEAR(<*expD*>)

Examples

`? YEAR({12/31/95})`	Returns 1995
`? YEAR({12/31/99}+1)`	Returns 2000

► Summary

In this chapter, you've gotten a detailed breakdown of the operators and operands that make up dBASE for Windows expressions, and two organizations of the functions that make up a critical part of those expressions.

You reviewed the eight types of operands: constants, memory variables, fields, object properties, object references, subroutine references, function calls, and expressions.

You read about the six types of operators: arithmetic operators, date operators, string operators, logical operators, structure operators, and relational operators

As a special case, you looked at function calls, which are another way of combining operands with an operation.

You went on to learn about the functions available in dBASE for Windows. Although we eliminated the functions that are only useful to programmers, as well as the ones that are included just to support dBASE IV-style applications, there are plenty of other functions that you might find useful in dBASE for Windows expressions.

We divided these functions first into a categorical reference, so you could see the functions grouped by their uses.

We concluded with an alphabetical list, with syntax and examples, for convenient reference when you need to use these functions.

▶ ▶ CHAPTER 13

Using Command Window Commands

▶▶ **The** commands covered in this chapter are the dBASE for Windows commands that are used in the Command window. dBASE 5 for Windows also includes dBASE IV compatibility commands, which are the ones you see in programs written before dBASE for Windows was available. We recommend that you avoid them. The dBASE IV compatibility commands are included in Appendix D, because sooner or later you will probably meet them in an old dBASE program. Also, you may see them in the dBASE for Windows on-line and printed documentation, which doesn't always tell you which commands to avoid.

We'll summarize the Command window commands by topic, and then provide an alphabetical reference.

▶▶ **NOTE**

You'll find that dBASE for Windows's on-line documentation on each of these is extensive. The program documentation comes with lots of examples of how each command is used. We haven't tried to duplicate that here, since it would fill a book every bit as long as this one. You may find some differences between the syntax shown in this chapter and the on-line documentation. In case of differences, the safe approach is to test the alternatives in the Command window.

►► Commands versus Statements

The two types of lines in dBASE for Windows program files, such as .PRG, .WFM, and .QBE files, are commands and statements.

The commands all start with verbs, such as REPLACE, APPEND, and SEEK, and they continue with the other information needed to perform the action. For example, this line holds a 20-percent-off sale:

```
REPLACE ALL product->price WITH product->price*0.80
```

The language statements are used to structure applications and to control the order of execution of the commands. These statements are covered in the next chapter. As you will see, the dBASE for Windows programming language is relatively small and simple.

►► **NOTE**

The dBASE for Windows documentation refers to both statements and commands as *commands*. We think the distinction helps you keep separate concepts separate.

►► Commands Listed by Topic

We have divided the dBASE for Windows commands into six categories:

- Data manipulation commands
- Data summary commands
- System related commands
- dBASE control commands
- Command window input/output commands
- Printer output commands

Table 13.1 lists the commands according to these categories.

TABLE 13.1: *dBASE for Windows Commands*

DATA MANIPULATION COMMANDS	
APPEND AUTOMEM	INDEX
APPEND FROM	INSERT
APPEND FROM ARRAY	INSERT AUTOMEM
APPEND MEMO	JOIN
BLANK	LABEL FORM
BROWSE	LIST
CHANGE	LIST STRUCTURE
CONTINUE	LOCATE
CONVERT	MODIFY STRUCTURE
COPY	OPEN DATABASE
COPY BINARY	PACK
COPY FILE	RECALL
COPY INDEXES	REINDEX
COPY MEMO	RENAME TABLE
COPY STRUCTURE	REPLACE
COPY TABLE	REPLACE AUTOMEM
COPY TAG	REPLACE BINARY
COPY TO ARRAY	REPLACE FROM ARRAY
COPY TO STRUCTURE EXTENDED	REPLACE MEMO
CREATE	REPLACE MEMO FROM
CREATE FROM STRUCTURE EXTENDED	REPLACE OLE
DELETE	SEEK
DELETE TABLE	SKIP
EDIT	SORT

TABLE 13.1: *dBASE for Windows Commands (continued)*

DATA MANIPULATION COMMANDS (continued)	
FIND	UPDATE
GENERATE	USE
IMPORT	ZAP
DATA SUMMARY COMMANDS	
AVERAGE	SUM
CALCULATE	TOTAL
COUNT	
SYSTEM-RELATED COMMANDS	
!	ERASE
CD	KEYBOARD
CLEAR TYPEAHEAD	LIST FILES
CLOSE ALTERNATE	MKDIR
CLOSE PRINTER	MODIFY FILE
DELETE FILE	RENAME
DIRECTORY	TYPE
DOS	
DBASE CONTROL COMMANDS	
CANCEL	LOAD DLL
CLEAR AUTOMEM	MODIFY APPLICATION
CLEAR FIELDS	MODIFY COMMAND
CLEAR MEMORY	MODIFY FORM
CLEAR PROGRAM	MODIFY LABEL
CLEAR ALL	MODIFY QUERY
CLOSE ALL	MODIFY REPORT
CLOSE DATABASES	MODIFY VIEW
CLOSE FORMS	OPEN FORM

TABLE 13.1: *dBASE for Windows Commands (continued)*

DBASE CONTROL COMMANDS (continued)	
CLOSE INDEXES	PLAY SOUND
CLOSE TABLES	QUIT
CLOSE PROCEDURE	REDEFINE
COMPILE	REFRESH
CONTINUE	RELEASE
CREATE APPLICATION	RELEASE AUTOMEM
CREATE CATALOG	RELEASE DLL
CREATE FORM	RELEASE OBJECT
CREATE LABEL	REPORT FORM
CREATE QUERY	RESTORE
CREATE REPORT	RESTORE IMAGE
CREATE SESSION	RESUME
CREATE VIEW	RETRY
DEBUG	SAVE
DEFINE	SELECT
DELETE TAG	SET … (all the SET commands)
DO	SHOW OBJECT
EXTERN	SLEEP
FLUSH	STORE
GO	STORE AUTOMEM
HELP	STORE MEMO
LIST COVERAGE	SUSPEND
LIST MEMORY	UNLOCK
LIST STATUS	WAIT

TABLE 13.1: *dBASE for Windows Commands (continued)*

COMMAND WINDOW INPUT/OUTPUT COMMANDS	
?	DISPLAY FILES
??	DISPLAY MEMO
???	DISPLAY STATUS
CLEAR	DISPLAY STRUCTURE
DISPLAY	INPUT
DISPLAY COVERAGE	
PRINTER OUTPUT COMMANDS	
EJECT	EJECT PAGE

►► Alphabetical Reference to Commands

The descriptions that follow include the use of the command, the command's syntax, and examples of the command's use (if examples clarify the use). The commands are listed in pure alphabetic order; they are not grouped in categories as they are in Table 13.1.

For an explanation of the format used for the command syntax, see the beginning of the alphabetical reference to functions in Chapter 12. We've used the same format here.

The ! Command

The ! command runs DOS commands and programs from the Command window.

Syntax

! <*DOS command*>

Example

```
!CHKDSK
```

The ? Command

The ? command lets you output the value of one or more expressions in the results pane of the Command window. The extensive formatting options are left over from the DOS versions, where ? output was a key part of reporting.

Syntax

```
? [<exp 1>
    [PICTURE <format expC>]
    [FUNCTION <function expC>]
    [AT <column expN>]
    [STYLE [<fontstyle expN>] [<fontstyle expC>] ]
    [,<exp 2>
    [PICTURE <format expC>]
    [FUNCTION <function expC>]
    [AT <column expN>]
    [STYLE [<fontstyle expN>] [<fontstyle expC>] ] ]...
  [,]
```

Example

```
? 'Send to results pane'
```

The ?? Command

The ?? command is identical to the ? command, except that the ? command precedes its output with a carriage return/line feed pair, putting you on a new line. The ?? command does not, so its output is appended to the output on the last line written.

Syntax

```
?? [<exp 1>
    [PICTURE <format expC>]
    [FUNCTION <function expC>]
    [AT <column expN>]
    [STYLE [<fontstyle expN>] [<fontstyle expC>] ]
    [,<exp 2>
    [PICTURE <format expC>]
    [FUNCTION <function expC>]
    [AT <column expN>]
    [STYLE [<fontstyle expN>] [<fontstyle expC>] ] ]   [,]
```

Examples

```
?? ' append to current line'
```

Here's an example of using ? and ?? in the Command window:

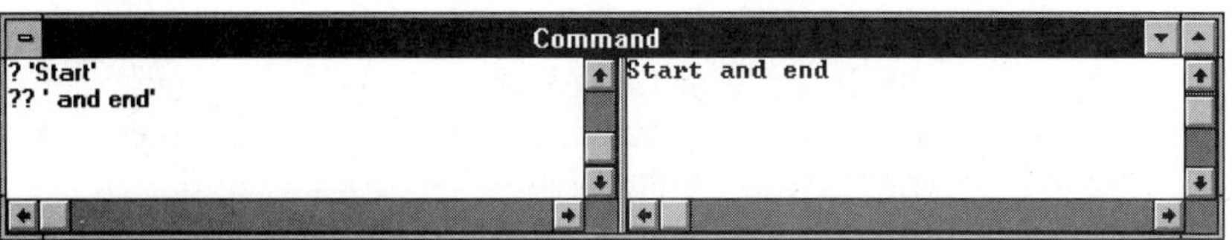

The ??? Command

The ??? command writes directly to a printer, bypassing the printer driver. In Microsoft Windows, this is totally unnecessary and bad programming practice. The command ??? may, however, come to your rescue in these cases:

- You have the printer manual, so you can look up printer control codes.
- You do *not* have an operable Microsoft Windows driver for the printer.
- You absolutely must print that report tonight. (We recommend putting on a fresh pot of coffee.)

Syntax

```
??? <expC>
```

Example

```
??? CHR(27)+'E'
```

CHR(27) is an Esc character.

The APPEND AUTOMEM Command

The automemory feature is used in programs to create a set of memory variables matching a table's fields. This lets the program have full control over the input process, prior to updating any data on disk. APPEND AUTOMEM is used when a valid new record has been entered. It adds the new record to the current table from the automemory variables.

Syntax

```
APPEND AUTOMEM
```

The APPEND FROM Command

APPEND FROM is used to add data in bulk to a table. It will read SDF (System Data Format, which are plain text files), Quattro Pro, dBASE III+, Paradox, and dBASE data files. The other options filter the incoming data (the FOR clause) and tune the efficiency (REINDEX). REINDEX turns the indexes off during the APPEND and does a full REINDEX after all the data has been appended. This is faster than indexing as you go for very large data sets.

Syntax

```
APPEND FROM <filename> ¦ ? ¦ <filename skeleton>
  [FOR <condition>]
  [[TYPE] SDF ¦ WB1 ¦ DBMEMO3 ¦ PARADOX ¦ DBASE ¦
    DELIMITED [WITH <char> ¦ BLANK] ]
  [POSITION]
  [REINDEX]
```

Example

In producing this book, we used a dBASE program to grab the figure labels, preparing a list of figures. We used a table called TEXT with a single field, also called text. These commands read our ASCII text files into our dBASE table:

```
USE text EXCLUSIVE
ZAP
APPEND FROM chap13.txt SDF
```

The APPEND FROM ARRAY Command

Arrays are used as an alternative to memory variables. The disadvantage of arrays is that they lead to less readable programs. However, memory variables can lead to name conflicts. For example, your Customer table and your Product table might both have a field called NAME.

Syntax

```
APPEND FROM ARRAY <array name>
  [FIELDS <field list>]
  [FOR <condition>]
```

```
[REINDEX]
```

The APPEND MEMO Command

APPEND MEMO appends into Memo fields from text files.

Syntax

```
APPEND MEMO <memo field>
  FROM <filename> ¦ ? ¦ <filename skeleton>
  [OVERWRITE]
```

Example

```
APPEND MEMO notes FROM t.txt
```

The AVERAGE Command

AVERAGE computes the average value of one or more expressions (typically just field names representing Numeric or Float data types). The additional options let you compute the average for only a specified part of your records and store the results in memory variables or an array.

TIP

The AVERAGE command is also available through the Table Utilities menu (see Chapter 9). Try an average calculation and examine the command echoed to the Command window.

Syntax

```
AVERAGE
  [<exp list>]
  [<scope>]
  [FOR <condition 1>]
  [WHILE <condition 2>]
  [TO <memvar list> ¦ ARRAY <array name>]
```

The BLANK Command

The BLANK command writes blank values into your tables. A *blank* number, for example, is one that is not filled in. This is different from a zero value.

Syntax

```
BLANK
  [<scope>]
  [FOR <condition 1>]
  [WHILE <condition 2>]
  [FIELDS <field list> ¦ [LIKE <skeleton 1>] [EXCEPT <skeleton 2>]]
  [REINDEX]
```

Example

```
BLANK NEXT 5
```

The BROWSE Command

The BROWSE command lets a program present the user with a selective Table Records tool. From the Command window, you can use BROWSE to see the current table.

Launching a table with a left double-click (or by pressing F2) in the Navigator initiates a BROWSE. You can examine the command in the Command window after you use the Navigator. Note that the choices in the Table Properties dialog box (discussed in Chapter 9) set the multitude of parameters available for the BROWSE command.

Syntax

```
BROWSE
  [<browse name>]
  [<scope>]
  [FOR <condition 1>]
  [WHILE <condition 2>]
  [COLOR [<standard text>]
    [, [<enhanced text>]
    [, [<perimeter color>]
    [, [<background color>]]]]]
    [FIELDS <field 1> [<field option list 1>] ¦     <calculated field 1> =
    <exp 1> [<calculated field option list 1>]
    [, <field 2> [<field option list 2>] ¦
    <calculated field 2> = <exp 2> [<calculated field option list 2>] ...]]
  [FORMAT]
  [FREEZE <field 3>]
  [KEY <exp 3>[, <exp 4>]]
  [LOCK <expN 2>]
  [NOAPPEND]
```

[NODELETE]
[NOEDIT ¦ NOMODIFY]
[NOFOLLOW]
[NOINIT]
[NOMENU]
[NOORGANIZE]
[NORMAL]
[NOTOGGLE]
[NOWAIT]
[TITLE <*expC 1*>]
[WIDTH <*expN 3*>]
[WINDOW <*window name*>]

The CALCULATE Command

The CALCULATE command performs multiple calculations more efficiently than if you use multiple individual commands, such as COUNT and TOTAL. If you COUNT, dBASE for Windows examines each record once. If you then TOTAL, dBASE examines each record again. If you CALCULATE, you can do both these chores (and a lot more) in a single pass through the data.

TIP

The CALCULATE command is also available through the Table Utilities menu (see Chapter 9). Try a calculation and examine the command echoed to the Command window.

Syntax

CALCULATE <*function list*>
[<*scope*>]
[FOR <*condition 1*>]
[WHILE <*condition 2*>]
[TO <*memvar list*> ¦ ARRAY <*array name*>]

The CANCEL Command

The CANCEL command terminates a program. You will typically use this after program errors. For example, your program may halt with an error message. You can use the SUSPEND command so you can check things out in the Command window. When you find the problem, you can use CANCEL to terminate the program.

Syntax

```
CANCEL
```

The CD Command

CD is the DOS CD (or CHDIR) command for changing directories. It is the same as setting the current directory in the Navigator. You can include a disk drive letter in the command.

Syntax

```
CD [<path>]
```

Example

```
CD D:\DBWORK
```

The CHANGE Command

CHANGE is a synonym for BROWSE. See the description of the BROWSE command for details.

Syntax

```
CHANGE
  [<edit name>]
  [<starting record expN 1> | <bookmark>]
  [<scope>]
  [FOR <condition 1>]
  [WHILE <condition 2>]
  [COLOR [<standard text>]
    [, [<enhanced text>]
    [, [<perimeter color>]
    [, <background color>]]]]
  [COLUMNAR]
  [COMPRESS]
  [FIELDS <field 1> [<field option list 1>] |   <calculated field 1> =
    <exp 1> [<calculated field option list 1>]
    [, <field 2> [<field option list 2>] |
    <calculated field 2> = <exp 2> [<calculated field option list 2>]
...]]
  [FORMAT]
```

```
[FREEZE <field 3>]
[KEY <exp 3>[, <exp 4>]]
[LOCK <expN 2>]
[NOAPPEND]
[NODELETE]
[NOEDIT | NOMODIFY]
[NOFOLLOW]
[NOINIT]
[NORMAL]
[NOTOGGLE]
[NOWAIT]
[TITLE <expC 1>]
[WIDTH <expN 3>]
[WINDOW <window name>]
```

The CLEAR Command

CLEAR clears the Command window results pane. Unless you specify a character, it clears the pane to blanks.

Syntax

```
CLEAR [CHARACTER <expC>]
```

The CLEAR ALL Command

CLEAR ALL clears everything, except open PROCEDURE and LIBRARY files, in the current session. It closes tables, clears the results pane, releases memory variables, and more.

Syntax

```
CLEAR ALL
```

The CLEAR AUTOMEM Command

CLEAR AUTOMEM provides a blank set of automemory variables for use with commands such as APPEND AUTOMEM.

Syntax

```
CLEAR AUTOMEM
```

The CLEAR FIELDS Command

CLEAR FIELDS is a synonym for SET FIELDS TO. It removes any fields lists.

Syntax

```
CLEAR FIELDS
```

The CLEAR MEMORY Command

CLEAR MEMORY releases all memory variables. If used from the Command window, it is the same as RELEASE ALL. It should not be used in programs.

Syntax

```
CLEAR MEMORY
```

The CLEAR PROGRAM Command

When dBASE for Windows loads a program into memory, it does not automatically free that memory when the program terminates. It retains the compiled program so that it can be run again, without reloading. CLEAR PROGRAM forces dBASE to free the memory allocated to programs, except the memory for LIBRARY and PROCEDURE files.

Syntax

```
CLEAR PROGRAM
```

The CLEAR TYPEAHEAD Command

dBASE for Windows allows you to set the length of the typeahead buffer (this buffer lets users type without waiting for the computer to process all their keystrokes). CLEAR TYPEAHEAD dumps any characters in the typeahead buffer, without processing them.

You cannot make constructive use of this command in the Command window, because everything you type in the Command window is entered through the typeahead buffer. Anything you've typed that you might want cleared has already been processed.

You can, however, use it in programs. Typically, this command is given when a program detects an error.

Syntax

CLEAR TYPEAHEAD

The CLOSE ALL Command

The CLOSE ALL command closes all open databases and tables, as well as related files, such as index and memo files. CLOSE ALL also closes other open files, such as text files.

NOTE

You'll need to use CLOSE ALL in the Command window when you want to create a report that does not use the current query or table choice.

Syntax

CLOSE ALL

The CLOSE ALTERNATE Command

The ALTERNATE file is a text file that has been set to receive output. CLOSE ALTERNATE closes that file.

Syntax

CLOSE ALTERNATE

The CLOSE DATABASES Command

The CLOSE DATABASES command allows you to close the current database, a named database, or all databases. Unlike CLOSE ALL, CLOSE DATABASES does not affect open text files.

Syntax

CLOSE DATABASES [<*database name*>][,<*database name*>]...

The CLOSE FORMS Command

The CLOSE FORMS command closes one or more forms.

Syntax

```
CLOSE FORMS [<form name list>]
```

Example

```
CLOSE FORMS my_form1, my_form3
```

The CLOSE INDEXES Command

The CLOSE INDEXES command closes all the .MDX and .NDX files in the current work area, except for the production .MDX file. CLOSE INDEXES does *not* close the production .MDX file.

Syntax

```
CLOSE INDEXES
```

The CLOSE PRINTER Command

The CLOSE PRINTER command closes a file opened to receive printer output. This command does not affect the printer itself. It just closes files that were receiving printer output.

Syntax

```
CLOSE PRINTER
```

The CLOSE PROCEDURE Command

The CLOSE PROCEDURE command closes a procedure file opened with a SET PROCEDURE TO command.

Syntax

```
CLOSE PROCEDURE <filename>
```

The CLOSE TABLES Command

The CLOSE TABLES command closes all tables in all work areas or, in an SQL database, all tables in the open database.

Syntax

```
CLOSE TABLES
```

The COMPILE Command

The COMPILE command invokes the dBASE for Windows built-in program compiler, without running the program. You can use COMPILE to check a new program for syntax errors, without running that program.

NOTE

If you run the program, it is automatically compiled when the source .PRG or .WFM file has been changed more recently than the compiled .PRO or .WFO file.

Syntax

COMPILE <*filename*> ¦ ? ¦ <*filename skeleton*>

The .PRG extension is implied. Other extensions, such as .QBE or .WFM, must be explicitly supplied.

Example

```
COMPILE tester
```

The CONTINUE Command

CONTINUE repeats the last LOCATE, beginning at the next record. When you LOCATE a particular record, dBASE for Windows stops at the first record it finds that matches your criteria. CONTINUE locates the next record matching your criteria. Used repeatedly, CONTINUE locates all the records that match your criteria.

Syntax

```
CONTINUE
```

The CONVERT Command

CONVERT updates a single-user table to multiuser status. The TO clause lets you fine-tune the update by setting the size of a multiuser field.

TIP

We recommend that you ignore the TO clause for CONVERT—potential disk space savings are slight—unless your files have more than a million records.

Syntax

```
CONVERT [TO <expN>]
```

The COPY Command

The COPY command lets you make a copy of your data into another table, or into a text file, Quattro Pro worksheet, dBASE III+ memo file, or other Paradox or dBASE file. The *scope*, FOR, and WHILE clauses let you select a portion of your data. The WITH PRODUCTION option copies the production .MDX file when your copy is to another dBASE table.

Syntax

```
COPY TO <filename> | ?
  [<scope>]
  [FOR <condition 1>]
  [WHILE <condition 2>]
  [FIELDS <field list>]
  [[TYPE] SDF | WB1 | DBMEMO3 | PARADOX | DBASE |
    DELIMITED [WITH <char> | BLANK] ] |
  [[WITH] PRODUCTION]
```

Example

You can use a dBASE for Windows program to manipulate a text file. This is simple if you first read the text into a table. We use a table called Text with a single, wide field, also called TEXT. These commands will read, process, and write a text file.

```
USE text EXCLUSIVE
ZAP
APPEND FROM mytext.txt SDF

* run program(s) that manipulate the text in the file

COPY TO mytext.txt SDF
```

The COPY BINARY Command

The COPY BINARY command lets you copy a Binary field to a file. This lets you write file types such as .BMP, .PCX, and .WAV from your data. The ADDITIVE clause specifies that the field be added to the file. Without ADDITIVE, the file is overwritten.

Syntax

```
COPY BINARY <field name> TO <filename> ¦ ? [ADDITIVE]
```

Example

```
COPY BINARY bit_map TO my_pic.bmp
```

The COPY FILE Command

The COPY FILE command is similar to the DOS copy command. It copies one file to another. It does not copy multiple files. The ? and <*filename skeleton*> options open the Open File dialog box so that the user can pick a file.

Syntax

```
COPY FILE <filename 1> ¦ ? ¦ <filename skeleton> TO
<filename 2 > ¦ ? ¦ <filename skeleton 2 >
```

The COPY INDEXES Command

The COPY INDEXES command moves a list of .NDX files into a single .MDX file.

Syntax

```
COPY INDEXES <.ndx filename list> [TO <.mdx filename> ¦ ? ]
```

The COPY MEMO Command

The COPY MEMO command lets you copy a memo field to an external text file. The ADDITIVE option lets you append to the external file.

Syntax

```
COPY MEMO <memo field> TO <filename> ¦ ? [ADDITIVE]
```

Example

Assume that you want a Memo field dumped to a temporary file, perhaps for transfer to a DOS word processor. You could use the COPY MEMO command like this:

```
COPY MEMO notes TO t.t
```

The COPY STRUCTURE Command

The COPY STRUCTURE command makes a copy of just the structure of the current table. You can select specific fields with the FIELDS clause, and also copy the index structure with the WITH PRODUCTION clause.

Syntax

```
COPY STRUCTURE TO <filename> ¦ ?
  [[TYPE] PARADOX ¦ DBASE]
  [FIELDS <field list>]
  [[WITH] PRODUCTION]
```

Example

These commands create an empty table that has the same fields as an active table.

```
USE active
COPY STRUCTURE TO empty
```

The COPY TABLE Command

COPY TABLE is like COPY FILE for tables. However, unlike COPY FILE, COPY TABLE will correctly copy index and memo files, along with the data table.

Syntax

```
COPY TABLE <source tablename> TO <target tablename>
  [[TYPE] DBASE ¦ PARADOX ]
```

The COPY TAG Command

The COPY TAG command copies individual index tags from an .MDX file into an individual .NDX file.

▶▶ **WARNING**

We don't recommend the use of single .NDX files. They date all the way back to 1981 and the beginning of dBASE, and they are not as good as today's .MDX files.

Syntax

COPY TAG <*tag name*> [OF *.mdx filename*] TO <*.ndx filename*>

The COPY TO ARRAY Command

The COPY TO ARRAY command makes a copy of all or a selected portion of your current table in an in-memory array.

Syntax

```
COPY TO ARRAY <array name>
  [<scope>]
  [FOR <condition 1>]
  [WHILE <condition 2 >]
  [FIELDS <field list >]
```

The COPY TO STRUCTURE EXTENDED Command

The COPY TO STRUCTURE EXTENDED command creates a table that resembles the ones you edit when you use the Table Structure tool. Its contents are the structure of the current table. This file is then used by a CREATE FROM STRUCTURE EXTENDED command.

Syntax

```
COPY TO <filename> ¦ ? STRUCTURE EXTENDED
[[TYPE] PARADOX ¦ DBASE]
```

or

```
COPY STRUCTURE EXTENDED TO <filename> ¦ ?
[[TYPE] PARADOX ¦ DBASE ]
```

The COUNT Command

The COUNT command counts the number of records in the current table, optionally counting just those that match your criteria. If SET

DELETED is off, records marked for deletion will be included in the count. If the TO clause is not specified, it reports its results in the Counted Records dialog box (see Chapter 9).

Syntax

```
COUNT
  [<scope>]
  [FOR <condition 1>]
  [WHILE <condition 2 >]
  [TO <memvar >]
```

The CREATE Command

The CREATE command opens the Table Structure tool, letting you create a new table. If you do not specify a file name, or you specify the ? option, it launches the Open File dialog box, so that you can choose a file.

►► **TIP**

If you are already in the Command window, the CREATE commands can be quicker than the equivalent Navigator commands.

Syntax

```
CREATE [<filename> ¦ ? ]
  [[TYPE] PARADOX ¦ DBASE]
```

Example

```
CREATE new_tabl
```

The CREATE APPLICATION Command

The CREATE APPLICATION command is a synonym for CREATE FORM. It launches the Form Designer. If you do not specify a file name, it will open the Open File dialog box so you can select a file.

Syntax

```
CREATE APPLICATION [<filename> ¦ ? ¦ <filename skeleton>]
```

The CREATE CATALOG Command

The CREATE CATALOG command first launches the Open File dialog box if you do not specify an individual file name. It then creates a catalog file and launches the Catalog tool so you can work with the new catalog.

Syntax

```
CREATE CATALOG
  [<filename> ¦ ? ¦ <filename skeleton>]
```

The CREATE FORM Command

CREATE FORM launches the Form Designer. If you do not specify an individual file name, it will open the Open File dialog box so you can select a file.

Syntax

```
CREATE FORM [<filename> ¦ ? ¦ <filename skeleton>]
```

Example

```
CREATE FORM people_c
```

The CREATE FROM STRUCTURE EXTENDED Command

The CREATE FROM STRUCTURE EXTENDED command uses the data file created by a COPY TO STRUCTURE EXTENDED command to create a new table. If any of the fields are specified as indexed, the production .MDX file is also created.

TIP

After you COPY TO STRUCTURE EXTENDED, the structure is in a normal .DBF file, which you can examine and modify with any of the normal Table tools. For an unmodified, exact copy, use COPY STRUCTURE.

Syntax

```
CREATE <filename> ¦ ?
  STRUCTURE EXTENDED
  [[TYPE] PARADOX ¦ DBASE]
```

The CREATE LABEL Command

The CREATE LABEL command launches the Crystal Reports label design tool.

Syntax

```
CREATE LABEL [<filename> ¦ ? ¦ <filename skeleton>]
```

Example

```
CREATE LABEL orgs_c
```

The CREATE QUERY Command

The CREATE QUERY command launches the Query Designer. If you do not specify a file name, it first opens the Open File dialog box.

Syntax

```
CREATE QUERY <filename> ¦ ?
```

The CREATE REPORT Command

The CREATE REPORT command launches the Crystal Reports report design tool.

Syntax

```
CREATE REPORT [CROSSTAB] [<filename> ¦ ? ¦ <filename
skeleton>]
```

The CREATE SESSION Command

The CREATE SESSION command creates a new session. Each session behaves as if you had switched to a separate computer and started dBASE for Windows as another user. This lets you open the same table in multiple windows.

▶▶ NOTE

You never explicitly close a session. Sessions are closed automatically by dBASE for Windows after the last open form or table in the session is closed.

Syntax

CREATE SESSION

The CREATE VIEW Command

CREATE VIEW is a synonym for CREATE QUERY. It launches the Query Designer. If you do not specify a file name, it first opens the Open File dialog box.

Syntax

CREATE VIEW [<*filename*> ¦ ? ¦ <*filename skeleton*>]

The DEBUG Command

The DEBUG command launches the dBASE for Windows Debugger.

Syntax

DEBUG [<*filename*> ¦ ? ¦ <*filename skeleton*> ¦ <*procedure name*> ¦ <*UDF name*>
  [WITH <*parameter list*>]]

The DEFINE Command

The DEFINE command creates and assigns properties to new objects.

Syntax

DEFINE <*class name*> <*object name* >
  [OF <*container object*>]
  [FROM <*row, col*> TO <*row, col*> > ¦ <AT <*row, col*>]
  [PROPERTY <*stock property list* >]
  [CUSTOM <*custom property list* >]
  [WITH <*parameter list* >]

Example

```
DEFINE Pushbutton OK_button OF my_form ;
  PROPERTY;
    Top 13, Left 15, Height 2, Width 12, Text "OK"
```

The DELETE Command

The DELETE command lets you mark for deletion individual or groups of records in dBASE tables.

Syntax

```
DELETE
  [<scope>]
  [FOR <condition 1>]
  [WHILE <condition 2 >]
```

The DELETE FILE Command

The DELETE FILE command deletes an individual file. If you use the ? or <*filename skeleton*> options, it launches the Erase File dialog box.

Syntax

```
DELETE FILE <filename> ¦ ? ¦ <filename skeleton>
```

Example

```
DELETE FILE t.tmp
```

The DELETE TABLE Command

Like DELETE FILE, DELETE TABLE deletes a specified table or one selected with the Erase File dialog box. It takes care of deleting associated index and memo files, as well as the data table.

Syntax

```
DELETE TABLE <table name> ¦ ?
  [[TYPE] PARADOX ¦ DBASE ]
```

The DELETE TAG Command

The DELETE TAG command deletes one or more tags from .MDX files.

Syntax

```
DELETE TAG <tag name 1>
    [OF <filename 1> ¦ ? ¦ <filename skeleton 1>]
    [, <tag name 2 >
    [OF <filename 2 > ¦ ? ¦ <filename skeleton 2 >] ... ]
```

The DIR Command

The DIR (or DIRECTORY) command is similar to the DOS DIR command. If given without any arguments, it defaults to DIR *.DBF. DIR *.* must be explicitly specified.

Syntax

```
DIR ¦ DIRECTORY
  [ON <drive>[ON <drive>[:]]]
  [LIKE [<path>\] <filename> ¦ <filename skeleton>]
  [[<drive>:] [<path>\] [<filename> ¦ <filename skeleton>]]
```

Example

```
DIR *.*
```

The DISPLAY Command

The DISPLAY command displays one or more records in the Command window's results pane, unless you explicitly direct output to a file or to your printer. DISPLAY is a synonym for LIST, except that DISPLAY defaults to the current record; LIST defaults to all records.

Syntax

```
DISPLAY
  [<scope>]
  [FOR<condition 1>]
  [WHILE<condition 2>]
  [[FIELDS] <exp list>]
  [OFF]
  [TO FILE <filename> ¦ ? ¦ [TO PRINTER]]
```

Example

Here is an example of using a DISPLAY command in the Command window:

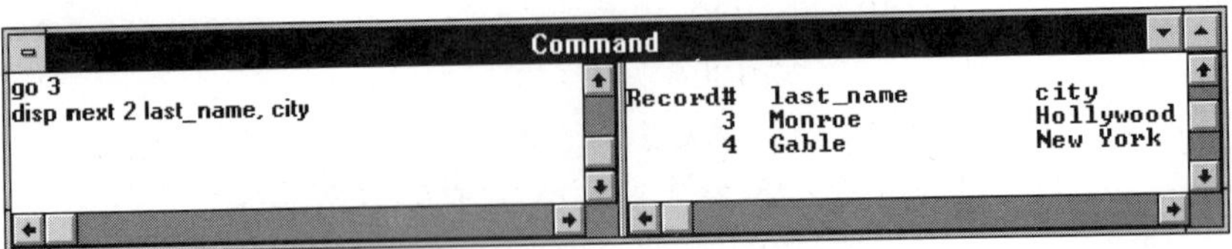

The DISPLAY COVERAGE Command

DISPLAY COVERAGE is used in programming to examine the results of program coverage—a detailed analysis of how much use each part of a program gets. This is used to tune a program for better performance.

Syntax

DISPLAY COVERAGE <*filename 1*> ¦ ? ¦ <*filename skeleton*>
[ALL]
[SUMMARY]
[TO FILE <*filename 2*> ¦ ?] ¦ <*filename skeleton*> ¦ [TO PRINTER]

The DISPLAY FILES Command

DISPLAY FILES provides the same service as DIR. Like DIR, it defaults to *.DBF.

Syntax

DISPLAY FILES
[[LIKE] <*filename 1*> ¦ <*filename skeleton*>]
[ON <*drive*>]
[TO FILE <*filename 2*> ¦ ?] ¦ [TO PRINTER]

The DISPLAY MEMORY Command

The DISPLAY MEMORY command sends a long list, describing the contents of memory, to the Command window's results pane, to a file, or to the printer. You can use DISPLAY MEMORY to send the list to a .TXT file, and then use the text editor (MODI FILE starts it) to examine it.

Syntax

DISPLAY MEMORY [TO FILE *<filename>* ¦ ? ¦ *<filename skeleton>* ¦ PRINTER]

Example

DISPLAY MEMORY TO t.txt

The DISPLAY STATUS Command

Like DISPLAY MEMORY, DISPLAY STATUS sends an extensive status report to the Command window's results pane. Again, you can use DISPLAY STATUS to send the report to a .TXT file, and then use the text editor to examine it.

Syntax

DISPLAY STATUS [TO FILE *<filename>* ¦ ? ¦ *<filename skeleton>* ¦ PRINTER]

The DISPLAY STRUCTURE Command

The DISPLAY STRUCTURE command shows the structure of a table in the results pane of the Command window or sends it to a file or to the printer.

▶▶ **TIP**

For a better look at your structure, use MODI STRU to launch the Table Structure tool.

Syntax

DISPLAY STRUCTURE
  [IN *<alias>*]
  [TO FILE *<filename>* ¦ ? ¦ *<filename skeleton>* ¦ PRINTER]

The DO Command

The DO command runs a program (usually a .PRG file).

Syntax

```
DO <filename> | ? | <filename skeleton> | <procedure name> |
<UDF name> [WITH <parameter list >]
```

Examples

```
DO my_prog
DO my_prog WITH 100, .05, 30
```

The DOS Command

The DOS command runs a DOS session under dBASE for Windows.

Syntax

```
DOS
```

The EDIT Command

The EDIT command is a synonym for BROWSE. EDIT or BROWSE instantly launches the Table Records tool. If you are in the Command window, using this command is quicker than returning to the Navigator.

Syntax

```
EDIT
  [<starting record expN > | <bookmark >]
  [<scope >]
  [FOR <condition 1 >]
  [WHILE <condition 2 >]
  [COLOR [<standard text >] [, [<enhanced text >] [, <border >]]]
  [COLUMNAR]
  [COMPRESS]
  [FIELDS <field 1> [<field option list 1 >] |   <calculated field 1> =
      <exp 1> [<calculated field option list 1 >]
     [, <field 2> [<field option list 2>] |
     <calculated field 2> = <exp 2>
      [<calculated field option list 2 >]... ]]
  [FORMAT]
  [FREEZE <field 3 >]
  [KEY <exp 3> [, <exp 4 >]]
  [LOCK <expN >]
  [NOAPPEND]
  [NOCLEAR]
  [NODELETE]
```

[NOEDIT ¦ NOMODIFY]
[NOFOLLOW]
[NOINIT]
[NORMAL]
[NOTOGGLE]
[NOWAIT]
[TITLE <*expC 1* >]
[WIDTH <*expN* >]
[WINDOW <*window name* >]

The EJECT Command

EJECT sends a form-feed to your printer.

Syntax

EJECT

The EJECT PAGE Command

The EJECT PAGE command sends a form-feed to your printer and calls any page handling set by an ON PAGE command.

Syntax

EJECT PAGE

The ERASE Command

The ERASE command erases a single file. Using the ? or <*filename skeleton*> option launches the Erase File dialog box.

NOTE

ERASE *.tmp does *not* erase all files with the .TMP extension. It opens the Erase File dialog box so that you can choose a particular .TMP file to erase. To erase a group of files, run the DOS ERASE command with `!ERASE *.tmp`.

Syntax

ERASE <*filename*> ¦ ? ¦ <*filename skeleton*>

The EXTERN Command

The EXTERN command is used in programs to gain full access to any routine in a .DLL file or another Microsoft Windows executable file, such as a Windows .EXE file. Routines in .DLL files include all of the Windows API (application programming interface). EXTERN lets advanced programmers interface directly with Windows and other libraries without using C or assembler code.

Syntax

```
EXTERN [CDECL] <return type> <function name>
  ([<parameter type 1>[<parameter type 2 >,...]])
  [<path >] <filename>
```

The FIND Command

The FIND command is a form of SEEK that saves some typing in the Command window. You FIND Smith (no quotation marks around Smith), in lieu of SEEK "Smith".

Syntax

```
FIND <search key literal>
```

The FLUSH Command

FLUSH sends the contents of dBASE for Windows' internal data buffers to the operating system.

▸▸ **WARNING**

FLUSH may not succeed in getting your critical data to disk. In a single-user setup, disk-buffering software may delay the actual writes to disk. On a network, considerable delays are possible. Unfortunately, there is no way for dBASE for Windows (or any database program) to tell our current operating systems, "Write it to disk, now!"

Syntax

```
FLUSH
```

The GENERATE Command

The GENERATE command adds random records to a table. This is useful for testing.

Syntax

```
GENERATE [<expN >]
```

Example

```
GENERATE 1000
```

The GO Command

The GO command moves the record pointer to either the BOTTOM, TOP, or a selected record number. SQL databases that do not have record numbers can use bookmarks instead.

Syntax

```
GO[TO] BOTTOM | TOP | <bookmark > | [RECORD] <expN> [IN
<alias >]
```

Examples

```
GO TOP
GO 300
GO BOTTOM
```

The HELP Command

The HELP command launches the dBASE for Windows Help program. If you supply a topic, the command launches Help's Search dialog box for that topic.

TIP

Using the HELP command in the Command window is often quicker than using the Windows Help Search dialog box.

Syntax

```
HELP [<help topic >]
```

Example

```
HELP class form
```

The IMPORT Command

The IMPORT command reads data into a table from another table or spreadsheet file.

Syntax

```
IMPORT FROM <filename> ¦ ?
  [[TYPE] WB1 ¦ WK1 ]
  [HEADING]
```

The INDEX Command

The INDEX command creates a new TAG in an .MDX file or a new .NDX file. You can index only unique values for a partial set of data and in ascending (the default) or descending sequence.

▶▶ **TIP**

If you have a large table, indexing on a small set of records makes access based on that index just as fast as if the table were small.

Syntax

```
INDEX ON <key expC list >
  TO <.ndx filename> ¦ ? ¦ <.ndx filename skeleton>
  [UNIQUE]
```

or

```
INDEX ON <key expC list >
  TAG <tag name> [OF <.mdx filename> ¦ ? ¦ <.mdx filename
skeleton >]
  [FOR <condition >]
  [DESCENDING]
  [UNIQUE]
```

Example

```
INDEX ON date_order DESCENDING
```

The INPUT Command

INPUT dates to the earliest days of dBASE II and its mainframe predecessors. It is a *very* old-fashioned way of getting data from a user. It is still popular for use in beginning programming classes.

Syntax

```
INPUT [<prompt expC>] TO <memvar>
```

The INSERT Command

The INSERT command inserts a blank record after (or optionally before) the current record. If BLANK is not specified, INSERT launches the currently selected view to edit the new record.

▶▶ **WARNING**

INSERT must physically move every record from the point of insertion to the end of the file. Always use APPEND [BLANK] except on tiny files.

Syntax

```
INSERT [BLANK] [BEFORE] [NOWAIT]
```

The INSERT AUTOMEM Command

We include this command only because we want to warn you never to use it. While INSERT can be handy for working on small files from the Command window, INSERT AUTOMEM is only useful in a program. INSERT should never be used in programs. You should use APPENDs and use indexes to keep your data logically ordered.

Syntax

```
INSERT AUTOMEM [BEFORE]
```

The JOIN Command

The JOIN command performs a physical joining of two tables. Use it when you want to combine two tables into one (say, for export to a spreadsheet). For most work, SET RELATION achieves the same effect with much higher efficiency.

Syntax

```
JOIN WITH <alias > TO <filename> ¦ ? ¦ <filename skeleton>
  [[TYPE] [PARADOX ¦ DBASE] ]
  FOR <condition>
  [FIELDS <field list >]
```

The KEYBOARD Command

The KEYBOARD command puts one or more characters into the typeahead buffer, as if you had typed them.

▸▸ TIP

KEYBOARD commands can be used to provide macro facilities for starting any program that can be run from the keyboard. Put a single KEYBOARD command in a .PRG file, then DO that .PRG instead of typing.

Syntax

```
KEYBOARD <expC> [CLEAR]
```

Example

In a program, this command can be used instead of pressing Ctrl-F to find records, because CHR(6) is Ctrl-F:

```
KEYBOARD CHR(6)
```

The LABEL FORM Command

The LABEL FORM command uses a label design you have created with Crystal Reports (an .RPL file) to write mailing labels.

Syntax

```
LABEL FORM <filename 1> ¦ ? ¦ <filename skeleton 1>
  [<scope >]
  [FOR <condition 1 >]
  [WHILE <condition 2 >]
  [SAMPLE]
  [TO FILE <filename 2 > ¦ ? ¦ <filename skeleton 2 > ¦ PRINTER]
```

Example

LABEL FORM phones_b

The LIST Command

The LIST command lists all, or selected, records to the results pane of the Command window, to a file, or to your printer. It is the same as DISPLAY, except that DISPLAY defaults to the current record; LIST defaults to all records. The OFF option eliminates record numbers from the listing.

Syntax

LIST
  [<*scope* >]
  [FOR <*condition 1* >]
  [WHILE <*condition 2* >]
  [[FIELDS] <*exp list* >]
  [OFF]
  [TO FILE <*filename*> ¦ ? ¦ <*filename skeleton*> ¦ PRINTER]

Example

Here's an example of using LIST in the Command window:

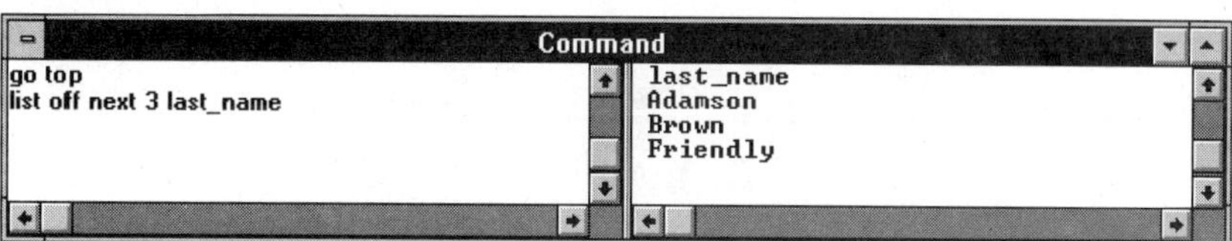

The LIST COVERAGE Command

LIST COVERAGE is used in programming to examine the results of program coverage—a detailed analysis of how much use each part of a program gets. This is used to tune a program for better performance.

Syntax

LIST COVERAGE
  [<*coverage filename*> ¦ ? ¦ <*coverage filename skeleton* >]
  [ALL]
  [SUMMARY]

[TO FILE <*text filename*> ¦ ? ¦ <*text filename skeleton*> ¦
[PRINTER]

The LIST FILES Command

LIST FILES provides the same service as DIR. Like DIR, it defaults to *.DBF.

Syntax

LIST FILES
[LIKE <*filename 1*> ¦ <*filename skeleton* >]
[ON <*drive* >]
[TO FILE <*filename 2* > ¦ ? ¦ <*filename skeleton 2* > ¦ PRINTER]

The LIST MEMORY Command

LIST MEMORY sends a long list, describing the contents of memory, to the Command window's results pane or to a file or the printer. You can use LIST MEMORY to send the list to a .TXT file, and then use the text editor (MODI FILE starts it) to examine it.

Syntax

LIST MEMORY [TO FILE <*filename*> ¦ ? ¦ <*filename skeleton*> ¦
PRINTER]

The LIST STATUS Command

Like LIST MEMORY, LIST STATUS sends an extensive status report to the Command window's results pane. Again, you can use LIST STATUS to send the report to a .TXT file, and then use the text editor to examine it.

Syntax

LIST STATUS [TO FILE <*filename*> ¦ ? ¦ <*filename skeleton*> ¦
PRINTER]

The LIST STRUCTURE Command

LIST STRUCTURE shows the structure of a table in the results pane of the Command window or sends it to a file or your printer.

▶▶ **TIP**

For a better look at your structure, use MODI STRU to launch the Table Structure tool.

Syntax

```
LIST STRUCTURE
  [IN <alias >]
  [TO FILE <filename> ¦ ? <filename skeleton> ¦ PRINTER]
```

The LOAD DLL Command

LOAD DLL is used by programmers who have created .DLL files using a language other than dBASE. It lets dBASE programs access the routines written in the other language. Among other uses, it allows access to specialized Visual Basic controls.

Syntax

```
LOAD DLL [<path >] <DLL filename>
```

The LOCATE Command

LOCATE is used to search for a record based on criteria that may not be available in an index.

▶▶ **TIP**

LOCATE is many times slower than SEEK if you do not have an index. Add an index on any criteria for which you do frequent searches.

Syntax

```
LOCATE
  [<scope >]
  [FOR <condition 1 >]
  [WHILE <condition 2 >]
```

Example

```
LOCATE FOR first_name = "Mary"
```

The MKDIR Command

The MKDIR command calls the DOS service of the same name.

Syntax

MD ¦ MKDIR <*directory*>

Example

MD new_subd

The MODIFY APPLICATION Command

MODIFY APPLICATION is a synonym for MODIFY FORM. It launches the Form Designer.

Syntax

MODIFY APPLICATION <*filename*> ¦ ? ¦ <*filename skeleton*>

The MODIFY COMMAND Command

MODIFY COMMAND starts the Program Editor. The default extension for the file is .PRG.

▸▸ TIP

If you are working in the Command window, using MODI COMM from the Command window is much quicker than switching back to the Navigator for the same service.

Syntax

MODIFY COMMAND [<*filename*> ¦ ? ¦ <*filename skeleton* >]

MODIFY FILE starts the Text Editor. The default extension for the file is .TXT.

Syntax

MODIFY FILE [<*filename*> ¦ ? ¦ <*filename skeleton* >]

Example

MODIFY FILE dbasewin.ini

The MODIFY FORM Command

MODIFY FORM launches the Form Designer. If you are working in the Command window, use this command to work on your .WFM files.

Syntax

MODIFY FORM *<filename>* ¦ ? ¦ *<filename skeleton>*

The MODIFY LABEL Command

MODIFY LABEL launches the Crystal Reports label design tool.

Syntax

MODIFY LABEL *<filename>* ¦ ? ¦ *<filename skeleton>*

The MODIFY QUERY Command

MODIFY QUERY launches the Query Designer.

Syntax

MODIFY QUERY *<filename>* ¦ ? ¦ *<filename skeleton>*

The MODIFY REPORT Command

MODIFY REPORT launches the Crystal Reports report design tool.

Syntax

MODIFY REPORT *<filename>* ¦ ? ¦ *<filename skeleton>*

The MODIFY STRUCTURE Command

MODIFY STRUCTURE launches the Table Structure tool. It is the same as selecting the table in the Navigator and pressing Shift-F2 or right double-clicking.

Syntax

MODIFY STRUCTURE

The MODIFY VIEW Command

MODIFY VIEW is a synonym for MODIFY QUERY. It launches the Query Designer.

Syntax

```
MODIFY VIEW <filename> ¦ ? ¦ <filename skeleton>
```

The OPEN DATABASE Command

The OPEN DATABASE command opens an SQL database.

Syntax

```
OPEN DATABASE <database name>
  [LOGIN <username>/<password >]
  [WITH <option string >]
```

The OPEN FORM Command

The OPEN FORM command launches a dBASE for Windows form, such as the ones you create in the Form Designer. The ON clause specifies which object on the form receives focus.

Syntax

```
OPEN FORM <form name 1> [ON <object name 1>
  [<form name 2> [ON <object name 2 >] ...]]
```

Example

```
OPEN FORM my_form ON ok_button
```

The PACK Command

The PACK command physically removes deleted records from a table. For larger tables, it is generally part of regular maintenance procedures.

▸▸ TIP

PACK is often used on network tables during weekend maintenance. A full backup should always be done before using the PACK command.

Syntax

```
PACK
```

The PLAY SOUND Command

The PLAY SOUND command plays a sound recorded in a .WAV file or stored in a Binary field.

Syntax

```
PLAY SOUND FILENAME <filename> ¦ ? ¦ <filename skeleton> ¦
BINARY <binary field>
```

The QUIT Command

The QUIT command terminates your dBASE for Windows session. The WITH clause will return a code to the operating system. From DOS, the WITH return value becomes ERRORLEVEL in a DOS batch file.

Syntax

```
QUIT [WITH <expN >]
```

The RECALL Command

The RECALL command defaults to the current record. Any record that was deleted (with DELETE) may be recalled (the Delete flag is turned off) with RECALL prior to using PACK on a table. After using PACK, the data is physically gone.

Syntax

```
RECALL
  [<scope >]
  [FOR <condition 1 >]
  [WHILE <condition 2 >]
```

Examples

```
RECALL ALL
RECALL FOR Balance > 0
```

The REDEFINE Command

The REDEFINE command modifies definitions of objects, such as those made by a DEFINE command or a prior REDEFINE command, or through a tool such as the Form Designer.

Syntax

```
REDEFINE <class name> <object name>
  [OF <container object >]
  [FROM <row, col> TO <row, col> > ¦ <AT <row, col >]
  [PROPERTY <stock property list >]
  [CUSTOM <custom property list >]
  [WITH <parameter list >]
```

The REFRESH Command

REFRESH is used in multiuser situations. It causes dBASE for Windows to reread any data in its buffers. Any changes made by other users are read during a REFRESH.

▸▸ **NOTE**

You operate as multiple users if you use multiple sessions, so you may need to REFRESH to keep all your windows current.

Syntax

```
REFRESH [<alias >]
```

The REINDEX Command

The REINDEX command rebuilds all open indexes for the table currently in use.

▸▸ **WARNING**

On a network, using REINDEX generates a storm of network traffic if your table is large. To avoid this, issue the REINDEX command in a dBASE for Windows session on the server itself.

Syntax

```
REINDEX
```

Example

A common maintenance procedure, generally run in the evening or over a weekend, is to back up the data in the table, and then issue these commands:

```
PACK
REINDEX
```

The RELEASE Command

The RELEASE command deletes memory variables and arrays, freeing the memory they took.

Syntax

RELEASE <*memvar list*> ¦
  ALL [LIKE <*memvar skeleton* 1 >] [EXCEPT <*memvar skeleton 2* >]

Example

```
RELEASE ALL LIKE temp*
```

The RELEASE AUTOMEM Command

The RELEASE AUTOMEM command releases only the automemory (AUTOMEM) variables.

Syntax

```
RELEASE AUTOMEM
```

The RELEASE DLL Command

RELEASE DLL releases a .DLL file previously loaded with a LOAD DLL command.

Syntax

RELEASE DLL <*DLL filename list*>

The RELEASE OBJECT Command

RELEASE OBJECT deletes objects from memory, freeing the memory they took. If you release a Form, all objects on that form are automatically released before the Form object itself is released.

Syntax

RELEASE OBJECT *<object parent>.<object name>*

Example

RELEASE OBJECT Form.Pushbutton1

The RENAME Command

Similar to the DOS command of the same name, RENAME changes the name of a file.

Syntax

RENAME *<filename 1>* ¦ ? ¦ *<filename skeleton 1>* TO *<filename 2>* ¦ ? ¦ *<filename skeleton 2>*

Example

RENAME people.dbf TO people.sav

The RENAME TABLE Command

RENAME TABLE is an intelligent RENAME command, for use with tables. It takes care of the table name, as well as related index and memo files.

Syntax

RENAME *<old table name>* ¦ ? ¦ *<filename skeleton 1>* TO *<new table name>* ¦ ? ¦ *<filename skeleton 2>* [TYPE PARADOX ¦ DBASE]

Example

This command renames ORGS.DBF, ORGS.MDX, and ORGS.DBT:

RENAME TABLE orgs TO orgs_1

The REPLACE Command

A REPLACE command can update just the current record, a whole table, or part of a table.

▶▶ **TIP**

Using REPLACE from the Command window can do mass updates very easily. This is often quicker than using the Table menu Replace Records ...choice.

Syntax

```
REPLACE
  <field 1> WITH <exp 1> [ADDITIVE]
  [, <field 2> WITH <exp 2> [ADDITIVE]...
  [<scope >]
  [FOR <condition 1 >]
  [WHILE <condition 2 >]
  [REINDEX]
```

Examples

```
REPLACE ALL Orgs_ID WITH RECNO()+1000
REPLACE last_name WITH "Smythe"
REPLACE ALL PRICE WITH PRICE * 0.80
```

The REPLACE AUTOMEM Command

The REPLACE AUTOMEM command transfers the values in your automemory (AUTOMEM) variables into the equivalent fields in your table's current record.

Syntax

```
REPLACE AUTOMEM
```

The REPLACE BINARY Command

The REPLACE BINARY command replaces a Binary field with a file. This is used to load data such as .WAV, .BMP, and .PCX files.

Syntax

```
REPLACE BINARY <binary field name> FROM <filename> | ? |
<filename skeleton> [TYPE <binary type user number >]
```

Example

```
REPLACE BINARY pic_field FROM my_pic.bmp
```

The REPLACE FROM ARRAY Command

The REPLACE FROM ARRAY command updates the current record, or a range of records, with data stored in a memory array.

Syntax

```
REPLACE FROM ARRAY <array name>
  [<scope >]
  [FOR <condition 1 >]
  [WHILE <condition 2 >]
  [FIELDS <field list >]
  [REINDEX]
```

The REPLACE MEMO Command

The REPLACE MEMO command is used when you have a memory array in which each line of the array is one line of text. This array will be written to the Memo field by a REPLACE MEMO command.

Syntax

```
REPLACE MEMO <memo field> WITH ARRAY <array name> [ADDITIVE]
```

The REPLACE MEMO FROM Command

The REPLACE MEMO FROM command lets you replace the contents of a Memo field with the contents of a file.

▸▸ **NOTE**

Memo fields work, but Binary fields are the preferred method for storing binary data types, such as .WAV, .BMP, and .PCX files.

Syntax

```
REPLACE MEMO <memo field> FROM <filename> | ? | <filename
skeleton> [ADDITIVE]
```

The REPLACE OLE Command

The REPLACE OLE command lets you put an OLE document in an OLE field (the default) or a link to an OLE document.

Syntax

```
REPLACE OLE <OLE field name>
    <filename> ¦ ? ¦ <filename skeleton>
  [LINK [CLASS <class name >]]
```

The REPORT FORM Command

The REPORT FORM command provides data to a report format you have defined in Crystal Reports. You can specify a regular report (.RPT) or a cross-tab report (.RPC).

Syntax

```
REPORT FORM <filename 1> ¦ ? ¦ <filename skeleton 1>
  [<scope >] [FOR <condition 1 >] [WHILE <condition 2 >]
  [CROSSTAB]
  [HEADING <expC >]
  [NOEJECT]
  [PLAIN]
  [SUMMARY]
  [TO FILE <filename 2> ¦ ? ¦ <filename skeleton 2>
```

The RESTORE Command

RESTORE is used to restore data, such as memory variables, previously saved with a SAVE command.

Syntax

```
RESTORE FROM <filename> ¦ ? ¦ <filename skeleton> [ADDITIVE]
```

The RESTORE IMAGE FROM Command

The RESTORE IMAGE FROM command restores an image to your screen or printer. It will get the image from a file or a Binary field. The default type is .BMP.

Syntax

```
RESTORE IMAGE FROM
  <filename> ¦ ? ¦ <filename skeleton> ¦ BINARY <binary field>
  [TIMEOUT <expN >]
  [TO PRINTER]
  [[TYPE] PCX]
```

The RESUME Command

The RESUME command may be given after a SUSPEND command, to start a program at the point at which it was suspended. Typically, this command is issued in the Command window after an error, such as a file not being open, has been fixed.

Syntax

```
RESUME
```

The RETRY Command

The RETRY command attempts to access a record to which access was previously denied because another user had locked it.

Syntax

```
RETRY
```

The SAVE Command

The SAVE command stores one or more memory variables in a file. They can later be restored with a RESTORE command.

Syntax

```
SAVE TO <filename> ¦ ? ¦ <filename skeleton>
  [ALL]
  [LIKE <memvar skeleton 1 >]
  [EXCEPT <memvar skeleton 2 >]
```

Example

```
SAVE TO mem_file ALL LIKE *_saved_var
```

The SEEK Command

The SEEK command is similar to the FIND command. SEEK is usually preferred in programs. It locates values in the master index.

Syntax

```
SEEK <expC> ¦ <expN> ¦ <expD>
```

The SELECT Command

The SELECT command lets you choose any work area from 1 to 225, or name an area by an alias assigned to a table. Each work area can have one open table and as many related .MDX and .NDX files as needed. Each session can have up to 225 work areas.

WARNING

dBASE for Windows has a virtually unlimited capacity for open tables and associated files. DOS does not. Your real limit on sessions and work areas will be your DOS files limit.

Syntax

```
SELECT <alias>
```

Examples

```
SELECT 2
SELECT orgs
```

The SET Command

The SET command launches the Desktop Properties multi-tab dialog box.

Syntax

```
SET
```

The SET ALTERNATE Command

The SET ALTERNATE command turns output to an alternate device or file ON. It routes output of the ?, ??, and dBASE IV-style output commands to this device or file.

Syntax

```
SET ALTERNATE ON ¦ OFF
```

The SET ALTERNATE TO Command

The SET ALTERNATE TO command sets a device or file to receive alternate output, when you SET ALTERNATE ON. If no file or device is specified, it closes the former alternate device or file.

Syntax

```
SET ALTERNATE TO [<filename> ¦ ? ¦ <filename skeleton>
[ADDITIVE]]
```

The SET AUTOSAVE Command

The SET AUTOSAVE command sets the autosave feature on or off. With AUTOSAVE ON, dBASE flushes its buffers to the operating system more frequently than with AUTOSAVE OFF. You can gain some safety at the cost of some speed. (With AUTOSAVE either ON or OFF, saving is automatic.)

Syntax

```
SET AUTOSAVE ON ¦ OFF
```

The SET BELL Command

The SET BELL command sets the bell feature on or off. With BELL OFF, the beeps (when you fill a field completely, for instance) are turned off.

Syntax

```
SET BELL ON ¦ OFF
```

The SET BELL TO Command

The SET BELL TO command lets you adjust the pitch and duration of the bell. The 256 setting is about middle C on the piano. Duration is measured in clock ticks; each tick occurs 18.2 times per second. One or two ticks makes a decent bell.

▸▸ **NOTE**

The word *bell* dates back to the dawn of dBASE, when there really was a bell in typical terminals.

Syntax

SET BELL TO [<*frequency expN*>, <*duration expN* >]

The SET BLOCKSIZE TO Command

The SET BLOCKSIZE TO command sets the size of blocks in index and memo files. The BLOCKSIZE is given in multiples of 512 bytes (1 is 512, 2 is 1024, and so on). The maximum BLOCKSIZE is 63.

Syntax

SET BLOCKSIZE TO <*expN*>

The SET CARRY Command

The SET CARRY command turns the CARRY property on or off. When ON, values for a newly appended record are carried forward from the previous record.

Syntax

SET CARRY ON ¦ OFF

The SET CARRY TO Command

The SET CARRY TO command allows the user to select the fields that participate in the CARRY.

Syntax

SET CARRY TO [<*field list*> [ADDITIVE]]

Example

SET CARRY TO City, State, Zip

The SET CATALOG Command

The SET CATALOG command turns cataloging on and off. When ON, files opened are automatically added to the current catalog.

Syntax

SET CATALOG ON ¦ OFF

The SET CATALOG TO Command

The SET CATALOG TO command opens a catalog file. Without a file name, it closes the current catalog. The ? option or using a skeleton calls the Open Catalog dialog box.

Syntax

SET CATALOG TO [<*filename*> ¦ ? ¦ <*filename skeleton* >]

The SET CENTURY Command

The SET CENTURY command, when ON, includes all four year digits in date displays.

Syntax

SET CENTURY ON ¦ OFF

Example

Here's an example of using the SET CENTURY command in the Command window:

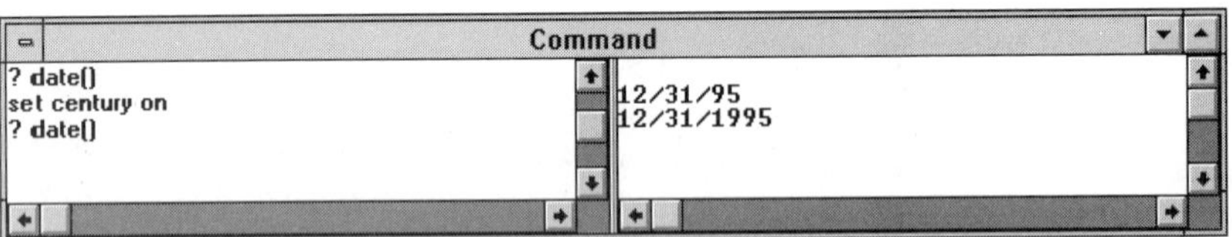

The SET CONFIRM Command

The SET CONFIRM command controls the behavior of dBASE for Windows when you type the last character in a field. With CONFIRM ON, dBASE for Windows waits for you to press Tab or Enter to confirm that you have finished, which makes fixing errors very easy. With CONFIRM OFF, dBASE immediately moves to the next field. This behavior is better for high-volume data-entry work.

Syntax

SET CONFIRM ON ¦ OFF

The SET CONSOLE Command

The SET CONSOLE command, when ON, uses the results pane of the Command window for output from commands such as LIST and ?.

Syntax

```
SET CONSOLE ON ¦ OFF
```

The SET COVERAGE Command

The SET COVERAGE command is used when you want an extended analysis of which portions of a program are used most often. This is useful when your program is not as fast as you would like and you want to know where you can gain the most speed.

Syntax

```
SET COVERAGE ON ¦ OFF
```

The SET CUAENTER Command

The SET CUAENTER command controls the behavior of the Enter key. According to the CUA definition, pressing Enter submits a form (is the same as clicking OK). However, for much data-entry work, people are used to pressing Enter to complete a single field, which is the behavior when you set CUAENTER OFF.

Syntax

```
SET CUAENTER ON ¦ OFF
```

The SET CURRENCY Command

The SET CURRENCY command specifies the side of a number for placement of the currency symbol.

Syntax

```
SET CURRENCY LEFT ¦ RIGHT
```

The SET CURRENCY TO Command

The SET CURRENCY TO command specifies the symbol that is used for currency amounts.

Syntax

SET CURRENCY TO [<*expC* >]

The SET DATABASE Command

The SET DATABASE TO command selects a database in an SQL database environment.

Syntax

SET DATABASE TO [<*database name* >]

The SET DATE TO Command

The SET DATE [TO] command specifies the format used for the display of dates. The choices are as follows:

American	MM/DD/YY
ANSI	YY.MM.DD
British	DD/MM/YY
French	DD/MM/YY
German	DD.MM.YY
Italian	DD-MM-YY
Japanese	YY/MM/DD
USA	MM-DD-YY
MDY	MM/DD/YY
DMY	DD/MM/YY

▸▸ **NOTE**

The YY form is used when CENTURY is OFF. YYYY is used when CENTURY is ON.

Syntax

SET DATE [TO]
AMERICAN ¦ ANSI ¦ BRITISH ¦ FRENCH ¦ GERMAN ¦ ITALIAN
¦ JAPAN ¦ USA ¦ MDY ¦ DMY ¦ YMD

Example

```
SET DATE TO JAPAN
```

The SET DATE TO Command

The SET DATE TO command accepts a date as a character string and assigns its value to the system date. This is the same as using the DOS DATE command.

NOTE

The SET DATE TO argument is a character string. The string "12/31/95" works, but {12/31/95} is not accepted.

Syntax

SET DATE TO *<expC>*

Example

```
SET DATE TO "12/31/95"
```

The SET DBTYPE TO Command

The SET DBTYPE TO command selects .DB tables (Paradox) or .DBF tables (dBASE) as the default type for tables.

Syntax

```
SET DBTYPE TO [PARADOX ¦ DBASE]
```

The SET DECIMALS Command

The SET DECIMALS TO command specifies the number of decimals to display.

Syntax

SET DECIMALS TO [*<expN >*]

Example

Here's an example of using SET DECIMALS TO in the Command window:

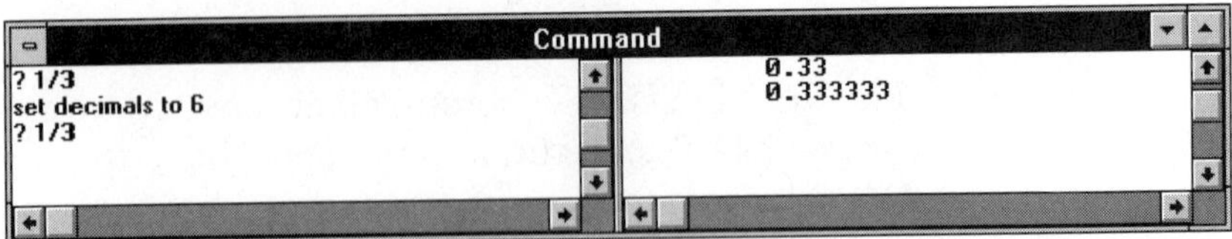

The SET DEFAULT Command

The SET DEFAULT TO command selects a disk drive.

Syntax

```
SET DEFAULT TO [<drive>[:]]
```

Example

```
SET DEFAULT TO D:
```

The SET DELETED Command

When ON, SET DELETED treats deleted records as if they were physically deleted. When OFF, it treats deleted records as if they were only flagged for deletion. Pressing the default status is saved in DBASE WIN.INI and may be seen in the Desktop Properties dialog box.

Syntax

```
SET DELETED ON ¦ OFF
```

The SET DELIMITERS Command

When ON, SET DELIMITERS adds delimiter characters to older screen input/output (I/O) commands.

Syntax

```
SET DELIMITERS ON ¦ OFF
```

The SET DELIMITERS TO Command

The SET DELIMITERS TO command specifies the character to be used for delimiters when SET DELIMITERS is ON.

Syntax

SET DELIMITERS TO [*<expC>* ¦ DEFAULT]

The SET DESIGN Command

The SET DESIGN command, when ON, allows the use of Design mode. If OFF, only Run mode is permitted.

Syntax

SET DESIGN ON ¦ OFF

The SET DEVELOPMENT Command

The SET DEVELOPMENT command, if OFF, suppresses automatic recompilation of programs that have source forms more recent than their object forms. If SET DEVELOPMENT is ON, dBASE for Windows compares the date and time a .WFO file, for example, was last updated to the date and time of the corresponding .WFM file. If the .WFM file is more recent, it is recompiled.

►► **TIP**

The date/time comparisons take very little time. Leave DEVELOPMENT ON whenever possible.

Syntax

SET DEVELOPMENT ON ¦ OFF

The SET DEVICE TO Command

The SET DEVICE TO command selects the destination for streaming output, such as output from the ? command.

Syntax

SET DEVICE TO SCREEN ¦ PRINTER ¦ FILE *<filename>* ¦ ? ¦ *<filename skeleton>*

The SET DIRECTORY TO Command

The SET DIRECTORY TO command specifies the current directory.

Syntax

```
SET DIRECTORY TO [<path >]
```

Example

```
SET DIRECTORY TO \DBWORK
```

The SET DISPLAY TO Command

The SET DISPLAY TO command selects a display type. This provides compatibility with older text-mode programs.

Syntax

```
SET DISPLAY TO MONO ¦ COLOR ¦ EGA25 ¦ EGA43 ¦ MONO 43 ¦
VGA25 ¦ VGA43 ¦ VGA50
```

The SET ECHO Command

The SET ECHO command is a synonym for DEBUG. (In older versions of dBASE, it echoed commands to the console, which was useful in debugging programs.)

Syntax

```
SET ECHO ON ¦ OFF
```

The SET EDITOR TO Command

The SET EDITOR TO command sets the editor used for text files to the specified executable file.

Syntax

```
SET EDITOR TO [<expC >]
```

The SET ERROR TO Command

The SET ERROR TO command specifies a string to precede, and, optionally, one to follow, run-time error messages from dBASE for Windows.

Syntax

```
SET ERROR TO [<precedingexpC>[, <followingexpC >]]
```

The SET ESCAPE Command

The SET ESCAPE command, if ON, lets you press the Esc key to interrupt a running program.

WARNING

Never set ESCAPE OFF until you are absolutely sure that your program doesn't have any errors that could cause an infinite loop (such as forgetting to SKIP in a DO WHILE .NOT. EOF() loop).

Syntax

```
SET ESCAPE ON ¦ OFF
```

The SET EXACT Command

The SET EXACT command controls string comparisons. With EXACT OFF, *Smith* equals *S*. With EXACT ON, comparison is made to the length of the longer string. A longer string matches a shorter one only if the extra characters in the longer string are all space characters (blank).

Syntax

```
SET EXACT ON ¦ OFF
```

The SET EXCLUSIVE Command

The SET EXCLUSIVE command, if ON, opens all tables for exclusive use.

WARNING

In Microsoft Windows your sessions are individual users of the table. Setting EXCLUSIVE ON will cause your forms to conflict if the users try to use the same table.

Syntax

```
SET EXCLUSIVE ON ¦ OFF
```

The SET FIELDS Command

The SET FIELDS command, if OFF, uses all the fields, not the fields specified in a SET FIELDS command. The SET FIELDS TO command automatically sets FIELDS ON.

Syntax

SET FIELDS ON ¦ OFF

The SET FIELDS TO Command

The SET FIELDS TO command establishes the list of fields that are active in subsequent data table commands.

Syntax

SET FIELDS TO [<*field list*> ¦ ALL [LIKE <*skeleton 1* >] [EXCEPT <*skeleton 2* >]]

Example

SET FIELDS TO Last_name, Full_name, City, Phone

The SET FILTER TO Command

The SET FILTER TO command establishes a condition that records must meet to appear in the table.

Syntax

SET FILTER TO [<*condition* >] ¦ [FILE <*filename*> ¦ ? ¦ <*filename skeleton* >]

Example

SET FILTER TO State = 'CA'

The SET FULLPATH Command

When ON, the SET FULLPATH command causes functions such as CATALOG() and MDX() to return a full path specification with the file name.

Syntax

SET FULLPATH ON ¦ OFF

The SET FUNCTION Command

The SET FUNCTION command causes the specified key to be equal to typing the character expression. If the last character in the expression is a semicolon, an Enter keypress is substituted for the semicolon.

Syntax

SET FUNCTION <*key*> TO <*expC*>

Example

```
SET FUNCTION F9 TO 'DO people.wfm;'
```

The SET HEADINGS Command

The SET HEADINGS command controls the use of default (field name) headings for commands such as DISPLAY and SUM. If ON, the headings are used.

Syntax

SET HEADINGS ON ¦ OFF

The SET HELP TO Command

The SET HELP TO command is used to change Help files. If you build a Help file for your own system (with a Help file builder, such as Borland's ForeHelp), you can activate it with this command.

Syntax

SET HELP TO [<*help filename*> ¦ ? ¦ <*help filename skeleton* >]

The SET IBLOCK TO Command

The SET IBLOCK TO command overrides the BLOCKSIZE setting for index blocks only. It sets the size of index blocks. The number given is the number of 512-byte blocks to allocate for each index blocks. The minimum is 2 (1024 bytes).

Syntax

SET IBLOCK TO <*expN*>

The SET INDEX TO Command

The SET INDEX TO command opens one or more index files or specifies the master index tag in an open index file.

Syntax

```
SET INDEX TO [<filename list> ¦ ? ¦ <filename skeleton list >]
  [ORDER [TAG] <filename 1> ¦ <tag name> [OF
  <filename 2> ¦ ? ¦ <filename skeleton >]]
```

Examples

```
SET INDEX TO TAG Last_name
SET INDEX TO special.mdx
```

The SET KEY Command

The SET KEY command sets a key to call a program file or subroutine in a program file.

Syntax

```
SET KEY <expN> ¦ <expC> TO [<program name> ¦ <procedure
name >]
```

Examples

```
SET KEY "F2" TO open_it
SET KEY "F3" TO close_it
```

The SET KEY TO Command

The SET KEY TO command specifies a value or range of values for the master index.

Syntax

```
SET KEY TO [<exp list 1> ¦ RANGE <exp 2> [,] ¦ , <exp 3> ¦ <exp
2 >, <exp 3 > [LOW <exp list 2> [,] ] [HIGH [,] <exp list 3 >]
[EXCLUDE]
```

Examples

These examples assume a master index on the STATE field:

SET KEY TO 'CA', 'NY'	California and New York
SET KEY TO RANGE ,'CA'	Start through California
SET KEY TO RANGE 'NY'	New York to end
SET KEY TO RANGE 'CA','NY'	California through New York

The SET LDCHECK Command

The SET LDCHECK command tells dBASE for Windows that you do, or do not, want it to check that the language driver conforms to the DOS code page.

▶▶ NOTE

LDCHECK is a necessary check if you are preparing a system to be used in multiple countries.

Syntax

```
SET LDCHECK ON ¦ OFF
```

The SET LIBRARY TO Command

The SET LIBRARY TO command specifies a file of subroutines that will be accessed by your other program files. The LIBRARY file is the last place that dBASE for Windows will look for a subroutine that it needs.

Syntax

SET LIBRARY TO [<*filename*> ¦ ? ¦ <*filename skeleton* >]

The SET LOCK Command

The SET LOCK command affects the locking status of certain commands, such as SUM, that read values from a table. With LOCK ON, the table is locked, which prevents other users from accessing it but ensures that the returned value is correct as of the instant it is calculated. With LOCK OFF, another user can update a value just before or after the SUM command reads a record.

Syntax

```
SET LOCK ON ¦ OFF
```

The SET MARGIN TO Command

The SET MARGIN TO command sets the left margin for printed reports.

Syntax

```
SET MARGIN TO <expN>
```

The SET MARK TO Command

The SET MARK TO command sets the character used in formatting dates.

Syntax

```
SET MARK TO [<expC >]
```

Example

```
SET MARK TO '/'
```

The SET MBLOCK TO Command

The SET MBLOCK TO command sets the size of Memo field blocks. Its value is in units of 64 bytes each (1 is 64, 2 is 128, and so on).

TIP

Smaller memo blocks waste less disk space; larger ones run faster if you have large Memo fields. With today's disk-compression technology, the wasted space is for the most part insignificant, so opt for efficiency.

Syntax

SET MBLOCK TO <*expN*>

The SET MEMOWIDTH TO Command

The SET MEMOWIDTH TO command sets the display width for Memo fields.

Syntax

SET MEMOWIDTH TO [<*expN* >]

The SET MESSAGE TO Command

The SET MESSAGE TO command sets the message that is displayed on the left side of the status bar.

Syntax

SET MESSAGE TO [<*message expC* >]

The SET NEAR Command

The SET NEAR command determines the position of the record pointer after a SEEK command that does not find its target value. With NEAR OFF, the pointer is set at EOF (end of file). With NEAR ON, the record pointer stops at the first record after the SEEK value.

Syntax

SET NEAR ON ¦ OFF

The SET ODOMETER TO Command

The SET ODOMETER TO command controls the display of record counts in the status bar for commands such as APPEND and COPY. The odometer setting is the increment at which the odometer is updated.

Syntax

```
SET ODOMETER TO [<expN >]
```

Example

```
SET ODOMETER TO 100
```

Updates the status bar with every 100 records processed.

The SET ORDER TO Command

The SET ORDER TO command specifies an index tag in the production index, or selects a tag by number or specifies a new .MDX file for the master index and picks a tag in the new .MDX file.

Syntax

```
SET ORDER TO [<index position expN >] ¦
        [<.ndx filename 1 >] [NOSAVE] ¦
        [TAG] <tag name> [OF <filename> ¦ ? ] [NOSAVE]
```

Examples

```
SET ORDER TO 3
```

Uses the third tag

```
SET ORDER TO Last_name
```

The SET PATH TO Command

The SET PATH TO command sets one or more paths to search for files, or, with the path list omitted, turns off the former path settings.

Syntax

```
SET PATH TO [<path list >]
```

Examples

```
SET PATH TO D:\DBWORK, C:\GENERAL
SET PATH TO
```

The SET PCOL TO Command

The SET PCOL TO command sets the current printer column (horizontal position).

Syntax

```
SET PCOL TO <expN>
```

The SET POINT TO Command

The SET POINT TO command specifies the character to use between the whole and fractional parts of a number.

Syntax

```
SET POINT TO [<expC >]
```

The SET PRECISION TO Command

The SET PRECISION TO command sets the number of decimal places dBASE for Windows uses when it compares numbers. The range is 10–19.

Syntax

```
SET PRECISION TO [<expN >]
```

The SET PRINTER Command

The SET PRINTER command turns files or devices that are receiving printer output on or off. (It does not turn the physical printer on or off.)

Syntax

```
SET PRINTER ON ¦ OFF
```

The SET PRINTER TO Command

The SET PRINTER TO command establishes an alternate file of device for printer output.

Syntax

```
SET PRINTER TO [[FILE] <filename> ¦ ? ¦ <filename skeleton >] ¦
[<device >]
```

Example

```
SET PRINTER TO FILE print.tmp
```

The SET PROCEDURE TO Command

The SET PROCEDURE TO command establishes a file (usually a .PRG file) where dBASE for Windows will look for subroutines that it cannot find in its main program. The ADDITIVE clause adds the subroutines in the specified PROCEDURE file to any others that are already available. Without ADDITIVE, the PROCEDURE file replaces any other PROCEDURE files. When searching for subroutines, dBASE for Windows looks in PROCEDURE files before it looks in the LIBRARY file.

Syntax

```
SET PROCEDURE TO [<filename> ¦ ? ¦ <filename skeleton >]
[ADDITIVE]
```

Example

```
SET PROCEDURE TO my_subrs.prg ADDITIVE
```

The SET PROW TO Command

The SET PROW TO command sets the printer's row (vertical position).

Syntax

```
SET PROW TO <expN>
```

The SET REFRESH TO Command

The SET REFRESH TO command specifies the number of seconds (0 to 3600) that elapse between dBASE for Windows refreshing client screens with data from the file server. Frequent refreshes ensure that each simultaneous user is looking at the same data, but they slow overall performance.

Syntax

```
SET REFRESH TO <expN>
```

The SET RELATION TO Command

The SET RELATION TO command establishes relationships between two or more tables. The Query Designer writes SET RELATION commands for you, based on a visual representation. Its output is a .QBE file, which includes SET RELATION commands. For more information about setting relations, refer to Chapter 5.

WARNING

Writing SET RELATION commands is tricky, at best, and terrifying, at worst. Running the Query Designer makes designing the relationships simple. When you save your work, dBASE for Windows does the hard work of writing SET RELATION commands.

Syntax

```
SET RELATION TO
    [<key exp list 1> ¦ <expN 1>
    INTO <child table alias 1>
    [, <key exp list 2> ¦ <expN 2>
    INTO <child table alias 2 >] ... ]
    [ADDITIVE]]
```

For dBASE for Windows tables only:

```
SET RELATION TO
    [<key exp list 1> ¦ <expN 1>
    INTO <child table alias 1>
    [CONSTRAIN]
    [INTEGRITY]
      [CASCADE ¦ RESTRICTED] ]
    [, <key exp list 2> ¦ <expN 2>
        INTO <child table alias 2 >]
        [CONSTRAIN]
        [INTEGRITY]
        [CASCADE ¦ RESTRICTED] ] ... ]
    [ADDITIVE]
```

The SET REPROCESS TO Command

The SET REPROCESS TO command specifies the number of times dBASE for Windows will repeat an attempt to get access to a locked record or file before giving up and reporting a locking error. The default is 0; the maximum is 32000. A count of –1 tells dBASE to keep trying and never give up.

▸▸ **WARNING**

Avoid large retry numbers. If someone else has locked a record or table, you can always try again yourself after dBASE for Windows gives you an error message. Never use –1, unless you want to "hang" your computer.

Syntax

```
SET REPROCESS TO <expN>
```

The SET SAFETY Command

When the SET SAFETY command is ON, it causes dBASE for Windows to prompt you before overwriting a file or deleting all the records in a table or other activities about which you might want to think twice.

▸▸ **WARNING**

The only time to set SAFETY OFF is when you know that you are going to overwrite a scratch, temporary file, with another one. When your program turns it off, be sure it turns it back on again almost immediately.

Syntax

```
SET SAFETY ON | OFF
```

Example

```
SET SAFETY OFF
SET ALTERNATE TO t.tmp
SET ALTERNATE ON
```

```
SET SAFETY ON
```

The SET SEPARATOR Command

The SET SEPARATOR command specifies the character that is used to separate the whole part of numbers into groups of three digits each.

Syntax

SET SEPARATOR TO [<*expC* >]

The SET SKIP TO Command

The SET SKIP TO command specifies the record pointer advancement order when you have two or more related tables. Although the SET SKIP command is much simpler than the SET RELATION command, if you use (as we recommend) the Query Designer to define your tables' relationships, your SET SKIP commands will be correctly written for you by the Query Designer. See the SET RELATION command for more on this subject.

Syntax

SET SKIP TO [<*alias 1*> [, <*alias 2* >] ...]

The SET SPACE Command

The SET SPACE command, if set ON, has dBASE for Windows include a space between fields in an output field list in commands such as ? and ??.

Syntax

SET SPACE ON ¦ OFF

The SET STATUS Command

The SET STATUS command turns the status bar on or off.

Syntax

SET STATUS ON ¦ OFF

The SET STEP Command

The SET STEP command is a synonym for DEBUG. Earlier versions of dBASE, which lacked a real debugging tool, let you SET STEP ON, which meant running a program one line at a time, pausing after each command.

Syntax

```
SET STEP ON ¦ OFF
```

The SET TALK Command

The SET TALK command turns the echo of command results to the results pane of the Command window on or off.

Syntax

```
SET TALK ON ¦ OFF
```

The SET TIME TO Command

The SET TIME TO command is similar to the DOS TIME command. It sets the system time.

Syntax

```
SET TIME TO <expC>
```

Example

```
SET TIME TO "13:30:30"
```

The SET TITLE Command

When the SET TITLE command is ON, it asks dBASE to prompt you for title and comment information when CATALOG is ON. (This adds descriptive information to each file in the catalog.)

Syntax

```
SET TITLE ON ¦ OFF
```

The SET TOPIC TO Command

The SET TOPIC TO command specifies the current Help topic. This is not useful in the Command window, since the HELP command itself takes a topic parameter (for example, HELP CLASS BROWSE), but it can be useful in a program to control the results you get when you press F1.

Syntax

```
SET TOPIC TO [<expC >]
```

Example

```
SET TOPIC TO "CLASS BROWSE"
```

The SET TYPEAHEAD TO Command

The SET TYPEAHEAD TO command sets the size of the typeahead buffer. The range is 0–1600 characters.

Syntax

```
SET TYPEAHEAD TO <expN>
```

The SET UNIQUE Command

When the SET UNIQUE command is ON, it suppresses entry of multiple records with identical key values in an index file. If it is OFF, every record is indexed. If ON, only the first record that has a key value is entered into the index. Subsequent records with the same value are not indexed.

Syntax

```
SET UNIQUE ON ¦ OFF
```

The SET VIEW Command

The SET VIEW command specifies a query file (.QBE) to be used as the current database view.

Syntax

```
SET VIEW TO <filename> ¦ ? ¦ <filename skeleton>
```

Example

```
SET VIEW TO phones_b.qbe
```

The SET WP TO Command

The SET WP TO command specifies the executable file to be used as the editor for Memo fields.

Syntax

SET WP TO [<*expC* >]

The SHOW OBJECT Command

The SHOW OBJECT command refreshes the display of an object on a form. If you changed a bitmap, you could refresh the display of an Image or Pushbutton object that used the bitmap.

Syntax

SHOW OBJECT <*form name*>.<*object name*>

The SKIP Command

The SKIP command moves the record pointer the specified number of records forward (backward if the number is negative). If you have multiple tables open, the IN <*alias*> clause lets you specify a table other than the one in the currently selected work area as the one to skip.

Syntax

SKIP [<*expN* >] [IN <*alias* >]

Examples

SKIP	Current table, defaults to 1
SKIP -1	Back up one
SKIP 5 IN orgs	5 forward in the Orgs table

The SLEEP Command

The SLEEP command causes dBASE for Windows to "go to sleep" (be inactive) for the specified number of seconds, or until the specified time on the specified date. If the date is omitted, the UNTIL time applies to today.

This command can be used to have dBASE wait a bit (for example, when a necessary table is locked), or it can be used to set up a program that should be run later (such as a backup process that you want to run after midnight).

Syntax

SLEEP <*seconds expN*> ¦ UNTIL <*time expC*> [, <*date expC* >]

Example

This example tells dBASE for Windows to get up late tomorrow morning:

```
SLEEP UNTIL "11:00:00", DATE()+1
```

The SORT Command

The SORT command sorts one table into another table. (Sorting is covered in Chapter 4.)

TIP

Use the Table Utilities menu to sort a table. You should almost never need to put a SORT command into a program. If you do, use Table Utilities and copy the command it writes into the Command window.

Syntax

SORT TO <*filename*> ¦ ? ¦ <*filename skeleton*>
[[TYPE] PARADOX ¦ DBASE]
ON <*field 1*> [/A ¦ /D [/C]]
[,<*field 2*> [/A ¦ /D [/C]] ...]
[<*scope* >]
[FOR <*condition 1* >]
[WHILE <*condition 2* >]
[ASCENDING ¦ DESCENDING]

The STORE Command

The STORE command is synonymous with the assignment statement. Both of these are the same:

```
STORE 123 TO x
```

```
x = 123
```

The STORE command is the handier form when you want to store one value into more than one memory variable or array element.

Syntax

STORE <*exp*> TO <*memvar list*> ¦ <*array element list*>

or

<*memvar*> ¦ <*array element*> = <*exp*>

Example

In this example, we initialize variables prior to doing a calculation:

```
STORE 0 TO qty_on_hand, sales_to_date, taxes_due
```

The STORE AUTOMEM Command

The STORE AUTOMEM command copies every field in the current record to a memory variable with the same name as the field. This lets you build forms that use the memory variables as DataLink properties.

Using fields, if you make changes and then decide to quit without saving (clicking a Cancel button, for example), your program must go to considerable trouble to undo the changes. If the form used memory variables, no additional work is needed.

Syntax

```
STORE AUTOMEM
```

The STORE MEMO Command

The STORE MEMO command puts a Memo field into an array. Each element of the array is filled with text from the Memo field, up to the length set with MEMOWIDTH.

Syntax

STORE MEMO <*memo field*> TO ARRAY <*array name*>

The SUM Command

The SUM command lets you sum one or more fields or expressions over part or all of a table, optionally storing the results to one or more memory variables or an array.

Syntax

```
SUM
  [<exp list >]
  [<scope >]
  [FOR <condition 1 >]
  [WHILE <condition 2 >]
  [TO <memvar list > ¦ ARRAY <array name >]
```

Example

```
SUM Price*Quantity TO M->sales
```

The SUSPEND Command

The SUSPEND command halts program execution and places you in the Command window. You place a SUSPEND command in a program when it is not working as you planned and you want to investigate the possible cause of an error.

You insert the SUSPEND command near your suspected problem area and then run the program. When it is suspended, you can use ? commands to examine your data, or type in the following program commands one at a time to see what is going wrong.

Syntax

```
SUSPEND
```

The TOTAL Command

The TOTAL command sums all records with matching key values from one table into a single record in a second table.

Syntax

```
TOTAL ON <key expC> TO <filename> ¦ ? ¦ <filename skeleton>
  [[TYPE] PARADOX ¦ DBASE]
  [<scope >]
  [FOR <condition 1 >]
  [WHILE <condition 2 >]
  [FIELDS <field list >]
```

Example

The following TOTAL command creates a new table, St_Tot, which will have one record for each value of the index "State" in the Custmers table. The St_Tot table will total each of the Numeric and Float fields from the Custmers table. The value in each will be the total of the records for each state in the Custmers table.

```
USE custmers ORDER state
TOTAL ON state TO st_tot
```

The TYPE Command

The TYPE command is analogous to the DOS TYPE command. It will display the contents of a text file in the Command window's results pane. The MORE clause is similar to the DOS more pipe; it pauses typing each time the results pane is filled with text. The NUMBER clause adds line numbers to the display. The TO clause lets you redirect output to a file or to the printer.

Syntax

```
TYPE <filename 1> ¦ ? ¦ <filename skeleton>
  [MORE]
  [NUMBER]
  [TO FILE <filename 2> ¦ ? ¦ PRINTER]
```

The UNLOCK Command

The UNLOCK command releases any file or record locks in the current work area and in tables related with SET RELATION commands to the current work area.

Syntax

```
UNLOCK [ALL ¦ IN <alias >]
```

The UPDATE Command

The UPDATE command copies values from a specified table into the current table, based on matching index values.

Syntax

```
UPDATE ON <key exp> FROM <alias>
  REPLACE <field 1> WITH <exp 1>
```

```
    [, <field 2> WITH <exp 2> ... ]
  [RANDOM]
  [REINDEX]
```

Example

Assume that you have an Invoic table and an Inv_Dtl table. The Inv_Dtl table contains multiple records for each Invoic record. The Inv_Dtl records contain a part ID, the quantity order, and the total cost for that part. Each invoice is related to one or more of these detail records. You could conveniently total the costs for each invoice with a TOTAL command:

```
USE inv_dtl ORDER Invoic_ID
TOTAL ON Invoic_ID TO temp
```

Then you could update your INVOIC file from the TEMP file you just created:

```
USE invoic ORDER Invoic_ID
UPDATE ON Invoic_ID FROM temp ;
  REPLACE tot_cost WITH temp->cost
```

The USE Command

The USE command opens a table. It defaults to a .DBF file unless one of the other types is specified. It will be opened in the current work area, unless the IN clause is used.

A dBASE for Windows table is automatically opened with the production index (the .MDX file that has the same name as the .DBF file) unless the INDEX clause is used to specify an alternate index.

No master index is used unless the ORDER clause is specified. The keyword TAG may be used if you find it more readable.

If you specify AGAIN, you can open a table that is also open in one or more other work areas.

The default alias name of a table is the table's name. With the ALIAS clause, you can specify an alternate name.

The AUTOMEM clause causes dBASE for Windows to create a set of memory variables whose names match the names of the fields in the table (see STORE AUTOMEM).

The EXCLUSIVE or SHARED clause overrides the setting of SET EXCLUSIVE.

NOSAVE opens the table for temporary use. It is deleted (along with related files) when it is closed.

NOUPDATE opens the table for read-only use.

Syntax

```
USE
  [<filename 1> ¦ ? ¦ <filename skeleton 1>
  [[TYPE] PARADOX ¦ DBASE] ¦ [DATABASE <database name >]
  [IN <alias >]
  [INDEX <index name list> ¦ <? list> ¦ <index name skeleton
  list >]
  [ORDER [TAG] <.ndx filename> ¦
      <tag name>[OF <.mdx filename >]]
  [AGAIN]
  [ALIAS <alias name >]
  [AUTOMEM]
  [EXCLUSIVE ¦ SHARED]
  [NOSAVE]
  [NOUPDATE]]
```

Example

Assume your system is for many stores, and you have a table for each store's sales. Your program could say:

```
USE store_1 ALIAS sales
DO my_prog

USE store_2 ALIAS sales
DO my_prog
```

Your my_prog routine would be programmed to use a Sales table and would work for any .DBF name.

The WAIT Command

The WAIT command can be used to pause output displayed in the Command window's results pane or program execution. The optional prompt replaces the default "Press any key to continue" message. The TO clause provides a memory variable to record the key pressed to continue.

Syntax

```
WAIT [<prompt expC >] [TO <memvar >]
```

Example

```
USE my_table
DO WHILE .NOT. EOF()
  LIST NEXT 10
  WAIT "Press Y to continue" TO key_pressed
  IF UPPER(key_pressed) <> 'Y'
    EXIT
  ENDIF
ENDDO
```

The ZAP Command

The ZAP command deletes every record in a table. (It is much faster than the equivalent DELETE ALL and PACK.) The ZAP command displays the Zap Records dialog box, which asks you if you want to delete every record in the table, unless SAFETY is off. The operation requires exclusive use of the table.

Syntax

```
ZAP
```

Example

```
USE scratch EXCLUSIVE
SET SAFETY OFF
ZAP
SET SAFETY ON
```

►► *Summary*

We divided all dBASE for Windows commands into two categories: programming statements and commands. The commands are lines that start with a verb, such as:

```
USE
LIST
SUM
```

The statements are the lines that control the execution of commands, and are covered separately in Chapter 14.

From the total set of commands, we placed those that are provided to support dBASE IV and older programs in Appendix D. In this chapter, we covered the commands that are used in the Command window and dBASE for Windows programs.

We divided the remaining commands into six categories. We listed the commands in each of these categories, and then gave you an alphabetical list showing the syntax and explaining the use of each command.

In the next chapter, we'll complete Part 4 with an overview of the programming statements.

▶ ▶ CHAPTER 14

Basics of Programming Statements

▶▶ **In** Chapter 12 we looked at dBASE for Windows expressions and functions. In Chapter 13 you met the Command window commands. The commands give you tremendous data-manipulation power, and the expressions let you specify indexes, data scopes, and more.

Although you don't need to be a dBASE for Windows programmer to handle your databases, you'll want to be able to put together simple programs to handle events, as you've already been doing in the Form Designer.

So far, you've let the Procedure Editor handle the details for you. In this chapter, you'll learn to use the basic dBASE for Windows program statements. These are program lines that provide structure and control, making decisions on which commands to execute at what times. Let's skip ahead a bit to look at a simple example:

```
IF total_sales <= slow
  REPLACE ALL product->price WITH product->price*0.9
ENDIF
```

The IF statement is one of the block statements. It controls *conditional* execution—one or more commands will be executed if the condition following the word IF evaluates to True. Here, we assume that a variable, *total_sales*, has been calculated, and another variable, *slow*, has been assigned some level of sales that we don't like.

If our sales have been slow, we'll do an across-the-board 10 percent price cut. (This is an example of dBASE programming, not an example of smart retail practice.)

As you can see, these statements are almost self-explanatory. The IF/ENDIF block does just what you might guess. The other good news about dBASE statements is that there aren't very many of them, so you won't have trouble keeping track of all of them.

We'll start with the block statements that you'll use frequently in the Form Designer's Procedure Editor. There are only four blocks to learn. After we're done with blocks, we'll show you the rest, so that you'll be able to read the output from the Form Designer and the Query Designer. But bear in mind that the block statements are the ones you'll need for your mental tool kit. The others are for reference, not daily use.

▶▶ **NOTE**

You may notice that our syntax is not always the syntax that you'll find in the software's language reference or in the on-line documentation. We think that ours is the most accurate documentation available at this time. Of course, we expect that the on-line documentation will be corrected and updated, so it should eventually become the best source.

▶▶ Block Statements

When you use the Procedure Editor in the Form Designer, you'll be developing a single subroutine. Within any routine, the basic order of execution is sequential: the first command is executed, then the second, and so on.

The dBASE for Windows block statements let you vary this in two ways. First, you may wish to execute one or more commands conditionally, as you saw in the example in this chapter's introduction.

The other type of nonsequential operation is called *looping*. If you wanted to perform some operation on each of a dozen items, you could write the logic a dozen times. This is tedious, and gets unreasonable when a dozen items grow to hundreds or thousands of items. Looping lets you write the logic once and apply it to as many items as needed.

Let's start with the conditional statement blocks.

▸ Conditional Execution

There are two conditional execution blocks. The basic IF can be used for any conditional need, but the DO CASE is much easier to write when it applies. We'll begin with IF.

IF

The IF block begins with an IF statement and ends with an ENDIF. You've seen it used to execute a single command. Any number of commands can be placed between the IF and the ENDIF. They are all executed if the IF condition is True. None are executed if the IF condition is False.

The IF block can also contain an ELSE statement, which divides the block into two parts. Commands in the first part are executed if the IF condition is True. Commands in the second part are executed if the IF condition is False.

The syntax of the IF/ELSE command is:

```
IF <condition expL>
    <statements>
  [ELSEIF <condition expL>
    <statements>]...
  [ELSE
    <statements>]
ENDIF
```

This is an example:

```
IF total_sales <= slow

  REPLACE ALL product->price WITH product->price*0.9
  LIST OFF ALL product->name, product->price

ELSE

  REPLACE FOR produce->price > 100 ;
    product->price WITH product->price*1.05
  LIST OFF FOR product->price > 100 ;
    product->name, product->price

ENDIF
```

In this example, all product prices are reduced by 10 percent, and a new price list is printed when *total_sales* is bad. If *total_sales* is greater than *slow*, the products priced over 100 are increased by 5 percent, and a new list of just those product prices is printed.

We've shown two common uses of "white space" (blank lines and spaces within lines). We've indented the commands inside the IF block, and we've set them off with blank lines. Both of these improve the readability of the block. White space has no effect on the execution of the program and has very little effect on the program's size (a blank line adds two bytes to the file size). Use white space generously.

▶▶ **TIP**

Always write the entire block statement before you begin to fill in the details. Write the IF and ENDIF lines, with the ELSE if you want one, for example. Then go back and put the commands in between the IF and ENDIF.

DO CASE

In some situations, you want to implement a variety of rules, covering different possibilities. For these, you could write lots of IF blocks:

```
IF total_sales <= slow

   REPLACE ALL product->price WITH product->price*0.9

ENDIF

IF total_sales > slow .AND. ;
   total_sales <= OK

   REPLACE ALL product->price WITH product->price*0.95

ENDIF

IF total_sales > OK .AND. ;
   total_sales <= fast

   REPLACE ALL product->price WITH product->price*1.05
```

```
ENDIF

IF total_sales > fast

   REPLACE ALL product->price WITH product->price*1.1

ENDIF
```

Although this type of programming works, it isn't much fun to type, and it's error-prone. The DO CASE block does a better job. Here's the same example:

```
DO CASE
   CASE total_sales <= slow
      REPLACE ALL product->price WITH product->price*0.9

   CASE total_sales <= OK
      REPLACE ALL product->price WITH product->price*0.95

   CASE total_sales <= fast
      REPLACE ALL product->price WITH product->price*1.05

   OTHERWISE
      REPLACE ALL product->price WITH product->price*1.1

ENDCASE
```

In a DO CASE block, each CASE is evaluated until one is True. The first one that is True is executed and that completes the block. If none are True, the optional OTHERWISE statement does just what it looks like: it heads a block of commands that execute if none of the CASEs is True.

As you can see in this example, this form simplifies the relational expressions. The second case here, for example says:

```
CASE total_sales <= OK
```

The comparable IF test was:

```
IF total_sales > slow .AND. ;
   total_sales <= OK
```

The CASE is simpler because the test immediately before was:

```
CASE total_sales <= slow
```

If *total_sales* was less than or equal to *slow*, the previous CASE would have been True, its command(s) executed, and the DO CASE terminated. A DO CASE only gets to the second CASE if the first one isn't True. It only gets to the third CASE if both the first and second ones are False, and so on.

The syntax for the DO CASE command is:

```
DO CASE
  [CASE <condition expL>
    <statements>]...
  [OTHERWISE
    <statements>]
ENDCASE
```

▶ Looping

There are three looping blocks in dBASE for Windows. They are the FOR, the DO WHILE, and the DO UNTIL loops. FOR loops are used when you can count a specific number of repetitions. DO WHILE and DO UNTIL loops are used when you want to keep looping as long as some condition is True.

FOR

FOR loops were introduced into the Xbase family from BASIC. The Clipper compiler adopted them, and they were later copied by FoxPro. The DOS and Windows 5.0 products are the first to bring FOR loops into dBASE. We're glad to have them.

The syntax of the FOR command is:

```
FOR <memvar> = <start expN> TO <end expN> [STEP <step expN>]
    <statements>
  [LOOP | EXIT
    <statements>]...
ENDFOR | NEXT
```

There is nothing that the FOR loop can do that the DO WHILE loop can't handle. But since they are more limited, they can get their job done more efficiently than DO WHILE.

Here's a sample FOR loop that writes the numbers 1 through 10 into the Command window's results pane:

```
FOR i = 1 TO 10
   ? i
ENDFOR
```

BASIC's FOR loop is terminated with the NEXT statement. dBASE also allows NEXT as a synonym for ENDFOR. We like ENDFOR because all the other blocks are terminated with an END statement.

By adding the optional STEP clause, you can have the FOR loop work backward, and by units other than 1. Here's one that counts backward from 10 to 1 by halves:

```
FOR i = 10 TO 1 STEP -0.5
   ? i
ENDFOR
```

You can try a simple FOR loop in the Command window, entering it on a single line. Here's how:

```
FOR i = 1 TO 10; ? i; ENDFOR
```

►► **NOTE**

To enter a block command in the Command window, you must put it all on a single line. Use the semicolon to separate the components.

DO WHILE and DO UNTIL

The DO WHILE and DO UNTIL loops are very general. The most common use is to process each record in a table:

```
GO TOP
DO WHILE .NOT. EOF()
   * process the record here
   SKIP
ENDDO
```

You could also write:

```
GO TOP
DO
   * process the record here
   SKIP
UNTIL EOF()
```

The GO TOP command forces the record pointer to the top of the table. The SKIP command advances the pointer by one record. The comment "* process the record here" shows where you would place whatever commands or calculations you would like to do.

You can think of the flow of control in the DO WHILE as starting at the logical expression following the DO WHILE. If it evaluates to True, control passes to the commands inside the DO WHILE. The ENDDO transfers control back to the top, where this repeats.

```
DO WHILE <condition expL>
    <statements>
  [LOOP ¦ EXIT
    <statements>]...
ENDDO
```

The DO UNTIL construct always executes the enclosed commands once. At the UNTIL statement, the logical expression is tested. If it is False, control passes back up to the top of the loop, and the commands in the loop are repeated until the UNTIL expression is True. The syntax is:

```
DO
MS  <statements>
  [LOOP ¦ EXIT
    <statements>]...
UNTIL <condition expL>
```

Use DO WHILE unless you want to be sure your commands get executed at least once. In that case, use DO UNTIL.

The DO WHILE construct tests its condition at the top, so it can execute zero or more times. The DO UNTIL tests at the bottom, so it executes one or more times.

In fact, the second version or our example may have a bug.

```
GO TOP
DO
  * process the record here
  SKIP
UNTIL EOF()
```

This code will probably fail if the table is empty. The DO WHILE version will correctly handle an empty table (by doing nothing).

▸▸ **WARNING**

If you had a dollar for every time a dBASE session was "hung" because someone forgot the SKIP command in a DO WHILE .NOT. EOF(), you would be very rich. If you omit the SKIP, the DO WHILE loop will execute forever (or until you reboot your computer).

LOOP and EXIT

There are two statements that apply inside DO WHILE, DO UNTIL, and FOR loops: LOOP and EXIT. They are usually found inside IF/ENDIF blocks. LOOP transfers control back to the beginning of the loop. EXIT terminates execution of the loop.

Here's an example, with comments in lieu of logic:

```
GO TOP
DO WHILE .NOT. EOF()

  IF && the current record isn't of interest
    SKIP && to the next record
    LOOP && back to the beginning
  ENDIF

  * This is the logic that applies to
  * the right sort of record.

  IF && the current record is the last one of interest
    EXIT && we're done
  ENDIF

  SKIP
ENDDO
```

Although LOOP can occur anywhere in a DO WHILE or FOR loop, it is most common at the top. You know that only some records get special treatment, so you SKIP and LOOP back to the top for the records that you don't want to process.

Similarly, the EXIT statement can be placed anywhere in a DO WHILE, DO UNTIL, or FOR loop, but it is most common near the end. You check for some condition that tells you that you have processed all the records you are interested in.

Combined, these give you the general capability that FOR and WHILE clauses do on commands. LOOPing back to the top if the record doesn't meet a condition is like executing a command FOR that condition. EXITing when a record doesn't meet a condition is like executing WHILE that condition is True.

LOOP and EXIT control the innermost loop in which they occur.

▶ Nesting

The example of LOOP and EXIT statements in the previous section used *nesting*, which is including one block statement within another. There is no limit to the level or kind of nesting that you can do. When you nest block statements, it is particularly important to keep using progressively more indentation levels, or you could easily fall into crossed-block conditions.

Here's the right way:

```
FOR i = 1 TO 5 && loop over 5 work areas

   GO TOP
   DO WHILE .NOT. EOF()

      * do some interesting calculations

      IF && last record of interest?
         EXIT
      ENDIF

      SKIP

   ENDDO

ENDFOR
```

You can use a block statement anywhere that you can use a simple command. What you cannot do is cross them up like this:

```
FOR i = 1 TO 5 && loop over 5 work areas

  GO TOP
  DO WHILE .NOT. EOF()

    * do some interesting calculations

    IF && last record of interest?
      EXIT
ENDFOR && Error!

  ENDDO && Error!

    ENDIF && Error!
```

The last block statement you started must be completed before any prior block statement can be completed. If you start a FOR and then a DO WHILE, you must complete the DO WHILE before you complete the FOR. If you start other block statements inside the DO WHILE, they must all be completed before you finish the DO WHILE.

This is where you'll see that the indentation custom is vitally important. The errors in our example above were fairly obvious. But suppose we weren't in the habit of using white space so generously. Is this example correct?

```
FOR i = 1 TO 5 && loop over 5 work areas
GO TOP
DO WHILE .NOT. EOF()
* do some interesting calculations
IF && last record of interest?
EXIT
SKIP
ENDDO
ENDIF
ENDFOR
```

It's not correct, and dBASE's compiler will tell you so. The good news is that these mistakes are caught when the program is compiled, so it won't start executing and then get into a thorough tangle.

▸▸ Intra-file Program Structure

Within a program file, you can have a mainline and multiple subroutines. When you are in the Procedure Editor in the Form Designer, you are working on a subroutine.

A subroutine begins when you declare it, and it ends at the end of the file or class, or when another subroutine is declared.

▸ Subroutine Declarations

The two types of subroutines that you can declare in dBASE for Windows are PROCEDURE and FUNCTION. The PROCEDURE subroutine does not return a value; the FUNCTION subroutine does return a value. (See Chapter 12 for a discussion of the dBASE for Windows built-in functions.)

We should point out that the above rule can be broken, if you like. FUNCTIONs *must* return values, but PROCEDUREs may be used just like functions. We don't use PROCEDUREs to return values, though, just so that it's easier for us to read our own programs.

The PROCEDURE Statement

A PROCEDURE begins with a PROCEDURE statement. The documentation suggests that a PROCEDURE ends with an optional RETURN statement, but this is not true. RETURN statements are covered a little later. As you'll see, they can be used anywhere.

The syntax for the PROCEDURE command is

```
PROCEDURE <procedure name>[(<parameter list>)]
  [PARAMETERS <parameter list>]
  [[<statements>] RETURN <return exp>]...
```

Here's a simple procedure that prints a full name when first and last names are in the open table:

```
PROCEDURE say_full_name

? RTRIM(first_name)+' '+RTRIM(last_name)

* end of say_full_name
```

When your program does a procedure or function, it temporarily halts and passes control to the subroutine. The subroutine executes its statement, and then returns control to the calling routine. The calling routine resumes executing after the call to the subroutine.

When a PROCEDURE ends (at the end of the file, the class, or when another subroutine is declared), it passes control back to the routine that called it. A RETURN statement can be used to make this explicit. Here's the same example with an explicit RETURN:

```
PROCEDURE say_full_name

? RTRIM(first_name)+' '+RTRIM(last_name)

RETURN && end of say_full_name
```

The syntax of the RETURN command is:

```
RETURN [<return exp> ¦ TO MASTER ¦ TO <routine name> ]
```

Sometimes we use RETURNs, and sometimes we don't. It makes no difference in the program. We always use a comment that identifies the end of the procedure and names the procedure that is ending. In the above examples, this may seem a little redundant. But many procedures grow over time as you add more logic. When the end of the procedure is not on the same page or screen as the start, you'll see that this is a valuable habit.

FUNCTION

The other type of subroutine is the function, declared with the FUNCTION statement. As we noted earlier, FUNCTIONs must return values.

The syntax of the FUNCTION command is:

```
FUNCTION <function name>[(<parameter list>)]
  [PARAMETERS <parameter list>]
  [ [<statements>]
  RETURN <return exp>]...
```

Here is a function that prepares a full name from first and last names, but returns it to the calling program instead of displaying it on the screen:

```
FUNCTION make_full_name
LOCAL s
```

```
s = RTRIM(first_name)+' '+RTRIM(last_name)

RETURN s

* end of make_full_name
```

Functions written this way can be used just like the dBASE for Windows built-in functions. They are used as parts of expressions, just as you see RTRIM used in this function. Here's an example of code that uses that make_full_name( ) function above:

```
* List employees:
USE emps
LIST ALL emp_id, make_full_name()
```

Note that you need the parentheses. These identify the item as a subroutine call.

▶ Other Subroutine Statements

The subroutines above did not have parameters, which sometimes is the case in running code. Frequently, however, functions have parameters.

RETURN statements may mark the end of procedures and functions, but they have other uses, too. These are covered here.

Including Parameters

In a very confusing bit of terminology, you pass *arguments* to functions, and the functions receive *parameters*, which are the same values that you called *arguments* when you were thinking about calling the function.

The syntax of the PARAMETERS command is:

```
PARAMETERS <parameter list>
```

Here is a mainline and function for calculating the cubic volume of cartons:

```
? 'Little one: ' + STR( carton_volume(2, 3, 4) )
? 'Big one: ' + STR( carton_volume(20, 30, 40) )

FUNCTION carton_volume
PARAMETERS height, length, width

RETURN height * length * width
```

```
* end of carton_volume
```

This code will report:

```
Little one:     24
Big one:        24000
```

The call carton_volume(2, 3, 4) is said to *pass the arguments* 2, 3, and 4 to the carton_volume function. In turn, the carton_volume function is said to *receive the parameters* height, length, and width. In this case, height is 2, length is 3, and width is 4.

Parameters may be specified by enclosing them in parentheses in the function declaration line. Here's the same example, with this alternate form:

```
? 'Little one: ' + STR( carton_volume(2, 3, 4) )
? 'Big one: ' + STR( carton_volume(20, 30, 40) )

FUNCTION carton_volume(height, length, width)

RETURN height * length * width

* end of carton_volume
```

There is a subtle difference between these forms that is unimportant if your function, such as this one, does not call other functions you have written. If you start writing functions that call your other functions, you'll want to carefully consider the different scoping.

RETURN

RETURN statements can be used anywhere in a dBASE for Windows program. Their primary use is to RETURN values from functions, or to specify the RETURN of control to the calling routine in procedures. You have seen both of these uses in the examples above.

Here we'll show some of their other uses. First, multiple RETURNs may be used. A typical case is to check for an error condition and RETURN immediately:

```
PROCEDURE long_complicated_proc

IF EOF() && can't do this at EOF()
```

```
   RETURN
ENDIF

* long, complicated set
* of statements here

RETURN && end of long_complicated_proc
```

Functions can also RETURN from different points in the function. Here's an example that returns an adjective describing business conditions:

```
* logic here calculates "unemp_rate"

? "Unemployment is "+unemp_descrip(unemp_rate)

FUNCTION unemp_descrip(urate)

DO CASE
   CASE urate < .02
      RETURN "dangerously low"

   CASE urate < .04
      RETURN "low"

   CASE urate < .06
      RETURN "moderate"

   OTHERWISE
      RETURN "high"

ENDCASE

* end of unemp_descrip
```

Note that some software-engineering theorists recommend that each subroutine have exactly one RETURN point. We disapprove of the indiscriminate use of RETURNs, but think that both the examples above are good examples of well-written, readable, and maintainable code.

►► **WARNING**

You should avoid burying a RETURN someplace in the middle of a complex function that looks like it returns a value from the end. If you have a nonobvious RETURN, put a comment at the end of the routine that says, "* under such and such conditions, there's a RETURN taken 25 lines above." Keep your RETURNs obvious.

DO

You've seen that your functions can be called by including them in expressions, just like the dBASE built-in functions. You call a procedure with the DO statement, giving a command as you would for any other dBASE command:

```
* start of SAY_HI.PRG

DO hello

* end of mainline

PROCEDURE hello
? "Hello, world!"
* end of hello

* end of SAY_HI.PRG
```

The above example is a complete program illustrating the DO command. The DO keyword can be eliminated if you use parentheses following the subroutine name, as in this example:

```
* start of SAY_HI.PRG

hello()

* end of mainline

PROCEDURE hello
? "Hello, world!"
* end of hello
```

```
* end of SAY_HI.PRG
```

In both cases, the subroutine you DO could be either a procedure or a function, but we think that calling functions this way (the value they return will be discarded) doesn't make much sense.

In both cases, parameters can be included with the call. Here's an example showing both ways:

```
* start of SAY_HI.PRG

DO hello WITH "DO/WITH form"
hello("parentheses form")

* end of mainline

PROCEDURE hello(string_to_report)
? string_to_report
* end of hello

* end of SAY_HI.PRG
```

Both calls to hello( ) report their respective argument strings. There is no difference in the compiled code that is produced for these two methods.

TIP

Adopt a consistent method of calling subroutines and stick with it. We like to use DO <*procname*> when there are no arguments and we use the form with parentheses when there are arguments (saves typing).

ON

In addition to explicitly calling your subroutine, you can use an ON command to notify dBASE for Windows that there is a condition to watch for and that your subroutine should be called when it occurs. The ON KEY and ON ERROR commands are two ON commands.

ON KEY is used to assign a dBASE command (a DO command or any other) to respond to a specific keystroke. The ON ERROR command assigns a dBASE command (almost always a DO command, but it could be any other) to execute in response to an error.

The primary use for ON KEY is to respond to an extended set of function keys (F1 is assigned to Help, automatically). ON ERROR's primary use is to gracefully handle multiuser situations, such as attempting to write to a record locked by another user.

The syntax of the ON commands is:

```
ON ERROR [<command>]

ON ESCAPE [<command>]

ON KEY [LABEL <key label>] [<command>]

ON NETERROR [<command>]

ON PAGE [AT LINE <expN> <command>]

ON READERROR [<command>]

ON SELECTION FORM <form name> [<expFP> | <expCB>]
```

▸ CLASS Blocks

Building your own classes is best left to major programming efforts, and we would like to say that they are beyond the scope of this book. But we can't say that.

The problem is that if you have generated your first Form Designer form, you have built your first class using CLASS blocks. That's precisely what a form is—a customized class inheriting the Form class's properties and adding the details specific to your form.

If you look at the generated .WFM file, it starts like this:

```
** END HEADER -- do not remove this line*
* Generated on 07/05/94
*
LOCAL f
f = NEW OBJECTSFORM()
f.Open()

CLASS OBJECTSFORM OF FORM
```

As discuss in Chapter 15, your commands and comments can precede the ** END HEADER line. The Two-Way-Tool capability requires this line. It lets the Form Designer know where its code starts and your code stops.

The next three lines after the comment establish a LOCAL variable (LOCALs are covered later in this chapter, in the section about variable declarations) and creates a NEW instance of your class. The third line launches the form.

The CLASS OBJECTSFORM OF FORM begins a CLASS/ENDCLASS block. The OF FORM tells dBASE for Windows that your OBJECTSFORM class should inherit all the properties (including data, event handlers, and methods) of the Form class.

The CLASS block has this structure:

```
CLASS
  * constructor code
  * method 1
  * method 2
  * ...
ENDCLASS
```


The *constructor code* is the part that runs when you create a member of your class. It will define the text labels, entry fields, pushbuttons, comboboxes, and whatever else builds your form.

The *methods* are subroutines that are specific to your class. For example, you could have an OnResize method that adjusted your form's components sizes when the user resizes the form. This is important when you remember that you could have many sorts of forms which all have their own OnResize methods.

As with the other blocks, you can have as many CLASS blocks as you like, and other blocks can nest inside the CLASS blocks. CLASS blocks themselves cannot be nested, however.

The syntax of the CLASS command is:

```
   CLASS <class name> [(parameters)] [CUSTOM]
   PARAMETERS [(parameters)]
   [OF <base class name>] [(parameters)]
   [<constructor code>]
   [<member functions>]
ENDCLASS
```

▸▸ Inter-file Program Structure

Two commands, SET PROCEDURE and SET LIBRARY, give you access to classes and subroutines spread over multiple files. Additionally, the DO command will also let you run code in a separate file.

▸ The SET PROCEDURE Command

The SET PROCEDURE command informs dBASE for Windows that your subroutines and classes may be found in a separate file. This example lets your program use code in the MY_LIB.PRG file:

```
SET PROCEDURE TO my_lib
```

The procedure file does not need to be in your current working directory. (Normally, you move your procedure files to a separate directory when all their programs are fully debugged.) This example uses a procedure file in another directory:

```
SET PROCEDURE TO \dbwork\lib\my_lib
```

These examples opened a single file as *the* procedure file. You may want to have more than one open. In this case, use the ADDITIVE keyword:

```
SET PROCEDURE TO my_lib
SET PROCEDURE TO another_lib ADDITIVE
```

▸▸ TIP

We always include the ADDITIVE keyword. If no other procedure files are open, it has no effect. Other routines elsewhere may be depending on open procedure files, so you want to be sure you don't inadvertently close them.

You may close all open procedure files with the simplest form of the SET PROCEDURE command:

```
SET PROCEDURE TO
```

Without a parameter, all open procedure files are closed.

▶ The SET LIBRARY Command

The LIBRARY file is a special case of a PROCEDURE file. You get exactly one library file, and it has a special place (last) in the search order. It has the same capabilities as the PROCEDURE file, except that it does not accept the ADDITIVE keyword.

Over time, you may find that you have created several subroutines that you use in different systems. These should be placed in your library file.

To open a library file:

```
SET LIBRARY TO my_lib
```

To open a library file in another directory:

```
SET LIBRARY TO \dbwork\lib\my_lib
```

To close the library file:

```
SET LIBRARY TO
```


▶ The DO Command

We have used DO to call a subroutine in the same file as itself. DO has much more power than that. First, the file name alone is the name of the code that comes before any subroutine or class declaration. It can be used as a subroutine. Here's an example, where the main routine calls another file as a subroutine. We'll start with the main routine:

```
* Start of MAIN.PRG

DO banger

* end of MAIN.PRG
```

This is the subroutine file:

```
* Start of BANGER.PRG

? 'BIIGGG BBBBAAAAANNNNNNGGGGGGG!!!!!!!!'

* end of BANGER.PRG
```

Running the mainline will get the big bang from BANGER.PRG. Both MAIN and BANGER could also have additional subroutines and classes.

This means, of course, that you could have two subroutines with the same name. How does dBASE decide which to use? The answer is that it knows by the search order.

The Search Order

dBASE for Windows searches for a subroutine in a specific order. First, it looks in the file where the subroutine (procedure or function) is called. All this searching stops as soon as dBASE finds the subroutine it's looking for. If it finds it in the current file, it looks no further.

If it can't find the subroutine in the current file, dBASE looks in any other running files. In the previous example, MAIN.PRG called BANGER.PRG. If BANGER called another subroutine, dBASE would look in BANGER first, then in MAIN.

Next, dBASE looks in any PROCEDURE files (files opened with SET PROCEDURE commands). It examines PROCEDURE files in the order they were opened with SET PROCEDURE commands.

If it still hasn't found the routine, dBASE looks in your LIBRARY file (if you have SET LIBRARY to a file). This means that your LIBRARY file has last priority, which is useful. If your LIBRARY file has a routine that you want to modify for just one application, put the modified version in a PROCEDURE file opened in that application. Your other applications will still access the standard LIBRARY version.

Finally, dBASE looks for a program file (.PRG extension) whose name matches the subroutine's name. It looks first in the current directory, and then follows your search path, if you've specified one.

And there's one more detail. dBASE looks for a .PRG and a .PRO file. The .PRO file is the compiled version of the .PRG file. If it finds both, it compares their time/date stamps. If the .PRG file has been modified (changed after the .PRO file was created), dBASE recompiles the .PRG file to create a new .PRO file. If dBASE can't find the .PRG file, it will use the .PRO file as is. If it finds a .PRG file but not a .PRO file, it will compile to .PRO and then use that .PRO.

Shortening the Search

If you specify a path with the DO command, dBASE assumes that you want to run the .PRG file you specified. In our big bang example, we could have written:

```
DO \dbwork\banger
```

In this form, there is no search. dBASE compares the .PRG file to the .PRO file, recompiles if necessary, and runs the program.

▶▶ **NOTE**

You can also put subroutines in classes. See a dBASE programming book for details.

▶▶ Variable Declarations

The final class of dBASE for Windows statements we'll consider is the group of variable declarations. In dBASE, these declarations restrict the scope of the variable.

▶ LOCAL Variables

LOCAL variables are new with dBASE for Windows 5.0. For experienced programmers, LOCALs will be by far the most popular data declarations.

The syntax of the LOCAL command is:

LOCAL <*memvar list*>

This example declares three LOCAL variables:

```
LOCAL i, j, summary_total
```

LOCAL variables exist just in the subroutine in which they are declared. No other routine can see them. (This means that no other routine can inadvertently change them.) Every subroutine you have could use the same name, but if the variables are LOCAL, they never conflict.

LOCAL variables are created when the subroutine begins, and they are discarded when the subroutine ends.

► STATIC Variables

STATIC variables are permanent. They are created when the subroutine that declares them starts for the first time. They are discarded when the whole program terminates.

The syntax of the STATIC command is:

```
STATIC <memvar list>
```

The declaration statement can assign a value:

```
STATIC x, y, z
STATIC background_color = 'N/W'
```

The STATIC declaration can mix assignments freely within its variable list. For instance:

```
STATIC x=1, y, z=.T.
```

STATIC variables are used when you want persistent values. You might use one to keep a session-wide total of records added to a file, or to store color specifications and other system settings.

► PRIVATE Variables

PRIVATE data is not in the least PRIVATE. Like a LOCAL, a PRIVATE variable is created by the subroutine that declares it and is discarded when that subroutine terminates. But it is visible to that subroutine and every subroutine called by it.

This is useful only when you have a specific reason for letting a lower-level routine modify a value in the current routine. Software-engineering theorists claim that this should never be done. We almost never use PRIVATEs anymore.

In the early days (before dBASE 5.0) the only scopes you could declare were PUBLIC and PRIVATE. Declaring a variable PRIVATE prevented that variable from inadvertently changing a value in a higher-level routine. So it provided a bit of privacy to the routines above it, but had no privacy with respect to routines that it called, which may not have always declared their variables PRIVATE.

The syntax of the PRIVATE command is:

```
PRIVATE <memvar list> | ALL
```

```
[LIKE <memvar skeleton 1>]
[EXCEPT <memvar skeleton 2>]
```

▶ PUBLIC Variables

PUBLIC data is available to every routine in the system. Importantly, the lifetime of a PUBLIC is the life of your dBASE session, not just the program that creates the variable.

The syntax of the PUBLIC command is:

```
PUBLIC <memvar list> |
  ARRAY <array name 1>"["<expN list 1>"]"
  [, <array name 2>"["<expN list 2>"]"]...
```

Let's look at an example:

```
PUBLIC myform
myform = NEW Form()
myform.Open()
```

When you run this code, you create a PUBLIC variable, assign a reference to a new default form to it, and then open the form. When your form is opened, your program is completed. By making *myform* a PUBLIC variable, you have it still available in the Command window, or to other programs.

In the Command window you could say, for example:

```
INSPECT(myform)
```

If *myform* were not PUBLIC, that INSPECT( ) function would only report that the variable *myform* was undefined. It would have been discarded when the program terminated.

▶ DECLARE Declarations

Arrays are created with DECLARE declarations. An array is a named, sized collection of memory variables.

The syntax of the DECLARE command is:

```
DECLARE <array name 1>"["<expN list 1>"]"
  [,<array name 2>"["<expN list 2>"]"...]
```

These are declarations of one- and two-dimensional arrays:

```
DECLARE names[10]
DECLARE square[5, 5]
DECLARE small[50], medium[500], large[5000]
```

These arrays are then used to store data. For example:

```
DECLARE names[10]

names[1] = "Tom"
names[2] = "Dick"
names[3] = "Harry"
```

►► Adding Comments

As you've seen in this and previous chapters, you can (and should) use comments generously in your program code. There are several ways you can put comments into a dBASE program:

```
&& <comment>

* <comment>

NOTE <comment>
```

►► Other Statements

Some other statements you may use are PRINTJOB and SCAN. The TEXT statement is used in earlier versions of dBASE.

► The PRINTJOB Command

The PRINTJOB block can be used to program the printer directly, without using Crystal Reports. Its syntax is:

```
PRINTJOB
  <commands>
ENDPRINTJOB
```

▶ The SCAN Command

SCAN provides an alternative to the DO WHILE or DO/UNTIL loops. Its syntax is:

```
SCAN... [WHILE <condition 2>]
    [<statements>]
  [LOOP ¦ EXIT
    <statements>]...
ENDSCAN
```

▶ The TEXT Command

The TEXT command is a block statement that is primarily used in dBASE IV and older programs. Its syntax is:

```
TEXT
    <text characters>
ENDTEXT
```

The TEXT block could contain a block of text from one to many lines long. This would be output to the output device. One application of the TEXT block was to write the body of form letters. With dBASE for Windows, the same function is provided by the text capability of Crystal Reports (see Chapter 11.)

▶▶ Summary

In this chapter, you've studied the commands that give the program structure. We call these commands *statements*.

You met the block statements. The conditional blocks are the IF/ELSE/ENDIF test and the DO CASE/CASE/OTHERWISE/ ENDCASE switch. The looping blocks are FOR/ENDFOR, DO WHILE/ENDDO, and DO/UNTIL. The loops can include LOOP and EXIT statements.

You also learned that all the block statements can be nested, and that indenting your code is a good way of making it clear and avoiding errors.

After the block statements, you looked at the structures that are used within a program file. These include the FUNCTION and PROCEDURE subroutine declarations. Other statements used in subroutines are PARAMETERS, RETURN, DO, and ON.

You also studied the CLASS/ENDCLASS blocks. These are always written by the Form Designer when it saves your designs.

You went on to examine the inter-file structure statements, including SET PROCEDURE, SET LIBRARY, and DO. You learned that a program could be used as a subroutine by another program. We discussed the order in which dBASE searches your files for subroutines, and learned to control the one it picks if you have more than one with the same name.

Finally, you met all the variable declaration statements. These are LOCAL, STATIC, PRIVATE, PUBLIC, and DECLARE.

This concludes Part 4. In Part 5, we'll delve into the Form Designer and its associated tools, such as the Menu Designer and the Procedure Editor.

▶ ▶ CHAPTER 15

Designing Forms and Menus

▶▶ **I***n* this chapter, we'll begin our in-depth look at the Form Designer and all its related tools. We'll start with the Form Designer itself, and then branch into the related tools:

- The Object Properties Inspector
- The Controls Palette
- The Procedure Editor

Finally, we'll close with a detailed look at the Menu Designer.

▶▶ *Is It Programming?*

Before we begin, let's consider dBASE for Windows programming. Some of you dove into Part 4 and devoured it with gusto. Others flipped on by it, afraid that it contained some contagious disease. The thought of programming tends to trigger strong reactions, one way or another.

Well, we would like you to think about this: between the two of us, we've logged almost half a century of programming experience, and now we're not sure what "programming" means.

Let's say you have a form with some controls that you want to group together. You go to the Controls palette and pick a Rectangle object. You drop it onto your form, and then put the controls in place inside the rectangle. You press Ctrl-W, and your work is saved.

What is saved is a computer program: your .WFM file. Were you programming? It's hard to find any reason to say that sizing your rectangle and putting some controls inside it wasn't programming. Its result was a precise definition in a form that the computer can understand.

Suppose you had your controls in place before you added the rectangle. You dragged the rectangle into position and saw that it impolitely sat on top of your controls, hiding them. This is not what you want; it's a bug.

So you reorder your controls, putting the rectangle on the bottom and the controls on top. Now it looks better. You've fixed the bug. You never ran the bad version—you could see instantly that it wasn't what you wanted. Programmers have fixed bugs for years by noticing them before they ran their programs.

When we get to reordering our controls, you'll see that the simplest way is *not* to use the Form Designer. It's much easier to shuffle the code around.

We'll show you how to use the Form Designer to reorder your controls, but it's a bit complicated and we recommend that only people who will be building lots and lots of forms (presumably, part- and full-time programmers) use the Form Designer. It's easier to use the Program Editor if you don't have much of this work to do.

Now there's a nice turn of events. We tell you to edit the program, like an old-fashioned programmer, if you don't do a lot of form-design work. The mouse-driven, never-touch-a-line-of-code technique is really only appropriate for programmers.

What's happening here? It seems that the skill called programming is rapidly changing. What used to be done by typing lines of code one at a time is now being done by dragging controls around until they look right.

If you've at least scanned the material in Part 4, you'll be able to put together event handlers—often just a line or two of code—and you'll do the rest of your work at the visual level, except when the simplest way to do something is to edit the .WFM file as a program.

If you really want to be a "programmer" in the old-fashioned way, there are lots of opportunities. After all, it was old-fashioned programming that made the dBASE for Windows table indexes run like greased lightning.

Now let's dive into the Form Designer and find out how to keep that rectangle from hiding our other objects.

▸▸ Working with the Form Designer

The Form Designer is the tool through which dBASE for Windows opens into a much wider world, extending well beyond the boundaries of dBASE for Windows. For example, through the Form Designer, we can add custom controls written in Visual Basic (.VBX files). Programming .VBX files is itself the subject of several books.

The Form Designer also can provide, through the EXTERN command, access to the complete Microsoft Windows application programming interface (API). The API is a subject that has never been adequately covered in a single volume. As you'll see, even within dBASE for Window's own set of objects and properties, there's quite a large universe.

In this section, we'll concentrate on the visual tools of the Form Designer and the Form object.

▸ Lassos and Layouts

First, let's build a form with four Pushbutton objects, which we'll use to explore the lasso and layout tools. Follow these steps:

1. From the Navigator, select the Untitled form. Double-click or press Shift-F2 to launch the Form Designer.
2. The Form Expert will ask you if you want its help or just a Blank Form. Choose the Blank Form and click on the Create button or press Enter. (The Next button changes to the Create button when you click the Blank Form radio button.)
3. Open the Controls palette, if it is not already open. (Use the View menu or the Speed menu.)
4. Click on the Pushbutton control, then drag the outline of a Pushbutton object onto your form.
5. Repeat step 4 three more times, until you have a form with four Pushbutton objects, as shown in Figure 15.1.

Now we want to try the alignment options from the speedbar and from the menus. Before we begin, let's try to align these buttons without help from the Form Designer.

FIGURE 15.1

A Form object with four Pushbutton objects

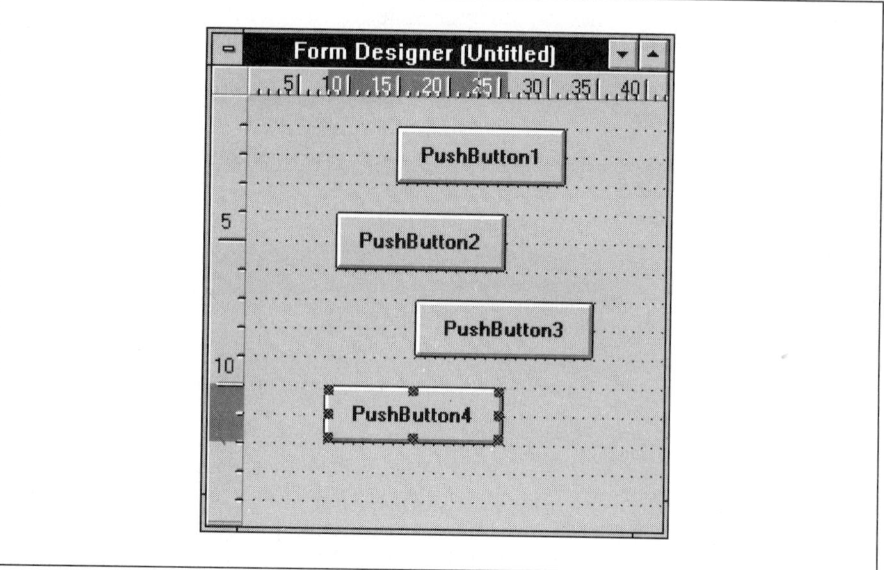

First, attempt to line up each of your pushbuttons' left edges, so that they're in a neat column. (Don't worry about the fact that their widths are different.) Try dragging each of them, in turn, into alignment with the leftmost button.

Don't spend too long trying. When you're convinced that there ought to be a better way, drag a couple of them back to the right so they are nicely messed up again.

Now let's get automated. Click on the top button to select it. Then use either Shift-click or Ctrl-click (there's no difference here) to click on each of the other three buttons to select them as well. To select every object on a form, you can also use Edit ➤ Select All. When you're finished, all four Pushbutton objects should be selected.

Now let's take a look at the speedbar icons for alignment:

As you can see, there are four buttons to align groups of controls on any of four edges: left, right, top, or bottom. If you click on the left-alignment button, for example, the selected controls will be lined up with the left-most control's left edge. Go ahead and try it.

If your controls are not all the same width, try aligning their right edges by clicking the next button.

The first four choices on the Layout menu are alternatives to the four speedbar alignment buttons:

Align Left
Align Right
Align Top
Align Bottom
Align Special ►

Try left- and right-aligning your pushbuttons using this menu.

Now let's go to the rodeo and lasso some controls. Start by clicking anywhere in the form outside the selected controls. This will deselect the controls and select the form. For good measure, drag one or two pushbuttons left or right, dramatically out of position.

Now visualize a rectangle surrounding the bottom three pushbuttons. Click and hold your mouse button down at the upper-right side of this rectangle and drag it to the lower-left. The completion of this lasso process is shown in Figure 15.2.

When you release the mouse button, all the controls that are inside your lasso are selected. In Figure 15.2, the bottom three pushbuttons are selected.

After selecting with the lasso, you can align your buttons with the appropriate choice from the speedbar or from the Layout menu.

►► **WARNING**

Alignments are done as you specify, so be sure you mean what you say. For example, using top or bottom alignment on our sample pushbuttons will create a messy heap of buttons.

FIGURE 15.2

Using the lasso to rope pushbuttons

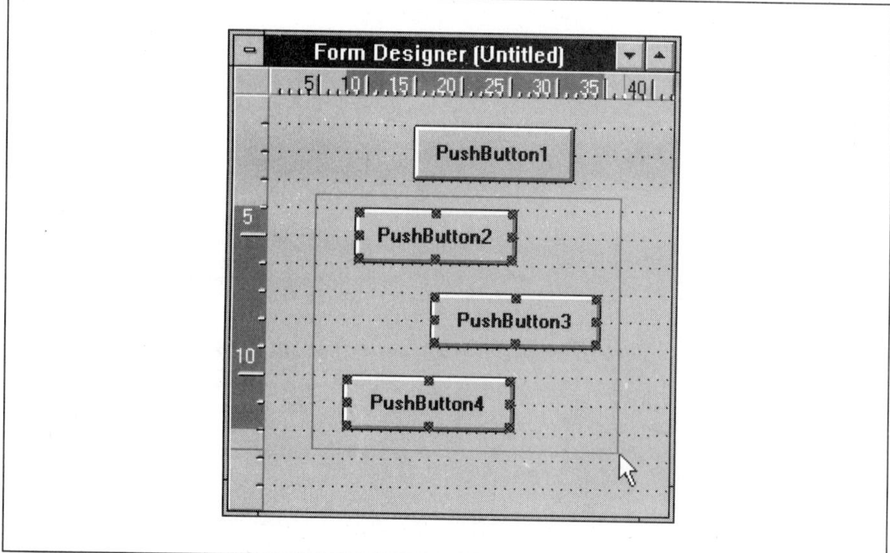

If you make a pile of controls, click in the form outside the selected controls to deselect all of them. Then click once on the pile of controls. That will select whichever one happens to be on top. Using your mouse, drag the selected control off the stack and drop it in an empty area of the form.

Repeat that process, dragging one control at a time off the pile, until you have cleared up the mess. Then use the layout tools (from the Layout menu or speedbar) to line up your controls in a useful fashion.

Before we go on to ordering, we want you to take a look at the Layout ➤ Align Special menu:

When you have selected a group of controls (using the lasso, or click and Shift-click), you can use this menu.

Absolute Horizontal Center
Relative Horizontal Center
Absolute Vertical Center
Relative Vertical Center

The Absolute Horizontal Center option centers each of your controls in the middle (from left to right) of the form. The Relative Horizontal Center option calculates the average center point for the selected items and lines them up on that center.

Similarly, the Absolute Vertical Center and Relative Vertical Center options place your controls in the center (from top to bottom) of the form, or on a center line calculated from the average center of the group.

To center a title, choose Layout ➤ Align Special ➤ Absolute Horizontal Center. The default Text Alignment property is 0, top left. Change this to 1, top center, or 4, center center, to center the text within the Text object. Your title will be perfectly centered.

▸ Ordering Your Controls

Just as our Table Records tool has three layouts, the Form Designer has two views, Layout view and Order view. You can toggle between these views by clicking on the speedbar buttons, or by choosing from the View menu:

Form	F2
√ Form Design	Shift+F2
√ Layout View	
Order View	
√ Controls	
√ Object Properties	
√ Procedures	

The Order view shows you the z-axis—the order in which your controls are stacked in your form. The axes are named in the old fashion, popular in high school algebra. A two-dimensional graph labels the horizontal axis the x-axis, and the vertical axis is called the y-axis.

The z-axis is the third dimension—in our case the dimension that comes out of the screen straight at you. Every control on your form has a unique place in the z-axis, even though they all appear to be in the same plane if you haven't stacked them.

Figures 15.3 and 15.4 show a stack of Form objects, tiled and cascaded. Their titles (and the cascaded form) show their places in the z-axis.

FIGURE 15.3

Forms on the z-axis

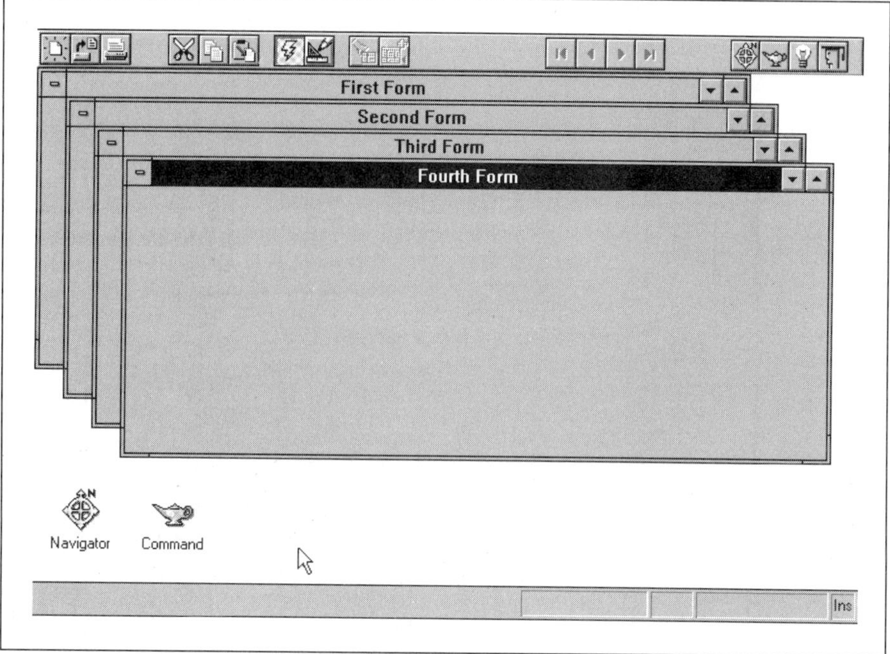

FIGURE 15.4

Tiled forms are still on the z-axis

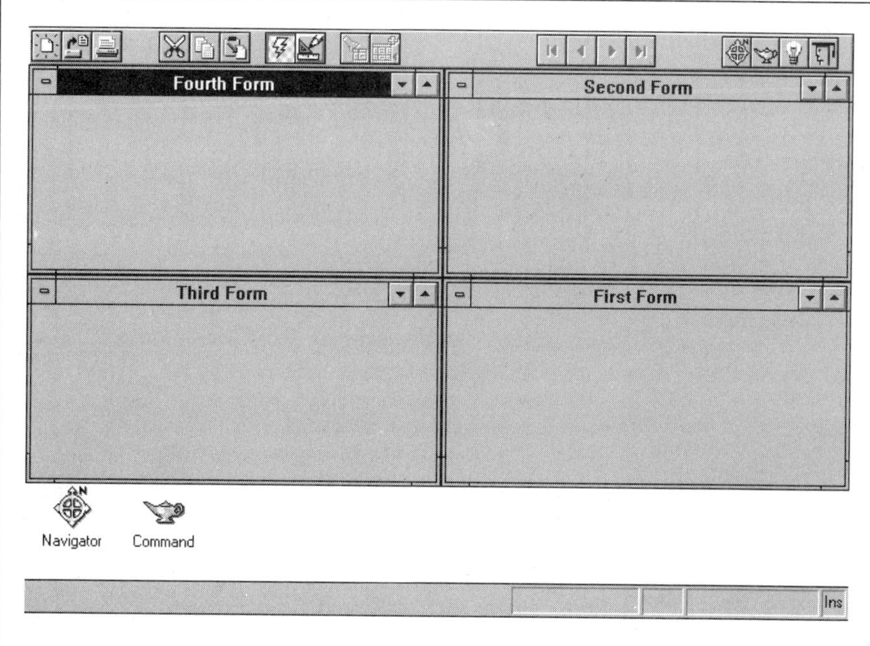

You can see in Figure 15.3 that the First Form is the deepest, and the Fourth Form is on top. This is the z-axis ordering in the Form Designer, too.

The z-axis is important for two reasons. First, it is the tabbing order—the order that your controls will be activated as you press the Tab key. Second, it is the order in which they are drawn on the form. This is not important until you want one control to overlap or be on top of another one (for example, placing check boxes or other controls on a rectangle).

All your form objects are in the z-axis, although not all of them are in the tabbing order. Objects such as Rectangles, Lines, and Images are never in the tabbing order. Other objects, such as Pushbuttons and Entryfields, are usually in the tabbing order, but you may choose to eliminate them at times (for example, making a pushbutton unavailable when its action is not appropriate).

The first z-order is established as you add controls to your form. In the sample form we used for learning the layout tools, we added four pushbuttons. The Form Designer gave them the default names Pushbutton1, Pushbutton2, and so on. The digits at the end of their names are also their positions in the z-order, until we change those positions.

If you have the sample form we built in the previous section, you can continue to use it. If you don't, go back and create it, and then continue here.

Overlap the four sample pushbuttons, but leave the numbers showing. Figure 15.5 shows our pushbuttons, overlapped so you can easily see their positions on the z-axis.

Of course, the reason we are interested in the z-axis, or z-order, is so that we can change it. One of the most common things to do as you build a form is to decide to add another pushbutton or other control. Until Murphy's Law is repealed, the one you add is *not* going to be the one that you want to be last in the z-order.

Adding a rectangle to enclose a set of controls is typical. Since the last object added is the last object in the z-order, your rectangle will initially cover the controls that you want on top (not underneath!) your rectangle.

FIGURE 15.5

Pushbuttons overlapped reveal their z-axis positions

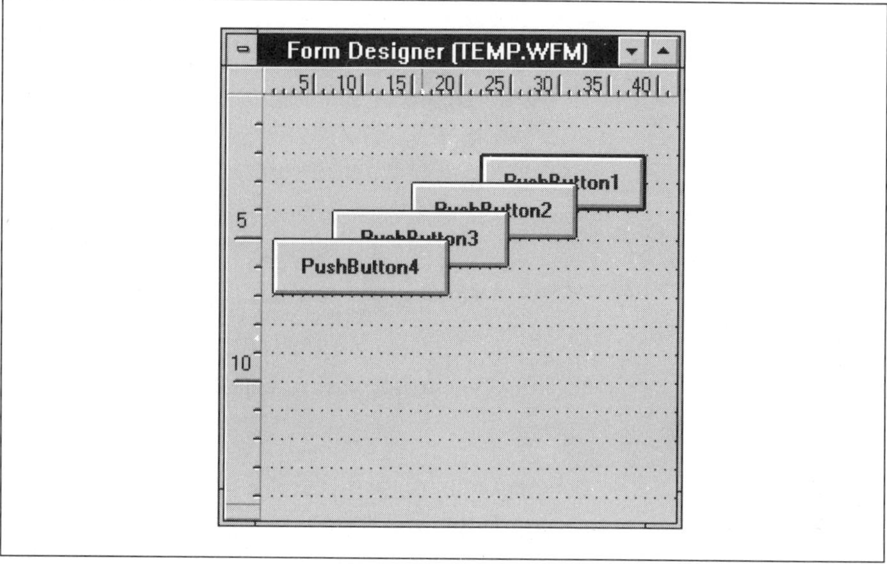

Ordering by Editing the .WFM

The simplest way to order controls on a form is to edit the .WFM file. To see this, save the form with the overlapped pushbuttons. We called ours TEMP so we know that we can throw it away tomorrow.

Here, with a great deal of detail omitted, is what the .WFM file looks like:

```
CLASS TEMPFORM OF FORM
   Set Procedure To E:\DBASEWIN\SAMPLES\BUTTONS.CC additive
   this.HelpFile = ""
   this.Height =        14.8818
   ...

   DEFINE PUSHBUTTON PUSHBUTTON1 OF THIS;
      PROPERTY;
         Height        2,;
         Left       22,;
         Text "PushButton1",;
         ...
```

```
DEFINE PUSHBUTTON PUSHBUTTON2 OF THIS;
  PROPERTY;
    Height        2,;
    Left        15,;
    Text "PushButton2",;
    ...

DEFINE PUSHBUTTON PUSHBUTTON3 OF THIS;
  PROPERTY;
    Height        2,;
    Left        7,;
    Text "PushButton3",;
    ...

DEFINE PUSHBUTTON PUSHBUTTON4 OF THIS;
  PROPERTY;
    Height        2,;
    Left        1,;
    Text "PushButton4",;
    ...

ENDCLASS
```

When you run this .WFM file (if you click the lightning icon, your .WFM file is written, then run), the z-order is the order in which the controls are defined. In this case, Pushbutton1 precedes Pushbutton2, and so on.

Let's try a sample correction. Suppose you decide that you really want Pushbutton3 to be first in the tabbing order. To change it, just take the DEFINE command and all the properties that are defined for Pushbutton3 and move that block ahead of the DEFINE command for Pushbutton1. These are the steps to take, working from the Navigator:

1. Select TEMP.WFM and click the right mouse button for the Speed menu.
2. Choose Edit as Program. This will launch the program in the Program Editor.

3. Use the vertical scroll bar to position the entire Pushbutton3 DEFINE command (it's about ten lines long) in the Program Editor window.

4. Select the entire Pushbutton3 DEFINE command. You can do this by dragging the mouse from the left margin at the start of the DEFINE command, to the same position at the start of the next DEFINE command. We like to use the keyboard—put the insertion point at the left margin at the start of the DEFINE command for Pushbutton3. Then hold the Shift key down while you press the ↓ key. Stop and release when the insertion point is at the start of the line that begins Pushbutton4's DEFINE command.

5. Cut this text to the Clipboard. (Press Shift-Del or Ctrl-X or choose Edit ➤ Cut.) Note that we have cut the DEFINE command plus the blank line that followed it.

6. Using PgUp and ↑ and ↓ as needed, position the insertion point at the left margin in front of the DEFINE command for Pushbutton1.

7. Paste the contents of the Clipboard (your previous cut) by pressing Shift-Ins or Ctrl-V, or by choosing Edit ➤ Paste. There are also speedbar buttons and Speed menu options for Cut, Copy, and Paste, if you prefer.

You should now have the DEFINE command for Pushbutton3 as the first control defined in your .WFM file. Pushbutton1 comes next.

If you've never moved a block of text in the Program Editor (or any similar Windows editor), we'll assume you've made a colossal mess of the entire file. No problem: press Ctrl-Q to quit without saving and start over.

On the other hand, maybe you only messed up the neat alignment of the code lines. You can fix the alignment (or if you're in a hurry, forget it; dBASE doesn't care about left margins). Perhaps you want to shuffle another DEFINE command or two into a new position. Be creative—try a shift using the keyboard and another using the mouse. Do one from the menu and another from the speedbar.

Once you have the pushbuttons ordered as you want them, press Ctrl-D to Do the program. If you just moved Pushbutton3 to the first position in the z-order, your result will look like Figure 15.6.

FIGURE 15.6

Pushbutton3 placed first in the z-order

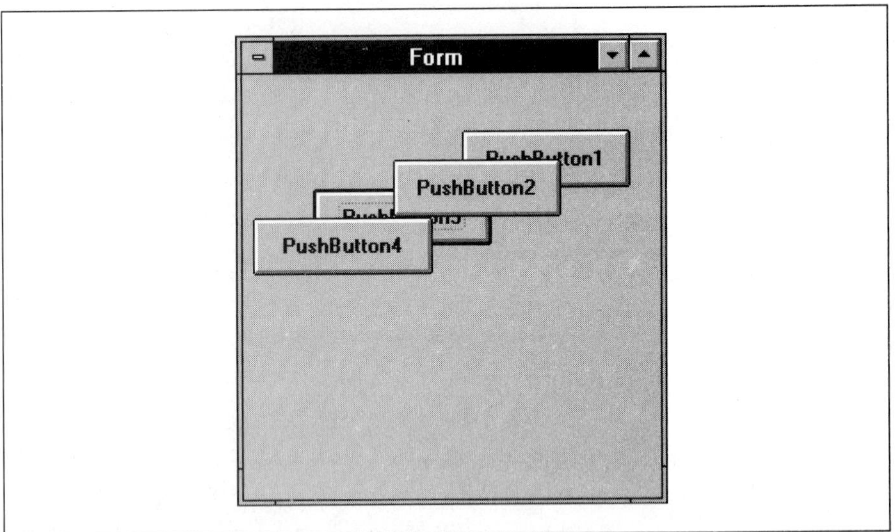

Of course, without overlap you can only see that pushbuttons 1 and 3 precede 2 and 4. To check the actual z-order, click on the drafting tools icon to switch from Run mode to Design mode. (You'll need to double-click the System button of the Program Editor before you can get to Design mode in the Form Designer.)

In Design mode, drag the buttons until they each overlap, but leave as many numbers visible as you can. You'll see that the z-order is exactly the one you set up using the Program Editor.

Working in the Order View

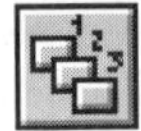

When you choose the Order view, by clicking on its speedbar button (shown in the margin) or choosing View ➤ Order Layout, the form changes to show labeled outline versions of each of your objects. You'll also see a new tool on the speedbar: the order spinbox. Figure 15.7 shows the Order view of our sample form and the order spinbox in the speedbar above the form.

In the Order view, if you click on an object, its number will be set to the number in the spinbox. All the numbers between the new number and the control's original number are adjusted appropriately. For example, if you change object 4 to 2, the former 2 will become 3 and the former 3 will become 4.

FIGURE 15.7

The Order view and the order spinbox

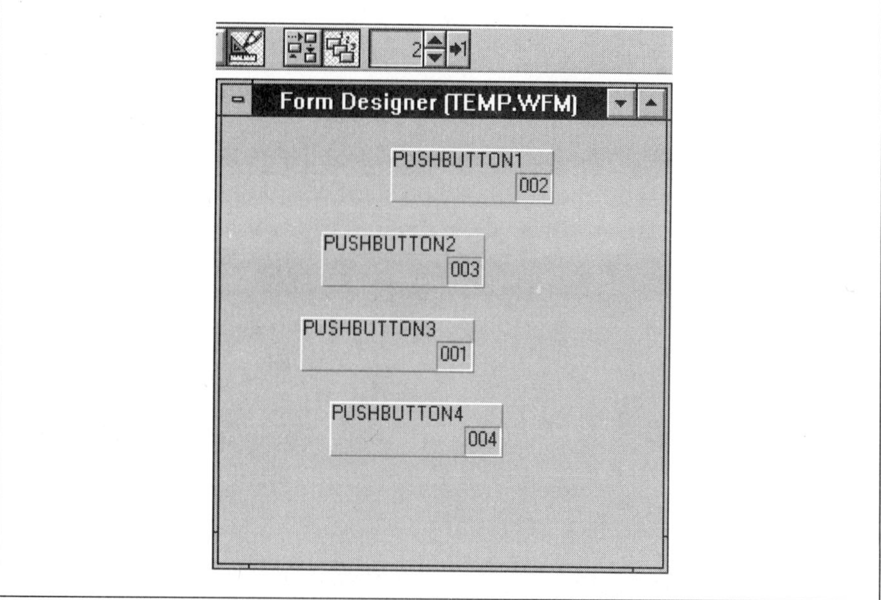

The large, right-pointing arrow in the order spinbox resets the counter to 1. If you click on objects on your form, starting with 1, the counter advances each time you click. This means that you can simply click on each control in turn, and you will set the order of your clicks as the new z-order.

This is a very workable method for setting the z-order in our simple, four-pusbutton form. However, if you had a normal table with, perhaps, 20 fields, you would have at least 20 Entryfields or other control objects, 20 Text objects labeling these controls, a Title object, and perhaps some Pushbutton objects. With a well-populated form, it becomes very difficult to click each in the right order. (If you're good at this sort of thing, you might get it right, but even so, it's not a quick process.)

We suggest that you experiment with the Order view and the order spinbox with the simple, four-pushbutton form. You'll probably decide, as we did, that adding a control and then moving its DEFINE command in the Program Editor is a straightforward way of setting the z-order.

If you are a full-time programmer, however, we suggest that you spend enough time with this tool to be able to use it proficiently. If you do a lot of form work, the time it takes to learn to use the Order view will be repaid by time saved adjusting your form's z-orders.

Working in Layout View

There are four perfectly sensible speedbar buttons and equivalent Layout menu choices that you can use to adjust the z-order without leaving Layout view. Toggle back to Layout view by clicking on its speedbar button (shown in the margin) or by choosing View ➤ Layout. Then choose Layout to see these choices at the bottom of the menu:

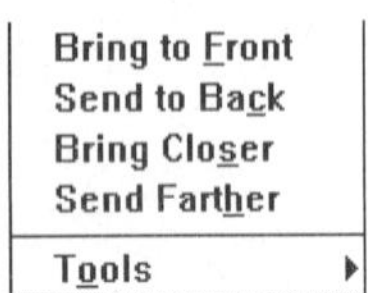

To use the menu choices (or the equivalent speedbar buttons), you must first select an object on your form. These are the speedbar buttons and commands:

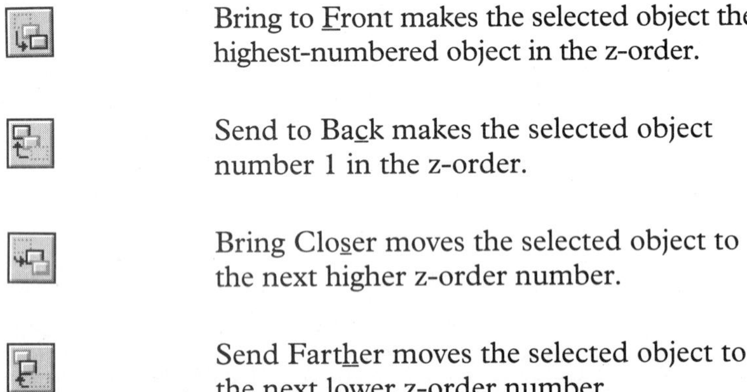

Bring to Front makes the selected object the highest-numbered object in the z-order.

Send to Back makes the selected object number 1 in the z-order.

Bring Closer moves the selected object to the next higher z-order number.

Send Farther moves the selected object to the next lower z-order number.

There is one serious problem with using these choices, however. If your objects don't overlap, you can't see any difference as you click these buttons. Changing object 13 to 12 or 14 is an invisible change in Layout view, unless your object 13 overlapped 12 or 14.

Without overlap, these choices are very subtle. You need to keep a mental picture of the z-order and adjust that order as you click these buttons.

Again, we recommend just editing the .WFM file and moving the DEFINE blocks into whatever order you like, unless you are spending a lot of your working day building forms.

▶ Form Designer Properties

The Form Designer Properties dialog box is shown in Figure 15.8. You get to this dialog box by choosing Properties ➤ Form Designer.

FIGURE 15.8

Setting the Form Designer's properties

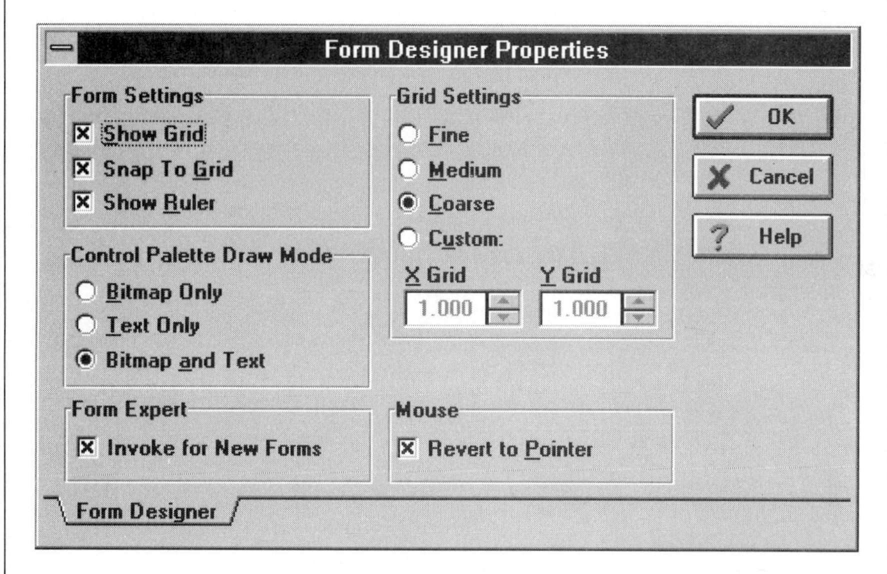

The Form Settings Choices

In the Form Settings section, you choose whether the grid (dotted lines) should show on your form and whether the rules (rulers at the top and left sides of the form) should be shown. Less obvious, perhaps, is the critical Snap To Grid check box.

For almost all your work, the Snap To Grid choice should be checked. Then, every time you place, move, or size an object on your form, its edges are moved to the nearest grid lines. If you do not check Snap To Grid, the edges are left where you drop them.

The advantage of using the snap feature is that you have a fair chance of getting your controls aligned vertically and horizontally without a lot of trouble. If you have any doubts, uncheck this box and then move four or five Entryfield objects onto your form. Use four or five Text

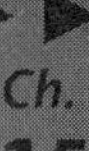

objects as labels for the Entryfield objects, and try to get a good-looking alignment. It's nearly impossible.

The Control Palette Draw Mode Selections

The Controls palette shows icons, representing the objects you can select, with text labels for the icons. Its default is to show both text and icons.

If you want to turn the icons off, you can select Text Only in the Form Designer Properties dialog box. You can also turn the text off (with Bitmap Only), but that would make selecting very tricky indeed. In the Controls palette Custom tab, you may have many identical icons, so we consider the text a necessity.

The Form Expert Choice

You have a single choice for the Form Expert: Invoke for New Forms. We're not sure why anyone would want to turn this option off, since exactly two clicks are required to go through the Form Expert to a blank form when you don't want Expert help.

When you have a new table for which you need a form, the Expert is an invaluable time saver. We recommend that you leave this checked.

The Grid Settings

dBASE uses its own coordinates, called Turpins (after Borland's head of dBASE development, Bill Turpin). A Turpin is a cell as large as a single character in the default ScaleFont. Before dBASE for Windows, characters were the standard mode for addressing the screen. The standard screen was 25 lines high by 80 characters wide. The Turpin-based coordinates approximate this way of addressing the screen.

The Grid Settings choices let you specify the type of grid that you want (the grid that your placements will snap to, assuming you have Snap To Grid selected):

- Fine is 0.5 Turpin, each way.
- Medium is 0.75 Turpin, tall and wide.
- Coarse (the default grid) is 1 Turpin high and 1 Turpin wide.
- Custom lets you choose your own size with the X Grid and Y Grid spinbuttons.

In a coarse grid, each character is about twice as tall as it is wide. This means that the grid is about twice as fine horizontally as it is vertically, which turns out to be quite convenient in practice. We suggest that you do almost all your work with the coarse grid, and then pick a finer setting to fine-tune your work.

▶▶ **TIP**

We find that most of our fine-tuning work is easier when we edit the .WFM file as a program and adjust the Top, Left, Height, and Width properties, rather than going to a very fine grid or turning Snap To Grid off.

The Mouse Choice

You have one choice for your mouse, somewhat cryptically called Revert to Pointer. If you check this box, after you grab a control and place it on your form, the mouse switches back to a pointer.

If you do not check this box, the mouse will stay set to whatever object you last selected. This is very handy if you want to drag a large number of the same type of object onto your form. When you are finished, you can switch to the pointer by choosing the Pointer option from the Controls palette.

▶▶ **TIP**

For most work, the Revert to Pointer behavior is far more convenient than having to explicitly go back and choose the pointer before you can begin work on the object you just placed.

▶▶ *Using the Form Designer and Menu Designer Tools*

In your work with the Form Designer, you may use the Object Properties Inspector, Controls palette, and Procedure Editor. The Object

Properties Inspector and the Procedure Editor are also available when you work with the Menu Designer. In the following sections, we'll look at each of these tools in turn. For the first two, we'll highlight some points that you might have missed, even though you already have been using these tools. For the Procedure Editor, we'll study the overall form of the .WFM file in more depth and see how this relates to the Procedure Editor.

You may select each of these tools from the Form Designer's Speed menu (right-click over the form) or from the View menu. From either source, if your tool is available, the menu choice will be checked. Choosing a checked menu choice deselects (removes the check) the choice. Choosing an unchecked menu choice both selects it (adds the check) and launches it as the active window.

▸▸ TIP

If your tool is checked (this is useful when it is hidden behind other objects), you can use the Window menu to bring it immediately to the front.

▸ Setting Properties with the Object Properties Inspector

You use the Object Properties Inspector to examine and to set properties for your on-form objects. It has three tabs, corresponding to three main types of properties:

- Properties (data properties)
- Events (event properties)
- Methods (non-event method properties)

Properties can be data or methods. Methods are subroutines that your object can execute. Events, or event handlers, are methods that are executed in response to an event, such as a mouse click.

Outline and Non-Outline Options

You've seen how the Object Properties Inspector is organized in outline form, with the properties grouped under headings that can be expanded or contracted. The outline-style makes it easier to find all of an object's properties. When the Object Properties Outline setting isn't checked, the properties are simply shown in alphabetical order. Figure 15.9 shows Object Properties Inspectors in both formats.

FIGURE 15.9

Object Properties Inspectors in outline and non-outline styles

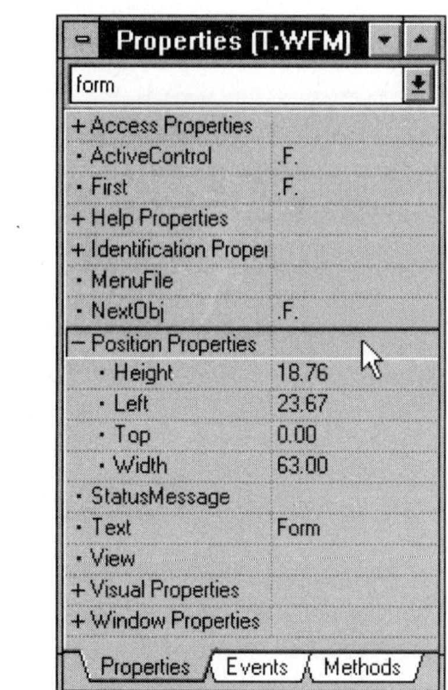

In both of these examples, the object being inspected is a Form, with no controls. In the outline style, all the controls you add are grouped under dBASE Variable Properties. In the non-outline form, your controls are placed alphabetically by their names, mingled with the built-in properties.

Manipulating the Object Properties Inspector

You can size the Object Properties Inspector by dragging its borders and corners or from its System menu, just as you can manipulate any other MDI child window. You can drag the centerline (the separator between property names and values) left or right, just as you can in the Table Records tool's Browse Layout view.

►► TIP

We give our Object Properties Inspectors about one-third the width and the full height of the dBASE for Windows client area. We place the centerline so that a third of the Object Properties Inspector's space is available for property names, leaving two-thirds for data. With full height, if we can keep our forms from going all the way down to the status bar, we always have the Object Properties Inspector's tabs peeking out at the bottom, where we can click on them to get straight to the tab.

From the keyboard, pressing Tab or Shift-Tab cycles between the menus at the top, the properties area, and the tabs. In the properties area, ↑ and ↓ select individual properties. In the tabs, ← and → select tabs. The properties area is adjusted automatically as you shift between tabs.

You've been double-clicking outline topics to expand those with a + symbol and to contract those with a – symbol. You can also toggle the expanded state by pressing the gray + key on the numeric keypad.

►► TIP

Ctrl-+ (gray plus, on the numeric keypad) expands all outline categories, if you have selected any outline category. Ctrl-– (gray minus, on the numeric keypad) contracts all outline categories, if you have selected any outline category.

Selecting Objects from the Drop-Down List

As you select different objects in the Form Designer, the Object Properties Inspector is set to show the properties of the selected item. You can also select items through the drop-down list at the top of the Object Properties Inspector.

Clicking on the selected list item, or on the drop-down arrow, displays the list. The list shows your Form object and each of the objects placed on the form. Clicking on any list entry selects that object as the one whose properties are displayed in the Object Properties Inspector.

With the keyboard, use Alt-↓ to drop down the list. After the list is dropped, you can use ↓ and ↑ to move between objects and Enter to select the currently highlighted object. To close the list, press Alt-↑.

Events and Methods

Before you assign your own events and methods, the Events tab will list all the available events, and their data properties will all be blank (there are no default event handlers). On the other hand, the Methods tab will list all available methods, which will all be filled in with an entry in this form:

<classname>::*<eventname>*

These are two examples:

```
FORM::CLOSE
PUSHBUTTON::MOVE
```

If you add an event handler through the Procedure Editor, you create a new method and you assign a *function pointer*, a reference to the method, to the event handler. Your reference to the method is the new value in the Events properties list, and your method is a new value in the Methods properties list.

WARNING

The Methods tab is *not* updated when you add or delete a method. It is updated when you start the Form Designer. This bug only affects the list in the Methods tab, however. The code is handled correctly.

► Adding Controls with the Controls Palette

You've also already used the Controls palette, a two-tab form:

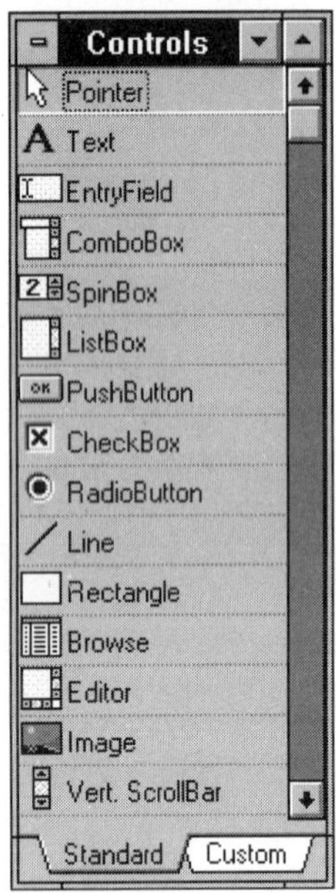

The first tab lists the Pointer plus each of dBASE for Windows' built-in objects that can be placed on a form. The second tab lists the custom controls that you have installed. The default custom controls are the Borland-style pushbuttons defined in \DBASEWIN\SAMPLES\BUTTONS.CC. You can create your own custom controls or purchase add-on sets from Borland and a wide variety of third-party vendors.

►► **WARNING**

dBASE for Windows supports .VBX controls. Not all .VBX controls are equally good at supporting dBASE for Windows, however. Only purchase .VBX add-ons if the vendor guarantees compatibility with dBASE for Windows.

From the keyboard, pressing Tab or Shift-Tab toggles between the tabs. PgUp and PgDn adjust the display of available tools. (But we recommend that you stick to the mouse, since you will need it to drag your control into position on the form.)

Pressing Enter or double-clicking on a control sends that control to the form immediately. It is placed in its default position (the upper-left corner). From there, you can drag it into place when you're ready. This lets you select several controls at once before returning to your form.

TIP

We do the same thing with our Controls palette that we do with the Object Properties Inspector: we give it the full height of the client area and let at least the tabs stick out on the bottom. That way, we can always click on a tab to get right to the Controls palette.

As discussed earlier, if the Revert to Pointer box in the Form Designer Properties dialog box is not checked, use the Control palette's Pointer selection to select objects on your form.

Working with the Procedure Editor

The Procedure Editor has two jobs. First, it provides an editor that lets you add statements and commands to your .WFM file and to the methods in the .WFM file. Equally important, it ties your events to your methods. The process of attaching a method to an event is one of those repetitive, detailed tasks that a computer does well.

Procedure Editor Properties

We'll begin by looking at the Editor Properties dialog box, shown in Figure 15.10. This dialog box is available through the Properties ➤ Procedure Editor ... choice. It's also the first choice on the Procedure Editor's Speed menu (right-click in the Procedure Editor).

As is true of the Program Editor, Text Editor, and Memo Editor, the Procedure Editor is a specialized version of a single editor that you can customize to suit your needs.

FIGURE 15.10

Setting the Procedure Editor's properties

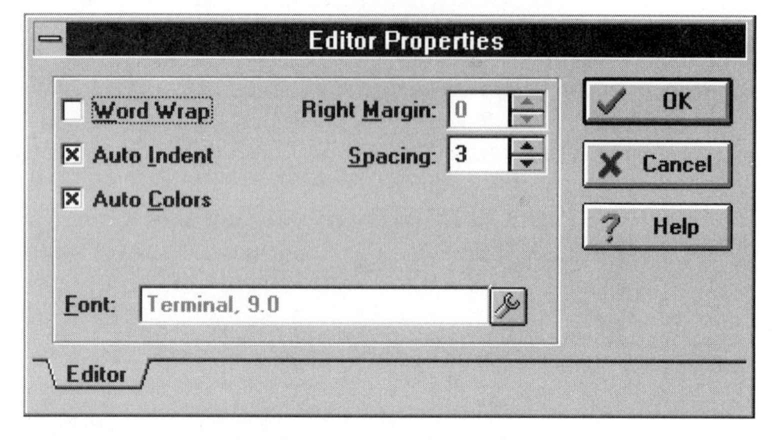

The Word Wrap check box turns word wrapping on at the right margin. You can set the Right Margin with the spinbutton only if the Word Wrap box is checked.

You may think that word wrapping is just about useless in a programming editor. Since the editor supports that choice (clearly needed for editing memo fields), the dBASE for Windows designers left it in all the editors.

▸▸ **NOTE**

We appreciate word wrapping in the Program Editor. Books and magazines have a strict limit on line length. When we write about program code, we routinely set the word wrap on, just to remind us. If we go too far and our code wraps, we know we need to trim it before we can run it. We point this out to suggest that extra features, no matter how apparently worthless, just might be handy to someone. When a feature has already been programmed, you might as well leave it available.

The Auto Indent property handles indenting at the left side. If this is set on, and the previous line is indented, the insertion point doesn't go to the left margin—it returns to the point of the last indent. Tab and Shift-Tab indent and outdent the number of spaces set by the Spacing spinbutton.

Auto Colors turns color syntax highlighting on or off. We suggest you leave it on.

You can also set the Font through the entry field at the bottom of the box. Clicking the tool icon next to this field brings you to the Font dialog box. (For more about this dialog box, see Appendix B.)

Structure of the .WFM File

The Procedure Editor is your basic tool for adding to the .WFM file that dBASE for Windows writes. To understand this tool, you need to understand the .WFM file.

It has four areas:

- Header code (optional, you provide it)
- Startup code (fixed, dBASE for Windows provides it)
- Class code (variable, defines the form and objects you provide)
- General code (optional, you provide it)

This is an example of a .WFM file written by dBASE for Windows for a plain form. We've added nothing:

```
** END HEADER -- do not remove this line*
* Generated on 01/13/95
*
LOCAL f
f = NEW TEMPFORM()
f.Open()

CLASS TEMPFORM OF FORM
   Set Procedure To E:\DBASEWIN\SAMPLES\BUTTONS.CC additive
   this.Width =        63
   this.HelpID = ""
   this.HelpFile = ""
   this.Text = "Form"
   this.Height =        18
   this.Left =       1
   this.Top =       0

ENDCLASS
```


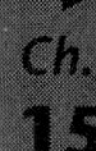

The header section that you may provide comes before the line:

```
** END HEADER—do not remove this line*
```

The Form Designer looks for this line when it reads the .WFM file and uses it to determine the location of the end of the header.

The startup code is the next six lines (counting the blank). The section that starts with the CLASS statement and ends with the ENDCLASS statement is the class code. Here you will find all the definitions for your form and its objects, as well as the class methods.

The general section (in this case, there is none) follows the END-CLASS statement.

Now we'll add an OK pushbutton (we'll use the Borland custom OK-BUTTON control). If you want to try this yourself, launch the Untitled form and tell the Form Expert to create a blank form. Add the OKBUTTON from the Custom tab of the Controls palette. Save your work as TEMP.WFM (overwrite any preexisting TEMP—that's what the name TEMP means).

From the Object Properties Inspector's Events tab, click on the On-Click event, and then click on the tool icon next to that event to get to the Procedure Editor. Add this line:

```
Form.Close()
```

Save your work. Except for the exact position of your Pushbutton object, your .WFM file should look like this:

```
** END HEADER -- do not remove this line*
* Generated on 01/13/95
*
LOCAL f
f = NEW TEMPFORM()
f.Open()

CLASS TEMPFORM OF FORM
  Set Procedure To E:\DBASEWIN\SAMPLES\BUTTONS.CC additive
  this.Width =        63
  this.HelpID = ""
  this.HelpFile = ""
  this.Text = "Form"
  this.Height =        18
  this.Left =        1
```

```
this.Top =        0

DEFINE OKBUTTON OKBUTTON1 OF THIS;
  PROPERTY;
    Width       13,;
    OnClick CLASS::OKBUTTON1_ONCLICK,;
    Group .T.,;
    Height       2,;
    Left      24,;
    Top       7

Procedure OKBUTTON1_OnClick
Form.Close()

ENDCLASS
```

As you add more objects to your form, you will have more DEFINE commands. All the DEFINE commands are grouped together, preceding the methods. Additional methods would follow the line:

```
Procedure OKBUTTON1_OnClick
```

Here you see the assignment of the function pointer (reference to the method) to the OnClick property of OKBUTTON1:

```
OnClick CLASS::OKBUTTON1_ONCLICK
```

The word CLASS and the scope resolution operator **::** tell you that this is a reference to a method found in the current class. The Form Designer builds the procedure name by tying the object name (OKBUTTON1) to the event name (ONCLICK) with an underscore character.

This name is then repeated in the Procedure statement that begins the method definition.

The Drop-Down Editor List

In the upper-left corner of the Procedure Editor, you see a drop-down list of the items known to the Procedure Editor, as in this example:

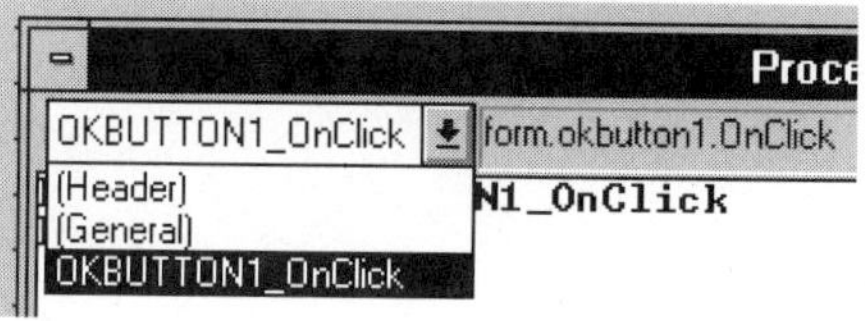

This list always includes the header and general areas. Additionally, it includes an entry for every method you have defined.

Use this list to add comments at the top and bottom of your file. We feel that these comments should be added to all your forms. In the header area, try at least something like this:

```
* TEMP.WFM -- a demonstration form
* Simpson and Rinehart, 8/31/95
*
```

Identify the name of the file, explain what it's for, credit yourself as the author, and note when it was first written. The trailing asterisk is needed since the Form Designer does not provide any space between the last header line and the ** END OF HEADER comment.

The end of the file should, at the very least, identify itself as the end of the file. This avoids mysterious bugs that could happen if the file were accidentally truncated. Add this, at a minimum, to the general section, using the Procedure Editor:

```
*
* end of TEMP.WFM
```

Again, the leading asterisk will separate your general code from the ENDCLASS statement.

If you find it easier, you may add the header and general section using the Program Editor. With these additions, your .WFM file should read like this:

```
* TEMP.WFM -- a demonstration form
* Simpson and Rinehart, 8/31/95
*
** END HEADER -- do not remove this line*
* Generated on 01/13/95
*
LOCAL f
f = NEW TEMPFORM()
f.Open()

CLASS TEMPFORM OF FORM

  ... code omitted
```

```
ENDCLASS
*
* end of TEMP.WFM
```

The Procedure Menu

The Procedure menu adds key capabilities to the Procedure Editor:

New Method
Remove Method
Verify Method

Edit Event
Link Event
Unlink Event

The options work as follows:

- The New Method choice lets you add another method, without linking it to a predefined event.
- The Remove Method lets you delete a method that you have defined.
- The Verify Method does a complete syntax check.
- The Edit Event method opens the Edit Event dialog box, which lets you edit your events.
- The Link Event choice opens the Link Event to Procedure dialog box, which lets you link an event to the procedure you have active in the Procedure Editor.
- The Unlink Event choice opens the Unlink Events dialog box, for unlinking events and procedures.

TIP

Always use Verify Method for important methods. It is much easier to correct a typo here than to wait until you run your form.

Editing Events

Figure 15.11 shows the Edit Event dialog box you see when you choose Procedure ➤ Edit Event. You can pick any object in the Object list on the left. When you pick an object, the menu in the Event section on the right changes to show the events you can edit. If you already have a property assigned to one of the events, a lightning icon appears next to the event name.

FIGURE 15.11 ►

Editing events through the Edit Event dialog box

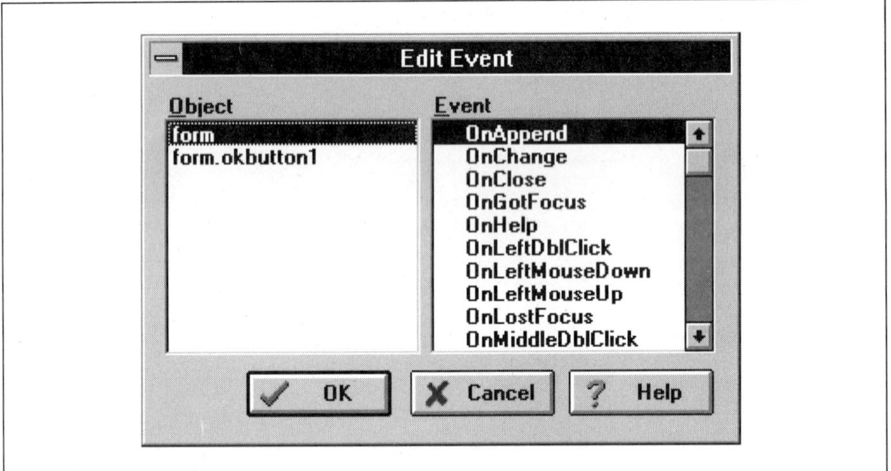

Linking and Unlinking Events

The Link Event choice in the Procedure menu launches the same dialog box as Edit Event, except that it's retitled Link Event to Procedure, followed by the name of the procedure you have active in the Procedure Editor.

The Unlink Event choice launches the Unlink Events dialog box, shown in Figure 15.12.

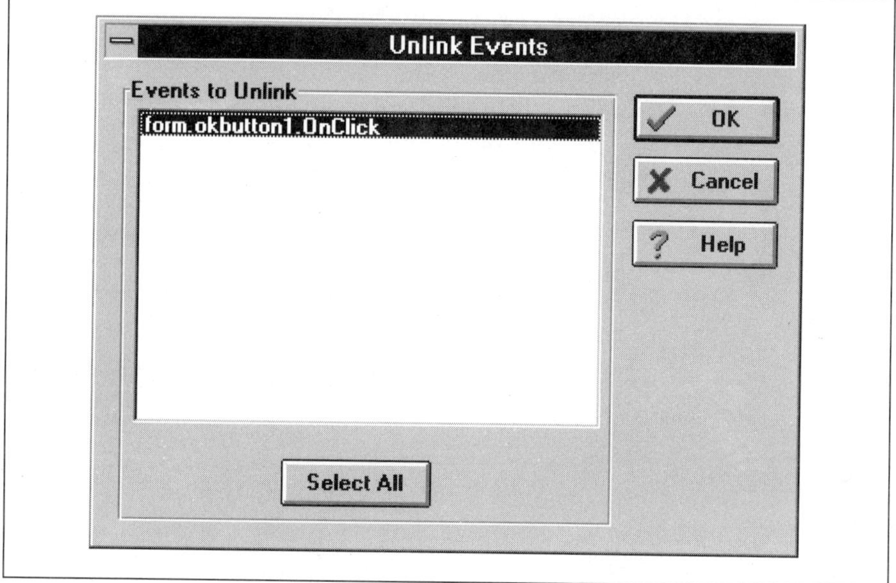

FIGURE 15.12

Unlinking events through the Unlink Events dialog box

The Unlink Events dialog box lists all the events for which you have supplied values. Choosing to unlink the event erases the data value. (You can also erase the value in the Events tab of the Object Properties Inspector.)

►► Using the Menu Designer

The Menu Designer is a simple tool, which we have already explored in Chapter 6. But there is another way to look at it: the Menu Designer is a sophisticated tool which draws its power from the Procedure Editor and the Object Properties Inspector tools.

Here, we'll fill in some details. Bear in mind that all the previous discussions of the two related tools apply equally to the Menu Designer, which also includes the Procedure Editor and the Object Properties Inspectors.

▸ The Menu Designer Menus

The menus for the Menu Designer are primarily the menus for the Procedure Editor. For example, the Edit menu has most choices grayed:

Undo	Ctrl+Z
Cut	Ctrl+X
Copy	Ctrl+C
Paste	Ctrl+V
Delete	Del
Select All	
Insert from File...	
Copy to File...	
Search	▸
Convert Case	▸
Join Text Lines	
Build Expression...	Ctrl+E

Of the choices, only the Select All choice actually applies. It will select the entire text of the current Menu object. The Search and Convert Case choices are not grayed, but they lead to other menus, with all their choices grayed.

If you have selected some or all of the Menu object's Text property, the appropriate Clipboard choices are made available. These are of limited use. (It would be more helpful if you could cut or copy the selected Menu object to the Clipboard, but you can't.)

The one menu that is unique to the Menu Designer is Menu:

Insert Menu Item	Ctrl+N
Insert Menu	Ctrl+M
Insert Separator	Ctrl+T
Delete Selected	Ctrl+U

The options on this menu let you manipulate either menu items or whole menus. There is only one Menu object, which is also a menu item. dBASE for Windows does not get confused, however.

Each menu item has a Before property, which is the Menu object that it is Before in the current menu. If there is a pull-down menu, or a cascading menu attached, this will show up as a Menu object in the dBASE Variable Properties.

The two choices for inserting items let you choose between menu items and menus explains to the Menu Designer how the new item should be included. Separators are only included as menu items. When you choose to delete a menu item, it is deleted from the menu. If it is the last item in the menu, the menu itself disappears.

▶ The Menu Designer Speedbar

The following speedbar buttons are unique to the Menu Designer:

Adds a menu item (same as Menu ➤ Insert Menu Item or Ctrl-N).

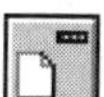

Deletes the currently selected item (same as Menu ➤ Delete Selected choice or Ctrl-U).

▶▶ Form and Menu Object Properties Reference

In this section, we provide an alphabetical listing of all the properties of the Form object and the Menu object. Each listing includes the default value (if one exists). If a property is read-only, you cannot assign a value to it. If a property is read-only, it is noted in its listing.

Data properties are called Properties; events and other methods are called Methods. Additionally, Methods' names are followed by parentheses; for example, ClassName is a data property, but Close( ) is a method. Some methods take parameters within their parentheses, as noted in their listings.

▶ Form Object Properties

This section lists and briefly explains the properties of the Form object.

The Form.ActiveControl Property

The ActiveControl is the object that currently has focus. You can examine this value to see where focus is in the form, and you can assign a different object to ActiveControl to change focus.

The Form.AutoSize Property

Default value: .F.

If True, AutoSize causes the Form object's size to be adjusted to fit its objects each time it is opened.

The Form.ClassName Property

Default value: FORM

This property is read-only. ClassName is assigned by dBASE for Windows for each of the built-in classes. This can be used to distinguish among multiple objects with the same name.

The Form.Close( ) Method

The Close method is executed when a Form object is closed. The form is not closed, and this event is not triggered, if Valid returns .F. for the current object. Close is executed after OnLostFocus and after removing the Form object from the screen.

The Form.ColorNormal Property

Default value: N/W

The ColorNormal property specifies the color of the Form object. ColorNormal may be a dBASE IV-style color specification, or it may be a color selected from the color palette with the Choose Color dialog box.

The Form.Enabled Property

Default value: .T.

If Enabled is True, the object is accessible. You can use the Enabled property to disable options in event handlers. For example, a Valid function could set some object's Enabled property to False if required conditions were not met.

The Form.EscExit Property

Default value: .T.

If True, the EscExit property lets the Esc keypress exit from the Form object.

The Form.First Property

Default value: "", or .F. is Form object is empty

This property is read-only. The First property is a reference to the first object in the Form object's tabbing order.

The Form.Height Property

Default value: 18

The Height property specifies the height of the object in characters.

The Form.HelpFile Property

Default value: ""

The HelpFile property names the Windows Help file that will be used when you press F1.

The Form.HelpID Property

Default value: –1

The HelpID specifies the individual Help screen that will be accessed in the Windows Help file specified by the HelpFile property.

The Form.hWnd Property

This property is read-only. The hWnd property is an arbitrary integer number that identifies the window's handle of the Form object. It is used when you access Windows functions directly via EXTERN commands.

The Form.Left Property

Default value: 0

The Left property specifies the location of the left side of the Form object in characters. The leftmost character is number 0.

The Form.Maximize Property

Default value: .T.

If Maximize is True, the Form object can be maximized.

The Form.MDI( ) Method

If MDI is True, the Form object is an MDI (multiple document interface), child form.

The Form.MenuFile Property

Default value: “”

The MenuFile property specifies the name of a menu definition file, which defines the menu to be used on the form. If it is blank, no menu appears.

The Form.Minimize Property

Default value: .T.

If Minimize is True, the Form object can be minimized (changed to an icon).

The Form.MousePointer Property

Default value: 0

Available Setttings: 0–11

The MousePointer property specifies the type of mouse pointer to use when the pointer is over the Form object. The settings are default (0), arrow (1), cross (2), I-beam (3), icon (4), size (5), size NESW (6), size S (7), size NWSE (8), size E (9), up-arrow (10), and wait (hourglass, 11).

The Form.Move( ) Method

Parameters: *<lft>*,*<tp>*,*<wdth>*,*<hght>*

Move is a method property that can move the Form object, resize the Form object, or both. You provide Move with four parameters, representing the new values for the properties Left, Top, Width, and Height, respectively.

The Form.Moveable Property

Default value: .T.

If Moveable is True, the Form object can be moved (by dragging the title bar with the mouse or choosing Move from the System menu).

The Form.NextCol( ) Method

The NextCol method of a Form object returns the next column, in character coordinates, at which a new object could be placed without overlapping previous objects.

The Form.NextObj( ) Method

This NextObj method returns an object reference to the next object in the Form object's tabbing order.

The Form.NextRow( ) Method

The NextRow method returns, in character coordinates, the next row on the Form object that can be used for a new object without overlapping existing objects.

The Form.OnAppend( ) Method

The OnAppend method is called when you append a record.

The Form.OnChange( ) Method

The OnChange method is called whenever you change a value in the Form object.

The Form.OnClose( ) Method

The OnClose method is called whenever you close a Form object.

The Form.OnGotFocus( ) Method

The OnGotFocus method is called when the Form object receives focus.

The Form.OnHelp( ) Method

The OnHelp method is called when the F1 key is pressed.

The Form.OnLeftDblClick( ) Method

Parameters: <*flags*>,<*col*>,<*row*>

The OnLeftDblClick event is called when you double-click with the left mouse button over the Form object. The parameters report the status of the Shift, Ctrl, and Alt keys, as well as the location at the time of the OnLeftDblClick event.

The Form.OnLeftMouseDown( ) Method

Parameters: <*flags*>,<*col*>,<*row*>

The OnLeftMouseDown event is called when you press the left mouse button over the Form object. The parameters report the status of the Shift, Ctrl, and Alt keys, as well as the location at the time of the On-LeftMouseDown event.

The Form.OnLeftMouseUp( ) Method

Parameters: <*flags*>,<*col*>,<*row*>

The OnLeftMouseUp handler is called whenever you release the left button over the Form object. (An up event over one object might have been preceded by a down event over another object.) The parameters report the status of the Shift, Ctrl, and Alt keys, as well as the location at the time of the OnLeftMouseUp event.

The Form.OnLostFocus( ) Method

The OnLostFocus method is called whenever the Form object loses focus.

The Form.OnMiddleDblClick( ) Method

Parameters: <*flags*>,<*col*>,<*row*>

The OnMiddleDblClick event is called when you double-click with the middle mouse button of a three-button mouse over the Form object. The parameters report the status of the Shift, Ctrl, and Alt keys, as well as the location at the time of the OnMiddleDblClick event.

The Form.OnMiddleMouseDown( ) Method

Parameters: <*flags*>,<*col*>,<*row*>

The OnMiddleMouseDown event is called when you press the middle mouse button of a three-button mouse over the Form object. The parameters report the status of the Shift, Ctrl, and Alt keys, as well as the location at the time of the OnMiddleMouseDown event.

The Form.OnMiddleMouseUp( ) Method

Parameters: <*flags*>,<*col*>,<*row*>

The OnMiddleMouseUp handler is called whenever you release the middle mouse button over the Form object. (An up event over one object might have been preceded by a down event over another object.) The parameters report the status of the Shift, Ctrl, and Alt keys, as well as the location at the time of the OnMiddleMouseUp event.

The Form.OnMouseMove( ) Method

Parameters: <*flags*>,<*col*>,<*row*>

The OnMouseMove event is called on any mouse movement detected over the Form object.

The Form.OnMove( ) Method

Parameters: <*left*>,<*top*>

The OnMove method executes a subroutine when a Form object is moved. The parameters specify the new location of the Form object.

The Form.OnNavigate( ) Method

The OnNavigate event is called after the record pointer is shifted.

The Form.OnOpen( ) Method

The OnOpen event is called when the Form object is opened.

The Form.OnRightDblClick( ) Method

Parameters: <*flags*>,<*col*>,<*row*>

The OnRightDblClick event is called when you double-click with the right mouse button over the Form object. (Right double-clicks are recognized by the Navigator as commands to design the object.) The parameters report the status of the Shift, Ctrl, and Alt keys, as well as the location at the time of the OnRightDblClick event.

The Form.OnRightMouseDown( ) Method

Parameters: <*flags*>,<*col*>,<*row*>

The OnRightMouseDown event is called when you press the right mouse button over the Form object. The parameters report the status of the Shift, Ctrl, and Alt keys, as well as the location at the time of the OnRightMouseDown event.

The Form.OnRightMouseUp( ) Method

Parameters: <*flags*>,<*col*>,<*row*>

The OnRightMouseUp handler is called whenever you release the right button over the Form object. (An up event over one object might have been preceded by a down event over another object.) The parameters report the status of the Shift, Ctrl, and Alt keys, as well as the location at the time of the OnRightMouseUp event.

The Form.OnSelection( ) Method

Parameter: <*controlid*>

The OnSelection method executes a subroutine when a Form object is submited.

The Form.OnSize( ) Method

The OnSize method is called after the Form object is resized by dragging its edges or corners, or by choosing Size from the System menu.

The Form.Open( ) Method

Parameters: <*flags*>,<*col*>,<*row*>

The Open method opens the Form object as a modeless window. It is called from programs, the Command window, or the Navigator.

The Form.Print( ) Method

The Print method is called from a program or the File ➤ Print menu. It opens the Print dialog box.

The Form.ReadModal( ) Method

The ReadModal method opens the Form object as a modal window. It has exclusive focus until it is explicitly closed.

The Form.Release( ) Method

The Release method removes the Form object from memory. Releasing a Form also releases all of the Form's objects.

The Form.ScaleFontName Property

Default value: MS Sans Serif

The ScaleFontName property is the name of the ScaleFont.

The Form.ScaleFontSize Property

Default value: 8

The ScaleFontSize property is the size, in points, of the ScaleFont.

The Form.Scrollbar Property

Default value: 0 or 1

Available settings: 0–3

The Scrollbar property defaults to on for Editor objects and off for Form objects. Its values are off (0), on (1), auto (2), and disabled (3). An auto scroll bar appears only when the data exceeds the visible area of the Form or Editor object. A disabled scroll bar is visible but does not respond to mouse clicks.

The Form.SetFocus( ) Method

The SetFocus method changes focus to the Form object.

The Form.Sizeable Property

Default value: .T.

If Sizeable is True, the Form object may be sized by dragging its edges or corners, or by choosing Size from the System menu.

The Form.StatusMessage Property

Default value: ""

The StatusMessage appears in the left portion of the status bar when the mouse pointer is over the Form object and when the Form object has focus.

The Form.SysMenu Property

Default value: .T.

If SysMenu is True, the Form object has a System menu accessed by a System button in the upper-left corner, or by pressing Alt-hyphen (modeless form) or Alt-spacebar (modal form). MDI forms always have a System menu, regardless of the status of SysMenu.

The Form.Text Property

Default value: "FORM"

The Text property specifies the title of a Form object.

The Form.Top Property

Default value: 0

The Top property is the location of the top of the Form object, in characters sized by the Form object's ScaleFont. The top-left corner of the dBASE for Windows client area is 0,0.

The Form.View Property

Default value: ""

The View property names a .DBF or .QBE file that provides access to data referenced by objects on the Form object.

The Form.Visible Property

Default value: .T.

If Visible is True, the Form object is shown.

The Form.Width Property

Default value: 63.0

The Width property specifies the width of the Form object in characters. The width of each character is determined by the Form object's ScaleFont properties.

The Form.WindowState Property

Default value: 0

Available settings: 0–2

The WindowState property specifies that the window is normal (0), minimized (1), or maximized (2).

▶ Menu Object Properties

The following listings briefly explain the properties of Menu objects.

The Menu.Before Property

Before is an object reference to the object that this Menu object precedes in the Form's tabbing order. If this Menu object is the last one in the Form's tabbing order, Before is a reference to the first object in the tabbing order (Form.First).

The Menu.Checked Property

Default value: .F.

If True, Checked specifies that a check mark is placed to the left of a menu item.

The Menu.ClassName Property

Default value: MENU

This property is read-only. ClassName is assigned by dBASE for Windows for each of the built-in classes. This can be used to distinguish among multiple objects with the same name.

The Menu.Enabled Property

Default value: .T.

If Enabled is True, the Menu object is accessible. You can use the Enabled property to disable options in event handlers. For example, a Valid function could set some object's Enabled property to False if required conditions were not met.

The Menu.HelpFile Property

Default value: ""

The HelpFile property names the Windows Help file that will be used when you press F1.

The Menu.HelpID Property

Default value: –1

The HelpID specifies the individual Help screen that will be accessed in the Windows Help file specified by the HelpFile property.

The Menu.Name Property

Default value: Text, capitalized

The Name property is the property name given to this Menu on the parent Form. If the text is File, the name is FILE.

The Menu.OnClick( ) Method

The OnClick property is called whenever you click a button or menu choice.

The Menu.OnHelp( ) Method

The OnHelp method is called when the F1 key is pressed with focus on the Menu object.

The Menu.Parent Property

The Parent property is an object reference to the parent Form of the Menu object. It is usually a read-only property assigned when the object is created via a DEFINE command or a NEW call to the constructor. For menus, which may be moved from one Form to another by changing the Parent property, it is not read-only.

The Menu.Release( ) Method

The Release method removes the Menu object from memory. Releasing a Form also releases all of the Form's objects.

The Menu.Separator Property

Default value: .F.

If Separator is True, the Separator property specifies that this Menu object is a separator between other menu choices, not a menu choice.

The Menu.Shortcut Property

The Shortcut property names the accelerator key used to trigger a menu choice.

The Menu.StatusMessage Property

Default value: ""

The StatusMessage appears in the left portion of the status bar when the mouse pointer is over the Menu object and when the Menu object has focus.

The Menu.Text Property

Default value: ""

The Text property of a Menu object is the prompt that appears on the menu. If you precede a letter in the text with an ampersand, that letter will be its selection key; it will be underscored, and pressing the letter with the Alt key will immediately select that choice.

Working with Forms

PART FIVE

In this final part, we'll dive into the Form Designer. As you have already seen, the Form Designer is a tool of almost unlimited depth and breadth.

In earlier parts, you've learned that simple forms can be built quite easily. On the other hand, you may want to build forms with more sophisticated elements, such as drop-down list boxes, multiple radio button groups, text editors, and more. All these capabilities are available.

In each chapter in this part, we'll start with an explanatory section, showing examples working with the more important and commonly used features of the objects that we're discussing. Then we'll finish each chapter with reference material that discusses every property of each object covered in the chapter.

For example, we don't want you to memorize the various states of a Scrollbar object. On your first reading of the chapter, we want you to find out that you can put scroll bars on a form, leave them off, or let them appear automatically when they are needed. You can always return to the chapter when you need to control the Scrollbar objects on an actual form.

In Chapter 15, Designing Forms and Menus, we'll cover the Form and Menu object classes. You'll get an in-depth look at the Form Designer and its related tools: the Object Properties Inspector, the Controls palette, and the Procedure Editor. This chapter also includes a thorough inspection of all the capabilities of the Menu Designer.

In Chapter 16, Working with Static Form Objects, you'll learn about the simplest types of objects you can put on a form—the ones that do not allow you to enter data. They are Image, Line, Rectangle, and Text objects. Images let you dress your forms with graphics. Lines let you draw lines on your forms, but if you think that's all, we urge you to take a look! Rectangles are commonly used to enclose a group of related controls on a form. Text is used, of course, to label the components of a form.

Chapter 17, Working with Data-Entry Form Objects, will cover Checkbox, Entryfield, Radiobutton, and Spinbox objects. These are the primary objects for getting data into your tables, and for reporting the contents of your tables.

The more complex objects available for data entry will be covered in Chapter 18, Working with Advanced Form Objects. Here, you'll learn about Browse, Combobox, Editor, and Listbox objects. The Browse object lets you use part or all of the facilities of the Table Records tool right in a form. Combobox and Listbox objects allow you to select from one or more choices, singly or in groups. Editor objects let you edit text files and Memo fields on your forms. Using these more advanced objects can add great power to your forms.

The final chapter, Chapter 19, Putting the System Together, will cover two more objects used to hold forms together and relate pieces of your system: Pushbutton and Scrollbar objects. In addition to detailed coverage of these objects, the chapter includes an additional section, Using What You've Learned, in which you'll put the more advanced topics to use by tying your forms and tables together into a working system.

▶ ▶ CHAPTER 16

Working with Static Form Objects

▶▶ **This** chapter covers static objects: Image, Line, Rectangle, and Text objects. We call these *static* objects not because they cannot move or change, but because you cannot manipulate them directly (in contrast to Entryfield or Checkbox objects, for example).

Image objects display graphics on the form. Images can come from bitmap files, from resources in Windows code files such as .DLL and .EXE files, or from Binary fields in your tables.

Line objects are, as their name suggests, used to draw lines on forms. When we get to Line objects, you'll see that they are more interesting than you might imagine.

Rectangle objects are typically used in the background to group related controls. By setting their borders, you can have raised and lowered panels on your forms, creating a variety of interesting and subtle effects.

Text objects are used to display fixed text on the form, for titles, and to label controls. You can vary the fonts and font sizes, as well as text colors. If you don't get carried away, this capability can produce good-looking, effective forms.

▶▶ Working with Image Objects

To prepare Figure 16.1, we changed our working directory to \DBASEWIN\SAMPLES and launched the image DIVESHOP.BMP half a dozen times (selecting the Image file type in the Navigator).

FIGURE 16.1

Six ways to show DIVESHOP.BMP

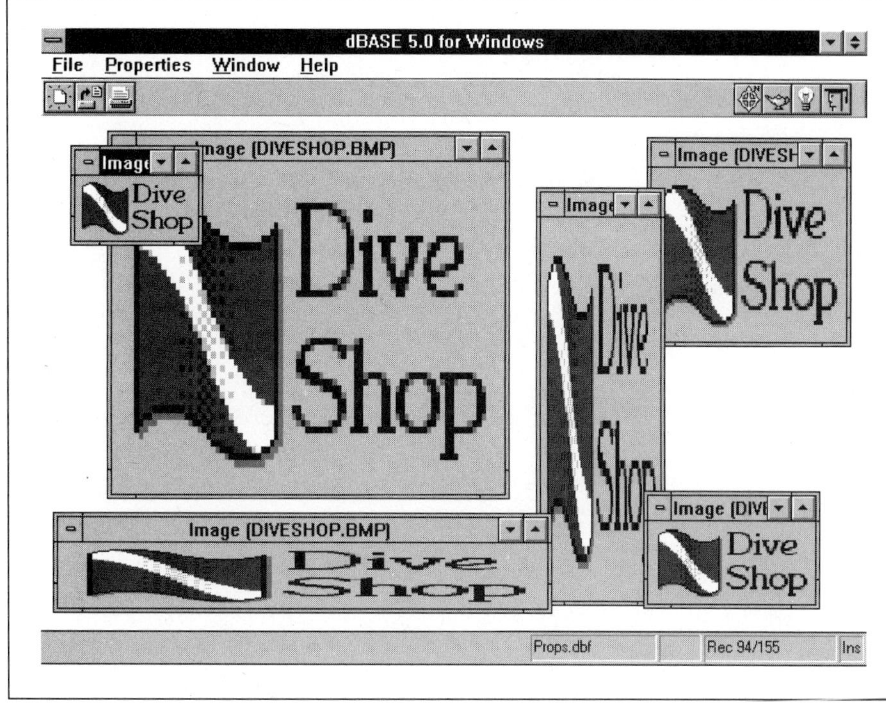

The smallest image is the original size of the DIVESHOP image. The others are stretched in one or both directions. The first point we want to make about images is that Windows supports stretching them, and dBASE for Windows lets you take advantage of this fact.

In the following sections, we'll examine the Alignment property, and then make a simple program that turns an image on and off.

▶ Aligning Images

When you open an image file from the Navigator, the image is enclosed in a window, with its borders "glued" to the borders of the window. As you change the window's size and shape, the image stretches or compresses to fit. This is the *stretch* alignment.

For our work with Image objects, change to the \DBASEWIN\SAMPLES directory and use one of the .BMP files in that directory. If you prefer, you can create an image for yourself in your \DBWORK directory.

►► **NOTE**

Microsoft Paintbrush, which is included with Windows, can be used to create .BMP files. However, if you plan to do a lot of artwork, you'll find that a full-fledged paint program is a good investment.

Follow these steps to experiment with image alignment:

1. With an image file available, launch the Untitled form.
2. Select the Image control from the Controls palette and put an Image object on your form.
3. Choose the Object Properties Inspector's Properties tab and select the DataSource property.
4. Click the tool icon to go to the Choose Bitmap dialog box. In the Location drop-down list, choose the Filename option, as shown in Figure 16.2.

FIGURE 16.2

Choosing a bitmap in a file

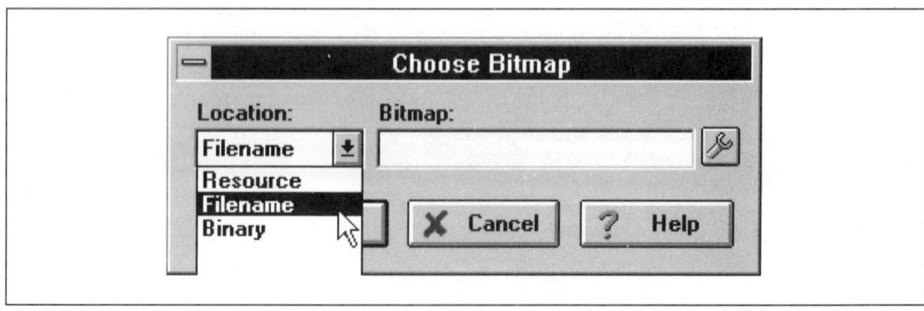

The Filename option is used to choose a bitmap stored as an individual file, with an extension of .BMP. The Resource choice lets you choose bitmaps that are used by dBASE for Windows in your own system. The Binary option lets you choose a Binary field in one of your tables.

5. Repeat the image selection process, putting two more Image objects on your form and using the same .BMP file as the DataSource property for all three.
6. Stretch the three images into different shapes. Our form is shown in Figure 16.3. (We've selected all three with the lasso, so you can see their boundaries clearly.)

FIGURE 16.3

Three stretched images on a form

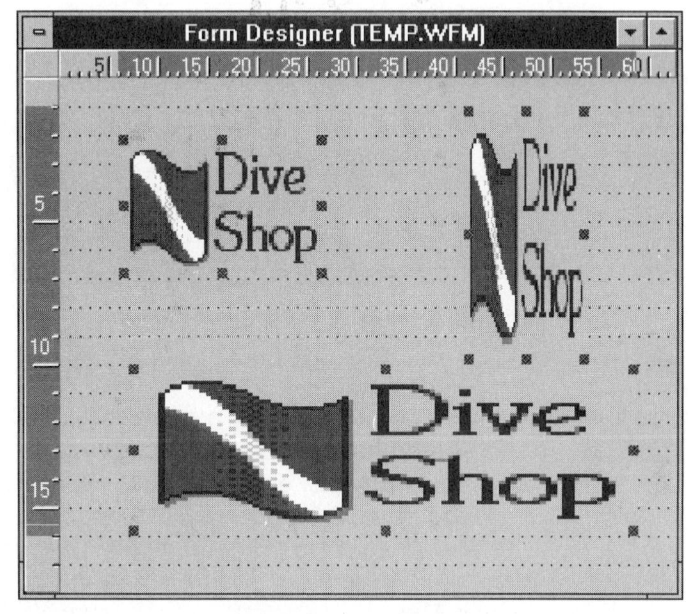

Each of these images has the default stretch alignment, which is one of the three possible alignments. Let's reset two of them to use the other two alignments.

7. Select one of your larger Image objects and then click the Properties tab of your Object Properties Inspector.

8. Click on the Alignment property in the Position Properties group. Select 1 - Top Left alignment for one of your Image objects:

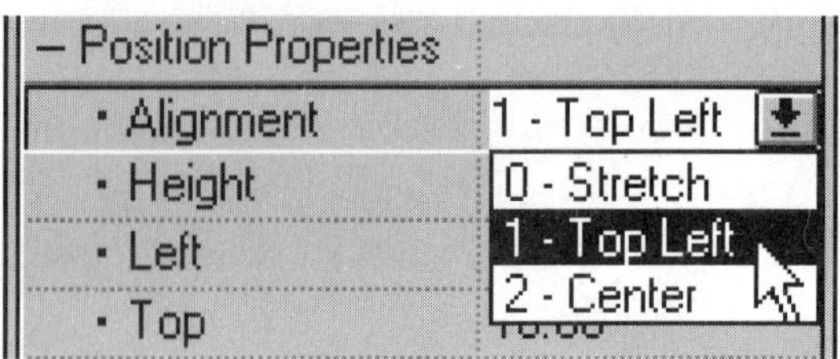

►► **NOTE**

When you pick Top Left, the Alignment property is assigned the value 1 (Alignment is a numeric property). The Object Properties Inspector is nice enough to tell you that 1 means Top Left, but when you edit your .WFM file as a program, you'll see just the 1 assigned to the Alignment property.

9. Select 2 - Center alignment for one of your Image objects. You should have one Image using each of the three Alignment settings. Our work is shown in Figure 16.4, again with all three selected so you can see their borders.

Examine the image in the upper-right part of our form, which uses the center Alignment. We made the Image object too skinny to entirely fit the original bitmap. As you can see, the image is centered, and the parts that don't fit are chopped off. This gives you a limited capability for cropping an image, as you might crop a photograph. (More detailed cropping can be done with a good paint program.)

For a fun effect, you can put the following lines in a Form's OnNavigate method:

```
IF image1.Alignment < 2
    image1.Alignment = image1.Alignment + 1
```

FIGURE 16.4

Three different Alignment properties

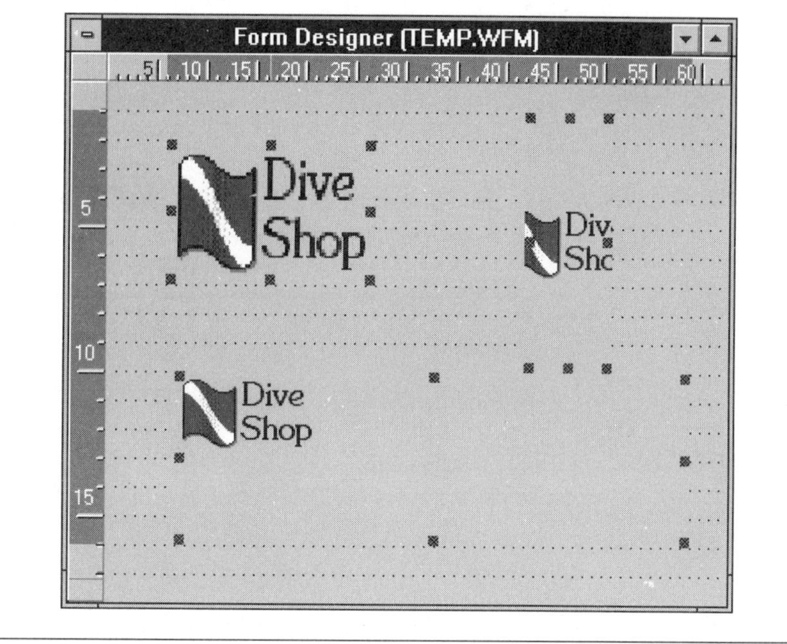


```
   ELSE
      image1.Alignment = 0
ENDIF
```

This bit of code will make the "static" Image object quite active! It changes your Alignment property every time you change from one record to the next. (Please don't do nonsense like this unless this type of variety is appropriate for your application.)

▶ Visible and Invisible Objects

Now let's have some fun. The code we'll add is totally useless, unless, of course, you're learning to work with Image objects, which is precisely what you're doing. (That means you shouldn't feel guilty about having this bit of fun, regardless of how busy you are.)

In the previous section, we explored the Alignment property. Text objects also have an Alignment property, but with a different set of choices than those available for Image objects. Here, we'll look at the Visible property, which is shared by 15 other object classes. All of the Visible properties work the same way.

Visible is a data property that takes a logical value. Whenever we say a *value*, it means that you can place any expression that returns the appropriate value type in the property.

When an object has a True value (.T.) in the Visible property, you can see it. If Visible is False (.F.), you can't see it. Now, what do you think happens to the object's event handlers when Visible is False?

Do you suppose that an invisible object will still handle, for example, an OnLeftMouseDown event? No reference material answers the question we pose here. In fact, the interplay of the various properties and events is so potentially complex that no reference work could even begin to tell you how all combinations interact. If you want to know how an event handler is affected by the setting of a data property, the only reliable method is to try it. Which is exactly what we'll do here.

Think about the following line for a moment:

```
This.Visible = .NOT. This.Visible
```

If you are used to algebraic equations, you'll probably think that line is an error. Not so. The equal sign in this statement is an assignment operator, not a check for equality. That statement reverses the setting of a logical property every time it is executed. If This.Visible starts True, it is changed to False. If it starts False, it is changed to True. This is the underlying statement beneath all toggles (switches that alternately set something on and off) in computer programs.

Let's try this statement in the OnLeftMouseDown event handler of our Image object. First, you need a form with a single Image object. If you have the form used in the previous section, just delete two of the Image objects. If you haven't got this form, go back to the start of the section about aligning images and follow steps 1 through 4 to put a single image on your form.

Select your object and click on the Events tab of the Object Properties Inspector. Click on the OnLeftMouseDown event and then click on the tool icon to launch the Procedure Editor. Add this line to add the toggle to the OnLeftMouseDown event handler:

```
This.Visible = .NOT. This.Visible
```

Click on the lightning icon to run your form. Ready for the experiment? Click on the image. It will disappear. Without moving your mouse, click again. What happens?

For us, nothing happens. That image is dead as a doornail. It's history. Or is it?

Click on the design icon (or press Shift-F2) to return to the Form Designer. When you get back, your image is still on the form. So what happened? The image turned invisible when your mouse click triggered the toggle statement you entered. And further clicking didn't do any good because an invisible image does not respond to mouse events.

Well, the Form object should still be responding to mouse events. Let's add the same toggle to OnLeftMouseDown anyplace in the form. However, there is something to bear in mind: the "This" object is the object that traps the event. In an event handler for the Image, it is the Image object. In an event handler for the Form, it is the Form object. So the correct statement in the Form's OnLeftMouseDown is this:

```
This.image1.Visible = .NOT. This.image1.Visible
```

Enter that line in the Procedure Editor as the handler for the Form's OnLeftMouseDown event. Did you create the current form by deleting two of the Image objects created in the previous section? If you did, then the name might be image1, image2, or image3. Check the Name property in the Identification Properties outline topic.

With that line in place, click on the lightning icon or press F2 to run your form. Now click on the image. It disappears. Click anyplace in the form—your image reappears! In fact, click anywhere in the form, and the image is toggled from visible to invisible or back.

If you are not getting the right result, check your .WFM file against ours. Your coordinates (Top, Left, Height, and Width) and DataSource property may not match ours, but the OnLeftMouseDown handlers and methods should match these:

```
** END HEADER -- do not remove this line*
* Generated on 01/14/95
*
LOCAL f
f = NEW TEMPFORM()
f.Open()
```

```
CLASS TEMPFORM OF FORM
  Set Procedure To BUTTONS.CC additive
  this.HelpID = ""
  this.Width =         63
  this.OnLeftMouseDown = CLASS::FORM_ONLEFTMOUSEDOWN
  this.HelpFile = ""
  this.Text = "Form"
  this.Left =         13.5
  this.Top =          0.0586
  this.Height =         18

  DEFINE IMAGE IMAGE1 OF THIS;
    PROPERTY;
      Width        16,;
      OnLeftMouseDown CLASS::IMAGE1_ONLEFTMOUSE-
DOWN,;
      DataSource "FILENAME E:\DBASEWIN\SAMPLES\
DIVESHOP.BMP",;
      Left        24,;
      Top         6,;
      Height        5

  Procedure IMAGE1_OnLeftMouseDown(flags, col, row)
  This.Visible = .NOT. This.Visible

  Procedure Form_OnLeftMouseDown(flags, col, row)
  This.Image1.Visible = .NOT. This.Image1.Visible

ENDCLASS
```

If you click your mouse quickly, you won't see your image flash on and off (or off and on). Why? The first click triggers an OnLeftMouse-Down. Another in rapid succession triggers OnLeftMouseDblClick, not another OnLeftMouseDown.

To experiment with events like this, put a line like this in all the events you might be triggering:

```
? 'Caught an OnLeftMouseDown in the Image'
```

When you run the form, be sure to have the results pane of the Command window visible. Then click away, and you'll see the reports of your activity in the results pane.

We hope you enjoyed that little program, as well as learning from it. Now let's go on to explore Line objects.

▶▶ Working with Line Objects

A Line object in dBASE for Windows is certainly more than just the shortest distance between two points. In this section, we'll explore the shape of the Line object.

▶ Exploring the Line's Possibilities

Figure 16.5 is *not* our attempt to copy Mondrian's art—it's a demonstration of the shapes you can get with Line objects.

FIGURE 16.5 ▶

These are all Line objects

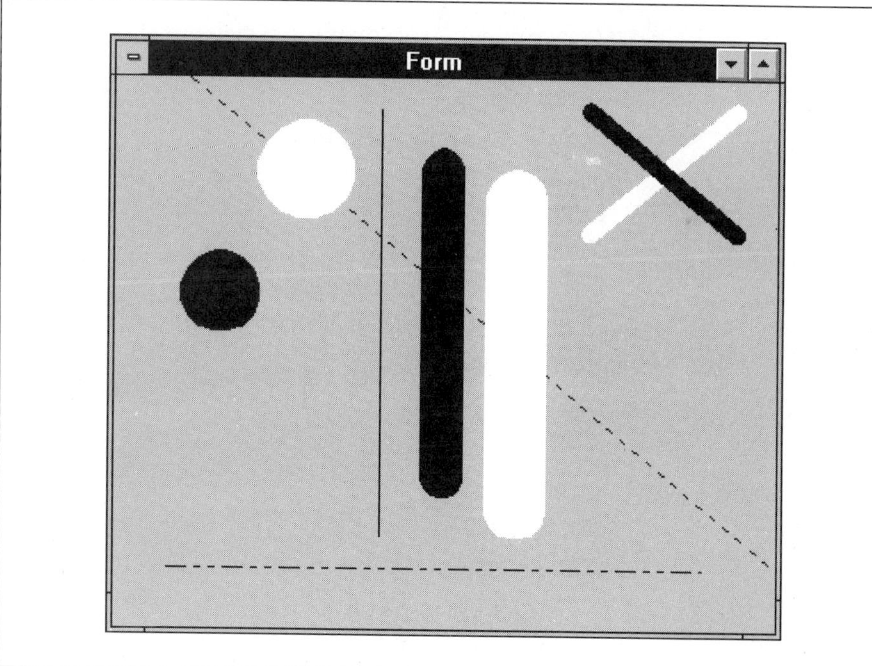

As you can see, lines can be solid, dotted, or patterned lines; oblong shapes; and even circles (well, close to circles). The following is the

.WFM file that defines Figure 16.5:

```
** END HEADER -- do not remove this line*
* Generated on 01/14/95
*
LOCAL f
f = NEW TEMPFORM()
f.Open()

CLASS TEMPFORM OF FORM
   Set Procedure To E:\DBASEWIN\SAMPLES\BUTTONS.CC additive
   this.Width =      63
   this.Text = "Form"
   this.HelpId = ""
   this.HelpFile = ""
   this.Height =      18
   this.Left =      12.666
   this.Top =      0.1758

   DEFINE LINE LINE1 OF THIS;
      PROPERTY;
      Width      55,;
      ColorNormal "+W",;
      Right      18,;
      Bottom      3,;
      Left      18,;
      Top      3

   DEFINE LINE LINE2 OF THIS;
      PROPERTY;
      Width      45,;
      ColorNormal "N",;
      Right      10,;
      Bottom      7,;
      Left      10,;
      Top      7

   DEFINE LINE LINE3 OF THIS;
      PROPERTY;
      Width      35,;
      ColorNormal "+W",;
      Right      38,;
      Bottom      14,;
```

```
    Pen       4,;
    Left      38,;
    Top       4

DEFINE LINE LINE4 OF THIS;
    PROPERTY;
    Width       25,;
    ColorNormal "N",;
    Right       31,;
    Bottom      13,;
    Left        31,;
    Top         3

DEFINE LINE LINE5 OF THIS;
    PROPERTY;
    Width       1,;
    ColorNormal "N",;
    Right       56,;
    Bottom      16,;
    Pen         4,;
    Left        5,;
    Top         16

DEFINE LINE LINE6 OF THIS;
    PROPERTY;
    Width       1,;
    ColorNormal "N",;
    Right       25,;
    Bottom      15,;
    Left        25,;
    Top         1

DEFINE LINE LINE7 OF THIS;
    PROPERTY;
    Width       1,;
    ColorNormal "N",;
    Right       63,;
    Bottom      16,;
    Pen         2,;
    Left        7,;
    Top         0
```

```
DEFINE LINE LINE8 OF THIS;
   PROPERTY;
   Width      10,;
   ColorNormal "N",;
   Right      59,;
   Bottom      5,;
   Left      45,;
   Top      1

DEFINE LINE LINE9 OF THIS;
   PROPERTY;
   Width      10,;
   ColorNormal "+W",;
   Right      45,;
   Bottom      5,;
   Left      59,;
   Top      1

ENDCLASS
```

► Exploring the Shape of the Line

Let's begin by examining the shape of a Line object. We'll prepare a test form that will make this dramatically apparent.

Grabbing a Line

To look at a line, start by drawing a cross-hair pattern with two sensible lines, as you see in Figure 16.6. Again, we've used the lasso to select both Line objects, so you can see the ends.

Launch a blank form and grab two lines. After you fiddle a bit trying to get a good-looking set of cross-hairs, read on—we'll tell you the easy way.

When you try working with your first line, you'll find that it is different from the other screen objects. Instead of having eight boxes to grab in a resize rectangle, there are only two: one at either end. If you grab one or the other of these, you can move the end of the line while the other stays anchored.

You can grab the Line object to move it as you grab other objects, but you must get the mouse pointer positioned exactly on the line, between the resize rectangles. Ready for the cross-hair hints?

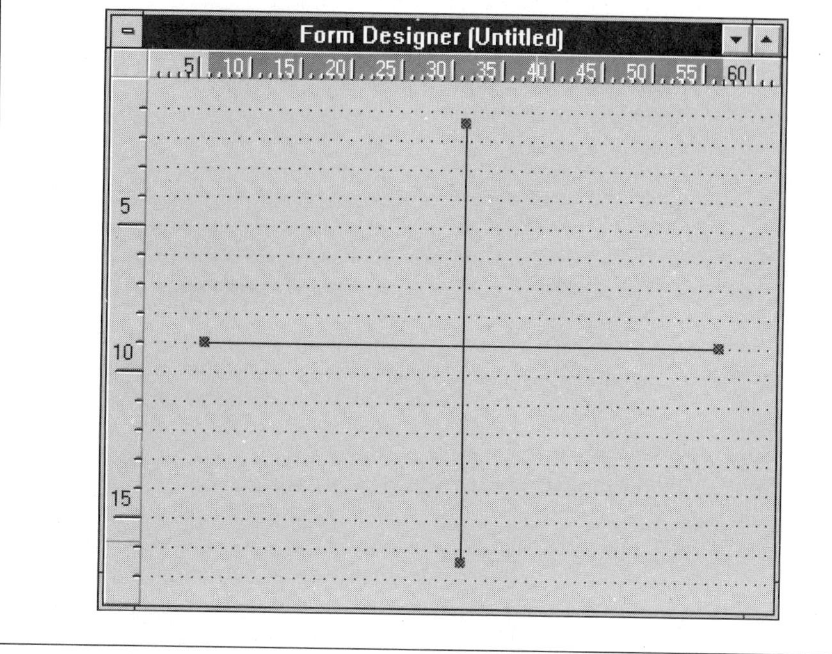

FIGURE 16.6

Cross-hairs for examining line shapes

First, vertical and horizontal lines are quite easy if you have checked Snap To Grid in the Form Designer Properties dialog box (choose Properties ➤ Form Designer, or use the Form Designer's Speed menu).

Second, in Chapter 15 we pointed out the Layout menu's Align Special cascaded pull-down menu. If you have one vertical and one horizontal line, choose Layout ➤ Align Special ➤ Absolute Vertical Center, and then Layout ➤ Align Special ➤ Absolute Horizontal Center. Presto—instant cross-hairs, neatly centered in your form.

Put the Line in Your Sight

With the cross-hairs in place, draw a third line, starting from the exact point where the cross-hairs meet and extending to the right. (With Snap To Grid checked, you'll hit the "exact" point where the cross-hairs meet if you come within half a character, or Turpin, of the point.)

After you place this third line, go immediately to the Object Properties Inspector. Click on the Width property (it's one of the Visual Properties, near the bottom). Using the spinbutton, click the up arrow to increase the width. Pay attention to the exact shape of your line when it is two and three units wide.

Jumping ahead, Figure 16.7 shows our line when we reached 21 pixels wide.

FIGURE 16.7

A wide, white line on the cross-hairs

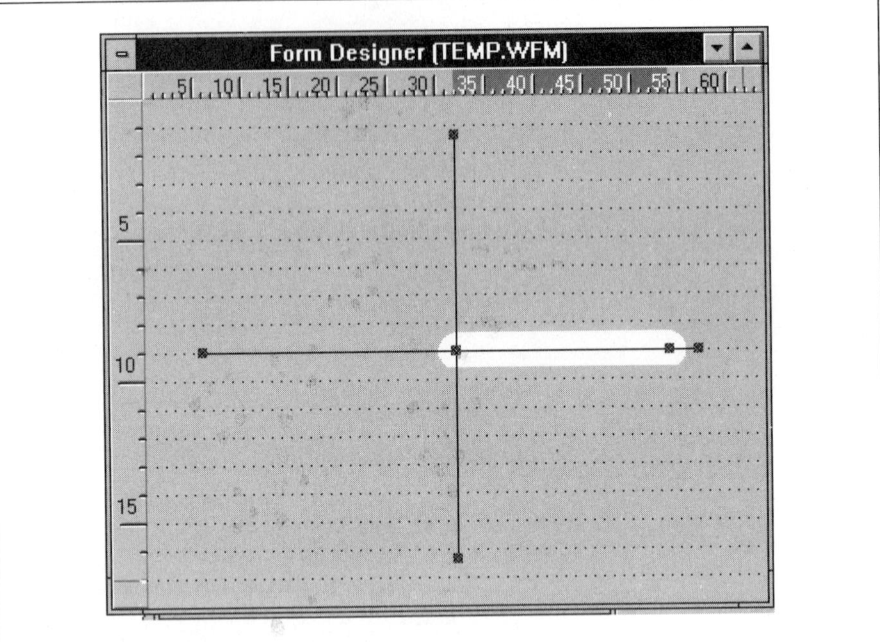

We've also colored our line white (see the discussion of setting the colors) and used the lasso to select all three lines, so you can see as much as possible. One of the things you can see is that the black cross-hairs are on top of the white line, although they were drawn first. Unlike everything else in dBASE for Windows forms, lines are drawn in reverse order—last first. We're not sure if this is a feature you can count on, or a bug that may be corrected soon.

Grow your own line slowly, clicking the up arrow on the Width spinbutton.

As you can see, the line's Width property is in pixels, not Turpins. You'll also notice as you increase the width that the redrawing process is somewhere between slow and very slow. Bear in mind that dBASE for Windows is drawing an individual line for every pixel in width of your Line object.

The other thing we want you to examine carefully is the shape of the end of the line. Watch it closely where the cross-hairs meet.

As your line expands, you clearly see that the "end" of your line isn't the end at all. The end point is the center of a semicircle whose diameter is the width of your line.

▶ Drawing a Circle

We're not sure that everybody who has this book should know all about lines. Wide lines eat hideous helpings of Windows' limited resources. Someone at Microsoft had a bad day when the Windows resource pools were designed: key resources such as GDI (Graphics Device Interface) resources were given a single 64 KB pool. Your machine may have 64 MB of RAM, but you have only 64 KB for graphics resources.

Since each line breaks down into one line per pixel of the Line object's width, fat lines are great resource consumers. In a small system, making circles out of Line objects is fun. In a large system, you shouldn't waste the resources.

▶▶ **NOTE**

If you get serious about circles, you'll need to get into the Windows API (Application Programming Interface). Using dBASE for Windows' EXTERN command, it's very easy to interface directly to the Windows API. Unfortunately, all the documentation on the Windows API assumes that you are an experienced C and C++ programmer, so learning your way around is vastly more difficult than actually using what you learn.

Now, with that said, let's go back to having some fun with our lines. First, select and delete the cross-hairs on your form. Leave just the wide line.

Both ends of a line are semicircles. To make a circle, you need a line without a midsection. One way to do that is to select your line; grab an end and move it in to the other end. If you are *very* good with your mouse, you can do this, getting the two ends precisely together.

The simple way to make a circle is to edit the Position Properties directly. Every on-form object in dBASE for Windows has Top, Left, Height, and Width properties defining its position and shape—except for the Line object. Line obects have Top, Left, Bottom, and Right coordinates.

Actually, the Top and Left coordinates locate the point at the center of one end; the Bottom and Right coordinates locate the center of the other end. The Top could be below the Bottom, and the Left could be to the right of the Right. Unlike the Width, which is measured in pixels, the end coordinates are given in the standard Turpins.

To make a circle, use the Object Properties Inspector as you see us doing in Figure 16.8.

FIGURE 16.8

Setting the Line object's ends together

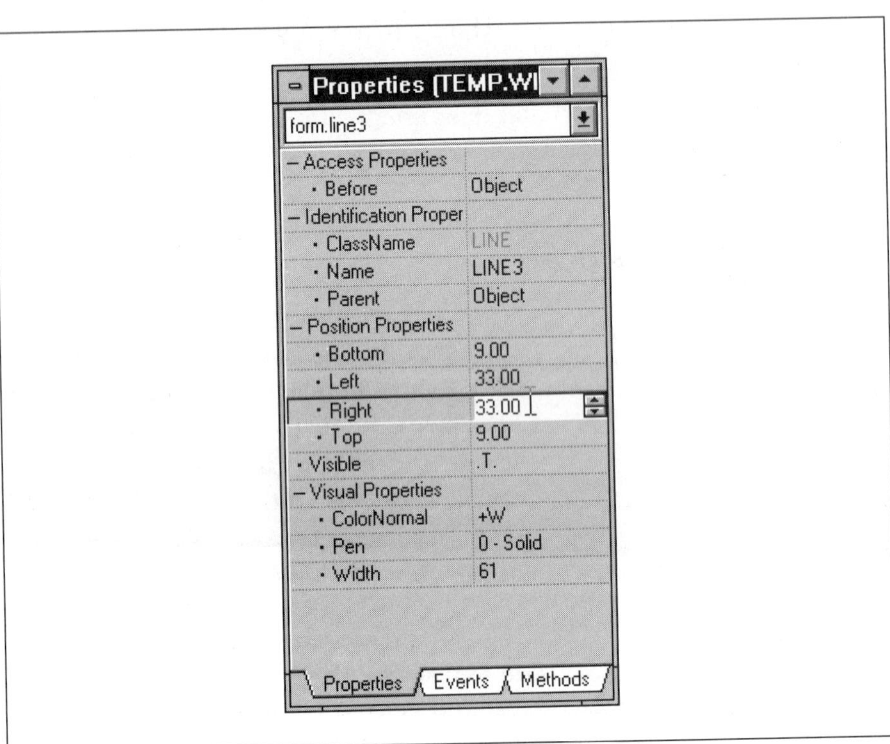

Set the Bottom equal to the Top (if your line was horizontal, these two are already equal) and set the Left equal to the Right. Now go to the Width property and make it very fat!

This will give you a circle. Nothing in the dBASE documentation suggests that this is possible, so don't depend on this behavior lasting into future versions of the product.

▶ Setting the Colors

dBASE for Windows supports both the Windows color scheme and the older dBASE color specifications. The original dBASE color specification used the 16 colors available on the original CGA (Color Graphics Adapter) monitor, which IBM introduced with the first PCs in 1981.

The common Windows color scheme lets you select a palette of 256 colors from a universe whose size is bounded by the pixel depth of your graphics card. A 16-bit card gives you 64 thousand colors; a 24-bit card gives you 16 million colors.

For most database work, however, the older scheme is more than adequate. If your table stores color pictures, dBASE and Windows will handle complexities of displaying them to the full capabilities of your hardware. You can still build your forms with the simple color scheme.

The original colors are as follows:

W	White (or light gray)
N	Black (no color)
R	Red
G	Green
B	Blue
RG	Brown or yellow (red and green)
BG	Cyan (blue and green)
RB	Maroon (red and blue)

The two-letter combinations can be specified in either order. BG is the same as GB, for example. Any of these colors can be specified as shown, or with an added plus sign (+). The plus sign originally meant high-intensity on the CGA adapter. For example, to turn the normal light gray of W into a true white, use +W. The plus sign can precede or follow the color—+W is the same as W+.

We routinely use the W setting, which is the common light-gray background for Windows. It is easy on the eyes and provides good contrast for either black (the N setting) or white (the +W setting) letters, which are also colors we use frequently.

The other colors should be used sparingly for decorative effects and for emphasis. Red is good for warnings. Borland's pushbuttons make good use of small amounts of color.

Our line in Figure 16.7 used the +W specification in its ColorNormal property. All on-form objects have a ColorNormal property. Entryfield, Listbox, and Spinbutton objects also have a ColorHighlight property.

▸▸ Working with Rectangle Objects

In all of the dBASE for Windows dialog boxes, Rectangle objects are used to divide the dialog box into logical sections. This is their primary function.

When you add a Rectangle object, it will cover the objects underneath it, which you probably don't want. As we discussed in Chapter 15, to control the order of objects in your form, you need to work with their z-order. You want to put your Rectangle objects at or near the start of the z-order. (If you use the Program Editor, moving all the rectangle DEFINE commands to the top will generally get what you want.)

There are some very interesting properties of the Rectangle object that you might overlook if you just use this object to divide your dialog boxes into panels. As you might expect, using the techniques suggested here without some restraint will produce garish results. Using these techniques for emphasis and occasional variety adds interest to your forms.

▸ Adding a Label with the Text Property

The first property of a Rectangle object that is, perhaps, unexpected is the Text property. In addition to the Text property, there are all the Font properties normally associated with text (FontName, FontSize, and so on).

The text is placed in the upper-left corner of the Rectangle object, where you would normally want to use it to label a panel in a dialog box.

Figure 16.9 shows a form with two Rectangle objects. In this example, we've done a couple tricks with the Text property.

FIGURE 16.9

Using fancy Text properties in Rectangle objects

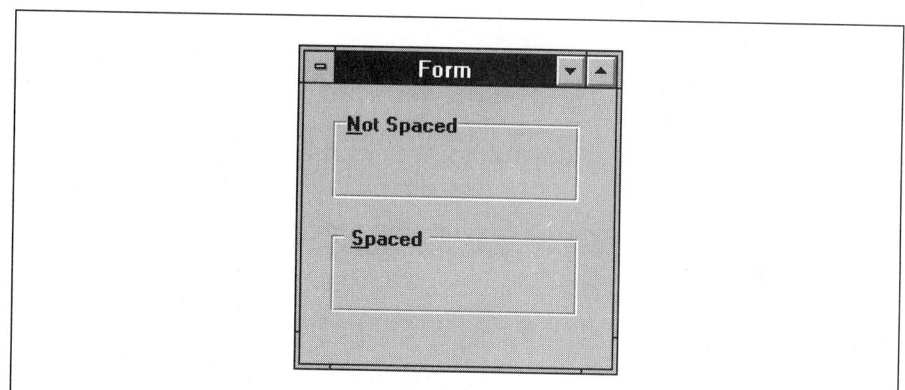

First, you see that we have chosen letters to underscore. These are the letters that are used in combination with the Alt key to go immediately to a particular panel or input control. In the Text property, precede the letter with an ampersand to have it underscored and used as an Alt-key combination.

The text names suggest the next item we are showing. The default is to insert the text into the Rectangle object's border, without spacing to the left or right. We think a single space on either side of the text makes a better-looking label for Rectangle objects.

We added the spacing by editing the assignment to the Text property in the .WFM file. This is our .WFM:

```
** END HEADER -- do not remove this line*
* Generated on 01/15/95
*
LOCAL f
f = NEW TEMPFORM()
f.Open()

CLASS TEMPFORM OF FORM
   Set Procedure To E:\DBASEWIN\SAMPLES\BUTTONS.CC additive
```

```
this.Left =      18
this.Top =       0
this.Text = "sample"
this.Width =       31.5
this.HelpID = ""
this.HelpFile = ""
this.Height =       9.7051

DEFINE RECTANGLE RECTANGLE1 OF THIS;
   PROPERTY;
   Left      3,;
   Top       1,;
   ColorNormal "N/W",;
   Text "&Not Spaced",;
   Width      25,;
   Border .T.,;
   Height      3

DEFINE RECTANGLE RECTANGLE2 OF THIS;
   PROPERTY;
   Left      3,;
   Top       5,;
   ColorNormal "N/W",;
   Text " &Spaced ",;
   Width      25,;
   Border .T.,;
   Height      3

ENDCLASS
```

You can see the difference between the character strings in this .WFM file. The ampersands establish the underscored letter, and the spaces inside the quotation marks establish the spacing we want between the border and the title.

Note that you can add both the ampersands and the spaces using the Object Properties Inspector, if you prefer. Be careful typing trailing spaces, since there is no way to see exactly what you have created.

▸ Checking Out the OldStyle Property

We always try out the OldStyle property, because we're curious people. Every time we take a look, we conclude that the old style is not nearly as nice as the replacement, and we never set OldStyle to True after we take a look. See if you agree:

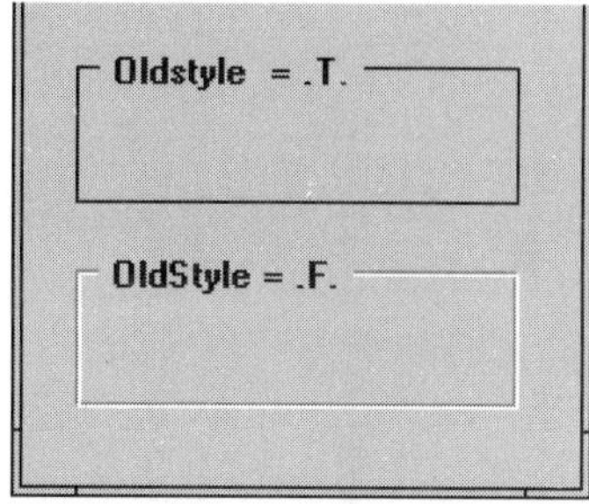

We're not going to mention OldStyle anymore. It's a property of six other objects, and changing it from the default False to True has a similar effect as you see in our example.

Adding Border Styles

So far, we've left the BorderStyle property set to 0, which means Normal. It can also be raised or lowered. Figure 16.10 shows Rectangle objects with the three border styles.

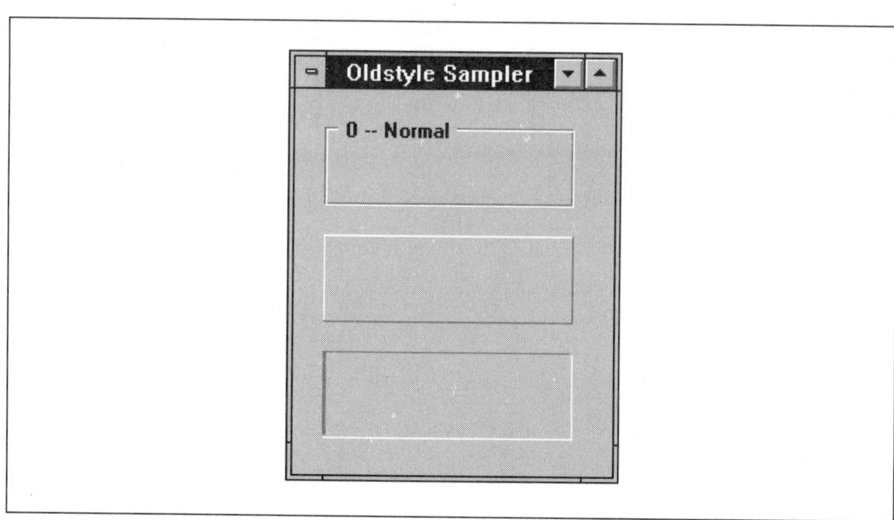

FIGURE 16.10

Carving panels with doubled Rectangle objects

We didn't forget the Text property for the raised and lowered borders. dBASE for Windows only shows Text on a normal border. If you want to have raised or lowered borders and a label, too, you need to provide a Text object, if you want a label.

We really like old-fashioned woodwork, with lots of carved panels. You can do your own woodworking with dBASE for Windows by slipping one Rectangle object inside another and manipulating the BorderStyle property. Figure 16.11 shows four combinations of two rectangles each.

FIGURE 16.11

Normal, raised, and lowered Rectangle borders

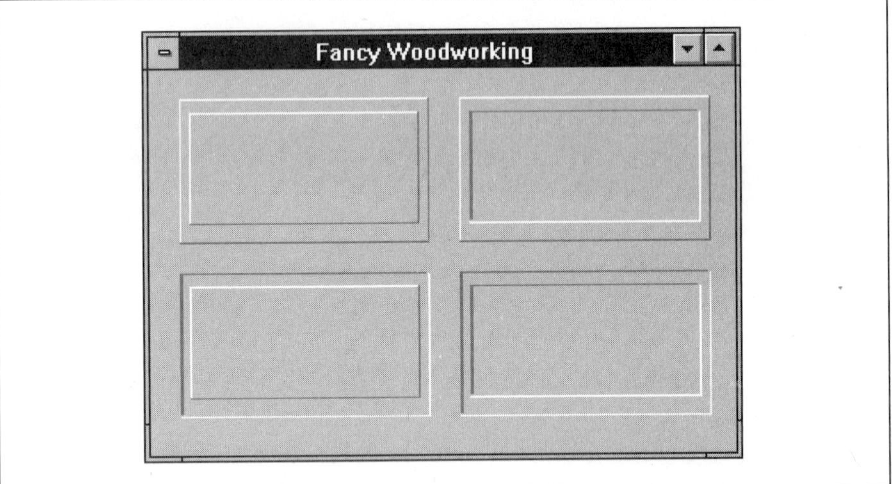

In each of the examples in Figure 16.11, we drew the interior rectangle from the top of the outside rectangle down to one Turpin above the bottom. We drew it one Turpin inside on both the left and right. Then we used the Object Properties Inspector to add 0.5 to the Top property of the inside rectangle.

With some care, we think you can get even better-looking results than the ones we show in Figure 16.11. These effects can add a lot to your forms, and they don't run so quickly into the world of garish distractions as using too many colors or fonts does.

About the only downside to using these effects is that you can spend so much time making great-looking forms that you forget that your form is supposed to be working for you in handling your data.

▶ Adding a Pattern

The PatternStyle property is probably a reflection of the internal capabilities of Windows graphics. The Windows API calls that let you draw a rectangle also let you choose a style. dBASE for Windows brings those styles to us as the PatternStyle property.

We've yet to use any of these in practice, but they're here if you want them. Figure 16.12 shows the possibilities.

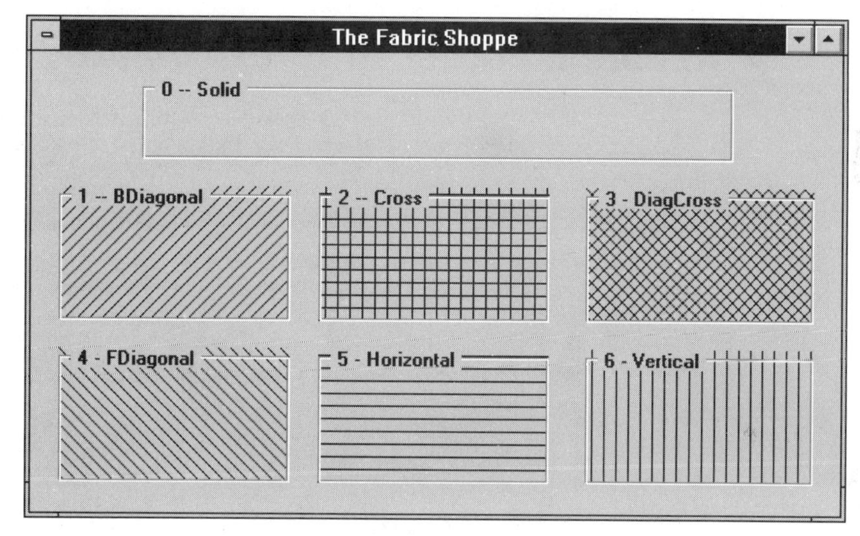

FIGURE 16.12

Settings of the PatternStyle property

Since these styles are built into Windows graphics interface, using them does not extract a big penalty in available GDI resources. Of course, not everything that is free is valuable. The window title in Figure 16.12 suggests the application that comes most readily to mind.

You can also see that the pattern extends to the border of the rectangle, but the visible border of a rectangle with a normal border is somewhat below the top of the rectangle. This allows for the height of the text label. It also lets the pattern bleed over the edge. Using a raised or lowered border traps the pattern wholly within the visible border.

►► Working with Text Objects

The Text object is your basic means for putting text on your forms. Browse, Checkbox, Form, Menu, Pushbutton, Radiobutton, Rectangle, and Text objects all have a Text property. Except for the Text object, however, each of these serves to label the object to which it is attached. For example, a Form object's Text property is in the window title bar. A Checkbox object's Text property is just to the right of the check box.

Text objects can do anything you like with text, anywhere on your form.

► Adding a Border to a Text Object

A Text object can have a border, which makes it a near-relative of the Rectangle object. Figure 16.13 shows the possibilities.

FIGURE 16.13

Text borders

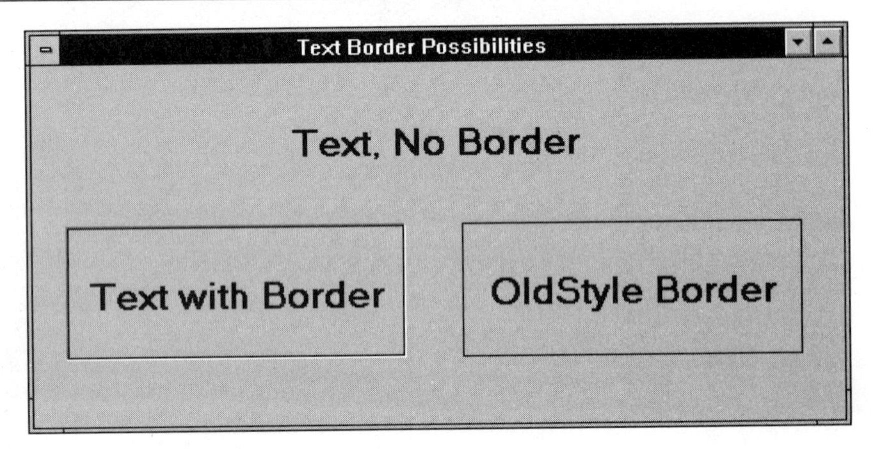

Unlike a Rectangle object, a Text object gives you full control of the location of the text within it. Each of the samples in Figure 16.13 is aligned in the center of the Text object.

▶ The Many Ways to Align a Text Object

While dBASE for Windows is not a complete desktop publishing package, the Alignment property of the Text object gives you a lot of possibilities. Figure 16.14 shows what can be done with the Alignment property of a Text object.

FIGURE 16.14

Twelve ways to align your text

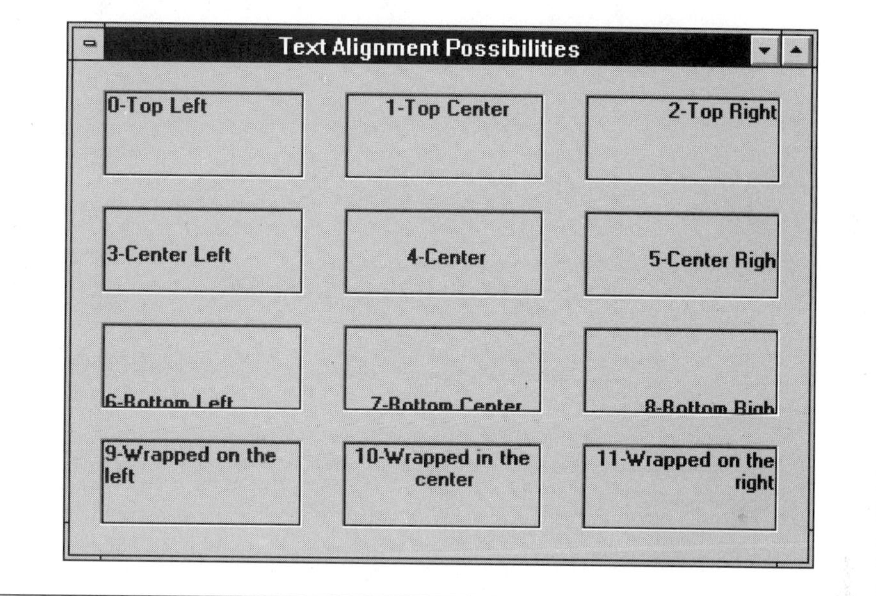

You can place your text where you want it within the Text object. The Text object can even accommodate text that is too long and needs to be wrapped to fit. However, as you can see, the Alignment property is not always intelligent about avoiding the border.

▶ Choosing Fonts and Type Families

We wouldn't have a true Windows product if we couldn't use various fonts, sizes, and styles of type. dBASE for Windows gives you a fine selection, limited only by the fonts you have installed for Windows. All the examples in this section will use only the fonts that come with Windows.

The FontSize Property

With scalable fonts, such as Microsoft's TrueType fonts, you can get any size you like. The older fonts came in just one size or in a limited range of sizes. The Font dialog box shows you the available sizes for each font. Here's a range of sizes, beginning with the default 8-point size.

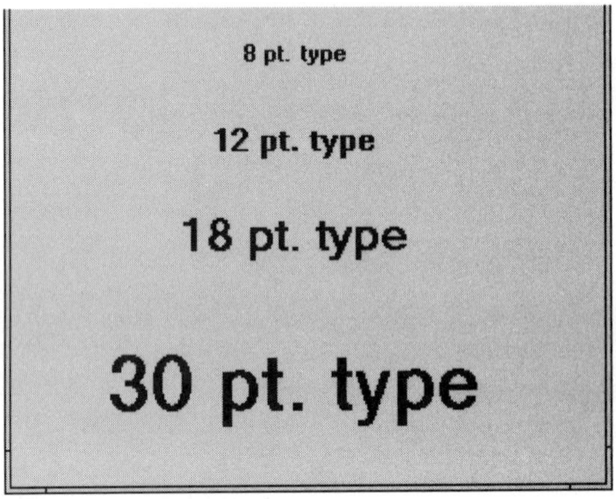

8 pt. type

12 pt. type

18 pt. type

30 pt. type

In American typesetting, a point is a twelfth of a pica, and a pica is a sixth of an inch, so there are 72 points per inch. The Europeans adopted a metric measurement, much easier to deal with and quite close to our point. American dominance in computer software, however, has stuck us with this oddball unit of measure.

You can set any size you like by typing directly in the FontSize property, using the spinbutton in the FontSize property, or clicking on the tool icon (in FontSize or any other Font property) and setting the size in the Font dialog box.

You can learn a lot by clicking the spinbutton and watching the text change on your form, one point at a time. You'll see that even scalable fonts don't look equally good in even very close point sizes. It's not unusual to see a text label that is handsome in 24-point type become only barely legible in 25-point type.

The FontName Property

Along with changing sizes, you can also change fonts. If you know the font's name, you can type it directly into the FontName property, but you are generally better off clicking on the tool icon and choosing the FontName through the Font dialog box.

These are samples of four TrueType fonts that come with Windows:

This is Arial

This is MS Sans Serif

This is Courier New

This is Times New Roman

On paper, such as in this book, fonts with serifs (the decorative bits around the edges of letters) are considered more readable, so they are usually used for the body text. On screen, the opposite is true. Fonts without serifs are more readable.

Times New Roman is a very readable font on the printed page, but should only be used for special effects in larger sizes on a form. The Courier fonts, including Courier New, are *monospaced* fonts; the letter *i* is as wide as a *W*. The other fonts are *proportional* fonts; each letter is as wide as the type designer thought was attractive.

Monospaced fonts are a good choice when you want to line up text in neat columns, such as in a computer program. A monospaced font would be a good choice for the Program Editor's font. We don't otherwise recommend them. (Numerals are all the same width in any one font, so columns of numbers will line up.)

In addition to the TrueType fonts in our example, you might consider the special Small Fonts set, which provides fonts from 7 points down to

2 points. Screen fonts that are 6 or 7 points are barely legible—good for copyright notices and other noncritical text.

The FontStyle Property

One of the endless (and probably pointless) debates that we computer people engage in is the one over the definition of a font. Is bold Arial one font and normal Arial a second, or is Arial a font and normal and bold just two font styles?

If a font vendor sells you a normal, bold, italic, and bold italic font, it tends to call that four fonts. The dBASE for Windows property names suggest that Borland's designers aren't in the business of selling fonts.

The four common styles (or fonts?) are normal, bold, italic, and bold italic. On the printed page, **boldface** should be reserved for emphasis or other special uses. On the screen, however, most fonts are more readable if you choose bold. (Each of the TrueType samples is bold.) These are the available font styles:

This is regular Arial
This is bold Arial
This is italic Arial
This is bold italic Arial
Underlined bold Arial
Srikeout bold Arial

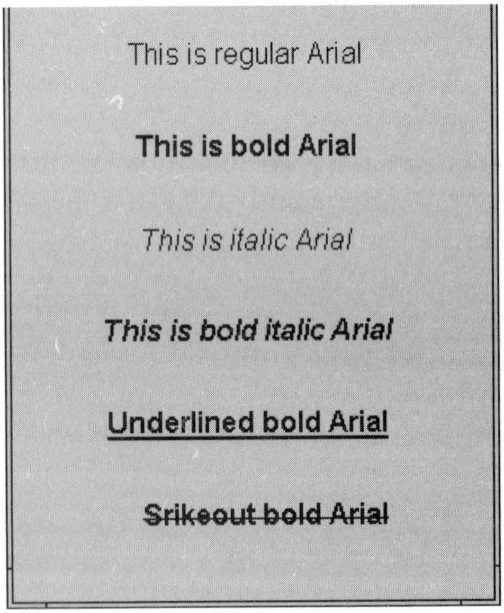

The underlining and strikeout are two of the things that are built into Windows, so the dBASE for Windows designers decided that they might as well let us specify them. The underlined style can be useful, but we haven't yet used the FontStrikeOut property, except in this example.

Static Form Object Properties Reference

In this section, we provide an alphabetical listing of all the properties of the Image, Line, Rectangle, and Text objects. The listing includes the default value of the item (if it has one). If an item is read-only, you cannot assign a value to it via the Object Properties Inspector or in a program. If a property is read-only, it is noted in the listing.

Data properties are called Properties; events and other methods are called Methods. Additionally, Methods' names are followed by parentheses. For example, ClassName is a data property, but Close( ) is a method.

NOTE

You can find similar reference material in the on-line Help and in the *Language Reference* manual. However, as this is written, our reference is more reliable. (We expect that the on-line reference material will improve with later releases, but that won't help you much if you want to browse through the properties while you wait for your train.)

Image Object Properties

This section lists and briefly explains the properties of the Image object.

The Image.Alignment Property

Default value: 0

With the Alignment property, an image can be aligned at the top left (1), centered (2), or stretched to fit (0).

The Image.Before Property

Before is an object reference to the object that this Image precedes in the form's tabbing order. If this Image object is the last one in the form's tabbing order, Before is a reference to the first object in the tabbing order (Form.First).

The Image.ClassName Property

Default value: IMAGE

ClassName is read-only. This property is assigned by dBASE for Windows for each of the built-in classes. ClassName can be used to distinguish among multiple objects with the same name.

The Image.DataSource Property

The DataSource property specifies the source of data for the Image object. An Image can come from a resource, Binary field, or file.

The Image.Height Property

Default value: 5.5

The Height property specifies the height of the Image object in characters.

The Image.hWnd Property

The hWnd property is read-only. This property is an arbitrary integer number that identifies the window to which the Image object belongs. This is called the window's *handle*. It is used when you access Windows functions directly via EXTERN commands.

The Image.ID Property

Default value: -1

ID is a number that can be used to distinguish between otherwise identical Image objects. It is typically used when a program creates a set of similar objects in a FOR loop.

The Image.Left Property

Default value: 1

The Left property specifies the location of the left side of the Image object within its form, in characters. The leftmost character is number 0.

The Image.MousePointer Property

Default value: 0

Available settings: 0–11

The MousePointer property specifies the type of mouse pointer to use when the pointer is over the Image object. For example, the mouse pointer is an arrow over a form, but turns to an I-beam in an editor. The settings are default (0), arrow (1), cross (2), I-beam (3), icon (4), size (5), size NESW (6), size S (7), size NWSE (8), size E (9), up arrow (10), and wait (hourglass, 11).

The Image.Move( ) Method

Parameters: <*lft*>,<*tp*>,<*wdth*>,<*hght*>

Move is a method property which can move the Image object, resize the Image object, or both. You provide Move with four parameters, representing the new values for the properties Left, Top, Width, and Height, respectively.

The Image.Name Property

Default value: IMAGE<*n*>

The Name property is the property name given to this Image on the parent form. If the name is IMAGE1, for example, specifying Parent.IMAGE1 specifies this Image object.

The Image.OnLeftDblClick( ) Method

Parameters: <*flags*>,<*col*>,<*row*>

The OnLeftDblClick event is called when you double-click with the left mouse button over the Image object. The parameters report the status of the Shift, Ctrl, and Alt keys, as well as the location at the time of the left double-click event.

The Image.OnLeftMouseDown( ) Method

Parameters: <*flags*>,<*col*>,<*row*>

The OnLeftMouseDown event is called when you press the left mouse button over the Image object. The parameters report the status of the Shift, Ctrl, and Alt keys, as well as the location at the time of the left mouse-down event.

The Image.OnLeftMouseUp( ) Method

Parameters: <*flags*>,<*col*>,<*row*>

The OnLeftMouseUp handler is called whenever you release the left button over the Image object. (An up event over one object might have been preceded by a down event over another object.) The parameters report the status of the Shift, Ctrl, and Alt keys, as well as the location at the time of the event.

The Image.OnMiddleDblClick( ) Method

Parameters: <*flags*>,<*col*>,<*row*>

The OnMiddleDblClick event is called when you double-click with the middle mouse button of a three-button mouse over the Image object. The parameters report the status of the Shift, Ctrl, and Alt keys, as well as the location at the time of the middle double-click event.

The Image.OnMiddleMouseDown( ) Method

Parameters: <*flags*>,<*col*>,<*row*>

The OnMiddleMouseDown event is called when you press the middle mouse button of a three-button mouse over the Image object. The parameters report the status of the Shift, Ctrl, and Alt keys, as well as the location at the time of the middle mouse-down event.

The Image.OnMiddleMouseUp( ) Method

Parameters: <*flags*>,<*col*>,<*row*>

The OnMiddleMouseUp handler is called whenever you release the middle mouse button over the Image object. (An up event over one object might have been preceded by a down event over another object.) The parameters report the status of the Shift, Ctrl, and Alt keys, as well as the location at the time of the middle mouse-up event.

The Image.OnMouseMove( ) Method

Parameters: <*flags*>,<*col*>,<*row*>

The OnMouseMove event is called when any mouse movement is detected over the Image object.

The Image.OnOpen( ) Method

The OnOpen event is called when the form containing the Image object is opened.

The Image.OnRightDblClick( ) Method

Parameters: <*flags*>,<*col*>,<*row*>

The OnRightDblClick event is called when you double-click with the right mouse button over the Image object. (Right double-clicks are recognized by the Navigator as commands to design the object.) The parameters report the status of the Shift, Ctrl, and Alt keys, as well as the location at the time of the right double-click event.

The Image.OnRightMouseDown( ) Method

Parameters: <*flags*>,<*col*>,<*row*>

The OnRightMouseDown event is called when you press the right mouse button over the Image object. The parameters report the status of the Shift, Ctrl, and Alt keys, as well as the location at the time of the right mouse-down event.

The Image.OnRightMouseUp( ) Method

Parameters: <*flags*>,<*col*>,<*row*>

The OnRightMouseUp handler is called whenever you release the right button over the Image object. (An up event over one object might have been preceded by a down event over another object.) The parameters report the status of the Shift, Ctrl, and Alt keys, as well as the location at the time of the right mouse-up event.

The Image.Parent Property

The Parent property is read-only. This property is an object reference to the parent form of the Image object. It is assigned when the Image is created via a DEFINE command or a NEW call to the constructor.

The Image.Release( ) Method

The Release method removes the Image object from memory.

The Image.Top Property

Default value: 0.5

The Top property is the location of the top of the Image object, in characters sized by the form's ScaleFont. The top-left corner of the form is 0,0.

The Image.Visible Property

Default value: .T.

If Visible is True, the Image object is shown. Manipulating the Visible property lets you choose among alternative objects on a form.

The Image.Width Property

Default value: 9.0

The Width property specifies the width of the Image object in characters. The width of each character is determined by the form's ScaleFont properties.

▸ Line Object Properties

This section lists and briefly explains the properties of the Line object.

The Line.Before Property

Before is an object reference to the object that this Line precedes in the form's tabbing order. If this object is the last one in the form's tabbing order, Before is a reference to the first object in the tabbing order (Form.First).

The Line.Bottom Property

Default value: 5

The Bottom and Right properties together locate one end of a Line object. (Note that the Bottom is not necessarily below the Top of a Line object.)

The Line.ClassName Property

Default value: LINE

ClassName is read-only. This property is assigned by dBASE for Windows for each of the built-in classes. It can be used to distinguish among multiple objects with the same name.

The Line.ColorNormal Property

Default value: N

The ColorNormal property specifies the color of the object, or, for objects that also have a ColorHighlight property, it specifies the color when the object does not have focus. ColorNormal may be a dBASE IV-style color specification, or it may be a color selected from the color palette with the Choose Color dialog box.

The Line.Left Property

Default value: 0

The Left property specifies the location of the left side of the Line object within its form, in characters. The leftmost character is number 0.

The Line.Name Property

Default value: LINE<*n*>

The Name property is the property name given to this Line on the parent form. If the name is LINE1, for example, specifying Parent.LINE1 specifies this Line object.

The Line.OnOpen( ) Method

The OnOpen event is called when the form containing the Line object is opened.

The Line.Parent Property

The Parent property is read-only. This property is an object reference to the parent form of the Line object. It is assigned when the Line object is created via a DEFINE command or a NEW call to the constructor.

The Line.Pen Property

Default value: 0

Available settings: (0–4)

The Pen property specifies the pen style for line drawing. It is solid (0), dash (1), dot (2), dash dot (3), or dash dot dot (4).

The Line.Release( ) Method

The Release method removes the Line object from memory.

The Line.Right Property

Default value: 10

The Right property, together with Bottom, specifies one end of a Line. The Right property is not necessarily greater than the Left property.

The Line.Top Property

Default value: 8.0

The Top property is the location of the top of the Line object, in characters sized by the form's ScaleFont. The top-left corner of the form is 0,0.

The Line.Visible Property

Default value: .T.

If Visible is True, the Line object is shown. Manipulating the Visible property lets you choose among alternative objects on a form.

The Line.Width Property

Default value: 1

The Width property specifies the width of the Line object in characters. The width of each character is determined by the form's ScaleFont properties.

▶ Rectangle Object Properties

This section lists and briefly explains the properties of the Rectangle object.

The Rectangle.Before Property

Before is an object reference to the object that the Rectangle object precedes in the form's tabbing order. If this object is the last one in the form's tabbing order, Before is a reference to the first object in the tabbing order (Form.First).

The Rectangle.Border Property

Default value: .T.

If Border is True, the object is surrounded by a border. The border is plain, raised, or lowered, depending on the setting of BorderStyle.

The Rectangle.BorderStyle Property

Default value: 0

The BorderStyle may be normal (0), which appears surrounded by a chiseled line; raised (1), which appears elevated above the form; or lowered (2), which appears sunk into the form.

The Rectangle.ClassName Property

Default value: RECTANGLE

ClassName is read-only. This property is assigned by dBASE for Windows for each of the built-in classes. It can be used to distinguish among multiple objects with the same name.

The Rectangle.ColorNormal Property

Default value: N/W

The ColorNormal property specifies the color of the object. For objects that also have a ColorHighlight property, it specifies the color when the object does not have focus. ColorNormal may be a dBASE IV-style color specification, or it may be a color selected from the color palette with the Choose Color dialog box.

The Rectangle.FontBold Property

Default value: .T.

If True, FontBold specifies that the object's font is boldface.

The Rectangle.FontItalic Property

Default value: .F.

If True, FontItalic specifies that the object's font is italic.

The Rectangle.FontName Property

Default value: MS Sans Serif

The FontName property specifies the name of the font. This may be set from the Font dialog box, accessed via the tool icon in the Form Designer's Properties dialog box.

The Rectangle.FontSize Property

Default value: 8

The FontSize property specifies the size of the font, in points.

The Rectangle.FontStrikeOut Property

Default value: .F.

If FontStrikeOut is True, the characters will be displayed with strikeout slashes.

The Rectangle.FontUnderline Property

Default value: .F.

If True, FontUnderline specifies that the characters are underlined.

The Rectangle.Height Property

Default value: 5.5

The Height property specifies the height of the Rectangle object in characters.

The Rectangle.hWnd Property

The hWnd property is read-only. This property is an arbitrary integer number that identifies the window to which the Rectangle object belongs. This is called the window's *handle*. It is used when you access Windows functions directly via EXTERN commands.

The Rectangle.Left Property

Default value: 1

The Left property specifies the location of the left side of the Rectangle object within its form, in characters. The leftmost character is number 0.

The Rectangle.MousePointer Property

Default value: 0

Available settings: 0–11

The MousePointer property specifies the type of mouse pointer to use when the pointer is over the Rectangle object. For example, the mouse pointer is an arrow over a form, but turns to an I-beam in an editor. The settings are default (0), arrow (1), cross (2), I-beam (3), icon (4), size (5), size NESW (6), size S (7), size NWSE (8), size E (9), up arrow (10), and wait (hourglass, 11).

The Rectangle.Move( ) Method

Parameters: <*lft*>,<*tp*>,<*wdth*>,<*hght*>

Move is a method property that can move the Rectangle object, resize the Rectangle object, or both. You provide Move with four parameters, representing the new values for the properties Left, Top, Width, and Height, respectively.

The Rectangle.Name Property

Default value: RECTANGLE<*n*>

The Name property is the property name given to this object on the parent form. If the name is RECTANGLE1, for example, specifying Parent.RECTANGLE1 specifies this Rectangle object.

The Rectangle.OldStyle Property

Default value: .F.

Setting OldStyle to True lets you use the older Windows application style. (This is generally a less attractive look than you get with OldStlye set False.)

The Rectangle.OnLeftDblClick( ) Method

Parameters: <*flags*>,<*col*>,<*row*>

The OnLeftDblClick event is called when you double-click with the left mouse button over the Rectangle object. The parameters report the status of the Shift, Ctrl, and Alt keys, as well as the location at the time of the left double-click event.

The Rectangle.OnLeftMouseDown( ) Method

Parameters: <*flags*>,<*col*>,<*row*>

The OnLeftMouseDown event is called when you press the left mouse button over the Rectangle object. The parameters report the status of the Shift, Ctrl, and Alt keys, as well as the location at the time of the left mouse-down event.

The Rectangle.OnLeftMouseUp( ) Method

Parameters: <*flags*>,<*col*>,<*row*>

The OnLeftMouseUp handler is called whenever you release the left button over the Rectangle object. (An up event over one object might have been preceded by a down event over another object.) The parameters report the status of the Shift, Ctrl, and Alt keys, as well as the location at the time of the event.

The Rectangle.OnMiddleDblClick( ) Method

Parameters: <*flags*>,<*col*>,<*row*>

The OnMiddleDblClick event is called when you double-click with the middle mouse button of a three-button mouse over the Rectangle object. The parameters report the status of the Shift, Ctrl, and Alt keys, as well as the location at the time of the middle double-click event.

The Rectangle.OnMiddleMouseDown( ) Method

Parameters: <*flags*>,<*col*>,<*row*>

The OnMiddleMouseDown event is called when you press the middle mouse button of a three-button mouse over the Rectangle object. The parameters report the status of the Shift, Ctrl, and Alt keys, as well as the location at the time of the middle mouse-down event.

The Rectangle.OnMiddleMouseUp( ) Method

Parameters: <*flags*>,<*col*>,<*row*>

The OnMiddleMouseUp handler is called whenever you release the middle mouse button over the Rectangle object. (An up event over one object might have been preceded by a down event over another object.) The parameters report the status of the Shift, Ctrl, and Alt keys, as well as the location at the time of the middle mouse-up event.

The Rectangle.OnMouseMove( ) Method

Parameters: <*flags*>,<*col*>,<*row*>

The OnMouseMove event is called when any mouse movement is detected over the Rectangle object.

The Rectangle.OnOpen( ) Method

The OnOpen event is called when the form containing the Rectangle object is opened.

The Rectangle.OnRightDblClick( ) Method

Parameters: <*flags*>,<*col*>,<*row*>

The OnRightDblClick event is called when you double-click with the right mouse button over the Rectangle object. (Right double-clicks are recognized by the Navigator as commands to Design the object.) The parameters report the status of the Shift, Ctrl, and Alt keys, as well as the location at the time of the right double-click event.

The Rectangle.OnRightMouseDown( ) Method

Parameters: <*flags*>,<*col*>,<*row*>

The OnRightMouseDown event is called when you press the right mouse button over the Rectangle object. The parameters report the status of the Shift, Ctrl, and Alt keys, as well as the location at the time of the right mouse-down event.

The Rectangle.OnRightMouseUp( ) Method

Parameters: <*flags*>,<*col*>,<*row*>

The OnRightMouseUp handler is called whenever you release the right button over the Rectangle object. (An up event over one object might have been preceded by a down event over another object.) The parameters report the status of the Shift, Ctrl, and Alt keys, as well as the location at the time of the right mouse-up event.

The Rectangle.Parent Property

The Parent property is read-only. This property is an object reference to the parent form of the Rectangle object. It is assigned when the Rectangle object is created via a DEFINE command or a NEW call to the constructor.

The Rectangle.PatternStyle Property

Default value: 0

Available settings: 0–6

The PatternStyle property sets the background for a rectangle. It can be solid (0); BDiagonal, which is SW–NE lines (1); cross, which is a tic-tac-toe pattern (2); diagcross, which is SW–NE and SE–NW lines (3); Fdiagonal, which is SE–NW lines (4); horizontal, which is horizontal lines (5); or vertical, which is vertical lines (6).

The Rectangle.Release( ) Method

The Release method removes the Rectangle object from memory.

The Rectangle.Text Property

Default value: "<*objectname*><*n*>"

The Text property specifies the title of a form or the text in an on-form object. The default text for a form is *Form*. The default text on an on-form object is the object name followed by a number, as in *Text1* and *Text2*.

The Rectangle.Top Property

Default value: 0.5

The Top property is the location of the top of the Rectangle object, in characters sized by the form's ScaleFont. The top-left corner of the form is 0,0.

The Rectangle.Visible Property

Default value: .T.

If Visible is True, the Rectangle object is shown. Manipulating the Visible property lets you choose among alternative objects on a form.

The Rectangle.Width Property

Default value: 16.0

The Width property specifies the width of the Rectangle object in characters. The width of each character is determined by the form's ScaleFont properties.

▶ Text Object Properties

This section lists and briefly explains the properties of the Text object.

The Text.Alignment Property

Default value: 0

A Text object can be aligned at the top left, the top center, and so on, through the bottom right. A Text object may also use "wrap" alignment, wrapping its Text property to fit.

The Text.Before Property

Before is an object reference to the object that this Text object precedes in the form's tabbing order. If this object is the last one in the form's tabbing order, Before is a reference to the first object in the tabbing order (Form.First).

The Text.Border Property

Default value: .F.

If Border is True, the object is surrounded by a border. The border is plain, raised, or lowered, depending on the setting of BorderStyle.

The Text.ClassName Property

Default value: TEXT

ClassName is read-only. This property is assigned by dBASE for Windows for each of the built-in classes. It can be used to distinguish among multiple objects with the same name.

The Text.ColorNormal Property

Default value: N/W

The ColorNormal property specifies the color of the object, or, for objects that also have a ColorHighlight property, it specifies the color when the object does not have focus. ColorNormal may be a dBASE IV-style color specification, or it may be a color selected from the color palette with the Choose Color dialog box.

The Text.FontBold Property

Default value: .T.

If True, FontBold specifies that the object's font is boldface.

The Text.FontItalic Property

Default value: .F.

If True, FontItalic specifies that the object's font is italic.

The Text.FontName Property

Default value: MS Sans Serif

The FontName property specifies the name of the font. This may be set from the Font dialog box, accessed via the tool icon in the Form Designer's Properties dialog box.

The Text.FontSize Property

Default value: 8

The FontSize property specifies the size of the font, in points.

The Text.FontStrikeOut Property

Default value: .F.

If Font StrikeOut is True, the characters will be displayed with strike-out slashes.

The Text.FontUnderline Property

Default value: .F.

If True, FontUnderline specifies that the characters are underlined.

The Text.Function Property

Default value: ""

Function is a string of function symbols that control the display of the object's text. For example, a ! forces all alphabetic characters to uppercase, and a (places negative numbers in parentheses.

The Text.GetTextExtent( ) Method

Parameter: <*string*>

The GetTextExtent method returns the length of the parameter string, in characters, based on the parent form's ScaleFont.

The Text.Height Property

Default value: 1.0

The Height property specifies the height of the Height object in characters.

The Text.hWnd Property

The hWnd property is read-only. This property is an arbitrary integer number that identifies the window to which the Text object belongs. This is called the window's *handle*. It is used when you access Windows functions directly via EXTERN commands.

The Text.ID Property

Default value: –1

ID is a number than can be used to distinguish between otherwise identical Text objects. It is typically used when a program creates a set of similar objects in a FOR loop.

The Text.Left Property

Default value: 0

The Left property specifies the location of the left side of the Text object within its form, in characters. The leftmost character is number 0.

The Text.MousePointer Property

Default value: 0

Available settings: 0–11

The MousePointer property specifies the type of mouse pointer to use when the pointer is over the Text object. For example, the mouse pointer is an arrow over a form, but turns to an I-beam in an editor. The settings are default (0), arrow (1), cross (2), I-beam (3), icon (4), size (5), size NESW (6), size S (7), size NWSE (8), size E (9), up arrow (10), and wait (hourglass, 11).

The Text.Move( ) Method

Parameters: <*lft*>,<*tp*>,<*wdth*>,<*hght*>

Move is a method property that can move the Text object, resize the Text object, or both. You provide Move with four parameters, representing the new values for the properties Left, Top, Width, and Height, respectively.

The Text.Name Property

Default value: TEXT<*n*>

The Name property is the property name given to this object on the parent form. If the name is TEXT1, for example, specifying Parent.TEXT1 specifies this Text object.

The Text.OldStyle Property

Default value: .F.

Setting OldStyle to True lets you use the older Windows application style. (This is generally a less attractive look than you get with OldStlye set False.)

The Text.OnLeftDblClick( ) Method

Parameters: <*flags*>,<*col*>,<*row*>

The OnLeftDblClick event is called when you double-click with the left mouse button over the Text object. The parameters report the status of the Shift, Ctrl, and Alt keys, as well as the location at the time of the left double-click event.

The Text.OnLeftMouseDown( ) Method

Parameters: <*flags*>,<*col*>,<*row*>

The OnLeftMouseDown event is called when you press the left mouse button over the Text object. The parameters report the status of the Shift, Ctrl, and Alt keys, as well as the location at the time of the left mouse-down event.

The Text.OnLeftMouseUp( ) Method

Parameters: <*flags*>,<*col*>,<*row*>

The OnLeftMouseUp handler is called whenever you release the left button over the Text object. (An up event over one object might have been preceded by a down event over another object.) The parameters report the status of the Shift, Ctrl, and Alt keys, as well as the location at the time of the event.

The Text.OnMiddleDblClick( ) Method

Parameters: <*flags*>,<*col*>,<*row*>

The OnMiddleDblClick event is called when you double-click with the middle mouse button of a three-button mouse over the Text object. The parameters report the status of the Shift, Ctrl, and Alt keys, as well as the location at the time of the middle double-click event.

The Text.OnMiddleMouseDown( ) Method

Parameters: *<flags>*,*<col>*,*<row>*

The OnMiddleMouseDown event is called when you press the middle mouse button of a three-button mouse over the Text object. The parameters report the status of the Shift, Ctrl, and Alt keys, as well as the location at the time of the middle mouse-down event.

The Text.OnMiddleMouseUp( ) Method

Parameters: *<flags>*,*<col>*,*<row>*

The OnMiddleMouseUp handler is called whenever you release the middle mouse button over the Text object. (An up event over one object might have been preceded by a down event over another object.) The parameters report the status of the Shift, Ctrl, and Alt keys, as well as the location at the time of the middle mouse-up event.

The Text.OnMouseMove( ) Method

Parameters: *<flags>*,*<col>*,*<row>*

The OnMouseMove event is called when any mouse movement is detected over the Text object.

The Text.OnOpen( ) Method

The OnOpen event is called when the form containing the Text object is opened.

The Text.OnRightDblClick( ) Method

Parameters: *<flags>*,*<col>*,*<row>*

The OnRightDblClick event is called when you double-click with the right mouse button over the Text object. (Right double-clicks are recognized by the Navigator as commands to design the object.) The parameters report the status of the Shift, Ctrl, and Alt keys, as well as the location at the time of the right double-click event.

The Text.OnRightMouseDown( ) Method

Parameters: *<flags>*,*<col>*,*<row>*

The OnRightMouseDown event is called when you press the right mouse button over the Text object. The parameters report the status of the Shift, Ctrl, and Alt keys, as well as the location at the time of the right mouse-down event.

The Text.OnRightMouseUp( ) Method

Parameters: <*flags*>,<*col*>,<*row*>

The OnRightMouseUp handler is called whenever you release the right button over the Text object. (An up event over one object might have been preceded by a down event over another object.) The parameters report the status of the Shift, Ctrl, and Alt keys, as well as the location at the time of the right mouse-up event.

The Text.Parent Property

The Parent property is read-only. This property is an object reference to the parent form of the Text object. It assigned when the Text object is created via a DEFINE command or a NEW call to the constructor.

The Text.Picture Property

Default value: ""

The Picture property controls the display of the value in the object. For example, it can be used to put negative numbers in parentheses, to insert separator characters between groups of three digits, or to force all letters to display in uppercase.

The Text.Release( ) Method

The Release method removes the Text object from memory.

The Text.Text Property

Default value: "<*objectname*><*n*>"

The Text property specifies the title of a form or the text in an on-form object. The default text for a form is *Form*. The default text for an on-form object is the object name followed by a number, as in *Text1* and *Text2*.

The Text.Top Property

Default value: 0

The Top property is the location of the top of the Text object, in characters sized by the form's ScaleFont. The top-left corner of the form is 0,0.

The Text.Visible Property

Default value: .T.

If Visible is True, the Text object is shown. Manipulating the Visible property lets you choose among alternative objects on a form.

The Text.Width Property

Default value: 6.0

The Width property specifies the width of the Text object, in characters. The width of each character is determined by the form's ScaleFont properties.

► ► CHAPTER 17

Working with Data-Entry Form Objects

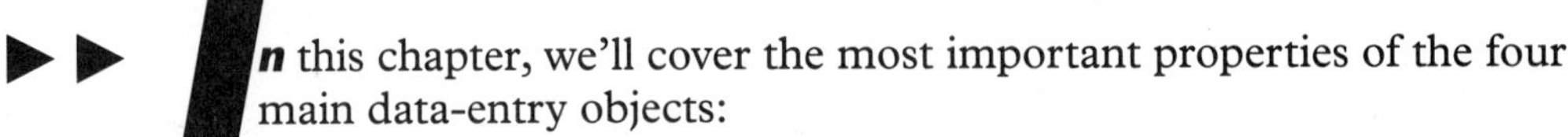

In this chapter, we'll cover the most important properties of the four main data-entry objects:

- Checkbox objects, which are used for logical values, for selecting Yes/No or On/Off options
- Entryfield objects, which are general-purpose but especially well-suited for text fields
- Radiobutton objects, which are used in lieu of Checkbox objects when the choices are mutually exclusive (selecting one means de-selecting the others in a set)
- Spinbox objects, which can be useful for numeric and date values

Following the discussion of the most important properties, we'll give you a reference section where you can look up all the properties for each object.

TIP

These objects are all easy to position if you use the Coarse grid setting in the Form Designer Properties dialog box.

Working with Checkbox Objects

The Checkbox object is the one that the Form Expert selects for Logical fields. To try these out, let's begin by building a fragment of a database table.

How's your appetite? We've just arranged a small job for you: you're building a simple system for your local pizza parlor. The owner is going to provide you with a free pie whenever you drop in, in return for your help. (This is a great deal only if they make great pizza!)

We'll have a form that lists all the pizza toppings, where the clerk checks the appropriate ones as the customers place their orders.

Figure 17.1 shows the definition of TEMP.DBF. It has a few toppings that would be part of a Pizza table if we were working out all the details of this system. For this example, we'll use just a few toppings.

Build your own table with a handful of your personal favorites. Each field should be a Logical type. Save your table definition as TEMP.DBF. (Delete any other TEMP.DBF file first.)

FIGURE 17.1

Some of our favorite pizza toppings

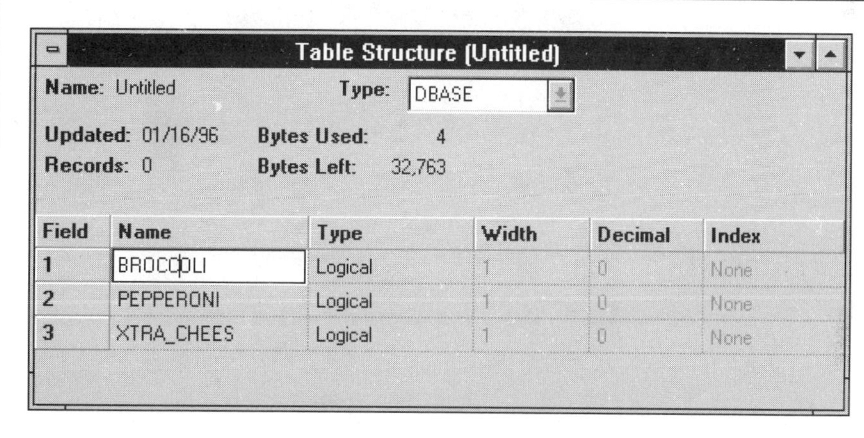

▶ Linking the Checkbox Object

To begin working with the Checkbox, delete any TEMP.WFM file you already have, and launch the Form Expert in the Form Designer. Use all the fields in TEMP.DBF. Our initial form is shown in Figure 17.2.

You see that the Form Expert created a Checkbox object for each of our logical fields. This is precisely what we want for this application.

When you have built your version of the pizza form, select one of your Checkbox objects, and then select the Object Properties Inspector. In

FIGURE 17.2

Designing the pizza form

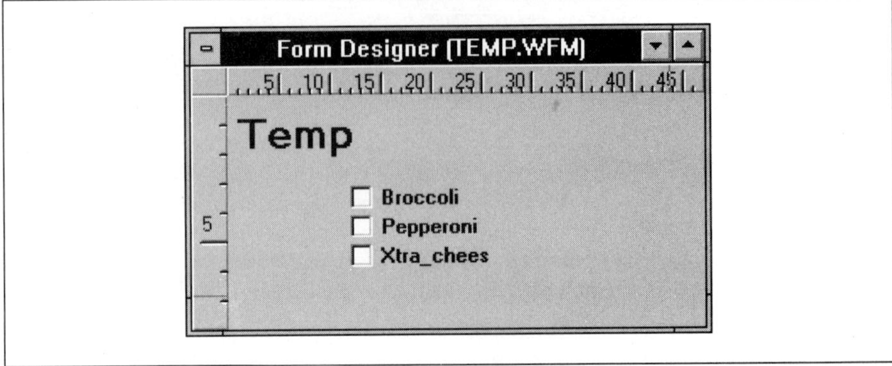

the Properties tab, select the DataLink property. Our DataLink property is TEMP->BROCCOLI:

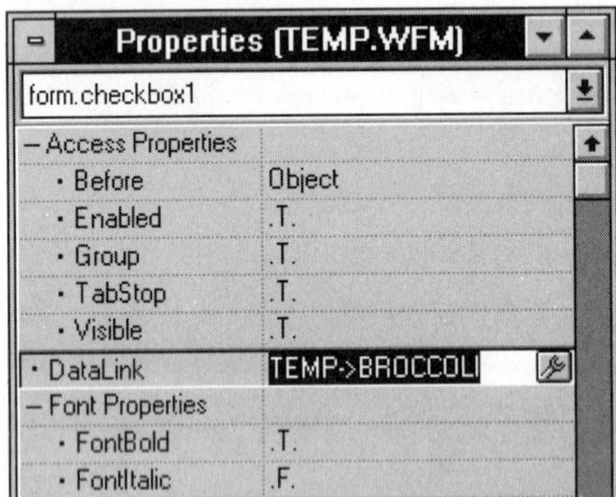

This is the name of the table (TEMP), the **->** arrow (hyphen and greater-than sign), followed by the name of the field. The property tells dBASE for Windows that this Checkbox object is linked to the BROCCOLI field in TEMP.DBF, which is precisely what we want.

Now we'll sidetrack for just a minute to see just how much flexibility we have in the form-design process. Click on the tool icon to the right of the name you've given for the DataLink property. You'll go to the Choose Field dialog box, shown in Figure 17.3.

FIGURE 17.3

dBASE for Windows lets you link to a different pizza topping

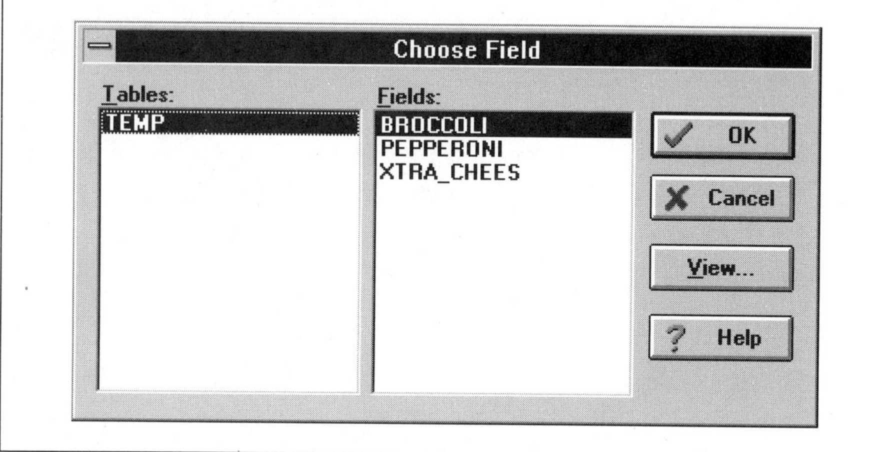

Notice that this dialog box has a View… pushbutton in addition to the standard pushbuttons (OK, Cancel, and Help). The Form Expert established the TEMP table as your view when you selected it from the list of tables and .QBE files. If you click on the View… pushbutton, you move to the Choose Field dialog box, shown in Figure 17.4. Here you can choose a different view.

Now we can get back on track. Our original choice was just fine, so click on Cancel (or press Esc) to return to the Form Designer. When you are in the Form Designer, click on the lightning icon or press F2 to run the form.

When the form is running, click on the add records icon in the speedbar (or press Ctrl-A), and select your favorite toppings. Repeat this for a few pizzas. Return to the Form Designer (click on the design button or press Shift-F2), and you will see the check boxes reflect the choices you made for your first pizza.

When you establish a data link (or when the Form Expert establishes a data link), two things happen:

- The check box (or other data-entry field) is updated every time the linked data changes.
- The underlying data is changed every time you check or uncheck the box.

FIGURE 17.4 ▶

dBASE for Windows lets you choose a different view

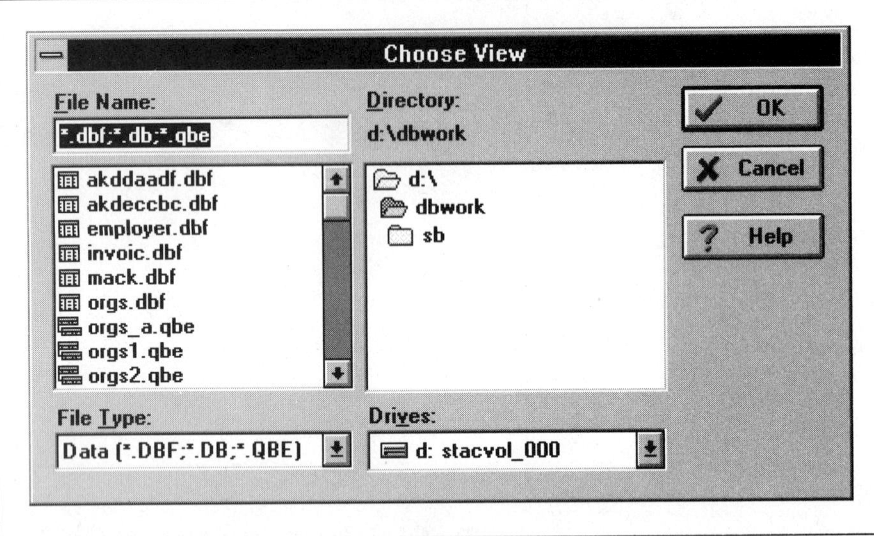

Actually, the second part is not quite that simple. When you check or uncheck the box, the Value property is changed. If you quit the record (by using Ctrl-Q, Esc, or File ➤ Abandon and Close), the underlying data is not updated. If you close the form or exit the record by any other means (such as by going to another record), the underlying data is updated.

▶ Improving Checkbox Labels

Our Form Expert did a fine job establishing the DataLink property that we wanted. For labeling the Checkbox objects, it did the best that we can expect. For a field named PEPPERONI, the default Text property, the field name, is a fine choice.

However, when we have a field named XTRA_CHEES, we should take the trouble to improve on the work of the Form Expert. (After all, what does the Form Expert know about pizza?) This is simply a matter of changing the Text property.

In the Form Designer, select a Checkbox for which you can improve the label and then choose the Properties tab of the Object Properties Inspector. The Text property is near the bottom, just above the Value property. Change something weak, like Xtra_Chees, to something strong, like More Mozzarella.

Along with the Text property is the full set of Font properties for you to manipulate the text. Choose your favorite topping and increase the FontSize from its default 8-point size to something larger. Figure 17.5 shows one way to emphasize the extra cheese option.

FIGURE 17.5

Biasing the choices with extra emphasis

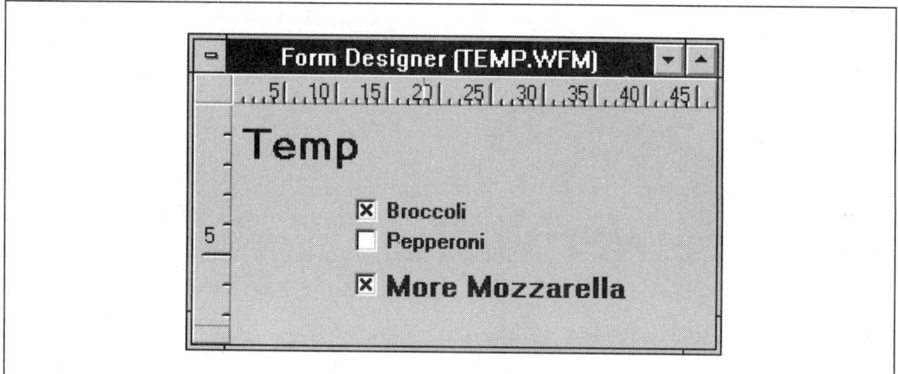

Increasing the size of particular text is a valuable technique for emphasizing the key items on a form. You might do this just because you like extra cheese. On the other hand, this would be a good way to reinforce the owner's desire to have his clerks always ask, "Would you like extra cheese?"

You can change the FontName, the styles, or any other characteristic of the Text property for your own form.

Adding Checkbox Object Values

The check boxes on your form were blank when you first entered the Form Designer. This is because the Checkbox object shows its Value property in the check box square. The Value defaults to False. If you have checks in some but not all of your Checkbox objects on your form, you can use the Object Properties Inspector to examine each of their Value properties to see that this is true.

When you click on the check box, your Checkbox object internally executes a line like this one:

```
CHECKBOX1.Value = .NOT. CHECKBOX1.Value
```

This is another toggle, which reverses itself every time you click on the check box (or tap the spacebar when the check box has focus). The DataLink property actually establishes a link between the Value property and the external data source. For example, when you change records, the DataSource is used to set the Value property. The routine that sets the Value property redisplays the check box appropriately checked or unchecked.

►► **NOTE**

The next time you set the DataSource property for a bitmap—Image or Pushbutton objects—check the Resource icons. You'll see that the checked and unchecked boxes are icons.

Immediately before leaving the current record, the DataLink property is updated from the Value property of the Checkbox object. (If you quit the record, DataLink is not updated.)

You can have a Checkbox object without a DataLink property. If you grab a Checkbox from the Controls palette, you will have one without a DataLink. You can establish a DataLink property using the Object Properties Inspector, but you do not need to do this. You can let the Checkbox object's Value property store its state.

Any event handler can refer to CHECKBOX1.Value to examine the value of the first Checkbox object. If you're going to use a Checkbox object this way, we recommend that you change the Name property to something more meaningful, such as Zap_Records. Then your event handler could have more readable code, such as this:

```
IF zap_records.value = .T.
   ZAP
ENDIF
```

►► Working with Entryfield Objects

The Entryfield object is the all-purpose workhorse of the data-entry objects. To work with it, let's build a .DBF file with one field of each of five primary types:

- Character
- Numeric
- Float
- Date
- Logical

Figure 17.6 shows our table structure. As you can see, we've named each of our five fields after the type we chose for it.

FIGURE 17.6 ►

Five field types, clearly labeled

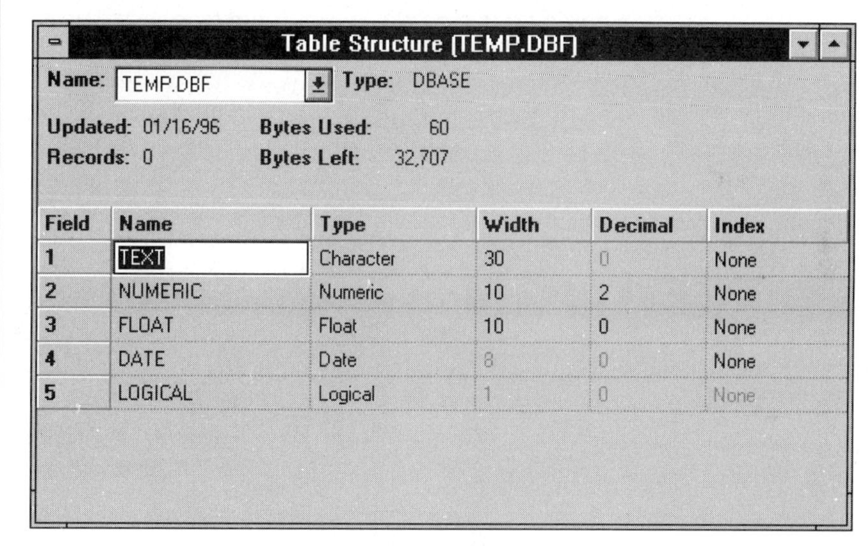

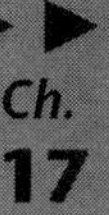

Create a TEMP.DBF table that duplicates this one, and then launch the Form Expert in the Form Designer. Choose TEMP.DBF and all the fields in it. When the Form Designer creates your form, it should look like the one shown in Figure 17.7.

FIGURE 17.7

The Form Expert's form

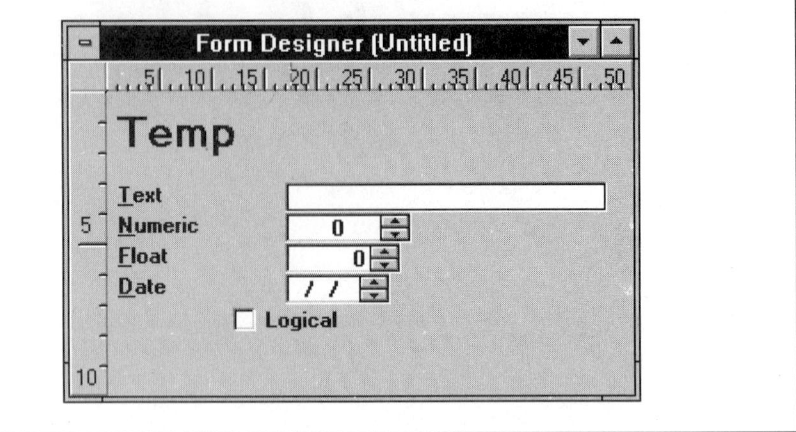

This is a good start, but it's not exactly what we had in mind. We want to use Entryfield objects for all of the fields. We'll replace the Spinbox objects with Entryfield objects.

Start by deleting the three Spinbox objects (lasso them and press Del to do it all at once). When they are gone, add three Entryfield objects in their place. Then delete the Checkbox object. Replace it with a Text object on the left and an Entryfield object lined up with the others. Replace the Text object's Text property with the word **Logical**. When you have gone this far, your form should look like the one in Figure 17.8.

FIGURE 17.8

The form rebuilt with Entryfield objects

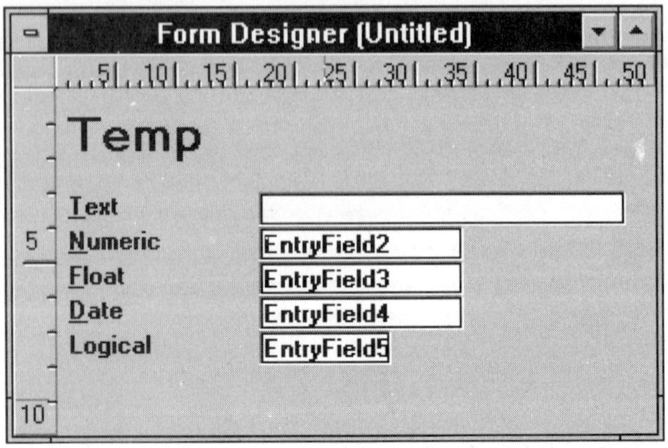

The final step in preparing our form is to use the DataLink property to connect the new Entryfield objects to our table's fields. Select the field opposite the Numeric 1, click on the Properties tab of the Object Properties Inspector, and then click on the DataLink property.

Click on the tool icon next to the DataLink property to see the Choose Field dialog box, and choose the Numeric field from the list, as shown in Figure 17.9.

FIGURE 17.9

Choosing the Numeric field for a DataLink

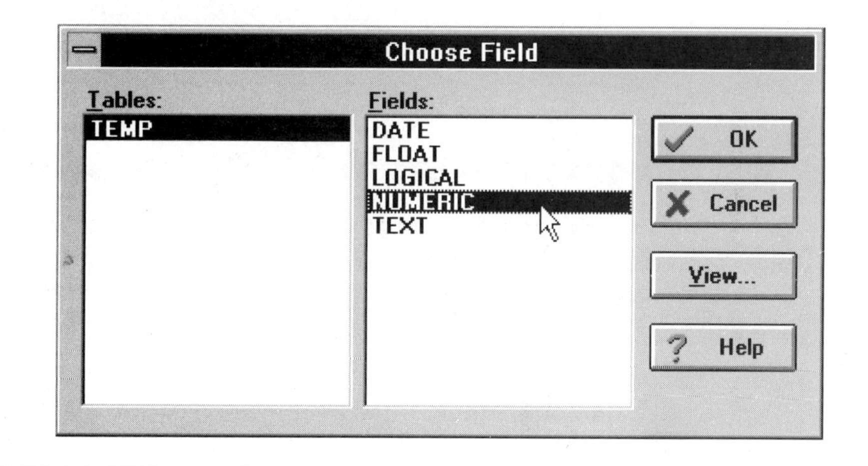

When you return to the Form Designer, the Value property of the Entryfield object (which shows in the Entryfield input area) changes from the default text string to 0.00, the default value for an empty Numeric field.

Repeat this process, assigning each of the Entryfield's DataLink properties to the fields that match the text labels on your form. Your Float field value will start with 0. Your Date and Logical fields will be blank.

Run the form and fill in data in the first record, as you see in Figure 17.10.

With this test form prepared, let's explore some properties of the Entryfield object.

FIGURE 17.10

Seeding the first record with data

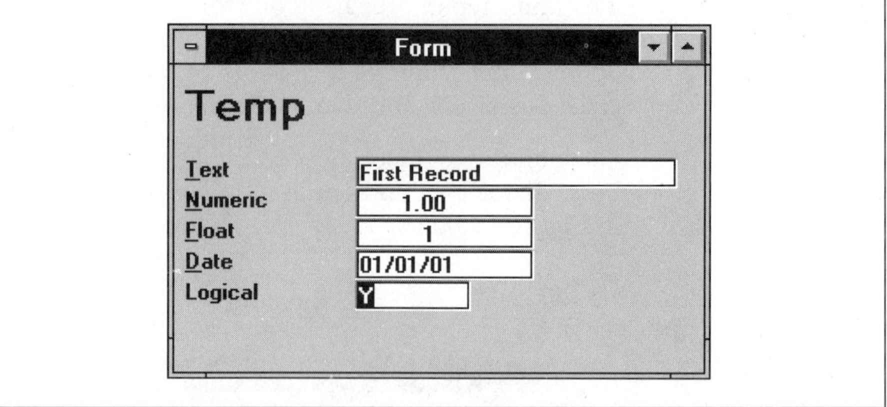

▸ Changing the Entryfield Object Border

The attractive sunken borders placed around Entryfield objects by default correspond to a True value for the Border property. In Figure 17.11 we have put more room between the fields and turned the Border property to False for alternate Entryfield objects.

We think you'll agree that the Border property should be left set to True for a more attractive form.

FIGURE 17.11

Alternate Border properties turned False

Form Designer (TEMP.WFM)

Temp First Record

Text 1.00

Numeric

Float 1

Date

Logical 01/01/01

T

If you get a very large application and are running out of GDI resources (see Help ➤ About dBASE 5.0 for Windows), turning off everything fancy—such as Entryfield borders—may save enough resources to let you proceed.

▶ *Setting the Entryfield Object's Maximum Length*

The MaxLength property gives you an alternative to using the field's length in the table. If you have set a DataLink property, the Max-Length property is set to the length of the underlying field. Without a DataLink property, the MaxLength is set to its default value of 25.

Consider the various field lengths:

- MaxLength, which is the maximum number of characters you can type
- Width, which is the width of the field in average width characters
- Display width, which is the characters that are displayed in the field

When the Form Expert creates an Entryfield object for an underlying Character field, it gives it a width equal to the width of the linked field. The width on the form is then wide enough to accommodate the correct number of characters, provided that the Entryfield object's font is the same as the Form's ScaleFont (in both name and size) and that the characters you enter are average width.

Assuming that you use default fonts, 8-point MS Sans Serif bold will be the ScaleFont for the Form object, as well as the font for the Entry-field object.

A 30-character field, such as our Text field, will fill with *i* letters long before we come to its right edge. In Figure 17.12, we've added an extra Entryfield object at the top of the form to show that 8 *W* characters are slightly wider than our maximum 30 *i* characters.

In the table on disk, any letter is stored in a single 8-bit byte. (This will probably expand to 16 bits to accommodate Asian languages, but Western

FIGURE 17.12

Excess i's or a dearth of W's

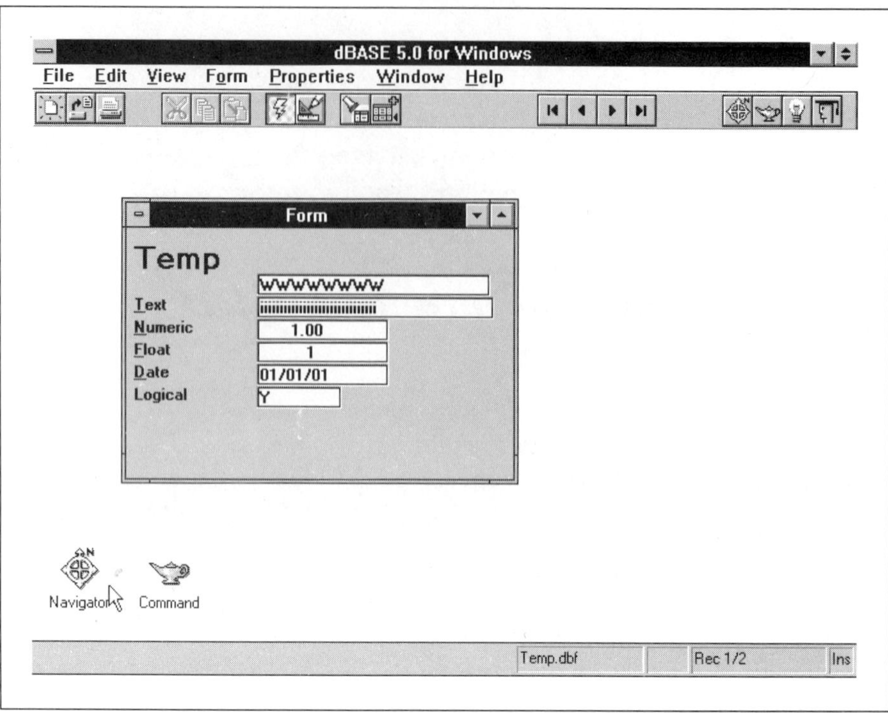

languages all work with 8-bit characters.) In storage, the capital *W* takes the same amount of space as the lowercase *i*.

The MaxLength property lets you specify the number of characters allowed in the field. dBASE for Windows will scroll the display within the Width property specified for the Entryfield object, or stop accepting characters when the value of the MaxLength property is reached, to keep the actual character count equal to or less than MaxLength.

▸ Selecting All the Entryfield's Contents

The SelectAll property works as if you entered the field and then dragged the mouse from one end to the other, to select the field (for cutting or copying to the Clipboard, for instance). As with a mouse drag, the contents of the field are in reverse colors to show that they are selected. If you press Backspace, or just start typing, the selected characters are deleted. Since SelectAll selects all the characters, all of them are deleted.

SelectAll defaults to True, which makes it easy to replace the entire contents of a field. If you just start typing, the old value is immediately deleted. On the other hand, to edit a field which is all selected, you need to press either the ← or → key, or click the mouse where you want to start editing, to deselect the contents. Then you can begin normal editing procedures.

If you will do more editing than total replacing, change SelectAll to False. Then the insertion point will start at the left side of the field, and nothing will be selected. This makes it far simpler to do routine editing, such as correcting the spelling of a name.

▶ Controlling Valid Values in Entryfields

If you run the sample form, you see that it's impossible to type any value that does not fit the type of the field. You can place letters and digits in a Text field, but you can only place a number in a Numeric or Float field. The Date field accepts only a date, and the Logical field insists on a T or F (or Y or N) choice.

The Valid properties give you additional control over the values allowed in a field. There are three Valid properties:

- Valid
- ValidErrorMsg
- ValidRequired

The Valid property accepts any expression that returns a True or False value. It does not let focus leave the Entryfield object until it returns a True value. (This includes shifting to another control, changing focus to another form, or closing the form.) Since you can write a function that returns True or False, there is literally no limit to the extent of the checking you can do in a Valid property.

The ValidErrorMsg will be displayed in the status bar when a Valid property returns a False value.

▸▸ **TIP**

Always supply a ValidErrorMsg when you supply a Valid. Otherwise, users will see dBASE for Windows refuse to proceed, but they will have no idea why.

Normally, Valid applies to data you enter. However, if you have the ValidRequired property set to True, dBASE for Windows will make the Valid check for every record that you look at. It will stop and refuse to proceed if the Valid property does not return True, just as if you had just entered the value.

You might also want to consider the StatusMessage property when working with Valid properties. StatusMessage displays a message in the status bar when the Entryfield object receives focus. You may want to put an appropriate suggestion here, so that users are reminded of what is acceptable.

Let's work through an example. Suppose that our Numeric field is the price of an item for sale in the shop we manage. The owner lets us vary this price between $11.99 and $14.99 based on our judgment.

Begin by selecting the Numeric field, and then click on the Events tab of the Object Properties Inspector. Enter this expression for the Valid event:

numeric >= 11.99 .and. numeric <= 14.99

Do not go to the Procedure Editor to enter this expression. Just type it into the Valid event's entry area.

Next, click on the Properties tab and enter some text like this in the ValidErrorMsg property (it's one of the Edit Properties):

11.99 thru 14.99, please

Last, it would be nice to see this message before you started typing a wrong value, so add text like the following to the StatusMessage property (it's one of the Help Properties):

Price between 11.99 and 14.99

Now run your form. We ran ours and entered the value 15. Figure 17.13 shows the Alert box that pops up to advise us of our error. Notice the status bar message, which clearly spells out the acceptable input.

TIP

The status bar in Figure 17.13 is *not* in the default 8-point type. We changed to 10-point type and made it boldface. (Use the Properties ➤ Desktop, Applications tab to set this font.)

FIGURE 17.13

A bad entry is refused

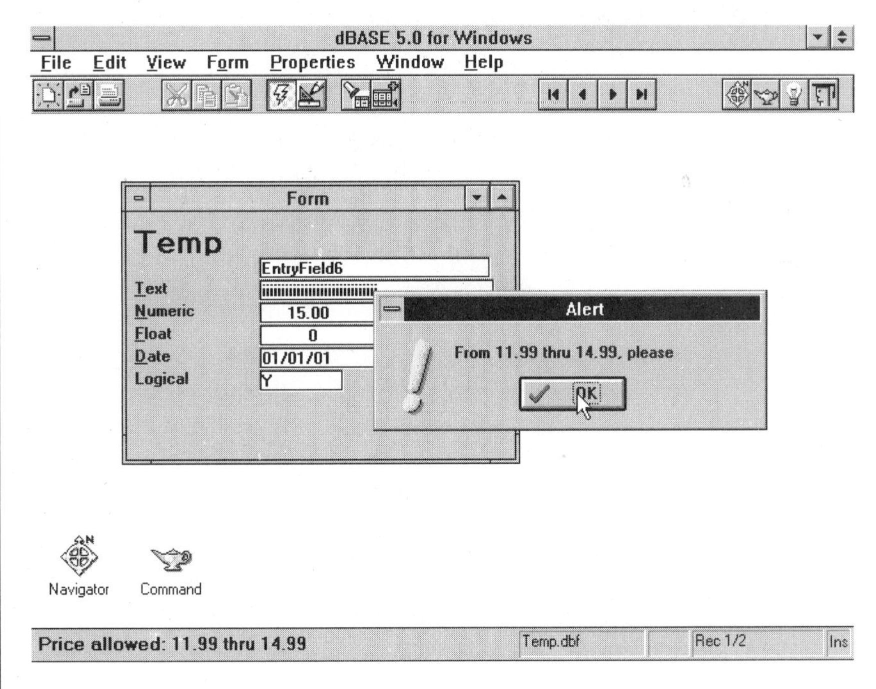

▸ Controlling When an Entryfield Object Is Available

In some cases, you may not want to be able to use an entry field at all. Suppose that our shop has fixed prices on smaller items, but allows a certain amount of negotiating on some “big-ticket” items. Again, let’s use our sample form to see how to set this up.

This time, suppose again that the Numeric field is the price of an item, and the following Float field is the maximum discount we’ll allow on big-ticket items. We define big-ticket as any item where the price (Numeric field) exceeds 100.

If the price is below 100, we don’t want to allow any use of the Float field. To do this, remove the Valid expression from the Numeric field and add this expression to the Float field’s When property:

Numeric > 100

▸▸ **WARNING**

We said that discounts weren’t allowed unless the price exceeded 100, which is exactly what our logical expression says. However, this precludes discounts if the price is exactly 100. Whenever you use a relational operator, ask yourself what you actually want to include. For example, do you want just greater than, or do you really mean greater than or equal to.

When you run your form, you will see that the Float field is *not* in the tabbing order (you skip right past it) when the value in the Numeric field is 100 or less. Put 101 into the Numeric field and the Float field is again available.

There is one problem that you may notice. If you put a value higher than 100 into Numeric, you can enter a value in Float. If you subsequently change the value in Numeric to something less than 100, the value in Float is still there, but is not available.

If you want the value in Float to be zero when the value in Numeric is less than 100, add an event handler to the OnLostFocus property of the Numeric field:

```
IF numeric <= 100
   float = 0
ENDIF
```

►► Working with Radiobutton Objects

The easy way to use Radiobutton objects is to use them like Checkbox objects: attach each one to a Logical field in your table. Let's go back to our pizza parlor and provide entries for small, medium, and large pies.

Obviously, you can add any or none of the extra toppings on a pizza. On the other hand, any pizza must be one—and only one—of small, medium, or large. (This presumes that those are the only sizes the pizza parlor makes.)

Again, let's use our TEMP.DBF table to model this fragment of our pizza system. Figure 17.14 shows our new table structure.

FIGURE 17.14 ►

The pie-size table fragment

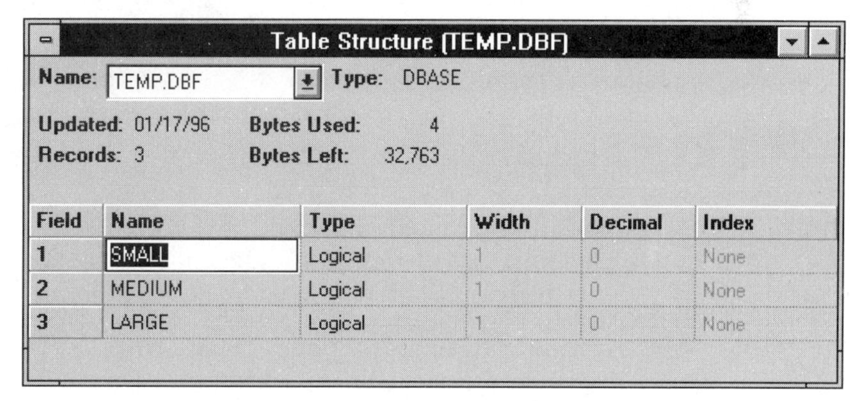

With this table built (delete the former TEMP.DBF table before launching the Untitled table from the Navigator), you are ready to build a form with radio buttons to choose the pie's size.

Delete the old TEMP from the Forms section of the Navigator, and then launch Untitled to get to the Form Expert. Again, choose TEMP.DBF and all its fields. After your final color selections, the Form Expert will create a form with a title and three Checkbox objects, which is not what we want.

Lasso the Checkbox objects and press Del to get rid of all three. Then add three Radiobutton objects in their place. Select the first Radiobutton, change its DataLink property to Small, and change its Text property to **Small**. Then change the DataLink and Text properties for the Medium and Large buttons.

When you're finished, your form should look like the one shown in Figure 17.15.

FIGURE 17.15

Adding Radiobutton objects to choose pie size

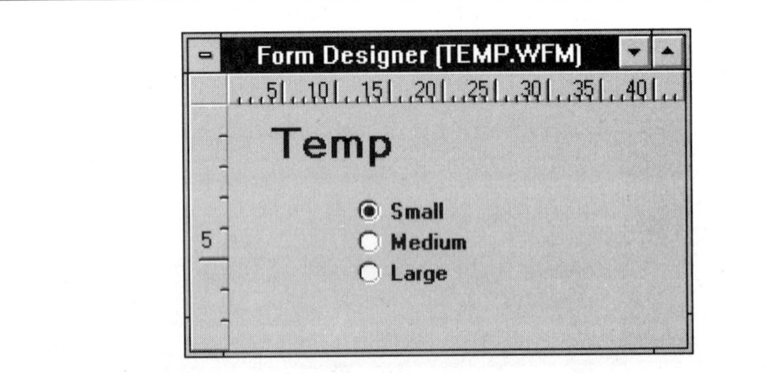

Note that as you are working in the Form Designer, the first Radiobutton object is selected and the subsequent ones are not. This is the major difference between Radiobutton and Checkbox objects.

Run your form at this point. Press Ctrl-A to add a few records, selecting a size for each. Then return to Design mode.

The default behavior of these Radiobutton objects is exactly what we wanted. They behave as a group. If you punch one in, the previously punched one comes back out. How does this work?

It's set up by the Group property. A more descriptive name for this property might have been StartOfGroup. The default for the first Radiobutton is True, which means that it starts a group. The default for subsequent Radiobutton objects is False, which means that they do not start a group—the existing group continues.

If you want to test the working of the Group property, change the Group setting to True for the Large pie Radiobutton object. This will give you two groups: one for Small and Medium, the other for just Large.

When you run the form, clicking either Small or Medium deselects the other of this pair. Clicking the button for Large does nothing, which is the correct behavior. In a group of Radiobutton objects, the definition is that one and only one member of the group is selected, so you cannot deselect the button of a one-member group.

▸▸ Working with Spinbox Objects

As you saw when we started to work on the Entryfield object, the Form Expert is very fond of Spinbox objects. It uses them for Numeric, Float, and Date field types. We're not as fond of spinboxes as the Form Expert, but we like them some of the time. They work best for whole numbers and dates where the value you'll choose is not too far from the default value at which the spinbox starts.

To look at Spinbox objects, let's build a table with Numeric and Date fields. Figure 17.16 shows the structure of our new TEMP table.

With that table built, go on to have the Form Expert build a form from all the fields in TEMP.DBF. Our form is shown in Figure 17.17.

We now have a form with four Spinbox objects: two each for Numeric and Date fields.

▸ Choosing the Spinbox Object's Border

Like an Entryfield object, a Spinbox object defaults to an attractive sunken border style. This border is optional. In Figure 17.18, we've added space between the Spinbox objects and turned off the borders of alternate Spinboxes.

FIGURE 17.16

A table for testing Spinbox objects

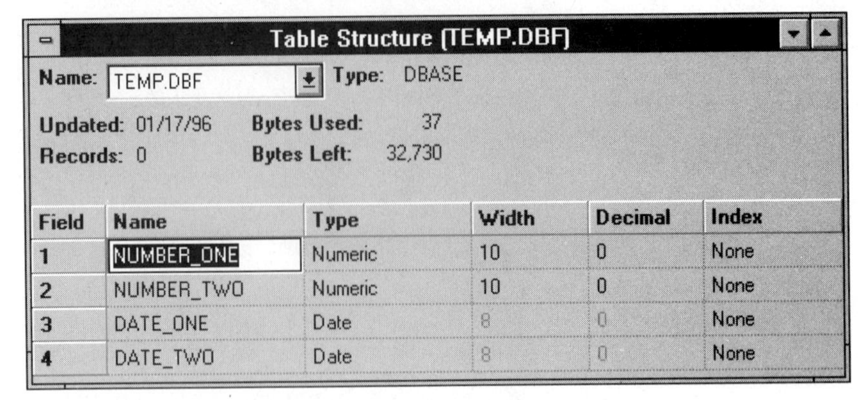

FIGURE 17.17

The Form Expert's default form

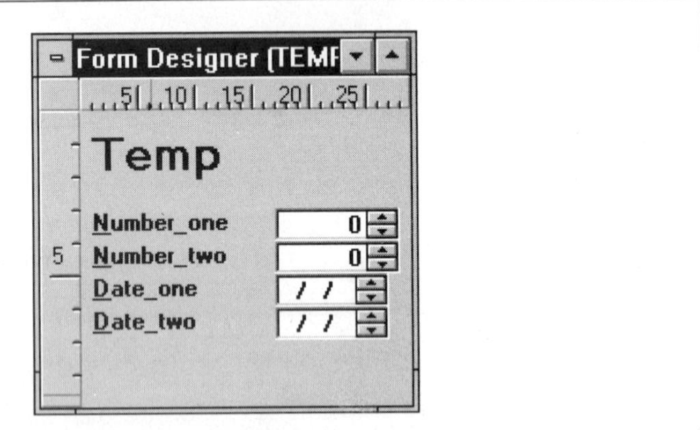

FIGURE 17.18

Bordered and borderless Spinbox objects

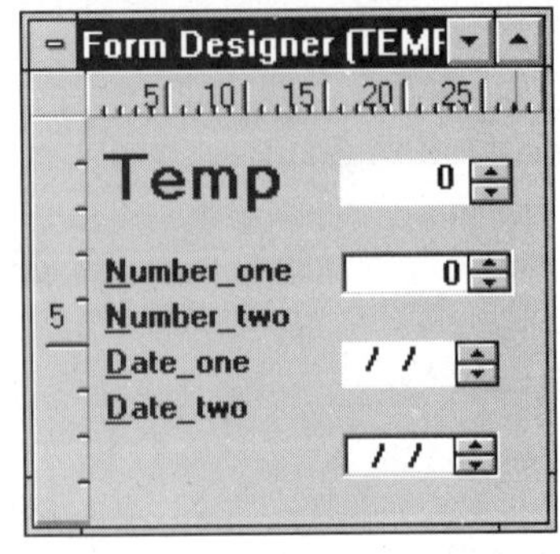

TIP

The default Border setting makes a more attractive control. If you are very short on resources, turning off the border may help. It might be more helpful to switch from using a Spinbox to using a plain Entryfield.

► *Setting the Spinbox Object's Range*

The Range properties of the Spinbox object let you control the minimum and maximum values that can be set. They can simplify the effort that you would otherwise put into an Entryfield's Valid properties.

The RangeMin and RangeMax properties are just what their names suggest: the lowest and highest values which can be entered with the Spinbox object. Here's how we can use the Object Properties Inspector to limit the range of Spinbox1 to 10 through 20, inclusive:

– Edit Properties	
· Function	
· Picture	
· Rangemax	20
· Rangemin	10
· RangeRequired	.F.
· SelectAll	.T.
· ValidErrorMsg	Invalid input
· ValidRequired	.F.
– Font Properties	
· FontBold	.T.
· FontItalic	.F.

Properties / Events / Methods

All properties within each category are listed alphabetically, which places RangeMax before RangeMin. We would have been tempted to sacrifice alphabetical order in this case.

The default range for a date is 100 days, starting with the current day. You'll probably want to adjust the range to suit your application.

▸ Allowing Spinning Only

The default setting for SpinOnly is False, which means that the Spinbox is a combination object. You can type a value into the data field, or you can use the spinner to set a value. If you change the SpinOnly property to True, you will not be able to type in the field. The SpinOnly property is located between the Position Properties and the Step property in the Object Properties Inspector.

▸▸ **WARNING**

Do not set the SpinOnly property to True unless the range of your Spinbox is fairly small.

For a good example of why both spinning and typing are valuable, try to set the bell to a pitch of 1000 in the Desktop Properties dialog box, Data Entry tab. You'll see that minor adjustments are fine with the spinner, but spinning by a few hundred takes far too long.

▸ Using the Spinbox Object's Picture Property

You can use a Picture property with a Spinbox object, just as you can with an Entryfield object. For example, you may want to use a Picture property to shift a number to the left. This Picture property shows three digits at the left side of the Spinbox object's display area:

```
999
```

Make sure that you use RangeMin and RangeMax to keep the values in the Spinbox object within the limits of a picture such as this one.

▸ Increasing the Spin Steps

In some cases, you may want to spin more than just one increment at a time. To increase the increments, change the Step property from its default value of 1. For a wide-ranging value such as the bell's pitch (values from under 100 to over 2000 could be used), a Step property of 25 would make sense to us.

If you combine a high step value with a False SpinOnly property, fast movements are possible and typing still allows you absolute control.

►► Data-Entry Form Properties Reference

In this section, we provide an alphabetical listing of all the properties of the Checkbox, Entryfield, Radiobutton, and Spinbox objects. Each listing includes the default value (if one exists). If a property is read-only, you cannot assign a value to it. If a property is read-only, this is noted in its listing.

Data properties are called Properties; events and other methods are called Methods. Additionally, Methods' names are followed by parentheses; for example, ClassName is a data property, but Close( ) is a method. Some methods take parameters within their parentheses, as noted in their listings.

► Checkbox Object Properties

This section lists and briefly explains the properties of the Checkbox object.

The Checkbox.Before Property

Before is an object reference to the object that this Checkbox precedes in the form's tabbing order. If this Checkbox object is the last one in the form's tabbing order, Before is a reference to the first object in the tabbing order (Form.First).

The Checkbox.ClassName Property

Default value: CHECKBOX

ClassName is read-only. This property is assigned by dBASE for Windows for each of the built-in classes. It can be used to distinguish among multiple objects with the same name.

The Checkbox.ColorNormal Property

Default value: N/W

The ColorNormal property specifies the color of the Checkbox object. ColorNormal may be a dBASE IV-style color specification, or it may be a color selected from the color palette with the Choose Color dialog box.

The Checkbox.DataLink Property

Default value: ""

The DataLink property links the object's value to a memory variable or a table field. When you change the data value in this Checkbox object, it changes the value in the associated memory variable or table field.

The Checkbox.Enabled Property

Default value: .T.

If Enabled is True, the Checkbox object is accessible. You can use the Enabled property to disable options in event handlers. For example, a Valid function could set some object's Enabled property to False if required conditions were not met.

The Checkbox.FontBold Property

Default value: .T.

If True, FontBold specifies that the Checkbox object's font is boldface.

The Checkbox.FontItalic Property

Default value: .F.

If True, FontItalic specifies that the Checkbox object's font is italic.

The Checkbox.FontName Property

Default value: MS Sans Serif

The FontName property specifies the name of the font. This may be set from the Font dialog box, accessed via the tool icon in the Form Designer's Properties dialog box.

The Checkbox.FontSize Property

Default value: 8

The FontSize property specifies the size of the font, in points.

The Checkbox.FontStrikeOut Property

Default value: .F.

If FontStrikeOut is True, the characters will be displayed with strikeout slashes.

The Checkbox.FontUnderline Property

Default value: .F.

If True, FontUnderline specifies that the characters are underlined.

The Checkbox.Group Property

Default value: .T., then .F.

The Group property really specifies Beginning of Group. If True, this begins a group. The group continues until the next object with a True value for the Group property. To group a set of radio buttons, for instance, set all but the first button's Group property to False. The first Radiobutton object added to a form has a True Group property by default. Subsequent Radiobutton objects have a False Group property by default.

The Checkbox.Height Property

Default value: 2.0

The Height property specifies the height of the Checkbox object in characters. If you use 10-point Courier as your form's ScaleFont, 1 character in height is 15 pixels.

The Checkbox.HelpFile Property

Default value: ""

The HelpFile property names the Windows Help file that will be used when you press F1.

The Checkbox.HelpID Property

Default value: –1

The HelpID specifies the individual Help screen that will be accessed in the Windows Help file specified by the HelpFile property.

The Checkbox.hWnd Property

The hWnd property is read-only. This property is an arbitrary integer number that identifies the window to which the Checkbox object belongs. This is called the window's *handle*. It is used when you access Windows functions directly via EXTERN commands.

The Checkbox.ID Property

Default value: –1

ID is a number than can be used to distinguish between otherwise identical objects. It is typically used when a program creates a set of similar objects in a FOR loop.

The Checkbox.Left Property

Default value: 0

The Left property specifies the location of the left side of the Checkbox object within its form, in characters. The leftmost character is number 0.

The Checkbox.MousePointer Property

Default value: 0

Available settings; 0–11

The MousePointer property specifies the type of mouse pointer to use when the pointer is over the Checkbox object. For example, the mouse pointer is an arrow over a form, but turns to an I-beam in an editor. The settings are default (0), arrow (1), cross (2), I-beam (3), icon (4), size (5), size NESW (6), size S (7), size NWSE (8), size E (9), up arrow (10), and wait (hourglass, 11).

The Checkbox.Move( ) Method

Parameters: *<lft>*,*<tp>*,*<wdth>*,*<hght>*

Move is a Method property that can move the Checkbox object, resize the Checkbox object, or both. You provide Move with four parameters, representing the new values for the properties Left, Top, Width, and Height, respectively.

The Checkbox.Name Property

Default value: CHECKBOX<*n*>

The Name property is the property name given to this Checkbox object on the parent form. If the name is CHECKBOX1, for example, specifying Parent.CHECKBOX1 specifies this Checkbox object.

The Checkbox.OldStyle Property

Default value: .F.

Setting OldStyle to True lets you use the older Windows application style. (This is generally a less attractive look than you get with OldStlye set False.)

The Checkbox.OnChange( ) Method

The OnChange method is called whenever the user changes a value in the Checkbox object.

The Checkbox.OnGotFocus( ) Method

The OnGotFocus method is called when the Checkbox object receives focus.

The Checkbox.OnHelp( ) Method

The OnHelp method is called when the F1 key is pressed with focus on the Checkbox object.

The Checkbox.OnLeftDblClick( ) Method

Parameters: <*flags*>,<*col*>,<*row*>

The OnLeftDblClick event is called when the user double-clicks with the left mouse button over the Checkbox object. The parameters report the status of the Shift, Ctrl, and Alt keys, as well as the location at the time of the OnLeftDblClick event.

The Checkbox.OnLeftMouseDown( ) Method

Parameters: <*flags*>,<*col*>,<*row*>

The OnLeftMouseDown event is called when the user presses the left mouse button over the Checkbox object. The parameters report the status of the Shift, Ctrl, and Alt keys, as well as the location at the time of the OnLeftMouseDown event.

The Checkbox.OnLeftMouseUp( ) Method

Parameters: <*flags*>,<*col*>,<*row*>

The OnLeftMouseUp handler is called whenever the user releases the left button over the Checkbox object. (An up event over one object might have been preceded by a down event over another object.) The parameters report the status of the Shift, Ctrl, and Alt keys, as well as the location at the time of the OnLeftMouseUp event.

The Checkbox.OnLostFocus( ) Method

The OnLostFocus method is called whenever the Checkbox object loses focus.

The Checkbox.OnMiddleDblClick( ) Method

Parameters: <*flags*>,<*col*>,<*row*>

The OnMiddleDblClick event is called when the user double-clicks with the middle mouse button of a three-button mouse over the Checkbox object. The parameters report the status of the Shift, Ctrl, and Alt keys, as well as the location at the time of the OnMiddleDblClick event.

The Checkbox.OnMiddleMouseDown( ) Method

Parameters: <*flags*>,<*col*>,<*row*>

The OnMiddleMouseDown event is called when the user presses the middle mouse button of a three-button mouse over the Checkbox object. The parameters report the status of the Shift, Ctrl, and Alt keys, as well as the location at the time of the OnMiddleMouseDown event.

The Checkbox.OnMiddleMouseUp( ) Method

Parameters: <*flags*>,<*col*>,<*row*>

The OnMiddleMouseUp handler is called whenever the user releases the middle mouse button over the Checkbox object. (An up event over one object might have been preceded by a down event over another object.) The parameters report the status of the Shift, Ctrl, and Alt keys, as well as the location at the time of the OnMiddleMouseUp event.

The Checkbox.OnMouseMove( ) Method

Parameters: <*flags*>,<*col*>,<*row*>

The OnMouseMove event is called on any mouse movement detected over the Checkbox object.

The Checkbox.OnOpen( ) Method

The OnOpen event is called when the form containing the Checkbox object is opened.

The Checkbox.OnRightDblClick( ) Method

Parameters: <*flags*>,<*col*>,<*row*>

The OnRightDblClick event is called when the user double-clicks with the right mouse button over the Checkbox object. (Right double-clicks are recognized by the Navigator as commands to design the object.) The parameters report the status of the Shift, Ctrl, and Alt keys, as well as the location at the time of the OnRightDblClick event.

The Checkbox.OnRightMouseDown( ) Method

Parameters: <*flags*>,<*col*>,<*row*>

The OnRightMouseDown event is called when the user presses the right mouse button over the Checkbox object. The parameters report the status of the Shift, Ctrl, and Alt keys, as well as the location at the time of the OnRightMouseDown event.

The Checkbox.OnRightMouseUp( ) Method

Parameters: <*flags*>,<*col*>,<*row*>

The OnRightMouseUp handler is called whenever the user releases the right button over the Checkbox object. (An up event over one object might have been preceded by a down event over another object.) The parameters report the status of the Shift, Ctrl, and Alt keys, as well as the location at the time of the OnRightMouseUp event.

The Checkbox.Parent Property

The Parent property is read-only. This property is an object reference to the parent form of the Checkbox object. It is assigned when the object is created via a DEFINE command or a NEW call to the constructor.

The Checkbox.Release() Method

The Release method removes the Checkbox object from memory. Releasing a form also releases all of the form's objects.

The Checkbox.SetFocus() Method

The SetFocus method changes focus to the Checkbox object on the form.

The Checkbox.StatusMessage Property

Default value: ""

The StatusMessage appears in the left portion of the status bar when the mouse pointer is over the Checkbox object and when the Checkbox object has focus.

The Checkbox.TabStop Property

Default value: .T.

If TabStop is True, the Checkbox object is part of the tabbing order. If False, Tab and Shift-Tab will bypass the Checkbox object.

The Checkbox.Text Property

Default value: "CHECKBOX<*n*>"

The Text property specifies the text to the right of the check box in the Checkbox object.

The Checkbox.Top Property

Default value: 0

The Top property is the location of the top of the Checkbox object, in characters sized by the form's ScaleFont. The top-left corner of the form is 0,0.

The Checkbox.Value Property

Default value: .F.

The Value property is the value held by the Checkbox object. Its type can be any type appropriate to the data link.

The Checkbox.Visible Property

Default value: .T.

If Visible is True, the Checkbox object is shown. Manipulating Visible lets you choose among alternative objects on a form.

The Checkbox.When( ) Method

If When is False, the user cannot give focus to the Checkbox object.

The Checkbox.Width Property

Default value: 15.00

The Width property specifies the width of the Checkbox object in characters. The width of each character is determined by the form's ScaleFont properties.

Entryfield Object Properties

This section lists and briefly explains the properties of the Entryfield object.

The Entryfield.Before Property

Before is an object reference to the object that Entryfield precedes in the form's tabbing order. If this Entryfield object is the last one in the form's tabbing order, Before is a reference to the first object in the tabbing order (Form.First).

The Entryfield.Border Property

Default value: .T.

If Border is True, the Entryfield object is surrounded by a border.

The Entryfield.ClassName Property

Default value: ENTRYFIELD

ClassName is read-only. This property is assigned by dBASE for Windows for each of the built-in classes. ClassName can be used to distinguish among multiple objects with the same name.

The Entryfield.ColorHighlight Property

Default value: N/W+

The ColorHighlight property is the color of the Entryfield object when it has focus. ColorHighlight may be a dBASE IV-style color string, or it may be a color selected from the color palette.

The Entryfield.ColorNormal Property

Default value: N/W

The ColorNormal property specifies the color when the Entryfield object does not have focus. ColorNormal may be a dBASE IV-style color specification, or it may be a color selected from the color palette with the Choose Color dialog box.

The Entryfield.DataLink Property

Default value: “”

The DataLink property links the Entryfield object’s value to a memory variable or a table field. When you change the data value in this Entryfield, it changes the value in the associated memory variable or table field.

The Entryfield.Enabled Property

Default value: .T.

If Enabled is True, the Entryfield object is accessible. You can use the Enabled property to disable options in event handlers. For example, a Valid function could set some Entryfield object's Enabled to False if required conditions were not met.

The Entryfield.FontBold Property

Default value: .T.

If True, FontBold specifies that the Entryfield object's font is boldface.

The Entryfield.FontItalic Property

Default value: .F.

If True, FontItalic specifies that the Entryfield object's font is italic.

The Entryfield.FontName Property

Default value: MS Sans Serif

The FontName property specifies the name of the font. This may be set from the Font dialog box, accessed via the tool icon in the Form Designer's Properties dialog box.

The Entryfield.FontSize Property

Default value: 8

The FontSize property specifies the size of the font, in points.

The Entryfield.FontStrikeOut Property

Default value: .F.

If FontStrikeOut is True, the characters will be displayed with strikeout slashes.

The Entryfield.FontUnderline Property

Default value: .F.

If True, FontUnderline specifies that the characters are underlined.

The Entryfield.Function Property

Default value: ""

Function is a string of function symbols that control the display of the Entryfield object's text. For examples, ! forces all alphabetic characters to uppercase, and (places negative numbers in parentheses.

The Entryfield.Height Property

Default value: 2.0

The Height property specifies the height of the Entryfield object in characters.

The Entryfield.HelpFile Property

Default value: ""

The HelpFile property names the Windows Help file that will be used when you press F1.

The Entryfield.HelpID Property

Default value: –1

The HelpID specifies the individual Help screen that will be accessed in the Windows Help file specified by the HelpFile property.

The Entryfield.hWnd Property

The hWnd property is read-only. This property is an arbitrary integer number that identifies the window to which the Entryfield object belongs. This is called the window's *handle*. It is used when you access Windows functions directly via EXTERN commands.

The Entryfield.ID Property

Default value: –1

ID is a number than can be used to distinguish between otherwise identical Entryfield objects. It is typically used when a program creates a set of similar Entryfield objects in a FOR loop.

The Entryfield.Key( ) Method

Parameters: <*nchar*>,<*nposition*>

Key is a reference to a subroutine. If not null, the subroutine referred to by Key is called each time you press a key. This could be used, as one example, to create a password entry field, where each keypress shows only an asterisk in the field.

The Entryfield.Left Property

Default value: 0

The Left property specifies the location of the left side of the Entryfield object within its form, in characters. The leftmost character is number 0.

The Entryfield.MaxLength Property

Default value: 25

The MaxLength property specifies the maximum number of characters that can be entered in a character field. For data entered into a memory variable, this could be use to ensure that the data will later fit into a table field.

The Entryfield.MousePointer Property

Default value: 0

Available settings: 0–11

The MousePointer property specifies the type of mouse pointer to use when the pointer is over the Entryfield object. The settings are default (0), arrow (1), cross (2), I-beam (3), icon (4), size (5), size NESW (6), size S (7), size NWSE (8), size E (9), up arrow (10), and wait (hourglass, 11).

The Entryfield.Move( ) Method

Parameters: <*lft*>,<*tp*>,<*wdth*>,<*hght*>

Move is a Method property that can move the Entryfield object, resize the Entryfield object, or both. You provide Move with four parameters, representing the new values for the properties Left, Top, Width, and Height, respectively.

The Entryfield.Name Property

Default value: ENTRYFIELD<*n*>

The Name property is the property name given to this Entryfield on the parent form. If the name is Entryfield1, for example, specifying Parent.Entryfield1 specifies this Entryfield object.

The Entryfield.OldStyle Property

Default value: .F.

Setting OldStyle to True lets you use the older Windows application style. (This is generally a less attractive look than you get with OldStlye set False.)

The Entryfield.OnChange( ) Method

The OnChange method is called whenever the user changes a value in the Entryfield object.

The Entryfield.OnGotFocus( ) Method

The OnGotFocus method is called when Entryfield object receives focus.

The Entryfield.OnHelp( ) Method

The OnHelp method is called when the F1 key is pressed with focus on the Entryfield object.

The Entryfield.OnLeftDblClick( ) Method

Parameters: <*flags*>,<*col*>,<*row*>

The OnLeftDblClick event is called when the user double-clicks with the left mouse button over the Entryfield object. The parameters report the status of the Shift, Ctrl, and Alt keys, as well as the location at the time of the OnLeftDblClick event.

The Entryfield.OnLeftMouseDown( ) Method

Parameters: <*flags*>,<*col*>,<*row*>

The OnLeftMouseDown event is called when the user presses the left mouse button over the Entryfield object. The parameters report the status of the Shift, Ctrl, and Alt keys, as well as the location at the time of the OnLeftMouseDown event.

The Entryfield.OnLeftMouseUp() Method

Parameters: <*flags*>,<*col*>,<*row*>

The OnLeftMouseUp handler is called whenever the user releases the left button over the Entryfield object. (An up event over one object might have been preceded by a down event over another object.) The parameters report the status of the Shift, Ctrl, and Alt keys, as well as the location at the time of the OnLeftMouseUp event.

The Entryfield.OnLostFocus() Method

The OnLostFocus method is called whenever the Entryfield object's parent form loses focus.

The Entryfield.OnMiddleDblClick() Method

Parameters: <*flags*>,<*col*>,<*row*>

The OnMiddleDblClick event is called when the user double-clicks with the middle mouse button of a three-button mouse over the Entryfield object. The parameters report the status of the Shift, Ctrl, and Alt keys, as well as the location at the time of the OnMiddleDblClick event.

The Entryfield.OnMiddleMouseDown() Method

Parameters: <*flags*>,<*col*>,<*row*>

The OnMiddleMouseDown event is called when the user presses the middle mouse button of a three-button mouse over the Entryfield object. The parameters report the status of the Shift, Ctrl, and Alt keys, as well as the location at the time of the OnMiddleMouseDown event.

The Entryfield.OnMiddleMouseUp() Method

Parameters: <*flags*>,<*col*>,<*row*>

The OnMiddleMouseUp handler is called whenever the user releases the middle mouse button over the Entryfield object. (An up event over one object might have been preceded by a down event over another object.) The parameters report the status of the Shift, Ctrl, and Alt keys, as well as the location at the time of the OnMiddleMouseUp event.

The Entryfield.OnMouseMove( ) Method

Parameters: <*flags*>,<*col*>,<*row*>

The OnMouseMove event is called on any mouse movement detected over the Entryfield object.

The Entryfield.OnOpen( ) Method

The OnOpen event is called when the form containing the Entryfield object is opened.

The Entryfield.OnRightDblClick( ) Method

Parameters: <*flags*>,<*col*>,<*row*>

The OnRightDblClick event is called when the user double-clicks with the right mouse button over the Entryfield object. (Right double-clicks are recognized by the Navigator as commands to design the object.) The parameters report the status of the Shift, Ctrl, and Alt keys, as well as the location at the time of the OnRightDblClick event.

The Entryfield.OnRightMouseDown( ) Method

Parameters: <*flags*>,<*col*>,<*row*>

The OnRightMouseDown event is called when the user presses the right mouse button over the Entryfield object. The parameters report the status of the Shift, Ctrl, and Alt keys, as well as the location at the time of the OnRightMouseDown event.

The Entryfield.OnRightMouseUp( ) Method

Parameters: <*flags*>,<*col*>,<*row*>

The OnRightMouseUp handler is called whenever the user releases the right button over the Entryfield object. (An up event over one object might have been preceded by a down event over another object.) The parameters report the status of the Shift, Ctrl, and Alt keys, as well as the location at the time of the OnRightMouseUp event.

The Entryfield.Parent Property

The Parent property is read-only. This property is an object reference to the parent form of the Entryfield object. It is assigned when the Entryfield object is created via a DEFINE command or a NEW call to the constructor.

The Entryfield.Picture Property

Default value: ""

The Picture property controls the display of the value in the Entryfield object. For example, it can be used to put negative numbers in parentheses, insert separator characters between groups of three digits, or force all letters to display in uppercase.

The Entryfield.Release( ) Method

The Release method removes the Entryfield object from memory. Releasing a form also releases all of the form's objects.

The Entryfield.SelectAll Property

Default value: .T.

If True, SelectAll causes the entire value in a field to appear selected (highlighted). If the entire value is highlighted, typing or pressing Backspace deletes it. Pressing ← or →, or clicking the mouse where you want to edit, unselects it for normal editing. If SelectAll is False, the value in the field is not selected. Then Backspace deletes just one character, and typing adds new characters.

The Entryfield.SetFocus( ) Method

The SetFocus method changes focus to the Entryfield object.

The Entryfield.StatusMessage Property

Default value: ""

The StatusMessage appears in the left portion of the status bar when the mouse pointer is over the Entryfield object and when the Entryfield object has focus.

The Entryfield.TabStop Property

Default value: .T.

If TabStop is True, the Entryfield object is part of the tabbing order. If it is False, Tab and Shift-Tab will bypass the Entryfield object.

The Entryfield.Top Property

Default value: 0

The Top property is the location of the top of the Entryfield object, in characters sized by the form's ScaleFont. The top-left corner of the form is 0,0.

The Entryfield.Valid( ) Method

The Valid method is called whenever an attempt is made to remove focus from the object with focus. (Tabbing, clicking on another object, or submitting a form are examples.) The Valid method is a function or code block that returns a logical value. If it returns .F., focus is not moved from the Entryfield object.

The Entryfield.ValidErrorMsg Property

Default value: "Invalid Input"

The ValidErrorMsg is a text string that will be displayed in the left part of the status bar when the Entryfield object's Valid method returns False.

The Entryfield.ValidRequired Property

Default value: .F.

If ValidRequired is False, the Valid property applies only to new and changed values. If ValidRequired is True, all existing values are rechecked.

The Entryfield.Value Property

Default value: Entryfield1

The Value property is the value held by the Entryfield object. Its type can be any type appropriate to the data link. For scroll bars, value can be set by moving the thumb, or the thumb can be positioned by changing the Value property.

The Entryfield.Visible Property

Default value: .T.

If Visible is True, the Entryfield object is shown. Manipulating Visible lets you choose among alternative objects on a form.

The Entryfield.When( ) Method

If When is False, the user cannot give focus to the Entryfield object.

The Entryfield.Width Property

Default value: 12.00

The Width property specifies the width of the Entryfield object in characters. The width of each character is determined by the form's ScaleFont properties.

▶ Radiobutton Object Properties

This section lists and briefly explains the properties of the Radiobutton object.

The Radiobutton.Before Property

Before is an object reference to the Radiobutton object that this one precedes in the form's tabbing order. If this Radiobutton object is the last one in the form's tabbing order, Before is a reference to the first object in the tabbing order (Form.First).

The Radiobutton.ClassName Property

Default value: RADIOBUTTON

ClassName is read-only. This property is assigned by dBASE for Windows for each of the built-in classes. ClassName can be used to distinguish among multiple objects with the same name.

The Radiobutton.ColorNormal Property

Default value: N/W

The ColorNormal property specifies the color of the Radiobutton object. ColorNormal may be a dBASE IV-style color specification, or it may be a color selected from the color palette with the Choose Color dialog box.

The Radiobutton.DataLink Property

Default value: ""

The DataLink property links the Radiobutton object's value to a memory variable or a table field. When you change the data value in this Radiobutton object, it changes the value in the associated memory variable or table field.

The Radiobutton.Enabled Property

Default value: .T.

If enabled is True, the Radiobutton object is accessible. You can use the Enabled property to disable options in event handlers. For example, a Valid function could set some object's Enabled to False if required conditions were not met.

The Radiobutton.FontBold Property

Default value: .T.

If True, FontBold specifies that the Radiobutton object's font is boldface.

The Radiobutton.FontItalic Property

Default value: .F.

If True, FontItalic specifies that the Radiobutton object's font is italic.

The Radiobutton.FontName Property

Default value: MS Sans Serif

The FontName property specifies the name of the font. This may be set from the Font dialog box, accessed via the tool icon in the Form Designer's Properties dialog box.

The Radiobutton.FontSize Property

Default value: 8

The FontSize property specifies the size of the font, in points.

The Radiobutton.FontStrikeOut Property

Default value: .F.

If FontStrikeOut is True, the characters will be displayed with strikeout slashes.

The Radiobutton.FontUnderline Property

Default value: .F.

If True, FontUnderline specifies that the characters are underlined.

The Radiobutton.Group Property

Default value: .T., then .F.

The Group property really specifies Beginning of Group. If True, this begins a group. The group continues until the next object with a True value for the Group property. To group a set of radio buttons, for instance, set all but the first button's Group property to False. By default, the first Radiobutton object begins a group.

The Radiobutton.Height Property

Default value: 2.0

The Height property specifies the height of the object in characters.

The Radiobutton.HelpFile Property

Default value: ""

The HelpFile property names the Windows Help file that will be used when you press F1.

The Radiobutton.HelpID Property

Default value: –1

The HelpID specifies the individual Help screen that will be accessed in the Windows Help file specified by the HelpFile property.

The Radiobutton.hWnd Property

The hWnd property is read-only. This property is an arbitrary integer number that identifies the window to which the Radiobutton object belongs. This is called the window's *handle*. It is used when you access Windows functions directly via EXTERN commands.

The Radiobutton.ID Property

Default value: –1

ID is a number than can be used to distinguish between otherwise identical Radiobutton objects. It is typically used when a program creates a set of Radiobutton objects in a FOR loop.

The Radiobutton.Left Property

Default value: 0

The Left property specifies the location of the left side of the Radiobutton object within its form, in characters. The leftmost character is number 0.

The Radiobutton.MousePointer Property

Default value: 0

Available settings: 0–11

The MousePointer property specifies the type of mouse pointer to use when the pointer is over the Radiobutton object. For example, the mouse pointer is an arrow over a form, but turns to an I-beam in an editor. The settings are default (0), arrow (1), cross (2), I-beam (3), icon (4), size (5), size NESW (6), size S (7), size NWSE (8), size E (9), up arrow (10), and wait (hourglass, 11).

The Radiobutton.Move( ) Method

Parameters: <*lft*>,<*tp*>,<*wdth*>,<*hght*>

Move is a Method property that can move the Radiobutton object, resize the Radiobutton object, or both. You provide Move with four parameters, representing the new values for the properties Left, Top, Width, and Height, respectively.

The Radiobutton.Name Property

Default value: RADIOBUTTON<*n*>

The Name property is the property name given to this Radiobutton object on the parent form. If the name is Radiobutton1, for example, specifying Parent.Radiobutton1 specifies this Radiobutton object.

The Radiobutton.OldStyle Property

Default value: .F.

Setting OldStyle to True lets you use the older Windows application style. (This is generally a less attractive look than you get with OldStlye set False.)

The Radiobutton.OnChange( ) Method

The OnChange method is called whenever the user changes the value of the Radiobutton object.

The Radiobutton.OnGotFocus( ) Method

The OnGotFocus method is called when the Radiobutton object receives focus.

The Radiobutton.OnHelp( ) Method

The OnHelp method is called when the F1 key is pressed with focus on the Radiobutton object.

The Radiobutton.OnLeftDblClick( ) Method

Parameters: <*flags*>,<*col*>,<*row*>

The OnLeftDblClick event is called when the user double-clicks with the left mouse button over the Radiobutton object. The parameters report the status of the Shift, Ctrl, and Alt keys, as well as the location at the time of the OnLeftDblClick event.

The Radiobutton.OnLeftMouseDown( ) Method

Parameters: <*flags*>,<*col*>,<*row*>

The OnLeftMouseDown event is called when the user presses the left mouse button over the Radiobutton object. The parameters report the status of the Shift, Ctrl, and Alt keys, as well as the location at the time of the OnLeftMouseDown event.

The Radiobutton.OnLeftMouseUp( ) Method

Parameters: <*flags*>,<*col*>,<*row*>

The OnLeftMouseUp handler is called whenever the user releases the left button over the Radiobutton object. (An up event over one object might have been preceded by a down event over another object.) The parameters report the status of the Shift, Ctrl, and Alt keys, as well as the location at the time of the OnLeftMouseUp event.

The Radiobutton.OnLostFocus( ) Method

The OnLostFocus method is called whenever the Radiobutton object loses focus.

The Radiobutton.OnMiddleDblClick( ) Method

Parameters: <*flags*>,<*col*>,<*row*>

The OnMiddleDblClick event is called when the user double-clicks with the middle mouse button of a three-button mouse over the Radiobutton object. The parameters report the status of the Shift, Ctrl, and Alt keys, as well as the location at the time of the OnMiddleDblClick event.

The Radiobutton.OnMiddleMouseDown( ) Method

Parameters: <*flags*>,<*col*>,<*row*>

The OnMiddleMouseDown event is called when the user presses the middle mouse button of a three-button mouse over the Radiobutton object. The parameters report the status of the Shift, Ctrl, and Alt keys, as well as the location at the time of the OnMiddleMouseDown event.

The Radiobutton.OnMiddleMouseUp( ) Method

Parameters: <*flags*>,<*col*>,<*row*>

The OnMiddleMouseUp handler is called whenever the user releases the middle mouse button over the Radiobutton object. (An up event over one object might have been preceded by a down event over another object.) The parameters report the status of the Shift, Ctrl, and Alt keys, as well as the location at the time of the OnMiddleMouseUp event.

The Radiobutton.OnMouseMove( ) Method

Parameters: <*flags*>,<*col*>,<*row*>

The OnMouseMove event is called on any mouse movement detected over the Radiobutton object.

The Radiobutton.OnOpen( ) Method

The OnOpen event is called when the form containing the Radiobutton object is opened.

The Radiobutton.OnRightDblClick( ) Method

Parameters: <*flags*>,<*col*>,<*row*>

The OnRightDblClick event is called when the user double-clicks with the right mouse button over the Radiobutton object. (Right double-clicks are recognized by the Navigator as commands to design the object.) The parameters report the status of the Shift, Ctrl, and Alt keys, as well as the location at the time of the OnRightDblClick event.

The Radiobutton.OnRightMouseDown( ) Method

Parameters: <*flags*>,<*col*>,<*row*>

The OnRightMouseDown event is called when the user presses the right mouse button over the Radiobutton object. The parameters report the status of the Shift, Ctrl, and Alt keys, as well as the location at the time of the OnRightMouseDown event.

The Radiobutton.OnRightMouseUp( ) Method

Parameters: <*flags*>,<*col*>,<*row*>

The OnRightMouseUp handler is called whenever the user releases the right button over the Radiobutton object. (An up event over one object might have been preceded by a down event over another object.) The parameters report the status of the Shift, Ctrl, and Alt keys, as well as the location at the time of the OnRightMouseUp event.

The Radiobutton.Parent Property

The Parent property is read-only. This property is an object reference to the parent form of the Radiobutton object. It is assigned when the object is created via a DEFINE command or a NEW call to the constructor.

The Radiobutton.Release( ) Method

The Release method removes the Radiobutton object from memory. Releasing a form also releases all of the form's objects.

The Radiobutton.SetFocus( ) Method

The SetFocus method changes focus to the Radiobutton object on the form.

The Radiobutton.StatusMessage Property

Default value: ""

The StatusMessage appears in the left portion of the status bar when the mouse pointer is over the Radiobutton object and when the Radiobutton object has focus.

The Radiobutton.TabStop Property

Default value: .T.

If TabStop is True, the Radiobutton object is part of the tabbing order. If it is False, Tab and Shift-Tab will bypass the Radiobutton object.

The Radiobutton.Text Property

Default value: "RADIOBUTTON<*n*>"

The Text property specifies the text to the right of the Radiobutton object. The default text for a Radiobutton object is the Radiobutton object's name.

The Radiobutton.Top Property

Default value: 0

The Top property is the location of the top of the Radiobutton object, in characters sized by the form's ScaleFont. The top-left corner of the form is 0,0.

The Radiobutton.Value Property

Default value: .T., then .F.

The Value property is the value held by the Radiobutton object. Its type is logical. By default, the first Radiobutton object is selected (.T.).

The Radiobutton.Visible Property

Default value: .T.

If Visible is True, the Radiobutton object is shown. Manipulating Visible lets you choose among alternative objects on a form.

The Radiobutton.When( ) Method

If When is False, you cannot give focus to the Radiobutton object.

The Radiobutton.Width Property

Default value: 16.00

The Width property specifies the width of the object in characters. The width of each character is determined by the form's ScaleFont properties.

► Spinbox Object Properties

This section lists and briefly explains the properties of the Spinbox object.

The Spinbox.Before Property

Before is an object reference to the object that this Spinbox object precedes in the form's tabbing order. If this Spinbox object is the last one in the form's tabbing order, Before is a reference to the first object in the tabbing order (Form.First).

The Spinbox.Border Property

Default value: .T.

If Border is True, the Spinbox object is surrounded by a border.

The Spinbox.ClassName Property

Default value: SPINBOX

ClassName is read-only. This property is assigned by dBASE for Windows for each of the built-in classes. ClassName can be used to distinguish among multiple objects with the same name.

The Spinbox.ColorHighlight Property

Default value: N/W*

The ColorHighlight property is the color of the Spinbox object when it has focus. ColorHighlight may be a dBASE IV-style color string, or it may be a color selected from the color palette.

The Spinbox.ColorNormal Property

Default value: N/W+

The ColorNormal property specifies the color when the Spinbox object does not have focus. ColorNormal may be a dBASE IV-style color specification, or it may be a color selected from the color palette with the Choose Color dialog box.

The Spinbox.DataLink Property

Default value: ""

The DataLink property links the Spinbox object's value to a memory variable or a table field. When you change the data value in this Spinbox object, it changes the value in the associated memory variable or table field.

The Spinbox.Enabled Property

Default value: .T.

If Enabled is True, the Spinbox object is accessible. You can use the Enabled property to disable options in event handlers. For example, a Valid function could set some object's Enabled to False if required conditions were not met.

The Spinbox.FontBold Property

Default value: .T.

If True, FontBold specifies that the Spinbox object's font is boldface.

The Spinbox.FontItalic Property

Default value: .F.

If True, FontItalic specifies that the Spinbox object's font is italic.

The Spinbox.FontName Property

Default value: MS Sans Serif

The FontName property specifies the name of the font. This may be set from the Font dialog box, accessed via the tool icon in the Form Designer's Properties dialog box.

The Spinbox.FontSize Property

Default value: 8

The FontSize property specifies the size of the font, in points.

The Spinbox.FontStrikeOut Property

Default value: .F.

If FontStrikeOut is True, the characters will be displayed with strikeout slashes.

The Spinbox.FontUnderline Property

Default value: .F.

If True, FontUnderline specifies that the characters are underlined.

The Spinbox.Function Property

Default value: ""

Function is a string of function symbols that control the display of the Spinbox object's value.

The Spinbox.Height Property

Default value: 2.0

The Height property specifies the height of the Spinbox object in characters.

The Spinbox.HelpFile Property

Default value: ""

The HelpFile property names the Windows Help file that will be used when you press F1.

The Spinbox.HelpID Property

Default value: –1

The HelpID specifies the individual Help screen that will be accessed in the Windows Help file specified by the HelpFile property.

The Spinbox.hWnd Property

The hWnd property is read-only. This property is an arbitrary integer number that identifies the window to which the Spinbox object belongs. This is called the window's *handle*. It is used when you access Windows functions directly via EXTERN commands.

The Spinbox.ID Property

Default value: –1

ID is a number than can be used to distinguish between otherwise identical Spinbox objects. It is typically used when a program creates a set of Spinbox objects in a FOR loop.

The Spinbox.Left Property

Default value: 0

The Left property specifies the location of the left side of the Spinbox object within its form, in characters. The leftmost character is number 0. If you use 10-point Courier for your form's ScaleFont, each character is 8 pixels wide.

The Spinbox.MousePointer Property

Default value: 0

Available settings: 0–11

The MousePointer property specifies the type of mouse pointer to use when the pointer is over the Spinbox object. For example, the mouse pointer is an arrow over a form, but turns to an I-beam in an editor. The settings are default (0), arrow (1), cross (2), I-beam (3), icon (4), size (5), size NESW (6), size S (7), size NWSE (8), size E (9), up arrow (10), and wait (hourglass, 11).

The Spinbox.Move( ) Method

Parameters: *<lft>*,*<tp>*,*<wdth>*,*<hght>*

Move is a Method property that can move the Spinbox object, resize the Spinbox object, or both. You provide Move with four parameters, representing the new values for the properties Left, Top, Width, and Height, respectively.

The Spinbox.Name Property

Default value: SPINBOX<n>

The Name property is the property name given to this Spinbox object on the parent form. If the name is SPINBOX1, for example, specifying Parent.SPINBOX1 specifies this Spinbox object.

The Spinbox.OldStyle Property

Default value: .F.

Setting OldStyle to True lets you use the older Windows application style. (This is generally a less attractive look than you get with OldStlye set False.)

The Spinbox.OnChange( ) Method

The OnChange method is called whenever the user changes the value of the Spinbox object.

The Spinbox.OnGotFocus( ) Method

The OnGotFocus method is called when the Spinbox object receives focus.

The Spinbox.OnHelp( ) Method

The OnHelp method is called when the F1 key is pressed with focus on the Spinbox object.

The Spinbox.OnLeftDblClick( ) Method

Parameters: <*flags*>,<*col*>,<*row*>

The OnLeftDblClick event is called when the user double-clicks with the left mouse button over the Spinbox object. The parameters report the status of the Shift, Ctrl, and Alt keys, as well as the location at the time of the OnLeftDblClick event.

The Spinbox.OnLeftMouseDown( ) Method

Parameters: <*flags*>,<*col*>,<*row*>

The OnLeftMouseDown event is called when the user presses the left mouse button over the Spinbox object. The parameters report the status of the Shift, Ctrl, and Alt keys, as well as the location at the time of the OnLeftMouseDown event.

The Spinbox.OnLeftMouseUp( ) Method

Parameters: <*flags*>,<*col*>,<*row*>

The OnLeftMouseUp handler is called whenever the user releases the left button over the Spinbox object. (An up event over one object might have been preceded by a down event over another object.) The parameters report the status of the Shift, Ctrl, and Alt keys, as well as the location at the time of the OnLeftMouseUp event.

The Spinbox.OnLostFocus( ) Method

The OnLostFocus method is called whenever the Spinbox loses focus.

The Spinbox.OnMiddleDblClick( ) Method

Parameters: <*flags*>,<*col*>,<*row*>

The OnMiddleDblClick event is called when the user double-clicks with the middle mouse button of a three-button mouse over the Spinbox object. The parameters report the status of the Shift, Ctrl, and Alt keys, as well as the location at the time of the OnMiddleDblClick event.

The Spinbox.OnMiddleMouseDown( ) Method

Parameters: <*flags*>,<*col*>,<*row*>

The OnMiddleMouseDown event is called when the user presses the middle mouse button of a three-button mouse over the Spinbox object. The parameters report the status of the Shift, Ctrl, and Alt keys, as well as the location at the time of the OnMiddleMouseDown event.

The Spinbox.OnMiddleMouseUp( ) Method

Parameters: <*flags*>,<*col*>,<*row*>

The OnMiddleMouseUp handler is called whenever the user releases the middle mouse button over the Spinbox object. (An up event over one object might have been preceded by a down event over another object.) The parameters report the status of the Shift, Ctrl, and Alt keys, as well as the location at the time of the OnMiddleMouseUp event.

The Spinbox.OnMouseMove( ) Method

Parameters: <*flags*>,<*col*>,<*row*>

The OnMouseMove event is called on any mouse movement detected over the Spinbox object.

The Spinbox.OnOpen( ) Method

The OnOpen event is called when the form containing the Spinbox object is opened.

The Spinbox.OnRightDblClick( ) Method

Parameters: <*flags*>,<*col*>,<*row*>

The OnRightDblClick event is called when the user double-clicks with the right mouse button over the Spinbox object. (Right double-clicks are recognized by the Navigator as commands to design the object.) The parameters report the status of the Shift, Ctrl, and Alt keys, as well as the location at the time of the OnRightDblClick event.

The Spinbox.OnRightMouseDown( ) Method

Parameters: <*flags*>,<*col*>,<*row*>

The OnRightMouseDown event is called when the user presses the right mouse button over the Spinbox object. The parameters report the status of the Shift, Ctrl, and Alt keys, as well as the location at the time of the OnRightMouseDown event.

The Spinbox.OnRightMouseUp( ) Method

Parameters: <*flags*>,<*col*>,<*row*>

The OnRightMouseUp handler is called whenever the user releases the right button over the Spinbox object. (An up event over one object might have been preceded by a down event over another object.) The parameters report the status of the Shift, Ctrl, and Alt keys, as well as the location at the time of the OnRightMouseUp event.

The Spinbox.Parent Property

The Parent property is read-only. This property is an object reference to the parent form of the Spinbox object. It is assigned when the Spinbox object is created via a DEFINE command or a NEW call to the constructor.

The Spinbox.Picture Property

Default value: ""

The Picture property controls the display of the value in the Spinbox object. It can be used to put negative numbers in parentheses, for example.

The Spinbox.RangeMax Property

Default value: 100

The RangeMax property specifies the upper limit to a range. Scroll bars use the Range along with Value to position the thumb.

The Spinbox.RangeMin Property

Default value: 0

The RangeMin property specifies the lower limit to a range. Scroll bars use the Range along with Value to position the thumb.

The Spinbox.RangeRequired Property

Default value: .F.

If RangeRequired is True, all data values are checked for compliance with your specified range. If it is False, values are only checked when they are changed.

The Spinbox.Release() Method

The Release method removes the Spinbox object from memory. Releasing a form also releases all of the form's objects.

The Spinbox.SelectAll Property

Default value: .T.

If True, SelectAll causes the entire value in a field to appear selected (highlighted). If the entire value is highlighted, typing or pressing Backspace deletes it. Pressing ← or →, or clicking the mouse where you want to edit, unselects it for normal editing. If SelectAll is False, the value is not selected. Then Backspace deletes just one character, and typing adds new characters.

The Spinbox.SetFocus() Method

The SetFocus method changes focus to the Spinbox object on the form.

The Spinbox.SpinOnly Property

Default value: .F.

If True, the SpinOnly property disallows typing the value in a Spinbox object.

The Spinbox.StatusMessage Property

Default value: ""

The StatusMessage appears in the left portion of the status bar when the mouse pointer is over the Spinbox object and when the Spinbox object has focus.

The Spinbox.Step Property

Default value: 1

The Step property specifies the increment added (subtracted) with each click on the Spinbox's up and down arrows.

The Spinbox.TabStop Property

Default value: .T.

If TabStop is True, the Spinbox object is part of the tabbing order. If it is False, Tab and Shift-Tab will bypass the object.

The Spinbox.Top Property

Default value: 0

The Top property is the location of the top of the Spinbox object, in characters sized by the form's ScaleFont. The top-left corner of the form is 0,0.

The Spinbox.Valid( ) Method

The Valid method is called whenever an attempt is made to remove focus from the object with focus. (Tabbing, clicking on another object, or submitting a form are examples.) The Valid method is a function or code block that returns a logical value. If it returns .F., focus is not moved from the Spinbox object.

The Spinbox.ValidErrorMsg Property

Default value: "Invalid Input"

The ValidErrorMsg property is a text string that will be displayed in the left part of the status bar when the Spinbox object's Valid method returns False.

The Spinbox.ValidRequired Property

Default value: .F.

If ValidRequired is False, the Valid property applies only to new and changed values. If ValidRequired is True, all existing values are rechecked.

The Spinbox.Value Property

Default value: 1.00, 1, or blank date

The Value property is the value held by the Spinbox object. Its type can be numeric or date.

The Spinbox.Visible Property

Default value: .T.

If Visible is True, the Spinbox object is shown. Manipulating Visible lets you choose among alternative objects on a form.

The Spinbox.When( ) Method

If When is False, the user cannot give focus to the Spinbox object.

The Spinbox.Width Property

Default value: 11.00

The Width property specifies the width of the Spinbox object in characters. The width of each character is determined by the form's ScaleFont properties.

▶ ▶ CHAPTER 18

Working with Advanced Form Objects

▶▶ **I** **n** this chapter, we'll cover the properties of the advanced form objects: Browse, Combobox, Editor, and Listbox objects.

▶▶ Working with Browse Objects

The Browse object lets you build most of the capabilities of the Table Records tool into your forms. The less work you do after dropping a Browse object onto your form, the more fully it reflects the full capabilities of the Table Records tool.

However, the most important uses for the Browse object are not simply to imitate the Table Records tool. We saw one key use when we built our phone list system in Part 2. We used Browse objects as another alternative for navigating among the records of a table.

The Browse objects we used let us navigate based on people's last names and on employer's names. These are the common handles that we would expect to use to look up a person or employer in any database, computerized or otherwise.

Among the data-entry objects covered in Chapter 17 and the advanced objects covered in this chapter, the Browse object has a particularly meaningful unique feature: it has no Value property. The purpose of the Browse is to move the record pointer in your tables. You can think of your table's record as the value that the Browse object is assuming.

In this section, we'll highlight some of the more commonly used properties of the Browse object.

▶ Using Aliases with Browse Objects

In Chapter 6, we covered the use of the View property of the Browse object. With View, you can specify either a table or a .QBE file that is automatically used by your Browse object. A .QBE file may have multiple tables, so the Alias property is provided to let you specify a particular table.

You can use a Browse object to look at multiple linked tables, just as we have done with the Table Records tool. In a Form object, however, a Browse object is more commonly used to access just one of the tables used in a query. For example, you could use our PHONES_A.QBE file as the View property for a Form object, and within that form use PEOPLE.DBF as the Alias property for a Browse object that let us look at the people who are related to an employer.

▶ Editing Properties of Browse Objects

We will consider three Edit properties in this section: Append, Delete, and Modify. The controlling Edit property is the Modify property. It defaults to True, which means that you can change data within the Browse object.

▶▶ **NOTE**

Consider a Browse object with Modify and Delete set to False as a kind of dictionary. The printed version that we have cannot be modified.

With Modify and Delete set to False, you cannot add or delete records. Additionally, you cannot change records. If you set Modify to False, you don't need to set Append to False.

The Append property lets you add records to your table if it is left in its default True state. If you are thinking of tables such as our People table, you may wonder why you would ever want to set Append to False.

But in some cases, you'll find that a static table is helpful. Suppose your company does business in half a dozen countries. You might have a table for the countries, from which you will select the country for a transaction.

In your Browse object, you'll just show the country name, but to use a country, you must fill its table with mandatory information.

The information you might need would include the shipper, the currency, the current exchange rate, and so on. One of your forms would allow you to enter and edit all of this data, including appending to the table. It would include needed Valid properties to make sure, for example, that you filled in the currency and exchange rate.

You would only edit your country information through its form. On the form that you use for routine transactions, you would browse through the country names, assuming that the rest of the data would be available. From the point of view of the transaction form, the country table is a static list, with no appending permitted.

The default Delete property value is True, which allows deletions when you are in the Browse object. Setting Delete to False prevents you from deleting records. In the example that follows, we set Delete to False, just to be sure we don't make a mistake! When we are sure that we want to delete a record, we make very careful use of the Table Records tool.

▸ The Browse Object's Field Properties

The Field properties are Fields and FieldWidth. In the Object Properties Inspector, the Fields property is one of the Data Linkage Properties. The FieldWidth property is found in the Visual Properties section.

The Fields property is a character string, analogous to the one you set with the Table Records Properties dialog box Fields tab. Figure 18.1 shows the Choose Fields dialog box that is launched from the tool icon beside the Fields property.

As in the Table Records Properties dialog box, you can select a field here and then click the on Properties… pushbutton to launch the Field Properties dialog box, shown in Figure 18.2.

All the properties you set for each field are inserted into a single character string, so the Fields property actually selects the fields to use in the Browse object and optionally specifies properties for each field.

The FieldWidth property is analogous to the Table Records tool's Width setting in the Table Records Properties dialog box, Window tab. It specifies the width for Character and Logical fields that will be used

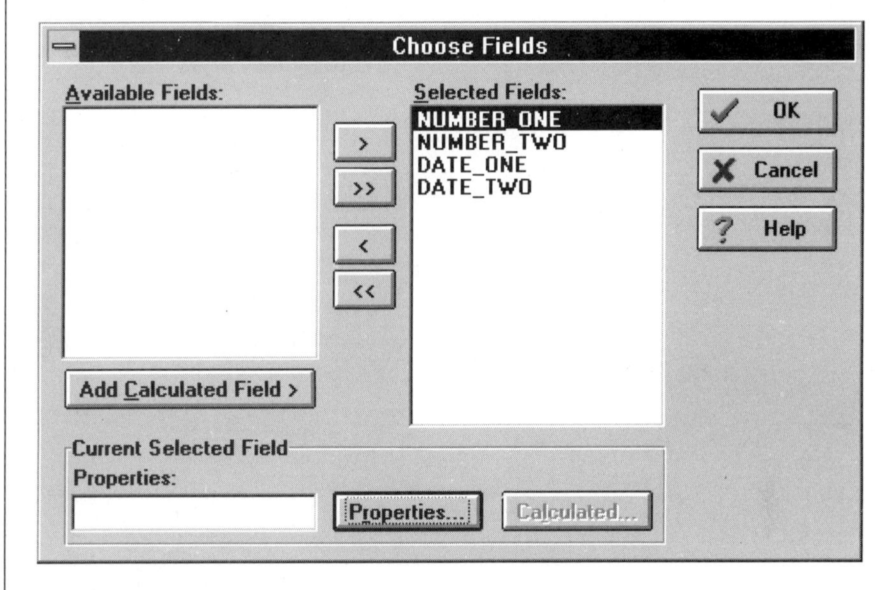

FIGURE 18.1

Adding to the Fields property

if no width is specified for the individual fields. When this property is set to the default zero value, the table's field width is used when individual widths are not specified in the Fields property.

Setting the Browse Object's Mode and Toggle Properties

The Browse object's Mode property sets the inital mode to one of the three views available in the Table Records tool: Browse Layout, Form Layout, or Columnar Layout. The available values are as follows:

Mode 0	Browse
Mode 1	Form Edit
Mode 2	Columnar Edit

The Toggle property is one of the Edit properties in the Object Properties Inspector. It defaults to True, which means that you can change the Browse object from one to the other of the Browse, Form, and Columnar Layout views. (The changes are done by clicking on the appropriate speedbar button or by pressing F2 to toggle between the three layouts.)

FIGURE 18.2

Setting properties for an individual field

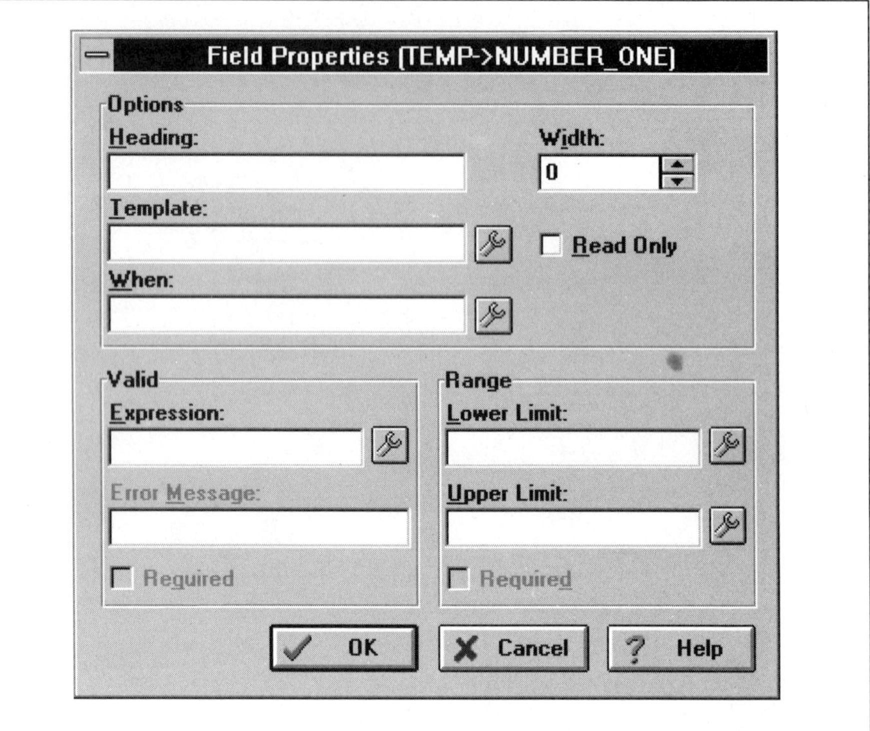

▸▸ NOTE

In practice, we always leave Mode set to its default zero value. We're not sure why you would want a Form Layout, for instance, within a Browse object in a Form object. But we're sure that somewhere, somebody will find a perfectly good reason for doing this. Since the code to implement this is already in place, we're glad that dBASE for Windows' designers left us the option. Similarly, we always set the Toggle property to False, so that the Browse object shows just a Browse Layout view, but again, we're sure that somebody, somewhere will find a use for this.

▶ Showing Items in Browse Objects

There are three Show properties: ShowDeleted, ShowHeading, and ShowRecNo.

The ShowDeleted property is related to the setting of Deleted (set by using the SET DELETED ON/OFF command in the Command window, or by the Deleted checkbox in the Desktop Properties dialog box, Table tab). If Deleted is on, the ShowDeleted setting is ignored.

If Deleted is off, the ShowDeleted property controls the display of deleted records. When ShowDeleted is True, deleted records are shown (with the Del column on the left side of each record in the Browse object). If ShowDeleted is False, deleted records are not shown (and neither is the Del column).

The ShowHeading property, if True, shows headings above each column in the Browse object. The heading specified in the Fields property is used. If there is no Fields heading, the field name is used as a column heading.

The ShowRecNo property controls the display of record numbers to the left of each record in the Browse object. If it is True, the record numbers are shown.

▶ A Browse Example

The Browse objects we added in our phone list system in Part 2 are typical of the Browse objects you'll add. However, sometimes a more complex Browse object is called for.

Early in our work with dBASE for Windows (long before the product was released), we used the on-line Help system to make a list of the available objects and the properties available for each object. Then we compared our list to the documentation for each property, which, among other things, listed the objects in which each property was found. The two didn't match.

We realized that a database would help us to be sure that we didn't make the same mistake. In fact, generating the cross-referencing from a single database seemed to us to be the only possible way to be sure that we were consistent. So we built a database.

The database has two tables: one for objects and one for properties. Both have common information, such as the name. The cross-referencing is done by an extended set of Logical fields in the Properties table. There is one Logical field for each object type. If it is True, that property is contained in the appropriate object. For example, the Browse field in the Properties table is True in the ShowRecNo property, but False in the Alignment property.

We built a couple of forms to help us work with this database. One of them contains just one Browse object—nothing else. The following listing shows just the DEFINE command for that Browse object from this database:

```
DEFINE BROWSE BROWSE1 OF THIS;
  PROPERTY;
    Left        0,;
    Top         0,;
    Height        20,;
    Width      101,;
    ShowRecNo .F.,;
    FontBold .F.,;
    Alias "PROPS",;
    Fields "PROP_ID\H='ID'\4\R," + ;
        "NAME\16," + ;
        "TYPE\4," + ;
        "DEFAULT\6," + ;
        "PARAMS\6," + ;
        "READ_ONLY\H='RO'\3\P='Y'," + ;
        "NOTES\3," + ;
        "BROWSE\2\P='Y'," + ;
        "CHECKBOX\2\P='Y'," + ;
        "COMBOBOX\2\P='Y'," + ;
        "DDELINK\2\P='Y'," + ;
        "DDETOPIC\3\P='Y'," + ;
        "EDITOR\2\P='Y'," + ;
        "ENTRYFIELD\2\P='Y'," + ;
        "FORM\2\P='Y'," + ;
        "IMAGE\2\P='Y'," + ;
        "LINE\3\P='Y'," + ;
        "LISTBOX\2\P='Y'," + ;
        "MENU\2\P='Y'," + ;
        "OLE\2\P='Y'," + ;
        "PUSHBTN\2\P='Y'," + ;
```

```
        "RADIOBTN\3\P='Y'," + ;
        "RECTANGLE\2\P='Y'," + ;
        "SCROLLBAR\2\P='Y'," + ;
        "SPINBOX\2\P='Y'," + ;
        "TEXT\2\P='Y'",;
    ColorNormal "N/W",;
    Toggle .F.,;
    Delete .F.
```

For this listing, we've divided the Fields property into one line per field. (In the .WFM file, this property extends in a single line that would need a book about 3 feet wide to print.)

Figure 18.3 shows us using this Browse to check the Show properties of Browse objects.

FIGURE 18.3

We check that ShowRecNo is only a Browse property

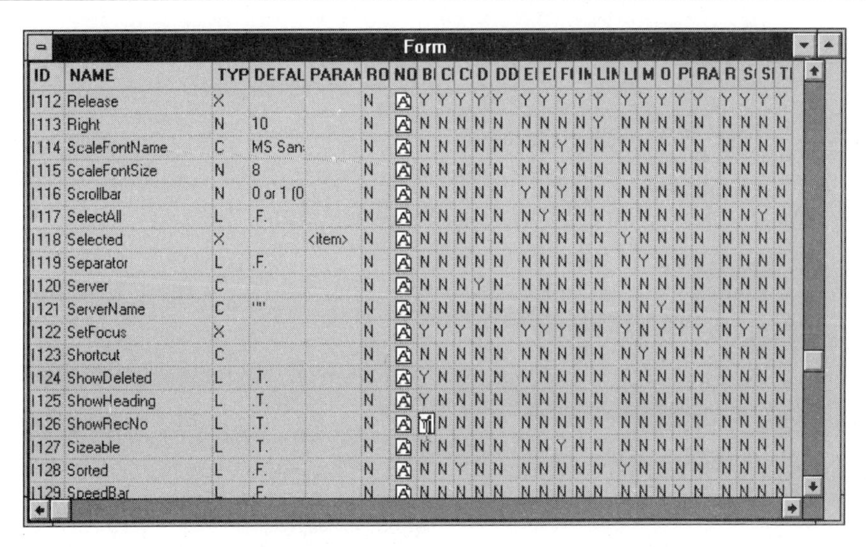

Form

ID	NAME	TYP	DEFAL	PARAM	RO	NO	B	C	C	D	DD	E	E	F	IN	LIN	LI	M	O	P	RA	R	S	SI	T
1112	Release	X			N	A	Y	Y	Y	Y	Y	Y	Y	Y	Y	Y	Y	Y	Y	Y	Y	Y	Y	Y	Y
1113	Right	N	10		N	A	N	N	N	N	N	N	N	N	N	Y	N	N	N	N	N	N	N	N	N
1114	ScaleFontName	C	MS San		N	A	N	N	N	N	N	N	N	Y	N	N	N	N	N	N	N	N	N	N	N
1115	ScaleFontSize	N	8		N	A	N	N	N	N	N	N	N	Y	N	N	N	N	N	N	N	N	N	N	N
1116	Scrollbar	N	0 or 1 (0		N	A	N	N	N	N	N	Y	N	Y	N	N	N	N	N	N	N	N	N	N	N
1117	SelectAll	L	.F.		N	A	N	N	N	N	N	N	Y	N	N	N	N	N	N	N	N	N	N	Y	N
1118	Selected	X		<item>	N	A	N	N	N	N	N	N	N	N	N	N	Y	N	N	N	N	N	N	N	N
1119	Separator	L	.F.		N	A	N	N	N	N	N	N	N	N	N	N	N	Y	N	N	N	N	N	N	N
1120	Server	C			N	A	N	N	N	Y	N	N	N	N	N	N	N	N	N	N	N	N	N	N	N
1121	ServerName	C	""		N	A	N	N	N	N	N	N	N	N	N	N	N	N	Y	N	N	N	N	N	N
1122	SetFocus	X			N	A	Y	Y	Y	N	N	Y	Y	Y	N	N	Y	N	Y	Y	Y	N	Y	Y	N
1123	Shortcut	C			N	A	N	N	N	N	N	N	N	N	N	N	N	Y	N	N	N	N	N	N	N
1124	ShowDeleted	L	.T.		N	A	Y	N	N	N	N	N	N	N	N	N	N	N	N	N	N	N	N	N	N
1125	ShowHeading	L	.T.		N	A	Y	N	N	N	N	N	N	N	N	N	N	N	N	N	N	N	N	N	N
1126	ShowRecNo	L	.T.		N	A	Y	N	N	N	N	N	N	N	N	N	N	N	N	N	N	N	N	N	N
1127	Sizeable	L	.T.		N	A	N	N	N	N	N	N	N	Y	N	N	N	N	N	N	N	N	N	N	N
1128	Sorted	L	.F.		N	A	N	N	Y	N	N	N	N	N	N	N	Y	N	N	N	N	N	N	N	N
1129	SpeedBar	L	.F.		N	A	N	N	N	N	N	N	N	N	N	N	N	N	N	Y	N	N	N	N	N

You can see that we took a lot of time setting up each field so that it was no wider than necessary (2 characters) and formatted correctly (P='Y' is the Y picture, that formats Logical fields as a Y or N value).

The Toggle and Delete properties are turned off. The result of all this work is that we have a Browse object that shows us a snapshot of each property's objects, and each object's properties. This database was used in the preparation of all the reference material in this part of the book.

▸▸ **NOTE**

Appendixes G and H were written with the help of dBASE for Windows programs that we created to read this data and format the output appropriately. This is why we can be certain that the material here is correctly cross-referenced. (Borland is now using this database, so we expect that the on-line help, if not the printed manuals, will be consistent, perhaps by the time you read this.)

▸▸ Working with Combobox Objects

The Combobox object in Windows interfaces combines an entry field with a list box. The dBASE for Windows Combobox object may, or may not, support this combination.

The Combobox object can be used to select from field values in a table, from a list of files in a directory, or from other sources. The Combobox object may be linked to a field through a DataLink property, as our other data-entry objects are.

In this section we explore some of the key properties of the Combobox object.

▸ Setting the Combobox Object's Data Properties

There are two data properties of the Combobox object: DataLink and DataSource. The DataLink property links the Value property of the Combobox object to a field in a table. This works like the other DataLink properties for objects such as Checkboxes and Entryfields. The DataSource property provides the list of items from which you can select the Value.

We'll build an example that demonstrates these properties. To begin, we'll use a table that has a field to store a file name and another field to store a field name. Figure 18.4 shows the structure of another TEMP.DBF file.

FIGURE 18.4

A table to store a file name and a field name

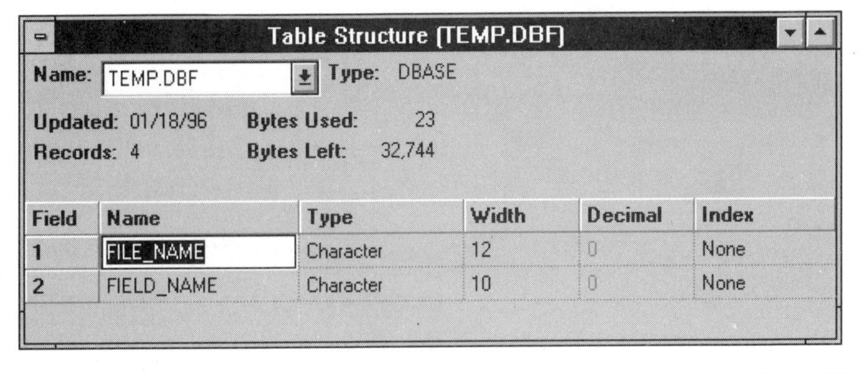

Note that the width of the FILE_NAME field is 12, to accommodate the 8.3 character form of DOS file names. As you've done before, launch the Form Expert in the Form Designer and have it construct a form using both the fields in TEMP.DBF.

Once your .WFM file is available in the Form Designer, use the lasso to rope both Entryfield objects, and then press Del to delete them. Stretch the form to make it wider, and then add two Combobox objects, side by side. Drag the *Field_name* text into position so that your form looks like the one shown in Figure 18.5.

FIGURE 18.5

Two fresh Combobox objects

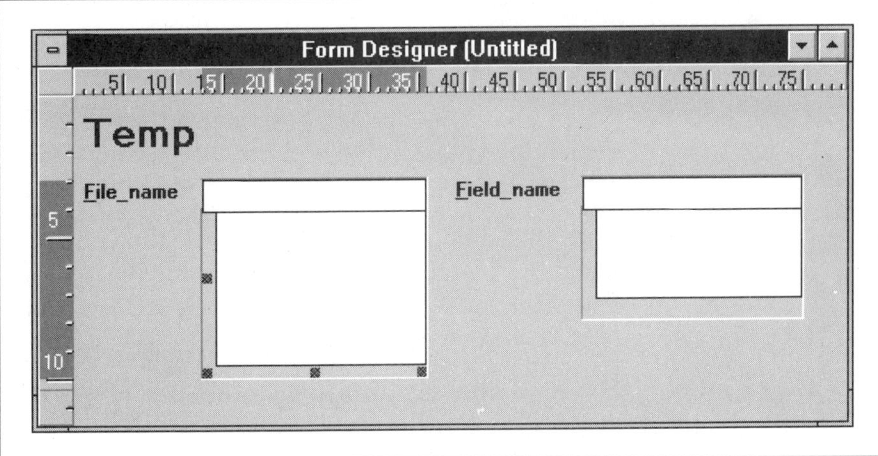

In one Combobox, we'll choose a file name from the names of our .DBF files. Select the Combobox object on the left, and then click on the Properties tab of the Object Properties Inspector. Click on the DataSource property, and then click on the tool icon on the right.

This will launch the Choose Data Source dialog box, shown in Figure 18.6.

FIGURE 18.6

Choosing the .DBF files for a Combobox's DataSource property

The Type: drop-down list defaults to File, which is what we want. For files, the tool icon next to the Data Source entry field is inactive. You type whatever file mask you want in this field. We've used *.DBF, which has its normal DOS meaning.

This will let us choose an entry from the list of the .DBF files in the current directory. You could also use a drive and path specification, or specify *.DB for Paradox-type tables. If you're using tables from an SQL database, there is a Tables choice in the Type: drop-down list.

When you choose a DataSource property, the Form Designer accesses the source you selected and populates your Combobox object, so you get an idea of what the finished product will look like.

With this choice made, return to the Object Properties Inspector and select the DataLink property. Clicking on the tool icon on the right of DataLink launches the Choose Field dialog box. Select the FILE_NAME field.

You have now established a Combobox object that will show you a list of all .DBF files. It will enter the one you choose into the FILE_NAME field of your TEMP table.

Now let's enter a field name from the structure of our TEMP table into the FIELD_NAME field. Select the second Combobox object and click the tool icon next to the DataSource property. From the Choose Data Source dialog box, select Structure from the Type: drop-down list. With this choice, there is nothing to put into the Data Source: entry field. Leave it blank.

Select the DataLink property and link this Combobox object to the FIELD_NAME field in your TEMP table. With that done, we're almost ready to run the form.

There is one problem with this form as we have built it so far. When you navigate, you will have almost no clue as to which record you are working with. Let's add a Text object to report the current record number.

Grab a Text object from the Controls palette and place it over the Combobox objects. At this point, our form is shown in Figure 18.7. Yours should look similar.

As you see in Figure 18.7, the Text object we added is named Text4. You'll need to know this name to add the event handlers that will report the record number as you move through your table. While this text is selected, choose the Properties tab of the Object Properties Inspector and set two Visual Properties: set Border to True and set ColorNormal to N/W+ (black on pure white).

FIGURE 18.7

Adding a Text object to report the record number

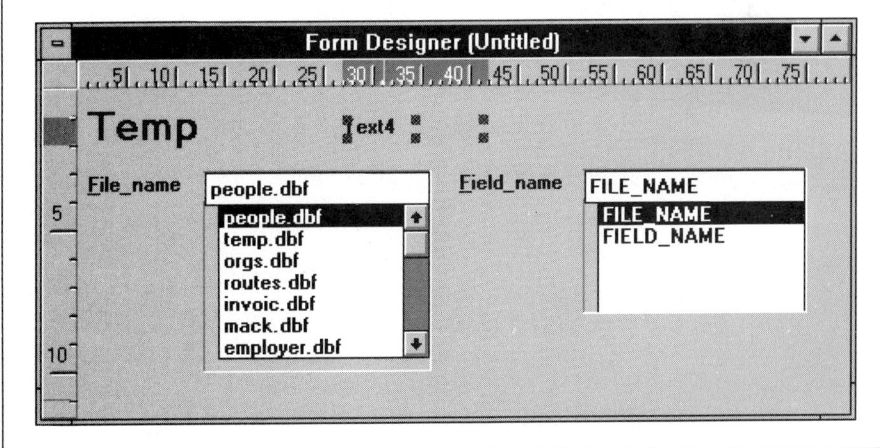

With the Text4 object ready, add the following line to the Form's event handlers OnAppend, OnNavigate, and OnOpen:

```
This.text4.Text = STR( RECNO( ) )
```

Be sure that you have selected the Form, not the Text4 object, when you add these three event handlers.

Now you're ready to run your form. Click on the lightning icon. To begin, use the Combobox object on the left to select the first file in its list. Click on the append record icon, or press Ctrl-A, and select the second file for the second record. Put the third file name in the third record, and so on.

You'll have two choices on the right: the File_name and Field_name, which are the names of the fields in your TEMP file's structure. You can experiment with these (selecting them will place their values into your Field_name field, which is the DataLink for this Combobox object).

You can link the Structure as a DataSource property for advanced applications where you will actually manipulate table structures. But you can also use this Combobox option to put small, relatively static lists into tables that are used just for reference. For instance, one table might have fields named Dollar, Pound, Franc, Mark, and so on. This table would be in a .QBE file but not linked to other tables.

▸▸ **WARNING**

In an early release of dBASE for Windows, multiple Combobox objects were not correctly supported. Values correctly data-linked only for the last Combobox you used if you had more than one. Check before you use multiple Combobox objects in a form.

▸ *Putting Combobox Entries in Order*

The Sorted property puts your Combobox object entries into ascending sort order. If you return to Design mode and select the left Combo-box object, you can see the effect of the Sorted property (it's one of the Data Linkage Properties). Change it from the default .F. to .T., and you will see your list redisplayed in alphabetical order. Most Combo-box lists are improved by setting Sorted to True.

The Sorted property does *not* sort lists of values from fields in a table. Use an index on the field, so the Combobox object entries start sorted.

▶ Choosing Combobox Object Styles

The Combobox object supports three separate Style settings:

Style 0	Simple combination box (the default)
Style 1	Drop-down combination box
Style 2	Drop-down list

We've been working with the default simple combination box (Style 0). This is the most convenient combination form. However, if your form is crowded, you may not have room to leave the Combobox object dropped down. Choose Style 1 for a drop-down box, which shows only the current selection until you click on the drop-down arrow.

The Style 2 setting is not a combination box at all. It is a drop-down list. This type of drop-down list shares all the other characteristics of the combination box, but it doesn't let you type in the entry field portion (although you can type the first letter of the desired entry to jump to that portion of the list). This means that your choice must be one of the items in the list; you cannot type something else, as you can with the other forms.

Go ahead and experiment with these styles. Figure 18.8 shows the drop-down combination box on the left and the drop-down list on the right.

▶▶ **NOTE**

You may notice a subtle difference between the drop-down combination box and the drop-down list. The combination box separates the drop-down arrow from the entry field. In the drop-down list, the two components are adjacent.

FIGURE 18.8

A drop-down combination box and a drop-down list

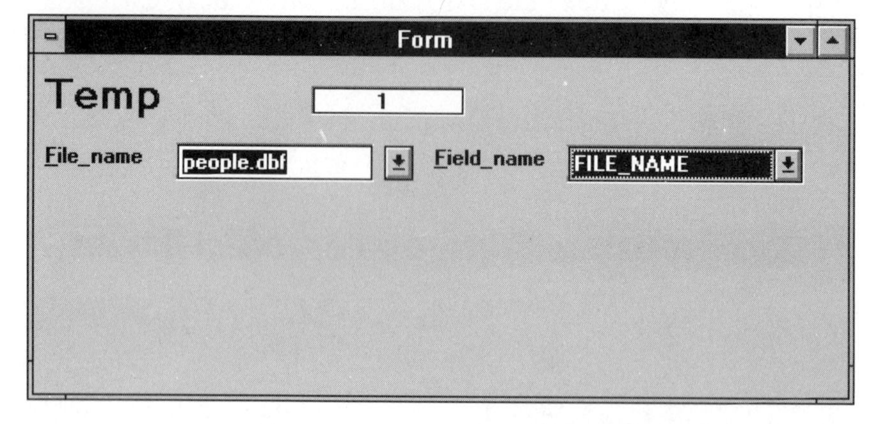

▶ Setting the Combobox Object's Value

Comboboxes do not need to be attached to a table field via the DataLink property. They have a Value property that is the currently selected choice. Your event handlers can use the value by specifying Form.combobox1.Value (or combobox2, or whatever the number is).

▸▸ Working with Editor Objects

In this section, we'll explore some of the key properties of the Editor object. Editors can be used to handle Memo fields in a file or text files, such as program files. To explore the characteristics of the Editor object, we'll build a text editor for our .WFM files.

If you thought that building a text editor was a job for advanced programmers, you would have been right not too long ago. Now, however, it is as simple as putting an Editor object on a form and using its properties.

Let's begin with a program template. We'll call our program WEDIT.PRG, because it is a .WFM editor. In the Navigator, select Programs and launch the Untitled file. Enter these two comment lines, as shown in Figure 18.9.

```
* WEDIT.PRG--an editor for .WFM files
* end of WEDIT.PRG
```

FIGURE 18.9

Beginning the WEDIT program in the Program Editor

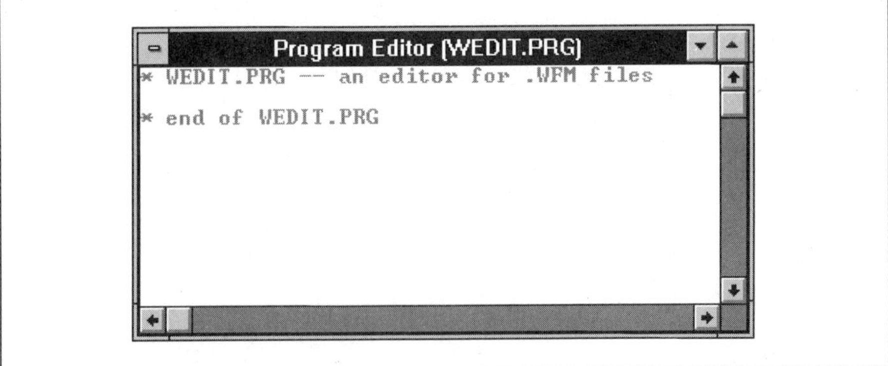
Program Editor (WEDIT.PRG)
* WEDIT.PRG -- an editor for .WFM files
* end of WEDIT.PRG

We begin all our programs with a comment that names the program and states its purpose. We end all our programs with the comment that tells us this is the end of the file. You should put similar lines into the Header and General sections of each of your .WFM files.

With the start and end comments in place, press Ctrl-D to Do your program. When you are asked for a name for the program, give the name **WEDIT** (the .PRG extension is supplied automatically if you omit an extension). You are returned to the Command window after giving the name.

Actually, a lot more happened after you supplied the name. First, your program text was saved. Next, dBASE for Windows ran its compiler to produce WEDIT.PRO—the object program that is actually run. Then it executed the .PRO file.

The reason that you may have missed all this is that it probably took less than a second. Since our program consists of two comments, there is absolutely nothing for it to do, yet. If you check your directory (use DIR *.PRO in the Command window), you'll see that the .PRO file was written.

Ready to get started? The first thing an editor should do is let us choose the file we want to edit. An Open File dialog box would be a good way to choose a file. Fortunately, this takes exactly one line of code.

We'll use two lines. The first will do the work, and the second will tell us what happened. Add these two lines in the middle of your program:

```
fname = GETFILE( "*.WFM", "Choose Form" )
? fname
```

The first line calls the GETFILE( ) function, which launches an Open File dialog box. The first argument, "*.WFM," is the file skeleton you want the Open File dialog box to use. The second argument, "Choose Form," is the title you want the Open File dialog box box to display.

The second line, ? fname, will write the value of the variable fname into the Command window's results pane. We use lots of lines like this as we are programming; otherwise, we wouldn't see what is going on in our program.

Press Ctrl-D after you have entered those lines. If you typed them correctly, an Open File dialog box, titled Choose Form, is launched, with *.WFM as the file skeleton. Select a file, and you will be returned to the Command window. If you look in the Command window's results pane, you'll see the name of the file you selected.

That's an amazingly simple program for such a sophisticated result. One of the essential goals of object-oriented programming is to let you reuse existing objects, such as the Open File dialog box. In this instance, that goal is beautifully realized.

Now let's get on to launching the file we chose in an Editor object. We'll need a Form object to contain the Editor object. Then we'll need to assign the file name we chose to the Editor's DataLink property. All of this is less work to do than to explain. Our new program is shown in full in Figure 18.10.

FIGURE 18.10

Our first text editor program

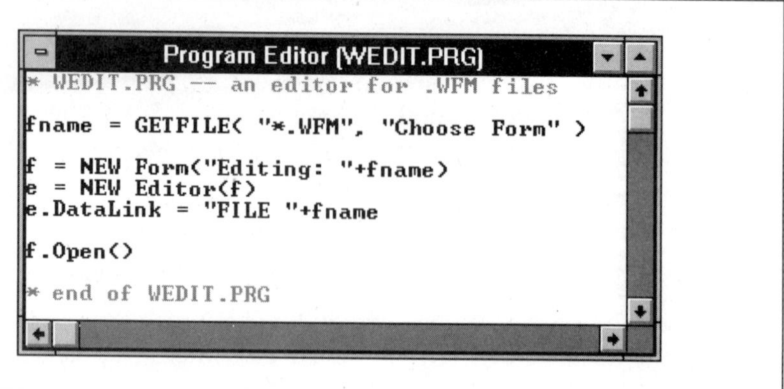
Program Editor (WEDIT.PRG)
* WEDIT.PRG -- an editor for .WFM files
fname = GETFILE("*.WFM", "Choose Form")
f = NEW Form("Editing: "+fname)
e = NEW Editor(f)
e.DataLink = "FILE "+fname
f.Open()
* end of WEDIT.PRG

Let's go through these lines one at a time. First, you should have deleted the line that read ? fname. (Once you use one of these lines and check the results in the Command window, you can delete it.)

We begin with:

```
f = NEW Form("Editing: "+fname)
```

This line opens a NEW Form object. The argument in parentheses is the title to display in the window's title bar.

The next line is

```
e = NEW Editor(f)
```

This creates a NEW Editor object. The argument inside parentheses is the Form object to which this Editor is attached.

The line:

```
e.DataLink = "FILE "+fname
```

assigns the word "FILE " plus the name returned from GETFILE( ) to the DataLink property. Note that Editors have a DataLink, not a DataSource. DataLinks are two-way links—they read the current value and, if you modify it, write it back. DataSource properties are ones that are read-only.

The last of our four new lines:

```
f.Open()
```

calls the Open method of the Form object named f. The parentheses are used to tell dBASE for Windows that we are invoking a method property.

When you press Ctrl-D, you should get a result similar to the one we show in Figure 18.11.

Well, what do you think? It's not precisely what you had in mind, is it? But on the other hand, we bet you didn't think that you could do any sort of text editor in a program of five lines, did you?

Your .WFM editor is now a full, working editor. It will scroll, let you enter text, respond to Ctrl-F to find text, Ctrl-R to replace text, and so on. Of course, the default Editor object dimensions make working with this editor less than useful.

FIGURE 18.11

Our first Editor is a bit cramped

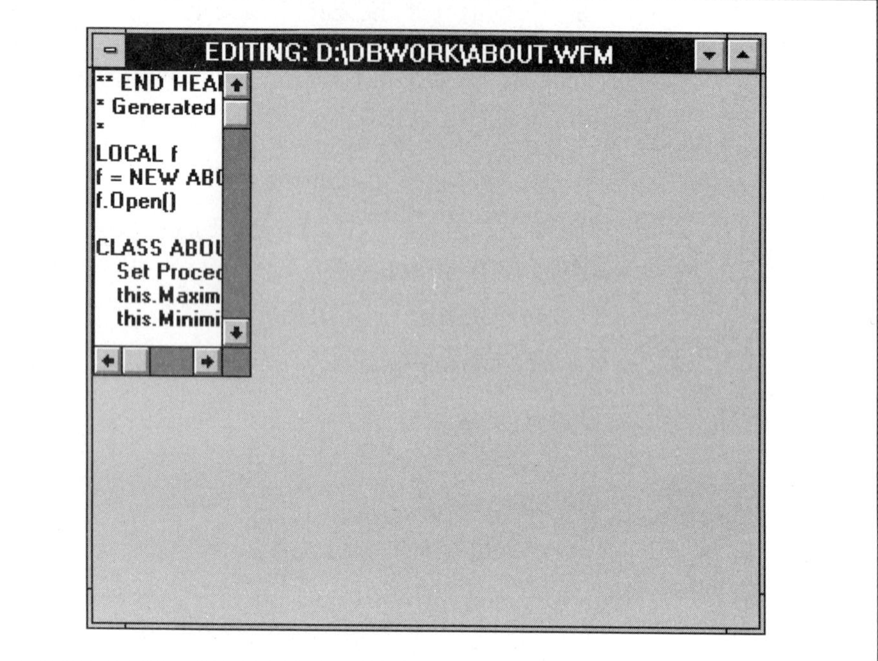

▸▸ TIP

If you check the reference sections that conclude the chapters in Part 5 before you start, you can find the default dimensions. That way, you'll know what's coming when you place an object on a form.

Let's expand the Editor object to match the dimensions of the form. Before the f.Open() line, add these two lines:

```
e.Height = f.Height
e.Width = f.Width
```

Figure 18.12 shows these lines added to our program.

With the addition of these two lines, you've set the Height and Width properties of the Editor object to match the Height and Width of the Form object that contains it. Now when you press Ctrl-D, you get the very good-looking, useful editor shown in Figure 18.13.

FIGURE 18.12

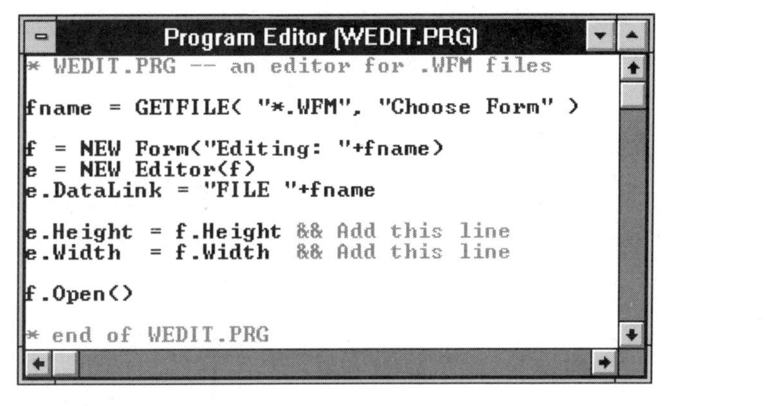

Adding Height and Width settings

FIGURE 18.13

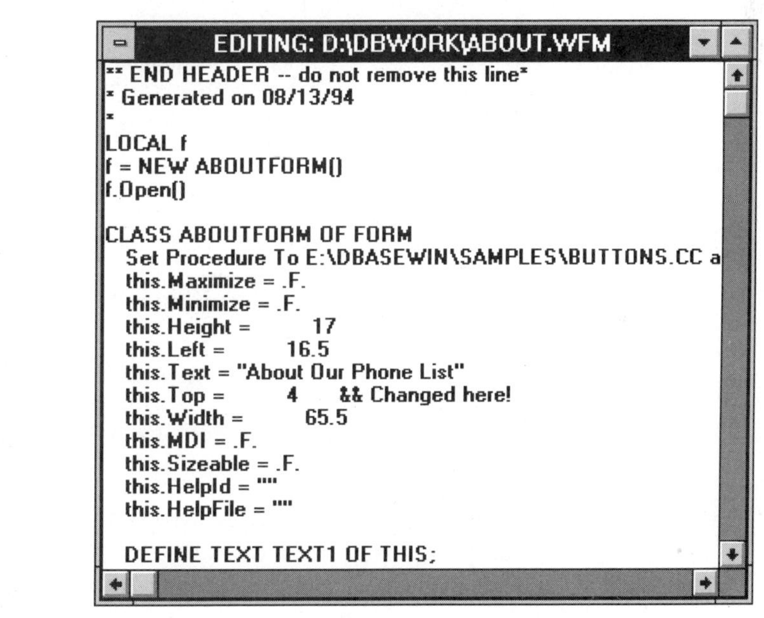

The resized text editor

Now we're up to seven lines of program (not counting blank lines and comments), and we've built a useful .WFM editor. We think you're probably convinced by now that this is no longer the province of advanced programmers.

There is one serious problem we haven't addressed. If you grab the lower-right corner of your editor and stretch, you'll get the result shown in Figure 18.14.

FIGURE 18.14

Resizing is not what you wanted

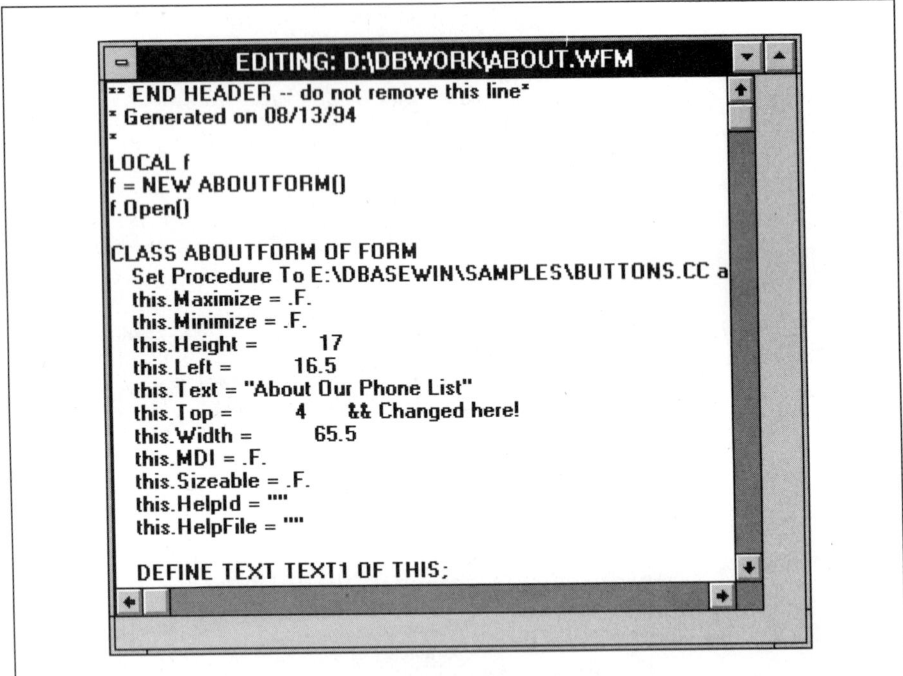

You can see that the Editor object stays the same size; it does not resize itself when the form is resized. Let's make one more improvement to correct this before we move on.

To have the Editor object resized when the Form object is resized, we need to add a resizing method to our program. Since we're working without the benefit of the Procedure Editor, we'll need to handle the linking lines and the header on our own. All of this adds only four lines to the program. The completed program is shown in Figure 18.15.

Let's look at the new lines. The first new line is:

```
f.OnSize = resizer
```

This line assigns the resizer routine to the Form's OnSize event. Whenever you resize the Form, the resizer routine will be called.

FIGURE 18.15

A complete editor for .WFM files

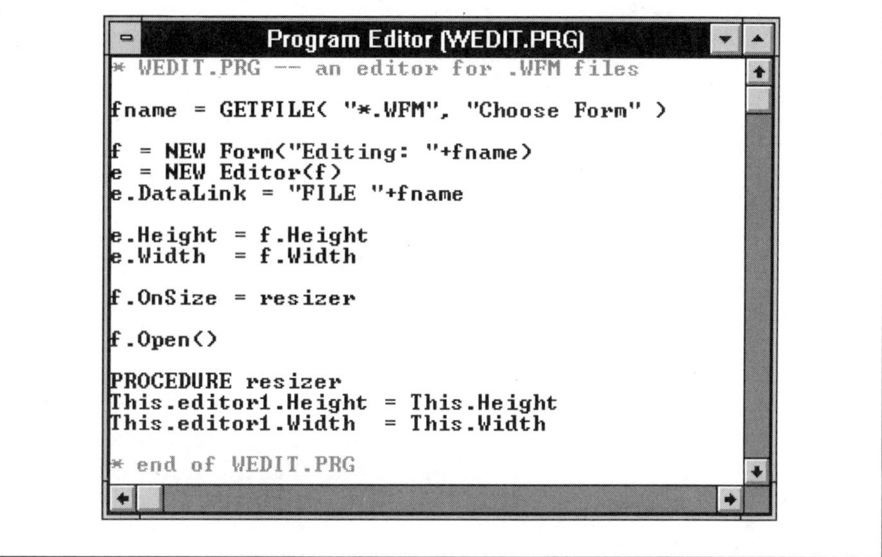

Program Editor (WEDIT.PRG)
* WEDIT.PRG -- an editor for .WFM files
fname = GETFILE("*.WFM", "Choose Form")
f = NEW Form("Editing: "+fname)
e = NEW Editor(f)
e.DataLink = "FILE "+fname
e.Height = f.Height
e.Width = f.Width
f.OnSize = resizer
f.Open()
PROCEDURE resizer
This.editor1.Height = This.Height
This.editor1.Width = This.Width
* end of WEDIT.PRG

And here's that routine:

```
PROCEDURE resizer
This.editor1.Height = This.Height
This.editor1.Width  = This.Width
```

The resizer routine is simple. It assigns the Form's Height to the Editor's Height, and does the same for Width. In an event handler, This is the object that is handling the event. Here, it is the Form object (it's the form that is resized when you grab the borders and drag or use the System menu).

The Editor object, since it's the first one (the only one, too) is named Editor1 by default, so This.editor1 is the Editor object.

With this addition, our program has now grown to 11 working lines, and makes a very useful editor.

Some other properties that you may find useful include the following:

- Modify, which allows editing if set to True (otherwise, only reading)
- Scrollbar, which defaults to 1 (on)
- Wrap, which turns word wrapping on if it is set to True

▸▸ Working with Listbox Objects

The Listbox object is similar to the Combobox object, which we explored earlier in this chapter. See the Combobox section for a discussion of the DataSource and the Value properties, which are the same for Listbox objects.

The Listbox does not drop down, as the Combobox does. However, it has one very important property: it allows multiple choices in the list. One drawback is that programming is required to use these choices.

In this section, we'll develop a small program that creates a Form object with a Listbox object and a Pushbutton object that triggers a report of the selected entries. Although it is not a complex program, you may be surprised to find that it is not quite as simple as the .WFM editor we developed in the previous section.

Before you begin any programming, go to the Programming tab of the Desktop Properties dialog box and be sure that Talk is *not* checked and that Ensure Compilation *is* checked.

Let's begin with two comment lines in a general-purpose shell program:

```
* TEMP.PRG -- a temporary program for testing

* end of TEMP.PRG
```

▸▸ TIP

We keep a copy of TEMP.PRG permanently. When we've finished testing something, we delete all the lines between these comments and leave it for our next test. If you invent a new name and .PRG file for each test use, you'll quickly clutter up your work directory.

With the TEMP.PRG shell program ready for use, let's create a form with a Listbox object on it and launch the form. Since we already looked up the default size of the Listbox object (see the reference section at the end of this chapter), we know that we'll need to adjust it.

We'll also need to assign a DataSource property. Figure 18.16 shows the program with these features.

As you can see, we used the semicolon to put separate program statements on a single line, in these lines:

```
lb.Top = 3; lb.Left = 5
lb.Height = 8; lb.Width = 15
```

FIGURE 18.16

Our starting Listbox program

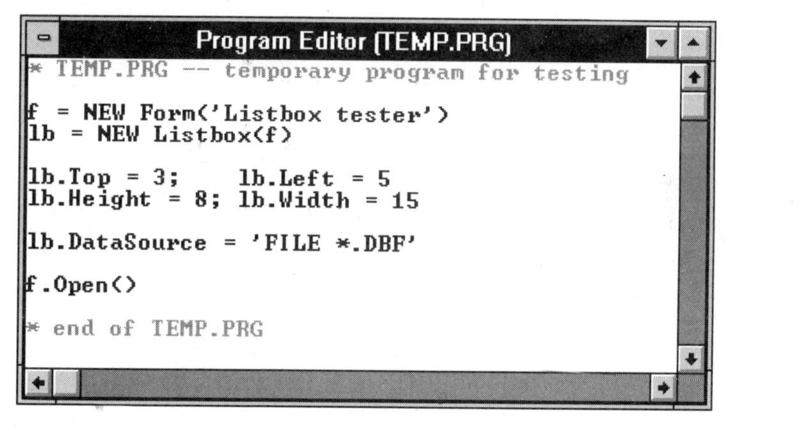

NOTE

We use multiple statements on a line only when the statements are very closely related, such as assigning coordinates and dimensions to an object.

When you run your program, it should look like ours, which is shown in Figure 18.17.

If you click on your Listbox object, you'll see that you are selecting a single choice. As with radio buttons, if you click on one choice, the previously selected choice is deselected. We'll get to multiple selections, but first, let's add a reporter routine hooked to a Pushbutton object.

This is the bottom of the new program:

```
pb = NEW pushbutton(f)
pb.OnClick = reporter
```

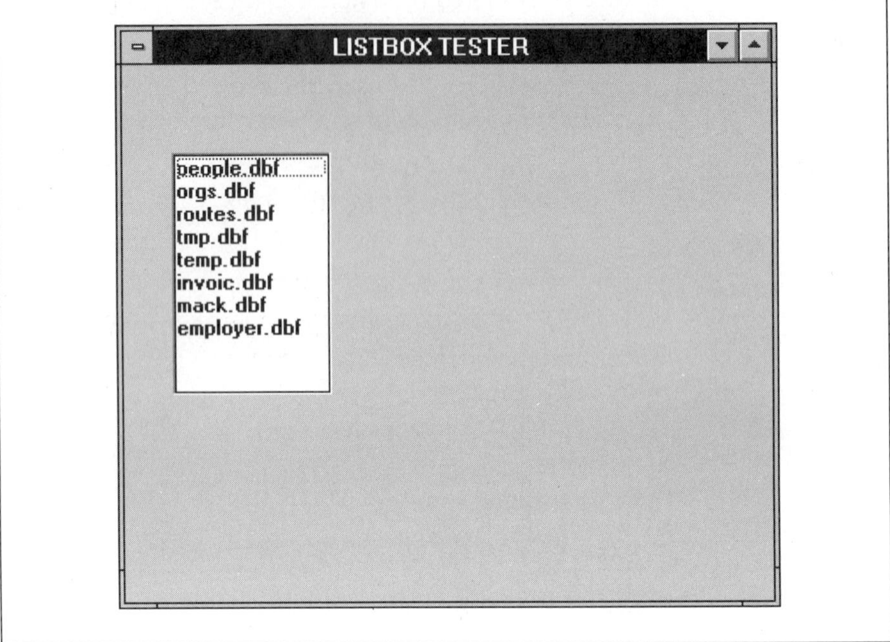

FIGURE 18.17 *Our starting Listbox program in operation*

```
f.Open()

PROCEDURE reporter
CLEAR
? Form.Listbox1.Value

* end of TEMP.PRG
```

The two lines that define the Pushbutton and assign reporter to its OnClick event are new. The PROCEDURE reporter line and the two following ones are also new.

With these lines in place, run your program again. Adjust your form and your Command window so that you can see the results pane as well as your Form and Listbox objects at the same time. When you select an entry in the list box, the Value property of the Listbox object is recorded. When you click on the pushbutton, the Value property is reported in your Command window's results pane.

Figure 18.18 shows us selecting a .DBF file and having it reported in the Command window.

FIGURE 18.18

Getting a report with a button click

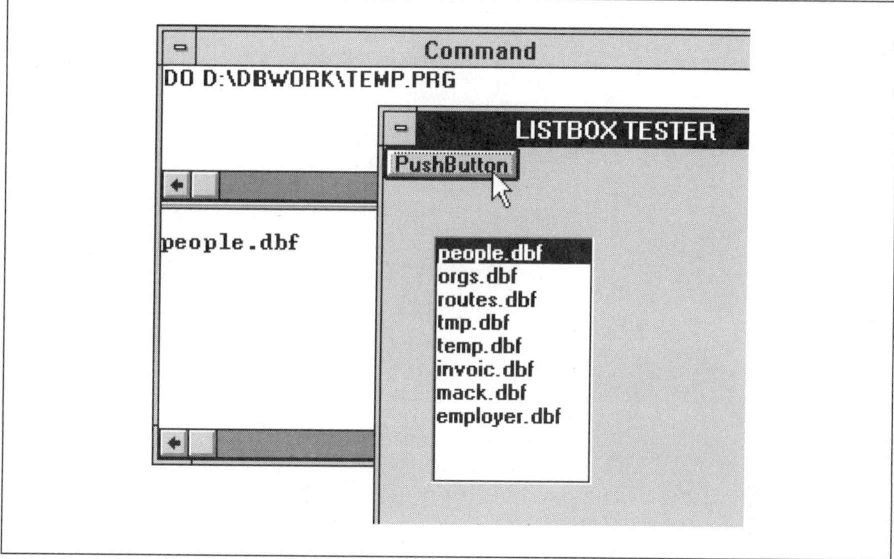

Now let's get the list sorted and allow multiple selections. This takes two new lines—the ones we've commented in the following listing:

```
lb.DataSource = 'FILE *.DBF'

lb.Sorted = .T. && add this line
lb.Multiple = .T. && and this one, too

pb = NEW pushbutton(f)
```

With those two lines added, your list will be sorted and you will be able to select as many items as you like. Add them and test your new program. Do you see a small problem?

The problem is that our reporter routine does not show multiple items, it just reports the Value property. The Value is the last choice you made, not all the choices you've made. We'll need to add a loop to our reporter to handle all the choices we've made.

To do this, we'll use the LISTCOUNT( ) function, which returns the number of items in the Listbox, and the LISTSELECTED( ) function. The LISTSELECTED( ) function is called with the list box you want to examine and an item number. It returns a blank string if the item is not selected; it returns the item itself if it is selected.

This is the new reporter routine:

```
PROCEDURE reporter
LOCAL i, fname

CLEAR

FOR i = 1 TO LISTCOUNT(Form.Listbox1)
   fname = LISTSELECTED(Form.Listbox1, i)
   IF .NOT. EMPTY(fname)
      ? fname
   ENDIF
ENDFOR
```

This version of the reporter will work for any number of choices. It loops from 1 to however many choices there are in your Listbox object. Inside the loop it assigns the LISTSELECTED() value of each choice to the variable fname. If fname is not empty (the EMPTY() function returns True if fname is all blank), the value of fname is reported to the Command window's results pane.

Figure 18.19 shows us running this program, selecting multiple files, and clicking the pushbutton when we are content with our selections.

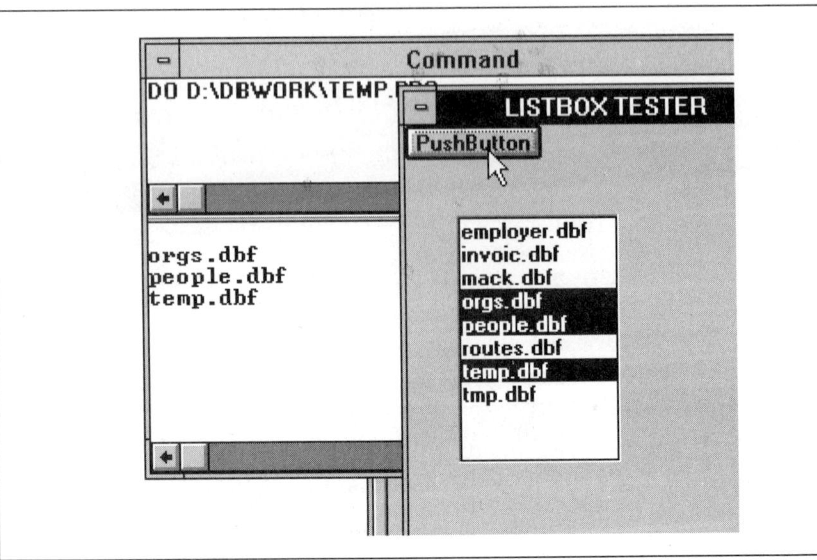

FIGURE 18.19

Selecting and reporting multiple items

The technique of looping over all the choices and picking those which are not EMPTY() is the one you will use whenever you need multiple selections from a Listbox object. Obviously, you could be doing something more interesting.

If the choices were .DBF files, you could open them or close them. If the choices were field names, you could create a total or other calculation for the selected ones. The only limit is your imagination.

If you are having trouble, the full listing of our program follows. Compare yours to this one:

```
* TEMP.PRG -- temporary program for testing

f = NEW Form('Listbox tester')
lb = NEW Listbox(f)

lb.Top = 3;    lb.Left = 5
lb.Height = 8; lb.Width = 15

lb.DataSource = 'FILE *.DBF'

lb.Sorted   = .T. && add this line
lb.Multiple = .T. && and this one, too

pb = NEW pushbutton(f)
pb.OnClick = reporter

f.Open()

PROCEDURE reporter
LOCAL i, fname

CLEAR

FOR i = 1 TO LISTCOUNT(Form.Listbox1)
   fname = LISTSELECTED(Form.Listbox1, i)
   IF .NOT. EMPTY(fname)
      ? fname
   ENDIF
ENDFOR

* end of TEMP.PRG
```

►► Advanced Form Objects Properties Reference

In this section, we provide an alphabetical listing of all the properties of the Browse, Combobox, Editor, and Listbox objects. Each listing includes the default value (if one exists). If a property is read-only, you cannot assign a value to it. If a property is read-only, this is noted in its listing.

Data properties are called Properties; events and other methods are called Methods. Additionally, Methods' names are followed by parentheses; for example, ClassName is a data property, but Close() is a method. Some methods take parameters within their parentheses, as noted in their listings.

► Browse Object Properties

This section lists and briefly explains the properties of the Browse object.

The Browse.Alias Property

Default value: ""

The Alias is the name or alias of the table that is accessed.

The Browse.Append Property

Default value: .T.

If Append is True, you can append data using the Browse object.

The Browse.Before Property

Before is an object reference to the object that this Browse object precedes in the form's tabbing order. If this Browse object is the last one in the form's tabbing order, Before is a reference to the first object in the tabbing order (Form.First).

The Browse.ClassName Property

Default value: BROWSE

ClassName is read-only. This property is assigned by dBASE for Windows for each of the built-in classes. ClassName can be used to distinguish among multiple objects with the same name.

The Browse.ColorNormal Property

Default value: N/W

The ColorNormal property specifies the color of the Browse object. ColorNormal may be a dBASE IV-style color specification, or it may be a color selected from the color palette with the Choose Color dialog box.

The Browse.Delete Property

Default value: .T.

If Delete is False, the Browse object will not allow marking records for deletion.

The Browse.Enabled Property

Default value: .T.

If Enabled is True, the Browse object is accessible. You can use the Enabled property to disable options in event handlers. For example, a Valid function could set some object's Enabled to False if required conditions were not met.

The Browse.Fields Property

Default value: ""

The Fields property is a single string (possibly hundreds or more characters long) that encodes all the information entered through the Browse Field Picker.

The Browse.FieldWidth Property

Default value: 0

If supplied, the FieldWidth property limits the display width of Character fields. If not specified, the display length of a Character field is the greater of its length or the length of its name. Display lengths for individual fields override these considerations.

The Browse.Follow Property

Default value: .T.

If Follow is True, the Browse's record display is adjusted when a value in the active index tag is changed. If it is False, the changed data could "disappear" when the record is relocated.

The Browse.FontBold Property

Default value: .F.

If True, FontBold specifies that the Browse object's font is boldface.

The Browse.FontItalic Property

Default value: .F.

If True, FontItalic specifies that the Browse object's font is italic.

The Browse.FontName Property

Default value: MS Sans Serif

The FontName property specifies the name of the font. This may be set from the Font dialog box, accessed via the tool icon in the Form Designer's Properties dialog box.

The Browse.FontSize Property

Default value: 8

The FontSize property specifies the size of the font, in points.

The Browse.Height Property

Default value: 8.5

The Height property specifies the height of the Browse object, in characters.

The Browse.HelpFile Property

Default value: ""

The HelpFile property names the Windows Help file that will be used when you press F1.

The Browse.HelpID Property

Default value: ""

The HelpID specifies the individual Help screen that will be accessed in the Windows Help file specified by the HelpFile property.

The Browse.hWnd Property

The hWnd property is read-only. This property is an arbitrary integer number that identifies the window to which the Browse object belongs. This is called the window's *handle*. It is used when you access Windows functions directly via EXTERN commands.

The Browse.ID Property

Default value: –1

ID is a number than can be used to distinguish between otherwise identical Browse objects.

The Browse.Left Property

Default value: 1.0

The Left property specifies the location of the left side of the Browse object within its form, in characters. The leftmost character is number 0.

The Browse.Mode Property

Default value: 0

Available settings: 0–2

The Mode property specifies one of Browse mode (0), Form Edit (1), or Columnar Edit (2).

The Browse.Modify Property

Default value: .T.

If Modify is False, the Browse object will not let you make any changes to the data.

The Browse.MousePointer Property

Default value: 0

Available settings: 0–11

The MousePointer property specifies the type of mouse pointer to use when the pointer is over the Browse object. For example, the mouse pointer is an arrow over a form, but turns to an I-beam in an editor. The settings are default (0), arrow (1), cross (2), I-beam (3), icon (4), size (5), size NESW (6), size S (7), size NWSE (8), size E (9), up arrow (10), and wait (hourglass, 11).

The Browse.Move( ) Method

Parameters: *<lft>*,*<tp>*,*<wdth>*,*<hght>*

Move is a method property that can move the Browse object, resize the Browse object, or both. You provide Move with four parameters, representing the new values for the properties Left, Top, Width, and Height, respectively.

The Browse.Name Property

Default value: BROWSE*<n>*

The Name property is the property name given to this Browse object on the parent form. If the name is BROWSE1, for example, specifying Parent.BROWSE1 specifies this Browse object.

The Browse.OnAppend( ) Method

The OnAppend method is called when you append a record.

The Browse.OnChange( ) Method

The OnChange method is called whenever you change a value in the Browse object.

The Browse.OnGotFocus( ) Method

The OnGotFocus method is called when the Browse object receives focus.

The Browse.OnHelp( ) Method

The OnHelp method is called when the F1 key is pressed with focus on the Browse object.

The Browse.OnLeftDblClick( ) Method

Parameters: <*flags*>,<*col*>,<*row*>

The OnLeftDblClick event is called when you double-click with the left mouse button over the Browse object. The parameters report the status of the Shift, Ctrl, and Alt keys, as well as the location at the time of the OnLeftDblClick event.

The Browse.OnLeftMouseDown( ) Method

Parameters: <*flags*>,<*col*>,<*row*>

The OnLeftMouseDown event is called when you press the left mouse button over the Browse object. The parameters report the status of the Shift, Ctrl, and Alt keys, as well as the location at the time of the OnLeftMouseDown event.

The Browse.OnLeftMouseUp( ) Method

Parameters: <*flags*>,<*col*>,<*row*>

The OnLeftMouseUp handler is called whenever you release the left button over the Browse object. (An up event over one object might have been preceded by a down event over another object.) The parameters report the status of the Shift, Ctrl, and Alt keys, as well as the location at the time of the OnLeftMouseUp event.

The Browse.OnLostFocus( ) Method

The OnLostFocus method is called whenever the Browse object loses focus.

The Browse.OnMiddleDblClick( ) Method

Parameters: <*flags*>,<*col*>,<*row*>

The OnMiddleDblClick event is called when you double-click with the middle mouse button of a three-button mouse over the Browse object. The parameters report the status of the Shift, Ctrl, and Alt keys, as well as the location at the time of the OnMiddleDblClick event.

The Browse.OnMiddleMouseDown( ) Method

Parameters: <*flags*>,<*col*>,<*row*>

The OnMiddleMouseDown event is called when you press the middle mouse button of a three-button mouse over the Browse object. The parameters report the status of the Shift, Ctrl, and Alt keys, as well as the location at the time of the OnMiddleMouseDown event.

The Browse.OnMiddleMouseUp( ) Method

Parameters: <*flags*>,<*col*>,<*row*>

The OnMiddleMouseUp handler is called whenever you release the middle mouse button over the Browse object. (An up event over one object might have been preceded by a down event over another object.) The parameters report the status of the Shift, Ctrl, and Alt keys, as well as the location at the time of the OnMiddleMouseUp event.

The Browse.OnMouseMove( ) Method

Parameters: <*flags*>,<*col*>,<*row*>

The OnMouseMove event is called when any mouse movement is detected over the Browse object.

The Browse.OnNavigate( ) Method

The OnNavigate event is called after the record pointer is shifted.

The Browse.OnOpen( ) Method

The OnOpen event is called when the form containing the Browse object is opened.

The Browse.OnRightDblClick( ) Method

Parameters: <*flags*>,<*col*>,<*row*>

The OnRightDblClick event is called when you double-click with the right mouse button over the Browse object. (Right double-clicks are recognized by the Navigator as commands to design the object.) The parameters report the status of the Shift, Ctrl, and Alt keys, as well as the location at the time of the OnRightDblClick event.

The Browse.OnRightMouseDown( ) Method

Parameters: <*flags*>,<*col*>,<*row*>

The OnRightMouseDown event is called when you press the right mouse button over the Browse object. The parameters report the status of the Shift, Ctrl, and Alt keys, as well as the location at the time of the OnRightMouseDown event.

The Browse.OnRightMouseUp( ) Method

Parameters: <*flags*>,<*col*>,<*row*>

The OnRightMouseUp handler is called whenever you release the right button over the Browse object. (An up event over one object might have been preceded by a down event over another object.) The parameters report the status of the Shift, Ctrl, and Alt keys, as well as the location at the time of the OnRightMouseUp event.

The Browse.Parent Property

The Parent property is read-only. This property is an object reference to the parent form of the Browse object. It is assigned when the Browse object is created via a DEFINE command or a NEW call to the constructor.

The Browse.Release( ) Method

The Release method removes the Browse object from memory. Releasing a form also releases all of the form's objects.

The Browse.SetFocus( ) Method

The SetFocus method changes focus to the Browse object on the form.

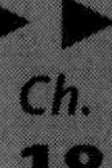

The Browse.ShowDeleted Property

Default value: .T.

If True, the ShowDeleted property makes deleted records visible in a Browse object when Deleted is on. If Deleted is off, (set through the Desktop Properties dialog box, Table tab), ShowDeleted has no effect.

The Browse.ShowHeading Property

Default value: .T.

If ShowHeading is True, the top line of the Browse object shows field names or headings.

The Browse.ShowRecNo Property

Default value: .T.

If True, the ShowRecNo property specifies that record numbers are displayed on the left side of each Browse row.

The Browse.StatusMessage Property

Default value: ""

The StatusMessage appears in the left portion of the status bar when the mouse pointer is over the Browse object and when the Browse object has focus.

The Browse.TabStop Property

Default value: .T.

If TabStop is True, the Browse object is part of the tabbing order. If it is False, Tab and Shift-Tab will bypass the Browse object.

The Browse.Text Property

Default value: ""

The Text property specifies a title line at the top of the Browse object.

The Browse.Toggle Property

Default value: .T.

If True, the Toggle property lets you change between Browse, Record, and Columnar Layout views in a Browse object.

The Browse.Top Property

Default value: 12.5

The Top property is the location of the top of the Browse object, in characters sized by the form's ScaleFont. The top-left corner of the form is 0,0.

The Browse.Visible Property

Default value: .T.

If Visible is True, the Browse object is shown. Manipulating Visible lets you choose among alternative objects on a form.

The Browse.When( ) Method

If When is False, you cannot give focus to the Browse object.

The Browse.Width Property

Default value: 13.0

The Width property specifies the width of the Browse object, in characters. The width of each character is determined by the form's Scale-Font properties.

▶ Combobox Object Properties

This section lists and briefly explains the properties of the Combobox object.

The Combobox.Before Property

Before is an object reference to the object that this Combobox precedes in the form's tabbing order. If this Combobox object is the last one in the form's tabbing order, Before is a reference to the first object in the tabbing order (Form.First).

The Combobox.ClassName Property

Default value: COMBOBOX

ClassName is read-only. This property is assigned by dBASE for Windows for each of the built-in classes. ClassName can be used to distinguish among multiple objects with the same name.

The Combobox.DataLink Property

Default value: ""

The DataLink property links the Combobox object's value to a memory variable or a table field. When you change the data value in this Combobox object, it changes the value in the associated memory variable or table field.

The Combobox.DataSource Property

The DataSource property specifies the source of data for the Combobox object. For example, a Combobox object could have an array source for its choices, or it could have a .BMP file as a source for its image bitmap.

The Combobox.Enabled Property

Default value: .T.

If Enabled is True, the Combobox object is accessible. You can use the Enabled property to disable options in event handlers. For example, a Valid function could set some object's Enabled to False if required conditions were not met.

The Combobox.FontBold Property

Default value: .T.

If True, FontBold specifies that the Combobox object's font is boldface.

The Combobox.FontItalic Property

Default value: .F.

If True, FontItalic specifies that the Combobox object's font is italic.

The Combobox.FontName Property

Default value: MS Sans Serif

The FontName property specifies the name of the font. This may be set from the Font dialog box, accessed via the tool icon in the Form Designer's Properties dialog box.

The Combobox.FontSize Property

Default value: 8

The FontSize property specifies the size of the font, in points.

The Combobox.FontStrikeOut Property

Default value: .F.

If FontStrikeOut is True, the characters will be displayed with strikeout slashes.

The Combobox.FontUnderline Property

Default value: .F.

If True, FontUnderline specifies that the characters are underlined.

The Combobox.Height Property

Default value: 6.5

The Height property specifies the height of the Combobox object, in characters.

The Combobox.HelpFile Property

Default value: ""

The HelpFile property names the Windows Help file that will be used when you press F1.

The Combobox.HelpID Property

Default value: –1

The HelpID specifies the individual Help screen that will be accessed in the Windows Help file specified by the HelpFile property.

The Combobox.hWnd Property

The hWnd property is read-only. This property is an arbitrary integer number that identifies the window to which the Combobox object belongs. This is called the window's *handle*. It is used when you access Windows functions directly via EXTERN commands.

The Combobox.ID Property

Default value: –1

ID is a number than can be used to distinguish between otherwise identical Combobox objects.

The Combobox.Left Property

Default value: 1.0

The Left property specifies the location of the left side of the Combobox object within its form, in characters. The leftmost character is number 0.

The Combobox.MousePointer Property

Default value: 0

Available settings: 0–11

The MousePointer property specifies the type of mouse pointer to use when the pointer is over the Combobox object. For example, the mouse pointer is an arrow over a form, but turns to an I-beam in an editor. The settings are default (0), arrow (1), cross (2), I-beam (3), icon (4), size (5), size NESW (6), size S (7), size NWSE (8), size E (9), up arrow (10), and wait (hourglass, 11).

The Combobox.Move( ) Method

Parameters: <*lft*>,<*tp*>,<*wdth*>,<*hght*>

Move is a method property that can move the Combobox object, resize the Combobox object, or both. Your provide Move with four parameters, representing the new values for the properties Left, Top, Width, and Height, respectively.

The Combobox.Name Property

Default value: COMBOBOX<*n*>

The Name property is the property name given to this property on the parent form. If the name is COMBOBOX1, for example, specifying Parent.COMBOBOX1 specifies this Combobox object.

The Combobox.OnChange( ) Method

The OnChange method is called whenever you change a value in the Combobox object.

The Combobox.OnGotFocus( ) Method

The OnGotFocus method is called when the Combobox object receives focus.

The Combobox.OnHelp( ) Method

The OnHelp method is called when the F1 key is pressed with focus on the Combobox object.

The Combobox.OnLeftDblClick( ) Method

Parameters: <*flags*>,<*col*>,<*row*>

The OnLeftDblClick event is called when you double-click with the left mouse button over the Combobox object. The parameters report the status of the Shift, Ctrl, and Alt keys, as well as the location at the time of the OnLeftDblClick event.

The Combobox.OnLeftMouseDown( ) Method

Parameters: <*flags*>,<*col*>,<*row*>

The OnLeftMouseDown event is called when you press the left mouse button over the Combobox object. The parameters report the status of the Shift, Ctrl, and Alt keys, as well as the location at the time of the OnLeftMouseDown event.

The Combobox.OnLeftMouseUp( ) Method

Parameters: <*flags*>,<*col*>,<*row*>

The OnLeftMouseUp handler is called whenever you release the left button over the Combobox object. (An up event over one object might have been preceded by a down event over another object.) The parameters report the status of the Shift, Ctrl, and Alt keys, as well as the location at the time of the OnLeftMouseUp event.

The Combobox.OnLostFocus( ) Method

The OnLostFocus method is called whenever the Combobox loses focus.

The Combobox.OnMiddleDblClick( ) Method

Parameters: <*flags*>,<*col*>,<*row*>

The OnMiddleDblClick event is called when you double-click with the middle mouse button of a three-button mouse over the Combobox object. The parameters report the status of the Shift, Ctrl, and Alt keys, as well as the location at the time of the OnMiddleDblClick event.

The Combobox.OnMiddleMouseDown( ) Method

Parameters: <*flags*>,<*col*>,<*row*>

The OnMiddleMouseDown event is called when you press the middle mouse button of a three-button mouse over the Combobox object. The parameters report the status of the Shift, Ctrl, and Alt keys, as well as the location at the time of the OnMiddleMouseDown event.

The Combobox.OnMiddleMouseUp( ) Method

Parameters: <*flags*>,<*col*>,<*row*>

The OnMiddleMouseUp handler is called whenever you release the middle mouse button over the Combobox object. (An up event over one object might have been preceded by a down event over another object.) The parameters report the status of the Shift, Ctrl, and Alt keys, as well as the location at the time of the OnMiddleMouseUp event.

The Combobox.OnMouseMove( ) Method

Parameters: <*flags*>,<*col*>,<*row*>

The OnMouseMove event is called when any mouse movement is detected over the Combobox object.

The Combobox.OnOpen( ) Method

The OnOpen event is called when the form containing the Combobox object is opened.

The Combobox.OnRightDblClick( ) Method

Parameters: <*flags*>,<*col*>,<*row*>

The OnRightDblClick event is called when you double-click with the right mouse button over the Combobox object. (Right double-clicks are recognized by the Navigator as commands to design the object.) The parameters report the status of the Shift, Ctrl, and Alt keys, as well as the location at the time of the OnRightDblClick event.

The Combobox.OnRightMouseDown( ) Method

Parameters: <*flags*>,<*col*>,<*row*>

The OnRightMouseDown event is called when you press the right mouse button over the Combobox object. The parameters report the status of the Shift, Ctrl, and Alt keys, as well as the location at the time of the OnRightMouseDown event.

The Combobox.OnRightMouseUp( ) Method

Parameters: <*flags*>,<*col*>,<*row*>

The OnRightMouseUp handler is called whenever you release the right button over the Combobox object. (An up event over one object might have been preceded by a down event over another object.) The parameters report the status of the Shift, Ctrl, and Alt keys, as well as the location at the time of the OnRightMouseUp event.

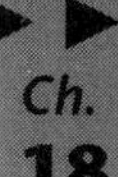

The Combobox.Parent Property

The Parent property is read-only. This property is an object reference to the parent form of the Combobox object. It is assigned when the

Combobox object is created via a DEFINE command or a NEW call to the constructor.

The Combobox.Release( ) Method

The Release method removes the Combobox object from memory. Releasing a form also releases all of the form's objects.

The Combobox.SetFocus( ) Method

The SetFocus method changes focus Combobox object on the form.

The Combobox.Sorted Property

Default value: .F.

If Sorted is True, the prompts in the Listbox or Combobox object are sorted before being displayed.

The Combobox.StatusMessage Property

Default value: ""

The StatusMessage appears in the left portion of the status bar when the mouse pointer is over the Combobox object and when the Combobox object has focus.

The Combobox.Style Property

Default value: 0

Available settings: 0–2

The Style property of a Combobox specifies simple (0), drop-down (1) or drop-down list (2) behavior. A simple Combobox is always open. A drop-down combobox drops in response to a click on its down button or a ↓ keypress. A drop-down list is a drop-down that disallows typing the value into the field.

The Combobox.TabStop Property

Default value: .T.

If TabStop is True, the Combobox object is part of the tabbing order. If it is False, Tab and Shift-Tab will bypass the Combobox object.

The Combobox.Top Property

Default value: 0.5

The Top property is the location of the top of the Combobox object, in characters sized by the form's ScaleFont. The top-left corner of the form is 0,0.

The Combobox.Value Property

The Value property is the value held by the Combobox object. Its type can be any type appropriate to the data link.

The Combobox.Visible Property

Default value: .T.

If Visible is True, the Combobox object is shown. Manipulating Visible lets you choose among alternative objects on a form.

The Combobox.When( ) Method

If When is False, you cannot give focus to the Combobox object.

The Combobox.Width Property

Default value: 9.0

The Width property specifies the width of the Combobox object, in characters. The width of each character is determined by the form's ScaleFont properties.

▶ Editor Object Properties

This section lists and briefly explains the properties of the Editor object.

The Editor.Before Property

Before is an object reference to the object that this Editor precedes in the form's tabbing order. If this Editor object is the last one in the form's tabbing order, Before is a reference to the first object in the tabbing order (Form.First).

The Editor.Border Property

If Border is True, the Editor object is surrounded by a border.

The Editor.ClassName Property

Default value: EDITOR

ClassName is read-only. This property is assigned by dBASE for Windows for each of the built-in classes. ClassName can be used to distinguish among multiple objects with the same name.

The Editor.ColorNormal Property

Default value: N/W*

The ColorNormal property specifies the color of the Editor object. ColorNormal may be a dBASE IV-style color specification, or it may be a color selected from the color palette with the Choose Color dialog box.

The Editor.DataLink Property

Default value: ""

The DataLink property links the Editor object's value to a memory variable or a table field. When you change the data value in this Editor object, it changes the value in the associated memory variable or table field.

The Editor.Enabled Property

Default value: .T.

If Enabled is True, the Editor object is accessible. You can use the Enabled property to disable options in event handlers. For example, a Valid function could set some object's Enabled to False if required conditions were not met.

The Editor.FontBold Property

Default value: .T.

If True, FontBold specifies that the Editor object's font is boldface.

The Editor.FontItalic Property

Default value: .F.

If True, FontItalic specifies that the Editor object's font is italic.

The Editor.FontName Property

Default value: MS Sans Serif

The FontName property specifies the name of the font. This may be set from the Font dialog box, accessed via the tool icon in the Form Designer's Properties dialog box.

The Editor.FontSize Property

Default value: 8

The FontSize property specifies the size of the font, in points.

The Editor.FontStrikeOut Property

Default value: .F.

If FontStrikeOut is True, the characters will be displayed with strikeout slashes.

The Editor.FontUnderline Property

Default value: .F.

If True, FontUnderline specifies that the characters are underlined.

The Editor.Height Property

Default value: 8.5

The Height property specifies the height of the Editor object, in characters.

The Editor.HelpFile Property

Default value: ""

The HelpFile property names the Windows Help file that will be used when you press F1.

The Editor.HelpID Property

Default value: –1

The HelpID specifies the individual Help screen that will be accessed in the Windows Help file specified by the HelpFile property.

The Editor.hWnd Property

The hWnd property is read-only. This property is an arbitrary integer number that identifies the window to which the Editor object belongs. This is called the window's *handle*. It is used when you access Windows functions directly via EXTERN commands.

The Editor.ID Property

Default value: –1

ID is a number than can be used to distinguish between otherwise identical Editor objects.

The Editor.Left Property

Default value: 1.0

The Left property specifies the location of the left side of the Editor object within its form, in characters. The leftmost character is number 0.

The Editor.LineNo Property

Default value: 1

The LineNo property moves the insertion point to the specified line in the Editor object.

The Editor.Modify Property

Default value: .T.

If Modify is False, the Editor object will not let you make any changes to the data.

The Editor.MousePointer Property

Default value: 0

Available settings: 0–11

The MousePointer property specifies the type of mouse pointer to use when the pointer is over the Editor object. For example, the mouse pointer is an arrow over a form, but turns to an I-beam in an editor. The settings are default (0), arrow (1), cross (2), I-beam (3), icon (4), size (5), size NESW (6), size S (7), size NWSE (8), size E (9), up arrow (10), and wait (hourglass, 11).

The Editor.Move( ) Method

Parameters: *<lft>*,*<tp>*,*<wdth>*,*<hght>*

Move is a method property that can move the Editor object, resize the Editor object, or both. You provide Move with four parameters, representing the new values for the properties Left, Top, Width, and Height, respectively.

The Editor.Name Property

Default value: EDITOR*<n>*

The Name property is the property name given to this Editor object on the parent form. If the name is EDITOR1, for example, specifying Parent.EDITOR1 specifies this Editor object.

The Editor.OnChange( ) Method

The OnChange method is called whenever you change a value in the Editor object.

The Editor.OnGotFocus( ) Method

The OnGotFocus method is called when the Editor object receives focus.

The Editor.OnHelp( ) Method

The OnHelp method is called when the F1 key is pressed with focus on the Editor object.

The Editor.OnLeftDblClick( ) Method

Parameters: <*flags*>,<*col*>,<*row*>

The OnLeftDblClick event is called when you double-click with the left mouse button over the Editor object. The parameters report the status of the Shift, Ctrl, and Alt keys, as well as the location at the time of the OnLeftDblClick event.

The Editor.OnLeftMouseDown( ) Method

Parameters: <*flags*>,<*col*>,<*row*>

The OnLeftMouseDown event is called when you press the left mouse button over the Editor object. The parameters report the status of the Shift, Ctrl, and Alt keys, as well as the location at the time of the OnLeftMouseDown event.

The Editor.OnLeftMouseUp( ) Method

Parameters: <*flags*>,<*col*>,<*row*>

The OnLeftMouseUp handler is called whenever you release the left button over the Editor object. (An up event over one object might have been preceded by a down event over another object.) The parameters report the status of the Shift, Ctrl, and Alt keys, as well as the location at the time of the OnLeftMouseUp event.

The Editor.OnLostFocus( ) Method

The OnLostFocus method is called whenever the Editor object loses focus.

The Editor.OnMiddleDblClick( ) Method

Parameters: <*flags*>,<*col*>,<*row*>

The OnMiddleDblClick event is called when you double-click with the middle mouse button of a three-button mouse over the Editor object.

The parameters report the status of the Shift, Ctrl, and Alt keys, as well as the location at the time of the OnMiddleDblClick event.

The Editor.OnMiddleMouseDown( ) Method

Parameters: <*flags*>,<*col*>,<*row*>

The OnMiddleMouseDown event is called when you press the middle mouse button of a three-button mouse over the Editor object. The parameters report the status of the Shift, Ctrl, and Alt keys, as well as the location at the time of the OnMiddleMouseDown event.

The Editor.OnMiddleMouseUp( ) Method

Parameters: <*flags*>,<*col*>,<*row*>

The OnMiddleMouseUp handler is called whenever you release the middle mouse button over the Editor object. (An up event over one object might have been preceded by a down event over another object.) The parameters report the status of the Shift, Ctrl, and Alt keys, as well as the location at the time of the OnMiddleMouseUp event.

The Editor.OnMouseMove( ) Method

Parameters: <*flags*>,<*col*>,<*row*>

The OnMouseMove event is called on any mouse movement detected over the Editor object.

The Editor.OnOpen( ) Method

The OnOpen event is called when the form containing the Editor object is opened.

The Editor.OnRightDblClick( ) Method

Parameters: <*flags*>,<*col*>,<*row*>

The OnRightDblClick event is called when you double-click with the right mouse button over the Editor object. (Right double-clicks are recognized by the Navigator as commands to design the object.) The parameters report the status of the Shift, Ctrl, and Alt keys, as well as the location at the time of the OnRightDblClick event.

The Editor.OnRightMouseDown( ) Method

Parameters: <*flags*>,<*col*>,<*row*>

The OnRightMouseDown event is called when you press the right mouse button over the Editor object. The parameters report the status of the Shift, Ctrl, and Alt keys, as well as the location at the time of the OnRightMouseDown event.

The Editor.OnRightMouseUp( ) Method

Parameters: <*flags*>,<*col*>,<*row*>

The OnRightMouseUp handler is called whenever you release the right mouse button over the Editor object. (An up event over one object might have been preceded by a down event over another object.) The parameters report the status of the Shift, Ctrl, and Alt keys, as well as the location at the time of the OnRightMouseUp event.

The Editor.Parent Property

The Parent property is read-only. This property is an object reference to the parent form of the Editor object. It is assigned when the Editor object is created via a DEFINE command or a NEW call to the constructor.

The Editor.Release( ) Method

The Release method removes the Editor object from memory. Releasing a form also releases all of the form's objects.

The Editor.Scrollbar Property

Default value: 0 or 1

Available settings: 0–3

The Scrollbar property defaults to on (1) for editors and off (0) for forms. The other values are auto (2) and disabled (3). An auto scroll bar appears only when the data exceeds the visible area of the form or editor. A disabled scroll bar is visible but does not respond to mouse clicks.

The Editor.SetFocus( ) Method

The SetFocus method changes focus to the Editor object on the form.

The Editor.StatusMessage Property

Default value: ""

The StatusMessage appears in the left portion of the status bar when the mouse pointer is over the Editor object and when the Editor object has focus.

The Editor.TabStop Property

Default value: .T.

If TabStop is True, the Editor object is part of the tabbing order. If it is False, Tab and Shift-Tab will bypass the Editor object.

The Editor.Top Property

Default value: 0.5

The Top property is the location of the top of the Editor object, in characters sized by the form's ScaleFont. The top-left corner of the form is 0,0.

The Editor.Valid( ) Method

The Valid method is called whenever an attempt is made to remove focus from the object with focus. (Tabbing, clicking on another object, or submitting a form are examples.) The Valid method is a function or code block that returns a logical value. If it returns .F., focus is not moved from the Editor object.

The Editor.Value Property

The Value property is the value held by the Editor object. Its type can be any type appropriate to the data link. For scroll bars, value can be set by moving the thumb, or the thumb can be positioned by changing the Value property.

The Editor.Visible Property

Default value: .T.

If Visible is True, the Editor object is shown. Manipulating Visible lets you choose among alternative objects on a form.

The Editor.When( ) Method

If When is False, you cannot give focus to the Editor object.

The Editor.Width Property

Default value: 13.0

The Width property specifies the width of the Editor object, in characters. The width of each character is determined by the form's ScaleFont properties.

The Editor.Wrap Property

Default value: .F.

If Wrap is True, word wrapping is turned on in the Editor.

▸ Listbox Object Properties

This section lists and briefly explains the properties of the Listbox object.

The Listbox.Before Property

Before is an object reference to the object that this Listbox object precedes in the form's tabbing order. If this Listbox object is the last one in the form's tabbing order, Before is a reference to the first object in the tabbing order (Form.First).

The Listbox.ClassName Property

Default value: LISTBOX

ClassName is read-only. This property is assigned by dBASE for Windows for each of the built-in classes. ClassName can be used to distinguish among multiple objects with the same name.

The Listbox.ColorHighlight Property

Default value: W+/B

The ColorHighlight property is the color of the Listbox object when it has focus. ColorHighlight may be a dBASE IV-style color string, or it may be a color selected from the color palette.

The Listbox.ColorNormal Property

Default value: N/W*

The ColorNormal property specifies the color when the Listbox object does not have focus. ColorNormal may be a dBASE IV-style color specification, or it may be a color selected from the color palette with the Choose Color dialog box.

The Listbox.Count( ) Method

The Count method returns the number of items in a Listbox object's data source. For example, you could ask for the number of items in a file or the number of files in a directory listing.

The Listbox.CurSel Property

Default value: 0

The CurSel property specifies which Listbox item is highlighted.

The Listbox.DataSource Property

The DataSource property specifies the source of data for the Listbox object.

The Listbox.Enabled Property

Default value: .T.

If Enabled is True, the Listbox object is accessible. You can use the Enabled property to disable options in event handlers. For example, a Valid function could set some object's Enabled to False if required conditions were not met.

The Listbox.FontBold Property

Default value: .T.

If True, FontBold specifies that the Listbox object's font is boldface.

The Listbox.FontItalic Property

Default value: .F.

If True, FontItalic specifies that the Listbox object's font is italic.

The Listbox.FontName Property

Default value: MS Sans Serif

The FontName property specifies the name of the font. This may be set from the Font dialog box, accessed via the tool icon in the Form Designer's Properties dialog box.

The Listbox.FontSize Property

Default value: 8

The FontSize property specifies the size of the font, in points.

The Listbox.FontStrikeOut Property

Default value: .F.

If FontStrikeOut is True, the characters will be displayed with strikeout slashes.

The Listbox.FontUnderline Property

Default value: .F.

If True, FontUnderline specifies that the characters are underlined.

The Listbox.Height Property

Default value: 5.5

The Height property specifies the height of the Listbox object, in characters.

The Listbox.HelpFile Property

Default value: ""

The HelpFile property names the Windows Help file that will be used when you press F1.

The Listbox.HelpID Property

Default value: ""

The HelpID specifies the individual Help screen that will be accessed in the Windows Help file specified by the HelpFile property.

The Listbox.hWnd Property

The hWnd property is read-only. This property is an arbitrary integer number that identifies the window to which the Listbox object belongs. This is called the window's *handle*. It is used when you access Windows functions directly via EXTERN commands.

The Listbox.ID Property

Default value: –1

ID is a number than can be used to distinguish between otherwise identical Listbox objects.

The Listbox.Left Property

Default value: 1.0

The Left property specifies the location of the left side of the Listbox object within its form, in characters. The leftmost character is number 0.

The Listbox.MousePointer Property

Default value: 0

Available settings: 0–11

The MousePointer property specifies the type of mouse pointer to use when the pointer is over the Listbox object. The settings are default (0), arrow (1), cross (2), I-beam (3), icon (4), size (5), size NESW (6), size S (7), size NWSE (8), size E (9), up arrow (10), and wait (hourglass, 11).

The Listbox.Move( ) Method

Parameters: *<lft>*,*<tp>*,*<wdth>*,*<hght>*

Move is a method property that can move the Listbox object, resize the Listbox object, or both. You provide Move with four parameters, representing the new values for the properties Left, Top, Width, and Height, respectively.

The Listbox.Multiple Property

Default value: .F.

If Multiple is True, the Listbox object allows the selection of zero or more items. If it is False, exactly one item is selected.

The Listbox.Name Property

Default value: LISTBOX<*n*>

The Name property is the property name given to this property on the parent form. If the name is LISTBOX1, for example, specifying Parent.LISTBOX1 specifies this Listbox object.

The Listbox.OldStyle Property

Default value: .F.

Setting OldStyle to True lets you use the older Windows application style. (This is generally a less attractive look than you get with OldStlye set False.)

The Listbox.OnChange( ) Method

The OnChange method is called whenever you change a value in the Listbox object.

The Listbox.OnGotFocus( ) Method

The OnGotFocus method is called when the Listbox object receives focus.

The Listbox.OnHelp( ) Method

The OnHelp method is called when the F1 key is pressed with focus on the Listbox object.

The Listbox.OnLeftDblClick( ) Method

Parameters: <*flags*>,<*col*>,<*row*>

The OnLeftDblClick event is called when you double-click with the left mouse button over the Listbox object. The parameters report the status of the Shift, Ctrl, and Alt keys, as well as the location at the time of the OnLeftDblClick event.

The Listbox.OnLeftMouseDown( ) Method

Parameters: <*flags*>,<*col*>,<*row*>

The OnLeftMouseDown event is called when you press the left mouse button over the Listbox object. The parameters report the status of the Shift, Ctrl, and Alt keys, as well as the location at the time of the OnLeftMouseDown event.

The Listbox.OnLeftMouseUp( ) Method

Parameters: <*flags*>,<*col*>,<*row*>

The OnLeftMouseUp handler is called whenever you release the left button over the Listbox object. (An up event over one object might have been preceded by a down event over another object.) The parameters report the status of the Shift, Ctrl, and Alt keys, as well as the location at the time of the OnLeftMouseUp event.

The Listbox.OnLostFocus( ) Method

The OnLostFocus method is called whenever the Listbox object loses focus.

The Listbox.OnMiddleDblClick( ) Method

Parameters: <*flags*>,<*col*>,<*row*>

The OnMiddleDblClick event is called when you double-click with the middle mouse button of a three-button mouse over the Listbox object. The parameters report the status of the Shift, Ctrl, and Alt keys, as well as the location at the time of the OnMiddleDblClick event.

The Listbox.OnMiddleMouseDown( ) Method

Parameters: <*flags*>,<*col*>,<*row*>

The OnMiddleMouseDown event is called when you press the middle mouse button of a three-button mouse over the Listbox object. The parameters report the status of the Shift, Ctrl, and Alt keys, as well as the location at the time of the OnMiddleMouseDown event.

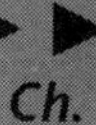

The Listbox.OnMiddleMouseUp( ) Method

Parameters: <*flags*>,<*col*>,<*row*>

The OnMiddleMouseUp handler is called whenever you release the middle mouse button over the Listbox object. (An up event over one object might have been preceded by a down event over another object.) The parameters report the status of the Shift, Ctrl, and Alt keys, as well as the location at the time of the OnMiddleMouseUp event.

The Listbox.OnMouseMove( ) Method

Parameters: <*flags*>,<*col*>,<*row*>

The OnMouseMove event is called when any mouse movement is detected over the Listbox object.

The Listbox.OnOpen( ) Method

The OnOpen event is called when the form containing the Listbox object is opened.

The Listbox.OnRightDblClick( ) Method

Parameters: <*flags*>,<*col*>,<*row*>

The OnRightDblClick event is called when you double-click with the right mouse button over the Listbox object. (Right double-clicks are recognized by the Navigator as commands to design the object.) The parameters report the status of the Shift, Ctrl, and Alt keys, as well as the location at the time of the OnRightDblClick event.

The Listbox.OnRightMouseDown( ) Method

Parameters: <*flags*>,<*col*>,<*row*>

The OnRightMouseDown event is called when you press the right mouse button over the Listbox object. The parameters report the status of the Shift, Ctrl, and Alt keys, as well as the location at the time of the OnRightMouseDown event.

The Listbox.OnRightMouseUp( ) Method

Parameters: <*flags*>,<*col*>,<*row*>

The OnRightMouseUp handler is called whenever you release the right button over the Listbox object. (An up event over one object might have been preceded by a down event over another object.) The parameters report the status of the Shift, Ctrl, and Alt keys, as well as the location at the time of the OnRightMouseUp event.

The Listbox.OnSelChange( ) Method

The OnSelChange method executes a subroutine when a Listbox object's selection is changed.

The Listbox.Parent Property

The Parent property is read-only. This property is an object reference to the parent form of the Listbox object. It is assigned when the object is created via a DEFINE command or a NEW call to the constructor.

The Listbox.Release( ) Method

The Release method removes the Listbox object from memory. Releasing a form also releases all of the form's objects.

The Listbox.Selected( ) Method

Parameter: <*item*>

The Selected method returns the value of the selected item in a Listbox.

The Listbox.SetFocus( ) Method

The SetFocus method changes focus to the Listbox object on the form.

The Listbox.Sorted Property

Default value: .F.

If Sorted is True, the prompts in the Listbox or Combobox are sorted before being displayed.

The Listbox.StatusMessage Property

Default value: ""

The StatusMessage appears in the left portion of the status bar when the mouse pointer is over the Listbox object and when the Listbox object has focus.

The Listbox.TabStop Property

Default value: .T.

If TabStop is True, the Listbox object is part of the tabbing order. If it is False, Tab and Shift-Tab will bypass the object.

The Listbox.Top Property

Default value: 0.5

The Top property is the location of the top of the Listbox object, in characters sized by the form's ScaleFont. The top-left corner of the form is 0,0.

The Listbox.Value Property

The Value property is the value held by the Listbox object. Its type can be any type appropriate to the data link. For scroll bars, Value can be set by moving the thumb, or the thumb can be positioned by changing the Value property.

The Listbox.Visible Property

Default value: .T.

If Visible is True, the Listbox object is shown. Manipulating Visible lets you choose among alternative Listbox objects on a form.

The Listbox.When( ) Method

If When is False, you cannot give focus to the Listbox object.

The Listbox.Width Property

Default value: 9.0

The Width property specifies the width of the Listbox object, in characters. The width of each character is determined by the form's Scale-Font properties.

▶ ▶ CHAPTER 19

Putting the System Together

▶▶ **In** this chapter, we'll cover two more objects: the Pushbutton and the Scrollbar. Then we'll use everything we've learned about forms to revisit our phone list system and make the sort of improvements that you'll probably want for all your systems.

These improvements include the maintenance of keys and the automation of relationships between the tables. When we get there, you'll see that these methods can increase the efficiency of any database system.

▶▶ Working with Pushbutton Objects

We've already added Pushbutton objects while we were building our phone system. Our Append buttons append a record to their tables, and our Close buttons close their forms. In many ways, Pushbutton objects help you control the use of your systems.

▶ Assigning OnClick Event Handlers

The most important property of the Pushbutton object is the OnClick event handler. We've used this property with the Procedure Editor to add the behaviors that we wanted, such as appending a record or closing a form. When you use the Procedure Editor, this is an example of what it will assign to the OnClick property:

```
DEFINE PUSHBUTTON PUSHBUTTON1 OF THIS;
   PROPERTY;
     OnClick CLASS::PUSHBUTTON1_ONCLICK,;
     Text "Append",;
     ...
```

The OnClick event is assigned a reference to the class PUSHBUTTON1_ONCLICK method. The name of the method is built from the name of the Pushbutton object and the name of the event handler. Unfortunately, this does help make the method's use readily apparent, even if you're not looking at the assignment to an event handler. Here's the method called in the previous example:

```
Procedure PUSHBUTTON1_OnClick
APPEND BLANK
```

As you can see, this method has exactly two lines. The first is the Procedure statement (see Chapter 14). The second line is the command that does the work (see Chapter 13). When a method is this simple, it can be a better practice to use a code block.

Using Code Blocks

A *code block* is a subroutine programmed within a single line of the source file. It is enclosed in braces and begins with the value it should return. Semicolons separate additional commands. For a process such as appending a blank line, you don't have a value to return, so the code block starts with a semicolon, meaning there is no return value. Here's the code block equivalent of the PUSHBUTTON1_ONCLICK routine:

```
{ ; APPEND BLANK }
```

Unlike Procedures, code blocks don't have names. You just put them where you want to use them. In this case, the OnClick assignment could have been done this way:

```
DEFINE PUSHBUTTON PUSHBUTTON1 OF THIS;
   PROPERTY;
     OnClick { ;APPEND BLANK}
     Text "Append",;
     ...
```

To add a code block such as this one, don't click on the tool icon that takes you to the Procedure Editor. Just type the code block into the Object Properties Inspector next to the event you are defining.

The advantage of the code block is that when you look at either the .WFM code or look at the Object Properties Inspector, you see instantly what your event does. Compare this line:

```
OnClick CLASS::PUSHBUTTON1_ONCLICK,;
```

to this line:

```
OnClick { ;APPEND BLANK}
```

In the first form, you see that the event calls a subroutine. You don't have any idea what the subroutine does—you must look for it.

In the second form, you see exactly what the event does. There is nothing to look for. When we assign simple events, we prefer the code block form.

▸ Pushbuttons and the Speedbar Property

The Speedbar property of a Pushbutton object defaults to False. When you create a Pushbutton, it is part of the tabbing order. You can give focus to it, and you can access it by pressing Tab or Shift-Tab.

A speedbar button, on the other hand, cannot be reached from the keyboard. It is only works with a mouse.

Consider these two buttons in our PHONES_A.WFM form:

Here we've given focus to the Append button. Notice that there are two subtle differences between the Pushbutton object with focus and the other one: the one with focus is surrounded with an extra thick black border, and its text is surrounded with a fine rectangle.

If you use the Tab and Shift-Tab keystrokes to alternate between the two buttons, you'll see that the button that has focus appears to shrink slightly. That's because the extra black space around it is stolen from the button, not from the surrounding form (which is a necessity if you want your buttons to live peacefully with the other controls on a crowded form).

If you change a Pushbutton's Speedbar property to True, it will no longer behave this way when it has focus. The button stops being a tab stop and it has no "focus" visual effect. In essence, your pushbuttons become speedbar buttons, accessible only by mouse clicks. Figure 19.1 shows a little speedbar that we built onto our People form.

FIGURE 19.1

A custom-built speedbar

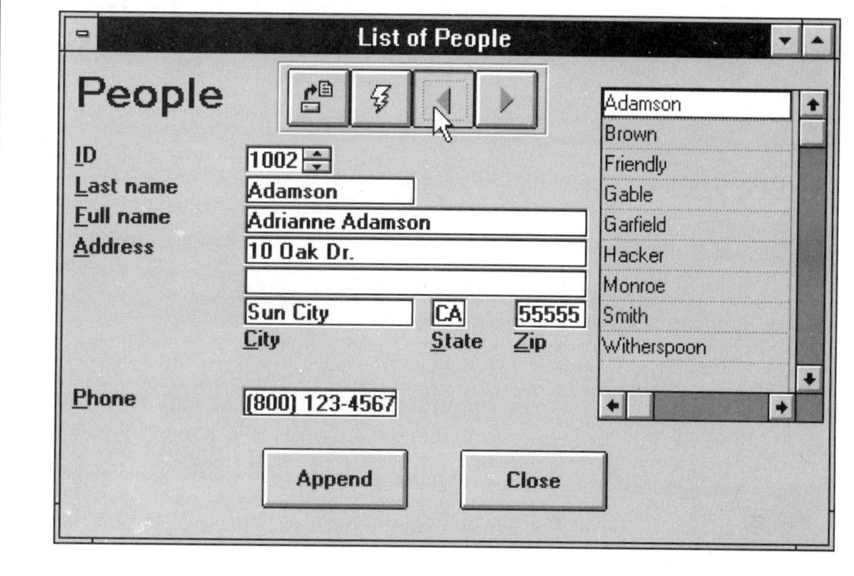

The four buttons here all have the Speedbar property set to True. We put a Rectangle object on the form first, then started adding Push-button objects. With the buttons in place, we used the Resource file to get icons.

After we set the icons, we added event handlers to each button's On-Click property. (Actually, that's what we would have done if this were really a speedbar, but we haven't decided what these buttons should do, other than look good.)

To make your own speedbar, leave the grid set to Coarse. Adjust the Top property of each Pushbutton to 0.5, and set the Top of the Rectangle to 0.25. Our Pushbutton objects are 2 Turpins tall, and the Rectangle object behind them is 2.5 Turpins tall.

TIP

Whatever function is performed by a speedbar button should also be available from the menus. That way, you can reach the option from the keyboard if you need to.

▸ Adding Conditions with the When Property

In some cases, you may want a Pushbutton object to be accessible only under certain conditions. The When property can be set by events to include or exclude a Pushbutton from the tabbing order.

For example, suppose that we want to make the Close button inaccessible if the LAST_NAME field of a People table record is blank. We could disable the OnClick event handler by an addition such as this:

```
IF .NOT. EMPTY(Last_name)
   Form.Close()
ENDIF
```

But that's not necessarily the best way to handle the situation. You'll be clicking on an active button, but nothing will happen. Instead, you can use the When property to make sure that the button is not accessible.

The When property must return a True or False, which makes it an ideal candidate for a code block. Try this one in the Close button's When property:

```
{ .NOT. EMPTY(Last_name) }
```

Note that this code block returns the value of the expression, so it does not begin with a semicolon.

With this When property, if the LAST_NAME field is empty, pressing Tab or Shift-Tab will bypass the Close button completely. You can point at it with the mouse, but clicking has no effect—the button cannot be pressed.

▸▸ Working with Scrollbar Objects

The last Form object we'll discuss is the Scrollbar, although, for reasons that will become clear, we won't actually use it.

Two objects have a Scrollbar property: the Form and Editor. Although the Browse, Combobox, and Listbox objects have scroll bars, they don't have a Scrollbar property. This means that in the Form and Editor, you have some control over what is done with scroll bars. In the other three objects, dBASE for Windows takes care of the scroll bars for you. Since we have all these objects with automatic scroll bars, what use is a separate Scrollbar object?

Well, it's not of much use unless you are doing a lot of programming. If you're building more complex systems, you may need a new control that dBASE for Windows does not include.

For example, we built an Outline object that expands and contracts outline items. The Object Properties Inspector has only one level of outline expansion. Our outline goes to as many levels as you like. With an outline, sooner or later you'll have more items than will fit in whatever space you've provided. When you run out of space, you'll need to begin scrolling.

In case you want to try it, we'll give you the general idea of how to use the Scrollbar object properties.

Your program sets the Value property within the RangeMin and RangeMax properties. For example, setting a Value of 50 with a 1 to 100 range would position the elevator's (scroll bar's) thumb (the center square) in the middle of the elevator. As you scrolled up and down in your data, you would continue to set the Value property to properly position the elevator.

On the other side of the elevator, you could be clicking on it or dragging the thumb. Your data must take frequent looks at the elevator and reposition itself appropriately. If you are in the middle of your data (50 in a 1 to 100 range) but you find that the Value is 25, you need to reposition your display halfway back to the beginning.

If you want to try working with a Scrollbar object, an interesting application is to use it as a slide switch. Figure 19.2 shows a survey form using sliders (horizontal elevators) to capture results.

The Controls palette features both horizontal and vertical elevators. The only difference is the setting of the Vertical property: True for Vertical and False for Horizontal. We suspect that when you fill in this survey, Form and Pushbutton objects are going to win ease-of-use prizes but Scrollbar objects might not.

FIGURE 19.2

Scroll bars used as slide switches

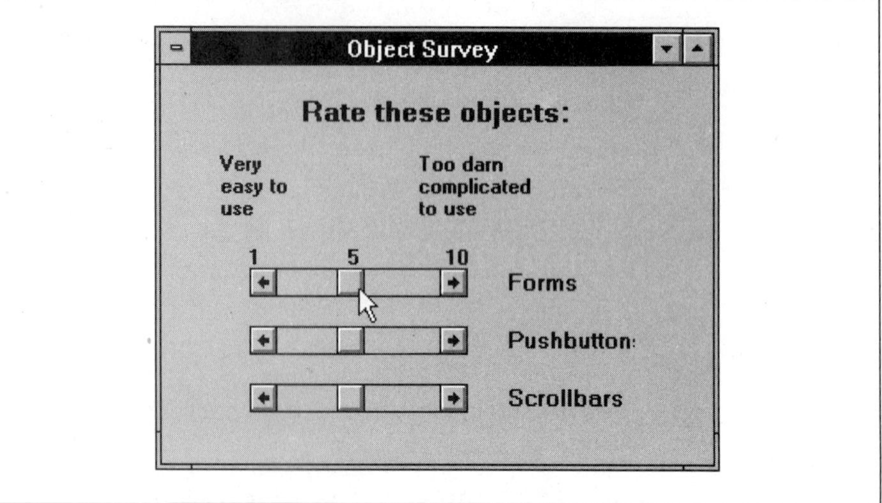

▸▸ Using What You've Learned

As you work with more databases, you'll find that the single-table ones are not a problem. But they're not common, either. You'll find that almost all useful databases have multiple tables.

As you work with multiple-table databases, you'll find that they are nothing but repetitions of a single pattern: the parent-child (or, if you prefer, one-to-many) relationship.

If you can make these one-to-many relationships smooth, your multiple table systems won't present any more problems than your single-table systems. The secret to getting them right is to have record IDs properly assigned and used.

In Part 2 we built a phone list system that depended on your filling in these keys correctly. This is *not* the way to get the best long-term results. We human beings are notoriously error-prone. Maintaining correct keys is a job we can delegate to our computers, which we will now proceed to do.

First, let's begin by explaining to dBASE for Windows that we want new keys automatically assigned when we add records.

▶ Automating Key Assignments

Let's begin with a couple bits of jargon that we really enjoy. Don't get put off; these are very simple concepts with very fancy names. (Sort of like calling your mustard *Grey Poupon*, even though your factory's in New Jersey—who would want to buy it if you called it New Jersey Factory mustard?)

So let's dive into *entity integrity* and its cousin, *primary key integrity*. Entity integrity is what you've got if everything in each record is about a single entity. In our People table, we can't put Mary's address together with Bill's phone number and Sam's name, can we?

More subtly, though not by a lot, you don't have a single entity when you put Bill's name and address in along with BigCo's name and address, even if Bill works for BigCo. These are two separate entities. If you have any doubts about structuring your tables, you might give Chapter 3 another look.

Now that we've decided to put facts about just one entity, and no shuffling please, in each record, we've got entity integrity. Primary key integrity means that we have a unique tag, or ID number, or *key* if you like the relational jargon, for each record.

The requirements for the ID are not subtle. Each record must have a key, and no two records in any one table can have the same key. Our goal is to be able to say that Bill works for employer 1234 (or whatever) and be sure that 1234 is the key to one and only one employer. Obviously, if two employers are given the ID 1234, we won't know who Bill works for.

There is only one not-so-obvious requirement for primary keys: the requirement for uniqueness is dynamic, not static. If you assign an ID and later delete the record, don't think that the ID can be reassigned. It can't.

Well, actually, you can sometimes get away with reassigning keys, but in most cases, this will cause all sorts of problems. For example, suppose you have a customer billing system. You stop doing business with a customer, and a year later reassign that ID to a new customer.

Then you get a letter from an attorney for the old customer suggesting that your billings were erroneous. You must reconstruct the records for that customer.

How are you going to do this if your file of invoices has another customer with that customer number? It may be possible to separate the billing by dates, but at the least it's a headache, especially if the old customer's attorney challenges your system's accuracy. If you never reassigned keys, you would have no problem with presenting your evidence.

As we suggested in Chapter 3, you should select keys with expansion in mind. We use keys that have at least a digit more than we think we'll need, so we never need to reassign. If you think you'll have maybe a few hundred names in your People table, use a four-digit key so you'll have IDs for a few thousand.

As it stands now, we can enter a new ID field value that is not unique. Equally bad, or worse, we can enter a record without entering the ID field. A much better way is to have dBASE for Windows enter a unique number every time we append a record.

If you use Paradox tables, the .DB table type has just what you need. It's called the *auto-increment* field. The first one is given the number 1, the next one you add is number 2, and so on. The field is read-only, so you can't make it fail.

Unfortunately, dBASE for Windows is not as adept at handling Paradox .DB files as it is at handling its native .DBF format. For example, the Form Expert assigns a spinbox to the auto-increment field, which is quite unsuitable for a read-only field.

Let's create our own auto-increment field for a .DBF table. If you are using an SQL database, you will probably have a field type that is designed as a unique key. Check it carefully! Some SQL databases assign random numbers, and check that they are unique. This method is guaranteed to cause problems since it will reassign keys that have been deleted. If your SQL database does this, use the technique shown here for .DBF files.

We want the OnAppend event to create the key for us. Then we will need to be sure that we don't use the Table Records tool to append new records. We must use only our forms that know how to properly Append.

When you press Ctrl-A, or otherwise append a record, dBASE for Windows appends a new, blank record to your table. It then moves the record pointer to point at this record and returns control to you.

However, we want to have the blank record's ID filled in. The right value is the previous record's ID plus one. This would be simple:

```
* the blank was just appended
* the record pointer is at the blank record

SKIP -1
LOCAL new_id
new_id = people->people_id + 1

SKIP
REPLACE people->people_id WITH new_id
```

Your record pointer is at the last record in the table (the blank record that was just appended). You want to SKIP –1 to back up one record. Then you add one to the ID you find there, storing the result in a LOCAL variable. With the new value stored, you SKIP back to the new, blank record and replace the ID field with this new value.

If you try this without reading on, you'll have *no* primary key integrity. In fact, you'll have nothing but problems. Why? Because your records are ordered by an index. The People table is indexed on the UPPER() of the LAST_NAME field for a true alphabetic sort. When you SKIP –1 from the last record, you're not backing up to the second-to-last record in the table—you're following an alphabetic index.

What you want is to skip back to the prior record in natural order, not index order. (Natural order is the order in which you added the records; it's the physical order of the table on disk.)

The commands to turn the index off and then on are:

```
SET ORDER TO
SET ORDER TO Last_name
```

The first command turns the indexes off before we start SKIPping through the table. The next command turns the index by last name back on before we add the new data. This is the algorithm with the indexes correctly handled:

```
SET ORDER TO

SKIP –1
LOCAL new_id
new_id = people->people_id + 1
```

```
SKIP
REPLACE people->people_id WITH new_id

SET ORDER TO Last_name
```

If you have any doubts about these commands, use them in the Command window. Use the DISPLAY command (abbreviate it to disp) to look at the current record. Figure 19.3 shows us using the Command window to take a look at the bottom record after an APPEND BLANK, both with and without the LAST_NAME index tag set.

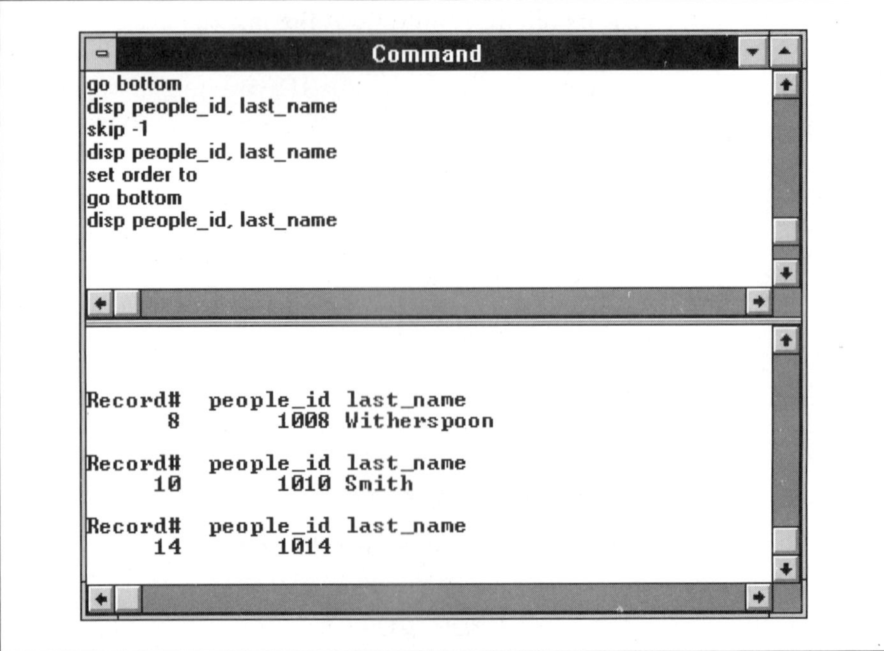

FIGURE 19.3 ►

Checking SET ORDER in the Command window

The algorithm we're using now is still not perfect, although it's good. The problem is that it will not correctly handle deleted records if they are at the bottom of the table. (If you are using SQL databases or Paradox tables, you won't be able to solve this problem without some fancy programming.)

If you append a record, fill in the data, and then change your mind and delete it, our algorithm will skip right over the deleted record to the last nondeleted record. (We assume that you've used a SET DELETED

ON command or checked the Deleted checkbox in the Desktop Properties dialog box, Table tab, so that deleted records appear to disappear from your table.)

This will normally be quite acceptable. On the other hand, let's assume that your table is relatively inactive. You might have used the last physical record (remember that the index sorts your data from Aardvark to Zebra, but the physical file could end with Monkey) for a month or so, and then deleted it. A couple more weeks went by before you wanted to add another record. You might very well be adding a new record with an ID that duplicates one that was in service for a while. This is particularly troublesome if you have the type of data that deals regularly with a small but active group of customers (for example, the customer list of a business).

What you really want to do is to go to the last physical record in the table, whether or not it was deleted. To do this, you want to turn Deleted off temporarily. These are the commands to do that:

```
SET DELETED OFF   && include deleted records
SET DELETED ON    && go back to excluding them
```

With that improvement, here is the finished algorithm, written in dBASE code:

```
SET ORDER TO
SET DELETED OFF

SKIP -1
LOCAL new_id
new_id = people->people_id + 1

SKIP
REPLACE people->people_id WITH new_id

SET ORDER TO Last_name
SET DELETED ON
```

Figure 19.4 shows the Procedure Editor with the new code added to the form's OnAppend event handler. We have done this in PHONE_A.WFM.

With this code in place, our ID values are almost automated. We need to be sure that our table starts correctly to use code like this. If you will

FIGURE 19.4 ►

Automating the ID values

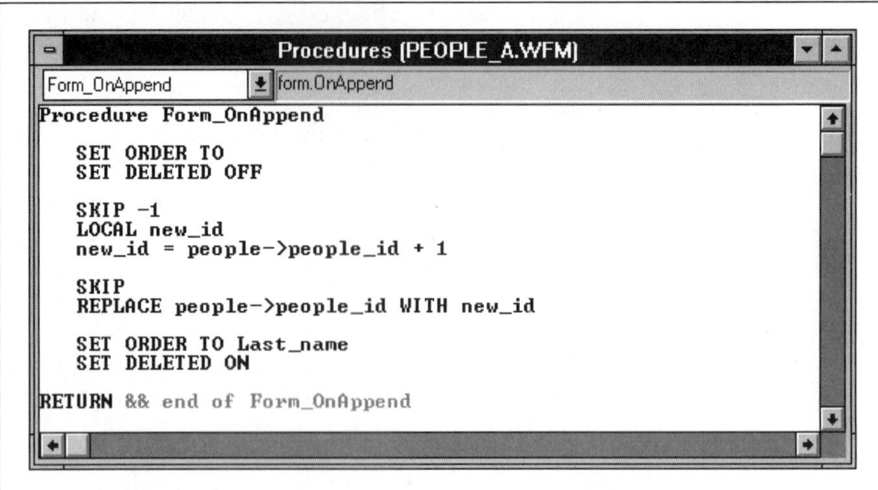

be using this technique from the start, manually add the ID 1001 to the first record when you create your table.

►► **TIP**

If your ID is four digits wide, use 1001 for your first ID number. If it is five digits, use 10001, and so on. This makes all your IDs the same width, which guarantees that your listings will line up neatly, no matter what software you might export your data to.

If you have been using the People table for a while, you need to make sure that it starts clean. The simplest way to do this is to use the Command window. These commands will give you a clean start:

```
USE people EXCLUSIVE
PACK
REPLACE ALL people_id WITH RECNO()+1000
USE
```

These commands pack out all deleted records and make sure that all the ID values are 1001, 1002, and so on. The first USE command opens the table for EXCLUSIVE use, which you need for the PACK command. Since we don't specify an index tag, the table is opened in natural order, which is what we want when we assign the starting IDs. The final USE closes the table.

Now you are ready to run the People_A form. Try it, and your ID values should be automated. When you add a record, a new ID value will appear without any effort on your part.

There's one more change to make to your form. Now that the ID is an auto-incrementing field, you don't want to let yourself edit the value. Let dBASE assign the values sequentially, and you'll never need to worry about them again.

We want a field that displays our ID, but doesn't permit editing. A Spinbox object is definitely not appropriate. Delete the Spinbox and replace it with an Entryfield object. Set the DataLink property to:

```
PEOPLE->PEOPLE_ID
```

Then set the Enabled property (it's one of the Access Properties at the top) to False. When you set Enabled to False, there is no access to Entryfield object. It is automatically removed from the tabbing order, and it won't say hello to your mouse, either.

We also think it's a good idea to move the object up and out of the way, where we won't confuse it with the real entry fields. While we're at it, there's an ampersand in the Text property of the Text object that labels the ID. This should be removed, since pressing Alt-P won't get us to this read-only field.

Now we've got a fully automated ID for our PEOPLE_A.WFM file. We leave it to you to upgrade your ORGS_A.WFM and other forms to have equally intelligent OnAppend handlers. Here's a hint about the easy way to do this.

Fire up ORGS_A.WFM in the Form Designer. Go to the Procedure Editor via the Form's OnAppend event. But don't start typing all those lines of code. Type something that you can easily recognize, such as *** copy the code here!**. Then save your work and exit from the Form Designer.

In the Program Editor, open the PEOPLE_A.WFM file. Find the OnAppend code and copy it to the Clipboard. Then open ORGS_A.WFM in the Editor. Find the "* copy the ..." comment you added. Paste the code from the Clipboard.

Now read your copied code, and you'll remember that PEOPLE> PEOPLE_ID is not exactly what you want for the Orgs table. Change the tag name from LAST_NAME to just NAME, too.

▶ Automating Foreign Key Entry

Did we say that we were going to "automate foreign key entry?" This jargon stuff sure catches on fast. We want to show a list of employers from which we can pick one. For example, if we click on BigCo, our form will fill in BigCo's ID in Bill's record.

For this to work, you need to make sure that the ID that gets into Bill's ORG_ID field is the ID of an employer in the Orgs table. If you click on an employer's name and the underlying event handlers take care of transferring the ID value, you won't be able to get a bad ID.

If every ID that refers to another record is correct, you have *referential integrity*. We're going to develop a way of automating the handling of foreign keys so that we always maintain referential integrity. In other words, we're going to be able to point and click, and let dBASE for Windows worry about getting the IDs right.

Begin with a Query

As usual, you begin a multi-table form by building a query. The only unusual thing about this query is that we will *not* link the tables in the Query Designer. We will be handling the linkage in our form with our own event handlers, so we will not want dBASE for Windows to be throwing in its two cents.

Launch the Untitled query in the Query Designer. Use the People table and the Orgs table. For the People table, select the LAST_NAME tag as the index. For the Orgs table, select the NAME tag as the index. We want all the fields from both tables, which is the default.

We saved our query as PEOPLE_B.QBE.

Put the Form Expert to Work

Once your query is designed and saved, put the Form Expert to work by launching the Untitled form in the Form Designer. Choose the query you just built, but don't select all the available fields. Instead, just choose all the fields that came from the People table. Leave the Orgs fields out of the form, for now.

Let the Form Expert build you a columnar form, using your colors and other preferences. When the form is ready, it should look something like the one in Figure 19.5.

FIGURE 19.5

The Form Expert's starting form

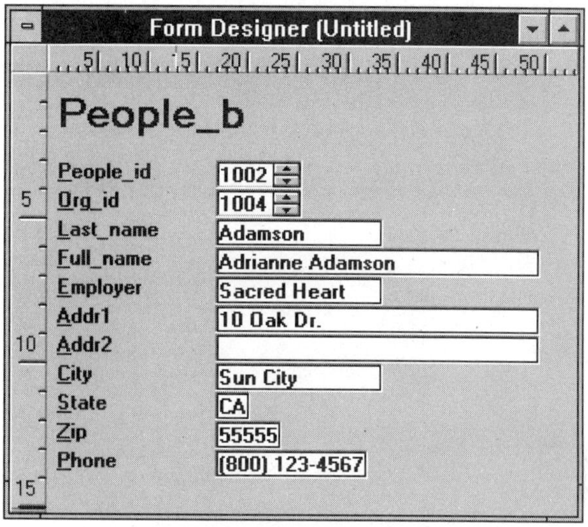

Add the OnAppend Logic

Begin by adding the OnAppend logic we added to our People_A and other forms. Click on Form, then the Events tab in the Object Properties Inspector. For OnAppend, click on the tool icon to go to the Procedure Editor. Type * **copy code here**, or something similar. Save and exit to the Navigator.

Launch both the PEOPLE_A.WFM and PEOPLE_B.WFM files in Program Editor windows. In People_A, look for the OnAppend procedure. Copy its code to the Clipboard and press Ctrl-Q to exit without saving. In People_B, find your "* copy …" command and delete it. Then paste in the code from the Clipboard. It should run correctly without a single change. This time, exit with a Ctrl-W keypress and return to the Form Designer to continue working on People_B.

Improving the Form

You want to replace both spinboxes for PEOPLE_ID and ORG_ID with entry fields. Delete both Spinbox objects and add two Entryfield objects. Use the DataLink property's tool icon to choose PEOPLE->People_ID for the first one and PEOPLE->Org_ID for the second one. Set the Enabled property to False in both, so that they are read-only fields.

Now stretch the form and add a Browse object on the right. Move the read-only ID fields up and out of the way of the rest of your data. Adjust the Text objects to label the fields, and slide the fields in the address around to look their best.

Your result should look similar to the form shown in Figure 19.6.

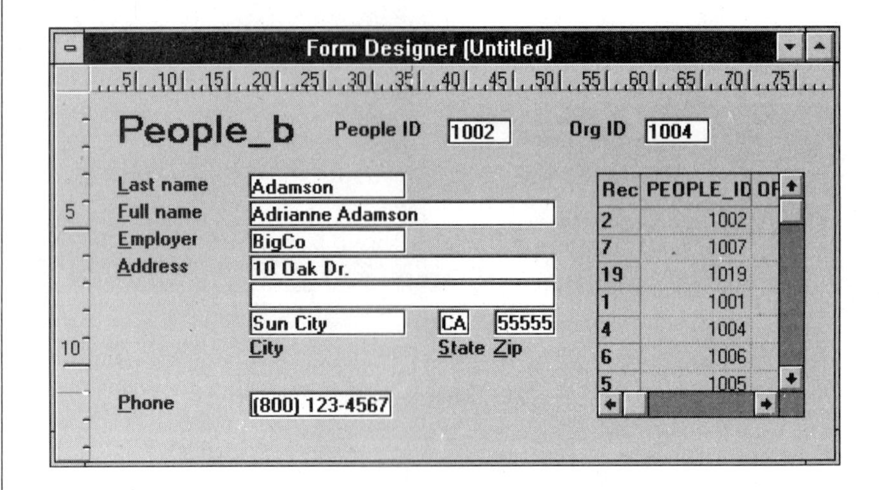

FIGURE 19.6 *The form with a Browse object and other improvements*

We have linked the EMPLOYER field, under the FULL_NAME field, to the Orgs table NAME field. The original default linkage for the Browse object is the People table, which is not what we want. Let's get the Browse object organized.

Setting Up the Browse Object

Begin by linking the Browse object to the ORGS Alias. The Alias property is one of the Data Linkage Properties. The tool icon next to it takes you to the Choose Alias dialog box.

Under the Alias property is the Fields property. Click on the tool icon next to Fields. You'll see that the default selection is every field in the view, which is not what we want. In the Choose Fields dialog box, click on the **<<** pushbutton to empty the Selected Fields list. Then choose just the ORGS->Name field.

Now we are ready to get on the other changes we made when we added Browse objects to our phone list system in Chapter 6. Begin by setting the Browse object's Edit Properties. Set Modify to False, so that this Browse is used just for selection. Then set Toggle to False, so you don't inadvertently try to squeeze a form or columnar layout into the rather small space available for browsing.

In the Visual Properties section, set each of ShowDeleted, ShowHeading, and ShowRecNo to False, since we don't want any of these. We want just a simple list of names.

Let's Go for a Test Drive

We're ready to test the work we've done so far. If you haven't already done so, save your form as PEOPLE_B.WFM. Clicking on the lightning icon or pressing F2 triggers the Save Form dialog box, before taking you into Run mode.

With the form running, you can see what you've done so far. When you add a new person, you should see the PEOPLE_ID field correctly updated with another sequential value. When you manipulate the Browse object, you should see the ORG_ID field change appropriately.

You also see that you can manipulate either the field or the Browse object without impacting the other. But it would be better if when you scroll through the people in your table, the Browse window is updated to highlight their employers.

There is no updating because we didn't establish any link in the Query Designer. Instead, we're going to provide our own event handlers.

Before you leave Run mode, select the Browse object and click on one of the speedbar's navigation buttons. You'll see your navigation reflected in the Browse object. Next, click on a field in the table, such as the FULL_NAME field. When you select one of the People table fields and click on a navigation button, your People table data changes.

Notice that you are navigating the People table on the left, and the Orgs table in the Browse object. We'll need to remember this.

The Event Handlers

Now it's time to put together those event handlers to make this work. There are actually two separate events that we want to handle.

When we navigate in the People table, we want to use the PEOPLE> Org_ID field to find the right employer in the Orgs table. This means that we'll use the PEOPLE->Org_ID to look up the employer with the matching ORGS->Org_ID.

On the other hand, with a person selected, if we navigate in the Employer table we'll want the PEOPLE->Org_ID field updated to hold the ID of whatever employer we select.

The only difficulty we face here is that navigating in either table will trigger the Form object's OnNavigate event. We really need two separate handlers: one for OnNavigateInThePeopleTable and the other for OnNavigateInTheEmployerBrowse. As you'll see, it's not difficult to distinguish one from the other, even though we have only a single OnNavigate event property.

From the Form Designer, click on the Events tab of the Object Properties Inspector, and then click on OnNavigate. We'll use the ActiveControl property of the Form to tell us where we are. The ActiveControl is the one that has focus. It is an object. The ActiveControl.Name property will tell us which control it is.

Add this code to the OnNavigate method:

```
IF Form.ActiveControl.Name = 'BROWSE1'
    ? 'Navigate in Browse'
  ELSE
    ? 'Navigate elsewhere'
ENDIF
```

With that addition, return to Run mode and set up your form and Command window so that you can see the Command window's results pane as you navigate in the form. Our setup is shown in Figure 19.7.

▸▸ **WARNING**

Never write too many lines of event commands without checking to see that they are working. Always put "? 'Tell me where I am'" commands in when you use IF statements, and be sure you're in the right place before you start adding other commands.

FIGURE 19.7

Checking our navigation reports

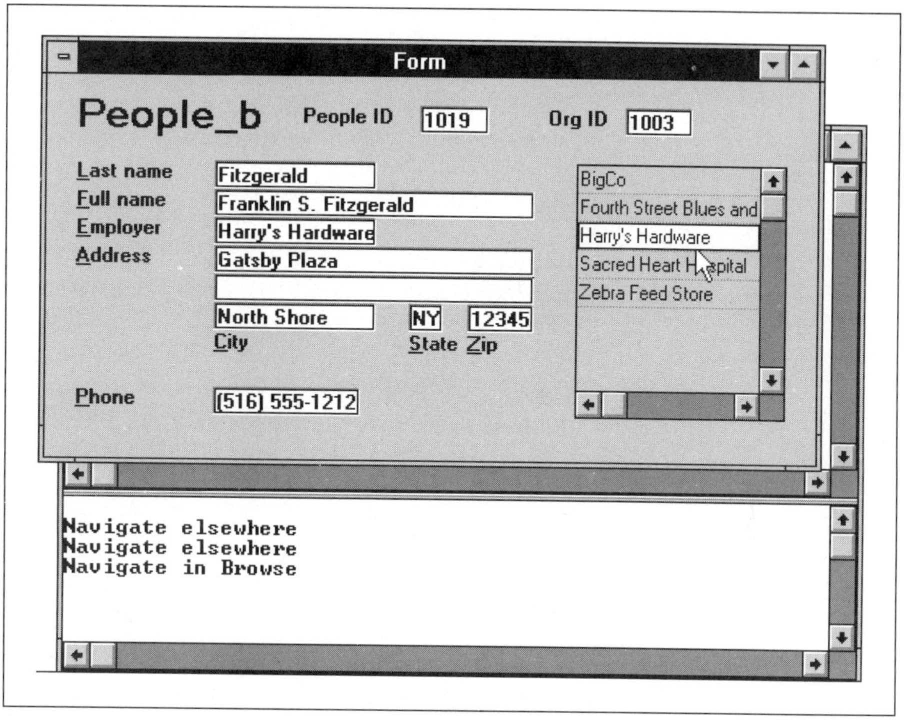

Coordinating the Navigation

The first challenge we meet is having the Browse object correctly positioned as we move from one person to another. We want the person's employer to be the highlighted record in the Browse window.

This will take a little work. The problem we'll need to overcome is that the Orgs table has indexes on both the NAME (actually, the UPPER( ) of the NAME) and on the ORG_ID field. We want to see the employers listed in order by name, but the computer will need the ORG_ID index to do the lookup. Here's the basic technique:

```
* switch to the Orgs table
* switch to the ID index

* do the lookup

* switch back to the Name index
* switch back to the People table
```

To switch from the People table to the Orgs table and back, we'll need to look at the query code, to see which work area the tables have been opened in. Here's our PEOPLE_B.QBE:

```
* dBASE Windows .QBE file 9
CLOSE DATABASES
SET EXACT ON
SELECT 1
USE PEOPLE.DBF ORDER TAG LAST_NAME OF PEOPLE.MDX
SET FIELDS TO PEOPLE_ID, ORG_ID, LAST_NAME, FULL_NAME,
EMPLOYER, ADDR1, ;
ADDR2, CITY, STATE, ZIP, PHONE, TAG01=UPPER(PEOPLE-
>LAST_NAME)
SELECT 2
USE ORGS.DBF ORDER TAG NAME OF ORGS.MDX
SET FIELDS TO ORG_ID, NAME, ADDRESS1, ADDRESS2, CITY,
STATE, ZIP, PHONE, ;
TAG01=UPPER(ORGS->NAME)
SELECT 1
GO TOP
```

As you see, work area 1 is selected. and the People table is opened. Then work area 2 is selected, and the Orgs table is opened.

This lets us replace some of our comments with working code:

```
SELECT 2 && ORGS
* switch to the ID index

* do the lookup

* switch back to the Name index
SELECT 1 && back to PEOPLE
```

Now we can look at the next issue, selecting the right index tags. Here's the code to correctly handle that problem:

```
SELECT 2 && ORGS
SET ORDER TO Org_ID

* do the lookup

SET ORDER TO Name
SELECT 1 && back to PEOPLE
```

We Fell Off the Edge of the World

When you write even simple programs, there is always the possibility that you will fall into what is known as an infinite loop. Here's a simple example:

```
DO WHILE 2 < 3
   ? "This won't stop!"
ENDDO
```

You can inspect this loop and realize immediately that 2 will always be less than 3. Even with only a dozen lines of event handlers for your background, you'll probably see that this is a mistake. Of course, if that expression involved variables or functions, it might be less obvious that the loop would run forever.

At the other extreme, you have the subtle ways of falling into an infinite loop. The one of us who wrote this code first (name withheld to protect the guilty!) fell into an infinite loop. See if you can spot it:

```
SELECT 2
SET ORDER TO Org_ID

SEEK PEOPLE->Org_ID

SET ORDER TO Name
SELECT 1
```

Here's a hint: think about where you are (or, more exactly, where dBASE for Windows is) when this code runs.

Give up? We're in an OnNavigate event handler. The SEEK command moves the record pointer—a type of navigation. So when you SEEK, the OnNavigate event is triggered, which calls this function again. When this function is called, it gets to the line that does a SEEK. The SEEK calls OnNavigate again, which gets to the line that does a SEEK, and so on.

If you don't turn the feature off, pressing Esc in the middle of a dBASE program will interrupt the program. So when we saw our program sit there blinking like crazy for several seconds, we pounced on the Esc key.

If you don't tap Esc, memory will fill up with the information dBASE records every time it calls a subroutine, such as an OnNavigate handler. (dBASE must write down where it was, so it knows what to resume when the subroutine is completed.) When you completely fill memory with return information, your computer won't like it. This may be something as simple as a "dBASE has become unstable" alert.

The worst result of this sort of error is the destruction of your hard disks file allocation table (FAT). A programmer would say, "You fried your FAT!" At its worst, this can cost you all the data and programs on your hard disk.

▸▸ **NOTE**

It may reassure you to know that we've never seen a fried FAT happen to anyone who had maintained a sound backup procedure. However, we have seen two occurrences—to careless programmers who had no backups. Murphy's Law hasn't been repealed.

With that in mind, we don't suggest you test the above version. To avoid the infinite loop, you need to save the value assigned to the OnNavigate event. Then you assign a dummy value (.F. is traditional) to the OnNavigate event, just while you do your own navigation. When you are finished, you replace the OnNavigate handler with the saved value. Here is the complete code that does that SEEK:

```
Form.SaveNav = Form.OnNavigate
Form.OnNavigate = .F.
SEEK PEOPLE->Org_ID
Form.OnNavigate = Form.SaveNav
```

Here is the OnNavigate method with the full handler for positioning the Browse:

```
Procedure Form_OnNavigate
IF Form.ActiveControl.Name = 'BROWSE1'

   * code to come

   ELSE

     SELECT 2
     SET ORDER TO Org_ID

     Form.SaveNav = Form.OnNavigate
```

```
        Form.OnNavigate = .F.
        SEEK PEOPLE->Org_ID
        Form.OnNavigate = Form.SaveNav

        SET ORDER TO Name
        SELECT 1

    ENDIF
```

Enter this using the Procedure Editor in place of the ? 'Navigate … code that we used to test our logic.

When you run this program, you'll see the Browse window updated as you move through the People table's data on the left side of your form.

NOTE

If you have an early release version of dBASE for Windows, your Browse object may flash as it positions itself. We trust that Borland will fix this in a maintenance release. It's not pretty, but it's harmless.

Choosing Employers with the Browse

Once we have selected a person, we want to be able to use the Browse object to choose an employer. With a person selected we should be able to just click on BigCo (or whatever employer you choose) and have that employer linked to the person.

That means that underneath your click, the event handler should look at the employer's ORG_ID field and enter its value as the value in the person's ORG_ID field.

The good news is that unlike the Browse lookup process, the code for this is just one simple line. Add this one line where the comment "* code to come" was placed.

```
REPLACE PEOPLE->Org_ID WITH ORGS->Org_ID
```

This statement will change your person's ORG_ID to each new ORG_ID in the Orgs table, as you navigate in the Browse window. Note that at every point, the ORG_ID field in the People table has been read from an ORG_ID field in the Orgs table, so there is no chance for error here.

Now test run your form. You've got almost complete referential integrity. Or, if you prefer, each person is correctly linked to a single employer by a valid ID. We've achieved our initial goal.

Final Touches

There are two more changes to make. First, the EMPLOYER field that comes after the FULL_NAME field should be read-only. You should use the z-order tools to have the Browse object located right at the EMPLOYER field.

That way, when you press Tab (or Enter) after the FULL_NAME field, you'll go right to the Browse window to select an employer. When you press Tab or Enter to leave the Browse window, you'll continue down your form, as if you had typed the employer's name in the appropriate spot.

The other change is to have the Browse lookup code executed when you open your form. Copy the ELSE part of the OnNavigate code into the OnOpen handler. (Hint: you can also copy through the Clipboard using just the Procedure Editor.)

▸ Where Do We Go from Here?

At this point, you're doing some simple dBASE for Windows programming in the Form Designer. The only limit to what you can get your forms to do is your knowledge and creativity.

You now have explored every part of dBASE for Windows and can call yourself an expert. But you've also seen that by using the dBASE for Windows powerful object-oriented programming language, you can reach far greater levels of expertise.

Before you go on with developing your own systems, allow us to remind you just once more about Chapter 3. When you set up a system that seems to give you nothing but trouble, go back to that chapter and think about how you designed your tables.

If you design good tables, you've got plenty of power to control every other aspect of your database.

►► Pushbutton and Scrollbar Properties Reference

In this section, we provide an alphabetical listing of all the properties of the Pushbutton and Scrollbar objects. Each listing includes the default value (if one exists). If a property is read-only, you cannot assign a value to it. If a property is read-only, it is noted in its listing.

Data properties are called Properties; events and other methods are called Methods. Additionally, Methods' names are followed by parentheses; for example, ClassName is a data property, but Close( ) is a method. Some methods take parameters within their parentheses, as noted in their listings.

► Pushbutton Object Properties

This section lists and briefly explains the properties of the Pushbutton object.

The Pushbutton.Before Property

Before is an object reference to the object that this Pushbutton precedes in the form's tabbing order. If this Pushbutton object is the last one in the form's tabbing order, Before is a reference to the first object in the tabbing order (Form.First).

The Pushbutton.ClassName Property

Default value: PUSHBUTTON

ClassName is read-only. This property is assigned by dBASE for Windows for each of the built-in classes. ClassName can be used to distinguish among multiple objects with the same name.

The Pushbutton.ColorNormal Property

Default value: N/W

The ColorNormal property specifies the color of the Pushbutton object. ColorNormal may be a dBASE IV-style color specification, or it may be a color selected from the color palette with the Choose Color dialog box.

The Pushbutton.Default Property

Default value: .F.

The default pushbutton (if there are multiple pushbuttons on a form) is the first one in the tabbing order. You can change the default to another button by setting the Default property of that button to True.

The Pushbutton.DisabledBitmap Property

The DisabledBitmap is shown on the Pushbutton object if the Pushbutton's Enabled property is False.

The Pushbutton.DownBitmap Property

The DownBitmap property specifies the source of the bitmap that is displayed when the button is pushed down.

The Pushbutton.Enabled Property

Default value: .T.

If Enabled is True, the Pushbutton object is accessible. You can use the Enabled property to disable options in event handlers. For example, a Valid function could set some object's Enabled property to False if required conditions were not met.

The Pushbutton.FocusBitmap Property

Default value: ""

The FocusBitmap property specifies the source of the bitmap that is displayed when the Pushbutton object has focus.

The Pushbutton.FontBold Property

Default value: .T.

If True, FontBold specifies that the Pushbutton object's font is boldface.

The Pushbutton.FontItalic Property

Default value: .F.

If True, FontItalic specifies that the Pushbutton object's font is italic.

The Pushbutton.FontName Property

Default value: MS Sans Serif

The FontName property specifies the name of the font. This may be set from the Font dialog box, accessed via the tool icon in the Form Designer's Properties dialog box.

The Pushbutton.FontSize Property

Default value: 8

The FontSize property specifies the size of the font, in points.

The Pushbutton.FontStrikeOut Property

Default value: .F.

If True, FontStrikeOut specifies that the characters will be displayed with strikeout slashes.

The Pushbutton.FontUnderline Property

Default value: .F.

If True, FontUnderline specifies that the characters are underlined.

The Pushbutton.Group Property

Default value: .T.

The Group property actually specifies Beginning of Group. If True, this begins a group. The group continues until the next object with a True value for the Group property.

The Pushbutton.Height Property

Default value: 0.0

The Height property specifies the height of the Pushbutton object in characters.

The Pushbutton.HelpFile Property

Default value: ""

The HelpFile property names the Windows Help file that will be used when you press F1.

The Pushbutton.HelpID Property

Default value: –1

The HelpID specifies the individual Help screen that will be accessed in the Windows Help file specified by the HelpFile property.

The Pushbutton.hWnd Property

The hWnd property is read-only. This property is an arbitrary integer number that identifies the window to which the Pushbutton object belongs. This is called the window's *handle*. It is used when you access Windows functions directly via EXTERN commands.

The Pushbutton.ID Property

Default value: –1

ID is a number than can be used to distinguish between otherwise identical Pushbutton objects.

The Pushbutton.Left Property

Default value: 0

The Left property specifies the location of the left side of the Pushbutton object within its form, in characters. The leftmost character is number 0.

The Pushbutton.MousePointer Property

Default value: 0

Available settings: 0–11

The MousePointer property specifies the type of mouse pointer to use when the pointer is over the Pushbutton object. For example, the mouse pointer is an arrow over a form, but turns to an I-beam in an editor. The settings are default (0), arrow (1), cross (2), I-beam (3), icon (4), size (5), size NESW (6), size S (7), size NWSE (8), size E (9), up arrow (10), and wait (hourglass, 11).

The Pushbutton.Move( ) Method

Parameters: *<lft>*,*<tp>*,*<wdth>*,*<hght>*

Move is a method property that can move the Pushbutton object, resize the Pushbutton object, or both. You provide Move with four parameters, representing the new values for the properties Left, Top, Width, and Height, respectively.

The Pushbutton.Name Property

Default value: PUSHBUTTON*<n>*

The Name property is the property name given to this property on the parent form. If the name is PUSHBUTTON1, for example, specifying Parent.PUSHBUTTON1 specifies this Pushbutton object.

The Pushbutton.OnClick( ) Method

The OnClick method is called whenever you click a button or menu choice.

The Pushbutton.OnGotFocus( ) Method

The OnGotFocus method is called when a Pushbutton object receives focus.

The Pushbutton.OnHelp( ) Method

The OnHelp method is called when the F1 key is pressed with focus on the Pushbutton object.

The Pushbutton.OnLeftDblClick( ) Method

Parameters: *<flags>*,*<col>*,*<row>*

The OnLeftDblClick event is called when you double-click with the left mouse button over the Pushbutton object. The parameters report the status of the Shift, Ctrl, and Alt keys, as well as the location at the time of the OnLeftDblClick event.

The Pushbutton.OnLeftMouseDown( ) Method

Parameters: <*flags*>,<*col*>,<*row*>

The OnLeftMouseDown event is called when you press the left mouse button over the Pushbutton object. The parameters report the status of the Shift, Ctrl, and Alt keys, as well as the location at the time of the OnLeftMouseDown event.

The Pushbutton.OnLeftMouseUp( ) Method

Parameters: <*flags*>,<*col*>,<*row*>

The OnLeftMouseUp handler is called whenever you release the left button over the Pushbutton object. (An up event over one object might have been preceded by a down event over another object.) The parameters report the status of the Shift, Ctrl, and Alt keys, as well as the location at the time of the OnLeftMouseUp event.

The Pushbutton.OnLostFocus( ) Method

The OnLostFocus method is called whenever the Pushbutton object loses focus.

The Pushbutton.OnMiddleDblClick( ) Method

Parameters: <*flags*>,<*col*>,<*row*>

The OnMiddleDblClick event is called when you double-click with the middle mouse button of a three-button mouse over the Pushbutton object. The parameters report the status of the Shift, Ctrl, and Alt keys, as well as the location at the time of the OnMiddleDblClick event.

The Pushbutton.OnMiddleMouseDown( ) Method

Parameters: <*flags*>,<*col*>,<*row*>

The OnMiddleMouseDown event is called when you press the middle mouse button of a three-button mouse over the Pushbutton object. The parameters report the status of the Shift, Ctrl, and Alt keys, as well as the location at the time of the OnMiddleMouseDown event.

The Pushbutton.OnMiddleMouseUp( ) Method

Parameters: <*flags*>,<*col*>,<*row*>

The OnMiddleMouseUp handler is called whenever you release the middle mouse button over the Pushbutton object. (An up event over one object might have been preceded by a down event over another object.) The parameters report the status of the Shift, Ctrl, and Alt keys, as well as the location at the time of the OnMiddleMouseUp event.

The Pushbutton.OnMouseMove( ) Method

Parameters: <*flags*>,<*col*>,<*row*>

The OnMouseMove event is called when any mouse movement is detected over the Pushbutton object.

The Pushbutton.OnOpen( ) Method

The OnOpen event is called when the form containing the Pushbutton object is opened.

The Pushbutton.OnRightDblClick( ) Method

Parameters: <*flags*>,<*col*>,<*row*>

The OnRightDblClick event is called when you double-click with the right mouse button over the Pushbutton object. (Right double-clicks are recognized by the Navigator as commands to design the object.) The parameters report the status of the Shift, Ctrl, and Alt keys, as well as the location at the time of the OnRightDblClick event.

The Pushbutton.OnRightMouseDown( ) Method

Parameters: <*flags*>,<*col*>,<*row*>

The OnRightMouseDown event is called when you press the right mouse button over the Pushbutton object. The parameters report the status of the Shift, Ctrl, and Alt keys, as well as the location at the time of the OnRightMouseDown event.

The Pushbutton.OnRightMouseUp( ) Method

Parameters: *<flags>*,*<col>*,*<row>*

The OnRightMouseUp handler is called whenever you release the right button over the Pushbutton object. (An up event over one object might have been preceded by a down event over another object.) The parameters report the status of the Shift, Ctrl, and Alt keys, as well as the location at the time of the OnRightMouseUp event.

The Pushbutton.Parent Property

The Parent property is read-only. This property is an object reference to the parent form of the Pushbutton object. It is assigned when the Pushbutton object is created via a DEFINE command or a NEW call to the constructor.

The Pushbutton.Release( ) Method

The Release method removes the Pushbutton object from memory. Releasing a form also releases all of the form's objects.

The Pushbutton.SetFocus( ) Method

The SetFocus method changes focus to the Pushbutton object on the form.

The Pushbutton.Speedbar Property

Default value: .F.

If the Speedbar property is True, the Pushbutton object is excluded from the form's tabbing order.

The Pushbutton.StatusMessage Property

Default value: ""

The StatusMessage appears in the left portion of the status bar when the mouse pointer is over the Pushbutton object and when the Pushbutton object has focus.

The Pushbutton.TabStop Property

Default value: .T.

If TabStop is True, the Pushbutton object is part of the tabbing order. If it is False, Tab and Shift-Tab will bypass the Pushbutton object.

The Pushbutton.Text Property

Default value: "PUSHBUTTON<*n*>"

The Text property specifies the text in the Pushbutton object.

The Pushbutton.Top Property

Default value: 0

The Top property is the location of the top of the Pushbutton object, in characters sized by the form's ScaleFont. The top-left corner of the form is 0,0.

The Pushbutton.UpBitmap Property

Default value: ""

The UpBitmap property specifies the source of the bitmap to display when the Pushbutton is up and enabled.

The Pushbutton.Visible Property

Default value: .T.

If Visible is True, the Pushbutton object is shown. Manipulating the Visible property lets you choose among alternative objects on a form.

The Pushbutton.When( ) Method

If When is False, you cannot give focus to the Pushbutton object.

The Pushbutton.Width Property

Default value: 13.0

The Width property specifies the width of the Pushbutton object in characters. The width of each character is determined by the form's ScaleFont properties.

► Scrollbar Object Properties

This section lists and briefly explains the properties of the Scrollbar object.

The Scrollbar.Before Property

Before is an object reference to the object that this Scrollbar object precedes in the form's tabbing order. If this Scrollbar object is the last one in the form's tabbing order, Before is a reference to the first object in the tabbing order (Form.First).

The Scrollbar.ClassName Property

Default value: SCROLLBAR

ClassName is read-only. This property is assigned by dBASE for Windows for each of the built-in classes. ClassName can be used to distinguish among multiple objects with the same name.

The Scrollbar.DataLink Property

Default value: ""

The DataLink property links the field's value to a memory variable or a table field. When you change the data value in this field, it changes the value in the associated memory variable or table field.

The Scrollbar.Enabled Property

Default value: .T.

If Enabled is True, the Scrollbar object is accessible. You can use the Enabled property to disable options in event handlers. For example, a Valid function could set some object's Enabled property to False if required conditions were not met.

The Scrollbar.Height Property

Default value, vertical scrollbar: 7.5

Default value, horizontal scrollbar: 1.5

The Height property specifies the height of the Scrollbar object, in characters.

The Scrollbar.HelpFile Property

Default value: ""

The HelpFile property names the Windows Help file that will be used when you press F1.

The Scrollbar.HelpID Property

Default value: –1

The HelpID specifies the individual Help screen that will be accessed in the Windows Help file specified by the HelpFile property.

The Scrollbar.hWnd Property

The hWnd property is read-only. This property is an arbitrary integer number that identifies the window to which the Scrollbar object belongs. This is called the window's *handle*. It is used when you access Windows functions directly via EXTERN commands.

The Scrollbar.ID Property

Default value: –1

ID is a number than can be used to distinguish between otherwise identical Scrollbar objects.

The Scrollbar.Left Property

Default value: 1.0

The Left property specifies the location of the left side of the Scrollbar object within its form, in characters. The leftmost character is number 0.

TIP

Since a Scroll bar object is 2 characters wide, to locate a vertical scroll bar at the right side of a Form object, you would assign Left this expression: Form.Width-2.

The Scrollbar.MousePointer Property

Default value: 0

Available Settings: 0–11

The MousePointer property specifies the type of mouse pointer to use when the pointer is over the Scrollbar object. For example, the mouse pointer is an arrow over a form, but turns to an I-beam in an editor. The settings are default (0), arrow (1), cross (2), I-beam (3), icon (4), size (5), size NESW (6), size S (7), size NWSE (8), size E (9), up arrow (10), and wait (hourglass, 11).

The Scrollbar.Move( ) Method

Parameters: *<lft>*,*<tp>*,*<wdth>*,*<hght>*

Move is a method property that can move the Scrollbar object, resize the Scrollbar object, or both. You provide Move with four parameters, representing the new values for the properties Left, Top, Width, and Height, respectively.

The Scrollbar.Name Property

Default value: SCROLLBAR*<n>*

The Name property is the property name given to this property on the parent form. If the name is SCROLLBAR1, for example, specifying Parent.SCROLLBAR1 specifies this Scrollbar object.

The Scrollbar.OnChange( ) Method

The OnChange method is called whenever you manipulate the Scrollbar object.

The Scrollbar.OnGotFocus( ) Method

The OnGotFocus method is called when the Scrollbar object receives focus.

The Scrollbar.OnHelp( ) Method

The OnHelp method is called when the F1 key is pressed with focus on the Scrollbar object.

The Scrollbar.OnLeftDblClick( ) Method

Parameters: <*flags*>,<*col*>,<*row*>

The OnLeftDblClick event is called when you double-click with the left mouse button over the Scrollbar object. The parameters report the status of the Shift, Ctrl, and Alt keys, as well as the location at the time of the OnLeftDblClick event.

The Scrollbar.OnLeftMouseDown( ) Method

Parameters: <*flags*>,<*col*>,<*row*>

The OnLeftMouseDown event is called when you press the left mouse button over the Scrollbar object. The parameters report the status of the Shift, Ctrl, and Alt keys, as well as the location at the time of the OnLeftMouseDown event.

The Scrollbar.OnLeftMouseUp( ) Method

Parameters: <*flags*>,<*col*>,<*row*>

The OnLeftMouseUp handler is called whenever you release the left button over the Scrollbar object. (An up event over one object might have been preceded by a down event over another object.) The parameters report the status of the Shift, Ctrl, and Alt keys, as well as the location at the time of the OnLeftMouseUp event.

The Scrollbar.OnLostFocus( ) Method

The OnLostFocus method is called whenever the Scrollbar object loses focus.

The Scrollbar.OnMiddleDblClick( ) Method

Parameters: <*flags*>,<*col*>,<*row*>

The OnMiddleDblClick event is called when you double-click with the middle mouse button of a three-button mouse over the Scrollbar object. The parameters report the status of the Shift, Ctrl, and Alt keys, as well as the location at the time of the OnMiddleDblClick event.

The Scrollbar.OnMiddleMouseDown( ) Method

Parameters: <*flags*>,<*col*>,<*row*>

The OnMiddleMouseDown event is called when you press the middle mouse button of a three-button mouse over the Scrollbar object. The parameters report the status of the Shift, Ctrl, and Alt keys, as well as the location at the time of the OnMiddleMouseDown event.

The Scrollbar.OnMiddleMouseUp( ) Method

Parameters: <*flags*>,<*col*>,<*row*>

The OnMiddleMouseUp handler is called whenever you release the middle mouse button over the Scrollbar object. (An up event over one object might have been preceded by a down event over another object.) The parameters report the status of the Shift, Ctrl, and Alt keys, as well as the location at the time of the OnMiddleMouseUp event.

The Scrollbar.OnMouseMove( ) Method

Parameters: <*flags*>,<*col*>,<*row*>

The OnMouseMove event is called when any mouse movement is detected over the Scrollbar object.

The Scrollbar.OnOpen( ) Method

The OnOpen event is called when the form containing the Scrollbar object is opened.

The Scrollbar.OnRightDblClick( ) Method

Parameters: <*flags*>,<*col*>,<*row*>

The OnRightDblClick event is called when you double-click with the right mouse button over the Scrollbar object. (Right double-clicks are recognized by the Navigator as commands to design the object.) The parameters report the status of the Shift, Ctrl, and Alt keys, as well as the location at the time of the OnRightDblClick event.

The Scrollbar.OnRightMouseDown( ) Method

Parameters: <*flags*>,<*col*>,<*row*>

The OnRightMouseDown event is called when you press the right mouse button over the Scrollbar object. The parameters report the status of the Shift, Ctrl, and Alt keys, as well as the location at the time of the OnRightMouseDown event.

The Scrollbar.OnRightMouseUp( ) Method

Parameters: <*flags*>,<*col*>,<*row*>

The OnRightMouseUp handler is called whenever you release the right button over the Scrollbar object. (An up event over one object might have been preceded by a down event over another object.) The parameters report the status of the Shift, Ctrl, and Alt keys, as well as the location at the time of the OnRightMouseUp event.

The Scrollbar.Parent Property

The Parent property is read-only. This property is an object reference to the parent form of the Scrollbar object. It is assigned when the Scrollbar object is created via a DEFINE command or a NEW call to the constructor.

The Scrollbar.RangeMax Property

Default value: 100

The RangeMax property specifies the upper limit to a range. Scrollbar objects use the Range along with Value to position the thumb.

The Scrollbar.RangeMin Property

Default value: 1

The RangeMin property specifies the lower limit to a range. Scrollbar objects use the Range along with Value to position the thumb.

The Scrollbar.Release( ) Method

The Release method removes the Scrollbar object from memory. Releasing a form also releases all of the form's objects.

The Scrollbar.SetFocus( ) Method

The SetFocus method changes focus to the Scrollbar object.

The Scrollbar.StatusMessage Property

Default value: ""

The StatusMessage appears in the left portion of the status bar when the mouse pointer is over the Scrollbar object and when the Scrollbar object has focus.

The Scrollbar.TabStop Property

Default value: .T.

If TabStop is True, the Scrollbar object is part of the tabbing order. If it is False, Tab and Shift-Tab will bypass the object.

The Scrollbar.Top Property

Default value: 0.5

The Top property is the location of the top of the Scrollbar object, in characters sized by the form's ScaleFont. The top-left corner of the form is 0,0.

The Scrollbar.Value Property

Default value: 1.0

The Value property is the value held by the Scroll bar object. The value is the location of the elevator thumb relative to the RangeMin and RangeMax values.

The Scrollbar.Vertical Property

Default value: .T.

If Vertical is True, the Scrollbar object is a vertical one. The Scrollbar is horizontal if Vertical is set to False.

The Scrollbar.Visible Property

Default value: .T.

If Visible is True, the Scrollbar object is shown. Manipulating the Visible property lets you choose among alternative objects on a form.

The Scrollbar.When( ) Method

If When is False, you cannot give focus to the Scrollbar object.

The Scrollbar.Width Property

Default value, vertical scroll bar: 3

Default value, horizontal scroll bar: 9

The Width property specifies the width of the Scrollbar object, in characters. The width of each character is determined by the form's ScaleFont properties.

▶ ▶ APPENDIX A

Installing dBASE for Windows

If you haven't installed dBASE for Windows yet, or if you ever might have to install another copy for yourself or a co-worker, this appendix is for you.

In the normal installation, you answer a handful of questions (regarding where the program should be installed and which features to include), and then sit quietly feeding floppy disks into your drive as the installation program requests them.

While you're waiting (25 minutes or so, depending on your computer) for the installation program to read, unpack, and write the programs and data, you stare at a nice highway scene (see Figure A.7 for a preview). Unfortunately, your car is stuck in one place—the scene doesn't change.

What does change is the contents of a billboard that alternately extols the virtues of dBASE for Windows' many features (quite honestly so, we think) and urges you to register your copy, which you can do by calling the 800 number shown on one of the billboards.

We love the virtues of this product, and we highly recommend that you register. Still, sitting and reading billboards isn't our idea of fun. Here's how to get around it.

Preload Your Hard Disk to Save Time

dBASE for Windows will take about 22 megabytes (MB) for a total installation. If you have an extra 10 MB beyond that on any available disk, the technique discussed here will allow you to install the software in less than half the time that installation usually takes.

First, make a directory where you have about 10 MB of extra disk space (space that you won't need for dBASE for Windows). Then copy each of the distribution disks (copy everything: *.*) into this directory. When you have read all the disks into your installation directory, back up this directory using your favorite backup program and media. Save the backup copy in a location separate from where you store the dBASE for Windows original disks.

Now you're ready to begin the installation process, which we discuss in the next section. From the Program Manager, run INSTALL.EXE from your installation directory. (It doesn't need to be on the drive where dBASE for Windows gets installed.)

Answer the questions, as described in the next section, and you are finished! Your computer isn't finished—it's got a good 10 or 15 minutes worth of work to complete. But you're free to get on to something else while your computer is hard at work.

►► The Installation Questions

If you have enough disk space, proceed to run the INSTALL.EXE program from the installation directory where you copied all the installation disks, as discussed in the previous section. If you don't have enough space, put Disk 1 into a drive and run INSTALL.EXE from that drive.

To run INSTALL.EXE, choose File ➤ Run ... from the Program Manager. Type the drive and path, plus **INSTALL.EXE** into the dialog box. Alternatively, launch the File Manager, pick the drive and path, and double-click on INSTALL.EXE.

► Pick an Appropriate Installation

Once the installation process begins, you will see the screen shown in Figure A.1. If you have 22 MB available for a full installation, accept the Complete default.

If you don't have enough space for a full installation, choose Custom or Minimum to specify which parts you want. See the section about customizing your installation for some advice on what to include and exclude.

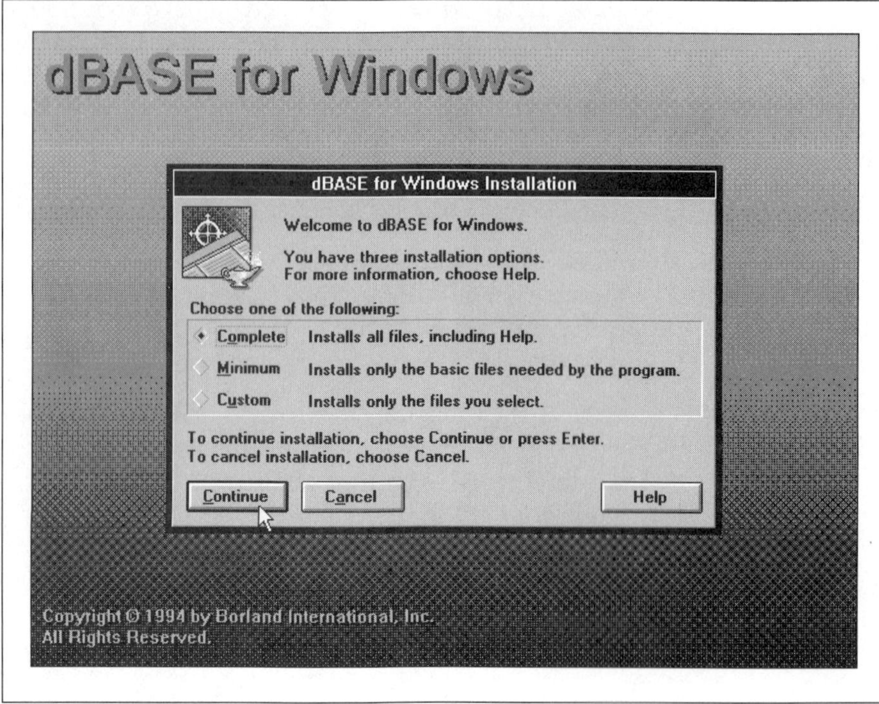

FIGURE A.1

Choosing full installation

► Direct Installation to Your Drive

After you've picked the appropriate type of installation, you will be asked to choose a drive and directory. The default is C:\DBASEWIN.

For simplicity in following the examples in the manual, don't choose a directory other than \DBASEWIN. We found space on our E: drive, so we changed the drive, but not the directory. Figure A.2 shows the dBASE for Windows Destination Drive dialog box.

► Claiming Ownership of Your Copy

The dBASE for Windows Registration dialog box, shown in Figure A.3, insists that you type your name and also lets you add a company name.

This has nothing to do with registering your copy of dBASE for Windows with Borland, which you can do by calling the 800 number or by returning the registration card. Choose whichever means you prefer, but by all means register.

FIGURE A.2

Choosing a disk drive with available space

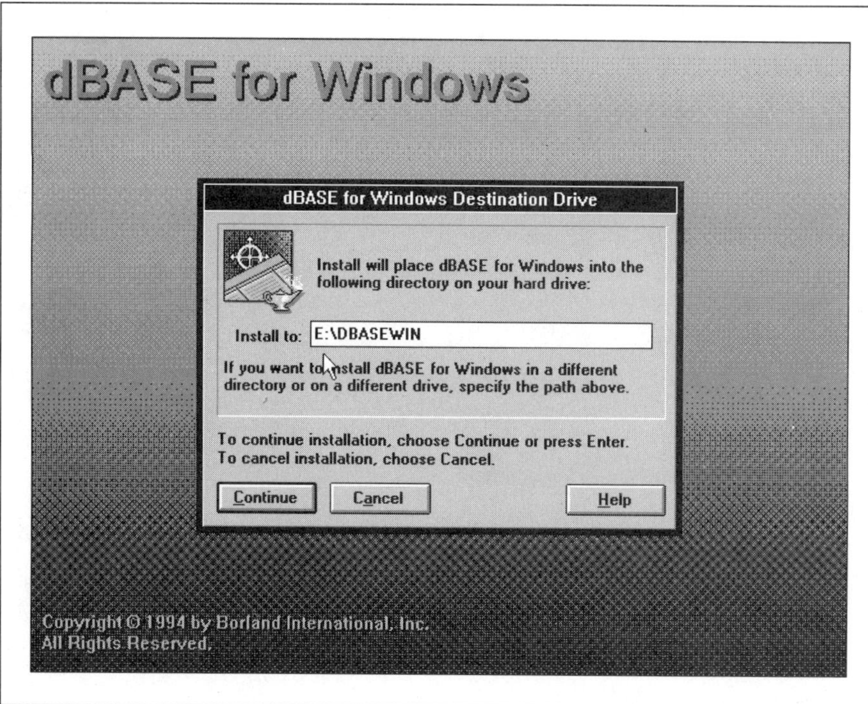

TIP

The name and company you enter here are logged in your DBASEWIN.INI file. You can change them by editing that file. It's a plain text file. Search for "Company" to find this data.

Customizing Your Installation to Save Space

The only really optional part of the full installation is the Component Builder. Unfortunately, that's only about 1 percent of the total space requirement, so not selecting it won't save you very much space. These instructions are for those who simply haven't got enough space for a full installation, or are installing a copy on a laptop before leaving on a trip.

FIGURE A.3

"Registering" your copy of dBASE for Windows

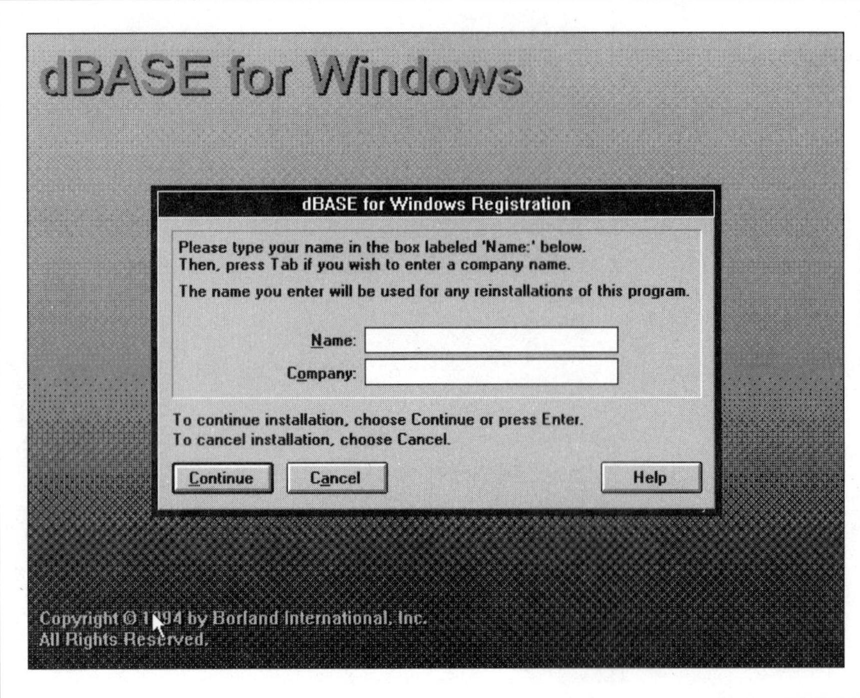

When you choose a Minimum or Custom installation, you see the dBASE for Windows Custom Installation dialog box, shown in Figure A.4. The instructions at the top of the dialog box explain how to select file groups for installation. The following sections discuss your alternatives.

▸▸ **NOTE**

You must have dBASE for Windows, at a minimum. The dBASE for Windows choice is on the Custom Installation menu for those who are doing a second installation. For example, you may have installed dBASE for Windows and the Tutors. After running the Tutors, you delete them and return to install the sample files. In this second installation, there is no need to reinstall dBASE for Windows.

FIGURE A.4

Choosing Custom Installation

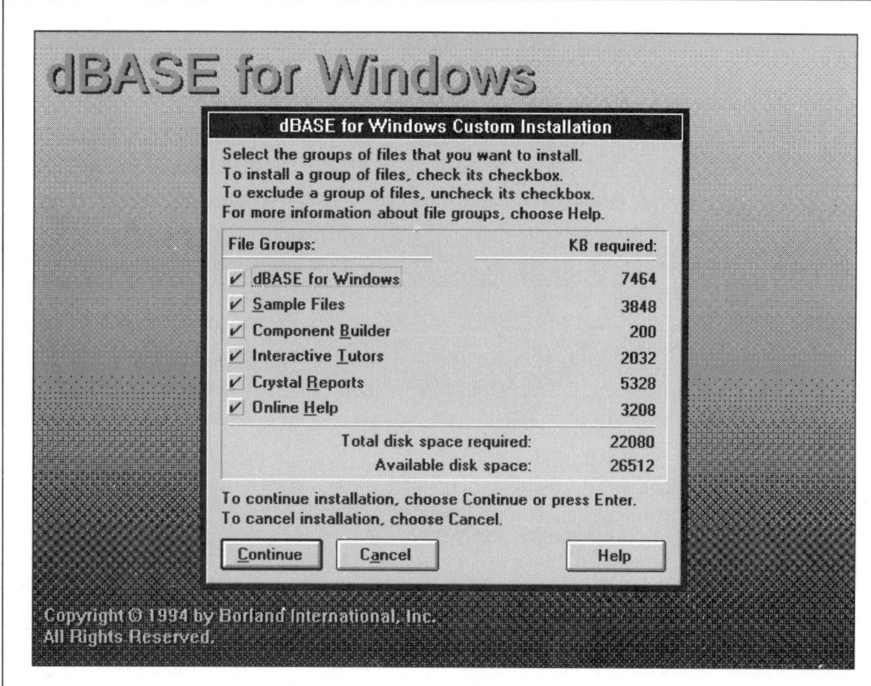

Sample Files

The sample files are just what their name suggests: samples. They include sample data tables, forms, queries, and reports. We have avoided them in this book, so that we could accommodate people who have a minimum installation. If you have space enough to include them, by all means do so.

Component Builder

The Component Builder is strictly optional. Its job is to help convert older dBASE IV-style applications to dBASE for Windows code. If you have these older applications, it is vital. If you are starting with dBASE for Windows, it has no value.

Interactive Tutors

The Tutors are not necessary if you have another source of tutorial material, such as this book. On the other hand, they are extremely well done and we used them ourselves to get started.

For better or worse, the programmers who built these Tutors added a magnificent look and feel which goes well beyond current Windows standards, and beyond what you can readily achieve with dBASE for Windows forms. You'll want to take a look and see for yourself, if you can afford the 2 MB of disk space.

Crystal Reports

Crystal Reports is the report writer. You will definitely want Crystal Reports. Of course, that spare copy of dBASE for Windows that you place on your laptop for quick reference on the road—when you don't even have a printer—that installation may not have much use for Crystal Reports.

On-line Help

We found the on-line Help system to be indispensable. Of course, we started using dBASE for Windows before books like this were available, and even before there were printed manuals. Back then it was truly indispensable.

Today, you may choose to skip the convenience of on-line help. We still strongly recommend it if you can afford the 3 MB of disk space.

► IDAPI Needs Space, Too

Borland's Independent Database Application Programming Interface, IDAPI, is the tool that lets you access data from SQL servers, as well as from dBASE and Paradox tables. It can be shared by multiple applications. The IDAPI Location Settings dialog box is shown in Figure A.5.

If you have changed your drive, the IDAPI location defaults to the drive you specified for \DBASEWIN. You could change that drive selection here if you needed to.

After you've made your choices, you move onto the dBASE for Windows Installation dialog box, shown in Figure A.6. Unless you decide that you did something wrong, go ahead and choose Install.

FIGURE A.5 

IDAPI defaults to the disk drive you choose for dBASE for Windows.

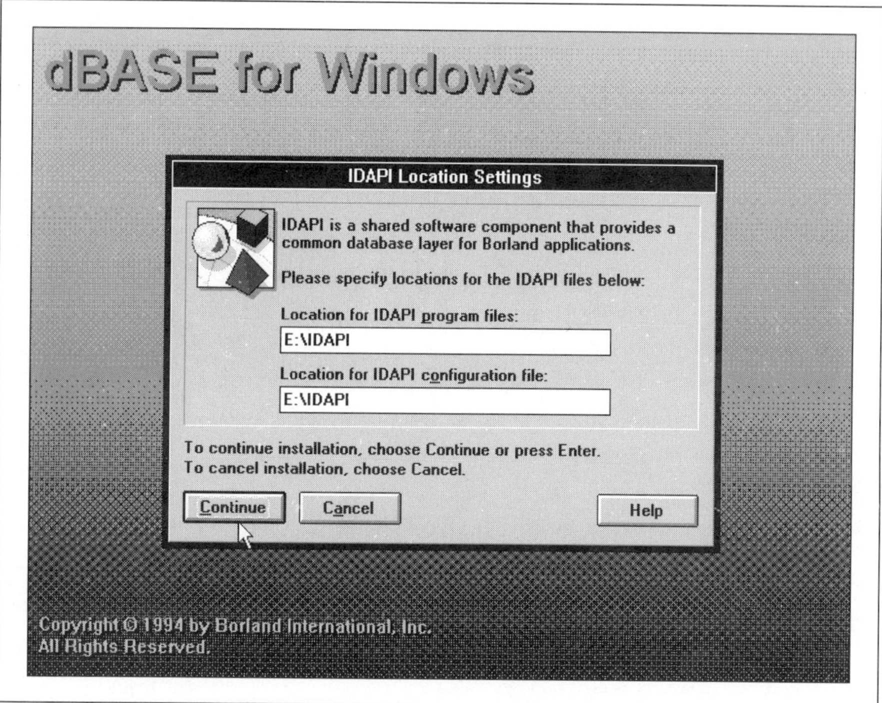

FIGURE A.6 

Choosing to install

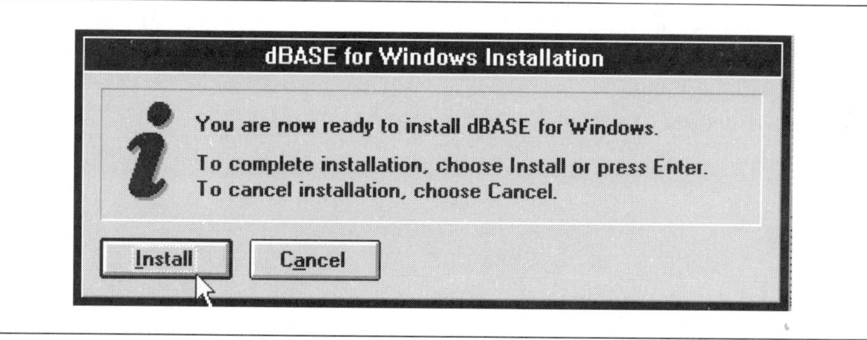

▶▶ The Installation Process

Figure A.7 shows the dashboard, scenery, and billboard that you can watch during the installation. If you followed our tip on speeding the process by copying everything into an installation directory on your hard disk, you can leave now.

FIGURE A.7 ►

The scene that doesn't change

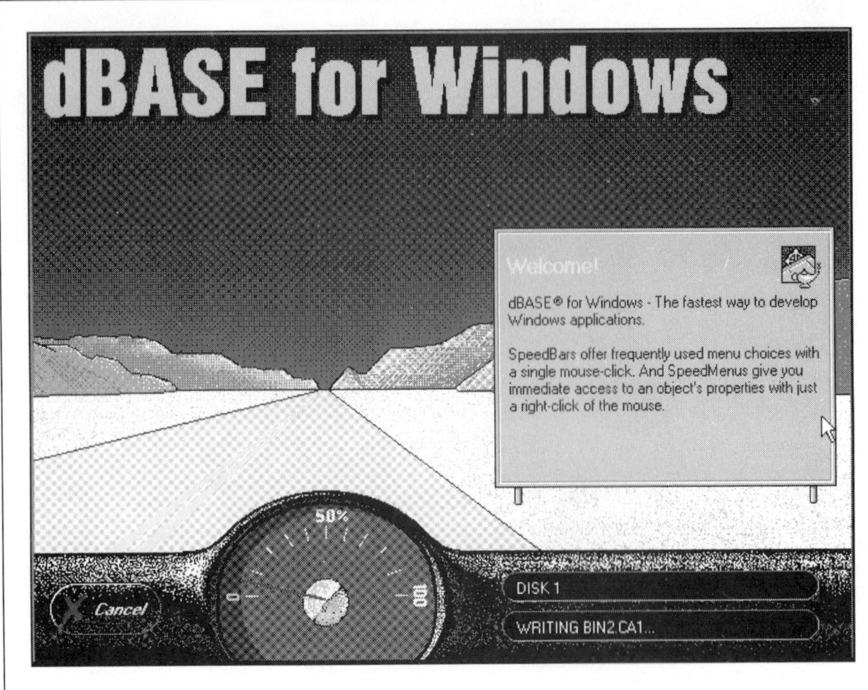

If your installation files are all available in the directory from which you ran INSTALL.EXE, busy yourself for 15 minutes with some other project. If you're still at your desk, jiggle the mouse from time to time to get rid of the screen saver (it slows down the install process).

If you didn't have the disk space and are installing direct from floppies, we hope you enjoy the billboards! Every few minutes, you will be prompted to remove one disk and insert another. Follow the instructions and in perhaps 25 minutes (more or less depending on your equipment), you'll have completed the installation process.

►► Post-Installation Choices

After dBASE for Windows has been installed, the installation program asks you if you would like a dBASE for Windows group built for the Program Manager. This dialog box is shown in Figure A.8. We suggest that you choose Continue to have this group created for you.

FIGURE A.8 

Choosing to have a new group created

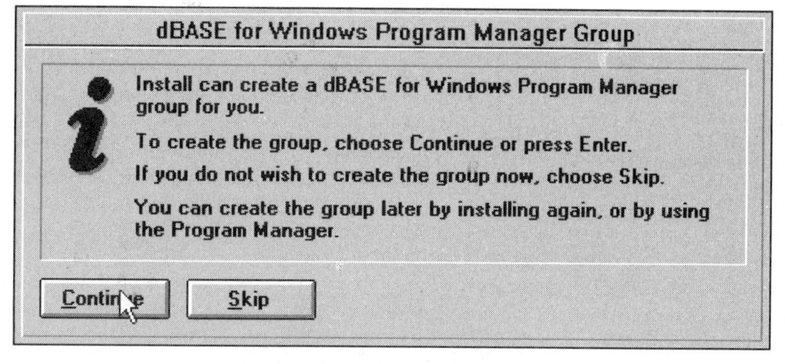

Even if you intend to move the dBASE for Windows program icons into other groups, it's easiest to start with all of them available. Dragging the icons from the dBASE for Windows group into other groups is easier than setting them up from scratch.

If you don't want this group, you can Skip this step, or you can Continue, and then delete the group once you have moved the icons into whatever groups you choose.

The next dialog box, shown in Figure A.9, gives you an opportunity to examine the READ.ME file. This will show you any last-minute changes that Borland has made in your version of the product, so we strongly urge you to spend some time with this file.

FIGURE A.9 

A chance to check last-minute changes

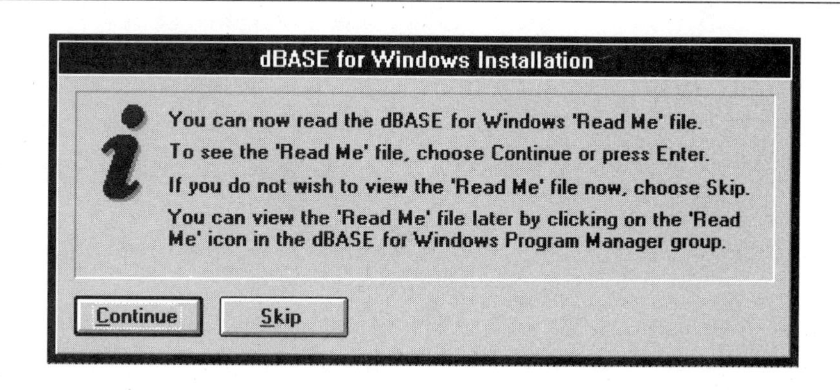

If you don't have time right now (or simply don't have patience) you can Skip the READ.ME file. It's available as an icon in the dBASE for Windows group, which you can click anytime. You may prefer to print the file and read it from the printed copy at a more opportune time.

Finally, the dBASE for Windows Install Notification dialog box tells you that your installation is complete, as you see in Figure A.10.

FIGURE A.10

Your installation is complete.

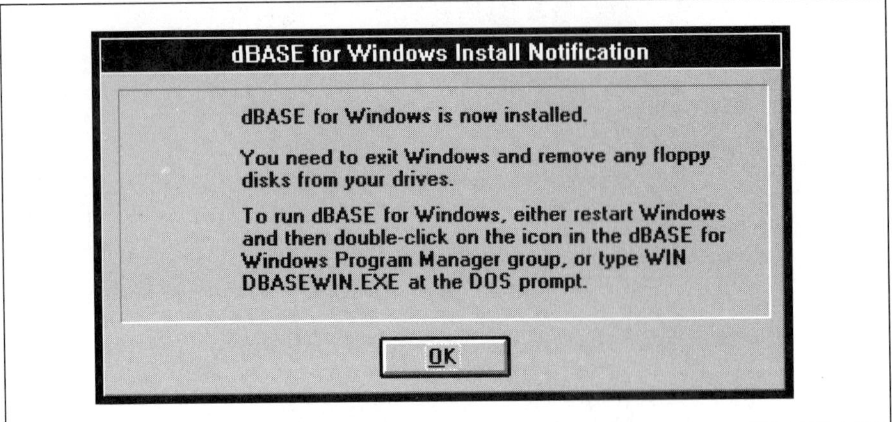

This screen explains the next steps you need to take to begin using dBASE for Windows.

APPENDIX B

The Common Dialog Boxes

▶▶ **In** your work with dBASE for Windows, you'll see lots of dialog boxes. Many of them are covered under their related topics. For example, the Navigator Properties dialog box is covered along with the rest of the Navigator in Chapter 8.

Other dialog boxes are used throughout dBASE for Windows. For example, the Open File dialog box is used by almost every design tool and run process. You'll see an Open File dialog under many titles, such as:

- Open Table
- Open Catalog
- Insert from File
- Copy to File
- Execute Program

All of these are actually variations of the same dialog box. This appendix covers these common dialog boxes. It also covers dialog box components, such as the field-selector and the Scope panel, which are used in many different dialog boxes.

Before we get to the specifics, however, we'll begin with a general discussion of the various types of dialog boxes.

▶▶ *Dialog Box Types*

The dialog boxes appear in three types of windows:

- Parent windows

- Modal child windows
- Modeless child windows

▶ Parent Windows

Figure B.1 shows the dBASE for Windows application window. Other parent windows are also available from dBASE for Windows, such as the dBASE for Windows Help and Crystal Reports for dBASE.

You can minimize, maximize, and resize a parent window. It can share the screen with other parent windows. Its client area hosts its child windows.

FIGURE B.1 ▶

dBASE 5.0 for Windows parent window

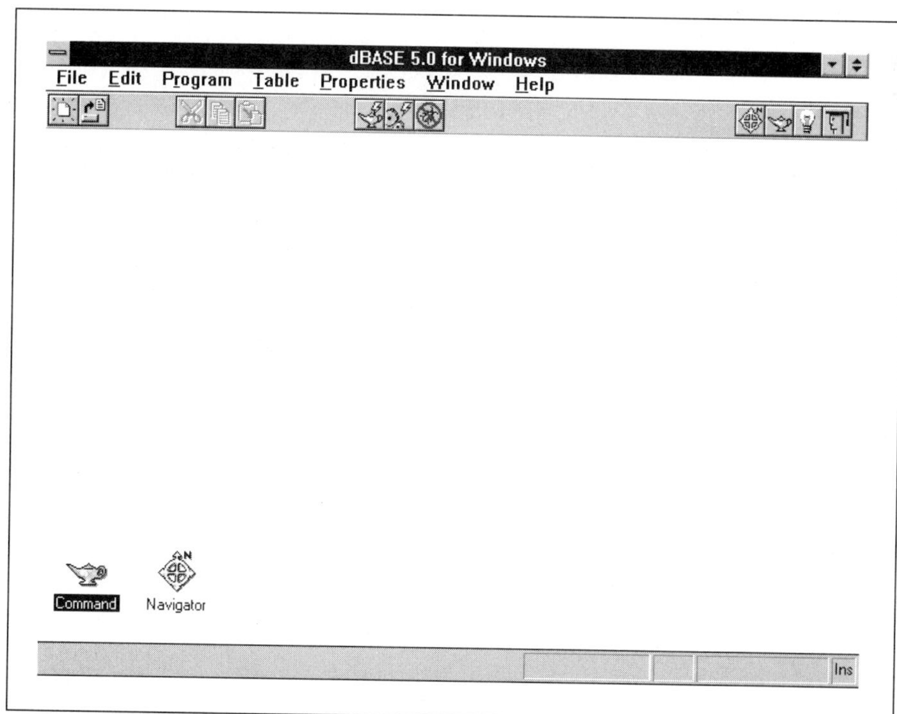

The System menu of a parent window is opened by clicking on the System button, or from the keyboard by pressing Alt-spacebar. It includes these options:

- Restore
- Move

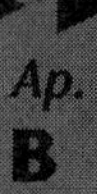

- Size
- Minimize
- Maximize
- Close (Alt-F4)
- Switch To … (Ctrl-Esc)

You cannot create a parent window with the Form Designer, but a programmer can add commands to make a Form Designer window into a parent window.

▶ Modal Child Windows

Figure B.2 shows a typical modal child window with its System menu opened.

A modal child dialog box must be acted on. You need to select OK or Cancel before you continue your work. The modal child does not have a Minimize or Maximize button. It cannot be resized.

FIGURE B.2 ▶

The Open File dialog box in a modal child window

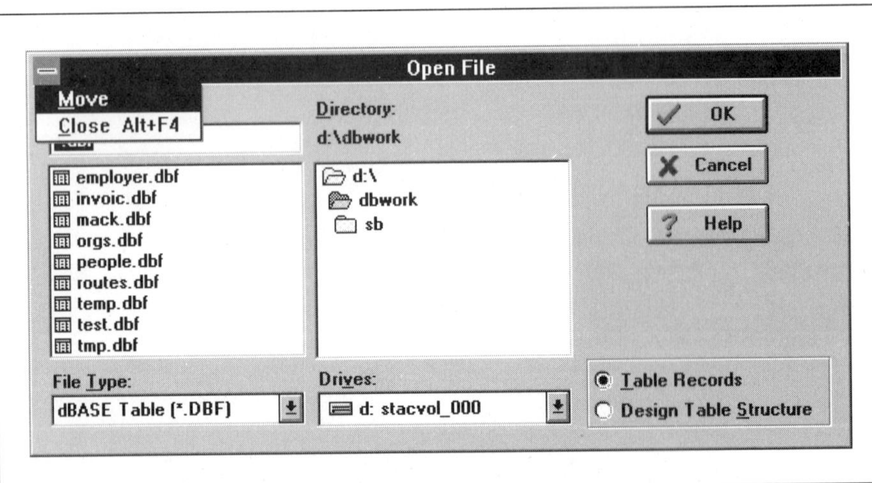

You can open the System menu of a modal child by pressing Alt-spacebar or by clicking on the System menu button in the upper-left corner. The two System menu choices are Move and Close.

▶▶ TIP

Parent keystrokes work in modal child dialog boxes. Alt-spacebar opens a modal System menu. Alt-F4 closes the modal child window.

You can create a modal child window in the Form Designer by specifying .F. for the MDI property.

▶ MDI Child Windows

An MDI child window is flexible. You can leave it in the client area, minimize it, maximize it, or close it. You can size it to meet your needs. You work with it when you want.

Figure B.3 shows the Navigator and Command windows, which are typical MDI child windows. In the figure, the Navigator's System menu is open.

The System menu of an MDI child window has these options:

- Restore
- Move
- Size
- Minimize
- Maximize
- Close (Ctrl-F4)
- Next (Ctrl-F6)

You can reach the System menu of an MDI child by clicking on its System button, or from the keyboard by pressing Alt-hyphen.

MDI child windows are the default window type created by the Form Designer.

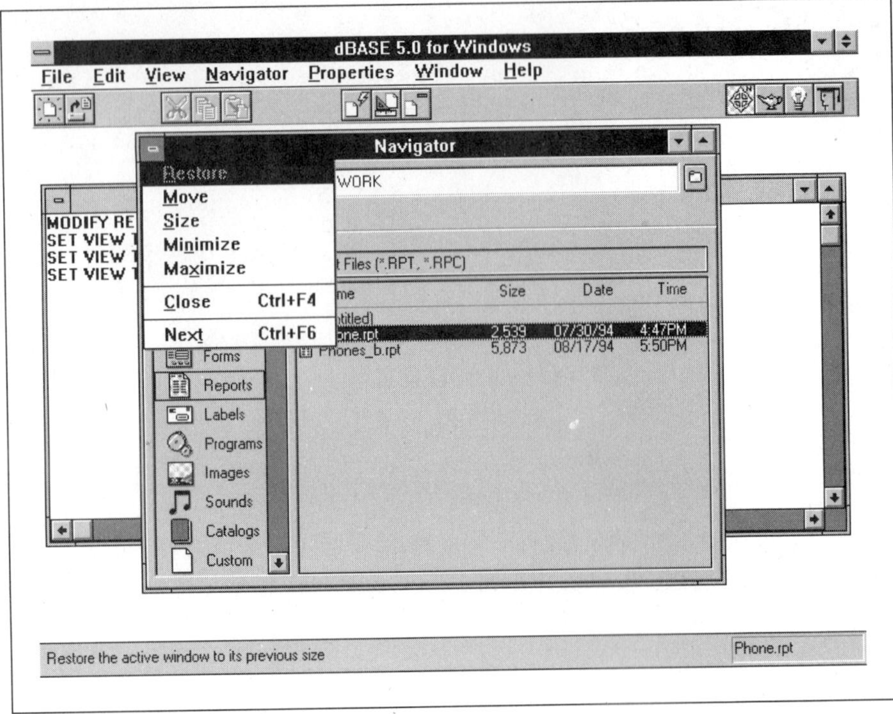

FIGURE B.3 ▶

The Navigator, an MDI child window, and its System menu

▸▸ The Open File Dialog Box

As we mentioned earlier, the Open File dialog box is a modal child dialog box. This dialog box is shown in Figure B.4.

The following dialog boxes are instances of the Open File dialog box, with the indicated file type initially highlighted.

- Open File: Various
- Open Table: .PRG
- Open Catalog: .CAT
- Insert from File: *.*
- Copy to File: *.*
- Execute Program: *.PRG

FIGURE B.4

Open File dialog box

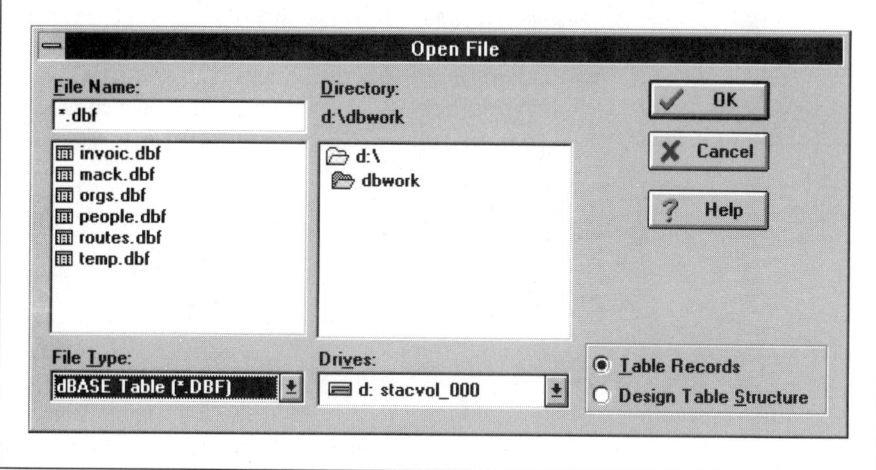

- Import File: *.DBF, *.DB, *.TXT
- Save File: Various

▶ Tabbing Order

The standard Open File dialog box has nine controls. This is the tab order:

- File Name entry field
- File Name rectangle
- Directory rectangle
- File Type drop-down list
- Disk Drive drop-down list
- Radio buttons (if present)
- OK pushbutton
- Cancel pushbutton
- Help pushbutton

Note that in the Choose Program Editor and Choose Memo Editor dialog boxes, the File Types drop-down list is replaced by a single choice: *.EXE.

▸ File Name Entry Field and Rectangle

You can type a file name or a DOS file mask (such as *.DBF) in the File Name entry field. With a name or a mask, you can optionally specify a path, including either or both drive and directory specifications.

In the File Name rectangle, clicking on a file selects the file. Double-clicking selects and completes (implies an OK click) the file selection. A vertical scroll bar appears if there are more files listed than fit in the rectangle.

▸ The Directory Rectangle

In the Directory rectangle, clicking on any entry expands the entry. Clicking on a directory, for instance, immediately shows the subdirectories of that directory and updates the list in the File Name rectangle. A vertical scroll bar appears if there are more directories and subdirectories than fit in the rectangle.

▸ Available File Types

The File Type drop-down list shows the available choices. This is a cramped box, with a miniscule elevator covering a lot of choices. We prefer to type the mask into the File Name entry field.

The following file types are available:

- All (*.*)
- dBASE Table (*.DBF)
- Paradox Table (*.DB)
- Query by Example (*.QBE)
- View (*.VUE)
- Filter (*.QRY)
- Form (*.WFM)
- Format (*.FMT)
- Crystal Report (*.RPT)
- Crystal Cross-Tab (*.RPC)

- dBASE ➤ DOS Report (*.FRM)
- dBASE ➤ DOS Label (*.LBG)
- Crystal Label (*.RPL)
- dBASE ➤ DOS Label (*.LBL)
- dBASE ➤ DOS Report (*.FRG)
- Program Source (*.PRG)
- Bitmap (*.BMP)
- PC Paintbrush TM (*.PCX)
- Sound (*.WAV)
- Catalog (*.CAT)
- Menu (*.MNU)

These file types disappear if Older File Types is not checked in the Properties ➤ Desktop, Files tab:

- View (*.VUE)
- Filter (*.QRY)
- Format (*.FMT)
- dBASE/DOS Report (*.FRM)
- dBASE/DOS Label (*.LBG)
- dBASE/DOS Label (*.LBL)
- dBASE/DOS Report (*.FRG)

You gain the following compiled file types:

- *.QBO
- *.FRO
- *.WFO
- *.MNO
- *.LBO

► The Disk Drive Drop-down List

The Disk Drive list lets you choose from your disk drives. The list includes drive letters and drive volume names (if your drives have volume names).

► The Radio Buttons

For most file types, the radio buttons let you choose between Design and Run modes, but this varies, depending on the file type. These are the choices:

- *.*: No radio buttons
- .DBF and .DB: Table Records and Design Table Structure
- .QBE: Run Query and Design Query
- .VUE and .QRY: Run Query
- .FMT: Run Form and Design Form
- .FRM: Run Report
- .RPT, .RPC, and .FRG: Run Report and Design Report
- .LBG and .RPL: Run Labels and Design Labels
- .LBL: Run Labels
- .PRG: Do and Design Program
- .BMP and .PCX: Display Image and Design Image
- .WAV: Play Sound and Design Sound
- .CAT: Open Catalog
- .MNU: Design Menu

►► The Choose Directory Dialog Box

The Choose Directory dialog box is a modal child window. It has three entry rectangles: Directories, Files, and Drives, as shown in Figure B.5.

The Directories rectangle works in the same way as its sibling in the Open File dialog box. The name that is selected is also reported in the upper-left, above this rectangle.

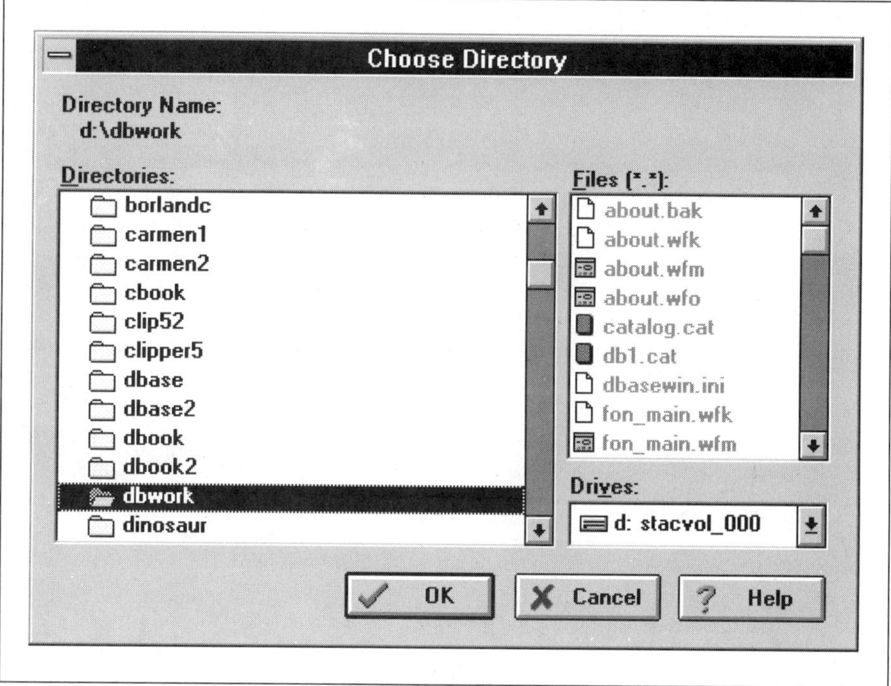

FIGURE B.5

The Choose Directory dialog box

The Files box shows the files (*.*) in the directory, for your reference. The Drives rectangle also works as does its sibling in the Open File dialog box.

The Font Dialog Box

The Font dialog box, shown in Figure B.6, is part of Microsoft Windows, not dBASE for Windows. It is used whenever you want to make or change a font selection. For its use, consult your Windows documentation.

WARNING

Although the Font dialog box will not allow you to choose an invalid Font name or Font Style, it will accept any number in the Size box. Except for scalable fonts, such as TrueType fonts, only the sizes in the Size combination list box are actually available.

FIGURE B.6

Font dialog box

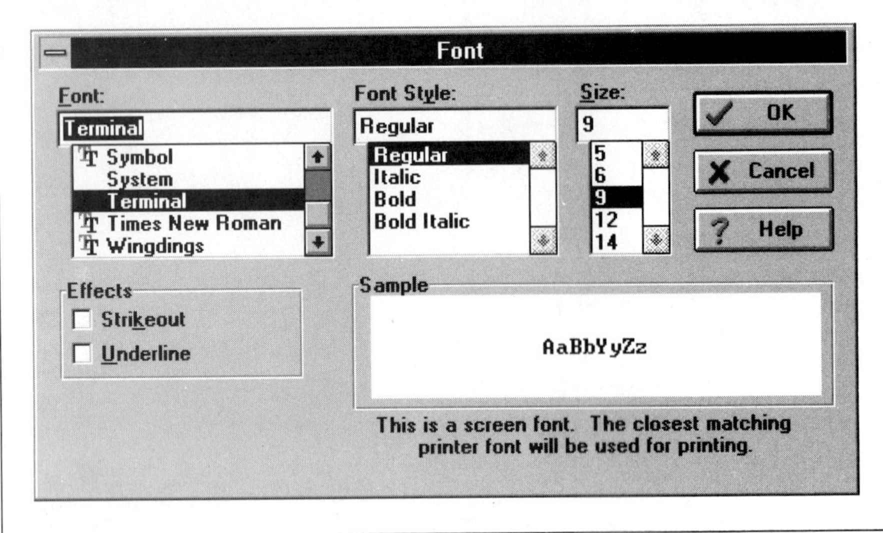

▸▸ Select Window Dialog Box

The Select Window dialog box is shown in Figure B.7. It appears when you use more than seven dBASE for Windows child windows (nine, counting Navigator and Command) and choose Window ➤ More Windows….

With this box, you can choose from any of your open windows. A window is listed here whether it is open in the client area or minimized as an icon.

▸▸ Manage Indexes Dialog Box

The Manage Indexes dialog box is available from several different places:

- From the Table Utilities menu, which is a Table menu choice when a form or the Table Records tool is active
- From the Structure menu when the Table Structure tool is active
- From the Query menu when the Query Designer is active

The Manage Indexes dialog box lets you control the contents of each table's production .MDX file, which is the one whose name matches

FIGURE B.7 

Select Window dialog box

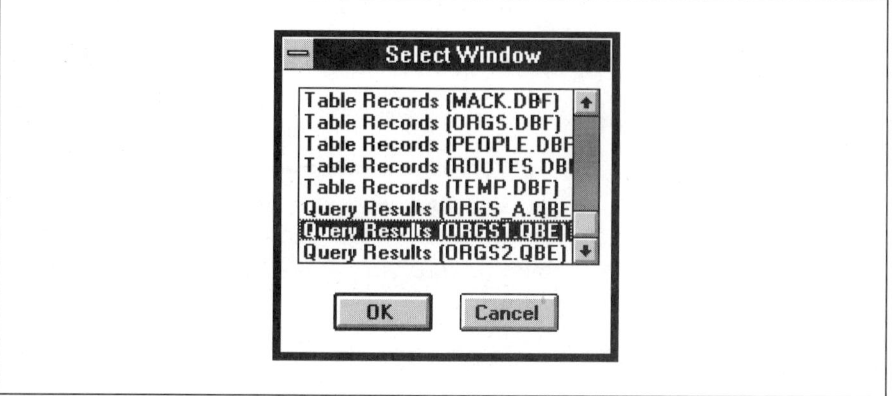

the .DBF file name. This .MDX file is opened automatically when you open the .DBF file. If the Natural Order choice is not the main choice, it assigns a default index to the table.

The title bar of the Manage Indexes dialog box shows the name of the .DBF file in parentheses, as you see in Figure B.8.

FIGURE B.8

Manage Indexes dialog box

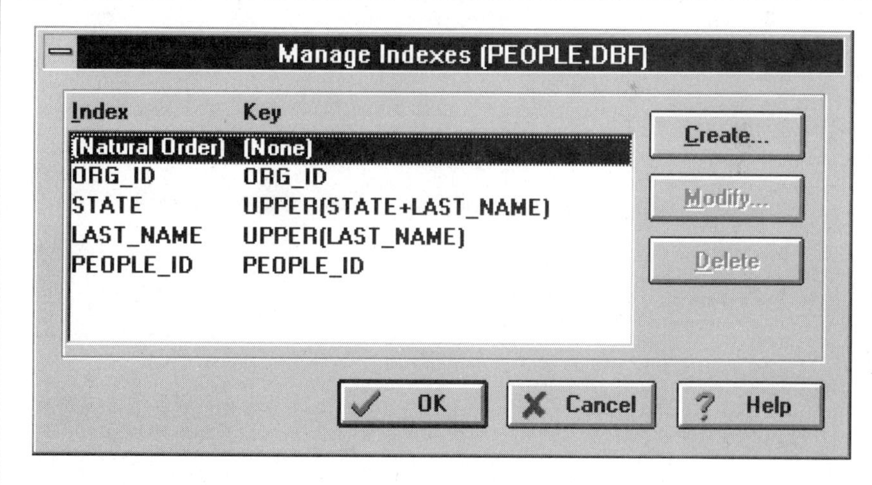

The Manage Indexes dialog box has Create ..., Modify ..., and Delete buttons. If the (Natural Order) index is highlighted, the Modify and Delete choices are grayed (not available). When an index is highlighted, those choices become available. The Create and Modify buttons both

open the Index type of dialog box, which will be labeled Create Index or Modify Index.

▸▸ **WARNING**

When you choose OK, the currently highlighted index tag becomes the default index. Be sure that the main index (which might not be the last one you created or modified) is highlighted before leaving this dialog box.

▸▸ Index Dialog Box

The Index dialog box, which appears when you choose Create … or Modify … in the Manage Indexes dialog box, is shown in Figure B.9.

FIGURE B.9 

The Index dialog box used to modify an index

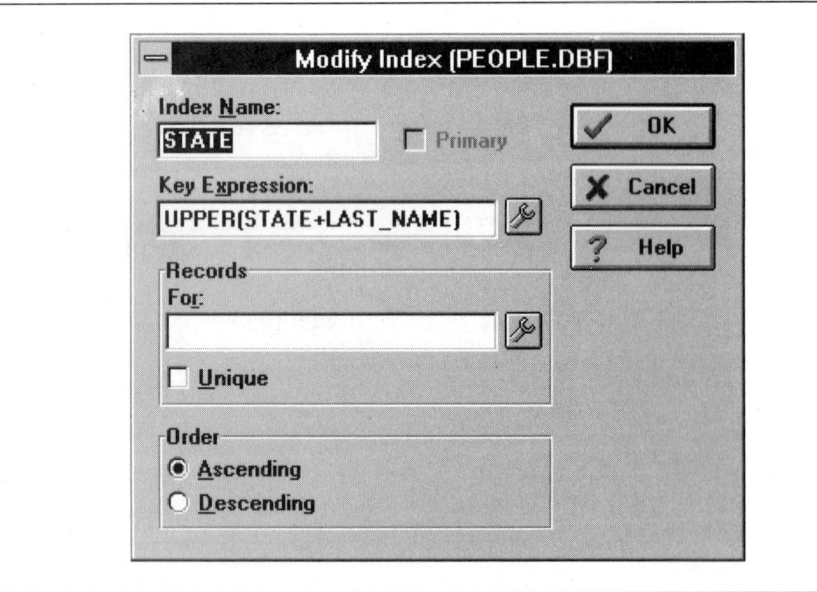

▸ Name and Key Expression

The Index dialog box includes entry fields for Index Name and Key Expression. You assign a name to each index tag and enter an expression.

(See Chapter 12 for more information about dBASE for Windows expressions.)

A check box to the right of the Name field allows you to select an index as the primary one if the table type supports primary indexing. (Paradox and some databases do; .DBF tables do not support this feature.)

To the right of the key expression is a pushbutton with the tool icon. Clicking this icon calls the Build Expression dialog box (see Chapter 8).

▶ For and Unique Records Options

The Records rectangle includes a For entry field, the tool icon pushbutton, and a Unique check box. Assigning a For expression indexes only those records for which the expression is True. For example, if the expression "state = 'CA'" were entered, only those records where the "state" value was "CA" would be indexed.

Note that the For expression need not be related to the index expression. Clicking on the tool icon pushbutton lets you use the Build Expression dialog box to create this expression.

When you use an index with a For clause, your data table will appear to contain only those records where the expression is True.

▶▶ TIP

If you regularly use the same subset of your records, indexing with a For clause will be much more efficient than using a query to select the same records.

Checking Unique gives you an index that includes only unique values. Once a value is entered into the index, the index will not add another record having the same index expression value. Use this when you want only a single instance.

Assume that you wanted to maintain a list of those countries in which you have customers, and that your customer table has a COUNTRY field. A Unique index on that field would show only one record in each country. Using that index, this Command window command would give you a list

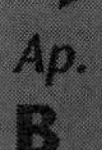

of the countries in which you have customers (the OFF clause eliminates the record numbers):

```
LIST OFF country
```

▶ The Order Options

The Order rectangle has two radio buttons: Ascending and Descending. Ascending indexes *A*s before *B*s, *1*s before *2*s, and today before tomorrow. Ascending is the default choice. The Descending choice indexes in the opposite order.

▶▶ TIP

Descending indexes can be very useful, too. If you have a descending index by total purchases, you will sort your customer list with your most important customers at the top. You may find more use for descending indexes than for ascending when you deal with dates. (Descending gets the most recent dates first.)

▶▶ The Scope Panel

The Scope panel isn't a dialog box, but this same panel appears within several dBASE for Windows dialog boxes. One place it appears is in the Find Records dialog box in the Table Records tool (see Chapter 9), as shown in Figure B.10.

The Scope Panel's four radio buttons let you select a scope for the operation. The entry fields let you impose conditions on that scope. The scope choices are as follows:

- All
- Rest
- Next:
- Record:

FIGURE B.10

The Scope panel in the Find Records dialog box

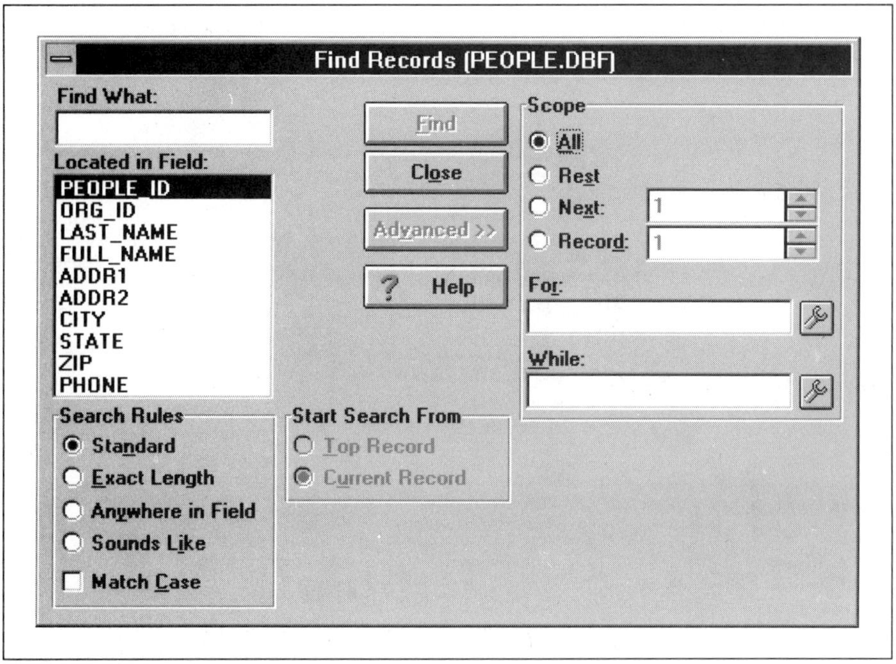

All and Rest let you specify the entire table, or just the table starting with the current record.

The Next option limits the scope to the number of records specified with the spinbox. If the current record is 100 and you specify Next 10, the scope is records 100 through 109. (If the Deleted flag is on or a filter is set, the last record would be the tenth record not eliminated.)

The Record button lets you select a particular record via the associated spinbutton. Note that using this option lets you select a record absolutely. For instance, a deleted record could be selected even though you had specified elsewhere that deleted records should be ignored.

The For: entry field specifies a condition that must be True for the record to be included. The While: entry field specifies a condition that will end the scope as soon as it evaluates to False. For example, the condition:

```
Country='UK'
```

in the For: field would cause the action to ignore any records for other countries. The same condition in the While: entry field would cause whatever action to stop as soon as it came to a record for another country.

There is a precedence order to bear in mind:

- While
- Scope
- For

The action is stopped as soon as the While condition is False. As long as the While condition is True, the scope (all, rest, next, and record) limits the action. As long as the While is true and the record is within the scope, the For condition (if any) is used to decide whether or not to include the record.

Clicking on the tool icons next to the For: and While: entry fields launches the Build Expression dialog box (see Chapter 8).

▸▸ The Choose Template Dialog Box

The Choose Template dialog box, shown in Figure B.11, is launched from both the Picture and Function properties of the Form Designer's Object Properties Inspector.

The Picture and Function properties are properties of Entryfield, Spinbox, and Text objects.

As you see in Figure B.11, the Choose Template dialog box is a three-tab form. Choosing another tab changes the set of choices available for template symbols and format functions.

▸ The Choose Template Panels

From top to bottom, the Template entry field is the target of your work. You construct an appropriate set of functions and a template in this area. The functions and template can be typed in, or they can be selected in the Template Symbols and Format Functions window and Pasted into the Template. The Description panel describes the template symbol or format function highlighted in the window below.

The Template Symbols and Format Functions window shows all the available symbols and functions for the data type selected by the tab at

FIGURE B.11

The Choose Template dialog box, for a Character field

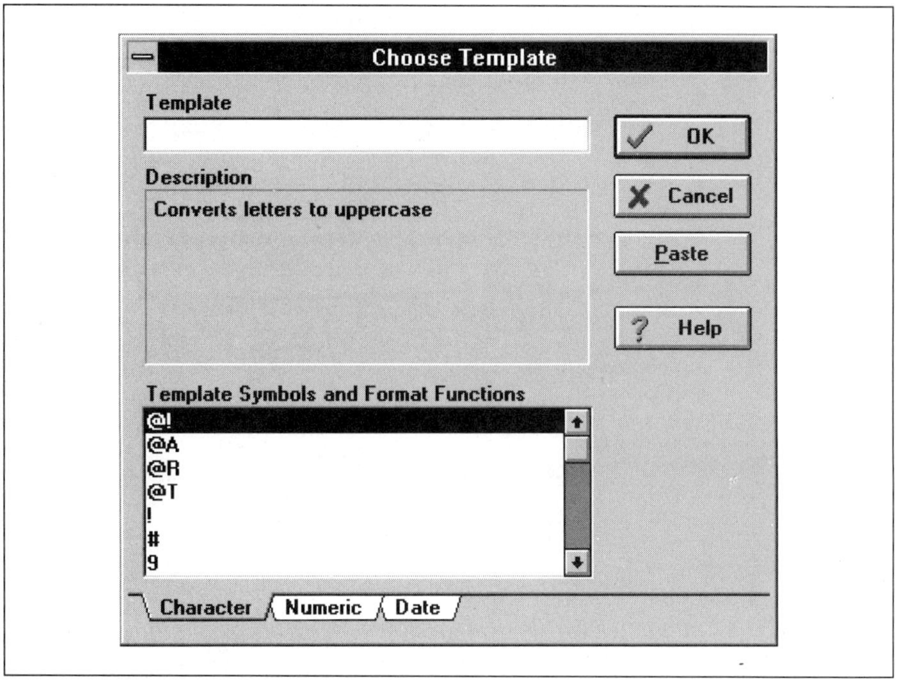

Choose Template

Template

OK

Description

Converts letters to uppercase

Cancel

Paste

Help

Template Symbols and Format Functions

@!
@A
@R
@T
!
#
9

Character | Numeric | Date

the bottom. As you select different symbols and functions, the Description panel changes to describe the highlighted item.

▶ Available Functions and Symbols

A function affects the entire entry. For example, choosing the @! function (uppercase) will convert all character entries to uppercase, regardless of its case when you type it. (When you enter a field name in the Table Structure tool, a "@!" format is active.)

A template, on the other hand, accepts (and possibly converts) one input character at a time. For example, this is a template for an American telephone number (assuming the underlying field is a character string):

```
(999) 999-9999
```

In this template, only the 9 characters are valid entry symbols, so each keystroke is sent to the next 9; a total of 10 keystrokes are allowed. The 9 symbol for character data accepts only digits, so any other keystroke is ignored. You must press a digit for each 9.

When you enter the data, you see blank spaces where the 9s are in the template, as well as the blank between the area code (the first three 9s) and the exchange (the next group of 9s). The template directs your typing into the appropriate character positions.

The set of applicable template symbols and functions changes depending on the type of data being formatted. In the case of the 9 symbol, the meaning also changes depending on the data type.

Formatting Character Data

The following functions are available to format character data:

- @!: Capitalize all letters; allow all characters
- @A: Allow only letter characters
- @R: Expand to fill template
- @T: On display, trim leading blanks

If you supply an @R function, the field need be only as long as the number of typed characters in the template. For example, consider the phone number template (999) 999-9999 again. There are 14 characters in the field, but only 10 characters can be typed. If you use the @R format, you can store this data in a 10-byte field. The template will expand the stored bytes into the format you see here. In storage, however, the punctuation marks and the interior blank space will be discarded.

@R saves data table space, but it can make your tables harder to read. Consider these two phone numbers:

```
(212) 445-1379
2124451379
```

The first was stored in a 14-character field, not using the @R function. The latter was stored in a 10-character field, using the @R function.

The following symbols are available for character data templates:

- !: Capitalize, if the character is a letter
- #: Allow digit, space, +, or - only
- 9: Allow digit only

- A: Allow any alphabetic character
- L: Allow T, t, Y, y, F, f, N, or n.
- Y: Accept any logical, but always display Y, y, N, or n
- X: Accept any character

The L and Y template symbols may also be used if the associated entry field's type is Logical.

Formatting Numeric Data

Numbers may also be formatted with functions and templates. The templates are always given using the American symbol conventions: the currency symbol is a dollar sign ($), the numeric separator is a comma (,) and the decimal point is a period (.). When the number is displayed, these symbols are replaced by the ones specified in the Desktop Properties dialog box, Country tab, or specified by these Command window commands:

- SET CURRENCY TO
- SET SEPARATOR TO
- SET POINT TO

The numeric functions are as follows:

- @$: Show the currency symbol
- @Z: Replace a zero value with all spaces
- @^: Use scientific notation

The following template symbols are available:

- *: Fill leading spaces with the asterisk (*) character
- ,: Insert the separator character
- .: Insert the decimal point character
- 9: Allow any digit, or leading sign (+ or –)

Formatting Dates

The primary means of formatting dates is through the specifications in the Desktop Properties dialog box, Country tab, or through the Command window with a SET DATE TO command (see Chapter 13).

The following two functions are allowed in the Choose Template dialog box:

- @D: Use the currently selected date format
- @E: Use the European format, *DD/MM/YY*

►► Field Selectors

Many dialog boxes allow you to choose fields by selecting from a list. Available fields are shown in a rectangle on the left, and selected fields are displayed in a rectangle on the right. Figure B.12 shows the Table Records Properties dialog box, which includes a field selector.

FIGURE B.12 ►

A typical field selector in a dialog box

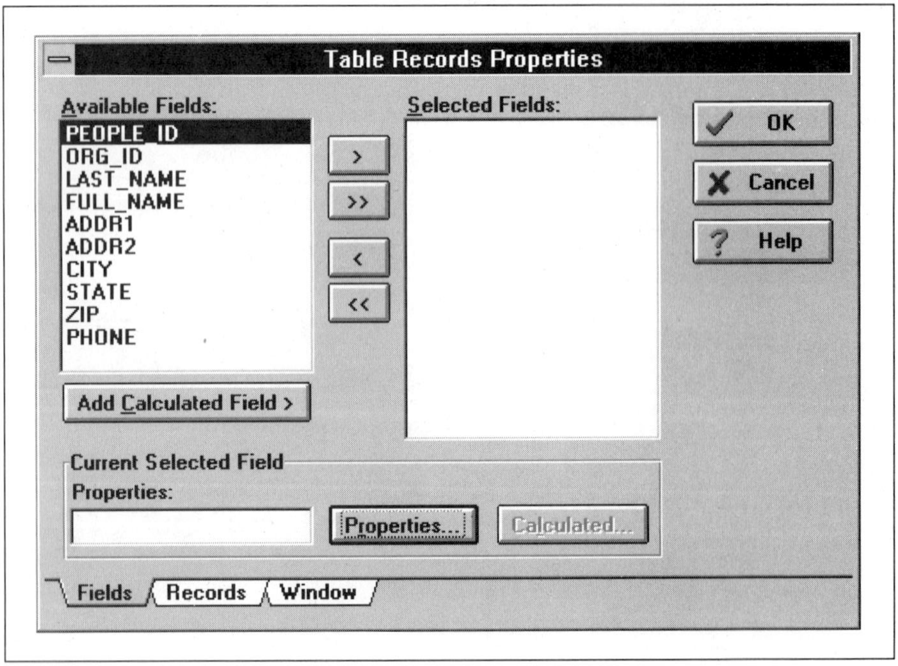

In most field selectors, the Available Fields: rectangle and the Selected Fields: rectangle (the names and hot keys change, but the purpose is always the same) are the same size. In this field selector, the Add Calculated Field pushbutton reduces the size of the Available Fields rectangle.

But this is typical of most field selectors—they all have minor variations based on their purpose. There are two keys to understanding the field selector:

- Using the pushbuttons
- Selecting to control order

▶ Using the Pushbuttons

The angle symbols on the pushbuttons between the Available and Selected rectangles suggest their intended use:

- The **>** pushbutton sends a field from left to right (Available to Selected).
- The **<** pushbutton does the reverse, sending a file from right to left.
- The **>>** pushbutton sends all the fields on the left to the right (selects all fields).
- The **<<** pushbutton clears the Selected rectangle, sending all fields back to Available.

▶ Selecting to Control Order

It is obvious that you need to select a field in the Available Fields rectangle to use the **>** pushbutton. What is less obvious is that the selected field in the destination rectangle is also important.

The destination of the field or fields sent from one rectangle to another is immediately below the selected field in the receiving rectangle. Consider the situation shown in Figure B.13.

We wanted to browse the table, looking at the last name and phone numbers. We didn't care at all about the ID fields, and we were happy to leave the other fields over on the right, where we could look at them if we chose (and not be too concerned about trying to make them all fit).

FIGURE B.13 ►

Putting the PHONE field after the FULL_NAME field

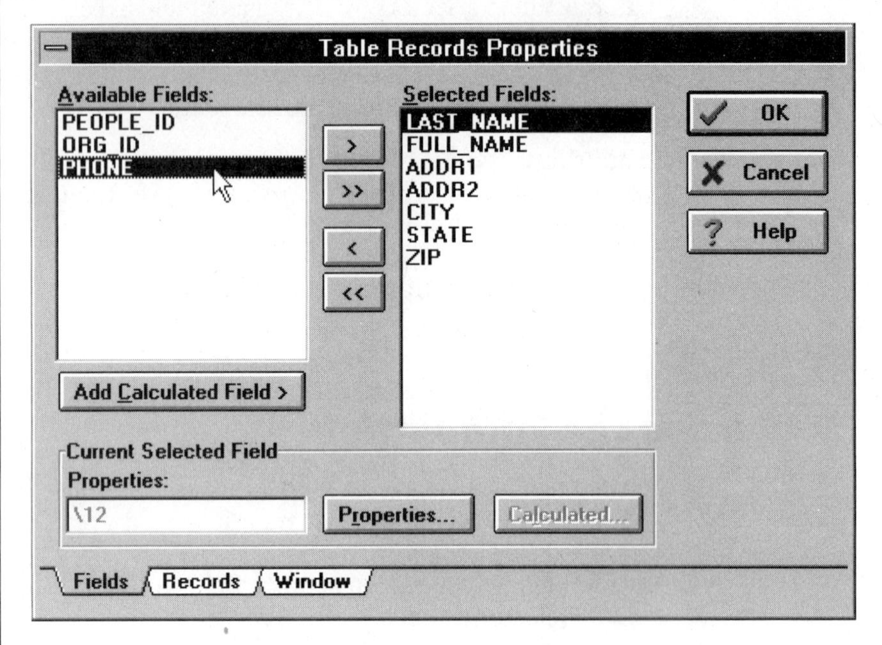

We first selected all fields. Then we used the **<** pushbutton to put the ID fields back into the Available list. Next, we wanted to move the PHONE field from the bottom, where it started, to just under the LAST_NAME field.

To do this, we first selected it (in the Selected rectangle) and clicked < to move it back to Available. Then we selected the LAST_NAME field in the Selected rectangle, as you see in Figure B.13.

When we click on the PHONE field now, it will land just under the LAST_NAME field, which is exactly where we want it.

APPENDIX C

Configuring with DBASEWIN.INI

▶▶ **dBASE** for Windows reads its initial settings from the DBASEWIN.INI file. As you use the program, dBASE updates this file to reflect your current settings. This way, dBASE very agreeably learns your tastes and habits, and conforms to your way of doing things. This appendix describes the DBASEWIN.INI file's uses and settings.

▶▶ What Can You Do with DBASEWIN.INI?

In general, we don't worry about DBASEWIN.INI—dBASE for Windows takes care of it for us. But there are some important reasons for understanding this file:

- You can have multiple DBASEWIN.INI files for multiple projects.
- You can restore DBASEWIN.INI if you lose it (or damage it).
- Sometimes, the *only* way to do something is through DBASEWIN.INI.

▶ Multiple DBASEWIN.INIs for Multiple Projects

Among the data stored in DBASEWIN.INI is the location of your data and other files. If you are working on several different projects, you will probably find it convenient to keep your work in different directories.

We'll show you how to create multiple copies of DBASEWIN.INI, which you can register in Microsoft Windows with separate icons. Each icon can represent a different dBASE for Windows project.

▶ Recovering the Original DBASEWIN.INI

If you edit DBASEWIN.INI directly, there is always a chance that you will inadvertently damage or destroy the file. Hardware failures, software failures, or simply deleting the wrong file by mistake could also destroy DBASEWIN.INI.

You might experiment with different fonts and other settings while you run dBASE for Windows. If you later decide that you hate your results and want it all put back like it was, you might want to restore the original DBASEWIN.INI.

▶ Things You Can't Do Without Editing DBASEWIN.INI

If you let dBASE for Windows create a new DBASEWIN.INI, your name and company will not be filled in. There is no way to update the sign-on screen without editing DBASEWIN.INI, unless you reinstall dBASE for Windows.

▶▶ Using Multiple Copies of DBASEWIN.INI

One way to use multiple copies of DBASEWIN.INI is to have a DBASEWIN.INI file in a working directory, where it will be used when you start dBASEWIN with that directory as the working directory.

We assume that you have set up a \DBWORK directory to work on the examples in this book. Suppose you also want to build your own project as you acquire the skills. Mixing your own project into the \DBWORK directory will get clumsy as you accumulate more files. A better way to work would be to have a separate directory.

Create a \MYWORK (or another name that suits you) directory with these steps:

1. If you are in dBASE for Windows or another program, hold the Alt key down and press Tab until the Program Manager nameplate shows.

2. Release the Alt key, and you will be in the Program Manager.
3. Double-click on the File Manager icon to start the File Manager. From the keyboard, press Ctrl-Tab until you get to the group, use the arrow keys to select the File Manager icon, and then press Enter.
4. In the File Manager, choose File ➤ Create Directory....
5. Type **\MYWORK** in the name box, and press Enter or click on OK.
6. Select the dBASE for Windows icon in the dBASE for Windows group. Then choose File ➤ Copy. In the Copy Program Item dialog box, choose the dBASE for Windows group. You now have two dBASE for Windows icons in your group.
7. Select the new dBASE for Windows icon and press Alt-Enter (or choose File ➤ Properties). In the Program Item Properties dialog box, change the Description line to something appropriate, such as **dBASE for \MYWORK**.
8. Enter **\MYWORK** in the Working Directory field. Then click on OK or press Enter.

You now have two icons in your group, which will use dBASE for Windows in different working directories. You can make as many of these as you like. (These entries only take a few bytes each in your group file.)

▸▸ **NOTE**

Alternatively, you may be able to have multiple .INI files, which you can use within one or more directories, via a command line switch when you start DBASEWIN.EXE in Windows. The switch is DBASEWIN.EXE -C<dbwinini.fil>**. This switch is documented in the 5.0 release, but it does not appear to be implemented. Being able to mix multiple DBASEWIN.INI files with multiple working directories will provide great power to tune dBASE for Windows to the precise requirements of each of your tasks.**

▸▸ DBASEWIN.INI in Detail

DBASEWIN.INI has 25 groups, including the following:

Fonts	ControlsWindow
CommandSettings	FormDesigner
Custom Classes	TableRecords
Install	ProgramEditor
Desktop	Dialogs
CommandWindow	Catalog
Navigator	TextEditor
MRU_Files	MemoEditor
OnOffCommandSettings	QueryDesigner
ObjectProperties	ProcedureEditor
DLL	ExpressionBuilder
Printer	Table Structure
IDAPI	

▸ The Structure of DBASEWIN.INI

DBASEWIN.INI is a set of sections. Each section has a heading line and then a series of relevant settings. This is the format:

```
[first section]
FirstSetting=1
SecondSetting=2

[next section 2]
FirstSection2Setting=
```

In the following sections, we'll discuss the settings in each group.

▸ The Fonts Section

The Fonts section of DBASEWIN.INI assigns fonts to style numbers. These keep compatibility with dBASE IV. This is a sample:

```
[Fonts]
1=Times New Roman,12,ROMAN
2=Arial,10,SWISS
3=Arial,24,SWISS
4=Ariston,24,SCRIPT
```

The number is assigned a font name, point size, and font family.

▸▸ **TIP**

These font numbers predate DBASEWIN.INI. Use the Form Designer and Crystal Reports to have complete control of fonts, sizes, and styles—both on screen and on paper.

▸ The CommandSettings Section

The CommandSettings section of DBASEWIN.INI provides one of three ways of setting certain values:

- These values can be set here in DBASEWIN.INI.
- These values can be set through the tab pages in the Desktop Properties dialog box.
- These values can be set through commands given in the Command window or by a program.

The settings you provide here will be overridden by a setting entered into the Desktop Properties dialog box, or given by a SET command. Those settings will be written back to DBASEWIN.INI so your next use of dBASE for Windows will maintain your latest settings.

Dbwinhome

Dbwinhome is a global variable that specifies the drive and root directory for your dBASE for Windows installation. A sample setting is:

```
dbwinhome=C:\DBASEWIN
```

Directory

The Directory variable contains the drive and full path of the current directory. This is the directory you select using the Navigator. A sample setting is:

```
directory=E:\DBWORK
```

Path

The Path variable holds your alternate search path, as provided to the Navigator or in the Command window via a SET PATH TO command. The path is set off by:

```
path=
```

Separator

The Separator character is the one displayed between groups of three digits to the left of the decimal character. In American notation, it is the comma in *1,000*. You can set this in the Command window with the SET SEPARATOR TO command. A sample setting is:

```
SEPARATOR=,
```

Point

The Point character is the character that separates the whole and fractional parts of a decimal number. In American notation, it is the period in *123.45*. You can set this in the Command window with the SET POINT TO command. A sample setting is:

```
POINT=.
```

Currency

The Currency symbol is the one used to denote money. In American notation, it is the dollar sign ($). You can also set this in the Desktop

Properties dialog box or from the Command window with a SET CURRENCY TO command. A sample setting is:

```
CURRENCY=$
```

▸▸ **NOTE**

You can specify the side of the number on which the currency symbol appears from either the Desktop Properties dialog box or the Command window, with a SET CURRENCY LEFT (or RIGHT) command. In the DBASEWIN.INI file, you can specify CURRENCY=LEFT **in the OnOffCommandSettings section.**

Date

The Date format specifies the display characteristics of Date fields and variables. You can choose one of the following:

- AMERICAN
- ANSI
- BRITISH
- FRENCH
- ITALIAN
- GERMAN
- JAPAN
- USA
- YMD
- MDY
- DMY

You can also set these in the Desktop Properties dialog bpx, or via a SET DATE TO command in the Command window. A sample setting is:

```
DATE=MDY
```

Mark

The Mark is the character used to separate date components. It is the slash (/) character in *12/31/95*. You can also set this in the Desktop Properties dialog box, or via a SET MARK TO command in the Command window. A sample setting is:

```
MARK=/
```

Refresh

The Refresh setting is the number of seconds to wait between automatic refresh commands. (See SET REFRESH TO in Chapter 13.) A sample setting is:

```
REFRESH=0
```

Reprocess

The Reprocess setting specifies the number of attempts dBASE for Windows will make to gain access to a record locked by another user before reporting an error. A sample setting is:

```
REPROCESS=0
```

Dbtype

The Dbtype setting specifies the use of dBASE or Paradox tables as the default. A sample setting is:

```
DBTYPE=DBASE
```

The other acceptable value is:

```
DBTYPE=PARADOX
```

Iblock

The Iblock setting is the index block size setting (see the SET IBLOCK TO command in Chapter 13). A sample setting is:

```
IBLOCK=1
```

Mblock

The Mblock setting is the Memo field block size setting (see the SET MBLOCK TO command in Chapter 13). A sample setting is:

```
MBLOCK=8
```

Typeahead

The Typeahead setting specifies the size of the typeahead buffer, in characters. You can also set this in the Desktop Properties dialog box or via a SET TYPEAHEAD TO command in the Command window. A sample setting is:

```
TYPEAHEAD=50
```

Delimiters

The Delimiters setting is retained for compatibility with dBASE IV and earlier applications that use the Command window's results pane for data entry. Delimiters are optional characters that surround input fields. (These date back to the early days of dBASE, when it ran on dumb terminals without even monochrome shading capabilities.) A sample setting is:

```
DELIMITERS=::
```

Bell

The two numbers for the Bell setting represent the frequency and duration of the bell tone if Bell is on. The frequency is in cycles per second. Middle C on the piano is about 256 cycles per second. The duration is given in PC clock ticks, about 18.2 clock ticks occur every second. These may be set in the Desktop Properties dialog box or via a SET BELL TO command in the Command window. A sample setting is:

```
BELL=512,2
```

WP

The WP setting selects a word processor for editing Memo fields. If you leave it blank, it defaults to the dBASE for Windows Text Editor. You can also set this value in the Desktop Properties dialog box. This setting uses the built-in editor:

```
WP=
```

Editor

The Editor setting selects an external editor. This setting uses the built-in editor:

```
EDITOR=
```

Decimals

The Decimals setting specifies the default number of decimals to display for numeric output. You can also specify this value in the Desktop Properties dialog box or via a SET DECIMALS TO command in the Command window. A sample setting is:

```
DECIMALS=2
```

TIP

The dBASE for Windows default for decimals is 2. We think 4 is more generally useful.

Precision

The Precision setting specifies the internal precision for Numeric data, in number of decimal places. You can also specify this value in the Desktop Properties dialog box or via a SET PRECISION TO command in the Command window. A sample setting is:

```
PRECISION=16
```

Margin

The Margin setting specifies the default left margin for printed output. You can also specify this value in the Desktop Properties dialog box or via a SET MARGIN TO command in the Command window. A sample setting is:

```
MARGIN=0
```

Sample CommandSettings Section

A sample CommandSettings section of DBASEWIN.INI is:

```
[CommandSettings]
dbwinhome=E:\DBASEWIN
directory=E:\DBOOK0\WORK
path=
SEPARATOR=,
POINT=.
CURRENCY=$
DATE=MDY
MARK=/
REFRESH=0
REPROCESS=0
DBTYPE=DBASE
IBLOCK=1
MBLOCK=8
TYPEAHEAD=50
DELIMITERS=::
BELL=512,2
WP=
EDITOR=
DECIMALS=2
PRECISION=16
MARGIN=0
```

▶ The CustomClasses Section

The CustomClasses section lists your installed dBASE for Windows custom classes. The default installation installs one custom class file that includes the Borland-style pushbuttons (with a check mark graphic for OK, question mark graphic for Help, and so on).

Each custom class setting has the same format:

```
CCn=<drive><path><filename and extension>
```

The *n* in CC*n* is replaced by a number, starting with 0 for the first custom class, 1 for the second, and so on.

A sample CustomClasses in DBASEWIN.INI is:

```
[CustomClasses]
CC0=E:\DBASEWIN\SAMPLES\BUTTONS.CC
```

► The Install Section

The Install section has just two settings: your name and company as you gave them during the installation. Editing DBASEWIN.INI is the only way to change these, or to add them to a new DBASEWIN.INI file without reinstalling dBASE for Windows. A sample Install section is:

```
[Install]
Username=Alan Simpson and
Company=Martin L. Rinehart
```

► The Desktop Section

The Desktop section of DBASEWIN.INI provides access to some of the settings you can make in the Desktop Properties dialog box.

Position

The Position setting provides the resized (not maximized) position of the desktop. The coordinates are top, left, bottom, and right, respectively. They are given in pixels, relative to the dBASE for Windows client area. A sample setting is:

```
Position= 0 0 640 400
```

CurrentTab

The CurrentTab setting selects one of the six tabs in the Desktop Properties dialog box (choose Properties ➤ Desktop, anytime). You can easily change tabs by clicking on whichever tab you want. A sample setting is:

```
CurrentTab=2
```

The tabs are as follows:

0	Country
1	Table
2	Data Entry
3	Files
4	Application
5	Programming

EditRecordsLayout

The setting of EditRecordsLayout specifies the layout of tables for editing and browsing. You can change this setting by clicking the appropriate speedbar button. A sample setting is:

```
EditRecordsLayout=0
```

The choices are as follows:

0	Browse
1	Form
2	Columnar

AddRecordsLayout

The setting of AddRecordsLayout specifies the layout of tables for appending data. You can change this setting by clicking the appropriate speedbar button. A sample setting is:

```
AddRecordsLayout=1
```

The choices are as follows:

0	Form
1	Columnar

OlderFileTypes

The OlderFileTypes setting corresponds to the Use Older File Types check box in the Desktop Properties dialog box (choose Properties ➤ Desktop, anytime). If it is on (set to 1) the older file types are used. A sample setting is:

```
OlderFileTypes=1
```

The older file types were used in dBASE IV and earlier versions. They are:

- View (*.VUE)
- Filter (*.QRY)
- Format (*.FMT)
- dBASE ➤ DOS Report (*.FRM)
- dBASE ➤ DOS Label (*.LBG)
- dBASE ➤ DOS Label (*.LBL)
- dBASE ➤ DOS Report (*.FRG)

Sessions

The Sessions setting turns sessions on (set to 1) or off (set to 0). With sessions on, you can access a single file in multiple windows, as if you are multiple users. A sample setting is:

```
Sessions=1
```

SpeedBarStyle

The SpeedBarStyle setting specifies the location of the speedbar. This can also be set in the Desktop Properties dialog box (choose Properties ➤ Desktop, anytime). A sample setting is:

```
SpeedBarStyle=0
```

The choices are as follows:

0	Horizontal Top
1	Horizontal Bottom

2	Vertical Right
3	Vertical Left
4	Horizontal Float
5	Vertical Float

StatusMessageFont

The StatusMessageFont setting specifies the font name, size, and style of the messages in the status bar. A sample setting is:

```
StatusMessageFont=MS Sans Serif, 8.0
```

FormExpert

If on (set to 1), the FormExpert setting starts the Form Expert when you enter Design mode for a new form. This corresponds to the Invoke for New Forms check box in the Form Designer Properties dialog box (choose Properties ➤ Form Designer when the Form Designer is active). A sample setting is:

```
FormExpert=1
```

Don't change this one. With FormExpert=1, launching the Form Designer with a blank form requires exactly one extra mouse click. Forgetting the Form Expert for a new table could cost you a half hour.

A Sample Desktop Section

A sample Desktop section is:

```
[Desktop]
Position=
CurrentTab=1
EditRecordsLayout=0
```

```
AddRecordsLayout=1
OlderFileTypes=0
Sessions=1
SpeedBarStyle=0
StatusMessageFont=MS Sans Serif, 8.0
FormExpert=1
```

▶ The CommandWindow Section

As its name implies, the CommandWindow section controls the setup of the Command window.

Window Size Settings

The Maximized and Minimized settings determine whether the Command window will be shown maximized, minimized (as an icon), or neither. These settings cannot both be set on (equal to 1). Your Command window's setting is recorded in these values when you exit dBASE for Windows. Sample settings are:

```
Maximized=0
Minimized=0
```

Position

The Position setting provides the resized (not maximized) position of the Command window. The coordinates are top, left, bottom, and right, respectively. They are given in pixels, relative to the dBASE for Windows client area. A sample setting is:

```
Position=-1 2 513 328
```

PaneRatio

The PaneRatio setting might better be called the InputPaneRatio setting. It is the size of the input pane as a percentage of the size of the Command window. A PaneRatio of 33 would give one-third of the Command window to the input pane and two-thirds to the results pane. A sample setting is:

```
PaneRatio=50
```

PanePosition

A PanePostion setting of 0 puts the input pane above the results pane. Other legal values are as follows:

1	Input pane below the results pane
2	Input pane to the left of the results pane
3	Input pane to the right of the results pane

A sample setting is:

```
PanePosition=0
```

The Command Window Fonts

The InputPaneFont and ResultsPaneFont settings specify the fonts used in the respective panes. These may be set from the Command Windows Properties dialog box (choose Properties ➤ Command Window when the Command window is active). Sample settings are:

```
ResultsPaneFont=Terminal, 9.0
InputPaneFont=MS Sans Serif, 8.0 Bold
```

A Sample CommandWindow Section

This is a sample CommandWindow section:

```
[CommandWindow]
Maximized=0
Minimized=0
Position=6 42 629 155
PaneRatio=50
PanePosition=2
```

▶ The Navigator Section

The Navigator section controls the setup of the Navigator window.

Navigator Size Settings

The Maximized and Minimized settings determine whether the Navigator will be shown maximized, minimized (as an icon), or neither. These settings cannot both be set on (equal to 1). Your Navigator's setting is recorded in these values when you exit dBASE for Windows. Sample settings are:

```
Maximized=0
Minimized=0
```

Position

The Position setting provides the resized (not maximized) position of the Navigator. The coordinates are top, left, bottom, and right, respectively. They are given in pixels, relative to the dBASE for Windows client area. A sample setting is:

```
Position=112 13 526 361
```

IconType

The IconType setting selects Large, Small, or Detail settings for the Navigator. These can be selected in the View menu when the Navigator is active. A sample setting is:

```
IconType=3
```

The settings are as follows:

1	Use Large Icons
2	Use Small Icons
3	Details

CustomFilesSkeletonList

The CustomFilesSkeletonList is the list of file skeletons (such as *.H) you have supplied (if any) for the Navigator's Custom file type. A sample setting is:

```
CustomFilesSkeletonList=*.MNU
```

FileSort

The FileSort setting selects the order of files in the Navigator. It can be selected in the View menu when the Navigator is active. A sample setting is:

```
FileSort=2
```

The settings are:

1	Sort by name
2	Sort by extension
3	Sort by size
4	Sort by date and time

TablesFromDatabase

The TablesFromDatabase setting corresponds to the radio buttons in the Navigator that specify Tables from Directory or Tables from Database. If IDAPI.CFG contains aliases and TablesFromDatabase is on (set to 1), data tables are read from an SQL database. If TablesFromDatabase is off (0), the tables are read from .DBF or .DB files in the specified directory.

If there are no aliases in IDAPI.CFG, this setting is not meaningful—tables are only read from a directory. A sample setting is:

```
TablesFromDatabase=0
```

Icon Spacing Settings

The next five settings control the spacing of icons in the Navigator window. They correspond to the spinbuttons in the Navigator Properties dialog box (choose Properties ➤ Navigator when the Navigator is active). Sample settings are:

```
LargeIconXSpacing=85
LargeIconYSpacing=50
SmallIconXSpacing=105
SmallIconYSpacing=17
DetailsIconYSpacing=17
```

SearchPath

The SearchPath setting corresponds to the status of the Use Supplemental Search Path check box in the Navigator Properties dialog box (choose Properties ➤ Navigator, anytime). A setting of 1 corresponds to a check in the box. A sample setting is:

```
SearchPath=0
```

A Sample Navigator Section

A sample Navigator section is:

```
[Navigator]
Maximized=0
Minimized=0
Position=80 4 531 352
IconType=2
CustomFilesSkeletonList=*.MNU
FileSort=1
LargeIconXSpacing=100
LargeIconYSpacing=47
SmallIconXSpacing=117
SmallIconYSpacing=13
DetailsIconYSpacing=12
SearchPath=0
```

▶ The MRU_Files Section

The Most Recently Used Files section lists the five (or other number) files you have accessed most recently. This provides convenient mouse and keyboard access to the files you are using. You can choose File ➤ 1 to open your most recently used file, File ➤ 2 to get the next most recently used file, and so on.

Order

The first file (by file letter) to appear in the File menu MRU list (choice 1) is the first file in the Order. The next file in the MRU list (2) is the second file in Order, and so on. A sample setting is:

```
Order=deacb
```

MaximumSize

The MaximumSize setting specifies the number of files to be remembered in the MRU list. Five is the default setting. A sample setting is:

```
MaximumSize=5
```

The MRU Files List

The next settings list the MRU files. If there are five MRU files, the settings will be a through e. A sample setting is:

```
a=E:\DBOOK1\WORK\ORGS.DBF
b=E:\DBOOK1\WORK\BUGS.TXT
c=E:\DBOOK1\WORK\PEOPLE.DBF
d=E:\DBOOK0\DBWORK\PEOPLE.WFM
e=E:\DBOOK1\WORK\PHONES.RPT
```

A Sample MRU_Files Section

A sample MRU_Files section is:

```
[MRU_Files]
Order=bcaed
MaximumSize=5
a=E:\DBOOK1\WORK\T.BK,23,2
b=E:\DBOOK1\WORK\T.ASC,23,2
c=E:\DBOOK1\WORK\LINDA.PRG,14,2
d=E:\DBOOK0\WORK\TMP.DBF,0,2
e=E:\DBOOK1\WORK\T.PRG,14,2
```

▸ The OnOffCommandSettings Section

The settings in the OnOffCommandSettings section can all be made from the Desktop Properties dialog box (choose Properties ➤ Desktop, with any tool active). They can also be made from the Command window. In each case, the command is:

```
SET <name> ON
```

or

```
SET <name> OFF
```

The <*name*> in the SET command is the same as the name of the setting in this section.

The CURRENCY setting takes LEFT or RIGHT, not ON or OFF.

A sample OnOffCommandSettings section is:

```
[OnOffCommandSettings]
CURRENCY=LEFT
CENTURY=OFF
LOCK=ON
EXCLUSIVE=OFF
AUTOSAVE=OFF
DELETED=ON
EXACT=OFF
NEAR=OFF
LDCHECK=ON
CONFIRM=OFF
CUAENTER=ON
ESCAPE=ON
DELIMITERS=OFF
BELL=ON
FULLPATH=OFF
SPACE=ON
COVERAGE=OFF
DEVELOPMENT=ON
DESIGN=ON
SAFETY=ON
TALK=OFF
TITLE=ON
HEADINGS=ON
```

▶ The ObjectProperties Section

The ObjectProperties section controls the appearance of the Object Properties Inspector box.

Outline

The default setting (1) shows the Object Properties Inspector as an outline-based tool. Double-clicking headings with a plus sign (+) expands a topic; double-clicking items with a minus sign (–) contracts the topic.

If the outline property is set off (0), you are given an alphabetical list of properties.

A sample setting is:

```
Outline=1
```

CenterLine

The CenterLine setting positions the line between property names and property settings. (This line can be dragged left or right with the mouse.)

A sample setting is:

```
CenterLine=136
```

The CenterLine setting is given in pixels, from the left edge of the Object Properties Inspector box.

Position

The Position setting provides the position of the Object Properties Inspector box. The coordinates are top, left, bottom, and right, respectively. They are given in pixels, relative to the dBASE for Windows client area. A sample setting is:

```
Position=272 4 633 370
```

Minimized

If the Minimized setting is on (set to 1) the Object Properties Inspector box is minimized (shown as an icon). A sample setting is:

```
Minimized=0
```

ExpandedCategories

The ExpandedCategories setting is a bitmap of the expanded/contracted outline properties. It is shown here as an equivalent integer. There is no useful way to edit this setting. A sample setting is:

```
ExpandedCategories=722
```

CurrentTab

The CurrentTab setting selects the top tab of the Object Properties Inspector box.

A sample setting is:

```
CurrentTab=0
```

The settings are as follows:

0	Properties
1	Events
2	Methods

A Sample ObjectProperties Section

A sample ObjectProperties section is:

```
[ObjectProperties]
Outline=1
CenterLine=136
Position=385 -2 639 381
Minimized=0
ExpandedCategories=210
CurrentTab=0
```

▶ The ControlsWindow Section

The ControlsWindow section contains settings for the appearance of the Form Designer's Controls palette.

Position

The Position setting provides the position of the Controls box. The coordinates are top, left, bottom, and right, respectively. They are given in pixels, relative to the dBASE for Windows client area. A sample setting is:

```
Position=462 3 630 383
```

Minimized

If the Minimized setting is on (set to 1), the Controls window is minimized (shown as an icon). A sample setting is:

```
Minimized=0
```

Control

The Control setting is the currently set active control. If Mouse Revert to Pointer is checked in the Form Designer Properties dialog box (after dropping a control on your form, the mouse pointer returns to pointer status), this setting is not meaningful.

A sample setting is:

```
Control=0
```

A Sample ControlsWindow Section

A sample ControlsWindow section is:

```
[ControlsWindow]
Position=-2 -2 166 382
Minimized=0
Control=0
```

► The FormDesigner Section

The FormDesigner section establishes values for the Form Designer tool. You can also set these values in the Form Designer, but you cannot access them through Command window commands.

ShowGrid

A setting of 0 for ShowGrid specifies that grids are not shown. A 1 value specifies that grids are shown. A sample setting is:

```
ShowGrid=0
```

The Related Tools Settings

The Form Designer has three related tools:

- Object Properties Inspector
- Procedure Editor
- Controls window

The ObjectProperties, ProcedureEditor, and ControlsWindow settings determine whether or not these tools are launched with the Form Designer. A 1 value launches the tool. These can be set inside the Form Designer by right-clicking on the form and clicking on the corresponding menu items.

Sample settings are:

```
ObjectProperties=1
ProcedureEditor=0
ControlsWindow=1
```

SnapTo

The SnapTo setting of 1 causes each object you place on the form to adjust its edges to the nearest grid settings (by default, the nearest whole characters). A SnapTo setting of 0 leaves the objects precisely where you put them. A sample setting is:

```
SnapTo=1
```

TIP

We like SnapTo set on. For precise control, we set the values in the object's location properties.

GridOneCharacter

The GridOneCharacter setting selects character units if set to 1. A 0 specifies pixel units. This can also be set in the Form Designer Properties (choose Properties ➤ Form Designer with the Form Designer launched). A sample setting is:

```
GridOneCharacter=1
```

GridPixelUnits

The GridPixelUnits setting applies if GridOneCharacter is set to 1. The values correspond to the Coarse, Medium, and Fine grid choices, or to the values you can set for Custom choices in the Form Designer Properties dialog box. A Coarse grid is 6 by 17, a Medium grid is 4 by 12, and the Fine grid is 3 by 3. The first value is the number of pixels horizontally; the second is the number of pixels vertically.

A sample setting is:

```
GridPixelUnits=8 16
```

MouseRevertToPointer

If MouseRevertToPointer is on (set to 1), after you select an object from the Controls palette and drop the object on your form, the object is not automatically selected. The mouse pointer can be used to drop another tool of the same type. You can continue dropping objects until you return to the Controls palette to select the pointer object.

If MouseRevertToPointer is off (set to 0), the object you drop is automatically selected and the mouse pointer returns to a pointer.

A sample setting is:

```
MouseRevertToPointer=1
```

ShowRuler

The ShowRuler setting is 1 if the Show Ruler box is checked in the Form Designer Properties dialog box. Otherwise, it is set to 0. A sample setting is

```
ShowRuler=0
```

A Sample FormDesigner Section

A sample FormDesigner section is:

```
[FormDesigner]
ShowGrid=1
ObjectProperties=1
ProcedureEditor=1
SnapTo=1
GridOneCharacter=0
GridPixelUnits=6 17
MouseRevertToPointer=1
ShowRuler=0
```

▶ The TableRecords Section

The TableRecords section records the settings of selected entries in the Table Records Properties dialog box (choose Properties ➤ Table Records when the Table Records view is active).

CurrentTab

The CurrentTab setting specifies which of the three tabs in the Table Records Properties dialog box is active.

A sample setting is:

```
CurrentTab=2
```

The choices are as follows:

0	Fields
1	Records
2	Window

The Grid Settings

The Xgrid setting is 1 if the horizontal grids are on. The Ygrid setting is 1 if the vertical grids are on. If the grid is off, the setting is 0. These are available in the Table Records Properties dialog box (choose Properties ➤ Table Records, when the Table Records tool is active).

Sample settings are:

```
XGrid=0
YGrid=1
```

The File Settings

The other settings show the Fields property assigned to each of your tables. (This is the same as the Fields property of a Browse object.)

These settings are highly condensed. If you have made extensive use of the Table Records Properties tool to customize, for example, a Browse Layout view, these records can be hundreds of bytes long.

There is no practical way to edit these except through the Table Records Properties dialog box.

Sample settings are:

```
D:\DBWORK\PEOPLE.DBF=FIELDS PEO-
PLE_ID\H='ID'\4,ORG_ID\H='ORG'\4
D:\DBWORK\ROUTES.DBF=FIELDS DISTANCE,DEPOT_PKUP,
DEPOT_DROP
```

A Sample TableRecords Section

A sample TableRecords section is:

```
[TableRecords]
CurrentTab=1
XGrid=1
YGrid=1
D:\DBWORK\PEOPLE.DBF=FIELDS PEO-
PLE_ID\H='ID'\4,ORG_ID\H='ORG'\4
D:\DBWORK\ROUTES.DBF=FIELDS DISTANCE,DEPOT_PKUP,
DEPOT_DROP
```

▶ The ProgramEditor Section

The editors—Memo Editor, Program Editor, Procedure Editor, and Text Editor—are two instances of a single editor program. The differences between them reflect their different uses. For example, word wrap is normally on in the Text Editor and off in the Program Editor.

Position

The Position setting provides the resized (not maximized) position of the Program Editor. The coordinates are top, left, bottom, and right, respectively. They are given in pixels, relative to the dBASE for Windows client area. A sample setting is:

```
Position=2 22 566 378
```

AutoColors

The AutoColors setting of 1 specifies color syntax highlighting. Turning this off (set to 0) eliminates this feature. AutoColors may also be chosen from the Program Editor Properties dialog box (choose Properties ➤ Program Editor). A sample setting is:

```
AutoColors=1
```

AutoIndent

With AutoIndent on (set to 1) a carriage return sends the cursor to the position on the next line matching the indentation level of the line above. (If you have indented six spaces, following lines are also automatically indented six spaces.) An off setting (set to 0) sends all carriage returns to the left margin. AutoIndent may also be chosen from the Program Editor Properties dialog box (choose Properties ➤ Program Editor). A sample setting is:

```
AutoIndent=1
```

WordWrap

With WordWrap off (set to 0), lines extend horizontally to whatever length you enter. With WordWrap on (set to 1), lines are wrapped to fit within the specified right margin. WordWrap may also be chosen from the Program Editor Properties dialog box (choose Properties ➤ Program Editor). A sample setting is:

```
WordWrap=0
```

IndentSize

IndentSize determines the number of characters that the Tab key will move the insertion point to the right and the Shift-Tab keypress will move the insertion point to the left.

►► **NOTE**

The IndentSize setting applies to the left of any text on a line. Tab stops are automatically set every 8 spaces for tabs on the right of text.

IndentSize may also be chosen from the Program Editor Properties dialog box (choose Properties ➤ Program Editor). A sample setting is:

```
IndentSize=3
```

RightMargin

The RightMargin setting causes a line to appear at the specified position (if the editor is set so that this position is visible). If WordWrap is on, RightMargin also wraps paragraphs so this margin is observed. The RightMargin setting is not available when WordWrap is off.

RightMargin may also be chosen from the Program Editor Properties dialog box (choose Properties ➤ Program Editor). A sample setting is:

```
RightMargin=0
```

A right margin of 0 eliminates the vertical line from your screen, which is the common choice for programming.

Font

The Font setting specifies a font name, size, and style. You can select a font by clicking on the tool icon next to the Font entry field in the Program Editor Properties dialog box.

A sample setting is:

```
Font=Terminal, 9.0
```

A Sample ProgramEditor Section

This is a sample ProgramEditor section:

```
[ProgramEditor]
Position=2 22 566 378
AutoColors=1
AutoIndent=1
WordWrap=1
```

```
IndentSize=3
RightMargin=60
Font=Terminal, 9.0
```

▶ The Dialogs Section

The Dialogs section specifies the locations of dialog boxes. The dialog boxes set here are:

REPLACE	Replace Records dialog box
FIND	Find Records dialog box
FindText	Find Text dialog box (all text editors)
ReplaceText	Replace Text dialog box (all text editors)
More	More dialog box (Continue Display?) in the Command window

The Position settings provide the position of each dialog box. The coordinates are top, left, bottom, and right, respectively. They are given in pixels, relative to the dBASE for Windows client area.

You can edit these settings directly. They are recorded for you whenever you reposition one of these dialog boxes.

▶▶ **TIP**

We slide our Find Text and Replace Text dialog boxes to the upper-right corner of the screen, where they just might not be quite so much in the way.

A sample Dialogs section is:

```
[Dialogs]
REPLACE=32 72 639 446
FIND=184 112 688 464
FindText=176 112 611 250
ReplaceText=-8 216 427 408
More=56 264 269 382
```

▶ The Catalog Section

The Catalog section controls the settings of the specialized Navigator used for catalogs.

The first five settings control the spacing of icons in Catalog windows. They correspond to the spinbuttons in the Navigator Properties dialog box (Properties ➤ Navigator) when the Catalog file type is selected. Sample settings are:

```
LargeIconXSpacing=85
LargeIconYSpacing=50
SmallIconXSpacing=105
SmallIconYSpacing=17
DetailsIconYSpacing=17
```

The IconType settings are 0 for Large Icons, 1 for Small Icons, and 2 for Details. A sample setting is:

```
IconType=2
```

The FileSort setting is 0 for Name, 1 for Type, 2 for Size, or 3 for Date and Time.

A sample Catalog section is:

```
[Catalog]
LargeIconXSpacing=100
LargeIconYSpacing=47
SmallIconXSpacing=117
SmallIconYSpacing=13
DetailsIconYSpacing=12
IconType=2
FileSort=2
```

▶ The TextEditor Section

The Text Editor is the version of the editor that is launched when you give a MODIFY FILE command in the Command window or open a file with a .TXT type through File ➤ Open (or the corresponding speedbar icon).

These properties are the same as in the ProgramEditor section, described earlier, except that word wrap defaults to on.

A sample TextEditor section is:

```
[TextEditor]
Position=0 0 595 394
AutoColors=0
AutoIndent=0
WordWrap=1
IndentSize=3
RightMargin=70
Font=Terminal, 9.0
```

▶ The MemoEditor Section

Like the Text Editor, the Memo Editor is another version of the standard editor, used for editing Memo fields (unless another editor has been selected via the WP property in the CommandSettings section, above).

The default MemoEditor settings make this editor a smaller size than the Text Editor version. See the discussion of the ProgramEditor section for details on these properties.

A sample MemoEditor section is:

```
[MemoEditor]
Position=0 0 400 200
AutoColors=0
AutoIndent=0
WordWrap=1
IndentSize=3
RightMargin=0
Font=System, 8.0
```

▶ The QueryDesigner Section

The only choice in the QueryDesigner is the ComplexIndexes property. This corresponds to the single choice in the Query Designer Properties dialog box: Display Complex Indexes. If the Display Complex Indexes box is checked, the ComplexIndexes setting will be 1. Otherwise, it will be 0.

A sample QueryDesigner section is:

```
[QueryDesigner]
ComplexIndexes=1
```

▶ The ProcedureEditor Section

The Procedure Editor is another instance of the general editor. It has a specialized heading showing the procedure being edited (or other section of a .WFM). For more information about these settings, see the discussion of the the ProgramEditor section.

A sample ProcedureEditor section is:

```
[ProcedureEditor]
Position=0 207 640 388
Minimized=0
AutoColor=4
AutoIndent=4
Font=Terminal, 9.0
FontDefault=0
IndentSpacing=4
RightMargin=0
WordWrap=0
```

APPENDIX D

Other dBASE for Windows Commands

This appendix lists the commands in dBASE for Windows that provide compatibility with dBASE IV and older systems. See Chapter 13 for a discussion of the commands used in Command window and programs, as well as an explanation of the syntax used here.

The @ CLEAR Command

The @ CLEAR command cleared (set to blanks) a rectangular area of the screen.

Syntax

```
@ <row 1>,<col 1> [CLEAR [TO <row 2 >,<col 2 >]]
```

The @ FILL Command

The @ FILL command colored a rectangular area on the screen.

Syntax

```
@ <row 1>,<col 1> FILL TO <row 2 >,<col 2 > [COLOR <color>]
```

The @ SAY and @ GET Commands

The @ SAY, @ GET, and @ SAY... GET commands were used before we had Text and Entryfield objects.

Syntax

```
@ <row >,<col>
[SAY <exp>
[PICTURE <picture expC>
[FUNCTION <function expC>]]
[COLOR <color >]]
[GET <field name> ¦ <memvar name>
[PICTURE <picture expC>]
```

```
[FUNCTION <function expC >]
[DEFAULT <expC 1>]
[HELP <expC 2>]
[MESSAGE <expC list >]
[RANGE [REQUIRED] [<low exp>][,[<high exp>]]
[VALID [REQUIRED] <condition expL>
[ERROR <error expC>]]
[WHEN <condition expL>]
[[OPEN] WINDOW <window name>]
[COLOR <color >]]
```

The @ SCROLL Command

The @ SCROLL command scrolled the contents of a rectangular area of the screen.

Syntax

```
@ <row 1>,<col 1> TO <row 2 >,<col 2 > SCROLL
[UP ¦ DOWN ¦ LEFT ¦ RIGHT]
[BY <expN>]
[WRAP]
```

The @ TO Command

The @ TO command drew a box on the screen.

Syntax

```
@ <row 1>,<col 1> TO <row 2 >,<col 2 >
[DOUBLE ¦ PANEL ¦ <border definition list>]
[COLOR <color>]
```

The ACCEPT Command

The ACCEPT command dates back to the era of teletype-style (scrolling, like plain DOS commands) user interfaces. It prompts you and gets your answer into a memory variable.

Syntax

```
ACCEPT [<prompt expC>] TO <memvar>
```

The ACTIVATE MENU Command

dBASE IV had MENUs (horizontal, main menu style menus) and POPUPs (vertical menus, now normally used as pull-down or cascading menus). After a menu was defined, the ACTIVATE command painted it on the screen and gave it focus.

Syntax

ACTIVATE MENU <*menu name*> [PAD <*pad name*>] [RETRACTED]

The ACTIVATE POPUP Command

The ACTIVATE POPUP command painted and gave focus to a vertical menu (often a pull-down from the main menu).

Syntax

ACTIVATE POPUP <*pop-up name*>

The ACTIVATE SCREEN Command

The ACTIVATE SCREEN command countered the effect of an ACTIVATE WINDOW command. Subsequent @ SAY/GET-type commands referred to the full screen, not an active window.

Syntax

ACTIVATE SCREEN [SAVE]

The ACTIVATE WINDOW Command

After a WINDOW was defined, the ACTIVATE WINDOW command painted it and gave it focus. Subsequent @ SAY/GET commands were contained in the active window.

Syntax

ACTIVATE WINDOW <*window name* 1> [, <*window name 2* >...] ¦
ALL

The CLEAR GETS Command

Pending GETS (see the READ command in this appendix) were cleared by a CLEAR GETS command.

Syntax

```
CLEAR GETS
```

The CLEAR MENUS Command

The CLEAR MENUS command released active menus. (Menus were the horizontal menus.)

Syntax

```
CLEAR MENUS
```

The CLEAR POPUPS Command

The CLEAR POPUPS command released active pop-up menus (vertical menus).

Syntax

```
CLEAR POPUPS
```

The CLEAR SCREENS Command

The CLEAR SCREENS command released from memory screens that were saved with SAVE SCREEN commands.

Syntax

```
CLEAR SCREENS
```

The CLEAR WINDOWS Command

The CLEAR WINDOWS commands released all windows from memory.

Syntax

```
CLEAR WINDOWS
```

The CLOSE FORMAT Command

Format files (the predecessor to .WFM files) contained a set of @ SAY/GET and other screen read/write commands. They were closed with the CLOSE FORMAT command.

Syntax

```
CLOSE FORMAT
```

The CREATE SCREEN Command

The CREATE SCREEN command created a SAVE SCREEN file.

Syntax

CREATE SCREEN [<*filename*> ¦ ? ¦ <*filename skeleton*>]

The CREATE VIEW FROM ENVIRONMENT Command

The CREATE VIEW FROM ENVIRONMENT command created a .VUE file (earlier form of .QBE) from your working environment, remembering which tables were open in which work areas and how they were related.

Syntax

CREATE VIEW <*filename*> FROM ENVIRONMENT

The DEACTIVATE MENU Command

The DEACTIVATE MENU command deactivated (removed focus from and cleared) a horizontal menu, without releasing its definition from memory.

Syntax

```
DEACTIVATE MENU
```

The DEACTIVATE POPUP Command

This command deactivated (removed focus from and cleared) a vertical menu, without releasing its definition from memory.

Syntax

```
DEACTIVATE POPUP
```

The DEACTIVATE WINDOW Command

This command cleared the active window, retaining its definition in memory.

Syntax

DEACTIVATE WINDOW <*window name 1*> [, <*window name 2* >...]
¦ ALL

The DEFINE BAR Command

The BAR in a POPUP menu was the predecessor to our Menu object. The clauses here were an early way of defining what we now know as properties of the Menu object.

Syntax

DEFINE BAR <*expN*>
OF <*popup name*>
PROMPT <*prompt expC*>
[MESSAGE <*message expC*>]
[PICK <*character expC*>]
[SKIP [FOR <*condition expL*>]]

The DEFINE BOX Command

The DEFINE BOX command drew a box (bordered rectangle) on the screen.

Syntax

DEFINE BOX FROM <*left col*> TO <*right col*> HEIGHT <*expN 1*>
[AT LINE <*expN 2* >]
[SINGLE ¦ DOUBLE ¦ <*border definition list*>]

The DEFINE PAD Command

The PAD in a horizontal menu was a predecessor to our Menu object. The clauses here were an early way of defining what we now know as properties of the Menu object. They are analogous to the BARs in a dBASE IV-style POPUP menu.

Syntax

DEFINE PAD <*pad name*>
OF <*menu name*>
PROMPT <*prompt expC*>
[AT <*row*>,<*col*>]
[MESSAGE <*message expC*>]
[SKIP [FOR <*condition expL*>]]

The DEFINE POPUP Command

The DEFINE POPUP command defined a vertical menu. The PROMPT options are similar to the DataSource properties in our Listbox and Combobox objects.

Syntax

```
DEFINE POPUP <pop-up name>
FROM <row>,<col> [TO <row >,<col>]
[PROMPT
ARRAY <array name> ¦
FIELD <field> ¦
FILES [LIKE <filename skeleton>] ¦
STRUCTURE]
[COLOR <color >]
[MESSAGE <expC>]
```

The DEFINE WINDOW Command

The DEFINE WINDOW command created the predecessor to our Window objects.

Syntax

```
DEFINE WINDOW <window name>
FROM <row 1>, <col 1> TO <row 2>, <col 2>
[COLOR <standard text> ¦ <enhanced text > ¦ <frame>]
[DOUBLE ¦ NONE ¦ PANEL ¦ <border definition list >]
```

The MOVE WINDOW Command

The MOVE WINDOW command moved a window. It is analogous to our Form object's Move method.

Syntax

```
MOVE WINDOW <window name>
TO <row > [, <col>] ¦
BY <rows expN> [, <cols expN>]
```

The ON BAR Command

The ON BAR command executed a command when the user chose a bar in a pop-up menu.

Syntax

ON BAR <*bar expN*> OF <*popup menu*> [<*command* >]

The ON EXIT BAR Command

The ON EXIT BAR command established another old-style event handler. It specified a command to execute when the cursor moved off the BAR (prompt in a vertical menu). We would consider it an OnLostFocus event handler assignment.

Syntax

ON EXIT BAR <*bar expN*> OF <*popup menu*> [<*command* >]

The ON EXIT MENU Command

Similar to ON EXIT BAR, ON EXIT MENU set a command to be executed when the cursor moved off a menu. We would consider it an OnLostFocus event handler assignment.

Syntax

ON EXIT MENU <*menu name*> [<*command*>]

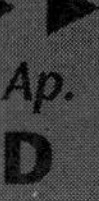

The ON EXIT PAD Command

The ON EXIT PAD command established another old-style event handler. It specified a command to execute when the cursor moved off the PAD (prompt in a horizontal menu). We would consider it an OnLostFocus event handler assignment.

Syntax

ON EXIT PAD <*pad name*> OF <*menu name*> [<*command*>]

The ON EXIT POPUP Command

Similar to ON EXIT PAD, ON EXIT POPUP set a command to be executed when the cursor moved off a vertical menu. We would consider it an OnLostFocus event handler assignment.

Syntax

ON EXIT POPUP <*pop-up name*> [<*command* >]

The ON MENU Command

The ON MENU command set a command to execute when the cursor moved into a horizontal menu. It's analogous to our OnGotFocus event handlers.

Syntax

ON MENU <*menu name*> [<*command* >]

The ON MOUSE Command

ON MOUSE provided a sort of universal, simple handler for the left mouse click. The command was any dBASE command, but almost invariably was a call to a subroutine. The mouse-handling subroutine would query the functions MROW( ) and MCOL( ) to find the location of the mouse, and decide what action to take based on that information.

Syntax

ON MOUSE [<*command* >]

The ON PAD Command

Like the ON BAR routine, ON PAD is an early form of event handler that allowed you to program a response to the cursor moving onto a menu pad (menu option in a horizontal menu). It is analogous to our OnGotFocus event properties.

Syntax

ON PAD <*pad name*> OF <*menu name* > [<*command*>] ¦ [ACTIVATE POPUP <*popup name*>]

The ON POPUP Command

The ON POPUP command specified a command to execute when your cursor entered a vertical menu. It is analogous to our OnGotFocus event properties.

Syntax

ON POPUP <*pop-up name*> [<*command* >]

The ON SELECTION BAR Command

The ON SELECTION BAR command let you associate a command with a selection event (mouse click or Enter keypress) for a BAR (menu prompt in a vertical menu). Today we would use an OnClick event property.

Syntax

ON SELECTION BAR <*bar expN*> OF <*pop-up name*> [<*command* >]

The ON SELECTION MENU Command

The ON SELECTION MENU command let you specify a default command to execute for any OnClick-type events on BARs (menu options) which did not have ON SELECTION BARs defined.

Syntax

ON SELECTION MENU <*menu name*> [<*command* >]

The ON SELECTION PAD Command

The ON SELECTION PAD command let you associate a command with a selection event (mouse click or Enter keypress) for a PAD (menu prompt in a horizontal menu). Today we would use an OnClick event property.

Syntax

ON SELECTION PAD <*pad name*> OF <*menu name*> [<*command* >]

The ON SELECTION POPUP Command

The ON SELECTION POPUP command let you specify a default command to execute for any OnClick-type events on BARs (menu options) which did not have ON SELECTION BARs defined.

Syntax

ON SELECTION POPUP <*pop-up name*> ¦ ALL> [BLANK] [<*command* >]

The READ Command

When you used @ GET or @ SAY … GET commands, you defined areas equivalent to our Entryfield objects. These areas were not activated until you issued the READ command. You entered data into any or all of them, and signaled you were done (returning control to the next line of the program) by pressing Ctrl-W, Ctrl-Q, or Esc.

Syntax

READ [SAVE]

The RELEASE MENUS Command

The RELEASE MENUS command released menus, freeing their memory.

Syntax

RELEASE MENUS [<*menu name list* >]

The RELEASE POPUPS Command

The RELEASE POPUPS command released pop-ups, freeing their memory.

Syntax

RELEASE POPUPS [<*pop-up name list* >]

The RELEASE SCREENS Command

The RELEASE SCREENS command released all saved screens from memory.

Syntax

RELEASE SCREENS [<memvar list>]

The RELEASE WINDOWS Command

The RELEASE WINDOWS command released all defined windows from memory.

Syntax

RELEASE WINDOWS [<*window name list*>]

The RESTORE SCREEN Command

The RESTORE SCREEN FROM command retrieved screens from files created with the SAVE SCREEN TO command.

Syntax

RESTORE SCREEN [FROM *<memvar>* ¦ FILE *<filename>* ¦ ? ¦ *<filename skeleton>*]

The RESTORE WINDOW Command

The RESTORE WINDOW command restored windows to memory that had previously been saved with a SAVE WINDOW command.

Syntax

RESTORE WINDOW *<window name list >* ¦ ALL
FROM *<filename>* ¦ ? ¦ *<filename skeleton>*

The SAVE SCREEN Command

The SAVE SCREEN command let you write a screen to a memory file, from which you could RESTORE SCREEN to retrieve it. This functionality dates to the days when DOS computers were strictly limited to 640 KB of physical memory.

Syntax

SAVE SCREEN [TO *<memvar>* ¦ FILE *<filename>* ¦ ? ¦ *<filename skeleton>*]

The SAVE WINDOW Command

The SAVE WINDOW command let you write a window to a memory file, from which you could RESTORE WINDOW to retrieve it. This functionality dates to the days when DOS computers were strictly limited to 640 KB of physical memory.

Syntax

SAVE WINDOW *<window name list>* ¦ ALL TO *<filename>* ¦ ? ¦ *<filename skeleton>*

The SET BORDER Command

The SET BORDER command provided a default border setting for objects such as windows and menus that were defined after the SET BORDER command.

Syntax

SET BORDER TO [SINGLE ¦ DOUBLE ¦ PANEL ¦ NONE ¦ *<border definition list>*]

The SET COLOR OF Command

The SET COLOR OF command picked a color for the item specified.

Syntax

SET COLOR OF
NORMAL ¦ HIGHLIGHT ¦ MESSAGES ¦ TITLES ¦ BOX ¦ INFORMATION ¦ FIELDS
TO [*<color>*]

The SET COLOR TO Command

The SET COLOR TO command set one or more of the colors that were available in dBASE IV-style systems.

Syntax

SET COLOR TO
[*<standard text>*
[, [*<enhanced text>*]
[, [*<perimeter>*]
[, *<background>*]]]]

The SET CURSOR Command

The SET CURSOR command controlled the display of the text-mode cursor. It would be set off when a menu was active, for example, and you would turn it back on for data entry.

Syntax

SET CURSOR ON ¦ OFF

The SET FORMAT TO Command

The SET FORMAT TO command specified a format (.FMT) file which would contain commands such as @ SAY and @ SAY... GET.

Syntax

```
SET FORMAT TO [<filename> ¦ ? ¦ <filename skeleton>]
```

The SET INTENSITY Command

The SET INTENSITY command specified the use of reverse video for data-entry fields or, for color-equipped computers, the use of an alternate color. The old DELIMITERS could be used to delimit fields when INTENSITY was off.

Syntax

```
SET INTENSITY ON ¦ OFF
```

The SET WINDOW OF MEMO TO Command

The SET WINDOW OF MEMO TO command specified a window to be used for editing Memo fields.

Syntax

```
SET WINDOW OF MEMO TO [<window name>]
```

The SHOW MENU Command

The SHOW MENU command made a menu visible but did not give it focus.

Syntax

```
SHOW MENU <menu name> [PAD <pad name>]
```

The SHOW POPUP Command

The SHOW POPUP command made a pop-up menu (vertical menu) visible but did not give it focus.

Syntax

```
SHOW POPUP <pop-up name>
```

APPENDIX E

Other dBASE for Windows Functions

▶▶ **This** appendix includes the dBASE for Windows functions that are useful primarily in advanced programming work or are carried over from earlier dBASE versions to support dBASE IV-style programs. For information about the functions that are used in expressions, such as index expressions, and the abbreviations used in the syntax, see Chapter 12.

The ACOPY Function

The ACOPY function copies part or all of an array.

Syntax

ACOPY(<*source array name*>, <*target array name*> [, <*starting element expN*> [, <*elements expN*> [, <*target element expN*>]]])

The ADEL Function

The ADEL function deletes a portion of an array.

Syntax

ADEL(<*array name*>, <*position expN*> [, 1 ¦ 2])

The ADIR Function

The ADIR function reads a disk directory into an array.

Syntax

ADIR(<*array name*> [, <*filename skeleton expC*> [, <*DOS file attribute list expC*>]])

The AELEMENT Function

The AELEMENT function converts row, column subscripts to a single subscript.

Syntax

AELEMENT(*<array name>*, *<subscript1 expN>*, [*<subscript2 expN>*])

The AFIELDS Function

The AFIELDS function stores a table structure in an array.

Syntax

AFIELDS(*<array name>*)

The AFILL Function

The AFILL function fills part or all of an array with a value.

Syntax

AFILL(*<array name>*, *<exp>* [, *<start expN>* [, *<count expN>*]])

The AINS Function

The AINS function inserts an element or row of elements with a value .F. into an array.

Syntax

AINS(*<array name>*, *<position expN>* [, 2])

The ALEN Function

The ALEN function returns the dimension of an array.

Syntax

ALEN(*<array name>*[, *<expN>*])

The ANSI Function

The ANSI function returns the ANSI equivalent of an OEM character.

Syntax

ANSI(*<expC>*)

The ASCAN Function

The ASCAN function searches an array for a value.

Syntax

ASCAN(*<array name>*, *<exp>* [, *<starting element expN>*
[, *<elements expN>*]])

The ASORT Function

The ASORT function sorts the values in an array.

Syntax

ASORT(*<array name>* [, *<starting element expN>* [,*<elements to sort expN>* [, *<sort order expN>*]]])

The ASUBSCRIPT Function

The ASUBSCRIPT function returns two-dimensional subscripts given an element number.

Syntax

ASUBSCRIPT(*<array name>*, *<element expN>*, *<row/column expN>*)

The BAR Function

The BAR function is an obsolete function maintained for dBASE IV compatibility. It returns a number representing the last bar chosen from a pop-up menu in dBASE IV.

Syntax

BAR()

The BARCOUNT Function

The BARCOUNT function is an obsolete function maintained for dBASE IV compatibility. It returns a number representing the total bars in a pop-up menu in dBASE IV.

Syntax

BARCOUNT ([*<pop-up name>*])

The BARPROMPT Function

The BARPROMPT function is an obsolete function maintained for dBASE IV compatibility. It displays a prompt from a pop-up menu bar in dBASE IV.

Syntax

```
BARPROMPT(<bar expN> [,<pop-up name>])
```

The BEGINTRANS Function

The BEGINTRANS function begins a transaction (for rollback, in case of error).

Syntax

```
BEGINTRANS([<database name expC>])
```

The BITAND Function

The BITAND function bitwise ANDs two integers.

Syntax

```
BITAND(<expN1>, <expN2>)
```

The BITLSHIFT Function

The BITLSHIFT function left-shifts bits in an integer.

Syntax

```
BITLSHIFT(<expN1>, <expN2 >)
```

The BITOR Function

The BITOR function bitwise ORs two integers.

Syntax

```
BITOR(<expN1>, <expN2 >)
```

The BITRSHIFT Function

The BITRSHIFT function right-shifts bits in an integer.

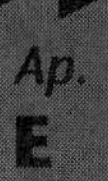

Syntax

```
BITRSHIFT(<expN1>, <expN2 >)
```

The BITSET Function

The BITSET function sets bits in an integer.

Syntax

```
BITSET(<expN1>, <expN2>)
```

The BITXOR Function

The BITXOR function performs a bitwise exclusive OR of two integers.

Syntax

```
BITXOR(<expN1>, <expN2>)
```

The CERROR Function

The CERROR function returns the number of the last compiler error.

Syntax

```
CERROR()
```

The CHANGE Function

The CHANGE function detects record changes made by another user.

Syntax

```
CHANGE([<alias>])
```

The CHARSET Function

The CHARSET function is used in applications supporting multiple languages.

Syntax

```
CHARSET([<alias>])
```

The CHOOSEPRINTER Function

The CHOOSEPRINTER function opens the Printer Setup dialog box.

Syntax

```
CHOOSEPRINTER()
```

The COL Function

The COL function is an obsolete function maintained for dBASE IV compatibility. It returns the current cursor position in a table according to the column number in dBASE IV.

Syntax

```
COL()
```

The COMMIT Function

The COMMIT function requests that internal buffers be sent to the operating system.

Syntax

```
COMMIT([<database name expC>])
```

The DBERROR Function

The DBERROR function returns the number of the last database error.

Syntax

```
DBERROR()
```

The DBMESSAGE Function

The DBMESSAGE function returns the last IDAPI error.

Syntax

```
DBMESSAGE()
```

The DISKSPACE Function

The DISKSPACE function returns the amount of space available on disk.

Syntax

```
DISKSPACE([<drive expN>])
```

The ERROR Function

The ERROR function returns the number of the last dBASE for Windows error.

Syntax

```
ERROR()
```

The FCLOSE Function

The FCLOSE function closes a low-level file.

Syntax

```
FCLOSE(<file identifier expN>)
```

The FCREATE Function

The FCREATE function creates a low-level file.

Syntax

```
FCREATE(<filename expC>[, <access expC>])
```

The FDATE Function

The FDATE function returns the date of a low-level file.

Syntax

```
FDATE(<filename expC>)
```

The FEOF Function

The FEOF function returns the EOF status of a low-level file.

Syntax

```
FEOF(<file identifier expN>)
```

The FERROR Function

The FERROR function returns the error number from low-level file I/O.

Syntax

```
FERROR()
```

The FFLUSH Function

The FFLUSH function flushes low-level file buffers to the operating system.

Syntax

FFLUSH(<*file identifier expN*>)

The FGETS Function

The FGETS function gets strings from a low-level file.

Syntax

FGETS(<*file identifier expN*> [, <*characters expN*>][, <*end-of-line exp*>])

The FIXED Function

The FIXED function was used in dBASE IV functions to convert floating-point data to fixed-point data. You may see it in index expressions created under dBASE IV.

Syntax

FIXED(<*expN*>)

The FKLABEL Function

The FKLABEL function returns the name of a programmable function key.

Syntax

FKLABEL(<*expN*>)

The FKMAX Function

The FKMAX function returns the number of programmable function keys.

Syntax

```
FKMAX()
```

The FLOCK Function

The FLOCK function locks a low-level file.

Syntax

FLOCK([<*alias* >])

The FOPEN Function

The FOPEN function opens a low-level file.

Syntax

FOPEN(<*filename expC*>[, <*access expC*>])

The FPUTS Function

The FPUTS function writes a string to a low-level file.

Syntax

FPUTS(<*file identifier expN*>, <*string expC*> [, <*characters expN*>]
[, <*end-of-line exp*>])

The FREAD Function

The FREAD function reads characters from a low-level file.

Syntax

FREAD(<*file identifier expN*>, <*characters expN*>)

The FSEEK Function

The FSEEK function positions the pointer of a low-level file.

Syntax

FSEEK(<*file identifier expN*>, <*bytes expN*>[, <*position expN*>])

The FSIZE Function

The FSIZE function returns the size of a low-level file.

Syntax

FSIZE(<*filename expC*>)

The FTIME Function

The FTIME function returns the time of the last update for a low-level file.

Syntax

```
FTIME(<filename expC>)
```

The FUNIQUE Function

The FUNIQUE function creates a unique file name.

Syntax

```
FUNIQUE(<expC>)
```

The FWRITE Function

The FWRITE function writes to a low-level file.

Syntax

```
FWRITE(<file identifier expN>, <string expC> [, <characters expN>])
```

The GETCOLOR Function

The GETCOLOR function is an obsolete function maintained for dBASE IV compatibility. It opens the Choose Color window.

Syntax

```
GETCOLOR([<title expC>])
```

The GETDIR Function

The GETDIR function launches the Choose Directory dialog box. It is a synonym for GETDIRECTORY( ).

Syntax

```
GETDIR([<directory expC>])
```

The GETENV Function

The GETENV function gets the value of a DOS environment variable.

Syntax

```
GETENV(<expC>)
```

The GETEXPR Function

The GETEXPR function launches the Expression Builder.

Syntax

GETEXPR([<*expression expC*> [, <*title expC*>[, <*data type expC*>]]])

The GETFILE Function

The GETFILE function launches an Open File dialog box.

Syntax

GETFILE([<*filename skeleton expC*> [, <*title expC*> [, <*file type expL*> [, <*change file type expL*>]]]])

The GETFONT Function

The GETFONT function launches the Font dialog box.

Syntax

GETFONT([<*title expC*>]))

The HOME Function

The HOME function returns the directory of DBASEWIN.EXE.

Syntax

HOME()

The HTOI Function

The HTOI function converts a hexadecimal string to an integer number.

Syntax

HTOI(<*expC*>)

The ID Function

The ID function returns the network ID of a LAN user.

Syntax

ID()

The INKEY Function

The INKEY function is an obsolete function maintained for dBASE IV compatibility. It identifies and deletes entries in a keyboard buffer in dBASE IV.

Syntax

```
INKEY([<seconds expN>] [, <mouse expC>])
```

The ISMOUSE Function

The ISMOUSE function returns .T. if a mouse is available.

Syntax

```
ISMOUSE()
```

The ITOH Function

The ITOH function converts an integer number to a hexadecimal string.

Syntax

```
ITOH(<expN 1>[, <expN 2> ])
```

The LASTKEY Function

The LASTKEY function is an obsolete function maintained for dBASE IV compatibility. It stores the last key pressed in dBASE IV.

Syntax

```
LASTKEY()
```

The LDRIVER Function

The LDRIVER function returns the name of a language driver.

Syntax

```
LDRIVER([<alias >])
```

The LINENO Function

The LINENO function returns the current line number of the active program.

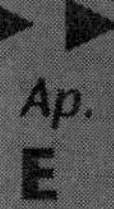

Syntax

```
LINENO()
```

The LISTCOUNT Function

The LISTCOUNT function returns the number of entries in a list box.

Syntax

```
LISTCOUNT(<form name>, <list box name>)
```

The LISTSELECTED Function

The LISTSELECTED function evaluates the user's choice in a list box.

Syntax

```
LISTSELECTED(<form name>, <list box name> [, expN])
```

The LKSYS Function

The LKSYS function gets information about a locked record.

Syntax

```
LKSYS(<expN>)
```

The LOCK Function

The LOCK function locks one or more records.

Syntax

```
LOCK([<list expC>] | [<bookmark 1>[, <bookmark 2> ...]] [,]
[<alias>])
```

The MCOL Function

The MCOL function is an obsolete function maintained for dBASE IV compatibility. It returns the current mouse pointer column position in dBASE IV.

Syntax

```
MCOL()
```

The MDOWN Function

The MDOWN function is an obsolete function maintained for dBASE IV compatibility. It records a mouse button click in dBASE IV.

Syntax

```
MDOWN()
```

The MEMLINES Function

The MEMLINES function returns the number of editor lines in a memo.

Syntax

```
MEMLINES(<memo field>[, <line length expN>])
```

The MEMORY Function

The MEMORY function returns the amount of available memory (RAM).

Syntax

```
MEMORY([<expN>])
```

The MENU Function

The MENU function is an obsolete function maintained for dBASE IV compatibility. It records the title of the current menu bar in dBASE IV.

Syntax

```
MENU()
```

The MESSAGE Function

The MESSAGE function gets the message of the most recent dBASE for Windows error.

Syntax

```
MESSAGE()
```


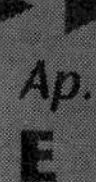

The MLINE Function

The MLINE function gets a single line from a memo variable.

Syntax

MLINE(<*memo field*> [, <*line number* expN >[, <*line length expN*>]])

The MROW Function

The MROW function is an obsolete function maintained for dBASE IV compatibility. It returns the current mouse pointer row position.

Syntax

MROW()

NDX

The NDX function is included here because you may see it in dBASE IV and earlier programs running under dBASE for Windows. Its current equivalent is MDX.

Syntax

NDX([<*index position expN*>[,<*alias*>]])

The NETWORK Function

The NETWORK function returns .T. if running on a network.

Syntax

NETWORK()

The NEXTKEY Function

The NEXTKEY function gets the decimal value of the next key in the typeahead buffer.

Syntax

NEXTKEY(<*expN*>)

The OEM Function

The OEM function returns the OEM value of an ANSI character.

Syntax

OEM(<*expC*>)

The OS Function

The OS function returns the name of the operating system.

Syntax

```
OS()
```

The PAD Function

The PAD function is an obsolete function maintained for dBASE IV compatibility. It returns the pad name last highlighted or selected in dBASE IV.

Syntax

```
PAD()
```

The PADPROMPT Function

The PADPROMPT function is an obsolete function maintained for dBASE IV compatibility. It returns the prompt associated with the pad selected in dBASE IV.

Syntax

```
PADPROMPT(<pad name> [, <menu name>])
```

The PCOL Function

The PCOL function is used for programming printer output.

Syntax

```
PCOL()
```

The PCOUNT Function

The PCOUNT function gets the number of parameters passed to a subroutine.

Syntax

```
PCOUNT()
```

The POPUP Function

The POPUP function is an obsolete function maintained for dBASE IV compatibility. It returns the pop-up menu name currently active in dBASE IV.

Syntax

```
POPUP()
```

The PRINTSTATUS Function

The PRINTSTATUS function determines if a printer is online and ready.

Syntax

```
PRINTSTATUS([<port name expC>])
```

The PROGRAM Function

The PROGRAM function gets the name of the currently running program.

Syntax

```
PROGRAM([expN])
```

The PROMPT Function

The PROMPT function is an obsolete function maintained for dBASE IV compatibility. It returns the prompt of the currently selected menu item in dBASE IV.

Syntax

```
PROMPT()
```

The PROW Function

The PROW function is used for programming printer output.

Syntax

```
PROW()
```

The PUTFILE Function

The PUTFILE function opens the Save File dialog box.

Syntax

```
PUTFILE([<title expC> [, <filename expC> [, <extension expC>]]])
```

The READKEY Function

The READKEY function is an obsolete function maintained for dBASE IV compatibility. It returns the keypress sent to end editing in dBASE IV.

Syntax

```
READKEY()
```

The READMODAL Function

The READMODAL function opens a modal window.

Syntax

```
READMODAL(<object reference> [, <expL>])
```

The RESOURCE Function

The RESOURCE function gets a Windows resource from a .DLL file.

Syntax

```
RESOURCE(<resource id>, <DLL filename>)
```

The RLOCK Function

The RLOCK function locks a record.

Syntax

```
RLOCK([<list expC>] | [<bookmark 1>[, <bookmark 2>... ]] [,]
[<alias>])
```

The ROLLBACK Function

The ROLLBACK function rolls back a transaction (for error recovery).

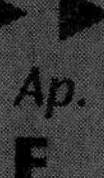

Syntax

ROLLBACK([<*database name expC*>])

The ROW Function

The ROW function is an obsolete function maintained for dBASE IV compatibility. It returns the current results pane row number position.

Syntax

ROW()

The SHELL Function

The SHELL function is used to run an application as a stand-alone Windows program.

Syntax

SHELL(<*expL*>)

The TYPE Function

The TYPE function returns the type of an expression.

Syntax

TYPE(<*exp*> | <*expC*>)

The UPDATED Function

The UPDATED function is an obsolete function maintained for dBASE IV compatibility.

Syntax

UPDATED()

The VALIDDRIVE Function

The VALIDDRIVE function checks if a drive exists.

Syntax

VALIDDRIVE(<*drive expC*>)[:]

The VARREAD Function

The VARREAD function is an obsolete function maintained for dBASE IV compatibility. It returns the memory variable name currently being read in dBASE IV.

Syntax

```
VARREAD()
```

The VERSION Function

The VERSION function returns the current dBASE version number.

Syntax

```
VERSION()
```

The WINDOW Function

The WINDOW function is an obsolete function maintained for dBASE IV compatibility. It returns the name of the active window in dBASE IV.

Syntax

```
WINDOW()
```

The WORKAREA Function

The WORKAREA function returns the number of the current work area.

Syntax

```
WORKAREA()
```

APPENDIX F

Properties of DDE and OLE Objects

▶▶ **This** appendix provides an alphabetical listing of all the properties of the DDELink, DDETopic, and OLE objects. DDE (Dynamic Data Exchange) allows multiple Microsoft Windows applications to share data. OLE (Object Linking and Embedding) has superseded DDE as a means for applications to share information. OLE programming is generally the province of advanced programmers.

Each listing includes the default value (if one exists). If a property is read-only, you cannot assign a value to it. If a property is read-only, it is noted in its listing.

Data properties are called Properties; events and other methods are called Methods. Additionally, Methods' names are followed by parentheses; for example, ClassName is a data property, but Close( ) is a method. Some methods take parameters within their parentheses, as noted in their listings.

▶▶ DDELink Object Properties

This section lists and briefly explains the properties of the DDELink object.

The DDELink.Advise( ) Method

Parameter: *<item>*

The Advise method establishes a hot link to an item in a DDE server topic.

The DDELink.ClassName Property

Default value: DDELINK

ClassName is read-only. This property is assigned by dBASE for Windows for each of the built-in classes. ClassName can be used to distinguish among multiple objects with the same name.

The DDELink.Execute( ) Method

Parameter: <*command*>

The Execute method sends the command parameter as a macro command to the DDE server.

The DDELink.Initiate( ) Method

Parameters: <*server*>, <*topic*>

The Initiate method opens a DDE link between your dBASE application and an external DDE application.

The DDELink.OnNewValue( ) Method

Parameters: <*item*>,<*value*>

The OnNewValue method executes a subroutine when a hot-linked item in a DDE server document has changed.

The DDELink.Peek( ) Method

Parameter: <*item*>

The Peek method requests the value of <*item*> from a DDE application server.

The DDELink.Poke( ) Method

Parameter: <*item*>, <*value*>

The Poke method writes a data item into a DDE server application.

The DDELink.Reconnect( ) Method

The Reconnect method attempts to restore a terminated DDE link.

The DDELink.Release() Method

The Release method removes the DDELink object from memory. Releasing a form also releases all of the form's objects.

The DDELink.Server Property

The Server property is the name of the server application in a DDELink.

The DDELink.Terminate() Method

The Terminate method terminates a conversation with a DDE server.

The DDELink.TimeOut Property

Default value: 10

The TimeOut property specifies the number of seconds dBASE for Windows will wait for the completion of a DDE request.

The DDELink.Topic Property

Default value: ""

The Topic property of a DDE link specifies the topic of the link, as specified in the Initiate( ) method.

The DDELink.Unadvise( ) Method

The Unadvise method tells the DDE server that dBASE wants to terminate a hot link.

▸▸ DDETopic Object Properties

This section lists and briefly explains the properties of the DDETopic object.

The DDETopic.ClassName Property

Default value: DDETOPIC

ClassName is read-only. This property is assigned by dBASE for Windows for each of the built-in classes. ClassName can be used to distinguish among multiple objects with the same name.

The DDETopic.Notify( ) Method

Parameter: <*item*>

The Notify method informs a DDE client application that an item in the dBASE server session has changed.

The DDETopic.OnAdvise( ) Method

Parameter: <*item*>

The OnAdvise method is executed when an external application requests a DDE hot link to an item in the server topic.

The DDETopic.OnExecute( ) Method

Parameter: <*cmd*>

The OnExecute method executes a subroutine when a DDE client sends <*cmd*> to a dBASE DDE server program.

The DDETopic.OnPeek( ) Method

Parameter: <*item*>

The OnPeek method executes a subroutine in response to a DDE client's peek request. The parameter, <*item*>, is the dBASE for Windows item that the client wants returned.

The DDETopic.OnPoke( ) Method

Parameters: <*item*>,<*value*>

The OnPoke method executes a subroutine in response to a DDE client application's request to insert a new value into your dBASE server application.

The DDETopic.OnUnadvise( ) Method

Parameter: <*item*>

The OnUnadvise method executes a subroutine in response to a DDE client application request for the termination of a hot link.

The DDETopic.Release( ) Method

The Release method removes the DDETopic object from memory. Releasing a form also releases all of the form's objects.

The DDETopic.Topic Property

Default value: ""

The Topic property of a DDE link specifies the topic of the link, as specified in the Initiate( ) method.

▸▸ OLE Object Properties

This section lists and briefly explains the properties of the OLE object.

The OLE.Before Property

Before is an object reference to the object that this OLE object precedes in the form's tabbing order. If this OLE object is the last one in the form's tabbing order, Before is a reference to the first object in the tabbing order (Form.First).

The OLE.Border Property

If Border is True, the OLE object is surrounded by a border.

The OLE.ClassName Property

Default value: OLE

ClassName is read-only. This property is assigned by dBASE for Windows for each of the built-in classes. ClassName can be used to distinguish among multiple objects with the same name.

The OLE.DataLink Property

Default value: ""

The DataLink property links the OLE object's value to a memory variable or a table field. When you change the data value in this OLE object, it changes the value in the associated memory variable or table field.

The OLE.DoVerb() Method

Parameters: <*OLE verb*>, <*title*>

The DoVerb method initiates the action specified by the first parameter.

The OLE.Enabled Property

Default value: .T.

If Enabled is True, the OLE object is accessible. You can use the Enabled property to disable options in event handlers. For example, a Valid function could set some object's Enabled property to False if required conditions were not met.

The OLE.Height Property

Default value: 5.0

The Height property specifies the height of the OLE object in characters.

The OLE.hWnd Property

The hWnd property is read-only. This property is an arbitrary integer number that identifies the window to which the OLE object belongs. This is called the window's *handle*. It is used when you access Windows functions directly via EXTERN commands.

The OLE.ID Property

Default value: –1

ID is a number that can be used to distinguish between otherwise identical OLE objects.

The OLE.Left Property

Default value: 0

The Left property specifies the location of the left side of the OLE object within its form, in characters. The leftmost character is number 0.

The OLE.LinkFileName Property

Default value: ""

The LinkFileName property specifies the name of the file linked with the current OLE field for display in an OLE viewer.

The OLE.MousePointer Property

Default value: 0

Available settings: 0–11

The MousePointer property specifies the type of mouse pointer to use when the pointer is over the OLE object. For example, the mouse pointer is an arrow over a form, but turns to an I-beam in an editor. The settings are default (0), arrow (1), cross (2), I-beam (3), icon (4), size (5), size NESW (6), size S (7), size NWSE (8), size E (9), up arrow (10), and wait (hourglass, 11).

The OLE.Name Property

Default value: OLE<*n*>

The Name property is the property name given to this property on the parent form. If the name is OLE1, for example, specifying Parent. OLE1 specifies this OLE object.

The OLE.OLEType Property

Default value: 0

Available settings: 0–2

The OLEType property is read-only. This property specifies that there is no link to an OLE document (0), there is an embedded document (1), or there is a link to a document file (2).

The OLE.OnChange( ) Method

The OnChange method is called whenever you change a value in the OLE object.

The OLE.OnClose( ) Method

The OnClose method is called whenever you close the OLE object.

The OLE.OnGotFocus( ) Method

The OnGotFocus method is called when the OLE object receives focus.

The OLE.OnLostFocus( ) Method

The OnLostFocus method is called whenever the OLE object loses focus.

The OLE.OnOpen( ) Method

The OnOpen event is called when the form containing the OLE object is opened.

The OLE.Parent Property

The Parent property is read-only. This property is an object reference to the parent form of the OLE object. It is assigned when the object is created via a DEFINE command or a NEW call to the constructor.

The OLE.Release( ) Method

The Release method removes the OLE object from memory. Releasing a form also releases all of the form's objects.

The OLE.ServerName Property

Default value: ""

The ServerName property is the name of the server application in an OLE viewer.

The OLE.SetFocus( ) Method

The SetFocus method changes focus to the OLE object.

The OLE.StatusMessage Property

Default value: ""

The StatusMessage appears in the left portion of the status bar when the mouse pointer is over the OLE object and when the OLE object has focus.

The OLE.TabStop Property

Default value: .T.

If TabStop is True, the OLE object is part of the tabbing order. If it is False, Tab and Shift-Tab will bypass the OLE object.

The OLE.Top Property

Default value: 0

The Top property is the location of the top of the OLE object, in characters sized by the form's ScaleFont. The top-left corner of the form is 0,0.

The OLE.Visible Property

Default value: .T.

If Visible is True, the OLE object is shown. Manipulating the Visible property lets you choose among alternative objects on a form.

The OLE.Width Property

Default value: 8.0

The Width property specifies the width of the OLE object, in characters. The width of each character is determined by the form's ScaleFont properties.

APPENDIX G

A Quick Reference to Object Properties by Object

▶▶ **This** appendix lists the properties of each object class, excluding the Array and Object classes. The Array class is useful in advanced programming, which is beyond the scope of this book. The Object class has no properties.

The information presented here is based on one of the first production applications built in dBASE for Window: our database of objects and properties.

Browse Object Properties

Append	HelpFile	OnLeftDbl Click	Release
Before	HelpID	OnLeft MouseDown	SetFocus
ClassName	hWnd	OnLeft MouseUp	ShowDeleted
ColorNormal	ID	OnLost Focus	Show Heading
Delete	Left	OnMiddle DblClick	ShowRecNo
Enabled	Mode	OnMiddle MouseDown	Status Message
Fields	Modify	OnMiddle MouseUp	TabStop
FieldWidth	MousePointer	OnMouse Move	Text
Follow	Move	OnNavigate	Toggle
FontBold	Name	OnOpen	Top

- FontItalic
- FontName
- FontSize
- OnAppend
- OnChange
- OnGotFocus
- OnRight DblClick
- OnRight MouseDown
- OnRight MouseUp
- Visible
- When
- Width

Checkbox Object Properties

- Before
- ClassName
- Color Normal
- DataLink
- Enabled
- FontBold
- FontItalic
- FontName
- FontSize
- Font-StrikeOut
- Font Underline
- Group
- Height
- HelpFile
- HelpID
- hWnd
- ID
- Left
- Mouse Pointer
- Move
- Name
- OldStyle
- OnChange
- OnGotFocus
- OnHelp
- OnLeftDbl Click
- OnLeft MouseDown
- OnLeft MouseUp
- OnLostFocus
- OnMiddle DblClick
- OnMiddle MouseDown
- OnMiddle MouseUp
- OnMouse Move
- OnOpen
- OnRightDbl Click
- OnRight MouseDown
- OnRight MouseUp
- Parent
- Release
- SetFocus
- Status Message
- TabStop
- Text
- Top
- Value
- Visible
- When
- Width

Combobox Object Properties

Before	HelpFile	OnLeft MouseDown	Release
ClassName	HelpID	OnLeft MouseUp	SetFocus
DataLink	hWnd	OnLost Focus	Sorted
DataSource	ID	OnMiddle DblClick	Status Message
Enabled	Left	OnMiddle MouseDown	Style
FontBold	Mouse Pointer	OnMiddle MouseUp	TabStop
FontItalic	Move	OnMouse Move	Top
FontName	Name	OnOpen	Value
FontSize	OnChange	OnRightDbl Click	Visible
Font-StrikeOut	OnGotFocus	OnRight MouseDown	When
Font Underline	OnHelp	OnRight MouseUp	Width
Height	OnLeftDbl Click	Parent	

DDELink Object Properties

Advise	OnNewValue	Release	Topic
ClassName	Peek	Server	Unadvise
Execute	Poke	Terminate	
Initiate	Reconnect()	TimeOut	

DDETopic Object Properties

ClassName	OnAdvise	OnPeek	OnUnadvise
Notify	OnExecute	OnPoke	Release
			Topic

Editor Object Properties

Before	HelpFile	OnLeftDbl Click	Release
Border	HelpID	OnLeft MouseDown	Scrollbar
ClassName	hWnd	OnLeft MouseUp	SetFocus
Color Normal	ID	OnLost Focus	Status Message
DataLink	Left	OnMiddle DblClick	TabStop
Enabled	LineNo	OnMiddle MouseDown	Top
FontBold	Modify	OnMiddleMo useUp	Valid
FontItalic	Mouse Pointer	OnMouse Move	Value
FontName	Move	OnOpen	Visible
FontSize	Name	OnRightDbl Click	When
Font-StrikeOut	OnChange	OnRight MouseDown	Width
Font Underline	OnGotFocus	OnRight MouseUp	Wrap
Height	OnHelp	Parent	

Entryfield Object Properties

- Before
- Border
- ClassName
- Color Highlight
- Color Normal
- DataLink
- Enabled
- FontBold
- FontItalic
- FontName
- FontSize
- Font-StrikeOut
- Font Underline
- Function
- Height
- HelpFile
- HelpID
- hWnd
- ID
- Key
- Left
- MaxLength
- Mouse Pointer
- Move
- Name
- OldStyle
- OnChange
- OnGotFocus
- OnHelp
- OnLeftDbl Click
- OnLeft MouseDown
- OnLeft MouseUp
- OnLost Focus
- OnMiddle DblClick
- OnMiddle MouseDown
- OnMiddle MouseUp
- OnMouse Move
- OnOpen
- OnRight DblClick
- OnRight MouseDown
- OnRight MouseUp
- Parent
- Picture
- Release
- SelectAll
- SetFocus
- Status Message
- TabStop
- Top
- Valid
- ValidError Msg
- Valid Required
- Value
- Visible
- When
- Width

Form Object Properties

- Active Control
- AutoSize
- MenuFile
- Minimize
- OnLeft MouseUp
- OnLost Focus
- Print
- ReadModal

ClassName	Mouse Pointer	OnMiddle DblClick	Release
Close	Move	OnMiddle MouseDown	ScaleFont Name
Color Normal	Moveable	OnMiddle MouseUp	ScaleFont Size
Enabled	NextCol	OnMouse Move	Scrollbar
EscExit	NextObj	OnMove	SetFocus
First	NextRow	OnNavigate	Sizeable
Height	OnAppend	OnOpen	Status Message
HelpFile	OnChange	OnRightDbl Click	SysMenu
HelpID	OnClose	OnRight MouseDown	Text
hWnd	OnGotFocus	OnRight MouseUp	Top
Left	OnHelp	OnSelection	View
Maximize	OnLeftDbl Click	OnSize	Visible
MDI	OnLeft MouseDown	Open	Width
			WindowState

Image Object Properties

Alignment	Left	OnMiddle DblClick	OnRight MouseUp
Before	Mouse Pointer	OnMiddle MouseDown	Parent
ClassName	Move	OnMiddle MouseUp	Release
DataSource	Name	OnMouse Move	Top

Height	OnLeftDbl Click	OnOpen	Visible
hWnd	OnLeft MouseDown	OnRightDbl Click	Width
ID	OnLeft MouseUp	OnRight MouseDown	

Line Object Properties

Before	Color Normal	OnOpen	Release
Bottom	Left	Parent	Right
ClassName	Name	Pen	Top
			Visible
			Width

Listbox Object Properties

Before	Font Underline	OnHelp	OnSel Change
ClassName	Height	OnLeftDbl Click	Parent
Color Highlight	HelpFile	OnLeft MouseDown	Release
Color Normal	HelpID	OnLeft MouseUp	Selected
Count	hWnd	OnLost Focus	SetFocus
CurSel	ID	OnMiddle DblClick	Sorted
DataSource	Left	OnMiddle MouseDown	Status Message
Enabled	Mouse Pointer	OnMiddle MouseUp	TabStop

FontBold	Move	OnMouse Move	Top
FontItalic	Multiple	OnOpen	Value
FontName	Name	OnRightDbl Click	Visible
FontSize	OldStyle	OnRight MouseDown	When
Font-StrikeOut	OnGotFocus	OnRight MouseUp	Width

Menu Object Properties

Before	HelpFile	OnClick	Separator
Checked	HelpID	OnHelp	Shortcut
ClassName	ID	Parent	Status Message
Enabled	Name	Release	Text

OLE Object Properties

Before	hWnd	OnChange	ServerName
Border	ID	OnClose	SetFocus
ClassName	Left	OnGotFocus	Status Message
DataLink	LinkFile Name	OnLost Focus	TabStop
DoVerb	Mouse Pointer	OnOpen	Top
Enabled	Name	Parent	Visible
Height	OLEType	Release	Width

Pushbutton Object Properties

Before	Font Underline	OnHelp	Parent
ClassName	Group	OnLeftDbl Click	Release
Color Normal	Height	OnLeft MouseDown	SetFocus
Default	HelpFile	OnLeft MouseUp	SpeedBar
DisabledBit-map	HelpID	OnLost Focus	Status Message
Down Bitmap	hWnd	OnMiddle DblClick	TabStop
Enabled	ID	OnMiddle MouseDown	Text
Focus Bitmap	Left	OnMiddle MouseUp	Top
FontBold	Mouse Pointer	OnMouse Move	UpBitmap
FontItalic	Move	OnOpen	Visible
FontName	Name	OnRightDbl Click	When
FontSize	OnClick	OnRight MouseDown	Width
Font-StrikeOut	OnGotFocus	OnRight SMouseUp	

Radiobutton Object Properties

Before	Height	OnLeftDbl Click	OnRight MouseUp
ClassName	HelpFile	OnHelp	Parent
Color Normal	HelpID	OnLeft MouseDown	Release

DataLink	hWnd	OnLeft MouseUp	SetFocus
Enabled	ID	OnLost Focus	Status Message
FontBold	Left	OnMiddle DblClick	TabStop
FontItalic	Mouse Pointer	OnMiddle MouseDown	Text
FontName	Move	OnMiddle MouseUp	Top
FontSize	Name	OnMouse Move	Value
Font-StrikeOut	OldStyle	OnOpen	Visible
Font Underline	OnChange	OnRightDbl Click	When
Group	OnGotFocus	OnRight MouseDown	Width

Rectangle Object Properties

Before	FontStrike Out	OnLeftDbl Click	OnRight MouseDown
Border	Font Underline	OnLeft MouseDown	OnRight MouseUp
BorderStyle	Height	OnLeft MouseUp	Parent
ClassName	hWnd	OnMiddle DblClick	PatternStyle
Color Normal	Left	OnMiddle MouseDown	Release
FontBold	Mouse Pointer	OnMiddle MouseUp	Text
FontItalic	Move	OnMouse Move	Top

FontName	Name	OnOpen	Visible
FontSize	OldStyle	OnRightDbl Click	Width

Scrollbar Object Properties

Before	Mouse Pointer	OnMiddle DblClick	RangeMin
ClassName	Move	OnMiddle MouseDown	Release
DataLink	Name	OnMiddle MouseUp	SetFocus
Enabled	OnChange	OnMouse Move	Status Message
Height	OnGotFocus	OnOpen	TabStop
HelpFile	OnHelp	OnRightDbl Click	Top
HelpID	OnLeftDbl Click	OnRight MouseDown	Value
hWnd	OnLeft MouseDown	OnRight MouseUp	Vertical Vertical
ID	OnLeft MouseUp	Parent	When
Left	OnLost Focus	RangeMax	Width

SpinBox Object Properties

Before	HelpFile	OnLost Focus	SelectAll
Border	HelpID	OnMiddle DblClick	SetFocus
ClassName	hWnd	OnMiddle MouseDown	SpinOnly

Color Highlight	ID	OnMiddle MouseUp	Status Message
Color Normal	Left	OnMouse Move	Step
DataLink	Mouse Pointer	OnOpen	TabStop
Enabled	Move	OnRightDbl Click	Top
FontBold	Name	OnRight MouseDown	Valid
FontItalic	OldStyle	OnRight MouseUp	ValidError Msg
FontName	OnChange	Parent	Valid Required
FontSize	OnGotFocus	Picture	Value
Font-StrikeOut	OnHelp	RangeMax	Visible
Font Underline	OnLeftDbl Click	RangeMin	When
Function	OnLeftMouse Down	Range Required	Width
Height	OnLeft MouseUp	Release	

Text Object Properties

Alignment	Font Underline	OldStyle	OnRight MouseDown
Before	Function	OnLeftDbl Click	OnRight MouseUp
Border	GetText Extent	OnLeft MouseDown	Parent
ClassName	Height	OnLeft MouseUp	Picture

Color Normal	hWnd	OnMiddle DblClick	Release
FontBold	ID	OnMiddle MouseDown	Text
FontItalic	Left	OnMiddle MouseUp	Top
FontName	Mouse Pointer	OnMouse Move	Visible
FontSize	Move	OnOpen	Width
Font-StrikeOut	Name	OnRightDbl Click	

APPENDIX H

A Quick Reference to Object Properties by Property

▶▶ **This** appendix lists each property and the objects that include it, excluding the Array class. The Array class is useful in advanced programming, which is beyond the scope of this book.

The information presented here is based on one of the first production applications built in dBASE for Windows: our database of objects and properties.

ActiveControl Property

Form

Advise Property

DDELink

Alias Property

Browse

Alignment Property

Image, Text

Append Property

Browse

AutoSize Property

Form

Before Property

Browse, Checkbox, Combobox, Editor, Entryfield, Image, Line, Listbox, Menu, OLE, Pushbutton, Radiobutton, Rectangle, Scrollbar, SpinBox, Text

Border Property

Editor, Entryfield, OLE, Rectangle, SpinBox, Text

BorderStyle Property

Rectangle

Bottom Property

Line

Checked Property

Menu

ClassName Property

Browse, Checkbox, Combobox, DDELink, DDETopic, Editor, Entryfield, Form, Image, Line, Listbox, Menu, OLE, Pushbutton, Radiobutton, Rectangle, Scrollbar, SpinBox, Text

Close Property

Form

ColorHighlight Property

Entryfield, Listbox, SpinBox

ColorNormal Property

Browse, Checkbox, Editor, Entryfield, Form, Line, Listbox, Pushbutton, Radiobutton, Rectangle, SpinBox, Text

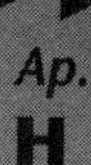

Count Property

Listbox

CurSel Property

Listbox

DataLink Property

Checkbox, Combobox, Editor, Entryfield, OLE, Radiobutton, Scrollbar, SpinBox

DataSource Property

Combobox, Image, Listbox

Default Property

Pushbutton

Delete Property

Browse

DisabledBitmap Property

Pushbutton

DoVerb Property

OLE

DownBitmap Property

Pushbutton

Enabled Property

Browse, Checkbox, Combobox, Editor, Entryfield, Form, Listbox, Menu, OLE, Pushbutton, Radiobutton, Scrollbar, SpinBox

EscExit Property

Form

Execute Property

DDELink

Fields Property

Browse

FieldWidth Property

Browse

First Property

Form

FocusBitmap Property

Pushbutton

Follow Property

Browse

FontBold Property

Browse, Checkbox, Combobox, Editor, Entryfield, Listbox, Pushbutton, Radiobutton, Rectangle, SpinBox, Text

FontItalic Property

Browse, Checkbox, Combobox, Editor, Entryfield, Listbox, Pushbutton, Radiobutton, Rectangle, SpinBox, Text

FontName Property

Browse, Checkbox, Combobox, Editor, Entryfield, Listbox, Pushbutton, Radiobutton, Rectangle, SpinBox, Text

FontSize Property

Browse, Checkbox, Combobox, Editor, Entryfield, Listbox, Pushbutton, Radiobutton, Rectangle, SpinBox, Text

FontStrikeOut Property

Checkbox, Combobox, Editor, Entryfield, Listbox, Pushbutton, Radiobutton, Rectangle, SpinBox, Text

FontUnderline Property

Checkbox, Combobox, Editor, Entryfield, Listbox, Pushbutton, Radiobutton, Rectangle, SpinBox, Text

Function Property

Entryfield, SpinBox, Text

GetTextExtent Property

Text

Group Property

Checkbox, Pushbutton, Radiobutton

Height Property

Browse, Checkbox, Combobox, Editor, Entryfield, Form, Image, Listbox, OLE, Pushbutton, Radiobutton, Rectangle, Scrollbar, SpinBox, Text Property

HelpFile

Browse, Checkbox, Combobox, Editor, Entryfield, Form, Listbox, Menu, Pushbutton, Radiobutton, Scrollbar, SpinBox

HelpID Property

Browse, Checkbox, Combobox, Editor, Entryfield, Form, Listbox, Menu, Pushbutton, Radiobutton, Scrollbar, SpinBox

hWnd Property

Browse, Checkbox, Combobox, Editor, Entryfield, Form, Image, Listbox, OLE, Pushbutton, Radiobutton, Rectangle, Scrollbar, SpinBox, Text

ID Property

Browse, Checkbox, Combobox, Editor, Entryfield, Image, Listbox, Menu, OLE, Pushbutton, Radiobutton, Scrollbar, SpinBox, Text

Initiate Property

DDELink

Key Property

Entryfield

Left Property

Browse, Checkbox, Combobox, Editor, Entryfield, Form, Image, Line, Listbox, OLE, Pushbutton, Radiobutton, Rectangle, Scrollbar, SpinBox, Text

LineNo Property

Editor

LinkFileName Property

OLE

Maximize Property

Form

MaxLength Property

Entryfield

MDI Property

Form

MenuFile Property

Form

Minimize Property

Form

Mode Property

Browse

Modify Property

Browse, Editor

MousePointer Property

Browse, Checkbox, Combobox, Editor, Entryfield, Form, Image, Listbox, OLE, Pushbutton, Radiobutton, Rectangle, Scrollbar, SpinBox, Text

Move Property

Browse, Checkbox, Combobox, Editor, Entryfield, Form, Image, Listbox, Pushbutton, Radiobutton, Rectangle, Scrollbar, SpinBox, Text

Moveable Property

Form

Multiple Property

Listbox

Name Property

Browse, Checkbox, Combobox, Editor, Entryfield, Image, Line, Listbox, Menu, OLE, Pushbutton, Radiobutton, Rectangle, Scrollbar, SpinBox, Text

NextCol Property

Form

NextObj Property

Form

NextRow Property

Form

Notify Property

DDETopic

OldStyle Property

Checkbox, Entryfield, Listbox, Radiobutton, Rectangle, SpinBox, Text

OLEType Property

OLE

OnAdvise Property

DDETopic

OnAppend Property

Browse, Form

OnChange Property

Browse, Checkbox, Combobox, Editor, Entryfield, Form, OLE, Radiobutton, Scrollbar, SpinBox

OnClick Property

Menu, Pushbutton

OnClose Property

Form, OLE

OnExecute Property

DDETopic

OnGotFocus Property

Browse, Checkbox, Combobox, Editor, Entryfield, Form, Listbox, OLE, Pushbutton, Radiobutton, Scrollbar, SpinBox

OnHelp Property

Browse, Checkbox, Combobox, Editor, Entryfield, Form, Listbox, Menu, Pushbutton, Radiobutton, Scrollbar, SpinBox

OnLeftDblClick Property

Browse, Checkbox, Combobox, Editor, Entryfield, Form, Image, Listbox, Pushbutton, Radiobutton, Rectangle, Scrollbar, SpinBox, Text

OnLeftMouseDown Property

Browse, Checkbox, Combobox, Editor, Entryfield, Form, Image, Listbox, Pushbutton, Radiobutton, Rectangle, Scrollbar, SpinBox, Text

OnLeftMouseUp Property

Browse, Checkbox, Combobox, Editor, Entryfield, Form, Image, Listbox, Pushbutton, Radiobutton, Rectangle, Scrollbar, SpinBox, Text

OnLostFocus Property

Browse, Checkbox, Combobox, Editor, Entryfield, Form, Listbox, OLE, Pushbutton, Radiobutton, Scrollbar, SpinBox

OnMiddleDblClick Property

Browse, Checkbox, Combobox, Editor, Entryfield, Form, Image, Listbox, Pushbutton, Radiobutton, Rectangle, Scrollbar, SpinBox, Text

OnMiddleMouseDown Property

Browse, Checkbox, Combobox, Editor, Entryfield, Form, Image, Listbox, Pushbutton, Radiobutton, Rectangle, Scrollbar, SpinBox, Text

OnMiddleMouseUp Property

Browse, Checkbox, Combobox, Editor, Entryfield, Form, Image, Listbox, Pushbutton, Radiobutton, Rectangle, Scrollbar, SpinBox, Text

OnMouseMove Property

Browse, Checkbox, Combobox, Editor, Entryfield, Form, Image, Listbox, Pushbutton, Radiobutton, Rectangle, Scrollbar, SpinBox, Text

OnMove Property

Form

OnNavigate Property

Browse, Form

OnNewValue Property

DDELink

OnOpen Property

Browse, Checkbox, Combobox, Editor, Entryfield, Form, Image, Line, Listbox, OLE, Pushbutton, Radiobutton, Rectangle, Scrollbar, SpinBox, Text

OnPeek Property

DDETopic

OnPoke Property

DDETopic

OnRightDblClick Property

Browse, Checkbox, Combobox, Editor, Entryfield, Form, Image, Listbox, Pushbutton, Radiobutton, Rectangle, Scrollbar, SpinBox, Text

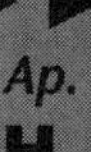

OnRightMouseDown Property

Browse, Checkbox, Combobox, Editor, Entryfield, Form, Image, Listbox, Pushbutton, Radiobutton, Rectangle, Scrollbar, SpinBox, Text

OnRightMouseUp Property

Browse, Checkbox, Combobox, Editor, Entryfield, Form, Image, Listbox, Pushbutton, Radiobutton, Rectangle, Scrollbar, SpinBox, Text

OnSelChange Property

Listbox

OnSelection Property

Form

OnSize Property

Form

OnUnadvise Property

DDETopic

Open Property

Form

Parent Property

Browse, Checkbox, Combobox, Editor, Entryfield, Image, Line, Listbox, Menu, OLE, Pushbutton, Radiobutton, Rectangle, Scrollbar, SpinBox, Text

PatternStyle Property

Rectangle

Peek Property
DDELink

Pen Property
Line

Picture Property
Entryfield, SpinBox, Text

Poke Property
DDELink

Print Property
Form

RangeMax Property
Scrollbar, SpinBox

RangeMin Property
Scrollbar, SpinBox

RangeRequired Property
SpinBox

ReadModal Property
Form

Reconnect() Property
DDELink

Release Property

Browse, Checkbox, Combobox, DDELink, DDETopic, Editor, Entryfield, Form, Image, Line, Listbox, Menu, OLE, Pushbutton, Radiobutton, Rectangle, Scrollbar, SpinBox, Text

Right Property

Line

ScaleFontName Property

Form

ScaleFontSize Property

Form

Scrollbar Property

Editor, Form

SelectAll Property

Entryfield, SpinBox

Selected Property

Listbox

Separator Property

Menu

Server Property

DDELink

ServerName Property

OLE

SetFocus Property

Browse, Checkbox, Combobox, Editor, Entryfield, Form, Listbox, OLE, Pushbutton, Radiobutton, Scrollbar, SpinBox

Shortcut Property

Menu

ShowDeleted Property

Browse

ShowHeading Property

Browse

ShowRecNo Property

Browse

Sizeable Property

Form

Sorted Property

Combobox, Listbox

SpeedBar Property

Pushbutton

SpinOnly Property

SpinBox

StatusMessage Property

Browse, Checkbox, Combobox, Editor, Entryfield, Form, Listbox, Menu, OLE, Pushbutton, Radiobutton, Scrollbar, SpinBox

Step Property

SpinBox

Style Property

Combobox

SysMenu Property

Form

TabStop Property

Browse, Checkbox, Combobox, Editor, Entryfield, Listbox, OLE, Pushbutton, Radiobutton, Scrollbar, SpinBox

Terminate Property

DDELink

Text Property

Browse, Checkbox, Form, Menu, Pushbutton, Radiobutton, Rectangle, Text

TimeOut Property

DDELink

Toggle Property

Browse

Top Property

Browse, Checkbox, Combobox, Editor, Entryfield, Form, Image, Line, Listbox, OLE, Pushbutton, Radiobutton, Rectangle, Scrollbar, SpinBox, Text

Topic Property

DDELink, DDETopic

Unadvise Property

DDELink

UpBitmap Property

Pushbutton

Valid Property

Editor, Entryfield, SpinBox

ValidErrorMsg Property

Entryfield, SpinBox

ValidRequired Property

Entryfield, SpinBox

Value Property

Checkbox, Combobox, Editor, Entryfield, Listbox, Radiobutton, Scrollbar, SpinBox

Vertical Property

Scrollbar

View Property

Form

Visible Property

Browse, Checkbox, Combobox, Editor, Entryfield, Form, Image, Line, Listbox, OLE, Pushbutton, Radiobutton, Rectangle, Scrollbar, SpinBox, Text

When Property

Browse, Checkbox, Combobox, Editor, Entryfield, Listbox, Pushbutton, Radiobutton, Scrollbar, SpinBox

Width Property

Browse, Checkbox, Combobox, Editor, Entryfield, Form, Image, Line, Listbox, OLE, Pushbutton, Radiobutton, Rectangle, Scrollbar, SpinBox, Text

WindowState Property

Form

Wrap Property

Editor

▶ INDEX

Page numbers in *italics* refer to figures; page number in **bold** refer to primary topic discussions

▶ Symbols & Numbers

#, in templates, 1002
$ operator, 513
% button (Crystal format bar), 446
& (ampersand)
    for command variable, 234
    in menu name, 228
&& (ampersands), for comments in program, 195–196, 224–225
^ operator, 511
* (asterisk)
    in leading spaces of number, 1003
    for program comments, 160, 196
** operator, 511
... (three dots), to indicate dialog box, 230
+ operator, for concatenation, 168
:: (scope resolution operator), 721
< button, in Form Expert, 51
< (less than) operator, 516
<< button, in Form Expert, 51
<> (not equal to) operator, 143, 516
= (equal to) operator, 516
!, in templates, 1002
> button, in Form Expert, 51
> (greater than) operator, 516
>> button, in Form Expert, 51
. (period), as "property of" operator, 222, 514
[] (brackets), as subscript operator, 514
! command, **581**
? ("What is") command, 168, 220, **328**, 499, 506–507, **582**
?? command, **582–583**
??? command, **583**
@$ function, 1003
@&& function, 1003
@! function, 1001, 1002
\ symbol, 526

▶ A

@A function, 1002
abbreviations, for commands, 329
ABC button, 60
About box
    creating, **204–225**
    as modal form, 201
    text objects in, 219
About dBASE 5.0 for Windows (Help menu), 309, *310*
About form, formatting memory report, 223–225
ABOUT.WFM program file, 223, *224*, *226*
ABS function, 522, **527**
Absolute Horizontal Center option, for control alignment, 699
absolute value, of numbers, 527
Absolute Vertical Center, for control alignment, 700
ACCEPT command, 1049
Access properties, for Browse objects, 238
ACOPY function, 1064
ACOS function, 524, **527**
ACTIVATE MENU command, 1050
ACTIVATE POPUP command, 1050
ACTIVATE SCREEN command, 1050
ACTIVATE WINDOW command, 1050

ActiveControl property, for Form object, 728, 944
Add Column to Cross-tab button (Cross-Tab window), 471
Add Records (File properties), 299
Add Records (Navigator menu), 41
Add Records (Table menu), 365
Add Row to Cross-tab button (Cross-Tab window), 471
Add Summarized Field button (Cross-Tab window), 471
Add Table (Speed menu), 158
ADDITIVE keyword, 682
AddRecordsLayout setting, in DBASEWIN.INI file, 1022
address fields, in form letters, 488–491
addressing letters, 481
ADEL function, 1064
ADIR function, 1064
Advanced >> pushbutton (Replace Records dialog box), 138, *139*
Advise() method, for DDELink objects, 1086
AELEMENT function, 1064–1065
AFIELDS function, 1065
AFILL function, 1065
AINS function, 1065
ALEN function, 1065
alias, 504
  in SELECT function, 558
ALIAS function, 519, **528**
Alias property, 239, 249
  for Browse objects, **861**, 888, 942
alignment
  of cross-tab report fields, 465
  with Crystal Format bar buttons, 445
  of image objects, **745–749**
  of Text objects, **769**
Alignment (Crystal Format String dialog box), 405
Alignment property
  for Image object, 773
  for text object, 208, 220, 787
alphabetic sorting, 115–116. *See also* sorting
Alt key
  with function keys for shortcut key, 235
  with underscored letter, 763
ALTERNATE file, closing, 591
ALTERNATE setting
  SET function and, 559
  SETTO function and, 561
ampersand (&)
  for command variable, 234
  in menu name, 228
  for underscore in Text property, 763
ampersands (&&), for comments in program, 195–196, 224–225
AND conditions
  evaluating, 176
  in queries, 172, 175
.AND. operator, 513–514
angles, converting radians to degrees, 556
ANSI function, 1065
Append (Table Record Properties dialog box), 373
APPEND AUTOMEM command, **583–584**
APPEND BLANK command, 243
Append field record button (Table Structure speedbar), 357
APPEND FROM ARRAY command, **484–485**
APPEND FROM command, **584**
APPEND MEMO command, **585**
Append property, 240
  for Browse objects, 861, 888
Append Records from File (Table Utilities menu), 383–384
Append Records from File dialog box, *383*, 383
Append to Alias dialog box, 191–192
Application properties, **300–302**
arccosine, 527
arcsine, 528–529
arctangent, 524, **529**
arguments for functions, 675
arithmetic operators, 509–511
Arrange Icons (Window menu), *308*
arranging windows, 305
arrays
  command to append from, **484–485**
  command to place memo field in, 654
  coping, 1064
  copying table to, 597
  creating, 687
  dimensions of, 1065
  searching, 1066
  sorting, 1066
  subscript operator for, 514–515
ASC function, 525, **528**
ASCAN function, 1066
ascending index, 353
ASCII character set
  function to return character from number, 525, **532**

function to return number for character in, 525, **528**
sorting, 115
ASIN function, 524, **528–529**
ASORT function, 1066
aspect ratio of graphic, 432
associated files, deleting when deleting .DBF files, 125
asterisk (*)
in leading spaces of number, 1003
for program comments, 160, 196
ASUBSCRIPT function, 1066
AT function, 522, **529**
ATAN function, 524, **529**
ATN2 function, 524, **530**
Auto Colors (Editor Properties dialog box), 719
AutoColors setting, for Program Editor, 1039
auto-increment field, 934–935
preventing editing of, 939
Auto Indent (Editor Properties dialog box), 718
AutoIndent setting, in DBASEWIN.INI file, 1039
automemory variables, 583
command to provide blank set, 589–590
releasing, 621
transferring values to current record, 623
Autosave (Table properties), 295
autosave feature, 628
AUTOSAVE setting, SET function and, 559
AutoSize property, for Form object, 728
Available Fields box (Sort Records dialog box), 125
average, 146
calculating, 389
AVERAGE command, **585**
Avery labels, 278, 279, 476

► B

background color, in reports, 430
backup copies
before table structure editing, 358
and packing tables, 381
of tables, 144
balancing index, 378
BAR function, 1066
BARCOUNT function, 1066
BARPROMPT function, 1067
Before property, 506
for Browse objects, 888
for Checkbox object, 821
for Combobox objects, 897
for Editor objects, 905
for Entryfield objects, 829
for Image object, 774
for Line objects, 778
for Listbox objects, 914
for Menu object, 737
for OLE objects, 1090
for Pushbutton objects, 951
for Radiobutton objects, 839
for Rectangle object, 781
for Scrollbar objects, 960
for Spinbox objects, 848
for Text object, 787
BEGINTRANS function, 1067
bell, turning on or off, 628
Bell Selections, settings for, 297
Bell setting
in DBASEWIN.INI file, 1018
SET function and, 559
SETTO function and, 561
binary field types, 352
copying to file, 595
editor for, 365
function to return type, 519, **530**
replacing with file, **623**
BINTYPE function, 519, **530**
BITAND function, 1067
BITLSHIFT function, 1067
BITOR function, 1067
BITRSHIFT function, 1067–1068
BITSET function, 1068
BITXOR function, 1068
blank, function to test for, 522, **543–544**
BLANK command, **585–586**
blank fields, as zero value, 361
blank form
adding text objects to, 204–208
attaching menu to, 227–228
in Form Designer, 201
in Form Expert, 50, *202*
blank lines, suppressing, 435, 489–490
blank record, inserting, 611
Blank Selected Record, (Table menu), 365
blank spaces
function to remove leading, 523, **548–549**
function to remove trailing, 523, **556–557**
removing from form letter, 487
block command, in Command window, 668
Block Sizes (Table properties), 295

block statements, **663–672**
conditional execution, **664–667**
BLOCKSIZE setting, SETTO function and, 561
.BMP file extension, 314, 623, 625
creating files, 746
inserting file in report, 426
for pushbutton icon, 216
BOF function, 519, **530–531**
boldface type, 772
in reports, 61, 62, 263, 445
BOOKMARK function, 519, **531**
Border property
for Editor objects, 906
for Entryfield objects, 830
for OLE objects, 1090
for Rectangle object, 781
for Spinbox objects, 848
for Text object, 788
BORDER setting, SETTO function and, 561
borders
for Entryfield objects, **808–809**
formatting in reports, 430–431
for Rectangle objects, *765*, 765–766, *766*
of Spinbox objects, 817, *818*, 819
for Text objects, **768**
BorderStyle property, for Rectangle object, 781
Bottom property, for Line objects, 778–779
Bottom Record (Table menu), 366
bottom totals, formatting in cross-tab reports, 466–467
Box Format dialog box, 271, *272*, 433–434, *434*
boxes
formatting, **433**
inserting in reports, **426**
speed menu in Crystal Reports for, 452
to surround data, 270–273
Boyce-Codd Normal form, 72–73
braces ({ }), for date constants, 502
brackets ([ ]), as subscript operator, 514
Bring Closer speedbar button, 708
Bring to Front speedbar button, 708
Browse area, in Table Structure tool, **354**
BROWSE command, 161, **586–587**
Browse Field Data (Crystal Edit menu), 419
Browse Layout (View menu), 41
Browse Layout view, *112*
bug in record number column display, 128
bug in vertical elevator, 115
customizing, **43–44**
customizing table appearance in, 110–111
editing files in, 45
navigation buttons for, 44, 368
for People form, **237–240**
selecting record in, 363–364
speedbar button for, 367
updating to add field, 182
Browse objects, **860–867**, 942–943
adding, *239*
to choose record, 949–950
disabling toggling between layouts, 365
editing properties of, **861–862**
example of, **865–868**
field properties of, **862–863**
Mode property of, **863–864**
properties of, 1098–1099
ShowDeleted property for, 865
Toggle property for, 863–864
using aliases with, **861**
Browse window, for Table Structure tool, 350, *351*
B-tree index structure, 117, 378
bugs, 200–201, 695
in Browse Layout view vertical elevator, 115
in Crystal Reports, 276
in Form Designer, 211, 223
in Form Designer Methods tab, 715
multiple Combobox objects and, 872
in record number column in Browse Layout view, 128
Build Expression (Edit menu), for Command window, 333
Build Expression dialog box, 338, *339*, 489
buttons, descriptions on status bar, 43

▶ C

CALCULATE command, **587**
CALCULATE MAX() command, 359
Calculate Records (Table Utilities menu), 389–390
Calculate Records dialog box, 359
Calculated Field dialog box, *369*, 369–370
calculated fields
in single-table queries, **178–179**
in Table Records Properties dialog box, 369
Calculation Results dialog box, *147*
calculations, **146–148**
calling functions, **517–518**

calling routine, 674
CANCEL command, **587–588**
candidate keys, 73
capitalization, of commands in Query Designer, 163
CARRY property, 629
CARRY setting
- SET function and, 559
- SETTO function and, 561

Cascade Delete Alert box, 192
cascade deletes, 97–98, 191
cascading menu, creating, 230–231
cascading windows, 13, *305*
.CAT file extension, 314, 325
CATALOG function, 519, **531**
Catalog Item Description dialog box, *323*, 323, 324
Catalog menu, ➤ Add Item, 324
Catalog Properties dialog box, 325
Catalog section, in DBASEWIN.INI file, **1042**
CATALOG setting
- SET function and, 559
- SETTO function and, 561

catalogs, **321–325**, *326*
- adding items to, **324**
- command for descriptive information in, 650
- creating, **323–324**, 599
- deleting item from, 324
- Navigator menu for, 318
- opening file, 630
- speed menus for, 320
- turning off and on, 629
- using, **325**

Category list, in Expression Builder, **340–342**, *341*
CD command, 234, **588**
CDOW function, 341–342, 520, **531**
CD-ROMs, 5
CEILING function, 522, **531–532**
CENTER function, 522, **532**
centering titles, 700
CenterLine setting, for Object Properties Inspector, 1032
CENTURY setting, 550, 571
- SET function and, 559

CERROR function, 1068
CGA (Color Graphics Adapter) monitor, 761
CHANGE command, **588–589**
CHANGE function, 1068
Change Icon dialog box, *414*
Changes Made - Table Structure dialog box, 106
character field types, 352
- changing type, 360–361
- determining width, 359
- and indexes, 353

character string constants, 501–502
characters
- converting uppercase to lower, 523, **548**
- function to test for, 522, **543**
- functions to format, 1002

Character-Separated Values dialog box, *398*
CHARSET function, 1068
check marks, in query field tables, 48
Checkbox objects, **798–804**
- adding values to, **803–804**
- labels for, **802–803**
- linking, **799–802**
- properties of, **821–829**, 1099
- vs. Radiobutton objects, 816

Checked property, for Menu object, 737
Cheshire labels, 476
child records, deleting, 97
child tables, 186
- inverting order with parent table, 247

child windows
- and File menu, 12
- MDI, 987, *988*
- modal, **986–987**
- in Window menu, 306

Choose Alias dialog box, 942
Choose Bitmap dialog box, 216, *217*, *746*, 746
Choose Data Source dialog box, *870*, 870
Choose Directory dialog box, 35, 298, **992–993**, *993*
Choose Field dialog box, 800–801, *801*, 862, *863*, 870
Choose Graphic File dialog box, 426
Choose Mailing Label Type list, 279
Choose New Location dialog box, 437
Choose Template dialog box, 371, **1000–1004**, *1001*
Choose View dialog box, *802*
CHOOSEPRINTER function, 1069
CHR function, 525, **532**
circles, drawing, **759–761**
CLASS blocks, 680–681
class code, 720
CLASS command, 681, 721
CLASS OBJECTSFORM OF FORM, 681
classes, separate file for, 682
ClassName property

for Browse objects, 888–889
for Checkbox object, 821
for Combobox objects, 898
for DDELink objects, 1086
for DDETopic objects, 1088–1089
for Editor objects, 906
for Entryfield objects, 830
for Form object, 728
for Image object, 774
for Line objects, 779
for Listbox objects, 914
for Menu object, 737–738
for OLE objects, 1090
for Pushbutton objects, 951
for Radiobutton objects, 839
for Rectangle object, 781
for Scrollbar objects, 960
for Spinbox objects, 848
for Text object, 788
Clear (Crystal Edit menu), 414
CLEAR ALL command, **589**
CLEAR AUTOMEM command, 589–590
CLEAR command, **589**
@CLEAR command, 1048
CLEAR FIELDS command, **590**
CLEAR GETS command, 1050–1051
CLEAR MEMORY command, **590**
CLEAR MENUS command, 1051
CLEAR POPUPS command, 1051
CLEAR PROGRAM command, **590**
Clear Results (Edit menu), for Command window, 333
CLEAR SCREENS command, 1051
CLEAR TYPEAHEAD command, 590–591
CLEAR WINDOWS command, 1051
client area, 9, *9*
Clipboard, 13, 363–364
to copy program code, 939
copying form letter to, 484
speedbar buttons for, 16
CLOSE ALL command, 278, **591**
Close All Tables (Table Utilities menu), 379
Close All Windows (Window menu), 305–306
CLOSE ALTERNATE command, **591**
CLOSE DATABASES command, 160, **591**
CLOSE FORMAT command, 1051–1052
CLOSE FORMS command, **591–592**
CLOSE INDEXES command, **592**
Close() method, for Form object, 728
CLOSE PRINTER command, **592**
CLOSE PROCEDURE command, **592**
Close Table (Table Utilities menu), 379
CLOSE TABLES command, **592**
closing
dBASE for Windows, 10, 274
non-MDI or MDI forms, 211
sessions, 601
CMONTH function, 520, **533**
Codd, E.F., 6
code blocks, 927–928
COL function, 1069
color
for forms, 52
function to test computer capability, 522, **544**
for Line objects, **761–762**
in reports, 430–431
syntax in Procedure Editor, 719
COLOR setting, SETTO function and, 561
ColorHighlight property, 762
for Entryfield objects, 830
for Listbox objects, 914
for Spinbox objects, 848
ColorNormal property, 762
for Browse objects, 889
for Checkbox object, 822
for Editor objects, 906
for Entryfield objects, 830
for Form object, 728
for Line objects, 779
for Listbox objects, 915
for Pushbutton objects, 951
for Radiobutton objects, 840
for Rectangle object, 781
for Spinbox objects, 848
for Text object, 788
column headings, deleting from report, 259
column titles, formatting in cross-tab report, 464–466
Columnar Layout (View menu), 42
Columnar Layout view, 189
editing files in, 45
navigation buttons for, 44, 368
speedbar button for, 367
columns
changing order in Table Structure Browse area, 354
in relational database, 7, *8*
combined form creation, **247–250**
Combobox objects, **868–874**
properties of, **897–905**, 1100
Sorted property for, **872–873**
styles for, 873, *874*
Value property for, 874

comma button (Crystal format bar), 446
Command Output (Programming properties), 302–303
command variable, ampersand (&) for, 234
Command window, *9*, 9, **10**, *31*, 129, 162, **326–338**, *326*
- block command in, 668
- to change state codes, 138
- checking output in results pane, **330**
- command entry in input pane, **327–330**
- cross-tab report from, 460
- to delete files, 126
- Edit menu for, **332–334**
- and File menu, 12
- fonts for, 1026
- input pane position in, 336–337
- input/output commands, 581
- launching Expression Builder from, 339
- Main menu, 332
- pasting to and from, **345**
- Program menu for, **334–335**
- Properties menu for, **336–337**, *336*
- speed menus, **337–338**
- speedbar, **331**
- speedbar button for, 16
- Table menu for, 335
- in Window menu, 306

Command window Properties dialog box, *336*, 336–337
commands, **576–660**
- abbreviations for, 329
- for Command window input/output, 581
- to control dBASE, 579–580
- for data manipulation, 578–579
- for data summary, 579
- entry in input pane, **327–330**
- indentation in program, 665
- for printer output, 581
- repeating, 330
- system-related, 579
- vs. statements, **577**

CommandWindow section, in DBASEWIN.INI file, **1025–1026**
comma-separated values, exporting to, 398
commenting out program sections, 224–225
comments
- for beginning and end of program, 874–875
- for program statements, **688**
- in .WFM file, 722

comments in program
- ampersands (&&) for, 195–196, 224–225
- asterisk (*) for, 160, 196
- to identify procedures, 674
- for RETURN statements, 678

COMMIT function, 1069
Common User Access (CUA) standard menus, 12
Compile (Program menu), for Command window, 335
COMPILE command, **593**
Compile Program dialog box, 335
compiling
- command to suppress automatic, 635
- forms, 200

Complete default installation, 971
Component Builder, 973
- installing, 975

concatenation of strings, 512
- + operator for, 168

conditional execution, 662
- of block statements, **664–667**

Confirm option (Data Entry properties), 296
CONFIRM setting, SET function and, 559
CONSOLE setting, SET function and, 559
constants
- editing in Expression Builder, **342–343**
- in expressions, 500–502

constructor code, 681
Contents (Help), 309
contiguous records, counting, 146
CONTINUE command, **593**
Control Palette draw mode (Form Designer Properties dialog box), 710
controls, order on form, 703
Controls Palette, **716–717**
- DBASEWIN.INI file settings for, **1033–1034**
- in Form Designer, 202
- Standard tab, 204, *205*
- Standard tab, Pushbutton object, 212, 243

ControlsWindow section, of DBASEWIN.INI file, **1033–1034**
ControlsWindow setting, in DBASEWIN.INI file, 1035
CONVERT command, **593–594**
Copy (Edit menu), 292
COPY BINARY command, **595**
COPY command, **594**
COPY FILE command, **595**
COPY INDEXES command, **595**
COPY MEMO command, **595–596**
COPY STRUCTURE command, **596**
COPY TABLE command, **596**

COPY TAG command, **596–597**
COPY TO ARRAY command, **597**
Copy to File (Edit menu), for Command window, 333
COPY TO STRUCTURE EXTENDED command, **597**
copyright line, in About box, *209*, 210
COS function, 524, **533**
cosine, 533
count
  of contiguous records, 146
  of records matching condition, 145
  of total records in table, 145
COUNT command, **597–598**
Count() method, for Listbox objects, 915
Count Records (Table Utilities menu), 387–388
Count Records dialog box, *388*, 388
Counted Records dialog box, 388
country properties, **293**
Country tab, in Desktop Properties dialog box, *33*
Courier font, 771
.COV file extension, 335
Coverage (Programming properties), 303
coverage file, 335
COVERAGE setting, SET function and, 559
CREATE APPLICATION command, **598**
CREATE CATALOG command, **599**
Create Catalog dialog box, 323
Create Catalog process, starting, 291
CREATE command, **598**
CREATE FORM command, **599**
CREATE FROM STRUCTURE EXTENDED command, **599–600**
Create Index dialog box, 121, *169*
CREATE LABEL command, **600**
Create Query (Table menu), 365
CREATE QUERY command, **600**
CREATE REPORT command, 484, **600**
CREATE REPORT CROSSTAB command, 460
CREATE SCREEN command, 1052
CREATE SESSION command, **600–601**
CREATE VIEW command, **601**
CREATE VIEW FROM ENVIRONMENT command, 1052
cropping graphics, 432, 748
cross-tab reports, **458–473**
  adding dimension, **467–473**
  adding formula to group, 468–470
  changing layout, 467–468
  formatting, **464–467**
  page headers and footers for, **464**
  previewing, **464**
  table structure for, *459*
  viewing, **463**
Cross-Tab window, in Crystal Reports, *461*
Crystal Reports, 57, **254–285**, *257*, **394–492**. *See also* cross-tab reports; form letters
  bugs in, 276
  and closing dBASE for Windows, 274
  command to launch label design tool, 600
  Cross-Tab window in, *461*
  Database menu in, **437–438**
  dragging fields in, 61
  Edit menu in, **412–421**
  File menu in, **395–411**
  font size and style in, **269–270**
  Format bar, **444–446**
  Format menu in, **428–437**, *429*
  Help menu in, **441–442**
  installing, 976
  launching, 255, 291, 484
  for mailing labels, **278–284**, **473–480**
  main menu, 394
  preview in, *63*, **261**, **266–267**
  report embellishments, **269–277**
  Report menu in, **438–440**
  sorting by, **63–64**
  speed menus, **448–453**
  speedbar in, 62, **442–444**
  two-table grouped report, **264–269**
  two-table report, **254–264**
  use of open tables, 256
  Window menu in, 441
CTOD function, 525, **533**
Ctrl key, with function keys for shortcut key, 235
CUA Enter (Data Entry properties), 296–297
CUA ENTER setting, SET function and, 559
CURRENCY setting
  SET function and, 559
  SETTO function and, 561
Currency symbol, 293, 407, 446, 631
  in DBASEWIN.INI file, 1015–1016
  function to display, 1003
  placement of, 631
Current Directory (File properties), 298
Current Directory (Navigator), 35, 312
current session, clearing, 589
CurrentTab setting in DBASEWIN.INI file
  for Desktop, 1021
  for Object Properties Inspector, 1033

for Table Records Properties dialog box, 1037
CurSel property, for Listbox objects, 915
cursor, as "stop" shape circle, 460, 462
CURSOR setting, SET function and, 559
Custom (Navigator menu), 318
custom controls, in Controls Palette, 716
Custom files, 314
custom forms, creating, **50–56**
Custom installation, 971, **973–976**
Custom Installation dialog box, 974–976, *975*
Custom Speed menu, 320
CustomClasses section, of DBASEWIN.INI file, **1020–1021**
CustomFilesSkeletonList, in DBASEWIN.INI file, 1027
customizing
  Browse Layout view, **43–44**
  Table Records tool, **109–113**
Cut (Edit menu), 292

▶ D

@D function, 1004
dashed line styles, 433
data
  arrangement in tables, **7–8**
  commands for manipulating, 578–579
  editing, **44–45**
  preventing loss during table restructure, **358–362**
  types, 7–8
data buffer, command to send contents to operating system, 608
Data Directory (Crystal Options dialog box), 403
data entry, **41–42**
  automating for foreign keys, **940–950**
  in query view, 189
  restrictions on, 371
  selecting single field for, 375
  SET CONFIRM command and, 630
  templates for, **244–245**
Data Entry properties, **296–297**
data groups, locating and updating, **128–131**
Data Interchange Format (DIF), exporting to, 398
Data Loss Potential warning box, *358*, 358, 360
data summary, commands for, 579
data table, created by Crystal Reports, 396
database design, **68–73**
  art of, **71–72**
  eliminating tables in, 84
  field lists, 77
  hotel guest registration example, 80–84
  phone and mail list example, 79–80
  science of, **72–73**
  TED Design method, 73, **74–89**
  wholesale supplier example, 84–89
database fields, speed menu for, 450
Database File dialog box, 474
DATABASE function, 519, **534**
database integrity, **90–98**
  constraints, **90–91**
Database menu (Crystal Reports), **437–438**
  Verify Before Printing, 438
Database Selector (Crystal Options dialog box), 403
DATABASE setting, SETTO function and, 561
database-related functions, 519–520
databases
  command to close all, 591
  origins, **4–5**
  relational, **5–7**
data-entry objects, **798–857**
  Checkbox objects, **798–804**, 821–829
  Entryfield objects, **805–815**, 829–839
  properties of, **821–857**
  Radiobutton objects, **815–817**, 839–847
  Spinbox objects, **817–821**, 847–857
DataLink property
  for Checkbox objects, 800, 822
  for Combobox objects, 868–872, 898
  for Editor objects, 876, 877, 906
  for Entryfield objects, 830, 939
  for OLE objects, 1090
  for Radiobutton objects, 840
  for Scrollbar objects, 960
  for Spinbox objects, 848
data-linkage properties, 239
DataSource property, 804
  for Combobox objects, 868–872, 898
  for Editor objects, 877
  for Entryfield objects, 807
  for Image object, 746, 774
  for Listbox objects, 915
date constants, 502
Date field types, 352
  changing type, 360–361
Date format, 1004
  command to set, 632

- in DBASEWIN.INI file, 1016
- default, 408–409
- setting character for, 642
- setting number of digits for year, 630
- setting options, 293

DATE function, 133, 507, 520, **534**
date operator, adding in Expression Builder, **343–344**
DATE setting, SETTO function and, 561
dates
- function to return for last table update, 520, **549**
- functions to manipulate, 520–521
- inserting special field in report, 427
- sorting, 122
- style options for, 563

DAY function, 521, **534**
day of week
- function to return number representing, 521, **536**
- function to return string for, 531

.DB file extension, 149, 314
dBASE commands, shortening, 161
dBASE expression, in Find Records dialog box, 133
"dBASE has become unstable" alert, 948
dBASE III+ compatible .DBF format, 384
dBASE internal global variable names, underscore character for, 503
dBASE sessions, variables declared for, 687
dBASE tables, setting as default type, 1017
dBASE for Windows
- built-in program compiler, 593
- closing, 10, 274
- command to terminate session, 619
- commands to control, 579–580
- Custom installation, 971, **973–976**
- exiting, 30–31, 40, 46
- file categories for, 36
- importing data to, 151
- installing, **970–980**
- menus for, **11–15**
- overview, **8–23**
- Registration dialog box, **972–973**, *974*
- starting, 30

dBASE for Windows Bitmaps dialog box, 217
dBASE for Windows Debugger
- command to launch, 601
- launching, 335

DBASEWIN.EXE file, directory of, 1074
DBASEWIN.INI file, 111, **1010–1044**
- Catalog section, **1042**
- CommandSettings section, **1014–1020**
- CommandWindow section, **1025–1026**
- ControlsWindow section, **1033–1034**
- CustomClasses section, **1020–1021**
- Desktop section, **1021–1025**
- Dialogs section, **1041**
- Field Properties dialog box and, 372
- Font section, **1014**
- FormDesigner section, **1034–1037**
- Install section, **1021**
- MemoEditor section, **1043**
- MRU_Files section, **1029–1030**
- multiple for multiple projects, 1010, **1011–1012**
- Navigator section, **1026–1029**
- ObjectProperties section, **1031–1033**
- OnOffCommandSettings section, **1030–1031**
- Procedure Editor section, **1044**
- ProgramEditor section, **1038–1041**
- QueryDesigner section, **1043**
- recovering original, 1011
- structure, **1013**
- TableRecords section, **1037–1038**
- TextEditor section, **1042–1043**

\DBASEWIN\SAMPLES\BUTTONS.CC file, 716
DBERROR function, 1069
.DBF file extension, 39, 314
- as default table type, 633
- deleting records from, 381
- for reports, 58
- and USE command, 329

DBF function, 519, **534**
.DBK file extension, 125
DBMESSAGE function, 1069
Dbtype setting
- in DBASEWIN.INI file, 1017
- SETTO function and, 561

Dbwinhome global variable, 1015
DDE (Dynamic Data Exchange), 1086
DDELink objects, properties of, **1086–1088**, 1100
DDETopic objects, properties of, **1088–1090**, 1101
DEACTIVATE MENU command, 1052
DEACTIVATE POPUP command, 1052
DEACTIVATE WINDOW command, 1052–1053
Debug (Program menu), for Command window, 335
DEBUG command, **601**

Decimal field, in Table Structure tool, 353
decimal fractions, as numeric constants, 500–501
decimal places, function to return number for field, 519, **538**
decimal selection buttons (Crystal format bar), 446
decimal separator, setting for, 407
Decimals field, in Table Structure tool, 106
Decimals setting, 302, 407, 633–634
  in DBASEWIN.INI file, 1019
  SETTO function and, 561
DECLARE declarations, **687–688**
Default property, for Pushbutton objects, 952
DEFAULT setting, SETTO function and, 561
default settings
  for alignment in report, 405
  changing window title, 374
  for character-based fields in Crystal Reports, 404
  for date format, 408–409
  for file extension for exporting, 148–149
  for path, 36
default settings. *See also* DBASEWIN.INI file
Default Table type, options for, 294–295
default values, for empty Numeric field, 807
DEFINE BAR command, 1053
DEFINE BOX command, 1053
DEFINE command, **601–602**, 721, 762, 866
  for objects, 515
DEFINE PAD command, 1053
DEFINE POPUP command, 1054
Define Relation dialog box, 186, 190, *191*, 193, *248*, 255, *256*
  Every Parent box, 192
DEFINE WINDOW command, 1054
degrees
  converting radians to, 556
  converting to radians, 524, **536**
Del column, 140, *141*
Delete (Edit menu), 292
Delete (Table Record Properties dialog box), 373
DELETE command, **602**
Delete field record button (Table Structure speedbar), 357
DELETE FILE command, **602**
Delete property, for Browse objects, 240, 861, 889
Delete Records (Table Utilities menu), 379–380
Delete Records dialog box, 141, *142*, *380*, 380
Delete Section dialog box (Crystal Reports), 418–419, *419*
Delete Selected Record (Table menu), 365
DELETE TABLE command, **602**
DELETE TAG command, **602–603**
Deleted (Table properties), 295
deleted column, removing from display, 240
Deleted flag
  and Count Records dialog box, 388
  for records, 140
DELETED function, 519, **535**
deleted records
  and auto-increment ID fields, 936–937
  command to recall, 619
  PACK command to remove, 618
  and record IDs, 92
  setting status for, 634, 865
DELETED setting, SET function and, 559
deleting
  column headings from report, 259
  to control mailing, 143
  .DBK file and associated files, 125–126
  every record in table, 659
  fields in table structure, **39–40**
  files, 316
  groups of records, **140–144**
  indexes, 121
  items from catalogs, 324
  making action permanent, 143–144
  .QBE file, 157
  record counts after, 145
  records, relational integrity and, 97
  report sections, **418–419**
  with ZAP command, 144
delimited data files, 149–150
delimited files, 384
delimiter characters, command to set, 634–635
Delimiters choices (Data Entry properties), 297
Delimiters setting
  in DBASEWIN.INI file, 1018
  SET function and, 559
  SETTO function and, 561
DESCENDING function, 519, **535**
descending indexes, 353, 998
design. *See also* database design
  font selection, 270, 411
  for form letters, **481–483**
  format features and, 429
  of menu, **226–236**
  of tables offline, 37

Design check box (Programming properties), 304
Design Current Menu (Modify Menu Property dialog box), 227
design icon, 17
Design mode, **20**, 291
 command to control use, 635
 in Form Designer, 56
 launching file in, 315
 launching table in, 105
DESIGN setting, SET function and, 559
desktop
 layout for Form Designer, 201–203, *204*
 setting preferences, 14
Desktop Properties dialog box
 Country tab, *33*
 and DBASEWIN.INI settings, 1014, 1030
 Files tab, *34*
 Programming tab, 882
Detail table, 78, 87, *88*, 88–89
Details, in TED database design, 74, 78
Details option, for Navigator, 315, 318
DetailsIconYSpacing setting, in DBASEWIN.INI file, 1028
DEVELOPMENT setting, SET function and, 559
DEVICE setting, SETTO function and, 561
.DFF files, Windows resource from, 1081
dialog boxes, **984–1006**. *See also specific names*
 field selectors in, **1004–1006**
 MDI child windows, 987, *988*
 modal child windows, **986–987**
 parent windows, **985–986**, *985*
 rectangle objects in, 762
 three dots (...) to indicate, 230
 types, **984–987**
Dialogs section, in DBASEWIN.INI file, **1041**
DIFFERENCE function, 522, **535**
DIR command, **603**
directories
 command to change, 588
 command to set, 635–636
 creating, 1012
 creation menu object to change, 234
 for installation, 972
 reading into array, 1064
 separate for each project, 1011–1012
 working, **32–34**
Directory Area, in Navigator, **312–313**
Directory rectangle (Open File dialog box), **990**
DIRECTORY setting, SETTO function and, 562
Directory variable, 1015
DisabledBitmap property, for Pushbutton objects, 952
disk-buffering software, 608
disk drive, command to select, 634
Disk Drive drop-down list (Open File dialog box), **992**
disk space
 for dBase for Windows, 970
 field width and, 77
 for generated records, 387
DISKSPACE function, 1069–1070
Display As Icon (Crystal Paste Special dialog box), 413
DISPLAY command, **603–604**, 936
Display Coverage (Program menu), for Command window, 335
DISPLAY COVERAGE command, **604**
Display Coverage dialog box, 335
DISPLAY FILES command, **604**
DISPLAY MEMORY command, **604–605**
DISPLAY setting, SETTO function and, 562
DISPLAY STATUS command, **605**
DISPLAY STRUCTURE command, 605
display type, command to select, 636
distribution disks, preloading to hard disk, 971
division, function to return remainder, 522, **550–551**
.DLL file
 command to access routines, 608, 615
 command to release, 621
DMY function, 525, **535–536**
Do (Program menu), for Command window, 334
DO CASE block, **665–667**
DO command, 161, 233, 329, **605–606**
DO statement, 678–679
DO UNTIL loops, 668–670
DO WHILE loops, 668–670
documentation. *See also* comments in program
 printing for report, 399
domain of field, 8
domain integrity, 90–91
Domain-Key Normal form, 73
DOS clock tick, for bell, 297
DOS command, **606**
DOS commands, running from Command window, 581
DOS environment variable, 1073

DOS file handle, and number of open tables, 558
DOS program, function to run, 524, **557**
dot prompt, 10, 328
dots (…), to indicate dialog box, 230
dotted line styles, 433
double-clicking, System button to exit dBASE, 31
DoVerb() method, for OLE objects, 1091
DOW function, 521, **536**
DownBitmap property, for Pushbutton objects, 952
dragging fields, in Crystal Reports, 61
drawing in reports, **270–271**
drive, for installation, 972
drop shadow, 273
DTOR function, 524, **536**
DTOS function, 122, 525, **537**
duration of bell, 628
Duration spinbutton, for bell, 297
Dynamic Data Exchange (DDE), 1086

► E

@E function, 1004
ECHO setting, SET function and, 559
Edit (Table Record Properties dialog box), 373
EDIT command, **606–607**
Edit Event dialog box, *724*
Edit Event method (Procedure Editor Procedure menu), 723, 724
Edit Group Section dialog box, *418*
Edit menu, 13, **292**
  for Command window, **332–334**
  ➤ Delete, 125
  ➤ Paste, 484
  ➤ Paste Add Records, 364
  ➤ Select All, 697
  for Table Records tools, 363–364
Edit menu (Crystal Reports), **412–421**
  ➤ Browse Field Data, 419
  ➤ Clear, 414
  ➤ Delete Section, 418–419
  ➤ Formula, 415
  ➤ Group Section, 418
  ➤ Links, 420
  ➤ Objects, 420
  ➤ Paste Special, **412–414**
  ➤ Select Fields, 415
  ➤ Show Field Names, 419
  ➤ Show/Hide Sections, 417
  ➤ Summary Operation, 415, 416
  ➤ Text Field, 415
Edit as Program (Speed menus), 159, 195, 223, 704
Edit properties, 240
Edit Records (File properties), 299
Edit Report Title dialog box, 435–436, *436*
Edit Text Field dialog box, 262–263, 415, *416*, 422, 464
editing
  data, **44–45**
  query program, **194–196**
  relational integrity and, 96–97
editor
  command to specify, 636, 652
  setting preferences, **298–299**
Editor objects, **874–881**
  changing dimensions of, 878, *879*
  DataLink property, 876
  properties of, **905–914**
  resizing method for, 880–881
Editor setting
  in DBASEWIN.INI file, 1019
  SETTO function and, 562
EditRecordsLayout setting, in DBASEWIN.INI file, 1022
Einstein button, 338
EJECT command, **607**
EJECT PAGE command, **607**
ELAPSED function, 524, **537**
ELSE statement, in IF block, 664
EMPTY function, 522, **537**, 886
empty string, 490
empty table, DO WHILE loop for, 669
Enabled property
  for Browse objects, 889
  for Checkbox object, 822
  for Combobox objects, 898
  for Editor objects, 906
  for Entryfield objects, 830–831, 939
  for Form object, 728
  for Listbox objects, 915
  for Menu object, 738
  for OLE objects, 1091
  for Pushbutton objects, 952
  for Radiobutton objects, 840
  for Scrollbar objects, 960
  for Spinbox objects, 849
end of file
  comment to identify in .WFM file, 722
  function to test for, 519, **537**

ENDIF statement, 664
Ensure Compilation (Programming properties), 303–304, 882
Enter key, 32
  command to control behavior, 631
  and directory list, 312
  setting options for, 296
entity integrity, 933
entity and primary key integrity, 90
Entryfield objects, **805–815**
  border for, **808–809**
  controlling availability, **814–815**, 939
  controlling valid values, **811–813**
  DataSource property for, 807
  MaxLength property for, **809–810**
  properties of, **829–839**, 1102
  SelectAll property for, **810–811**
EOF function, 507, 519, **537**
EOF status, function to return, 1070
equal sign (=), 174
equal to (=) operator, 516
ERASE command, **607–608**
ERROR function, 1070
ERROR setting, SETTO function and, 562
errors, function to return, 1069
Esc key
  to interrupt program, 637, 947
  setting for, 297
ESCAPE setting, SET function and, 559
EscExit property, for Form object, 729
event handlers, 943–944
  attaching to OnClick event, 215
  and data property, 750
  object to trap, 751
events, 712
  attaching method to, 717
  in TED database design, 74, 75–76
Events tab (Object Properties Inspector), 715
EXACT
  SET function and, 559
  setting on or off, 193, 194–195
Exact (Table properties), 295
Excel, exporting to, 398
ExcExit property, 211
Exclude check box (Table Record Properties dialog box), 373
exclusive access, 119
Exclusive Access Required dialog box, 168
Exclusive setting, 294
  SET function and, 559
exclusive use, and zapping files, 382
executable form, compiling source program into, 335
Execute() method, for DDELink objects, 1087
Execute Program dialog box, 334, 335
Execute Selection (Edit menu), for Command window, 334
EXIT statement, 670–671
exiting
  creating functioning menu option for, 232–233
  from dBASE for Windows, 30–31, 40, 46
  Query Designer, **49–50**
  Table Structure tool, 40
EXP function, 522, **538**
ExpandedCategories setting, for Object Properties Inspector, 1032
Expert Assistance, in Form Expert, 50
Experts, speedbar button for, 16
Experts (Help menu), 309
exponentiation, 510–511
Export dialog box, *397*
Export Records (Table Utilities menu), 384
Export Records dialog box, *149*, 276, *277*, 384, *385*
  Scope, 150
exporting data, **148–150**
  by printing to file, 397–399
Expression Builder, **338–345**
  adding date operator, **343–344**
  Category, Type, and Paste lists, **340–342**, *341*
  editing constants, **342–343**
  launching, 333–334, 337, 338
  launching in Crystal Reports, 415, 422, 439
  pasting expression from, 345
expressions, **498–518**
  object properties in, 505
  as operands, 508–509
  operands in, **500–509**
  operators in, **509–517**
EXTERN command, **608**, 696, 759

▶ F

.F. logical constant, 502
FCLOSE function, 1070
FCREATE function, 1070
FDATE function, 1070
FDECIMAL function, 519, **538**
FEOF function, 1070

FERROR function, 1070–1071
FFLUSH function, 1071
FGETS function, 1071
Field Contents (View menu), 365
field definitions, in Table Structure tool, *38*, 38–39
FIELD function, 519, **538**
field lists
  command to remove, 590
  designing, 77
field names, 504–505
  displaying for columns from commands, 303
  in Table Structure tool, 351
Field options (Table Records Properties dialog box), 374
Field Picker, for exporting records, 150
Field Properties dialog box, *112*, 183, *184*, *370*, 370–372
field selection
  in Form Expert, 51
  for reports, **58–59**, *60*
  single for data entry, 375
  for single-table queries, **162–164**
  for sorting, *64*
field selector
  in dialog boxes, **1004–1006**
  in Table Records Properties dialog box, 368
field types
  changing, 360–361
  in Table Structure tool, 352
field value operator (->), 514
field width, 38, 77
  changing in Browse Layout view, 43
  changing in Table Structure, 358–359
  checking maximum, 359
  fitting on label, 480
  in Table Structure tool, 352–353
fields, 7, *8*
  adding to form letter, **485–486**
  adding to report, 257–261
  adding to table structure, **351–354**
  changing order in Query Designer, 164
  controlling order in field selectors, **1005–1006**
  domain integrity for, 90–91
  dragging for cross-tab report, 460, *462*, 462
  dragging in Crystal Reports, 61
  emphasizing, 273
  excluding from printed report, 405, 407
  formatting in Crystal Reports, **429–430**
  frozen, 374, 375
  function to return length, **539**
  function to return name, 519, **538**
  function to return number in table, 519, **539**
  inserting in Crystal Reports, 421
  maximum display width, 374, 375
  rearranging and deleting in table structure, **39–40**
  restrictions on values, 8
  speed menus for, 450–451
  updating Browse Layout view to add, 182
  verifying existence for report, 437–438
  width for Entryfield objects, 809
Fields list, adding new fields to, 107
Fields property, for Browse objects, 862, 889
FIELDS setting
  SET function and, 559
  SETTO function and, 562
FieldWidth property, for Browse objects, 862, 889
Fifth Normal Form, 73
file allocation table, 948
file categories, for dBASE for Windows, 36
file extensions, in Navigator lists, 314
FILE function, 524, **538–539**
File Item Properties dialog box, *319*
File Location (Crystal Database menu), 437
File Manager (Windows), to create directory, 32, 1012
File menu, 12, **290–292**
  ➤ Append Records, 151
  ➤ Create Directory, 32
  ➤ Exit, 31
  ➤ Import, 151
  Most Recently Used files in, 291, 302
  ➤ New, 291
  ➤ Open, 291
  ➤ Print, 45
  ➤ Run, 32
  ➤ Save, 40
  ➤ Save As, 56
  in Table Records tools, 362–363
File menu (Crystal Reports), **395–411**
  ➤ New, Cross-Tab, 460
  ➤ New, Mailing Label, 474
  ➤ Options, 259, **400–411**
  ➤ Page Margins, 399–400
  ➤ Print, **396–400**
  ➤ Print, Report Definition, 399, 436
  ➤ Printer Setup, 399

➤ Set Label Layout, 281
File Name entry field (Open File dialog box), 990
file names, for sorted tables, 124
File properties, **298–300**
file server, setting elapsed time for refresh from, 646
File settings, for Table Records Properties tool, 1038
File Type drop-down list (Open File dialog box), **990–991**
File Types menu, in Navigator, **313**
files
command to change name, 622
command to copy, 595
command to delete, 602
deleting, 316
double-clicking to launch in Run mode, 315
exporting by printing, 397–398
Files list, in Navigator, **313–315**, 320
Files tab, in Desktop Properties dialog box, *34*
FileSort setting, in DBASEWIN.INI file, 1028
fill color, in reports, 430
@FILL command, 1048
FILTER setting, SETTO function and, 562
filters, 170–171
command to set, 638
financial functions, 521
FIND command, **608**
table properties for, 295
Find Records dialog box, *132*, 132
position of, 1041
speedbar button for, 367
Find What entry field (Find Records dialog box), 133
finding records, **131–134**
keyboard for, 133
finding and replacing, groups of records, **134–140**
fine-tuning forms, 711
First Normal Form, 72
First property, for Form object, 729
First record, speedbar button for, 367
fixed field lengths, 384
FIXED function, 1071
fixed-length character fields, 77
FKLABEL function, 1071
FKMAX function, 1071
FLDCOUNT function, 519, **539**
FLDLIST function, 519, **539**
FLENGTH function, 521, **539**
float field types, 352
changing type, 360–361
FLOAT function, 522, **539**
floating-point number, 510
floating speedbars, 301
FLOCK function, 1072
FLOOR function, 522, **540**
floppy disks, 5
FLUSH command, **608**
.FMT file extension, 300, 314
focus
ActiveControl property and, 728
for pushbutton, 928
FocusBitmap property, for Pushbutton objects, 952
Follow Index (Table Record Properties dialog box), 373
Follow property, for Browse objects, 890
Font dialog box, 410, **993**, *994*
function to launch, 1074
Font section, in DBASEWIN.INI file, **1014**
Font setting, for Program Editor, 1040
FontBold property
for Browse objects, 890
for Checkbox object, 822
for Combobox objects, 898
for Editor objects, 906
for Entryfield objects, 831
for Listbox objects, 915
for Pushbutton objects, 952
for Radiobutton objects, 840
for Rectangle object, 782
for Spinbox objects, 849
for Text object, 788
FontItalic property
for Browse objects, 890
for Checkbox object, 822
for Combobox objects, 898
for Editor objects, 907
for Entryfield objects, 831
for Listbox objects, 915–916
for Pushbutton objects, 953
for Radiobutton objects, 840
for Rectangle object, 782
for Spinbox objects, 849
for Text object, 788
FontName property
for Browse objects, 890
for Checkbox object, 822
for Combobox objects, 899
for Editor objects, 907
for Entryfield objects, 831

for Listbox objects, 916
for Pushbutton objects, 953
for Radiobutton objects, 840–841
for Rectangle object, 782
for Spinbox objects, 849
for Text objects, 771–772, 788

fonts
for Command window, 337, 1026
in Crystal Reports, 445
for forms, 52
for report title, 60
size of, 993
size and style in Crystal Reports, **269–270**
for Text objects, **769–773**

FontSize property, 208
for Browse objects, 890
for Checkbox object, 823
for Combobox objects, 899
for Editor objects, 907
for Entryfield objects, 831
for Listbox objects, 916
for Pushbutton objects, 953
for Radiobutton objects, 841
for Rectangle object, 782
for Spinbox objects, 849
for Text objects, 770, 789

FontStrikeOut property
for Checkbox object, 823
for Combobox objects, 899
for Editor objects, 907
for Entryfield objects, 831
for Listbox objects, 916
for Pushbutton objects, 953
for Radiobutton objects, 841
for Rectangle object, 782
for Spinbox objects, 849
for Text object, 789

FontStyle property, for Text objects, 772

FontUnderline property
for Checkbox object, 823
for Combobox objects, 899
for Editor objects, 907
for Entryfield objects, 831
for Listbox objects, 916
for Pushbutton objects, 953
for Radiobutton objects, 841
for Rectangle object, 782
for Spinbox objects, 849–850
for Text object, 789

footers for reports, **261–264**
in cross-tab report, **464**
page numbers in, 264

FOPEN function, 1072

For entry field
in Count Records dialog box, 145–146
in Index dialog box, 997
in Replace Records dialog box, 138, *139*
in Scope panel, 999

FOR function, 519, **540**

FOR loops, 667–668

foreground color, in reports, 430

foreign keys, 94, 181–182
automating entry, **940–950**
changes to, 96–97
and relational integrity, 95

Form Designer, 18, 50, **52–55**, *53*, **200–251**, **694–711**
and CLASS blocks, 680
command to launch, 598, 599, 617
Controls palette, *18*, 19
desktop layout for, 201–203, *204*
launching, 201
Layout view, 708
mouse for, 53
Object Properties Inspector for selected object in, 714–715
Order view, 706–707, *707*
and parent windows, 986
speed menu for, 712

Form Designer Properties dialog box, *709*, 709–711
Revert to Pointer, 717

Form Expert, 18–20, *20*, **50–52**, 237, 940
Blank Form, *202*
field selection panel, *51*
launching, 291
and Spinbox objects, 817

Form Expert (Form Designer Properties dialog box), 710

Form Layout (View menu), 42

Form Layout view, 189
editing files in, 45
navigation buttons for, 44, 368
speedbar button for, 367

form letters, **480–491**
adding fields to, **485–486**
address fields in, 488–491
creating, **483–485**
eliminating blank lines from, 489–490
formula fields in, **486–491**
removing blank space from, 487

Form objects, 18
properties of, **727–737**, 1102–1103

mixed-type, 521
numeric, 522
string-related, 522–523
system-related, 524
time-related, 524
trigonometric, 524
type-conversion, 525
FUNIQUE function, 524, **540–541**, 1073
future value, function for, 521, **541**
FV function, 521, **541**
FWRITE function, 1073

▶ G

Gap Between Labels (Mailing Labels dialog box), 478
GDI (Graphics Device Interface) resources, 759
conserving, 809
general section, of .WFM file, 720
GENERATE command, **609**
Generate Records (Table Utilities menu), 386–387
Generate Records dialog box, 127
@GET command, 1048–1049
GETCOLOR function, 1073
GETDIR function, 1073
GETDIRECTORY command, 234
GETENV function, 1073
GETEXPR function, 1074
GETFILE command, 875–876
GETFILE function, 1074
GETFONT function, 1074
GetTextExtent() method, for Text object, 789
.GIF file extension, inserting file in report, 426
GO command, **609**
Go to Field dialog box, in Table Structure tool, 355
GO TOP command, 161, 669
Goto Record Number (Table menu), 366
grand total
adding in Crystal Reports, 425
speed menu for, 449
Graphic Device Interface (GDI) resources, 759
Graphic Format dialog box, *431*, 431–432
Graphic Position dialog box, 432
graphics
formatting, 431–432
inserting in reports, **426**
OLE for, 412
speed menu in Crystal Reports for, 453
gray areas, and print speed, 272–273
greater than (>) operator, 516
grid
in Form Designer, 709
settings for, 710–711
Grid settings, in DBASEWIN.INI file, 1037–1038
GridOneCharacter setting, in DBASEWIN.INI file, 1036
GridPixelUnits setting, in DBASEWIN.INI file, 1036
Group button, in Expression Builder, 340
group of fields, moving, 265
Group header, putting data in, 265–266
group number, inserting special field in report, 427
Group property
for Checkbox object, 823
for Pushbutton objects, 817, 953
for Radiobutton objects, 841
group section, inserting in report, **428**
Group Section (Crystal Edit menu), 418
Group Selection Formula (Crystal Report menu), 439
Group Sort Order (Crystal Report menu), 440
groups
creating in reports, **264–265**
sorting records within, 440
groups of records
deleting and recovering, **140–144**
finding and replacing, **134–140**
updating, **126–148**

▶ H

handles, *54*, 54
hard disks, 5
header, of .WFM file, 720
headers for reports, **261–264**
for cross-tab reports, **464**
field names in, 258
title in, 262–263
Heading entry field (Field Properties dialog box), 371
Headings (Programming properties), 303
HEADINGS setting, SET function and, 560
height of labels, 478
Height property
for Browse objects, 890

for Checkbox object, 823
for Combobox objects, 899
for Editor objects, 907
for Entryfield objects, 831
for Form object, 729
for Image object, 774
for Listbox objects, 916
for OLE objects, 1091
for Pushbutton objects, 953–954
for Radiobutton objects, 841
for Rectangle object, 782
for Scrollbar objects, 960–961
for Spinbox objects, 850
for Text object, 789
Help, on-line reference for object properties, 773
HELP command, **609–610**
Help files, command to change, 639
Help menu, 12–13, **308–309**
Windows Tutorial, 29
Help menu (Crystal Reports), **441–442**
HELP setting, SETTO function and, 562
Help topic, command to specify current, 651
HelpFile property
for Browse objects, 890
for Checkbox object, 823
for Combobox objects, 899
for Editor objects, 907
for Entryfield objects, 831
for Form object, 729
for Listbox objects, 916
for Menu object, 738
for Pushbutton objects, 954
for Radiobutton objects, 841
for Scrollbar objects, 961
for Spinbox objects, 850
HelpID property
for Browse objects, 891
for Checkbox object, 824
for Combobox objects, 899–900
for Editor objects, 908
for Entryfield objects, 831
for Form object, 729
for Listbox objects, 916–917
for Menu object, 738
for Pushbutton objects, 954
for Radiobutton objects, 842
for Scrollbar objects, 961
for Spinbox objects, 850
hexadecimal string
function to convert integer to, 1075
function to convert to integer, 1074
hi-bit characters, 403–404
Hide when Printing (Crystal Format String dialog box), 405
Hide when printing (Crystal Graphic Format dialog box), 432
hiding, report sections, 417, 434
HOME function, 1074
Horizontal Grid (Table Records Properties dialog box), 374
horizontally tiling windows, *306*
How to Use Help (Help menu), 309
HTOI function, 1074
hWnd property
for Browse objects, 891
for Checkbox object, 824
for Combobox objects, 900
for Editor objects, 908
for Entryfield objects, 831
for Form object, 729
for Image object, 774
for Listbox objects, 917
for OLE objects, 1091
for Pushbutton objects, 954
for Radiobutton objects, 842
for Rectangle object, 783
for Scrollbar objects, 961
for Spinbox objects, 850
for Text object, 789

 **I**

Iblock setting
in DBASEWIN.INI file, 1017
SETTO function and, 562
icons
adding to pushbuttons, 216–217
spacing settings in DBASEWIN.INI file, 1028
turning off in Control Palette, 710
IconType setting, in DBASEWIN.INI file, 1027
ID fields
adding to table structure, **105–107**
data entry by dBASE, **107–109**
as Read-only, 371
reestablishing unique, 129–131
for relating tables, 180
requirements for, 933–934
setting first, 937–938
ID function, 1074
ID property

for Browse objects, 891
for Checkbox object, 824
for Combobox objects, 900
for Editor objects, 908
for Entryfield objects, 831
for Image object, 774
for Listbox objects, 917
for OLE objects, 1091
for Pushbutton objects, 954
for Radiobutton objects, 842
for Scrollbar objects, 961
for Spinbox objects, 850
for Text object, 790
IDAPI (Independent Database Application Programming Interface), 976
IDAPI.CFG file, 1028
IDAPI Location Settings dialog box, 976, *977*
IDCHECK setting, SET function and, 560
IDs, *See* record IDs
IF statement, 662, 664–665
IIF function, 122, 490, 521, **541**
Image objects, **744–752**
aligning, **745–749**
properties of, 773–778, 1103–1104
visible and invisible, **749–752**
images
and catalogs, 322
Navigator menu for, 318
speed menus for, 320
IMPORT command, **610**
Import dialog box, 362, *363*
imported files, appending records from, 383–384
importing
data to dBASE for Windows, 151
spreadsheets, 362, *363*
indentation
of commands, 665
for nested blocks, 671–672
in Procedure Editor, 718
IndentSize setting, in DBASEWIN.INI file, 1039–1040
Independent Database Application Programming Interface (IDAPI), 976
index blocks, setting size, 295, 629, 639, 1017
INDEX command, **610**
Index dialog box, **996–998**
index expressions, 518
Index field, for table structure, 39, 106, 353
index files, opening, 640
Index Range (Table Record Properties dialog box), 373
Index Selector (Crystal Options dialog box), 403
INDEX setting, SETTO function and, 562
index tags, 118, 644
copying from .MDX file to .NDX file, 596–597
deleting from .MDX files, 602–603
function to return name, 520, **567**
selecting multiple, 167–168
selecting single, 165–167
in USE command, 167
indexed fields, updating, 129
indexes, **116–117**, **376–379**
adding and deleting, 121
balancing, 378
command to rebuild, 620–621
commands to turn off and on, 130, 935
descending, 998
function to return key expression for, 520, **545**
function to search for value in, 520, **558**
function to test for expression in, 520, **545**
managing from Query Designer, **164–168**
modifying, 119–120
storing, **117–119**
of unique records only, 651
infinite loops, 947–948
.INI files, multiple, 1012
Initiate() method, for DDELink objects, 1087
INKEY function, 1075
input. *See also* data entry
INPUT command, 611
input pane
copying contents to program file, 333
position in Command window, 336–337
running commands from, 330
input templates, **244–245**
InputPaneFont setting, in DBASEWIN.INI file, 1026
INSERT AUTOMEM command, **611**
INSERT command, **611**
Insert Database Field dialog box, 59, 257, 421, *422*, 485
Insert Detail Field Titles (Crystal Options dialog box), *259*, 259–260, 402
Insert field record button (Table Structure speedbar), 357
Insert Formula dialog box, 422, *423*, 487
Insert from File (Edit menu), for Command window, 333
Insert Group Section dialog box, *264*, 264, *428*
Insert menu (Crystal Reports), 421–428

  ➤ Box, 270, 426
  ➤ Database Field, 421, 485
  ➤ Formula Field, 422, 487
  ➤ Graphic, 426
  ➤ Group Section, 264, 428
  ➤ Line, 426
  ➤ Special Field, 264, 427, 464
  ➤ Summary Field, 423, *424*
  ➤ Summary Field, Grand Total, 425
  ➤ Summary Field, Subtotal, 424
  ➤ Text Field, 262, 422, 464
Insert mode, 45
Insert Object dialog box, 426, *427*
inserting, subtotal in Crystal Reports, 424–425
INSPECT function, 521, **541–542**
installing dBASE for Windows, **970–980**
  post-installation choices, **978–980**
  preloading hard disk, **970–971**
INT function, 469, 522, **542–543**
integers
  arithmetic operations and, 510
  as numeric constants, 500
INTENSITY setting, SET function and, 560
interactive tutors, installing, 975–976
Interactive Tutors (Help menu), 309
international list, and formatting, 245
inverted queries, 247–248
inverted relationship, running report with, **276**
invisible Image objects, **749–752**
  mouse events and, 751
ISALPHA function, 522, **543**
ISBLANK function, 522, **543–544**
ISCOLOR function, 522, **544**
ISLOWER function, 522, **544**
ISMOUSE function, 1075
ISTABLE function, 520, **544**
ISUPPER function, 523, **545**
italics, for report text, 263, 445
ITOH function, 1075

J

JOIN command, **611–612**
joining tables, 70–71

K

Keep Section Together (Format Section dialog box), *268*, 268, 435
key assignments, automating, **933–939**
key expression, in Index dialog box, 996–997
Key Fields box (Sort Records dialog box), 125
KEY function, 520, **545**
Key() method, for Entryfield objects, 833
KEY setting, SETTO function and, 562
keyboard, 31. *See also* typeahead buffer
  and Form Designer, 203
  for searching, 133
  and speedbar button, 928
  vs. mouse, 11
Keyboard (Data Entry properties), 296
Keyboard (Help menu), 309
KEYBOARD command, **612**
KEYMATCH function, 520, **545**
keys, unique, 73, 91–92

L

LABEL FORM command, **612–613**
labels. *See also* mailing labels
  adding to Rectangle object, **762–764**
  for Checkbox objects, **802–803**
  Navigator menu for, 318
  need for, in forms, 260
  speed menus for, 320
Language (Help menu), 309
language driver, 641, 1075
Language Driver Check (Table properties), 295
Large Icons, for Navigator, 318
LargeIconXSpacing setting, in DBASEWIN.INI file, 1028
lasso tool
  and button alignment, 698
  in Crystal reports, 415, 465
  in Form Designer, 415
  to move group of fields, 265
LASTKEY function, 1075
launching
  Crystal Reports, 255, 291, 484
  dBASE for Windows, 30
  dBASE for Windows Debugger, 335
  Expression Builder, 333–334, 337
  Expression Builder in Crystal Reports, 415, 422, 439
  files in Run mode, 315
  Form Designer, 201
  Form Expert, 291
  Menu Designer, 232, 246
  Procedure Editor, 222
  Program Editor, 291

Query Designer, 158, 291
Table Structure tool, 105, 291
Layout menu
➤ Align Special, 699
➤ Align Special, Absolute Vertical Center, 757
➤ Align Special Absolute Horizontal Center, 757
Layout view, in Form Designer, 700
layouts
disabling toggling between, 365
for forms, 52
.LBG file extension, 300, 314
.LBL file extension, 300, 314
LDRIVER function, 1075
leading zeros, in numeric constants, 501
LEFT function, 523, **546**
left margin, command to set, 642
Left property
for Browse objects, 891
for Checkbox object, 824
for Combobox objects, 900
for Editor objects, 908
for Entryfield objects, 833
for Form object, 729
for Image object, 774–775
for Line objects, 779
for Listbox objects, 917
for OLE objects, 1091
for Pushbutton objects, 954
for Radiobutton objects, 842
for Rectangle object, 783
for Scrollbar objects, 961
for Spinbox objects, 851
for Text object, 790
left-handed mouse, 30
LEN() command, 359
LEN function, 138, 523, **546**
LENNUM function, 523, **546**
less than operator (<), 516
LIBRARY file for subroutines, 641
LIBRARY setting, SETTO function and, 562
lightning bolt icon (run icon), 17
LIKE function, 523, **547**
Line Format dialog box, *433*
Line objects, **753–762**
color for, **761–762**
drawing circle, **759–761**
properties of, **778–780**, 1104
shape of, **756–759**
LINENO function, 1075–1076
LineNo property, for Editor objects, 908
lines
formatting, **433**
grabbing, 756–757
inserting in reports, **426**
speed menu in Crystal Reports for, 452
lines (menu separators), adding to menu, 230
lines per label, 480
Link Event (Procedure Editor Procedure menu), 723, 724–725
LinkFileName property, for OLE objects, 1091–1092
linking Checkbox objects, **799–802**
linking field, for relating tables, 181
Links dialog box, *420*, 420
LIST command, **613–614**
LIST COVERAGE command, **613–614**
LIST FILES command, **614**
LIST MEMORY command, 614
LIST STATUS command, **614**
LIST STRUCTURE command, **614–615**
Listbox objects, **882–887**
multiple selections from, 887
properties of, **914–923**, 1104–1105
LISTCOUNT function, 885–886, 1076
lists, of available windows, 13
LISTSELECTED function, 885, 1076
literal strings, quotation marks for, 134
LKSYS function, 1076
LOAD DLL command, 615
LOCAL variables, 681, **685**, 935
LOCATE command, **615**
and CONTINUE command, 593
Location (File properties), 298
LOCK function, 1076
Lock option, 294
Lock Selected Record, (Table menu), 365–366
LOCK setting, SET function and, 560
Lock spinbutton (Table Records Properties dialog box), 374
locked records
information about, 1076
setting attempts to access, 648
locking status of commands, 642
LOG10 function, 522, **547–548**
LOG function, 522, **547**
logical constants, 502
logical expression, for record selection in query, 170
Logical field types, 352
Checkbox object for data entry, 798
default settings for, 410
sorting values, 122–123

logical operators, 513–514
looking glass icon, to preview report, 261
LOOKUP function, 521, **548**
LOOP statement, 670–671
looping, 663, **667–671**
  infinite, 947–948
Lotus 1-2-3
  exporting to, 398
  importing spreadsheets from, 363
LOWER function, 523, **548**
  and $ operator, 513
lowercase characters, function to test for, 522, **544**
lowered border style, 765
LTRIM function, 523, **548–549**
LUPDATE function, 520, **549**

▶ M

macro facilities, 612
mailing, deletions to control, 143
mailing labels, **278–284**
  Crystal Reports for, **473–480**
  margins for, 283
  multi-column layout for, 435
  multiple-table set, **282–284**
  page margins for, 478
  printing, 281–282, **479–480**
  from single-table, **278–282**
Mailing Labels dialog box, 279, *280*, *474*, 474–478
  Choose Mailing Label Type, 474–476
  Define Mailing Label Layout section, **477–478**
  Gap Between Labels, 478
  Label Size section, 474
  leaving and returning to, **469**
  Number of Labels section, 477
  Printing Direction section, **476**
main menu
  creating, 228, *229*, 230
  for Navigator, **315–318**
Manage Indexes dialog box, 106–107, *114*, 114, 119, 353, 354, 356, *377*, 377, **994–995**, *995*
many-to-many relationships, 93
Margin (Programming properties), 303
Margin setting
  in DBASEWIN.INI file, 1019–1020
  SETTO function and, 562
margins
  command to set left, 642
  and label printing problems, 479–480
  for labels, 283
Mark, in DBASEWIN.INI file, 1017
MARK setting, SETTO function and, 562
master index, 117–119, 167
  picking, 131
master index tag, function to return name, 520, **551**
MAX function, 521, **549**
Maximize property, for Form object, 729
Maximized setting in DBASEWIN.INI file
  for Command window, 1025
  for Navigator, 1027
maximum, 146
  calculating, 389
MaximumSize setting, in DBASEWIN.INI file, 1030
MaxLength property, for Entryfield objects, 809–810, 833
Mblock setting
  in DBASEWIN.INI file, 1018
  SETTO function and, 562
MCOL function, 1076
MDI child windows, 987, *988*
MDI forms
  closing, 211
  menu for, 227
MDI() method, for Form object, 729
MDI property, for form, 210, 227, 241
MDOWN function, 1077
.MDT file extension, USE command and, 129
.MDX file extension, 117, 376. *See also* production indexes
  closing file with, 592
  controlling file contents, 994
  deleting tags from files, 602–603
  function to return number of active indexes in, 520, **568**
MDX function, 520, **549**
MDY function, 525, **549–550**
MEMLINES function, 1077
Memo Block, adjusting size, 295
Memo Editor, 298
memo field blocks, setting size, 642–643, 1018
memo field types, 352
  changing type, 361
  text editor for, 365
Memo fields, 82
  command to append to, 585
  command to place in array, 654
  copying to external text file, 595–596

Editor objects for, 874
replacing with file contents, 624
selecting word processor to edit, 1019
setting display width, 643
memo files, blocksize in, 629
MemoEditor section, in DBASEWIN.INI file, **1043**
memory
command to describe contents, 604–605
freeing after program termination, 590
MEMORY function, 220–221, 1077
memory variables, 503–504
command to release, 590
copying record fields to, 654
names vs. field names, 504–505
saving, 626
MEMOWIDTH setting, SETTO function and, 562
menu design, **226–236**
Menu Designer, 228, **725–727**
cascading menu creation, 230–231
launching, 232, 246
main menu creation, 228, *229*, 230
menus in, 726–727
pull-down menu creation, 230
speedbars for, 727
MENU function, 1077
Menu menu
➤ Delete Selected, 231
➤ Insert Menu Item, 276
➤ Insert Separator, 230
Menu objects
attaching form to, 246
attaching shortcut keys to, **234–236**
launching form from, 233
program code for, 228
properties of, **737–739**, 1105
MenuFile property, 227–228
for Form object, 730
menus
adding line separators to, 230
attaching actions to choices, 231–233
attaching to blank form, 227–228
choices from, **29–30**
creating functioning Exit option on, 232–233
for dBASE for Windows, **11–15**
non-MDI window vs. MDI window, 241
running report from, **275–276**
for Table Records tools, **362–366**
for Table Structure tool, **355–356**
for Table Utilities, 376
MESSAGE function, 1077
MESSAGE setting, SETTO function and, 562
methods, 712. *See also specific names*
attaching to event, 717
for class, 681
Methods tab (Object Properties Inspector), 214, 715
Microsoft Paintbrush, 746
Microsoft Windows, *See* Windows (Microsoft)
middle mouse button, 30
MIN function, 521, **550**
Minimize button, *9*, 11
Minimize property, for Form object, 730
Minimized setting in DBASEWIN.INI file
for Command window, 1025
for Controls palette, 1034
for Navigator, 1027
for Object Properties Inspector, 1032
minimum, 146
calculating, 389
Minimum installation, 971
miscellaneous functions, 521
mixed-type functions, 521
MKDIR command, **616**
MLINE function, 1077–1078
.MNU file extension, 228
MOD function, 522, **550–551**
modal forms, **201–211**
setting as modal, 210–211
modal windows
child windows, **986–987**
function to open, 1081
Mode property, for Browse objects, **863–864**, 891
modem, registering via, 442
MODIFY APPLICATION command, **616**
MODIFY command, 328–329
MODIFY COMMAND command, 159, **616**
MODIFY FILE command, 484
MODIFY FORM command, **617**
Modify Index dialog box, 121, *378*
MODIFY LABEL command, **617**
Modify Menu Property dialog box, 227
Modify property, 240
for Browse objects, 861, 891–892
for Editor objects, 881, 908
MODIFY QUERY command, 162, **617**
MODIFY REPORT command, 617
MODIFY STRUCTURE command, **617**
MODIFY VIEW command, **617–618**
MON() function, 468–469

monospaced fonts, 771
month, function to return as string from date, 533
MONTH function, 521, **551**
More Windows (Window menu), 306–307
Most Recently Used files
  DBASEWIN.INI file and, 1030
  in File menu, 291
mouse, 30, 1075
  for Form Designer, 53
  right button for speed menus, 21
  setting in Form Designer Properties dialog box, 711
  and speedbar button, 928
  vs. keyboard, 11
MOUSE setting, SET function and, 560
MousePointer property
  for Browse objects, 892
  for Checkbox object, 824
  for Combobox objects, 900
  for Editor objects, 909
  for Entryfield objects, 833
  for Form object, 730
  for Image object, 775
  for Listbox objects, 917
  for OLE objects, 1092
  for Pushbutton objects, 954–955
  for Radiobutton objects, 842
  for Rectangle object, 783
  for Scrollbar objects, 962
  for Spinbox objects, 851
  for Text object, 790
MouseRevertToPointer setting, in DBASEWIN.INI file, 1036
Move() method
  for Browse objects, 892
  for Checkbox object, 824–825
  for Combobox objects, 900–901
  for Editor objects, 909
  for Entryfield objects, 833
  for Form object, 730
  for Image object, 775
  for Listbox objects, 917
  for Pushbutton objects, 955
  for Radiobutton objects, 842–843
  for Rectangle object, 783
  for Scrollbar objects, 962
  for Spinbox objects, 851
  for Text object, 790
MOVE WINDOW command, 1054
Moveable property, for Form object, 731
moving
  fields in table structure, **39–40**
  group of fields, 265
  multiple objects, 219
  objects, 54
MROW function, 1078
MRU Files List, in DBASEWIN.INI file, 1030
MRU_Files section, in DBASEWIN.INI file, **1029–1030**
MRU Size spinbutton, 302
Multi-Column Layout dialog box, 435, *436*
multiple objects, selecting in form, 219
multiple projects, multiple DBASEWIN.INI file files for, 1010, **1011–1012**
Multiple property, for Listbox objects, 918
multiusers
  REFRESH command and, 620
  setting choices, 294

▶ N

Name property
  for Browse objects, 892
  for Checkbox object, 825
  for Combobox objects, 901
  for Editor objects, 909
  for Entryfield objects, 834
  for Image object, 775
  for Line objects, 779
  for Listbox objects, 918
  for Menu object, 738
  for OLE objects, 1092
  for Pushbutton objects, 955
  for Radiobutton objects, 843
  for Rectangle object, 783
  for Scrollbar objects, 962
  for Spinbox objects, 851
  for Text object, 790
name tags, 474
names, for memory variables, 503–504
natural logarithm, function for, 522, **547**
Natural order, for records, 114, 119, 935
navigation
  coordinating, 945–946
  in forms, 56
  of records, Browse objects for, 860
  in tables, 44
Navigator, **310–320**, *311*
  adding *.MNU files to, *246*
  catalog as, *322*

O

appearance of, 301–302, **1031–1033**
for Browse object, 238–240
for Checkbox objects, 799–800, *800*
Events tab, 214–215, 715
Events tab, for Exit menu option, 232
in Form Designer, 202
function to open, 521, **541–542**
to make circle, 760–761
in Menu Designer, 228
Methods tab, 214, 715
outline for, 712–713
Properties tab, Bitmap Properties, 216
Properties tab, spinbutton, 244, *245*
for pushbuttons, 213
for selected object in Form Designer, 714–715
sizing, 713–714
for text object, 206, 207
Object Properties Outline checkbox, 301–302
object reference variable, 506
object references, 505–506
ObjectProperties, in DBASEWIN.INI file, **1031–1033**, 1035
objects, 17
command to create and assign properties, 601–602
command to modify definitions, 619–620
creating, 515
deleting from memory, 621–622
forms as, 53
inserting in reports, **426**
moving, 54
refreshing display on form, 652
selecting on form, 219, 697
speed menu in Crystal Reports for, 453
Objects (Crystal Edit menu), 420
ODOMETER setting, 644
SETTO function and, 562
OEM characters, ANSI equivalent, 1065
OEM function, 1078
OF clause, in USE command, 167
OK pushbutton, adding to .WFM file, 720–721
OKBUTTON Custom Control, 212
Older File Types (File properties), 299, 300, 314, 991
OlderFileTypes setting, in DBASEWIN.INI file, 1023
OldStyle property
for Checkbox object, 825
for Entryfield objects, 834
for Listbox objects, 918
for Radiobutton objects, 843
for Rectangle objects, **764–765**, 784
for Spinbox objects, 851
for Text object, 791
OLE field types, 352, 624
editor for, 365, 420
properties of, **1090–1094**, 1105
OLE programming, 1086
OLEType property, for OLE objects, 1092
ON BAR command, 1054–1055
ON command, 679–680
ON ERROR command, 679
ON EXIT BAR command, 1055
ON EXIT MENU command, 1055
ON EXIT PAD command, 1055
ON EXIT POPUP command, 1055
ON KEY command, 679–680
ON MENU command, 1056
ON MOUSE command, 1056
ON PAD command, 1056
ON POPUP command, 1056
ON SELECTION BAR command, 1057
ON SELECTION MENU command, 1057
ON SELECTION PAD command, 1057
ON SELECTION POPUP command, 1057
OnAdvise() method, for DDETopic objects, 1089
OnAppend() method
and auto-increment field, 934–935
for Browse objects, 892
for Form object, 731, 872, 939, 941
OnChange() method
for Browse objects, 892
for Checkbox object, 825
for Combobox objects, 901
for Editor objects, 909
for Entryfield objects, 834
for Form object, 731
for Listbox objects, 918
for OLE objects, 1092
for Radiobutton objects, 843
for Scrollbar objects, 962
for Spinbox objects, 852
OnClick() method, 241, 243
attaching event handler to, 215
for Menu object, 738
for Pushbutton objects, **926–928**, 955
OnClick property, 232
OnClose() method
for Form object, 731
for OLE objects, 1092
one-to-many relationships, 93, 932

for Text object, 792–793
OnRightMouseUp() method
for Browse objects, 895
for Checkbox object, 827–828
for Combobox objects, 903
for Editor objects, 912
for Entryfield objects, 836
for Form object, 734
for Image object, 777
for Listbox objects, 921
for Pushbutton objects, 958
for Radiobutton objects, 846
for Rectangle object, 786
for Scrollbar objects, 965
for Spinbox objects, 854
for Text object, 793
OnSelChange() method, for Listbox objects, 921
OnSelection() method, for Form object, 734
OnSize() method, for Form objects, 734, 880
OnUnadvise() method, for DDETopic objects, 1089
OPEN DATABASE command, **618**
Open File dialog box, 291, *986*, **988–992**
Directory rectangle, **990**
Disk Drive drop-down list, **992**
File Name entry field, 990
File Type drop-down list, **990–991**
function to launch, 1074
program code for, 875
radio buttons, **992**
tabbing order, **989**
OPEN FORM command, **618**
Open() method, for Form object, 734, 877
Open Table Required dialog box, *57*, 57, 185, 236
for labels, 282
for Query Designer, 47
opening table, command for, 129
operands
in expressions, **500–509**
expressions as, 508–509
operating system, 1079
operators, in expressions, **509–517**
Options dialog box (Crystal Reports), *259*, **400–411**
Database options, 402–404, *403*
Font options, 410–411, *411*
Format options, *404*, 404–410
General options, 400–402, *401*
OR conditions
evaluating, 176
for queries, 173, 175
.OR. operator, 513–514
ORDER clause, for USE command, 167, 657
ORDER function, 520, **551**
order of precedence, 508
Order setting
in DBASEWIN.INI file, 1029
SETTO function and, 562
Order view, in Form Designer, 700
Orgs form, **242–247**, *242*
adding pushbuttons, **242–243**
Orgs table, creating, 180, *181*
OS function, 1079
OTHERWISE statement, in DO CASE block, 666
outline, for Object Properties Inspector, 712–713
Outline setting, for Object Properties Inspector, 1031–1032
output, setting device for, 635
Overstrike mode, 45

 **P**

PACK command, 143, **618**, 938
Pack Records (Table Utilities menu), 381–382
PAD function, 1079
PADPROMPT function, 1079
page footer, speed menu for, 450
Page header, *See* headers for reports
page margins, for labels, 478
page numbers
inserting special field in report, 427
in report footer, 264
page size, for mailing labels, 477
pages, speedbar buttons to move between, 367
PanePosition setting, in DBASEWIN.INI file, 1026
PaneRatio setting, in DBASEWIN.INI file, 1025
Paradox tables, 934
continuous packing of, 381
as default type, 294–295, 633
setting as default type, 1017
parallel ports, 4
parameters, for functions, 675
PARAMETERS command, 675–676
parent-child relationship, 93
Parent property, 506
for Browse objects, 895
for Checkbox object, 828

for Combobox objects, 903–904
for Editor objects, 912
for Entryfield objects, 837
for Image object, 777–778
for Line objects, 779–780
for Listbox objects, 921
for Menu object, 739
for OLE objects, 1093
for Pushbutton objects, 958
for Radiobutton objects, 846
for Rectangle object, 786
for Scrollbar objects, 965
for Spinbox objects, 854
for Text object, 793

parent records
deletion and relational integrity, 97
showing every, 192

parent table, 186
inverting order with child table, 247
and referential integrity, 190

parent windows, **985–986**, *985*

parentheses
for expressions, 508–509
inserting with Expression Builder, 340
and logical operators, 514
for method property, 877
for negative values, 407

Paste (Edit menu), 292
Paste button (Crystal Paste Special dialog box), 413
Paste lists, in Expression Builder, **340–342**, *341*
Paste Special button (Crystal Paste Special dialog box), 413
Paste Special dialog box, 412, *413*

pasting
from Clipboard, 364
to and from Command window, **345**

path, specifying full, 638
PATH setting, SETTO function and, 562
Path variable, 1015
paths, setting for file search, 644
PatternStyle property, for Rectangle objects, **767**, 786
PAYMENT function, 507, 521, **551–552**
PCOL function, 1079
PCOL setting, SETTO function and, 562
PCOUNT function, 1079
.PCX file extension, 314, 623
inserting file in report, 426
Peek() method, for DDELink objects, 1087
peel-and-stick labels, 476
Pen property, for Line objects, 780

People form creation, **236–241**
base form for, 237, *238*
Browse Layout view for, **237–240**
building query, **236–237**
completed form, *240*
tying form into system, 241

percent sign, displaying, 446
period (.), as "property of" operator, 222, 514
phone list form, *249*
physical sorting, of tables, **123–126**
PI function, 524, **552**
pica, 770
Picture property, 244–245, *245*
bug in Form Designer handling of, 223
for Entryfield objects, 837
for Spinbox objects, **820**, 854
for text in forms, 224
for Text object, 793

picture string, function to format input string with, 523, **569**
pictures, field types for, 352
pitch of bell, 628
PLAY SOUND command, **619**
Point, setting options for decimal number, 293
Point character, in DBASEWIN.INI file, 1015
point and click, in Navigator window, 10
point (measurement), 770
POINT setting, SETTO function and, 562
point size, for report title, 60
Poke() method, for DDELink objects, 1087
population, 416
POPUP function, 1080
pop-up menus, *See* Speed menus

Position setting in DBASEWIN.INI file
for Command window, 1025
for Controls palette, 1033
for Desktop, 1021
for Navigator, 1027
for Object Properties Inspector, 1032
for Program Editor, 1039

Precision (Programming properties), 303

Precision setting
in DBASEWIN.INI file, 1019
SETTO function and, 563

preferences, setting for Desktop, 14
present value, function for, 521, **553**
presorting mail, 279
preview window (Crystal Reports), **63**, **261**, *262*, **266–267**, 397
for cross-tab report, **464**
speedbar for, **447–448**
working in, 269

Previous Record (Table menu), 366
.PRG file extension, 314, 593, 684
Primary key integrity, 933
primary keys, 73, 94
  changes to, 96
principal, function to return payment required to repay, 521, **551–552**
Print at Bottom of Page (Format Section dialog box), 434
Print Date dialog box, 440, *441*
Print() method, for Form object, 735
Print Records dialog box, 45
Print Setup dialog box, 399
printer
  command to write directly to, 583
  directly programming, 688
printer column, command to set, 645
Printer Margins dialog box, 399–400, *400*
printer output
  closing file receiving, 592
  commands for, 581
printer row, setting, 646
PRINTER setting
  SET function and, 560
  SETTO function and, 563
Printer Setup dialog box, 1069
printing
  in Crystal Reports, **396–400**
  default margin for, 303
  excluding fields from, 405, 407
  gray areas and speed of, 272–273
  labels, 281–282
  mailing labels, 281–282, 284, **479–480**
  reports, 275
  table structure, 614
  tables, **45–46**
Printing Reports dialog box, 275
PRINTJOB command, **688**
PRINTSTATUS function, 1080
PRIVATE variables, **686–687**
Procedure Editor, 202, 215–216, 232, **717–725**
  to create working button, 213–216
  drop-down list, 721–723
  in Form Designer, 202
  launching, 222
  OnClick event, 241
  Procedure menu, 723
  properties of, 717–719
procedure files, closing, 592, 682
PROCEDURE setting, SETTO function and, 563
PROCEDURE statement, 673–674
PROCEDURE subroutine, vs. FUNCTION subroutine, 673
ProcedureEditor section, in DBASEWIN.INI file, **1044**
ProcedureEditor setting, in DBASEWIN.INI file, 1035
procedures, calling with DO statement, 678
production indexes, 117, 376
  rebuilding, 378–379
program code
  Clipboard to copy, 939
  for Open File dialog box, 875
  semicolon for multiple statements on single line, 883
program compiler, 593
Program Development (Programming properties), 303–304
Program Editor, 159, 195, 298
  command to start, 616
  launching, 291
  starting Expression Builder from, 338
Program Editor Properties dialog box, *160*
PROGRAM function, 1080
Program Manager
  building dBASE group in, 978–979
  dBASE for Windows group in, *29*
  keystrokes to move between groups, 31
Program menu, for Command window, **334–335**
program statements, **662–690**
  block statements, **663–672**
  commenting out during testing, 224–225
  comments for, **688**
  conditional execution of, 662
  inter-file structure, **682–685**
  intra-file structure, **673–681**
  nesting, **671–672**
  variable declarations, **685–688**
ProgramEditor section, in DBASEWIN.INI file, **1038–1041**
Programming properties, **302–304**
programs, **694–695**
  analysis with SET COVERAGE command, 631
  command to run, 605–606
  command to terminate, 587–588
  information on frequently used sections, 335
  Navigator menu for, 318
  readability of, 665
  setting Esc key to interrupt, 637
  speed menus for, 320

stopping execution, 655
Projection-Join Normal form, 73
PROMPT function, 1080
PROPER function, 523, **552**
for replacing records, 136
properties, 18, 712
of Browse objects, 1098–1099
of Checkbox objects, **821–829**, 1099
of Combobox objects, **897–905**, 1100
of data-entry objects, **821–857**
of DDELink objects, **1086–1088**, 1100
of DDETopic objects, **1088–1090**, 1101
of Editor objects, **905–914**, 1101
of Entryfield objects, **829–839**, 1102
of Form objects, **727–737**, 1102–1103
of Image objects, **773–778**, 1103–1104
of line objects, **778–780**, 1104
of Listbox objects, **914–923**, 1104–1105
of Menu objects, **737–739**, 1105
objects including specific, 1114–1130
of OLE objects, **1090–1094**, 1105
of Procedure Editor, 717–719
of Pushbutton objects, **951–959**, 1106
of radiobutton objects, **839–847**, 1106–1107
of rectangle objects, **781–787**, **1107–1108**
for Scrollbar objects, **960–967**, 1108
of Spinbox objects, **847–857**, 1108–1109
Static objects reference for, **773–794**
of Text objects, **787–794**, 1109–1110
Properties menu, 14, **292–304**
➤ Catalog Window, 325
for Command window, **336–337**, *336*
➤ Desktop, 22, 33
➤ Desktop, Applications tab, 291, **300–302**, *300*, 813
➤ Desktop, Country, 293
➤ Desktop, Data Entry, **296–297**
➤ Desktop, Deleted feature, 141
➤ Desktop, Files, **298–300**
➤ Desktop, Files, Edit Records box, 159
➤ Desktop, Files, Older File types, 299, 300, 314, 991
➤ Desktop, Programming, **302–304**, *302*
➤ Desktop, Table tab, 140, **294–295**
➤ Form Designer, 709
➤ Navigator, **318–319**
➤ Navigator, Use Supplemental Search Path, 36, 318
➤ Procedure Editor, 717
➤ Program Editor, 159
➤ Selected File Item, 319
➤ Table Records Properties, 368
for Table Records Tools, 366
➤ Table Records Window, 107, 109, 182
for Table Structure tool, 356
➤ Table Structure window, 356
➤ Text Editor, 484
"property of" operator, period (.) as, 222, 514
proportional fonts, 771
PROW function, 1080
PROW setting, SETTO function and, 563
PUBLIC variables, **687**
pull-down menus, creating, 230
PUSHBUTTON1_ONCLICK method, 927
Pushbutton objects, 696, **926–930**
properties of, **951–959**, 1106
and Speedbar property, **928–929**
pushbuttons
adding icon to, 216–217
adding to form, **242–243**
alignment of, 697–698
attaching to form, **212–225**
and field selectors in dialog boxes, **1005**
PUTFILE function, 1081
PV function, 521, **553**

➤ Q

.QBE file extension, 50, 314
aliases and, 861
deleting, 157
for reports, 58
.QBO file extension, deleting file with, 157
.QRY file extension, 300, 314
Quattro Pro
exporting to, 398
importing spreadsheets from, 363
queries, **46–50**. *See also* single-table queries
building consolidated results table from, 276–277
building for form, **236–237**
to define table relationships, 23
editing program, **194–196**
inverted, 247–248
multiple conditions for multiple fields, 173–176
multiple conditions for one field, 172–173, *173*
for multi-table forms, 940
Navigator menu for, 317
relating tables for two-table database, **185–186**

relational operator in, 49
running, 158
saving, 50, 193
setting conditions on multiple fields, 171–172
speed menus for, 320
for two-table reports, **254–255**
Query Designer, **47–50**, **156–197**, 236–237
capitalization of commands in, 163
command to launch, 600, 601, 617
Conditions box, 177
dragging fields to change orders, 164
exiting, **49–50**
launching, 158, 291
managing indexes, **164–168**
SET RELATION command from, 647
speedbar button to launch, 367
switching to, 49
query files, specifying for current database view, 651
Query menu
➤ Add Table, 185, 254
➤ Create Calculated Field, 178
➤ Manage Indexes, 168
➤ Modify Relation, 190
Query Results Table view, *48*
query view, using, 189–190
QueryDesigner section, in DBASEWIN.INI file, **1043**
QUIT command, **619**
quotation marks, for strings, 49, 134, 135, 501

► R

@R function, 1002
"R" function, for Text object, 224
radians, converting degrees to, 524, **536**
Radiobutton objects, **815–817**
properties of, **839–847**, 1106–1107
vs. Checkbox objects, 816
raised border style, 765
random-access storage, 5
RANDOM function, 522, **553**
random numbers and text, generating for testing, 128
Range option (Field Properties dialog box), 371
Range properties, of Spinbox objects, 819
RangeMax property
for Scrollbar objects, 965
for Spinbox objects, 819, 855
for spinbutton, 244
RangeMin property
for Scrollbar objects, 965
for Spinbox objects, 244, 819, 855
RangeRequired property, for Spinbox objects, 855
RAT function, 523, **554**
READ command, 1057–1058
READ.ME file, 979–980
Read Only check box (Field Properties dialog box), 371
Read Only primary keys, 96
readability of programs, 665
READKEY function, 1081
READMODAL function, 1081
ReadModal() method, for Form object, 735
read-only property, 727, 821
RECALL command, **619**
Recall Records dialog box, *142*, *381*
Recall Selected Record (Table menu), 366
RECCOUNT function, 388, 520, **554**
RECNO function, 109, 507, 520, **554**
Reconnect() method, for DDELink objects, 1087
record IDs, 78
and database integrity, 90
deleted records and, 92
record number, inserting special field in report, 427
record number column, removing from display, 240
record pointer
command to move, 609, 649, 652
SET NEAR command for position after SEEK, 643
Record Selection Formula (Crystal Report menu), 439
Record Sort Order dialog box, 64, *439*, 439–440
records, 7, *8*. *See also* groups of records
command to count in current table, 597–598
command to delete, 602
command to insert blank, 611
command to retry access, 626
command to update, 622–623
counting active, 145
counting contiguous, 146
counting those matching condition, 145
counting total in table, 145
deleting all in table, 144, 659
finding, **131–134**

function to count, 520, **554**
Natural order for, 114, 119
preventing appending, editing or deleting, 373
pushbutton to add blank, 243
relational integrity and adding, 94–95
saving, 46
selecting for single-table queries, **169–177**
updating from array data, 624
using replace on all, 134–135
viewing single, 42
zapping all, 382
recovering, deleted groups of records, **140–144**
RECSIZE function, 520, **554–555**
rectangle objects, **762–767**
border styles for, *765*, 765–766, *766*
OldStyle property, **764–765**
PatternStyle property for, **767**
properties of, **781–787**, 1107–1108
Text property to add label, **762–764**
REDEFINE command, **619–620**
redundant data, 82
referential integrity, 940
REFRESH command, **620**
Refresh counter, 294
Refresh data on every print (Crystal Options dialog box), 402
Refresh Items (Navigator menu), 317–318
Refresh Report Data (Crystal Report menu), 440
Refresh setting
in DBASEWIN.INI file, 1017
SETTO function and, 563
refuse deletes, 97
registration information, for Crystal Computer Services, 442
REINDEX command, **620–621**
related tables, using, **188–194**
RELATION function, 520, 555
RELATION setting, SETTO function and, 563
relational databases, **5–7**
relational integrity, 91
maintaining, **92–98**, 190–192
relational operators, 516–517
in query, 49, 174
Relative Horizontal Center option, for control alignment, 699
Relative Vertical Center, for control alignment, 700
RELEASE AUTOMEM command, 621
RELEASE command, **621**
RELEASE DLL command, **621**
RELEASE MENUS command, 1058
Release() method
for Browse objects, 895
for Checkbox object, 828
for Combobox objects, 904
for DDELink objects, 1088
for DDETopic objects, 1090
for Editor objects, 912
for Entryfield objects, 837
for Form object, 735
for Image object, 778
for Line objects, 780
for Listbox objects, 921
for Menu object, 739
for OLE objects, 1093
for Pushbutton objects, 958
for Radiobutton objects, 846
for Rectangle object, 786
for Scrollbar objects, 965
for Spinbox objects, 855
for Text object, 793
RELEASE OBJECT command, **621–622**
RELEASE POPUPS command, 1058
RELEASE SCREENS command, 1058
RELEASE WINDOWS command, 1058
Remove Method (Procedure Editor Procedure menu), 723
RENAME command, **622**
RENAME TABLE command, **622**
REPLACE AUTOMEM command, **623**
REPLACE BINARY command, **623**
REPLACE command, 129, **622–623**
REPLACE FROM ARRAY command, **624**
REPLACE MEMO command, **624**
REPLACE MEMO FROM command, **624**
REPLACE OLE command, **624–625**
Replace Records dialog box, 108–109, *110*, **134–140**, *135*, *136*
Advanced >> pushbutton, 138, *139*
For clause, 138, *139*
position of, 1041
While clause, 139–140
REPLICATE function, 523, **555**
report bands
for Grand total, 425
speed menus for, **449–450**
report data, Crystal Report copy of, 267
REPORT FORM command, 276, **625**
Report menu (Crystal Reports), **438–440**
➤ Record Sort Order, 64, 439
report sections

deleting, **418–419**
hiding, 417
report titles, formatting, 435–436
reports, **57–64**. *See also* Crystal Reports
adding fields to, 257–261
creating groups in, **264–265**
deleting column headings from, 259
drawing in, **270–271**
emphasizing names in, **273–274**
field names in Page Header, 258
font size in, 263
headers and footers for, **261–264**
lines and boxes in, **426**
Navigator menu for, 317
preventing section splitting in, **267–269**
printing, 275
running from menu, **275–276**
running from Navigator, **274–275**
sorting data, **63–64**
speed menus for, 320
titles for, **60–62**
two-table, **254–264**
verifying field existence for, 437–438
ReportSmith report writer, 57, 254
Reprocess button, 294
Reprocess setting
in DBASEWIN.INI file, 1017
SETTO function and, 563
Reset Page Number After (Format Section dialog box), 435
Resize/Maximize button, *9*, 11
resolution of screen, 11
RESTORE command, **625**
RESTORE IMAGE FROM command, **625**
RESTORE SCREEN command, 1059
RESTORE WINDOW command, 1059
results pane, 631
checking output in, **330**
clearing, 333
command to clear, 589
command to write expression results in, 328
displaying table structure in, 605
echo command results to, 650
listing records to, 613
pausing output in, 658
Speed menu for, 338
ResultsPaneFont setting, in DBASEWIN.INI file, 1026
RESUME command, **626**
RETRY command, **626**
Return key, 32. *See also* Enter key
RETURN statement, 673, 674, 675, 676–678
Revert to Pointer (Form Designer Properties dialog box), 711, 717
Rich Text Format, exporting to, 398
RIGHT function, 523, **555–556**
right-handed mouse, 30
Right Margin (Editor Properties dialog box), 718
right mouse button, for speed menus, 21
Right property, for Line objects, 780
RightMargin settings, in DBASEWIN.INI file, 1040
RLOCK function, 1081
ROLLBACK function, 1081–1082
ROUND function, 522, **556**
rounding
CEILING function to round up, 522, **531–532**
FLOOR function to round down, 522, **540**
INT function for, 522, **542–543**
setting default for, 407
ROW function, 1082
rows
label formatting in cross-tab reports, 466
in relational database, 7, *8*
.RPC file extension, 314
.RPL file extension, 281, 314
.RPT file extension, 314
RTOD function, 524, **556**
RTRIM function, 138, 487, 488, 512, 523, **556–557**
RUN function, 524, **557**
run icon (lightning bolt), 17
for query, 48
Run Mode, **20**
default layout for, 299
in Form Designer, 56
launching files in, 105, 315
running, form including menu, 231
running commands, from input pane, 330
running queries, 158, 188
running reports
with inverted relationship, **276**
from menus, **275–276**
from Navigator, **274–275**
run-time error messages, 636

▶ S

Safety check box (Programming properties), 304

Safety Net, for Expression Builder, 339, 340
SAFETY setting
    command to set, 648
    SET function and, 560
salutation field, in form letter, 487
sample, 416
sample files, installing, 975
SAVE command, **626**
Save Data with Closed Report (Crystal Options dialog box), 402
Save Data with Closed Report (Crystal Report menu), 440
Save Form dialog box, 210
SAVE SCREEN command, 1059
Save Table dialog box, 39
SAVE WINDOW command, 1059
Saved Data dialog box, *396*, 396, 402
saving
    before closing window, 306
    forms, 55
    queries, 50, 193
    records, 46
    table definition, 39
    in Table Records tools, 362
@SAY command, 1048–1049
ScaleFontName property, for Form object, 735
ScaleFontSize property, for Form object, 735
scaling graphics, 432
SCAN command, **689**
scientific notation, 501, 1003
Scope (Export Records dialog box), 150
Scope panel, **998–1000**, *999*
scope resolution operator (::), 721
screen resolution, 11
@SCROLL command, 1049
Scrollbar objects, **930–931**
    properties for, **960–967**, 1108
Scrollbar property
    for Editor objects, 881, 912
    for Form object, 735
SDF files, 149, 384
Search (Edit menu), for Command window, 333
Search (Help menu), 309
Search Path (File properties), 298
Search Path (Navigator), 312–313
Search Rules panel (Find Records dialog box), 134
searches. *See also* SEEK command
    LOCATE command for, 615
    operator for, 513
SearchPath setting, in DBASEWIN.INI file, 1029
Second Normal Form, 72
SECONDS function, 524, **557**
section splitting, preventing in reports, **267–269**
sections, formatting, 267, 434–435, *435*
SEEK command, **626**, 947, 948
    table properties for, 295
    vs. FIND command, 608
SEEK function, 520, **558**
SELECT 1 command, 160
Select All (Edit menu), for Command window, 332
SELECT command, **627**
Select Fields (Crystal Edit menu), 415
SELECT function, 520, **558**
Select Window dialog box, **994**, *995*
SelectAll property
    for Entryfield objects, **810–811**, 837
    for Spinbox objects, 855
Selected() method, for Listbox objects, 921
selecting. *See also* field selection
    file in Navigator list, 315
    multiple objects in form, 219
    objects on form, 697
    record in Browse Layout view, 363–364
    records for single-table queries, **169–177**
    title on reports, 263
semicolon, for multiple program statements on single line, 883
Send Behind Others (Crystal Format menu), 437
Send Farther speedbar button, 708
Send to Back speedbar button, 708
Separator character
    in DBASEWIN.INI file, 1015
    setting option, 293
Separator property, for Menu object, 739
SEPARATOR setting, SETTO function and, 563
serial data access, 4–5
serial ports, 4
serifs, 771
Server property, for DDELink objects, 1088
ServerName property, for OLE objects, 1093
sessions
    closing, 601
    command to create, 600–601
Sessions (File properties), 299
Sessions setting, in DBASEWIN.INI file, 1023

SET ALTERNATE command, **627**
SET ALTERNATE TO command, **628**
SET AUTOSAVE command, **628**
SET BELL command, **628**
SET BELL TO command, **628–629**
SET BLOCKSIZE TO command, **629**
SET BORDER command, 1060
SET CARRY command, **629**
SET CARRY TO command, **629**
SET CATALOG command, **629**
SET CATALOG TO, **630**
SET CENTURY command, **630**
SET COLOR OF command, 1060
SET COLOR TO command, 1060
SET command, 627
  and DBASEWIN.INI file settings, 1030
SET CONFIRM command, 630
SET CONSOLE command, **631**
SET COVERAGE command, **631**
SET CUAENTER command, **631**
SET CURRENCY command, **631**
SET CURRENCY TO command, **631–632**, 1003
SET CURSOR command, 1060
SET DATABASE command, **632**
SET DATE TO command, **632–633**
SET DBTYPE TO command, **633**
SET DECIMALS command, **633–634**
SET DEFAULT command, **634**
SET DELETED command, **634**, 865
SET DELIMITERS command, **634**
SET DELIMITERS TO command, **634–635**
SET DESIGN command, **635**
SET DEVELOPMENT command, **635**
SET DEVICE TO command, **635**
Set Directory dialog box, *402*, 402, 403
SET DIRECTORY TO command, **635–636**
SET DISPLAY TO command, **636**
SET ECHO command, **636**
SET EDITOR TO command, **636**
SET ERROR TO command, **636**
SET ESCAPE command, **637**
SET EXACT command, 160, **637**
SET EXACT ON command, 166, 193
SET EXCLUSIVE command, **637**
SET FIELDS command, 163, 164, **638**
SET FIELDS TO command, 638
  FLDLIST function and, 539
SET FILTER TO command, 170–171, **638**
SET FORMAT TO command, 1061
SET FULLPATH command, **638**
SET function, 521, **559–561**
SET FUNCTION command, **639**
SET HEADINGS command, **639**
SET HELP TO command, **639**
SET IBLOCK TO command, **639**
SET INDEX TO command, 130–131, **640**
SET INTENSITY command, 1061
SET KEY command, **640**
SET KEY TO command, **640–641**
SET LDCHECK command, **641**
SET LIBRARY TO command, **641**
Set Location dialog box, 437, *438*
SET LOCK command, **642**
SET MARGIN TO command, **642**
SET MARK TO command, **642**
SET MBLOCK TO command, **642–643**
SET MEMOWIDTH TO command, **643**
SET MESSAGE TO command, **643**
SET NEAR command, **643**
SET ODOMETER TO command, **644**
SET ORDER TO command, **644**, 935
SET PATH TO command, **644**
SET PCOL TO command, **645**
SET POINT TO command, **645**, 1003
SET PRECISION TO command, **645**
Set Print Date (Crystal Report menu), 440
SET PRINTER command, **645**
SET PRINTER TO command, **645**
SET PROCEDURE command, **682–683**
SET PROCEDURE TO command, **646**
SET PROW TO command, **646**
SET REFRESH TO command, **646**
SET RELATION command, vs. JOIN command, 611–612
Set Relation icon, 186
SET RELATION TO command, **647**
SET REPROCESS TO command, **648**
SET SAFETY command, **648**
SET SEPARATOR command, **649**
SET SEPARATOR TO command, 1003
SET SKIP TO command, 194, **649**
SET SPACE command, **649**
SET STATUS command, **649**
SET STEP command, **650**
SET TALK command, **650**
SET TIME TO command, **650**
SET TITLE command, **650**
SET TOPIC TO command, **651**
SET TYPEAHEAD TO command, **651**
SET UNIQUE command, **651**
SET VIEW command, **651**
SET VIEW TO command, 276

SET WINDOW OF MEMO TO command, 1061
SET WP TO command, **652**
SetFocus() method
  for Browse objects, 895
  for Checkbox object, 828
  for Combobox objects, 904
  for Editor objects, 912
  for Entryfield objects, 837
  for Form object, 735
  for Listbox objects, 921
  for OLE objects, 1093
  for Pushbutton objects, 958
  for Radiobutton objects, 846
  for Scrollbar objects, 965
  for Spinbox objects, 855
SETTO function, 521, **561–564**
shared access, 119
SHELL function, 1082
shortcut keys, attaching to menu object, **234–236**
Shortcut property, for Menu object, 739
Show Field Names (Crystal Edit menu), 419
Show Field Names (Options dialog box), 401, 419
Show/Hide Sections dialog box (Crystal Reports), *417*
SHOW MENU command, 1061
SHOW OBJECT command, **652**
SHOW POPUP command, 1061
ShowDeleted property, 240
  for Browse objects, 865, 896, 943
ShowGrid setting, in DBASEWIN.INI file, 1034
ShowHeading property, 240
  for Browse objects, 865, 896, 943
ShowRecNo property, 240
  for Browse objects, 865, 896, 943
ShowRuler setting, in DBASEWIN.INI file, 1036
SIGN function, 522, **564**
SIN function, 524, 564
single-table queries, **157–179**
  calculated fields, **178–179**
  selecting fields for, **162–164**
  selecting records, **169–177**
size of font, in reports, 263, 445
size of windows, changing, 11
Sizable property, for Form object, 736
sizing
  graphics, 432
  Object Properties Inspector, 713–714
  objects, 54
SKIP command, 168, **652**, 669, 935
  in DO WHILE .NOT. EOF(), 670
SKIP setting, SETTO function and, 563
SLEEP command, **652–653**
slide switch, Scrollbar object for, 931, *932*
Small Fonts set, 771
Small Icons, for Navigator, 318
SmallIconXSpacing setting, in DBASEWIN.INI file, 1028
Snap to Grid check box (Form Designer Properties dialog box), 709, 757
SnapTo setting, in DBASEWIN.INI file, 1035
Social Security number, 92
SORT command, **653**
Sort Records (Table Utilities menu), 385–386
Sort Records dialog box, *124*, 124–125, 385–386, *386*
Sorted property, for Combobox objects, **872–873**, 904
sorting
  arrays, 1066
  dates, 122
  files in Navigator, 1028
  logical values, 122–123
  physical for tables, **123–126**
  report data, **63–64**
  speed of, 116
SOUNDEX function, 523, **565**
SOUNDEX search, 134
sounds
  and catalogs, 322
  field types for, 352
  Navigator menu for, 318
  speed menus for, 320
source code, 157
Space (Programming properties), 303
SPACE function, 523, **565**
SPACE setting, SET function and, 560
spacebar, and directory list, 312
special fields
  inserting in reports, **427**
  speed menu in Crystal Reports for, 452
speed
  index rebuilding and, 378
  of printing, gray areas and, 272–273
  of sorting, 116
  While clause in Find & Replace, 139–140
Speed menus, **21**, 30, 315
  Add Records, 41
  Add Table, 158
  for Command window, **337–338**

for Crystal Reports, **448–453**
Design Menu, 246
Edit as Program, 159, 195, 223, 704
for fields, 450–451
Find Records, 132
Navigator, **319–320**
for results pane, 338
for Table Structure tool, **356–357**
Speedbar property, for Pushbutton objects, **928–929**, 958
speedbars, *9*, 9, **15–17**
ABC button, 60
for Command window, **331**
creating, 929
for Crystal preview window, **447–448**
in Crystal Reports, 62, **442–444**
Einstein icon, 487
icons to switch views, 43
for Menu Designer, 727
positioning, 22
print icon, 45
setting position, 301
for Table Records tools, **366–368**
for Table Structure tool, **357**
turning off or on for Crystal Reports, 400
z-order changes with, 708
SpeedBarStyle setting, in DBASEWIN.INI file, 1023–1024
Spinbox objects, **817–821**
borders of, 817, *818*, 819
increment for, 820–821
properties of, **847–857**, 1108–1109
range for, **819**
spinbuttons, 244
SpinOnly property, for Spinbox objects, 820, 855–856
spreadsheets, importing, 362, *363*
SQL database
command to open, 618
function to test for table in, 520, **544**
unique key in, 934
SQL tables
BOOKMARK function for, 531
continuous packing of, 381
SQLEXEC function, 520, **565–566**
SQRT function, 522, **566**
square brackets, for string constants, 501
square root, 566
standard deviation, 146
calculating, 389
Start Search From box, 133
starting. *See also* launching
dBASE for Windows, 30
startup code, of .WFM file, 720
state codes, converting to uppercase, 137–138
statements, vs. commands, **577**
static data table, physical sorting, 123
static objects, **744–794**
image objects, **744–752**, 773–778
line objects, **753–762**, 778–780
properties reference, **773–794**
rectangle objects, **762–767**, 781–787
Text objects, **768–773**, 787–794
static tables, 861–862
STATIC variables, **686**
status bar, *9*, 9, **17**
button descriptions on, 43
command to turn off and on, 649
font size for, 813
message for invalid data entry, 812
mode indicator in, 45
setting message displayed, 643
setting options, 301
turning off and on for Crystal Reports, 400
turning off and on, , 22
StatusMessage property
for Browse objects, 896
for Checkbox object, 828
for Combobox objects, 904
for Editor objects, 913
for Entryfield object, 812, 813
for Entryfield objects, 837
for Form object, 736
for Listbox objects, 922
for Menu object, 739
for OLE objects, 1093
for Pushbutton objects, 958
for Radiobutton objects, 846
for Scrollbar objects, 966
for Spinbox objects, 856
StatusMessageFont setting, in DBASEWIN.INI file, 1024
STEP clause, in FOR loop, 668
Step property, for Spinbox objects, 856
STEP setting, SET function and, 560
"stop" shape circle, cursor as, 460, 462
STORE AUTOMEM command, **654**
STORE command, **653–654**
STORE MEMO command, **654**
STR function, 221, 507, 525, **566**
stretch alignment, 745–749, *747*
strikeout type, 772–773
string operators, 512–513
string-related functions, 522–523

PROPER function, 523, **552**
to remove leading blanks, 523, **548–549**
to remove trailing blanks, 523, **570**
to return characters from right side, 523, **555–556**
to return left portion, 523, **546**
to return length, 138, 523, **546**
to return number of spaces as, **565**
to return time as, 524, **569**
STUFF function, 523, **567**

strings
converting numbers to, 221
converting to date, 525, **533**
empty, 490
function to center, 532
quotation marks for, 49, 134, 135
SET EXACT command and comparison, 637

Structure menu
➤ Insert Field, 105
➤ Manage Indexes, 106
in Table Structure tool, 355

structure operators, 514–516
STUFF function, 523, **567**
Style property, for Combobox objects, 904
subroutines, 673
code blocks as, **927–928**
dBASE search order for, 684
declarations, **673–675**
LIBRARY file for, 641
LOCAL variables for, 685
separate file for, 682
setting file to search for, 646

subscript operator, brackets ([ ]) as, 514
SUBSTR function, 523, **567**
substring
function to extract, 523, **567**
function to find, 523, **554**
function to return location in string, 522, **529**

subtotal, inserting in Crystal Reports, 424–425
sum, 146
calculating, 389

SUM command, **654–655**
summary field
inserting, 423, *424*
speed menu for, 451

Summary Field dialog box, *416*
Summary Operation (Crystal Edit menu), 415, 416
Suppress Blank Lines (Format Section dialog box), 435
Suppress if Duplicated option
in Crystal Format Number dialog box, 407
in Crystal Format String dialog box, 405

SUSPEND command, 587, **655**
symbols. *See also* currency symbol
in Choose Template dialog box, **1001–1004**

syntax of functions, 526–527
SysMenu property, for Form object, 736
system, attaching forms to, 246–247, 250
System button, *9*, 10
System menu
Alt-spacebar to access, 10
Close, 30
➤ Edit, Mark, 484
of MDI child window, 987
opening for modal child window, 986

system time, command to set, **650**
system-related commands, 579
system-related functions, 524

➤ T

@T function, 1002
.T. logical constant, 502
tab stops, 1040
tabbing order
for Open File dialog box, **989**
and z-axis, 702

table alias specifications, 504
Table of Contents, for Help, 309
table fields, speed menu for, 450
Table menu, 14
for Command window, 335
➤ Delete Selected Record, 140
➤ Find Records, 131
➤ Replace Records, 108, 134
for Table Records tools, 365–366
➤ Table Utilities, 375. *See also* Table Utilities menu

Table properties, **294–295**, *294*
Table Properties dialog box, custom Fields list, 107
Table Records Properties dialog box, 109, 182, *183*, **368–375**, *1006*
active tab in, 1037
Fields tab, *369*, 368–371
for Read Only primary keys, 96
Records tab, *372*, 372–373

Window tab, *374*, 374–375
Table Records tool, **41**, **362–375**
Browse objects and, 860
command to launch, 606–607
customizing, **109–113**
menus, **362–366**
speedbars, **366–368**
table structure
adding fields to, **351–354**
adding ID fields to, **105–107**
copying, 596
for cross-tab reports, *459*
displaying in results pane, 605, 614
storing in array, 1065
Table Structure tool, *16*, **37–39**, 105–106, *106*, 180, **350–362**
avoiding data loss during restructure, **358–362**
Browse area, **354**
CREATE command to open, 598
exiting from, 40
field definitions in, *38*, 38–39
file name in combo box, 354
launching, 105, 291
menus, **355–356**
record length given in, 387
speed menu, **356–357**
speedbar for, 17, **357**
Table Utilities, **375–390**
indexes, **376–379**
Table Utilities (Table menu), 365
Table Utilities menu, 375, 376
Append Records from File, 151, 383–384
Calculate, 359
Calculate Records, 147, 389–390
Close All Tables, 379
Close Table, 379
Count Records, 145, 387–388
Delete Records, 141, 379–380
Export Records, 148–150, 276, 384
Generate Records, 127, 386–387
Manage Indexes, 113–116, 168, 376–378
Pack Records, 143, 381–382
Recall Records, 141
Reindex, 378–379
Sort Records, 124, 385–386
Zap Records, 382
TableRecords section, in DBASEWIN.INI file, **1037–1038**
tables
approximating size of, 555
backup copies of, 144
catalogs as, **325**
command to add bulk data to, 584
command to close, 129, 592
command to close all, 591
command to delete, 602
command to physically join, 611–612
command to set relationships, 647
command to update, 622–623
converting single-user to multi-user, 593–594
creating, **35–40**
data arrangement in, **7–8**
default type for, **633**
deleting every record in, 144, 659
designing offline, 37
eliminating in database design, 84
function to return date of last update, 520, **549**
function to return number of fields in, 519, **539**
joining, 70–71
LOOKUP function for, 521, **548**
moving through, **55**
Navigator menu for, 317
opening for exclusive use, 637
physical sorting, **123–126**
printing, **45–46**
queries to define relationships, 23
selecting for Query Designer, *158*
speed menus for, 320
updating, 566–567
USE command to open, 657
TablesFromDatabase setting, in DBASEWIN.INI file, 1028
Tab-separated text, exporting to, 398
TabStop property, 238–239, 249
for Browse objects, 896
for Checkbox object, 828
for Combobox objects, 904
for Editor objects, 913
for Entryfield objects, 838
for Listbox objects, 922
for OLE objects, 1094
for Pushbutton objects, 959
for Radiobutton objects, 846
for Scrollbar objects, 966
for Spinbox objects, 856
TAG, in USE command, 167
TAG function, 520, **567**
TAGCOUNT function, 520, **568**
TAGNO function, 520, **568**
tags, *See* index tags

Talk (Programming properties), 303, 882
TALK setting, SET function and, 560
TAN function, 524, **568**
TARGET function, 520, **568**
TED Design method, 73, **74–89**
TEMP file name, for sorted data, 124
Template entry field (Field Properties dialog box), 371
templates, **1000–1004**
  for input, **244–245**
temporary data table, created by Crystal Reports, 396
Terminate() method, for DDELink objects, 1088
testing
  commenting out program sections, 224–225
  expanding table for, 127–128, 387
  mailing labels, 278, 284
  temporary program for, 882
text. *See also* strings
  color of, 430
  for pushbutton, 213
text areas, speed menu in Crystal Reports for, 452
TEXT command, **689**
text editor, for form letter creation, 484
Text field (Crystal Edit menu), 415
Text field (Crystal Insert menu), 422
text fields
  to label grand total field, 425
  permitting multiple print lines for, 405
  speed menu for, 451
Text files, exporting to, 398
Text objects, *54*, 54, *206*, **768–773**
  in About form, 219
  adding properties with program, 224
  adding to blank form, 204–208
  aligning, **769**
  borders for, **768**
  for Combobox objects, 871–872
  FontName property for, 771–772
  fonts for, **769–773**
  FontSize property for, 770
  FontStyle property for, 772
  Object Properties Inspector for, 206, *207*
  properties of, **787–794**, 1109–1110
Text property, 768
  ampersand (&) for underscore in, 763
  for Browse objects, 896
  for Checkbox object, 828
  for Checkbox objects, 802–803
  for Form object, 736
  for Menu object, 739
  for Pushbutton objects, 243, 959
  for Radiobutton objects, 846–847
  for Rectangle object, 763–764, 766, 786
  for Text object, 793
TextEditor section, in DBASEWIN.INI file, **1042–1043**
.TGA file extension, inserting file in report, 426
Things, in TED database design, 74–75
Third Normal Form, 72
thousands separator
  command to specify, 649
  displaying or hiding, 446
  setting option, 293, 407
.TIF file extension, inserting file in report, 426
tiling windows, 13
  horizontally, *306*
  vertically, *307*
time, function to return difference, 524, **537**
TIME function, 524, **569**
TIME setting, SETTO function and, 563
TimeOut property, for DDELink objects, 1088
time-related functions, 524
Times New Roman, 771
title
  in report header, 262
  of window, changing, 374
Title (File properties), 299
Title (Table Records Properties dialog box), 374
TITLE setting, SET function and, 560
titles
  centering, 700
  for reports, **60–62**
@TO command, 1049
today's date, function to return, 520, **534**
Toggle Layout check box (Table Records Properties dialog box), 374
Toggle property
  for Browse objects, 863–864, 896
  to switch views, 240
toggles, 750
Top property
  for Browse objects, 897
  for Checkbox object, 828–829
  for Combobox objects, 905
  for Editor objects, 913
  for Entryfield objects, 838
  for Form object, 736

for Image object, 778
for Line objects, 780
for Listbox objects, 922
for OLE objects, 1094
for Pushbutton objects, 959
for Radiobutton objects, 847
for Rectangle object, 787
for Scrollbar objects, 966
for Spinbox objects, 856
for Text object, 794
Top Record (Table menu), 366
Topic property
for DDELink objects, 1088
for DDETopic objects, 1090
TOPIC setting, SETTO function and, 563
TOTAL command, **655–656**
total records, counting in table, 145
trailing blanks, function to remove, 523, **556–557**
TRANSFORM function, 523, **569**
Translate DOS Memos (Crystal Options dialog box), 403
Translate DOS Strings (Crystal Options dialog box), 403
trigonometric functions, 524
TRIM command, 359
TRIM function, 523, **570**
trimming operation, for strings, 512–513
TrueType fonts, 770, 993
tuple, 7, *8*
Turpins, 710
Tutors
installing, 975–976
speedbar button for, 16
two-table database, **180–194**
preparing, **180–183**
relating tables with queries, **185–186**
two-table report, **254–264**
definition, **255–257**
grouped, **264–269**
query for, **254–255**
Two-Way-Tool
Menu Designer as, 228
Query Designer as, 156, 194
.TXT file extension, 149
Type: lists
in Choose Data Source dialog box, 870
in Expression Builder, **340–342**, *341*
TYPE command, **656**
TYPE function, 221, 1082
typeahead buffer
clearing, 590–591
size of, 297, 651
Typeahead setting
in DBASEWIN.INI file, 1018
SETTO function and, 563
Typeahead spinbutton, 297
type-conversion functions, 525
typehead buffer, KEYBOARD command and, 612

▶ U

UDFs (user-defined functions), 508
Unadvise() method, for DDELink objects, 1088
unary negation, 510
underlined type, 772–773
for report text, 263, 445
underscore character, for dBASE internal global variable names, 503
Undo (Edit menu), 292
Unique check box, (Index dialog box), 997
UNIQUE function, 520, **570**
unique keys, 73
assigning, 91–92
command to set, 129
reestablishing, 129–131
UNIQUE setting, SET function and, 560
uniqueness, of ID field, 933–934
Unlink Event (Procedure Editor Procedure menu), 723, 724–725, *725*
UNLOCK command, **656**
UNTIL statement, in DO UNTIL loop, 669
Untitled icon
in Navigator, 36
for Table Structure tool, 38
UpBitmap property, 216
for Pushbutton objects, 959
update anomalies, 72
UPDATE command, **565–567**
UPDATED function, 1082
updating
data groups, **128–131**
groups of records, **126–148**
indexed fields, 129
UPPER function, 523, **570–571**
and $ operator, 513
and alphabetic sorting, 120
uppercase characters
converting state codes to, 137–138
function to test for, 523, **545**

USE command, 129, 161, 167, 325, 329, **657–658**
Use Default Margins check box (Printer Margins dialog box), 400
Use Indexes For Speed (Crystal Options dialog box), 403
Use Short Section Names (Options dialog box), 401
Use Supplemental Search Path check box (Navigator Properties dialog box), 312, 318
Use Windows Default Format (Crystal Format Date dialog box), 408
Use Windows Default Format (Crystal Format Number dialog box), 407
user-defined functions (UDFs), 508
user input, command for, 611
user interfaces, objects in, 17

V

VAL function, 361, 525, **571**
VALID handlers, 91
Valid() method
  for Editor objects, 913
  for Entryfield objects, 838
  for Spinbox objects, 856
Valid option (Field Properties dialog box), 371
Valid property, for Entryfield object, 811–812
VALIDDRIVE function, 1082
ValidErrorMsg property
  for Entryfield objects, 812, 838
  for Spinbox objects, 856–857
ValidRequired property
  for Entryfield objects, 838
  for Spinbox objects, 857
Value property
  for Checkbox objects, 803–804, 829
  for Combobox objects, 874, 905
  for Entryfield objects, 838–839
  for Listbox objects, 922
  for Radiobutton objects, 847
  for Scrollbar objects, 931, 966
  for Spinbox objects, 857
variable declarations, in programs, **685–688**
variance, 146
  calculating, 389
VARREAD function, 1083
.VBX file extension, 696, 716
VCR labels, 474
Verify Before Printing (Crystal Database menu), 438
Verify Database (Crystal Database menu), 437–438
Verify Method (Procedure Editor Procedure menu), 723
VERSION function, 1083
Vertical Grid (Table Records Properties dialog box), 374
Vertical property, for Scrollbar objects, 966
vertically tiling windows, *307*
View menu
  ➤ Browse Layout, 41, 107
  ➤ Columnar Layout, 42, 189
  in Form Designer, 700
  ➤ Form Layout, 42, 189
  in Navigator, 316–317
  ➤ Object Properties, 52
  ➤ Order Layout, 706
  ➤ Query Results, 49, 188
  in Table Records tools, 364–365
  in Table Structure tool, 355
View property, for Form object, 736
VIEW setting, SETTO function and, 563
viewing, single record, 42
views, 156, 179–180
  creating with Query Designer, 47
Views and Tools (Help menu), 309
Visible property
  for Browse objects, 897
  for Checkbox objects, 829
  for Combobox objects, 905
  for Editor objects, 913
  for Entryfield objects, 839
  for Form object, 737
  for Image object, 778
  for Image objects, **749–752**
  for Line objects, 780
  for Listbox objects, 922
  for OLE objects, 1094
  for Pushbutton objects, 959
  for Radiobutton objects, 847
  for Rectangle object, 787
  for Scrollbar objects, 966
  for Spinbox objects, 857
  for Text object, 794
Visual Basic, 696
visual properties, for Browse object, 240
.VUE file extension, 300, 314

▶ W

WAIT command, **658–659**
warning dialog box, 304
.WAV file extension, 314, 623
  command to play file, 619
WEDIT.PRO file, 875
.WFM file extension, 200, 210, 223, 314, 505–506, 694
  building text editor for files, **874–881**
  CLASS blocks in, 680–681
  editing file to change control order, 703–706
  file for line objects, *753*, 754–756
  for form, 233
  structure of file, 719–721
.WFO file extension, 201
"What is" (?) command, 168, 220, **328**, 499, 506–507, **582**
When entry field (Field Properties dialog box), 371
When() method
  for Browse objects, 897
  for Checkbox objects, 829
  for Combobox objects, 905
  for Editor objects, 914
  for Entryfield objects, 839
  for Listbox objects, 922
  for Pushbutton objects, **930**, 959
  for Radiobutton objects, 847
  for Scrollbar objects, 967
  for Spinbox objects, 857
While: entry field (Count Records dialog box), 145–146
While clause (Replace Records dialog box), 139–140
white space, in programs, 665
width of fields, 38
  maximum display, 374, 375
width of labels, 478
Width property
  for Browse objects, 897
  for Checkbox objects, 829
  for Combobox objects, 905
  for Editor objects, 914
  for Entryfield objects, 839
  for Form object, 737
  for Image object, 778
  for Line objects, 758, 780
  for Listbox objects, 922–923
  for OLE objects, 1094
  for Pushbutton objects, 959
  for Radiobutton objects, 847
  for Rectangle object, 787
  for Scrollbar objects, 967
  for Spinbox objects, 857
  for Text object, 794
WINDOW function, 1083
Window menu, 13, **304–306**
  ➤ Navigator, 35
Window menu (Crystal Reports), 441
Window properties, setting for form, 211
Window size settings, in DBASEWIN.INI file, 1025
windows
  arranging, 305
  changing size, 11
  losing when closing form, 241
Windows (Microsoft), 28–29. *See also* Program Manager
  application programming interface (API), 696, 759
  File Manager to create directory, 32, 1012
  Font dialog box, 410
  function to run program, 524, **557**
  graphics interface and PatternStyle property, 767
  special keys and shortcut key assignment in dBASE, 236
  System button, *9*, 10
Windows Control Panel
  using date default format, 408
  using number default format, 407
Windows (Microsoft) resources, 759
  and Spinboxes, 819
Windows Print dialog box, 397
Windows Tutorial (Help menu), 29
WindowState property, for Form object, 737
word processor
  mail-merge capabilities of, 481
  selecting to edit Memo fields, 1019
word wrap, 406
Word Wrap check box (Editor Properties dialog box), 718
WordWrap setting, in DBASEWIN.INI file, 1039
work area, 946
  function to return number of next available, 520, **558**
work areas
  command to select, 160–161
  selecting, 627
WORKAREA function, 1083

working directory, **32–34**
WP setting
  in DBASEWIN.INI file, 1019
  SETTO function and, 563
Wrap property, for Editor objects, 881, 914

Y

YEAR function, 521, **571–572**

Z

@Z function, 1003
ZAP command, **659**
Zap Records (Table Utilities menu), 382
z-axis
  in form, 700, *701*, 702
  and tabbing order, 702
zero-length string, 135
zeros, leading, in numeric constants, 501
zoom, in Preview window, 261
z-order, 437
  adjusting in Layout view, 708
  setting in Order view, 707

Table Records Window Speedbar

Table Structure Window Speedbar

Button	Function
1 New File	Create new file
2 Open File	Open existing file
3 Save File	Save table to disk
4 Print	Print table
5 Cut	Cut text to Clipboard
6 Copy	Copy text to Clipboard
7 Paste	Paste text from Clipboard
8 Run	Run table (view and edit data) [Table Structure window]
9 Design	Design table (use Table Structure tool) [Table Records window]
10 Browse Layout [Table Records window]	View multiple records in columns
10 Append [Table Structure window]	Add field at end of structure
11 Form Layout [Table Records window]	View single records as forms
11 Insert [Table Structure window]	Insert field in middle of structure
12 Columnar Layout [Table Records window]	View single records, fields in column
12 Delete [Table Structure window]	Delete current field
13 Find	Search for data
14 Append	Add new records
15 New Query	Create new query for this table
16 Beginning of File	Go to first record
17 Previous Page	Go back screenful of records
18 Previous Record	Go back one record
19 Next Record	Go forward one record
20 Next Page	Go forward screenful of records
21 End of File	Go to last record
22 Navigator	Open Navigator
23 Command	Open Command window
24 Expert	Choose Expert
25 Tutor	Run interactive tutorial